Women's America

WOMEN'S AMERICA

Refocusing the Past

SIXTH EDITION

Edited by

Linda K. Kerber
University of Iowa

Jane Sherron De Hart
University of California, Santa Barbara

New York   Oxford
Oxford University Press
2004

Oxford University Press

Oxford New York
Auckland Bangkok Buenos Aires Cape Town Chennai
Dar es Salaam Delhi Hong Kong Istanbul Karachi Kolkata
Kuala Lumpur Madrid Melbourne Mexico City Mumbai
Nairobi São Paulo Shanghai Taipei Tokyo Toronto

Copyright © 1982, 1987, 1991, 1995, 2000, 2004 by Oxford University Press, Inc.

Published by Oxford University Press, Inc.
198 Madison Avenue, New York, New York 10016
http://www.oup-usa.org

Oxford is a registered trademark of Oxford University Press

Library of Congress Cataloging-in-Publication Data
    Women's America : refocusing the past / edited by Linda K. Kerber,
Jane Sherron De Hart. — 6th ed.
        p. cm.
    Includes bibliographical references.
    ISBN 0-19-515982-9 (pbk.)
        1. Women—United States—History—Sources. 2. Women—Employment—
United States—History—Sources. 3. Women in politics—United
States—History—Sources. 4. Women—Health and hygiene—United
States—History—Sources. 5. Feminism—United States—History—
Sources. I. Kerber, Linda K. II. De Hart, Jane Sherron.
HQ1426.W663 2003
    305.4'0973—dc21   2003042971

Printing (last digit): 10 9 8 7 6 5 4 3

Printed in the United States of America on acid-free paper

For

Christel Villela Vidal (b. 1998)

Hannah Jewell Kerber (b. 2000)

Ruth Elinor Kerber (b. 2002)

the littlest feminists,
with love

CONTENTS

ACKNOWLEDGMENTS

As we've made selections for this book, we have been awed by the strength of feminist scholar-ship in recent years. New subjects have been engaged, complex social relationships scrutinized, analytical challenges met.

Good authors take pride in their writing; it is not easy to give up carefully crafted sentences. We have been especially touched by the generosity of spirit and understanding with which the authors in this volume have coped with our limitations of space. We thank the six anonymous consultants who responded generously and forthrightly to Oxford University Press's request for their appraisal of the fifth edition. We hope this volume reflects their good counsel.

Our collaborators—Carolyn Herbst Lewis of the University of California, Santa Barbara, and Catherine Denial of the University of Iowa—threw themselves into the making of this edition with extraordinary vigor and creativity. We came to rely on their good judgment, managerial skills, and ingenuity. We greatly admire their sensitivity to an undergraduate audience. Alexan-der Rondón has been an energetic and precise assistant. Sharon Wood, now of the University of Nebraska, Omaha, and Rachel Bohlmann, now of the Newberry Library, who assisted us in the past, intervened at important moments. Malinda Ellwood and Sarah Case offered their energy and splendid research skills at a critical moment; this book could not have met its press dead-lines without them. We are grateful for the shrewd copyediting of Matt Hannafin.

We feel especially fortunate to have this manuscript in the good hands of Elias Muhanna, Christine D'Antonio, and Peter Coveney. It has been wonderful to work with them.

Linda K. Kerber   Jane Sherron De Hart
University of Iowa   *University of California, Santa Barbara*

contributory history can be very important in connecting women to major movements in the past: the women of Hull House "contribute" to Progressive reforms, the women in cotton factories in Lowell, Massachusetts, are an important part of the story of the industrialization of America. Pioneering historians in the late 1920s and 1930s, among them Julia Cherry Spruill, Mary Beard, and Caroline Ware, wrote important books that firmly established women's participation in and contribution to significant developments in American history: frontier settlement, abolition, urbanization and industrialization, populism and progressivism.

It could be said that a third stage of women's history—which developed as a vigorous field of study and research in the 1970s and 1980s—is to move past a recounting of women's "contributions" and to seek to test familiar generalizations and to rewrite the historical narrative. Things we thought we "knew" about American history turn out to be more complex than we had suspected. For example, most textbooks suggest that the frontier meant opportunity for Americans, "a gate of escape from the bondage of the past." But it was men who more readily found on the frontier compensation for their hard work; many women found only drudgery. (In fact, women were more likely to find economic opportunity in cities than on the frontier.) Other generalizations turn out to be equally suspect. We have often assumed that American slaves were provided with at least adequate diets, but the generalization holds better for male slaves than for pregnant women and nursing mothers; for them, the slaves' diet meant semistarvation. The new women's history challenges us to re-examine the social relations of the sexes, to *reconstruct* many historical generalizations, and to *reconfigure* the historical narrative.

Finally, women's history challenges us to understand that gender itself is a social construction. Historians increasingly ask questions about how people construct meaning for their historical experience, and how difference between the sexes operates to shape the construction of meaning. Women's history also suggests a more complex understanding of traditional categories of historical interpretation. Conventional periodization has used presidential administrations or wars as major guideposts in organizing our description of the past: the Revolutionary Era, the Age of Jackson, the Civil War, the Eisenhower Years. Conventional interpretations have tended to emphasize the accomplishments of men, whether they be presidents, generals, farmers, or ranch hands. But all men had women for contemporaries, and women experienced the same great social phenomena that men did.

This book is divided into four major chronological sections. Because dates that mark major turning points in traditional historical accounts do not automatically coincide with those dates that mark significant changes in the lives of American women, women's history challenges us to re-examine conventional periodization. Our sections are generally congruent with familiar periodization; they also reflect changing realities in women's experience. The dividing date between traditional and industrial America is 1820, by which time forces were in motion that would erode the domestic economy of an agrarian society, slowly transforming women's lives in the process. The long period of industrialization that followed 1820 may conveniently be broken at 1880, by which time large-scale industries in which women were employed were firmly established. By this time, too, women's rights leaders had come to recognize that suffrage would not be granted by the courts on the basis of a fresh interpretation of the Constitution, and they demanded a spe-

cific constitutional amendment. The second major period ends at 1900, when the necessary ingredients for emancipation were present. Gerda Lerner has identified these as
"urbanization; industrialization with technology permitting society to remove food
preparation and care of the sick from the home; the mechanization of heating and laundry; spread of health and medical care sufficient to lower infant mortality and protect
maternal health; birth control; . . . and availability of education on all levels to all children."[8] These conditions existed in varying measure by 1900.

It should be noted, however, that industrialization was never a uniform process
occurring simultaneously in all of the United States. Industrialized areas in the East and
upper Midwest coexisted with frontier conditions in the West. There, encounters between
Anglos, Native Americans, and Hispanics accentuated disparities just as had earlier contact in the East among British immigrants, Native Americans, and Africans, prompting
us to call this section, "The Many Frontiers of Industrializing America." Although the
frontiers of industrializing America extended throughout the nineteenth century, the
onset of the twentieth marks a convenient break. In the next half century, American life
would be reshaped by an influx of immigrants, increasing urbanization, rapid technological advances, and a growing consumer culture. In the midst of these changes, progressives at the turn of the century and New Dealers during the 1930s worked to redefine the federal government's responsibility to its citizens, spurred by major events with
seismic impacts—a crippling depression and two world wars. We have headed this third
section "Creating a State in an Industrialized Nation, 1900–1945." Women were in the
forefront of state-building just as they played an indispensable role in the struggle to
organize unions, to hold their families together amid the onslaught of depression at home
and Nazism in Europe, to keep production lines rolling so as to keep the troops fighting
abroad, and—not least—to achieve full citizenship for themselves. For some women,
however, a war waged in the name of freedom did not mean freedom in their own country. The state could be an instrument of injustice, as Japanese Americans discovered during World War II when they were forced out of their homes on the West Coast and placed
in internment camps inland because of concerns about their loyalties. However misguided specific policies such as internment were, the United States emerged from World
War II a true superpower. What we discover in this third section is how the perspective
of women's history allows us to re-examine male-dominated structures such as the state,
gaining new insights into the role women played in its creation. We also see once again
how the perspectives of women of color and their communities call into question old
notions about citizenship and about the nation as an organic entity.

The second half of the twentieth century consisted of decades dominated by the
Cold War, the rights revolution, and the resurgence of conservatism. It stands as a separate section, the fourth, and is titled "Struggles against Injustice, 1945–2000." While
these struggles involving racial justice, civil rights, welfare rights, workers' rights,
women's rights (including reproductive rights), and the nuclear arms race took place
within the United States, they cannot be separated from those waged on an international stage. For those women engaged, politicization and participation in movement-
building reached new heights during this period. Movements bred counter-movements
as pro-choice women found themselves confronted by pro-life women.

However historical experience is periodized, women shared in that experience. The
history of industrialization, for example, is a history that involves female workers quite

as much as it does male. Like their male counterparts, most women workers relied on their wages for their own support and that of their families. In the first factory labor force—the mill hands of Samuel Slater's first textile factory in Pawtucket, Rhode Island, in 1790—women and children actually outnumbered men. Extensively employed in manufacturing by the nineteenth century, they worked in a wide variety of trades as bookbinders, printers, shoemakers, seamstresses, laundresses, glass painters, button makers. In the twentieth century they worked in shipyards, airplane factories, and automobile plants turning out the military equipment essential to allied victory in two world wars.

Women were at the forefront of working-class protest. Women weavers in Pawtucket, Rhode Island, who walked off work in 1824 were among the first American workers to strike against low wages and long hours; a significant number of strikes by women workers followed in the 1830s.[9] Women at the textile mills in Lowell, Massachusetts, in the 1840s were the first industrial workers in the nation to demand state regulation of the length of the workday. In the twentieth century, large-scale strikes organized by men in mines and railroads had their counterparts in large-scale strikes organized by women in textile mills and garment factories.[10]

Similarly, enslaved workers—primarily Africans but also, in the early centuries, Indians—were as likely to be women as men. Enslaved women workers were to be found in the fields, toiling alongside men, in the same jobs.

THE DIFFERENT HISTORICAL EXPERIENCE OF WOMEN AND MEN

The historical experience of the two sexes, for all its similarities, was in many important ways profoundly different. Difference itself is a comparative term. As legal scholar Martha Minow writes, "I am no more different from you than you are from me. A short person is different only in relation to a tall one." While making distinctions helps people cope with complexity, descriptions of difference usually carry with them unstated assumptions of value and hierarchy. As Minow puts it, "Women are compared to the unstated norm of men, 'minority' races to white, handicapped persons to the able-bodied, and 'minority' religions to 'majorities.'"[11] Difference, therefore, is not a neutral term.

Differences among women are also multiple. Differences of culture, nationality, and historical memory are exacerbated by distinctions of race, class, ethnicity, and sexual preference. Because women are apt to live with men—husbands, fathers, sons—who share their racial, class, and ethnic identities, commonalities with women who don't share that identity are often obscured. Because each of these differences carries with it implications of hierarchy, further distancing can develop. Affluent women may feel superior to poor women; white women may feel hostile to black women; Asian American women may feel that they have little in common with Hispanic women.

Hispanic women, who are often identified as a single ethnic group, are in fact people of many nationalities: Puerto Ricans, Cubans, Mexicans, Brazilians—to name a few. Moreover, most are of Central American Indian descent and share the gene pool of North American Indians. They learned to speak Spanish—hence the name "Hispanic"— only because their original land was conquered by Spain. "Hispanic" women differ from each other not only with respect to ethnicity but also class. Affluent women who are part of the Miami Cuban community may feel that they have little in common with migrant agricultural workers from Mexico. By the same token, Asian American women who came from such countries as China, Japan, the Philippines, Korea, Thailand, or Vietnam are separated by diverse heritages, various languages, and disparate economic resources. So are white women who are separated by multiple ethnic backgrounds, religious affiliations, and class positions.

Differences in sexual preference further divide women, stigmatizing lesbians and obscuring the commonalities they share with heterosexual women. Even those heterosexual women who reject negative stereotypes of homosexuals may view their lesbian counterparts with ambivalence. Women who are able to tolerate same-sex relationships as long as they remain discreetly hidden are often uncomfortable with open displays of homosexual preference and distance themselves from the women involved. Lesbians who have struggled for self-validation and a life-style that allows them to express same-sex love, affection, and sexuality feel no less alienated from women whose discomfort is a measure of their identification with a system that has stigmatized and oppressed other women.

That the factors which women share with men and which separate them from other women have been so powerful and persistent should not blind us to fundamental divergence in the historical experience of women and men. Gender differences in life cycles and family experiences have been a central factor in that divergence. Employment patterns of white women in a large New England textile factory make this clear. As young single women at the turn of the century, they went into the mill to supplement family income, often allowing brothers to improve their job prospects by staying in school; as wives, they withdrew when children were born and returned as mothers of small children when the perilous state of family finances required them to do so. As mothers of grown children, they returned to stay. Thus family responsibilities were a crucial factor not only in determining at what stage in their life cycle women were gainfully employed but also in explaining why their employment patterns differed from those of male workers.

Once in the work force, the jobs to which women were assigned, the wages they were paid, the opportunities for unionization they encountered, and the relationship they forged with governmental regulators all reinforced fundamental differences between the sexes. Even when they entered the factory together, with comparable skills, men and women were assigned by management to different tasks at markedly different pay scales. Despite the low wages, which should have made them ripe recruits for unionization, most unions were loath to organize women workers. In part because women lacked the leverage that unions afforded skilled male workers, federal and state governments reluctantly agreed to regulate women's hours, wages, and working conditions long before they regulated men's.

Most people, male and female, particularly if they were white and middle class, understood difference to mean advantage. They assumed that women were spared heavy physical labor and fierce competitive pressures. Excused from primary responsibility for family support, wives and daughters could spend most of their adult lives at home rather than in the work force, devoting their time to such congenial tasks as caring for children, doing charitable deeds, and socializing with friends. Those who were employed outside the home were thought to work for "pin money," which they could use to indulge their whims as consumers.

Recent research makes clear that most of these "advantages" were class-specific and illusory. Exhausting labor performed in hazardous conditions characterized many women's jobs. Responsibility for supporting other family members was not limited to men, especially among the working class. Unmarried women often returned their wages to their parents, who relied on daughters' wages for essentials. Most adult women—whether they were single, widows, or wives—worked to feed and shelter themselves, their children, other members of their families. Their expenditure of money was rarely capricious; in fact they accepted low wages in nonunionized jobs because they were so likely to be in desperate need.

The notion that the home protected working-class housewives from the competitive pressures of the marketplace and all housewives from real work was also an illusion. The home has always been less a haven than a workplace. It was the site of housework—heavy physical labor and unremitting toil—work that was no less strenuous for all the denial that it was work at all since it was performed for love of family rather than wages. Even the middle-class housewife who enjoyed the conveniences of nineteenth-century town life and possibly a servant to help with the laundry and cooking struggled with an exhausting array of tasks that included washing, starching, ironing, sorting, and putting away laundry; scrubbing, sweeping, and dusting floors, walls, windows, furniture, and accessories; growing, pickling, preserving, and baking food; sewing, mending, and knitting clothes, towels, pillowcases, quilts, curtains, carpets, and rugs; birthing, nursing, tending, instructing, and disciplining children. According to one harried antebellum housewife, every day was "hurry, hurry, hurry, and drive, drive, drive."[12] For rural women the workload was even heavier. There were farm-related chores to perform and raw materials such as soap and cloth to produce in addition to core household tasks. Through much of the nineteenth century rural black women were enslaved; after the Civil War most lived in sharecropping families in which the level of subsistence was scarcely higher and the physical work load almost as heavy, although the psychological conditions were generally better. Reflecting on the workload of her mother's generation, a nineteenth-century daughter spoke for millions when she lamented that her mother had been robbed of "her health, her strength, and her life."[13] In some respects, little has changed. In the 1980s, a farm woman in northern Iowa told an interviewer, "I plant the garden, I feed the chickens, I sell the eggs, I put up a year's worth of vegetables. I don't have *time* to work!"[14]

Although twentieth-century technology has lightened the onerous physical burden, the equation of homemaking with leisure remains an illusion carefully nurtured by the advertising industry. From the introduction of the electrical washing machine in the 1920s—"an entire new day will be added to your week"—to the dishwashers, ranges, and microwave ovens of the 1990s that will do the work "whether you are at home or not," promises of relief from drudgery through the purchase of new products have been accompanied by new expectations that entailed more work.[15] Laundry—and there was more of it—had to be done more frequently; cooking demanded more creativity; clothing necessitated hours spent shopping; child care involved properly sterilized bottles, regular feeding schedules, greater attention to toilet training, nutrition, hygiene, and properly supervised play. If the nature of housework had changed, the time spent doing it did not. In 1960, nonemployed urban women were spending 55 hours per week in housework—three hours more than rural homemakers in the 1920s. Fully employed women in the 1980s each week pack an additional 25 hours of work—housework—into evenings and weekends. While there is evidence to suggest that some younger men may be doing more, the gender disparity in terms of housework is likely to persist well into the twenty-first century.[16]

If women seldom found the home that tranquil center of repose depicted in popular literature, they had equal difficulty finding in it the much celebrated "haven" from the competitive pressures of a "heartless world." We have long understood that severe downturns in the market have enormous economic and psychic impact on family life. During the Great Depression of the 1930s, for example, many homemakers were thrust into the work force, joining the long lines of men desperate for work. Refusing to sit by passively when their families lacked basic necessities, others opened their homes to boarders and applied their sewing skills to piecework—measures that wives of laborers had long used to supplement family income even in periods of prosperity. Resorting to the home production that had engaged their grandmothers, middle- and working-class women alike raised and canned vegetables and patched, mended, and recycled clothes in order to keep cash outlays at a minimum.

What historians have only begun to appreciate is the extent to which in more prosperous times such enterprise and frugality benefited not only the household economy but the national economy as well. By helping out husbands in shops, buying in bulk, taking in boarders, doing piecework, taking in wash, peddling goods on the street, scavenging for food and fuel, wives in laboring-class households throughout the nineteenth and early twentieth century managed to transform a husband's wages below subsistence level into subsistence wages. Because of such efforts, businesses employing those husbands were able to stay afloat in an undercapitalized and volatile economy. Among the emerging middle class where a husband's income was sufficient for maintenance, it was the value of the wife's labor that frequently provided the kind of savings and investments that buffered the family against market vicissitudes and fueled economic growth in an industrializing nation. In sum, even in the nineteenth century, the boundaries between home and market, domestic sphere and public sphere, were far more permeable than once assumed.

GENDER AS A SOCIAL CONSTRUCTION

The adverse economic implications for women associated with the old perception that housework was not real work suggest that in this instance, as in many others, difference has meant disadvantage. Women's historians have not only documented this disadvantage, but have sought to explain it. The factors involved in this explanation are very complex and still imperfectly understood. The explanation traditionally offered has been a variant of biological essentialism. As Supreme Court Justice David Brewer put it in 1908, "The two sexes differ in the structure of the body, in the functions to be performed by each, in the amount of physical strength, in the capacity for long continuing labor . . . , [in] the self reliance which enables one to assert full rights, and in the capacity to maintain the struggle for subsistence." Woman's "physical structure and a proper discharge of her maternal functions" place her at a disadvantage in that struggle, he continued, and justify legislation to protect her.[17]

Justice Brewer's statement reveals a common confusion of sex and gender. To the extent that his view of difference is based on anatomical and hormonal features that differentiate males and females biologically, he is talking about *sexual* difference. When, however, he speaks of "the self-reliance that enables . . . [men] to assert full rights," "the capacity [of men] to maintain the struggle for subsistence," and the "proper discharge of [woman's] maternal functions," he is referring to *gender* difference. The assumption that men are self-reliant and that women are not, that men struggle for subsistence and women do not, that women nurture their children and men cannot, reflects the ways in which Justice Brewer and most of his generation understood the implications of being male or female.

In antebellum America, for example, white southern males, whether members of the low-country planter class or the backcountry working class, identified masculinity with a concept of personal honor, in defense of which duels were fought and fists flew. In the cities of the North, many young working-class males shared their southern counterparts' obsession with physical prowess and bellicosity. So synonymous were masculinity and toughness for those New Yorkers known as "Bowery boys" that when the Bowery boy was represented on stage, he was immediately recognizable by his swaggering gait and aggressive persona. Although the black abolitionist Frederick Douglass would not have been comfortable with the flamboyant aggressiveness and virility flaunted by the Bowery boys as a badge of working-class masculinity, the identification of force and power with manhood was a concept he well understood. In *Narrative of the Life of Frederick Douglass* (1845), Douglass's autobiographical account of his life as a slave and his escape to freedom, the author prefaced a description of his brutal fight with the vicious slave breaker Covey with a single sentence: "You have seen how a man was made a slave; you shall see how a slave was made a man."

Not all social groups defined masculinity in this fashion, even in antebellum America. Although aggressiveness, self-reliance, and competitiveness were cultivated in most boys because these traits were needed in the work world of adult males, families whose values were shaped by evangelical Protestantism emphasized that manliness also involved self-restraint, moral self-discipline, and sobriety. These qualities became even more important in the new urban bourgeois culture of the late nineteenth century. A bureaucratized corporate capitalism would require of the middle class a model of masculinity different from the rougher, more "macho" ideal characteristic of the frontier. A "real" man, while projecting a virile and, if necessary, tough demeanor, also needed to be a "team player"—an attribute cultivated in boyhood games and team sports. Indeed, competitive sports, virility, and masculinity have become so intertwined in the twentieth century . . . that "the boy or man who dislikes competitive sports or virile postures has little choice but to affect 'manly' interests and behavior and to hope these affectations will not be exposed."[18] To behave otherwise was to risk being called a "sissy" or a "queer." Such labels reflected popular assumptions that "real" men were sportsmen and that nonathletes, whether heterosexual or not, were males who wished to have sexual relations only with males, were effeminate, and/or wished to be women. In other words, sex refers to biological differences that are unchanging; gender involves the *meaning* that a particular society and culture attach to sexual difference. Because that meaning varies over time and among cultures, gender differences are both socially constructed and subject to change. Definitions of what is masculine and feminine are learned as each society instructs its members from infancy through adulthood as to what behavior and personality attributes are appropriate for males and females of that generation.

Sexuality is also socially constructed. Anatomical and hormonal characteristics set certain boundaries within which we operate. Within those boundaries socially constructed scripts provide cues as to how we respond sexually—what or who arouses our desire. How sexual preference is first determined or chosen—and when—is a matter experts do not fully understand. But here, too, culture plays a part. It is helpful, writes historian Carroll Smith-Rosenberg, to "view sexual and emotional impulses as part of a continuum or spectrum. . . . At one end of the continuum lies committed heterosexuality, at the other uncompromising homosexuality; between, a wide latitude of emotions and sexual feelings."[19] Where we place ourselves on that continuum and whether we move within it is affected by cultural norms as well as a strong biological component.

Sexuality has its own history. Conceptions of sexuality, attitudes as to how sexual feelings should be expressed, with whom, and where, have been continually reshaped by the changing nature of the economy and politics. In the seventeenth century, for example, women were believed to be more lustful and carnal than men. Female sexuality was seen as a source of power and corruption to be feared and controlled. By the nineteenth century, when sexual restraints had to be internalized, sexuality was redefined. Women—at least white, native-born, middle- and upper-class women—were viewed as having weaker sexual desires than men. Sensuality was attached to poor or "darker" women—who, by definition, "invited" male advances.

As we begin to uncover the history of sexuality, we can better understand what part sexuality played in women's subordination. We can also see how women tried to devise ways to enhance sexual control and expression. In the nineteenth century, for example, some married women used the concept of women as passionless to reduce the frequency of sexual intercourse so as to reduce the likelihood of pregnancy and enhance sexual pleasure. Women who wished to express themselves sexually as well as emotionally in single-sex relationships constructed life-styles that opened up new realms of freedom. Indeed, we are just beginning to understand the ways in which these private relationships sustained the public activism of women such as Jane Addams or Lillian Wald.

Like gender and sexuality, race, too, is a social construction, despite the fact that we have long believed it to be an indisputable biological marker. Indeed, it was not until the nineteenth century that the idea of race was fully conceptualized in the way we understand it: human beings connected to or separated from other human beings by virtue of physical characteristics that are presumably genetic, such as skin pigmentation, hair texture, proportion, facial structure, and so on. In fact, however, there are no genetic characteristics possessed by all blacks but not non-blacks; similarly, there is no gene or cluster of genes common to all whites but not to non-whites. It is law and custom that are critical determinants of how individuals are classified with respect to race. In colonial Virginia, for example, a child born of a black mother and white father was classified as black. In the wake of American Revolution, the legal definition changed so that a person was defined as black if he or she had a black parent or grandparent; anyone less than one-quarter black was white. In practice, however, even a more distant black member in one's family tree resulted in the classification "black." In 1910, Virginians changed the law to define as black anyone who was one-sixteenth black. Twenty years later, the state adopted the notorious "one-drop" law, which defined as black anyone with one drop of African blood, however that might have been determined.

Mexican Americans have also been subject to changing classifications. In the early nineteenth century, the term referred to nationality, not to race. Those persons who lived in Mexico might be white, Native American, black, or Asian. Once land that had originally belonged to Mexico became a part of the Southwestern United States, "Mexican" became a racial category. In 1855, the California legislature defined Mexicans as people with Spanish and Indian blood. Called a "mixed breed," they were seen as an indolent, cowardly people—an inferior "mongrel" race. Yet in the twentieth century, the Supreme Court determined that Mexican Americans were "white."

Just how arbitrary and confusing racial classification could become is illustrated in the case of people from India. Uniformly classified as Caucasian by anthropologists, which should have earned them the designation "white," many were dark-skinned and therefore regarded by the American public as "non-white." In a 1922 Supreme Court decision, *United States* v. *Thind*,[20] the justices, reasoning that "the average well informed white American would learn with some degree of astonishment that the race to which he belongs is made up of such heterogenous elements," concluded that common knowledge rather than science prevailed. Bhagat Singh Thind, the plaintiff in the case, was not, as he claimed, "white." That a concept with no scientific significance that has been understood in such varied and often irrational ways retains such force as a source of meaning, identity, and (dis)advantage is a reminder of how powerfully social constructions function in how we organize and understand our social world.

Class is yet another category that is socially constructed. Differences in wealth and property are transformed into class by a set of institutional practices that allows a small propertied elite to retain property within that group. For example, the practice of restricting marriages to people within the same propertied group assured the retention of wealth within that group. Arranged marriages served this function, as did the internalization of cultural definitions of who might be a suitable marriage partner. Consider the example of Eliza Lucas, who at the age of 17 ran her father's South Carolina plantation while he served as royal governor of Antigua, a small island in the Caribbean. Rejecting the first two suitors her father selected, she made her own decision as to whom to marry. She chose a wealthy planter, Charles Pinckney—a choice consistent with the marital strategy of her class.

Miscegenation laws that prohibited racial intermarriage and, therefore, transmission of property to heirs of "mixed blood" have been a device designed to preserve property of a particular racial group. The interpenetration of class and race was most evident in the South, where, in the decades after the Civil War, lynching and other forms of terror were often directed at black men who managed to secure some degree of economic independence. When race and class intersected, as it did for those black women who had the financial resources to purchase a ticket entitling them to sit in the "Ladies" car of the train, race trumped class. Women such as Ida Wells Barnett and Charlotte

Hawkins Brown suffered the humiliation of being physically ejected—a reminder of how spatial segregation can reinforce social distinctions. For upper-class Mexican American women, on the other hand, class could trump race. When marriage brought with it significant property, Anglo suitors, eager to consolidate their own class position, could easily be persuaded that the young woman was of "pure" Spanish ancestry. Such practices exemplify the meaning of the phrase "money whitens."

Understanding how differences associated with gender, sexuality, race, and class interacted—and continue to interact—in the lives of women to privilege as well as to exclude and oppress is key to understanding the varied experiences of American women. The place to begin is with gender.

GENDER AND ITS IMPLICATIONS

Understanding the difference between sex and gender provides a key to understanding the differences in men's and women's historical experience. In the workplace, for example, women and men were assigned jobs that reflected the employers' beliefs about the kind of work each sex should do. In a society whose understanding of gender included the conviction that women's primary obligations were familial and their basic talents domestic, female wage earners were persistently channeled into jobs that corresponded with the kind of work done in the domestic sphere or with characteristics long associated with women.

In the preindustrial domestic economy, women did both heavy physical labor— hauling water, slaughtering chickens—and skilled tasks—spinning, weaving, nursing. When women sought new avenues through which to gain economic independence they followed these chores into the marketplace. As slaves and as "hired help" they toiled on other people's farms; as "mill girls" they tended dangerous spinning machinery for twelve hours a day; as packinghouse workers they labored amid stench and slime. Upwardly mobile women laid claim to the teaching and nursing professions by emphasizing that the personality characteristics and skills required for such work were precisely those believed to be unique to the female sex. Thus nursing, considered in pre-Civil War years an occupation no respectable woman would enter, was eventually touted as a profession eminently suited to women. Providence, after all, had endowed the fairer sex with that "compassion which penetrate[s] the heart, that instinct which divines and anticipates the wants of the sick, and the patience which pliantly bends to all their caprices."[21] As the economy grew more complex, middle-class women infiltrated the ranks of librarians and secretaries. These occupations had been primarily male, but, like teaching and nursing, were redefined so as to emphasize the nurturing, service-oriented qualities ascribed to women—with a corresponding decrease in pay. Newer industries provided new job titles but old work categories. Receptionists and social workers were hired by employers still convinced that the tasks required in these jobs were consistent with the personality characteristics and skills traditionally associated with women. New white-collar jobs were also segregated by race, even in the North where segregation was not officially practiced. White women were overwhelmingly hired as stewardesses on national airlines until after the civil rights legislation of the 1960s. Because gender rather than individual talent or capability has been the primary consideration, the result of this kind of stereotyping has been to segregate women into certain kinds of work, whether in the professions or in industry. Most women workers are employed as waitresses, salespersons, secretaries, nurses, and teachers.

Once a form of work has been identified with women, it has invariably become associated with low pay and minimal prestige. "Theoretically, the market treats men and women neutrally, judging only the characteristics of their labor," writes the historian Alice Kessler-Harris. "In the world of economists, the wage is rooted in the play of supply and demand." In practice, she continues, "the wage is neither neutral nor natural, but reveals a set of social constructs . . . that convey messages about the nature of the world, and about . . . men and women and . . . the relations between them."[22] Low pay was appropriate for people assumed to be marginal workers, whose place was in the home where purity and virtue could be protected and family duties fulfilled. In this way the home subsidized the factory.

Gender was embedded not only in economic relations but in legal relations as well. In the legal tradition English colonists brought to America, the husband was understood to be the head of the family and to represent it in its dealings with the world. Upon marriage, the woman lost her separate civil identity; it was assumed that she had voluntarily forsworn the claim to make choices at odds with those of her husband. In a powerful legal fiction, man and wife were understood to be one person; the married woman was the *feme covert*, "covered" with her husband's legal identity for virtually all purposes except crime.[23] All personal property she brought to the marriage became her husband's; he could sell her jewelry, gamble away her money. He could not sell her real estate unless she consented, but he could decide how it was to be used: whether land was to be farmed, rented out, planted in corn or vegetables, whether trees on it were to be cultivated or cut down. Since married women did not own property they could not make legal contracts affecting it; they could not buy and sell without their husband's consent. A married woman could not decide whether their children were to be kept at home or apprenticed or, if apprenticed, who their masters would be. She could not sign a contract independently; not until she was a widow could she leave a will. So powerful was the fiction that husband and wife are one person that marital rape was inconceivable. Indeed, marital rape was not outlawed anywhere in the world until 1978, when New York State passed a statute prohibiting forced sexual intercourse whether by a stranger, an acquaintance, or a spouse. As of 1990, only nine states have followed New York's lead. Congress attempted to remedy the situation in 1990s, offering block grants to all states that would outlaw marital rape, but the recent date of the incentive, 1993, is a reminder of what a long struggle it has been to rid the law of remnants of coverture and obtain for women the bodily integrity that men enjoy.[24]

Gender also defined political relationships. In Anglo-American tradition the right to participate in political activities—voting, office-holding, jury duty—was conditioned on the holding of property. Since married women could not direct the use of their property, it seemed to follow that they could be neither jurors, nor voters, nor officeholders. That politics was considered a male domain, that women were not political beings, is an understanding as old as Western civilization. Aristotle, whose classic work provided the basic terms by which westerners have understood politics, said that men alone realized themselves as citizens. It is no accident that the civic *virtue* he extolled derives from the same root as the word *virile*. Women, Aristotle maintained, realized themselves only within the confines of the household. Their relationship to the world of politics, like their legal status, was derivative—through fathers, husbands, and sons.

This derivative relationship forced women to carve out a political role that rested upon their ability to influence those who held political power. A time-honored tradition, this use of influence was employed in the interests of a wide range of important social issues and philanthropic causes in the years before 1920. Women found that the wielding of influence benefited their communities and enlarged their political skills. The uses of influence continued to be exploited by American women even after they got the vote. As primary adviser to Al Smith, governor of New York and presidential candidate in the 1920s, Belle Moskowitz had enormous impact both on the policies of his administration and on the politics of the Democratic party. But she was uncomfortable claiming power for herself and never ran for political office. Mary McLeod Bethune, a prominent African American educator, was equally adept in the uses of influence. As president of the National Association of Colored Women and the National Council of Negro Women, Bethune met Eleanor Roosevelt. The first lady, admiring the effectiveness with which this forceful, articulate black woman championed the needs of her people, used her own influence to secure for Bethune appointments to a number of positions, notably in the National Youth Administration. From her position within the administration, Bethune in turn organized the Federal Council on Negro Affairs, a group of black leaders who worked effectively to focus the attention of the media as well as the administration on the desperate problems facing blacks in the Depression.

The gendering of politics forced women to clothe their political claims in domestic language. Deflecting male hostility to their entry into the political arena, they argued that women should have the vote in order to elect city officials who would see to it that rotting garbage was removed from homes, decaying meat taken out of markets, and polluted water purified; otherwise, the best efforts of mothers to assure their children clean homes and wholesome food were to no avail. Women in the nuclear disarmament movement also used gendered language, naming their organization "Women Strike for Peace."

THE DIFFICULTIES OF UNDERSTANDING GENDER AS A SYSTEM

Economics, law, politics—each, as we have seen, was permeated by assumptions, practices, and expectations that were deeply gendered. So widely shared were these assumptions, practices, and expectations and so much a part of the ordinary, everyday experience that they acquired an aura of naturalness, rightness, even inevitability. Common sense dictated that "this is simply the way things are." But "common sense," as anthropologist Clifford Geertz has shrewdly observed, "is not what the mind cleared of cant spontaneously apprehends; it is what the mind filled with presuppositions . . . concludes."[25] The consequence of comprehending the world in this way—whether in the nineteenth century or in our own time—is that it obscures the workings of a system in which economic, political, and cultural forces interact and reinforce each other in ways that benefit one group and disadvantage the other. Unable to recognize the system, failing to understand that what shapes and defines our lives has been constructed piece by interlocking piece over time by other human beings, we constantly reproduce the world we know believing we have no other choice. As a result the inequities persist, becoming more difficult to challenge because they, too, seem as natural and inevitable as the system that has produced them.

To develop a way of looking that allows one to "see" economic and social relationships, which are presumed to be neutral and natural, as socially constructed arrangements which in fact benefit one group at the expense of others is always a difficult task. That task is made even more difficult by the fact that language itself has embedded within it the values, norms, and assumptions of the dominant group. Consequently it reflects and re-creates reality as it is perceived by that group. Using language that is not one's own to expose unequal relationships or to create an alternative to those relationships challenges the ingenuity and analytical abilities of even the most clearheaded and imaginative thinkers.

Analytical skills, however, are not inborn. They are developed slowly and painfully within an educational process that values and encourages those skills as contrasted, for example, with simple memorization or rote learning. Throughout history, women have been explicitly excluded from the intellectual community. Prior to the seventeenth century when most people were illiterate, elite families in which sons learned to read and write rarely provided such opportunities for their daughters. A major literacy gap existed until well into the nineteenth century throughout the world and, in many underdeveloped countries, persists today. At the time of the American Revolution, when it has been estimated that 70 percent of the men in Northern cities could read, only 35 percent of their female counterparts could do so. Slaves were denied by law access to instruction in reading and writing lest they learn about alternatives to slavery. Not until the second half of the nineteenth century were white women admitted to major state universities. Between 1870 and 1890 a few elite colleges were founded that were designed to provide upper middle-class young women an education equivalent to that which their brothers were receiving at Harvard, Yale, and Princeton universities. These new women's colleges reluctantly admitted a few black students. It was left to black women with meager resources in a rigidly segregated society—notably Mary McLeod Bethune and Charlotte Hawkins Brown—to develop their own institutions. Because public schools served black children so badly, these private institutions often began not as colleges, but as elementary or secondary schools and later grew into larger and higher-level colleges. Only in recent generations have women in substantial numbers been able to acquire not only a basic education, but the rigorous training that would facilitate their ability to analyze and question the social and cultural arangements within which they lived.

Another consequence of women's educational deprivation was their ignorance of history and, therefore, their lack of an intimate acquaintance with other historical actors—male or female—who had faced challenges that in some way resembled their own. Lacking a history of their own, they had few models—heroes to emulate or strategies to adopt. The lack of a history in which women were actors made it particularly difficult for even educated women to envision a world other than one in which men— their experiences and needs—were the norm. Marginality in the past thus confirmed and reinforced marginality in the present.

Understanding economic and social relationships that benefit one sex at the expense of another, developing language with which to critique those hierarchical relationships and articulate an alternative vision, and forging the group solidarity necessary to realize that vision, have been the tasks of feminism. The term *feminism* came into use in the United States around 1910 at a time when women were engaged in the fight for suffrage as well as a host of other reforms. As historian Nancy Cott has pointed out, feminism included suffrage and other measures to promote women's welfare that had emerged out of the nineteenth-century women's movement.[26] However, feminism encompassed a wider range of fundamental changes, amounting to a revolution in the relation of the sexes. "As an *ism* (an ideology)," Cott notes, "[feminism] presupposed a set of principles not necessarily belonging to every woman—nor limited to women."[27] In other words, not all women would oppose a sex hierarchy that privileged men as a group nor would they feel compelled to struggle for sexual equality. Some men would, joining feminist women in their efforts to dismantle a system that conferred on one sex the power to define the other. While this system has been partially dismantled—the goal of suffrage was realized in law in 1920[28]—the wider revolution remains to be accomplished.

RETHINKING THE SOCIAL CONSTRUCTION OF GENDER

Embracing the goals of their feminist predecessors and enriched by current scholarship on gender, contemporary feminists seek to reconstruct social relations between the sexes. To do so, they believe, requires change in both public life and private behavior. This double agenda has a long history.

In 1848, when American feminists drafted their first manifesto, Elizabeth Cady Stanton demanded change in both law and custom. She called for legal change in the form of property rights for married women and voting rights for all women. Recognizing the ways in which women's self-esteem and autonomy were undermined, she also urged women to work for wide-ranging cultural change, such as equal standards of sexual behavior and equal roles in churches.

When twentieth-century feminists began to understand gender as a social construction, they too realized that the feminist revolution had to be waged in personal life as well as public life; in home as well as in workplace; in the most intimate relationships as well as the most remote. "It must be womanly as well as manly to earn your own living, to stand on your own feet," observed the feminist Crystal Eastman shortly after the national suffrage amendment was passed in 1920. "And it must be manly as well as womanly to know how to cook and sew and clean and take care of yourself in the ordinary exigencies of life. . . . [T]he second part of this revolution will be more passionately resisted than the first. Men will not give up their privilege of helplessness without a struggle. The average man has a carefully cultivated ignorance about household matters . . . a sort of cheerful inefficiency."[29] But it was fifty years before Eastman's insights became an agenda for action.

Feminists of the 1970s captured national attention with bitter criticisms of parents who gave nurses' kits to their daughters and doctors' bags to their sons and of guidance counselors who urged mathematically talented girls to become bookkeepers and boys to become engineers. Feminists condemned stereotypes that fit children to conventional roles in their adult life and encouraged the publication of books and toys designed to demonstrate to both boys and girls that they need not shape their aspirations to gendered stereotypes. (The popular TV show, record, and book *Free to Be You and Me* encapsulated these themes.) Feminists also urged a new set of private decisions in the family, so that both sexes would share more equitably the burdens and pleasures associated with earning a living, maintaining a household, and rearing a family. But gender stereotypes turned out to be more resilient than many had anticipated; socialization is a lifetime process.

Feminists themselves had to wrestle with a culture that maintained a hierarchy of values, reserving strength, competence, independence, and rationality for men and nurture, supportiveness, and empathy for women. Questioning both the hierarchy and the dualisms embedded in this gendering of values, feminists argued that these should be viewed as shared human qualities that are not sex-specific.

Sexual hierarchy was not the only cultural hierarchy that posed problems. There were also hierarchies of race and class. White feminists in the 1970s were criticized for promoting a vision of feminism that ignored black women and assumed that all women who were impatient with contemporary culture were white and middle-class. The upwardly mobile vision was a contested vision; the priorities of women of different classes and races did not necessarily converge. Many black women supported many elements of the agenda of middle-class white feminists of the 1970s—equal pay for equal work, access to jobs—but they disagreed on priorities. They were skeptical of those who placed the needs of middle-class women ahead of the needs of working women. Middle-class white women, the employers of domestic workers, were markedly more enthusiastic about the elimination of quotas for female students in law and medical schools than they were about the establishment of minimum wage and social security protection for domestic workers. The first generation of white radical feminists fought vigorously for the repeal of all abortion laws and for safe access to birth control; for black feminists the need for access to abortion was only one of a wide range of medical services for which many black women struggled.

Differences in sexual preference also posed problems for this generation of feminists. Challenges to traditional gender arrangements have always inspired charges of sexual deviance from those seeking to discredit the movement and trivialize grievances; the 1960s were no exception. Concerned about the movement's image, many feminists, rejecting the charge, attempted to push lesbians out of sight. They insisted that equality, not sexual preference, was the issue. Lesbian feminists disagreed, arguing that autonomy in sexual matters involved more than access to reproductive control. In time, tensions eased as many heterosexual feminists accepted the legitimacy of lesbian involvement and the validity of their contention that straight/gay divisions also constituted a form of cultural hierarchy that reinforced male supremacy.

THE COMPLEXITY OF CREATING EQUALITY

Recognizing the magnitude of cultural and personal change required if each woman was to realize her full human potential, feminists of the 1970s simultaneously challenged the institutions and the laws that denied women equal treatment. They launched a barrage of test cases in state and federal courts challenging practices of unequal responsibility for jury service, unequal benefits for dependents, unequal age requirements for drinking and marriage. In 1971, in an Idaho case testing who was to be the administrator of a will, feminists persuaded the Supreme Court for the first time in American history to treat discrimination on the basis of sex as a denial of equal protection under the law.[30] But the Supreme Court was reluctant to build on this precedent in subsequent cases. The Court's refusal to apply as strict a standard to sex discrimination as to racial discrimination prompted feminists to try to insert a ban on sex discrimination in the Constitution. The Equal Rights Amendment, passed overwhelmingly by Congress in 1972, failed to garner the last three states necessary for the three-quarter majority required for ratification. A contributing factor in its failure was basic disagreement on whether equality under law requires equality of military obligation.

Lobbying vigorously with both Congress and the executive branch, feminists won guarantees of equal pay for equal work, equal employment opportunities, equal access to credit and to education.[31] Building on the tactics and achievements of the civil rights movement, feminists secured major gains in the 1960s and 1970s. In the process, however, they discovered that guarantees of equality in a system structured with men's needs as the norm does not always produce a gender-neutral result. In many professions, for example, there is enormous pressure to demonstrate mastery of one's field in the early stages of a career, precisely when the physical hazards of childbearing are relatively minimal. Although the standard appears to be gender-neutral, it presents young women with excruciating choices that do not confront their male peers.

Nowhere was the challenge of achieving gender-neutrality in the workplace greater than on the matter of pregnancy. Aware of the long history of discrimination against pregnant employees, feminists successfully attacked regulations that prevented women from making their own decisions about whether and how long to work when pregnant. But initial legislative "solutions" raised new complexities challenging the assumption that equality always requires identical treatment. If employers could no longer fire pregnant women, they could still exclude from the company's disability program those temporarily unable to work during some portion of their pregnancy or at childbirth. Pregnancy, according to the Supreme Court, was not temporary disability but a "voluntary physical condition."[32] Outraged at the Court's ruling, feminists and their allies demanded congressional action that would require pregnancy and childbirth be treated like any other physical event that befalls workers. Responding in 1978 with model legislation mandating *equal* treatment in the workplace, Congress required employers to give physically disabled pregnant workers the same benefits given to other disabled workers. The problem, however, was not yet resolved.

If employers denied disability leave to all employees as a matter of company policy, federal legislation mandating equal treatment for both sexes with respect to pregnancy disability would, in effect, penalize female employees unable to work because of pregnancy-related illness. Equality, in this instance, seemed to require *special* treatment. Law makers in California and a few other states agreed and required employers to provide pregnant workers disability coverage even if no other illnesses were covered. Employers complained that this constituted "preferential treatment" for women. Some feminists, aware of the ways in which legislation designating women as a special class of employees because of their reproductive capacity had penalized female workers in the past, questioned whether such legislation was in the best interests of women. Would it reinforce sexist stereotypes of men as "natural" breadwinners and women as "natural" childbearers and rearers, making employers reluctant to hire married women of childbearing age and further marginalizing women as workers? Wouldn't it be better strategy to concentrate on extending disability benefits to workers of both sexes? Other feminists were untroubled. Pregnancy is unique to women, they argued, and calls for "special treatment" in recognition of that uniqueness. Such legislation, they insisted, acknowledges reality at a time when growing numbers of women become pregnant within one year of their employment.

Writing for the majority in a 1987 decision upholding a controversial California law on pregnancy disability benefits, Justice Thurgood Marshall went to the heart of the equality/difference dilemma. He noted that "while federal law mandates the same treatment of pregnant and non-pregnant employees, it would be violating the spirit of the law to read it as barring preferential treatment of pregnancy." The California law, he reasoned, "promotes equal employment opportunities because it allows women as well as men to have families without losing their jobs."[33]

The difficulty of determining what is fair treatment for pregnant women dramatically illustrates the complexities involved in reconciling equality and sexual difference. Part of the difficulty has to do with the meaning of equality. Is equality to be thought of, as it has been throughout American history, as equality of opportunity? Or is equality to be defined as equality of results? In either case, do the methods used to achieve equality demand the same treatment or different treatment? The stakes in this debate are high, as the debate over pregnancy in the workplace illustrates, because childbearing impacts so directly on women's struggle for economic independence.

Childbearing is only one aspect of sexual difference that complicates efforts to achieve equality between the sexes. Closely related are other issues surrounding reproduction. In the first half of the twentieth century, access to birth control was the contested issue. Feminists argued that the right to choose if and when to bear children was the foundation on which authentic equality between men and women must rest. The debate was intense and emotionally charged because reproductive issues involve sexuality, ethical and religious values, medical technology, constitutional rights to privacy, as well as matters of economic dependence, physical vulnerability, and state power. In the second half of the twentieth century, particularly in the wake of the Supreme Court's decision in *Roe* v. *Wade* (1973), these issues were fought out over policies governing access to abortion. Issues of race, class, and gender intersected. For many white middle-class feminists, preserving abortion rights was a top priority. Advocates of birth control, they saw abortion as a measure of last resort. Without that option, women's efforts to plan their lives, to set priorities, and to make choices were severely constrained, and constrained in ways that men's were not. For poor women and women of color who had been the subject of involuntary sterilization and who lacked access to a wide range of medical services, abortion was only one among many essential needs, and not necessarily the most pressing one. For many other women, abortion was not an essential need at all. Believing that the fetus is a human being from the moment of conception and that motherhood is women's key reason for being, they denied any connection between equality and access to abortion. They rejected the feminist contention that denying women access to abortion is a way in which men use the power of the state to reinforce their own power over women. Whether the state should permit and/or fund abortions for teen-age victims of incest is the most dramatic of the issues in conflict.

Incest is only one aspect of the larger problem of sexual violence that feminists contend is the ultimate expression of male dominance. Sexual violence, they insist, is violence, not sex, and it is a public, not a private, matter. Rape crisis centers, battered women's shelters, and "Take Back the Night" marches are expressions of their insistence that government respond to male violence against women. Feminists also attack directly the notion that female victims of violence are in some measure to blame by virtue of provocative dress and behavior or prior sexual experience. In the late 1970s they convinced policymakers that sexual harassment was a form of economic discrimination and that those who maintained workplaces were legally obliged to take action to prevent it.

Feminists also exposed the link between sexual violence and pornography. Many of them argued that material that objectifies women and equates violence against them with sexual pleasure is an invasion of their civil liberties. This interpretation represents a radical reformulation of traditional civil liberties arguments and a willingness on the part of some feminists to entertain reconsideration of the boundaries of protected speech. Other feminists strenuously object. They argue that some pornography can give people pleasure and enable them to learn about their sexuality, that causes of male violence against women are multiple, and that the likely effects of real-world enforcement of restrictions on pornography would serve neither the interests of women nor the cause of free speech. They fear, for example, that laws would be so vaguely written as to ensnare sexually explicit material that all feminists would agree should not be censored.

THE ANGUISH OF FUNDAMENTAL CHANGE

Reconciling equality and difference, equity and justice, involves feminists in a task as consequential as any in human history. Relationships assumed to be the result of choice, even of love, were now exposed as hierarchical relationships involving power and control. Such exposures are always traumatic. "All the decent drapery of life is . . . rudely torn off," complained the British legislator Edmund Burke when revolutionaries in France challenged the divine right of kings two hundred years ago. "When ancient opinions and rules of life are taken away, the loss cannot possibly be estimated. From that moment we have no compass to govern us; nor can we know distinctly to what port we steer."[34]

Even those in the vanguard of change can appreciate its difficulty; old habits are hard to break even for those determined to break them. For those who are not the initiators, challenges to long-standing beliefs and behaviors, whether issued now or in the past, can be, at best, unwelcome and, at worst, profoundly threatening. Feminism is no exception. Demands for equality in terms of power, resources, and prestige are usually seen as redistributive. Giving one party its share of the pie may result in a smaller share for the others. Even individuals who believe in equality in the abstract may find themselves loath to share power and privileges in practice, especially when their own lives are affected intimately. Moreover, new governmental policies designed to provide women equal protection in the law, equity in the workplace, and parity in politics were only part of what feminists were about. Cultural values as well as social institutions were under scrutiny. Even the definition of family was being tampered with as the 1980 White House Conference on Families made clear. Family had always meant that members were related by blood, marriage, or adoption. The term was now being applied to two mothers with children or an unmarried heterosexual couple who were childless; "anybody living under the same roof that provides support for each other *regardless* of blood, marriage, or adoption" seemed to qualify. To recognize these arrangements as multiple family forms, which many feminists did, was to legitimate people who, from the viewpoint of traditionalists, were living "illegitimate lifestyles."[35]

From this perspective it is hardly surprising that gender changes that feminists saw as expanding options for women and men alike, were seen by traditionalists as rejecting cherished beliefs and practices—"neuterizing society."[36] Women who believe they have lived useful and admirable lives by the old rules often regard feminists' attacks on traditional gender roles as an attack on a way of life they have mastered—and hence an attack on them personally. They fear that "a woman who has been a good wife and homemaker for decades" will be "turned out to pasture with impunity" by "a new, militant breed of women's liberationist" prepared to sacrifice justice for equality.[37] At issue are not just economic security and personal identity of individuals but the larger social order. Convinced that biological differences between the sexes dictate "natural" roles, traditionalists see the maintenance of these roles as socially and morally necessary—a source of stability in a world of flux. Thus feminist insistence that women should be able to seek fulfillment in the public world of work and power as well as in the private world of home and family is viewed by traditionalists as an egocentric demand that places personal gratification above familial duty. "Feminists praise self-centeredness and call it liberation," observed activist Connie Marshner.[38] By the same token, the demand that women themselves be the ultimate judge of whether and when to bear children is seen by some not as a legitimate desire to ensure a good life for those children who are born but as an escape from maternal obligations that threatens the future of the family and ultimately, therefore, society itself.

To suggest that some women find feminism an essential part of their identity and that other women define themselves and their lives in terms of traditionalism is not to suggest that the ideological history of women is bipolar. It embraces many variants. Nor do we suggest that there is little on which the two groups agree. Traditionalist women may be as suspicious of male-controlled institutions as feminists. Traditionalists may also be as vocal and publicly active on behalf of their goals. Feminists may be just as dedicated to family as traditionalists. Both groups identify with "sisterhood" and see "women's issues" as special ones, although they do not consistently agree on what they are or how they should be addressed. Partisans of these issues may unite or divide along class, occupational, or political lines. But no matter where they fall on the ideological spectrum, *all* women are a part of women's history.

"Woman has always been acting and thinking . . . at the center of life," wrote Mary Beard three-quarters of a century ago;[39] but the significance of women's activities has, until recent years, often been discounted and rarely been understood. The scholarship of the past decades has spotlighted much that has lain in the shadows of history unnoticed and unappreciated. As we have examined that scholarship, we find ourselves less impressed by gender-based constraints—which were very real—than by the vigor and subtlety with which women have defined the terms of their existence. These creative experiences show how the private lives of historical persons can help us understand the rich complexities of change. To study women's history, then, is to take part in a bold enterprise that can eventually lead us to a new history, one that, by taking into account both sexes, should tell us more about each other and, therefore, our collective selves.

NOTES

1. Frantz Fanon, *The Wretched of the Earth*, trans. Constance Farrington (New York: Grove Press, 1963), p. 170.

2. Christine de Pizan, *The Book of the City of Ladies*, trans. Earl Jeffrey Richards (New York: Persea Books, 1982), pp. 6–8, 10–11.

3. Jane Austen, *Northanger Abbey and Persuasion*, ed. John Davie (London: Oxford University Press, 1971), pp. 97–99.

4. Elizabeth Cady Stanton, Susan B. Anthony and Matilda Joslyn Gage, *History of Woman Suffrage*, vol. 1. (New York: Fowler & Wells, 1881), pp. 7–8.

5. Mary R. Beard, *Woman as Force in History: A Study in Traditions and Realities* (New York: Macmillan, 1946), pp. 59–60.

6. "Placing Women in History: Definitions and Challenges," *Feminist Studies* III (1975):5–14; reprinted in Gerda Lerner, *The Majority Finds Its Past: Placing Women in History* (New York: Oxford University Press, 1979), pp. 145–59.

7. Edward T. James, Janet Wilson James, and Paul Boyer, eds. *Notable American Women, 1607–1950: A Biographical Dictionary*, 3 vols. (Cambridge, Mass.: Belknap Press of Harvard University Press, 1971); and Barbara Sicherman and Carol Hurd Green, eds., *Notable American Women: The Modern Period* (Cambridge, Mass. Belknap Press of Harvard University Press, 1980).

8. Lerner, *The Majority Finds Its Past*, pp. 49–50.

9. Alice Kessler-Harris, *Out to Work: A History of Wage-Earning Women in the United States* (New York: Oxford University Press, 1982), p. 40.

10. For detailed essays on the wave of garment workers' strikes of the early twentieth century, see Joan M. Jensen and Sue Davidson, eds., *A Needle, a Bobbin, a Strike: Women Needleworkers in America* (Philadelphia: Temple University Press, 1984), pp. 81–182.

11. Martha Minow, "The Supreme Court—1986 Term. Foreword: Justice Engendered," *Harvard Law Review* 101 (1987):13. Minow points out that "'Minority' itself is a relative term. . . . Only in relation to white Westerners are [people of color] minorities."

12. Quoted from Harriet Beecher Stowe in Jeanne Boydston, *Home and Work: Housework, Wages, and the Ideology of Labor in the Early Republic* (New York: Oxford University Press, 1991), chap. 4.

13. *Reminiscences and Letters of Caroline C. Briggs*, ed. George S. Merriam (New York: Houghton Mifflin and Co., 1897), pp. 21–23. Quoted in Boydston, *Home and Work*, chap. 4.

14. See Deborah Fink, *Open Country, Iowa: Rural Women, Tradition and Change* (Albany, N.Y.: State University of New York Press, 1986), pp. 62–65.

15. Quoted in Susan Strasser, *Never Done: A History of American Housework* (New York: Pantheon Books, 1982), pp. 268, 278.

16. Joann Vanek, "Time Spent in Housework," *Scientific American* 231 (1974):116–20.

17. *Mueller* v. *Oregon*, 208 U.S. 412.

18. Mark C. Carnes and Clyde Griffin, eds., *Meanings for Manhood: Constructions of Masculinity in Victorian America* (Chicago: University of Chicago Press, 1990), p. 203.

19. Carroll Smith-Rosenberg, "The Female World of Love and Ritual: Relations between Women in Nineteenth Century America," *Signs: Journal of Women in Culture and Society* 1 (1975):29–30.

20. On *United States* v. *Thind*, see Ian F. Haney Lopez, "White by Law," in *Critical Race Theory: The Cutting Edge*, ed. Richard Delgado (Philadelphia: Temple University Press, 1995), pp. 542–50.

21. For purposes of these calculations, predominantly female occupations were defined as those hiring 70% or more women; predominantly male occupations were defined as those hiring 30% or less women. The calculations were made by Jennifer Lettieri on the basis of materials supplied by the U.S. Department of Labor, Bureau of Labor Statistics. See especially *Employment and Earnings* (Washington, D.C., January 1989), pp. 183–88.

22. Alice Kessler-Harris, *A Woman's Wage* (Lexington, Ky.: University Press of Kentucky, 1990).

23. If, however, she committed a crime under his direction or surveillance, it was understood that he was the culprit. In most elements of criminal law, however, even married women were understood to have independent moral and ethical responsibilities; women could be charged with murder or treason.

24. New York Penal Law, Sec. # 130.00 1978. *McKinney's Consolidated Laws of New York Annotated* (Buffalo, N.Y.: W.S. Heint Co., 1987). For a basic review of the laws, see Herma Hill Kay, ed., *Sex-Based Discrimination* (St. Paul: West, 1988), pp. 239–62; and Raquel Kennedy Bergen, *Wife Rape: Understanding the Response of Survivors and Service Providers* (Thousand Oaks, Cal.: Sage Publications, 1996), p. 150. Remaining states enacted laws against marital rape in 1993 in order to qualify for funds under the Violence Against Women Act, which was finally passed in 1994. See U.S. Statutes at Large 108 (1994): 1796.

25. Clifford Geertz, *Local Knowledge: Further Essays in Interpretive Anthropology* (New York: Basic Books, 1983), p. 84.

26. Nancy F. Cott, *The Grounding of Modern Feminism* (New Haven: Yale University Press, 1987), pp. 13–16.

27. Ibid., p. 3.

28. But in a segregated South, poll taxes and other devices barred black women (as well as men) from voting; not until the civil rights revolution of the 1950s and 1960s did the suffrage slowly and irregularly become available.

29. "Now We Can Begin," in Blanche Weisen Cook, ed., *Crystal Eastman on Women and Revolution* (New York: Oxford University Press, 1978), pp. 54–55. Originally published in *The Liberator* (December 1920).

30. *Reed* v. *Reed* 404 U.S. 71 (1971).

31. Equal Pay Act of 1963; Equal Credit Opportunity Act of 1974; Title VII of the Civil Rights Act of 1964; Title IX of the Educational Amendments Act of 1974.

32. *Geduldig* v. *Aiello* 417 U.S. 484 (1974); and *General Electric* v. *Martha Gilbert* 97 S. Ct. 401 (1976).

33. *California Federal Savings and Loan Association* v. *Guerra* 479 U.S. 272 (1987). "Promoting equal employment opportunities" requires new child care policies. Giving men and women equal access to a workplace that lacks provisions for child care is not gender neutral in its results when over 50% of these women have children under six. Working mothers, whatever the ages of their children and whatever their income level, currently spend 25 hours per week on domestic work compared with only 11 hours spent by their male partners. With less time and energy available for the kind of job-related activities and training programs that would improve their economic position, many are penalized with respect to both pay and promotion. Others who accept low-paying jobs for which they are overqualified because the hours or location allow them to more easily integrate wage work and family responsibilities find themselves similarly immobilized. For women who are single parents and heads of household, the penalties are especially severe.

34. Edmund Burke, *Reflections on the Revolution in France* (London, 1910), pp. 74–75.

35. Paul Weyrich, "Debate with Michael Lerner," speech presented at the Family Forum II conference, Washington, D.C., July 28, 1982. Quoted in Rebecca Klatch, *Women of the New Right* (Philadelphia: Temple University Press, 1987), pp. 125–26.

36. Phyllis Schlafly, *The Power of the Positive Woman* (New Rochelle, N.Y.: Arlington House, 1977), p. 25.

37. Ibid., p. 81.

38. Connaught Marshner, *The New Traditional Woman* (Washington, D.C., 1982), pp. 1, 3–4, 12. See also Klatch, *Women of the New Right*, p. 129.

39. Mary R. Beard, ed., *America through Women's Eyes* (New York: Macmillan, 1933), pp. 4–5.

I

TRADITIONAL AMERICA, 1600–1820

Many American histories treat the colonial period as a time when government and order were imposed upon a wilderness. The important subjects have tended to be Indian wars, international trade, the establishment of legislatures, and rivalries between British colonies and those of other nations. The first woman mentioned is usually Pocahontas, the innocent Indian princess who allegedly saved the life of the hero of Jamestown, Captain John Smith. The second woman who appears is often Anne Hutchinson, who was banished from the Massachusetts Bay Colony for heresy. Both met premature and unpleasant deaths. Unaccustomed to the climate of England, where she had been taken to be shown to Queen Anne, Pocahontas died of pneumonia. Hutchinson was massacred by Indians during a raid on her lonely dwelling in what is now Westchester County, New York. The reader may be pardoned for concluding from these examples that the few women we remember are likely to have been troublesome and to have come to a bad end.

But suppose we ask Mary Beard's question: What did colonial America look like, seen through women's eyes? The picture changes. More constructive than troublesome, women were among the founders of every colony. Indeed, a settlement counted itself as having passed the stage of a temporary camp only after it had attracted a reasonable number of women. A sex ratio approaching 100 (that is, 100 women to every 100 men) was taken to be evidence that the settlement was here to stay. Once founded, communities were maintained in large part by women's labor. The productivity of housekeepers is not easily measured, but over sixty years ago Julia Cherry Spruill established the complexity of the tasks performed in frontier households.[1]

It may be that America seemed to European women less radical a change from the Old World than it did to men. The terrors of the ocean crossing and of the wilderness were shared by all. In the farming communities Europeans established, daily tasks proceeded in the manner of England, whether the agricultural laborer were farmer or farmer's wife. The rituals of childbirth were transmitted intact from Old World to New, although it appears that the rate of survival for mothers and infants was better in the American countryside, where the dangers of infection were far fewer than in the towns and cities of Europe. By contrast, the innovations that made the colonies most distinctive from the Old World—especially governmental institutions like town meetings and provincial legislatures—were settings from which women were barred.

For African women, in sharp contrast, America meant violence and vulnerability. Slavery and the slave trade to the Americas had been established by the Spanish and the Dutch long before Virginians bought their first African slaves in 1619. In an era in which white working people often sold their labor for a term of years, African workers seem at first to have been treated not very differently from European indentured servants. But although white women servants were not generally required to do field labor, black women were. By the mid–seventeenth century, Africans were increasingly being treated as property. In 1662 the system was solidified: A Virginia law established that the children of an enslaved woman and an English man should follow "the condition of the mother." This rule made slaves out of mixed-race children and prevented the gradual erosion of slavery.

New England was largely settled by Protestant dissenters, and in the earliest days of their formation, radical Protestant groups often welcomed women as equals to men— not only in their moral selves, but also in some of their social roles. In the earliest days of Puritan settlement, women as well as men signed covenants establishing new churches; women as well as men made public professions of faith when they joined. (By the second generation of settlement, however, women's profession of faith was likely to be made privately, or read out loud by the minister.) Peripheral churches retained participatory, even disruptive roles for women longer; among the Quakers it was established that women could prophesy, that women would speak in public, and that women would have a significant role in the institutional decisions of the community. Among Baptists and Methodists in the eighteenth century, radical evangelical faith also could translate into shared governance and public participation.

But despite repeated quotation of St. Paul's rule that "in Christ there is neither man nor woman," believers of every faith were very conscious of gender distinctions. Anne Hutchinson's heresy was compounded by the fact that it was formulated by a woman. Many of the questions in her trial were grounded in the objection that she had stepped out of her proper place. As Baptist and Methodist communities became more solidly established, more "mainstream," they narrowed the space they offered "disorderly" women.[2]

English colonists brought with them English legal practices, including the English system of domestic law. The old law of domestic relations began from the principle that at marriage the husband controlled the physical body of the wife. (There was no concept of marital rape in American statutes until the mid-1970s; at present, not all states recognize the concept.) If he controlled her body, then he could easily force her into agreement with him on every other aspect of their lives. There followed from this premise the elaborate system of coverture. The practice of coverture transferred a woman's civic identity to her husband at marriage, giving him the use and direction of her property throughout the marriage.

When the United States purchased the Louisiana Territory in 1803, it acquired vast expanses of land that had been ruled by Spanish and French law, systems not marked by coverture, in which the property husbands and wives brought to their marriage became "community property." Although husbands were "head and master" of their households and had wide discretion in their use of family property, married women

This portrait of a Carolina Algonquin woman was drawn at her home settlement in Virginia during the summer of 1585 by John White, the official artist of the English expedition to Roanoke. His drawings are rare representations of Algonquin life before extensive European contact. The woman, who looks skeptically at the viewer, is the wife of a leading male chief or counselor. Her body is decorated with gray, brown, and blue tattoos on the face, neck, arms, and legs. Women's tattoos simulated elaborate necklaces and other ornamentation; men used body paint for ceremonial purposes. (Courtesy of The British Museum. See also Paul Hulton, America 1585: The Complete Drawings of John White *[Chapel Hill: University of North Carolina Press and British Museum Publications, 1984].)*

could keep separate property in their own names and pass it on to whomever they chose as heirs. These practices were not erased when the land passed to the United States. Louisiana, Texas, New Mexico, as well as Arizona, Idaho, Nevada, California, and Washington would be community-property states, offering significant legal advantages to married women deep into the twentieth century.

The right to participate in the political system was conditioned on holding property outright. Since married women normally did not hold property outright, it seemed logical to colonists that political rights be granted only to men. (Even this logic would not have explained the practice of excluding single women and widows from political rights.) Since girls could not grow up to be legislators or ministers or lawyers, little care was taken to provide them with any but the most elementary forms of schooling. "How many female minds, rich with native genius and noble sentiment, have been lost to the world, and all their mental treasures buried in oblivion?" mourned one writer.[3]

Like it or not, women were part of the community. What they chose to do or not to do set constraints on men's options. The Revolutionary army, lacking an effective quartermaster corps, was dependent on women for nursing, cooking, and cleaning. The army, in turn, could not move as quickly as Washington would have liked because provision had to be made for the "woemin of the army." The task of the recruiting officer was eased when men could rely on their female relatives to keep family farms and mills in operation, fend off squatters, and protect family property by their heavy labor, often at grave physical risk. We have no simple calculus for measuring the extent to which women's services made it possible for men to act in certain ways during the Revolution, but it is clear that women's work provided the civilian context in which the war was carried on.

When the war was over and the political structure of the new nation was being reshaped in federal and state constitutions, legislators made many radical changes in the system of government they had inherited from England. The new republic promised to protect "life, liberty and property," but it maintained the old law that deprived a married woman of her property and her earnings, and also the liberties that property permitted. If women had had the vote in 1789, they might well have used it to claim independent property rights for themselves or to claim custody of their children in the event of divorce. Almost certainly they would have used the vote to establish pensions for widows of veterans. But women's distinctive needs continued to be discounted as trivial. It was left to women of succeeding generations to accomplish for themselves what the Revolution had not.

NOTES

1. Julia Cherry Spruill, *Women's Life and Work in the Southern Colonies* (Chapel Hill, N.C.: University of North Carolina Press, 1938).

2. Mary Maples Dunn, "Saints and Sisters: Congregational and Quaker Women in the Early Colonial Period" in Janet Wilson James, ed., *Women in American Religion* (Philadelphia: University of Pennsylvania Press, 1980), pp. 27–46. For Methodists, see Donald Mathews, *Religion in the Old South* (Chicago: University of Chicago Press, 1977), chs. 1 and 2; for Baptists, see Susan Juster, *Disorderly Women: Sexual Politics and Evangelicalism in Revolutionary New England* (Ithaca, N.Y.: Cornell University Press, 1994).

3. Clio [pseud.], "Thoughts on Female Education," *Royal American Magazine,* Jan. 1774, pp. 9–10.

ANN MARIE PLANE

Creating a Blended Household: Christian Indian Women and English Domestic Life in Colonial Massachusetts

The household has long been central to our understanding of human society. Native American communities had their own definition of home, family, economy, and political order that was often at odds with arrangements that Europeans thought were the "common sense" and ought to be universal.

The English settlers of the seventeenth century northern colonies understood households to be "little commonwealths," mirroring the gendered political and religious hierarchies of their communities. Men and women each had a distinct place within the household, although boundaries could overlap. Custom allowed women to act as their husbands' representative in legal and business matters, for example, and their labor was as crucial to the family economy as that of men. (See essay by Laurel Thatcher Ulrich, pp. 45–54.)

In this essay, Ann Marie Plane expands our understanding of the variety of household types in seventeenth-century New England by studying the practices of the region's "praying Indians." Despite their close proximity to the English colonists and their frequent adoption of some form of Christianity, these Native families resisted modeling their households after those of their neighbors. In that resistance lay a great deal of confusion for English settlers, and ultimately an opportunity for Native women to enjoy greater power within their homes than Englishwomen could attain.

Maria, a pregnant Indian servant, hurried away from her master's home in Weymouth, Massachusetts, a town just south of Boston, sometime during a Saturday in the late winter of 1678.[1] She told her mistress only that she, "woud go to the Indians wigwam." As Hannah French recalled, "I used all meanes I coud to persuade her to the contrary [but] I coud not prevent her Going: my husband being not at home."[2]

Feeling the onset of premature labor pains, Maria chose to abandon her mistress for the company of other Indians—local Indians, even though she herself was a "Spanish" Indian, not a native of New England. She left the home of her master, Stephen French, for a very different sort of house. The "Indians' wigwam" was apparently headed by a married couple—Charles and his wife—who were central to Maria's tale. Two days after Maria's hasty departure, Charles came to French's house and told Hannah French that he was "much sory yor sqwa Lost her piganiny [pickaninny: i.e., baby] yesterday a little before sunsett." He hastened to explain his delay: "And she no tell me tell [until] this morning [when] she tell my wife." When he had asked Maria why she had said nothing, the unfortunate woman responded, "Great many Indian[s] me much shamed."[3] Immediately, Charles and his

Excerpted from "In Their Families," ch. 4 of *Colonial Intimacies: Indian Marriage in Early New England* (Ithaca: Cornell University Press, 2000). Condensed and reprinted by permission of the author and Cornell University Press. Notes have been revised and renumbered.

wife looked for the infant's body but found only "something all Rotten: me thinke English women call Bagg."[4] Later that same day, Thomas Deake, an important man of mature years, found the Indian man at his door with the same news, delivered gravely, in the same broken English.

In the aftermath of [King Philip's War], the English community was primed to believe the worst of Charles and his compatriots. An Englishman named John Vining had already alarmed the neighborhood with the report that he had seen "an Indian diging hole as he thought to bury the child."[5]

. . . The gossipy John Vining visited Goodwife Sarah Pratt to tell her "that there was a child borne at the Indian wigwam and that it was throwed out to the hogges and they had eat some of it and the child Lay by the wigwam Dore." With this hideous news, Pratt "went & told goody Whitmarsh and she and I went forthwith to the wigwam," launching their own investigation. They found both "Stephen French his Indian woman & Charles['s] Squa," and closely "examined them where the Child was." But "charles squa said they could not tell for they no see no child." The three women proceeded to search the field all around. Eventually Charles's wife brought something to the English women to examine "which we did judge to be most like . . . [an] after birth."[6] Pratt and Whitmarsh reported their findings in the crucial depositions that respected goodwives commonly made before English courts investigating suspected infanticides.[7] Their testimonies offer an enduring picture of two English goodwives and one Indian "squaw" pacing through a clearing near a wigwam, searching for evidence to be presented before an English judge.

Interestingly enough, no one ever made an issue of the fact that Maria was apparently not married. Her story exposes a crucial conflict between English household ideology and native practices. For the English, marriage and household were deeply connected. Good family governance was seen as the key to good social order, and households centered on a married couple, their children, and their dependents.[8] Maria's flight bridged the distance between Stephen French's household and the Indians' wigwam, a cultural gap that had only widened during and after the war. Vining's rumors—unsubstantiated and effervescent though his charges would prove—

exposed an English fear or fantasy of Indian wigwams as places of deep disorder. What sort of people, he asked, would have a newborn child "throwed out to the hogges" and leave the child's body to lie unburied "by the wigwam Dore"? Moreover, by locating the infant's body at the doorway (the place where outside and inside met), Vining's story marked the disorder and chaos of the "Indian wigwam."[9] Even Thomas Deake, whose investigation discredited Vining's wild fancies, shared a sense of the wigwam's disorder. Deake reported that he interviewed only as many Indians as he could "understand did belong to the wigwam at that time." His vagueness suggests a loosely assembled group of individuals, perhaps pretty much anyone of native descent who had reason to stop for a while in Weymouth. Someone who, like Maria, had crossed between English and Indian worlds thus warranted careful supervision, as did the wigwam itself. Its disorder might best be contained in this instance by the vigorous "investigations" and "examinations" of English magistrates and goodwives.[10]

Pejorative views of native households reveal much about colonists' biases but relatively little about either the structures of life in native communities or the ways in which natives interpreted, transformed, or resisted English household ideologies. . . . The "household" (that peculiar bundle of rights and responsibilities, co-residence and kinship, productive and reproductive functions which the English gathered together under this rubric) affected native lives very unevenly. Because native residential groups were not necessarily founded on a marriage, their continuity over time may have had little to do with the conjugal couple. Indeed, the relative ease with which native couples could separate may have resulted in part from the fact that marriage did *not* lie at the center of these households—or, at least, did not affect the maintenance and patrimony of children, the ability to obtain food, and other important rights that marriage ensured among the English. Thus, divorce or separation may not have had the dire effects it often did for English families, whose women and children would be left without male provision.[11]

The legal codes of early Indian praying towns reveal efforts to stabilize the considerable fluidity of native household composition. They ordered that any unmarried man who was not a servant should "not live shifting up and downe to other Wigwams" but "set up a Wigwam and plant for himselfe."[12] Similarly, menstruating women, who had traditionally separated themselves from the rest of their families, now found a twenty-shilling fine set upon this "old Ceremony of the Maide walking alone and living apart so many dayes."[13] Provisions like these indicate the traditionally easy movement of adolescent men and mature women in and out of dwellings, unguided by the adult male who, in English notions of family governance, anchored the household—in theory if not always in practice. Indeed, according to Roger Williams, when a man or woman died, his or her spouse would "break up house, and live here and there a while with Friends." Williams said this was intended "to allay their excessive sorrows," but his remark that "commonly a single person hath no house" implied that no adult—even when widowed—lived alone.[14] Their impermanent wigwam structures—built to allow people to move from season to season and to rebuild their homes altogether as necessary—offered a strong contrast to the fixed, "orderly" houses of the English.

Ezra Stiles's 1761 sketch of "Phebe & Eliza Mohege's Wigwaum" offers a rare glimpse into a New England "praying Indian" household. This "wigwaum" was somewhat typical Native dwelling for the region. Note, however, the influence of English culture in the objects recorded in the bottom left corner: "A. Tea Table, B. Shelf with Plates, C&D. Chests, E&F. Pots Hanging, G. a Table, H. a Dresser, I. a Chair, where I took View, K. Mats for Beds, L. Fire, M. Door." (Ezra Stiles Papers. Courtesy of the Beinecke Rare Book and Manuscript Library, Yale University.)

Native defeat in the war of 1675–76 heightened the impact of English household ideology on southeastern New England's Indian peoples. The postwar period brought rapid changes to their economic, political, and demographic circumstances, and the English household served as a metaphor through which relations of gender, status, religion, and race could be mediated and naturalized. Although the ambitious reform programs launched by first-generation missionaries were largely abandoned in the wake of the war, a few evangelists continued this earlier work. They stressed more moderate goals, however: the principles of industry, temperance, and "family prayer." The focus of conversion thus shifted from a wholesale remaking of native culture to more limited and practical aims centered on establishing "orderly" households and communities. Although some converts tried to implement these English teachings, native households by and large remained distinctive. Indian wives and mothers were more active and visible than English women in maintaining their families, while native men often sought distant or dangerous employment that took them away from their communities. . . .

Before the war some colonists had hoped that servitude would be a quick way to teach Indians about orderly (that is, English) household life. Roger Williams thought that service might help natives by "training [them] up to labor," and John Eliot and other missionaries commonly argued that it might accustom natives to "civilized" ways.[15] One 1653 account observed that "the Godly Counsels, and Examples they [the Indians] have had in all our Christian Families, have been of great use . . . to prepare them for the Gospel."[16] In 1674, Gookin put the missionaries' goals still more forthrightly, recommending that as many Indian children as possible—"with the free consent of their parents and relations"— be placed in "sober and christian families," where the boys would be taught a trade, and the girls "good housewifery of all sorts." Gookin also insisted that they should be taught to read and write English. He thought, rather optimistically, that these aims could be easily accomplished "because servants are scarce in New England." If he foresaw a difficulty, it was with the Indian parents, "for they are generally so indulgent to their children, that they

are not easily persuaded to put them forth to the English."[17]

It is clear, in short, that the use of Indian servants was well established before the war of 1675–76. The war had a dramatic effect, however, on the experiences of Indian servants under English masters, and the subsequent surge in Indian servitude reworked local understandings of race. After 1676, as the missionaries almost entirely abandoned their dreams for the total reformation of the Indians, servitude replaced old-style evangelization as a means of assimilating individual Indians to English ways. Servitude would hasten cultural assimilation in particular, Gookin reminded the masters to whom he assigned the war orphans; he cited the orders of the Massachusetts Bay General Court that "the children bee religiously educated and taught to read the english tounge."[18] Another ostensible goal of service was the training of Indian youth to become proper husbands and wives at the end of their indenture.

Second- and third-generation missionaries (those men active from 1677 to 1730 and later) increasingly shifted their focus on full conversion to such lesser matters as temperance, industry, sexual continence, and family prayer. As the evangelist Grindall Rawson stressed in 1699, the war had "proved an unhappy occasion of obstructing and hindring the progress of the Gospel," both because it had opened a "fatal door . . . unto those corrupting and ruining Temptations" that "too much prevailed" among the Indians, and also because it had unleashed "those radicated prejudices against the Indians in general, which have occasioned many [Englishmen] to have too great an aversion for them." With all these "growing vices and abominations, which like a land flood threaten to overwhelm us," it was not surprising that progress was slow, that it was certainly "a day of small things amongst them." Still, Rawson asked hopefully, "who hath despised the day of small things?"[19]

. . . Evangelists could point to a few notable successes. Experience Mayhew especially praised one seventeenth-century native family, the Hannits of Martha's Vineyard. Japhet Hannit left a rare documentary trail that traces the impact of English household ideology on native domestic lives. Hannit was a Christian minister who preached at Gay Head, at the west end of the island. He had absorbed and implemented English ideas about household more fully than anyone else among the praying Indians.... Yet closer examination suggests that even those Christian natives who assimilated English ideology most fully nevertheless continued to carve out distinctive patterns in marriage, household, and gender roles in practice.

The child of early Christian converts, Hannit had proved a trusted informer during King Philip's War, reassuring Englishmen who were mightily nervous about an Indian uprising against their tiny island settlement.[20] By about 1690 he had begun to take a leading role in the Indian church, completing a preaching apprenticeship with his uncle, Janawanit, and with the pastor at Chilmark, John Tackanash, whom he soon succeeded.[21] Hannit's influence was not limited to Martha's Vineyard; he also served as an itinerant missionary on the mainland, receiving compensation from the New England Company (the missionary society) to preach among unchurched Narragansett, Pequot, and Mohegan groups.[22]

Complementing this exemplary work was Hannit's orderly household, ably managed by his industrious wife, Sarah, whom Mayhew described as "chaste, a keeper at home, that minded her own Business, and ... no Busybody, or Tale-bearer." The Hannits lived in a large wigwam in Christiantown, the Indian community near Tisbury. Mayhew commended Sarah Hannit's attention to housewifery. Like the best English goodwife, she worked hard to keep her husband's linens clean, and she raised her children carefully. She performed customary indigenous tasks as well, such as making beautiful mats for the inner walls of the wigwam, "neatly embroidered with the inner Barks of Walnut-Trees, artificially softened, and dyed of several Colours." Their wigwam was nicer than most, "neither was it inferior to those the chief Sachems lived in."[23] Like other Christian Indians on the island at this time, the family was probably "well habited [i.e., clothed].... [The] women especially ... [were] attired with a very Surprising Gravity and Decency."[24]

Like Sarah's equal facility with linens and bark mats, the Hannit family's blend of native with English household practices produced a distinctive new form of Indian family life. They adapted to new economic and political exigencies, at the same time keeping the best

of Indian culture. If Japhet no longer left home to hunt for food, he nevertheless still spent much of his time far away, hunting for souls. His missionary activities did bring in some cash—as when Samuel Sewall made him a present of "two Arabian pieces of Gold ... to buy Corn"[25]—but it seems that Sarah may have been left, as Indian women had been in former days, to support their children from their lands. Further, like nearly all their neighbors in Christiantown, the Hannits continued to live in a wigwam, perhaps the most visible profession of their creative blending of old with new ways.

Natives on both the island and the mainland would continue to build and live in wigwams well into the eighteenth and nineteenth centuries, although they often modified them by adding European elements such as boards, brick, stone, and glass windows.... At Mashpee [in 1807], a visitor described some eighty houses, "either wigwams or cottages." The wigwams were "about fifteen or eighteen feet square; and others, of nearly the same dimensions, are of an octagon shape." Served by a smokehole above a central firepit, these impermanent structures were "built of sedge; and [would] last about ten years." The more numerous cottages were "dirty, unfinished huts."[26] Dwellings that were neither "traditional" wigwams nor exact copies of English houses gave visual expression to the vast cultural differences that set native communities apart from those of their English neighbors.

The Hannits' ... had six children, but only their daughters—Bethiah, Hannah, and Jerusha—survived to maturity.[27] When Bethiah's husband died in a military campaign, she "went to live with her father," along with her only son, Japhet, who had already been under the "special Care and Charge" of his grandfather. Mayhew described the younger Japhet "as being also instead of an own son to him [the grandfather], and one called by his name."[28] One of Hannit's other daughters married Job Soomanan, a weaver who "provided comfortably for his Family, tho lame in one of his Legs." They had only one child, a daughter.[29] In 1712 the elder Japhet left all his "Land and Goods" to his daughters for their use after his wife's death, cautioning, "but I do really Will it to my Grand Children unto all theire generations"; however, if "Bethiah's Son die before her, then that part shall be firmly

Enjoyed by Bethiah."[30] Indeed, the younger Japhet suffered from a "consumptive illness" and died shortly after his grandfather, in 1715, when he was twenty-six years old.[31] As the will suggests, the household of Japhet Hannit did not die with him but was carried on in the female line.[32] . . .

If these had been English women, they might have expected to remarry with ease. But there is good reason to suspect that particular demographic patterns, including low fertility and high mortality, conspired to turn Indian enclaves into communities of women. Robert V. Wells notes that in Massachusetts Indian communities by 1764, there was a clear "preponderance of women, with only 76 men present for each 100 females."[33] Mayhew gives several examples of women who never married: Abigail Sekitchahkomun, who lived with her mother and her mother's sister; Assanooshque, also known as "Old Sarah," who chose not to remarry after her husband died, "saying, that if she married again, she might thereby bring such Troubles upon her self, as living a single Life she might be free from." Certainly this implies that it was economically feasible for an Indian woman who "chose to live in a State of Widowhood" to support herself.[34] . . .

Clearly, crucial changes in native households resulted from new economic and social challenges, rather than from religious and ideological prescription alone. Decades of encroachments by land-hungry English colonists had seriously disrupted the old Indian land-use patterns and, with them, the old gendered division of labor.[35] By the eighteenth century, native women and men were making their way as day laborers, itinerant peddlers of baskets and brooms, and maritime hands or in other pursuits just short of outright servitude.[36] And death was always present, always demanding that survivors step into new roles and reach out both to others among their kin and to neighbors. Given such circumstances, how did native Christians reinvent household and family (or, as modern scholars would call them, co-residence and kinship), and how did such structures affect marriages in Indian communities?

To answer these questions, one needs to look at some individual lives. Experience Mayhew's biographical sketches of "a considerable number" of the most exemplary Indian Christians on Martha's Vineyard—though intended to convince readers as close as Boston and as far away as London that the progress of the gospel on the island had been truly remarkable and was therefore deserving of financial support—give an unparalleled view of life inside Indian households on the island.

James P. Ronda has noted that Mayhew's accounts show Indian wives playing a remarkably active role within their families.[37] Perhaps they were simply taking on the sort of "deputy husbanding"—the temporary shouldering of properly masculine burdens—that made up the everyday responsibility of many a wife under New England patriarchy.[38] If so, their burdens may have been exacerbated by the limited economic opportunities available to Indians in a labor market increasingly segregated by race. Whatever the cause, women posed something of a paradox for missionaries intent on instilling patriarchy into Indian households of the late seventeenth century: In order to establish the proper relations of female dependence that undergirded the ideal household, evangelists found that they would have to rely heavily upon the efforts of women to reform their husbands.

Hannah Charles, for example, was a "believing Wife" who conquered her own drinking problem and then aggressively tried to save her husband: "She prevail'd with him to worship God in his Family," and for a time people "began to entertain good Hopes concerning him." Although all her efforts eventually came to naught, she never allowed herself to be drawn again into temptation by her husband but supported her children and raised them as Christians. Similarly, Rachel Ompany Wompanummoo worked to reform her husband, who, "tho a child of praying Parents, and one that had been well instructed, yet . . . would frequently drink to Excess, nor could he be persuaded to pray in his Family." Rachel "was much grieved, yet she would bring no railing Accusations against him" but rather did so gently "intreat him to reform" that "she did after some time so far overcome his Evil by her Goodness, that there appeared to be a sensible Reformation in him."[39] . . .

Jonathan Amos, a notable convert on Chappaquiddick Island, encouraged his daughter when she despaired because her husband, William Taphus, spent his family's resources on liquor. After the daughter made

This detail from one of two painted buffalo hides sent from New Mexico to Lucerne, Switzerland by Father Phillipe von Segesser in the 1750s shows raiding activities common in the early southwestern borderlands. The Spanish horses and weaponry used by the attackers provide evidence of the contact between Native and European cultures in the region. Note the women behind the protective palisades in the far right of the picture. These women were likely the focus of this confrontation—valuable cultural commodities to be taken hostage and exchanged between Native, mixed-heritage, and European men. (Segesser Hide 1. Photo by Blair Clark. Courtesy of the Museum of New Mexico, Neg. No. 146448.)

St. Louis to become the matriarch of an increasingly prominent family. Her New Mexican son, José Juliano, would visit her there. . . . María finally died at the home of her daughter, Hélène, in 1830, at well over ninety years of age. For María Rosa Villalpando, captivity yielded a painful, yet paradoxically successful, passage across cultures into security and longevity.[1]

. . . During the Spanish and Mexican periods (c. 1600–1847), thousands of Indian and hundreds of Spanish women and children "crossed cultures" through the workings of a captive-exchange system that knit diverse communities into vital, and violent, webs of interdependence. These captives, whether of Spanish origin, or Native Americans "ransomed" by the Spanish at *rescates* (trade fairs), . . . utilized human beings in far-reaching social and economic exchange.

. . . Prolonged, intensive interaction between New Mexican *pobladores* (village settlers) and nomadic or pastoral Indian societies required some mutually intelligible symbols through which cultural values, interests, and needs could be defined. Horses, guns, and animal hides spring immediately to mind as customary symbols of exchange, but women and children proved even more valuable (and valorized) as agents (and objects) of cultural negotiations. In New Mexico, as elsewhere in North America, the "exchange of women" through systems of captivity, adoption, and marriage seem to have provided European and Native men with mutually understood symbols of power with which to bridge cultural barriers.

. . . In New Spain, under the *Recopilación* of 1680 (a compendium of laws governing colonial/Indian relations), Spanish subjects had been encouraged to redeem indigenous captives from their captors, baptize them into the Catholic faith, and acculturate them as new "detribalized" colonial subjects. These redem-ptions occurred in roughly two forms—either through formal "ransoming" at annual trade fairs (*ferias* or *rescates*) or small-scale bartering (*cambalaches*) in local villages or at trading places on the Great Plains. Trade fairs at Taos, Pecos, and Picuris Pueblos had long fostered the exchange of bison meat for corn, beans, and squash between Plains Indians and the Río Grande Pueblos and had probably included some exchanges of people as well.[2]

These seasonal events continued after the Spanish reconquest of New Mexico in 1692–96. Throughout the eighteenth century, Spanish church and secular authorities vied to gain control of this trade, variously blaming each other or local *alcaldes* (village mayors) for "the saddest of this commerce." In 1761 Fray Pedro Serrano chided Spanish governors, who "when the fleet was in" scrambled to gather as many horses, axes, hoes, wedges, picks, bridles, and knives in order to "gorge themselves" on the "great multitude of both sexes offered for sale." Fifteen years later, Fray Anatasio Domínguez

reported that the Comanches brought to Taos for sale "pagan Indians, of both sexes, whom they capture from other nations." The going rate of exchange, which held quite steady until the mid–nineteenth century, was "two good horses and some trifles" for an "Indian girl twelve to twenty years old." Male captive boys usually brought a "she mule" or one horse and a "poor bridle . . . garnished with red rags."[3] . . .

After 1800 these formal *rescates* decline, replaced with smaller, more frequent on-the-spot bartering. This seems due to several factors—Plains Indians wishing to avoid possible exposure to Euroamerican disease, a desire on the part of New Mexican villagers to escape taxation of their Indian trade, and a geographical expansion of the borderlands economy. By the 1850s local traders like José Lucero and Powler Sandoval would purchase Mexican captives from Comanches at Plains outposts like "Quitaque" in Floyd County, Texas, giving, for example, "one mare, one rifle, one shirt, one pair of drawers, thirty small packages of powder, some bullets, and one buffalo robe" in exchange for ten-year-old Teodoro Martel of Saltillo, Mexico.[4]

Judging from extant New Mexican parochial registers, between 1700 and 1850, nearly 3,000 members of nomadic or pastoral Indian groups entered New Mexican society as *indios de rescate* (ransomed Indians), *indios genízaros* ("slaves"), *criados* (servants), or *huerfanos* (orphans), primarily through the artifice of "ransom" by colonial purchasers.[5] Usually the cost of ransom would be repaid by ten to twenty years of service to the redeemers, but in practice there were many exceptions.

Ransomed captives comprised an important component in colonial society, averaging about 10 to 15 percent of the colonial population, and especially in outlying villages, where they may have represented as much as 40 percent of the "Spanish" residents.[6] Girls and boys under the age of fifteen composed approximately two-thirds of these captives, and about two-thirds of all captives were women "of serviceable age" or prepubescent girls.[7]

This commerce in women and children proved more than a one-way traffic, however. . . . Nomadic groups like Comanches and Navajos made regular raids on the scattered *poblaciones* (settlements), at times seizing as many as fifty women and children. In 1780,

Spanish authorities estimated that the *Naciones del Norte* (Plains tribes of the northern frontier) held more than 150 Spanish citizens captive, and by 1830 the figure for the Comanches alone may have exceeded 500. Among the Navajos, as late as 1883 U.S. Indian agent Dennis M. Riordan estimated that there were "300 slaves in the hands of the tribe," many of whom were "Mexicans captured in infancy."[8] Like their Indian counterparts, these women and children found themselves most often incorporated into their host society through indigenous systems of adoption. As fictive kin, they experienced a range of treatment. . . .

. . . Shortly before the Pueblo Revolt in the summer of 1680, a band of *Apaches del Nabajo* ("Navajos") swept down upon the *rancho* of Captain Andrés Hurtado and took captive his seven-year-old daughter, Juana.[9] For the next twelve years, her life among the Navajos lies concealed, a blank in the historical record that can only be reconstructed by inference and imagination. But those years of captivity seem to hold the key to understanding much of Juana's subsequent life, a long and controversial career that ended in 1753. When she died, Juana owned her own *rancho* with three houses and managed extensive herds and flocks. Her illegitimate son, Juan Galván, served as the *teniente* (assistant magistrate) of the Zia district.[10] . . . Juana's family linked her to both Spanish and Pueblo society, and in her captivity she developed linguistic and kinship ties with the Navajos. Throughout her life, her experience as a captive woman would afford her special negotiating skills with which she pursued security for her lineage.

Juana's mother had come from the Pueblo of Zia, probably as a *criada* (domestic servant) of Captain Hurtado, but we know little more about her life.[11] No doubt sexually used by Hurtado, the daughter she bore in 1673 was just one among hundreds of such *coyotas* (children of mixed Spanish/Indian parentage) resulting from the Spanish colonization of New Mexico. The mother's connection with Zia Pueblo, however, remained central to her daughter's story. After Juana's half-brother, Martín, a soldier in the Spanish *reconquista* of 1692, ransomed Juana from captivity, the young woman petitioned for and received a private *merced* (land grant) at the northwest corner of the Zia Pueblo lands, near the village known today as San Ysidro.[12] This *rancho*

proved a key locus of trade among Navajos, Pueblos, and Spanish villagers for the next half-century and was the source of Juana's wealth and influence.

Although restored to colonial society, Juana never severed connections with her one-time captors. Frequent visits by Navajos to her *rancho* suggest that she had experienced adoption into a Navajo clan. She may even have married in captivity, as she never formalized any future conjugal relationship. Kinship aside, her trilingual skills and cultural expertise facilitated economic exchanges between potential enemies. Her affinity with Navajos remained so close that Fray Miguel de Menchero commended her usefulness in assisting proselytization efforts: "They had kept her for so long [that] the Indians of said Nation make friendly visits to her, and in this way the father of the said mission has been able to instruct some of them."[13]

Juana's conduct, however, also attracted criticism from church authorities. Throughout her life, she persisted in maintaining a long-term liaison with a married man of Zia, presumably named Galván. By 1727, this relationship had resulted in four children and charges of scandalous behavior leveled against her by Franciscan *padres*. When authorities sought to place Juana in stocks, however, the people of Zia "threatened that the whole pueblo would move to the mesa tops, rather than have her mistreated."[14] Like the Navajos, the people of Zia apparently saw tangible benefits in the presence of this kinswoman on their borders. Defining kinship more broadly than did the Spanish, they seemed willing to provoke conflict in defense of their relationship with someone who provided a bridge across three cultures. As she drew upon her qualities and talents as a negotiator, Juana "La Galvana" utilized her experience as a captive to carve out an intermediate niche in the complex power relations of colonial New Mexico.

. . . The Navajo were not the only indigenous group to take women captive. Warfare among the Jicarilla Apache often involved the seizure of captives, either for vengeance satisfaction or cultural integration. Adult male captives "were tied to posts and slain by women with lances," but captive women and children found themselves incorporated into the band. A captive woman "could not be molested until she had been brought back and a ceremony . . . performed over her," probably some form of adoption that established her subordination within Apache society. Even with this adoption, captive women "were not considered fit wives. They were sexually used, and sent from camp to camp to do the heavy work. Their children by Apache men, however, were recognized as Jicarilla" and "accepted into Apache life."[15] . . . This second-generation integration appears nearly universal among the indigenous groups in the region. . . .

No other Plains society engaged in captive raiding as vigorously as did the Comanches. This seems a result of both individual status competition and the need to replace a population ravaged by warfare and epidemic disease.[16] Comanche society offered several social spaces into which captives could be integrated, ranging from chattels to kinsmen and women. Ralph Linton suggests that the prestige value of captives reflected their "importance in the social and economic life of the tribe. Mostly Mexican, they tended the horse herds and practiced most of the specialized industries such as gun repairing and saddle-making." The honored position of center-pole cutter in the Comanche Sun Dance went either to a "virtuous Comanche woman, a virtuous captive woman, [or] a captive man who had a number of war-deeds to his credit."[17] . . .

Captive women often found themselves under the protection of Comanche women. Rosita Rodrigues, writing in 1846, reported she "remained a prisoner among the Comanche Indians about one year, during which time I was obliged to work very hard, but was not otherwise badly treated as I became the property of an old squaw who became much attached to me."[18] Similarly, Sarah Ann Horn, taken captive in 1837, reported that she was taken in "by an old widow woman . . . a merciful exception to the general character of these merciless beings." Although she was "set to work to dress buffalo hides," she did not suffer sexual abuse.[19] It appears that at least some captive women were informally adopted by older women, by which action they received the protection of the Comanche incest taboo.[20] By extension, it bears consideration that in some cases, Comanche women may have identified and acted upon interests counter to those of Comanche men, protecting captive women either for their value as "chore sisters" or through basic empathy.

Rodrigues and Horn are among the very few women who, when repatriated, wrote of their experiences among the Comanche. Most captive women seem to have remained with their captors, marrying and establishing families in the host society.[21] Rodrigues herself left a son behind among the Comanche, reporting that she "heard from him a short time ago— he is well and hearty but he is pure Indian now." Josiah Gregg noted the presence of Mexican women among the Comanche when he began traveling the Santa Fe Trail in the 1830s. He remarked with surprise that some of these "preferred remaining with [their captors], rather than encounter the horrible ordeal of ill-natured remarks on being restored to civilized life." One woman refused to return even after the offer of $1,000 for her ransom. She sent word that the Comanche "had disfigured her by tatooing; that she was married, and perhaps *enceinte* (pregnant), and she would be more unhappy returning . . . under these circumstances than remaining where she was."[22]

These women had good reason to fear rejection if they returned to Spanish society. When authorities introduced an alms-gathering plan in 1780 to raise funds for the ransom of Spanish captives, Teodoro de Croix declared with alarm that "this evil [captivity] extends especially . . . to the feminine sex . . . on account of the lascivious vice of sensuality in which they are now afforded the greatest liberty to indulge themselves."[23] This may have been a rhetorical flourish to heighten interest in the plan, but it suggests that the conjugal arrangements of Comanche women might entail certain attractions to captive Spanish women as well. . . .

In addition to the life-cycle labor of family reproduction, these women engaged in subsistence and market production. . . . With the horse and gun, one Indian man could procure fifty to sixty buffalo hides per season, twice as many as one Indian woman could tan for use or exchange. An increase in polygamy, and raiding for captive women, served to counteract this labor shortage.[24] The captivity narratives quoted earlier make it clear that captive women were "set to work to tan hides" almost immediately. . . .

Navajo and Apache women held captive in New Mexican households also worked as weavers, both of basketry and textiles. H. P. Mera has described the nineteenth-century

"Slave Blanket" as a crossover style between Navajo and New Mexican techniques, using New Mexican yarns and designs, but produced on the distinctive upright looms of Navajo women.[25] These early New Mexican *serapes* became important trade items at *rescates*, given in exchange for buffalo hides and dried pemmican. Although today in villages like Chimayo, men weave the distinctive Rio Grande blankets, this seems the result of a concerted effort early in the nineteenth century to develop a commercial textile industry.

Captive women and children played important roles in one last area, that of Spanish-Indian diplomacy. Their cross-cultural experience made them valuable as interpreters, translators, and envoys for Spanish military leaders. By 1750 the Comanche had obtained French guns, and Governor Vélez declared that unless a peace were negotiated they might prove "the ruin of this province." In order to communicate with several Comanche hostages held in Santa Fe, Vélez utilized the interpretive services of a Kiowa woman who had been captured by the Comanche, lost to the Utes in a raid, then purchased as a *criada* by Antonio Martín. This negotiation resulted in a temporary truce, sealed by the exchange of several prisoners.[26]

When the peace collapsed in 1760, captive women again served in a diplomatic capacity, this time as emissaries. Unable to find the appropriate Comanche leaders with whom to bargain, Vélez "dispatched six Comanche women prisoners as ambassadors to their nation." Within a month, four of the women had returned, along with nine Comanche captains, and another truce was affirmed by the return to the Comanche of "thirty-one women and children, among whom, fortunately, were their relatives."[27] Similarly, when Governor Juan Bautista de Anza and Ecueracapa (Leather Jacket) negotiated the Spanish-Comanche Peace of 1786, which lasted until 1846, they sealed their agreement by exchanging a Comanche boy, "José Chiquito," for Alejandro Martín, "eleven years a captive among the band of Captain Tosapoy."[28]

NEGOTIATING CAPTIVITY IN THE NEW MEXICAN BORDERLANDS

Often deemed invisible commodities in the "slave trade" of the Spanish borderlands, the captive women and children discussed here emerge as historical actors.... Their stories begin in a moment of abject powerlessness, where subordination serves as a substitute for violent death. But from that moment forward, we see them taking tentative steps toward autonomy and security. Captive women worked within the limits set by their captors, yet through the creation of kinship, their daily labors, and their diplomatic usefulness, they managed to carve out a future for themselves and their lineages....

Beginning with an indigenous tradition of captive taking, and intensified by Spanish military and economic exploitation, the captive-exchange system developed as one important component of a borderlands political economy that produced conflict *and* coexistence.... In New Mexico, Spanish and Indian men found that even more than horses, guns, or hides, their counterparts valued women and children; and they established some nominal agreement that these would serve as objects and agents of intersocietal exchange....

Despite the exploitative quality of the captive-exchange system, its victims found ways to exercise agency and achieve some measure of security and comfort for themselves and their descendants....

Although the American conquest of 1846–48 resulted in the erosion of shared values and interests between New Mexicans and southwestern Indians, vestiges of the borderlands communities of interest still survive. As Miguel Montoya, historian of the village of Mora, observes, "We were Spanish by law, but Indian by thought-world and custom."[29] ...

NOTES

1. Jack B. Tykal, "Taos to St. Louis: The Journey of María Rosa Villalpando," *New Mexico Historical Review* (April 1990):161–74.

2. See the essays in Katherine Spielmann, ed., *Farmers, Hunters, and Colonists: Interaction between the Southwest and the Southern Plains* (Tucson: University of Arizona Press, 1991).

3. "Report of the Reverend Father Provincial, Fray Pedro Serrano . . . to the Marquis de Cruillas . . . 1761," in *Historical Documents Relating to New Mexico, Nueva Vizcaya, and Approaches Thereto, to 1773*, trans. and ed. Charles Wilson Hackett (Washington, D.C.: Carnegie Institution of Washington, 1937), pp. 486–87; Fray Anatasio Domínguez, *The Missions of New Mexico, 1776*, trans. and ed. Eleanor B. Adams and Fray Angélico-Chávez (Albuquerque: University of New Mexico Press, 1956), p. 252.

4. James S. Calhoun to Commissioner Brown, 31 Mar. 1850, in *The Official Correspondence of James S. Calhoun, Indian Agent at Santa Fe*, ed. Annie Heloise Abel (Washington, D.C.: Government Printing Office, 1915), p. 181–83.

5. Because only about 75 percent of baptismal registers still exist, the actual figures are probably somewhat higher. David M. Brugge, *Navajos in the Catholic Church Records of New Mexico, 1694–1875* (Tsaile, Ariz.: Navajo Community College Press, 1985), p. 2; for breakdown by tribal derivation and date, see pp. 22–23.

6. "Analysis of the Spanish Colonial Census of 1750," Eleanor Olmsted, comp., New Mexico State Records Center, indicates a rural village population of 1,052, of whom 447 are recorded as having some Indian blood.

7. Brugge (116) estimates a sixty-to-forty female-male ratio for the Navajo captives he has studied. In 1770, Don Augustín Flores de Vargara donated "for the sermon of the day" at the Chapel of San Miguel in Santa Fe "one Indian girl of serviceable age valued at 80 pesos." See "Certified copy of the Expenditures made by Captain Don Augustín Flores de Vargara for the Chapel of Glorious San Miguel . . . ," Crawford Buel Collection, New Mexico States Records Center, Santa Fe.

8. "*Bando* of Don Phelipe De Neve, Governor and Commander-General of the Interior Provinces of New Spain, May 8, 1784," Bexar Archives, University of Texas, Austin. For the 1830s' estimate, see Jean Luis Berlandier in *The Indians of Texas in 1830*, ed. John C. Ewers (Washington, D.C.: Smithsonian Institution Press, 1969), p. 119. Also see Dennis M. Riordan to Commissioner, Aug. 14 1883, *Annual Report of the Commissioner of Indian Affairs for the Year 1883* (U.S. Department of the Interior, Washington, D.C.).

9. See Fray Angélico Chávez, *Origins of New Mexico Families* (1954; rpt., Santa Fe: Museum of New Mexico Press, 1992), p. 49–50.

10. I thank Frances Swadesh Quintana for suggesting Juana Hurtado as a case study in captivity and for sharing her notes with me.

11. *Spanish Archives of New Mexico* [hereafter SANM] 2, no. 367, reel 6, frames 1010–23.

12. The journal of Don Diego de Vargas records Martín ransoming Juana at the Zuni Pueblo of Halona, along with her fourteen-year-old daughter María Naranjo, as well as a younger daughter and a son "about three years-old." This raises some confusion as to Juana's age at her capture in 1680 and suggests that at least one and probably two of her children were born to her during her captivity. As we will see, if true, this would have given Juana and her "Navajo" children membership in a Navajo clan and may help explain her long-term good relations with Navajos in the years to come. See J. Manuel Espinosa, ed. and trans., *First Expedition of Vargas into New Mexico, 1692* (Albuquerque: University of New Mexico Press, 1940), p. 237.

13. "Declaration of Fray Miguel de Menchero, Santa Barbara, May 10, 1744," in *Historical Documents*, vol. 3, p. 404–5.

14. Abandonment of the Pueblo for defensible mesa-top positions often preceded Pueblo-Spanish conflict. See Swadesh, "They Settled . . . " See *SANM* 2, no. 345, for details of the incident.

15. Morris E. Opler, "A Summary of Jicarilla Apache Culture," *American Anthropologist*, n.s., 38 (1936):213. This information, gathered by Opler in the 1930s, may reflect an intensification of social stratification following the American conquest of the 1850s.

16. Stanley Noyes, *Los Comanches: The Horse People* (Albuquerque: University of New Mexico Press, 1993); Brooks, pp. 133–35.

17. Ernest Wallace and E. Adamson Hoebel, *The Comanche: Lords of the Southern Plains* (Norman: University of Oklahoma Press, 1952), pp. 241–42; Ralph Linton, "The Comanche Sun Dance," *American Anthropologist*, n.s., 37 (1935):420–28.

18. Rosita Rodrigues to Don Miguel Rodrigues, Jan. 13, 1846, Bexar Archives, Barker History Center, University of Texas, Austin.

19. "A Narrative of the Captivity of Mrs. Horn and Her Two Children" (St. Louis, 1839), reprinted in C. C. Rister, *Comanche Bondage* (Glendale, Calif.: Arthur H. Clarke Co., 1955), p. 157.

20. On the incest taboo, see E. Adamson Hoebel, "The Political organization and Law Ways of the Comanche Indians," *Memoirs of the American Anthropological Association*, 1940), p. 108. I am indebted to Tressa L. Berman for suggesting the association between captive women's low incidence of sexual abuse and the adoptive incest taboo. For similar examples among other Indian groups, see James Axtell, "The White Indians of Colonial America," *William and Mary Quarterly* 32 (January 1975):55–88.

21. Cynthia Ann Parker, the mother of Quanah Parker, the last Comanche war chief, is the most famous example of women who remained with their captors. See Margaret Schmidt Hacker, *Cynthia Ann Parker* (El Paso: Texas Western Press, University of Texas at El Paso, 1990). Parker lived thirty-four years among the Comanche and died "of heartbreak" shortly after her "rescue."

22. Josiah Gregg, *The Commerce of the Prairies*, ed. Milo Milton Quaife (1844; rpt., Lincoln: University of Nebraska Press, 1967), p. 208.

23. "*Expediente* of de Croix, June 6, 1780; Bonilla's Certification of June 15, 1780," Bexar Archives.

24. Alan M. Klein, "The Political Economy of Gender: A Nineteenth-Century Plains Indian Case Study," in *The Hidden Half: Studies of Plains Indian Women*, ed. Patricia Albers and Beatrice Medicine (Lanham, Md.: University Press of America, 1983), pp. 143–74; for a study of the bison economy, see Dan Flores, "Bison Ecology and Bison Diplomacy: The Southern Plains from 1800–1850," *Journal of American History* 78 (September 1991):465–85.

25. H. P. Mera, *The Slave Blanket*, General Series Bulletin No. 5 (Santa Fe: New Mexico Laboratory of Anthropology, 1938).

26. "General Campaign: Report of Governor Vélez Cachupín to Conde de Revilla Gigedo, Nov. 27, 1751," in Alfred B. Thomas, *The Plains Indians and New Mexico, 1751–1778* (Norman: University of Oklahoma Press, 1940), p. 74. "Juan José Lobato to Vélez, August 28, 1752," ibid., 114–15.

27. "Report of Governor Vélez to Marqués de Cruillas, 1762," ibid., 152–53.

28. "Abstract of Report Offered by de Anza, as Written by Pedro Garrido y Durran, Chihuahua,

December 21, 1786," in Alfred B. Thomas, *Forgotten Frontiers: A Study of the Spanish Indian Policy of Don Juan Bautista de Anza, Governor of New Mexico, 1777–1787* (Norman: University of Oklahoma Press, 1932), p. 296; Elizabeth A. John, *Storms Brewed in Other Men's Worlds* (Lincoln: University of Nebraska Press, 1975), p. 732.

29. Author's field notes, Aug. 17, 1990.

LAUREL THATCHER ULRICH
The Ways of Her Household

One of the greatest barriers to an accurate assessment of women's role in the community has been the habit of assuming that what women did was not very important. Housekeeping has long been women's work, and housework has long been regarded as trivial. Laurel Thatcher Ulrich shows, however, that housekeeping can be a complex task and that real skill and intelligence might be exercised in performing it. The services house-keepers perform, in traditional as well as contemporary America, are an important part of the economic arrangements that sustain the family and need to be taken into account when describing any community or society. Note the differences Ulrich finds between rural and urban women, and between middle-class and impoverished women.

By English tradition, a woman's environment was the family dwelling and the yard or yards surrounding it. Though the exact composition of her setting obviously depended upon the occupation and economic status of her husband, its general outlines were surprisingly similar regardless of where it was located. The difference between an urban "houselot" and a rural "homelot" was not as dramatic as one might suppose.

If we were to draw a line around the housewife's domain, it would extend from the kitchen and its appendages, the cellars, pantries, brewhouses, milkhouses, washhouses, and butteries which appear in various combinations in household inventories, to the exterior of the house, where, even in the city, a mélange of animal and vegetable life flourished among the straw, husks, clutter, and muck. Encircling the pigpen, such a line would surround the garden, the milkyard, the well, the hen-house, and perhaps the orchard itself— though husbands pruned and planted trees and eventually supervised the making of cider, good housewives strung their wash between the trees and in season harvested fruit for pies and conserves.

The line demarking the housewife's realm would not cross the fences which defined outlying fields of Indian corn or barley, nor would it stretch to fishing stages, mills, or wharves, but in berry or mushroom season it would extend into nearby woods or marsh and in spells of dearth or leisure reach to the shore. Of necessity, the boundaries of each woman's world would also extend into the houses of neighbors and into the cartways of a village or town. Housewives commanded a limited domain. But they were neither isolated nor self-sufficient. Even in farming settlements, families found it essential to bargain for needed goods and services. For prosperous and socially prominent women, interdependence took on another meaning as well. Prosperity meant charity, and in early New England charity meant personal responsibility for nearby neighbors. . . .

. . . For most historians, as for almost all antiquarians, the quintessential early American woman has been a churner of cream and a spinner of wool. Because home manufacturing has all but disappeared from modern housekeeping, many scholars have assumed that the key change in female economic life has been a shift from "production" to "consumption," a shift precipitated by the industrial revolution.[1] This is far too simple, obscuring the variety which existed even in the preindustrial world. . . .

. . . Beatrice Plummer, Hannah Grafton, and Magdalen Wear lived and died in New England in the years before 1750. One of them lived on the frontier, another on a farm, and a third in town. Because they were real women, however, and not hypothetical examples, the ways of their households were shaped by personal as well as geographic factors. A careful examination of the contents of their kitchens and chambers suggests the varied complexity as well as the underlying unity in the lives of early American women.

Let us begin with Beatrice Plummer of Newbury, Massachusetts.[2] Forgetting that death brought her neighbors into the house on January 24, 1672, we can use the probate inventory which they prepared to reconstruct the normal pattern of her work.

With a clear estate of £343, Francis Plummer had belonged to the "middling sort" who were the church members and freeholders of the Puritan settlement of Newbury. As an immigrant of 1653, he had listed himself as a "linnen weaver," but he soon became a farmer as well.[3] At his death, his loom and tackling stood in the "shop" with his pitchforks, his hoes, and his tools for smithing and carpentry. Plummer had integrated four smaller plots to form one continuous sixteen-acre farm. An additional twenty acres of salt marsh and meadow provided hay and forage for his small herd of cows and sheep. His farm provided a comfortable living for his family, which at this stage of his life included only his second wife, Beatrice, and her grandchild by a previous marriage. . . .

The house over which Beatrice presided must have looked much like surviving dwellings from seventeenth-century New England, with its "Hall" and "Parlor" on the ground floor and two "chambers" above. A space designated in the inventory only as "another Roome" held the family's collection of pots, kettles, dripping pans, trays, buckets, and earthenware. . . . The upstairs chambers were not bedrooms but storage rooms for foodstuffs and out-of-season equipment. The best bed with its bolster, pillows, blanket, and coverlet stood in the parlor; a second bed occupied one corner of the kitchen, while a cupboard, a "great chest," a table, and a backless bench called a "form" furnished the hall. More food was found in the "cellar" and in the "dairy house," a room which may have stood at the coolest end of the kitchen lean-to.[4]

The Plummer house was devoid of ornament, but its contents bespeak such comforts as conscientious yeomanry and good huswifery afforded. On this winter morning the dairy house held four and a half "flitches" or sides of bacon, a quarter of a barrel of salt pork, twenty-eight pounds of cheese, and four pounds of butter. Upstairs in a chamber were more than twenty-five bushels of "English" grain—barley, oats, wheat, and rye. (The Plummers apparently reserved their Indian corn, stored in another location, for their animals.) When made into malt by a village specialist, barley would become the basis for beer. Two bushels of malt were already stored in the house. The oats might appear in a variety of dishes, from plain breakfast porridge to "flummery," a gelatinous dish flavored with spices and dried fruit.[5] But the wheat and rye were almost certainly reserved for bread and pies. The fine hair sieves stored with the grain in the hall chamber suggest that Beatrice Plummer was particular about her baking, preferring a finer flour than came directly from the miller. A "bushell of pease & beans" found near the grain and a full barrel of cider in the cellar are the only vegetables and fruits listed in the inventory, though small quantities of pickles, preserves, or dried herbs might have escaped notice. Perhaps the Plummers added variety to their diet by trading some of their abundant supply of grain for cabbages, turnips, sugar, molasses, and spices. . . .

Since wives were involved with early-morning milking, breakfast of necessity featured prepared foods or leftovers—toasted bread, cheese, and perhaps meat and turnips kept from the day before, any of this washed down with cider or beer in winter, with milk in summer. Only on special occasions would there be pie or doughnuts. Dinner was the main meal of the day. Here a housewife with culinary aspirations and an ample larder could display her specialities. After harvest Beatrice Plummer might have served roast pork or goose with apples, in spring an eel pie flavored with parsley and winter savory, and in summer a leek soup or gooseberry cream; but for ordinary days the most common menu was boiled meat with whatever "sauce" the season provided—dried peas or beans, parsnips, turnips, onions, cabbage, or garden greens. A heavy pudding stuffed into a cloth bag could steam atop the vegetables and meat. The broth from this boiled dinner might reappear at supper as "pottage" with the addition of minced herbs and some oatmeal or barley for thickening. Supper, like breakfast, was a simple meal. Bread, cheese, and beer were as welcome at the end of a winter day as at the beginning. . . .

Preparing the simplest of these meals required both judgment and skill. . . . The most basic of the housewife's skills was building and regulating fires—a task so fundamental that it must have appeared more as habit than craft. Summer and winter, day and night, she kept a few brands smoldering, ready to stir into flame as needed. The cavernous fireplaces of early New England were but a century removed from the open fires of medieval houses, and they retained some of the characteristics of the latter. Standing inside one of these huge openings today, a person can see the sky above. Seventeenth-century housewives did stand in their fireplaces, which were conceived less as enclosed spaces for a single blaze than as accessible working surfaces upon which a number of small fires might be built. Preparing several dishes simultaneously, a cook could move from one fire to another, turning a spit, checking the state of the embers under a skillet, adjusting the height of a pot hung from the lug-pole by its adjustable trammel. The complexity of firetending, as much as anything else, encouraged the one-pot meal.[6]

The contents of her inventory suggest that Beatrice Plummer was adept not only at roasting, frying, and boiling but also at baking, the most difficult branch of cookery. Judging from the grain in the upstairs chamber, the bread which she baked was "maslin," a common type made from a mixture of wheat and other grains, usually rye. She began with the sieves stored nearby, carefully sifting out the coarser pieces of grain and bran. Soon after supper she could have mixed the "sponge," a thin dough made from warm water, yeast, and flour. Her yeast might have come from the foamy "barm" found on top of fermenting ale or beer, from a piece of dough saved from an earlier baking, or even from the crevices in an unwashed kneading trough. Like fire-building, bread-making was based upon a self-perpetuating chain, an organic sequence which if once interrupted was difficult to begin again. Warmth from the banked fire would raise the sponge by morning, when Beatrice could work in more flour, knead the finished dough, and shape the loaves, leaving them to rise again.

Even in twentieth-century kitchens with standardized yeast and thermostatically controlled temperatures, bread dough is subject to wide variations in consistency and behavior. In a drafty house with an uncertain supply of yeast, bread-making was indeed "an art, craft, and mystery." Not the least of the problem was regulating the fire so that the oven was ready at the same time as the risen loaves. Small cakes or biscuits could be baked in a skillet or directly on the hearth under an upside-down pot covered with coals. But to produce bread in any quantity required an oven. Before 1650 these were frequently constructed in dooryards, but in the last decades of the century they were built into the rear of the kitchen fireplace, as Beatrice Plummer's must have been. Since her oven would have had no flue, she would have left the door open once she kindled a fire inside, allowing the smoke to escape through the fireplace chimney. Moving about her kitchen, she would have kept an eye on this fire, occasionally raking the coals to distribute the heat evenly, testing periodically with her hand to see if the oven had reached the right temperature. When she determined that it had, she would have scraped out the coals and inserted the bread—assuming that it had risen enough by this time or had not risen too much and collapsed waiting for the oven to heat.[7]

Cooking and baking were year-round tasks. Inserted into these day-by-day routines were seasonal specialities which allowed a housewife to bridge the dearth of one period with the bounty of another. In the preservation calendar, dairying came first, beginning with the first calves of early spring. In colonial New England cows were all-purpose creatures, raised for meat as well as for milk. Even in new settlements they could survive by browsing on rough land; their meat was a hedge against famine. But only in areas with abundant meadow (and even there only in certain months) would they produce milk with sufficient butterfat for serious dairying.[8] Newbury was such a place.

We can imagine Beatrice Plummer some morning in early summer processing the milk which would appear as cheese in a January breakfast. Slowly she heated several gallons with rennet dried and saved from the autumn's slaughtering. Within an hour or two the curd had formed. She broke it, drained off the whey, then worked in a little of her own fresh butter. Packing this rich mixture into a mold, she turned it in her wooden press for an hour or more, changing and washing the cheesecloth frequently as the whey dripped out. Repacking it in dry cloth, she left it in the press for another thirty or forty hours before washing it once more with whey, drying it, and placing it in the cellar or dairy house to age. As a young girl she would have learned from her mother or a mistress the importance of thorough pressing and the virtues of cleanliness. . . .

The Plummer inventory gives little evidence of the second stage of preservation in the housewife's year, the season of gardening and gathering which followed quickly upon the dairy months. But there is ample evidence of the autumn slaughtering. Beatrice could well have killed the smaller pigs herself, holding their "hinder parts between her legs," as one observer described the process,"and taking the snout in her left hand" while she stuck the animal through the heart with a long knife. Once the bleeding stopped, she would have submerged the pig in boiling water for a few minutes, then rubbed it with rosin, stripped off the hair, and disemboweled it. Nothing was lost. She reserved the organ meats for immediate use, then cleaned the intestines for later service as sausage casing. Stuffed with meat scraps and herbs and smoked, these "links" were a treasured delicacy. The larger cuts could be roasted at once or preserved in several ways.[9] . . .

Fall was also the season for cider-making. The mildly alcoholic beverage produced by natural fermentation of apple juice was a staple of the New England diet and was practically the only method of preserving the fruit harvest. With the addition of sugar, the alcoholic content could be raised from five to about seven percent, as it usually was in taverns and for export. . . .

Prosaic beer was even more important to the Plummer diet. Although some housewives brewed a winter's supply of strong beer in October, storing it in the cellar, Beatrice seems to have been content with "small beer," a mild beverage usually brewed weekly or bi-weekly and used almost at once. Malting—the process of sprouting and drying barley to increase its sugar content—was wisely left to the village expert. Beatrice started with cracked malt or grist, processing her beer in three stages. "Mashing" required slow steeping at just below the boiling point, a sensitive and smelly process which largely determined the success of the beverage. Experienced brewers knew by taste whether the enzymes were working. If it was too hot, acetic acid developed which would sour the finished product. The next stage, "brewing," was relatively simple. Herbs and hops were boiled with the malted liquid. In the final step this liquor was cooled and mixed with yeast saved from last week's beer or bread. Within twenty-four hours—if all had gone well—the beer was bubbling actively.[10]

. . . A wife who knew how to manage the ticklish chemical processes which changed milk into cheese, meal into bread, malt into beer, and flesh into bacon was a valuable asset, though some men were too churlish to admit it. After her husband's death, Beatrice married a man who not only refused to provide her with provisions, but insisted on doing his own cooking. He took his meat "out of ye pickle" and broiled it directly on the coals, and when she offered him "a cup of my owne Sugar & Bear," he refused it. When the neighbors testified that she had been a dutiful wife, the Quarterly Court fined him for "abusive carriages and speeches." Even the unhappy marriage that thrust Beatrice Plummer into court helps to document the central position of huswifery in her life.[11] . . .

Beatrice Plummer represents one type of early American housewife. Hannah Grafton represents another.[12] Chronology, geography, and personal biography created differences between the household inventories of the two women, but there are obvious similarities as well. Like Beatrice Plummer, Hannah Grafton lived in a house with two major rooms on the ground floor and two chambers above. At various locations near the ground-floor rooms were service areas—a washhouse with its own loft or chamber, a shop, a lean-to, and two cellars. The central rooms in the Grafton house were the "parlour," with the expected featherbed, and the "kitchen," which included much of the same collection of utensils and iron pots which appeared in the Plummer house. Standing in the corner of the kitchen were a spade and a hoe, two implements useful only for chipping away ice and snow on the December day on which the inventory was taken, though apparently destined for another purpose come spring. With a garden, a cow, and three pigs, Hannah Grafton clearly had agricultural responsibilities, but these were performed in a strikingly different context than on the Plummer farm. The Grafton homelot was a single acre of land standing just a few feet from shoreline in the urban center of Salem.[13]

Joshua Grafton was a mariner like his father before him. His estate of £236 was modest, but he was still a young man and he had firm connections with the seafaring elite who were transforming the economy of Salem. When he died late in 1699, Hannah had three living children—Hannah, eight; Joshua, six; and Priscilla, who was just ten months.[14] This young family used their space quite differently than had the Plummers. The upstairs chambers which served as storage areas in the Newbury farmhouse were sleeping quarters here. In addition to the bed in the parlor and the cradle in the kitchen, there were two beds in each of the upstairs rooms. One of these, designated as "smaller," may have been used by young Joshua. It would be interesting to know whether the mother carried the two chamber pots kept in the parlor upstairs to the bedrooms at night or whether the children found their way in the dark to their parents' sides as necessity demanded. But adults were probably never far away. Because there are more bedsteads in the Grafton house than members of the immediate family, they may have shared their living quarters with unmarried relatives or servants.

Ten chairs and two stools furnished the kitchen, while no fewer than fifteen chairs, in two separate sets, crowded the parlor with its curtained bed. The presence of a punch bowl on a square table in the parlor reinforces the notion that sociability was an important value in this Salem household. Thirteen ounces of plate, a pair of gold buttons, and a silver-headed cane suggest a measure of luxury as well—all of this in stark contrast to the Plummers, who had only two chairs and a backless bench and no discernible ornamentation at all. Yet the Grafton house was only slightly more specialized than the Newbury farmhouse. It had no servants' quarters, no sharp segregation of public and private spaces, no real separation of sleeping, eating, and work. A cradle in the kitchen and a go-cart kept with the spinning wheels in the upstairs chamber show that little Priscilla was very much a part of this workaday world.

How then might the pattern of Hannah Grafton's work have differed from that of Beatrice Plummer? Certainly cooking remained central. Hannah's menus probably varied only slightly from those prepared in the Plummer kitchen, and her cooking techniques must have been identical. But one dramatic difference is apparent in the two inventories. The Grafton house contained no provisions worth listing on that December day when Isaac Foot and Samuel Willard appeared to take inventory. Hannah had brewing vessels, but no malt; sieves and a meal trough, but no grain; and a cow, but no cheese. What little milk her cow gave in winter probably went directly into the children's mugs. Perhaps she would continue to breast-feed Priscilla until spring brought a more secure supply.... Trade, rather than manufacturing or agriculture, was the dominant motif in her meal preparations.

In colonial New England most food went directly from processer or producer to consumer. Joshua may have purchased grain or flour from the mill near the shipbuilding center called Knocker's Hole, about a mile away from their house. Or Hannah may have eschewed bread-making altogether, walking or sending a servant the half-mile to Elizabeth Haskett's bakery near the North River. Fresh meat for the spits in her washhouse may have come from John Cromwell's slaughterhouse on Main Street near the Congregational meetinghouse, and soap for her washtubs from the soap-boiler farther up the street near the

Quaker meetinghouse.[15] Salem, like other colonial towns, was laid out helter-skelter, with the residences of the wealthy interspersed with the small houses of carpenters or fishermen. Because there was no center of retail trade, assembling the ingredients of a dinner involved many transactions. Sugar, wine, and spice came by sea; fresh lamb, veal, eggs, butter, gooseberries, and parsnips came by land. Merchants retailed their goods in shops or warehouses near their wharves and houses. Farmers or their wives often hawked their produce door to door.[16] . . .

In such a setting, trading for food might require as much energy and skill as manufacturing or growing it. One key to success was simply knowing where to go. Keeping abreast of the arrival of ships in the harbor or establishing personal contact with just the right farmwife from nearby Salem village required time and attention. Equally important was the ability to evaluate the variety of unstandardized goods offered. An apparently sound cheese might teem with maggots when cut.[17] Since cash was scarce, a third necessity was the establishment of credit, a problem which ultimately devolved upon husbands. But petty haggling over direct exchanges was also a feature of this barter economy.

Hannah Grafton was involved in trade on more than one level. The "shop" attached to her house was not the all-purpose storage shed and workroom it seems to have been for Francis Plummer. It was a retail store, offering door locks, nails, hammers, gimlets, and other hardware as well as English cloth, pins, needles, and thread. As a mariner, Joshua Grafton may well have sailed the ship which brought these goods to Salem. In his absence, Hannah was not only a mother and a housewife but, like many other Salem women, a shopkeeper as well.

There is another highly visible activity in the Grafton inventory which was not immediately apparent in the Plummer's—care of clothing. Presumably, Beatrice Plummer washed occasionally, but she did not have a "washhouse." Hannah did. The arrangement of this unusual room is far from clear. On December 2, 1699, it contained two spits, two "bouldishes," a gridiron, and "other things." Whether those other things included washtubs, soap, or a beating staff is impossible to determine. . . .

But on any morning in December the washhouse could . . . have been hung with the family wash. Dark woolen jackets and petticoats went from year to year without seeing a kettle of suds, but linen shifts, aprons, shirts, and handkerchiefs required washing. Laundering might not have been a weekly affair in most colonial households, but it was a well-defined if infrequent necessity even for transient seamen and laborers. One can only speculate on its frequency in a house with a child under a year. When her baby was only a few months old, Hannah may have learned to hold little Priscilla over the chamber pot at frequent intervals, but in early infancy, tightly wrapped in her cradle, the baby could easily have used five dozen "clouts" and almost as many "belly bands" from one washing to another. Even with the use of a "pilch," a thick square of flannel securely bound over the diaper, blankets and coverlets occasionally needed sudsing as well.[18]

Joshua's shirts and Hannah's own aprons and shifts would require careful ironing. Hannah's "smoothing irons" fitted into their own heaters, which she filled with coals from the fire. As the embers waned and the irons cooled, she would have made frequent trips from her table to the hearth to the fire and back to the table again. At least two of these heavy instruments were essential. A dampened apron could dry and wrinkle while a single flatiron replenished its heat.

As frequent a task as washing was sewing. Joshua's coats and breeches went to a tailor, but his shirts were probably made at home. Certainly Hannah stitched and unstitched the tucks which altered Priscilla's simple gowns and petticoats as she grew. The little dresses which the baby trailed in her go-cart had once clothed her brother. Gender identity in childhood was less important in this society than economy of effort. It was not that boys were seen as identical to girls, only that all-purpose garments could be handed from one child to another regardless of sex, and dresses were more easily altered than breeches and more adaptable to diapering and toileting. At eight years of age little Hannah had probably begun to imitate her mother's even stitches, helping with the continual mending, altering, and knitting which kept this growing family clothed.[19]

In some ways the most interesting items in the Grafton inventory are the two spinning wheels kept in the upstairs chamber. Beatrice Plummer's wheel and reel had been key components in an intricate production chain. The Plummers had twenty-five sheep in the fold and a loom in the shed. The Graftons had neither. Children—not sheep—put wheels in Hannah's house. The mechanical nature of spinning made it a perfect occupation for women whose attention was engrossed by young children. This is one reason why the ownership of wheels in both York and Essex counties had a constancy over time unrelated to the ownership of sheep or looms. In the dozen inventories taken in urban Salem about the time of Joshua Grafton's death, the six non-spinners averaged one minor child each, the six spinners had almost four. Instruction at the wheel was part of the almost ritualistic preparation mothers offered their daughters.[20] Spinning was a useful craft, easily picked up, easily put down, and even small quantities of yarn could be knitted into caps, stockings, dishcloths, and mittens.

. . . a cluster of objects in the chamber over Hannah Grafton's kitchen suggests a fanciful but by no means improbable vignette. Imagine her gathered with her two daughters in this upstairs room on a New England winter's day. Little Priscilla navigates around the end of the bedstead in her go-cart while her mother sits at one spinning wheel and her sister at the other. Young Hannah is spinning "oakum," the coarsest and least expensive part of the flax. As her mother leans over to help her wind the uneven thread on the bobbin, she catches a troublesome scent from downstairs. Have the turnips caught on the bottom of the pot? Has the maid scorched Joshua's best shirt? Or has a family servant returned from the wharf and spread his wet clothes by the fire? Hastening down the narrow stairs to the kitchen, Hannah hears the shop bell ring. Just then little Priscilla, left upstairs with her sister, begins to cry. In such pivotal but unrecorded moments much of the history of women lies hidden.

The third inventory can be more quickly described.[21] Elias Wear of York, Maine, left an estate totaling £92, of which less than £7 was in household goods—including some old pewter, a pot, two bedsteads, bedding, one chest, and a box. Wear also owned a saddle, three guns, and a river craft called a gundalow. But his wealth, such as it was, consisted of land (£40) and livestock (£36). It is not just relative poverty which distinguished Elias Wear's

inventory from that of Joshua Grafton or Francis Plummer. Every settlement in northern New England had men who owned only a pot, a bed, and a chest. Their children crowded in with them or slept on straw. These men and their sons provided some of the labor which harvested barley for farmers like Francis Plummer or stepped masts for mariners like Joshua Grafton. Their wives and their daughters carded wool or kneaded bread in other women's kitchens. No, Elias Wear was distinguished by a special sort of frontier poverty.

His father had come to northern New England in the 1640s, exploring and trading for furs as far inland in New Hampshire as Lake Winnipesaukee. By 1650 he had settled in York, a then hopeful site for establishing a patrimony. Forty years later he died in the York Massacre, an assault by French and Indians which virtually destroyed the town, bringing death or captivity to fully half of the inhabitants. Almost continuous warfare between 1689 and 1713 created prosperity for the merchant community of Portsmouth and Kittery, but it kept most of the inhabitants of outlying settlements in a state of impecunious insecurity.[22]

In 1696, established on a small homestead in the same neighborhood in which his father had been killed, Elias Wear married a young widow with the fitting name of Magdalen. When their first child was born "too soon," the couple found themselves in York County court owning a presentment for fornication. Although New England courts were still sentencing couples in similar circumstances to "nine stripes a piece upon the Naked back," most of the defendants, like the Wears, managed to pay the not inconsequential fine. The fifty-nine shillings which Elias and Magdalen pledged the court amounted to almost half of the total value of two steers. A presentment for fornication was expensive as well as inconvenient, but it did not carry a permanent onus. Within seven years of their conviction Elias was himself serving on the "Jury of Tryalls" for the county, while Magdalen had proved herself a dutiful and productive wife.[23]

Every other winter she gave birth, producing four sons—Elias, Jeremiah, John, and Joseph—in addition to the untimely Ruth. A sixth child, Mary, was just five months old when her father met his own death by Indians in August of 1707 while traveling between their Cape Neddick home and the more densely settled York village. Without the benefits of a cradle, a go-cart, a spinning wheel, or even a secure supply of grain, Magdalen raised these six children. Unfortunately, there is little in her inventory and nothing in any other record to document the specific strategies which she used, though the general circumstances of her life can be imagined.

Chopping and hauling for a local timber merchant, Elias could have filled Magdalen's porridge pot with grain shipped from the port of Salem or Boston. During the spring corn famine, an almost yearly occurrence on the Maine frontier, she might have gone herself with other wives of her settlement to dig on the clam flats, hedging against the day when relief would come by sea.[24] Like Beatrice Plummer and Hannah Grafton, she would have spent some hours cooking, washing, hoeing cabbages, bargaining with neighbors, and, in season, herding and milking a cow. But poverty, short summers, and rough land also made gathering an essential part of her work. We may imagine her cutting pine splinters for lights and "cattails" and "silkgrass" for beds. Long before her small garden began to produce, she would have searched out a wild "sallet" in the nearby woods, in summer turning to streams and barrens for other delicacies congenial to English taste—eels, salmon, berries, and plums. She would have embarked on such excursions with caution, however, remembering the wives of nearby Exeter who took their children into the woods for strawberries "without any Guard" and narrowly avoided capture.[25] . . .

. . . The Wears probably lived in a single-story cottage which may or may not have been subdivided into more than one room. A loft above provided extra space for storage or sleeping. With the addition of a lean-to, this house could have sheltered animals as well as humans, especially in harsh weather or in periods of Indian alarm. Housing a pig or a calf in the next room would have have simplified Magdalen's chores in the winter. If she managed to raise a few chickens, these too would have thrived better near the kitchen fire.[26]

Thus, penury erased the elaborate demarcation of "houses" and "yards" evident in yeoman inventories. It also blurred distinctions between the work of a husbandman and the work of his wife. At planting time and at harvest Magdalen Wear undoubtedly went into the fields to help Elias, taking her babies with

her or leaving Ruth to watch them as best she could.[27] A century later an elderly Maine woman bragged that she "had dropped corn many a day with two governors: a judge in her arms and a general on her back."[28] None of the Wear children grew up to such prominence, but all six of them survived to adulthood and four married and founded families of their own. Six children did not prevent Magdalen Wear from remarrying within two years of her husband's death. Whatever her assets—a pleasant face, a strong back, or lifetime possession of £40 in land—she was soon wed to the unmarried son of a neighboring millowner.[29]

Magdalen Wear, Hannah Grafton, and Beatrice Plummer were all "typical" New England housewives of the period 1650–1750. Magdalen's iron pot represents the housekeeping minimum which often characterized frontier life. Hannah's punch bowl and her hardware shop exemplify both the commerce and the self-conscious civilization of coastal towns. Beatrice's brewing tubs and churn epitomize home manufacturing and agrarian self-sufficiency as they existed in established villages. Each type of housekeeping could be found somewhere in northern New England in any decade of the century. Yet these three women should not be placed in rigidly separate categories. Wealth, geography, occupation, and age determined that some women in any decade would be more heavily involved in one aspect of housekeeping than another, yet all three women shared a common vocation. Each understood the rhythms of the seasons, the technology of fire-building, the persistence of the daily demands of cooking, the complexity of home production, and the dexterity demanded from the often conflicting roles of housekeeper, mother, and wife.

The thing which distinguished these women from their counterparts in modern America was not, as some historians have suggested, that their work was essential to survival. "Survival," after all, is a minimal concept. Individual men and women have never needed each other for mere survival but for far more complex reasons, and women were essential in the seventeenth century for the very same reasons they are essential today— for the perpetuation of the race. . . . Nor was it the narrowness of their choices which really set them apart. Women in industrial cities have lived monotonous and confining lives, and they may have worked even harder than early American women. The really striking differences are social.

... [T]he lives of early American housewives were distinguished less by the tasks they performed than by forms of social organization which linked economic responsibilities to family responsibilities and which tied each woman's household to the larger world of her village or town.

For centuries the industrious Bathsheba has been pictured sitting at a spinning wheel— "She layeth her hands to the spindle, and her hands hold the distaff." Perhaps it is time to suggest a new icon for women's history. Certainly spinning was an important female craft in northern New England, linked not only to housework but to mothering, but it was one enterprise among many. Spinning wheels are such intriguing and picturesque objects, so resonant with antiquity, that they tend to obscure rather than clarify the nature of female economic life, making home production the essential element in early American huswifery and the era of industrialization the period of crucial change. Challenging the symbolism of the wheel not only undermines the popular stereotype, it questions a prevailing emphasis in women's history.

An alternate symbol might be the pocket. In early America a woman's pocket was not attached to her clothing, but tied around her waist with a string or tape. (When "Lucy Locket lost her pocket, Kitty Fisher found it.") Much better than a spinning wheel, this homely object symbolizes the obscurity, the versatility, and the personal nature of the housekeeping role. A woman sat at a wheel, but she carried her pocket with her from room to room, from house to yard, from yard to street. The items which it contained would shift from day to day and from year to year, but they would of necessity be small, easily lost, yet precious. A pocket could be a mended and patched pouch of plain homespun or a rich personal ornament boldly embroidered in crewel. It reflected the status as well as the skills of its owner. Whether it contained cellar keys or a paper of pins, a packet of seeds or a baby's bib, a hank of yarn, or a Testament, it characterized the social complexity as well as the demanding diversity of women's work.

NOTES

1. [See] William H. Chafe, *Women and Equality: Changing Patterns in American Culture* (New York: Oxford University Press, 1977), p. 17; ... and Nancy F. Cott, *The Bonds of Womanhood* (New Haven and London: Yale University Press, 1977), p. 21.

2. Unless otherwise noted, the information which follows comes from the Francis Plummer will and inventory, *The Probate Records of Essex County* (hereafter *EPR*) (Salem, Mass.: Essex Institute, 1916–1920), II:319–22.

3. Joshua Coffin, *A Sketch of the History of Newbury, Newburyport, and West Newbury* (Boston, 1845; Hampton, N.H.: Peter E. Randall, 1977), p. 315.

4. Abbott Lowell Cummings, *The Framed Houses of Massachusetts Bay, 1625–1725* (Cambridge, Mass., and London: Harvard University Press, 1979), pp. 29–32.

5. Darrett B. Rutman, *Husbandmen of Plymouth* (Boston: Beacon Press, 1967), pp. 10–11. ... *Records and Files of the Quarterly Courts of Essex County, Massachusetts* (hereafter *ECR*) (Salem, Mass.: Essex Institute, 1911–1975), III:50; ... Massachusetts Historical Society (hereafter MHS) *Collections*, 5th Ser., I:97; and Jay Allen Anderson, "A Solid Sufficiency: An Ethnography of Yeoman Foodways in Stuart England" (Ph.D. diss., University of Pennsylvania, 1971), pp. 171, 203–04, 265, 267, 268.

6. Cummings, *Framed Houses*, pp. 4, 120–22; ... Jane Carson, *Colonial Virginia Cookery* (Charlottesville: University Press of Virginia, 1968), p. 104; ...

7. Carson, *Colonial Virginia Cookery*, pp. 104–06.

8. Anderson, "Solid Sufficiency," pp. 63, 65, 118; ... New Hampshire Historical Society *Collections*, V (1837), p. 225.

9. Anderson, "Solid Sufficiency," pp. 99–108, 120–32.

10. Sanborn C. Brown, *Wines and Beers of Old New England* (Hanover, N.H.: University Press of New England, 1978). ...

11. *ECR*, IV:194–95, 297–98.

12. Unless otherwise noted, the information which follows comes from the Joshua Grafton will and inventory, Manuscript Probate Records, Essex County Probate Court, Salem, Mass. (hereafter Essex Probate), vol. CCCVII, pp. 58–59.

13. "Part of Salem in 1700," pocket map in James Duncan Phillips, *Salem in the Seventeenth Century* (Boston: Houghton Mifflin, 1933), H-6.

14. Sidney Perley, *The History of Salem, Massachusetts* (Salem, 1924), I:435, 441.

15. Phillips, *Salem in the Seventeenth Century*, pp. 328, 314, 318, 317; and James Duncan Phillips, *Salem in the Eighteenth Century* (Boston: Houghton Mifflin, 1937), pp. 20–21.

16. [See] Karen Friedman, "Victualling Colonial Boston," *Agricultural History* XLVII (July 1973): 189–205, and ... Benjamin Coleman, *Some Reasons and Arguments Offered to the Good People of Boston and Adjacent Places, for the Setting Up Markets in Boston* (Boston, 1719), pp. 5–9.

17. ... *The Salem Witchcraft Papers*, ed. Paul Boyer and Stephen Nissenbaum (New York: Da Capo Press, 1977), I:117–29.

18. [See] . . . e.g., *Province and Court Records of Maine* (hereafter *MPCR*) (Portland: Maine Historical Society, 1928–1975), IV:205–06; . . . and Essex Probate, CCCXXI:96. . . .

19. Susan Burrows Swan, *Plain and Fancy: American Women and Their Needlework, 1700–1850* (New York: Holt, Rinehart and Winston, 1977), pp. 18–19, 34–38.

20. "Letter-Book of Samuel Sewall," MHS *Collections,* 6th Ser., I:19. . . .

21. Unless otherwise noted, the information which follows comes from the Elias Wear will and inventory, Manuscript Probate Records, York County Probate Court, Alfred, Me., . . . II:26.

22. Charles Clark, *The Eastern Frontier* (New York: Alfred A. Knopf, 1970), pp. 67–72.

23. *MPCR,* IV:91–92, 175, 176, 206, 263, 307, 310.

24. Maine Historical Society *Collections,* IX:58–59, 457, 566; MHS *Collections,* 6th Ser., I:126–65, 182–84, 186–89; . . .

25. Cotton Mather, *Decennium Luctuosum* (Boston, 1699), reprint Charles H. Lincoln, ed., *Narratives of the Indian Wars* (New York: Charles Scribner's Sons, 1913), pp. 266–67.

26. Richard M. Candee, "Wooden Buildings in Early Maine and New Hampshire: A Technological and Cultural History, 1600–1720" (Ph.D. diss., University of Pennsylvania, 1976), pp. 18, 42–48. . . .

27. . . . MHS *Proceedings* (1876), p. 129. Also see *ECR,* II:372–73, 22, 442; . . .

28. Sarah Orne Jewett, *The Old Town of Berwick* (Berwick, Me.: Old Berwick Historical Society, 1967), n.p., . . .

29. Sybil Noyes, Charles Thornton Libby, and Walter Goodwin Davis, *A Genealogical Dictionary of Maine and New Hampshire* (Portland, Me.: Southworth-Anthoensen Press, 1928), pp. 726, 729.

DOCUMENTS: The Law of Domestic Relations: Marriage, Divorce, Dower

Examples from Colonial Connecticut

Marriage is an intimate relationship that is result of private choice. But marriage is also a public act and has important social, political, and legal implications for women and for men. Indeed, deep into our own time, the law of marriage has shaped how men and women relate to each other and how they act in the world—when people want to change those relationships, they often begin by challenging the rules of marriage. (At the beginning of the twenty-first century, for example, the question of whether marriage should be available to same-sex couples is strongly debated.) If we want to understand the systems of gender in a culture, the rules of marriage are the place to begin.

Europeans were startled by the patterns of intimate relations among Native Americans. Although there were many differences among native cultures, marriage was generally situated within complex matrifocal systems of kinship in which husbands moved into the dwellings of the wife's kin; in which sisters and brothers remained close even in adulthood; and in which uncles and aunts could play important roles in the upbringing of nieces and nephews. In these kin networks, premarital sex, polygamy, marital separation, and divorce were not necessarily frowned upon, dissolute, and there was often a space for homosexual practice. For Europeans, different rules of intimacy were signs of weakness of civilization; pressures on Native Americans to become "civilized" regularly took the form of pressures for Christian marriage practice.

"Husband and wife are one person in law, that is, the very being or legal existence of the woman is suspended during the marriage, or at least is incorporated and consolidated into that of the husband; under whose wing, protection, and *cover,* she performs every thing; and is therefore called . . . *a feme covert.*" This understanding, known as *coverture,* was the foundation of the English law of domestic relations. When an Englishwoman married, her husband became the owner of all the movable things she possessed and of all the property or wages she might earn during their marriage. He also received the right to manage and collect the rents and profits on any real estate she owned; if they had a child, the child could not inherit the dead mother's lands until after the death of the father. (For more details of the system of coverture, see Kerber, pp. 119–27.)

French law and Spanish law both derived from Roman law, a considerably different legal tradition than the Anglo-Saxon tradition from which the English common law had developed. Roman law recognized the husband and wife to be separate persons, who could each continue to own separately the property they brought to the marriage, who were co-owners of the property they acquired during their marriage, and who passed the property down evenly to their heirs. The husband, however, was "the head and master" of the household, with broad powers over wife and children and over the use of the property during the duration of the marriage. In practice, women living under community-property rules were somewhat better situated than those who lived under

English legal systems. The concept of "community property" was unknown in the English colonies and the states that succeeded them, but when as a result of the Louisiana Purchase in 1803 the United States absorbed thousands of people who were already engaged in complex property and commercial relationships, it seemed wisest to maintain established property law. Community property continued to be the norm not only in Louisiana but in other states that developed from French or Spanish settlement—California, New Mexico, Arizona, Texas.

All colonies placed in their statutes a law regulating marriage. This step reflected a concern that marriage be celebrated publicly in order to guard against bigamy. Connecticut did not forbid interracial marriage, but many other colonies did. Laws also defined incest; note the large number of relatives prohibited from marrying in the statute from colonial Connecticut that follows. In the course of the next century the list of prohibited relatives was gradually reduced. Note that the Connecticut marriage law included a provision against cross-dressing.

AN ACT FOR REGULATING AND ORDERLY CELEBRATING OF MARRIAGES. . . . 1640,
WITH REVISIONS 1672, 1702

Forasmuch as the ordinance of marriage is honourable amongst all; so it is meet it should be orderly and decently solemnized:

Be it therefore enacted . . . That no persons shall be joined in marriage, before the purpose or intention of the parties proceeding therein, hath been sufficiently published in some public meeting or congregation on the Lord's day, or on some public fast, thanksgiving, or lecture-day, in the town, parish, or society where the parties, or either of them do ordinarily reside; or such purpose or intention be set up in fair writing, upon some post or door of their meeting-house, or near the same, in public view, there to stand so as it may be read, eight days before such marriage.

. . . And in order to prevent incestuous and unlawful marriages, be it further enacted, That no man shall marry . . . his grand-father's wife, wife's grandmother, father's sister, mother's sister, father's brother's wife, mother's brother's wife, wife's father's sister, wife's mother's sister, father's wife, wife's

mother, daughter, wife's daughter, son's wife, sister, brother's wife, son's daughter, daughter's daughter, son's son's wife, daughter's son's wife, wife's son's daughter, wife's daughter's daughter, brother's daughter, sister's daughter, brother's son's wife, sister's son's wife.

And if any man shall hereafter marry, or have carnal copulation with any woman who is within the degrees before recited in this act, every such marriage shall be . . . null and void; And all children that shall hereafter be born of such incestuous marriage or copulation, shall be forever disabled to inherit by descent, or by being generally named in any deed or will, by father or mother. . . .

And that if any man shall wear women's apparel, or if any woman shall wear men's apparel, and be thereof duly convicted; such offenders shall be corporally punished or fined at the discretion of the county court, not exceeding *seventeen* dollars . . .

Early America was a divorceless society. South Carolina boasted that it granted no divorce until 1868. Most colonies followed the British practice of treating marriage as a moral obligation for life. Occasional special dissolutions of a marriage were granted by legislatures in response to individual petitions or by courts of equity, but these were separations from bed and board, which normally did not carry with them freedom to marry again.

The Puritan settlers of Massachusetts and Connecticut were unusual in treating marriage as a civil contract, which might be broken if its terms were not carried out. Connecticut enacted the earliest divorce law in the colonies. It made divorce available after a simple petition to the superior court under certain circumstances. People who did not fit these circumstances were able to present special petitions to the legislature. Normally a divorce in Connecticut implied that the innocent party had the right to marry again.

Most petitioners for divorce in early America were women. On what grounds might Connecticut women petition for divorce?

AN ACT RELATING TO BILLS OF DIVORCE, 1667

Be it enacted . . . that no bill of divorce shall be granted to any man or woman, lawfully married, but in case of adultery, or fraudulent contract, or wilful desertion for three years with total neglect of duty; or in case of seven years absence of one party not heard of: after due enquiry is made, and the matter certified to the superior court, in which case the other party may be deemed and accounted single and unmarried. And in that case, and in all other cases afore-mentioned, a bill of divorce may be granted by the superior court to the aggrieved party; who may then lawfully marry or be married again.

Perhaps no statutes were more important to women in the first 250 years after settlement of the English colonies than the laws protecting their claims to dower. The "widow's dower" should be distinguished from the dowry a bride might bring with her into marriage. "The widow's dower" or the "widow's third" was the right of a widow to use one-third of the real estate that her husband held at the time of his death. She was also entitled to one-third of the personal property he had owned, after the debts were paid. It was an old English tradition that he might leave her more in his will, but he could not leave her less. If a man died without a will, the courts would ensure that his widow received her "thirds."

It is important to note that she only had the right to use the land and buildings. She might live on this property, rent it out, farm the land, and sell the produce. But she could not sell or bequeath it. If the real estate was simply the family home and her children were adults, she had a claim only to a *portion* of the house. (Occasionally husbands wrote that they intended the widow to have the "best" bedroom, a sign that they could not always trust their own sons to care well for their mothers.) After the widow's death the property reverted to her husband's heirs, who normally would be their children, but in the event of a childless marriage was likely to revert to his brothers or nephews.

In Lousiana law, community property was acquired during the marriage; the wife had her own separate claim to the property she brought to the marriage. "Dotal" property, or dowry, was intended to help with the expenses of the marriage; the husband could manage this property and spend its income, but at the end of the marriage it was restored to the wife or her heirs, thus keeping it in her own family line of succession. She also kept her own "paraphernalia"—personal clothing and other items—which she could trade as a merchant without her husband's consent or dispose of in her own will.

In the Connecticut statute, printed below, note the provisions protecting the widow's interests. Normally colonial courts were scrupulous about assigning the widow's portion. Observe, however, that widows could not claim dower in "movable" property, which might represent a larger share of their husband's wealth than real estate. As time passed and the American economy became more complex, it became increasingly likely that a man's property would not be held in the form of land. If the land were heavily mortgaged, the widow's prior right to her "third" became a barrier to creditors seeking to collect their portion of a husband's debts. By the early nineteenth century courts were losing their enthusiasm for protecting widows' thirds.

By the middle of the century the married women's property acts began to reformulate a definition of the terms by which married women could claim their share of the property of wife and husband. But between 1790 and 1840, when the right to dower was more and more laxly enforced and the new married women's property acts had not yet been devised, married women were in a particularly vulnerable position. See Keziah Kendall, pp. 198–200.

AN ACT CONCERNING THE DOWRY OF WIDOWS, 1672

That there may be suitable provision made for the maintenance and comfortable support of widows, after the decease of their husbands, Be it enacted . . . that every married woman, living with her husband in this state, or absent elsewhere from him with his consent, or through his mere default, or by inevitable providence; or in case of divorce where she is the innocent party, that shall not before marriage be estated by way of jointure in some houses, lands, tenements or hereditaments for term of life . . . shall immediately upon, and after the death of her husband, have right, title and interest by way of dower, in and unto one third part of the real estate of her said deceased husband, in houses and lands which he stood possessed of in his own right, at the time of his decease, to be to her during her natural life: the remainder of the estate shall be disposed of according to the will of the deceased. . . .

And for the more easy, and speedy ascertaining such rights of dower, It is further enacted, That upon the death of any man possessed of any real estate . . . which his widow . . . hath a right of dower in, if the person, or persons that by law have a right to inherit said estate, do not within sixty days next after the death of such husband, by three sufficient freeholders of the same county; to be appointed by the judge of probate . . . and sworn for that purpose, set out, and ascertain such right of dower, that then such widow may make her complaint to the judge of probate . . . which judge shall decree, and order that such woman's dowry shall be set out, and ascertained by three sufficient freeholders of the county . . . and upon approbation thereof by said judge, such dower shall remain fixed and certain. . . .

And every widow so endowed . . . shall maintain all such houses, buildings, fences, and inclosures as shall be assigned, and set out to her for her dowry; and shall leave the same in good and sufficient repair.

CAROL BERKIN
African American Women in Colonial Society

There was much in the slave experience that women and men shared. Denied any legal ability to control the conditions of their lives, both men and women labored according to their masters' demands. Both women and men were vulnerable to brutal punishment and to the separation of families; neither men nor women had any choice but to accept marginal food and clothing. Enslaved men and women were part of the productive system of the colonial economy; they were found on tobacco plantations, in rice fields, in urban households in Charleston and Savannah, and, though in fewer numbers, throughout farms and towns in the North.

But women also did reproductive work. By this we mean not only the actual bearing and nurturing of children but also the domestic work within slave quarters that fed husbands, fathers, and children and gave them the strength to persevere at the productive work of the masters' economy. As childbearing women, they were physically vulnerable in ways that men were not; indeed, slaves suffered a heavy proportion of deaths due to Sudden Infant Death Syndrome because of the malnutrition and overwork of mothers.* The law did not protect enslaved women against rape or seduction. Because the children of enslaved women followed "the condition of the mother," the legal system actually offered advantages to men of the master class who seduced or raped them. In the lives of slave women, economics and biology intersected in complex, forceful, and sorrowful ways.

Still, as Carol Berkin shows, enslaved women built strong bonds of family and community. Note the wide range of work that slave women did. Compare and contrast the work they did on plantations and in cities, North as well as South. Consider the pervasiveness of slavery throughout the colonies.

Mary came to Virginia aboard the *Margrett and John* in the spring of 1622, soon after the Powhatan Indians launched an attack on the English tidewater settlers. She entered a community still reeling from the violent death of 350 colonists killed in a single morning. That the slaughter took place on Good Friday added to the horror these colonial survivors felt, but the day carried no special meaning for Mary. She was, after all, neither English nor Christian. She was one of a handful of Africans brought against her will to this struggling Chesapeake colony.

We can say very little about Mary; her age when she arrived in Virginia, her physical appearance, her temperament, her abilities are all unknown. Yet her experiences before arriving in Virginia could not have differed greatly from those of other Africans wrenched from their homeland and carried to America. The accounts we have of the brutality of the slave traders, from both black and white witnesses,

*Michael P. Johnson, "Smothered Slave Infants: Were Slave Mothers at Fault?" *Journal of Southern History* 47 (1981): 495–509.

of the painful forced march to the Atlantic coast of Africa in which women and men were chained together, of the humiliation of branding, and of the horrors of the "middle passage" allow us to envision her distress even if we lack her personal testimony on such matters. The knowledge we have of her adjustment to America—mastering a foreign tongue, adapting to a new climate, to strange clothing and food, a new physical environment, and a culture whose customs and values were alien—make the loneliness and isolation of her situation certain even if it is undocumented. Her circumstances, then, are more vivid than her personality.

Mary was taken to Richard Bennett's large tobacco plantation on the south side of the James River. Here she witnessed the full consequences of hostile relations between the English and the Indians, for only five of the fifty-seven servants who worked Bennett's Warresquioake plantation had survived the Good Friday assault. Although her English master needed every able-bodied worker he could muster, Bennett may not have set Mary to work in the tobacco fields. His culture identified agriculture with masculinity, and in these earliest decades of Chesapeake society, some masters may have been unwilling to overturn the gendered division of labor they held to be natural. Mary surely demurred from such notions, for in most West African societies women dominated agriculture. These very different traditions produced a surprising harmony in the matter of slave importation. Faced with demands for captives, African villages preferred to surrender up their males and protect their female agriculturists; faced with a need for fieldworkers, Europeans preferred to purchase men.

What we do know of Mary's life in the colonies is that she had good fortune. Despite the scarcity of Africans of either sex in the Chesapeake, one of Warresquioake's five lucky survivors of the Good Friday attack was a black man named Antonio. Mary took him as her husband, in fact if not in English law. In a society where early deaths routinely interrupted marriages, Mary and Antonio enjoyed a forty-year relationship. Together they made the transition from bound service to freedom, although how and when is unclear, and together they raised four children, whom they baptized in the Christian faith.

Like most freed servants, Mary and her husband—known in their freedom as Mary and Anthony Johnson—migrated from Bennett's plantation, seeking arable land of their own. The Johnsons settled on the Pungoteague River, in a small farming community that included black and white families. By mid-century, they had accumulated an estate of over 250 acres on which they raised cattle and pigs. In 1653, their good luck was threatened by a fire which ravaged their plantation and brought the Johnson family close to ruin. Mary's neighbors responded with sympathy, and local authorities helped by granting the Johnsons' petition that Mary and her two daughters be exempt from local taxes for their lifetimes.

This considerate act by the courts is the first concrete evidence that race set Mary and her family apart from their English neighbors. In seventeenth-century Virginia, taxes were assessed on people rather than on possessions, and Virginia's taxable citizens were those "that worke in the grounde." Such a definition was intended to exempt the wives and daughters of Virginia planters, whose proper occupation was domestic. By the time of the Johnsons' devastating fire, however, the earlier unity of gender had been severed by race and "Negro women" were denied this exemption. And yet the racial distinction was not so rigid, the practice was not so uniform that Mary's neighbors could not embrace her as a proper woman if they chose. . . .

In the 1660s, the Johnsons, like other eastern shore colonists, pulled up stakes and moved to Maryland in search of fresh land. The Johnsons may have arranged to have someone else finance their move, for they were claimed as the headrights of two wealthy planters. They were not, however, claimed as servants. Instead, Anthony was a tenant, leasing a 300-acre farm in Somerset County, Maryland, which he named Tonies Vineyard. Anthony and Mary's now grown sons and daughters soon joined them in Maryland, establishing farms nearby. Thus when Anthony died shortly after the move, Mary Johnson was surrounded by her family.

In 1672, when Mary sat down to write her will, a new generation of Johnsons was making its mark in this farming community. But a new generation of English colonists was making their task harder. Bad signs were everywhere:

in a new colonial policy that forbade free blacks to employ white indentured servants, and in the Virginia and Maryland laws that lengthened terms for servants without indenture, a category to which almost every new African immigrant belonged. Mary's grandchildren, to whom she lovingly willed her cows and their calves, would grow to adulthood in a strikingly biracial society, for the number of African immigrants was rapidly growing. But few of these Africans would enter the world of free men and women as Mary and Anthony had done. The society that had once found room for "Mary a Negro," to become the matriarch of a comfortable family, could spare no such space for Mary's descendants. If it was accidental, it is apt that when Mary's grandson John died in 1706, the Johnson family disappeared from the historical record. . . .

In 1623 Mary Johnson was one of only twenty-three Africans in Virginia. By 1650, she was one of perhaps three hundred. . . . In the decade of Mary Johnson's death, the African population in the Chesapeake began to rise sharply, reaching 3,000 in Virginia by 1680 and continuing to grow until, by 1700, the colony had almost 6,000 black settlers. African population growth in Maryland was no less dramatic: in 1658 there were only 100 blacks in four Maryland counties, but by 1710 the number had risen to over 3,500, or almost one-quarter of the local population. Nearly 8,000 of Maryland's 43,000 colonists that year were black. Yet the mass involuntary migration of Africans had only begun. Between 1700 and 1740, 54,000 blacks reached the Chesapeake, the overwhelming majority imported directly to these colonies from Biafra and Angola rather than coming by way of the West Indies. Immigrants from the west, or "windward," coast of Africa poured into South Carolina as well. By the time of the American Revolution, over 100,000 Africans had been brought to the mainland colonies. For the overwhelming majority, their destination was the plantation fields of the upper and lower South.

The relentless demand for cheap agricultural labor spurred this great forced migration. As the English economy improved in the 1680s and 1690s, the steady supply of desperate young men and women willing to enter indentured servitude in the colonies dwindled. . . . Planters were forced to abide by customs that prevented labor after sunset, allotted five

hours' rest in the heat of the day during the summer months, and forbade work on Saturday, Sunday, and many religious holidays. On the other hand, local courts would not acknowledge or uphold any claims to such "customary rights" by African servants . . .

Slavery—as a permanent and inheritable condition—developed unevenly across the colonies and within individual colonies. In the Chesapeake, the laws that sharply distinguished black bound labor from white were accompanied by laws that limited the economic and social opportunity of free blacks. Together, these laws established race as a primary social boundary. The process began before the greatest influx of Africans to the region. The 1672 law forbidding free black planters to purchase the labor of white servants squeezed those planters out of the competitive tobacco market. This disarming of African Americans in the economic sphere was echoed in Chesapeake laws that forbade blacks to carry or possess firearms or other weapons. In 1691, Chesapeake colonial assemblies passed a series of laws regulating basic social interaction and preventing the transition from servitude, or slavery, to freedom. Marriage between a white woman and a free black man was declared a criminal offense, and the illegitimate offspring of interracial unions were forced into bound service until they were thirty years old. A master could still choose to manumit a slave, but after 1691 he was required to bear the cost of removing the freed woman or man from the colony. Such laws discouraged intimacy across racial lines and etched into social consciousness the notion that African origins were synonymous with the enslaved condition. By 1705, political and legal discrimination further degraded African immigrants and their descendants, excluding them from officeholding, making it a criminal offense to strike a white colonist under any circumstances, and denying them the right to testify in courts of law. While Mary Johnson had never enjoyed the rights of citizenship available to her husband, Anthony, eighteenth-century African-American men of the Chesapeake lost their legal and political identity as well. Thus, the history of most African Americans in the Chesapeake region, as in the lower South, is the history of women and men defined by slavery, even in their freedom.

Much of a newly arrived slave woman's

energy was devoted to learning the language of her masters, acquiring the skills of an agriculture foreign to her, and adjusting to the climate and environment of the Chesapeake. Weakened by the transatlantic voyage, often sick, disoriented, and coping with the impact of capture and enslavement to an alien culture, many women as well as men died before they could adjust to America. Until well into the eighteenth century, a woman who survived this adjustment faced the possibility of a lifetime as the solitary African on a farm, or as the solitary woman among the planter's African slaves. . . .

Under such circumstances, African women found it difficult to re-create the family and kinship relations that played as central a part in African identity as they did in Native American identity. In fact, the skewed sex ratio—roughly two to one into the early eighteenth century—and the wide scattering of the slave population, as much as the heterogeneity of African cultures and languages, often prevented any satisfactory form of stable family. Until the 1740s, those women and men who did become parents rarely belonged to the same master and could not rear their children together. The burden of these problems led many African-born women to delay childbearing until several years after their arrival in America. Most bore only three children, and of these, only two were likely to survive. With twice as many male slaves as female, delayed childbearing, and high mortality among both adults and infants, there was no natural increase among the Chesapeake slaves in the late seventeenth or early eighteenth century.

There was little any Chesapeake slave woman could do to rectify the circumstances of her personal life. While women of any race or class in colonial society lacked broad control over their person or their actions, the restraints of slavery were especially powerful. A woman deprived of physical mobility and unable to allocate the use of her time could take few effective steps to establish her own social world.

Although Mary Johnson may never have worked the fields at Warresquioake plantation, the slave women who came to the Chesapeake after 1650 were regularly assigned to field labor. Organized into mixed-sex work gangs of anywhere from two to a rare dozen laborers, slave women and men worked six days a week and often into the night. Daylight

work included planting, tending, and harvesting tobacco and corn by hand, without the use of draft animals. In the evening, male and female slaves stripped the harvested tobacco leaves from stems or shucked and shelled corn. The crops were foreign to most African-born slave women, but the collective organization of workers was not. Indeed, slaves resisted any effort to deny them this familiar, cooperative form of labor.

By the middle of the eighteenth century, slave women on the largest Chesapeake plantations would wake to a day of labor that segregated them from men. As the great planters shifted from cultivation by the hoe to the plow, and as they branched out into wheat and rye production, lumbering, milling, and fishing, they reinstituted a gendered division of labor. Male slaves were assigned to the new skilled and semi-skilled tasks. While men plowed and mastered crafts, women remained in the fields, left to hoe by hand what the plows could not reach, to weed and worm the tobacco, and to carry the harvested grain to the barns on their heads or backs. When new tasks were added to women's work repertoire, they proved to be the least desirable: building fences, grubbing swamps in the winter, cleaning seed out of winnowed grain, breaking new ground too rough for the plow, cleaning stables, and spreading manure.

If many male slaves were drawn out of the fields and into the workshops or iron mills, few black women in their prime were assigned to domestic duty in the planter's house or taught housewifery skills. Instead, throughout the eighteenth century, young girls not yet strong enough for field labor and elderly women past their productive years in the hoeing gang were assigned to cleaning, child care, and other domestic tasks in the planter's home. Thus, much of the work done by Chesapeake slave women in 1750 differed little from the work done by slave women a half century earlier.

Slave women's work may have remained constant, but other aspects of their lives did not. By 1750, some of these women had the opportunity to create stable families and to participate in a cohesive slave community. These opportunities were linked to changes in the size of plantations and in the composition of their labor forces. Throughout the eighteenth century, great plantations developed, and the number of slaves on these plantations grew, too, ending the isolation the earliest generations had experienced. Many of these slaves were native-born rather than "saltwater," and their energies were not drained by the efforts of adjustment and acculturation. As English-speakers, they shared a common language, and in Christianity, many shared a common religion as well. Both were factors in helping creole slaves begin to create a distinctive community. The gradual equalization of the sex ratio among creoles also helped, and, so did the lower mortality rate. Finally, the evolution of this slave community and slave culture in the Chesapeake was aided by a growing opportunity for slaves to live away from the intrusive eyes of their white masters. The retreat from contact was mutual: many white colonists sought relief from the alien impact of Africanisms by creating separate slave quarters. In these slave quarters blacks acquired a social as well as a physical space in which to organize everyday domestic activities, establish rituals, and develop shared values and norms. Most important, they were able to establish families through which to sustain and uphold this shared culture. . . .

Black women delivered their children in the company of other women, just as English colonists continued to do throughout most of the eighteenth century, and midwives saw the mother through these births. The differences are perhaps more telling than the similarities, however. African nursing customs, retained by many slave women, produced wider intervals between children than English weaning patterns. Slave women bore an average of nine children, giving birth every twenty-seven to twenty-nine months. The power of masters to

Although white masters seem to have hesitated to require field work of indentured white women servants, they felt no hesitancy in requiring enslaved women to work in the fields at heavy labor. In this rare eyewitness testimony, Benjamin Henry Latrobe's watercolor documents the practice in late-eighteenth-century Virginia. He gave it the ironic title "An Overseer doing his duty." (Watercolor, ink, and ink wash on paper, 1798. Papers of Benjamin Henry Latrobe. Courtesy of the Maryland Historical Society, Baltimore, Maryland.)

separate wives and husbands—through hiring-out practices or sales—led to wide gaps in many slave women's childbearing histories. Conception and birth cycles in King William Parish, Virginia, reveal other ways in which race interposed upon gender. Two-thirds of the black births in King William Parish occurred between February and July, while white women bore their children in the fall and early winter months. For black women, this meant that the most disabling months of pregnancy often fell in the midst of heavy spring planting chores. Perhaps this accounts for the greater risk of childbirth for slave mothers and the higher infant mortality rate among slave children. . . .

Thus, after 1750, a Chesapeake slave woman might be able to live out her life in the company of her family, as Mary Johnson had done. Yet she knew that powerful obstacles stood in her way. Husbands often lived on other plantations. Children between the ages of ten and fourteen, especially sons, were commonly sold. Sisters and brothers were moved to different slave quarters. And on a master's death, slaves were often dispensed along with other property to his heirs. A master who might never separate a family during his lifetime thought it his obligation to his survivors to divide them at his death. Hard times could prompt a master to sell a slave woman's family members in order to provide for his own. A planter's widow might keep her family intact by hiring out her slave's sons or daughters. Even the wedding celebration of a planter's daughter might mean the tragic separation of a slave woman and her own young daughter, sent to serve in the bride's new home. In the 1770s, the westward expansion of agriculture into the Piedmont and beyond led to mass dispersal of slave families among the new farms and plantations. Slave women, and their men, could succeed in creating effective family structures despite the many demands of slavery, but they could not ensure their permanence. . . .

The planters of the Lower South also relied on an African slave-labor force. Indeed, the slave-based agriculture of this region developed with remarkable speed in the early eighteenth century. . . . Despite clear laws against slaveholding, the Georgia settlers were, as one observer put it, "stark Mad after Negroes." Illegal sale of slaves took place right under the nose of colonial authorities, eventually forcing the ban to be lifted. Between 1751 and 1770, the slave population of Georgia rose from 349 to 16,000; these slaves were imported directly from Africa or purchased from traders in South Carolina.

In the region's showplace city, Charleston, a largely creole population of African Americans swelled to over half the population, filling positions as house servants, boatmen, dockworkers, and artisans of all kinds. The highly acculturated Charleston slave women shared little in common with their rural sisters, for the slaves who worked the large rice plantations had almost no contact with white society. The plantation slave society that developed was the product of an isolation more pronounced than in the Chesapeake. And because of the steady importation of Africans throughout the eighteenth century, this community differed significantly from the creole-dominated world of the Chesapeake slaves. West African traditions shaped the rice and indigo culture in fundamental ways. Plantation slaves spoke Gullah, a language which combined English and several West African dialects, and they preserved the African custom of naming children for the day of the week on which they were born. Chesapeake girls and boys came to recognize themselves in the diminutives of English names—Lizzie, Betty, or Billy—but among slave children in the Lower South names like Quaco, Juba, and Cuba linked them to their African past.

Like Chesapeake slave women, Lower South women worked the fields. But as rice growers, the women of Carolina and Georgia labored under a task system rather than in gangs. This system assigned specific tasks to each slave but did not regulate the time in which it was to be completed. Thus, slaves on the rice plantations controlled the pace of their workday. The task system did provide a measure of autonomy, but no slave who worked the rice plantations would call their occupation an enviable one. "The labor required for the cultivation [of rice] is fit only for slaves," wrote one frank observer, "and I think the hardest work I have seen them engaged in." The most grueling of all the tasks was the pounding of grain with mortar and pestle—and this was a woman's job. It was also the deadliest; mortality rates were higher in the Lower South than in the Chesapeake, and the women who beat the rice were more likely to die than the men who spent hours stooping in the stagnant rice-paddy waters.

By the middle-of the eighteenth century, each slave was responsible for a quarter of an acre. Other activities on the plantation—pounding the rice, making fences, and later, in tidal rice cultivation, digging critical irrigation systems—were tasked as well. . . . The task system was not designed-to-accommodate the women and men who worked in the rice fields or paddies, of course. Its logic lay in the fact that effective rice cultivation did not require the constant supervision of workers. Yet the task system allowed slaves to develop a lively domestic or internal economy. South Carolina and Georgia slaves were given land on which to grow a variety of crops, including corn, potatoes, tobacco, peanuts, melons, and pumpkins, all of which they marketed. This agriculture within an agriculture quickly became entrenched, despite efforts by lawmakers to curtail it. By 1751 Lower South authorities were fighting a staying action, insisting that slaves could sell their rice, corn, or garden crops only to their own masters. These restrictions were ignored. Slave women and men continued to sell everything from corn to catfish, baskets, canoes, and poultry products. But here, unlike in the Piedmont, slave agriculture reflected the community's active African tradition, for Low Country slaves grew tania, bene, peppers, and other African crops. When local slave crops reached Charleston, slave women took charge of their marketing. These female traders were known for their shrewdness in bargaining with customers of both races, to whom they hawked poultry, eggs, and fruit at sometimes shocking prices. Slave women willingly paid their masters a fee for the privilege of selling the pies, cakes, handicrafts, or dry goods they made or brokered, for any profits after the fee was met belonged to them. These women drew on a West African tradition of female traders not unlike the female market-town traders of England. . . .

Slavery in the North was an accepted tradition but not a widespread habit. The Dutch had employed slave labor extensively when New York was New Netherlands, using African labor to compensate for the scarcity of colonists from Holland. The small farmers of New England, on the other hand, had little practical use for slave labor, and where slaves were employed it was often because of their master's close tie to the transatlantic slave trade. For example, the merchant-landowners of Rhode Island who made their riches in trade liked to flaunt their prosperity by retaining anywhere from five to forty slaves. One merchant magnate boasted a holding of 238 slaves. But the majority of New England slaves, like the slaves of the middle colonies, were found in the cities, where shortages of white labor in artisan shops, on the docks, and in household or personal service were a periodic problem. The greatest influx of African slaves to Pennsylvania, for example, came during the Seven Years War, when the flow of English and other European servants was seriously disrupted. By mid-century, roughly 10 percent of the population of Boston, Philadelphia, and New York was black, although only one out of every five families owned a slave.

A slave woman in these Northern cities spent her days engaged in housework—cooking, cleaning, washing and ironing, tending the fires and the gardens, and looking after her master's children. She passed her nights sleeping in the garret or the kitchen. She might be hired out to nurse the sick, to put in a neighbor's garden, to preserve food or wait on tables for a special occasion, but few urban slave women were ever hired out to learn a craft. Colonial artisans considered their shops a male domain. Ironically, the "black mammy" so often associated with plantation life was not an authentic figure of the colonial South, but she could be found in the fashionable homes of Philadelphia and New York. Slaves in the countryside also did housework, but more of their time was spent tending larger gardens, raising poultry, milking cows, and spinning cloth than in cooking, cleaning, or serving as personal maids to farm family members. At harvest time, these women were assigned to fieldwork.

As they worked in the wheat fields of southern Pennsylvania or in the kitchens of Boston, Northern slave women experienced constant, intimate contact with white society. Whether their owners were kind or callous, their values and customs were ever present, and a solitary black servant, working, eating, sleeping in a crowded Pennsylvania farmhouse, or in the close quarters of a merchant's home, lacked the steady reinforcement of her African heritage. Not surprisingly, Northern slave women were more likely to acculturate than their sisters in the plantation South.

Urban slave women had little hope of creating a family that could remain intact. Slaveholdings were too small for a woman to choose a husband from the household, and few urban colonists were willing to shoulder the costs of raising a slave child in their midst. Rural slaveholders could set a slave's child to work in the garden or field, but in the cities youngsters were simply a drain on resources and living space. At least one master preferred to sell his pregnant slave rather than suffer having her child underfoot. Other masters solved the problem of an extra mouth to feed by selling infants—or, in one case, giving his slave's baby away. Slave women who dared to start or add to their families were sometimes separated from the men who fathered their children. In Boston, a pregnant woman and her husband chose to commit suicide rather than endure the dissolution of their family. Urban slave women who were allowed to keep their children often lost them quickly. Communicable diseases and cramped quarters combined in deadly fashion in every household in eighteenth-century colonial cities, but black infant mortality rates were two to three times higher than white.

A slave woman's life—like a slave man's—could be enriched by a family, an independent culture and community, and the autonomous spaces created by the task system or wrested from the gang-labor system of the Chesapeake. In a sense, these were all forms of resistance to enslavement. But there were other forms of resistance as well—rebellion, suicide, murder, escape, self-mutilation, disobedience, the destruction of tools and equipment, arson, theft of supplies, feigned illness, feigned pregnancy, and feigned ignorance or stupidity. Colonial English society rarely assumed that slaves were docile or content, and slaveholders preferred to rely on repressive laws, a show of force, and harsh reprisals rather than a belief in the passivity or contentedness of their slaves . . .

The work demanded of Northern slave women was less grueling than the work done with mortar and pestle in the Carolinas or with hoes and hands in the Chesapeake tobacco fields. Indeed, slavery in the North was generally less brutal than in the Southern colonies. Yet enslaved women in the middle colonies and New England also resisted, ran away, and rebelled. Here, too, women fled their master's home, determined to reunite with their husband or children. And here, too, women participated in the rare but violent uprisings of slaves seeking to overthrow their oppressors. When authorities moved against participants in the 1712 Slave Revolt in New York City, several women were among those arrested and convicted. And when a slave presented the first petition for freedom to the newly formed state legislature of Massachusetts in 1782, she was a woman. The woman, Belinda, pressed these Revolutionaries to make good on their state constitution's pledge to discontinue slavery, stating her case with eloquence: "I have not yet enjoyed the benefits of creation . . . I beg freedom."

DOCUMENTS: The Law of Slavery

> *"According to the condition of the mother . . . "*

The system of slavery relied heavily on marking differences of status (slave or free)—by visible bodily difference (black or white). Free blacks and enslaved mulattoes undermined the simplicity of these signals, displaying in their very beings the fact that it was power, not nature, that placed any particular individual in one status or another.

How to interpret the status of children whose fathers were white and whose mothers were black? Might they make a claim for free status or support from their free parent? Could white fathers be obliged to take responsibility for such children? In Spanish colonies in South America, a complex system of godparenting made it possible for white fathers to maintain a wide variety of relationships with their mixed-blood children.

The Virginia Law of 1662 established a different set of rules for the English colony; Maryland passed a similar statute two years later. How does the 1662 law challenge traditional English inheritance practices? What do the two sections of the law reveal about how Virginia legislators wished to shape interracial sexual relations? What are the implications of the law for children whose fathers were free black men and whose mothers were enslaved?

Whereas some doubts have arrisen whether children got by any Englishman upon a negro woman should be slave or free, *Be it therefore enacted and declared by this present grand assembly,* that all children borne in this country shalbe held bond or free only according to the condition of the mother, *And* that if any christian shall committ fornication with a negro man or woman hee or shee soe offending shall pay double the [usual] fines. . . . *

*The usual fine for fornication was 500 pounds of tobacco.

Assembly of Virginia, Act XVI, December 1691, in William Waller Hening, *The Statutes at Large: Being a Collection of All the Laws of Virginia, from the First Session of the Legislature, in the Year 1619,* 13 vols. (New York: R & W & G Bartow, 1823), 2:170.

"For prevention of that abominable mixture . . ."

By the late seventeenth century, Virginia and Maryland attempted to punish interracial sexual relations, even among free men and women. What relationships does the Virginia law of 1691 make illegal? What does it prescribe for interracial children? Why did the legislators think the law would be self-enforcing? A restatement of the statute in 1705 also punished ministers for officiating at interracial marriages.

[1691] . . . for prevention of that abominable mixture and spurious issue which hereafter may encrease in this dominion, as well by negroes, mulattoes, and Indians intermarrying with English, or other white women, as by their unlawful accompanying with one another, *Be it enacted* . . . that . . . whatsoever English or other white man or woman being free shall intermarry with a negroe, mulatto or Indian man or woman bond or free shall within three months after such marriage be banished and removed from this dominion forever. . . .

And be it further enacted . . . That if any English woman being free shall have a bastard child by any negro or mulatto, she pay the sume of fifteen pounds sterling, within one moneth after such bastard child shall be born, to the Church wardens of the parish . . . and in default of such payment she shall be taken into the possession of the said Church wardens and disposed of for five yeares, and the said fine of fifteen pounds, or whatever the woman shall be disposed of for, shall be paid, one third

part to their majesties . . . and one other third part to the use of the parish . . . and the other third part to the informer, and that such bastard child be bound out as a servant by the said Church wardens untill he or she shall attaine the age of thirty yeares, and in case such English woman that shall have such bastard child be a servant, she shall be sold by the said church wardens, (after her time is expired that she ought by law to serve her master) for five yeares, and the money she shall be sold for divided as is before appointed, and the child to serve as aforesaid.

[1705] *And be it further enacted,* That no minister of the church of England, or other minister, or person whatsoever, within this colony and dominion, shall hereafter wittingly presume to marry a white man with a negro or mulatto woman; or to marry a white woman with a negro or mulatto man, upon pain of forfeiting or paying, for every such marriage the sum of ten thousand pounds of tobacco; one half to our sovereign lady the Queen . . . and the other half to the informer. . . .

Assembly of Virginia, Act XVI, April 1691, in William Waller Hening, *The Statutes at Large: Being a Collection of All the Laws of Virginia, from the First Session of the Legislature, in the Year 1619,* 13 vols. (New York: R & W & G Bartow, 1823), vol. 3, pp. 86–87; and Assembly of Virginia, Chap. XLIX, Sec. XX, October 1705 in Hening, vol. 3, p. 453.

MARY BETH NORTON
"Searchers again Assembled": Gender Distinctions in Seventeenth-Century America

The story that Mary Beth Norton tells is one that demonstrates that gender is a a social as well as a biological construction. It is very rare that newborn is hermaphrodite, or intersexed, displaying "some combination of 'female' and 'male' reproductive and sexual features." Later in life, hormonal abnormalities may mask clear distinctions between male and female. In our own time, "sexual reassignment" surgery is generally performed while an intersexed child is an infant; for adults, hormonal treatments, sometimes accompanied by surgery, can be used to clarify the gender identity of an individual.*

In one seventeenth-century Virginia community, the presence of a person who dressed as man and also as a woman, who behaved alternately like a woman and like a man, and whose physical formation was vulnerable to multiple interpretations was deeply disconcerting. How did T. Hall's neighbors respond to gossip that this person's sex was unclear? What authority did women claim in assessing the situation? What authority did men claim? What does the struggle to mark T. Hall's gender identity suggest about the structure of community life and the roles of men and women?

On April 8, 1629, a person named Hall was brought before the General Court of the colony of Virginia. Hall was not formally charged with a crime, although witnesses alluded to a rumor about fornication. Yet Hall's case is one of the most remarkable to be found in the court records of any colony. If no crime was involved, why was Hall in court?

Hall had been reported to the authorities for one simple reason: people were confused about Hall's sexual identity. At times Hall dressed as a man; at other times, evidently, as a woman. What sex was this person? other colonists wanted to know. The vigor with which they pursued their concerns dramatically underscores the significance of gender distinctions in seventeenth-century Anglo-America. The case also provides excellent illustrations of the powerful role the community could play in individuals' lives and of the potential influence of ordinary folk, both men and women, on the official actions of colonial governments.

The Hall case offers compelling insights into the process of defining gender in early American society. Hall was an anomalous individual, and focusing on such anomalies can help to expose fundamental belief systems. Since in this case sex was difficult to determine, so too was gender identity. Persons of indeterminate sex, such as the subject of this discussion, pose perplexing questions for any society. The process through which the culture categorizes these people is both complex and revealing. The analysis here will examine the ways in which seventeenth-century Virginians

---

*Suzanne Kessler, "The Medical Construction of Gender: Case Management of Intersexed Infants." *Signs: Journal of Women in Culture and Society* XVI (1990): 3–26.

attempted to come to grips with the problems presented to them by a sexually ambiguous person.[1] ...

Describing my usage of personal pronouns and names is essential to the analysis that follows. The other historians who have dealt with the case have referred to Hall as "Thomas" and "he," as do the court records (with one significant exception). Yet the details of the case, including Hall's testimony, make such usage problematic. Therefore the practice here shall be the following: when Hall is acting as a female, the name "Thomasine" and the pronoun "she" will be used. Conversely, when Hall is acting as a male, "Thomas" and "he" are just as obviously called for. In moments of ambiguity or generalization (as now) "Hall," or the simple initial "T" will be employed (the latter as an ungendered pronoun).

Thomasine Hall was born "at or neere" the northeastern English city of Newcastle upon Tyne.[2] As the name suggests, Hall was christened and raised as a girl. At the age of twelve, Thomasine went to London to stay with her aunt, and she lived there for ten years. But in 1625 her brother was pressed into the army to serve in an expedition against Cadiz. Perhaps encouraged by her brother's experience (or perhaps taking his place after his death, for that expedition incurred many casualties), Hall subsequently adopted a new gender identity. Thomas told the court that he "Cut of[f] his heire and Changed his apparell into the fashion of man and went over as a souldier in the Isle of Ree being in the habit of a man."[3] Upon returning to Plymouth from army service in France, probably in the autumn of 1627, Hall resumed a feminine identity. Thomasine donned women's clothing and supported herself briefly by making "bone lace" and doing other needlework. That she did so suggests that Thomasine had been taught these valuable female skills by her aunt during her earlier sojourn in London.

Plymouth was one of the major points of embarkation for the American colonies, and Hall recounted that "shortly after" arriving in the city Thomasine learned that a ship was being made ready for a voyage to Virginia. Once again, Hall decided to become a man, so he put on men's clothing and sailed to the fledgling colony. Thomas was then approxi-

mately twenty-five years old, comparable in age to many of the immigrants to Virginia, and like most of his fellows he seems to have gone to the Chesapeake as an indentured servant.

By December, Hall was settled in Virginia, for on January 21, 1627/8, a man named Thomas Hall, living with John and Jane Tyos (T's master and mistress), was convicted along with them for receiving stolen goods from William Mills, a servant of one of their neighbors. According to the testimony, Hall and the Tyoses had encouraged Mills in a series of thefts that began before Christmas 1627. Some of the purloined items—which included tobacco, chickens, currants, a shirt, and several pairs of shoes—were still in the possession of Hall and the Tyoses at the time their house was searched by the authorities on January 14. Although Thomas Hall is a common name (indeed, John Tyos knew another Thomas Hall, who had arrived with him on the ship Bona Nova in 1620), a significant piece of evidence suggests that T and the man charged with this crime were one and the same. William Mills had difficulty carrying the currants, which he piled into his cap during his initial theft. Since that was clearly an unsatisfactory conveyance, when Mills was about to make a second foray after the desirable dried fruits he asked his accomplices to supply him with a better container. Thomas Hall testified that Jane Tyos then "did bring a napkin unto him and willed him to sowe it & make a bagg of it to carry currants." It is highly unlikely that an ordinary male servant would have had better seamstressing skills than his mistress, but Thomasine was an expert at such tasks.[4]

Although thus far in Hall's tale the chronology and the sequence of gender switches have been clear—for T specifically recounted the first part of the tale to the Virginia General Court, and the timing of the thefts and their prosecution is clearly described in court testimony—the next phase of the story must be pieced together from the muddled testimony of two witnesses and some logical surmises.

A key question not definitively answered in the records is: what happened to raise questions in people's minds about Hall's sexual identity? Two possibilities suggest themselves. One is that John and Jane Tyos, who obviously recognized that Hall had "feminine" skills shortly after T came to live with them, spoke of that fact to others, or perhaps visitors to their plantation observed Hall's activities and drew their own conclusions. Another possibility is that, after traveling to Virginia as a man, Hall reverted to the female clothing and role that T appears to have found more comfortable. The court records imply that Hall did choose to dress as a woman in Virginia, for Francis England, a witness, reported overhearing a conversation in which another man asked T directly: why do you wear women's clothing? T's reply—"I goe in weomans aparell to gett a bitt for my Catt"—is difficult to interpret and will be analyzed later. In any event, a Mr. Stacy (who cannot be further identified) seems to have first raised the issue of T's anomalous sexual character by asserting to other colonists that Hall was "as hee thought a man and woeman." Just when Mr. Stacy made this statement is not clear, but he probably voiced his opinion about a year after T arrived in the colony.

In the aftermath of Mr. Stacy's statement, a significant incident occurred at the home of Nicholas Eyres, perhaps a relative of Robert Eyres, who had recently become John Tyos's partner. "Uppon [Mr Stacy's] report," three women—Alice Longe, Dorothy Rodes, and Barbara Hall—scrutinized Hall's body. Their action implied that T was at the time dressed as a woman, for women regularly searched other women's bodies (often at the direction of a court) to look for signs of illicit pregnancy or perhaps witchcraft. They never, however, performed the same function with respect to men—or anyone dressed like a man. Moreover, John Tyos both then and later told Dorothy Rodes that Hall was a woman. Even so, the female searchers, having examined Hall, declared that T was a man. As a result of the disagreement between Tyos and the women about T's sex, T was brought before the commander of the region, Captain Nathaniel Basse, for further examination.[5]

Questioned by Mr. Basse, T responded with a description of a unique anatomy with ambiguous physical characteristics. (The text of the testimony is mutilated, and the remaining fragments are too incomplete to provide a clear description of T's body.) Hall then refused to choose a gender identity, instead declaring that T was "both man and woeman." Captain Basse nevertheless decided that Hall was female and ordered T "to bee putt in weomans apparell"—thus implying that T was, at

that moment at least, dressed as a man. The three women who had previously searched T's body were shaken by the official ruling that contradicted their own judgment; after being informed of the commander's decision, they reportedly "stood in doubte of what they had formerly affirmed."

John Tyos then sold Hall, now legally a maidservant named Thomasine, to John Atkins, who was present when Captain Basse questioned T. Atkins must have fully concurred with Mr. Basse's decision; surely he would not have purchased a female servant about whose sex he had any doubts. Yet on February 12, 1628/9, questions were again raised about T, for Alice Longe and her two friends went to Atkins's house to scrutinize Thomasine's body for a second time. They covertly examined her while she slept and once more decided that the servant was male. But Atkins, though summoned by the searchers to look at his maid's anatomy, was unable to do so, for Hall's "seeming to starre as if shee had beene awake" caused Atkins to leave without viewing her body.

The next Sunday, the three women returned with two additional female helpers.[6] On this occasion, the searchers had the active cooperation and participation of John Atkins, who ordered Thomasine to show her body to them. For a third time the women concluded that Hall was a man. Atkins thereupon ordered his servant to don men's clothing and informed Captain Basse of his decision.

By this time not only Hall but also everyone else was undoubtedly confused. Since Hall was now deemed to be male, the next curiosity-seekers to examine T's body were also male. One of them was Roger Rodes, probably the husband of Dorothy, who had joined in all the previous searches of Hall's body. Before forcefully throwing Thomas onto his back and checking his anatomy, Roger told Hall, "thou hast beene reported to be a woman and now thou art proved to bee a man, i will see what thou carriest." Like the female searchers before them, Roger and his associate Francis England concluded that T was male.

A rumor that Hall "did ly with a maid of Mr Richard Bennetts called great Besse" must have added considerably to the uncertainty. Hall accused Alice Longe, one of the persistent female searchers, of spreading the tale. She denied the charge, blaming the slander instead on an unnamed male servant of John Tyos's. If the story was true, what did it imply about Hall's sexual identity? Whether Hall was male or female would obviously have a bearing on the interpretation of any relationship with Bennett's maid Bess. Clearly, Virginians now had reason to seek a firm resolution of the conflict. Since Captain Basse, the local commander, had been unable to find an acceptable solution, there was just one remaining alternative—referring the dilemma to the General Court.

That court, composed of the governor and council, was the highest judicial authority in the small colony. The judges heard from Hall and considered the sworn depositions of two male witnesses (Francis England and John Atkins), who described the events just outlined. Remarkably, the court accepted T's own self-definition and, although using the male personal pronoun, declared that Hall was "a man and a woeman, that all the Inhabitants there may take notice thereof and that hee shall goe Clothed in mans apparell, only his head to bee attired in a Coyfe and Crosecloth with an Apron before him." Ordering Hall to post bond for good behavior until formally released from that obligation, the court also told Captain Basse to see that its directives were carried out. Since most court records for subsequent years have been lost (they were burned during the Civil War), it is impossible to trace Hall's story further.

What can this tale reveal about gender definitions and the role of the community in the formative years of American society? Six different but related issues emerge from the analysis of Hall's case.

First, the relationship of sexual characteristics and gender identity. All those who examined T, be they male or female, insisted T was male. Thus T's external sex organs resembled male genitals. Roger Rodes and Francis England, for example, pronounced Thomas "a perfect man" after they had "pulled out his members." Still, T informed Captain Basse "hee had not the use of the mans parte" and told John Atkins that "I have a peece of an hole" (a vulva). Since T was identified as a girl at birth, christened Thomasine, and raised accordingly, T probably fell into that category of human beings who appear female in infancy but at puberty develop what seem to be male genitalia. Such

individuals were the subjects of many stories in early modern Europe, the most famous of which involved a French peasant girl, Marie, who suddenly developed male sex organs while chasing pigs when she was fifteen, and who in adulthood became a shepherd named Germain. It is not clear whether early Virginians were aware of such tales, but if they understood contemporary explanations of sexual difference, the narrative of Marie-Germain would not have surprised them. Women were viewed as inferior types of men, and their sexual organs were regarded as internal versions of male genitalia. In the best scientific understanding of the day, there was just one sex, and under certain circumstances women could turn into men.[7]

What, then, in the eyes of Virginia's English residents, constituted sufficient evidence of sexual identity? For the male and female searchers of T's body, genitalia that appeared to be normally masculine provided the answer. But that was not the only possible contemporary response to the question. Leaving aside for the moment the persons who saw T as a combination of male and female (they will be considered later), it is useful to focus on those who at different times indicated that they thought T was female. There were three such individuals, all of them men: Captain Nathaniel Basse, who ordered T to wear women's clothing after T had appeared before him; John Atkins, T's second master, who purchased Thomasine as a maidservant and referred to T as "shee" before bowing to the contrary opinion of the female searchers and changing the pronoun to "him"; and, most important of all, T's first master, John Tyos.

It is not clear from the trial record why Captain Basse directed T to dress as a woman, for T asserted a dual sexual identity in response to questioning and never claimed to be exclusively female. Perhaps the crucial fact was T's admission that "hee had not the use of the mans parte." Another possibility was that Mr. Basse interpreted T's anatomy as insufficiently masculine. As was already indicated, the partial physical description of T included in this portion of the record survives only in fragmentary form and so is impossible to interpret, especially in light of the certainty of all the searchers.

John Atkins acquired T as a servant after Captain Basse had issued his order, and he at first accepted Thomasine as a woman, referring to how "shee" seemed to awaken from sleep. Yet Atkins changed his mind about his servant after he and the five women subjected T's body to the most thorough examination described in the case record. It involved a physical search by the women, then questioning by Atkins, followed by an order from Atkins to Hall to "lye on his backe and shew" the "peece of an hole" that T claimed to have. When the women "did againe finde him to bee a man," Atkins issued the directive that contradicted Captain Basse's, ordering T to put on men's clothes. For Atkins, Hall's anatomy (which he saw with his own eyes) and the women's testimony were together decisive in overriding his initial belief that T was female, a belief presumably based at least in part on his presence at Mr. Basse's interrogation of T.

Unlike Atkins, John Tyos had purchased T as Thomas—a man. And for him the interpretive process was reversed. After just a brief acquaintance with Thomas, John and his wife learned that he had female skills. Approximately a year later Tyos "swore" to Dorothy Rodes that Hall "was a woman," a conclusion that contradicted the opinion of the female searchers. It also seemingly flew in the face of what must have been his own intimate knowledge of Hall's physical being. The lack of space in the small houses of the seventeenth-century Chesapeake is well known to scholars.[8] It is difficult to imagine that Tyos had never seen Hall's naked body—the same body that convinced searchers of both sexes that T was male. So why would Tyos insist that T was Thomasine, even to Dorothy Rodes, who forcefully asserted the contrary? The answer must lie not in T's sexual organs but in T's gender—that is, in the feminine skills and mannerisms that would have been exhibited by a person born, raised, and living as a female until reaching the age of twenty-two, and which would have been immediately evident to anyone who, like John Tyos, lived with T for any length of time.

Thus, for these colonists, sex had two possible determinants. One was physical: the nature of one's genitalia. The other was cultural: the character of one's knowledge and one's manner of behaving. The female and male searchers used the former criterion, John Tyos, the latter. John Atkins initially adopted the second approach, but later switched to the first. Nathaniel Basse may have agreed with

Tyos, or he may have refused to interpret T's anatomy as unambiguously as did the searchers: it is not clear which. But it is clear that two quite distinct tests of sexual identity existed in tandem in early Virginia. One relied on physical characteristics, the other on learned, gendered behavior. On most occasions, of course, results of the two tests would accord with each other. Persons raised as females would physically appear to be females; persons raised as males would look like other males. Hall acted like a woman and physically resembled a man. Thus in T's case the results of the two independent criteria clashed, and that was the source of the confusion.

Second, the importance of clothing. Many of the key questions about Hall were couched in terms of what clothing T should wear, men's or women's. Captain Basse and John Atkins did not say to T, "you are a man," or "you are a woman," but instead issued instructions about what sort of apparel T was to put on. Likewise, although the General Court declared explicitly that Hall was both male and female, its decision also described the clothing T was to wear in specific detail. Why was clothing so important?

The answer lies in the fact that in the seventeenth century clothing was a crucial identifier of persons. Not only did males and females wear very different garb, but persons of different ranks also were expected to reveal their social status in their dress. In short, one was supposed to display visually one's sex and rank to everyone else in the society. Thus, ideally, new acquaintances would know how to categorize each other even before exchanging a word of greeting. In a fundamental sense, seventeenth-century people's identity was expressed in their apparel. Virginia never went so far as Massachusetts, which passed laws regulating what clothing people of different ranks could wear, but the Virginia colonists were clearly determined to uphold the same sorts of rules.[9]

Clothing, which was sharply distinguished by the sex of its wearer, served as a visual trope for gender. And gender was one of the two most basic determinants of role in the early modern world (the other was rank, which was never at issue in Hall's case—T was always a servant). People who wore skirts nurtured children; people who wore pants did not. People who wore aprons could take no role in governing the colony, whereas other people could, if they were of appropriate status. People who wore headdresses performed certain sorts of jobs in the household; people who wore hats did other types of jobs in the fields. It is hardly surprising, therefore, that Virginians had difficulty dealing with a person who sometimes dressed as a man and other times as a woman—and who, on different occasions, did both at the direction of superiors. Nor, in light of this context, is it surprising that decisions about T's sexual identity were stated in terms of clothing.[10]

Third, the absence of a sense of personal privacy throughout the proceedings. To a modern sensibility, two aspects of the case stand out. First, seventeenth-century Virginians appear to have had few hesitations about their right to examine the genitalia of another colonist, with or without official authorization from a court and regardless of whether that activity occurred forcibly, clandestinely, or openly. The physical examinations were nominally by same-sex individuals (women when T was thought to be female, men when T had been declared to be male), with one key exception: John Atkins joined the women in scrutinizing the body of his maidservant. A master's authority over the household, in other words, extended to the bodies of his dependents. If a master like Atkins chose to search the body of a subordinate of either sex, no barrier would stand in his way.

Second, Hall seems not to have objected to any of the intrusive searches of T's body nor to the intimate questioning to which T was subjected by Captain Basse and the General Court. Hall too appears to have assumed that T's sexual identity was a matter of concern for the community at large. Such an attitude on Hall's part was congruent with a society in which the existing minimal privacy rights were seen as accruing to households as a unit or perhaps to their heads alone. Subordinates like Hall neither expected nor received any right to privacy of any sort.

Fourth, the involvement of the community, especially women, in the process of determining sexual identity. One of the most significant aspects of Hall's story is the initiative taken throughout by Hall's fellow colonists. They not only brought their doubts about Hall's sex to the attention of the authorities, they also refused to accept Captain Basse's determination that Hall was female. Both men and women joined in the effort to convince Virginia's leaders that T was male. Nearly uniformly rejecting T's self-characterization as "both" (the only exception outside the General Court being Mr. Stacy), Virginians insisted that Hall had to be either female or male, with most favoring the latter definition. They wanted a sexual category into which to fit T, and they did not hesitate to express their opinions about which category was the more appropriate.

Women in particular were active in this regard. Three times groups of women scrutinized T's body, whereas a group of men did so only once. After each examination, women rejected T as one of their number. Because of the vigorous and persistent efforts of female Virginians, Hall was deprived of the possibility of adopting unambiguously the role with which T seemed most comfortable, that of Thomasine. Here Hall's physical characteristics determined the outcome. Accustomed to searching the bodies of other females, women thought T did not physically qualify as feminine—regardless of the gendered skills T possessed—and they repeatedly asserted that to any man who would listen. For them, T's anatomy (sex) was more important than T's feminine qualities (gender).

Male opinion, on the other hand, was divided. The three male searchers of T's body—Roger Rodes, Francis England, and John Atkins—agreed with the women's conclusion. Other men were not so sure. John Tyos and Nathaniel Basse thought T more appropriately classified as a woman, while Mr. Stacy and the members of the General Court said T displayed aspects of both sexes. It seems plausible to infer from their lack of agreement about T's sex that men as a group were not entirely certain about what criteria to apply to create the categories "male" and "female." Some relied on physical appearance, others on behavior.

Moreover, the complacency of the male searchers can be interpreted as quite remarkable. They failed to police the boundaries of their sex with the same militance as did women. That T, if a man, was a very unusual sort of man indeed did not seem to bother Rodes, Atkins, and England. For them, T's physical resemblance to other men was adequate evidence of masculinity, despite their knowledge of T's feminine skills and occasional feminine dress. That opinion was, however, in the end overridden by the doubts of higher-ranking men on the General Court, who were not so willing to overlook T's peculiarities.

Fifth, the relationship among sex, gender, and sexuality. Twice, and in quite different ways, the case record raises issues of sexuality rather than of biological sex or of gendered behavior. Both references have been alluded to briefly: the rumor of Thomas's having committed fornication with "greate Besse," and T's explanation for wearing women's clothing—"to gett a bitt for my Catt."

A judgment about T's body would imply a judgment about T's sexuality as well. Yet was it possible to reach a definitive conclusion about T's sexuality? If T were Thomas, then he could potentially be guilty of fornicating with the maidservant Bess; if T were Thomasine, then being in the same bed with Bess might mean nothing—or it could imply "unnatural" acts, the sort of same-sex coupling universally condemned when it occurred between men. The rumor about Bess, which for an ordinary male servant might have led to a fistfight (with the supposed slanderer, Tyos's servant), a defamation suit, or a fornication presentment, thus raised perplexing questions because of T's ambiguous sexual identity, questions that had to be resolved in court.[11]

T's phrase "to gett a bitt for my Catt," as reported by Francis England, was even more troubling. What did it mean, and was that meaning evident to England and the members of the General Court? As an explanation for wearing female apparel, it could have been straightforward and innocent. One historian reads it literally, as indicating that Hall wore women's clothing to beg scraps for a pet cat. Hall might also have been saying that because T's skills were feminine, dressing as a woman was the best way for T to earn a living, "to get a bit (morsel) to eat." But some scholars have read erotic connotations into the statement. Could T, speaking as a man, have been saying that wearing women's clothing allowed T to get close to women, to—in modern slang—"get a piece of pussy" by masquerading as a female?[12]

There is another more likely and even more intriguing erotic possibility. Since Hall had served in the English army on an expedition to France, T could well have learned a contemporary French slang phrase—"pour avoir une bite pour mon chat"—or, crudely put in English, "to get a penis for my cunt." Translating the key words literally into English equivalents (bite=bit, chat=cat) rather than into their metaphorical meanings produced an answer that was probably as opaque and confusing to seventeenth-century Virginians as it has proved to be to subsequent historians.[13] Since much of Francis England's testimony (with the exception of his report of this statement and the account of his and Roger Rodes's examination of T's anatomy) duplicated John Atkins's deposition, England could have been called as a witness primarily to repeat such a mysterious conversation to the court.

If T was indeed employing a deliberately misleading Anglicized version of contemporary French slang, as appears probable, two conclusions are warranted. First, the response confirms T's predominantly feminine gender, for it describes sexual intercourse from a woman's perspective. In light of the shortage of women in early Virginia, it moreover would have accurately represented T's experience: donning women's garb unquestionably opened sexual possibilities to Thomasine that Thomas lacked. Second, at the same time, Hall was playing with T's listeners, answering the question about wearing women's apparel truthfully, but in such an obscure way that it was unlikely anyone would comprehend T's meaning. In other words, Hall was having a private joke at the expense of the formal and informal publics in the colony. Hall's sly reply thus discloses a mischievous aspect of T's character otherwise hidden by the flat prose of the legal record.

Sixth, the court's decision. At first glance, the most surprising aspect of the case is the General Court's acceptance of Hall's self-definition as both man and woman. By specifying that T's basic apparel should be masculine, but with feminine signs—the apron and the coif and cross-cloth, a headdress commonly worn by women at the time—Virginia officials formally recognized that Hall contained elements of both sexes. The elite men who sat as judges thereby demonstrated their ability to transcend the dichotomous sexual categories that determined the thinking of ordinary Virginians. But their superficially astonishing verdict becomes explicable when the judges' options are analyzed in terms of contemporary understandings of sex and gender.

First, consider T's sexual identity. Could the court have declared Hall to be female? That alternative was effectively foreclosed. Women had repeatedly scrutinized T's anatomy and had consistently concluded that T was male. Their initial determination that T was a man (in the wake of Mr. Stacy's comment that T was both) first brought the question before Captain Basse. Subsequently, their adamant rejection of Captain Basse's contrary opinion and their ability to convince John Atkins that they were correct, coupled with the similar assessment reached by two men, were the key elements forcing the General Court to consider the case. A small community could not tolerate a situation in which groups of men and women alternately stripped and searched the body of one of its residents, or in which the decisions of the local commander were so openly disobeyed. Declaring T to be female was impossible; ordinary Virginians of both sexes would not accept such a verdict.

Yet, at the same time, could anyone assert unconditionally that Hall was sexually a man? Francis England, Roger Rodes, John Atkins, and the five female searchers thought so, on the basis of anatomy; but John Tyos, who was probably better acquainted with T than anyone else, declared unequivocally that Hall was a woman. And T had testified about not having "the use of the mans parte." Hall, in other words, revealed that although T had what appeared to be male genitalia, T did not function sexually as a man and presumably could not have an erection. To Captain Basse and the members of the General Court, that meant that (whatever T's physical description) Hall would not be able to father children or be a proper husband to a wife.

. . . The ability to impregnate a woman was a key indicator of manhood in seventeenth-century Anglo-America. Childless men were the objects of gossip, and impotence served as adequate grounds for divorce. A person who could not father a child was by that criterion alone an unsatisfactory male. T had admitted being incapable of male orgasm. Given that admitted physical incapacity and its implications, declaring Hall to be a man was as impossible as declaring T to be a woman.[14]

Second, consider T's gender identity. In seventeenth-century Anglo-America, as in all other known societies, sexual characteristics carried with them gendered consequences. In Hall's life history those consequences were especially evident, because what T did and how T did it were deeply affected by whether T chose to be Thomas or Thomasine.

Whenever Hall traveled far from home, to France in the army or to Virginia, T became Thomas. Men had much more freedom of movement than did women. Unlike other persons raised as females, Hall's unusual anatomy gave T the opportunity to live as a male when there was an advantage to doing so. Even though T seemed more comfortable being Thomasine—to judge by frequent reversions to that role—the option of becoming Thomas must have been a welcome one. It permitted Hall to escape the normal strictures that governed early modern English women's lives and allowed T to pursue a more adventurous lifestyle.[15]

Thus whether T chose to be male or female made a great difference in T's life. As Thomas, Hall joined the army and emigrated to the colonies; as Thomasine, Hall lived quietly in London with an aunt, did fancy needlework in Plymouth, and presumably performed tasks normally assigned to women in Virginia. T's most highly developed skills were feminine ones, so T was undoubtedly more expert at and familiar with "women's work" in general, not just seamstressing.

It was, indeed, Hall's feminine skills that convinced some men that T was female; and those qualities, coupled with Hall's physical appearance, must have combined to lead to the court's decision. T's gender was feminine but T's sex seemed to be masculine—with the crucial exception of sexual functioning. Given T's sexual incapacity, all indications pointed to a feminine identity—to Thomasine. But Virginia women's refusal to accept T as Thomasine precluded that verdict. On the other hand, the judges could not declare a person to be male who had admitted to Captain Basse an inability to consummate a marriage. Ordinary men might possibly make a decision on the basis of physical appearance alone, but the members of the General Court had a responsibility to maintain the wider social order. If they said Hall was a man, then Thomas theoretically could marry and become a household head once his term of service was complete. That alternative was simply not acceptable for a person of T's description.

So, considering sex (incompletely masculine) and gender (primarily feminine), the Virginia General Court's solution to the dilemma posed by Hall was to create a unique category that combined sex and gender for T alone. Unable to fit Hall into the standard male/female dichotomy, the judges preferred to develop a singular definition that enshrined T's dual identity by prescribing clothing that simultaneously carried conflicting messages.

The court's decision to make Hall unique in terms of clothing—and thus gender identity—did not assist the community in classifying or dealing with T. After the verdict, Virginians were forced to cope with someone who by official sanction straddled the dichotomous roles of male and female. By court order, Hall was now a dual-sexed person. T's identity had no counterpart or precedent; paradoxically, a society in which gender—the outward manifestation of sex—served as a fundamental dividing line had formally designated a person as belonging to both sexes. Yet at the same time it was precisely because gender was so basic a concern to seventeenth-century society that no other solution was possible.

Hall's life after the court verdict must have been lonely. Marked as T was by unique clothing, unable to adopt the gender switches that had previously given T unparalleled flexibility in choosing a way of life, Hall must have had a very difficult time. T, like other publicly marked deviants—persons branded for theft or adultery or mutilated for perjury or forgery—was perhaps the target of insults or assaults. The verdict in T's case, in its insistence that T be constantly clothed as both sexes rather than alternating between them, was therefore harsh, though it nominally accorded with T's own self-definition. Hall's identity as "both" allowed movement back and forth across gender lines. The court's verdict had quite a different meaning, insisting not on the either/or sexual ambiguity T had employed to such great advantage, but rather on a definition of "both" that required duality and allowed for no flexibility.

It is essential to re-emphasize here what necessitated this unusual ending to a remarkable case: the opinions and actions of the female neighbors of John Tyos and John Atkins. Captain Nathaniel Basse, confronted with basically the same information that the General Court later considered, concluded that Hall should be dressed and treated as a woman. In a sexual belief system that hypothesized that women were inferior men, any inferior man—that is, one who could not function adequately in sexual terms—was a woman. Thus, charged the women at an Accomack cow pen in 1637, John Waltham "hade his Mounthly Courses as Women have" because his wife had not become pregnant.[16] Undoubtedly the General Court's first impulse would have been the same as Captain Basse's: to declare that T, an inferior man, was female and should wear women's clothing. But Virginia women had already demonstrated forcefully that they would not accept such a verdict. Hall's fate therefore was determined as much by a decision reached by ordinary women as it was by a verdict formally rendered by the elite men who served on the General Court.

NOTES

1. Anthropologists have been in the forefront of the investigation of the various relationships of sex and gender. A good introduction to such work is Sherry Ortner and Harriet Whitehead, eds., *Sexual Meanings: The Cultural Construction of Gender and Sexuality* (New York: Cambridge University Press, 1981). . . . For an account of how contemporary American society handles sexually ambiguous babies at birth, see Suzanne J. Kessler, "The Medical Construction of Gender: Case Management of Intersexed Infants," *Signs*, XVI (1990), 3–26.

2. Unless otherwise indicated, all quotations and details in the account that follows are taken from the record in the case, *Va Ct Recs*, 194–95.

3. The expedition in which Thomas took part was an ill-fated English attack on the Isle de Ré during the summer of 1627. The troops who futilely tried to relieve the French Protestants besieged in the city of La Rochelle embarked on July 10, 1627; most of them returned to Plymouth in early November.

4. *Va Ct Recs*, 159, 162–64 (quotation 163). Yet it is possible that the Thomas Hall in this case was the other man, the one who came to Virginia in 1620. (For him, see Virginia M. Meyer and John F. Dorman, eds., *Adventurers of Purse and Person Virginia 1607–1624/5*, 3d ed. [Richmond: Order of First Families of Virginia, 1987]. The Virginia muster of 1624/5 [ibid., 42] lists Thomas Hall and John Tyos as residents of George Sandys's plantation in James City. . . .

5. Little can be discovered about the three women. . . .

6. The two newcomers were the wife of Allen Kinaston and the wife of Ambrose Griffen. . . .

7. The best discussion of the one-sex model of humanity and its implications is Thomas Laqueur, *Making Sex: Body and Gender from the Greeks to Freud* (Cambridge, Mass.: Harvard University Press, 1990). See 126–30 for an analysis of Marie-Germain. . . .

8. See Lois Green Carr et al., *Robert Cole's World: Agriculture & Society in Early Maryland* (Chapel Hill: University of North Carolina Press, 1991), 90–114, on "the standard of life" in the early Chesapeake.

9. See *Mass Col Recs*, IV, pt 1, 60–61, IV, pt 2, 41–42. . . .

10. Laqueur observes, in *Making Sex*, 124–25, that "in the absence of a purportedly stable system of two sexes, strict sumptuary laws of the body attempted to stabilize gender—woman as woman and man as man—and punishments for transgression were quite severe." A relevant recent study is Marjorie Garber, *Vested Interests: Cross-Dressing and Cultural Anxiety* (New York: Routledge, 1991).

11. A good general discussion of the colonists' attitudes toward sexuality is John D'Emilio and Estelle B. Freedman, *Intimate Matters: A History of Sexuality in America* (New York: Harper & Row, 1988), 1–52, especially (on the regulation of deviance) 27–38.

12. Brown interprets the statement literally in

her "Gender and the Genesis of Race and Class System," I, 88. The suggestion that the phrase might have meant "earning a living" is mine, developed after consulting the *OED* (q.v. "bit"). Katz speculates that T's phrase had the erotic meaning suggested here, though he recognizes that such an interpretation is problematic (*Gay/Lesbian Almanac*, 72).

13. I owe the identification of the probable French origin of this phrase to Marina Warner and, through her, to Julian Barnes, whom she consulted (personal communication, 1993). My colleague Steven Kaplan, a specialist in the history of early modern France (and scholars he consulted in Paris), confirmed that "bite" and "chat" were used thus in the late sixteenth century and that the interpretation appears plausible.

14. On the importance of marital sexuality in the colonies: D'Emilio and Freedman, *Intimate Matters*, 16–27.

15. See, on this point, Rudolf M. Dekker and Lotte C. van de Pol, *The Tradition of Female Transvestism in Early Modern Europe* (London: Macmillan, 1989).

16. Susie M. Ames, ed., *County Court Records of Accomack-Northampton, Virginia, 1632–1640* (American Legal Records, VII), (Washington, D.C., 1954), p. 85.

DOCUMENT: The Trial of Anne Hutchinson, 1637

> *"What law have I broken?"*

In 1989, in a solemn ceremony soaked with irony and bitter humor, the leaders of the Newport Rhode Island Congregational Church announced that injustice had been done more than 350 years before when Anne Hutchinson had been expelled from Boston's Congregational Church for blasphemy and perjury. The minister who took the initiative, and who coincidentally bore the same name as the John Wilson who had read the formal excommunication in the seventeenth century, thought that the Hutchinson affair raised questions that remained central to religion in the present: questions "of spiritual freedom, the role of women in the church, the issue of individual freedom versus being part of a covenant community, and the church-state issue." In a public ceremony, the president of the Rhode Island Conference of the United Church of Christ burned a copy of the writ of excommunication.*

The Antinomian heresy of 1637–38 threw the Puritan colony of Massachusetts Bay into turmoil for years and forced its leaders to reconsider the nature of their experiment. Antinomians placed greater emphasis on religious feeling than did orthodox Puritans. They tended to be suspicious (*anti*) of law (*nomos*) or formal rules and came close to asserting that individuals had access to direct revelation from the Holy Spirit. They criticized ministers who seemed to argue that it was possible to *earn* salvation by good deeds rather than leaving it to God freely to decide who was to be saved by their faith, a distinction between the "covenant of works" and a "covenant of faith" which they thought separated authentic Puritans from ones who remained too close to the Anglican Church. The close relationship between church and state in Massachusetts Bay meant that challenge to the ministers was quickly interpreted as challenge to established authority of all kinds.

One leading dissenter was Anne Hutchinson, a woman who had migrated to the colony in 1634, four years after its founding, and who commanded great respect for her competence as a midwife. At meetings held in her home after Sunday church services she summarized, discussed, and criticized ministers' sermons. The meetings became very popular; soon she was holding separate gatherings for men as well as for women. Women who followed Hutchinson were often those who respected her medical knowledge and also shared her criticisms of the ministers. The men who came to the meetings were often those who were critical of the Puritan leadership on political and economic as well as religious grounds.

*Madeline Pecora Nugent, "Apologizing to Anne Hutchinson," *The Christian Century* 106 (March 22, 1989):304–305.

Excerpted from "Examination of Mrs. Anne Hutchinson before the court at Newton, 1637," in David D. Hall, ed., *The Antinomian Controversy, 1636–1638: A Documentary History* (Middletown, Conn.: Wesleyan University Press, 1968), pp. 312–16. Copyright © 1968 by David D. Hall. Reprinted by permission of the editor. Notes have been renumbered.

Tensions were high in Massachusetts Bay through 1636 and 1637 as colonists violently attacked the Pequot Indians and decimated the tribe, capturing and enslaving their women and children. In a context in which Pastor John Wilson linked the destruction of "barbarous Indians" with God's will, religious and political dissent seemed easily to merge.* Rumor spread that criticism of the governor and council as well as ministers was voiced in the Hutchinson home, and she was challenged, first by a convocation of ministers and then, in November 1637, by the magistrates of the colony, in a "court" held in Newtown (now Cambridge). The proceedings were not a trial in the contemporary sense with modern safeguards; they were instead a colonial version of the "magisterial examination," an inquisition conducted without a jury. Hutchinson, who was pregnant, had no lawyer. Her trial was conducted by the governor of the colony, John Winthrop. (His house was directly across the path from the Hutchinson's home; he could not have avoided seeing the people coming and going to her meetings.) Winthrop was joined in his questioning by the deputy governor and other members of the legislature; at the end, they handed down the very heavy sentence of banishment from the colony.

Hutchinson's secular trial before the General Court was followed by an examination before a board of ministers, who handed down the heaviest sentence in their arsenal, excommunication. When Hutchinson was held up to public ridicule and exiled, explicit dissent by women was firmly squelched in the Puritan community. In Winthrop's memoir of the events, published in 1644, miscarriages suffered by Hutchinson and her closest colleague, Mary Dyer, were offered as evidence of God's "displeasure against their opinions and practises, as clearly as if he had pointed with his finger, in causing the two fomenting women in the time of the height of the Opinions to produce out of their wombs, as before they had out of their braines, such monstrous births as no Chronicle . . . hardly ever recorded the like."[†]

Hutchinson and her husband fled to Rhode Island, where Roger Williams offered toleration to dissenters; several years later they moved on to the forests of what is now Westchester County, north of New York City. Hutchinson died at the hands of Indians in 1643.

In reading this excerpt from Anne Hutchinson's trial in 1637, note the extent to which criticism of her religious and political behavior merge with the complaint that she is challenging gender roles. Note also the shrewdness with which Hutchinson defends her actions; at one point she challenges Winthrop that if he thinks it "not lawful for me to teach women . . . why do you call me to teach the court?"

---

*Sandra F. Van Burkleo, "'To Bee Rooted Out of Her Station': The Ordeal of Anne Hutchinson," in *American Political Trials* (Westport, Conn.: Greenwood Press, 1994), p. 8.

[†]John Winthrop, *A Short Story of the Rise, Reign, and Ruine of the Antinomians, Familists & Libertines*, in David D. Hall, ed. *The Antinomian Controversy, 1636–1638: A Documentary History* (Middletown, Conn.: Wesleyan University Press, 1968), p. 214.

NOVEMBER 1637

The Examination of Mrs. Ann Hutchinson at the Court at Newtown

Mr. Winthrop, governor. Mrs. Hutchinson, you are called here as one of those that have troubled the peace of the commonwealth and the churches here; you are known to be a woman that hath had a great share in the promoting and divulging of those opinions that are causes of this trouble, and to be nearly joined not only in affinity and affection with some of those the court had taken notice of and passed censure upon, but you have spoken divers things as we have been informed very prejudicial to the honour of the churches and ministers thereof, and you have maintained a meeting and an assembly in your house that hath been condemned by the general assembly as a thing not tolerable nor comely in the sight of God nor fitting for your sex, and notwith standing that was cried down you have continued the same, therefore we have thought good to send for you to understand how things are, that if you be in an erroneous way we may reduce you that so you may become a profitable member here among us, otherwise (if you be obstinate in your course that then the court may take such course that you may trouble us no further) therefore I would intreat you to express whether you do not hold and assent in practice to those opinions and factions that have been handled in court already, that is to say, whether you do not justify Mr. Wheelwright's sermon and the petition.

Mrs. Hutchinson. I am called here to answer before you but I hear no things laid to my charge.

Gov. I have told you some already and more I can tell you.

Mrs. H. Name one, Sir.

Gov. Have I not named some already?

Mrs. H. What have I said or done?

Gov. Why for your doings, this you did harbour and countenance those that are parties in this faction that you have heard of.

Mrs. H. That's matter of conscience, Sir.

Gov. Your conscience you must keep or it must be kept for you. . . . Say that one brother should commit felony or treason and come to his other brother's house, if he knows him guilty and conceals him he is guilty of the same. It is his conscience to entertain him, but if his conscience comes into act in giving countenance and entertainment to him that hath broken the law he is guilty too. So if you do countenance those that are transgressors of the law you are in the same fact.

Mrs. H. What law do they transgress?

Gov. The law of God and of the state.

Mrs. H. In what particular?

Gov. Why in this among the rest, whereas the Lord doth say honour thy father and thy mother.

Mrs. H. Ey Sir in the Lord.

Gov. This honour you have broke in giving countenance to them. . . .

Mrs. H. What law have I broken?

Gov. Why the fifth commandment.

Mrs. H. I deny that for [Mr. Wheelwright] saith in the Lord.

Gov. You have joined with them in the faction.

Mrs. H. In what faction have I joined with them?

Gov. In presenting the petition[1]. . .

Mrs. H. But I had not my hand to the petition.

Gov. You have councelled them.

Mrs. H. Wherein?

Gov. Why in entertaining them.

Mrs. H. What breach of law is that Sir?

Gov. Why dishonouring of parents.

Mrs. H. But put the case Sir that I do fear the Lord and my parents, may not I entertain them that fear the Lord because my parents will not give me leave?

Gov. If they be the fathers of the commonwealth, and they of another religion, if you entertain them then you dishonour your parents and are justly punishable.

Mrs. H. If I entertain them, as they have dishonoured their parents I do.

Gov. No but you by countenancing them above others put honor upon them.

Mrs. H. I may put honor upon them as the children of God and as they do honor the Lord.

Gov. We do not mean to discourse with those of your sex but only this; you do adhere unto them and do endeavour to set forward this faction and so you do dishonour us.

Mrs. H. I do acknowledge no such thing neither do I think that I ever put any dishonour upon you.

Gov. Why do you keep such a meeting at your house as you do every week upon a set day?

Mrs. H. It is lawful for me so to do, as it is all your practices and can you find a warrant for yourself and condemn me for the same thing? [I]t was in practice before I came therefore I was not the first.

Gov. For this, that you appeal to our practice you need no confutation. If your meeting had answered to the former it had not been offensive, but I will say that there was no meeting of women alone, but your meeting is of another sort for there are sometimes men among you.

Mrs. H. There was never any man with us.

Gov. Well, admit there was no man at your meeting and that you was sorry for it, there is no warrant for your doings, and by what warrant do you continue such a course?

Mrs. H. I conceive there lyes a clear rule in Titus, that the elder women should instruct the younger[2] and then I must have a time wherein I must do it.

Gov. All this I grant you, I grant you a time for it, but what is this to the purpose that you Mrs. Hutchinson must call a company together from their callings to come to be taught of you?

Mrs. H. Will it please you to answer me this and to give me a rule for then I will willingly submit to any truth. If any come to my house to be instructed in the ways of God what rule have I to put them away?

Gov. But suppose that a hundred men come unto you to be instructed will you forbear to instruct them?

Mrs. H. As far as I conceive I cross a rule in it.

Gov. Very well and do you not so here?

Mrs. H. No Sir for my ground is they are men.

Gov. Men and women all is one for that, but suppose that a man should come and say Mrs. Hutchinson I hear that you are a woman that God hath given his grace unto and you have knowledge in the word of God I pray instruct me a little, ought you not to instruct this man?

Mrs. H. I think I may.—Do you think it not lawful for me to teach women and why do you call me to teach the court?

Gov. We do not call you to teach the court but to lay open yourself.

Mrs. H. I desire you that you would then set me down a rule by which I may put them away that come unto me and so have peace in so doing.

Gov. You must shew your rule to receive them.

Mrs. H. I have done it.

Gov. I deny it because I have brought more arguments than you have.

Mrs. H. I say, to me it is a rule.

Mr. Endicot. You say there are some rules unto you. I think there is a contradiction in your own words. What rule for your practice do you bring, only a custom in Boston.

Mrs. H. No Sir that was no rule to me but if you look upon the rule in Titus it is a rule to me. If you convince me that it is no rule I shall yield.

Gov. . . . [T]his rule crosses that in the Corinthians.[3] But you must take it in this sense that elder women must instruct the younger about their business, and to love their husbands and not to make them to clash.

Mrs. H. I do not conceive but that it is meant for some publick times.

Gov. Well, have you no more to say but this?

Mrs. H. I have said sufficient for my practice.

Gov. Your course is not to be suffered for, besides that we find such a course as this to be greatly prejudicial to the state, besides the occasion that it is to seduce many honest persons that are called to those meetings and your opinions being known to be different from the word of God may seduce many simple souls that resort unto you, besides that the occasion which hath come of late hath come from none but such as have frequented your meetings, so that now they are flown off from magistrates and ministers and this since they have come to you, and besides that it will not well stand with the commonwealth that families should be neglected for so many neighbours and dames and so much time spent, we see no rule of God for this, we see not that any should have authority to set up any other exercises besides what authority hath already set up and so what hurt comes of this you will be guilty of and we for suffering you.

Mrs. H. Sir I do not believe that to be so.

Gov. Well, we see how it is we must therefore put it away from you, or restrain you from maintaining this course.

Mrs. H. If you have a rule for it from God's word you may.

Gov. We are your judges, and not you ours and we must compel you to it.

Mrs. H. If it please you by authority to put it down I freely let you for I am subject to your authority.

Notes

1. The petition the Antinomian party presented to the General Court in March 1637.

2. Titus 2.3, 4, 5.

3. 1 Corinthians 14.34, 35.

CAROL F. KARLSEN

The Devil in the Shape of a Woman: The Economic Basis of Witchcraft

Puritan ministers stressed the equality of each soul in the eyes of God and the responsibility of each believer to read the Bible. They urged women as well as men toward literacy and taking responsibility for their own salvation. One distinguished minister, Cotton Mather, writing at the end of the seventeenth century, observed that since women came close to the experience of death in repeated childbirth, their religiosity was likely to be greater than that of men. In being "helpmeets" to their husbands, women were encouraged to strengthen their ability to be competent and capable. There was much in Puritan thought that could be appealing to women.

But, as we have seen in the case of Anne Hutchinson, the Puritan community was unforgiving to women who failed to serve the needs of godly men in their strictly hierarchical community. Lurking in their imagination—as it lurked throughout the Judeo-Christian tradition—was the cautionary biblical story of Eve, who, by her disobedience, brought evil into the world. (Puritans paid no attention to other elements of that complicated tale: Eve's disobedience, after all, was in quest of Knowledge; the biology of birth is reversed, with Eve emerging from Adam's body.) Witchcraft prosecutions were endemic throughout the Puritan colonies in America and exploded into the famous outbreak in Salem, Massachusetts, in 1692, during which nearly 200 people, three-quarters of them women, were accused, and 20 people, nearly three-quarters of them women, were executed. Carol Karlsen argues that an older view of women as a necessary evil had been only superficially superseded by a new view of women as a necessary good.

Anthropologists have long understood that communities define as witches people whose behavior enacts the things the community most fears; witchcraft beliefs, wrote Monica Hunter Wilson, are "the standardized nightmare of a group, and . . . the comparative analysis of such nightmares . . . [is] one of the keys to the understanding of society."* If the most cherished values of the Puritan community were hierarchy and order, then it was an easy step to the condemnation of those who did not accept—or in some cases could not accept—their place in it. In what ways do the women described in the following essay fail to fit the values of the Puritan community?

---

*Quoted in Carol F. Karlsen, *The Devil in the Shape of a Woman* (New York: W. W. Norton, 1987), p. 181.

Excerpted from "The Economic Basis of Witchcraft," chap. 3 of *The Devil in the Shape of a Woman: Witchcraft in Colonial New England* by Carol F. Karlsen (New York: W. W. Norton, 1987). Copyright © 1987 by Carol F. Karlsen. Condensed and reprinted by permission of the author and W. W. Norton & Co., Inc. Notes have been revised and renumbered and tables renumbered.

Most observers now agree that witches in the villages and towns of late sixteenth- and early seventeeth-century England tended to be poor. They were not usually the poorest women in their communities, one historian has argued; they were the "moderately poor." Rarely were relief recipients suspect; rather it was those just above them on the economic ladder, "like the woman who felt she ought to get poor relief, but was denied it."[1] This example brings to mind New England's Eunice Cole, who once berated Hampton selectmen for refusing her aid when, she insisted, a man no worse off than she was receiving it.[2]

Eunice Cole's experience also suggests the difficulty in evaluating the class position of the accused. Commonly used class indicators such as the amount of property owned, yearly income, occupation, and political offices held are almost useless in analyzing the positions of women during the colonial period. While early New England women surely shared in the material benefits and social status of their fathers, husbands, and even sons, most were economically dependent on the male members of their families throughout their lives. Only a small proportion of these women owned property outright, and even though they participated actively in the productive work of their communities, their labor did not translate into financial independence or economic power. Any income generated by married women belonged by law to their husbands, and because occupations open to women were few and wages meager, women alone could only rarely support themselves. Their material condition, moreover, could easily change with an alteration in their marital status. William Cole, with an estate at his death of £41 after debts, might be counted among the "moderately poor," as might Eunice Cole when he was alive. But the refusal of the authorities to recognize the earlier transfer of this estate from husband to wife ensured, among other things, that as a widow Eunice Cole was among the poorest of New England's poor. . . .

Despite conceptual problems and sparse evidence, it is clear that poor women, both the destitute and those with access to some resources, were surely represented, and very probably overrepresented, among the New England accused. Perhaps 20 percent of accused women . . . were either impoverished or living at a level of bare subsistence when

they were accused.[3] Some, like thirty-seven-year-old Abigail Somes, worked as servants a substantial portion of their adult lives. Some supported themselves and their families with various kinds of temporary labor such as nursing infants, caring for sick neighbors, taking in washing and sewing, or harvesting crops. A few, most notably Tituba, the first person accused during the Salem outbreak, were slaves. Others, like the once-prosperous Sarah Good of Wenham and Salem, and the never-very-well-off Ruth Wilford of Haverhill, found themselves reduced to abject poverty by the death of a parent or a change in their own marital status.[4] Accused witches came before local magistrates requesting permission to sell family land in order to support themselves, to submit claims against their children or executors of their former husbands' estates for nonpayment of the widow's lawful share of the estate, or simply to ask for food and fuel from the town selectmen. Because they could not pay the costs of their trials or jail terms, several were forced to remain in prison after courts acquitted them. The familiar stereotype of the witch as an indigent woman who resorted to begging for her survival is hardly an inaccurate picture of some of New England's accused.

Still, the poor account for only a minority of the women accused. Even without precise economic indicators, it is clear that women from all levels of society were vulnerable to accusation. . . . Wives, daughters, and widows of "middling" farmers, artisans, and mariners were regularly accused, and (although much less often) so too were women belonging to the gentry class. The accused were addressed as Goodwife (or Goody) and as the more honorific Mrs. or Mistress, as well as by their first names.

Prosecution was a different matter. Unless they were single or widowed, accused women from wealthy families—families with estates valued at more than £500—could be fairly confident that the accusations would be ignored by the authorities or deflected by their husbands through suits for slander against their accusers. Even during the Salem outbreak, when several women married to wealthy men were arrested, most managed to escape to the safety of other colonies through their husbands' influence. Married women from moderately well-off families—families with estates valued at between roughly £200 and £500—

did not always escape prosecution so easily, but neither do they seem, as a group, to have been as vulnerable as their less prosperous counterparts. When only married women are considered, women in families with estates worth less than £200 seem significantly over-represented among convicted witches—a pattern which suggests that economic position was a more important factor to judges and juries than to the community as a whole in its role as accuser.[5]

Without a husband to act on behalf of the accused, wealth alone rarely provided women with protection against prosecution. Boston's Ann Hibbens, New Haven's Elizabeth Godman, and Wethersfield's Katherine Harrison, all women alone, were tried as witches despite sizable estates. In contrast, the accusations against women like Hannah Griswold of Say-brook, Connecticut, Elizabeth Blackleach of Hartford, and Margaret Gifford of Salem, all wives of prosperous men when they were accused, were simply not taken seriously by the courts.[6] . . .

Economic considerations, then, do appear to have been at work in the New England witchcraft cases. But the issue was not simply the relative poverty—or wealth—of accused witches or their families. It was the special position of most accused witches vis-à-vis their society's rules for transferring wealth from one generation to another. To explain why their position was so unusual, we must turn first to New England's system of inheritance.

Inheritance is normally thought of as the transmission of property at death, but in New England, as in other agricultural societies, adult children received part of their father's accumulated estates prior to his death, usually at the time they married.[7] Thus the inheritance system included both pre-mortem endowments and post-mortem distributions. While no laws compelled fathers to settle part of their estates on their children as marriage portions, it was customary to do so. Marriages were, among other things, economic arrangements, and young people could not benefit from these arrangements unless their fathers provided them with the means to set up households and earn their livelihoods. Sons' portions tended to be land, whereas daughters commonly received movable goods and/or money. The

exact value of these endowments varied to a father's wealth and inclination, but it appears that as a general rule the father of the young woman settled on the couple roughly half as much as the father of the young man.[8]

Custom, not law, also guided the distribution of a man's property at his death, but with two important exceptions. First, a man's widow, if he left one, was legally entitled "by way of dower" to one-third part of his real property, "to have and injoy for term of her natural life." She was expected to support herself with the profits of this property, but since she held only a life interest in it, she had to see that she did not "strip or waste" it.[9] None of the immovable estate could be sold, unless necessary for her or her children's maintenance, and then only with the permission of the court. A man might will his wife more than a third of his real property—but not less. Only if the woman came before the court to renounce her dower right publicly, and then only if the court approved, could this principle be waived. In the form of her "thirds," dower was meant to provide for a woman's support in widowhood. The inviolability of dower protected the widow from the claims of her children against the estate and protected the community from the potential burden of her care.

The second way in which law determined inheritance patterns had to do specifically with intestate cases.[10] If a man died without leaving a will, several principles governed the division of his property. The widow's thirds, of course, were to be laid out first. Unless "just cause" could be shown for some other distribution, the other two-thirds were to be divided among the surviving children, both male and female.[11] A double portion was to go to the eldest son, and single portions to his sisters and younger brothers. If there were no sons, the law stipulated that the estate was to be shared equally by the daughters. In cases where any or all of the children had not yet come of age, their portions were to be held by their mother or by a court-appointed guardian until they reached their majorities[12] or married. What remained of the widow's thirds at her death was to be divided among the surviving children, in the same proportions as the other two-thirds.

Although bound to conform to laws concerning the widow's thirds, men who wrote wills were not legally required to follow the principles of inheritance laid out in intestate cases. Individual men had the right to decide for themselves who would ultimately inherit their property.... [T]he majority seem to have adhered closely (though not always precisely) to the custom of leaving a double portion to the eldest son. Beyond that, New England men seem generally to have agreed to a system of partible inheritance, with both sons and daughters inheriting.

When these rules were followed, property ownership and control generally devolved upon men. Neither the widow's dower nor, for the most part, the daughter's right to inherit signified more than access to property. For widows, the law was clear that dower allowed for "use" only. For inheriting daughters who were married, the separate but inheritance-related principle of coverture applied. Under English common law, "feme covert" stipulated that married women had no right to own property—indeed, upon marriage, "the very being or legal existence of the woman is suspended."[13] Personal property which a married daughter inherited from her father, either as dowry or as a post-mortem bequest, immediately became the legal possession of her husband, who could exert full powers of ownership over it. A married daughter who inherited land from her father retained title to the land, which her husband could not sell without her consent. On her husband's death such land became the property of her children, but during his life her husband was entitled to the use and profits of it, and his wife could not devise it to her children by will.[14] The property of an inheriting daughter who was single seems to have been held "for improvement" for her until she was married, when it became her dowry.[15]

This is not to say that women did not benefit when they inherited property. A sizable inheritance could provide a woman with a materially better life; if single or widowed, inheriting women enjoyed better chances for an economically advantageous marriage or remarriage. But inheritance did not normally bring women the independent economic power it brought men.

The rules of inheritance were not always followed, however. In some cases, individual men decided not to conform to customary practices; instead, they employed one of several legal devices to give much larger shares of their estates to their wives or daughters, many times

for disposal at their own discretion. Occasionally, the magistrates themselves allowed the estate to be distributed in some other fashion. Or, most commonly, the absence of male heirs in families made conformity impossible. In all three exceptions to inheritance customs, but most particularly the last, the women who stood to benefit economically also assumed a position of unusual vulnerability. They, and in many instances their daughters, became prime targets for witchcraft accusations.

Consider first the experience of witches who came from families without male heirs.... [T]hese histories begin to illuminate the subtle and often intricate manner in which anxieties about inheritance lay at the heart of most witchcraft accusations.

KATHERINE HARRISON

Katherine Harrison first appears in the Connecticut colonial records in the early 1650s, as the wife of John Harrison, a wealthy Wethersfield landowner.[16] Her age is unknown[17] and her family background is obscure. We know that she called John, Jonathan, and Josiah Gilbert, three prominent Connecticut Valley settlers, her cousins, but her actual relationship to them is ambiguous.[18] ... She may have been the daughter or niece of Lydia Gilbert, who was executed as a witch in Hartford in 1654, but we can be reasonably certain only that the two women were members of the same Connecticut family.[19] ...

It has been said that Katherine Harrison was first tried as a witch in October 1668.[20] If so, then she must have been acquitted, because she was indicted in the Court of Assistants in Hartford on 25 May 1669, on the same charge.[21] The jury was unable to agree upon a verdict, however, and the court adjourned to the next session. Meantime, Harrison was supposed to remain in jail, but for some reason she was released in the summer or early fall, and she returned home to Wethersfield. Shortly thereafter, thirty-eight Wethersfield townsmen filed a petition, complaining that "shee was suffered to be at libertie," since she "was lately prooved to be Deaply guiltie of *suspicion* of Wichcrafte" and that "the Juerie (the greater part of them) judged or beleaved that she was guilty of such high crimes" and "ought to be put to death." Among the petition's signers were several of the town's most prominent citizens, including John Blackleach,

Sr., who had "taken much paines in the prosecution of this cause from the beginninge," and John Chester, who was then involved in a legal controversy with Harrison concerning a parcel of land.[22] When the Court of Assistants met again in October, all of the jury members found her guilty of witchcraft.[23]

The Hartford magistrates, however, were reluctant to accept the verdict. Perhaps remembering how accusations had gotten out of hand during the Hartford outbreak seven years before, they put Harrison back in prison and appealed to local ministers for advice on the use of evidence. The response was ambiguous enough to forestall execution.[24] At a special session of the Court of Assistants the following May, the magistrates reconsidered the verdict, determined that they were not able to concur with the jury "so as to sentance her to death or to a longer continuance in restraynt," and ordered Harrison to pay her fees and leave the colony for good.[25]

If witnesses testifying against her in her 1669 trial can be believed, Katherine Harrison's neighbors had suspected that she was a witch sixteen or eighteen years earlier. Elizabeth Simon deposed that as a single woman, Harrison was noted to be "a great or notorious liar, a Sabbath breaker and one that told fortunes"—and that her predictions frequently came to pass. Simon was also suspicious of Harrison for another reason: because she "did often spin so great a quantity of fine linen yarn as the said Elizabeth did never know nor hear of any other woman that could spin so much."[26] Other witnesses testified to the more recent damage she did to individuals and their property. Harrison was also a healer, and although many of her neighbors called upon her skills, over the years some of them came to suspect her of killing as well as curing.[27] Or so they said in 1668–69; she was not formally accused of any witchcraft crimes until after her husband's death.

John Harrison had died in 1666, leaving his wife one of the wealthiest, if not *the* wealthiest woman in Wethersfield. In his will he bequeathed his entire estate of £929 to his wife and three daughters. Rebecca, age twelve, was to have £60, and his two younger daughters, eleven-year-old Mary and nine-year-old Sarah, were to have £40 each. The remaining £789 was to go to his widow.[28] Unlike many widows in colonial New England, Katherine Harrison chose not to remarry. Instead she lived alone, managing her extensive holdings herself, with the advice and assistance of her Hartford kinsman, Jonathan Gilbert.

In October 1668, not long after her adversaries began gathering their witchcraft evidence against her, Harrison submitted a lengthy petition to "the Fathers of the Comonweale" asking for relief for the extensive vandalism of her estate since her husband's death. Among other damage, she spoke of oxen beaten and bruised to the point of being "altogether unserviceable"; of a hole bored into the side of her cow; of a three-year-old heifer slashed to death; and of the back of a two-year-old steer broken. Her corn crop was destroyed, she said, "damnified with horses, they being staked upon it," and "30 poles of hops cutt and spoyled." Twelve of her relatives and neighbors, she said, including Jonathan and Josiah Gilbert, could testify to the damage done. The response of the court went unrecorded, but there is no indication that provision was made for the "due recompense" Harrison requested or that her grievances were even investigated.[29]

The Court of Assistants also seems to have been unsympathetic to another petition Harrison submitted in the fall of 1668, in which she complained that the actions of the magistrates themselves were depleting her estate.[30] Indeed, the local court had recently fined her £40 for slandering her neighbors, Michael and Ann Griswold—a fine greatly in excess of the normal punishment in such cases.[31] The exact circumstances of the incident are unknown, but the Griswolds were among Harrison's witchcraft accusers, and she apparently considered Michael Griswold central in the recruiting of additional witnesses against her, for she said that "the sayd Michael Griswold would Hang her though he damned a thousand soules," adding that "as for his own soule it was damned long agoe." Griswold, a member of Wethersfield's elite, but not as wealthy as Harrison, sued her for these slanderous remarks and for calling his wife Ann "a savadge whore."[32] Besides levying the fine, the court ordered Harrison to confess her sins publicly.[33] She made the required confession, but she appealed the exorbitant fine.

Harrison's petition, which she filed within the month, was a peculiar mixture of justification for her actions, concession to the magistrates' insistence on deference in women, determination in her convictions, and desperation in her attempt to salvage her estate.

Acknowledging herself to be "a female, a weaker vessell, subject to passion," she pleaded as the source of her frustration and anger the vicious abuse to which she had been subjected since her husband's death. She admitted her "corruption," but pointed out that it was well known that she had made "a full and free confession of [her] fault" and had offered "to repair the wound that [she] had given to [the Griswolds'] names by a plaster as broad as the sore, at any time and in any place where it should content them." At the same time, she indicated Michael Griswold for being less interested in the reparation of his name than in her estate and did not hesitate to call the fine oppressive, citing the laws of God and the laws of the commonwealth as providing "that noe mans estate shal be deminished or taken away by any colony or pretence of Authority" in such an arbitrary manner. In her final statements, however, she returned to a more conciliatory stance: "I speake not to excuse my fault," she said, "but to save my estate as far as Righteousness will permit for a distressed Widow and Orphanes."[34]

Fear of losing her estate is a recurring theme in the records of Harrison's life during this period. Almost immediately after her husband's death in 1666, she petitioned the court to change the terms of her husband's will. Arguing that the bequests to the children were "inconsiderate" (by which she probably meant inconsiderable), she asked that the magistrates settle on her eldest daughter £210, and £200 on each of her younger daughters, reserving the house and lot for herself during her lifetime.[35] Since her husband had left her full ownership of most of his estate, she could simply have given her daughters larger portions, but she must have felt that the court's sanction rendered the inheritances less vulnerable. Several months later, she appealed directly to Connecticut's governor, John Winthrop, Jr., requesting that Hartford's John and Jonathan Gilbert, and John Riley of Wethersfield, be appointed overseers of her estate.[36] Winthrop must not have granted her request, because in 1668 Harrison signed over the rest of the estate she had inherited from her husband to her daughters and appointed Jonathan and John Gilbert her daughters' guardians.[37] By the following year, her neighbors reported, she had "disposed of great part of her estate to others in trust."[38]

In June 1670, Katherine Harrison moved to Westchester, New York, to begin her life anew.

Her reputation for witchcraft followed her, however, in the form of a complaint, filed in July by two of her new neighbors, that she had been allowed to resettle in Westchester. Noting that suspicion of her in Connecticut "hath given some cause of apprehension" to the townspeople, in order to "end their jealousyes and feares" a local New York magistrate told her to leave the jurisdiction.[39] Harrison refused. Before any action could be taken against her, her eldest daughter was fortuitously betrothed to Josiah Hunt, a son of Thomas Hunt, one of the men who had protested her presence in Westchester. The elder Hunt became a supporter and appeared in court on her behalf, with his son and three other influential men. Though she was required to give security for her "Civill carriage and good behaviour," the General Court of Assizes in New York ordered "that in regard there is nothing appears against her deserving the continuance of that obligacion shee is to bee releast from it, and hath Liberty to remaine in the Towne of Westchester where shee now resides, or any where else in the Government during her pleasure."[40]

Evidently Harrison continued to live with recurring witchcraft suspicion, but after 1670 there is no further evidence of official harassment.[41] Early in 1672, she reappeared in Hartford to sue eleven of her old Connecticut Valley neighbors, in most cases for debt, and to release her "intrusted overseer" Jonathan Gilbert from his responsibilities for her estate (although he continued to act as guardian to her two younger daughters).[42] A month later, she signed at least some of her remaining Wethersfield land over to Gilbert.[43] After that, she fades from view. She may have returned to Connecticut for good at that time, for some evidence suggests that she died at Dividend, then an outlying section of Wethersfield, in October 1682.[44]

SUSANNA MARTIN

Born in England in 1625, Susanna North was the youngest of three daughters of Richard North. Her mother died when Susanna was young and her father subsequently remarried. The family migrated to New England in or just prior to 1639, the year in which Richard North was listed as one of the first proprietors of Salisbury, Massachusetts. Susanna's sister Mary had married Thomas Jones and was living in

Gloucester by 1642. Of her sister Sarah we know only that she married a man named Oldham, had a daughter named Ann, and died before the child was grown. In August 1646, at the age of twenty-one, Susanna married George Martin, a Salisbury man whose first wife had recently died. In June of the following year, she gave birth to her son Richard, the first of nine children. One of these children, a son, died in infancy.[45] . . .

Early in 1668, less than a year after the birth of her last child, Susanna Martin's father died, leaving a modest estate of about £150. As the only surviving children, the then forty-three-year-old Susanna and her sister Mary anticipated receiving a major portion of the property, to posses either immediately or after the death of their stepmother, Ursula North. They were disappointed. According to the will probated shortly after he died, Richard North had voided all previous wills and written a new one—*nearly two decades* before his death. In this document, dated January 1649, he left all but £22 of his estate directly to his wife. Twenty-one pounds was to be divided among Mary Jones, Susanna Martin, and Ann Bates (Sarah Oldham's daughter). Susanna's share was 20 shillings and the cancellation of a £10 debt George Martin owed his father-in-law. Listed as witnesses to this will were Thomas Bradbury of Salisbury and Mary Jones's daughter, Mary Winsley.[46] But the will raised problems. In 1649, Ann Bates was still Ann Oldham (she did not marry Francis Bates until 1661) and the Mary Winsley listed as witness to the will was still Mary Jones, at most eleven or twelve years old when it was allegedly written.[47] Despite the obvious irregularities, Thomas Bradbury and Mary Winsley attested in court that this was indeed Richard North's last will and testament.

Whether Susanna Martin and her sister saw or protested this will when it was probated cannot be determined. Susanna, at least, may have had more pressing concerns on her mind. In April 1669, a bond of £100 was posted for her appearance at the next Court of Assistants "upon suspicion of witchcraft." That was the same day that George Martin sued William Sargent for slandering his wife. According to George Martin, Sargent had not only said that Susanna "was a witch, and he would call her witch," but also accused her of having "had a child" while still single and of "wringing its neck" shortly after. George Martin also sued

William Sargent's brother Thomas for saying "that his son George Marttin was a bastard and that Richard Marttin was Goodwife Marttin's imp."[48] . . .

Meanwhile, the magistrates bound Susanna Martin over to the higher court to be tried for witchcraft. Although the records have not survived, she must have been acquitted, because several months later she was at liberty. In October 1669, George Martin was again bound for his wife's appearance in court, not for witchcraft this time but for calling one of her neighbors a liar and a thief.[49]

By April 1671, George and Susanna Martin (Susanna's sister Mary Jones would later join them) were involved in what would become protracted litigation over the estate of Susanna's father. Ursula North had died a month or two before, leaving a will, dated shortly after her husband's death, that effectively disinherited her two stepdaughters by awarding them 40 shillings apiece. She left the rest of the original North estate first to her granddaughter, Mary Winsley, and secondarily to Mary and Nathaniel Winsley's only child, Hepzibah.[50]

The exact sequence of the numerous court hearings that followed is less clear. Evidently, Susanna and George Martin initiated legal proceedings against Mary and Nathaniel Winsley in April 1671, for unwarranted possession of the North estate. . . . In October 1672, the General Court responded, giving Susanna Martin liberty to sue for her inheritance a second time at the local level.

In April 1673, the recently widowed Mary Jones and George Martin, acting for his wife, sued Nathaniel Winsley "for withholding the inheritance of housing, lands and other estate . . . under color of a feigned or confused writing like the handwriting of Mr. Thomas Bradbury and seemingly attested by him, and Mary Winsly." The court declared the case nonsuited, and again Susanna Martin appealed to the General Court, requesting that the case be reheard at the local level. The General Court consented in May 1673, and the following October, Susanna and George Martin instituted proceedings against the Winsleys for the third time. Again the county court decided for the defendants, and the Martins appealed to the Court of Assistants. For a while it looked as though things were finally going their way. The higher court, which "found for the plaintiff there being no legall prooffe of Richard

North's will," ordered that "the estate the said North left be left to the disposall of the county court." . . .

[In 1674] Susanna, George, and Mary appealed a final time to the General Court, this time for "a hearing of the whole case" by the highest court itself. The magistrates agreed to hear the case, remitting the usual court fees, as they had done before, on the basis of Susanna's pleas of poverty. But in October 1674, after "perusall of what hath binn heard and alleadged by both parties," the court found for Nathaniel Winsley.[51] In what Susanna Martin and Mary Jones believed was a flagrant miscarriage of justice, they had lost what they considered their rightful inheritances.

For almost the next two decades, Susanna Martin's name rarely appears in the public records of the colony. Her sister Mary died in 1682, followed by her husband George in 1686.[52] Early in 1692, she was again accused of witchcraft, this time by several of the possessed females in Salem. They claimed that her apparition "greviously afflected" them, urging them to become witches themselves. Summoned before the court as witnesses against her were eleven men and four women, all old neighbors of the now sixty-seven-year-old widow.[53]

Unnerved by neither the agonies of the possessed or the magistrates' obvious belief in her guilt, Martin insisted that she was innocent. To Cotton Mather, she "was one of the most impudent, scurrilous, wicked Creatures in the World," who had the effrontery to claim "that she had lead a most virtuous and holy life."[54] Years of living as a reputed witch had left Martin well-versed on the subject of the Devil's powers. "He that appeared in sam[uel]s shape, a glorifyed saint," she said, citing the Bible in her own defense, "can appear in any ones shape." She laughed at the fits of her young accusers, explaining: "Well I may at such folly." When asked what she thought the possessed were experiencing, she said she did not know. Pressed to speculate on it, she retorted: "I do not desire to spend my judgment upon it" and added (revealing what must have been her long-standing opinion of the magistrates' bias), "my thoughts are my own, when they are in, but when they are out they are anothers."[55] . . .

Susanna Martin was found guilty of witch-craft and was one of five women executed on 19 July 1692. One week later, another Salisbury woman was indicted on the same charge. She was Mary Bradbury, the now elderly wife of the man Susanna Martin believed had written her father's "will" nearly twenty-five years before. Mary Bradbury was sentenced to hang too, but friends helped her to escape. No explicit connection between the accusations of the two women is discernible. Rumors circulated, however, that because Thomas Bradbury had friends in positions of authority, there had been little real effort to capture his fugitive wife.[56] . . .

These . . . short histories . . . suggest the diverse economic circumstances of witches in early New England. . . . The . . . women featured in these histories were either (1) daughters of parents who had no sons (or whose sons had died), (2) women in marriages which brought forth only daughters (or in which the sons had died), or (3) women in marriages with no children at all. These patterns had significant economic implications. Because there were no legitimate male heirs in their immediate families, each of these . . . women stood to inherit, did inherit, or were denied their apparent right to inherit substantially larger portions of their fathers' or husbands' accumulated estates than women in families with male heirs. Whatever actually happened to the property in question—and in some cases we simply do not know—these women were aberrations in a society with an inheritance system designed to keep property in the hands of men.

These . . . cases also illustrate fertility and mortality patterns widely shared among the families of accused witches. A substantial majority of New England's accused females were women without brothers, women with daughters but no sons, or women in marriages with no children at all (see Table 1). Of the 267 accused females, enough is known about 158 to identify them as either having or not having brothers or sons to inherit: only 62 of the 158 (39 percent) did, whereas 96 (61 percent) did not. More striking, *once accused*, women without brothers or sons were even more likely than women with brothers or sons to be tried, convicted, and executed: women from families without male heirs made up 64 percent of the females prosecuted, 76 percent of those who were found guilty, and 89 percent of those who were executed.

These figures must be read with care, however, for two reasons. First, eighteen of the sixty-two accused females who *had* brothers or sons to inherit were themselves daughters and granddaughters of women who did not. It appears that these eighteen females, most of whom were young women or girls, were accused because their neighbors believed that their mothers and grandmothers passed their witchcraft on to them. Therefore they form a somewhat ambiguous group. Since they all had brothers to inherit, it would be inaccurate to exclude them from this category in Table 1, yet including them understates the extent to which inheritance-related concerns were at issue in witchcraft accusations. At the same time, the large number of cases in which the fertility and mortality patterns of witches' families are unknown (109 of the 267 accused females in New England) makes it impossible to assess precisely the proportion of women among the accused who did not have brothers or sons.

Table 2 helps clarify the point. It includes as a separate category the daughters and granddaughters of women without brothers or sons and incorporates the cases for which this information is unknown. Although inclusion of the unknowns renders the overall percentages meaningless, this way of representing the available information shows clearly the particular vulnerability of women without brothers or sons. Even if *all* the unknown cases involved women from families *with* male heirs—a highly unlikely possibility—women from families without males to inherit would still form a majority of convicted and executed witches. Were the complete picture visible, I suspect that it would not differ substantially

from that presented earlier in Table 1—which is based on data reflecting 60 percent of New England's witches and which indicates that women without brothers and sons were more vulnerable than other women at all stages of the process.

Numbers alone, however, do not tell the whole story. More remains to be said about what happened to these inheriting or potentially inheriting women, both before and after they were accused of witchcraft.

It was not unusual for women in families without male heirs to be accused of witchcraft shortly after the deaths of fathers, husbands, brothers, or sons. Katherine Harrison [and] Susanna Martin . . . exemplify this pattern. So too does elderly Ann Hibbens of Boston, whose execution in 1656 seems to have had a profound enough effect on some of her peers to influence the outcome of subsequent trials for years to come. Hibbens had three sons from her first marriage, all of whom lived in England; but she had no children by her husband William Hibbens, with whom she had come to Massachusetts in the 1630s. William died in 1654; Ann was brought to trial two years later. Although her husband's will has not survived, he apparently left a substantial portion (if not all) of his property directly to her: when she wrote her own will shortly before her execution, Ann Hibbens was in full possession of a £344 estate, most of which she bequeathed to her sons in England.[57]

Similarly, less than two years elapsed between the death of Gloucester's William Vinson and the imprisonment of his widow Rachel in 1692. Two children, a son and a daughter, had been born to the marriage, but the son had died in 1675. Though William Vinson had had four sons (and three daughters) by a previous marriage, the sons were all dead by 1683. In his will, which he wrote in 1684, before he was certain that his last son had been lost at sea, William left his whole £180 estate to Rachel for her life, stipulating that she could sell part of the lands and cattle if she found herself in need of resources. After Rachel's death, "in Case" his son John "be Living and returne home agayne," William said, most of the estate was to be divided between John and their daughter Abigail. If John did not return, both shares were to be Abigail's.[58] . . .

In other cases, many years passed between the death of the crucial male relative

TABLE 1. Female Witches by Presence or Absence of Brothers or Sons, New England, 1620–1725 (A)

Action	Women without Brothers or Sons	Women with Brothers or Sons	Total
Accused	96 (61%)	62 (39%)	158
Tried	41 (64%)	23 (36%)	64
Convicted	25 (76%)	8 (24%)	33
Executed	17 (89%)	2 (11%)	19

TABLE 2. Female Witches by Presence or Absence of Brothers or Sons, New England, 1620–1725 (B)

Action	Women without Brothers or Sons	Daughters and Granddaughters of Women without Brothers or Sons	Women with Brothers or Sons	Unknown Cases	Total
Accused	96 (36%)	18 (7%)	44 (16%)	109 (41%)	267
Tried	41 (48%)	6 (7%)	17 (20%)	22 (26%)	86
Convicted	25 (56%)	0 (0%)	6 (13%)	12 (27%)	45
Executed	17 (61%)	0 (0%)	2 (7%)	9 (32%)	28

and the moment when a formal witchcraft complaint was filed.

. . . Mary English of Salem was charged with witchcraft seven years after she came into her inheritance. Her father, merchant William Hollingworth, had been declared lost at sea in 1677, but at that time Mary's brother William was still alive. Possibly because the younger William was handling the family's interests in other colonies, or possibly because the father's estate was in debt for more than it was worth, the magistrates gave the widow Elinor Hollingworth power of attorney to salvage what she could. With her "owne labor," as she put it, "but making use of other mens estates," the aggressive and outspoken Mistress Hollingworth soon had her deceased husband's debts paid and his wharf, warehouse, and tavern solvent again.[59] She had no sooner done so, however, than she was accused of witchcraft by the wife of a Gloucester mariner.[60] Though the magistrates gave little credence to the charge at the time, they may have had second thoughts later. In 1685, her son William died, and Elinor subsequently conveyed the whole Hollingworth estate over to Mary English, who was probably her only surviving child.[61]

Elinor Hollingworth had died by 1692, but Mary English was one of the women cried out upon early in the Salem outbreak. Her husband, the merchant Philip English, was accused soon after. Knowing their lives were in grave danger, the Englishes fled to the safety of New York. But as one historian of witchcraft has pointed out, flight was "the legal equivalent of conviction."[62] No sooner had they left than close to £1200 of their property was confiscated under the law providing attainder for witchcraft.[63]

Not all witches from families without male heirs were accused of conspiring with the Devil *after* they had come into their inheritances. On the contrary, some were accused prior to the death of the crucial male relative, many times before it was clear who would inherit. . . . [O]ne of these women . . . was Martha Corey of Salem, who was accused of witchcraft in 1692 while her husband was still alive. Giles Corey had been married twice before and had several daughters by the time he married the widow Martha Rich, probably in the 1680s. With no sons to inherit, Giles's substantial land holdings would, his neighbors might have assumed, be passed on to his wife and daughters. Alice Parker, who may have been Giles's daughter from a former marriage, also came before the magistrates as a witch in 1692, as did Giles himself. Martha Corey and Alice Parker maintained their innocence and were hanged. Giles Corey, in an apparently futile attempt to preserve his whole estate for his heirs, refused to respond to the indictment. To force him to enter a plea, he was tortured: successively heavier weights were placed on his body until he was pressed to death.[64]

What seems especially significant here is that most accused witches whose husbands were still alive were, like their counterparts who were widows and spinsters, over forty years of age—and therefore unlikely if not unable to produce male heirs. Indeed, the fact that witchcraft accusations were rarely taken seriously by the community until the accused stopped bearing children takes on a special meaning when it is juxtaposed with the anomalous position of inheriting women or potentially inheriting women in New England's social structure.

Witches in families without male heirs sometimes had been dispossessed of part or all of their inheritances before—sometimes long before—they were formally charged with witchcraft. Few of these women, however, accepted disinheritance with equanimity. Rather, like Susanna Martin, they took their battles to court, casting themselves in the role of public challengers to the system of male inheritance. In most instances, the authorities sided with their antagonists. . . .

. . . The property of women in families without male heirs was vulnerable to loss in a variety of ways, from deliberate destruction by neighbors (as Katherine Harrison experienced) to official sequestering by local magistrates. In nearly every case, the authorities themselves seem hostile or at best indifferent to the property claims of these women. One final example deserves mention here, not only because it indicates how reluctant magistrates were to leave property in the control of women, but because it shows that the property of convicted witches was liable to seizure even without the benefit of an attainder law.

Rebecca Greensmith had been widowed twice before her marriage to Nathaniel Greensmith. Her first husband, Abraham Elsen of Wethersfield, had died intestate in 1648, leaving an estate £99. After checking the birth dates of the Elsens' two children, three-year-old Sarah and one-year-old Hannah, the court initially left the whole estate with the widow. When Rebecca married Wethersfield's Jarvis Mudge the following year, the local magistrates sequestered the house and land Abraham Elsen had left, worth £40, stating their intention to rent it out "for the Use and Benefit of the two daughters."[65] The family moved to New London shortly after, but Jarvis Mudge died in 1652 and Rebecca moved with Hannah and Sarah to Hartford. Since Rebecca was unable to support herself and her two daughters, the court allowed her to sell the small amount of land owned by her second husband (with whom she had had no children) "for the paing of debts and the Bettering the Childrens portyons."[66]

Sometime prior to 1660, Rebecca married Nathaniel Greensmith. During the Hartford outbreak, Rebecca came under suspicion of witchcraft. After Nathaniel sued his wife's accuser for slander, Nathaniel himself was named. Both husband and wife were convicted and executed.[67]

Respecting Nathaniel's £182 estate, £44 of which was claimed by the then eighteen-year-old Sarah and seventeen-year-old Hannah Elsen, the court ordered the three overseers "to preserve the estate from Waste" and to pay "any just debts," the only one recorded being the Greensmiths' jail fees. Except for allowing the overseers "to dispose of the 2 daughters," presumably to service, the magistrates postponed until the next court any decision concerning the young women's portions. First, however, they deducted £40 to go "to the Treasurer for the County."[68] No reason was given for this substantial appropriation and no record of further distribution of the estate has survived.

Aside from these many women who lived or had lived in families without male heirs, there were at least a dozen other witches who, despite the presence of brothers and sons, came into much larger shares of estates than their neighbors would have expected. In some cases, these women gained full control over the disposition of property. We know about these women because their fathers, husbands, or other relatives left wills, because the women themselves wrote wills, or because male relatives who felt cheated out of their customary shares fought in the courts for more favorable arrangements.

Grace Boulter of Hampton, one of several children of Richard Swain, is one of these women. Grace was accused of witchcraft in 1680, along with her thirty-two-year-old daughter, Mary Prescott. Twenty years earlier, in 1660, just prior to his removal to Nantucket, Grace's father had deeded a substantial portion of his Hampton property to her and her husband Nathaniel, some of which he gave directly to her.[69]

Another witch in this group is Jane James of Marblehead, who left an estate at her death in 1669 which was valued at £85. While it is not clear how she came into possession of it, the property had not belonged to her husband Erasmus, who had died in 1660, though it did play a significant role in a controversy between her son and son-in-law over their rightful shares of both Erasmus's and Jane's estates. Between 1650 and her death in 1669, Jane was accused of witchcraft at least three times by her Marblehead neighbors.[70] . . .

Looking back over the lives of these many

women—most particularly those who did not have brothers or sons to inherit—we begin to understand the complexity of the economic dimension of New England witchcraft. Only rarely does the actual trial testimony indicate that economic power was even at issue. Nevertheless it is there, recurring with a telling persistence once we look beyond what was explicitly said about these women as witches. Inheritance disputes surface frequently enough in witchcraft cases, cropping up as part of the general context even when no direct link between the dispute and the charge is discernible, to suggest the fears that underlay most accusations. No matter how deeply entrenched the principle of male inheritance, no matter how carefully written the laws that protected it, it was impossible to insure that all families had male offspring. The women who stood to benefit from these demographic "accidents" account for most of New England's female witches.

The amount of property in question was not the crucial factor in the way these women were viewed or treated by their neighbors, however. Women of widely varying economic circumstances were vulnerable to accusation and even to conviction. Neither was there a direct line from accuser to material beneficiary of the accusation: others in the community did sometimes profit personally from the losses sustained by these women . . . , but only rarely did the gain accrue to the accusers themselves. Indeed, occasionally there was no direct temporal connection: in some instances several decades passed between the creation of the key economic conditions and the charge of witchcraft; the charge in other cases even anticipated the development of those conditions.

Finally, inheriting or potentially inheriting women were vulnerable to witchcraft accusations not only during the Salem outbreak, but from the time of the first formal accusations in New England at least until the end of the century. . . . The Salem outbreak created only a slight wrinkle in this established fabric of suspicion. If daughters, husbands, and sons of witches were more vulnerable to danger in 1692 than they had been previously, they were mostly the daughters, husbands, and sons of inheriting or potentially inheriting women. As the outbreak spread, it drew into its orbit increasing numbers of women, "unlikely" witches in that they were married

to well-off and influential men, but familiar figures to some of their neighbors nonetheless. What the impoverished Sarah Good had in common with Mary Phips, wife of Massachusetts's governor, was what Eunice Cole had in common with Katherine Harrison. . . . However varied their backgrounds and economic positions, as women without brothers or women without sons, they stood in the way of the orderly transmission of property from one generation of males to another.

NOTES

1. Alan Macfarlane, *Witchcraft in Tudor and Stuart England: A Regional and Comparative Study* (New York, 1970), pp. 149–51. See also Keith Thomas, *Religion and the Decline of Magic* (New York, 1971), pp. 457, 520–21, 560–68.

2. See Trials for Witchcraft in New England (unpaged), dated 5 September 1656 (manuscript volume, Houghton Library, Harvard University, Cambridge, Mass.).

3. Relying on very general indicators (a married woman who worked as a servant, a widow whose husband had left an estate of £39, and so forth), I was able to make rough estimates about the economic position of 150 accused women. Twenty-nine of these women seem to have been poor. . . .

4. For Abigail Somes, see *The Salem Witchcraft Papers: Verbatim Transcripts of the Legal Documents of the Salem Witchcraft Outbreak of 1692*, 3 vols., ed. Paul Boyer and Stephen Nissenbaum (New York, 1977), 3:733–37 (hereafter cited as *Witchcraft Papers*). For Tituba, see *Witchcraft Papers* 3:745–57. Documents relating to Ruth Wilford are in *Witchcraft Papers* 2:459; 3:961; *The Probate Records of Essex County, Massachusetts, 1635–1681*, 3 vols. (Salem, 1916–20), 3:93–95 (hereafter cited as *Essex Probate Records*).

5. Most families in seventeenth-century New England had estates worth less than £200. However, since only a very small proportion of convicted witches who were married seem to have come from families with estates worth *more* than £200, it seems reasonable to conclude that married women from families with less than £200 estates were overrepresented among the accused. Nearly all of the convictions of married women from families with estates worth more than £200 occurred during the Salem outbreak. . . .

6. For accusations against Hannah Griswold and Margaret Gifford, see Norbert B. Lacy, "The Records of the Court of Assistants of Connecticut, 1665–1701" (M.A. thesis, Yale University, 1937), pp. 6–7 (hereafter cited as "Conn. Assistants Records"); and *Records and Files of the Quarterly Courts of Essex County, Massachusetts*, 9 vols. (Salem, 1912–75), 7:405; 8:23 (hereafter cited as *Essex Court Records*).

7. This discussion of the inheritance system of seventeenth-century New England is drawn from the following sources: *The Book of the General Lawes and Libertyes Concerning the Inhabitants of the Massa-*

chusetts, ed. Thomas G. Barnes (facsimile from the 1648 edition, San Marino, Calif., 1975); *The Colonial Laws of Massachusetts. Reprinted from the Edition of 1672, with the Supplements through 1686*, ed. William H. Whitmore (Boston, 1887); John D. Cushing, comp., *The Laws and Liberties of Massachusetts, 1641–91: A Facsimile Edition*, 3 vols. (Wilmington, Del., 1976); *Massachusetts Province Laws, 1692–1699*, ed. John D. Cushing (Wilmington, Del., 1978); *New Hampshire Probate Records; Essex Probate Records: A Digest of the Early Connecticut Probate Records*, vol. 1, ed. Charles W. Manwaring (Hartford, 1904) (hereafter cited as *Conn. Probate Records*); Marylynn Salmon, *Women and the Law of Property in Early America* (Chapel Hill, 1986); George L. Haskins, "The Beginnings of Partible Inheritance in the American Colonies," in *Essays in the History of American Law*, ed. David H. Flaherty (Chapel Hill, 1969); Edmund S. Morgan, *The Puritan Family: Religion and Domestic Relations in Seventeenth-Century New England* (1944; reprint New York, 1966).

8. See Morgan, *The Puritan Family*, pp. 81–82.

9. Barnes, *Book of the General Lawes*, pp. 17–18....

10. Since only a small proportion of men left wills during the colonial period, intestacy law played a significant role in determining inheritance practices. See Salmon, *Women and the Law of Property*, p. 141.

11. Barnes, *The Book of the General Lawes*, p. 53.

12. Young women officially came of age in New England when they reached 18; young men when they reached 21.

13. William Blackstone, *Commentaries on the Laws of England*, 4 vols. (Oxford, 1765–69), 1:433.

14. Once widowed, a woman who inherited land from her father (or who had bought land with her husband in both of their names) could make a will of her own, as could a single woman who came into possession of land.... See Salmon, *Women and the Law of Property*, pp. 144–45 and passim.

15. Evidence suggests that in seventeenth-century New England, daughters of fathers who died relatively young (and possibly most sons) did not normally come into their inheritances until they married. If daughters had received their shares when they came of age, we would expect to find probate records for single women who died before they had the opportunity to marry. Though there are many existing intestate records and wills for single men who died in early adulthood, I have located only one record involving a young, single woman.

16. Wethersfield Land Records (manuscript volume, Town Clerk's Office, Town Hall, Wethersfield, Conn.) 1:19, 38.

17. Given the ages of her children, Katherine Harrison had to have been between her late twenties and her mid-fifties when she was first accused of witchcraft in 1668. I suspect that she was in her forties.

18. See Wethersfield Land Records 2:149; Katherine Harrison to John Winthrop, Jr., undated letter (probably early 1667), and Katherine Harrison's Testimony, undated document (probably October 1669), in the Winthrop Papers, Massachu-

setts Historical Society, Boston (hereafter cited as Winthrop Papers)....

19. Samuel Wyllys Papers: Depositions on Cases of Witchcraft, Assault, Theft, Drunkenness and Other Crimes, Tried in Connecticut, 1663–1728 (manuscript volume, Archives, History and Genealogy Unit, Connecticut State Library, Hartford, doc. 15) (hereafter cited as Wyllys Papers).

20. See Sherman W. Adams and Henry R. Stiles, *The History of Ancient Wethersfield*, 2 vols. (New York, 1904), 1:682; and Lacy, "Conn. Assistants Records," p. 12.

21. Lacy, "Conn. Assistants Records," p. 13.

22. Petition for the Investigation of Katherine Harrison, Recently Released after Imprisonment, Signed by John Chester and Thirty-Eight Other Citizens of Wethersfield (Manuscript Collections, Connecticut Historical Society, Hartford [hereafter cited as Petition for the Investigation of Katherine Harrison]) (emphasis mine). See also Order about Katherine Harrison's Land, in the Winthrop Papers....

23. Lacy, "Conn. Assistants Records," pp. 13–14, 18–19.

24. "The Answers of Some Ministers to the Questions Propounded to Them by the Honored Magistrates," dated 20 October 1669, Samuel Wyllys Papers, Supplement: Depositions on Cases of Witchcraft Tried in Connecticut, 1662–1693, photostat copies of original documents from the Wyllys Papers, Annmary Brown Memorial Brown University Library, Providence, R.I....

25. Lacy, "Conn. Assistants Records," p. 23....

26. Wyllys Papers Supplement, p. 11.

27. Depositions submitted against Harrison in 1668 and 1669 are in the Wyllys Papers, docs. 6–17; Wyllys Papers Supplement, pp. 46–63.... For Harrison's response to these accusations, see Katherine Harrison's Testimony, Winthrop Papers.

28. Manwaring, *Conn. Probate Records* 1:206.

29. "A Complaint of Severall Greevances of the Widdow Harrison's," Wyllys Papers Supplement, p. 53.

30. "The Declaration of Katherine Harrison in Her Appeal to This Court of Assistants," dated September 1668, in Connecticut Archives, Crimes and Misdemeanors, 1st ser. (1662–1789) (manuscript volume, Archives, History and Genealogy Unit, Connecticut State Library, Hartford), vol. 1 (pt. 1):34 (hereafter cited as Crimes and Misdemeanors).

31. Connecticut Colonial Probate Records 56:80; Records of the Colony of Connecticut, Connecticut Colonial Probate Records, County Court, vol. 56, 1663–77 (Archives, History and Genealogy Unit, Connecticut State Library, Hartford, 56:79–81 (hereafter cited as Connecticut Colonial Probate Records).

32. Ibid., pp. 78–79. For the Griswolds as accusers, see Katherine Harrison's Testimony, Winthrop Papers.

33. Connecticut Colonial Probate Records 56:80.

34. "The Declaration of Katherine Harrison," Crimes and Misdemeanors, 1 (pt. 1):34.

35. Manwaring, *Connecticut Probate Records*, p. 206.

36. Katherine Harrison to John Winthrop, Jr., "Letter," *Winthrop Papers*.

37. Wethersfield Land Records 2:149.

38. Petition for the Investigation of Katherine Harrison.

39. See "The Cases of Hall and Harrison," in *Narratives of the Witchcraft Cases, 1648–1706*, ed. Charles Lincoln Burr (New York, 1914), pp. 48–49.

40. Ibid., pp. 48–52.

41. See Samuel D. Drake, *Annals of Witchcraft in New England* (New York, 1869), pp. 133–34.

42. Connecticut Colonial Probate Records 56:118; Wethersfield Land Records 2:249.

43. Wethersfield Land Records 2:210.

44. See Gilbert Collection.

45. See Joseph Merrill, *History of Amesbury, Including the First Seventeen Years of Salisbury. . . .* (Haverhill, Mass., 1880), pp. 11–13, 28; *Vital Records of Salisbury . . .* (Topsfield, Mass., 1915), pp. 151, 415.

46. *Essex Probate Records* 2:125–27.

47. James Savage, *A Genealogical Dictionary of the First Settlers of New England*, 4 vols. (Boston, 1860–62), 1:138; 4:483.

48. See *Essex Court Records* 4:129, 133.

49. *Essex Court Records* 4:184, 187, 239.

50. *Essex Probate Records* 2:223–24.

51. See *Records of the Governor and Company of the Massachusetts Bay in New England*, 6 vols., ed. Nathaniel B. Shurtleff (Boston, 1853–54), 5:6, 26–27.

52. Savage, *Genealogical Dictionary* 2:566. . . . When he died, George Martin left an estate valued at £75, most of which he left to Susanna "during her Widowhood."

53. See *Witchcraft Papers* 2:549–79.

54. Cotton Mather, *The Wonders of the Invisible World* (1693; facsimile of the 1862 London edition, Ann Arbor, Mich., 1974), p. 148.

55. *Witchcraft Papers* 2:551.

56. *Witchcraft Papers* 1:115–29.

57. Ann Hibbens' will is reprinted in *New England Historical and Genealogical Register*, vol. 6 (1852), pp. 287–88.

58. See *Witchcraft Papers* 3:880–81.

59. *Essex Probate Records* 3:191–93.

60. *Essex Court Records* 7:238.

61. *New England Historical and Genealogical Register*, vol. 3 (1849), p. 129.

62. Marion L. Starkey, *The Devil in Massachusetts* (New York, 1949), p. 185.

63. *Witchcraft Papers* 3:988–91.

64. For Martha and Giles Corey and Alice Parker, see *Witchcraft Papers* 1:239–66; 2:623–28, 632–33; 3:985–86, 1018–19.

65. Manwaring, *Conn. Probate Records* 1:7–8.

66. *Records of the Particular Court of Connecticut, 1639–1663*, *Collections of the Connecticut Historical Society*, vol. 22 (1928), p. 119.

67. Ibid., p. 258.

68. Manwaring, *Conn. Probate Records* 1:121–22.

69. Norfolk Deeds (manuscript volume, Registry of Deeds, Essex County Courthouse, Salem, Mass.), 1:116, 154.

70. *Essex Probate Records* 1:314–16; 2:160; *Essex Court Records* 1:199, 204, 229; 2:213; 3:292, 342, 413.

CORNELIA HUGHES DAYTON
Taking the Trade:
Abortion and Gender Relations in an Eighteenth-Century New England Village

Some pregnancies end spontaneously, probably because of an abnormality in the fetus or in the way it is implanted in the womb. Colonial Americans made little distinction between spontaneous and induced abortion; no law attempted to regulate the practice. Efforts to end pregnancies by the use of herbs like savin were generally understood to be efforts to "restore" the regular menstrual cycle. Experienced midwives had impressive records of safe deliveries that are comparable to pre-penicillin twentieth-century experience; Martha Ballard of rural Maine brought some 900 women safely through childbirth in the late eighteenth century.*

In the course of the eighteenth century, male physicians were increasingly involved with midwifery, a practice that had been monopolized by women. Men were also more likely than women midwives to use instruments; indeed only men were trained in the use of the first forceps. In the following essay, Cornelia Hughes Dayton carefully reconstructs the narrative of the abortion and death of Sarah Grosvenor in a Connecticut village in 1742. How does Dayton interpret the meaning of abortion for Sarah Grosvenor and her friends? If it was not illegal, why did they seek to keep it secret? In what ways does Dayton think that relations between young women and young men changed in the mid-eighteenth century? In what ways does Dayton think that relations between young people and their parents changed? How was the memory of Sarah Grosvenor's death transmitted in the histories of the town?

In 1742 in the village of Pomfret, perched in the hills of northeastern Connecticut, nineteen-year-old Sarah Grosvenor and twenty-seven-year-old Amasa Sessions became involved in a liaison that led to pregnancy, abortion, and death. Both were from prominent yeoman families, and neither a marriage between them nor an arrangement for the support of their illegitimate child would have been an unusual event for mid-eighteenth-century New England. Amasa Sessions chose a different course; in consultation with John Hallowell, a self-proclaimed "practitioner of physick," he coerced his lover into taking an abortifacient. Within two months, Sarah fell ill. Unbeknownst to all but Amasa, Sarah, Sarah's sister Zerviah, and her cousin Hannah, Hallowell made an attempt to "Remove her Conseption" by a "manual opperation." Two days later Sarah miscarried, and her two young relatives secretly buried the fetus in the woods. Over the next month, Sarah struggled against a "Malignant fever" and was attended by several physicians, but on September 14, 1742, she died.[1]

Most accounts of induced abortions among seventeenth- and eighteenth-century

*Laurel Thatcher Ulrich, "'The Living Mother of a Living Child': Midwifery and Mortality in Post-Revolutionary New England," *William and Mary Quarterly* 3rd Ser., XLVI (1989): 27–48.

Excerpted from "Taking the Trade: Abortion and Gender Relations in an Eighteenth-Century New England Village" by Cornelia Hughes Dayton in *William and Mary Quarterly*, 3rd Ser., 48 (1991):19–49. Notes have been edited.

Obstetrical Instruments Case, circa 1780.
The case includes forceps, a double lever, two double blunt hooks, and a perforator. Perhaps no technological invention in traditional America had more direct connection to women's lives than these. Skillfully employed, forceps (invented in the eighteenth century) could be lifesaving. Hooks were used to dismember and remove a fetus that had died during delivery. Professional training in the use of instruments was monopolized by male physicians, to whom the middle class turned in the late eighteenth and early nineteenth centuries. Advances in medical technology were accompanied by the exclusion of midwives from advanced training and, increasingly, from the birthing room itself. (Courtesy of the Smithsonian Institution's Division of Science, Medicine & Society.)

whites in the Old and New Worlds consist of only a few lines in a private letter or court record book; these typically refer to the taking of savin or pennyroyal—two common herbal abortifacients. While men and women in diverse cultures have known how to perform abortions by inserting an instrument into the uterus, actual descriptions of such operations are extremely rare for any time period. Few accounts of abortions by instrument have yet been uncovered for early modern England, and I know of no other for colonial North America.[2] Thus the historical fragments recording events in a small New England town in 1742 take on an unusual power to illustrate how an abortion was conducted, how it was talked about, and how it was punished.

We know about the Grosvenor-Sessions case because in 1745 two prominent Windham County magistrates opened an investigation into Sarah's death. Why there was a three-year gap between that event and legal proceedings, and why justices from outside Pomfret initiated the legal process, remain a mystery. In November 1745 the investigating magistrates offered their preliminary opinion that Hallowell, Amasa Sessions, Zerviah Grosvenor, and Hannah Grosvenor were guilty of Sarah's murder, the last three as accessories. From the outset, Connecticut legal officials concentrated not on the act of abortion per se, but on the fact that an abortion attempt had led to a young woman's death.[3]

The case went next to Joseph Fowler, king's attorney for Windham County. He dropped charges against the two Grosvenor women, probably because he needed them as key witnesses and because they had played cover-up roles rather than originating the scheme. A year and a half passed as Fowler's first attempts to get convictions against Hallowell and Sessions failed either before grand juries or before the Superior Court on technical grounds. Finally, in March 1747, Fowler presented Hallowell and Sessions separately for the "highhanded Misdemeanour" of to destroy both Sarah Grosvenor's health and "the fruit of her womb."[4] A grand jury endorsed the bill against Hallowell but rejected a similarly worded presentment against Sessions. At Hallowell's trial before the Superior Court in Windham, the jury brought in a guilty verdict and the chief judge sentenced the physician to twenty-nine lashes and two

hours of public humiliation standing at the town gallows. Before the sentence could be executed, Hallowell managed to break jail. He fled to Rhode Island; as far as records indicate, he never returned to Connecticut. Thus, in the end, both Amasa Sessions and John Hallowell escaped legal punishment for their actions, whereas Sarah Grosvenor paid for her sexual transgression with her life.

Nearly two years of hearings and trials before the Superior Court produced a file of ten depositions and twenty-four other legal documents. This cache of papers is extraordinarily rich, not alone for its unusual chronicle of an abortion attempt, but for its illumination of the fault lines in Pomfret dividing parents from grown children, men from women, and mid-eighteenth-century colonial culture from its seventeenth-century counterpart.

The depositions reveal that in 1742 the elders of Pomfret, men and women alike, failed to act as vigilant monitors of Sarah Grosvenor's courtship and illness. Instead, young, married householders—kin of Sarah and Amasa—pledged themselves in a conspiracy of silence to allow the abortion plot to unfold undetected. The one person who had the opportunity to play middleman between the generations was Hallowell. A man in his forties, dogged by a shady past and yet adept at acquiring respectable connections, Hallowell provides an intriguing and rare portrait of a socially ambitious, rural medical practitioner. By siding with the young people of Pomfret and keeping their secret, Hallowell betrayed his peers and elders and thereby opened himself to severe censure and expulsion from the community.

Beyond depicting generational conflict, the Grosvenor-Sessions case dramatically highlights key changes in gender relations that reverberated through New England society in the eighteenth century. One of these changes involved the emergence of a marked sexual double standard. In the mid-seventeenth century, a young man like Amasa Sessions would have been pressured by parents, friends, or the courts to marry his lover. Had he resisted, he would most likely have been whipped or fined for the crime of fornication. By the late seventeenth century, New England judges gave up on enjoining sexually active couples to marry. In the 1740s, amid shifting standards of sexual behavior and growing concern over the evidentiary impossibility of establishing paternity, prosecutions of young men for premarital sex ceased. Thus fornication was decriminalized for men, but not for women. Many of Sarah Grosvenor's female peers continued to be prosecuted and fined for bearing illegitimate children. Through private arrangements, and occasionally through civil lawsuits, their male partners were sometimes cajoled or coerced into contributing to the child's upkeep.[5]

What is most striking about the Grosvenor-Sessions case is that an entire community apparently forgave Sessions for the extreme measures he took to avoid accountability for his bastard child. Although he initiated the actions that led to his lover's death, all charges against him were dropped. Moreover, the tragedy did not spur Sessions to leave town; instead, he spent the rest of his life in Pomfret as a respected citizen. Even more dramatically than excusing young men from the crime of fornication, the treatment of Amasa Sessions confirmed that the sexually irresponsible activities of men in their youth would not be held against them as they reached for repute and prosperity in their prime.

The documents allow us to listen in on the quite different responses of young men and women to the drama unfolding in Pomfret. Sarah Grosvenor's female kin and friends, as we shall see, became preoccupied with their guilt and with the inevitability of God's vengeance. Her male kin, on the other hand, reacted cautiously and legalistically, ferreting out information in order to assess how best to protect the Grosvenor family name. The contrast reminds us yet again of the complex and gendered ways in which we must rethink conventional interpretations of secularization in colonial New England.

Finally, the Grosvenor case raises more questions than it answers about New Englanders' access to and attitudes toward abortion. If Sarah had not died after miscarriage, it is doubtful that any word of Sessions's providing her with an abortifacient or Hallowell's operation would have survived into the twentieth century. Because it nearly went unrecorded and because it reveals that many Pomfret residents were familiar with the idea of abortion, the case supports historians' assumptions that abortion attempts were far from rare in colonial America.[6] We can also infer from the case that the most dangerous

abortions before 1800 may have been those instigated by men and performed by surgeons with instruments.[7] But both abortion's frequency and the lineaments of its social context remain obscure. . . .

Perhaps the most intriguing question centers on why women and men in early America acted *covertly* to effect abortions when abortion before quickening was legal. The Grosvenor case highlights the answer that applies to most known incidents from the period: abortion was understood as blameworthy because it was an extreme action designed to hide a prior sin, sex outside of marriage.[8] Reading the depositions, it is nearly impossible to disentangle the players' attitudes toward abortion itself from their expressions of censure or anxiety over failed courtship, illegitimacy, and the dangers posed for a young woman by a secret abortion. Strikingly absent from these eighteenth-century documents, however, is either outrage over the destruction of a fetus or denunciations of those who would arrest "nature's proper course." Those absences are a telling measure of how the discourse about abortion would change dramatically in later centuries.

THE NARRATIVE

Before delving into the response of the Pomfret community to Sarah Grosvenor's abortion and death, we need to know just who participated in the conspiracy to cover up her pregnancy and how they managed it. . . .

The chronicle opens in late July 1742 when Zerviah Grosvenor, aged twenty-one, finally prevailed upon her younger sister to admit that she was pregnant. In tears, Sarah explained that she had not told Zerviah sooner because "she had been taking [the] trade to remove it."[9] "Trade" was used in this period to signify stuff or goods, often in the deprecatory sense of rubbish and trash. The *Oxford English Dictionary* confirms that in some parts of England and New England the word was used to refer to medicine. In Pomfret trade meant a particular type of medicine, an abortifacient, thus a substance that might be regarded as "bad" medicine, as rubbish, unsafe and associated with destruction. What is notable is that Sarah and Zerviah, and neighboring young people who also used the word, had no need to explain to one another the meaning of "taking the trade."

Perhaps only a few New Englanders knew how to prepare an abortifacient or knew of books that would give them recipes, but many more, especially young women who lived with the fear of becoming pregnant before marriage, were familiar with at least the *idea* of taking an abortifacient.

Sarah probably began taking the trade in mid-May when she was already three-and-a-half-months pregnant.[10] It was brought to her in the form of a powder by Amasa.[11] Sarah understood clearly that her lover had obtained the concoction "from docter hollowel," who conveyed "directions" for her doses through Amasa. Zerviah deposed later that Sarah had been "loath to Take" the drug and "Thot it an Evil," probably because at three and a half months she anticipated quickening, the time from which she knew the law counted abortion an "unlawful measure."[12] At the outset, Sarah argued in vain with Amasa against his proposed "Method." Later, during June and July, she sometimes "neglected" to take the doses he left for her, but, with mounting urgency, Amasa and the doctor pressed her to comply. "It was necessary," Amasa explained in late July, that she take "more, or [else] they were afraid She would be greatly hurt by what was already done." To calm her worries, he assured her that "there was no life [left] in the Child" and that the potion "would not hurt her." Apparently, the men hoped that a few more doses would provoke a miscarriage, thereby expelling the dead fetus and restoring Sarah's body to its natural balance of humors.

Presumably, Hallowell decided to operate in early August because Sarah's pregnancy was increasingly visible, and he guessed that she was not going to miscarry. An operation in which the fetus would be removed or punctured was now the only certain way to terminate the pregnancy secretly.[13] To avoid the scrutiny of Sarah's parents, Hallowell resorted to a plan he had used once before in arranging a private examination of Sarah. Early one afternoon he arrived at the house of John Grosvenor and begged for a room as "he was weary and wanted Rest." John, Sarah's thirty-one-year-old first cousin, lived with his wife, Hannah, and their young children in a homestead only a short walk down the hill but out of sight of Sarah's father's house. While John and Hannah were busy, the physician sent one of the little children to fetch Sarah.

The narrative of Sarah's fateful meeting with Hallowell that August afternoon is best told in the words of one of the deponents. Abigail Nightingale had married and moved to Pomfret two years earlier, and by 1742 she had become Sarah's close friend. Several weeks after the operation, Sarah attempted to relieve her own "Distress of mind" by confiding the details of her shocking experience to Abigail. Unconnected to the Grosvenor or Sessions families by kinship, and without any other apparent stake in the legal uses of her testimony, Abigail can probably be trusted as a fairly accurate paraphraser of Sarah's words.[14] If so, we have here an unparalleled eyewitness account of an eighteenth-century abortion attempt.

This is how Abigail recollected Sarah's deathbed story:

> On [Sarah's] going down [to her cousin John's], [Hallowell] said he wanted to Speake with her alone; and then they two went into a Room together; and then sd. Hallowell told her it was necessary that something more should be done or else she would Certainly die; to which she replyed that she was afraid they had done too much already, and then he told her that there was one thing more that could easily be done, and she asking him what it was; he said he could easily deliver her. but she said she was afraid there was life in the Child, then he asked her how long she had felt it; and she replyed about a fortnight; then he said that was impossible or could not be or ever would; for that the trade she had taken had or would prevent it; and that the alteration she felt Was owing to what she had taken. And he farther told her that he verily thought that the Child grew to her body to the Bigness of his hand, or else it would have Come away before that time. and that it would never Come away, but Certainly Kill her, unless other Means were used.[15] On which she yielded to his making an Attempt to take it away; charging him that if he could percieve that there was life in it he would not proceed on any Account. And then the Doctor openning his portmantua took an Instrument out of it and Laid it on the Bed, and she asking him what it was for, he replyed that it was to make way; and that then he tryed to remove the Child for Some time in vain putting her to the Utmost Distress, and that at Last she observed he trembled and immediately perceived a Strange alteration in her body and thought a bone of the Child was broken; on which she desired him (as she said) to Call in some body, for that she feared she was a dying, and instantly swooned away.

With Sarah's faint, Abigail's account broke off, but within minutes others, who would testify later, stepped into the room. Hallowell reacted to Sarah's swoon by unfastening the door and calling in Hannah, the young mistress of the house, and Zerviah, who had followed her sister there. Cold water and "a bottle of drops" were brought to keep Sarah from fainting again, while Hallowell explained to the "much Surprized" women that "he had been making an Attempt" to deliver Sarah. Despite their protests, he then "used a further force upon her" but did not succeed in "Tak[ing] the Child . . . away." Some days later Hallowell told a Pomfret man that in this effort "to distroy hir conception" he had "either knipt or Squeisd the head of the Conception." At the time of the attempt, Hallowell explained to the women that he "had done so much to her, as would Cause the Birth of the Child in a Little time." Just before sunset, he packed up his portmanteau and went to a nearby tavern, where Amasa was waiting "to hear [the outcome of] the event." Meanwhile, Sarah, weak-kneed and in pain, leaned on the arm of her sister as the young women managed to make their way home in the twilight.

After his attempted "force," Hallowell fades from the scene, while Zerviah and Hannah Grosvenor become the key figures. About two days after enduring the operation, Sarah began to experience contractions. Zerviah ran to get Hannah, telling her "she Tho't . . . Sarah would be quickly delivered." They returned to find Sarah, who was alone "in her Father's Chamber," just delivered and rising from the chamber pot. In the pot was "an Untimely birth"—a "Child [that] did not Appear to have any Life In it." To Hannah, it "Seemed by The Scent . . . That it had been hurt and was decaying," while Zerviah later remembered it as "a perfect Child," even "a pritty child." Determined to keep the event "as private as they Could," the two women helped Sarah back to bed, and then "wr[ap]ed . . . up" the fetus, carried it to the woods on the edge of the farmstead, and there "Buried it in the Bushes."

. . . [A]bout ten days after the miscarriage, Sarah grew feverish and weak. Her parents consulted two college-educated physicians who hailed from outside the Pomfret area. Their visits did little good, nor were Sarah's symptoms—fever, delirium, convulsions—relieved by a visit from Hallowell, whom Amasa "fetcht" to Sarah's bedside. In the end, Hallowell, who had decided to move from nearby Killingly to more distant Providence, washed his hands of the case. A few days before Sarah died, her cousin John "went after" Hallowell, whether to bring him back or to express his rage, we do not know. Hallowell predicted "that She woul[d] not live."

Silence seems to have settled on the Grosvenor house and its neighborhood after Sarah's death on September 14. It was two and a half years later that rumors about a murderous abortion spread through and beyond Pomfret village, prompting legal investigation. The silence, the gap between event and prosecution, the passivity of Sarah's parents—all lend mystery to the narrative. But despite its ellipses, the Grosvenor case provides us with an unusual set of details about one young couple's extreme response to the common problem of failed courtship and illegitimacy. To gain insight into both the mysteries and the extremities of the Grosvenor-Sessions case, we need to look more closely at Pomfret, at the two families centrally involved, and at clues to the motivations of the principal participants. Our abortion tale, it turns out, holds beneath its surface a complex trail of evidence about generational conflict and troubled relations between men and women.

THE POMFRET PLAYERS

In 1742 the town of Pomfret had been settled for just over forty years. Within its central neighborhood and in homesteads scattered over rugged, wooded hillsides lived probably no more than 270 men, women, and children.[16] During the founding decades, the fathers of Sarah and Amasa ranked among the ten leading householders; Leicester Grosvenor and Nathaniel Sessions were chosen often to fill important local offices.

Grosvenor, the older of the two by seven years, had inherited standing and a choice farmstead from his father, one of the original six purchasers of the Pomfret territory. When the town was incorporated in 1714, he was elected a militia officer and one of the first selectmen. He was returned to the latter post nineteen times and eventually rose to the highest elective position—that of captain—in the local trainband. Concurrently, he was appointed many times throughout the 1710s and 1720s to ad hoc town committees, often alongside Nathaniel Sessions. But unlike Sessions, Grosvenor went on to serve at the colony level. Pomfret freemen chose him to represent them at ten General Assembly sessions between 1726 and 1744. Finally, in the 1730s, when he was in his late fifties, the legislature appointed him a justice of the peace for Windham County. Thus, until his retirement in 1748 at age seventy-four, his house would have served as the venue for petty trials, hearings, and recordings of documents. After retiring from public office, Grosvenor lived another eleven years, leaving behind in 1759 an estate worth over £600.[17]

Nathaniel Sessions managed a sizable farm and ran one of Pomfret's taverns at the family homestead. Town meetings were sometimes held there. Sessions was chosen constable in 1714 and rose from ensign to lieutenant in the militia—always a step behind Leicester Grosvenor. He could take pride in one exceptional distinction redounding to the family honor: in 1737 his son Darius became only the second Pomfret resident to graduate from Yale College, and before Sessions died at ninety-one he saw Darius elected assistant and then deputy governor of Rhode Island.[18]

The records are silent as to whether Sessions and his family resented the Grosvenors, who must have been perceived in town as more prominent, or whether the two families . . . enjoyed a close relationship that went sour for some reason *before* the affair between Sarah and Amasa. Instead, the signs (such as the cooperative public work of the two fathers, the visits back and forth between the Grosvenor and Sessions girls) point to a long-standing friendship and dense web of interchanges between the families. Indeed, courtship and marriage between a Sessions son and a Grosvenor daughter would hardly have been surprising.

What went wrong in the affair between Sarah and Amasa is not clear. Sarah's sisters and cousins knew that "Amasy" "made Sute to" Sarah, and they gave no indication of disapproving. The few who guessed at Sarah's condition in the summer of 1742 were not so much surprised that she was pregnant as that the couple "did not marry." It was evidently routine in this New England village, as in others, for courting couples to post banns for their nuptials soon after the woman discovered that she was pregnant.

Amasa offered different answers among his Pomfret peers to explain his failure to marry his lover. When Zerviah Grosvenor told Amasa that he and Sarah "had better Marry," he responded, "That would not do," for "he was afraid of his parents . . . [who would] always make their lives [at home] uncomfortable." Later, Abigail Nightingale heard rumors that Amasa was resorting to the standard excuse of men wishing to avoid a shotgun marriage—denying that the child was his.[19] Hallowell, with whom Amasa may have been honest, claimed "the Reason that they did not marry" was "that Sessions Did not Love her well a nough for [he] saith he did not believe it was his son and if he Could Cause her to gitt Red of it he would not Go near her again." Showing yet another face to a Grosvenor kinsman after Sarah's death, Amasa repented his actions and extravagantly claimed he would "give All he had" to "bring Sarah . . . To life again . . . and have her as his wife."

The unusual feature of Amasa's behavior was not his unwillingness to marry Sarah, but his determination to terminate her pregnancy before it showed. Increasing numbers of young men in eighteenth-century New England weathered the temporary obloquy of abandoning a pregnant lover in order to prolong their bachelorhood or marry someone else. What drove Amasa, and an ostensibly reluctant Sarah, to resort to abortion? Was it fear of their fathers? Nathaniel Sessions had chosen Amasa as the son who would remain on the family farm and care for his parents in their old age. An ill-timed marriage could have disrupted these plans and threatened Amasa's inheritance.[20] For his part, Leicester Grosvenor may have made it clear to his daughter that he would be greatly displeased at her marrying before she reached a certain age or until her older sister wed. Rigid piety, an authoritarian nature, an intense concern with being seen as a good household governor—any of these traits in Leicester Grosvenor or Nathaniel Sessions could have colored Amasa's decisions.

Perhaps it was not family relations that proved the catalyst but Amasa's acquaintance with a medical man who boasted about a powder more effective than the herbal remedies that were part of women's lore. Hallowell himself had fathered an illegitimate child fifteen years earlier, and he may have encouraged a rakish attitude in Amasa, beguiling the younger man with the promise of dissociating sex from its possible consequences. Or the explanation may have been that classic one: another woman. Two years after Sarah's death, Amasa married Hannah Miller of Rehoboth, Massachusetts. Perhaps in early 1742 he was already making trips to the town just east of Providence to see his future wife.[21]

What should we make of Sarah's role in the scheme? It is possible that she no longer loved Amasa and was as eager as he to forestall external pressures toward a quick marriage. However, Zerviah swore that on one occasion before the operation Amasa reluctantly agreed to post banns for their nuptials and that Sarah did not object.[22] *If* Sarah was a willing and active participant in the abortion plot all along, then by 1745 her female kin and friends had fabricated and rehearsed a careful and seamless story to preserve the memory of the dead girl untarnished.

In the portrait drawn by her friends, Sarah reacted to her pregnancy and to Amasa's plan first by arguing and finally by doing her utmost to protect her lover. She may have wished to marry Amasa, yet she did not insist on it or bring in older family members to negotiate with him and his parents. Abigail Nightingale insisted that Sarah accepted Amasa's recalcitrance and only pleaded with him that they not "go on to add sin to sin." Privately, she urged Amasa that there was an alternative to taking the trade—a way that would enable him to keep his role hidden and prevent the couple from committing a "Last transgression [that] would be worse then the first." Sarah told him that "she was willing to take the sin and shame to her self, and to be obliged never to tell whose Child it was, and that she did not doubt but that if she humbled her self on her Knees to her Father he would take her and her Child home." Her lover, afraid that his identity would become known, vetoed her proposal.[23]

According to the Pomfret women's reconstruction, abortion was not a freely chosen and defiant act for Sarah. Against her own desires, she reluctantly consented in taking the trade only because Amasa "So very earnestly perswaided her." In fact, she had claimed to her friends that she was coerced; he "would take no denyal." Sarah's confidantes presented her as being aware of her options, shrinking from abortion as an unnatural and immoral deed, and yet finally choosing the strategy consistent

with her lover's vision of what would best protect their futures. Thus, if Amasa's hubris was extreme, so too was Sarah's internalization of those strains of thought in her culture that taught women to make themselves pleasing and obedient to men.

While we cannot be sure that the deponents' picture of Sarah's initial recoil and reluctant submission to the abortion plot was entirely accurate, it is clear that once she was caught up in the plan she extracted a pledge of silence from all her confidantes. Near her death, before telling Abigail about the operation, she "insist[ed] on . . . [her friend's] never discovering the Matter" to anyone. Clearly, she had earlier bound Zerviah and Hannah on their honor not to tell their elders. Reluctant when faced with the abortionist's powder, Sarah became a leading co-conspirator when alone with her female friends.

One of the most remarkable aspects of the Grosvenor-Sessions case is Sarah and Amasa's success in keeping their parents in the dark, at least until her final illness. If by July Sarah's sisters grew suspicious that Sarah was "with child," what explains the failure of her parents to observe her pregnancy and to intervene and uncover the abortion scheme? Were they negligent, preoccupied with other matters, or willfully blind? . . .

In terms of who knew what, the events of summer 1742 in Pomfret apparently unfolded in two stages. The first stretched from Sarah's discovery of her pregnancy by early May to some point in late August after her miscarriage. In this period a determined, collective effort by Sarah and Amasa and their friends kept their elders in the dark.[24] When Sarah fell seriously ill from the aftereffects of the abortion attempt and miscarriage, rumors of the young people's secret activities reached Leicester Grosvenor's neighbors and even one of the doctors he had called in. It is difficult to escape the conclusion that by Sarah's death in mid-September her father and stepmother had learned of the steps that had precipitated her mortal condition and kept silent for reasons of their own.

Except for Hallowell, the circle of intimates entrusted by Amasa and Sarah with their scheme consisted of young adults ranging in age from nineteen to thirty-three. Born between about 1710 and 1725, these young people had grown up just as the town attracted enough settlers to support a church, militia,

and local market. They were second-generation Pomfret residents who shared the generational identity that came with sitting side by
side through long worship services, attending
school, playing, and working together at children's tasks. By 1740, these sisters, brothers,
cousins, courting couples, and neighbors, in
their visits from house to house—sometimes
in their own households, sometimes at their
parents'—had managed to create a world of
talk and socializing that was largely exempt
from parental supervision.[25] In Pomfret in
1742 it was this group of young people in their
twenties and early thirties, not the cluster of
Grosvenor matrons over forty-five, who monitored Sarah's courtship, attempted to get
Amasa to marry his lover, privately investigated the activities and motives of Amasa and
Hallowell, and, belatedly, spoke out publicly
to help Connecticut juries decide who should
be blamed for Sarah's death.

That Leicester Grosvenor made no public
move to punish those around him and that he
avoided giving testimony when legal proceedings commenced are intriguing clues to social
changes underway in New England villages in
the mid-eighteenth century. Local leaders like
Grosvenor, along with the respectable yeomen
whom he represented in public office, were
increasingly withdrawing delicate family problems from the purview of their communities.
Slander, illegitimacy, and feuds among neighbors came infrequently to local courts by mid-
century, indicating male householders' growing preference for handling such matters
privately.[26] Wealthy and ambitious families
adopted this ethic of privacy at the same time
that they became caught up in elaborating their
material worlds by adding rooms and acquiring luxury goods.[27] . . . But all the fine accou-
trements in the world would not excuse Justice
Grosvenor from his obligation to govern his
household effectively. Mortified no doubt at his
inability to monitor the young people in his
extended family, he responded, ironically, by
extending their conspiracy of silence. The best
way for him to shield the family name from
scandal and protect his political reputation in
the county and colony was to keep the story of
Sarah's abortion out of the courts.

THE DOCTOR

John Hallowell's status as an outsider in Pomfret and his dangerous, secret alliance with the

town's young adults may have shaped his destiny as the one conspirator sentenced to suffer
at the whipping post. Although the physician
had been involved in shady dealings before
1742, he had managed to win the trust of many
patients and a respectable social standing.
Tracking down his history . . . tells us something of the uncertainty surrounding personal
and professional identity before the advent of
police records and medical licensing boards. It
also gives us an all-too-rare glimpse into the
fashion in which an eighteenth-century country doctor tried to make his way in the world.

Hallowell's earliest brushes with the law
came in the 1720s. In 1725 he purchased land
in Killingly, a Connecticut town just north of
Pomfret and bordering both Massachusetts
and Rhode Island. Newly married, he was
probably in his twenties at the time. Seven
months before his wife gave birth to their first
child, a sixteen-year-old Killingly woman
charged Hallowell with fathering her illegitimate child. Using the alias Nicholas Hallaway,
he fled to southeastern Connecticut, where he
lived as a "transient" for three months. He was
arrested and settled the case by admitting to
paternity and agreeing to contribute to the
child's maintenance for four years.[28]

Hallowell resumed his life in Killingly.
Two years later, now referred to as "Dr.," he
was arrested again; this time the charge was
counterfeiting. Hallowell and several confederates were hauled before the governor and
council for questioning and then put on trial
before the Superior Court. Although many
Killingly witnesses testified to the team's suspect activities in a woodland shelter, the
charges against Hallowell were dropped when
a key informer failed to appear in court.[29]

Hallowell thus escaped conviction on a
serious felony charge, but he had been tainted
by stories linking him to the criminal subculture of transient, disorderly, greedy, and manually skilled men who typically made up
gangs of counterfeiters in eighteenth-century
New England.[30] After 1727 Hallowell may
have given up dabbling in money-making
schemes and turned to earning his livelihood
chiefly from his medical practice. Like two-
thirds of the male medical practitioners in
colonial New England, he probably did not
have college or apprentice training, but his
skill, or charm, was not therefore necessarily
less than that of any one of his peers who

might have inherited a library of books and a fund of knowledge from a physician father. All colonial practitioners, as Richard D. Brown reminds us, mixed learned practices with home or folk remedies, and no doctor had access to safe, reliable pharmacological preparations or antiseptic surgical procedures.[31]

In the years immediately following the counterfeiting charge. Hallowell appears to have made several deliberate moves to portray himself as a sober neighbor and reliable physician. At about the time of his second marriage, in 1729, he became a more frequent attendant at the Killingly meetinghouse, where he renewed his covenant and presented his first two children for baptism. He also threw himself into the land and credit markets of northeastern Connecticut, establishing himself as a physician who was also an enterprising yeoman and a frequent litigant.[32]

These activities had dual implications. On the one hand, they suggest that Hallowell epitomized the eighteenth-century Yankee citizen—a man as comfortable in the courtroom and countinghouse as at a patient's bedside; a man of restless energy, not content to limit his scope to his fields and village; a practical, ambitious man with a shrewd eye for a good deal.[33] On the other hand, Hallowell's losses to Boston creditors, his constant efforts to collect debts, and his farflung practice raise questions about the nature of his activities and medical practice. He evidently had clients not just in towns across northeastern Connecticut but also in neighboring Massachusetts and Rhode Island. Perhaps rural practitioners normally traveled extensively, spending many nights away from their wives and children. It is also possible, however, either that Hallowell was forced to travel because established doctors from leading families had monopolized the local practice or that he chose to recruit patients in Providence and other towns as a cover for illicit activities.[34] Despite his land speculations and his frequent resort to litigation, Hallowell was losing money. In the sixteen years before 1742, his creditors secured judgments against him for a total of £1,060, while he was able to collect only £700 in debts.[35] The disjunction between his ambition and actual material gains may have led Hallowell in middle age to renew his illicit money-making schemes. By supplying young men with potent abortifacients and dabbling in schemes to counterfeit New England's paper money, he betrayed the very gentlemen whose respect, credit, and society he sought.

What is most intriguing about Hallowell was his ability to ingratiate himself throughout his life with elite men whose reputations were unblemished by scandal. Despite the rumors that must have circulated about his early sexual dalliance, counterfeiting activities, suspect medical remedies, heavy debts, and shady business transactions, leading ministers, merchants, and magistrates welcomed him into their houses. . . .

Lacking college degree and family pedigree, Hallowell traded on his profession and his charm to gain acceptability with the elite. In August 1742 he shrewdly removed himself from the Pomfret scene, just before Sarah Grosvenor's death. In that month he moved, possibly without his wife and children, to Providence, where he had many connections. Within five years, Hallowell had so insinuated himself with town leaders such as Stephen Hopkins that fourteen of them petitioned for mitigation of what they saw as the misguided sentence imposed on him in the Grosvenor case.[36]

Hallowell's capacity for landing on his feet, despite persistent brushes with scandal, debt, and the law, suggests that we should look at the fluidity of New England's eighteenth-century elite in new ways.[37] What bound sons of old New England families, learned men, and upwardly mobile merchants and professionals in an expanded elite may partly have been a reshaped, largely unspoken set of values shared by men. We know that the archetype for white New England women as sexual beings was changing from carnal Eve to resisting Pamela and that the calculus of accountability for seduction was shifting blame solely to women.[38] But the simultaneous metamorphosis in cultural images and values defining manhood in the early and mid-eighteenth century has not been studied. The scattered evidence we do have suggests that, increasingly, for men in the more secular and anglicized culture of New England, the lines between legitimate and illegitimate sexuality, between sanctioned and shady business dealings, and between speaking the truth and protecting family honor blurred. Hallowell's acceptability to men like minister Ebenezer Williams and merchant Stephen Hopkins hints at how changing sexual and moral standards shaped the economic and social alliances made by New England's male leadership in the 1700s.

WOMEN'S TALK AND MEN'S TALK

If age played a major role in determining who knew the truth about Sarah Grosvenor's illness, gender affected how the conspiring young adults responded to Sarah's impending death and how they weighed the issue of blame. Our last glimpse into the social world of eighteenth-century Pomfret looks at the different ways in which women and men reconstructed their roles in the events of 1742.

An inward gaze, a strong consciousness of sin and guilt, a desire to avoid conflict and achieve reconciliation, a need to confess—these are the impulses expressed in women's intimate talk in the weeks before Sarah died. The central female characters in the plot, Sarah and Zerviah Grosvenor, lived for six weeks with the daily fear that their parents or aunts might detect Sarah's condition or their covert comings and goings. Deposing three years later, Zerviah represented the sisters as suffering under an intensifying sense of complicity as they had passed through two stages of involvement in the concealment plan. At first, they were passive players, submitting to the hands of men. But once Hallowell declared that he had done all he could, they were left to salvage the conspiracy by enduring the terrors of a first delivery alone, knowing that their failure to call in the older women of the family resembled the decision made by women who committed infanticide.[39] While the pain and shock of miscarrying a five-and-one-half-month fetus through a possibly lacerated vagina may have been the experience that later most grieved Sarah, Zerviah would be haunted particularly by her stealthy venture into the woods with Hannah to bury the shrouded evidence of miscarriage.[40]

The Grosvenor sisters later recalled that they had regarded the first stage of the scheme—taking the trade—as "a Sin" and "an Evil" not so much because it was intended to end the life of a fetus as because it entailed a protracted set of actions, worse than a single lie, to cover up an initial transgression: fornication. According to their religion and the traditions of their New England culture, Sarah and Zerviah knew that the proper response to

the sin of "uncleanness" (especially when it led to its visible manifestation, pregnancy) was to confess, seeking to allay God's wrath and cleanse oneself and one's community. Dire were the consequences of hiding a grave sin, so the logic and folklore of religion warned.[41] Having piled one covert act upon another, all in defiance of her parents, each sister wondered if she had not ventured beyond the pale, forsaking God and in turn being forsaken. . . .

. . . [V]isions of judgment and of their personal accountability to God haunted Sarah and Zerviah during the waning days of summer—or so their female friends later contended. Caught between the traditional religious ethic of confession, recently renewed in revivals across New England, and the newer, status-driven cultural pressure to keep moral missteps private, the Grosvenor women declined to take up roles as accusers. By focusing on their own actions, they rejected a portrait of themselves as helpless victims, yet they also ceded to their male kin responsibility for assessing blame and mediating between the public interest in seeing justice done and the private interests of the Grosvenor family. Finally, by trying to keep the conspiracy of silence intact and by allowing Amasa frequent visits to her bedside to lament his role and his delusion by Hallowell, Sarah at once endorsed a policy of private repentance and forgiveness *and* indicated that she wished her lover to be spared eventual public retribution for her death.

Talk among the men of Pomfret in the weeks preceding and following Sarah's death centered on more secular concerns than the preoccupation with sin and God's anger that ran through the women's conversations. Neither Hallowell nor Sessions expressed any guilt or sense of sin, as far as the record shows, *until* Sarah was diagnosed as mortally ill.[42] Indeed, their initial accounts of the plot took the form of braggadocio, with Amasa (according to Hallowell) casting himself as the rake who could "gitt Red" of his child and look elsewhere for female companionship, and Hallowell boasting of his abortionist's surgical technique to Sarah's cousin Ebenezer. Later, anticipating popular censure and possible prosecution, each man "Tried to Cast it" on the other. The physician insisted that "He did not do any thing but What Sessions Importuned him to Do," while Amasa exclaimed "That he could freely be Strip[p]ed naked provided he could bring Sarah . . . To life again . . . , but Doct Hallowell had Deluded him, and Destroyed her."[43] While this sort of denial and buck-passing seems very human, it was the antithesis of the New England way—a religious way of life that made confession its central motif. The Grosvenor-Sessions case is one illustration among many of how New England women continued to measure themselves by "the moral allegory of repentance and confession" while men, at least when presenting themselves before legal authorities, adopted secular voices and learned self-interested strategies.[44]

For the Grosvenor men—at least the cluster of Sarah's cousins living near her—the key issue was not exposing sin but protecting the family's reputation. In the weeks before Sarah died, her cousins John and Ebenezer each attempted to investigate and sort out the roles and motives of Amasa Sessions and John Hallowell in the scheme to conceal Sarah's pregnancy. Grilled in August by Ebenezer . . . , Hallowell revealed that "Sessions had bin Interseeding with him to Remove her Conseption." On another occasion, . . . Hallowell was more specific. He "[did] with her [Sarah] as he did . . . because Sessions Came to him and was So very earnest . . . and offered him five pounds if he would do it." "But," Hallowell boasted, "he would have twenty of[f] of him before he had done."[45] . . .

John and Ebenezer, deposing three or four years after these events, did not . . . explain why they did not act immediately to have charges brought against the two conspirators. Perhaps these young householders were loath to move against a male peer and childhood friend. More likely, they kept their information to themselves to protect John's wife, Hannah, and their cousin Zerviah from prosecution as accessories. They may also have acted, in league with their uncle Leicester, out of a larger concern for keeping the family name out of the courts. Finally, it is probable that the male cousins, partly because of their own complicity and partly because they may have believed that Sarah had consented to the abortion, simply did not think that Amasa's and Hallowell's actions added up to the murder to their relative.

Three years later, yet another Grosvenor cousin intervened, expressing himself much more vehemently than John or Ebenezer ever had. In 1742, John Shaw at age thirty-eight may have been perceived by the younger Grosvenors as too old—too close to the age when men took public office and served as grand jurors—to be trusted with their secret. Shaw seems to have known nothing of Sarah's taking the trade or having a miscarriage until 1745 when "the Storys" suddenly surfaced. Then Hannah and Zerviah gave him a truncated account. Shaw reacted with rage, realizing that Sarah had died not of natural causes but from "what Hollowell had done," and he set out to wring the truth from the doctor. Several times he sought out Hallowell in Rhode Island to tell him that "I could not look upon him otherwise Than [as] a Bad man Since he had Destroyed my Kinswoman." When Hallowell countered that "Amasa Sessions . . . was the Occasion of it," Shaw's fury grew. "I Told him he was like old Mother Eve When She said The Serpent beguild her, . . . [and] I Told him in my Mind he Deserved to dye for it."

Questioning Amasa, Shaw was quick to accept his protestations of sincere regret and his insistence that Hallowell had "Deluded" him. Shaw concluded that Amasa had never "Importuned [Hallowell] . . . to lay hands on her" (that is, to perform the manual abortion). Forged in the men's talk about the Grosvenor-Sessions case in 1745 and 1746 appears to have been a consensus that, while Amasa Sessions was somewhat blameworthy "as concerned in it," it was only Hallowell—the outsider, the man easily labeled a quack—who deserved to be branded "a Man of Death." Nevertheless, it was the stories of *both* men and women that ensured the fulfillment of a doctor's warning to Hallowell in the Leicester Grosvenor house just before Sarah died: "The Hand of Justice [will] Take hold of [you] sooner or Later."[46]

THE LAW

The hand of justice reached out to catch John Hallowell in November 1745. . . . *Something* had caused Zerviah and Hannah Grosvenor to break their silence. Zerviah provided the key to the puzzle, as she alone had been present at the crucial series of incidents leading to Sarah's death. The only surviving account of Zerviah's belated conversion from silence to public confession comes from the stories told by Pomfret residents into the nineteenth century. In Ellen Larned's melodramatic prose, the "whispered" tale recounted Zerviah's increasing discomfort thus: "Night after night, in her solitary chamber, the surviving sister was awakened by the rattling of the rings on which her bed-curtains were suspended, a ghostly knell continuing and intensifying till she was convinced of its preternatural origin; and at length, in response to her agonized entreaties, the spirit of her dead sister made known to her, 'That she could not rest in her grave till her crime was made public.'"[47]

Embellished as this tale undoubtedly is, we should not dismiss it out of hand as a Victorian ghost story. In early modern English culture, belief persisted in both apparitions and the supernatural power of the guiltless victim to return and expose her murderer.[48] Zerviah in 1742 already fretted over her sin as an accomplice, yet she kept her pledge of silence to her sister. It is certainly conceivable that, after a lapse of three years, she could no longer bear the pressure of hiding the acts that she increasingly believed amounted to the murder of her sister and an unborn child. Whether Zerviah's sudden outburst of talk in 1745 came about at the urging of some Pomfret confidante, or perhaps under the influence of the revivals then sweeping Windham County churches, or indeed because of her belief in nightly visitations by her dead sister's spirit, we simply cannot know.[49]

The Pomfret meetinghouse was the site of the first public legal hearing into the facts behind Sarah Grosvenor's death. We can imagine that townsfolk crowded the pews over the course of two November days to watch two prominent county magistrates examine a string of witnesses before pronouncing their preliminary judgment. The evidence, they concluded, was sufficient to bind four people over for trial at the Superior Court: Hallowell, who in their opinion was "Guilty of murdering Sarah," along with Amasa Sessions, Zerviah Grosvenor, and Hannah Grosvenor as accessories to that murder.[50] The inclusion of Zerviah and Hannah may have been a ploy to pressure these crucial, possibly still reluctant, witnesses to testify for the crown. When Joseph Fowler, the king's attorney, prepared a formal indictment in the case eleven months later, he dropped all charges against Zerviah and Hannah. Rather than stand trial, the two women traveled frequently during 1746 and

1747 to the county seat to give evidence against Sessions and Hallowell.

The criminal process recommenced in September 1746. A grand jury empaneled by the Superior Court at its Windham session first rejected a presentment against Hallowell for murdering Sarah "by his Wicked and Diabolical practice." Fowler, recognizing that the capital charges of murder and accessory to murder against Hallowell and Sessions were going to fail before jurors, changed his tack. He presented the grand jury with a joint indictment against the two men not for outright murder but for endangering Sarah's health by trying to "procure an Abortion" with medicines and "a violent manual opperation"; this time the jurors endorsed the bill. When the Superior Court trial opened in November, two attorneys for the defendants managed to persuade the judges that the indictment was faulty on technical grounds. However, upon the advice of the king's attorney that there "appear reasons vehemently to suspect" the two men "Guilty of Sundry Heinous Offenses" at Pomfret four years earlier, the justices agreed to bind them over to answer charges in March 1747.[51]

Fowler next moved to bring separate indictments against Hallowell and Sessions for the "highhanded misdemeanour" of endeavoring to destroy Sarah's health "and the fruit of her womb." This wording echoed the English common law designation of abortion as a misdemeanor, not a felony or capital crime. A newly empaneled grand jury of eighteen county yeomen made what turned out to be the pivotal decision in getting a conviction: they returned a true bill against Hallowell and rejected a similarly worded bill against Sessions.[52] Only Hallowell, "the notorious physician," would go to trial.[53]

On March 20, 1747, John Hallowell stepped before the bar for the final time to answer for the death of Sarah Grosvenor. He maintained his innocence, the case went to a trial jury of twelve men, and they returned with a guilty verdict. The Superior Court judges, who had discretion to choose any penalty less than death, pronounced a severe sentence of public shaming and corporal punishment. Hallowell was to be paraded to the town gallows, made to stand there before the public for two hours "with a rope visibly hanging about his neck," and then endure a public whipping of twenty-nine lashes "on the naked back."[54]

Before the authorities could carry out this sentence, Hallowell escaped and fled to Rhode Island. From Providence seven months after his trial, he audaciously petitioned the Connecticut General Assembly for a mitigated sentence, presenting himself as a destitute "Exile." As previously noted, fourteen respected male citizens of Providence took up his cause, arguing that this valued doctor had been convicted by prejudiced witnesses and hearsay evidence and asserting that corporal punishment was unwarranted in a misdemeanor case. While the Connecticut legislators rejected these petitions, the language used by Hallowell and his Rhode Island patrons is yet another marker of the distance separating many educated New England men at mid-century from their more God-fearing predecessors. Never mentioning the words "sin" or "repentance," the Providence men wrote that Hallowell was justified in escaping the lash since "every Person is prompted [by the natural Law of Self-Preservation] to avoid Pain and Misery."[55]

In the series of indictments against Hallowell and Sessions, the central legal question became who had directly caused Sarah's death. To the farmers in their forties and fifties who sat as jurors, Hallowell clearly deserved punishment. By recklessly endangering Sarah's life he had abused the trust that heads of household placed in him as a physician.[56] Moreover, he had conspired with the younger generation to keep their dangerous activities secret from their parents and elders.

Several rationales could have been behind the Windham jurors' conclusion that Amasa Sessions ought to be spared the lash. Legally, they could distinguish him from Hallowell as not being *directly* responsible for Sarah's death. Along with Sarah's male kin, they dismissed the evidence that Amasa had instigated the scheme, employed Hallowell, and monitored all of his activities. Perhaps they saw him as a native son who deserved the chance to prove himself mature and responsible. They may have excused his actions as nothing more than a misguided effort to cast off an unwanted lover. Rather than acknowledge that a culture that excused male sexual irresponsibility was responsible for Sarah's death, the Grosvenor family, the Pomfret community, and the jury men of the county persuaded themselves that Sessions had been ignorant of the potentially deadly consequences of his actions.

MEMORY AND HISTORY

No family feud, no endless round of recriminations followed the many months of deposing and attending trials that engaged the Grosvenor and Sessions clans in 1746 and 1747. Indeed, as Sarah and Amasa's generation matured, the ties between the two families thickened. . . . In 1775 Amasa's third son, and namesake, married sixteen-year-old Esther Grosvenor, daughter of Sarah's brother, Leicester, Jr.[57]

It is clear that the Grosvenor clan was not willing to break ranks with their respectable yeoman neighbors and heap blame on the Sessions family for Sarah's death. It would, however, be fascinating to know what women in Pomfret and other Windham County towns had to say about the outcome of the legal proceedings in 1747. Did they concur with the jurors that Hallowell was the prime culprit, or did they, unlike Sarah Grosvenor, direct their ire more concertedly at Amasa, insisting that he too was "a Bad man"? Nearly a century later, middle-class New England women would organize against the sexual double standard. However, Amasa's future career tells us that female piety in the 1740s did not instruct Windham County women to expel the newly married, thirty-two-year-old man from their homes.[58]

Amasa, as he grew into middle age in Pomfret, easily replicated his father's status. He served as militia captain in the Seven Years' War, prospered in farming, fathered ten children, and lived fifty-seven years beyond Sarah Grosvenor. His handsome gravestone, inscribed with a long verse, stands but twenty-five feet from the simpler stone erected in 1742 for Sarah.

After his death, male kin remembered Amasa fondly; nephews and grandsons recalled him as a "favorite" relative, "remarkably capable" in his prime and "very corpulent" in old age. Moreover, local story-telling tradition and the published history of the region, which made such a spectacular ghost story out of Sarah's abortion and death, preserved Amasa Sessions's reputation unsullied: the *name* of Sarah's lover was left out of the tale.[59]

If Sarah Grosvenor's life is a cautionary tale in any sense for us in the late twentieth century, it is as a reminder of the historically distinctive ways in which socialized gender roles, community and class solidarity, and legal culture combine in each set of generations to excuse or make invisible certain abuses and crimes against women. The form in which Sarah Grosvenor's death became local history reminds us of how the excuses and erasures of one generation not unwittingly become embedded in the narratives and memories of the next cultural era.

NOTES

1. The documentation is found in the record books and file papers of the Superior Court of Connecticut: *Rex* v. *John Hallowell et al.*, Superior Court Records, Book 9, pp. 113, 173, 175, and Windham County Superior Court Files, box 172, Connecticut State Library, Hartford. Hereafter all loose court papers cited are from *Rex* v. *Hallowell*, Windham Country Superior Court Files, box 172, unless otherwise indicated. . . .

2. . . . On the history of abortion practices see . . . Angus McLaren, *Reproductive Rituals: The Perception of Fertility in England from the Sixteenth Century to the Nineteenth Century* (London, 1984), chap. 4; Linda Gordon, *Woman's Body, Woman's Right: A Social History of Birth Control in America* (New York, 1976), pp. 26–41, 49–60. . . .

For specific cases indicating use of herbal abortifacients in the North American colonies, see Julia Cherry Spruill, *Women's Life and Work in the Southern Colonies* (New York, 1972: orig. pub. Chapel Hill, N.C., 1938), pp. 325–26; Roger Thompson, *Sex in Middlesex: Popular Mores in a Massachusetts County, 1649–1699* (Amherst, Mass., 1986), pp. 11, 24–26, 107–8, 182–83. I have found two references to the use of an abortifacient in colonial Connecticut court files.

3. Abortion before quickening (defined in the early modern period as the moment when the mother first felt the fetus move) was not viewed by the English or colonial courts as criminal. No statute law on abortion existed in either Britain or the colonies. To my knowledge, no New England court before 1745 had attempted to prosecute a physician or other conspirators for carrying out an abortion.

On the history of the legal treatment of abortion in Europe and the United States see . . . James C. Mohr, *Abortion in America: The Origins and Evolution of National Policy, 1800–1900* (New York, 1978); Michael Grossberg, *Governing the Hearth: Law and the Family in Nineteenth-Century America* (Chapel Hill, N.C., 1985), chap. 5; and Carroll Smith-Rosenberg, "The Abortion Movement and the AMA, 1850–1880," in *Disorderly Conduct: Visions of Gender of Victorian America* (New York, 1985), pp. 217–244.

4. Indictment against John Hallowell, Mar. 1746/47.

5. The story of the decriminalization of fornication for men in colonial New England is told most succinctly by Carol F. Karlsen, *The Devil in the Shape of a Woman: Witchcraft in Colonial New England* (New York, 1987), pp. 194–96, 198–202, 255. Laurel

Thatcher Ulrich describes a late eighteenth-century Massachusetts jurisdiction in *A Midwife's Tale: The Life of Martha Ballard, Based on Her Diary, 1785–1812* (New York, 1990), 147–60. . . . A partial survey of fornication prosecutions in the Windham County Court indicates that here, too, the local JPs and annually appointed grand jurymen stopped prosecuting men after the 1730s. The records for 1726–31 show that fifteen men were prosecuted to enjoin child support and twenty-one single women were charged with fornication and bastardy, while only two women brought civil suits for child maintenance. Nearly a decade ahead, in the three-year period 1740–42, no men were prosecuted while twenty-three single women were charged with fornication and ten women initiated civil paternity suits.

6. For a recent summary of the literature see Brief for American Historians as *Amicus Curiae* Supporting the Appellees 5–7, *William L. Webster et al.* v. *Reproductive Health Services et al.*, 109 S. Ct. 3040 (1989).

7. In none of the cases cited in n. 2 above did the woman ingesting an abortifacient die from it. . . .

8. Married women may have hidden their abortion attempts because the activity was associated with lewd or dissident women.

9. Deposition of Zerviah Grosvenor. [All direct quotations from witnesses come from Depositions (see n. 1).] . . . Hallowell's trade may have been an imported medicine or a powder he mixed himself, consisting chiefly of oil of savin, which could be extracted from juniper bushes found throughout New England.

10. So her sister Zerviah later estimated. . . .

11. After she was let into the plot, Zerviah more than once watched Amasa take "a paper or powder out of his pockett" and insist that Sarah "take Some of it." . . .

12. . . . "Unlawful measure" was Zerviah's phrase for Amasa's "Method." Concerned for Sarah's well-being, she pleaded with Hallowell not to give her sister "any thing that should harm her"; Deposition of Zerviah Grosvenor. At the same time, Sarah was thinking about the quickening issue. She confided to a friend that when Amasa first insisted she take the trade, "she [had] feared it was too late". . . .

13. Hallowell claimed that he proceeded with the abortion in order to save Sarah's life. If the powder had had little effect and he knew it, then this claim was a deliberate deception. On the other hand, he may have sincerely believed that the potion had poisoned the fetus and that infection of the uterine cavity had followed fetal death. Since healthy babies were thought at that time to help with their own deliveries, Hallowell may also have anticipated a complicated delivery if Sarah were allowed to go to full term—a delivery that might kill her. . . .

14. Hearsay evidence was still accepted in many eighteenth-century Anglo-American courts. . . . Sarah's reported words may have carried special weight because in early New England persons on their deathbeds were thought to speak the truth.

15. Twentieth-century obstetrical studies show an average of six weeks between fetal death and spontaneous abortion; J Robert Willson and Elsie

Reid Carrington, eds., *Obstetrics and Gynecology*, 8th ed. (St. Louis, Mo., 1987), p. 212. Hallowell evidently grasped the link between the two events but felt he could not wait six weeks, either out of concern for Sarah's health or for fear their plot would be discovered.

16. I am using a list of forty heads of household in the Mashamoquet neighborhood of Pomfret in 1731, presuming five persons to a household, and assuming a 2.5 percent annual population growth. See Ellen D. Larned, *History of Windham County, Connecticut* (Worcester, Mass., 1874), vol. I, p. 342, and Bruce C. Daniels, *The Connecticut Town: Growth and Development, 1635–1790* (Middletown, Conn., 1979), pp. 44–51. Pomfret village had no central green or cluster of shops and small house lots around its meeting-house. No maps survive for early Pomfret apart from a 1719 survey of proprietors' tracts. See Larned, *History of Windham County* (1976 ed.), I, foldout at p. 185.

17. . . . Larned, *History of Windham County*, I:200–202, 208–9, 269, 354, 343–44. . . .

18. Larned, *History of Windham County*, I:201, 204, 206, 208–9, 344; Ellen D. Larned, *Historic Gleanings in Windham County, Connecticut* (Providence, R. I., 1899), pp. 141, 148–49. . . .

19. . . . Contradicting Amasa's attempt to disavow paternity were both his investment in Hallowell's efforts to get rid of the fetus and his own ready admission of paternity privately to Zerviah and Sarah.

20. Two years later, in Feb. 1744 (nine months before Amasa married), the senior Sessions deeded to his son the north part of his own farm for a payment of £310. Amasa, in exchange for caring for his parents in their old age, came into the whole farm when his father died in 1771. Pomfret Land Records, III:120; Estate Papers of Nathaniel Sessions, 1771, Pomfret Probate District. On the delay between marriage and "going to housekeeping" see Ulrich, *A Midwife's Tale*, pp. 138–44.

21. Francis G. Sessions, comp, *Materials for a History of the Sessions Family in America* (Albany, N.Y., 1890), p. 60; Pomfret Vit. Rec., I:29. All vital and land records cited hereafter are found in the Barbour Collection, Connecticut State Library.

22. The banns never appeared on the meetinghouse door. . . .

23. . . . I have argued elsewhere that this is what most young New England women in the eighteenth century did when faced with illegitimacy. Their parents did not throw them out of the house but instead paid the cost of the mother and child's upkeep until she managed to marry. Dayton, *Women Before the Bar*. ch. 4.

24. In Larned's account, the oral legend insisted that Hallowell's "transaction" (meaning the abortion attempt) and the miscarriage were "utterly unsuspected by any . . . member of the household" other than Zerviah. *History of Windham County*. I:363.

25. The famous "bad books" incident that disrupted Jonathan Edwards's career in 1744 involved a similar group of unsupervised young adults ages twenty-one to twenty-nine. See Patricia J. Tracy, *Jonathan Edwards, Pastor: Religion and Society in Eigh-teenth-Century Northampton* (New York, 1980), pp. 160–64. The best general investigation of youth culture in early New England is Thompson's *Sex in Middlesex*, pp. 71–96. . . .

26. Helena M. Wall, *Fierce Communion: Family and Community in Early America* (Cambridge, Mass., 1990); Bruce H. Mann, *Neighbors and Strangers: Law and Community in Early Connecticut* (Chapel Hill, N.C., 1987).

27. . . . For recent studies linking consumption patterns and class stratification see . . . T. H. Breen, "'Baubles of Britain': The American and Consumer Revolutions of the Eighteenth Century," *Past and Present* 119 (May 1988): 73–104. . . .

28. Killingly Land Records, II:139; *Rex v. John Hallowell and Mehitable Morris*, Dec. 1726, Windham County Court Records, Book I:43, and Windham County Court Files, box 363. . . .

29. Hallowell was clearly the mastermind of the scheme, and there is little doubt that he lied to the authorities when questioned. . . . The case is found in Charles Hoadley, ed., *Public Records of the Colony of Connecticut*, 15 vols. (Hartford, Conn., 1873), vol. VII, p. 118.

30. The authority on counterfeiting in the colonies is Kenneth Scott . . . *Counterfeiting in Colonial America* [(New York, 1957),] esp. pp. 125, 35, 10, 36. See also Scott's more focused studies, *Counterfeiting in Colonial Connecticut* (New York, 1957) and *Counterfeiting in Colonial Rhode Island* (Providence, R.I., 1960).

For an illuminating social profile of thieves and burglars who often operated in small gangs, see Daniel A. Cohen, "A Fellowship of Thieves: Property Criminals in Eighteenth-Century Massachusetts," *Journal of Social History* XXII (1988):65–92.

31. Richard D. Brown, "The Healing Arts in Colonial and Revolutionary Massachusetts: The Context for Scientific Medicine," in Publications Col. Soc. Mass., *Medicine in Colonial Massachusetts 1620–1820* (Boston, 1980), esp. pp. 40–42. . . .

32. Between 1725 and 1742, Hallowell was a party to twenty land sales and purchases in Killingly. . . .

33. For example, in early 1735 Hallowell made a £170 profit from the sale of a sixty-acre tract with mill and mansion house that he had purchased two months earlier. Killingly Land Rec., IV:26, 36.

34. For a related hypothesis about the mobility of self-taught doctors in contrast to physicians from established medical families see Christianson, "Medical Practitioners of Massachusetts," in Col. Soc. Mass., *Medicine in Colonial Massachusetts*, p. 61. . . .

35. These figures apply to suits in the Windham County Court record books, 1727–42. Hallowell may, of course, have prosecuted debtors in other jurisdictions.

36. The petition's signers included Hopkins, merchant, assembly speaker, and Superior Court justice, soon to become governor; Daniel Jencks, judge, assembly delegate, and prominent Baptist; Obadiah Brown, merchant and shopkeeper; and George Taylor, justice of the peace, town schoolmaster, and Anglican warden. Some of the signers

stated that they had made a special trip to Windham to be "Earwitnesses" at Hallowell's trial. . . .

37. For discussions of the elite see Jackson Turner Main, *Society and Economy in Colonial Connecticut* (Princeton, N.J., 1985), esp. pp. 317–66. . . .

38. Laurel Thatcher Ulrich, *Good Wives: Image and Reality in the Lives of Women in Northern New England, 1650–1750* (New York, 1982), pp. 103–5, 113–17.

39. See Ulrich, *Good Wives*, pp. 195–201. . . .

40. Burying the child was one of the key dramatic acts in infanticide episodes and tales, and popular beliefs in the inevitability that "murder will out" centered on the buried corpse. . . . For more on "murder will out" in New England culture, see David D. Hall, *Worlds of Wonder, Days of Judgment: Popular Religious Belief in Early New England* (New York, 1989), pp. 176–78. . . .

41. Hall, *Worlds of Wonder*, pp. 172–78.

42. . . . Abigail Nightingale recalled a scene when Sarah "was just going out of the world." She and Amasa were sitting on Sarah's bed, and Amasa "endeavour[ed] to raise her up &c. He asked my thought of her state &c. and then leaning over her used these words: poor Creature, I have undone you[!]"; Deposition of Abigail Nightingale.

43. . . . For discussions of male and female speech patterns and the distinctive narcissistic bravado of men's talk in early New England, see Robert St. George, "'Heated' Speech and Literacy in Seventeenth-Century New England," in David Grayson Allen and David D. Hall, eds., *Seventeenth-Century New England*, Publications of the Colonial Society of Massachusetts, LXIII (Boston, 1984), pp. 305–15. . . .

44. On the centrality of confession see Hall, *Worlds of Wonder*, pp. 173, 241. . . . On the growing gap between male and female piety in the eighteenth century see Mary Maples Dunn, "Saints and Sisters: Congregational and Quaker Women in the Early Colonial Period," *American Quarterly* XXX (1978): 582–601. . . .

45. Deposition of Ebenezer Grosvenor; Deposition of John Grosvenor.

46. . . . Shaw here was reporting Dr. [Theodore?] Coker's account of his confrontation with Hallowell during Sarah's final illness. . . .

47. Larned reported that, according to "the legend," the ghostly visitations ceased when "Hallowell fled his country." *History of Windham County*, I:363.

48. For mid-eighteenth-century Bristol residents who reported seeing apparitions and holding conversations with them see Jonathan Barry, "Piety and the Patient: Medicine and Religion in Eighteenth Century Bristol," in Roy Porter, ed., *Patients and Practitioners: Lay Perceptions of Medicines in Pre-Industrial Society* (Cambridge, [Eng.,] 1985), p. 157.

49. None of the depositions produced by Hallowell's trial offers any explanation of the three-year gap between Sarah's death and legal proceedings. . . .

50. Record of the Inferior Court held at Pomfret, Nov. 5–6, 1745. . . .

51. Indictment against Hallowell, Sept. 4, 1746; Indictment against Hallowell and Sessions, Sept. 20, 1746; Pleas of Hallowell and Sessions before the adjourned Windham Superior Court, Nov. [18], 1746; Sup. Ct. Rec., bk. 12, pp. 112–17, 131–33.

52. Sup. Ct. Rec., bk. 12, pp. 173, 175; Indictment against John Hallowell, Mar. 1746/47; *Rex* v. *Amasa Sessions*, Indictment, Mar. 1746/47, Windham Sup. Ct. Files, box 172. See William Blackstone, *Commentaries on the Laws of England* (Facsimile of 1st ed. of 1765–69) (Chicago, 1979), I:125–26, IV:198.

53. Larned, *History of Windham County*, I:363.

54. Even in the context of the inflation of the 1740s, Hallowell's bill of costs was unusually high: £110.2s6d. Sessions was hit hard in the pocketbook too; he was assessed £83.14s.2d. in costs.

55. Petition of John Hallowell, Oct. 1747, Conn. Archives, Crimes and Misdemeanors, Ser. I, IV: 108. . . .

56. Note Blackstone's discussion of the liability of "a physician or surgeon who gives his patient a portion . . . to cure him, which contrary to expectation kills him." *Commentaries*, IV:197.

57. Pomfret Vit. Rec., II:67.

58. Carroll Smith-Rosenberg, "Beauty, the Beast and the Militant Woman: A Case Study in Sex Roles and Social Stress in Jacksonian America," *American Quarterly* XXIII (1971):562–84. . . .

59. Sessions, *Sessions Family*, pp. 31, 35; Larned, *History of Windham County*, I:363–64.

DOCUMENTS: Supporting the Revolution

"The ladies going about for money exceeded everything . . ."

This broadside of 1780 announced a women's campaign to raise contributions for patriot soldiers. Organized and led by Esther DeBerdt Reed, wife of the president of Pennsylvania, and by Benjamin Franklin's daughter Sarah Franklin Bache, the campaign was large and effective. "Instead of waiting for the Donations being sent the ladys of each Ward go from dore to dore and collect them," wrote one participant. Collecting contributions this way invited confrontation. One loyalist wrote to her sister, "Of all absurdities, the ladies going about for money exceeded everything; they were so extremely importunate that people were obliged to give them something to get rid of them."* The campaign raised $300,000 in paper dollars in inflated war currency. Rather than let George Washington merge it with the general fund, the women insisted on using it to buy materials for making shirts so that each soldier might know he had received an extraordinary contribution from the women of Philadelphia. The broadside itself is an unusually explicit justification for women's intrusion into politics.

On the commencement of actual war, the Women of America manifested a firm resolution of contribute . . . to the deliverance of their country. Animated by the purest patriotism, they are sensible of sorrow at this day, in not offering more than barren wishes for the success of so glorious a Revolution. They aspire to render themselves more really useful; and this sentiment is universal from the north to the south of the Thirteen United States. Our ambition is kindled by the fame of those heroines of antiquity, who have rendered their sex illustrious, and have proved to the universe, that, if the weakness of our Constitution, if opinion and manners did not forbid us to march to glory by the same paths as the Men, we should at least equal, and sometimes surpass them in our love for the public good. I glory in all that which my sex has done great and commendable. I call to mind with enthusiasm and with admiration, all those acts of courage, of constancy and patriotism, which history has transmitted to us: The people favoured by Heaven, preserved from destruction by the virtues, the zeal and the resolution of Deborah, of Judith, of Esther! The fortitude of the mother of the Macchabees, in giving up her sons to die before her eyes: Rome saved from the fury of a victorious enemy by the efforts of Volumnia, and other Roman Ladies: So many famous sieges where the Women have been seen forgetting the weakness of their sex, building new walls, digging trenches with their feeble hands, furnishing arms to their defenders, they themselves darting the missile weapons on the enemy, resigning the ornaments of their apparel, and their fortune, to fill the public treasury, and to hasten the deliverance of their country; burying themselves under its ruins; throwing themselves into the flames rather than submit to the disgrace of humiliation before a proud enemy.

Born for liberty, disdaining to bear the irons of a tyrannic Government, we associate ourselves to the grandeur of those Sovereigns, cherished and revered, who have held with so much splendour the scepter of the greatest States, The Batildas, the Elizabeths, the Maries,

*Mary Morris to Catharine Livingston, June 10 [1780], Ridley Family Papers, Massachusetts Historical Society, Boston; Anna Rawle to Rebecca Rawle Shoemaker, June 30, 1780, in *Pennsylvania Magazine of History and Biography* 35 (1911):398.

Excerpted from *The Sentiments of an American Woman* ([Philadelphia]: John Dunlap, 1780).

the Catharines, who have extented the empire of liberty, and contented to reign by sweetness and justice, have broken the chains of slavery, forged by tyrants in times of ignorance and barbarity....

We know that at a distance from the theatre of war, if we enjoy any tranquility, it is the fruit of your watchings, your labours, your dangers. . . . Who, amongst us, will not renounce with the highest pleasure, those vain ornaments, when she shall consider that the valiant defenders of America will be able to draw some advantage from the money which she may have laid out in these.... The time is arrived to display the same sentiments which animated us at the beginning of the Revolution, when we renounced the use of teas, however agreeable to our taste, rather than receive them from our persecutors; when we made it appear to them that we placed former necessaries in the rank of superfluities, when our liberty was interested; when our republican and laborious hands spun the flax, prepared the linen intended for the use of our soldiers; when [as] exiles and fugitives we supported with courage all the evils which are the concomitants of war....

Sarah Osborn, "The bullets would not cheat the gallows . . ."

Sarah Osborn was eighty-one years old when Congress made it possible for dependent survivors of Revolutionary war veterans to claim their pensions. She testified to her own service as well as to her husband's in the following deposition, sworn before the Court of Common Pleas in Wayne County, New Jersey, in 1837. Osborn's husband was a commissary guard; like many thousands of women, Osborn traveled with him, cooking and cleaning for troops at a time when there was no formal quartermaster corps and in which cleanliness was virtually the only guard against disease. Her account tells of working when the army was at West Point in 1780; of the long expedition south, marching proudly on horseback into Philadelphia, and then continuing to Yorktown. Osborn is the only one of the "women of the army" who has left us a narrative of her experiences. At Yorktown she brought food to soldiers under fire. When she told George Washington that she did not fear the bullets because they "would not cheat the gallows," she was conveying her understanding that her challenge to royal authority was congruent with his; if the soldiers risked being hanged for treason, so would she.

[In the march to Philadelphia in 1781?] Deponent was part of the time on horseback and part of the time in a wagon. Deponent's . . . husband was still serving as one of the commissary's guard.... They continued their march to Philadelphia, deponent on horseback through the streets.... Being out of bread, deponent was employed in baking the afternoon and evening ... they continued their march ... [at Baltimore she] embarked on board a vessel and sailed ... until they had got up the St. James River as far as the tide would carry them.... They ... marched for Yorktown.... Deponent was on foot.... Deponent took her stand just back of the American tents, say about a mile from the town, and busied herself washing, mending, and cooking for the soldiers, in which she was assisted by the other

Excerpted from John C. Dann, ed., *The Revolution Remembered: Eyewitness Accounts of the American Revolution* (Chicago: University of Chicago Press, 1980), pp. 240–45.

DEBORAH SAMPSON;

Drawn by Joseph Stone Framingham 1797.

Women like Sarah Osborn, who served in an informal quartermaster corps, were not the only women on or near Revolutionary War battlefields. In 1782, Deborah Sampson, who was already notable in her community of Middleborough, Massachusetts, for her height and strength, adopted men's clothing and the name of Robert Shurtleff. She enlisted for service with the Fourth Massachusetts Regiment. Like many young women from impoverished families, Deborah Sampson had been bound out to domestic service as a young teenager. When her term was up, she taught school briefly in Middleborough and joined the First Baptist Church there. She was expelled from the church before her enlistment. She served with her regiment in New York and possibly in Pennsylvania until she was wounded at a battle near Tarrytown, New York.

After her return to Massachusetts, Sampson married and bore three children. The fame of her exploits persisted. After a fictionalized biography was published by Herman Mann, she went on a wide-ranging speaking tour, perhaps the first American woman to undertake such an enterprise, and applied for the pensions to which her wartime service entitled her. These were awarded slowly and grudgingly, and she died impoverished in 1827. (Joseph Stone, "Deborah Sampson (Gannett)" 1797, oil on panel. Courtesy of the Rhode Island Historical Society.)

females; some men washed their own clothing. She heard the roar of the artillery for a number of days.... Deponent's ... husband was there throwing up entrenchments, and deponent cooked and carried in beef, and bread, and coffee (in a gallon pot) to the soldiers in the entrenchment.

On one occasion when deponent was thus employed carrying in provisions, she met General Washington, who asked her if she "was not afraid of the cannonballs?"

She replied, "No, the bullets would not cheat the gallows," that "It would not do for the men to fight and starve too."

They dug entrenchments nearer and nearer to Yorktown every night or two till the last. While digging that, the enemy fired very heavy till about nine o'clock next morning, then stopped, and the drums from the enemy beat excessively. Deponent was a little way off in Colonel Van Shaick's or the officers' marquee and a number of officers were present....

The drums continued beating, and all at once the officers hurrahed and swung their hats, and deponent asked them, "What is the matter now?"

One of them replied, "Are not you soldier enough to know what it means?"

Deponent replied, "No."

They then replied, "The British have surrendered."

Deponent, having provisions ready, carried the same down to the entrenchments that morning, and four of the soldiers whom she was in the habit of cooking for ate their breakfasts.

Deponent stood on one side of the road and the American officers upon the other side when the British officers came out of the town and rode up to the American officers and delivered up [their swords, which the deponent] thinks were returned again, and the British officers rode right on before the army, who marched out beating and playing a melancholy tune, their drums covered with black handkerchiefs and their fifes with black ribbands tied around them, into an old field and there grounded their arms and then returned into town again to await their destiny.... The British general at the head of the army was a large, portly man, full face, and the tears rolled down his cheeks as he passed along.

Rachel Wells, "I have Don as much to Carrey on the Warr as maney . . ."

Rachel Wells was probably sixty-five years old when she wrote the following words. She had bought loan office certificates from the state of New Jersey during the Revolution: subsequently she had moved to Philadelphia, but returned to Bordentown, New Jersey, after the war. In an effort to curb speculation, the New Jersey legislature decided that only state residents had a claim on interest payments; Rachel Wells's claim on her money was turned down because she had not been in the state at the war's end in 1783. She appealed directly to the Continental Congress. Although her petition was tabled, it remains—despite its bad spelling—as perhaps the most moving witness to the Revolution left to us by a woman. What did Rachel Wells think had been her contribution to the Revolution? What did she think the government owed to her?

Rachel Wells, Petition to Congress, May 18, 1786, Microfilm Papers of the Continental Congress, National Archives, Washington, D.C., microfilm M247, roll 56, item 42, vol. 8, pp. 354–55.

To the Honnorabell Congress I rachel do make this Complaint Who am a Widow far advanced in years & Dearly have ocasion of ye Interst for that Cash I Lent the States. I was a Sitisen in ye jersey when I Lent ye State a considerable Sum of Moneys & had I justice dun me it mite be Suficant to suporte me in ye Contrey whear I am now, near burdentown. I Leved hear then . . . but Being . . . so Robd by the Britans & others i went to Phila to try to get a Living . . . & was There in the year 1783 when our assembley was pleasd to pas a Law that No one Should have aney Interest that Livd out of jearsey Stats . . .

Now gentelmen is this Liberty, had it bin advertised that he or She that Moved out of the Stat should Louse his or her Interest you mite have sum plea against me. But I am Innocent Suspected no Trick. I have Don as much to Carrey on the Warr as maney that Sett now at ye healm of government. . . . your asembly Borrowed £300 in gould of me jest as the Warr Comencd & Now I Can Nither git Intrust nor principall Nor Even Security. . . . My dr Sister . . . wrote to me to be thankfull that I had it in my Power to help on the Warr which is well enough but then this is to be Considerd that others gits their Intrust & why then a poor old widow to be put of[f]. . . . I hartely pity others that ar in my Case that Cant Speak for themselves. . . .

god has Spred a plentifull table for us & you gentelmen are ye Carvers for us pray forgit Not the Poor weaklings at the foot of the Tabel ye poor Sogers has got Sum Crumbs That fall from their masters tabel. . . . Why Not Rachel Wells have a Little intrust?

if She did not fight She threw in all her mite which bought ye Sogers food & Clothing & Let Them have Blankets & Since that She has bin obligd to Lay upon Straw & glad of that. . . .

LINDA K. KERBER
The Republican Mother and the Woman Citizen: Contradictions and Choices in Revolutionary America

"I expect to see our young women forming a new era in female history," wrote Judith Sargent Murray in 1798. Her optimism was part of a general sense that all possibilities were open in the post-Revolutionary world. The experience of war had given words like *independence* and *self-reliance* personal as well as political overtones; among the things that ordinary people had learned from wartime had been that the world could, as the song played during the British surrender at Yorktown put it, turn upside down. The rich could quickly become poor; wives might suddenly have to manage farms and businesses; women might even, as the famous Deborah Sampson Gannett had done, shoulder a gun. Revolutionary experience taught that it was useful to be prepared for a wide range of unusual possibilities; political theory taught that republics rested on the virtue of their citizens. The stability and competence on which republican government relied required a highly literate and politically sophisticated constituency. Maintaining the republic was an intellectual and educational as well as a political challenge.

Murray herself, born into an elite family in Salem, Massachusetts, had felt the dislocations of the Revolution severely. Widowed, remarried to a Universalist minister of modest means, she understood what it was to be thrown on her own resources. "I would give my daughters every accomplishment which I thought proper," she wrote,

> and to crown all, I would early accustom them to habits of industry and order. They should be taught with precision the art economical; they should be enabled to procure for themselves the necessaries of life; independence should be placed within their grasp. . . . The SEX should be taught to depend on their own efforts, for the procurement of an establishment in life.[1]

The model republican woman was competent and confident. She could resist the vagaries of fashion; she was rational, independent, literate, benevolent, and self-reliant. Nearly every writer who described this paragon prepared a list of role models, echoing the pantheon of heroines admired by the fund-raising women of Philadelphia in 1780 (see pp. 114–15). There were women of the ancient world, like Cornelia, the mother of the Gracchi; rulers like Elizabeth of England and the Empress Catherine the Great of

This essay has been written for *Women's America*. It is drawn from *Women of the Republic: Intellect and Ideology in Revolutionary America* (Chapel Hill, N.C.: University of North Carolina Press, 1980), chs. 7 and 9; and *No Constitutional Right to Be Ladies: Women and the Obligations of Citizenship* (New York: Hill and Wang, 1998), introduction and ch. 1 © Linda K. Kerber.

Russia; and a long list of British intellectuals: Lady Mary Wortley Montagu, Hannah More, Mary Wollstonecraft, and the historian Catherine Macaulay. Those who believed in these republican models demanded that their presence be recognized and endorsed and that a new generation of young women be urged to find in them patterns for their own behavior.

The Revolutionary years had brought some women close to direct criticism of political systems. Women had signed petitions, they had boycotted imported tea and textiles, they had made homespun and "felt nationly," as one young woman put it. In some places they had signed oaths of loyalty to patriot or loyalist forces. Rachel Wells bought £300 of government bonds to support the war and had a keen sense of her own contribution: "I did my Posabels every way . . . Ive Don as much to help on this war as Though I had bin a good Soger," she told the New Jersey legislature.[2] Women were citizens of the new republic. They could be naturalized; they were required to refrain from treason on pain of punishment; if single, they paid taxes. Women could develop their own agendas; when Abigail Adams wrote the now-famous letter in which she urged her husband and his colleagues in the Continental Congress to "remember the ladies," she urged that domestic violence should be on the republican agenda: "Put it out of the power of our husbands to use us with impunity," she demanded. "Remember all men would be tyrants if they could."[3]

Expressions of women's desire to play a frankly political role were regularly camouflaged in satire, a device that typically makes new ideas and social criticism seem less threatening and more palatable. In 1791, for example, a New Jersey newspaper published a pair of semiserious satires in which women discuss the politics of excise taxes and national defense. "Roxana" expresses a feminist impatience:

> In fifty quarto volumes of ancient and modern history, you will not find fifty illustrious female names; heroes, statesmen, divines, philosophers, artists, are all of masculine gender. And pray what have they done during this long period of usurpation? . . . They have written ten thousand unintelligible books. . . . They have been cutting each other's throats all over the globe.[4]

Some years later, the students at Sarah Pierce's famous school for girls in Litchfield, Connecticut, prepared a "Ladies Declaration of Independence" for the Fourth of July. Alongside the frivolous phrasing is earnest comment on the unfilled promises of the republic. Less than ten years after that, Elizabeth Cady Stanton would use the same technique. "When in the Course of Human Events," the Litchfield declaration begins,

> it becomes necessary for the Ladies to dissolve those bonds by which they have been subjected to others, and to assume among the self styled Lords of Creation that separate and equal station to which the laws of nature and their *own talents* entitle them, a decent respect to the opinions of mankind requires, that they should declare the causes which impel them to the separation.
> We hold these truths to be self evident. That all *mankind* are created equal.

The Litchfield women wished to change "social relations." They complained about men who "have undervalued our talents, and disparaged our attainments; they have combined with each other, for the purpose of excluding us from all participation in Legislation and in the administration of Justice."[5]

As these young women understood, American revolutionaries had brilliantly and radically challenged the laws governing the relationship between ruler and ruled, subjects and the king. Republican ideology was antipatriarchal. It voiced the claim of adult men to be freed from the control of kings and political "fathers" in an antique monarchical system. "Is it in the interest of a man to be a boy all his life?" Tom Paine asked in *Common Sense*, the great political manifesto of the era.

But the men who modeled the new American republic after the war remodeled it in their own image. They did not eliminate the political father immediately or completely. George Washington quickly became the "Father of his Country"; at the Governor's Palace in Williamsburg, Virginia, the life-size portrait of George III was quickly replaced by a life-size portrait of George Washington in a similar pose. American revolutionary men understood that two major elements of prerevolutionary social and political life—the system of slavery and the system of domestic relations—directly clashed with the egalitarian principles of the Revolution. But they kept both systems in place. By embedding the three-fifths compromise and the Fugitive Slave Law in the federal Constitution of 1787, the founders actually strengthened and stabilized the system of slavery. And they left virtually intact the old English law governing relations between husbands and wives.

In traditional English practice, at marriage a husband gained access to the body of his wife; it followed that he could easily pressure her into agreement with him on all other matters. A married woman was understood to be "covered" by her husband's civic identity, as though they were walking together under an umbrella that the husband held. There were relatively few constraints on what he could do with her body and her property, though she was nearly always guaranteed the use of one-third of their combined real estate and the ownership of one-third of the moveable property throughout her widowhood. The rules of coverture made it seem logical that fathers be the guardians of the children and that husbands manage the property that wives brought to marriage and earned during it. So long as she was married, she could not make a contract without his permission; she could not make a will until she was a widow. She could not make choices—for example, about to whom a child was to be apprenticed—that challenged the choices made by her husband. The revolutionary republic promised to protect "life, liberty and property," but under the old law a married woman was deprived of her property and had none to protect. Coverture was theoretically incompatible with revolutionary ideology and with the newly developing liberal commercial society. But patriot men carefully sustained it. Recognizing that husbands could easily pressure the electoral choices of married women, legislators concluded not that husbands should be controlled, but that women—unmarried as well as married—should not vote.

Yet the fact of women's citizenship in a democratic republic contained deep within it an implicit challenge to coverture. Patriot men rarely spoke about this issue, but their actions speak for them. In England, the killing of a husband by a wife was *petit treason*, analogous to regicide, although the killing of a wife by a husband was murder. The penalties for *petit treason* were worse than those for murder. The concept was not much enforced in colonial America, but it remained in the statutes. It was the only element of the old law of domestic relations that legislators of the early republic eliminated. Legislators were conscious of what they intended; they carefully retained the concept of *petit treason* for the killing of the master by a slave. With that single exception, neither the Revolutionary government under the Articles of Confederation nor the federal government of the Constitution directly challenged the legal system of coverture.[6] Every free man, rich or poor, white or black, gained something from the system of domestic relations already in place; they had no need to renegotiate it.

The best introduction to the old system of thinking about relations between women and men is to read the treatises on which judges and lawyers relied. They even continued to refer to the body of law of domestic relations by its traditional name, "the law of baron et feme"—not "husband and wife" or "man and woman" but "lord and woman." The same treatises that described the law of baron and feme invariably went on to laws of parent and child, master and servant.

In an era before law schools were attached to universities, and when prospective lawyers "read law" as apprentices in the offices of practitioners, Tapping Reeve conducted perhaps the most respected legal training in the nation. Students came from all over the country to study in his Litchfield, Connecticut, home; among them were Reeve's own brother-in-law Aaron Burr and, years later, John C. Calhoun from South Carolina. There were also future U.S. congressmen and senators, judges and Supreme Court justices. Reeve's treatise on the law of baron and feme, first published in 1816, was reprinted with up-to-date annotations in 1846, a testament to its continued vitality. Reeve offers us pithy accounts of what the early generations of American jurists took to be the common sense of the matter of relations between men and women. Nothing that he wrote would have surprised his contemporaries.

To follow the law of marriage, as Reeve delicately spun out its implications, is to watch the playing out of a stacked deck. Reeve began his book with the forthright statement that "the husband, by marriage, acquires an absolute title to all the personal property of the wife." Husbands also gained extensive power over her real estate; wives gained no advantages "in point of property" from marriage.

Once these asymmetrical property relations were established, personal implications wound their way throughout the law. The husband's control of all property gave him such coercive power over the wife that she could not defy him. Instead of revising the law to remove its coercive elements, jurists simply ensured that the coerced voices would not speak. Husbands were responsible for crimes committed by their wives in their presence or with their approval—except in the case of treason, a crime so severe that responsibility for it overrode obligation to the husband, or in the event that a wife kept a brothel with the husband's knowledge, since keeping a brothel "is an offense of which the wife is supposed to have the principal management."[7] Before married women signed away their right to dower property, judges were supposed to question them privately about whether their husbands had coerced them, although the law offered no protection against continued coercion. A wife could not normally make contracts in her own name; if she did, her husband was bound "to fulfill the contract of his wife, when it is such an one as wives in her rank of life usually purchase. . . . If however, she were to purchase a ship or yoke of oxen, no such presumption would arise, for wives do not usually purchase ships or oxen."[8]

This system of marriage presupposed the husband's right to sexual access to the wife's body. When Reeve explained why it was logical that wives could not enter into contracts, his reason was not only that wives did not control property that could serve as a guarantee; it was that wives could not enter into contracts involving their own labor.

"The right of the husband to the person of his wife," Reeve observed, " . . . is a right guarded by the law with the utmost solicitude; if she could bind herself by her contracts, she would be liable to be arrested, taken in execution, and confined in a prison; and then the husband would be deprived of the company of his wife, which the law will not suffer." If a husband were banished from the realm, however, then his wife "could contract, could sue and be sued in her own name; for, in this case, . . . he was already deprived of the company of his wife, and her confinement in prison would not deprive him of his wife to any greater extent than was already the case."[9]

That the system of marriage contradicted the basic tenets of republican thinking was obvious. But women who named the contradictions invited extraordinary hostility and ridicule. Among the most persistent themes was the link of female intellectual activity and political autonomy to an unflattering masculinity. "From all we read, and all we observe, we are authorized in supposing that there is a *sex of soul*," announced the Boston minister John Gardiner. "Women of masculine minds, have generally masculine manners. . . . Queen Elizabeth understood Latin and Greek, swore with the fluency of a sailor, and boxed the ears of her courtiers. . . . Mrs. Macaulay, the author of a dull democratic history, at a tolerably advanced age, married a boy." A "mild, dove-like remper is so necessary to Female beauty, is so natural a part of the sex," reflected Parson Mason Locke Weems wistfully. "A masculine air in a woman frightens us."[10]

When women addressed political issues, the attacks were similar. A good example of this response appears in a newspaper letter written in 1790 by a Marylander who signed himself as "Philanthropos." Warning against literal interpretations of the phrase "All mankind are born equal," "Philanthropos" thought the principle of equality could be "taken in too extensive a sense, and might tend to destroy those degrees of subordination which nature seems to point out," including the subordination of women to men. If women were inept, they were also somehow too effective.

> A Female Orator, in haranguing an Assembly, might like many crafty politicians, keep her *best argument* for last, and would then be sure of the victory—Men would be exposed to temptations too great for their strength, and those who could resist a bribe, offered in the common way, might reasonably yield to what it would be hardly possible for a *man* to refuse.

Selections from Mary Wollstonecraft's *Vindication of the Rights of Woman* were published in the American press shortly after the book was published in London in 1792. She had borne one illegitimate daughter (Fanny Imlay) and lived with William Godwin before marrying him; after marriage she maintained lodgings in another house so that she could be free to write. Once her life history became generally known, it could be used to link intellectual women to political feminism and to aggressive sexuality, as the Federalist writer Timothy Dwight did in his bitter "Morpheus" essays, which ran in a Boston newspaper in 1802. In a dream sequence in "Morpheus," Wollstonecraft has arrived in America and sets out to teach its inhabitants wisdom.

> Women . . . are entitled to all the rights, and are capable of all the energies, of men. I do not mean merely mental energies. If any dispute remained on this subject, I have removed it entirely by displaying, in my immortal writings, all the mental energy of LOCKE and BACON. I intend bodily energies. They can naturally run as fast, leap as high, and as far, and wrestle, scuffle, and box with as much success, as any of the . . . other sex.

That is a mistake (said an old man) . . .

It is no mistake, (said the Female Philosopher).

. . . Why then, (said the senior again), are women always feebler than men?

Because (said MARY) they are educated to be feeble; and by indulgence . . . are made poor, puny, baby-faced dolls; instead of the manly women, they ought to be.

Manly women! (cried the wag). Wheu! a manly woman is a hoyden, a non descript.

Am I a hoyden (interrupted MARY, with spirit.)

You used to be a strumpet.

Wollstonecraft tells him that she was not a strumpet but a sentimental lover, "too free to brook the restraints of marriage." Her interlocutor responds, "We call them strumpets here, Madam—no offense, I hope," and then argues that when a woman claims the rights of men and the character of a manly woman, she necessarily forgoes what he calls women's "own rights" to "refined consideration." The implication is that Wollstonecraft can be insulted with impunity.

Still (said the senior) you ought to remember that she is a woman.

She ought to remember it (said the young man.)

Thus political behavior, like abstract thought, continued to be specifically proscribed as a threat to sensual attractiveness.

Only the mother who promised to use her political knowledge to serve the republic was spared this hostility. The concept was a variant of the argument for the improved education of women that republicans such as Judith Sargent Murray and Wollstonecraft herself had demanded. It defended education for women not only for their autonomy and self-realization but also so that they could be better wives, rational household managers, and better mothers for the next generation of virtuous republican citizens—especially sons. In a widely reprinted speech, "Thoughts upon Female Education," originally given at the new Young Ladies Academy of Philadelphia, the physician and politician Benjamin Rush addressed the issue directly: "The equal share that every citizen has in the liberty and the possible share he may have in the government of our country make it necessary that our ladies should be qualified to a certain degree, by a peculiar and suitable education, to concur in instructing their sons in the principles of liberty and government." The Republican Mother was an educated woman who could be spared the criticism normally directed at the intellectually competent woman because she placed her learning at her family's service. That she had the leisure and opportunity for study located her solidly in the middle class.

It was commonly believed that republican government was fragile and rested on the presence of virtuous citizens. The Republican Mother was also a Republican Wife.[11] She chose a virtuous man for her husband; she condemned and corrected her husband's lapses from civic virtue; she educated her sons for it. The creation of virtuous citizens required wives and mothers who were well informed, "properly methodical," and free of "invidious and rancorous passions." The word *virtue* was derived from the Latin word for, man, with its connotations of virility. Political action was ideologically marked as masculine; as we have seen, if political voice required independent property holding, it was legally marked masculine as well. Virtue in a woman required another theater for its display. To that end, writers created a mother who had a political purpose and argued that her domestic behavior had a direct political function in the republic.

As one college orator put it,

> Let us then figure to ourselves the accomplished woman, surrounded by a sprightly band, from the babe that imbibes the nutritive fluid, to the generous youth. . . . Let us contemplate the mother distributing the mental nourishment to the fond smiling circle . . . watching the gradual openings of their minds . . . see, under her cultivating hand, reason assuming the reins of government, and knowledge increasing gradually to her beloved pupils. . . . Yes, ye fair, the reformation of a world is in your power. . . . It rests with you to make this retreat [from the corruptions of Europe] doubly peaceful, doubly happy, by banishing from it those crimes and corruptions, which have never yet failed of giving rise to tyranny, or anarchy. While you thus keep our country virtuous, you maintain its independence.[12]

Defined this way, the educated woman ceased to threaten the sanctity of marriage; the intellectual woman need not be masculine.

The ideology of Republican Motherhood was deeply ambivalent. On the one hand, it was a progressive ideology, challenging those who opposed women in politics by the proposal that women could—and should—play a political role through influencing their husbands and raising patriotic children. Within the dynamic relationships of the private family—between husbands and wives, mothers and children—it allocated an assertive role to women. Those who shared the vision of the Republican Mother usually insisted upon better education, clearer recognition of women's economic contributions, and a strong political identification with the republic. This ideology could complement the "fertility transition" under way in the postwar republic, a rapid fall in birthrates that would continue into our own time, and that was first found in urban areas that had experienced commercial and industrial as well as political revolution. Free women, the historian Susan Klepp has recently suggested, "applied egalitarian ideas and a virtuous, prudent sensibility to their bodies and to their traditional images of self as revolutions inspired discussion and debate. . . . On the household level, restricted fertility and high rates of literacy or years of education were persistently linked: the higher the educational attainment of women, the lower fertility rates."[13]

The idea that a mother can perform a political function represents the recognition that a citizen's political socialization takes place at an early age, that the family is a basic part of the system of political communication, and that patterns of family authority influence the general political culture. Most premodern political societies—and even some fairly modern democracies—maintain unarticulated, but nevertheless very firm, social restrictions that seem to isolate the family's domestic world from politics. The willingness of the American woman to overcome this ancient separation brought her into the political community.[14] In this sense, Republican Motherhood was an important and progressive invention congruent with revolutionary politics and the demographic transition. It altered the female domain in which most women had lived out their lives; it justified women's claims for participation in the civic culture. The ideology was strong enough to rout "Philanthropos" and "Morpheus" by redefining female political behavior as valuable rather than abnormal, as a source of strength to the republic rather than an embarrassment. The ideology would be revived as a rallying point for many twentieth-century women reformers, who saw their committment to honest politics, efficient urban sanitation, and pure food and drug laws as an extension of their responsibilities as mothers.

But Republican Motherhood flourished in the context of coverture. The old law of domestic relations hemmed it in at every turn. Republican motherhood could legitimize only a minimum of political sophistication and interest. It was an extension into the republic of conservative traditions, stretching back at least as far as the Renaissance, that put narrow limits on women's assertiveness.[15] Captured by marriage, which not only secured their intimate relations but also their relationship to the public authority, for most of their lives most women had no alternative but to perform the narrow political role they managed to claim for themselves. Just as white planters claimed that democracy in the antebellum South necessarily rested on the economic base of black slavery, so male egalitarian society was said to rest on the moral base of deference among a class of people—women—who would devote their efforts to service by raising sons and disciplining husbands to be virtuous citizens of the republic. The learned woman, who might very well wish to make choices as well as to influence attitudes, was a visible threat to this arrangement. Women were to contain their political judgments within their homes and families; they were not to bridge the world outside and the world within. The Republican Wife was not to tell her husband for whom to vote. She was a citizen but not really a constituent.

Restricting women's politicization was one of a series of conservative choices that Americans made in the postwar years as they avoided the full implications of their own Revolutionary radicalism. By these decisions Americans may well have been spared the agony of the French cycle of revolution and counterrevolution, which spilled more blood and produced a political system more regressive than had the American war. Nevertheless, the impact of these choices was to leave race equality to the mercies of a bloody century that stretched from the Civil War through Reconstruction and lynching into the civil rights movement of our own time. And the impact of these choices was also to leave in place the system by which marriage stood between women and civil society. For most of the history of the United States, deep into the twentieth century, the legal traditions of marriage would be used to deny women citizens juries drawn from a full cross-section of the community, deny them control over their own property and their own earnings, sometimes deny them custody of their children, even deny them their rights as citizens should they marry a foreign man.

The "new era in female history" that Judith Sargent Murray had predicted remained to be created by women, fortified by their memories and myths of female strength during the trials of war, politicized by their resentment of male legislators slighting the issues of greatest significance to women. The promises of the republic remained to be fulfilled; remembering the Revolution helped to keep confidence alive. "Yes, gentlemen," said Elizabeth Cady Stanton to the New York legislature in 1854, "in republican America . . . we, the daughters of the revolutionary heroes of '76 demand at your hands the redress of our grievances—a revision of your State constitution—a new code of laws." Stanton understood that the traditions of coverture positioned domesticity against civic activism, motherhood against citizenship. Not until 1992 did the U.S. Supreme Court rule that as a general principle, "Women do not lose their constitutionally protected liberty when they marry."[16]

NOTES

1. Murray's newspaper essays were reprinted in a collected edition, *The Gleaner*, III (Boston, 1798). These comments appear in III, pp. 189; 167–68. See also Sheila L. Skemp, *Judith Sargent Murray: A Brief Biography with Documents* (Boston, 1998).

2. "Rachel Wells Petition for Relief," Nov 15, 1785, New Jersey Archives, Trenton.

3. Abigail Adams to John Adams, Mar. 31, 1776, *Adams Family Correspondence* (Cambridge, Mass., 1963), I: 370. See Nancy F. Cott, "Passionlessness: An Interpretation of Victorian Sexual Ideology, 1790–1850," *Signs: Journal of Women in Culture and Society* 4 (1978): 219–36.

4. *Burlington* (N.J.) *Advertiser*, Feb 1, 1791.

5. Miss Pierce's School Papers, 1849, Litchfield His. Soc., Litchfield, Conn.

6. See, for example, "An Act for Annulling the Distinction between the Crimes of Murder and Petit Treason," March 16, 1785, in Asahel Stearns et al., eds., *The General Laws of Massachusetts* . . . I (Boston, 1823), p. 188.

7. Tapping Reeve, *The Law of Baron and Femme, Parent and Child, Guardian and Ward, Master and Servant, and of the Powers of the Courts of Chancery* (New Haven, 1816; Burlington, 1846), ch. v, p. 73.

8. Reeve, ch. vi, pp. 78–79.

9. Reeve, ch. viii, pp. 98–99.

10. *New-England Palladium*, Sept. 18, 1801; Parson Mason Locke Weems, *Hymen's Recruiting Sergeant* (Philadelphia, 1800).

11. Jan Lewis, "The Republican Wife: Virtue and Seduction in the Early Republic," *William and Mary Quarterly* ser. 3, vol. 44 (1987):689–721.

12. *New York Magazine*, May 1795, pp. 301–5.

13. Susan E. Klepp, "Revolutionary Bodies: Women and the Fertility Transition in the Mid-Atlantic Region, 1760–1820," *Journal of American History* vol. 85 (1998), pp. 916, 915 (I have reversed the order of the sentences).

14. See Gabriel Almond and Sidney Verba, *The Civic Culture* (Princeton, 1963), pp. 377–401.

15. Elaine Forman Crane emphasizes this dimension; see *Ebb-Tide in New England: Women, Seaports, and Social Change, 1630–1800* (Boston, 1998), ch. 6.

16. *Planned Parenthood of Pennsylvania* v. *Casey* 112 S. Ct. 2791 (1992).

II

THE MANY FRONTIERS OF INDUSTRIALIZING AMERICA, 1820–1900

In the nineteenth century, the American economy was transformed by the industrial revolution. Railroads and steamboats linked distant parts of the country and simplified economic interaction, even as the distinctive economies of North and South fostered a political dialogue that became increasingly bitter over the years. In the South, the cotton gin ensured the profitability of the crop and reinforced the system of slave labor. In the North, factories began installing steam-powered spinning and weaving equipment tended by a new class of wage workers. The position of legislators on issues as disparate as tariffs and free speech could be linked to the economic interests and distinctive cultures of their regions. By 1860, institutions that had helped connect the two cultures—political parties, churches, economic networks—had broken down completely. Once Civil War came, the North's control of modern transportation networks was a crucial ingredient in its success.

It has been relatively easy for historians to see that economic and political developments affected men's lives. The right to vote and hold office was extended to virtually every white man, whether or not he held property; after the Civil War it was extended to black men in many parts of the country. Congress was a national forum for debate among male political leaders; by the 1850s, speeches made there were rapidly diffused to the public by cheap newspapers, printed by newly efficient presses and distributed by railroads throughout the nation. A host of new careers opened to men as politicians, journalists, teachers, capitalists, physicians, and reformers. The expansion of the physical boundaries of the country, by treaty and by war, opened new frontiers and created new opportunities for farmers, merchants, civic promoters, and land speculators.

When we look at these developments through women's eyes, we find that women's lives also changed markedly. The transportation revolution, for example, had special significance for women. Single women rarely traveled independently in the colonial period; long trips meant nights in unfamiliar taverns and lodging houses where accommodations were uncertain and safety could not be assured. The railroad changed that. In the three weeks between January 5 and January 26, 1855, Antoinette Brown and Ernes-

I SELL THE SHADOW TO SUPPORT THE SUBSTANCE.

SOJOURNER TRUTH.

Sojourner Truth (c.1797–1883) is better known in the twentieth century for words she did not utter—"aren't I a woman?"—than for her fierce and exemplary insistence on asserting her rights to speak and act publicly, and to religious expression. This photograph of Sojourner Truth stand-ing wearing a shawl was made c. 1864; she sold copies of it to support herself: "I sell the shadow to support the substance." *Entered according to Act of Congress, in the year 1864, by S. T. in the clerk's office of the U.S. District court, for Eastern District of Michigan. (Courtesy Sophia Smith Collection, Smith College.)*

tine Rose spoke at woman suffrage meetings in eleven different counties in upstate New York.

Improvements in the printing technology and distribution of newspapers meant that women as well as men were no longer dependent on local sources of information and political guidance. Even if one's town lacked a temperance society or an abolition-ist organization, one could still subscribe to a temperance or abolitionist newspaper, reaching out past the local notables to make contact with a wider political community. Abolitionist newspapers like the *National Anti-Slavery Standard* (which was, for a time, edited by a woman, Lydia Maria Child) and women's rights newspapers like *Una* or *The Revolution* could come straight to a woman's mailbox, enlarging her political world.

The historian David Potter urged us to ask whether established generalizations about the past apply to women as accurately as they apply to men.[1] We often find that they do not. For example, although male as well as female slaves were exploited, women were especially vulnerable to sexual exploitation and to debilitating chronic ailments incidental to childbearing. In free households, female work—including taking in boarders, washing their clothes, and cooking meals for them—might account for as much income as working-class husbands gained from their own employment. If the husband's work was seasonal or erratic, the steady income from taking in boarders could be crucial to the family's survival.

Democracy expanded as suffrage was extended to most white men, but simultaneously constrained as the gap between white men and free black men grew, and with it the gap between white men and all women. As Gerda Lerner has pointed out, many of the new opportunities for men came in a form that closed options for women. When additional men were granted suffrage, for example, "women's political status, while legally unchanged . . . deteriorated relative to the advances made by men."[2] The frontier has traditionally been treated as a metaphor for unbounded opportunity. New scholarship in the last decade has emphasized the multicultural complexities of frontiers, and their capacity to be sites of tension, rivalry, and violence. The experience of married women in the trans-Mississippi West was likely to be one of hardship encountered at the urging of their husbands, not out of their own initiative and choice.

In the nineteenth century, women pressed at the limits of the ways in which nonvoting citizens could influence the political order. In antislavery petition campaigns, in effective lobbying to persuade legislatures to reform laws dealing with married women's property rights and child custody, in responding to the crisis of the Civil War, in freedwomen pressing charges against former Confederates who tried to intimidate them, in naming alcohol abuse as a leading cause of domestic violence, in inventing new institutions like settlement houses, in campaigning for the vote, women expressed political opinions and sought to shape political events. The lessons they learned in nineteenth-century struggles go a long way toward explaining the many successes they would have in the twentieth.

NOTES

1. "American Women and the American Character," (1962) in *History and American Society: Essays of David M. Potter*, ed. Don E. Fehrenbacher (New York: Oxford University Press, 1973), p. 279.
2. Gerda Lerner, "The Lady and the Mill Girl," in *The Majority Finds Its Past: Placing Women in History* (New York: Oxford University Press, 1979), pp. 18–20.

DOCUMENTS: The Testimony of Slave Women

Maria Perkins, "I am quite heartsick . . ."

Because masters understood the connection between literacy and rebelliousness, slaves were rarely taught to read and write. This anguished letter from Maria Perkins is unusual because it was written by an enslaved woman. We do not know whether Perkins's husband Richard managed to persuade his master to buy her and keep the family together. If a trader did buy Maria Perkins or her child, the likelihood of permanent separation was great. Scottsville, mentioned in the letter, is a small town near Charlottesville; Staunton is some forty miles away.

Charlottesville, Oct. 8th, 1852
Dear Husband I write you a letter to let you know my distress my master has sold albert to a trader on Monday court day and myself and other child is for sale also and I want you to let [me] hear from you very soon before next cort if you can I don't know when I don't want you to wait till Christmas I want you to tell dr Hamelton and your master if either will buy me they can attend to it know and then I can go afterwards. I don't want a trader to get me they asked me if I had got any person to buy me and I told them no they took me to the court houste too they never put me up a man buy the name of brady bought albert and is gone I don't know where they say he lives in Scottesville my things is in several places some is in staunton and if I should be sold I don't know what will become of them I don't expect to meet with the luck to get that way till I am quite heartsick nothing more I am and ever will be your kind wife Maria Perkins.

Maria Perkins to Richard Perkins, October 8, 1852, Ulrich B. Phillips Collection, Yale University Library, New Haven.

Rose, "Look for some others for to 'plenish de earth"

Letters like Maria Perkins's are very rare. Most firsthand evidence of the experience of being a slave comes from narratives prepared by ex-slaves after they were free. Some accounts were published by abolitionist societies before the Civil War; some people were interviewed by agents of the Freedmen's Bureau after the war. A large group of elderly ex-slaves was interviewed in the 1930s as part of the Federal Writers' Project. One of these speakers we know only as Rose.

Manuscript Slave Narrative Collection, Federal Writers' Project, 1941, vol. 17, Texas Narratives, part 4, pp. 174–78, Library of Congress, Washington, D.C.

Abolitionists accused masters of breeding slaves as they did cattle. Masters denied these charges and claimed that high birth rates among slave women should be taken as evidence of high levels of nutrition and good treatment. In Brazil, for example, where the treatment of slaves was more brutal, fewer children survived. There was some truth to this defense. But slave women lacked the normal legal protections against sexual coercion. It has long been known that Sally Hemings, one of Thomas Jefferson's slaves, was the half-sister of Jefferson's wife, Martha Wayles. In his own lifetime, Jefferson's political opponents had claimed that he had fathered at least one of Sally Hemings' children; family tradition among the descendants of Sally Hemings confirmed the point. In 1998, DNA tests established that the contemporary descendant of Eston Hemings Jefferson carries the same Y chromosome as that carried in Thomas Jefferson's own lineage.*

We are unlikely to know the emotional quality of the relationship between Sally Hemings and Thomas Jefferson; we do not know whether and to what extent it rested on coercion. But it is certain that Jefferson owned Hemings, and that she had no free choice in the matter. When Federalists denounced Jefferson for hypocritical denunciations of miscegenation, they were on the mark.

As Rose's moving narrative shows, on the average plantation, the line between "forced breeding" and "strong encouragement" could be a thin one.

What I say am de facts. If I's one day old, I's way over 90, and I's born in Bell Country, right here in Texas, and am owned by Massa William Black. He owns mammy and pappy, too. Massa Black has a big plantation but he has more niggers dan he need for work on dat place, 'cause he am a nigger trader. He trade and buy an sell all de time.

Massa Black am awful cruel and he whip de cullud folks and works 'em hard and feed dem poorly. We'uns have for rations de cornmeal and milk and 'lasses and some beans and peas and meat once a week. We'uns have to work in de field every day from daylight till dark and on Sunday we'uns do us washin'. Church? Shucks, we'uns don't know what dat mean.

I has de correct mem'randum of when de war start. Massa Black sold we'uns right den. Mammy and pappy powerful glad to get sold, and dey and I is put on de block with 'bout ten other niggers. When we'uns gits te de tradin' block, dere lots of white folks dere what come to look us over. One man shows de intres' in pappy. Him named Hawkins. He talk to pappy and pappy talk to him and say, "Dem my woman and chiles. Please buy all of us and have mercy on we'uns." Massa Hawkins say,

"Dat gal am a likely lookin' nigger, she am portly and strong, but three am more dan I wants, I guesses."

De sale start and 'fore long pappy a put on de block. Massa Hawkins wins de bid for pappy and when mammy am put on de block, he wins de bid for her. Den dere am three or four other niggers sold befo' my time comes. Den massa Black calls me to de block and de auction man say, "What am I offer for dis portly, strong young wench. She's never been 'bused and will make de good breeder."

I wants to hear Massa Hawkins bid, but him say nothin'. Two other men am biddin' 'gainst each other and I sho' has de worryment. Dere am tears comin' down my cheeks 'cause I's bein' sold to some man dat would make sep'ration from my mammy. One man bids $500 and de auction man ask, "Do I hear more? She am gwine at $500.00." Den someone say, $525.00 and de auction man say, "She am sold for $525.00 to Massa Hawkins." Am I glad and 'cited! Why, I's quiverin' all over.

Massa Hawkins takes we'uns to his place and it am a nice plantation. Lots better am dat place dan Massa Black's. Dere is 'bout 50 niggers what is growed and lots of chillen. De first thing massa do when we'uns gits home am

*Dinitia Smith and Nicholas Wade, "DNA Test Finds Evidence of Jefferson Child by Slave," *New York Times*, Nov. 1, 1998, p. A1.

give we'uns rations and a cabin. You mus' believe dis nigger when I says dem rations a feast for us. Dere plenty meat and tea and coffee and white flour. I's never tasted white flour and coffee and mammy fix some biscuits and coffee. Well, de biscuits was yum, yum, yum to me, but de coffee I doesn't like.

De quarters am purty good. Dere am twelve cabins all made from logs and a table and some benches and bunks for sleepin' and a fireplace for cookin' and de heat. Dere am no floor, jus' de ground.

Massa Hawkins am good to he niggers and not force 'em work too hard. Dere am as much diff'ence 'tween him and old Massa Black in de way of treatment as 'twixt de Lawd and de devil. Massa Hawkins 'lows he niggers have reason'ble parties and go fishin', but we'uns am never tooken to church and has no books for larnin'. Dere am no edumcation for de niggers.

Dere am one thing Massa Hawkins does to me what I can't shunt from my mind. I knows he don't do it for meanness, but I allus holds it 'gainst him. What he done am force me to live with dat nigger, Rufus, 'gainst my wants.

After I been at he place 'bout a year, de massa come to me and say, "You gwine live with Rufus in dat cabin over yonder. Go fix it for livin'." I's 'bout sixteen year old and has no larnin', and I's jus' igno'mus chile. I's thought dat him mean for me to tend de cabin for Rufus and some other niggers. Well, dat am start de pestigation for me.

I's took charge of de cabin after work am done and fixes supper. Now, I don't like dat Rufus, 'cause he a bully. He am big and 'cause he so, he think everybody do what him say. We'uns has supper, den I goes here and dere talkin', till I's ready for sleep and den I gits in de bunk. After I's in, dat nigger come and crawl in de bunk with me 'fore I knows it. I says, "What you mean, you fool nigger?" He say for me to hush de mouth. "Dis am my bunk, too," he say.

"You's teched in de head. Git out," I's told him, and I puts de feet 'gainst him and give him a shove and out he go on de floor 'fore he knows what I's doin'. Dat nigger jump up and he mad. He look like de wild bear. He starts for de bunk and I jumps quick for de poker. It am 'bout three feet long and when he comes at me I let him have it over de head. Did dat nigger stop in he tracks? I's say he did. He looks at me steady for a minute and you's could tell he thinkin' hard. Den he go and set on de bench and say, "Jus' wait. You thinks it am smart, but you's am foolish in de head. Dey's gwine larn you somethin'."

"Hush yous big mouth and stay 'way from dis nigger, dat all I wants," I say, and jus' sets and hold dat poker in de hand. He jus' sets, lookin' like de bull. Dere we'uns sets and sets for 'bout an hour and den he go out and I bars de door.

De nex' day I goes to de missy and tells her what Rufus wants and missy say dat am de massa's wishes. She say, "Yous am de portly gal and Rufus am de portly man. De massa wants you-uns for to bring forth portly chillen."

I's thinkin' 'bout what de missy say, but say to myse'f, "I's not gwine live with dat Rufus." Dat night when him come in de cabin, I grabs de poker and sits on de bench and says, "Git 'way from me, nigger, 'fore I busts yous brains out and stomp on dem." He say nothin' and git out.

De nex' day de massa call me and tell me, "Woman, I's pay big money for you and I's done dat for de cause I wants you to raise me chillens. I's put yous to live with Rufus for dat purpose. Now, if you doesn't want whippin' at de stake, yous do what I wants."

I thinks 'bout massa buyin' me offen de block and savin' me from bein' sep'rated from my folks and 'bout bein' whipped at de stake. Dere it am. What am I's to do? So I 'cides to do as de massa wish and so I yields.

When we'uns am given freedom, Massa Hawkins tells us we can stay and work for wages or share crop de land. Some stays and some goes. My folks and me stays. We works de land on shares for three years, den moved to other land near by. I stay with my folks till they dies.

If my mem'radum am correct, it am 'bout thirty year since I come to Fort Worth. Here I cooks for white folks till I goes blind 'bout ten year ago.

I never marries, 'cause one 'sperience am 'nough for dis nigger. After what I does for de massa, I's never wants no truck with any man. De Lawd forgive dis cullud woman, but he have to 'scuse me and look for some others for to 'plenish de earth.

SHARON BLOCK
Lines of Color, Sex, and Service: Sexual Coercion in the Early Republic

A long tradition of describing Northern society as "free" and Southern society as "slave" has had the unfortunate effect of making distinctions seem far more clear in retrospect than they were in experience. Manumission was gradual in most Northern states, and that meant that a mixture of slavery, indentured labor, and freedom persisted throughout the first half of the nineteenth century. The abolitionist Sojourner Truth (see pp. 218–19) was born into slavery as Isabella Van Wagenen in New York in the late 1790s. As a child she was sold twice; when she married it was under a New York state law that recognized marriages between slaves. When she became free on July 4, 1827, according to New York state law she owed no further service, but her children, born after 1799, were bound to service for as much as a decade longer. "Indentured," writes the historian Nell Painter, "the children could not follow Isabella into freedom. . . . When Sojourner Truth became an abolitionist, some of her children were not free."*

Children of poor families were put out to bound labor during the early republic; burdened by their work, they were also vulnerable to the power and authority of their masters. This included, as we see in the essay that follows, vulnerability to sexual coercion—a term Sharon Block uses to mark a wider range of experience than is suggested by the simple term rape. The essay that follows is based on a close reading of a Pennsylvania court record and on one of the great autobiographies of the nineteenth century, Harriet Jacobs's *Incidents in the Life of a Slave Girl*. Writing under a pseudonym after years as a fugitive, supported in her project by the abolitionist writer and editor Lydia Maria Child, Jacobs herself became invisible to historians. For many years her narrative was treated as fiction. Not until 1987, when historian Jean Fagan Yellin published an edition identifying virtually all the individuals and substantiating virtually all the events, has it been possible to understand the narrative as nonfiction. It is compelling reading.†

In what ways did Rachel Davis and Harriet Jacobs try to avoid the power of their masters? In whom did they find allies? In what ways were the experiences of these young women similar? What difference did slavery make?

---

*Nell Irvin Painter, *Sojourner Truth: A Life, a Symbol* (New York: W. W. Norton, 1996), p. 23.

†Harriet A. Jacobs, *Incidents in the Life of a Slave Girl: Written by Herself*, ed. Jean Fagan Yellin (Cambridge, Mass.: Harvard University Press, 1987).

Excerpted from "Lines of Color, Sex, and Service: Comparative Sexual Coercion in Early America," by Sharon Block, in Martha Hodes, ed., *Sex, Love, Race: Crossing Boundaries in North American History* (New York: New York University Press, 1999).

Note: First names are used for all actors in incidents of sexual coercion because first names more easily distinguish men from women and eliminate confusion in identifying members of the same family.

Rachel Davis was born a free white child in the Pennsylvania mountains in 1790. She was fourteen years old when she became an indentured servant to William and Becky Cress in Philadelphia County. By the time Rachel was fifteen, William had begun making sexual overtures to her. After months of continuing sexual assaults, William's wife, Becky, suspected that her husband was having a sexual relationship with their servant. Ultimately, Becky demanded that Rachel be removed from the house. William continued to visit Rachel at her new home, again trying to have sex with her. In 1807, Rachel's father found out what had occurred and initiated a rape prosecution against William, who was found guilty and sentenced to ten years in prison.[1]

Harriet Jacobs was born an enslaved black child in Edenton, North Carolina, in 1813. In 1825, she became a slave in James and Mary Norcom's household. By the time Harriet was sixteen, James had begun making sexual overtures toward her. After months of continuing sexual assaults, James's wife, Mary, suspected that her husband was having a sexual relationship with their slave. Ultimately, Mary demanded that Harriet be removed from the house. James continued to visit Harriet at her new home, again trying to have sex with her. In 1835, Harriet became a runaway slave, and spent the next seven years a fugitive, hiding in her free grandmother's attic crawlspace.[2]

If we were to focus on the conclusions to these stories, we would frame a picture of the contrasting consequences for masters who sexually coerced black and white women: the master of the white servant was sent to prison, while the black slave imprisoned herself to escape her abuser. But these opposing ends tell only part of the story. Until their conclusions, both women engaged in nearly parallel struggles with masters, mistresses, and unwanted sexual overtures. This contrast between the laborers' similar experiences and their stories' opposing conclusions suggests that the practice of sexual coercion and the classification of the criminal act of rape were differently dependent on status and race.

. . . Rachel had an opportunity for institutional intervention that was unequivocally denied to Harriet. Enslaved women in early America did not have access to legal redress against white men who raped them. While no colonial or early republic statute explicitly excluded enslaved women from being the victims of rape or attempted rape, many mid-Atlantic and Southern legislatures set harsh punishments for black men's sexual assaults on white women, thus implicitly privileging white women as victims of rape.[3] At the same time, enslaved people could only be witnesses against non-white defendants, so an enslaved woman could not testify against a white man who had raped her.[4] Accordingly, no historian has recorded a conviction of a white man for the rape of a slave at any point from 1700 to the Civil War, let alone a conviction of a master for raping his own slave. Rape in early America was a crime whose definition was structured by race.[5]

Even though the early American legal system segregated Rachel Davis and Harriet Jacobs into incomparable categories, their own presentations told nearly parallel stories of sexual coercion. In both women's stories, their masters attempted to control the parameters and meanings of sexual acts. Thus, rape in these situations was not just an act of power, it was also the power to define an act. Servants and slaves could not only be forced to consent, but this force was refigured as consent. At the same time, neither Harriet Jacobs nor Rachel Davis presented herself as an abject victim of her master's will.

Rather than a clear demarcation between the rape of slaves and the rape of servants, these narratives suggest that black and white laboring women interpreted and experienced a master's sexual coercion in strikingly similar ways. The parallels in these two stories, however, stopped at the courtroom door, where a racially based legal system ended the women's comparable negotiations of personal interactions.

CREATING MASTERY: THE PROCESS OF COERCION

How did a master sexually coerce a servant or slave in early America? A master did not have to rely on physical abilities to force his dependents into a sexual act. Instead, he might use the power of his position to create opportunities for sexual coercion, backing a woman into a corner where capitulation was her best option. A servant or enslaved woman often recognized this manipulation and tried to negotiate her way around her master's overtures rather than confront him with direct resistance. But that compromise came at a high price . . . negotiation implied willingness, and a woman's willingness contrasted with the early American legal and social code that rape consisted of irresistible force. Despite its surface counterintuitiveness, it was precisely women's attempts to bargain their way out of sexual assaults that made these sexual encounters seem consensual.[6]

Both Harriet Jacobs and Rachel Davis drew direct links between their status and their masters' sexual assaults on them. Each explained how her master had forced her into situations where he could sexually coerce her without being discovered. Rachel described how William ordered her to hold the lantern for him one night in the stable, where he "tried to persuade me to something." In the most blatantly contrived incident, when they were reaping in the meadow, William "handed me his sickle & bad me to lay it down. He saw where I put it." Later that night, William asked Rachel,

> where I put them sickles. I asked if he did not see—he said no, I must come & show him. I told him I cd go with my sister, or by myself. he said that was not as he bad me. I went. Before we got quite to sickles, he bad me stop—I told him I was partly to the sickles—he bad me stop—I did—he came up & threw me down. . . . I hallowed—he put his hand over my mouth . . . he pulled up my cloathes, & got upon me . . . he did penetrate my body. I was dreadfully injured.

According to Rachel's statement, William had forced her to accompany him into a dark field on a contrived search for a purposefully lost farm implement so that he could rape her. William's authority to control where she went and what she did was integral to his ability to force Rachel to have sex with him.

Harriet Jacobs was even more explicit about the connections between James Norcum's mastery and his ability to force her into sexually vulnerable positions. It seemed to Harriet that he followed her everywhere—in her words, "my master met me at every turn"—trying to force her to have sex with him. As William did with Rachel, James structured Harriet's work so that she was often alone with him. He ordered Harriet to bring his meals to him so that while she watched him eat he could verbally torture her with the consequences of refusing his sexual overtures. Harriet further recalled that "when I suc-

ceeded in avoiding opportunities for him to talk to me at home, I was ordered to come to his office, to do some errand." Tiring of Harriet's continued resistance, James ordered his four-year-old daughter to sleep near him, thus requiring that Harriet also sleep in his room in case the child needed attention during the night. James repeatedly used his position as a master who controlled his slave's labor to manipulate Harriet into sexually vulnerable situations.[7] Controlling a woman's daily routine, her work requirements, and her physical presence—in other words, control over her labor and her body—gave men in positions of mastery access to a particular means of sexually coercive behavior.

Each woman also recalled how she had challenged her master's right to force her into a sexual relationship. Rachel recounted how she had "resisted" and "cried" when William tried to pull her into a darkened bedroom after sending the rest of the servants to bed, and how she threatened that she would tell his wife what he was doing. When these forms of resistance did not end his overtures, Rachel tried to carry out her master's orders in ways that might prevent her own sexual vulnerability. Rachel's description of being raped in the dark field began by recollecting that she had suggested that William could find the sickle himself, and then offered to find it on her own or with her sister. Ultimately, William resorted to his position as a master—"he said that was not as he bad me"—and issued a direct order for Rachel to accompany him. Rachel portrayed an interactive relationship with William: she may not have been able to override her master's orders, but she forced him to change their content. Rather than sex in the bedroom while the other children slept and his wife was away, Rachel forced William to order her into the dark field, thereby disrupting his original attempts at a seamless consensual interaction.

Harriet Jacobs's story contained similar efforts to avoid her master's sexual overtures that forced him to refigure his behavior. When Mary Norcum's suspicions made her husband revert to physical gestures instead of words to convey his sexual desires to Harriet, Harriet responded by letting "them pass, as if I did not understand what he meant." When James realized that Harriet could read, he wrote her notes that expressed his sexual intentions. But

Harriet repeatedly pretended "'I can't read them, sir.'" Overall, "by managing to keep within sight of people, as much as possible during the day time, I had hitherto succeeded in eluding my master." Harriet forced James into baldly claiming his right for sexual access as a privilege of mastery: according to Harriet, James began constantly "reminding me that I belonged to him, and swearing by heaven and earth that he would compel me to submit to him" because "I was his property; that I must be subject to his will in all things." Like Rachel Davis, Harriet Jacobs engaged in an exchange of maneuvers with her master where each tried to foil the other's plans and counterplans. Despite her master's legal property in her body, Harriet did not portray herself as utterly powerless. By playing into his image of her as too stupid to understand his signs and too illiterate to read his notes, Harriet used her own position as a slave to avoid her master's sexual overtures, forcing him to raise the stakes of his desires toward her.[8]

Because he did not receive unquestioned acquiescence from a servant or slave, a master had to create situations in which his laborers had little choice but to have sexual relations with him. Rachel's attempted refusal to go alone into a dark field with her master and Harriet's feigned ignorance of her master's intentions forced each man to modify his route to sexual interactions. By not consenting to a master's more subtle attempts at sexual relations, a servant or slave might force her master into more overtly coerced sexual acts. Ironically, this compelled a master to enact his laborer's interpretation of his overtures. Rather than the sexual offers that the masters first proposed, the men were forced to use coercion to carry out their sexual plans. Theoretically, a master could coerce through his physical prowess, but most masters did not have to rely exclusively on fists or whips to commit rape. Instead, they could rely on the strength of their mastery.

Beyond the unadorned physical power that could compel a woman into a sexual act, a master had an array of indirect means to force a dependent to have sex with him that simultaneously denied her resistance to him. . . . Harriet characterized her master as "a crafty man, [who] resorted to many means to accomplish his purposes. Sometimes he had stormy, terrific ways, that made his victims

tremble; sometimes he assumed a gentleness that he thought must surely subdue." James promised Harriet that if she would give in to him sexually, "I would cherish you. I would make a lady of you." The possibility of a better life that transcended her racial and labor status was more than a bribe to induce Harriet's consent. It created a fiction that Harriet could voluntarily choose to have sexual relations with her master. By switching between the threats of physical harm and the gifts of courtship, James undercut the appearance of a forced sexual interaction. By theoretically allowing space for Harriet's consent to his sexual overtures, James was redefining coercion into consensual sexual relations.[9]

Similarly, William's verbal narration of consensual relations overlay his forceful attempts at sex. While he had Rachel trapped underneath his body, William told her that "he wd have the good will of me." William's modification of the classic legal description of rape as a man having carnal knowledge of a woman "against her will" verbally created a consensual act even as he used force to have sexual relations.[10] In the same incident, William called Rachel by her family nickname, telling her, "Nate you dear creature, I must fuck you." Even while forcing Rachel to have sex with him, William used terms of endearment toward her. William's presentation of an affectionate and therefore consensual sexual relationship with Rachel differentiated his actions from the brutality that early Americans would most easily recognize as rape.

Thus, the process of master–servant and master–slave sexual coercion was not exclusively tied to racial boundaries. Harriet Jacobs's and Rachel Davis's similarly recounted experiences suggest that their sexual interactions were more directly shaped by lines of status and dependency. These patterns would be repeated as masters and their servants or slaves struggled to control public perceptions of what had occurred.

CREATING MASTER NARRATIVES: THE PROCESS OF PUBLICITY

Given these different versions of events, how did families, other household members, and communities interpret evidence of a possibly coercive sexual interaction? How did assaulted women portray what had happened to them? Harriet Jacobs's and Rachel Davis's narratives show that the process of publicizing a master's sexual overtures was again structured by the woman's position as his personally dependent laborer. Words—the power to speak them and the power to construct their meaning—became the prize in a struggle among masters, mistresses, and the assaulted servant or slave.

After attempting sexual overtures toward their laborers, masters had to contend with the possibility that the women would tell others about their masters' behavior. Harriet Jacobs's and Rachel Davis's masters attempted to threaten their laborers into silence about their sexual interactions. Harriet wrote that her master "swore he would kill me, if I was not as silent as the grave."[11] Similarly, William told Rachel that if she told "any body, he wd be the death of me." When Rachel threatened to tell his wife what William had been doing, "he sd if I did, I shd repent." By demanding her silence, each master tried to dictate the parameters of his sexual interactions with his servant or slave without outside interference that might contradict his interpretation or stop his sexual pursuit.

But both women also believed that their masters were afraid of the damage that they could do by publicizing their sexual behavior. Besides his threats of physical violence, William promised Rachel a "gown if she would not tell" what he had done, and on another occasion, "begged [Rachel] not to tell" her new mistress because "it wd be the Ruin of him." Harriet similarly believed that her master "did not wish to have his villainy made public." Instead, he "deemed it prudent to keep up some outward show of decency." From each woman's vantage point, then, her master's concern about his public image again allowed her some room for negotiation: he needed his servant or slave to conceal their sexual interactions. But by not telling anyone about her master's sexual assaults, a woman increased the likelihood that their sexual relationship would not appear to be a rape. This double-edged sword made the servant or slave an unwilling accomplice in the masking of her own sexual coercion.[12]

If pressuring his servant or slave into silence through bribes or threats did not silence her, a master might try to control her description of their sexual interaction. William Cress enacted an elaborate punishment scene that forced Rachel Davis to claim responsibility for anything that may have passed between them. After Rachel's complaints to her mistress prompted Mary to confront her husband about Rachel's allegations, William immediately challenged Rachel. "'Well Rachael,'" William accused, "'what are this you have been scraping up about me?,'" denying even in his question the possibility of his own misdeeds. When Rachel could not present a satisfactory answer, William employed the power of physical correction allowed to him as her master to reform her story. According to Rachel, he "whipt me dreadfully & he said . . . that he never had such a name before. . . . I fell down—he damned me, & bad me beg his pardon. I said I did not know how—he bad me go on my knees . . . he bad me go to house & tell" his wife that she (Rachel) had lied. By whipping Rachel, William attempted to disprove her story of sexual assault: his wife had said that if Rachel's assertions of sexual relations between herself and William "was lies" as William claimed, "he ought to whip" Rachel for her dishonesty. This whipping was not just a punishment unfairly inflicted, it was a punishment that retroactively attempted to define the sexual interactions between a servant and a master. Once subjugated, Rachel was required to deny that William had forced her to have sex with him. Rachel's younger sister, also a servant to William, believed this new version of events: she admitted that "I do remember D[efendant] whipping my sister—it was for telling so many lies." William was using his position as master to rewrite the sexual act that had taken place between them.

Rachel ended her description of this incident by stating that after William had beaten her, "he went to church that day & I showed my back to [my] Sister." Those final words on her master's brutal punishment (a whipping that prevented Rachel from lying on her side for three weeks) revealed the irony of the situation: while William continued to appear as a publicly reverent and virtuous patriarch, Rachel secretly bore the signs of his sins, visible only to those most intimate with her. In the process of sexual coercion, force did not have a solely physical purpose: masters also used force to create an image of consent.

Harriet Jacobs also noted the discrepancy between her master's public image and private behavior, telling her readers how he had pre-served his image at her expense. When Har-riet's mistress confronted Harriet with suspi-cions of her husband's sexual improprieties, Harriet swore on a Bible that she had not had a sexual relationship with her master. When Mary questioned her husband, however, James contradicted Harriet's statements. And just like Rachel's mistress, Harriet's mistress "would gladly have had me flogged for my supposed false oath." But unlike William Cress, James Norcum did not allow Harriet to be whipped because "the old sinner was politic. The application of the lash might have led to remarks that would have exposed him" to his family and community.[13]

In Rachel's and Harriet's narratives, their mistresses—the wives of their abusers—played important roles in the categorization of the sexually abusive relationship. Each woman had to deal with a mistress who ultimately took her displeasure at her husband's sexual relationship out on her servant or slave. Each mistress also used her position of secondary mastery to create a temporary alliance with her servant or slave. Once this alliance outlived its usefulness, it became another tool with which the mistress could assist in redefining or deny-ing the sexual relationship between the mas-ter and the slave or servant.

In both women's stories, the masters' wives did not immediately take their hostility at their sexually aggressive husbands out on the objects of their husbands' overtures. When Rachel and William came back from retrieving the "lost" sickle, his wife, Becky, asked "where he had been—he said, after the sickles, with nate (so they called me in family) she sd it was very extraordinary, no body else could go." Perhaps Becky suspected some sort of sexual liaison between her husband and their servant, and her pointed questions let her husband know her of her suspicions. When Becky heard William trying to kiss Rachel in the cellar, she "said she had caught him & he wd deceive her no longer," but William denied any wrongdoing and Becky left in tears. These ver-bal confrontations apparently did not alter William's behavior; he continued to force him-self sexually upon Rachel. Finally, Rachel's mistress "saw something was the matter with me, & asked what it was. I told her." After questioning her husband had little visible effect, Becky turned to Rachel to find out about

her husband's actions. This temporary alliance brought Rachel some protection from Wil-liam's retribution, if not from his sexual over-tures: when William heard that Rachel had told another relative some of what he had done to her, "he whipt me again, but not so bad—his wife wd not let him & said, he was in Fault."

Similarly, Harriet Jacobs believed that her mistress suspected James's illicit behavior: "She watched her husband with unceasing vigilance; but he was well practised in means to evade it." After Mary heard that her hus-band planned to have Harriet sleep in his room, she began questioning Harriet, who told her how James had been sexually harassing her. Harriet claimed that Mary, like most slave mistresses "had no compassion for the poor victim of her husband's perfidy. She pitied herself as a martyr." But Harriet also admitted that Mary "spoke kindly, and promised to pro-tect me," ordering Harriet to sleep with her, rather than with James. This protective kind-ness also allowed Mary to try to obtain the "truth" of Harriet and James's relationship out of Harriet while Harriet slept: "she whispered in my ear, as though it was her husband who was speaking to me, and listened to hear what I would answer." When Harriet did not pro-vide any self-incriminating information, Mary confronted her husband, but Mary's interven-tions did not end James's sexual overtures toward Harriet.[14]

If mistresses could not personally control their husbands' behavior, how could they stop the sexual relationship between master and laborer that was making a mockery of their marital vows? Theoretically, mistresses could turn to the legal system to petition for a divorce from their husbands. By the early nine-teenth century, most states had divorce laws that allowed wives to apply for divorce on the grounds of their husbands' adultery, but women's petitions for divorce were more com-monly based on charges of desertion.[15] Fur-thermore, proving adultery with a slave might be difficult without firsthand witnesses to the sexual interactions, since the slave was limited in her ability to testify against the white man. Married women also had a vested interest in their husbands' social and economic standing. Divorce or incarceration would most probably result in a woman's economic downturn from the loss of her husband's labor.

Ultimately, Rachel Davis's and Harriet Jacobs's mistresses concentrated their energies on removing their laborers from the household. Instead of bringing charges against her husband or applying for a divorce on the grounds of adultery, Becky Cress told Rachel Davis that she must "leave the house." Rachel recalled that "they then hired me out." Rachel's mistress may have ultimately recognized that her husband was (at best) complicit in his sexual relations with Rachel, but she also recognized that she, as his wife, was in a poor position to mandate a reform in his behavior. She could, however, as a mistress, remove the more disposable partner in the sexual relationship, and so she ordered Rachel to leave their home. Whether or not Becky believed Rachel's story of rape, she did not hold Rachel entirely innocent of wrongdoing. At the very least, she spread blame equally between her servant and her husband, with much of the resulting punishment falling on the more vulnerable of the two parties. As Rachel stated, "Before I was hired out, [my mistress] used me very bad & said she would knowck me down if I came to table to eat." Because William was a master—both of Rachel and of his household—his wife could enact only limited direct retribution against him. She could watch his behavior, confront him, and let him know her displeasure, but ultimately, it was easier to remove the object of his overtures than publicly to accuse him of wrongdoing.

Mary Norcum demanded that Harriet Jacobs leave the house once she learned that Harriet was pregnant, believing that conception was proof of their slave's sexual relationship with her husband. Harriet was not the only slave who was reputed to have been kicked out of her house because of a sexual relationship with the master. Recalling a story told to her by her grandmother about another slave, Harriet wrote that "her mistress had that day seen her baby for the first time, and in the lineaments of its fair face she saw a likeness to her husband. She turned the bondswoman and her child out of doors, and forbade her ever to return." In both of these examples, the mistress felt herself in sexual competition with the slave—even if the slave were not a willing competitor for the master's affections.[16]

Thus, while a wife's place in the household hierarchy may have proscribed her options, it did not leave her entirely at her husband's mercy. By forcing her husband to prove his marital loyalty by whipping the laborer for telling untruths about his sexual conduct, each mistress tried to create her own version of household sexual alliances. When mistresses could not force husbands to modify their behavior, these wives turned to regulating their servant's or slave's actions: first, by using them as the source of incriminating information, and later, as a problem that could be eliminated. Mistresses would not permanently join forces with slave or servant women to overthrow the household patriarch; they might want to change their husbands' behavior, but these wives did not wish publicly to condemn or disassociate themselves from their husbands through divorce or other legal action.

The silencing of sexual coercion was more profound in Harriet Jacobs's autobiography than it was in Rachel Davis's court-ordered testimony specifically about rape. Harriet's representation of her conflict with her master centered on the power to create a singular version of reality through the privilege of public speech. Throughout her narrative, Harriet insisted that her master sexually assaulted her only with words, never with his body. She wrote that he "tried his utmost to corrupt the pure principles my grandmother had instilled. He peopled my mind with unclean images." Harriet silenced her own description of her master's actions by calling the sexual degradation of slavery "more than I can describe." Harriet's versions of her master's verbal actions may have stood in for the literally unspeakable physical sexual abuse she suffered at his hands. By describing only James's speech, Harriet turned his possibly physical assaults on her into verbal assaults that no reader could expect her to control.[17]

In a personal letter written a few years before the publication of *Incidents in the Life of a Slave Girl* in 1861, Harriet hinted that she had indeed concealed the extent of James's actions. While she had tried to give a "true and just" account of her life in slavery, she admitted that "there are somethings I might have made plainer I know—Woman can whisper—her cruel wrongs into the ear of a very dear friend—much easier than she can record them for the world to read." In this passage, Jacobs drew a distinction between the private version of her pain and the version she chose to present for public consumption. Victorian womanhood's emphasis on modesty and respectability as well as the established genre of sexual euphemism popularized in sentimental novels probably encouraged Harriet Jacobs to present a sanitized version of her master's assaults on her. But her decision may also have reflected a personal need to distance herself from painful events, and a difficulty in telling others about her suffering that was shared by other victims—black and white—of a master's sexual harassment.[18]

Both Harriet and Rachel first told those closest to them about their masters' unwelcome sexual overtures. Harriet originally hesitated to tell Molly Horniblow, her grandmother and closest living relative, how James was treating her. Harriet "would have given the world to have laid my head on my grandmother's faithful bosom, and told her all my troubles," but James's threats and her own fear of her grandmother's reaction made her stay silent. When Harriet eventually did talk to her grandmother, she told her only some of her difficulties: "I talked with my grandmother about it, and partly told her my fears. I did not dare to tell her the worst." Harriet also told her uncle about some of her suffering. He told another relative that "you don't know what a life they lead her. She has told me something about it, and I wish [her master] was dead, or a better man." Harriet's recollection of interactions with her grandmother and her uncle emphasized that neither relative knew the entire story of her master's abuses. Just as the reader was given a sanitized version in the public transcript of Harriet's life, her hesitancy to confess the full extent of sexual coercion was reiterated in Harriet's personal interactions. Her inability to confess "the worst" of her experiences may have maintained Harriet's image of sexual purity and self-identity, but it was at the cost of denying the full spectrum of her master's assaults on her.[19]

Similarly, Rachel eventually told people close to her—one of her sisters (a servant in another household), her aunt, and her new mistress—about what William was doing to her. She recounted that she was hesitant to tell the whole story even to them. Rachel told her new mistress "something of what passed in the meadow, but not the worst of it. I told my sister Becky . . . the whole of it." Like Harriet's claim that it was easier to tell a close friend

than to proclaim one's victimization publicly, Rachel had an easier time confessing her problems to her sister than to her new mistress. When Rachel spoke with her aunt, Elizabeth Ashton, she again refrained from disclosing the full extent of William's coercion. Elizabeth told the court that Rachel had explained how William had isolated her in the cellar, had told her to go to bed with him when his wife was away, had cornered her in the barn, and had forced her to go with him to retrieve the sickle in the meadow. But Rachel stopped short of telling her aunt that William had succeeded in raping her, that his manipulative maneuvers had led to forced sexual intercourse. Elizabeth specified under cross-examination that "*I did not understand from her that he had fully effected his purpose in the meadow.*"[20] By minimizing the extent of her master's abuse of her, Rachel created a public version of her master's actions that denied that she had been raped.

The victims of sexual coercion were not the only people who purposefully avoided discussions of sexual assaults. Elizabeth Ashton did not know that William had raped Rachel partly because, as she told the court, "I did not enquire whether he obtained his will in the meadow." When Rachel's sister told her own mistress that "Mr Cress wanted to be gret [great] with her sister Rachael," the mistress replied, "I wanted to hear no more." When this sister eventually told their father what had happened, Jacob Davis recalled that she "did not tell me directly, she did not tell me the worst—I did not think it was so bad." A voluntary conspiracy of silence—from the servant who had difficulty discussing what had happened, to the other women who wanted neither to hear nor tell the full extent of William's abuse of Rachel—worked to deny the sexual coercion that William committed on his servant.

Similarly, Harriet Jacobs's fellow slaves were hesitant to volunteer verbal or physical assistance. Harriet believed that while her friends and relatives knew that she was being sexually abused, they were unable to speak of it. Harriet recalled that "the other slaves in my master's house noticed" her changed behavior as a result of her master's treatment, but "none dared to ask the cause. . . . They knew too well the guilty practices under that roof; and they were aware that to speak of them was an offence that never went unpunished." Harriet's fellow slaves' silence, necessary for their own self-preservation, limited their ability to help Harriet resist their master's overtures. By controlling potential allies, a master enmeshed his original acts of sexual coercion in an ever-widening coercive web that structured his victim's possibilities for support or redress.[21]

By not telling others what had happened to her, Harriet was at the mercy of other people's versions of events. James's wife, Mary, went to the house of Harriet's free grandmother to tell her that Harriet was pregnant with James's baby. Molly Horniblow then turned on Harriet, apparently believing Mary's story that Harriet had consented to the relationship: "'I had rather see you dead than to see you as you now are,'" she told her granddaughter. "'You are a disgrace to your dead mother. . . . Go away . . . and never come to my house, again.'" Because Harriet had consistently denied or downplayed her master's sexual attempts on her, her grandmother believed Mary's story that Harriet had voluntarily had sexual relations with James. Later, Harriet's grandmother learned that Harriet had chosen to become pregnant with another man's baby to try to force her sexually abusive master to leave her alone or sell her. Once her grandmother understood "the real state of the case, and all I had been bearing for years. . . . She laid her old hand gently on my head, and murmured, 'Poor child! Poor child!'" Harriet's inability to speak about her master's sexual coercion temporarily isolated Harriet from the woman who was most able to support her. When Harriet ultimately received her grandmother's forgiveness, she also gained an ally in her fight against her master's sexual demands.[22]

Both Harriet and Rachel believed that an independently powerful figure outside of the household could counterbalance their masters' attempts at dominance. When Rachel's aunt questioned "why she did not go to a Squire to complain" about her master's sexual assaults, Rachel replied "she did not dare—she a bound girl & her father absent." After telling her sister what had happened, her sister "advised her to stay there & be a good girl. . . . I thought nothing could be done, as my father was away." Rachel herself told the court that "I did not know if I went to a Justice, he wd take notice of it. Enough people knew it, but waited till my Father came back." Without a patriarchal figure beside her, Rachel would not

directly confront her master, and did not believe herself entitled to legal justice, a belief encouraged (or at least not contradicted) by the women in whom she confided. For Rachel, her father's support was crucial to her ability to receive public redress for her master's sexual assaults on her.

Enslaved women ordinarily did not have access to the protection offered by a patriarchal figure. Harriet Jacobs's observed that enslaved men "strive to protect wives and daughter from the insults of their masters. . . . [but] Some poor creatures have been so brutalized by the lash that they will sneak out of the way to give their masters free access to their wives and daughters." Although Harriet Jacobs did not have a waiting patriarchal figure to whom she could turn for protection, supporters outside of the household were still crucial to her limited redress. Harriet repeatedly spoke of her free grandmother's respect in the community, of how James "dreaded" this woman's "scorching rebuke," so that "her presence in the neighborhood was some protection to me." Ultimately, her grandmother's home became a partial refuge from James's pursuit. Harriet also spoke of her white lover's assistance in combating her master's "persecutions" of her through his "wish to aid me." Harriet partly justified her decision to have sexual relations with this man (pseudonymously referred to as "Mr. Sands") because she was "sure my friend, Mr. Sands, would buy me . . . and I thought my freedom could be easily obtained from him." While Harriet could not hope for institutional retribution against her master, she could hope that her new lover would help provide freedom from her master.[23]

Both Harriet Jacobs and Rachel Davis fought similar battles against the veil of silence surrounding their masters' treatment of them. Both were confronted by relatives and neighbors who had limited authority over another household's problems. Both women turned to another powerful figure—father or free grandmother and elite white lover, respectively—to rescue them from their masters' sexual abuse. When Rachel finally told her father about her master's sexual assaults, Jacob Davis successfully encouraged the local legal system to begin a criminal prosecution. But neither Harriet Jacobs's ultimate confession to her grandmother nor her involvement with a white lover could lead to legal intervention. The legal system marked an irreversible disjuncture in the two women's experiences.

EPILOGUE: CREATING RAPE: THE LEGAL PROCESS

Following the process of sexual coercion has led us back to this essay's opening, as Harriet Jacobs's and Rachel Davis's parallel stories reach diametrically opposed conclusions: while Rachel's master was convicted of rape and served a substantial jail sentence, there is no evidence that Harriet's master was ever subject to legal repercussions for his behavior. When a master tried to define coercive sex as consensual sex, both servants and slaves could negotiate with his terms and battle against his actions. But when the legal system defined enslaved women outside the judicial parameters of rape, there was little room for negotiation. The parallels in Harriet Jacobs's and Rachel Davis's stories ended with the legal distinction of criminal behavior. Rachel Davis may not have had easy access to criminal justice—her master was convicted of rape several years after he had first assaulted her. Yet she ultimately received legal protections that were denied to Harriet Jacobs.

We need to understand not only the legal history of rape, but the social history of sexual coercion. By taking seriously the possibility that white and black women in early America could have some experiences in common, we can begin to reassemble the complicated interactions of race, gender, and social and economic status in American history. Certainly the comparative possibilities are not exhausted with these two stories. Historians could compare the sexual experiences of free and enslaved African American women or white and black free servants. Were similar strategies used outside of households, in any relationship between a powerful man and a less powerful woman? In all of these comparisons, we should think carefully about how sex was coerced and how the crime of rape was defined. If we frame our investigations using solely the legal judgment of rape, we not only miss much of the story, we again replace women's experiences—much as their coercers had tried to do—with external categorizations. Instead, by interrogating the multiple and contested meanings of sexual coercion, we can

better understand the historical relationships of social and sexual power.

NOTES

1. "Commonwealth v. William Cress, Feb. 1808," Pennsylvania Court Papers, 1807–1809, Historical Society of Pennsylvania, Philadelphia, Pa. Unless otherwise noted, all quotations regarding Rachel Davis are from these documents. For the criminal prosecution of William Cress, see "Commonwealth v. William Cress, Philadelphia, Feb. 15, 1808," Pennsylvania Oyer and Terminer Docket, 1778–1827, 261, 262, 263, 265, Pennsylvania Historic and Museum Commission, Harrisburg, Pa.

2. Harriet Jacobs, *Incidents in the Life of a Slave Girl Written by Herself*, ed. Jean Fagan Yellin (1861; reprint, Cambridge, Mass.: Harvard University Press, 1987).

3. For examples of statutes specifying the crime of black-on-white rape, see John D. Cushing, ed., *The Earliest Printed Laws of Pennsylvania 1681–1713* (Wilmington, Del.: Michael Glazier, 1978), 69; B.W. Leigh, ed., *The Revised Code of the Laws of Virginia* (n.p., 1819), 585–86. See also Peter Bardalgio, "Rape and the Law in the Old South: 'Calculated to Excite Indignation in Every Heart,'" *Journal of Southern History* 60 (1994): 756–58.

4. See Thomas D. Morris, "Slaves and the Rules of Evidence in Criminal Trials," *Chicago-Kent Law Review* 68 (1993): 1209–39.

5. For further discussion of the cultural definitions of rape in early America, see Sharon Block, *He Said I Must: Coerced Sex in Early America* (Chapel Hill, OIEAHC at University of North Carolina Press, forthcoming).

6. Much of the following discussion about resistance's reformulation into consent was inspired by Ellen Rooney, "'A Little More than Persuading': Tess and the Subject of Sexual Violence," in *Rape and Representation*, eds. Lynn A. Higgins and Brenda R. Silver (New York: Columbia University Press, 1991), 87–114, and the fictional exploration of twentieth-century household sexual coercion in J.M. Redmann's three-book series culminating in *The Intersection of Law and Desire* (New York: W. W. Norton, 1995).

7. Jacobs, *Incidents*, 28, 27, 31–32. See also p. 41.

8. Ibid., 31, 32, 28, 27.

9. Ibid., 27, 35.

10. Italics added.

11. Jacobs, *Incidents*, 28. See also 32.

12. Ibid., 29.

13. Ibid., 34, 35.

14. Ibid., 31, 33, 34.

15. On divorce in the antebellum South, see Jane Turner Censer, "'Smiling Through Her Tears': Ante-bellum Southern Women and Divorce," American *Journal of Legal History* 25 (1981): 24–47; for Pennsylvania, see Merril D. Smith, *Breaking the Bonds: Marital Discord in Pennsylvania, 1730–1830* (New York: New York University Press, 1991); Thomas Meehan, "'Not Made out of Levity': Evolu-

tion of Divorce in Early Pennsylvania," *Pennsylvania Magazine of History and Biography* 92 (1968): 441–64.

16. Jacobs, Incidents, 59, 122.

17. Ibid., 27–28.

18. Harriet Jacobs to Amy Post, June 21, 1857, in Jacobs, *Incidents*, 242. For a discussion of African American women's psychological reactions to systemic sexual exploitation, see Darlene Clark Hine,

"Rape and the Inner Lives of Black Women in the Middle West: Preliminary Thoughts on the Culture of Dissemblance," *Signs* 14 (1989), 265–277.

19. Jacobs, *Incidents*, 28, 38, 25.

20. Underlining in original.

21. Jacobs, *Incidents*, 28.

22. Ibid., 56, 57.

23. Ibid., 29, 54–55.

STEPHANIE MCCURRY

Women's Work: The Gender Division of Labor in Yeoman Households of South Carolina before the Civil War

Americans have long taken pride in individual accomplishment. In the nineteenth century there was much talk of "self-made men" and "self-working farmers." But the terms often clouded over the fact that the work of these individuals was likely supplemented by their household subordinates' labor: male farmers claimed the labor of their wives and children; free women and men claimed the labor of slaves.

The tradition of describing Southern farms as *either* "slave" or "free" has also had the effect of suggesting that this distinction was fixed. But as Stephanie McCurry shows, white farmers who generally relied on the labor of their own family members also occasionally turned to hired slaves; a farm that was part of a "free labor" economy one year could be part of the slave system the next.

By childbirth and childraising, women reproduced the family for the next generation. By their physical labor, farm women produced household goods for which their counterparts in towns and cities were shopping in stores; the labor of farm women kept their families out of debt. This work, Stephanie McCurry points out, had national implications. When the South Carolina legislature annulled the national tariffs of 1828 and 1832 and refused to collect these taxes on imports (especially on cloth), they participated in a southern challenge to the authority of the federal government—part of the long struggle that would end in Civil War. In that context, women's household production was crucial to the ability of the South to separate itself from the federal economy. This sort of household production faded only gradually: In the 1930s, Amish families escaped some of the harshest impact of the Depression because women, by their household pro-

Excerpted from "Producing Dependence: Women, Work, and Yeoman Households in Low-Country South Carolina," ch. 3 in *Neither Lady nor Slave: Working Women of the Old South*, edited by Susanna Delfino and Michele Gillespie (Chapel Hill: University of North Carolina Press, 2002). Notes have been revised and renumbered.

duction, by their use of horses instead of cars, of cows instead of milk delivery, kept their families out of debt.

Why does McCurry think that women's work in the fields has been invisible? Whose interests were served by that invisibility? To what extent did men and women live in different "spheres"? What difference did it make that it was easy for the Sloan family to put Manda, a slave, to work? What does McCurry mean by suggesting that "Dependence was the stuff of which independence was made"?

"Self-working farmer." That was the face . . . yeomen farmers in the South turned to the world beyond the fence. But it was only one profile of yeoman household economy, inseparable from the other, domestic one. Infinitely more difficult to see, the domestic face turned into the household, where the daily work of producing independence was conducted. But these men were not really "self-working farmers." On the contrary, the very term expressed their successful appropriation of the labor of others: the women, children, and, sometimes, slaves who peopled their households and tilled their fields. The vitality of male independence that characterized the public sphere of marketplace and ballot box was tied intimately to the legal and customary dependencies of the household.[1] Dependence was the stuff of which independence—and manhood—was made. . . .

Northern travelers often expressed their shock at the discomfort and apparent disorder of yeoman homes and . . . their disapproval of a gender division of labor that seemed to weigh unnaturally on women. . . .

Frederick Law Olmsted, the designer of New York's Central Park, who traveled through the slave states in the mid-1850s had more than sufficient opportunity to observe the domestic arrangements of yeoman households. Lacking letters of introduction to planter families, he was forced not infrequently to seek plain folks' hospitality. He was a miserable guest. Neither yeoman homes nor their inhabitants conformed to his standards of decency and comfort. He complained incessantly about filthy, vermin-infested cabins, "mere square pens of logs roofed over" with a "shed of boards before the door." He longed for the comforts of home: a private room with a "clean sweet bed" in which to sleep "alone and undisturbed"; hot water in the morning with which to wash; a parlor, curtained, carpeted, and "glowing softly with the light of

sperm candles or a shaded lamp"; an armchair; a "fragrant cup of tea" with refined sugar and wheat bread; and the soothing sound of a woman playing classical music or reading aloud from Shakespeare or Dickens. Instead, when he was forced into yeoman homes by the approach of nightfall, "nine times out of ten" he had to sleep in "a room with others, in a bed that stank, supplied with but one sheet if any," and to make his morning ablutions in a common washbasin that doubled as a bread bowl. He found no garden, no flowers, no fruit, no tea, no cream, sugar, or bread, no curtains, no lifting windows, no couch and no carpets, not to mention Shakespeare or sheet music.[2]

At a purely descriptive level, Olmsted's depiction was not inaccurate. Yeoman men and women did live mostly in crude, unchinked double log cabins with porches in front and kitchens behind and with chimneys of sticks and clay and unglazed windows. One former slave from a yeoman neighborhood in Marion District pointed out that there was little difference between her "one room pole house that wad daubed wid dirt" and the one "my white folks live in [which was] a pole house daubed wid dirt too."[3] Inventories of yeomen's household goods, moreover, confirm that they were few and basic: wood and pewter dishes, cast-iron pots, more homemade stools than "seting chares," and more "shuck mattresses" than the prized feather beds that, where they existed, were typically the most valuable household goods yeomen owned. Luxury items such as clocks, books, and mahogany furniture were rare even in yeoman slaveholders' households. Upholstered armchairs, pianos, couches, and carpets were nowhere to be found.[4]

Olmsted's tone of moral indignation suggests, however, that something more basic than his sense of comfort was assaulted in yeoman homes. . . . As he saw it, slavery had corrupted all it touched, including the "natural" relations of men and women. Unlike the newly privatized middle-class homes of the urban Northeast (Olmsted's point of reference), from which so-called productive labor had been largely expelled by the 1850s, yeoman households remained the locus of production as well as of reproduction and consumption.[5] They had not developed the familiar and superior spatial, material, or moral arrangements of bourgeois "homes" associated with separate spheres and domesticity. Instead, house spilled out into yard and yard into house in total disregard of privacy and hygiene, as basic notions of order and morality would suggest. There was no parlor, never mind a womanly parlor culture, and the kitchen, far from representing the emotional center of domestic life, was usually an outbuilding physically separate from the dwelling house.[6] . . .

Women's labor of all sorts has historically been obscured by the public representation of the household in the person of its male head and by definitions of work that focus on the value of market exchange.[7] Such a resolutely ungendered approach cannot even begin to explain how, for example, self-sufficiency was achieved on yeoman farms. Yeoman farmers were fully aware that they could aspire to self-sufficiency in large measure because, in addition to grain, virtually everything else their families ate was grown or raised, preserved, and cooked by women, and virtually everything they wore was spun and woven, dyed and sewed by women. What little milk and butter yeomen had, their wives or daughters produced. "Milk cow!" a slave man said incredulously, "I nebber bid to sich a ting in my life. Dat'oman work."[8] A farm household without a farm wife was a disadvantaged one indeed. Even planters sought married overseers to acquire women's labor in the dairy and poultry house and in the making of cloth and clothing.[9]

The value of women's work was clear. By their industry, wives and daughters ensured that nothing was purchased that could be produced at home, whatever the cost in labor and sweat. In antebellum yeoman households women contributed more than the services and skills that continue to represent the unpaid labor of wives and mothers; they contributed as well the production of goods for household consumption that had elsewhere passed into the realm of the market. "I have been down at York today," the up-country farm wife Mary Davis Brown noted in her diary, and "I did not by much of enything."[10] In the broadest sense, the women's "domestic" production played a critical role in limiting the extent of the home market in consumer goods in the antebellum South. Indeed, the continued high levels of household production throughout the antebellum period point to one local manifestation of the systematic difference between farm women's work North and South. If yeoman farmers escaped relations of debt and dependency with local merchants and planters, they knew that the accomplishment was as much their wives' as their own.

Women's contribution to subsistence notwithstanding, the gender division of labor in yeoman households did not conform to distinctions between domestic and market production. The reason is simple. All economy was "domestic economy," at least in comparative terms; none of the products of yeoman households was definitively a subsistence or a market crop. Even cotton, although it could not be eaten, could be marketed in the raw for cash or goods or, by virtue of women's traditional craft skills, be turned into cloth for use at home or for sale. Yeoman families kept their account balances with local merchants within manageable limits not just with the annual influx of credit from the sale of two or three bales of cotton or a few bushels of surplus corn but also with the steady trickle of "country produce" that testified to women's ability to turn household production to market exchange. Intended chiefly for use in the household, the products of women's labor regularly appeared on the credit side of the ledger in store accounts and in petty trade with local planters; presumably, they figured as well in the informal exchanges, virtually impossible to document, between yeoman households. Eggs, chickens, feathers, butter, tallow, and homespun cloth were sufficiently important to local trade to figure prominently in the advertisements of village and crossroads merchants. "I feel like eating chicken and eggs, please bring me some," one enterprising rural Orangeburg merchant bantered in an illustrated advertisement, promising in another that those who called at "Uncle Tom's Corner . . . will be certain to get as much for [their] money, eggs, chickens, rags, and Raw Hides as [they] can almost anywhere else."[11] The value of such transactions usually did not approach that of the annual sale of the cotton crop, but the $23.50 that Mary Davis Brown was paid for the "web of janes cloth" she sold in 1858 must have been a significant contribution to a typical perennially cash-poor household.[12] At least one household of women, a widowed Barnwell farm wife and her daughters, managed to eke out a living by making cloth for sale, and another low-country woman told federal officials that she had purchased her farm with the proceeds of her "weaving."[13] . . .

The significance of women's work in the production of independence was not lost on contemporary politicians. In periodic prescriptions for economic reform, politicians encouraged the products of women's labor to sustain self-sufficiency at the level of the household and independence at the sectional level. Domestic economy was a proslavery strategy. "True independence is to be found in your own farms," John Belton O'Neall, a prominent jurist and agricultural reformer, exhorted suffering cotton producers in 1844. "Raise my countrymen your own hogs, sheep, cattle, horses, and mules, clothe your own household by domestic wheel and loom . . . supply your own tables with flour, potatoes, butter, and cheese of your own crops . . . and you can bid defiance to all the tariffs in the world." The centrality of women's work in such admittedly ill-fated strategies was evident. In the midst of the nullification crisis, the Pendleton Farmers' Society had initiated an antitariff campaign by obliging their members to appear at the next meeting "dressed *entirely in the Homespun of the district.*" This gratifying acknowledgment of the yeomanry's true republican style (they usually wore homespun—planters did not) was, like O'Neall's invocation of the republican producer ideal, a tribute to women's traditional craft skills. . . . Prizes were awarded only for cuts of plain and twilled homespun of cotton or wool, for linen diapers, coverlets, and imitation gingham cloth, for wool and cotton stockings, and for butter and cheese. Women thus received all of the premiums that year in acknowledgment of their work in the production of independence.[14] . . .

There was, however, one aspect of women's work that contemporary southerners were entirely unwilling to acknowledge. That was their labor, and especially wives' labor, in the fields. It is an interesting historical omission, especially in light of the inordinate attention such field work drew from northern and European travelers. Frederick Law Olmsted, for one, insisted that he had "in fact, seen more white native American women at work in the hottest sunshine in a single month, and that near mid-summer, than in all my life in the free states." It was, he added, "not on account of an emergency, as in harvesting, either, but in the regular cultivation of cotton and of corn [but] chiefly of cotton." . . . Olmsted . . . admitted that confronted with the spectacle of slave women plowing, he had "watched with some interest to see if there was any indication that their sex unfitted them for the occupation." Southerners would never have held such essentialist views of gender as to separate it so completely from slave, and thus from class and racial, status.[15] . . .

Most historians have assumed that field work was men's work, and, of course, slaves'. In taking this position, they have inadvertently deepened a contemporary southern silence on the subject that derived from very different sensibilities about the gender conventions of slave society.[16] Contemporaries of all classes were aware that the labor yeoman farmers commanded in the field included that of their wives and daughters; most yeomen simply did not own enough slaves to free female family members from field work. In the safe confines of the Black Oak Agricultural Society, an association of largely planter citizens of St. Stephen's Parish in rural Charleston District, Samuel DuBose openly attributed the local yeomanry's success at short-staple cotton cultivation to the fact that it was "a labor in which wives and daughters may conveniently and safely share with the husband and father. While he traces the furrow, they, protected by their sun bonnets, eradicate the weeds with a light hoe." Few public men showed such poor political judgment as did DuBose in acknowledging white women's labor in the fields.[17] . . .

Planter David Gavin jabbed the danger spot when he noted that his neighbor William Salsberry "used to work [his older girls] in the fields like negroes." Everybody knew yeoman women and girls worked in the fields. . . . The issue for yeoman men and women was less the work women actually performed in the household than the representation of it to the community at large. . . .

Women's work in the fields, although customary, was customarily ignored and even denied. A collusive silence surrounded one of the labor practices that most clearly distinguished yeoman farms from plantations, that set yeoman wives and daughters apart from their planter counterparts, that dangerously eroded the social distinctions between free women and slaves, and that cut deeply into the pride of men raised in a culture of honor. It was indeed the necessity of denying class difference between white southern women in order to reinforce their racial solidarity that rendered yeoman women's field labor all but invisible. Out of respect for yeoman masters and particularly for their votes, planter politicians refrained from noticing it. . . .

Historians have found it difficult to know with any certainty how yeoman farmers deployed their families' labor, especially in the fields, and have been able only to speculate about how it shaped relations with household dependents—with the slaves whose labor they owned or hired and with other subordinates, including women, in their households and Black Belt communities. But one very rare treasure, a yeoman farmer's journal, permits the historian to cross the threshold of the household and take a look inside. It confirms some of the labor patterns discernible in the more intransigent public records, and, more important, it suggests how they supported the manly public identity of its author.

James F. Sloan . . . lived in the up-country district of Spartanburg South Carolina. . . . In 1854, when his journal begins, Sloan's household consisted of himself, a thirty-four-year-old native-born South Carolinian, his second wife, Dorcas Lee Sloan, three children from his first marriage (a son, Seth, who was fifteen or sixteen years old, and two daughters, Sarah-Jane and Barbara, who were about thirteen and fourteen years old, respectively), and at least two other children (James Haddon and an unnamed baby girl) from his marriage with Dorcas Lee. For only one year, 1859, did that household include a slave, an adolescent girl named Manda whom Sloan hired for four dollars per month.[18]

If there was ever any doubt about the strategies by which yeoman farmers produced independence in the absence of significant numbers of slaves, Sloan's journal puts it to rest, along with any lingering notions that field labor marked an absolute class and racial divide between southern women, slave and free. Sloan put his "wimmin" to work in the fields regularly throughout the year, from at least late spring to the end of picking season in December. In June 1856, for example, while he and his eldest son, Seth, harrowed the cotton and corn fields, "the wimmin commenced hoeing cotton in the lot field." Prior to that, since May, the "children" had been thinning out the cotton, and in June they were joined by "the wimmin," who hoed first the corn and then the cotton fields. By 5 July, Sloan noted, the "girls had finished the cotton," and by 15 July, his crop was laid by. The children went to school briefly in August, but by 15 September, the cotton was "right smartly open" and picking season began. Sloan did not note the length of the picking season in 1856, but in 1858, it started on 8 September and continued until 30 November, during which time the "children" and the "balance of the family" picked cotton while he and Seth periodically attended to other tasks.[19]

Each year the tempo of work differed slightly. In June 1857, in one tragic interruption of the seasonal cycle, Dorcas Lee Sloan took "very bad" and later that day gave birth to "a still born babe"; she stayed out of the fields for a time after that. A little more than a year later, she was again absent from the fields, but this time the reason was a joyous one. "Mrs Sloan sent out and presented me with a very fine girl child."[20] . . .

Mrs. Sloan did not work in the fields for some time after the baby was born; in fact, it is entirely possible that her husband hired the slave girl to compensate for the field labor lost as a consequence. But yeoman women like Mrs. Sloan made a fundamental contribution to the household economy at great cost to their own health. For household independence required above all else the reproduction of the labor force. Well might yeomen boast, then, as another up-country man did, of the recent "edition to our family," declaring himself "well satisfied" with his riches: "a fine garden . . . a nice little crop . . . a pretty little stock of hogs and Cattle . . . the Best neighbour," and children who were growing "powerful fast and Bids fare to be a smart help to me soon should they be sparrd."[21] Children were precious assets in the relentless struggle to keep the farm.

The particular allocation of labor and tasks changed along with the family life cycle and with the presence of other dependent laborers. Yet every year, Sloan's family, including his teenage daughters and, although with less regularity, his wife, worked in the fields steadily from May until December, enabling them to produce sufficient subsistence and market crops to maintain their status as a respectable yeoman family. And if, unlike some other farmers' daughters, Sloan's girls were spared the indignity of driving a plow, the farm task perhaps most clearly demarcated as masculine, it was, at least in 1859, because another young woman assumed that burden: the slave Manda, who joined Seth Sloan in the fields and matched him task for task the year round.[22] Manda's presence did not, needless to say, relieve the Sloan women of the burden of field work, never mind the housework.

It did, however, change the gender division of labor, although the point is not that the ownership of slaves relieved yeoman women of domestic drudgery but that it relieved wives of the necessity of combining it with regular field labor. Mrs. Sloan escaped the fields (if temporarily); her daughters did not. They continued to work the land with Manda and Seth. In this respect, the Sloan case suggests that the deployment of female family members' labor constituted a significant difference between those yeoman households with slaves and those without. The point is confirmed by comparison with small planters' operations. The most striking distinction between the Sloan household, with its one hired slave, and that of David Golightly Harris (another up-country man), who had eleven slaves of his own and access to more belonging to his planter father, was that unlike Sloan's, Harris's wife and children never worked in the fields, and his children attended school the year round.[23] This comparison is a more stark one, admittedly. But the pattern is clear. The presence of even one slave, even if hired and even if a young woman, changed the gender division of labor among family members in yeoman households; rarely, if ever, however, did it entirely relieve women family members of field labor.

It is startling how easily Sloan appeared to manage the adjustment to masterhood, however temporary, of a slave. With the exception of Mrs. Sloan's withdrawal from the fields, Manda was introduced to his established labor system with little apparent disruption, extending it but not transforming it. On the first day that Sloan put Manda to work, he simply noted, "Seth and Manda hauled wood and rails," and thereafter she worked alongside Seth. Sloan's was an adjustment facilitated, no doubt, by years of commanding the labor of his other dependents, the "wimmin," "girls," "boys," and "children" who peopled his journal and cultivated the fields.[24] . . .

While all members of yeoman families labored in the field, only young men were groomed to assume the same public identity as their fathers. Seth Sloan, for example, was not only . . . increasingly assigned independent jobs on the farm; he was gradually introduced to the community of independent men and that of their sons and heirs in the surrounding neighborhood. With increasing regularity, Seth Sloan took his father's place in labor exchanges with neighbors and kinsmen and on trips to the gristmill and cotton screw, county store and tavern. These were the sites of male sociability, some of which also provided the social location of electoral politics and rituals of manhood within which they were enacted. In such places, yeoman sons like Seth Sloan were initiated into the culture of freemen.

Although Seth still worked under his father, he gradually came to stand beside him as well, a coming-of-age perhaps ritually marked in Sloan's journal by the entry of April 6, 1859, when for the first time Seth accompanied him to court day at Spartanburg. It was almost certainly a moment of ritualistic significance when father and son first worked together cultivating cotton in the field called "Seth's patch" in April 1860. Finally, Seth became his father's surrogate in the household, commanding dependents in his absence. Thus, while Seth's own path to independence was surely a long one, he had plenty of opportunity to practice the arts and affectations of masterhood, in immediate supervision over Manda's labor and presumably over that of his sisters as well. The economic and political foundations of his own claim to independence—and masterhood—had been laid.[25]

By contrast, the only coming-of-age ritual

Sloan recorded for his daughter, Barbara, was a brief note of her marriage, a ritual that we can be sure conferred authority but of a different and far more circumscribed kind. Yeoman daughters did not enjoy a long apprenticeship in the culture of freemen. Instead, their entry into adulthood was most commonly marked by evangelical conversion—the struggle to submit to God's will, representing, perhaps, proper prologue to the submission required of Christian wives. Daughters came of age into their mothers' world, the world inside the enclosure, ushered in with a brief ceremony, commemorated with "sider" and perhaps a few "wedding trimens," and characterized by a model of female excellence that made the submission of self the apotheosis of womanhood.[26]

Assumptions about gender, race, and power were reproduced within yeoman households in inevitable conjunction with the material basis of independence. Some women, like Barbara Sloan and, in profoundly different ways, Manda, retained the identity of dependents permanently. They represented the foundations of masterhood for those, like Seth, who reproduced the paternal claim to independence and to the public recognition and privileged political position that accompanied it in the slave South.

NOTES

1. For one study that explores the relationship between domestic hierarchies and public, political ones, see Allen Tullos, *Habits of Industry: White Culture and the Transformation of the Carolina Piedmont* (Chapel Hill: University of North Carolina Press, 1989).

2. Frederick Law Olmsted, *The Cotton Kingdom*, ed. Arthur Schlesinger (New York: Random House, 1984), pp. 160–63; Frederick Law Olmsted, *A Journey in the Back Country* (Williamstown, Mass.: Corner House, 1972), pp. 393–96; Charles E. Beveridge and Charles Capen McLaughlin, eds., *The Papers of Frederick Law Olmsted*, vol. 2 (Baltimore: Johns Hopkins University Press, 1981), pp. 291–311.

3. George Rawick, ed., *The American Slave: A Composite Autobiography, South Carolina Narratives*, supplement, series 2, part 1 (Westport, Conn.: Greenwood Press, 1979), pp. 187–95.

4. For the inventories of yeoman estates used in this study, see Barnwell District, Court of Probate, Inventories, Appraisements and Sales Book, 1789–1840, South Carolina Department of Archives and History, Columbia, S.C.; and Darlington District, Court of Probate, Inventories, Appraisements and Sales Book, 1853–59, ibid.

5. Such distinctions as "productive" and "unproductive" or "domestic" work were as much ideological as anything else. As Jeanne Boydston and others have demonstrated, the notion of "productive" work underwent a process of redefinition in free-labor states in precisely this period. As capitalist relations extended their grip, work was increasingly defined as that labor exchanged in the market for a wage. See Jeanne Boydston, *Home and Work: Housework, Wages, and the Ideology of Labor in the Early Republic* (New York: Oxford University Press, 1990), and Nancy Folbre, "The Unproductive Housewife: Her Evolution in Nineteenth-Century Economic Thought," *Signs* 16, no. 3 (Spring 1991):463–84. This line of analysis, pioneered by feminist historians concerned about the consequences for women's labor in the Northeast, would be deepened by a greater attention to definitions of work and value in the household economy of the slave states.

6. The literature on bourgeois homes, domesticity, and separate spheres is now enormous, but for a few key contributions, see Barbara Welter, "The Cult of True Womanhood, 1820–1860," *American Quarterly* 18 (Summer 1966):151–74; Kathryn Kish Sklar, *Catharine Beecher: A Study in American Domesticity* (New Haven: Yale University Press, 1973); Nancy Cott, *The Bonds of Womanhood: Woman's Sphere in New England, 1780–1835* (New Haven: Yale University Press, 1977). See also Linda Kerber, "Separate Spheres, Female Worlds, Woman's Place: The Rhetoric of Women's History," *Journal of American History* 75, no. 1 (June 1988):9–39.

7. For an interesting discussion of the history of census categories and their effect on assessments of women's work, see Folbre, "Unproductive Housewife," and Boydston, *Home and Work*. The slave South presents an intriguing point of contrast to Folbre's argument about the gendering of use value as female in the antebellum North.

8. *The Old Pine Farm, or the Southern Side* (Nashville: Southwestern Publishing House, 1860), p. 93.

9. When C. C. Pinckney hired an unmarried overseer, he provided him with a "Boy and a Woman to wait on him, cook and wash, and another Woman to take care of the Dairy, his Garden, and Poultry." The terms of the overseer's contract make clear the value of women's labor and the gender division of labor customarily observed (contract of C. C. Pinckney and William Winningham, January 20, 1855, Charles Cotesworth Pinckney and Family Papers, Series III, Library of Congress, Washington, D.C.).

10. Mary Davis Brown Diary, January 13 and July 29, 1857, April 25 and August 7 and 31, 1858, and throughout, South Caroliniana Library, University of South Carolina, Columbia, S.C. (hereafter SCL). On the value of women's (and girls') work, see also Elizabeth Finisher to Nancy H. Cowen, August 23, 1846, and Eleibers Cowen and Martha Cowen to John Cowen, February 1846, Nancy H. Cowan Papers, Manuscript Division, Perkins Library, Duke University, Durham, N.C. (hereafter Cowen Papers).

11. *Orangeburg Southron*, June 11, May 21, 1856. On the sale of butter to planters, see the receipts of July 2, December 4, 1841, and November 17, 1842, in

Lawton Family Papers, SCL. On store accounts, see Lewis Eldon Atherton, *The Southern Country Store, 1800–1860* (Baton Rouge: Louisiana State University Press, 1949), pp. 48–54, 87–91.

12. Mary Davis Brown Diary, October 9, 1858, SCL.

13. John H. Cornish Diary, January 9, 1847, Southern Historical Collection, University of North Carolina, Chapel Hill (hereafter SHC); Claim of Ellender Horton, Beaufort, RG 217, File #8006, Southern Claims Commission Records, National Archives and Records Administration, Washington, D.C. (hereafter SCCR).

14. O'Neall quoted in Lacy K. Ford Jr., *Origins of Southern Radicalism: The South Carolina Upcountry, 1800–1860* (New York: Oxford University Press, 1988); 453; Pendleton Farmers' Society Records, Minutes, October 12, 1827, October 9, 1828, August 13, 1829, SCL; Black Oak Agricultural Society, Constitution and Proceedings, November 16, 1847, SCL. On homespun as a powerful symbol of southern resistance invoked in local political meetings, see *Charleston Mercury*, June 25 and July 9 and 16, 1828. I would like to thank John Campbell for bringing the Pendleton Farmers' Society to my attention.

15. Olmsted, *Journey in the Back Country*, p. 298; Frances Trollope, *Domestic Manners of the Americans* (1832; reprint, Gloucester, Mass.: Peter Smith, 1968), pp. 117, 243.

16. Many southern historians would admit that yeoman women worked in the fields during harvest. But they typically treat that activity as an exception to an otherwise clear gender division of labor, as if harvesting were a crisis or an emergency rather than a regular seasonal activity. In none of the studies cited below, however, did women's field work figure in the analysis of self-sufficiency or yeoman household economy. See Gavin Wright, *The Political Economy of the Cotton South: Households, Markets, and Wealth in the Nineteenth Century* (New York: W. W. Norton, 1978), pp. 82–83; Steven Hahn, *The Roots of Southern Populism: Yeoman Farmers and the Transformation of the Georgia Upcountry* (New York: Oxford University Press, 1983), p. 30; and Ford, *Origins of Southern Radicalism*, pp. 78–81. It would be interesting to know when this (mis)representation of the gender division of labor among free whites emerged in the South. Certainly no one bothered to deny that white female indentured servants worked the fields

in the early colonial period, but by the antebellum period few would have publicly acknowledged such a fact. The representation of a complete racial divide between slave and free women of all classes thus appears to have emerged as part of a larger ideology of slavery.

17. Samuel DuBose, *Address Delivered at the Seventeenth Anniversary of the Black Oak Agricultural Society* (Charleston, S.C.: A. E. Miller, 1858), p. 21.

18. James F. Sloan Journals, June 24, 1854 to March 27, 1861, SCL. I would like to thank Lacy Ford for bringing these journals to my attention. Sloan's property holdings are outlined in Ford, *Origins of Southern Radicalism*, pp. 78–80.

19. Sloan Journals, June 21, July 5, and September 15, 1856, and September 8, 1856 to November 30, 1858, SCL.

20. Ibid., June 4, 1857 and July 7, 1858, SCL.

21. William P. Benson to Mr. John Cowan, 1846, William Benson to Mr. John Cowan, August 13, 1841, and Elizabeth Finisher to Nancy H. Cowan, August 23, 1846, Cowan Papers.

22. On the global identification of plowing as primarily a male task, see Esther Bosrup, *Women's Role in Economic Development* (London: George Allen and Universal Ltd., 1970), pp. 19–34. The idea has persisted among historians that women, even slave women, did not plow. But there is considerable evidence that slave women plowed on many plantations and that, on yeoman farms where grown sons were in short supply, wives and daughters took their turn driving the plow. On slave women, see the list of field hands, by task, in James Henry Hammond, Plantation Records, August 7, 1850, James Henry Hammond Papers, in Kenneth Stampp, ed., *Records of Antebellum Southern Plantations*, ser. A, pt. 1, reel 3 (Frederick, Md.: University Publications of America, 1986).

23. Philip N. Racine, ed., *Piedmont Farmer: The Journal of David Golightly Harris, 1855–1870* (Knoxville: University of Tennessee Press, 1990), pp. 29–169.

24. Sloan Journals, October 14 and March 8, 1859, SCL.

25. Sloan Journals, April 6, 1859, April 13, 1860, SCL.

26. Ibid., August 9, 1860; and Mary Davis Brown Diary, July 14, 1859, April 25, 1858, August 11, 1859, all SCL.

JEANNE BOYDSTON
The Pastoralization of Housework

Having read fiction and advice literature directed to women in the years before the Civil War, in 1966 the historian Barbara Welter identified a pervasive stereotype, which she called the "Cult of True Womanhood." Women were encouraged to cultivate the virtues of domesticity, piety, purity, and submissiveness. Home was referred to as women's "proper sphere" and understood to be a shelter from the outside world in which men engaged in hard work and cutthroat competition. Other historians agreed that men's and women's spheres of activity were separated and suggested that this separation was somehow linked to the simultaneous growth of capitalism and industrialization. Historian Gerda Lerner argued, by contrast, that stressing the shelter of home was a way by which middle-class women distinguished themselves from mill girls, and so maintained class boundaries.

How does Jeanne Boydston describe the relationship between home and work in antebellum America? How does she describe the relationship between women's work and men's work? What does she think were the uses of the ideology of separate spheres? How do the middle-class households described by Boydston differ from the households in which Harriet Jacobs and Rachel Davis lived? How do they differ from the households described by Stephanie McCurry?

In the colonial period, family survival had been based on two types of resources: the skills of the wife in housewifery, and the skills and property of the husband in agriculture. Both sets of skills involved the production of tangible goods for the family—such items as furnishings, food, and fabrics. Both were likely to involve some market exchange, as husbands sold grain and wives sold eggs or cheese, for example. And both involved services directly to the household. By the early nineteenth century, however, husbands' contributions to their households were focused disproportionately on market exchange—on the cash they brought into the family—while their direct activities in producing both goods and services for the family had vastly decreased.

The meaning of this shift has often been misread, interpreted as an indication that households were no longer dependent on goods and services provided from within but had instead become reliant upon the market

for their survival. . . . [But] consumerism was sharply curtailed by the amount of available cash. Choices constantly had to be made: to purchase a new cloak or try to refurbish the old one for another season, to hire a woman to help with the wash or lay aside some money to buy a house. In these patterns of mundane decisions lay the essential economic character of antebellum households: they were in fact "mixed economies"—economic systems that functioned on the bases of both paid and unpaid labor and were dependent upon both. They required paid labor for the cash to purchase some goods and services. Equally, they depended on unpaid labor in the household to process those commodities into consumable form and to produce other goods and services directly without recourse to the cash market. . . .

[The] antebellum era was the last period during which most adult women shared the experience of having been, at some point in their lives, paid household workers. To an extent never repeated, even middle-class wives were likely to have worked as hired "help" in their youth. . . . [It is therefore possible to make a rough calculation] of the cost to a family to replace the unpaid labor of the wife by purchasing it on the market.[1] . . .

In northeastern cities in 1860, a woman hired both to cook and to do the laundry earned between $3 and $4 a week. Seamstresses and maids averaged two-and-a-half dollars a week. On the market, caring for children was at the lower end of the pay scale, seldom commanding more than $2 a week. If we assume that a woman did the full work of a hired cook and child's nurse, and also spent even an hour a day each sewing and cleaning (valued at about three cents an hour apiece), the weekly price of her basic housework would approximate $4.70. Even if we reduce this almost by half to $3 a week (to allow for variations in her work schedule and for the presence of assistance of some sort), taken at an average, this puts the price of a wife's basic housework at about $150 dollars a year.[2] . . .

To this should be added the value of goods a wife might make available within the family for free or at a reduced cost. Among poorer households, this was the labor of scavenging. A rag rug found among the refuse was worth half a dollar in money saved, an old coat, several dollars. Flour for a week, scooped from a broken barrel on the docks, could save the household almost a dollar in cash outlay.[3] In these ways, a wife with a good eye and a quick hand might easily save her family a dollar a week— or $50 or so over the course of the year. In households with more cash, wives found other ways to avoid expenditures. By shopping carefully, buying in bulk, and drying or salting extra food, a wife could save ten to fifty percent of the family food budget . . . this could mean a saving of from 40 cents to over $2 a week. Wives who kept kitchen gardens or chickens . . . could . . . produce food worth a quarter a week (the price of 1/4 bushel of potatoes in New York in 1851).[4]

But there was also the cash that working-class wives brought into the household, by their needlework, or vending, or by taking in boarders, running a grocery or a tavern from her kitchen, or working unpaid in her husband's trade. A boarder might pay $4 a week into the family economy. Subtracting a dollar and a half for food and rent, the wife's labor-time represented $2.50 of that amount, or $130 a year.[5] . . .

The particular labor performed by a given woman depended on the size and resources of her household. . . . Yet we can estimate a general market price of housework by combining the values of the individual activities that made it up: perhaps $150 for cooking, cleaning, laundry, and childrearing; another $50 or so saved through scavenging or careful shopping, another $50 or so in cash brought directly into the household. This would set the price of a wife's labor-time among the laboring poor at roughly $250 a year beyond maintenance. . . . In working-class households with more income, where the wife could focus her labor on money-saving and on taking in a full-time boarder, that price might reach over $500 annually. . . . These shifts in the nature of a wife's work, and in the value of that work, as a husband's income increased seems not to have been entirely lost on males, who advised young men that if they meant to get ahead, they should "get married."[6] . . .

But husbands were not the sole beneficiaries of the economic value of housework, or of its unique invisibility. Employers were enabled by the presence of this sizeable but uncounted labor in the home to pay both men and women wages which were, in fact, below the level of subsistence. The difference was critical to the development of industrialization in the antebellum Northeast.[7] . . . Occasionally, mill owners acknowledged that the wages they paid did not cover maintenance. One agent admitted: "So long as they can do my work *for what I choose to pay them*, I keep them, getting out of them all I can. . . . [H]ow they fare outside my walls I don't know, nor do I consider it my business to know. They must look out for themselves."[8] . . .

Even when employers paid high enough salaries to provide present security for a family, they seldom provided either the income or the job security to ensure a household's well-being against the erratic boom-and-bust cycles of business and the unemployment consequent upon those cycles. . . . Women's unremunerated labor in the household provided the needed "safety net," enabling middle-class families to maintain some degree of both material stability and healthfulness in a volatile economic environment. . . . Put simply, a wife was a good investment for a man who wanted to get ahead.

THE PASTORALIZATION OF HOUSEWORK

The culture of the antebellum Northeast recognized the role of wives in the making of contented and healthy families. Indeed, the years between the War of 1812 and the Civil War were a period of almost unabated celebration of women's special and saving domestic mission. "Grant that others besides woman have responsibilities at home. . . ." wrote the Reverend Jesse Peck in 1857, "[s]till we fully accord the supremacy of domestic bliss to the wife and mother."[9] . . .

As recent historians have recognized, this glorification of wife and motherhood was at the heart of one of the most compelling and widely shared belief systems of the early nineteenth century: the ideology of gender spheres. An elaborate set of intellectual and behavioral conventions, the doctrine of gender spheres expressed a worldview in which both the orderliness of daily social relations and the larger organization of society derived from and depended on the preservation of an all-encompassing gender division of labor. Consequently, in the conceptual and emotional universe of the doctrine of spheres, males and females existed as creatures of naturally and essentially different capacities. As the Providence-based *Ladies Museum* explained in 1825:

> Man is strong—woman is beautiful. Man is daring and confident—woman is diffident and unassuming. Man is great in action—woman i[n] suffering. Man shines abroad—woman at home. Man talks to convince—woman to persuade and please. Man has a rugged heart—woman a soft and tender one. Man prevents misery—woman relieves it. Man has science—woman taste. Man has judgment—woman sensibility. Man is a being of justice—woman of mercy.

These "natural" differences of temperament and ability were presumed to translate into different social roles and responsibilities for men and women. Clearly intended by the order of nature to "shine at home," Woman was deemed especially ill-equipped to venture into the world of nineteenth-century business, where "cunning, intrigue, falsehood, slander, [and] vituperative violence" reigned and

where "mercy, pity, and sympathy, are vagrant fowls."[10] . . .

[T]he ideology of gender spheres was partly a response to the ongoing chaos of a changing society—an intellectually and emotionally comforting way of setting limits to the uncertainties of early industrialization. . . . The traits that presumably rendered Woman so defenseless against the guiles and machinations of the business world not only served to confine her to the home as her proper sphere but made her presence there crucial for her family, especially for her husband. Even the most enthusiastic boosters of economic expansion agreed that the explosive opportunism of antebellum society created an atmosphere too heady with competition and greed to engender either social or personal stability. However great his wisdom or strong his determination, to each man must come a time

> when body, mind, and heart are overtaxed with exhausting labor; when the heavens are overcast, and the angry clouds portend the fearful storm; when business schemes are antagonized, thwarted by stubborn matter, capricious man, or an inauspicious providence; when coldness, jealousy, or slander chills his heart, misrepresents his motives, or attacks his reputation; when he looks with suspicion on all he sees, and shrinks from the frauds and corruptions of men with instinctive dread.[11] . . .

Whatever the proclivities or ambitions of individual women, the presumed contrasts between the sexes permitted Woman-in-the-abstract to be defined as the embodiment of all that was contrary to the values and behaviors of men in the marketplace, and thus, to the marketplace itself. Against its callousness, she offered nurturance. Against its ambition, she pitted her self-effacement and the modesty of her needs. Against its materialism, she held up the twin shields of morality and spiritual solace. If business was a world into which only men traveled and where they daily risked losing their souls, then wherever Woman was, was sanctuary. And Woman was in the Home.

The contrast between Man and Woman melted easily into a contrast between "workplace" and "home" and between "work" as Man engaged in it and the "occupations" of Woman in the home. Most writers of prescriptive literature did acknowledge that women were involved in activities of some sort in their households. For example, T. S. Arthur worried that a woman would be unable to keep the constant vigilance required to be a good mother if she also had to attend to "the operations of the needle, the mysteries of culinary science, and all the complicated duties of housekeeping." His language is revealing, however: housework consisted of "mysteries" and "duties"; it was a different order of activity from the labor that men performed. Indeed, some observers cautioned that the wife and mother should deliberately stay clear of employments which might seem to involve her in the economy.... William Alcott was among this group. Noting that a woman "... has duties to perform to the sick and to the well—to the young and to the aged; duties even to domestic animals," Alcott nevertheless cautioned that "[v]ery few of these duties are favorable to the laying up of much property, and some are opposed to it. So that while we commend industry—of the most untiring kind, too—we would neither commend nor recommend strong efforts to lay up property." The advice was not only consistent with, but reflected a critical aspect of the ideology of spheres: to the extent that workers in the household identified themselves with the labor of the marketplace, the function of the home as a place of psychological refuge would be undermined.[12]

Thus, the responsibilities of wives in their households were generally described in the prescriptive literature less as purposeful activities required and ordered by the welfare of their individual families than as emanations of an abstract but shared Womanhood. As Daniel C. Eddy explained:

> Home is woman's throne, where she maintains her royal court, and sways her queenly authority. It is there that man learns to appreciate her worth, and to realize the sweet and tender influences which she casts around her; there she exhibits the excellences of character which God had in view in her creation.

Underscoring the essentially passive nature of women's functions, Eddy concluded: "Her life should be a calm, holy, beautiful walk."[13]

... The consequence of this conflation of ideology with behavior was to obscure both the nature and the economic importance of women's domestic labor. It was not only Woman-in-the-abstract who did not labor in the economy, but also, by extension, individual women. It was not only Woman-in-the-abstract, but presumably, real women who guided the on-going functions of the home through the effortless "emanations" of their very being, providing for the needs of their families without labor, through their very presence in the household. As romantic narrative played against lived experience, the labor and economic value of housework ceased to exist in the culture of the antebellum Northeast. It became work's opposite: a new form of leisure....

William Alcott's description of the wife's labors in *The Young Wife* provides a striking illustration of the pastoralization of housework in descriptions of the antebellum home:

> Where is it that the eye brightens, the smile lights up, the tongue becomes flippant, the form erect, and every motion cheerful and graceful? Is it at home? Is it in doing the work of the kitchen? Is it at the wash-tub—at the oven—darning a stocking—mending a coat—making a pudding? Is it in preparing a neat table and table cloth, with a few plain but neat dishes? Is it in covering it with some of nature's simple but choice viands? Is it in preparing the room for the reception of an absent companion? Is it in warming and lighting the apartments at evening, and waiting, with female patience, for his return from his appointed labor? Is it in greeting him with all her heart on his arrival?[14]

Clearly, Alcott was quite familiar with the types of work performed by women in their own families, and his description is all the more interesting on this account: cooking, baking, washing clothes, mending and darning, serving meals, building fires, attending to lamps—it is a surprisingly accurate catalogue. It is also incomplete, of course. Missing from this picture is the making of the soap that the wash might be done, the lugging and heating of the water, the tiresome process of heating and lifting cast-iron irons, the dusting and sweeping of rooms, the cleaning of the stove, and the making of the stocking and the coat now in need of repair.

Even the domestic tasks which Alcott acknowledges, however, are not to be contemplated as true work, a point which is made explicit in his identification of only the husband's employments as "labor." With "labor," indeed, the wife's activities have no truck, for there is no labor here to perform. . . . the food appears virtually as a gift of nature, and the compliant fires and lamps seem to light and tend themselves. . . . All is ordered, and the ordering of it is not only *not* burdensome or tiring, but the certain vehicle of good health and a cheerful disposition. Far from labor, housework is positively regenerating. . . .

The pastoralization of housework, with its emphasis on the sanctified home as an emanation of Woman's nature, required the articulation of a new way of seeing (or, more exactly, of *not* seeing) women as actors, capable of physical exertion. Most specifically, this applied to women as laborers, but the "magical extraction" of physical activity from the concept of Womanhood in fact proceeded in much larger terms and was most apparent in the recurrent celebrations of female "influence." Typically invoked as the female counterpart to the presumably *male* formal political power,[15] the concept of indirect womanly "influence" supplanted notions of women as direct agents, and thus as laborers. [In an article entitled "Woman's Offices and Influences," J. H. Agnew argued that] the contrast between presumably male "power" (physical as well as moral) and female "influence" could be drawn quite explicitly:

> We may stand in awe, indeed, before the exhibition of *power*, whether physical or moral, but we are not won by them to the love of truth and goodness, while *influence* steals in upon our hearts, gets hold of the springs of action, and leads us into its own ways. It is the *inflowing* upon others from the nameless traits of character which constitute woman's idiosyncracy. Her heart is a great reservoir of love, the water-works of moral influence, from which go out ten thousand tubes, conveying the ethereal essences of her nature, and diffusing them quietly over the secret chambers of man's inner being.

Woman does not herself *act*. Rather, she "gets hold of the springs of action." An idiosyncrasy in the human order, she is not so much a physical as an ethereal being. Agnew concluded: "Let man, then, exercise power; woman exercise influence. By this she will best perform her offices, discharge her duties." It is the crowning touch on the pastoralization of housework: the home is not the setting of labor, but of "offices" and "duties." Therefore, what is required for the happy home is not a worker, but rather "a great reservoir of love."[16]

The pastoralization of household labor became a common feature of antebellum literature, both private and published. . . . [It] shaped much of the fiction of the period. In a piece entitled "The Wife" (published in the *Ladies' Literary Cabinet* in July of 1819 and included in *The Sketch Book* the following year), Washington Irving described the plight of a young couple forced by the husband's disastrous speculations to give up their fashionable life in the city and move to a modest country cottage. One might anticipate numerous headaches and a good deal of hard work in such a move, especially for the wife, but such was not the case for Irving's "Wife." Mary goes out to the cottage to spend the day "superintending its arrangement," but the substance of that process remains a mystery, for the packing and unpacking, cleaning, hanging of curtains, arranging of furniture, putting away of dishes, sorting of clothes, and adjusting of new domestic equipment which one might expect to be required under such circumstances remain undisclosed in the text. Indeed, all we learn is that, when next encountered by the narrator, Mary "'seems in better spirits than I have ever known.'" Transformed into a creature who is far more sylvan nymph than human female, Mary greets her husband and the narrator "singing, in a style of the most touching simplicity. . . . Mary came tripping forth to meet us; she was in a pretty rural dress of white, a few wild flowers were twisted in her fine hair, a fresh bloom was on her cheek, her whole countenance beamed with smile— I have never seen her look so lovely." To complete the pastoral scene, nature has obligingly provided "'a beautiful tree behind the cottage'" where the threesome picnic on a feast of wild strawberries and thick sweet cream.[17] . . .

In both its briefer and its more extended forms in fiction and in exposition, in prescription and in proscription, the pastoralization of housework permeated the culture of the antebellum Northeast. Often, it was expressed simply as a truism, as when the Reverend Hubbard Winslow reminded his Boston congregation that "[t]he more severe manual labors, the toils of the fields, the mechanics, the cares and burdens of mercantile business, the exposures and perils of absence from home, the duties of the learned professions devolve upon man. . . ." [H]e considered women's occupations to be of a "more delicate and retired nature." That same year, the shocked and angered Congregational clergy of Massachusetts drew upon the same assumptions and the same imagery of Womanhood to denounce the abolitionist activities of Sarah and Angelina Grimké. Reminding their female congregants that "the power of woman is in her dependence," the clergy spoke of the "unobtrusive and private" nature of women's "appropriate duties" and directed them to devote their energies to "those departments of life that form the character of individuals" and to embodying "that modesty and delicacy which is the charm of domestic life. . . ."[18]

As we have seen, working class husbands appear to have embraced the view that paid labor was economically superior to unpaid labor. They shared, too, a tendency to pastoralize the labor of their wives. The speeches of early labor activists, for example, frequently invoked both the rhetoric of the ideology of spheres and pastoral images of the household, implying a sharp contrast between "the odious, cruel, unjust and tyrannical system" of the factory, which "compels the operative Mechanic to exhaust his physical and mental powers," with the presumably rejuvenating powers of the home. Discouraging women from carrying their labor "beyond the home," working men called upon women to devote themselves to improving the quality of life within their families. . . . [A]s William Sylvis put it, it was the proper work of woman "to guide the tottering footsteps of tender infancy in the paths of rectitude and virtue, to smooth down the wrinkles of our perverse nature, to weep over our shortcomings, and make us glad in the days of our adversity. . . ."[19]

African-American newspapers of the antebellum Northeast also reflected and reaffirmed the pastoral conventions of women's domestic labor. *The Rights of All* compared women to ornamental creatures of nature, "as various in decorations as the insects, the birds, and the shells. . . ." In 1842, *The Northern Star and Freeman's Advocate* approvingly reprinted an article from the *Philadelphia Temperance Advocate* in which wives were described as deities "who preside over the sanctities of domestic life, and administer its sacred rights. . . ." That this perception ill fit the experiences of those female readers whose home was also their unpaid workplace, as well as those women who worked for money in someone else's home, appears not to have disturbed the paper's editors. Rather than as a worker, Woman was represented as a force of nature— and presumably one intended for man's special benefit: "The morning star of our youth— the day star of our manhood—the evening star of our age."[20]

For both middle-class and working-class men, the insecurities of income-earning during the antebellum period struck at the very heart of their traditional roles as husbands and fathers. Particularly since the late eighteenth century, manhood had been identified with wage-earning—with the provision of the cash necessary to make the necessary purchases of the household. In the context of the reorganization of paid work in the antebellum Northeast, the growing dependency of households on cash, and the roller-coaster business cycles against which few families could feel safe, that identification faced almost constant challenge. And as it was challenged, it intensified.

By the antebellum period, the late-eighteenth century association of manhood with wage-earning had flowered into the cult of the male "breadwinner." A direct response to the unstable economic conditions of early industrialization, this association crossed the lines of the emerging classes, characterizing the self-perceptions and social claims of both laboring and middle-class men.

Among laboring men, the identification of manhood with wage-earning melded easily with the traditional emphasis on the "manliness" of the crafts. . . . General Trades' Union leader Ely Moore warned that the unchecked industrial avarice of employers would create a class of "breadless and impotent" workers. When they struck for higher wages in 1860, the shoemakers of Massachusetts linked the encroachments of capital with an attack upon their manhood; in the "Cordwainers' Song," they called upon each other to "stand for your rights like men" and "Resolve by your fathers' graves" to emerge victorious and "like men" to "hold onto the last!"[21] Gender also provided the language for belittling the oppressor, for working men often expressed their rage—and reaffirmed the importance of their own manhood—by impugning the masculinity of their employers. The "Mechanic" sneered at "[t]he employers and those who hang on their skirts."[22]

In the midst of the upheavals of the antebellum economy, however, it was not only employers who threatened the old artisan definitions of manhood. Because an entire way of life was being undermined, so the dangers seemed to arise from everywhere in the new social order—including from wage-earning women themselves. In fact, women seldom directly imperiled men's jobs. The young women who went to Lowell were entering an essentially new industry. Moreover, in their families and hired out on an individual basis, carding, spinning, fulling, and even, to some extent, weaving had long been a part of women's work. . . .

But if wage-earning women did not directly challenge men's jobs, their very presence in the new paid labor force may have underscored the precariousness of men's position as wage-earners. Particularly given the post-Revolutionary emphasis on the importance of women's remaining in the home to cultivate the private virtues, females who were visible as outworkers and operatives may have seemed to bespeak an "unnaturalness" in society—an inability of wage-earning men to establish proper households. Like the witches of the seventeenth century, wage-earning women became symbols of the threats posed to a particular concept of manhood—in this instance, a concept that identified male claims to authority and power with the status of sole wage-earner. As they grappled with the precariousness of their own positions, laboring-class men focused their anxieties on the women who were their wives, daughters, and sisters, as well as on the men who were their employers.

They expressed these anxieties in two forms. First, wage-earning men complained that women were taking jobs—and thus the proper masculine role—away from men. An 1836 report of the National Trades Union charged that because women's wages were so low, a woman's "efforts to sustain herself and family are actually the same as tying a stone around the neck of her natural protector, Man, and destroying him with the weight she has brought to his assistance." Not uncommonly, working men suggested that women did not really need to work for money and castigated "the girl, or the woman, as the case may be, who being in a condition to live comfortably

at home by proper economy" selfishly took work from the truly needy. In 1831, the *Working Man's Advocate* called upon "those females who . . . are not dependent on their labor for a living" to withdraw from paid work so that men might have the jobs.[23]

At the same time, working men organized to call for "the family wage"—a wage packet for the male "breadwinner" high enough to permit his wife and children to withdraw from paid work. As Martha May has pointed out, the family wage "promised a means to diminish capitalists' control over family life, by allowing workingmen to provide independently for their families." But the demand for the family wage also signalled the gendering of the emerging class system, and, in this, the gendering of early industrial culture. Identifying the husband as the proper and "natural" wage-earner, the family wage ideal reinforced a distinctive male claim to the role of "breadwinner." By nature, women were ill-suited to wage-earning, many laboring-class men insisted. The National Trades' Union called attention to Women's "physical organization" and "moral sensibilities" as evidence of her unfitness for paid labor, and the anonymous "mechanic" focused on "the fragile character of a girl's constitution, [and] her peculiar liability to sickness."[24] Presumably, only men had the constitution for regular, paid labor.

It is tempting to see in the antebellum ideology of spheres a simple extension of the Puritan injunction to wives to be keepers at home and faithful helpmates to men. Certainly, the two sets of beliefs were related. The colonists brought with them a conviction that men and women were socially different beings, so created by God and so designated in the order of nature. Both were meant to labor, but they were meant to labor at different tasks. Perhaps even more important, they were meant to occupy quite different stations in social life and to exercise quite different levels of control over economic life. . . . "Labor" may have been a gender-neutral term in colonial culture, but "authority" and "property" were masculine concepts, while "dependence" and "subordination" were clearly feminine conditions. . . .

The origins of the antebellum gender culture were as much in the particular conditions of early industrialization as in the inherited past, however. . . . [T]he specific character of the nineteenth-century gender culture was dictated less by transformations in women's experience than by transformations in men's. To be sure, the principle of male dominance persisted into the nineteenth century. . . . Social power in the antebellum Northeast rested increasingly on the ability to command the instruments of production and to accumulate and reinvest profits. From these activities wives were legally barred, as they were from formal political processes that established the ground rules for the development of industrial capitalism. While most men were also eliminated from the contest on other grounds (race, class, and ethnicity, primarily), one had to be male to get into the competition at all. . . .

With the demise of the artisan system, and so of a man's hopes to pass along a trade to his sons, the practical grounds on which a laboring man might lay claim to the role of male head-of-household had altered. Increasingly, it was less his position as future benefactor of the next generation than his position as the provider of the present generation (that is, the "breadwinner") that established a man's familial authority.

For men of the emerging middle class, the stakes were equally high but somewhat different. Many of these were the sons and grandsons of middling farmers, forebears who, while not wealthy, had established their adulthood through the ownership of land, and whose role within the family had been centrally that of the "father." Their power residing in their control of inheritance to the next generation—these were men who might have been described with some degree of accuracy as "patriarchs." But by the second decade of the nineteenth century middling farms throughout much of the Northeast were scarcely capable of supporting the present generation; much less were they sizeable or fertile enough to establish patriarchal control of the family. Simultaneously, the emergence of an increasingly industrialized and urbanized society rendered the inheritance of land a less useful and less attractive investment in the future for sons. Even successful businessmen and professionals experienced diminishing control over their sons' economic futures. A son might still read the law with his father, but new law schools, like medical schools, foreshadowed the time when specialized education, rather than on-the-job training with his father or his father's friends,

would offer a young man the best chance for success. . . .

Early industrialization preserved the principle of male dominance, then, but in a new form: the "husband" replaced the "father." Men claimed social authority—and indeed exercised economic control—not because they owned the material resources upon which subsequent generations would be founded, but because they owned the resources upon which the present generations subsisted. More important, they had established hegemony over the definition of those resources. In the gender culture of the antebellum Northeast, subsistence was purchased by wages—and men were the wage-earners.

Early industrialization had simultaneously redefined the paradigm that guided the social and economic position of women. . . . [T]he paradigm of womanhood shifted from "goodwife" to "mother"—that is, from "worker" to "nurturer." . . . [W]hat-ever cultural authority women gained as "mothers" was at the direct cost of a social identity in the terms that counted most in the nineteenth century—that is, as workers. As Caroline Dall noted in 1860, most Americans cherished "that old idea, that all men support all women. . . ." Dall recognized this to be "an absurd fiction," but it was a fiction with enormous social consequences. Even when women did enter paid work, their preeminent social identity as "mothers" (in distinct contrast to "workers") made their status as producers in the economy suspect: the predisposition to consider women "unfit" helped to justify underpaying them.[25]

In all of this, the pastoralization of housework implicitly reinforced both the social right and the power of husbands and capitalists to claim the surplus value of women's labor, both paid and unpaid. It accomplished this by rendering the economic dimension of the labor invisible, thereby making pointless the very question of exploitation: one cannot confiscate what does not exist. Since the ideology of spheres made the non-economic character of housework a simple fact of nature, few observers in the antebellum Northeast felt compelled to argue the point.

The ideology of spheres did not affect all women in the same way, of course. Insisting that the domestic ideal was founded in the nature of Woman (and not in the nature of society), prescriptive writers saw its embodiments everywhere—from the poorest orphan on the streets, to the mechanic's daughter, to the merchant's wife. But their models transparently were meant to be the women of the emerging middle class. It was, after was, after all, in the middle classes that women had presumably been freed from the necessity for labor that had characterized the colonial helpmate; there, that mothers and wives had supposedly been enabled to express their fullest capacities in the service of family formation. In celebrations of middle-class "Motherhood" lay the fullest embodiments of the marginalization of housewives as workers.

But if middle-class women were encased in the image of the nurturant (and nonlaboring) mother, working-class women found that their visible inability to replicate that model worked equally hard against them. As historian Christine Stansell has vividly demonstrated, the inability (or unwillingness) of working-class women to remain in their homes—that is, their need to go out into the streets, as vendors, washerwomen, prostitutes, or simply as neighbors helping a friend out—provided the excuse for a growing middle-class intrusion into working-class households, as reformers claimed that women who could not (or did not wish to) aspire to middle-class standards were defined as poor mothers.[26]

In addition to its specific implications for women, the ideology of spheres, and the pastoralization of housework which lay at the heart of that ideology, both represented and supported larger cultural changes attendant upon the evolution of early industrial capitalism. The transition of industrialization was not purely material: it was ideological as well, involving and requiring new ways of viewing the relationship of labor to its products and of the worker to his or her work. In its denial of the economic value of one form of labor, the pastoralization of housework signalled the growing devaluation of labor in general in industrial America. Artisans were discovering, and would continue to discover, what housewives learned early in the nineteenth century: as the old skills were debased, and gradually replaced by new ones, workers' social claims to the fruits of their labor would be severely undercut. Increasingly, productivity was at-

tributed, not to workers, but to those "most wonderful machines."[27] It was in part against such a redefinition that the craft workers of New York and the shoemakers of Lynn, Massachusetts, struggled.[28]

The denial of the economic value of housework was also one aspect of a tendency, originating much earlier but growing throughout the eighteenth and nineteenth centuries, to draw ever-finer distinctions between the values of different categories of labor, and to elevate certain forms of economic activity to a superior status on the grounds of the income they produced. As with housework, these distinctions were rarely founded on the actual material value of the labor in question. Rather, they were based on contemporary levels of power and wealth, and served to justify those existing conditions. An industrialist or financier presumably deserved to earn very sizeable amounts of money, because in accumulating capital he had clearly contributed more labor and labor of a more valuable kind to society than had, for example, a drayman or a foundry worker. . . .

Finally, the ideology of spheres functioned to support the emergence of the wage system necessary to the development of industrial capitalism. The success of the wage system depends upon a number of factors—among them the perception of money as a neutral index of economic value and the acceptance of the wage as representing a fair "livelihood." The devaluation of housework was a part of a larger process of obscuring the continuation of and necessity for barter-based exchanges in the American economy. In this, it veiled the reliance of the family on resources other than those provided through paid labor and heightened the visibility of the wage as the source of family maintenance.

But how did women respond to the growing devaluation of their contributions as laborers in the family economy? . . . [I]n their private letters and diaries, wives quietly offered their own definition of what constituted the livelihood of their families, posing their own perception of the importance of conservation and stewardship against the cash-based index of the marketplace and easily integrating the family's periodic needs for extra cash into their understanding of their own obligations.

Nevertheless, among the public voices

affirming that Woman was meant for a different sphere than Man, and that the employments of Woman in the home were of a spiritual rather than an economic nature, were the voices of many women. In *Woman in America,* for example, Mrs. A. J. Graves declared: ". . . home is [woman's] appropriate sphere of action; and . . . whenever she neglects these duties, or goes out of this sphere . . . she is deserting the station which God and nature have assigned to her." Underscoring the stark contrast between Woman's duties in the household and Man's in "the busy and turbulent world," Graves described the refuge of the home in terms as solemn as any penned by men during the antebellum period: " . . . our husbands and our sons . . . will rejoice to return to its sanctuary of rest," she averred, "there to refresh their wearied spirits, and renew their strength for the toils and conflicts of life."[29]

Graves was not unusual in her endorsement of the ideology of spheres and of the pastoralization of housework. Even those women who most championed the continuing importance of women's household labor often couched that position in the language of spheres. No one more graphically illustrates this combination than Catharine Beecher, at once probably the most outspoken defender of the importance of women's domestic labor and one of the chief proponents of the ideology of female domesticity. . . . Beecher was clear and insistent that housework was hard work, and she did not shrink from suggesting that its demands and obligations were very similar to men's "business." In her *Treatise on Domestic Economy,* Beecher went so far as to draw a specific analogy between the marriage contract and the wage labor contract:

No woman is forced to obey any husband but the one she chooses for herself; nor is she obliged to take a husband, if she prefers to remain single. So every domestic, and every artisan or laborer, after passing from parental control, can choose the employer to whom he is to accord obedience, or, if he prefers to relinquish certain advantages, he can remain without taking a subordinate place to any employer.

Nevertheless, Beecher regularly characterized women's work in the home as the occupation merely of administering "the gentler charities of life," a "mission" chiefly of "self-denial" to

"lay up treasures, not on earth, but in heaven." This employment she contrasts with the "toils" of Man, to whom was "appointed the out-door labor—to till the earth, dig the mines, toil in the foundries, traverse the ocean, transport the merchandise, labor in manufactories, construct houses . . . and all the heavy work. . . ."[30]

Beecher's apparently self-defeating endorsement of a view that ultimately discounted the value of women's labor arose from many sources, not the least of which was her own identification with the larger middle-class interests served by the ideology of spheres. Beecher enjoyed the new standing afforded middle-class women by their roles as moral guardians to their families and to societies, and based much of her own claim to status as a woman on the presumed differences between herself and immigrant and laboring-class women. For example, she ended an extended discussion of "the care of Servants" in *The American Woman's Home* with the resigned conclusion that "[t]he mistresses of American families, whether they like it or not, have the duties of missionaries imposed upon them by that class from which our supply of domestic servants is drawn."[31]

But, also like many women in antebellum America, Catharine Beecher was sharply aware of the power difference between males and females. It was a theme to which she constantly returned in her writings, especially in her discussions of women's rights. . . . In her *Essay on Slavery and Abolitionism,* Beecher was quite explicit about the reasons why a woman might cloak herself and her positions in the language of dependency and subordination:

[T]he moment woman begins to feel the promptings of ambition, or the thirst for power, her aegis of defence is gone. All the sacred protection of religion, all the generous promptings of chivalry, all the poetry of romantic gallantry, depend upon woman's retaining her place as dependent and defenceless, and making no claims. . . .

It was much the same point that Elizabeth Ellet would later make in her *The Practical Housekeeper:* since men had many more alternatives than women, the smart woman made it her "policy" to create an appearance of domestic serenity.[32]

But it would be a mistake to read women's endorsement of the pastoralization of housework purely as a protective strategy. Women were not immune from the values of their communities, and many wives appear to have shared the perception of the larger society that their work had separated from the economic life of the community and that it was, in fact, not really work at all.

Those misgivings were nowhere more evident than in the letter that Harriet Beecher Stowe wrote to her sister-in-law, Sarah Beecher, in 1850. It was the first opportunity Harriet had had to write since the Stowes had moved to Brunswick, Maine, the spring before. Since her arrival with the children, she explained, she had "made two sofas—or lounges—a barrel chair—divers bedspreads— pillowcases—pillows—bolsters—matresses ... painted rooms ... [and] revarnished furniture." She had also laid a month-long siege at the landlord's door, lobbying him to install a new sink. Meanwhile, she had given birth to her eighth child, made her way through the novels of Sir Walter Scott, and tried to meet the obligations of her increasingly active career as an author—all of this while also attending to the more mundane work of running a household: dealing with tradespeople, cooking, and taking care of the children. From delivery bed to delivery cart, downstairs to the kitchen, upstairs to the baby, out to a neighbor's, home to stir the stew, the image of Stowe flies through these pages like the specter of the sorcerer's apprentice.

Halfway through the letter, Stowe paused. "And yet," she confided to her sister-in-law, "I am constantly pursued and haunted by the idea that I don't do anything."[33] It is a jarring note in a letter—and a life—so shaped by the demands of housework. That a skilled and loving mother could impart dignity and a sense of humane purpose to a family otherwise vulnerable to the degradations of the marketplace, Stowe had no doubt. But was that really "work"? She was less certain. In that uncertainty, to borrow Daniel Eddy's words, lay "a world of domestic meaning"—for housewives of the antebellum era, and for women since.

NOTES

1. See Luisella Goldschmidt-Clermont, *Unpaid Work in the Household: A Review of Economic Evaluation Methods* (Geneva, 1982).

2. See Edgar Martin, *The Standard of Living in 1860: American Consumption Levels on the Eve of the Civil War* (Chicago, 1942), p. 177; and Faye Dudden,

Serving Women: Household Service in Nineteenth-Century America (Middletown, Conn., 1983), p. 149.

3. This is calculated on the basis of an average weekly budget for a working-class family of five, as itemized in the New York *Daily Tribune*, May 27, 1851. See also Martin, *Standard of Living*, p. 122.

4. The New York *Daily Tribune*, May 27, 1851.

5. Martin, *Standard of Living*, p. 168.

6. Grant Thorburn, *Sketches from the Note-book of Lurie Todd* (New York, 1847), p. 12.

7. See Alice Kessler-Harris and Karen Brodlin Sacks, "The Demise of Domesticity in America," *Women, Households, and the Economy*, ed. Lourdes Beneria and Catherine R. Stimpson (New Brunswick, N.J., 1987), p. 67.

8. Quoted in Norman Ware, *The Industrial Worker, 1840–1860: The Reaction of American Industrial Society to the Advance of the Industrial Revolution* (New York, 1924; reprinted Gloucester, Mass., 1959), p. 77.

9. Jesse T. Peck, *The True Woman; or, Life and Happiness at Home and Abroad* (New York, 1857), p. 245.

10. *The Ladies Museum*, July 16, 1825, p. 3; Henry Ward Beecher, *Lectures to Young Men, on Various Important Subjects* (Boston, 1846), pp. 87, 91.

11. Peck, *The True Woman*, pp. 242–43.

12. *The Mother's Rule: or, The Right Way and the Wrong Way*, ed. T. S. Arthur (Philadelphia, 1856), p. 261; William A. Alcott, *The Young Wife, or, Duties of Woman in the Marriage Relation* (Boston, 1837), p. 149.

13. Daniel C. Eddy, *The Young Woman's Friend; or the Duties, Trials, Loves, and Hopes of Woman* (Boston, 1857), p. 23.

14. Alcott, *The Young Wife*, pp. 84–85.

15. For an excellent discussion of the concept of female "influence," see Lori D. Ginzburg, *Women and the Work of Benevolence: Morality and Politics in the Northeastern United States, 1820–1885* (New Haven, Conn., 1990).

16. J. H. Agnew, "Women's Offices and Influence," *Harper's New Monthly Magazine* 17:no. 3 (Oct. 1851):654–57, quote on p. 657.

17. Washington Irving, "The Wife," *Ladies Literary Cabinet*, July 4, 1819, pp. 82–84. Quotations are from Washington Irving, *The Sketch Book of Geoffrey Crayon, Gent.* (New York, 1961), pp. 34–36.

18. "Pastoral Letter of the Massachusetts Congregationalist Clergy" (1837) in *Up From the Pedestal: Selected Writings in the History of American Feminism*, ed. Aileen S. Kraditor (Chicago, 1968), pp. 51–52; Reverend Hubbard Winslow, *A Discourse Delivered in the Bowdoin Street Church* (Boston, 1837), p. 8.

19. *The Man*, May 13, 1835; *Life, Speeches, Labors, and Essays of William H. Sylvis*, ed. James C. Sylvis (Philadelphia, 1872), p. 120.

20. *The Rights of All*, June 12, 1829; *The Northern Star and Freeman's Advocate*, Dec. 8, 1842, and Jan. 2, 1843.

21. Moore is quoted in Sean Wilentz, *Chants Democratic: New York City and the Rise of the American Working Class, 1788–1850* (New York, 1986), p. 239. The "Cordwainers' Song" is printed in Alan Dawley, *Class and Community: The Industrial Revolution in Lynn* (Cambridge, Mass., 1976), pp. 82–83.

22. "A Mechanic," *Elements of Social Disorder: A Plea for the Working Classes in the United States* (Providence, R.I., 1844), p. 96.

23. Quoted in John Andrews and W. D. P. Bliss, *A History of Women in Trade Unions*, vol. 10 of *Report on Condition of Woman and Child Earners in the United States*, Senate Doc. 645, 61st Cong., 2d Sess. (Washington, D.C., 1911; reprint ed. New York, 1974), p. 48; "Mechanic," *Elements of Social Disorder*, p. 45; *Working Man's Advocate*, June 11, 1831.

24. Martha May, "Bread Before Roses: American Workingmen, Labor Unions and the Family Wage," in *Women, Work, and Protest: A Century of U.S. Women's Labor History*, ed. Ruth Milkman (Boston, 1985), p. 4; vol. 6 of *A Documentary History of American Industrial Society*, ed. John R. Commons et al. (New York, 1958), p. 281; "Mechanic," *Elements of Social Disorder*, p. 42.

25. Caroline Dall, *"Woman's Right to Labor"; or, Low Wages and Hard Work* (Boston, 1860), p. 57.

26. Christine Stansell, *City of Women: Sex and Class in New York, 1789–1860* (New York, 1986), pp. 193–216.

27. The phrase is from the title of Judith McGaw's study, *Most Wonderful Machine: Mechanization and Social Change in Berkshire Papermaking, 1801–1885* (Princeton, 1987).

28. See Wilentz, *Chants Democratic*; and Dawley, *Class and Community*, cited in n. 21 above.

29. Mrs. A. J. Garves, *Woman in America: Being an Examination into the Morals and Intellectual Condition of American Female Society* (New York, 1841), p. 156.

30. Catharine E. Beecher, *A Treatise on Domestic Economy, for the Use of Young Ladies at Home, and at School* (Boston, 1841), p. 26; Beecher, *An Essay on Slavery and Abolitionism, with Reference to the Duty of American Females* (Philadelphia, 1837), p. 128; Catharine E. Beecher and Harriet Beecher Stowe, *The American Woman's Home, or Principles of Domestic Science* (Hartford, Conn., 1975), p. 19.

31. Beecher and Stowe, *The American Woman's Home*, p. 327.

32. Beecher, *Essay on Slavery and Abolitionism*, pp. 101–2; *The Practical Housekeeper; a Cyclopaedia of Domestic Economy*, ed. Mrs. [Elizabeth] Ellet (New York, 1857), p. 17.

33. Harriet Beecher Stowe to Sarah Buckingham Beecher, Dec. 17 [1850], The Schlesinger Library, Radcliffe College, Cambridge, Mass.

DOCUMENT: Working Conditions in Early Factories, 1845

> *"She complained of the hours for labor being too many . . ."*

The textile factories of the first wave of industrialization might not have been built at all had their owners not believed they could count on a steady supply of cheap female labor. The history of industrialization as it affected both men and women needs to be understood in the context of the segmented labor market that women entered. Women were a major part of the first new work force that was shaped into "modern" work patterns: long, uninterrupted hours of labor in a mechanized factory with little or no room for individual initiative.

One of the earliest mill towns was Lowell, Massachusetts, where factory owners began recruiting young, unmarried women to work in six textile mills in 1823. Rural young women already toiled at home at farm labor and also at "outwork," goods that could be made at home and sold for cash. Compared to the work they had done at home, mill work at first seemed to pay well and to offer new opportunities. The Lowell mills developed a system of boardinghouses, which assured families that girls would live in wholesome surroundings. Letters sent home and fiction published by young women in the first wave of employment often testified to their pride in the financial independence that their new work brought.

Work in the mills was strictly segregated by sex: men were supervisors and skilled mechanics; women attended the spinning and weaving machinery. Women's wages ranged from one-third to one-half that of men; the highest-paid woman generally earned less than the lowest-paid man. Employers responded to economic downturns in the 1830s by adjusting their expenses. Women's wages in the Lowell mills dropped; piece rates forced increases in production without increases in pay. Mills established stricter discipline: those who were insubordinate were fired, workers who did not fulfill their year-long contracts were blacklisted. But boardinghouse life meant that the factory women developed strong support networks; when their wages were cut and work hours lengthened in the 1830s, those who lived together came together in opposition to the owners and staged some of the earliest industrial strikes in American history. In 1836, 1,500 women walked out in protest, claiming their inheritance as "Daughters of the Revolution." One manifesto stated: "As our fathers resisted unto blood the lordly avarice of the British ministry, so we, their daughters, never will wear the yoke which has been prepared for us."[*]

In January 1845, led by the indomitable worker Sarah Bagley, the Female Labor Reform Association organized a petition drive throughout the region, which forced the

---

[*]Thomas Dublin, *Women at Work* (New York: Columbia University Press, 1979), p. 98.

Excerpted from "The First Official Investigation of Labor Conditions in Massachusetts," in vol. 8 of *A Documentary History of American Industrial Society*, ed. John R. Commons, Ulrich B. Phillips, Eugene A. Gilmore, Helen L. Sumner, and John B. Andrews (Cleveland, 1910), pp. 133–142.

Women at textile machinery in a New England mill, approximately 1850. Note the poor lighting and the absence of anything to sit on during the long hours at the machines. (Courtesy of George Eastman House.)

Massachusetts legislature to hold the first public hearings on industrial working conditions ever held in the United States. On February 13, 1845, Eliza Hemmingway and Sarah Bagley had their chance to testify. What did they think it was important for the legislators to know?

... The first petitioner who testified was Eliza R. Hemmingway. She had worked 2 years and 9 months in the Lowell Factories ... Her employment is weaving—works by the piece. . . . and attends one loom. Her wages average from $16 to $23 a month exclusive of board. She complained of the hours for labor being too many, and the time for meals too limited. In the summer season, the work is commenced at 5 o'clock, a.m., and continued till 7 o'clock, p.m., with half an hour for breakfast and three quarters of an hour for dinner.

During eight months of the year, but half an hour is allowed for dinner. The air in the room she considered not to be wholesome. There were 293 small [oil] lamps and 61 large lamps lighted in the room in which she worked, when evening work is required. These lamps are also lighted sometimes in the morning. About 130 females, 11 men, and 12 children (between the ages of 11 and 14) work in the room with her ... The children work but 9 months out of 12. The other 3 months they must attend school. Thinks that there is no day when there are less than six of the females out of the mill from sickness. Has known as many as thirty. She herself, is out quite often, on account of sickness. . . .

She thought there was a general desire among the females to work but ten hours, regardless of pay. . . . She knew of one girl who last winter went into the mill at half past 4 o'clock, a.m. and worked till half past 7 o'clock, p.m. She did so to make more money. She earned from $25 to $30 per month. There is always a large number of girls at the gate wishing to get in before the bell rings. . . . They do this to make more wages. A large number come to Lowell to make money to aid their parents who are poor. She knew of many cases where married women came to Lowell and worked in the mills to assist their husbands to pay for their farms. . . .

Miss Sarah G. Bagley said she had worked in the Lowell Mills eight years and a half . . . She is a weaver, and works by the piece. . . . She thinks the health of the operatives is not so good as the health of females who do housework or millinery business. The chief evil, so far as health is concerned, is the shortness of time allowed for meals. The next evil is the length of time employed—not giving them time to cultivate their minds. . . . She had presented a petition, same as the one before the Committee, to 132 girls, most of whom said that they would prefer to work but ten hours. In a pecuniary point of view, it would be better, as their health would be improved. They would have more time for sewing. Their intellectual, moral and religious habits would also be benefited by the change. . . .

On Saturday the 1st of March, a portion of the Committee went to Lowell to examine the mills, and to observe the general appearance of the operatives. . . . [The Committee concluded:] Not only is the interior of the mills kept in the best order, but great regard has been paid by many of the agents to the arrangement of the enclosed grounds. Grass plats have been laid out, trees have been planted . . . everything in and about the mills, and the boarding houses appeared, to have for its end, health and comfort. . . . The [average hours of work per day throughout the year was $11\frac{1}{2}$; the workday was longest in April, when it reached $13\frac{1}{2}$ hours].

CARROLL SMITH-ROSENBERG
The Female World of Love and Ritual: Relations between Women in Nineteenth-Century America

Women's associations with each other have traditionally been ignored by historians. One reason for this has been a fascination with public life; only women who were powerful in the same fashion as men or whose lives were intertwined with the lives of powerful men attracted the historical spotlight. The world of women was treated as wholly private or domestic, encompassing only family responsibilities. Women's diaries and letters were used primarily as a source of illustrative anecdote.

Carroll Smith-Rosenberg has read the letters and diaries of women in a strikingly original way. She evaluates nineteenth-century American society in much the same way an anthropologist might observe a distant culture. She describes relations between women as intellectually active, personally rewarding, mutually supportive, and socially creative. Smith-Rosenberg offers a radically new account of the relationship between the sexes in Victorian America. What revision does she suggest ought to be made in our traditional understanding of Victorian sexuality?

The female friendship of the nineteenth century, the long-lived, intimate, loving friendship between two women, is an excellent example of the type of historical phenomena which most historians know something about, which few have thought much about, and which virtually no one has written about.[1] It is one aspect of the female experience which consciously or unconsciously we have chosen to ignore. Yet an abundance of manuscript evidence suggests that eighteenth- and nineteenth-century women routinely formed emotional ties with other women. Such deeply felt, same-sex friendships were casually accepted in American society. Indeed, from at least the late eighteenth through the mid-nineteenth century, a female world of varied and yet highly structured relationships appears to have been an essential aspect of American society. These relationships ranged from the supportive love of sisters, through the enthu- siasms of adolescent girls, to sensual avowals of love by mature women. It was a world in which men made but a shadowy appearance.[2]

Defining and analyzing same-sex relationships involves the historian in deeply problematical questions of method and interpretation. This is especially true since historians, influenced by Freud's libidinal theory, have discussed these relationships almost exclusively within the context of individual psychosexual developments or, to be more explicit, psychopathology.[3] Seeing same-sex relationships in terms of a dichotomy between normal and abnormal, they have sought the origins of such apparent deviance in childhood or adolescent trauma and detected the symptoms of "latent" homosexuality in the lives of both those who later became "overtly" homosexual and those who did not. Yet theories concerning the nature and origins of same-sex relationships are frequently contradictory or based on questionable or arbitrary data. In recent years such hypotheses have been subjected to criticism both from within and without the psychological professions. Historians who seek to work within a psychological framework, therefore, are faced with two hard questions: Do sound psychodynamic theories concerning the nature and origins of same-sex relationships exist? If so, does the historical datum exist which would permit the use of such dynamic models?

I would like to suggest an alternative approach to female friendships—one which would view them within a cultural and social setting rather than from an exclusively individual psychosexual perspective. Only by thus altering our approach will we be in the position to evaluate the appropriateness of particular dynamic interpretations. Intimate friendships between men and men and women and women existed in a larger world of social relations and social values. To interpret such friendships more fully they must be related to the structure of the American family and to the nature of sex-role divisions and of male-female relations both within the family and in society generally. The female friendship must not be seen in isolation; it must be analyzed as one aspect of women's overall relations with one another. The ties between mothers and daughters, sisters, female cousins and friends, at all stages of the female life cycle constitute the most suggestive framework for the historian to begin an analysis of intimacy and affection between women. Such an analysis would not only emphasize general cultural patterns rather than the internal dynamics of a particular family or childhood; it would shift the focus of the study from a concern with deviance to that of defining configurations of legitimate behavioral norms and options.[4]

This analysis will be based upon the correspondence and diaries of women and men in thirty-five families between the 1760s and the 1880s. These families, though limited in number, represented a broad range of the American middle class, from hard-pressed pioneer families and orphaned girls to daughters of the intellectual and social elite. It includes families from most geographic regions, rural and urban, and a spectrum of Protestant denominations ranging from Mormon to orthodox Quaker. Although scarcely a comprehensive sample of America's increasingly heterogeneous population, it does, I believe, reflect accurately the literate middle class to which the historian working with letters and diaries is necessarily bound. It was involved an analysis of many thousands of letters written to women friends, kin, husbands, brothers, and children at every period of life from adolescence to old age. Some collections encompass virtually entire life spans; one contains over 100,000 letters as well as diaries and account books. It is my contention that an analysis of women's private letters and diaries which were never intended to be published permits the historian to explore a very private world of emotional realities central both to women's lives and to the middle-class family in nineteenth-century America.[5]

The question of female friendships is peculiarly elusive; we know so little or perhaps have forgotten so much. An intriguing and almost alien form of human relationship, they flourished in a different social structure and amidst different sexual norms. Before attempting to reconstruct their social setting, therefore, it might be best first to describe two not atypical friendships. These two friendships, intense, loving, and openly avowed, began during the women's adolescence and, despite subsequent marriages and geographic separation, continued throughout their lives. For nearly half a century these women played a central emotional role in each other's lives, writing time and again of their love and of the pain of separation. Paradoxically to twentieth-century minds, their love appears to have been both sensual and platonic.

Sarah Butler Wister first met Jeannie Field Musgrove while vacationing with her family at Stockbridge, Massachusetts, in the summer of 1849.[6] Jeannie was then sixteen, Sarah fourteen. During two subsequent years spent together in boarding school, they formed a deep and intimate friendship. Sarah began to keep a bouquet of flowers before Jeannie's portrait and wrote complaining of the intensity and anguish of her affection.[7] Both young women assumed nom de plumes, Jeannie a female name, Sarah a male one; they would use these secret names into old age.[8] They frequently commented on the nature of their affection: "If the day should come," Sarah wrote Jeannie in the spring of 1861, "when you failed me either through your fault or my own, I would forswear all human friendship, thenceforth." A few months later Jeannie commented: "Gratitude is a word I should never use toward you. It is perhaps a misfortune of such intimacy and love that it makes one regard all kindness as a matter of course, as one has always found it, as natural as the embrace in meeting."[9]

Sarah's marriage altered neither the frequency of their correspondence nor their desire to be together. In 1864, when twenty-nine, married, and a mother, Sarah wrote to Jeannie: "I shall be entirely alone [this coming week]. I can give you no idea how desperately I shall want you. . . ." After one such visit Jeannie, then a spinster in New York, echoed Sarah's longing: "Dear darling Sarah! How I love you & how happy I have been! You are the joy of my life. . . . I cannot tell you how much happiness you gave me, nor how constantly it is all in my thoughts. . . . My darling how I long for the time when I shall see you. . . . " After another visit Jeannie wrote: "I want you to tell me in your next letter, to assure me, that I am your dearest. . . . I do not doubt you, & I am not jealous but I long to hear you say it once more & it seems already a long time since your voice fell on my ear. So just fill a quarter page with caresses & expressions of endearment. Your silly Angelina." Jeannie ended one letter: "Goodbye my dearest, dearest lover—ever your own Angelina." And another, "I will go to bed . . . [though] I could write all night—A thousand kisses—I love you with my whole soul—your Angelina."

When Jeannie finally married in 1870 at the age of thirty-seven, Sarah underwent a period of extreme anxiety. Two days before Jeannie's marriage Sarah, then in London, wrote desperately: "Dearest darling—How incessantly have I thought of you these eight days—all today—the entire uncertainty, the distance, the long silence—are all new features in my separation from you, grevious to be borne. . . . Oh Jeannie. I have thought & thought & yearned over you these two days. Are you married I wonder? My dearest love to you wherever and *who*ever you are."[10] Like many other women in this collection of thirty-five families, marriage brought Sarah and Jeannie physical separation; it did not cause emotional distance. Although at first they may have wondered how marriage would affect their relationship, their affection remained

unabated throughout their lives, underscored by their loneliness and their desire to be together.[11]

During the same years that Jeannie and Sarah wrote of their love and need for each other, two slightly younger women began a similar odyssey of love, dependence and—ultimately—physical, though not emotional, separation. Molly and Helena met in 1868 while both attended the Cooper Institute School of Design for Women in New York City. For several years these young women studied and explored the city together, visited each other's families, and formed part of a social network of other artistic young women. Gradually, over the years, their initial friendship deepened into a close intimate bond which continued throughout their lives. The tone in the letters which Molly wrote to Helena changed over these years from "My dear Helena," and signed "your attached friend," to "My dearest Helena," "My Dearest," "My Beloved," and signed "Thine always" or "thine Molly."[12]

The letters they wrote to each other during these first five years permit us to reconstruct something of their relationship together. As Molly wrote in one early letter:

> I have not said to you in so many or so few words that I was happy with you during those few so incredibly short weeks but surely you do not need words to tell you what you must know. Those two or three days so dark without, so bright with firelight and contentment within I shall always remember as proof that, for a time, at least—I fancy for quite a long time—we might be sufficient for each other. We know that we can amuse each other for many idle hours together and now we know that we can also work together. And that means much, don't you think so?

She ended: "I shall return in a few days. Imagine yourself kissed many times by one who loved you so dearly."

The intensity and even physical nature of Molly's love was echoed in many of the letters she wrote during the next few years, as, for instance in this short thank-you note for a small present: "Imagine yourself kissed a dozen times my darling. Perhaps it is well for you that we are far apart. You might find my thanks so expressed rather overpowering. I have that delightful feeling that it doesn't matter much what I say or how I say it, since we shall meet so soon and forget in that moment that we were ever separated. . . . I shall see you soon and be content."[13]

At the end of the fifth year, however, several crises occurred. The relationship, at least in its intense form, ended, though Molly and Helena continued an intimate and complex relationship for the next half-century. The exact nature of these crises is not completely clear, but it seems to have involved Molly's decision not to live with Helena, as they had originally planned, but to remain at home because of parental insistence. Molly was now in her late twenties. Helena responded with anger and Molly became frantic at the thought that Helena would break off their relationship. Though she wrote distraught letters and made despairing attempts to see Helena, the relationship never regained its former ardor—possibly because Molly had a male suitor.[14] Within six months Helena had decided to marry a man who was, coincidentally, Molly's friend and publisher. Two years later Molly herself finally married. The letters toward the end of this period discuss the transition both women made to having male lovers—Molly spending much time reassuring Helena, who seemed depressed about the end of their relationship and with her forthcoming marriage.[15]

It is clearly difficult from a distance of 100 years and from a post-Freudian cultural perspective to decipher the complexities of Molly and Helena's relationship. Certainly Molly and Helena were lovers—emotionally if not physically. The emotional intensity and pathos of their love becomes apparent in several letters Molly wrote Helena during their crisis: "I wanted so to put my arms round my girl of all the girls in the world and tell her . . . I love her as wives do love their husbands, as *friends* who have taken each other for life—and believe in her, as I believe in my God. . . . If I didn't love you do you suppose I'd care about anything or have ridiculous notions and panics and behave like an old fool who ought to know better. I'm going to hang on to your skirts. . . . You can't get away from [my] love." Or as she wrote after Helena's decision to marry: "You know dear Helena, I really was in love with you. It was a passion such as I had never known until I saw you. I don't think it was the noblest way to love you." The theme of intense female love was one Molly again expressed in a letter she wrote to the man Helena was to

marry: "Do you know sir, that until you came along I believe that she loved me almost as girls love their lovers. *I know I loved her so.* Don't you wonder that I can stand the sight of you." This was in a letter congratulating them on their forthcoming marriage.[16]

The essential question is not whether these women had genital contact and can therefore be defined as heterosexual or homosexual. The twentieth-century tendency to view human love and sexuality within a dichotomized universe of deviance and normality, genitality and platonic love, is alien to the emotions and attitudes of the nineteenth century and fundamentally distorts the nature of these women's emotional interaction. These letters are significant because they force us to place such female love in a particular historical context. There is every indication that these four women, their husbands and families—all eminently respectable and socially conservative—considered such love both socially acceptable and fully compatible with heterosexual marriage. Emotionally and cognitively, their heterosocial and their homosocial worlds were complementary.

One could argue, on the other hand, that these letters were but an example of the romantic rhetoric with which the nineteenth century surrounded the concept of friendship. Yet they possess an emotional intensity and a sensual and physical explicitness that is difficult to dismiss. Jeannie longed to hold Sarah in her arms; Molly mourned her physical isolation from Helena. Molly's love and devotion to Helena, the emotions that bound Jeannie and Sarah together, while perhaps a phenomenon of nineteenth-century society, were not the less real for their Victorian origins. A survey of the correspondence and diaries of eighteenth- and nineteenth-century women indicates that Molly, Jeannie, and Sarah represented one very real behavioral and emotional option socially available to nineteenth-century women.

This is not to argue that individual needs, personalities, and family dynamics did not have a significant role in determining the nature of particular relationships. But the scholar must ask if it is historically possible and, if possible, important, to study the intensely individual aspects of psychosexual dynamics. Is it not the historian's first task to explore the social structure and the world view which made intense and sometimes sensual female love both a possible and an acceptable emotional option? From such a social perspective a new and quite different series of questions suggests itself. What emotional function did such female love serve? What was its place within the hetero-and homosocial worlds which women jointly inhabited? Did a spectrum of love-object choices exist in the nineteenth century across which some individuals, at least, were capable of moving? Without attempting to answer these questions it will be difficult to understand either nineteenth-century sexuality or the nineteenth-century family.

Several factors in American society between the mid-eighteenth and the mid-nineteenth centuries may well have permitted women to form a variety of close emotional relationships with other women. American society was characterized in large part by rigid gender-role differentiation within the family and within society as a whole, leading to the emotional segregation of women and men. The roles of daughter and mother shaded imperceptibly and ineluctably into each other, while the biological realities of frequent pregnancies, childbirth, nursing, and menopause bound women together in physical and emotional intimacy. It was within just such a social framework, I would argue, that a specifically female world did indeed develop, a world built around a generic and unself-conscious pattern of single-sex or homosocial networks. These supportive networks were institutionalized in social conventions or rituals which accompanied virtually every important event in a woman's life, from birth to death. Such female relationships were frequently supported and paralleled by severe social restrictions on intimacy between young men and women. Within such a world of emotional richness and complexity devotion to and love of other women became a plausible and socially accepted form of human interaction.

An abundance of printed and manuscript sources exists to support such a hypothesis. Etiquette books, advice books on child rearing, religious sermons, guides to young men and young women, medical texts, and school curricula all suggest that late eighteenth- and most nineteenth-century Americans assumed the existence of a world composed of distinctly male and female spheres, spheres determined by the immutable laws of God and nature.[17] The unpublished letters and diaries of Americans during this same period concur, detailing the existence of sexually segregated worlds inhabited by human beings with different values, expectations, and personalities. Contacts between men and women frequently partook of a formality and stiffness quite alien to twentieth-century America and which today we tend to define as "Victorian." Women, however, did not form an isolated and oppressed subcategory in male society. Their letters and diaries indicate that women's sphere had an essential integrity and dignity that grew out of women's shared experiences and mutual affection and that, despite the profound changes which affected American social structure and institutions between the 1760s and the 1870s, retained a constancy and predictability. The ways in which women thought of and interacted with each other remained unchanged. Continuity, not discontinuity, characterized this female world. Molly Hallock's and Jeannie Field's words, emotions, and experiences have direct parallels in the 1760s and the 1790s.[18] There are indications in contemporary sociological and psychological literature that female closeness and support networks have continued into the twentieth century—not only among ethnic and working-class groups but even among the middle class.[19]

Most eighteenth- and nineteenth-century women lived within a world bounded by home, church, and the institution of visiting—that endless trooping of women to each other's homes for social purposes. It was a world inhabited by children and by other women.[20] Women helped each other with domestic chores and in times of sickness, sorrow, or trouble. Entire days, even weeks, might be spent almost exclusively with other women.[21] Urban and town women could devote virtually every day to visits, teas, or shopping trips with other women. Rural women developed a pattern of more extended visits that lasted weeks and sometimes months, at times even dislodging husbands from their beds and bedrooms so that dear friends might spend every hour of every day together.[22] When husbands traveled, wives routinely moved in with other women, invited women friends to teas and suppers, sat together sharing and comparing the letters they had received from other close women friends. Secrets were exchanged and cherished, and the husband's return at times viewed with some ambivalence.[23]

Summer vacations were frequently organized to permit old friends to meet at water spas or share a country home. In 1848, for example, a young matron wrote cheerfully to her husband about the delightful time she was having with five close women friends whom she had invited to spend the summer with her; he remained at home alone to face the heat of Philadelphia and a cholera epidemic.[24] Some ninety years earlier, two young Quaker girls commented upon the vacation their aunt had taken alone with another woman; their remarks were openly envious and tell us something of the emotional quality of these friendships: "I hear Aunt is gone with the Friend and wont be back for two weeks, fine times indeed I think the old friends had, taking their pleasure about the country . . . and have the advantage of that fine woman's conversation and instruction, while we poor young girls must spend all spring at home. . . . What a disappointment that we are not together. . . ."[25]

Friends did not form isolated dyads but were normally part of highly integrated networks. Knowing each other, perhaps related to each other, they played a central role in holding communities and kin systems together. Especially when families became geographically mobile women's long visits to each other and their frequent letters filled with discussions of marriages and births, illness and deaths, descriptions of growing children, and reminiscences of times and people past provided an important sense of continuity in a rapidly changing society.[26] Central to this female world was an inner core of kin. The ties between sisters, first cousins, aunts, and nieces provided the underlying structure upon which groups of friends and their network of female relatives clustered. Although most of the women within this sample would appear to be living within isolated nuclear families, the emotional ties between nonresidential kin were deep and binding and provided one of the fundamental existential realities of women's lives.[27] Twenty years after Parke Lewis Butler moved with her husband to Louisiana, she sent her two daughters back to Virginia to attend school, live with their grandmother and aunt, and be integrated back into Virginia society.[28] The constant letters between Maria Inskeep and Fanny Hampton,

sisters separated in their early twenties when Maria moved with her husband from New Jersey to Louisiana, held their families together, making it possible for their daughters to feel a part of their cousins' network of friends and interests.[29] The Ripley daughters, growing up in western Massachusetts in the early 1800s, spent months each year with their mother's sister and her family in distant Boston; these female cousins and their network of friends exchanged gossip-filled letters and gradually formed deeply loving and dependent ties.[30]

Women frequently spent their days within the social confines of such extended families. Sisters-in-law visited each other and, in some families, seemed to spend more time with each other than with their husbands. First cousins cared for each other's babies—for weeks or even months in times of sickness or childbirth. Sisters helped each other with housework, shopped and sewed for each other. Geographic separation was borne with difficulty. A sister's absence for even a week or two could cause loneliness and depression and would be bridged by frequent letters. Sibling rivalry was hardly unknown, but with separation or illness the theme of deep affection and dependency reemerged.[31]

Sisterly bonds continued across a lifetime. In her old age a rural Quaker matron, Martha Jefferis, wrote to her daughter Anne concerning her own half-sister, Phoebe: "In sister Phoebe I have a real friend—she studies my comfort and waits on me like a child. . . . She is exceedingly kind and this to all other homes (set aside yours) I would prefer—it is next to being with a daughter." Phoebe's own letters confirmed Martha's evaluation of her feelings. "Thou knowest my dear sister," Phoebe wrote, "there is no one . . . that exactly feels [for] thee as I do, for I think without boasting I can truly say that my desire is for thee."[32]

Such women, whether friends or relatives, assumed an emotional centrality in each other's lives. In their diaries and letters they wrote of the joy and contentment they felt in each other's company, their sense of isolation and despair when apart. The regularity of their correspondence underlies the sincerity of their words. Women named their daughters after one another and sought to integrate dear friends into their lives after marriage.[33] As one young bride wrote to an old friend shortly after her marriage: "I want to see you and talk with you and feel that we are united by the same bonds of sympathy and congeniality as ever."[34] After years of friendship one aging woman wrote of another: "Time cannot destroy the fascination of her manner . . . her voice is music to the ear. . . ."[35] Women made elaborate presents for each other, ranging from the Quakers' frugal pies and breads to painted velvet bags and phantom bouquets.[36] When a friend died, their grief was deeply felt. Martha Jefferis was unable to write to her daughter for three weeks because of the sorrow she felt at the death of a dear friend. Such distress was not unusual. A generation earlier a young Massachusetts farm woman filled pages of her diary with her grief at the death of her "dearest friend" and transcribed the letters of condolence other women sent her. She marked the anniversary of Rachel's death each year in her diary, contrasting her faithfulness with that of Rachel's husband who had soon remarried.[37]

These female friendships served a number of emotional functions. Within this secure and empathetic world women could share sorrows, anxieties, and joys, confident that other women had experienced similar emotions. One mid-nineteenth-century rural matron in a letter to her daughter discussed this particular aspect of women's friendships: "To have such a friend as thyself to look to and sympathize with her—and enter into all her little needs and in whose bosom she could with freedom pour forth her joys and sorrows—such a friend would very much relieve the tedium of many a wearisome hour. . . ." A generation later Molly more informally underscored the importance of this same function in a letter to Helena: "Suppose I come down . . . [and] spend Sunday with you quietly," she wrote Helena " . . . that means talking all the time until you are relieved of all your latest troubles, and I of mine. . . ."[38] These were frequently troubles that apparently no man could understand. When Anne Jefferis Sheppard was first married, she and her older sister Edith (who then lived with Anne) wrote in detail to their mother of the severe depression and anxiety which they experienced. Moses Sheppard, Anne's husband, added cheerful postscripts to the sisters' letters—which he had clearly not read—remarking on Anne's and Edith's contentment. Theirs was an emotional world to which he had little access.[39]

This was, as well, a female world in which hostility and criticism of other women were discouraged, and thus a milieu in which women could develop a sense of inner security and self-esteem. As one young woman wrote to her mother's longtime friend: "I cannot sufficiently thank you for the kind unvaried affection & indulgence you have ever shown and expressed both by words and actions for me. . . . Happy would it be did all the world view me as you do, through the medium of kindness and forbearance."[40] They valued each other. Women, who had little status or power in the larger world of male concerns, possessed status and power in the lives and worlds of other women.[41]

An intimate mother-daughter relationship lay at the heart of this female world. The diaries and letters of both mothers and daughters attest to their closeness and mutual emotional dependency. Daughters routinely discussed their mother's health and activities with their own friends, expressed anxiety in cases of their mother's ill health and concern for her cares.[42] Expressions of hostility which we would today consider routine on the part of both mothers and daughters seem to have been uncommon indeed. On the contrary, this sample of families indicates that the normal relationship between mother and daughter was one of sympathy and understanding.[43] Only sickness or great geographic distance was allowed to cause extended separation. When marriage did result in such separation, both viewed the distance between them with distress.[44] Something of this sympathy and love between mothers and daughters is evident in a letter Sarah Alden Ripley, at age sixty-nine, wrote her youngest and recently married daughter: "You do not know how much I miss you, not only when I struggle in and out of my mortal envelop and pump my nightly potation and no longer pour into your sympathizing ear my senile gossip, but all the day I muse away, since the sound of your voice no longer rouses me to sympathy with your joys or sorrows. . . . You cannot know how much I miss your affectionate demonstrations."[45] A dozen aging mothers in this sample of over thirty families echoed her sentiments.

Central to these mother-daughter relations is what might be described as an apprenticeship system. In those families where the daughter followed the mother into a life of traditional domesticity, mothers and other older women carefully trained daughters in the arts of housewifery and motherhood. Such training undoubtedly occurred throughout a girl's childhood but became more systematized, almost ritualistic, in the years following the end of her formal education and before her marriage. At this time a girl either returned home from boarding school or no longer divided her time between home and school. Rather, she devoted her energies on two tasks: mastering new domestic skills and participating in the visiting and social activities necessary to finding a husband. Under the careful supervision of their mothers and of older female relatives, such late-adolescent girls temporarily took over the household management from their mothers, tended their young nieces and nephews, and helped in childbirth, nursing, and weaning. Such experiences tied the generations together in shared skills and emotional interaction.[46]

Daughters were born into a female world. Their mother's life expectations and sympathetic network of friends and relations were among the first realities in the life of the developing child. As long as the mother's domestic role remained relatively stable and few viable alternatives competed with it, daughters tended to accept their mother's world and to turn automatically to other women for support and intimacy. It was within this closed and intimate female world that the young girl grew toward womanhood.

One could speculate at length concerning the absence of that mother-daughter hostility today considered almost inevitable to an adolescent's struggle for autonomy and self-identity. It is possible that taboos against female aggression and hostility were sufficiently strong to repress even that between mothers and their adolescent daughters. Yet these letters seem so alive and the interest of daughters in their mothers' affairs so vital and genuine that it is difficult to interpret their closeness exclusively in terms of repression and denial. The functional bonds that held mothers and daughters together in a world that permitted few alternatives to domesticity might well have created a source of mutuality and trust absent in societies where greater options were available for daughters than for mothers. Furthermore, the extended female network—a daughter's close ties with her own older sisters, cousins, and aunts—may well have permitted a diffusion and a relaxation of mother-daughter identification and so have aided a daughter in her struggle for identity and autonomy. None of these explanations are mutually exclusive; all may well have interacted to produce the degree of empathy evident in those letters and diaries.

At some point in adolescence, the young girl began to move outside the matrix of her mother's support group to develop a network of her own. Among the middle class, at least, this transition toward what was at the same time both a limited autonomy and a repetition of her mother's life seemed to have most frequently coincided with a girl's going to school. Indeed education appears to have played a crucial role in the lives of most of the families in this study. Attending school for a few months, for a year, or longer, was common even among daughters of relatively poor families, while middle-class girls routinely spent at least a year in boarding school.[47] These school years ordinarily marked a girl's first separation from home. They served to wean the daughter from her home, to train her in the essential social graces, and, ultimately, to help introduce her into the marriage market. It was not infrequently a trying emotional experience for both mother and daughter.[48]

In this process of leaving one home and adjusting to another, the mother's friends and relatives played a key transitional role. Such older women routinely accepted the role of foster mother; they supervised the young girl's deportment, monitored her health and introduced her to their own network of female friends and kin.[49] Not infrequently women, friends from their own school years, arranged to send their daughters to the same school so that the girls might form bonds paralleling those their mothers had made. For years Molly and Helena wrote of their daughters' meeting and worried over each other's children. When Molly finally brought her daughter east to school, their first act on reaching New York was to meet Helena and her daughters. Elizabeth Bordley Gibson virtually adopted the daughters of her school chum, Eleanor Custis Lewis. The Lewis daughters soon began to write Elizabeth Gibson letters with the salutation "Dearest Mama." Eleuthera DuPont, attending boarding school in Philadelphia at roughly the same time as the Lewis girls, developed a parallel relationship with her mother's friend, Elizabeth McKie Smith. Eleuthera went to the same school and became a close friend of the Smith girls and eventually married their first cousin. During this period she routinely called Mrs. Smith "Mother." Indeed Eleuthera so internalized the sense of having two mothers that she casually wrote her sisters of her "Mamma's" visits at her "mother's" house—that is, at Mrs. Smith's.[50]

Even more important to this process of maturation than their mother's friends were the female friends young women made at school. Young girls helped each other overcome homesickness and endure the crises of adolescence. They gossiped about beaux, incorporated each other into their own kinship systems, and attended and gave teas and balls together. Older girls in boarding school "adopted" younger ones, who called them "Mother."[51] Dear friends might indeed continue this pattern of adoption and mothering throughout their lives; one woman might routinely assume the nurturing role of pseudomother, the other the dependency role of daughter. The pseudomother performed for the other woman all the services which we normally associate with mothers; she went to absurd lengths to purchase items her "daughter" could have obtained from other sources, gave advice and functioned as an idealized figure in her "daughter's" imagination. Helena played such a role for Molly, as did Sarah for Jeannie. Elizabeth Bordley Gibson bought almost all Eleanor Parke Custis Lewis's necessities—from shoes and corset covers to bedding and harp strings—and sent them from Philadelphia to Virginia, a procedure that sometimes took months. Eleanor frequently asked Elizabeth to take back her purchases, have them redone, and argue with shopkeepers about prices. These were favors automatically asked and complied with. Anne Jefferis Sheppard made the analogy very explicitly in a letter to her own mother written shortly after Anne's marriage, when she was feeling depressed about their separation: "Mary Paulen is truly kind, almost acts the part of a mother and trys to aid and *comfort me,* and also to *lighten my new cares.*"[52]

A comparison of the references to men and women in these young women's letters is striking. Boys were obviously indispensable to the elaborate courtship ritual girls engaged in. In these teenage letters and diaries, however, boys appear distant and warded off—an effect produced both by the girl's sense of bonding and by a highly developed and deprecatory whimsy. Girls joked among themselves about the conceit, poor looks or affectations of suitors. Rarely, especially in the eighteenth and early nineteenth centuries, were favorable remarks exchanged. Indeed, while hostility and criticism of other women were so rare as to seem almost tabooed, young women permitted themselves to express a great deal of hostility toward peer-group men.[53] When unacceptable suitors appeared, girls might even band together to harass them. When one such unfortunate came to court Sophie DuPont she hid in her room, first sending her sister Eleuthera to entertain him and then dispatching a number of urgent notes to her neighboring sister-in-law, cousins, and a visiting friend who all came to Sophie's support. A wild female romp ensued, ending only when Sophie banged into a door, lacerated her nose, and retired, with her female cohorts, to bed. Her brother and the presumably disconcerted suitor were left alone. These were not the antics of teenagers but of women in their early and mid-twenties.[54]

Even if young men were acceptable suitors, girls referred to them formally and obliquely: "The last week I received the unexpected intelligence of the arrival of a friend in Boston," Sarah Ripley wrote in her diary of the young man to whom she had been engaged for years and whom she would shortly marry. Harriet Manigault assiduously kept a lively and gossipy diary during the three years preceding her marriage, yet did not once comment upon her own engagement nor indeed make any personal references to her fiancé— who was never identified as such but always referred to as Mr. Wilcox.[55] The point is not that these young women were hostile to young men. Far from it; they sought marriage and domesticity. Yet in these letters and diaries men appear as an other or out group, segregated into different schools, supported by their own male network of friends and kin, socialized to different behavior, and coached to a proper formality in courtship behavior. As a consequence, relations between young women and men frequently lacked the spontaneity and emotional intimacy that characterized the young girls' ties to each other.

Indeed, in sharp contrast to their distant relations with boys, young women's relations with each other were close, often frolicsome, and surprisingly long lasting and devoted. They wrote secret missives to each other, spent long solitary days with each other, curled up together in bed at night to whisper fantasies and secrets.[56] In 1862 one young woman in her early twenties described one such scene to an absent friend: "I have sat up to midnight listening to the confidences of Constance Kinney, whose heart was opened by that most charming of all situations, a seat on a bedside late at night, when all the household are asleep & only oneself & one's confidante survive in wakefulness. So she has told me all her loves and tried to get some confidences in return but being five or six years older than she, I know better. . . ."[57] Elizabeth Bordley and Nelly Parke Custis, teenagers in Philadelphia in the 1790s, routinely secreted themselves until late each night in Nelly's attic, where they each wrote a novel about the other.[58] Quite a few young women kept diaries, and it was a sign of special friendship to show their diaries to each other. The emotional quality of such exchanges emerges from the comments of one young girl who grew up along the Ohio frontier:

> Sisters CW and RT keep diaries & allow me the inestimable pleasure of reading them and in turn they see mine—but O shame covers my face when I think of it; theirs is so much better than mine, that every time. Then I think well now I *will* burn mine but upon second thought it would deprive me the pleasure of reading theirs, for I esteem it a very great privilege indeed, as well as very improving, as we lay our hearts open to each other, it heightens our love & helps to cherish & keep alive that sweet soothing friendship and endears us to each other by that soft attraction.[59]

Girls routinely slept together, kissed and hugged each other. Indeed, while waltzing with young men scandalized the otherwise flighty and highly fashionable Harriet Manigault, she considered waltzing with other young women not only acceptable but pleasant.[60]

Marriage followed adolescence. With increasing frequency in the nineteenth century, marriage involved a girl's traumatic removal from her mother and her mother's network. It involved, as well, adjustment to a husband, who, because he was male came to marriage with both a different world view and vastly different experiences. Not surprisingly, marriage was an event surrounded with supportive, almost ritualistic, practices. (Weddings are one of the last female rituals remaining in twentieth-century America.) Young women routinely spent the months preceding their marriage almost exclusively with other women—at neighborhood sewing bees and quilting parties or in a round of visits to geographically distant friends and relatives. Ostensibly they went to receive assistance in the practical preparations for their new home—sewing and quilting a trousseau and linen—but of equal importance, they appear to have gained emotional support and reassurance. Sarah Ripley spent over a month with friends and relatives in Boston and Hingham before her wedding; Parke Custis Lewis exchanged visits with her aunts and first cousins throughout Virginia.[61] Anne Jefferis, who married with some hesitation, spent virtually half a year in endless visiting with cousins, aunts, and friends. Despite their reassurance and support, however, she would not marry Moses Sheppard until her sister Edith and her cousin Rebecca moved into the groom's home, met his friends, and explored his personality.[62] The wedding did not take place until Edith wrote to Anne: "I can say in truth I am entirely willing thou shouldst follow him even away in the Jersey sands believing if thou are not happy in thy future home it will not be any fault on his part. . . ."[63]

Sisters, cousins, and friends frequently accompanied newlyweds on their wedding night and wedding trip, which often involved additional family visiting. Such extensive visits presumably served to wean the daughter from her family of origin. As such they often contained a note of ambivalence. Nelly Custis, for example, reported homesickness and loneliness on her wedding trip. "I left my Beloved and revered Grandmamma with sincere regret," she wrote Elizabeth Bordley. "It was sometime before I could feel reconciled to traveling without her." Perhaps they also functioned to reassure the young woman herself, and her friends and kin, that though marriage might alter it would not destroy old bonds of intimacy and familiarity.[64]

Married life, too, was structured about a host of female rituals. Childbirth, especially the birth of the first child, became virtually a *rite de passage,* with a lengthy seclusion of the woman before and after delivery, severe restrictions on her activities, and finally a dramatic reemergence.[65] This seclusion was supervised by mothers, sisters, and loving friends. Nursing and weaning involved the advice and assistance of female friends and relatives. So did miscarriage.[66] Death, like birth, was structured around elaborate unisexed rituals. When Nelly Parke Custis Lewis rushed to nurse her daughter who was critically ill while away at school, Nelly received support, not from her husband, who remained on their plantation, but from her old school friend, Elizabeth Bordley. Elizabeth aided Nelly in caring for her dying daughter, cared for Nelly's other children, played a major role in the elaborate funeral arrangements (which the father did not attend), and frequently visited the girl's grave at the mother's request. For years Elizabeth continued to be the confidante of Nelly's anguished recollections of her lost daughter. These memories, Nelly's letters make clear, were for Elizabeth alone. "Mr. L. knows nothing of this," was a frequent comment.[67] Virtually every collection of letters and diaries in my sample contained evidence of women turning to each other for comfort when facing the frequent and unavoidable deaths of the eighteenth and nineteenth centuries.[68] While mourning for her father's death, Sophie DuPont received elaborate letters and visits of condolence—all from women. No man wrote or visited Sophie to offer sympathy at her father's death.[69] Among rural Pennsylvania Quakers, death and mourning rituals assumed an even more extreme same-sex form, with men or women largely barred from the deathbeds of the other sex. Women relatives and friends slept with the dying woman, nursed her, and prepared her body for burial.[70]

Eighteenth- and nineteenth-century women thus lived in emotional proximity to each other. Friendships and intimacies followed the biological ebb and flow of women's lives. Marriage and pregnancy, childbirth and weaning, sickness and death involved physical and psychic trauma which comfort and sympathy made easier to bear. Intense bonds of love and intimacy bound together those women who, offering each other aid and sympathy, shared such stressful moments.

These bonds were often physical as well as emotional. An undeniably romantic and even sensual note frequently marked female relationships. This theme, significant throughout the stages of a woman's life, surfaced first during adolescence. As one teenager from a struggling pioneer family in the Ohio Valley wrote in her diary in 1808: "I laid with my dear R[ebecca] and a glorious good talk we had until about 4[A.M.]—O how hard I do *love* her. . . ."[71] Only a few years later Bostonian Eunice Callender carved her initials and Sarah Ripley's into a favorite tree, along with a pledge of eternal love, and then waited breathlessly for Sarah to discover and respond to her declaration of affection. The response appears to have been affirmative.[72] A half-century later urbane and sophisticated Katherine Wharton commented upon meeting an old school chum: "She was a great pet of mine at school & I thought as I watched her light figure how often I had held her in my arms—how dear she had once been to me." Katie maintained a long intimate friendship with another girl. When a young man began to court this friend seriously, Katie commented in her diary that she had never realized "how deeply I loved Eng and how fully." She wrote over and over again in that entry: "Indeed I love her!" and only with great reluctance left the city that summer since it meant also leaving Eng with Eng's new suitor.[73]

Peggy Emlen, a Quaker adolescent in Philadelphia in the 1760s, expressed similar feelings about her first cousin, Sally Logan. The girls sent love poems to each other (not unlike the ones Elizabeth Bordley wrote to Nellie Custis a generation later), took long solitary walks together, and even haunted the empty house of the other when one was out of town. Indeed Sally's absences from Philadelphia caused Peggy acute unhappiness. So strong were Peggy's feelings that her brothers began to tease about her affection for Sally and threatened to steal Sally's letters, much to both girls' alarm. In one letter that Peggy wrote the absent Sally she elaborately described the depth and nature of her feelings: "I have not words to express my impatience to see My Dear Cousin, what would I not give just now for an hours sweet conversation with her, it seems as if I had a thousand things to say to thee, yet when I see thee, everything will be forgot thro' joy. . . . I have a very great friendship for several Girls yet it dont give me so much uneasiness at being absent from them as from thee. . . . [Let us] go and spend a day down at our place together and there unmolested enjoy each others company."[74]

Sarah Alden Ripley, a young, highly educated woman, formed a similar intense relationship, in this instance with a woman somewhat older than herself. The immediate bond of friendship rested on their atypically intense scholarly interests, but it soon involved strong emotions, at least on Sarah's part. "Friendship," she wrote Mary Emerson, "is fast twining about her willing captive the silken hands of dependence, a dependence so sweet who would renounce it for the apathy of self-sufficiency?" Subsequent letters became far more emotional, almost conspiratorial. Mary visited Sarah secretly in her room, or the two women crept away from family and friends to meet in a nearby woods. Sarah became jealous of Mary's other young friends. Mary's trips away from Boston also thrust Sarah into periods of anguished depression. Interestingly, the letters detailing their love were not destroyed but were preserved and even reprinted in a eulogistic biography of Sarah Alden Ripley.[75]

Tender letters between adolescent women, confessions of loneliness and emotional dependency, were not peculiar to Sarah Alden, Peggy Emlen, or Katie Wharton. They are found throughout the letters of the thirty-five families studied. They have, of course, their parallel today in the musings of many female adolescents. Yet these eighteenth- and nineteenth-century friendships lasted with undiminished, indeed often increased, intensity throughout the women's lives. Sarah Alden Ripley's first child was named after Mary Emerson. Nelly Custis Lewis's love for and dependence on Elizabeth Bordley Gibson only increased after her marriage. Eunice Callender remained enamored of her cousin Sarah Ripley for years and rejected as impossible the suggestion by another woman that their love might some day fade away.[76] Sophie DuPont and her childhood friend, Clementina Smith, exchanged letters filled with love and dependency for forty years while another dear friend, Mary Black Couper, wrote of dreaming that she, Sophie, and her husband were all united in one marriage. Mary's letters to Sophie are filled with avowals of love and indications of ambivalence toward her own husband. Eliza Schlatter, another of Sophie's intimate friends, wrote to her at a time of crisis:

"I wish I could be with you present in the body as well as the mind & heart—I would turn your *good husband out of bed*—and snuggle into you and we would have a long talk like old times in Pine St.—I want to tell you so many things that are not *writable*. . . ."[77]

Such mutual dependency and deep affection is a central existential reality coloring the world of supportive networks and rituals. In the case of Katie, Sophie, or Eunice—as with Molly, Jeannie, and Sarah—their need for closeness and support merged with more intense demands for a love which was at the same time both emotional and sensual. Perhaps the most explicit statement concerning women's lifelong friendships appeared in the letter abolitionist and reformer Mary Grew wrote about the same time, referring to her own love for her dear friend and lifelong companion, Margaret Burleigh. Grew wrote, in response to a letter of condolence from another woman on Burleigh's death: "Your words respecting my beloved friend touch me deeply. Evidently . . . you comprehend and appreciate, as few persons do . . . the nature of the relation which existed, which exists, between her and myself. Her only surviving niece . . . also does. To me it seems to have been a closer union than that of most marriages. We know there have been other such between two men and also between two women. And why should there not be. Love is spiritual, only passion is sexual."[78]

How then can we ultimately interpret these long-lived intimate female relationships and integrate them into our understanding of Victorian sexuality? Their ambivalent and romantic rhetoric presents us with an ultimate puzzle: the relationship along the spectrum of human emotions between love, sensuality, and sexuality.

One is tempted, as I have remarked, to compare Molly, Peggy, or Sophie's relationships with the friendships adolescent girls in the twentieth century routinely form—close friendships of great emotional intensity. Helene Deutsch and Clara Thompson have both described these friendships as emotionally necessary to a girl's psychosexual development. But, they warn, such friendships might shade into adolescent and postadolescent homosexuality.[79]

It is possible to speculate that in the twentieth century a number of cultural taboos evolved to cut short the homosocial ties of girl hood and to impel the emerging women of thirteen or fourteen toward heterosexual relationships. In contrast, nineteenth-century American society did not taboo close female relationships but rather recognized them as a socially viable form of human contact—and, as such, acceptable throughout a woman's life. Indeed it was not these homosocial ties that were inhibited but rather heterosexual leanings. While closeness, freedom of emotional expression, and uninhibited physical contact characterized women's relationships with each other, the opposite was frequently true of male-female relationships. One could thus argue that within such a world of female support, intimacy, and ritual it was only to be expected that adult women would turn trustingly and lovingly to each other. It was a behavior they had observed and learned since childhood. A different type of emotional landscape existed in the nineteenth century, one in which Molly and Helena's love became a natural development.

Of perhaps equal significance are the implications we can garner from this framework for the understanding of heterosexual marriages in the nineteenth century. If men and women grew up as they did in relatively homogeneous and segregated sexual groups, then marriage represented a major problem in adjustment. From this perspective we could interpret much of the emotional stiffness and distance that we associate with Victorian marriage as a structural consequence of contemporary sex-role differentiation and gender-role socialization. With marriage both women and men had to adjust to life with a person who was, in essence, a member of an alien group.

I have thus far substituted a cultural or psychosocial for a psychosexual interpretation of women's emotional bonding. But there are psychosexual implications in this model which I think it only fair to make more explicit. Despite Sigmund Freud's insistence on the bisexuality of us all or the recent American Psychiatric Association decision on homosexuality, many psychiatrists today tend explicitly or implicitly to view homosexuality as a totally alien or pathological behavior—as totally unlike heterosexuality. I suspect that in essence they may have adopted an explanatory model similar to the one used in discussing schizophrenia. As a psychiatrist can speak of schizophrenia and of a borderline schizophrenic personality as both ultimately and fundamentally different from a normal or neurotic personality, so they also think of both homosexuality and latent homosexuality as states totally different from heterosexuality. With this rapid dichotomous model of assumption, "latent homosexuality" becomes the indication of a disease in progress—seeds of a pathology which belie the reality of an individual's heterosexuality.

Yet at the same time we are well aware that cultural values can affect choices in the gender of a person's sexual partner. We, for instance, do not necessarily consider homosexual-object choice among men in prison, on shipboard or in boarding schools a necessary indication of pathology. I would urge that we expand this relativistic model and hypothesize that a number of cultures might well tolerate or even encourage diversity in sexual and nonsexual relations. Based on my research into this nineteenth-century world of female intimacy, I would further suggest that rather than seeing a gulf between the normal and the abnormal we view sexual and emotional impulses as part of a continuum or spectrum of affect gradations strongly affected by cultural norms and arrangements, a continuum influenced in part by observed and thus learned behavior. At one end of the continuum lies committed heterosexuality, at the other uncompromising homosexuality; between, a wide latitude of emotions and sexual feelings. Certain cultures and environments permit individuals a great deal of freedom in moving across this spectrum. I would like to suggest that the nineteenth century was such a cultural environment. That is, the supposedly repressive and destructive Victorian sexual ethos may have been more flexible and responsive to the needs of particular individuals than those of mid-twentieth century.

Notes

1. The most notable exception to this rule is now eleven years old: William R. Taylor and Christopher Lasch, "Two 'Kindred Spirits': Sorority and Family in New England, 1839–1846," *New England Quarterly* 36 (1963):25–41.... I do not... accept the Taylor-Lasch thesis that female friendships developed in the mid-nineteenth century because of geographic mobility and the breakup of the colonial family. I have found these friendships as frequently in the eighteenth century as in the nine-

teenth and would hypothesize that the geographic mobility of the mid-nineteenth century eroded them as it did so many other traditional social institutions. . . .

2. I do not wish to deny the importance of women's relations with particular men. Obviously, women were close to brothers, husbands, fathers, and sons. However, there is evidence that despite such closeness relationships between men and women differed in both emotional texture and frequency from those between women. . . . I have discussed some aspects of male-female relationships in two articles: "Puberty to Menopause: The Cycle of Femininity in Nineteenth-Century America," Feminist Studies 1 (1973):58–72, and, with Charles Rosenberg, "The Female Animal: Medical and Biological Views of Women in 19th Century America," Journal of American History 59 (1973):331–56.

3. See Freud's classic paper on homosexuality, "Three Essays on the Theory of Sexuality," in The Standard Edition of the Complete Psychological Works of Sigmund Freud, trans. James Strachey (London: Hogarth Press, 1953), 7:135–72. The essays originally appeared in 1905. . . .

4. . . . [S]ee Charles Rosenberg, "Sexuality, Class and Role," American Quarterly 25 (1973): 131–53.

5. See, e.g., the letters of Peggy Emlen to Sally Logan, 1768–72, Wells Morris Collection, Box 1, Historical Society of Pennsylvania; and the Eleanor Parke Custis Lewis Letters, Historical Society of Pennsylvania, Philadelphia.

6. Sarah Butler Wister was the daughter of Fanny Kemble and Pierce Butler. In 1859 she married a Philadelphia physician, Owen Wister. The novelist Owen Wister is her son. Jeannie Field Musgrove was the half-orphaned daughter of constitutional lawyer and New York Republican politician David Dudley Field. Their correspondence (1855–98) is in the Sarah Butler Wister Papers, Wister Family Papers, Historical Society of Pennsylvania.

7. Sarah Butler, Butler Place, S.C., to Jeannie Field, New York, Sept. 14, 1855.

8. See, e.g., Sarah Butler Wister, Germantown, Pa., to Jeannie Field, New York, Sept. 25, 1862, Oct. 21, 1863; or Jeannie Field, New York, to Sarah Butler Wister, Germantown, July 3, 1861, Jan. 23 and July 12, 1863.

9. Sarah Butler Wister, Germantown, to Jeannie Field, New York, June 5, 1861, Feb. 29, 1864; Jeannie Field to Sarah Butler Wister, Nov. 22, 1861, Jan. 4 and June 14, 1863.

10. Sarah Butler Wister, London, to Jeannie Field Musgrove, New York, June 18 and Aug. 3, 1870.

11. See, e.g., two of Sarah's letters to Jeannie: Dec. 21, 1873, July 16, 1878.

12. This is the 1868–1920 correspondence between Mary Hallock Foote and Helena, a New York friend (the Mary Hallock Foote Papers are in the Manuscript Division, Stanford University). . . . In many ways these letters are typical of those women wrote to other women. Women frequently began letters to each other with salutations such as "Dearest," "My Most Beloved," "You Darling Girl," and signed them "tenderly" or "to my dear dear

sweet friend, good-bye." . . . She was by no means unique. See, e.g., Annie to Charlene Van Vleck Anderson, Appleton, Wis., June 10, 1871, Anderson Family Papers, Manuscript Division, Stanford University; Maggie to Emily Howland, Philadelphia, July 12, 1851, Howland Family Papers, Phoebe King Collection, Friends Historical Library, Swarthmore College; Mary Jane Burleigh to Emily Howland, Sherwood, N.Y., Mar. 27, 1872, Howland Family Papers, Sophia Smith Collection, Smith College; Mary Black Couper to Sophia Madeleine DuPont, Wilmington, Del.: n.d. [1834] (two letters), Samuel Francis DuPont Papers, Eleutherian Mills Foundation, Wilmington, Del. . . . in general the correspondence (1838–49) between Rebecca Biddle of Philadelphia and Martha Jefferis, Chester County, Pa., Jefferis Family Correspondence, Chester County Historical Society, West Chester, Pa.; Phoebe Bradford Diary, June 7 and July 13, 1832, Historical Society of Pennsylvania; . . . the Sarah Alden Ripley Correspondence, Schlesinger Library, Radcliffe College; . . . Anne Sterling Biddle Family Papers, Friends Historical Society, Swarthmore College; Harriet Manigault Wilcox Diary, Aug. 7, 1814, Historical Society of Pennsylvania; . . . Mrs. O. J. Wister and Miss Agnes Irwin, eds., Worthy Women of Our First Century (Philadelphia: J. B. Lippincott & Co., 1877), p. 195.

13. Mary Hallock [Foote] to Helena, n.d. [1869–70], n.d. [1871–72], Folder 1, Mary Hallock Foote Letters, . . .

14. Mary Hallock [Foote] to Helena, Sept. 15 and 23, 1873, n.d. [Oct. 1873], Oct. 12, 1873.

15. Mary Hallock [Foote] to Helena, n.d. [Jan. 1874], n.d. [Spring 1874].

16. Mary Hallock [Foote] to Helena, Sept. 23, 1873; Mary Hallock [Foote] to Richard, Dec. 13, 1873. Molly's and Helena's relationship continued for the rest of their lives. . . .

17. . . . [S]ee Barbara Welter, "The Cult of True Womanhood: 1820–1860," American Quarterly 18 (Summer 1966):151–74; Anne Firor Scott, The Southern Lady: From Pedestal to Politics, 1830–1930 (Chicago: University of Chicago Press, 1970), chaps. 1–2; Smith-Rosenberg and Rosenberg.

18. See, e.g., the letters of Peggy Emlen to Sally Logan, 1768–72. . . .

19. See, [e.g.,] Elizabeth Botts, Family and Social Network (London: Tavistock Publications, 1957); . . .

20. This pattern seemed to cross class barriers. . . . See Ann McGrann, Philadelphia, to Sophie M. DuPont, Philadelphia, July 3, 1834, Sophie Madeleine DuPont Letters, Eleutherian Mills Foundation.

21. [See, e.g.,] Harriet Manigault Diary, June 28, 1814, and passim; . . .

22. [See, e.g.,] . . . Ann Sterling Biddle Papers, passim, . . .

23. [See, e.g.,] Phoebe Bradford Diary, Jan. 13, Nov. 16–19, 1832, Apr. 26 and May 7, 1833; . . .

24. Lisa Mitchell Diary, 1860s, passim, Manuscript Division, Tulane University; . . . Jeannie McCall, Cedar Park, to Peter McCall, Philadelphia, June 30, 1849, McCall Section, Cadwalader Collection, Historical Society of Pennsylvania.

25. Peggy Emlen to Sally Logan, May 3, 1769.

26. For a prime example of this type of letter, see Eleanor Parke Custis Lewis to Elizabeth Bordley Gibson, Passim; . . .

27. Place of residence is not the only variable significance in characterizing family structure. Strong emotional ties and frequent visiting and correspondence can unite families that do not live under one roof. . . .

28. Eleanor Parke Custis Lewis to Elizabeth Bordley Gibson, Apr. 20 and Sept. 25, 1848.

29. Maria Inskeep to Fanny Hampton Correspondence, 1823–60, Inskeep Collection, Tulane University Library.

30. Eunice Callender, Boston, to Sarah Ripley [Stearns], Sept. 24 and Oct. 29, 1803, Feb. 16, 1805, Apr. 29 and Oct. 9, 1806, May 26, 1810.

31. Sophie DuPont filled her letters to her younger brother Henry (with whom she had been assigned to correspond while he was at boarding school) with accounts of family visiting (see, e.g., Dec. 13, 1827, Jan. 10 and Mar. 9, 1828, Feb. 4 and Mar. 10, 1832). . . . Mary B. Ashew Diary, July 11 and 13, Aug. 17, Summer and Oct. 1858. . . .

32. Martha Jefferis to Anne Jefferis Sheppard, Jan. 12, 1845; Phoebe Middleton to Martha Jefferis, Feb. 22, 1848. . . .

33. Rebecca Biddle to Martha Jefferis, 1838–49, passim; Martha Jefferis to Anne Jefferis Sheppard, July 6, 1846; Anne Jefferis Sheppard to Rachael Jefferis, Jan. 16, 1865; Sarah Foulke Farquhar [Emlen] Diary, Sept. 22, 1813, Friends Historical Library, Swarthmore College; . . .

34. Sarah Alden Ripley to Abba Allyn, n.d. . . .

35. Phoebe Bradford Diary, July 13, 1832.

36. Mary Hallock [Foote] to Helena, Dec. 23 [1868 or 1869]; Phoebe Bradford Diary, Dec. 8, 1832; Martha Jefferis and Anne Jefferis Sheppard letters, passim.

37. Martha Jefferis to Anne Jefferis Sheppard, Aug. 3, 1849; Sarah Ripley [Stearns] Diary, Nov. 12, 1808, Jan. 8, 1811. . . .

38. Martha Jefferis to Edith Jefferis, Mar. 15, 1841; Mary Hallock Foote to Helena, n.d. [1874–75?]; . . .

39. Anne Jefferis Sheppard to Martha Jefferis, Sept. 29, 1841.

40. Frances Parke Lewis to Elizabeth Bordley Gibson, Apr. 29, 1821.

41. [See, e.g.,] Mary Jane Burleigh, Mount Pleasant, S.C., to Emily Howland, Sherwood N.Y., Mar. 27, 1872, Howland Family Papers; . . .

42. [See, e.g.,] Harriet Manigault Diary, Aug. 15, 21, and 23, 1814, Historical Society of Pennsylvania; . . .

43. Mrs. S. S. Dalton, "Autobiography" (Circle Valley, Utah, 1876), pp. 21–22, Bancroft Library, University of California, Berkeley; Sarah Foulke Emlen Diary, Apr. 1809; Louisa G. Van Vleck, Appleton, Wis., to Charlena Van Vleck Anderson, Göttingen, n.d. [1875], . . .

44. Abigail Brackett Lyman, Boston, to Mrs. Abigail Brackett (daughter to mother), n.d. [1797], June 3, 1800; Sarah Alden Ripley wrote weekly to her daughter, Sophy Ripley Fisher, after the latter's

marriage (Sarah Alden Ripley Correspondence, passim); Phoebe Bradford Diary, Feb. 25, 1833, passim, 1832–33; Louisa G. Van Vleck to Charlena Van Vleck Anderson, Dec. 15, 1873, July 4, Aug. 15 and 29, Sept. 19, and Nov. 9, 1875. . . . Daughters evidently frequently slept with their mothers—into adulthood (Harriet Manigault [Wilcox] Diary, Feb. 19, 1815; Eleanor Parke Custis Lewis to Elizabeth Bordley Gibson, Oct. 10, 1832). Daughters also frequently asked mothers to live with them and professed delight when they did so. . . . We did find a few exceptions to this mother-daughter felicity (M. B. Ashew Diary, Nov. 19, 1857, Apr. 10 and May 17, 1858). Sarah Foulke Emlen was at first very hostile to her step-mother (Sarah Foulke Emlen Diary, Aug. 9, 1807), but they later developed a warm supportive relationship.

45. Sarah Alden Ripley to Sophy Thayer, n.d. [1861].

46. [See, e.g.,] Mary Hallock Foote to Helena [Winter 1873] (no. 52); Jossie, Stevens Point, Wis., to Charlena Van Vleck [Anderson], Appleton, Wis., Oct. 24, 1870; Pollie Chandler, Green Bay, Wis., to Charlena Van Vleck [Anderson], Appleton, n.d. [1870]; Eleuthera DuPont to Sophie DuPont, Sept. 5, 1829; . . .

47. . . . Sarah Foulke Emlen Journal, Sarah Ripley Stearns Diary, Mrs. S. S. Dalton, "Autobiography."

48. Maria Revere to her mother [Mrs. Paul Revere], June 13, 1801, Paul Revere Papers, Massachusetts Historical Society. In a letter to Elizabeth Bordley Gibson, Mar. 28, 1847, Eleanor Parke Custis Lewis from Virginia discussed the anxiety her daughter felt when her granddaughters left home to go to boarding school. . . .

49. . . . [See, e.g.,] the letters and diaries of three generations of Manigault women in Philadelphia: Mrs. Gabrielle Manigault, her daughter, Harriet Manigault Wilcox, and granddaughter, Charlotte Wilcox McCall. . . . Mrs. Henry Middleton, Charleston, S.C., to Mrs. Gabrielle Manigault, n.d. [mid 1800s]; Harriet Manigault Diary, vol. 1; Dec. 1, 1813, June 28, 1814; Charlotte Wilcox McCall Diary, vol. 1, 1842, passim. All in Historical Society of Philadelphia.

50. Frances Parke Lewis, Woodlawn, Va., to Elizabeth Bordley Gibson, Philadelphia, Apr. 11, 1821, Lewis Correspondence; Eleuthera DuPont, Philadelphia, to Victorine DuPont Bauday, Brandywine, Dec. 8, 1821, Jan. 31, 1822; Eleuthera DuPont, Brandywine, to Margaretta Lammont [DuPont], Philadelphia, May 1823.

51. [See, e.g.,] Sarah Ripley Stearns Diary, Mar. 9 and 25, 1810; Peggy Emlen to Sally Logan, Mar. and July 4, 1769; . . . Deborah Cope, West Town School, to Rest Cope, Philadelphia, July 9, 1828, Chester County Historical Society, West Chester, Pa.; . . .

52. Anne Jefferis Sheppard to Martha Jefferis, Mar. 17, 1841.

53. [See, e.g.,] Peggy Emlen to Sally Logan, Mar. 1769, Mount Vernon, Va.; . . .

54. Sophie M. DuPont and Eleuthera DuPont, Brandywine, to Victorine DuPont Bauday, Philadelphia, Jan. 25, 1832.

55. Sarah Ripley [Stearns] Diary and Harriet Manigault Diary, passim.

56. [See, e.g.,] Sophie Madeleine DuPont to Eleuthera DuPont, Dec. 1827; Clementina Beach Smith to Sophie Madeleine DuPont, Dec. 26, 1828; Sarah Faulke Emlen Diary, July 21, 1808, Mar. 30, 1809; . . .

57. Jeannie Field, New York, to Sarah Butler Wister, Germantown, Apr. 6, 1862.

58. Elizabeth Bordley Gibson, introductory statement to the Eleanor Parke Custis Lewis Letters [1850s], Historical Society of Pennsylvania.

59. Sarah Foulke [Emlen] Diary, Mar. 30, 1809.

60. Harriet Manigault Diary, May 26, 1815.

61. Sarah Ripley [Stearns] Diary, May 17 and Oct. 2, 1812; Eleanor Parke Custis Lewis to Elizabeth Bordley Gibson, Apr. 23, 1826; . . .

62. Anne Jefferis to Martha Jefferis, Nov. 22 and 27, 1840, Jan. 13 and Mar. 17, 1841; Edith Jefferis, Greenwich, N.J., to Anne Jefferis, Philadelphia, Jan. 31, Feb. 6 and Feb. 1841.

63. Edith Jefferis to Anne Jefferis, Jan. 31, 1841.

64. Eleanor Parke Custis Lewis to Elizabeth Bordley, Nov. 4, 1799. . . .

65. [See, e.g.,] Mary Hallock to Helena DeKay Gilder [1876] (no. 81); n.d. (no. 83), Mar. 3, 1884; Mary Ashew Diary, vol. 2, Sept.–Jan. 1860; . . .

66. [See, e.g.,] Fanny Ferris to Anne Biddle, Nov. 19, 1811; Eleanor Parke Custis Lewis to Elizabeth Bordley Gibson, Nov. 4, 1799, Apr. 27, 1827; . . .

67. Eleanor Parke Custis Lewis to Elizabeth Bordley Gibson, Oct.–Nov. 1820, passim.

68. [See, e.g.,] Emily Howland to Hannah, Sept. 30, 1866; Emily Howland Diary, Feb. 8, 11, and 27, 1880; Phoebe Bradford Diary, Apr. 12 and 13, and Aug. 4, 1833; . . .

69. Mary Black [Couper] to Sophie Madeleine DuPont, Feb. 1827 [Nov. 1, 1834], Nov. 12, 1834, two letters [late Nov. 1834]; Eliza Schlatter to Sophie Madeleine DuPont, Nov. 2, 1834.

70. For a few of the references to death rituals in

the Jefferis papers see: Martha Jefferis to Anne Jefferis Sheppard, Sept. 28, 1843, Aug. 21 and Sept. 25, 1844, Jan. 11, 1846, Summer 1848, passim; . . . This is not to argue that men and women did not mourn together. Yet in many families women aided and comforted women and men, men. . . .

71. Sarah Foulke [Emlen] Diary, Dec. 29, 1808.

72. Eunice Callender, Boston, to Sarah Ripley [Stearns], Greenfield, Mass., May 24, 1803.

73. Katherine Johnstone Brinley [Wharton] Journal, Apr. 26, May 30, and May 29, 1856, Historical Society of Pennsylvania.

74. A series of roughly fourteen letters written by Peggy Emlen to Sally Logan (1768–71) has been preserved in the Wells Morris Collection, Box 1, Historical Society of Pennsylvania (see esp. May 3 and July 4, 1769, Jan. 8, 1768).

75. . . . The eulogistic biographical sketch appeared in Wister and Irwin (n. 12 above). . . .

76. See Sarah Alden Ripley to Mary Emerson, Nov. 19, 1823. Sarah Alden Ripley routinely, and one must assume ritualistically, read Mary Emerson's letters to her infant daughter, Mary. Eleanor Parke Custis Lewis reported doing the same with Elizabeth Bordley Gibson's letters, passim. Eunice Callender, Boston, to Sarah Ripley [Stearns], Oct. 19, 1808.

77. Mary Black Couper to Sophie M. DuPont, Mar. 5, 1832. The Clementina Smith–Sophie DuPont correspondence is in the Sophie DuPont Correspondence. The quotation is from Eliza Schlatter, Mount Holly, N.J., to Sophie DuPont, Brandywine, Aug. 24, 1834. . . .

78. Mary Grew, Providence, R.I., to Isabel Howland, Sherwood, N.Y., Apr. 27, 1892, Howland Correspondence, Sophia Smith Collection, Smith College.

79. Helena Deutsch, *Psychology of Women* (New York: Grune & Stratton, 1944), 1: chaps. 1–3; Clara Thompson, *On Women*, ed. Maurice Green (New York: New American Library, 1971).

JAMES C. MOHR

Abortion in America

If we observe nineteenth-century society through women's eyes, surely no experience was as widely shared as the experience of childbirth. The biological act of maternity created powerful bonds among women as they coped with the experience of childbirth. Until the twentieth century, most births took place at home, where the birthing mother was likely to be surrounded by her mother, sisters, and cousins, a midwife and other experienced women, and her woman friends. The "female world of love and ritual" that Carroll Smith-Rosenberg describes "formed across the childbirth bed," writes historian Judith Walzer Leavitt. "When women had suffered the agonies of watching their friends die, when they had helped a friend recover from a difficult delivery, or when they had participated in a successful birthing they developed a closeness that lasted a lifetime." Leavitt finds that these circles of friendly support made significant choices. "The collectivity of women gathered around the birthing bed made sure that birth attendants were responsive to their wishes. They made decisions about when and if to call physicians to births that midwives were attending; they gave or withheld permission for physicians' procedures; and they created the atmosphere of female support in a room that might have contained both women and men." Leavitt argues that when in the twentieth century birthing moved to hospitals, much of this support evaporated; the reforms in hospital practices demanded by feminists since the 1970s have been an effort to reclaim what had been lost.*

During the centuries before reliable fertility control measures made it possible for women to set limits on reproduction, most married women and many unmarried women had to bear the physical and psychological burden of repeated pregnancies, childbirths, and postpartum recoveries. The cost in terms of time, energy, dreams, and bodies was high. If we observe nineteenth-century society through women's eyes, surely no statistic was as significant as the one that marked the decline in the average number of children borne by each woman. Childbirth was a time of terror.

During the early nineteenth century, a sharp decline took place in the birth rates; the decline was particularly marked in urban areas. No innovations in birth control technology appeared in this period; the decline was the result of choices—later marriage, abstinence from sexual intercourse—to limit the number of times women faced childbirth. In the mid-eighteenth century, the average rural woman could expect to face childbirth eight or nine times; by the early nineteenth century that number had dropped to six and in some urban areas to four. Except for occasional "baby booms," birth rates in the United States have fallen steadily and continue to stabilize in our own time.

When unsuccessful in avoiding pregnancies, many women attempted to abort them. The methods of the times were dangerous, but until the 1840s, the women were rarely censured by the community if fetal movement had not been felt. The vigorous attack on abortion after 1840 may well have been a response to the growing willingness of married women to attempt it. After 1840, an act that had been dealt with in a biological context was given ideological overtones.

What does the debate on abortion policy reveal about public attitudes toward women and their place in the family and in society? How had attitudes changed since Sarah Grosvenor's time? (See pp. 97–113.)

---

*Judith Walzer Leavitt, "Under the Shadow of Maternity: American Women's Responses to Death and Debility Fears in Nineteenth-Century Childbirth," *Feminist Studies* 12(1986):129–54.

ABORTION IN AMERICA 1800–1825

In the absence of any legislation whatsoever on the subject of abortion in the United States in 1800, the legal status of the practice was governed by the traditional British common law as interpreted by the local courts of the new American states. For centuries prior to 1800 the key to the common law's attitude toward abortion had been a phenomenon associated with normal gestation known as quickening. Quickening was the first perception of fetal movement by the pregnant woman herself. Quickening generally occurred near the midpoint of gestation, late in the fourth or early in the fifth month, though it could and still does vary a good deal from one woman to another. The common law did not formally recognize the existence of a fetus in criminal cases until it had quickened. After quickening, the expulsion and destruction of a fetus without due cause was considered a crime, because the fetus itself had manifested some semblance of a separate existence: the ability to move. The crime was qualitatively different from the destruction of a human being, however, and punished less harshly. Before quickening, actions that had the effect of terminating what turned out to have been an early pregnancy were not considered criminal under the common law in effect in England and the United States in 1800.[1]

Both practical and moral arguments lay behind the quickening distinction. Practically, because no reliable tests for pregnancy existed in the early nineteenth century, quickening alone could confirm with absolute certainty that a woman really was pregnant. Prior to quickening, each of the telltale signs of pregnancy could, at least in theory, be explained in alternative ways by physicians of the day. Hence, either a doctor or a woman herself could take actions designed to restore menstrual flow after one or more missed periods on the assumption that something might be unnaturally "blocking" or "obstructing" her normal cycles, and if left untreated the obstruction would wreak real harm upon the woman. Medically, the procedures for removing a blockage were the same as those for inducing an early abortion. Not until the obstruction moved could either a physician or a woman, regardless of their suspicions, be completely certain that it was a "natural"

blockage—a pregnancy—rather than a potentially dangerous situation. Morally, the question of whether or not a fetus was "alive" had been the subject of philosophical and religious debate among honest people for at least 5000 years. The quickening doctrine itself appears to have entered the British common law tradition by way of the tangled disputes of medieval theologians over whether or not an impregnated ovum possessed a soul.[2] The upshot was that American women in 1800 were legally free to attempt to terminate a condition that might turn out to have been a pregnancy until the existence of that pregnancy was incontrovertibly confirmed by the perception of fetal movement.

An ability to suspend one's modern preconceptions and to accept the early nineteenth century on its own terms regarding the distinction between quick and unquick is absolutely crucial to an understanding of the evolution of abortion policy in the United States. However doubtful the notion appears to modern readers, the distinction was virtually universal in America during the early decades of the nineteenth century and accepted in good faith. Perhaps the strongest evidence of the tenacity and universality of the doctrine in the United States was the fact that American courts pointedly sustained the most lenient implications of the quickening doctrine even after the British themselves had abandoned them. . . .

Because women believed themselves to be carrying inert non-beings prior to quickening, a potential for life rather than life itself, and because the common law permitted them to attempt to rid themselves of suspected and unwanted pregnancies up to the point when the potential for life gave a sure sign that it was developing into something actually alive, some American women did practice abortion in the early decades of the nineteenth century. One piece of evidence for this conclusion was the ready access American women had to abortifacient information from 1800 onward. A chief source of such information was the home medical literature of the era.

Home medical manuals characteristically contained abortifacient information in two different sections. One listed in explicit detail a number of procedures that might release "obstructed menses" and the other identified a number of specific things to be avoided in a suspected pregnancy because they were thought to bring on abortion. Americans probably consulted William Buchan's Domestic Medicine more frequently than any other home medical guide during the first decades of the nineteenth century.[3] Buchan suggested several courses of action designed to restore menstrual flow if a period was missed. These included bloodletting, bathing, iron and quinine concoctions, and if those failed, "a teaspoonful of the tincture of black hellebore [a violent purgative] . . . twice a day in a cup of warm water." Four pages later he listed among "the common causes" of abortion "great evacuations [and] vomiting," exactly as would be produced by the treatment he urged for suppressed menses. Later in pregnancy a venturesome, or desperate, woman could try some of the other abortion inducers he ticked off: "violent exercise; raising great weights; reaching too high; jumping, or stepping from an eminence; strokes [strong blows] on the belly; [and] falls."[4] . . .

Like most early abortion material, Buchan's . . . advice harked back to almost primordial or instinctual methods of ending a pregnancy. Bloodletting, for example, was evidently thought to serve as a surrogate period; it was hoped that bleeding from any part of the body might have the same flushing effect upon the womb that menstrual bleeding was known to have. This primitive folk belief lingered long into the nineteenth century, well after bleeding was abandoned as medical therapy in other kinds of cases, and it was common for abortionists as late as the 1870s to pull a tooth as part of their routine.[5] . . .

In addition to home medical guides and health manuals addressed to women, abortions and abortifacient information were also available in the United States from midwives and midwifery texts.[6] . . .

Herbal healers, the so-called Indian doctors, and various other irregular practitioners also helped spread abortifacient information in the United States during the early decades of the nineteenth century. Their surviving pamphlets, of which Peter Smith's 1813 brochure entitled "The Indian Doctor's Dispensary" is an example, contained abortifacient recipes that typically combined the better-known cathartics with native North American ingredients thought to have emmenagogic properties. For "obstructed menses" Smith recommended a concoction he called "Dr.

Reeder's chalybeate." The key ingredients were myrrh and aloes, combined with liquor, sugar, vinegar, iron dust, ivy, and Virginia or seneca snakeroot.[7] A sweet-and-sour cocktail like that may or may not have induced abortion, but must certainly have jolted the system of any woman who tried one. . . .

Finally, and most importantly, America's regular physicians, those who had formal medical training either in the United States or in Great Britain or had been apprenticed under a regular doctor, clearly possessed the physiological knowledge and the surgical techniques necessary to terminate a pregnancy by mechanical means. They knew that dilation of the cervix at virtually any stage of gestation would generally bring on uterine contractions that would in turn lead to the expulsion of the contents of the uterus. They knew that any irritation introduced into the uterus would have the same effect. They knew that rupturing the amniotic sac, especially in the middle and later months of pregnancy, would usually also induce contractions and expulsion, regardless of whether the fetus was viable. Indeed, they were taught in their lecture courses and in their textbooks various procedures much more complex than a simple abortion, such as in utero decapitation and fetal pulverization, processes they were instructed to employ in lieu of the even more horribly dangerous Caesarean section. Like the general public, they knew the drugs and herbs most commonly used as abortifacients and emmenagogues, and also like the general public, they believed such preparations to have been frequently effective.[8] . . .

This placed great pressure on physicians to provide what amounted to abortion services early in pregnancy. An unmarried girl who feared herself pregnant, for example, could approach her family doctor and ask to be treated for menstrual blockage. If he hoped to retain the girl and her family as future patients, the physician would have little choice but to accept the girl's assessment of the situation, even if he suspected otherwise. He realized that every member of his profession would testify to the fact that he had no totally reliable means of distinguishing between an early pregnancy, on the one hand, and the amenorrhea that the girl claimed, on the other. Consequently, he treated for obstruction, which involved exactly the same procedures he would have used to induce an early abortion, and wittingly or unwittingly terminated the pregnancy. Regular physicians were also asked to bring to a safe conclusion abortions that irregulars or women themselves had initiated. . . . And through all of this the physician might bear in mind that he could never be held legally guilty of wrongdoing. No statutes existed anywhere in the United States on the subject of abortion, and the common law . . . considered abortion actionable only after a pregnancy had quickened. No wonder then that Heber C. Kimball, recalling his courtship with a woman he married in 1822, claimed that she had been "taught . . . in our young days, when she got into the family way, to send for a doctor and get rid of the child"; a course that she followed.[9]

In summary, then, the practice of aborting unwanted pregnancies was, if not common, almost certainly not rare in the United States during the first decades of the nineteenth century. A knowledge of various drugs, potions, and techniques was available from home medical guides, from health books for women, from midwives and irregular practitioners, and from trained physicians. Substantial evidence suggests that many American women sought abortions, tried the standard techniques of the day, and no doubt succeeded some proportion of the time in terminating unwanted pregnancies. Moreover, this practice was neither morally nor legally wrong in the eyes of the vast majority of Americans, provided it was accomplished before quickening.

The actual number of abortions in the United States prior to the advent of any statutes regulating its practice simply cannot be known. But an equally significant piece of information about those abortions can be gleaned from the historical record. It concerns the women who were having them. Virtually every observer through the middle of the 1830s believed that an overwhelming percentage of the American women who sought and succeeded in having abortions did so because they feared the social consequences of an illegitimate pregnancy, not because they wanted to limit their fertility per se. The doctor who uncovered the use of snake root as an abortifacient, for example, related that in all of the many instances he heard about "it was taken by women who had indulged in illegitimate love. . . ."[10]

In short, abortion was not thought to be a means of family limitation in the United States, at least on any significant scale, through the first third of the nineteenth century. This was hardly surprising in a largely rural and essentially preindustrial society, whose birthrates were exceeding any ever recorded in a European nation.[11] One could, along with medical student [Thomas] Massie, be less than enthusiastic about such an "unnatural" practice as abortion, yet tolerate it as the "recourse . . . of the victim of passion . . . the child of nature" who was driven by "an unrelenting world" unable to forgive any "deviation from what they have termed virtue."[12] Consequently, Americans in the early nineteenth century could and did look the other way when they encountered abortion. Nothing in their medical knowledge or in the rulings of their courts compelled them to do otherwise, and, as Massie indicated, there was considerable compassion for the women involved. It would be nearly midcentury before the perception of who was having abortions for what reasons would begin to shift in the United States, and that shift would prove to be one of the critical developments in the evolution of American abortion policy.

A final point remains to be made about abortion in the United States during the first decades of the nineteenth century. Most observers appeared to consider it relatively safe, at least by the medical standards of the day, rather than extremely dangerous. . . . This too must have reassured women who decided to risk an abortion before quickening. According to the lecture notes of one of his best students, Walter Channing told his Harvard classes that abortion could be troublesome when produced by external blows, because severe internal hemorrhage would be likely, but that generally considered, "abortion [was] not so dangerous as commonly supposed."[13]

The significance of these opinions lay less in whether or not they were accurate than in the fact that writers on abortion, including physicians, saw no reason to stress the dangers attendant to the process. Far from it. They were skeptical about poisons and purgatives, but appear to have assessed physically induced abortions as medically acceptable risks by the standards of the day, especially if brought on during the period of pregnancy when both popular belief and the public courts condoned them anyhow. Here again was a significant early perception that would later change. That change, like the shift in the perception of who was having abortions for what purposes, would also have an impact on the evolution of American abortion policy. . . .

THE SOCIAL CHARACTER OF ABORTION IN AMERICA 1840–1880

Before 1840 abortion was perceived in the United States primarily as a recourse of the desperate, especially of the young woman in trouble who feared the wrath of an overexacting society. After 1840, however, evidence began to accumulate that the social character of the practice had changed. A high proportion of the women whose abortions contributed to the soaring incidence of that practice in the United States between 1840 and 1880 appeared to be married, native-born, Protestant women, frequently of middle- or upper-class status. The data came from disparate sources, some biased and some not, but in the end proved compelling.

Even before the availability of reliable evidence confirmed that the nation's birthrates were starting to plummet, observers noticed that abortion more and more frequently involved married women rather than single women in trouble. Professor Hugh L. Hodge of the University of Pennsylvania, one of the first physicians in the United States to speak out about abortion in anything approaching a public forum, lectured his introductory obstetrics students in 1839 that abortion was fast becoming a prominent feature of American life. Hodge still considered women trying "to destroy the fruit of illicit pleasure" to be the ones most often seeking abortions, but he alerted his students to the fact that "married women, also, from the fear of labor, from indisposition to have the care, the expense, or the trouble of children, or some other motive" were more and more frequently requesting "that the embryo be destroyed by their medical attendant." Hodge attributed a good deal of this activity to the quickening doctrine, which allowed "women whose moral character is, in other respects, without reproach; mothers who are devoted, with an ardent and self-denying affection, to the children who already constitute[d] their family [to be] perfectly indifferent respecting the foetus in the utero."[14] . . .

Opinion was divided regarding the social status of the women who accounted for the great upsurge of abortion during the middle period of the nineteenth century. While most observers agreed "all classes of society, rich and poor" were involved to some extent, many thought that the middle and upper classes practiced abortion more extensively than the lower classes.[15] The Michigan State Medical Society in 1859 declared that abortion "pervade[d] all ranks" in that state.[16] The Medical Society of Buffalo pointed out that same year "now we have ladies, yes, *educated and refined ladies*" involved as well.[17] On the other hand, court cases revealed at least a sprinkling of lower-class women, servant girls, and the like. . . .

Although the going price for an abortion varied tremendously according to place, time, practitioner, and patient, abortions appear to have been generally quite expensive. Regular physicians testified repeatedly throughout the period that the abortion business was enormously lucrative. Those doctors pledged not to perform abortions bitterly resented men like the Boston botanic indicted for manslaughter in an abortion case in 1851, who posted $8000 bond and returned to his offices, at a time when the average university professor in the United States earned under $2000 per year.[18] . . .

When women turned from regulars to the commercial abortionists, the prices were still not cheap. Itinerants and irregulars generally tried to charge whatever they judged the traffic would bear, which could vary anywhere from $5 to $500. During the 1840s, for example, Madame Restell charged $5 for an initial visit and diagnosis, then negotiated the price of the operation "according to the wealth and liberality of the parties." In a case for which she was indicted in 1846 she asked a young woman about "her beau's circumstances" before quoting a figure, and then tried to get $100 when she found out the man was a reasonably successful manufacturer's representative. The man thought that was too costly, and only after extensive haggling among go-betweens was a $75 fee agreed upon.[19] . . .

Despite the apparent gradual leveling of prices, however, the abortion business remained a profitable commercial venture well into the 1870s. Anthony Comstock, the single-minded leader of a massive anti-obscenity campaign launched in the United States during the 1870s, kept meticulous and extensive records of all of the people he helped arrest while operating as a special agent of the Post Office Department. Between 1872 and 1880 Comstock and his associates aided in the indictment of 55 persons whom Comstock identified as abortionists. The vast majority were very wealthy and posted large bonds with ease. . . .

. . . [A]bortion entered the mainstream of American life during the middle decades of the nineteenth century. While the unmarried and the socially desperate continued to have recourse to it as they had earlier in the century, abortion also became highly visible, much more frequently practiced, and quite common as a means of family limitation among white, Protestant, native-born wives of middle- and upper-class standing. These dramatic changes, in turn, evoked sharp comment from two ideologically opposed groups in American society, each of which either directly or indirectly blamed the other for the shift in abortion patterns. On one side of the debate were the antifeminists, led by regular physicians, and on the other side were the nation's feminists. Both groups agreed that abortion had become a large-scale and socially significant phenomenon in American life, but they disagreed over the reasons why.

Before examining the two chief explanations put forward by contemporaries for the striking shifts in the incidence and the character of abortion in the United States after 1840, two observations may be worth making. First, it is never easy to understand why people do what they do even in the most straightforward of situations; it is nearly impossible to know with certainty the different reasons, rational and irrational, why people in the past might have taken such a psychologically loaded action as the termination of a suspected pregnancy. Second, most participants on both sides of the contemporary debate over why so many American women began to practice abortion after 1840 actually devoted most of their attention to the question of why American women wanted to limit their fertility. This confirmed that abortion was important between 1840 and 1880 primarily as a means of family limitation, but such discussions offer only marginal help in understanding why so many American women turned to abortion itself as a means toward that end.

Cultural anthropologists argue that abortion has been practiced widely and frequently in preindustrial societies at least in part because "it is a woman's method [of limiting fertility] and can be practiced without the man's knowledge."[20] This implies a sort of women's conspiracy to limit population, which would be difficult to demonstrate in the context of nineteenth-century America. Nonetheless, there is some evidence, though it must be considered carefully, to suggest that an American variant of this proposition may have been at least one of the reasons why abortion became such a common form of family limitation in the United States during the period. A number of physicians, as will become evident, certainly believed that one of the keys to the upsurge of abortion was the fact that it was a uniquely female practice, which men could neither control nor prevent. . . .

Earlier in the century observers had alleged that the tract literature and lectures of the women's rights movement advocated family planning and disseminated abortifacient information.[21] In 1859 Harvard professor Walter Channing reported the opinion that "women for whom this office of foeticide, unborn-child-killing, is committed, are strongminded," and no later writer ever accused them of being weak-minded.[22] . . .

The most common variant of the view that abortion was a manifestation of the women's rights movement hinged upon the word "fashion." Over and over men claimed that women who aborted did so because they cared more about scratching for a better perch in society than they did about raising children. They dared not waste time on the latter lest they fall behind in the former. Women, in short, were accused of being aggressively self-indulgent. Some women, for example, had "the effrontery to say boldly, that they have neither the time nor inclination to nurse babies"; others exhibited "self-indulgence in most disgusting forms"; and many of the women practicing abortion were described as more interested in "selfish and personal ends" or "fast living" than in the maternity for which God had supposedly created them.[23] . . . For this reason, some doctors urged that feticide be made a legal ground for divorce.[24] A substantial number of writers between 1840 and 1880, in other words, were willing to portray women who had abortions as domestic subversives. . . .

Notwithstanding the possibility that recourse to abortion sometimes reflected the rising consciousness of the women who had them, and notwithstanding the fact that some males, especially regular physicians, were distinctly uneasy about the practice because of what its ultimate effects upon the social position of women might be, the relationship between abortion and feminism in the nineteenth century nevertheless remained indirect and ironical. This becomes evident when the arguments of the feminists themselves are analyzed. One of the most forceful early statements of what subsequently became the feminist position on abortion was made in the 1850s in a volume entitled *The Unwelcome Child*.[25] The author, Henry C. Wright, asserted that women alone had the right to say when they would become pregnant and blamed the tremendous outburst of abortion in America on selfishly sensual husbands. Wright's volume was more interesting than other similar tracts, however, because he published a large number of letters from women detailing the circumstances under which they had sought abortions.

One of Wright's letters was from a woman who had her first abortion in 1841, because her one-year-old firstborn was sick and her husband was earning almost nothing. She "consulted a lady friend, and by her persuasion and assistance, killed" the fetus she was carrying. When she found herself pregnant again shortly thereafter she "consulted a physician. . . . He was ready with his logic, his medicines and instruments, and told me how to destroy it. After experimenting on myself three months, I was successful. I killed my child about five months after conception." She steeled herself to go full term with her next pregnancy and to "endure" an addition to her impoverished and unhappy household. When pregnant again she "employed a doctor, to kill my child, and in the destruction of it . . . ended my power to be a mother." The woman's point throughout, however, was that abortion "was most repulsive" to her and her recourse to it "rendered [her] an object of loathing to [her]self." Abortion was not a purposeful female conspiracy, but an undesirable necessity forced by thoughtless men. As this woman put it: "I was the veriest slave alive."[26] . . .

The attitudes expressed by Wright's correspondents in the 1840s and 1850s became the basis of the official position of American feminists toward abortion after the Civil War. As Elizabeth Cady Stanton phrased it, the practice was one more result of "the degradation of woman" in the nineteenth century, not of woman's rising consciousness or expanding opportunities outside the home.[27] . . . The remedy to the problem of abortion in the United States, in their view, was not legalized abortion open to all but *"the education and enfranchisement of women"* which would make abortion unnecessary in a future world of egalitarian respect and sexual discretion.[28] In short, most feminists, though they agreed completely with other observers that abortion was endemic in America by midcentury, did not blame the increase on the rising ambitions of women but asserted with Matilda E. J. Gage "that this crime of 'child murder,' 'abortion,' 'infanticide,' lies at the door of the male sex."[29] The *Woman's Advocate* of Dayton, Ohio, put it even more forcefully in 1869: "Till men learn to check their sensualism, and leave their wives free to choose their periods of maternity, let us hear no more invectives against women for the destruction of prospective unwelcome children, whose dispositions, made miserable by unhappy ante-natal conditions, would only make their lives a curse to themselves and others."[30] . . .

Despite the blame and recrimination evoked by the great upsurge of abortion in the United States in the nineteenth century, some of which was directed at women and some at men, it appears likely that most decisions to use abortion probably involved couples conferring together, not just men imposing their wills or women acting unilaterally, and that abortion was the result of diffuse pressures, not merely the rising consciousness of women or the tyrannical aggressions of men. American men and women wanted to express their sexuality and mutual affections, on the one hand, and to limit their fertility, on the other. Abortion was neither desirable nor undesirable in itself, but rather one of the few available means of reconciling and realizing those two higher priorities. And it seems likely that the man and woman agreed to both of those higher priorities in most instances, thus somewhat mooting in advance the question of which one was more responsible for the decisions that made abortion a common phenomenon in mid-nineteenth-century America.[31]

Court records provide one source of evidence for the mutuality of most abortion decisions. Almost every nineteenth-century abortion case that was written up, whether in the popular press, in medical journals, or in the official proceedings of state supreme courts, involved the agreement of both the man and the woman. There is no record of any man ever having sued any woman for aborting his child. . . .

Perhaps the best evidence for the likely mutuality of most abortion decisions is contained in the diary that Lester Frank Ward, who later became one of America's most famous sociologists, kept as a newlywed in the 1860s. Though Ward was unique in writing down the intimate decisions that he and his wife had to make, the couple seemed otherwise typical young Americans, almost as Tocqueville might have described them, anxious for further education and ambitious to get ahead quickly. Both Ward and his wife understood that a child would overburden their limited resources and reduce the probability of ever realizing either their individual goals of self-improvement or their mutual goals as a couple. They avoided pregnancy in pre-marital intercourse, then continued to avoid it after their marriage in August 1862. Not until early in 1864 did Lizzie Ward become pregnant. In March, without consulting her husband, she obtained "an effective remedy" from a local woman, which made her very sick for two days but helped her to terminate her pregnancy. She probably took this action after missing three or four periods; it was still early enough in gestation that her husband did not realize she was pregnant but late enough that lactation had begun. Ward noted in his diary that "the proof" she had been pregnant was "the milk" that appeared after the abortion.[32]

Anti-feminists might have portrayed Lizzie Ward's action as diabolical, a betrayal of duty. Feminists might have viewed it as the only recourse open to a female who wanted both to further her own education and to remain on good terms with an ambitious spouse who would certainly have sacrificed his wife's goals to child-rearing, while he pursued his own. But the decision was really the result of a pre-existing consensus between the two of them. Though Ward had not been party to the process in a legal or direct sense, which may go some distance toward confirming the role of abortion as a more uniquely female method of family limitation than contraception, he was clearly delighted that his wife was "out of danger" and would not be having a child. After this brush with family responsibility, the Wards tried a number of new methods of contraception, which they presumably hoped would be more effective than whatever they had been using to avoid pregnancy before Lizzie had to resort to abortion. These included both "pills" and "instruments." Not until the summer of 1865, after Ward had obtained a decent job in Washington, did the couple have a baby.[33]

Abortion had been for the Wards what it apparently also was for many other American couples: an acceptable means toward a mutually desirable end, one of the only ways they had to allow themselves both to express their sexuality and affection toward each other with some degree of frequency and to postpone family responsibilities until they thought they were better prepared to raise children. The line of acceptability for most Americans trying to reconcile these twin priorities ran just about where Lizzie Ward had drawn it. Infanticide, the destruction of a baby after its birth, was clearly unacceptable, and so was abortion after quickening, though that was a much grayer area than infanticide. But abortion before quickening, like contraception itself, was an appropriate and legally permissible method of avoiding unwanted children. And it had one great advantage, as the Wards learned, over contraception: it worked. As more and more women began to practice abortion, however, and as the practice changed from being invisible to being visible, from being quantitatively insignificant to being a systematic practice that terminated a substantial number of pregnancies after 1840, and from being almost entirely a recourse of the desperate and the socially marginal to being a commonly employed procedure among the middle and upper classes of American society, state legislators decided to reassess their policies toward the practice. Between 1840 and 1860 law-makers in several states began to respond to the increase of abortion in American life.

NOTES

1. The quickening doctrine went back to the thirteenth century in England. . . . On quickening in

the common law see Cyril C. Means, Jr., "The Law of New York concerning Abortion and the Status of the Foetus, 1664–1968: A Case of Cessation of Constitutionality," *New York Law Forum* XIV, no. 3 (Fall 1968): 419–426.

2. Ibid., pp. 411–19, and John T. Noonan, Jr., "An Almost Absolute Value in History," in John T. Noonan, Jr., ed., *The Morality of Abortion* (Cambridge, Mass., 1970), pp. 1–59. . . .

3. . . . Buchan's volume was published in Philadelphia as early as 1782, where it went through many editions. . . . This remarkably successful book continued to be reprinted in America through 1850.

4. Buchan, *Domestic Medicine,* pp. 400, 403–4.

5. See, for example, Frederick Hollick, *Diseases of Women, Their Causes and Cure Familiarly Explained: With Practical Hints for Their Prevention, and for the Preservation of Female Health: For Every Female's Private Use* (New York, 1849), p. 150. . . .

6. . . . [See] George Ellington, *The Women of New York, or the Under-World of the Great City* (New York, 1869), pp. 399–400.

7. Peter Smith, "The Indian Doctor's Dispensary, Being Father Peter Smith's Advice Respecting Diseases and Their Cure; Consisting of Prescriptions for Many Complaints: And a Description of Medicines, Simple and Compound, Showing Their Virtues and How to Apply Them," [1813] reproduced in J. U. Lloyd, ed., *Bulletin of the Lloyd Library of Botany, Pharmacy and Materia Medica* (1901), Bull. #2, Reproduction Series #2, pp. 46–47.

8. John Burns, *Observations on Abortion: Containing an Account of the Manner in Which It Takes Place, the Causes Which Produce It, and the Method of Preventing or Treating It* (Troy, N.Y., 1808), pp. 73–81. . . .

9. Heber C. Kimball in the *Journal of Discourses,* 26 vols. (Liverpool, 1857), V:91–92.

10. Thomas Massie, "An Experimental Inquiry into the Properties of the Polygala Senega," in Charles Caldwell, ed., *Medical Theses, . . .* (Philadelphia, 1806), p. 203.

11. . . . William Petersen's widely used *Population* (New York, 3rd ed., 1975), p. 15, labels [the U.S. population from 1800 to 1830 as] the "underdeveloped" type and identifies its characteristics as a mixed economy, high fertility rates, falling mortality rates, and very high rates of population growth.

12. Massie, "Polygala Senega," p. 204.

13. John G. Metcalf, student notebooks written while attending Dr. Walter Channing's lectures of midwifery at Harvard Medical School, 1825–1826 (Countway Library, Harvard Medical School), entry for Dec. 27, 1825. . . .

14. Hugh L. Hodge in Francis Wharton and Moreton Stillé, *Treatise on Medical Jurisprudence* (Philadelphia, 1855), p. 270.

15. "Report on Criminal Abortion," *Transactions of the American Medical Association* XII (1859):75.

16. E. P. Christian, "Report to the State Medical Society on Criminal Abortions," *Peninsular & Independent Medical Journal* II:135.

17. "Criminal Abortions," *Buffalo Medical Journal and Monthly Review* XIV (1859):249.

18. *Boston Medical and Surgical Journal* XLIV, no. 14 (May 7, 1851):288. . . . Worthington Hooker, *Physician and Patient . . .* (New York, 1849), passim, and especially pp. 405–8. The estimate on income is from Colin B. Burke, "The Quiet Influence" (Ph.D. diss, Washington University of St. Louis, 1973):69, Table 2.19.

19. A Physician of New-York, *Trial of Madame Restell, For Producing Abortion on the Person of Maria Bodine, . . .* (New York, 1847), pp. 3–4, 10.

20. Kingsley Davis and Judith Blake, "Social Structure and Fertility: An Analytical Framework," *Economic Development and Cultural Change* IV, no. 3 (April 1956):230.

21. Hooker, *Physician and Patient,* p. 93; James Reed, *From Private Vice to Public Virtue: The Birth Control Movement and American Society since 1830* (New York, 1978), chaps. 1–5.

22. Walter Channing, "Effects of Criminal Abortion," *Boston Medical and Surgical Journal* LX (Mar. 17, 1859):135.

23. E. M. Buckingham, "Criminal Abortion," *Cincinnati Lancet & Observer* X (Mar. 1867):141; Channing, "Effects of Criminal Abortion," p. 135; J. C. Stone, "Report on the Subject of Criminal Abortion," *Transactions of the Iowa State Medical Society* I (1867):29; J. Miller, "Criminal Abortion," *The Kansas City Medical Record* I (Aug. 1884):296.

24. [See] H. Gibbons, Sr., "On Feticide," *Pacific Medical and Surgical Journal* (San Francisco) XXI, no. 3 (Aug. 1879):97–111; . . .

25. Henry C. Wright, *The Unwelcome Child; or, the Crime of an Undesigned and Undesired Maternity* (Boston, 1860). The volume was copyrighted in 1858.

26. Ibid., pp. 65–69.

27. E[lizabeth] C[ady] S[tanton], "Infanticide and Prostitution," *Revolution* I, no. 5 (Feb. 5, 1868):65.

28. Ibid. For the same point reiterated see "Child Murder," in ibid. I, no. 10 (Mar. 12, 1868):146–47. . . .

29. Ibid. I, no. 14 (Apr. 9, 1868):215–16.

30. E. V. B., "Restellism, and the N.Y. Medical Gazette," *Woman's Advocate* (Dayton, Ohio) I, no. 20 (Apr. 8, 1869):16. . . .

31. Carl N. Degler is one of those who have argued persuasively that nineteenth-century American women were very much aware of their own sexuality and desirous, morality books notwithstanding, of expressing it: "What Ought To Be and What Was: Women's Sexuality in the Nineteenth Century," *American Historical Review* LXXIX, no. 5 (Dec. 1974):1467–90.

32. Lester Ward, *Young Ward's Diary,* Bernhard J. Stern, ed. (New York, 1935), p. 140.

33. Ibid., pp. 150, 152–53, 174.

DOCUMENTS: Claiming Rights I

> *Sarah and Angelina Grimké: The Connection between Religious Faith, Abolition, and Women's Rights*

Sarah and Angelina Grimké were the first, and it seems likely the only, women of a slaveholding family to speak and write publicly as abolitionists. They were the first women agents of the American Anti-Slavery Society to tour widely and to speak to audiences of men and women. They were the first women who, from within the abolitionist movement, defended their rights *as women* to free speech. They were sustained in their work by a deep religious devotion, and their writings are examples of the spirit in which many women's rights advocates developed a wide-ranging critique of the relationship between the state, churches, and families.

The Grimké sisters grew up in Charleston, South Carolina. Their father was a distinguished legislator and judge; although he gave his daughters a traditional female education (lacking Greek, Latin, and philosophy), when he trained his sons for the law he included his daughters in the exercises. Both young women were sensitive to the injustices of slavery; as a young woman Sarah broke the law against teaching slaves to read and Angelina held prayer meetings for the family's slaves. When she was twenty-four years old Sarah accompanied her father to Philadelphia, where he sought medical treatment; after his death she returned there in 1821 to live among Quakers, who impressed her by their piety, simplicity, and refusal to hold slaves. In 1829 Angelina joined her; both joined a Quaker meeting. Sarah committed herself to boycott products made in slavery; Angelina joined the Philadelphia Female Antislavery Society. When reformers faced violence from proslavery mobs in the summer of 1835, William Lloyd Garrison wrote strong editorials in *The Liberator* denouncing what he called a "reign of terror." Angelina Grimké responded with a letter complimenting him on his fortitude: "The ground on which you stand is holy ground," she wrote, "never—never surrender it." Garrison surprised her by printing her letter; thus encouraged, Angelina went on to write *An Appeal to the Christian Women of the South*. The pamphlet sold widely in the North and made her reputation, but it was burned in Charleston.

When the American Anti-Slavery Society organized a group of "Agents" to travel and speak on slavery, Angelina and Sarah Grimké were among them. They began in late 1836, speaking to women in private parlors in New York City; by the turn of the year no private room was big enough and they held their sessions in a Baptist church. They involved themselves in founding women's antislavery societies and organizing women's antislavery petitions to Congress; they published their speeches as pamphlets. In mid-1837 they moved on to Boston, where an intense debate among factions of abolitionists was already under way. Sarah wrote a series of essays that appeared first in

From *The Public Years of Sarah and Angelina Grimké: Selected Writings, 1835–1839,* edited by Larry Ceplair. Copyright © 1989 by Columbia University Press. Reprinted with permission of the publisher.

newspapers and then as a pamphlet, *Letters on the Equality of the Sexes and the Condition of Women.*

In the summer of 1837, the Congregational ministers of Massachusetts published a "Pastoral Letter" attacking them as unwomanly. In the past they had offered their criticism of slavery in the context of religious faith; now they claimed that as moral individuals, women had as much right to take political positions as men. Though even some of their allies—including Theodore Dwight Weld, whom Angelina would soon marry—sought to dissuade them, they were forthright in their response. The term "feminist" had not yet been invented—it would be devised in the 1910s—but the ingredients of the concept were already present in the ideas of the Grimké sisters.*

ANGELINA GRIMKÉ, APPEAL TO THE CHRISTIAN WOMEN OF THE SOUTH (1836)

. . . Sisters in Christ I feel an interest in *you,* and often has the secret prayer arisen on your behalf, Lord "open thou their eyes that they may see wondrous things out of thy Law"—It is then, because I *do feel* and *do pray* for you, that I thus address you upon a subject about which of all others, perhaps you would rather not hear any thing; but, "would to God ye could bear with me a little in my folly, and indeed bear with me, for I am jealous over you with godly jealousy." Be not afraid then to read my appeal; it is *not* written in the heat of passion or prejudice, but in that solemn calmness which is the result of conviction and duty. It is true, I am going to tell you unwelcome truths, but I mean to speak those *truths in love,* and remember Solomon says, "faithful are the *wounds* of a friend." I do not believe the time has yet come when *Christian women* "will not endure sound doctrine," even on the subject of slavery, if it is spoken to them in tenderness and love, therefore I now address you. . . .

We must come back to the good old doctrine of our forefathers who declared to the world, "this self evident truth that *all* men are created equal, and that they have certain *inalienable* rights among which are life, *liberty,* and the pursuit of happiness." It is even a greater absurdity to suppose a man can be legally born a slave under *our free Republican* Government, than under the petty despotisms of barbarian Africa. If then, we have no right to enslave an African, surely we can have none to enslave an American; if it is a self evident truth that *all* men, every where and of every color are born equal, and have an *inalienable right to liberty,* then it is equally true that *no* man can be born a slave, and no man can ever *rightfully* be reduced to *involuntary* bondage and held as a slave, however fair may be the claim of his master or mistress through will and title-deeds. . . .

But perhaps you will be ready to query, why appeal to *women* on this subject? *We* do not make the laws which perpetuate slavery. No legislative power is vested in *us; we* can do nothing to overthrow the system, even if we wished to do so. To this I reply, I know you do not make the laws, but I also know that *you are the wives and mothers, the sisters and daughters of those who do;* and if you really suppose *you* can do nothing to overthrow slavery, you are greatly mistaken. You can do much in every way: four things I will name. Ist. You can read on this subject. 2d. You can pray over this subject. 3d. You can speak on this subject. 4th. You can *act* on this subject. I have not placed reading before praying because I regard it more important, but because, in order to pray aright, we must understand what we are praying for; it is only then we can "pray with the understanding and the spirit also."

1.   Read then on the subject of slavery. Search the Scriptures daily, whether the things I have told you are true. Other books and papers might be a great help to you in this investigation, but they are not necessary. . . .

2. Pray over this subject. When you have entered into your closets, and shut to the doors, then pray to your father, who seeth in

*See Gerda Lerner, *The Grimké Sisters from South Carolina: Rebels Against Slavery* (Boston, 1967), and *The Public Years of Sarah and Angelina Grimké: Selected Writings 1835–1839,* ed. Larry Ceplair (New York, 1989). The selections that follow are taken from the Ceplair edition, pp. 37–38, 54–56, 220–23, 268–69, 211, 216.

secret, that he would open your eyes to see whether slavery is *sinful*, and if it is, that he would enable you to bear a faithful, open and unshrinking testimony against it, and to do whatsoever your hands find to do . . .

3. Speak on this subject. It is through the tongue, the pen, and the press, that truth is principally propagated. Speak then to your relatives, your friends, your acquaintances on the subject of slavery; be not afraid if you are conscientiously convinced it is *sinful*, to say so openly, but calmly, and to let your sentiments be known. If you are served by the slaves of others, try to ameliorate their condition as much as possible; never aggravate their faults, and thus add fuel to the fire of anger already kindled in a master and mistress's bosom. . . .

4. Act on this subject. Some of you *own* slaves yourselves. If you believe slavery is *Sinful*, set them at liberty, "undo the heavy burdens and let the oppressed go free." If they wish to remain with you, pay them wages,if not let them leave you. Should they remain teach them, and have them taught the common branches of an English education; they have minds and those minds, *ought to be improved*. So precious a talent as intellect, never was given to be wrapt in a napkin and buried in the earth. It is the *duty* of all, as far as they can, to improve their own mental faculties, because we are commanded to love God with *all our minds*, as well as with all our hearts, and we commit a great sin, if we *forbid or prevent* that cultivation of the mind in others, which would enable them to perform this duty. Teach your servants then to read &c, and encourage them to believe it is their *duty* to learn, if it were only that they might read the Bible.

But some of you will say, we can neither free our slaves nor teach them to read, for the laws of our state forbid it. Be not surprised when I say such wicked laws *ought to be no barrier* in the way of your duty, and I appeal to the Bible to prove this position. What was the conduct of Shiphrah and Puah, when the king of Egypt issued his cruel mandate, with regard to the Hebrew children? "*They* feared *God*, and did *not* as the King of Egypt commanded them, but saved the men children alive." Did these *women* do right in disobeying that monarch? "*Therefore* (says the sacred text,) *God dealt well* with them, and made them houses."

SARAH M. GRIMKÉ, LETTERS ON THE EQUALITY OF THE SEXES AND THE CONDITION OF WOMEN (1837)

LETTER VIII: "ON THE CONDITION OF WOMEN IN THE UNITED STATES"

During the early part of my life, my lot was cast among the butterflies of the *fashionable* world; and of this class of women, I am constrained to say, both from experience and observation, that their education is miserably deficient; that they are taught to regard marriage as the one thing needful, the only avenue to distinction; hence to attract the notice and win the attentions of men, by their external charms, is the chief business of fashionable girls. They seldom think that men will be allured by intellectual acquirements, because they find, that where any mental superiority exists, a woman is generally shunned and regarded as step-ping out of her "appropriate sphere," which, in their view, is to dress, to dance, to set out to the best possible advantage her person, to read the novels which inundate the press, and which do more to destroy her character as a rational creature, than any thing else. . . .

There is another and much more numerous class in this country, who are withdrawn by education or circumstances from the circle of fashionable amusements, but who are brought up with the dangerous and absurd idea, that *marriage* is a kind of preferment; and that to be able to keep their husband's house, and render his situation comfortable, is the end of her being. Much that she does and says and thinks is done in reference to this situation; and to be married is too often held up to the view of girls as the sine qua non of human happiness and human existence. . . . I do long to see the time, when it will no longer be necessary for women to expend so many precious hours in furnishing "a well spread table," but that their husbands will forego some of the accustomed indulgences in this way, and encourage their wives to devote some portion of their time to mental cultivation, even at the expense of having to dine sometimes on baked potatoes, or bread and butter. . . .

There is another way in which the general opinion, that women are inferior to men, is manifested, that bears with tremendous effect on the laboring class, and indeed on almost all who are obliged to earn a subsistence, whether it be by mental or physical exertion—I allude to the disproportionate value set on the time and labor of men and of women. A man who is engaged in teaching, can always, I believe, command a higher price for tuition than a woman—even when he teaches the same branches, and is not in any respect superior to the woman. This I know is the case in boarding and other schools with which I have been acquainted, and it is so in every occupation in which the sexes engaged indiscriminately. As for example, in tailoring, a man has twice, or three times as much for making a waistcoat or pantaloons as a woman, although the work done by each may be equally good. In those employments which are peculiar to women, their time is estimated at only half the value of that of men. A woman who goes out to wash, works as hard in proportion as a wood sawyer, or a coal heaver, but she is not generally able to make more than half as much by a day's work. . . .

There is another class of women in this country, to whom I cannot refer, without feelings of the deepest shame and sorrow. I allude to our female slaves. Our southern cities are whelmed beneath a tide of pollution; the virtue of female slaves is wholly at the mercy of irresponsible tyrants, and women are bought and sold in our slave markets, to gratify the brutal lust of those who bear the name of Christians. In our slave States, if amid all her degradation and ignorance, a women desires to preserve her virtue unsullied, she is either bribed or whipped into compliance, or if she dares resist her seducer, her life by the laws of some of the slave States may be, and has actually been sacrificed to the fury of disappointed passion. Where such laws do not exist, the power which is necessarily vested in the master over his property, leaves the defenceless slave entiely at his mercy, and the sufferings of some females on this account, both physical and mental, are intense.

Letter XV: Man Equally Guilty with Woman in the Fall

. . . In contemplating the great moral reformations of the day, and the part which they are bound to take in them, instead of puzzling themselves with the harassing, because unnecessary inquiry, how far they may go without overstepping the bounds of propriety, which separate male and female duties, they will only inquire, "Lord, what wilt thou have us do?" They will be enabled to see the simple truth, that God has made no distinction between men and women as moral beings; that the distinction now so much insisted upon between male and female virtues is as absurd as it is unscriptural, and has been the fruitful source of much mischief—granting to man a license for the exhibition of brute force and conflict on the battle field; for sternness, selfishness, and the exercise of irresponsible power in the circle of home—and to woman a permit to rest on an arm of flesh, and to regard modesty and delicacy, and all the kindred virtues, as peculiarly appropriate to her. Now to me it is perfectly clear, that WHATSOEVER IT IS MORALLY RIGHT FOR A MAN TO DO, IT IS MORALLY RIGHT FOR A WOMAN TO DO; and that confusion must exist in the moral world, until woman takes her stand on the same platform with man, and feels that she is clothed by her Maker with the *same rights,* and, of course, that upon her devolve the *same duties.*

PASTORAL LETTER: THE GENERAL ASSOCIATION OF MASSACHUSETTS TO THE CHURCHES UNDER THEIR CARE

III.—We invite your attention to the dangers which at present seem to threaten the female character with wide spread and permanent injury.

The appropriate duties and influence of women are clearly stated in the New Testament. Those duties and that influence are unobtrusive and private, but the sources of mighty power. When the mild, dependant [sic], softening influence of woman upon the sternness of man's opinion is fully exercised, society feels the effects of it in a thousand forms. The power of woman is in her dependence, flowing from the consciousness of that weakness which God has given her for her protection, and which keeps her in those departments of life that form the character of individuals and of the nation. There are social influences which females use in promoting piety and the great objects of Christian benevolence which we cannot too highly commend. We appreciate the unostentatious prayers and efforts of woman in advancing the cause of religion at home and abroad; in Sabbath schools; in leading religious inquirers to the pastors for instruction; and in all such associated effort as becomes the modesty of her sex; and earnestly hope that she may abound more and more in these labors of piety and love.

But when she assumes the place and tone of man as a public reformer, our care and protection of her seem unnecessary; we put ourselves in self-defence against her; she yields the power which God has given her for protection, and her character becomes unnatural. If the vine, whose strength and beauty is to lean upon the trellis and half conceal its clusters, thinks to assume the independence and the overshading nature of the elm, it will not only cease to bear fruit, but fall in shame and dishonor into the dust. We cannot, therefore, but regret the mistaken conduct of those who encourage females to bear an obtrusive and ostentatious part in measures of reform, and countenance any of that sex who so far forget themselves as to itinerate in the character of public lecturers and teachers. We especially deplore the intimate acquaintance and promiscuous conversation of females with regard to things "which ought not to be named"; by which that modesty and delicacy which is the charm of domestic life, and which constitutes the true influence of woman in society is consumed, and the way opened, as we apprehend, for degeneracy and ruin . . .

SARAH M. GRIMKÉ, RESPONSE TO "THE PASTORAL LETTER . . ."

The motto of woman, when she is engaged in the great work of public reformation should be,—"The Lord is my light and my salvation; whom shall I fear? The Lord is the strength of my life; of whom shall I be afraid?" She must feel, if she feels rightly, that she is fulfilling one of the important duties laid upon her as an accountable being, and that her character, instead of being "unnatural," is in exact accordance with the will of Him to whom, and to no other, she is responsible for the talents and the gifts confided to her. As to the pretty simile, introduced into the "Pastoral Letter," "If the vine whose strength and beauty is to lean upon the trellis work, and half conceal its clusters, thinks to assume the independence and the overshadowing nature of the elm," & c. I shall only remark that it might well suit the poet's fancy, who sings of sparkling eyes and coral lips, and knights in armor clad; but it seems to me utterly inconsistent with the dignity of a Christian body, to endeavor to draw such an anti-scriptural distinction between men and women. Ah! how many of my sex feel in the dominion, thus unrighteously exercised over them, under the gentle appellation of *protection,* that what they have leaned upon has proved a broken reed at best, and oft a spear.

Thine in the bonds of womanhood,

Sarah M. Grimké.

Keziah Kendall, "What I have suffered, I cannot tell you"

We know nothing more about "Keziah Kendall" than what she revealed in this letter, which historians Dianne Avery and Alfred S. Konefsky discovered among the papers of Simon Greenleaf, a prominent Harvard law professor. It has not been possible to locate the author in the usual places—tax lists, land records, church lists. Keziah and her sisters carry the names of Job's daughters; whether the names are real or fictional, the writer assumed that her readers would remember the biblical reference: ". . . in all the land there were no women so fair as Job's daughters; and their father gave them inheritance among their brothers."

Kendall had been dismayed by what she heard at a public lycium lecture on women's rights given by Greenleaf in early 1839. At a time when the legal disabilities of inherited common law were increasingly being questioned—in Massachusetts, the abolitionists Sarah and Angelina Grimke had only recently delivered a forthright series of lectures on the rights of women—Greenleaf devoted his lecture to the claim that American women were well protected by American law as it stood. He argued that excluding women from politics saved society from "uproar" and impropriety, and that constraints on married women's use of their property was merely a technicality because in a happy marriage all property became part of "a common fund . . . it can make but little difference . . . by whose name it is called." And he insisted that except for "restriction in *political* matters" there were no significant "distinctions between the legal rights of unmarried women, and of men."

Keziah Kendall was unpersuaded, and wrote to demand that Greenleaf offer another lecture, acknowledging the "legal wrongs" of women. What are Kendall's objections to the law as she experienced it? What connections does she draw between paying taxes, voting, and officeholding? Why does she blame Massachusetts property law for her fiancé's death? Why is she worried about her sister's forthcoming marriage?

Keziah Kendall to Simon Greenleaf [1839?] I take the liberty to write to you on the subject of the Lyceum lecture you delivered last Feb. but as you are not acquainted with me I think I will introduce myself. My name is Kezia Kendall. I live not many miles from Cambridge, on a farm with two sisters, one older, one younger than myself. I am thirty two. Our parents and only brother are dead—we have a good estate—comfortable house—nice barn, garden, orchard & c and money in the bank besides. Jemima is a very good manager in the house, keeps everything comfortable—sees that the milk is nicely prepared for market—looks after everything herself, and rises before day, winter and summer,—but she never had any head for figures, and always expects me to keep all accounts, and attend to all business concerns. Keranhappuck, (who is called Kerry) is quite young, only nineteen, and as she was

---

Letter from Keziah Kendall to Simon Greenleaf (undated). Box 3, Folder 10, Simon Greenleaf Papers, Harvard Law School Library. Excerpted from Diane Avery and Alfred S. Konefsky. "The Daughters of Job: Property Rights and Women's Lives in Mid-Nineteenth-Century Massachusetts," *Law and History Review*, X (Fall 1992): 323–56. Notes have been renumbered and edited.

a little girl when mother died, we've always petted her, and let her do as she pleased, and now she's courted. Under these circumstances the whole responsibility of our property, not less than twenty five thousand dollars rests upon me. I am not over fond of money, but I have worked hard ever since I was a little girl, and tried to do all in my power to help earn, and help save, and it would be strange if I did not think more of it than those who never earned anything, and never saved anything they could get to spend, and you know Sir, there are many such girls nowadays. Well— our milkman brought word when he came from market that you were a going to lecture on the legal rights of women, and so I thought I would go and learn. Now I hope you wont think me bold when I say, I did not like that lecture much. I dont speak of the manner, it was pretty spoken enough, but there was nothing in it but what every body knows. We all know about a widow's thirds,[1] and we all know that a man must maintain his wife, and we all know that he must pay her debts, if she has any—but I never heard of a yankee woman marrying in debt. What I wanted to know, was good reasons for some of those laws that I cant account for. I do hope if you are ever to lecture at the Lyceum again, that you will give us some. I must tell my story to make you understand what I mean. One Lyceum lecture that I heard in C. stated that the Americans went to war with the British, because they were taxed without being represented in Parliament. Now we are taxed every year to the full amount of every dollar we possess—town, county, state taxes—taxes for land, for movables, for money and all. Now I dont want to go representative or any thing else, any more than I do to be a "constable or a sheriff," but I have no voice about public improvements, and I dont see the justice of being taxed any more than the "revolutionary heroes" did. You mention that woman here, are not treated like heathen and Indian women—we know that—nor do I think we are treated as Christian women ought to be, according to the Bible rule of doing to others as you would others should do unto you. I am told (not by you) that if a woman dies a week after she's married that her husband takes all her personal property and the use of her real estate as long as he lives[2]—if a man dies his wife can have her thirds—this does

not come up to the Gospel rule. Now the young fellow that is engaged to our Kerry, is a pleasant clever fellow, but he is not quite one and twenty, and I dont s'pose he ever earned a coat in his life. Uncle told me there was a way for a woman to have her property trustee'd,[3] and I told it to Kerry—but she, poor girl has romantic notions owing to reading too many novels,[4] and when I told her of it, she would not hear of such a thing—"What take the law to keep my property away from James before I marry him—if it was a million of dollars he should have it all." So you see I think the law is in fault here—to tell you the truth I do not think young men are near so careful about getting in debt as girls, and I have known more than one that used their wife's money to pay off old scores. . . . I had rather go to my mantua maker[5] to borrow twenty dollars if I needed it, than to the richest married woman I know.

Another thing I have to tell you—when I was young I had a lover, Jos. Thompson, he went into business in a neighboring town, and after a year or two while I was getting the wedding things—Joe failed, he met with misfortunes that he did not expect,—he could have concealed it from me and married, but he did not—he was honorable, and so we delayed. He lived along here two or three years, and tried all he could to settle with his creditors, but some were stiff and held out, and thought by and by we would marry, and they should get my property. Uncle said he knew if we were married, there were those who would take my cattle and the improvement of my land. Joseph used to visit me often those years, but he lost his spirits and he could not get into business again, and he thought he must go to sea. I begged him not to, and told him we should be able to manage things in time, but he said no— he must try his luck, and at least get enough to settle off old scores, and then he would come here and live and we would make the best of what I had. We parted—but it pleased God he should be lost at sea. What I have suffered, I cannot tell you. Now Joe was no sailor when I engaged with him, and if it had been a thing known that I should always have a right to keep possession of my own, he need never have gone to sea, and we might have lived happily together, and in time with industry and economy, he might have paid off all. I am one that cant be convinced without better reasons than I have heard of, that woman are dealt with by the "gospel rule." There is more might than right in such laws as far as I can see—if you see differently, do tell us next time you lecture. Another thing—you made some reflections upon women following the Anti's. . . . Women have joined the Antislavery societies, and why? women are kept for slaves as well as men—it is a common cause, deny the justice of it, who can! To be sure I do not wish to go about lecturing like the Misses Grimkie, but I have not the knowledge they have, and I verily believe that if I had been brought up among slaves as they were, and knew all that they know, and felt a call from humanity to speak, I should run the venture of your displeasure, and that of a good many others like you.[6] [See pp. 193–97.] I told Uncle that I thought your lecture was a onesided thing—and he said, "why Keziah, Squire Greenleaf is an advocate, not a judge, you must get him to take t'other side next time." Now I have taken this opportunity to ask you to give us a remedy for the "legal wrongs" of women, whenever you have a chance. The fathers of the land should look to these things—who knows but your daughter may be placed in the sad situation I am in, or the dangerous one Kerry is in. I hear you are a good man, to make it certain—do all the good you can, and justify no wrong thing.

Yours with regard
Keziah Kendall.

NOTES

1. She is, of course, referring to a widow's dower rights. [See "The Law of Domestic Relations" pp. 57–58.]

2. "Kendall" was correct in her understanding of a husband's rights in his wife's personal property if she should die as early as "a week after she's married." But under the common law he would not inherit a life interest in her real estate unless they were parents of a child.

3. This is a reference to the equitable device of placing the woman's property in a trust before marriage for the purpose of avoiding the husband's common law rights in her property as well as protecting it from the husband's creditors. Under the trust agreement, the trustee would be obligated to manage the property for the benefit of the married woman.

4. "Kendall" shared a widely held distrust of romantic novels.

5. In the early republic, mantua makers [i.e., skilled dressmakers] were often economically independent women.

6. "Kendall" is probably referring here to the "Pastoral Letter" issued by the Congregationalist ministers in the summer of 1837 denouncing the public lecturing of the Grimké sisters. [See pp. 196–97.]

JUDITH WELLMAN

The Seneca Falls Women's Rights Convention: A Study of Social Networks

In the familiar photographs, like the one reprinted on page 266, Elizabeth Cady Stanton comes to us as she appeared in her fifties and older: a plump, matronly woman with graying hair and a kindly face. But in 1848, when she wrote the great manifesto that set the agenda for the American woman's movement for the next 150 years, she was thirty-three years old, and the one photograph we have of her from that time shows

Excerpted from "The Seneca Falls Women's Rights Convention: A Study of Social Networks" by Judith Wellman, in *Journal of Women's History* 3 (1991): 9–37. Reprinted by permission of Indiana University Press. Notes have been edited and renumbered.

her to be slight and thin, her dark hair hanging in limp ringlets. Did she look tired because she was the mother of three boys under six? Her future—and ours—lay before her.

As Keziah Kendall and Sarah and Angelina Grimké had done, many people in the 1830s and 1840s had begun to criticize the way American law and custom defined gender relations. The 1848 Declaration of Sentiments (see pp. 214–16) gathered these complaints into a manifesto and offered an agenda for change that would shape a women's rights movement deep into our own time. But the Declaration itself has its own history, emerging out of the specific social conditions in western New York state, out of political and religious arguments, and out of the personal experiences of the women and men who wrote its words and signed their names to it.

At the time of the Seneca Falls Convention, Elizabeth Cady Stanton was the mother of three sons; the smallest, Gerrit, was a toddler. In this picture, taken around 1848, she is pictured with Daniel and Henry. (Courtesy of Elizabeth Cady Stanton Trust/Coline Jenkins-Sahlin.)

Judith Wellman's meticulous research has enabled us to know the class position, religious affiliation, kin relations, and political sympathies of many of the signers at Seneca Falls. Note the participation of Daniel Anthony, whose daughter, Susan, would soon become Stanton's colleague in women's rights activism. That partnership would last all their lives.

Although the initiative and imagination of Elizabeth Cady Stanton herself does much to account for the form of the final document, what other elements help explain the timing and content of the Seneca Falls Convention and the Declaration? How many of the political demands of the Declaration can be connected to political issues already being debated in the state legislature and within political parties? Why did the authors adopt the rhetoric of the Declaration of Independence of 1776, two generations before their time?

Shortly after 11:00 A.M. on the bright, sunlit morning of July 19, 1848, Elizabeth Cady Stanton walked to the front of the Wesleyan Chapel in Seneca Falls, New York. The time had come to take public action, to inaugurate, as Stanton later recalled, "the greatest rebellion the world has ever seen." She was so nervous, she remembered, that she "wanted to abandon all her principles" and run away. But she did not, and the first women's rights convention of modern North America began.[1]

For the next two days, perhaps three hundred people met in the Wesleyan Chapel to discuss not only the "social, civil, and religious condition and rights of woman" but also women's political rights, especially the right to vote. When the meeting was over, one hundred people (sixty-eight women and thirty-two men) had signed the Declaration of Sentiments, which was patterned after the Declaration of Independence, and asserted "that all men and women are created equal; they they are endowed by their Creator with certain inalienable rights; that among these are life, liberty, and the pursuit of happiness. . . ." Just as the colonists had brought charges against King George, so the signers at Seneca Falls brought charges against the men of America, against an establishment that legitimized male authority, denied women political rights (including the right to vote), gave husbands the power even to beat their wives, discriminated against women in employment, education, and property ownership, and took from women a sense of self-respect and of confidence in their own abilities.[2]

By using the Declaration of Independence as their model, women's rights advocates at

Seneca Falls drew immediate public attention to their cause, and they initiated a new, activist phase of the women's rights movement. As the historian Ellen Carol DuBois has argued, "For many years before 1848, American women had manifested considerable discontent with their lot. . . . Yet women's discontent remained unexamined, implicit, and above all, disorganized. . . . The women's rights movement crystallized these sentiments into a feminist politics . . . [and] began a new phase in the history of feminism."[3] . . .

This is the story of the one hundred signers of the Declaration of Sentiments. Who were they? And why did they sign a document that they agreed was "of the kind called radical"?[4] . . .

In 1888, Frederick Douglass, then editor of the *North Star* in Rochester, New York, and himself one of the signers, provided us a clue . . . at the fortieth anniversary of the convention, held by the International Council of Women in Washington, D.C.; [he said]

> Then who were we, for I count myself in, who did this thing? We were few in numbers, moderate in resources, and very little known in the world. The most that we had to commend us, was a firm conviction that we were in the right, and a firm faith that the right must ultimately prevail.[5]

For Douglass, it was shared values rather than a shared relationship to material resources that brought these women's rights advocates together at Seneca Falls. One value, that of equality, was central to all of their lives. "All men and women are created equal," they had affirmed. So we might hypothesize that the networks that linked the signers would reflect egalitarian values.[6] . . .

. . . [T]hose who signed the Seneca Falls Declaration of Sentiments were . . . very ordinary people. Only five of them—Frederick Douglass, Lucretia and James Mott, Martha Wright, and Stanton herself—ever became figures of national importance. Why did these relatively obscure people take such an early and unequivocal stand for women's rights? . . .

Beyond the simple act of signing the Declaration of Sentiments itself, few of these signers left any record of what shaped and sustained their egalitarian ideals. They did, however, leave imprints of their basic values on the social institutions in which they lived out their daily lives. . . .

. . . [T]hree major reform organizations linked these signers into value-oriented networks long before they knew about the Seneca Falls convention. These networks were composed of (1) legal reformers, who worked to implement the right of married women to own property and who also raised the question of political rights for women; (2) political abolitionists, who helped form the emerging Free Soil party; and (3) Quaker abolitionists, who supported Garrisonian abolitionism. . . .

Three networks, three events, three concerns. How did these develop? How did they coalesce in the summer of 1848 to motivate one hundred people to sign the Seneca Falls Declaration of Sentiments? . . .

ELIZABETH CADY STANTON

Elizabeth Cady Stanton was clearly the main organizer of the convention, and understanding her own story is key to understanding why the convention occurred in the first place. . . .

Three months before Stanton's eleventh birthday, in August 1826, her oldest brother, Eleazer, came home from Union College to die. Three more brothers died in infancy or early childhood, leaving Stanton's parents—Daniel and Margaret Cady—with six girls but no living sons. Daniel Cady never fully recovered, and he rebuffed Elizabeth's efforts to be as good as the sons he had lost. "I taxed every power," she remembered in her autobiography, "hoping some day to hear my father say: 'Well, a girl is as good as a boy, after all.' But he never said it."[7]

A few months later, Elizabeth's sister,

Tryphena, married Edward Bayard, and the newly wedded couple became surrogate parents for the remaining Cady children. Edward and his brother, Henry, studied law with Daniel Cady, Elizabeth's father, and she began to spend much of her time in her father's law office. With the revision of New York State's laws in 1828, the legal position of married women was suddenly clouded with doubt, and Daniel Cady's law students liked to tease Elizabeth about her powerlessness under the law. Contacts she made in her father's office would connect her with a significant network of legal reformers.

As she grew, Stanton began to spend considerable time with her cousin and his wife, Gerrit and Nancy Smith, at their home in Peterboro, New York. . . . One of the most famous was Henry B. Stanton, abolitionist orator and organizer. Against her father's wishes, Elizabeth married Henry in May 1840. Through Gerrit Smith and Henry Stanton, Elizabeth made important contacts among a second major network, that of political abolitionists.

On their honeymoon, Elizabeth and Henry attended the World Anti-Slavery convention in London. By refusing to seat women delegates, antislavery males unwittingly transformed their meeting into an episode in the development of the women's rights movement. As Stanton recalled:

> The action of this convention was the topic of discussion, in public and private, for a long time, and . . . gave rise to the movement for women's political equality both in England and the United States. As the convention adjourned, the remark was heard on all sides, "It is about time some demand was made for new liberties for women."[8]

Most important for Stanton was her introduction to Lucretia Mott and the circle of Quaker abolitionist women from Philadelphia. As an older woman, an abolitionist, and an accomplished public speaker, Mott represented "a new world of thought" to Stanton. She also connected Stanton to another wing of the antislavery movement, those who emphasized not political action but moral suasion. Often called Garrisonians after William Lloyd Garrison, perhaps the most vocal proponent of this view, these abolitionists embraced total equality for all people, "the *equal brotherhood* of the entire Human Family, without distinction of color, sex, or clime." It may have been in London that Elizabeth began to call herself a Garrisonian. Shortly afterward, she began to subscribe to the *Liberator,* Garrison's newspaper, and she continued to do so, in her own name, until the paper went out of existence.[9]

In 1840, just before the London meeting, political abolitionists had split with moral suasionist Garrisonians at the annual meeting of the American Anti-Slavery Society. They were never to be reconciled. Stanton, however, would maintain strong ties with both groups—with the political abolitionists through her husband, Henry, and her cousin, Gerrit Smith, and with the moral suasionists through her new mentor, Lucretia Mott.

All three of these networks—the legal reformers Stanton had met through her father's law office, the political abolitionists she knew so well through her husband, and the Garrisonian abolitionists that she herself belonged to and that she had come to know through Mott—came together in Stanton's life in the summer of 1848.

Stanton would be ready to take public action with these three networks in 1848, in part because of deeply disturbing events in her own personal life. Stanton had moved to Seneca Falls from Boston, and the change was both dramatic and depressing. With her husband almost always away from home, she struggled to maintain herself and her three rambunctious sons with little household help. Their house was on the outskirts of the village, in an Irish working-class neighborhood, overlooking the Seneca Turnpike, the Seneca and Cayuga Canal, and the mills along the Seneca River. Her life was made even more difficult when her children and servants all developed malaria. As she recalled, "Cleanliness, order, the love of the beautiful and artistic, all faded away in the struggle to accomplish what was absolutely necessary from hour to hour." . . . Increasingly frustrated, increasingly angry, Stanton tried to make sense of her feelings. She thought about cooperative housekeeping and about the advantages of Fourierist communities. . . . [She probably] suffered either a miscarriage or a still birth. . . . She was a woman in a state of siege.[10] At that critical point in her life, events outside her control would rouse her neighbors to organized action. The passage of the Married Women's Property Act in April

1848, the formation of the Free-Soil party, and the organization of dissident Quakers into the Congregational Friends in June 1848 set the stage to help Stanton transform her personal problems into political action through a convention for the rights of women.

BACKGROUND INFLUENCES

Although national in its impact, the Seneca Falls convention was local in its origins. Of the eighty-three known signers, 69 percent of them came either from Seneca Falls or the neighboring town of Waterloo. So many people attended the convention from Waterloo, in fact, that one newspaper called the meeting the "Waterloo Female Convention." A few people came from other townships in Seneca County, and a few more arrived from as far away as Rochester (forty miles west of Seneca Falls), Wayne County (just north of Seneca Falls), or Syracuse (forty miles east). Only three came from farther distances, and these were all on visits to relatives in central New York.[11]

In the 1840s, upstate New York, like the whole northeastern United States, was changing rapidly. Both Seneca Falls and Waterloo . . . lay on the country's major east–west transportation route, developed first as the Seneca Turnpike, then as the Erie Canal (connected to Seneca County by the Seneca and Cayuga Canal), and finally as a major rail route. Local industries epitomized the early industrial revolution. The 43-foot waterfall from which Seneca Falls took its name provided abundant water-power for mills and factories. Four miles west, Waterloo's woolen factory sustained production from the mid-1830s.

By the 1840s, Seneca Falls found itself economically in transition. Strongly affected by the depression of 1837, the town lost its older economy, which was based on milling local wheat into flour for eastern markets, as wheat production moved farther west. Local entrepreneurs had begun to manufacture both pumps and textiles, but these industries would not provide a dependable economic base until the 1850s.

Economic change eroded stable social institutions and challenged basic values of community cohesion. At the same time, it offered opportunities. On the one hand, signers of the Declaration of Sentiments were secure enough in their basic economic, social, and cultural positions to be willing to take risks. On the other hand, they found themselves on the shifting sands of change, where risk was not only possible but necessary. A complex mix—different for different signers—of personal characteristics, economic status, and family patterns set the stage for the involvement of these individuals in reform. By themselves, these elements do not explain why the signers became women's rights activists. They did, however, provide a context that promoted the growth of women's rights activism.[12]

Gender, for example, was an important variable but not a definitive one. Two-thirds of the signers were women. Whether or not men should sign the Declaration of Sentiments was, in fact, one of only two topics that occasioned disagreement at the convention.[13] . . .

Age did not link the signers, who ranged from fourteen-year-old Susan Quinn, the youngest signer, to sixty-eight-year-old George W. Pryor, the oldest. Their mean age was 38.7 years old.[14]

Ethnicity, race, and place of birth were also contributing but not defining factors. In race and ethnicity, the majority of signers reflected the majority of the surrounding population: they were native-born European Americans. Only one known signer, Frederick Douglass, was African American. Only one, Susan Quinn, was of Irish descent. Most had been born in New York State, New England, or Pennsylvania.[15]

Wealth, too, provided a context but not a cause for reform. According to the 1850 census, signers' families did, on average, own more property than did nonsigners' families. Variation among signers' families was so great, however, that wealth alone does not adequately distinguish the signers from the ordinary population. Excluding the four richest signatories from our calculations, the average value of property held by signers' families was $2,051. The average value of property held by nonsigning families in Seneca Falls and Waterloo, in contrast, was $1,117. (Seneca Falls had by far the lowest average amount of property ownership, with $869 per family, compared to $2,915 in Waterloo.[16] . . .

Occupations also provide clues about the relationship of signers to one another and to a new economic order. . . . Those who worked in manufacturing certainly had to confront

directly the possibility of dramatic changes in the way they earned their living. In fact, 39.6 percent of signers lived in households that derived their main income from manufacturing. Only 30.2 percent were involved in farming and 30.2 percent in services or trade. In Seneca Falls, most signers (55.2 percent) lived in manufacturing households.[17] . . .

Other signers, although they listed their occupations as farmers or as professionals, derived at least part of their income from industrialization. Richard P. Hunt, for example, told the census taker that he was a farmer. He did, indeed, own several farms in Waterloo, but he was also the major investor in the Waterloo woolen factory and one of the owners of Waterloo's main business district. Elisha Foote, a lawyer, specialized in patent law and himself held several patents.[18] . . .

Family networks give us another important clue about the relationship of these signers to other people. Almost half the identifiable signers (and perhaps almost two-thirds of the total) attended the convention with at least one other family member. Wives and husbands came together. Mothers brought their daughters, and fathers brought sons. Sisters and brothers came together, and so, in some cases, did uncles and cousins.[19]

. . . Some families did argue among themselves about women's rights. Henry Stanton, for example, refused to attend the convention at all. But many of the signers (including Stanton herself, who brought Harriet Cady Eaton, her sister, and Daniel Cady Eaton, her nephew) could count on at least one other family member to lend support. Women's rights may have divided some families, but it brought others together in a common cause.

. . . [T]hese family patterns lead us to suspect that husbands and wives had important ties not only with each other but with their own parents and siblings. While many husbands and wives signed the Declaration together, many women and men also signed the Declaration with members of their birth families. Sometimes these family relationships became very complicated. Richard P. Hunt, for example, signed not only with his wife, Jane, but with two sisters (Lydia Mount and Hannah Plant) and with Lydia's daughter, Mary E. Vail. . . .

Clearly, these signers valued their ties with sisters, brothers, parents, and children as much as those with husbands and wives. Links with their families of origin balanced marital relationships and provided women with a large network of support of "significant others." In spite of legal theory and emerging popular opinion, wives in this group did not define themselves solely by their relationship to their husbands.

Finally, for many signers, home was not simply a private place. It was also a public place, part of the world of work and of social interaction beyond the nuclear family. Many signers incorporated non-family members into their households, including apprentices, servants, boarders, and children. . . . The emerging distinction between women (whose place was in the home) and men (who worked outside the home) was blurred for these signers. Families and households were not peripheral to public activity but the very basis of community life itself.

All of these factors—sex, age, race and ethnicity, wealth and work, family and household—set the stage for the involvement of these people in the Seneca Falls convention. But these were contributing factors, not defining ones. I believe that the convention happened when and where it did primarily because these signers were linked together into three value-oriented networks and because Elizabeth Cady Stanton herself mobilized people in all three groups to create the Seneca Falls women's rights convention.

WOMEN AND LEGAL REFORM IN NEW YORK STATE

The first network emerged from a statewide debate about the legal rights of women in New York State. For almost two decades before the Seneca Falls convention, this debate was so widespread and so intertwined with fundamental questions of American identity that it engaged people at a grass-roots level all across New York State. And it framed the debate about women's rights in the language of the Declaration of Independence. Did the phrase "all men are created equal" include women? Were women, indeed, citizens? In effect, the debate over legal rights for married women provided a dress rehearsal for the Seneca Falls convention itself.[20]

In Seneca Falls, legal reform found its most ardent advocate in Ansel Bascom,

lawyer, abolitionist, legal reformer, and temperance man. Bascom did not sign the Declaration of Sentiments. He was a candidate for Congress in 1848 and perhaps did not want to commit himself to such a radical position. He did, however, attend the women's rights meeting, and he took a very active part in the discussion.[21]

Stanton herself formed a second member of this legal reform network. As a child, she had listened to her father and her father's law students debate women's legal rights. She had lobbied in Albany for legal reform in the 1840s. And she contributed in her own special way to the Declaration of Sentiments by emphasizing women's citizenship rights, especially the right of all women—married or single—to vote, which she articulated in terms of the statewide debate about women and the law.

Discussions about women's legal rights undoubtedly affected other signers, too. Elisha Foote, for example, a Seneca Falls lawyer and one of Stanton's father's former law students, quite likely took an active part. So, probably, did men such as Charles Hoskins and Jacob P. Chamberlain, who were politically aware, interested in questions of equality, financially well off, and worried about the future of their several daughters.[22] . . .

Two questions about legal rights for women roused considerable attention in New York State. The first was the right of married women to own property. The second concerned the right of women as citizens to participate in a democratic government. Particularly, should women be allowed to vote? Under the broad umbrella of republican rhetoric that dominated political discourse from the Revolution to the Civil War, these two questions, of property rights and citizenship rights, although often debated separately, were integrally intertwined. Only those with some material investment in the body politic, some argued, should be given a voice in public affairs. Such investment could be property ownership (which led to the payment of taxes) or militia service. As long as women were subject to neither, the rationale for denying them the vote remained intact. If laws were changed to allow married women to own property in their own names, then the whole legal and philosophical scaffolding of resistance to women's political power collapsed. As George Geddes, one of the supporters of a married women's property act, realized, such legislation raised "the whole question of woman's proper place in society, in the family and everywhere."[23]

New York State's citizens had publicly debated the question of women's rights at least since the 1821 state constitutional convention. There, opponents of universal male suffrage (i.e., of voting rights for all males, regardless of property ownership or race) argued that citizenship rights did not necessarily include voting rights. Over and over again, they used the exclusion of women from voting rights (as well as the exclusion of children, native Americans, foreigners, paupers, and felons) as a rationale for denying suffrage to others, including black males and white males without property. If women could legitimately be disfranchised, why could not others be excluded as well?[24]

In 1828, the question of married women's rights emerged in full force. Under the old law, based on English common law, wealthy New York families could protect property rights for their wives and married daughters by means of legal trusts, administered through equity courts. Many New Yorkers, however, viewed equity courts as fortresses of privilege for the wealthy. After 1828, New York State's Revised Statutes [cast in doubt] any sure protection for the right of married women to own property.

By the mid-1830s, considerable support existed across the state for a law protecting married women's right to own property. Men from wealthy families pushed for such a law most vigorously. They, after all, had most to lose, either to profligate sons-in-law or to ill-fated business ventures. Women's rights advocates, however, added their own small voice for reform. In 1836, Ernestine Rose, who was Polish American and Jewish, circulated a petition urging the passage of the married women's property act promoted by Thomas Herttell, a Democratic assemblyman from New York City. Although only six women signed this petition, it marked the first time that women themselves had taken public action for legal reform.[25]

Nowhere did the argument for full rights for women emerge more clearly than in a speech given in the late 1830s or early 1840s before the lyceum in Ogdensburg, New York. Arguing strenuously for married women's property rights, the author also raised the prospect both of the right to vote and the right

to hold office. The Declaration of Independence provided the key. "THAT ALL ARE CREATED FREE AND EQUAL; THAT THEY ARE ENDOWED BY THEIR CREATOR WITH CERTAIN UNALIENABLE RIGHTS; THAT AMONG THESE ARE LIFE, LIBERTY, AND THE PURSUIT OF HAPPINESS—is acknowledged to be the fundamental doctrine upon which this Republic is founded," the author asserted. Furthermore, this idea "is freedom's golden rule. . . . None should ever be allowed to restrict its universality. Women, as well as men, are entitled to the full enjoyment of its practical blessings." Clearly, women were citizens of this Republic, "amenable to the constitution and laws." Yet

> would any man be denominated free who was deprived of a representation in the government, under which he lived, who was thus disfranchised and had no voice in the affairs of his country? . . . He would be called a slave. Such, I blush for my country to say it—such is the degraded condition of women, in this boasted land of liberty. . . . Is this slavish condition of women compatible with the doctrine that all are created free and equal?[26] . . .

Discussion of women's rights—both property rights and political rights—reached a crescendo in 1846, when New York State called a new constitutional convention. The convention opened up once more the question of suffrage. Who should be allowed to vote in the State of New York? Should illiterates? Foreigners? Blacks? Even women? The issue seemed especially pressing because of recent unsuccessful efforts to legalize equal rights to suffrage for blacks in New York State.[27]

. . . At least three petitions (from Albany, Jefferson, and Wyoming counties, New York) asked for women's suffrage. Jefferson County petitioners argued, for example, that

> the present government of this state has widely departed from the true democratic principles upon which all just governments must be based by denying to the female portion of the community the right of suffrage and any participation in forming the government and laws under which they live, and to which they are amenable, and by imposing upon them burdens of taxation, both directly and indirectly, without admitting them the right of representation. . . . [28]

No taxation without representation constituted so powerful an argument that the convention could not entirely ignore it. Yet there was little sentiment in favor of doing anything about it. . . .

In April 1848, the New York State legislature again addressed the problem of married women's property rights. Again, they were prodded by petitions from citizens. One in particular revealed the importance of revolutionary rhetoric and grass-roots commitment in sustaining support for women's rights. In March 1848, forty-four "ladies" (married, as they were clear to assert), petitioned the legislature from the towns of Darien and Covington in Genesee and Wyoming counties, New York. Their petition argued, with potent sarcasm:

> That your Declaration of Independence declares, that governments derive their just powers from the consent of the governed. And as women have never consented to, been represented in, or recognized by this government, it is evident that in justice no allegiance can be claimed from them. . . . [29]

Perhaps inspired (or shamed) by such rhetoric, the New York State legislature did pass its first married women's property act just one month later, in April 1848. In creating a supportive climate for the Seneca Falls women's rights convention, discussion of the legal rights of women was extremely important. Passage of the Married Women's Property Act helped legitimize more radical action and prompted Stanton herself to promote women's right to vote. As Stanton noted, the Married Women's Property Act "encouraged action on the part of women, as the reflection naturally arose that, if the men who make the laws were ready for some onward step, surely the women themselves should express interest in legislation."[30]

FREE-SOIL ORGANIZATION

Passage of the Married Women's Property Act in April 1848 was the first major event in 1848 to set the stage for the Seneca Falls convention. Two more key events followed. Both occurred in June. Both linked local people to larger concerns. Both involved value-oriented networks, and both reflected major disruptions in those networks. One (in Seneca Falls) ripped apart political allegiances. It was the growth, in the late spring and early summer of 1848, of the new Free-Soil party. The other (in Waterloo

and beyond) mirrored a profound break in religious ties, when a group of Quaker abolitionists split away from the Genesee Yearly Meeting (Hicksite) to form the nucleus of the new Congregational or Progressive Friends. Both splits led directly to a confrontation over questions about equality in American life.

Both also involved people who were part of Elizabeth Cady Stanton's own personal circle. The Free-Soil movement drew support from men (and the women who had married these men) whom Stanton had met in her father's law office, as well as from political abolitionists she had met through her husband, Henry. The Quaker controversy deeply affected Friends who were linked to Lucretia Mott, Stanton's mentor and friend.

Political institutions in Seneca Falls were profoundly strained by debates surrounding the nomination of presidential candidates in 1848. Discussion centered on one question: Should slavery be allowed in the territories? In New York State, the question hit the Democratic party, already under stress from a decade of bickering, with particular force.[31] At a meeting in Syracuse in September 1847, the radical Barnburner wing of the party stalked out in anger when the conservative Hunkers refused to support resolutions against the extension of slavery. In May 1848, the national Democratic convention nominated Lewis Cass for president. For the Barnburners, now joined by former president Martin Van Buren, that was the last straw. They called a Barnburner state convention, to meet at Utica on June 22. Joined by antislavery Whigs and by men from the Liberty party, these dissident Democrats formed the nucleus of a new Free-Soil party, which would be organized formally at Buffalo in August. Championing "free soil, free labor, free men," they would rally behind Martin Van Buren for president.[32]

Electors in Seneca Falls found themselves swept into this national confrontation. On June 13, in preparation for the Utica meeting, 196 voters published an invitation in the *Seneca County Courier* to the "freemen of Seneca Falls" to meet in the Wesleyan Chapel to consider "the course of action which existing circumstances require of Northern Freemen." Chaired by Jacob Chamberlain, owner of a local flour mill, the attendees of the June 15 meeting agreed that slavery was "the chiefest curse and foulest disgrace" in America. The author of these stern resolutions? Ansel Bascom.[33]

Henry Stanton, too, leaped into the fight with gusto. He teamed up with Bascom to stump the state for the Free-Soil party. And he was one of 102 local delegates to the Buffalo Free-Soil convention, held in August.[34]

Old party issues were insignificant compared to the pressing need to find a presidential candidate who would restrict slavery. Such sentiments allied Seneca Falls Free-Soilers with the party's abolitionist wing. Nationally, many Free-Soil adherents supported the party not from antislavery principles but as a way to keep the west for whites only. People in Seneca Falls, however, considered slavery a moral evil and hoped the new party would strike a mortal blow against it.[35]

Some of them would go even further. They would take the idea of equality seriously enough to consider not only rights for black and white males but also for women. They would attend the Seneca Falls women's rights convention and would sign its Declaration of Sentiments.

. . . Of the twenty-six separate families of signers of the Declaration of Sentiments identifiable from Seneca Falls, eighteen of them also included a Free-Soil advocate. In Seneca Falls, not all Free-Soilers were women's rights advocates. But 69.2 percent of the households of women's rights advocates (compared to only 21.2 percent of nonsigners' households) were affiliated with the Free-Soilers.[36]

CONGREGATIONAL FRIENDS

Organizing for the Free-Soil party, combined with public discussion over women's legal rights, prepared citizens in Seneca Falls for the women's rights convention. Meanwhile, in Waterloo, four miles west of Seneca Falls, a different kind of excitement prevailed at just the same time. . . . [In June 1848] the Genesee Yearly Meeting of Friends, held at Farmington, in Ontario County, opened calmly enough, in spite of the heat. But tense disputes, left over from the year before, soon broke the Sabbath peace. On Sunday, June 11, the meeting house was filled to overflowing. Several speakers, "not very talented," as one observer commented, made the audience restive before Lucretia Mott rose and delivered an impressive sermon.[37]

. . . Disagreements were acrimonious and fundamental. Partly they centered on slavery. Conservative Quakers objected to the antislavery activities of many of their fellow Friends. Especially they did not want to open Quaker meeting houses for public discussion of abolitionism. . . .

Partly the disagreements involved the question of proper authority. Did essential authority reside within each individual person and then within each individual meeting? Or did the meeting of ministers and elders, along with quarterly and yearly meetings, have special power to determine the actions of local (i.e., monthly) meetings? . . .

For the Genesee Yearly Meeting, both these questions came to a head in June 1848. . . . About two hundred Friends ("something towards half," according to one observer) walked out, unhappy with what they felt was a manipulative and unfair action.[38]

With strong support from Quakers in Waterloo, Rochester, and Wayne County, these dissidents adjourned to a three-day conference of their own, held June 14–16. . . . Daniel Anthony, one of the few contemporaries to leave a detailed comment on the split, wrote to his daughter, Susan, that those who had left the "shriveled up nutshell" of the Genesee Yearly Meeting were those "who take the liberty of holding up to view the wickedness of War—Slavery—Intemperance—Hanging & c" and "who are of the opinion that each individual should have a right to even think as well as act for himself & in his own way to assist in rooling [sic] on the wheel of reform."[39]

Daniel Anthony reported, a month after the meeting, that "in Rochester they have commenced a new Meeting under the dictation of neither Priest deacon nor Elder."[40] We can assume that dissident Friends in the Waterloo area, affiliated with the Junius Monthly Meeting (after the original name of the township that once included Waterloo), did the same, for in Waterloo lived one of the main organizers of the walkout . . . Thomas McClintock. . . .

The McClintock family (Thomas and Mary Ann and their four children) had come to Waterloo by canal in 1837. Thomas ran a drugstore on Main Street, where, in a business block constructed by his brother-in-law, Richard P. Hunt, McClintock sold goods "free from the labor of slaves." Hunt also rented the family a comfortable brick house just behind the store.[41]

. . . As Quakers and as abolitionists, they took leadership roles in their own meeting. From 1839 to 1843, . . . [Thomas] was . . . clerk of the Genesee Yearly Meeting. Mary Ann was assistant clerk of the Women's Yearly Meeting. The whole family signed abolitionist petitions, helped organize antislavery fairs, and hosted antislavery lecturers.

When the split in the Genesee Yearly Meeting came in June 1848, Thomas was one of those who walked out. In the fall, this group would meet again. They would call themselves the Congregational Friends, and they would adopt a new form of organization. Men and women would meet together, not separately, as in traditional Quaker meetings. No person was to be subordinate to another. There were to be no ministers and no hierarchy of meetings. They were not to be tied to creeds or rituals, and they need not agree with one another on points of doctrine. They would focus instead on practical philanthropy. . . .

In mid-July, these Friends would become the single largest group to sign the Seneca Falls Declaration of Sentiments. At least twenty-three signers were affiliated with this wing of Friends. Most of them (nineteen) came from the Junius Monthly Meeting at Waterloo. One signer, Rhoda Palmer, remembered, in fact, that "every member" of that meeting attended the women's rights convention.[42]

Just as the Free-Soilers of Seneca Falls had broken out of traditional political parties, so had the Waterloo Quakers broken away from their traditional religious affiliation. Both had split away over issues of equality. Both did so in dramatic and emotionally wrenching ways.

In late June and early July, both groups were in the process of self-definition. They had many questions: Who were their members? What did they believe? In particular, how far did they want to carry this idea of equality?

THE RESULTS OF LOCAL AGITATION

At this critical juncture, in the midst of excitement caused by the Free-Soilers and the Congregational Friends, Lucretia Mott came with her sister, Martha Wright, to meet with Quaker women at the home of Jane and Richard Hunt. Elizabeth Cady Stanton was also invited. There, Stanton "poured out," as she remembered, "the torrent of my long-accumulating discontent, with such vehemence and indignation that I stirred myself, as well as the rest of the party, to do and dare anything." That evening, they wrote the call for a women's rights convention and published it on Tuesday, July 11, in the *Seneca County Courier.* Area newspapers (the *North Star* and the *Ovid Bee,* for example) printed the call in their own editions on Friday, July 14.[43]

Local people, concerned about women's legal rights, agitated about deep changes in their own institutional affiliations, and willing in this time of trial and transformation to expand their own boundaries, considered the purposes of the women's rights convention to be, as Stanton later remembered, "timely, rational and sacred." A core group of legal reformers, Free-Soilers, and Congregational Friends found the Declaration of Sentiments sensible, a logical extension of their own beliefs in ideals of liberty, equality, and independence.

But what about Elizabeth Cady Stanton? Can she still be called the convention's main organizer? Indeed she can. The convention would not have happened at all without her. Before the women's rights convention, Free-Soilers and advocates of legal reform in Seneca Falls had few identifiable contacts with the Congregational Friends of Waterloo and central New York. Stanton, however, knew leaders in all three movements. She knew Ansel Bascom, champion of legal reform. Among the Free-Soilers, she could count as friends not only Jacob Chamberlain (president of the June 13 Free-Soil meeting and Stanton's neighbor), and Charles Hoskins (secretary of that meeting and fellow attender of the Episcopal Church), but also her own husband, Henry. Finally, Stanton gained credibility among the Quakers of Waterloo, first, by her long-standing friendship with Lucretia Mott and, second, by her introduction to the McClintocks, who wholeheartedly endorsed her convention plans. Stanton persuaded these leaders to come to the convention. They, in turn, would attract their followers. She would become what network theorists call a broker, bringing together three networks at a critical juncture in their own development.[44]

Stanton willingly played this position, not because she wanted primarily to promote the Free-Soil party or Congregational Friends, nor even because she wanted to take up the challenge posed to women by passage of the Married Women's Property Act, to act on their own behalf. Instead, Stanton's most powerful motivation emerged from the stresses of her own personal life in 1848. The move to Seneca Falls, Henry's frequent absences, the lack of trained household help, and her family's sickness threatened to overwhelm her. Other women might have become depressed. Not Elizabeth Cady Stanton. Instead, she used her energy to enlist legal reformers, Free-Soilers, and Congregational Friends into a battle against social structures that oppressed women, rather than against individual oppressors.

People across the country reacted to the Seneca Falls convention. Many observers ridiculed the whole idea. The New York *Evening Post* squealed incredulously that the convention "had seriously resolved that all men and women are created equal!" Women's rights, said the *Mechanic's Advocate*, were "impracticable, uncalled for, and unnecessary," "a monstrous injury to all mankind," while *The Religious Recorder* of Syracuse simply dismissed it as "excessively silly."[45]

A few, however, endorsed women's rights with enthusiasm. "Success to the cause in which they have enlisted," cheered O.C.W. in the Herkimer *Freeman*. "Railroad speed to the ends they would accomplish!" The Rochester *National Reformer* encouraged continued agitation. "To the ladies we say," wrote editor George W. Cooper, "act—agitate—bid high, you will not get, in this age, more than you demand."[46]

It had been the genius of the convention's organizers, however, to couch their demands in terms of the Declaration of Independence. Americans found it difficult to repudiate the document upon which their nation had been founded. Many, therefore, would have agreed with Horace Greeley, the influential editor of the *New York Tribune*. Greeley, always logical, had to admit the justice of the cause, for

> when a sincere republican is asked to say in sober earnest, what adequate reason he can give for refusing the demand of women to an equal participation with men in political rights, he must answer, None at all.... However unwise and mistaken the demand, it is but the assertion of a natural right, and as such must be conceded.[47]

By using the language of the Declaration of Independence, the Seneca Falls Declaration

of Sentiments reached deep into the culture and conscience of many Americans. Although it may have been a historical accident that Stanton found herself in Seneca Falls in 1848, she seized the moment of agitation over married women's property rights, of political turmoil among the Free-Soilers, and of religious divisions among the Quakers to turn her personal vision into what would become a major political movement.

Notes

1. For references to weather, see Mary A. Bull, "Woman's Rights and 'Other Reforms' in Seneca Falls," *Seneca Falls Reville*, July 9, 1880, and manuscript diary of Jefferson Palmer, Montezuma, July 1848, in Seneca Falls Historical Society. Quotations about the convention are in *History of Woman Suffrage*, vol. 1 (New York: Fowler and Wells, 1881), p. 68....

2. Call to the convention, *Seneca County Courier*, July 11, 1848; *Report of the Woman's Rights Convention Held at Seneca Falls, N.Y., July 19th and 20th, 1848* (Rochester: John Dick at North Star, 1848). . . . Eleanor Flexner, *Century of Struggle: The Woman's Rights Movement in the United States* (Cambridge, Mass.: Harvard University Press, 1959), p. 76, notes that three hundred people attended the convention.... This is corroborated by calculations derived from the size of the Wesleyan Methodist Church building itself and from the arrangement of seats within it.

3. Ellen DuBois, *Feminism and Suffrage: The Emergence of an Independent Women's Movement in America, 1848–1869* (Ithaca: Cornell University Press, 1978), p. 21.

4. John Dick at the *North Star* office in Rochester printed a list of one hundred signers in the *Report of the Woman's Rights Convention*. This list may or may not contain the names of all those who originally signed the Declaration of Sentiments. In her autobiography, Stanton remembered that "so pronounced was the popular voice against us, in the parlor, press, and pulpit, that most of the ladies who had attended the convention and signed the declaration, one by one, withdrew their names and influence and joined our persecutors." *Eighty Years and More* reprint (New York: Schocken Books, 1971), p. 149. No manuscript of the Declaration has ever been found, and we do not know whether the printed list duplicates the original or omits those signers who later withdrew their names....

5. Frederick Douglass, *Report on the International Council of Women* (Washington, D.C.: Rufus H. Darby, 1888), p. 329.

6. For discussions of these issues, see, for example (listed in chronological order), Alma Lutz, *Created Equal: A Biography of Elizabeth Cady Stanton* (New York: John Day, 1940); Eleanor Flexner, *Century of Struggle*; Gerda Lerner, *The Grimke Sisters from South Carolina* (Boston: Houghton Mifflin, 1967); Ross Evans Paulson, *Women's Suffrage and Prohibition: A*

Comparative Study of Equality and Social Control (Glenview, Ill.: Scott, Foresman, 1973). . . . Lois Banner, *Elizabeth Cady Stanton: A Radical for Woman's Rights* (Boston: Little, Brown, 1980). . . . Nancy Hewitt, *Women's Activism and Social Change, Rochester, New York, 1822–1872* (Ithaca: Cornell University Press, 1984).

7. Stanton, *Eighty Years*, chap. 2.

8. Ibid., p. 82.

9. Ibid., p. 83; Minutes of Seventh Annual Meeting of the American Anti-Slavery Society, May 12–15, 1840, in Garrison Papers, Boston Public Library; *Liberator* subscription list, Garrison Papers, Boston Public Library. . . .

10. Stanton, *Eighty Years*, p. 47. Stanton's last living child, Gerrit, had been born in Sept. 1845; her next child, Theodore, would arrive on Feb. 10, 1851. . . .

11. Data on residence comes primarily from the 1850 federal census. . . .

12. The following brief analysis is based on preliminary results of a detailed statistical study, now under way, of all the residents of Seneca Falls and Waterloo in 1850, comparing the signers of the Declaration of Sentiments with the nonsigners in those two townships.

13. People signed the declaration in two groups, female and male, so we know the sex of the signers, even if no other information is available. . . .

14. Seneca Falls had the youngest average age, with 37.5; Waterloo had the oldest, with 41.

15. The sixteen signers about whom we have no reliable information may, of course, have been either black or foreign born. Seneca Falls had only twenty-four black residents in 1850 (.5 percent of the population), and Waterloo had sixty-one (1.7 percent). Of the 1,473 households in Seneca Falls in 1850, 196 of them (13.3 percent) were headed by Irish-born residents. Source: [U.S. Census for 1850].

16. Fifty-five signers' families appeared in the 1850 census. Average value of real estate for these families was $3,720. But these figures obscure considerable variation, both from family to family and from place to place. Overall, almost half (47.3 percent) of the signers' families held no property at all in 1850, varying from 64.3 percent in Waterloo to 59.3 percent in Seneca Falls to 7.1 percent elsewhere in central New York. Four families, in contrast, owned more than $15,000 of real estate. Those families of signers who owned more than $15,000 worth of property included the Hunts from Waterloo ($40,000), the father of S. D. Tillman, from Seneca Falls ($25,000), and Martha Wright's family in Auburn ($20,000). . . .

17. Information about occupations comes primarily from the 1850 census. For our purposes, this census has a major defect: It did not list occupations for women. Some of the women signers may also have been textile workers. . . .

18. Information about Elisha Foote's patents comes from *Appleton's Cyclopedia of American Biography*, vol. 2 (New York, 1887), p. 495. . . .

19. At least 47 percent of the signers (and perhaps as many as 62.7 percent) attended with at least one other family member. Sources: U.S. Census for 1850 and family genealogies.

20. For a more detailed discussion of debate over legal reform, see Norma Basch, *In the Eyes of the Law: Women, Marriage, and Property in Nineteenth-Century New York* (Ithaca: Cornell University Press, 1982); and Marylynn Salmon, *Women and the Law of Property in Early America* (Chapel Hill: University of North Carolina Press, 1986). . . .

21. Information on Bascom comes from many sources, including scattered copies of *The Memorialist*, a legal reform paper published by Bascom in Seneca Falls.

22. Martha Wright to Lucretia Mott, Mar. 11, 1841, in Garrison Papers, Smith College.

23. Geddes to Matilda Joslyn Gage, Nov. 25, 1880, in Stanton, Anthony, and Gage, eds., *History of Woman Suffrage*, I:65.

24. For examples of the debate, see Nathaniel H. Carter and William L. Stone, *Reports of the Proceedings and Debates of the Convention of 1821* (Albany: E. and E. Hosford, 1821), pp. 181, 190, 191, 248–49, 278. . . .

25. Basch, *In the Eyes of the Law*, pp. 115–19.

26. *Lecture Delivered Before the Ogdensburg Lyceum on the Political Rights of Women* (Ogdensburg, N.Y.: Tyler and James, 1837). This may have been delivered by Democratic politician and judge John Fine. . . . Angelina Grimke, for example, came right to the point in her *Appeal to the Women of the Nominally Free States* (Boston: Isaac Knapp, 1838): "Are we aliens because we are women?" she asked. "Are we bereft of citizenship because we are the mothers, wives, and daughters of a mighty people?" (p. 19). . . .

27. Phyllis Field, *Politics of Race in New York: The Struggle for Black Suffrage in the Civil War Era* (Ithaca: Cornell University Press, 1982). . . .

28. William G. Bishop and William H. Attree, *Report of the Debates and Proceedings of the Convention for the Revision of the Constitution of the State of New York* (Albany: Bishop and Attree, 1846), p. 646.

29. New York Assembly Documents, Mar. 15, 1848, no. 129:1–2. . . .

30. Theodore Stanton and Harriet Stanton Blatch, eds., *Elizabeth Cady Stanton as Revealed in Her Letters, Diary and Reminiscences*, 2 vols. (New York: Harper & Bros., 1992), I:149.

31. Judah Ginsberg, "The Tangled Web: The New York Democratic Party and the Slavery Controversy, 1844–1860," Ph.D. dissertation, University of Wisconsin, 1974, chap. 4.

32. Richard Sewall, *Ballots for Freedom: Anti-Slavery Politics in the United States, 1837–1860* (New York: Norton, 1976), pp. 145–69.

33. *Seneca County Courier*, June 13, 1848, and June 16, 1848.

34. Ibid., Aug. 4, 1848.

35. Sewall, *Ballots for Freedom*, pp. 160, 170–201, discusses the racial stance of Free-Soilers in general; Dwight Lowell Dumond, *Antislavery: The Crusade for Freedom in America*, reprint (New York: Norton, 1966), p. 304.

36. I identified Free-Soil advocates as those who signed one or more of three Free-Soil lists in the *Seneca County Courier* (June 13, Aug. 4, or Aug. 18, 1848).

37. For a thoughtful and detailed analysis of

Quakers who attended the Seneca Falls convention from Rochester and of differences between evangelical and Hicksite Quaker activism, see Nancy Hewitt, "Feminist Friends," *Feminist Studies* 12 (Spring 1986): 27–49. . . . Information about this meeting comes in bits and pieces from several sources. Most important is A. Day Bradley, "Progressive Friends in Michigan and New York," *Quaker History* 52 (Autumn 1963):95–101; John J. Cornell, *Autobiography* (Baltimore: Lord Baltimore Press, 1906), p. 22; Katharine Anthony, *Susan B. Anthony* (Garden City, N.Y.: Double-day, 1954), pp. 92–93. . . .

38. . . . Daniel Anthony to Susan B. Anthony, July 16, 1848, in Anthony Papers, Schlesinger Library, Radcliffe.

39. Daniel Anthony to Susan B. Anthony, July 16, 1848, Anthony Papers, Schlesinger Library.

40. Ibid.

41. Material on the McClintocks comes from John Becker, *History of Waterloo* (Waterloo: Waterloo Library and Historical Society, 1948), p. 135; Thomas McClintock, *Observations on the Articles Published in the Episcopal Recorder*. . . . (New York: Isaac T. Hopper, 1837); Ruth Ketring Nuermberger, *The Free-Produce Movement* (Durham, N.C.: Duke University Press, 1942), p. 14. . . .

42. Interview with Rhoda Palmer in *Geneva Daily Times,* Mar. 17, 1915; Lucretia Mott to Elizabeth Cady Stanton, July 16, 1848, in Stanton Papers, Library of Congress. . . .

43. Stanton, *Eighty Years*, p. 148.

44. Ronald S. Burt, "Models of Network Structure," *Annual Review of Sociology* 6 (1980):91, fn. 8, identifies a broker as one who is "the only connection between two subgroups of actors."

45. *Evening Post,* Aug. 12, 1848, quoted in Terpstra, "The 1848 Seneca Falls Women's Rights Convention," p. 46; *Mechanic's Advocate* [n.d.], quoted in *History of Woman Suffrage* I:803. . . .

46. *Herkimer Freeman,* as reprinted in the *Liberator,* Sept. 22, 1848; *National Reformer,* Aug. 10, 1848, in Alma Lutz notes, Vassar College.

47. *New York Tribune,* n.d., quoted from Alma Lutz notes, Vassar College.

DOCUMENTS: Claiming Rights II

Declaration of Sentiments, 1848

The Declaration of Sentiments, Stanton's indictment of the relations between men and women in her own society, is still stunning in its energy, its precision, and its foresight. It challenged many elements of American law and social practice which—thanks to five generations of political activism—no longer exist.

But the Declaration was only the beginning. Out of their vision of a community of equals, out of their discomfort with a social environment that privileged men and undermined women, the men and women at Seneca Falls dedicated themselves to Herculean political work. In one seventeen-day period in 1855 they held sixteen political meetings in fourteen different counties in upstate New York. In 1864, when it seemed possible that an end to slavery might also mean universal equal citizenship, they sent petitions with 100,000 signatures to the Senate and dreamed of getting a million.

They denounced the exclusion of women from learned professions and "nearly all the profitable employments." Male teachers earned $700 a year; women teachers earned $250. Susan B. Anthony would soon be demanding "equal pay for equal work," but there would be no federal equal pay act until 1963.

If Stanton and her Seneca Falls colleagues were to reappear in our own time, what changes would please them? What elements of their agenda would they believe are still alive?

Seneca Falls, New York,
July 19–20, 1848

When, in the course of human events, it becomes necessary for one portion of the family of man to assume among the people of the earth a position different from that which they have hitherto occupied, but one to which the laws of nature and of nature's God entitle them, a decent respect to the opinions of mankind requires that they should declare the causes that impel them to such a course.

We hold these truths to be self-evident: that all men and women are created equal; that they are endowed by their Creator with certain inalienable rights; that among these are life, liberty, and the pursuit of happiness; that to secure these rights governments are instituted, deriving their just powers from the consent of the governed. Whenever any form of government becomes destructive of these ends, it is the right of those who suffer from it to refuse allegiance to it, and to insist upon the institution of a new government, laying its foundation on such principles, and organizing its powers in such form, as to them shall seem most likely to effect their safety and happiness. Prudence, indeed, will dictate that governments long established should not be changed for light and transient causes; and accordingly all experience hath shown that mankind are more disposed to suffer, while evils are sufferable, than to right themselves by abolishing the forms to which they were accustomed. But when a long train of abuses and usurpations, pursuing invariably the same object evinces a design to reduce them under absolute despotism, it is their duty to throw off such government, and to provide new guards for their future security. Such has been the patient sufferance of the women under this government,

Declaration of Sentiments, in *History of Woman Suffrage*, edited by Elizabeth Cady Stanton, Susan B. Anthony, and Matilda Joslyn Gage, vol. 1 (New York: Fowler & Wells, 1881), pp. 70–71.

and such is now the necessity which constrains them to demand the equal station to which they are entitled.

The history of mankind is a history of repeated injuries and usurpations on the part of man toward woman, having in direct object the establishment of an absolute tyranny over her. To prove this, let facts be submitted to a candid world.

He has never permitted her to exercise her inalienable right to the elective franchise.

He has compelled her to submit to laws, in the formation of which she had no voice.

He has withheld from her rights which are given to the most ignorant and degraded men—both native and foreigners.

Having deprived her of this first right of a citizen, the elective franchise, thereby leaving her without representation in the halls of legislation, he has oppressed her on all sides.

He has made her, if married, in the eye of the law, civilly dead.

He has taken from her all right in property, even to the wages she earns.

He has made her, morally, an irresponsible being, as she can commit many crimes with impunity, provided they be done in the presence of her husband. In the covenant of marriage, she is compelled to promise obedience to her husband, he becoming, to all intents and purposes, her master—the law giving him power to deprive her of her liberty, and to administer chastisement.

He has so framed the laws of divorce, as to what shall be the proper causes, and in case of separation, to whom the guardianship of the children shall be given, as to be wholly regardless of the happiness of women—the law, in all cases, going upon a false supposition of the supremacy of man, and giving all power into his hands.

After depriving her of all rights as a married woman, if single, and the owner of property, he has taxed her to support a government which recognizes her only when her property can be made profitable to it.

He has monopolized nearly all the profitable employments, and from those she is permitted to follow, she receives but a scanty remuneration. He closes against her all the avenues to wealth and distinction which he considers most honorable to himself. As a teacher of theology, medicine, or law, she is not known.

He has denied her the facilities for obtaining a thorough education, all colleges being closed against her.

He allows her in Church, as well as State, but a subordinate position, claiming Apostolic authority for her exclusion from the ministry, and, with some exceptions, from any public participation in the affairs of the Church.

He has created a false public sentiment by giving to the world a different code of morals for men and women, by which moral delinquencies which exclude women from society, are not only tolerated, but deemed of little account in man.

He has usurped the prerogative of Jehovah himself, claiming it as his right to assign for her a sphere of action, when that belongs to her conscience and to her God.

He has endeavored, in every way that he could, to destroy her confidence in her own powers, to lessen her self-respect, and to make her willing to lead a dependent and abject life.

Now, in view of this entire disfranchisement of one-half the people of this country, their social and religious degradation—in view of the unjust laws above mentioned, and because women do feel themselves aggrieved, oppressed, and fraudulently deprived of their most sacred rights, we insist that they have immediate admission to all the rights and privileges which belong to them as citizens of the United States.

In entering upon the great work before us, we anticipate no small amount of misconception, misrepresentation, and ridicule; but we shall use every instrumentality within our power to effect our object. We shall employ agents, circulate tracts, petition the State and National legislatures, and endeavor to enlist the pulpit and the press in our behalf. We hope this Convention will be followed by a series of Conventions embracing every part of the country.

The following resolutions were discussed by Lucretia Mott, Thomas and Mary Ann McClintock, Amy Post, Catharine A. F. Stebbins, and others, and were adopted:

WHEREAS, The great precept of nature is conceded to be, that "man shall pursue his own true and substantial happiness." Blackstone in his Commentaries remarks, that this law of Nature being coeval with mankind, and dictated by God himself, is of course superior in obligation to any other. It is binding over all the globe, in all countries, and at all times; no human laws are of any validity if contrary to this, and such of them as are valid, derive all their force, and all their validity, and all their authority, mediately and immediately, from this original; therefore;

Resolved, That such laws as conflict, in any way, with the true and substantial happiness of woman, are contrary to the great precept of nature and of no validity, for this is "superior in obligation to any other."

Resolved, That all laws which prevent woman from occupying such a station in society as her conscience shall dictate, or which place her in a position inferior to that of man, are contrary to the great precept of nature, and therefore of no force or authority.

Resolved, That woman is man's equal— was intended to be so by the Creator, and the highest good of the race demands that she should be recognized as such.

Resolved, That the women of this country ought to be enlightened in regard to the laws under which they live, that they may no longer publish their degradation by declaring themselves satisfied with their present position, nor their ignorance by asserting that they have all the rights they want.

Resolved, That inasmuch as man, while claiming for himself intellectual superiority, does accord to woman moral superiority, it is preeminently his duty to encourage her to speak and teach, as she has an opportunity, in all religious assemblies.

Resolved, That the same amount of virtue, delicacy, and refinement of behavior that is required of woman in the social state, should also be required of man, and the same transgressions should be visited with equal severity on both man and woman.

Resolved, That the objection of indelicacy and impropriety, which is so often brought against woman when she addresses a public audience, comes with a very ill-grace from those who encourage, by their attendance, her appearance on the stage, in the concert, or in feats of the circus.

Resolved, That woman has too long rested satisfied in the circumscribed limits which corrupt customs and a perverted application of the Scriptures have marked out for her, and that it is time she should move in the enlarged sphere which her great Creator has assigned her.

Resolved, That it is the duty of the women of this country to secure to themselves their sacred right to the elective franchise.

Resolved, That the equality of human rights results necessarily from the fact of the identity of the race in capabilities and responsibilities.

Resolved, therefore, That, being invested by the Creator with the same capabilities, and the same consciousness of responsibility for their exercise, it is demonstrably the right and duty of woman, equally with man, to promote every righteous cause by every righteous means; and especially in regard to the great subjects of morals and religion, it is self-evidently her right to participate with her brother in teaching them, both in private and in public, by writing and by speaking, by any instrumentalities proper to be used, and in any assemblies proper to be held; and this being a self-evident truth growing out of the divinely implanted principles of human nature, any custom or authority adverse to it, whether modern or wearing the hoary sanction of antiquity, is to be regarded as a self-evident falsehood, and at war with mankind.

At the last session Lucretia Mott offered and spoke to the following resolution:

Resolved, That the speedy success of our cause depends upon the zealous and untiring efforts of both men and women, for the overthrow of the monopoly of the pulpit, and for the securing to woman an equal participation with men in the various trades, professions, and commerce.

Married Women's Property Acts, New York State, 1848, 1860

Ironically, the first married women's property acts, passed in Mississippi in 1839 and in New York in 1848, were supported by many male legislators out of a desire to preserve the estates of married daughters against spendthrift sons-in-law. Four out of the five sections of the Mississippi act broadened the rights of married women over their own slaves.

Note the limits of the 1848 New York law and the ways in which women's rights were extended by the 1860 revision. In 1860 married women were also confirmed in the joint guardianship of their children.

The statutes were narrowly interpreted by most courts, not only in New York but in other states that established similar legislation. For example, although married women were authorized to "carry on any trade or business, and perform any labor or services on her sole or separate account," that authorization was regularly interpreted as applying only when her work was not done on family property. She could rarely make claims for her earnings within the family or against her husband's estate; deep into the twentieth century farm women had, for example, no legal claim to the "butter and egg money" that customary practice enabled them to claim because they did the hard work of the barn and chicken coop.

1848

The real and personal property of any female [now married and] who may hereafter marry, and which she shall own at the time of marriage, and the rents issues and profits thereof shall not be subject to the disposal of her husband, nor be liable for his debts, and shall continue her sole and separate property, as if she were a single female. . . .

It shall be lawful for any married female to receive, by gift, grant, devise or bequest, from any person other than her husband and hold to her sole and separate use, as if she were a single female, real and personal property, and the rents, issues and profits thereof, and the same shall not be subject to the disposal of her husband, nor be liable for his debts. . . .

1860

[The provisions of the law of 1848 were retained, and others were added:]
A married woman may bargain, sell, assign, and transfer her separate personal property, and carry on any trade or business, and perform any labor or services on her sole and sep-

arate account, and the earnings of any married woman from her trade . . . shall be her sole and separate property, and may be used or invested by her in her own name. . . .

Any married woman may, while married, sue and be sued in all matters having relation to her . . . sole and separate property . . . in the same manner as if she were sole. And any married woman may bring and maintain an action in her own name, for damages, against any person or body corporate, for any injury to her person or character, the same as if she were sole; and the money received upon the settlement . . . shall be her sole and separate property.

No bargain or contract made by any married woman, in respect to her sole and separate property . . . shall be binding upon her husband, or render him or his property in any way liable therefor.

Every married woman is hereby constituted and declared to be the joint guardian of her children, with her husband, with equal powers, rights, and duties in regard to them, with the husband. . . .

Laws of the State of New-York, Passed at the Seventy-First Session of the Legislature . . . (Albany, 1848), pp. 307–8; *Laws of the State of New York, Passed at the Eighty-Third Session of the Legislature . . .* (Albany, 1860), pp. 157–59.

NELL IRVIN PAINTER
Sojourner Truth's Defense of the Rights of Women (as reported in 1851; rewritten in 1863)

Sojourner Truth (ca. 1797–1883) is often equated with the phrase "ar'n't I a woman?" which symbolizes black women in American history and strong women of any race. Truth, who was born a slave named Isabella in New York's Hudson River Valley, was emancipated by state law in 1827, moved to New York City in 1828, worked in private households to gain her living, became an unorthodox Methodist, and made a reputation as an exhorter. In 1843 divine inspiration directed her to take the name Sojourner Truth and become an itinerant preacher. Addressing outdoor camp meetings on Long Island and up the Connecticut River Valley, she reached the utopian Northampton [Massachusetts] Association in the winter of 1843–1844, where she settled and met abolitionists like William Lloyd Garrison and Frederick Douglass.

In 1845 Douglass published his first autobiography, which became a best-seller in England and the United States and inspired Sojourner Truth. Unlike Douglass, Truth was illiterate, and she dictated her narrative to Olive Gilbert, a teacher from Connecticut. In 1850 Truth paid to have *The Narrative of Sojourner Truth* published and began traveling the reform lecture circuit, speaking against slavery and for women's rights. Wherever she appeared she sold her *Narrative*, which provided her material support.

A women's rights convention in Akron, Ohio, in 1851 furnished Truth an opportunity to address a sympathetic gathering and sell books. The 1851 report by one of Truth's close associates in the Salem *Antislavery Bugle* runs like this:

One of the most unique and interesting speeches of the Convention was made by Sojourner Truth, an emancipated slave. It is impossible to transfer it to paper, or convey any adequate idea of the effect it produced upon the audience. Those only can appreciate it who saw her powerful form, her whole-souled, earnest gestures, and listened to her strong and truthful tones. She came forward to the platform and addressing the President said with great simplicity:

May I say a few words? Receiving an affirmative answer, she proceeded; I want to say a few words about this matter. I am a woman's rights. [sic] I have as much muscle as any man, and can do as much work as any man. I have plowed and reaped and husked and chopped and mowed, and can any man do more than that? I have heard much about the sexes being equal;

I can carry as much as any man, and can eat as much too, if I can get it. I am as strong as any man that is now. As for intellect, all I can say is, if a woman have a pint and man a quart—why cant she have her little pint full? You need not be afraid to give us our rights for fear we will take too much,—for we cant take more than our pint'll hold. The poor men seem to be all in confusion, and dont know what to do. Why children, if you have woman's rights give it to her and you will feel better. You will have your own rights, and they wont be so much trouble. I cant read, but I can hear. I have heard the bible and have learned that Eve caused man to sin. Well if woman upset the world, do give her a chance to set it right side up again. The Lady has spoken about Jesus, how he never spurned woman from him, and she was right. When Lazarus died,

Mary and Martha came to him with faith and love and besought him to raise their brother. And Jesus wept—and Lazarus came forth. And how came Jesus into the world? Through God who created him and woman who bore him. Man, where is your part? But the women are coming up blessed be God and a few of the man are coming up with them. But man is in a tight place, the poor slave is on him, woman is coming on him, and he is surely between a hawk and a buzzard.

The same newspaper also ran a report of the speech given by Frances Dana Gage (1808–1884), who chaired the convention. Gage was a lecturer, journalist, and poet who published mainly in the antislavery and feminist press. A more radical feminist and abolitionist than Harriet Beecher Stowe, Gage was less well known. In 1851 Gage used Sojourner Truth as a character called Winna in a story she serialized in a feminist newspaper, but she did not describe Truth's 1851 speech until a good deal later. In the meanwhile, Truth continued speaking and selling her books.

In the nineteenth century, as today, authors commonly asked celebrities for blurbs to use as advertisement. After the phenomenal success of *Uncle Tom's Cabin* in 1851–1852 made Harriet Beecher Stowe famous, Truth visited her to request a blurb, which was forthcoming. In subsequent years, Stowe mentioned Truth to her friends privately, but she did not publish anything until the 1860s. Once the Emancipation Proclamation and the acceptance of black men into the Union Army made the Civil War into an acknowledged struggle over slavery, "the Negro" became a popular topic of discourse; then Stowe tapped into her recollections of Truth to shape an essay in the *Atlantic Monthly*, one of the most respectable periodicals of the time. "Sojourner Truth, the Libyan Sibyl" appeared in April 1863.

The publication of Stowe's article inspired Gage to write her own essay and invent the phrase, "ar'n't I a woman?" As long as the values of consumers of journalism were more attuned to the sentimentalism of Stowe than the radicalism of Gage, Stowe's "Libyan Sibyl" remained more popular, but at the end of the nineteenth century, the balance began to tip in Gage's favor.

Susan B. Anthony (Gage's friend since the 1850s) and Elizabeth Cady Stanton included Gage's report, not Stowe's, in *The History of Woman Suffrage*, where woman suffragists found a figure of Sojourner Truth that was useful against antagonists. In the mid-twentieth century American tastes changed, rejecting Stowe's quaint little exotic and embracing Gage's bold feminist. The 1851 report of Truth's speech, however, still seems too moderate to be useful as symbolism, even though it captures the historic— as opposed to the emblematic—Sojourner Truth. At least for the time being, a symbol rather than an individual black woman's utterance is what American culture demands.

DREW GILPIN FAUST

Enemies in Our Households: Confederate Women and Slavery

The Civil War profoundly disrupted and reshaped American society; more people died in it than in all America's subsequent wars put together. It tested the stability of the Union and the meaning of democracy; Confederates insisted that their vision of a republic, which rested on racial hierarchy and the subordination of blacks, sustained the same claims to self-determination that had been central to the principles of the Revolution of 1776. The war would involve civilians in novel ways.

Because soldiers were recruited as companies from the same locality, it was not impossible for women to dress as men and enlist; buddies kept their secrets. A conservative estimate is that some 400 women joined in this way. A handful of women crossed military lines as spies, some disguising their race or their gender in the process. Thousands more women were recruited as hospital workers in both North and South; late in the war the Union recruited hundreds of freedwomen for this service. The bureaucracy of the federal government was vastly expanded during the war, and the personnel shortage was solved by hiring, for the first time in U.S. history, women to work in the same offices as men doing similar work.

Throughout the nation, North and South, familiar patterns of gender relations were disrupted, in a manner not unlike what had happened when men left for the Gold Rush, but on a far greater and more frightening scale. In the South, as Drew Faust explains, the departure of white men for war meant that white women were challenged to assume authority and to stabilize slavery despite the loss of the usual forms of force that had kept it in place. They discovered that they were living "with enemies in our own households." How they responded to this challenge varied; they were often profoundly transformed by their experiences.

What challenges did elite women face at the beginning of the war? What were some of the ways in which they responded? What allies did they have? What forms of resistance to authority did slaves engage in? How did the disruptions of the war bring into question traditional relations between white women and men?

When slaveholding men departed for battle, white women on farms and plantations across the South assumed direction of the region's "peculiar institution." In the antebellum years white men had borne overwhelming responsibility for slavery's daily management and perpetuation. But as war changed the shape of southern households, it necessarily transformed the structures of domestic authority, requiring white women to exercise unaccustomed—and unsought—power in defense of public as well as private order. Slavery was, as Confederate vice-president Alexander Stephens proclaimed, the "cornerstone" of the region's society, economy, and politics. Yet slavery's survival depended less on sweeping dictates of state policy than on tens of thousands of individual acts of personal domination exercised by particular masters over particular slaves. As wartime opportunity encouraged slaves openly to assert their desire for freedom, the daily struggle over coercion and control on hundreds of plantations and farms became just as crucial to defense of the southern way of life as any military encounter. Women called to manage increasingly restive and even rebellious slaves were in a significant sense garrisoning a second front in the South's war against Yankee domination.[1] . . .

Although white southerners—both male and female—might insist that politics was not, even in the changed circumstances of wartime, an appropriate part of woman's sphere, the female slave manager necessarily served as a pillar of the South's political order. White women's actions as slave mistresses were crucial to Confederate destinies, for the viability of the southern agricultural economy and the stability of the social order as well as the continuing loyalty of the civilian population all depended on successful slave control.

. . . The very meaning of mastery itself was rooted in the concepts of masculinity and male power. From the outset, Confederate leaders were uneasy about the transfer of such responsibility to women. . . .

As support grew in the fall of 1862 for some official draft exemption for slave managers, the *Macon Daily Telegraph* demanded, "Is it possible that Congress thinks . . . our women can control the slaves and oversee the farms? Do they suppose that our patriotic mothers, sisters and daughters can assume and discharge the active duties and drudgery of an overseer? Certainly not. They know better." In October Congress demonstrated that it did indeed know better, passing a law exempt-

ing from service one white man on each plantation of twenty or more slaves. But the soon infamous [law] . . . triggered enormous popular resentment, both from nonslaveholders who regarded it as valuing the lives of the elite over their own and from smaller slaveholders who were not included in its scope.[2]

In an effort to silence this threatening outburst of class hostility and at the same time meet the South's ever increasing manpower needs, the Confederate Congress repeatedly amended conscription policy, both broadening the age of eligibility and limiting exemptions. . . . This erosion of the statutory foundation for overseer exemptions greatly increased the difficulty of finding men not subject to military duty who could, as the original bill had phrased it, "secure the proper police of the country." Women across the Confederacy would find themselves unable to obtain the assistance of white men on their plantations and farms.

Conscription policy reveals fundamental Confederate assumptions, for it represents significant choices made by the Confederate leadership, choices that in important ways defined issues of class as more central to Confederate survival than those of gender. . . . White women in slaveowning households found their needs relegated to a position of secondary importance in comparison with the demands of nonslaveholding men. These men could vote, and the Confederacy required their service on the battlefield; retaining their loyalty was a priority. Minimizing class divisions within the Confederacy was imperative—even if ultimately unsuccessful. Addressing emerging gender divisions seemed less critical, because women—even the "privileged" ladies of the slaveowning elite—neither voted nor wrote editorials nor bore arms.[3]

With ever escalating military manpower demands, however, white women came to assume responsibility for directing the slave system that was so central a cause and purpose of the war. Yet they could not forget the promises of male protection and obligation that they believed their due. Women's troubling experiences as slave managers generated a growing fear and resentment of the burdens imposed by the disintegrating institution. Ultimately these tensions did much to undermine women's active support for both slavery and the Confederate cause. And throughout the South eroding slave control and diminishing plantation efficiency directly contributed to failures of morale and productivity on the homefront.

UNPROTECTED AND AFRAID

Women agreed with the Georgia newspaper that had proclaimed them unfit masters. "Where there are so many negroes upon places as upon ours," wrote an Alabama woman to the governor, "it is quite necessary that there should be men who can and will control them, especially at this time." Faced with the prospect of being left with sixty slaves, a Mississippi planter's wife expressed similar sentiments. "Do you think," she demanded of Governor John Pettus, "that this woman's hand can keep them in check?" Women compelled to assume responsibility over slaves tended to regard their new role more as a duty than an opportunity. Like many southern soldiers, they were conscripts rather than volunteers. As Lizzie Neblett explained to her husband, Will, when he enlisted in the 20th Texas Infantry, her impending service as agricultural and slave manager was "a coercive one."[4]

Women's reluctance derived in no small part from a profound sense of their own incapacities. One Mississippi woman complained that she lacked sufficient "moral courage" to govern slaves; another believed "managing negroes . . . beyond my power." "Master's eye and voice," Catherine Edmondston remarked, "are much more potent than mistress'." . . . Slaves themselves frequently seemed to share their mistresses' views of their own incapacities. Ellen Moore of Virginia complained that her laborers "all think I am a kind of usurper & have no authority over them." As war and the promise of freedom encouraged increasing black assertiveness, white women discovered themselves in charge of an institution quite different from the one their husbands, brothers, fathers, and sons had managed before military conflict commenced.[5]

Female apprehensions about slave mastery arose from fears of this very rebelliousness and from a sense of the special threat slave violence might pose to white women. Keziah Brevard, a fifty-eight-year-old South

Carolina widow, lived in almost constant fear of her sizable slave force. "It is dreadful to dwell on insurrections," she acknowledged. Yet "many an hour have I laid awake in my life thinking of our danger."[6] . . .

Early in the war, Mary Chesnut, who professed never to have had any fear of her slaves, felt compelled to reconsider her own safety when her cousin Betsey Witherspoon was smothered by her servants. An elderly widow who lived alone with her slaves, Witherspoon was well known as an ineffective and indulgent manager. Her murder underlined both the inadequacies and vulnerabilities of white women as slave masters; her fate was exactly what her South Carolina neighbor Keziah Brevard most feared. Another Carolina widow, Ada Bacot, contemplated Witherspoon's death and the prospects of her own slaves' loyalty with similar dismay. "I fear twould take very little to make them put me out of the way," she wrote.[7] . . .

. . . Reports of individual acts of violence proliferated as well. Ada Bacot was certain the fire in her neighbors' house was set by their slave Abel; Laura Lee was horrified when occupying troops released a Winchester slave convicted of murdering her mistress. In September 1862 the *Mobile Advertiser and Register* noted that a slave had succeeded in poisoning his master; the same month the *Richmond Enquirer* recorded the conviction of one Lavinia for torching her mistress's house.[8] . . .

By the middle years of the war, women had begun publicly to voice their fears, writing hundreds of letters to state and Confederate officials imploring that men be detailed from military service to control the slaves. A group of women living near New Bern petitioned North Carolina Governor Zebulon Vance for exemptions for the few men who still remained at home. "We pray your Excellency to consider that in the absence of all protection the female portion of this community may be subjected to a system of outrage that may be justly denominated the harrow of harrows more terrible to the contemplation of the virtuous maiden and matron than death." A petition to the Confederate secretary of war from a similar collection of "Ladies of the N.E. beat of Jas[per] County, Miss." sought male protection against an anticipated slave insurrection. If that was impossible, they requested arms and ammunition to defend themselves from "the demonic invasion" so that "we die with honor & innocence sustained."[9]

These women chose different euphemisms to express their anxieties—insult, outrage, "harrow of harrows," dishonor, stain, and molestation—but the theme was undeniably sexual. The Old South had justified white woman's subordination in terms of her biological difference, emphasizing an essential female weakness that rested ultimately in sexual vulnerability. In a society based on the oppression of a potentially hostile population of 4 million black slaves, such vulnerability assumed special significance. On this foundation of race, the white South erected its particular—and particularly compelling—logic of female dependence. Only the white man's strength could provide adequate and necessary protection. The very word *protection* was invoked again and again by Confederate women petitioning for what they believed [was] the fundamental right guaranteed them by the paternalistic social order of the South: "I feel unprotected and afraid," "unable to protect myself," "unable to stand up under her burden without the assistance of some white male to protect her." Denied such assurances of safety, many women would be impelled to question—even if implicitly—the logic of their willing acceptance of their own inferiority. In seeking, like the ladies of Jasper County, Mississippi, to protect themselves, Confederate women profoundly undermined the legitimacy of their subordination, demonstrating that they did not—indeed could not—depend on the supposed superior strength of white men.[10]

Significantly, the "demonic" invaders these Mississippi women most feared were not Yankees but rebellious slaves. In their terror of an insurgent black population, white southern women advanced their own definition of wartime priorities, one seemingly not shared by the Confederate leadership and government. "I fear the blacks more than I do the Yankees," confessed Mrs. A. Ingraham of besieged Vicksburg. . . . Living with slavery in wartime was, one Virginia woman observed, living with "enemies in our own households."[11]

The arrival of black soldiers in parts of the South represented the conjunction and culmination of these fears. Mary Lee of Winchester, Virginia, came "near fainting" when the troops appeared; she felt "more unnerved than by any sight I have seen since the war [began]."

These soldiers were at once men, blacks, and national enemies—her gender, racial, and political opposites, the quintessential powerful and hostile Other. Their occupying presence in Winchester reminded her so forcefully of her weakness and vulnerability that she responded with a swoon, an unwanted and unwonted display of the feminine impotence and delicacy she had struggled to overcome during long years of her own as well as Confederate independence.[12]

Yet women often denied or repressed these profound fears of racial violence, confronting them only in the darkest hours of anxious, sleepless nights. Constance Cary Harrison remembered that in the daytime, apprehensions about slave violence seemed "preposterous," but at night, "there was the fear . . . dark, boding, oppressive and altogether hateful . . . the ghost that refused to be laid."[13] . . .

Some women in fact regarded their slaves as protectors, hoping for the loyalty that the many tales of "faithful servants" would enshrine in Confederate popular culture and, later, within the myth of the Lost Cause. Elizabeth Saxon, in a typically rose-colored remembrance of slavery during the war, recalled in 1905 that "not an outrage was perpetrated, no house was burned. . . . [O]n lonely farms women with little children slept at peace, guarded by a sable crowd, whom they perfectly trusted. . . . [I]n no land was ever a people so tender and helpful." The discrepancy between this portrait and the anxieties of everyday life on Confederate plantations underscores how white southerners, both during the war and afterward, struggled to retain a view of slavery as a benevolent institution, appreciated by blacks as well as whites. During the war such "faithful servant" stories served to calm white fears. But examples of persisting white trust and confidence in slaves cannot be discounted entirely, nor can the stories themselves be uniformly dismissed as white inventions. There were in fact slaves who buried the master's silver to hide it from the enemy; there were slaves, like one Catherine Edmondston described, who drew knives to defend mistresses against Yankee troops. Such incidents reinforced white southerners' desire not to believe that men and women they thought they had known intimately—sometimes all their lives—had suddenly become murderers and revolutionaries.[14]

Much of the complexity of wartime relationships between white women and slaves arose because women increasingly relied on slaves' labor, competence, and even companionship at a time when slaves saw diminishing motivation for work or obedience. White women's dependence on their slaves grew simultaneously with slaves' independence of their owners, creating a troubling situation of confusion and ambivalence for mistresses compelled constantly to reassess, to interrogate, and to revise their assumptions as they struggled to reconcile need with fear. . . . Some slave mistresses, especially in isolated plantation settings, found that in changed wartime households, their closest adult connections were with female slaves. When Rhoda died in April 1862, her owner Anna Green wrote in despair to her sister. "I feel like I have lost my only friend and I do believe she was the most faithful friend I had [even] if she was a servant." Leila Callaway described the death from smallpox of her slave Susanna in almost identical terms. "Next to my own dear family Susanna was my warmest best friend." "I have no one now in your absence," she informed her husband, "to look to for protection." In the disruptions of the South's hierarchies of gender and race, Leila Callaway had invested a black woman with some of the responsibilities—emotional and otherwise—of the absent white man.[15]

. . . Maria Hawkins keenly felt the absence of her slave protector Moses and wrote to Governor Vance with a variation of the hundreds of letters to southern officials seeking discharge of husbands and sons. Hawkins requested Moses' release from impressment as a laborer on coastal fortifications. "He slept in the house, every night while at home, & protected everything in the house & yard & at these perilous times when deserters are committing depredations, on plantations every day, I am really so much frightened every night, that I am up nearly all night." In Hawkins's particular configuration of gender and racial anxieties, a black male protector was far preferable to no male at all.[16]

THE FRUITS OF THE WAR

Within the context of everyday life in the Confederacy, most women slaveholders confronted neither murderous revolutionaries nor the unfailingly loyal retainers of "moonlight and magnolias" tradition. Instead they faced complex human beings whose desires for freedom expressed themselves in ways that varied with changing means and opportunities as slavery weakened steadily under unrelenting northern military pressure.

Often opportunity was greatest in areas close to Union lines, and slave-owners in these locations confronted the greatest challenges of discipline. . . . Ada Bacot, widowed South Carolina plantation owner, believed her "orders disregarded more & more every day. I can do nothing so must submit, which is anything but pleasant." When she left Carolina for a nursing post at the Monticello Hospital in Charlottesville, however, she soon discovered "Virginia Negroes are not near so servile as those of S.C." . . . When an adolescent slave named William defied her order to clean up the dinner table in the house where she and the other nurses and doctors lodged, she called him to task. But the young slave was "so impertinent that I slaped him in the mouth before I knew what I did." His mother rushed from the kitchen to his defense, provoking Bacot to threaten both slaves with punishment. Unlike many Confederate slave managers, though, Bacot did not live in a world comprised exclusively of women. She turned for aid to the white male doctors who were also residents of the household, and they whipped both irate mother and insolent child.[17]

For many white women this physical dimension of slave control proved most troubling. . . .

Just as "paternalism" and "mastery" were rooted in concepts of masculinity, so violence was similarly gendered as male within the ideology of the Old South. Recourse to physical force in support of male honor and white supremacy was regarded as the right, even the responsibility, of each white man—within his household, on his plantation, in his community, and with the outbreak of war, for his nation. Women slave managers inherited a social order that depended on the threat and often the use of violence. Throughout the history of the peculiar institution, slave mistresses had in fact slapped, hit, and even brutally whipped their slaves—particularly slave women or children. But their relationship to this exercise of physical power was significantly different from that of their men. No gendered code of honor celebrated women's phys-ical power or dominance. A contrasting yet parallel ideology extolled female sensitivity, weakness, and vulnerability. In the prewar years, exercise of the violence fundamental to slavery was overwhelmingly the responsibil-ity and prerogative of white men. A white woman disciplined and punished as the mas-ter's subordinate and surrogate. Rationalized, systematic, autonomous, and instrumental use of violence belonged to men.

Ada Bacot surprised herself when she lashed out and slapped young William, and it was in just such moments of rage that many Confederate women embraced physical force. But for the kind of rationalized punishment intended to function as the mainstay of slave discipline, Bacot turned to men. Women alone customarily sought overseers, male relatives, or neighbors to undertake physical coercion of slaves, especially slave men. As white men disappeared to war, however, finding such help became increasingly difficult. . . .

As slaves grew more assertive in antici-pation of their freedom, their female managers regarded physical coercion as at once more essential and more impossible. Some white women began to bargain with violence, trying to make slavery seem benign in hopes of retaining their slaves' service, if not their loy-alty. Avoiding physical punishment even in the face of insolence or poor work, they endeavored to keep their slaves from depart-ing altogether. . . . [In Texas,] Lizzie Neblett urged her part-time overseer not to beat a slave in response to his insubordination. "I told him not to whip Joe, as long as he done his work well . . . that he might run away & we might never get him & if he never done me any good he might my children." Lizzie worried as well that whipping might provoke violent retalia-tion against managers who possessed the obvi-ous vulnerability of the Confederacy's white females. Many had, she noted, become "actu-ally affraid to whip the negros."[18]

The Old South's social hierarchies had created a spectrum of legitimate access to vio-lence, so that social empowerment was inex-tricably bound up with the right to employ physical force. Violence was all but required of white men of all classes, a cultural principle rendered explicit by the coming of war and conscription. Black slaves, by contrast, were forbidden the use of violence entirely, except within their own communities, where the dominant society chose to regard it as essen-tially invisible. White women stood upon an ill-defined middle ground, where behavior and ideology often diverged.

The Civil War exacerbated this very ten-sion . . . even on the homefront, women felt inadequate; their understanding of their gen-der undermined their effectiveness. Just as their inability to bear arms left Confederate women feeling "useless," so their inhibitions about violence made many females regard themselves as failures at slave management. As Lizzie Neblett wrote of her frustration in the effort to control eleven recalcitrant slaves, "I am so sick of trying to do a man's business when I am nothing but, a poor contemptible piece of multiplying human flesh tied to the house by a crying young one, looked upon as belonging to a race of inferior beings." The language she chose to describe her self-loathing is significant, for she borrowed it from the vocabulary of race as well as gender. Invoking the objective con-straints of biology—"multiplying flesh"—as well as the socially constructed limitations of status—"looked upon as belonging to a race of inferior beings"—she identified herself not with the white elite, not with those in whose interest the war was being fought, but with the South's oppressed and disadvantaged. Increas-ingly, even though self-indulgently, she came to regard herself as the victim rather than the beneficiary of her region's slave society. Lizzie Neblett's uniquely documented experience with violence and slavery deserves exploration in some detail, for it illustrates not simply the contradictions inherent in female management, but the profound personal crisis of identity gen-erated by her new and unaccustomed role.[19]

TROUBLED IN MIND

When her husband departed for war in the spring of 1863, Lizzie had set about the task of management committed to "doing my best" but was apprehensive both about her igno-rance of agriculture and about the behavior she might expect from her eleven slaves. Their initial response to her direction, however, seemed promising. "The negros," she wrote Will in late April, "seem to be mightily stirred up about making a good crop."[20]

By harvest, however, the situation had already changed. "The negros are doing nothing," Lizzie wrote Will at the height of first cotton picking in mid-August. . . . Lizzie harbored few illusions about the long-term loyalty of her own black family. "I dont think we have one who will stay with us."[21]

After a harvest that fell well below the previous year's achievement, Lizzie saw the need for new managerial arrangements. Will had provided for a male neighbor to keep a general supervisory eye over the Neblett slave force, but Lizzie wrote Will in the fall of 1863 that she had contracted to pay a Mr. Meyers to spend three half-days a week with her slaves. "He will be right tight on the negroes I think, but they need it. Meyers will lay down the law and enforce it." But Lizzie emphasized that she would not permit cruelty or abuse.[22]

Controlling Meyers would prove in some ways more difficult than controlling the slaves. His second day on the plantation Meyers whipped three young male slaves for idleness, and on his next visit, as Lizzie put it, "he undertook old Sam." Gossip had spread among slaves in the neighborhood—and from them to their masters—that Sam intended to take a whipping from no man.[23] Will Neblett had, in fact, not been a harsh disciplinarian, tending more to threatening and grumbling than whipping. But Meyers regarded Sam's challenge as quite "enough." When Sam refused to come to Meyers to receive a whipping he felt he did not deserve, Meyers cornered and threatened to shoot him. Enraged, Meyers beat Sam so severely that Lizzie feared he might die. She anxiously called the doctor, who assured her that Sam had no internal injuries and that he had seen slaves beaten far worse.

Lizzie was torn over how to respond—to Meyers or to Sam. "Tho I pity the poor wretch," she confided to Will, "I don't want him to know it." To the other slaves she insisted that "Meyers would not have whipped him if he had not deserved it," and to Will she defensively maintained, "somebody must take them in hand[.] they grow worse all the time[.] I could not begin to write you . . . how little they mind me." She saw Meyers's actions as part of a plan to establish control at the outset: "he lets them know what he is . . . & then has no more trouble." But Lizzie's very insistence and defensiveness suggest that this was not, even in her mind, slave management in its ideal form.[24]

Over the next few days, Lizzie's doubts about Meyers and his course of action grew. Instead of eliminating trouble at the outset, as he had intended, the incident seemed to have created an uproar. Sarah, a cook and house slave, reported to Lizzie that Sam suspected the whipping had been his mistress's idea, and that, when well enough, he would run away until Will came home.[25]

To resolve the volatile situation and to salvage her reputation as slave mistress, Lizzie now enlisted another white man, Coleman, to talk reasonably with Sam. Coleman had been her dead father's overseer and continued to manage her mother's property. In the absence of Will and Lizzie's brothers at the front, he was an obvious family deputy, and he had undoubtedly known Sam before Lizzie had inherited him from her father's estate. Coleman agreed to "try to show Sam the error he had been guilty of." At last Sam spoke the words Coleman sought, admitting he had done wrong and promising no further insubordination.[26]

Two weeks after the incident, Lizzie and Sam finally had a direct and, in Lizzie's view at least, comforting exchange: Meyers had ordered Sam back to work, but Lizzie had interceded in response to Sam's complaints of persisting weakness. Taking his cue from Lizzie's conciliatory gesture and acting as well in accordance with Coleman's advice, Sam apologized for disappointing Lizzie's expectations, acknowledging that as the oldest slave he had special responsibilities in Will's absence. Henceforth, he promised Lizzie, he was "going to do his work faithfully & be of as much service to me as he could. I could not help," Lizzie confessed to Will, "feeling sorry for the old fellow[.] . . . he talked so humbly & seemed so hurt that I should have had him whipped so."[27]

Sam's adroit transformation from rebel into Sambo helped resolve Lizzie's uncertainties about the appropriate course of slave management. Abandoning her defense of Meyers's severity, even interceding on Sam's behalf against her own manager, Lizzie assured Sam she had not been responsible for his punishment, had indeed been "astonished" by it. Meyers, she reported to Will with newfound assurance, "did wrong" and "knows nothing" about the management of slaves. He "don't," she noted revealingly, "treat them as moral beings but manages by brute force." Henceforth, Lizzie concluded, she would not feel impelled by her sense of helplessness to countenance extreme severity. Instead, she promised Sam, if he remained "humble and submissive," she would ensure "he would not get another lick."[28]

The incident of Sam's whipping served as the occasion for an extended negotiation between Lizzie and her slaves about the terms of her power. In calling upon Meyers and Coleman, she demonstrated that, despite appearances, she was not in fact a woman alone, dependent entirely on her own resources. Although the ultimate responsibility might be hers, slave management was a community concern. Pushed toward sanctioning Meyers's cruelty by fear of her own impotence, Lizzie then stepped back from the extreme position in which Meyers had placed her. But at the same time she dissociated herself from Meyers's action, she also reaped its benefit: Sam's abandonment of a posture of overt defiance for one of apparent submission. Sam and Lizzie were ultimately able to join forces in an agreement that Meyers must be at once deplored and tolerated as a necessary evil whom both mistress and slave would strive ceaselessly to manipulate. Abandoning their brief tryouts as Simon Legree and Nat Turner, Lizzie and Sam returned to the more accustomed and comfortable roles of concerned paternalist and loyal slave. Each recognized at last that his or her own performance depended in large measure on a complementary performance by the other.

Lizzie's behavior throughout the crisis demonstrated the essential part gender identities and assumptions played in master-slave relations. . . .

Accustomed to occasional strikes against female slaves, Lizzie called on a male slave to whip the adolescent Tom, then, later, she enlisted a male neighbor to dominate the venerable Sam. Yet even this structured hierarchy of violence was becoming increasingly "disagreeable" to her as she acted out her new wartime role as "chief of affairs." In part, Lizzie knew she was objectively physically weaker than both black and white men around her. But she confessed as well to a "troubled . . . mind," to uncertainties about her appropriate relationship to the ultimate exertion of force upon which slavery rested. As

wartime pressures weakened the foundations for the "moral" management that Lizzie preferred, what she referred to as "brute force" became simultaneously more attractive and more dangerous as an instrument of coercion.

Forbidden the physical severity that served as the fundamental prop of his system of slave management, Meyers requested to be released from his contract with Lizzie at the end of the crop year. Early in the agreement, Meyers had told Lizzie that he could "conquer" her slaves, "but may have to kill some one of them." It remained with Lizzie, he explained, to make the decision. In her moments of greatest exasperation, Lizzie was willing to consent to such extreme measures. "I say do it." But with calm reflection, tempered by Will's measured advice, considerations of humanity reasserted their claim. Repeatedly she interceded between Meyers and the slaves, protecting them from whippings or condemning Meyers when he disobeyed her orders and punished them severely. Yet despite her difficulties in managing Meyers and despite her belief that he was "deficient in judgment," Lizzie recognized her dependence on him and on the threat of force he represented. She was determined to "hold him on as long as I can." If he quit and the slaves found that no one was coming to replace him, she wrote revealingly, "the jig will be up." The game, the trick, the sham of her slave management would be over. Without a man—or a man part time for three half-days a week—without the recourse to violence that Meyers embodied, slavery was unworkable. The velvet glove of paternalism required its iron hand.[29]

Violence was the ultimate foundation of power in the slave South, but gender prescriptions carefully barred white women—especially those elite women most likely to find themselves responsible for controlling slaves—from purposeful exercise of physical dominance. Even when circumstances had shifted to make female authority socially desirable, it remained for many plantation mistresses personally unachievable. Lizzie's struggle with her attraction to violence and her simultaneous abhorrence of it embodied the contradictions that the necessary wartime paradox of female slave management imposed. Lizzie begged Will to hire out his slaves or even to "give your negros away and, I'll . . . work with my hands, as hard as I can, but my mind will rest." Lizzie wished repeatedly to die, to be a man, or to give up the slaves altogether—except, tellingly, for "one good negro to wait upon me." White women had reaped slavery's benefits throughout its existence in the colonial and antebellum South. But they could not be its everyday managers without in some measure failing to be what they understood as female. The authority of their class and race could not overcome the dependence they had learned to identify as the essence of their womanhood. [30] . . .

Beginning her duties as slave manager with optimism and enthusiasm, Mary Bell [of Franklin, North Carolina] came ultimately to share with Lizzie Neblett a profound sense of failure and personal inadequacy. As she repeatedly told [her husband], Alf, "unless you could be at home," "unless you were at home," the system would not work. "You say," Mary Bell wrote her husband in December 1864, "you think I am a good farmer if I only had confidence in myself. I confess I have very little confidence in my own judgment and management. wish I had more. perhaps if I had I would not get so out of heart. Sometimes I am almost ready to give up and think that surely my lot is harder than anyone else."[31]

A growing disillusionment with slavery among many elite white women arose from this very desire to "give up"—to be freed from burdens of management and fear of black reprisal that often outweighed any tangible benefits from the labor of increasingly recalcitrant slaves. Few slaveowning women had seriously questioned the moral or political legitimacy of the system, although many admitted to the profound evils associated with the institution. Gertrude Thomas noted its "terribly demoralising influence upon our men and boys," and Mary Chesnut's vehement criticisms similarly fixed on the almost unrestricted sexual access slavery gave white men to black women. Yet her concerns, like those of Gertrude Thomas, lay with the impact of these social arrangements on whites and their families rather than on exploited slaves. White southern women readily embraced the racism of their era. Blacks were, Chesnut remarked, "dirty—slatternly—idle—ill smelling by nature." Slaves were unquestionably inferior beings "blest," as one North Carolina woman wrote, "in having a home among Anglo Saxons." Jane Howison Beale of Virginia had no doubt that blacks "were ordained of High Heaven to serve the white man and it is only in that capacity they can be happy useful and respected."[32]

Southern slave mistresses began to convince themselves, however, that an institution that they were certain worked in the interest of blacks did not necessarily advance their own. Confederate women could afford little contemplation of slavery's merits "in the abstract," as its prewar defenders had urged. Slavery's meaning did not rest in the detached and intellectualized realms of politics or moral philosophy. The growing emotional and physical cost of the system to slaveholding women made its own forceful appeal, and many slave mistresses began to persuade themselves that the institution had become a greater inconvenience than benefit. . . . Like Lizzie Neblett, many white women focused on slavery's trials and yearned for the peculiar institution—and all the troublesome blacks constrained within its bonds—magically to disappear . . . . But . . . many women who entertained such fantasies at the same time longed for just "one good negro to wait upon me." For white women, this would be emancipation's greatest cost.[33]

AN ENTIRE RUPTURE OF OUR DOMESTIC RELATIONS

In the summer of 1862 a Confederate woman overheard two small girls "playing ladies." "Good morning, ma'am," said little Sallie to her friend. "How are you today?" "I don't feel very well this morning," four-year-old Nannie Belle replied. "*All my niggers have run away and left me.*"[34]

From the first months of the war, white women confronted yet another change in their households, one that a Virginia woman described as "an entire disruption of our domestic relations": the departure of their slaves. Sometimes, especially when Yankee troops swept through an area, the loss was total and immediate. Sarah Hughes of Alabama stood as a roadside spectator at the triumphant procession of hundreds of her slaves toward freedom. Her niece, Eliza Walker, en route to visit her aunt, described the scene that greeted her as she approached the Hughes plantation.

> Down the road [the Bluecoats] . . . came, and with them all the slaves . . . , journeying, as they thought, to the promised land. I saw them as they trudged the main road, many of the women with

babes in their arms . . . old and young, men, women and children. Some of them fared better than the others. A negro woman, Laura, my aunt's fancy seamstress, rode Mrs. Hughes' beautiful white pony, sitting [on] the red plush saddle of her mistress. The Hughes' family carriage, driven by Taliaferro, the old coachman, and filled with blue coated soldiers and negroes, passed in state, and this was followed by other vehicles.

With the trusted domestics leading the way, Sarah Hughes's slaves had turned her world upside down.[35]

Usually the departure of slaves was less dramatic and more secretive, as blacks simply stole away one by one or in groups of two or three when they heard of opportunities to reach Union armies and freedom. In Middleburg, Virginia, Catherine Cochran reported, "Scarcely a morning dawned that some stampede was not announced—sometimes persons would awake to find every servant gone & we never went to bed without anticipating such an occurrence." In nearby Winchester, Mary Lee presided over a more extended dissolution of her slave force. Her male slaves were the first to leave in the spring of 1862. Emily and Betty threatened to follow, and Lee considered sending them off to a more secure location away from Federal lines in order to keep from losing them altogether. Having regular help in the house seemed imperative, though, even if it was risky. "I despise menial work," Lee confessed. But she had no confidence she would retain her property. "It is an uncomfortable thought, in waking in the morning, to be uncertain as to whether you will have any servants to bring in water and prepare breakfast. . . . I dread our house servants going and having to do their work." When Betty talked again of leaving in June 1863, Laura Lee, Mary's sister-in-law, locked up the clothes the black woman had packed in anticipation of departure. Laura was determined "not to lose them too, if I could help it." Temporarily thwarted, Betty left for good the next summer, and the Lees lost slave and clothing after all.[36]

By the time of her exile from Winchester in February 1865, Mary Lee was surprised that her household still enjoyed the services of a mother and daughter, Sarah and Emily, who, despite repeated threats and stormy confrontations, had not yet fled to freedom. Mary Lee entertained few illusions about the continuing loyalty of her slaves. Early in the war, she made it clear that "I have never had the least confidence in the fidelity of any negro." Her grief at their gradual disappearance was highly pragmatic; she mourned their lost labor but did not seem to cherish an ideal of master-slave harmony to be shaken by the slaves' choice of freedom over loyalty.[37]

A South Carolina woman, by contrast, became "miserably depressed" when her three most dependable house slaves fled. "If they felt as I do," she explained, "they could not possibly leave me." The Jones family of Georgia, devout Presbyterians, reflected the tenacity of their evangelical proslavery vision in their indignant feelings of betrayal at the departure of their human property. Eva Jones was distraught when three female slaves seized their freedom "without bidding any of us an affectionate adieu." Mary Jones felt deeply wounded by what she regarded as slaves' "ingratitude." Committed to a conception of slavery as a Christian institution founded in reciprocal rights and duties, she could understand blacks' desire for freedom only as an unjust failure to appreciate her dedicated performance of her obligations within the system. "My life long . . . I have been laboring and caring for them, and since the war have labored with all my might to supply their wants, and expended everything I had upon their support, directly or indirectly, and this is their return." Even the shock of the blacks' behavior did not help Mary Jones to understand that her construction of slavery as an institution of mutual benevolence was not shared by her slaves. With their sights set on freedom, the blacks felt no duty to abide by the terms of the system as the white South had defined them.[38] . . .

In their reactions to slaves' departures, women revealed—to themselves as well as to posterity—the extent of their dependence on their servants. In our day of automated housework and prepared foods, it is easy to forget how much skill nineteenth-century housekeeping required. Many slave mistresses lacked this basic competence, having left to their slaves responsibility for execution of a wide range of essential domestic tasks. . . . Many white women felt themselves entirely ignorant about how to perform basic functions of everyday life.[39]

A Louisiana lady who had "never even so

much as washed out a pocket handkerchief with my own hands" suddenly had to learn to do laundry for her entire family. Kate Foster found that when her house servants left and she took on the washing, she "came near ruining myself for life as I was too delicately raised for such hard work." . . . Lizzie Carter of Petersburg gained a new understanding of motherhood when she was left without a nurse. "I never knew before the trouble of children," she complained to her sister. Martha Horne of Missouri remembered after the war that "I had never cooked a meal when the negro women left, and had a hard time learning." . . . When Henrietta Barr's cook departed, she assumed her place in the kitchen. "(Although a confession is humiliating)," she confided to her diary, "I must say I do not in the smallest particular fill the situation as creditably as she did. I certainly do not think my forte lies in cooking."[40]

The forte of the southern lady did not seem to lie in slave management either. These women were beginning to feel they could live neither with slaves nor without them. "To be without them is a misery & to have them is just as bad," confessed Amelia Barr of Galveston. Women already frustrated "trying to do a man's business" and direct slaves now discovered that they often felt equally incompetent executing the tasks that had belonged to their supposed racial inferiors. Like Henrietta Barr, many regarded the situation as "humiliating." "It is such a degradation," Matthella Page Harrison of Virginia wrote as she anticipated the imminent flight of her slaves, "to be so dependent upon the servants as we are."[41]

The concept of female dependence and weakness was not simply a prop of southern gender ideology; in the context of war, white ladies were finding it to be all too painful a reality. Socialized to believe in their own weakness and sheltered from the necessity of performing even life's basic tasks, many white women felt almost crippled by their unpreparedness for the new lives war had brought. Yet as they struggled to cope with change, their dedication to the old order faltered as well. Slavery, the "cornerstone" of the civilization for which their nation fought, increasingly seemed a burden rather than a benefit. White women regarded it as a threat as well. In failing to guarantee what white women believed to be their most fundamental right, in

failing to protect women or to exert control over insolent and even rebellious slaves, Confederate men undermined not only the foundations of the South's peculiar institution but the legitimacy of their power as white males, as masters of families of white women and black slaves.

NOTES

1. Alexander Stephens, *Southern Confederacy* [Atlanta], March 13, 1861.

2. *Macon Daily Telegraph*, September 1, 1862, quoted in Clarence Mohr, *On the Threshold of Freedom: Masters and Slaves in Civil War Georgia* (Athens: University of Georgia Press, 1986), 221.

3. See *The Statutes at Large of the Confederate States of America, passed at the Third Session of the First Congress* (Richmond: R. M. Smith, 1863), 158, 213–14; James M. Mathews, ed., *The Statutes at Large of the Confederate States of America* (Richmond: R. M. Smith, 1862), 30; *Acts of Congress in Relation to the Conscription and Exemption Laws* (Houston: Texas Book and Job Printing House, 1862), 8 (quotation); *Southern Historical Society Papers* 48 (1941): 104; Albert Burton Moore, *Conscription and Conflict in the Confederacy*, (New York: Macmillan, 1924), 83–113.

4. Mrs. B. A. Smith to Governor Shorter, July 18, 1862, Governor's Files, Alabama Dept. of Archives and History, Montgomery, Ala.; hereafter cited as ADAH; A Planter's Wife to Governor John J. Pettus, May 1, 1862, John J. Pettus Papers, Mississippi Dept. of Archives and History, Jackson, Miss.; hereafter cited as MDAH; see also Letitia Andrews to Governor John J. Pettus, March 28, 1863, Pettus Papers, MDAH, and Lizzie Neblett to Will Neblett, April 26, 1863, Lizzie Neblett Papers, Center for American History, University of Texas, Austin, Tex.; hereafter cited as UTA.

5. Lucy A. Sharp to Hon. John C. Randolph, October 1, 1862, Letters Received, Confederate Sec. of War; hereafter cited as LRCSW, S1000, RG 109, reel 72, M437, National Archives, Washington, D.C.; hereafter cited as NA; Sarah Whitesides to Hon. James Seddon, February 13, 1863, LRCSW, RG 109, reel 115, W136, NA; Catherine Edmondston, *Journal of a Secesh Lady: The Diary of Catherine Ann Devereux Edmondston, 1860–1866*, ed. Beth G. Crabtree and James W. Patton (Raleigh: North Carolina Department of Archives and History, 1979), 240; Frances Mitten to editors of the *Christian Index*, July 6, 1864, Thomas Watts, Governor's Papers, ADAH; Martha Fort to George Fort, October 7, 1861, Tomlinson Fort Papers, Special Collections, Woodruff Library, Emory Univ., Atlanta, GA; hereafter cited as EU; Amanda Walker to Secretary of War, October 31, 1862, LRCSW, RG 109, reel 79, W1106, NA.

6. Keziah Brevard Diary, November 28, 1860, April 4, 1861, December 29, 1860, South Caroliniana Library, University of South Carolina, Columbia, S.C.; hereafter cited as SCL.

7. C. Vann Woodward, ed., *Mary Chesnut's Civil*

War (New Haven: Yale University Press, 1981), 198–99; Ada Bacot Diary, September 21, 1861, SCL.

8. Laura Lee Diary, March 12, 1862, WM; Bacot Diary, February 27, 1861, SCL; *Mobile Advertiser and Register*, September 11, 1862; *Richmond Enquirer*, September 9, 1862.

9. Nancy Hall et al. to Governor Zebulon Vance, August 11, 1863, Zebulon Vance Papers, North Carolina Division of Archives and History, Raleigh, N.C.; hereafter cited as NCDAH; Miss Lettie Kennedy in behalf of the Ladies of the N.E. beat of Jas. County, Miss., September 15, 1862, LRCSW, RG 109, reel 56, K148, NA. See also Lida Sessums to Governor John J. Pettus, October 8, 1862, Pettus Papers, MDAH.

10. Lucy Watkins to Secretary of War Randolph, October 13, 1862, LRCSW, RG 109, reel 79, M1091, NA; Harriet Pipkin to S. Cooper, Adj Gen. and Insp Gen, series 12 (LR), box 18, H2636, NA; Mary Watts to Hon. James Seddon, May 15, 1863, LRCSW, RG 109, reel 116, W315, NA.

11. W. Maury Darst, "The Vicksburg Diary of Mrs. Alfred Ingraham," May 27, 1863, *Journal of Mississippi History* 44 (May 1982): 171; Catherine Broun Diary, May 11, 1862, Broun Family Papers, Woodson Research Center, Fondren Library, Rice Univ., Houston. Tex.; hereafter cited as RU.

12. Mary Greenhow Lee Diary, April 3, 1864, Winchester-Frederick County Historical Society, Handley Library, Winchester, Va.; hereafter cited as HL.

13. Constance Cary Harrison, "A Virginia Girl in the First Year of the War," *Century* 30 (August 1885): 606.

14. Elizabeth Saxon, *A Southern Woman's War Time Reminiscences* (Memphis: Pilcher, 1905), 33; Eugene D. Genovese, *Roll, Jordan, Roll: The World the Slaves Made* (New York: Pantheon, 1974), 99.

15. Anna Green to Martha Jones, April 16, 1862, Prescott-Jones Papers, Georgia Dept. of Archives and History, Atlanta, GA; hereafter cited as GDAH; Leila Callaway to Morgan Callaway, January 22, 19, 1863, Morgan Callaway Papers, EU.

16. Maria Hawkins to Governor Zebulon Vance, December 11, 1863, Vance Papers, NCDAH.

17. Edmondston, *Journal of a Secesh Lady*, 220; see also Octavia Stephens to Winston Stephens, July 15, 1862, Bryant-Stephens Papers, P.K. Yonge Library, University of Florida, Gainesville, Fla; hereafter cited as UFL; May, "Southern Elite Women," 255; and Bacot Diary, May 3, December 25, 1861, March 17, September 8, 1862, SCL.

18. Lizzie Neblett to Will Neblett, April 15, 1864, August 18, 1863, Neblett Papers, UTA.

19. Ibid., August 28, 1863, Neblett Papers, UTA. For a strikingly similar statement of female incapacity, see Carolina Pettigrew to Charles Pettigrew, June 19, 1862, Pettigrew Family Papers, Southern Historical College, University of North Carolina, Chapel Hill, N.C.; hereafter cited as SHC.

20. Lizzie Neblett to Will Neblett, April 26, 1863, Neblett Papers, UTA.

21. Ibid., August 18, 1863.

22. Ibid., November 17, 1863.

23. Ibid., November 23, 17, 1863.

24. Ibid., November 23, 1863.

25. Ibid., November 29, 1863.

26. Ibid.

27. Ibid., December 6, 1863.

28. Ibid.

29. Ibid., February 12, July 3, June 5, 1864.

30. Ibid., March 20, 1864, letter fragment [1864].

31. Mary Bell to Alfred Bell, November 24, December 16, 1864. See Elizabeth Fox-Genovese, *Within the Plantation Household: Black and White Women of the Old South* (Chapel Hill: University of North Carolina Press, 1988), 142, on women's desire for household slaves.

32. Ella Gertrude Clanton Thomas, *The Secret Eye: The Journal of Ella Gertrude Clanton Thomas, 1848–1889*, ed. Virginia Ingraham Burr (Chapel Hill: University of North Carolina Press, 1990), 236; Mary Chesnut quoted in Elisabeth Muhlenfeld, *Mary Boykin Chesnut: A Biography* (Baton Rouge: Louisiana State University Press, 1981), 109; Mary Brown to John B. Brown, June 20, 1865, W. Vance Brown Papers, NCDAH; Jane Howison Beale, *The Journal of Jane Howison Beale of Fredericksburg, Virginia, 1850–1862* (Fredericksburg: Historic Fredericksburg Foundation, 1979), 43.

33. Lizzie Neblett to Will Neblett, undated letter fragment [1864], Neblett Papers, UTA.

34. Betty Herndon Maury, *The Confederate Diary of Betty Herndon Maury, 1861–1863*, ed. Alice Maury Parmalee (Washington, D.C.: privately printed, 1938), 89.

35. Beale, *Journal*, June 1, 1862, 47; Eliza Kendrick Walker Reminiscences, 117–18, ADAH.

36. Catherine Cochran Reminiscences, March 1862, vol. 1, Virginia Historical Society, Richmond, Va.; hereafter cited as VHS; Mary Greenhow Lee Diary, June 29, July 15, 1862, HL; Laura Lee Diary, June 13, 1863, August 18, 1864, Manuscripts and Rare Books, Swem Library, College at William and Mary. Williamsburg, Va.; hereafter cited as WM. See also Sarah Fitch Poates Diary, July 6, 8, 23, November 1, 1863, Asa Fitch Papers, Dept. of Manuscripts, Library Cornell University, Ithaca, N.Y.; Hereafter cited as CU.

37. Mary Greenhow Lee Diary, March 22, 1862, HL.

38. Emma Mordecai Diary, May 6, 1865, Mordecai Family Papers, SHC; Genovese, *Roll, Jordan, Roll*, 105–6; Robert Manson Myers, ed., *The Children of Pride: A True Story of Georgia and the Civil War* (New Haven: Yale University Press, 1972), 1274, 1287, 1308.

39. On this point, see Fox-Genovese, *Within the Plantation Household*, 115, 128. See also Amanda Worthington Diary, April 25, 1863, MDAH.

40. George C. Rable, *Civil Wars: Women and the Crisis of Southern Nationalism* (Urbana: University of Illinois Press, 1989), 255; Kate Foster Diary, November 15, 1863, Manuscript Dept., Perkins Library, Duke University, Durham, N.C.; hereafter cited as DU; Lizzie Carter to her sister, March 23, 1863, W. Vance Brown Papers, NCDAH; Martha Horne, "War Experiences," in *Reminiscences of the Women of Missouri during the Sixties*, by Missouri Division, United Daughters of the Confederacy (Jefferson City, Mo.: Hugh Stephens, 192–), 43; *The Civil War Diary of Mrs. Henrietta Fitzhugh Barr, 1862–3*, ed. Sally Kiger Winn (Mari-

etta, Ohio: Marietta College Press, 1963), 25. See also Annie Harper Reminiscences, 46, MDAH; Emma Holmes, *The Diary of Miss Emma Holmes, 1861–1866,* ed. John Marszalek (Baton Rouge: Louisiana State University Press, 1979), 467; and Sarah Anne Grover Strickler Diary, August 12, 1862, Manuscripts Dept., Alderman Library, University of Virginia, Charlottesville, Va.; hereafter cited as UVA.

41. Amelia Barr to My Dear Jenny, March 3, [1866?], Amelia Barr Papers, UTA; Lizzie Neblett to Will Neblett, August 8, 1863, Neblett Papers, UTA; Matthella Page Harrison Diary, April 28, 1863, UVA.

DOCUMENTS: Counterfeit Freedom

> ### A. S. Hitchcock, "Young women particularly flock back & forth . . ."

Early in the Civil War, before the Emancipation Proclamation, the Union Army occupied the Sea Islands off the coast of Georgia; plantation owners fled and the army established base camps there. Although the Union forces expected former slaves to continue to work on their old plantations as contract laborers, freedpeople believed that the end of slavery should mean that they could travel freely and that they could choose other ways of supporting themselves.

How did the Union officials interpret the movement of women around the Islands?

A. S. HITCHCOCK, ACTING GENERAL SUPERINTENDENT OF CONTRABANDS, TO PROVOST MARSHAL GENERAL OF THE DEPARTMENT OF THE SOUTH, AUGUST 25, 1864 In accordance with a request made by you at this office . . . concerning measures to be instituted to lessen the number of idle & dissolute persons hanging about the central Posts of the Department & traveling to & from between them . . . I write this note. . . .

Had I the control of the negroes the first thing I would endeavor to do, & the thing I think of most importance to be done, is to Keep all the people possible on the farms or plantations at *honest steady* labor. As one great means to this end, I would make it as difficult as possible for them to get to the centres of population.—Young women particularly flock back & forth by scores to Hilton Head, to Beaufort, to the country simply to while away their time, or constantly to seek some new excitement, or what is worse to live by lasciviousness. . . . I would allow no peddling around camps whatsoever. . . . All rationing I would stop utterly, & introduce the poor house system, feeding none on any pretense who would not go to the place provided for all paupers to live. . . . All

persons out of the poor house running from place to place to beg a living I would treat as vagabonds, & also all persons, whether in town or on plantations, white or black, who lived without occupation should either go to the poor house or be put in a place where they *must work*—a work house or chain gang, & if women where they could wash iron & scrub for the benefit of the public. . . .

SEPTEMBER 6, 1864
GENERAL ORDERS NO. 130

Hilton Head, S.C. . . . The practice of allowing negro women to wander about from one plantation to another, and from one Post or District to another, on Government transports, for no other purpose than to while away their time, or visit their husbands serving in the ranks of the Army, is not only objectionable in every point of view, both to the soldiers and to themselves, but is generally subversive of moral restraint, and must be discontinued at once. All negro women, in future found wandering in this manner, will be immediately arrested, and compelled to work at some steady employment on the Plantations.

Excerpted from *Freedom: A Documentary History of Emancipation 1861–1867*, edited by Ira Berlin, Joseph P. Reidy, and Leslie S. Rowland, Ser. I, vol. 3, pp. 316–319. Reprinted with the permission of Cambridge University Press.

Roda Ann Childs, "I was more dead than alive"

In January 1865, before the Civil War was over, Congress and the states in the Union ratified the Thirteenth Amendment, putting an end to slavery and "involuntary servitude, except as punishment for crime whereof the party shall have been duly convicted." Once peace was established, it became clear that the states of the former Confederacy were quite creative in devising systems that maintained racial subordination (for example, broad definitions of what counted as "vagrancy" which, as crimes, could be punished by involuntary servitude). The Civil Rights Act of 1866 was designed to protect freedpeople; it promised "citizens of every race and color . . . full and equal benefit of all laws and proceedings for the security of person and property, as is enjoyed by white citizens. . . ." But the statute had been passed only over the veto of President Andrew Johnson, who denied that the states of the Confederacy had forfeited all civil rights and privileges by their rebellion. The Freedmen's Bureau was charged with protecting the rights of former slaves and assisting their transition to a market economy; it accomplished much, but it was always underfunded and understaffed, and many of its staff members were themselves deeply skeptical of freedpeople.

In a political climate marked by struggle between Congress and the President, the Ku Klux Klan and other vigilantes who wanted to intimidate freedpeople and take vengeance for their own defeat in war seized their opportunity. Not until 1871 did Congress pass the Ku Klux Klan Act, prescribing fines and imprisonment for those who went in disguise to terrorize others. The congressional committee that conducted a traveling inquiry into "the Condition of Affairs in the Late Insurrectionary States" filed a twelve-volume report. Its testimony of violence and intimidation, in excruciating detail, makes it clear that Roda Ann Childs's experience was replicated throughout the South.

Roda Ann Childs made her way to a Freedmen's Bureau agent in Griffin, Georgia, to swear this affidavit; she signed it with her mark. There is no evidence that her case was pursued. What clue does she offer for why she was a target for mob violence?

[*Griffin, GA*] Sept. 25, 1866 Rhoda Ann Childs came into this office and made the following statement:

"Myself and husband were under contract with Mrs. Amelia Childs of Henry County, and worked from Jan. 1, 1866, until the crops were laid by, or in other words until the main work of the year was done, without difficulty. Then, (the fashion being prevalent among the planters) we were called upon one night, and my husband was demanded; I Said he was not there. They then asked where he was. I Said he was gone to the water mellon patch. They then Seized me and took me Some distance from the house, where they 'bucked' me down across a log, Stripped my clothes over my head, one of the men Standing astride my neck, and beat me across my posterior, two men holding my legs. In this manner I was beaten until they were tired. Then they turned me parallel with the log, laying my neck on a limb which projected from the log, and one man placing his foot upon my neck, beat me again on my hip and thigh. Then I was thrown

---

Excerpted from *Freedom: A Documentary History of Emancipation, 1861–1876*, edited by Ira Berlin, Joseph P. Reidy and Leslie S. Rowland, Ser. 2, p. 807. Reprinted with the permission of Cambridge University Press.

upon the ground on my back, one of the men Stood upon my breast, while two others took hold of my feet and stretched My limbs as far apart as they could, while the man Standing upon my breast applied the Strap to my private parts until fatigued into stopping, and I was more dead than alive. Then a man, Supposed to be an ex-confederate Soldier, as he was on crutches, fell upon me and ravished me. During the whipping one of the men ran his pistol into me, and Said he had a hell of a mind to pull the trigger, and Swore they ought to Shoot me, as my husband had been in the 'God damned Yankee Army,' and Swore they meant to kill every black Son-of-a-bitch they could find that had ever fought against them. They then went back to the house, Seized my two daughters and beat them, demanding their father's pistol, and upon failure to get that, they entered the house and took Such articles of clothing as Suited their fancy, and decamped. There were concerned in this affair eight men, none of which could be recognized for certain.

her
Roda Ann × Childs
mark

TERA W. HUNTER
Reconstruction and the Meanings of Freedom

When the Civil War was ended at Appomatox, a long and complex struggle over its meaning had just begun. The Thirteenth Amendment technically ended slavery, but it left much room for interpretation about the meaning of servitude. It said nothing about equality, leaving resentful Southerners to conclude that the North would condone systems of racial hierarchy. Even after the passage of the Fourteenth Amendment, which provided that *All persons born or naturalized in the United States . . . are citizens of the United States and of the State wherein they reside*, the meanings of "citizenship" remained to be defined.

The aftermath of defeat is an internationally shared phenomenon. How did white southerners understand their defeat? What tensions marked postwar society? What would it mean to "reconstruct" the former Confederacy? Tera Hunter examines the experiences of freedpeople in the city of Atlanta, Georgia—Roda Ann Childs lived not far away. She finds that the process of rebuilding their lives could be quite different for men and for women. What opportunities did African American men have that African American women did not? What strategies might freedwomen use to stabilize their lives? In what ways did freedwomen participate in political life?

The Union victory at Appomattox in the spring of 1865 marked the official end of the war and inspired somber reflection, foot-stomping church meetings, and joyous street parades among the newly free. African Americans eagerly rushed into Atlanta in even greater

Excerpted from "Reconstruction and the Meanings of Freedom," ch. 2 of *To 'Joy My Freedom: Black Women's Lives and Labors after the Civil War* by Tera W. Hunter (Cambridge, Mass.: Harvard University Press, 1997). Copyright © 1997 by Tera W. Hunter. Reprinted by permission of the publisher. Notes have been numbered and edited.

numbers than before. Between 1860 and 1870, blacks in Atlanta increased from a mere nineteen hundred to ten thousand, more than doubling their proportion in the city's population, from 20 to 46 percent. Women made up the majority of this burgeoning population.[1] . . .

Wherever they came from, virtually all black women were compelled to find jobs as household workers once they arrived in the city. Some had acquired experience in such jobs as house slaves; others had worked in the fields or combined field and domestic chores. Whether or not they were working as domestics for the first time, black women had to struggle to assert new terms for their labor. The Civil War had exposed the parallel contests occurring in white households as the conflict on the battlefield, in the marketplace, and in the political arena unfolded. The war continued on the home front during Reconstruction after the Confederacy's military defeat. . . .

Just as black women and men in Atlanta had to reconstitute their lives as free people and build from the ground up, the city was faced with similar challenges. The legacy of physical desecration left by Sherman's invasion was everywhere. Tons of debris, twisted rails, dislodged roofs, crumbled chimneys, discharged cannon balls, and charred frame dwellings cluttered the streets.[2] Visitors to the city swapped remarks on the distinctive spirit of industry exemplified in the repair and rebuilding. . . . Atlanta aspired to construct a city in the New South in the image of established cities above the Mason-Dixon line.[3]

The capitalist zeal that impressed outsiders offered few benefits to the average person, however. Overwhelmed contractors could not keep up with demands, which added to housing shortages that sent prices for rents soaring beyond the means of most residents.[4] . . . Some builders took advantage of the shortage to offer makeshift huts and shanties to freedpeople at exorbitant prices.[5] Ex-slaves in more dire straits assembled scanty lodging that consisted of tents, cabins, and shanties made of tin, line, and cloth on rented parcels of land.[6] . . . The cost of food and other consumer goods likewise followed the pattern of scarcity, poor quality, and deliberate price gouging.[7]

The abrupt population growth and the inability of private charities or public coffers to relieve the migrants of want exacerbated postwar privation. Almost everyone in the city, regardless of race, shared the status of newcomer. It was not just African Americans who were migrating to the city in large numbers; so did many whites. In 1860, there were 7,600 whites living in Atlanta, ten years later there were 11,900.[8] White yeoman farmers fled to the city to find wage labor in the wake of the elimination of their rural self-sufficiency. White Northern and foreign industrial workers followed the prosperity promised by the railroad and construction boom.

Women and children, black and white, were particularly noticeable among the destitute sprawled over the desolate urban landscape. The indigent included elderly, single women, widows of soldiers, and wives of unemployed or underemployed men. White women seamstresses who numbered in the thousands during the war were reduced to poverty with the collapse of military uniform manufacturers.[9] Labor agents egregiously contributed to the disproportionate sex ratio among urban blacks by taking away men to distant agricultural fields, leaving the women and children deserted.[10] Those abandoned wandered the streets and scavenged for food, often walking between ten and forty miles per day. "Sometimes I gits along tolerable," stated a widow washerwoman with six children. "Sometimes right slim; but dat's de way wid everybody—times is powerful hard right now."[11]

The municipal government showed neither the capability nor the ambition to meet the needs of the poor. It allocated few resources for basic human services. Yet the Freedmen's Bureau, which was established by the federal government in 1865 to distribute rations and relief to ex-slaves, to monitor the transition to a free labor system, and to protect black rights, proved inadequate also. The bureau was preoccupied with stemming migration, establishing order, and restoring the economy, which led it to force blacks into accepting contracts without sufficient regard for the fairness of the terms. The federals evicted ex-slaves from contraband camps or pushed them further from the center of town to the edges—out of sight and out of mind.[12] Bureau officials urged their agents: "You must not issue rations or afford shelter to any person who can, and will not labor for his or her own support."[13] . . .

Ex-slaves who were evicted from the camps by the end of 1865 were more fortunate than they could appreciate initially. They escaped a smallpox epidemic in the city that devastated the enclaves. One missionary reported a horrifying scene she witnessed in the camps: "Men, women, and children lying on the damp ground suffering in every degree from the mildest symptoms to the most violent. The tents crowded, no fire to make them comfortable, and worse all the poor creatures were almost destitute of wearing apparel."[14] The dead who lay around the sick and suffering were buried in the ground half-naked or without clothes at all. . . .

African-American women and men were willing to endure the adversities of food shortages, natural disasters, dilapidated housing, and inadequate clothing in postwar Atlanta because what they left behind in the countryside, by comparison, was much worse. In the city at least there were reasons to be optimistic that their strength in numbers and their collective strategies of empowerment could be effective. In rural areas, however, their dispersion and separation by miles of uninhabited backwoods left them more vulnerable to elements intent on depriving them of life, liberty, and happiness. Abram Colby, a Republican legislator from Greene County, summed up the motivations for migration by stating that blacks went to Atlanta "for protection." He explained further: "The military is here and nobody interferes with us here . . . we cannot stop anywhere else so safely."[15]

African Americans moved to the city not only in search of safety, but also in search of economic self-sufficiency. Though most ex-slaves held dreams of owning farm land, many preferred to set up households in a city with a more diverse urban economy. In Atlanta they encountered an economy that was quickly recovering from the war and continuing to grow in the direction propelled by military demands and the promise of modernization.[16] . . .

Though the kaleidoscope of industry appeared to offer vast possibilities for workers, African Americans were slotted into unskilled and service labor. Black men filled positions with the railroads; as day workers, they groomed roads, distributed ballast, and shoveled snow off the tracks. As brakemen, they coupled and uncoupled stationary cars and ran along the roof of moving trains to apply the brakes, risking life and limb. Many others worked in rolling and lumber mills, mostly in

the lowest-paid positions as helpers to white men. Hotels employed black men as cooks, waiters, porters, bellhops, and barroom workers. A few ex-slaves worked in bakeries, small foundries, the paper mill, and candy factories. Slave artisans were high in number in the antebellum South, but in the postbellum era black men were rarely hired in skilled positions. They were able to benefit from the aggressive physical rebuilding of Atlanta, however, in the construction trades, as painters, carpenters, and brickmasons. Between 1870 and 1880, the proportion of black male shoemakers tripled to constitute the majority of the entire trade. A select few owned small businesses such as barber shops and grocery stores or worked in the professions as teachers and ministers.[17]

The range of job opportunities for black women was more narrow than for men. Black women were excluded from small manufacturing plants that hired white women, such as those that made candy, clothing, textiles, paper boxes, bookbinding, and straw goods. They were confined primarily to domestic labor in private homes as cooks, maids, and child-nurses. A few black women found related jobs in local hotels—a step above the same work performed in private households. Large numbers worked in their own homes in a relatively autonomous craft as laundresses, which had the advantage of accommodating family and community obligations. More desirable, yet less accessible, were skilled jobs outside domestic service as seamstresses or dressmakers. . . . Only a few black women were able to escape common labor and enter the professions as teachers.[18]

Reconstruction of the post-slavery South occurred on many levels. Just as the city's infrastructure had to be rebuilt for daily life to reach a new normalcy, so blacks had to rebuild their lives as free people by earning an independent living. Women's success or frustrations in influencing the character of domestic labor would define how meaningful freedom would be. Slave women had already demonstrated fundamental disagreements with masters over the principles and practices of free labor during the war. This conflict continued as workers and employers negotiated new terms. Even the most mundane and minute details of organizing a free labor system required rethinking assumptions about work that had previously relied on physical coercion. An employer acknowledged the trial-and-error nature of this process: "I had no idea what was considered a task in washing so I gave her all the small things belonging to the children taking out all the table cloths sheets counterpanes & c." The novice employer then decided in the same haphazard manner to pay the laundry worker 30 cents a day. But the laborer asserted her own understanding of fair work. "She was through by dinner time [and] appeared to work steady. I gave her dinner and afterwards told her that I had a few more clothes I wished washed out," the employer explained. "Her reply was that she was tired." The worker and employer held different expectations about the length of the work day and the quantity of the output of labor.[19]

African Americans labored according to their own sense of equity, with the guiding assumption that wage labor should not emulate slavery—especially in the arbitrariness of time and tasks. The experience of an ex-slave named Nancy illustrates this point. As some ex-slaves departed from their former masters' households, the burden of the work shifted to those who remained. Consequently, when the regular cook departed, Nancy's employer added cooking and washing to her previous child-care job, without her consent. Nancy faked illness on ironing days and eventually quit in protest against the extra encumbrance.[20] If workers and employers disagreed on the assignment of specific tasks, they also disagreed on how to execute them. Workers held to their own methods and preferences; employers held to theirs. . . .

If [a worker's] frustrations reached an intolerable level, she could exercise a new privilege as a free worker to register the ultimate complaint: she could quit and seek better terms for her work. Ex-slaves committed themselves to this precept of free labor with a firmness that vexed employers. "We daily hear of people who are in want of servants, and who have had in their employ in the last three or four months, a dozen different ones," stated a familiar news report. "The common experience of all is that the servants of the 'African-persuasion' can't be retained," it continued. "They are fond of change and since it is their privilege to come and go at pleasure, they make full use of the large liberty they enjoy."[21] . . .

African-American women decided to quit work over such grievances as low wages, long hours, ill treatment, and unpleasant tasks. Quitting could not guarantee a higher standard of living or a more pleasant work environment for workers, but it was an effective strategy to deprive employers of complete power over their labor. . . .

Employers did not share the same interpretations of labor mobility, however. They blamed the subversive influence of Yankees and "pernicious" Negroes for inciting "bad" work habits, or they explained quitting as a scientifically proven racial deficiency.[22] Whereas recently freed slaves often worked as much as they needed to survive and no more, white Southerners believed that if they refused to work as hard as slaves driven by fear they were mendicants and vagrants. "When a wench gets very hungry and ragged, she is ready to do the cooking for any sized family," a news report exclaimed. "But after she gets her belly well filled with provender, she begins to don't see the use of working all day and every day, and goes out to enjoy her freedom."[23]

Although many white Southerners resented the presence of the Freedmen's Bureau as the Northern overseer of Reconstruction, they readily sought its assistance to stem the revolving door of domestic workers. "What are persons to do when a 'freedman' that you hire as a nurse goes out at any time & against your direct orders?" one former master queried the bureau. "What must be done when they are hired and do only just what they please? orders being disregarded in every instance," he asked further. A bureau agent responded with an answer to alleviate the employer's frustrations and to teach him a lesson about the precepts of free labor. "Discharge her and tell her she dont suit you," the agent stated simply. "If you have a written contract with them and they quit you without good and sufficient cause—I will use all my power to have them comply," he reassured. But if these words provided comfort, the bureau agent made clear that the operative words were "without good and sufficient cause." He reiterated the employers' obligations and responsibilities to respect the liberties of workers: "You are expected to deal with them as Freemen and Freewomen. Individual exceptions there may be but as a whole where they are well treated they are faithful and work well."[24]

The federal government refused to return to white employers unilateral power to prohibit the mobility of black workers, leading employers to elicit the support of local laws. Quitting work became defined as "idleness" and "vagrancy"—prosecutable offenses. Southern state legislatures began passing repressive Black Codes in 1865 to obstruct black laborers' full participation in the marketplace and political arena. In 1866, the Atlanta City Council responded in a similar vein to stop the movement of household workers: it passed a law requiring employers to solicit recommendations from previous jobs in order to distinguish "worthy" from "worthless" laborers and to make it more difficult for workers to change jobs. Complaints continued long after the law took effect, which suggests its ineffectiveness.[25] . . .

Black women used the marginal leverage they could exercise in the face of conflict between employers to enhance their wages and to improve the conditions of work. When Hannah, "a cook & washer of the first character," was approached by Virginia Shelton in search of domestic help, she bargained for an agreement to match her needs. Hannah wanted to bring along her husband, a general laborer, and expected good wages for both of them. Shelton made an initial offer of $5 per month to Hannah and $10 per month to her husband. But the couple demanded $8 and $15, to which Shelton acceded. Shelton realized that it was worth making compromises with a servant she had traveled a long distance to recruit.[26]

Not all negotiations ended so pleasantly or in the workers' favor, however. . . . Domestic workers often complained of physical abuse by employers following disputes about wages, hours of work, or other work-related matters. . . . Samuel Ellison explained the argument that led to the death of his wife, Eliza Jane. Mrs. Ellison had argued with her employer, Mrs. L. B. Walton, about washing clothes. According to Ellison's husband, "My wife asked Mrs. Walton who would pay her for her washing extra clothes and which she was not bound to do by her contract." Walton's husband intervened and "abused" the laundress for "insulting" his wife. He left the house, returned and began another argument, insisting to Ellison, "shut up you God damn bitch." The fight ended when Walton shot Eliza Jane Ellison to death.[27]

African-American women like Ellison undoubtedly paid a high price for the simple desire to be treated like human beings. Incidents like this one made it apparent that freedom could not be secured through wage labor alone. The material survival of African Americans was critical, but they also needed to exercise their political rights to safeguard it. The political system had to undergo dramatic transformation to advance their interests, but here too they faced many obstacles.

The Ku Klux Klan, an anti-black terrorist organization founded by former Confederate soldiers in 1866, mounted the most bitter opposition to black rights. The KKK quickly became dominated by Democratic Party officials bent on preempting black participation in the electoral arena. The Klan sought to wrest economic and political power from the governing Republicans in order to restore it to the antebellum planter elite and to the Democrats. KKK members victimized Republican politicians like Abram Colby, whom they stripped and beat for hours in the woods. They harassed registered voters and independent landholders, ransacked churches and schools, intimidated common laborers who refused to bow obsequiously to planters, and tormented white Republicans sympathetic to any or all of the foregoing.[28]

African Americans' recalcitrance in commonplace disagreements with employers routinely provoked the vigilantes. Alfred Richardson, a legislator from Clarke County, suggested how labor relations continued to have strong political ramifications. The KKK assisted employers in securing the upper hand in conflicts with wage household workers. "Many times, you know, a white lady has a colored lady for cook or waiting in the house, or something of that sort," Richardson explained. "They have some quarrel, and sometimes probably the colored woman gives the lady a little jaw. In a night or two a crowd will come in and take her out and whip her." The Klan stripped and beat African Americans with sticks, straps, or pistol barrels when all else failed to elicit their compliance.[29]

If the KKK was determined to halt the reconstruction of a free labor system, it was most insistent about eliminating black political power. Though women were denied the right to vote in the dominant political system, they actively engaged in a grass-roots political culture that valued the participation of the entire community. Black women and children attended parades, rallies, and conventions; they voiced their opinions and cast their votes on resolutions passed at mass meetings. In the 1860s and 1870s, women organized their own political organizations, such as the Rising Daughters of Liberty Society, and stood guard at political meetings organized by men to allow them to meet without fear of enemy raids. They boldly tacked buttons on the clothing they wore to work in support of favorite candidates. They took time off from work to attend to their political duties, such as traveling to the polls to make sure men cast the right ballots. White housekeepers were as troubled by the dramatic absences of domestic workers on election day or during political conventions as were the planters and urban employers of men.[30] During an election riot in nearby Macon, a newspaper reported: "The Negro women, if possible, were wilder than the men. They were seen everywhere, talking in an excited manner, and urging the men on. Some of them were almost furious, showing it to be part of their religion to keep their husbands and brothers straight in politics."[31]

Whether they gave political advice and support to the men in their families and communities or carried out more directly subversive activities, black women showed courage in the face of political violence. Hannah Flournoy, a cook and laundress, ran a boardinghouse in Columbus well known as a gathering place for Republicans. When George Ashburn, a white party leader stalked by the KKK, looked to her for shelter she complied, unlike his other supporters in the town. Flournoy promised him, "You are a republican, and I am willing to die for you. I am a republican, tooth and toe-nail."[32] But neither Flournoy nor Ashburn could stop the Klan in its determination to take the life of freedom fighters. After Klansmen killed Ashburn, Flournoy escaped to Atlanta, leaving behind valuable property.

Republican activists like Ashburn and Flournoy were not the only victims of KKK violence. The Klan also targeted bystanders who happened to witness their misdeeds. In White County, Joe Brown's entire family was subjected to sadistic and brutal harassment because Brown had observed a murder committed by the Klan. "They just stripped me stark naked, and fell to beating us," Brown reported later. "They got a great big trace-chain, swung me up from the ground, and swung [my wife] up until she fainted; and they beat us all over the yard with great big sticks." The Klan continued its torture against his mother-in-law and sister-in-law. "They made all the women show their nakedness; they made them lie down, and they jabbed them with sticks." Indiscriminate in violating adults and children, the KKK lined up Brown's young daughters and sons "and went to playing with their backsides with a piece of fishing-pole."[33] . . .

Migrating to Atlanta certainly improved the personal safety of ex-slaves escaping the KKK and sexual assaults, but it did not ensure foolproof protection against bodily harm. Black women risked sexual abuse no matter where they lived. Domestics in white homes were the most susceptible to attacks. A year after the war ended, Henry McNeal Turner and other black men mounted the podium and wrote petitions to demand the cessation of sexual assaults upon black women. Freedom, they insisted, was meaningless without ownership and control over one's own body. Black men took great offense at the fact that while they were falsely accused of raping white women, white men granted themselves total immunity in the exploitation of black women. *"All we ask of the white man is to let our ladies alone,* and they need not fear us," Turner warned. "The difficulty has heretofore been *our ladies were not always at our disposal."*[34] In Savannah, black men mobilized the Sons of Benevolence "for the protection of female virtue" in 1865.[35] In Richmond, African Americans complained to military authorities that women were being "gobbled up" off the streets, thrown into the jail, and ravished by the guards. In Mobile, black men organized the National Lincoln Association and petitioned the Alabama State Constitutional Convention to enact laws to protect black women from assault by white civilians and the police.[36]

Most whites refused to acknowledge the culpability of white men in abusing black women. "Rape" and "black women" were words that were never uttered in the same breath by white Southerners. Any sexual relations that developed between black women and white men were considered consensual, even coerced by the seductions of black women's lascivious nature. Rape was a crime defined exclusively, in theory and in practice, as perceived or actual threats against white female virtue by black men, which resulted in lynchings and castrations of numbers of innocent black men. But Z. B. Hargrove, a white attorney, admitted with rare candor that the obsession with black men raping white women was misplaced. "It is all on the other foot," as he put it. The "colored women have a great deal more to fear from white men."[37]

Black Atlantans during Reconstruction were subjected to other kinds of physical violence, especially at the hands of white civilians and police. . . . When Mary Price objected to being called a "damned bitch" by a white neighbor, Mr. Hoyt, he brought police officer C. M. Barry to her door to reprimand her. Price's mother, Barbara, pregnant at the time, intervened and spoke to the police: "I replied that I would protect my daughter in my own house, whereupon he pulled me out of the house into the street. Here he called another man and the two jerked and pulled me along [the street] to the guard house and throwed me in there." When a Freedmen's Bureau agent complained to the mayor and city council on the Prices' behalf, the complaint was rebuffed by a unanimous vote acquitting the policeman of all charges against him. Meanwhile, mother and daughter were arrested, convicted for using profane language, and forced to pay $350 each in fines and court costs. Only after it became clear that the Bureau would persist in its efforts to get justice for the Price women did the mayor have a change of heart and fine the offending policeman. Barry was one of the worst officers on the force, and the Freedmen's Bureau eventually forced the city council to fire him, though he was rehired a year later.[38]

African Americans not only had to ward off physical threats; they were also challenged by the existence of perfectly legal abuses that diminished the meaning of freedom. Ex-slaves defined the reconstruction of their families torn asunder by slavery and war as an important aspect of the realization of the full exercise of their civil rights. But former masters seized upon the misery of African Americans, with the assistance of the law, to prolong the conditions of slavery and deny them the prerogative of reuniting their families. The Georgia legislature passed an Apprentice Act in 1866, ostensibly to protect black orphans by providing them

with guardianship and "good" homes until they reached the age of consent at twenty-one. Planters used the law to reinstate bondage through uncompensated child labor.[39] Aunts, uncles, parents, and grandparents inundated the Freedmen's Bureau with requests for assistance in rescuing their children, though this same agency also assisted in apprenticing black minors. Martin Lee, for example, a former slave living in Florence, Alabama, wrote to the chief of the Georgia bureau for help in releasing his nephew from bondage. He had successfully reunited part of his extended family, but could not gain the release of his nephew despite the fact that he and the child's mother, Lee's sister, were both willing and able to take custody.[40]

If admitted enemies of black freedom recklessly disregarded the unity of black families through apprenticeships, some of their friends operated just as wantonly. The American Missionary Association (AMA) sometimes impeded parents and relatives who wished to reclaim their children. In 1866, the AMA started an orphanage that operated out of a tent. Soon afterward they opened the Washburn Orphanage in a building to accommodate the large number of homeless black children who were surviving on the streets on scant diets of saltpork and hardtack. But the asylum functioned as a temporary way station for children before apprenticing them out as domestic help to white sponsors. "I succeeded in getting a little girl from the orphans asylum by the name of Mary Jane Peirce," one eager patron of the orphanage exclaimed. "Her father and mother are both dead. She has a step mother and a little step brother." Peirce's new guardian minced no words in disclosing reckless disregard for the reunion of the child's family. "I am glad she will have no outside influence exherted upon her," the guardian admitted.[41] . . .

African Americans persisted in pursuing the reconstitution of family ties, despite the obstacles put in their way. [Rebeca] Craighead [the matron of the asylum,] recognized the persistence of these ex-slaves, yet she showed neither respect nor sensitivity toward the virtues of their ambition. "Somehow these black people have the faculty of finding out where their children are," she acknowledged.[42] Both the uncle, Martin Lee, who used official channels to retrieve his nephew, and the anonymous aunt, who relied on her own resources to "steal" her niece, displayed no small measure of resourcefulness in achieving their aims. Men no less than women, non-kin as well as kin, sought to recreate the family bonds that had been strained or severed by slavery and the Civil War.

Not all missionaries were as insensitive as Craighead; there were others, like Frederick Ayers, who fully appreciated the significance of family to ex-slaves. "The idea of 'freedom' of independence, of calling their wives and their children, and little hut their *own*, was a soul animating one, that buoyed up their spirits," he observed.[43] . . .

Broad understandings of kinship encouraged black women to assume responsibility for needy children other than their natural offspring. Silvey, for example, could hardly survive on the minimal subsistence she earned, yet she extended compassion to the youngsters lost or deserted by other ex-slaves. "She was hard put to it, to work for them all," observed her former owner, Emma Prescott. But "of course, as our means were all limited, we could not supply her enough to feed them. Her life, was anything but ease & it was a pitiful sight."[44] . . .

The most complicated family issues involved romantic relationships between women and men. For generations slaves had married one another and passed on the importance of conjugal obligations, despite the absence of legal protection. Marriages between slaves were long-term commitments, usually only disrupted by forcible separation or the death of a spouse. Emancipation offered new opportunities to reaffirm marital vows and to reunite couples who had previously lived "abroad" in the households of different masters. Even before the last shots of gunfire ending the Civil War, thousands of husbands and wives sought the help of Union officers and Northern missionaries to register their nuptials and to conduct wedding ceremonies.[45] The significance of formalizing these ties was articulated by a black soldier: *"I praise God for this day! The Marriage Covenant is at the foundation of all our rights."*[46] Putting marriages on a legal footing bolstered the ability of ex-slaves to keep their families together, to make decisions about labor and education, and to stay out of the unscrupulous grasp of erstwhile masters.

The hardships of slavery and war that disrupted families, however, meant that in the postwar period spouses were not always reunited without problems and tensions. Slaves traveled long distances to reunite with spouses from whom they had been separated for years. They wrote love letters and mailed them to churches and to the Freedmen's Bureau, and retraced the routes of labor agents who had taken their partners away.[47] Emotional bonds were sometimes so intense that spouses would choose to suffer indefinitely if they could not be reunited with their lost loved ones. But affections undernourished by hundreds of miles and many years might be supplanted by other relationships. Many ex-slaves faced awkward dilemmas when spouses presumed to be dead or long-lost suddenly reappeared. Ex-slaves created novel solutions for the vexing moral, legal, and practical concerns in resolving marital relations disrupted by forces beyond their control. One woman lived with each of her two husbands for a two-week trial before making a decision. Some men felt obligated to two wives and stayed married to one wife while providing support to the other. In one case, perhaps unique, a wife resumed her relationship with her first husband, while the second husband, a much older man, was brought into the family as a "poor relation."[48]

The presence of children complicated marriages even further. Some spouses registered their marriages with the Freedmen's Bureau or local courts even when their spouses were dead or missing, in order to give legal recognition to their children. When both parents were present and unable to reconcile their differences, child custody became a point of contention. Madison Day and Maria Richardson reached a mutual agreement to separate after emancipation. The love between husband and wife may have changed, but the love that each displayed for their children did not. The Richardsons put the Freedmen's Bureau agent in a quandary in determining who should receive custody. "Neither husband nor wife seem to be in a condition to provide for the children in a manner better than is usual with the freedpeople," the agent noted. "Still both appear to have an affectionate regard for the children and each loudly demands them."[49] . . .

Sheer survival and the reconstruction of family, despite all the difficulties, were the highest priorities of ex-slaves in the postwar period. But the desire for literacy and education was closely related to their strategies for achieving economic self-sufficiency, political autonomy, and personal enrichment. By 1860, 5 percent of the slave population had defied the laws and learned to read and write. Some were taught by their masters, but many learned to read in clandestine sessions taught by other blacks. African Americans all over the South organized secret schools long before the arrival of Northern missionaries. When a New England teacher arrived in Atlanta in 1865, he discovered an ex-slave already running a school in a church basement.[50]

African Americans welcomed the support of New England teachers and the federal government in their education movement. But centuries of slavery had stirred the longing for self-reliance in operating schools and filling teaching staffs, with assistance, but without white control. Ex-slaves enthusiastically raised funds and donated in-kind labor for building, repairing, and maintaining school houses. They opened their spartan quarters to house teachers and shared vegetables from their gardens to feed them. Ex-slaves in Georgia ranked highest in the South in the amount of financial assistance donated to their own education.[51]

The education movement among African Americans in Georgia went hand in hand with the demand for political rights. In January 1865, black ministers formed the Savannah Education Association, which operated schools staffed entirely with black teachers. Despite the efforts of General Davis Tillson, the conservative head of the Freedmen's Bureau, to keep politics out of the organization, African Americans and more liberal white allies infused the group with political objectives. The name was changed to the Georgia Equal Rights and Education Association, explicitly linking equal rights in the political arena with the pursuit of education. The organization became an important training ground for black politicians and laypersons at the grass-roots level and functioned as the state's predecessor to the Republican Party.[52] . . .

African Americans' advocacy of universal public education did not fare well at the city level, because the municipal government was firmly controlled by Democrats and businessmen. William Finch, elected in 1870 as one of Atlanta's first black city councilmen, made universal education a hallmark of his election

campaign. Finch attempted, but failed, to galvanize the support of the white working class on this issue. City Hall's cold reception shifted the burden of basic education for blacks to private foundations. Finch did succeed in getting the council to absorb two primary schools run by the AMA. After his short term in office and unsuccessful bid for reelection in December 1871, he continued to be a strong advocate of public education and helped to negotiate a deal in 1872 whereby the city would pay nominal costs for some blacks to receive secondary training at Atlanta University. No publicly funded high school for blacks would be created until a half-century later, however.[53]

Former slaves of all ages were undeterred in their goals to achieve literacy, regardless of the obstacles imposed by municipal and state governments. "It is quite amusing to see little girls eight or ten years old lead up full-grown women, as well as children, to have their names enrolled," remarked a missionary. "Men, women, and children are daily inquiring when the 'Free School' is to commence, and whether all can come[.] There is a large class of married women who wish to attend, if the schools are not too crowded."[54] Household workers figured prominently among this group of older, eager scholars. Their eagerness to learn was not diminished, although often interrupted, by the pressing demands of gainful labor. In fact, these obstacles may have increased the value of education in the eyes of the ex-slaves. Sabbath schools operated by black churches and evening classes sponsored by the Freedmen's Bureau and Northern missionaries afforded alternatives for those who could not sacrifice time during the day. But black women also inventively stole time away from work by carrying their books along and studying during spare moments—even fastening textbooks to backyard fences to glimpse their lessons as they washed clothes.[55]

As parents, working-class adults were especially committed to the education of their children. The story of Sarah J. Thomas, a young woman from Macon, whose mother was a cook and washerwoman, is a poignant illustration. Thomas wrote Edmund Asa Ware, president of Atlanta University, to gain his support in her plans to enroll in the secondary school. "I exspected to come to Atlanta to morrow but I am dissappointed. The reason I can not come to morrow is this. You know how mothers are! I guess about their youngest children *girls* especially," she wrote. Mother Thomas was protective of her daughter and reluctant to send her away alone. "In order that I may *come* Mr. Ware! mother says can she get a place to work there in the family?" she asked. The younger Thomas boasted of her mother's fine skills and reputation and slipped in her salary history. She assured the president, surely swamped by requests for financial aid, that her matriculation depended upon parental supervision, not the need for money. "Mother says she dont mean not the least to work to pay for *my schooling?* father pays for that him self she dont have any thing to do with it she only want to be where she can see me."[56] The young scholar's astute strategizing swayed both her mother and the school's president; she entered Atlanta University and achieved a successful teaching career after graduation in 1875.

Clandestine antebellum activities and values had bolstered the exemplary efforts of African Americans to seek literacy and to build and sustain educational institutions after the war. Ex-slaves took mutual obligations seriously. Their belief in personal development was aided rather than hampered by ideals that emphasized broad definitions of kinship and community. Freedom meant the reestablishment of lost family connections, the achievement of literacy, the exercise of political rights, and the security of a decent livelihood without the sacrifice of human dignity or self-determination. Ex-slave women migrated to Atlanta, where they hoped they would have a better chance of fulfilling these expectations. They were faced with many challenges; uppermost among them were the white residents who were resentful of the abolition of slavery and persisted in thwarting the realization of the true meaning of freedom. Black women continued to struggle, resilient and creative, in pursuing their goals for dignity and autonomy. The character of the contest had already been cast, but the many guises of domination and resistance had yet to be exhausted as life in the New South unfolded.

Notes

1. . . . Franklin M. Garrett, *Yesterday's Atlanta* (Miami: E. A. Seeman, 1974), p. 38; Eric Foner, *Reconstruction: America's Unfinished Revolution, 1863–1877* (New York: Harper & Row, 1988), pp. 81–82; Leon

F. Litwack, *Been in the Storm So Long: The Aftermath of Slavery* (New York: Knopf, 1979), pp. 310–316; U.S. Department of the Treasury, Register of Signatures of Depositors in the Branches of the Freedman's Savings and Trust Company, Atlanta Branch, 1870–1874 (Microfilm Publication, M-544), National Archives (hereafter cited as Freedman's Bank Records). Frederick Ayer to George Whipple, 15 February 1866 (Georgia microfilm reels), American Missionary Association Archives, Amistad Research Center, Tulane University (hereafter cited as AMA Papers).

2. John Richard Dennett, *The South As It Is: 1865–1866,* ed. Henry M. Christman (New York: Viking, 1965), pp. 267–271; Sidney Andrews, *The South Since the War: As Shown by Fourteen Weeks of Travel and Observation in Georgia and the Carolinas* (Boston, 1866; reprint ed., New York: Arno, 1970), pp. 339–340; Don H. Doyle, *New Men, New Cities, New South: Atlanta, Nashville, Charleston, Mobile, 1860–1910* (Chapel Hill: University of North Carolina Press, 1990), p. 31.

3. Rebecca Craighead to [Samuel] Grant, 15 January 1866, Georgia, AMA Papers; Andrews, *South Since the War,* p. 340; Whitelaw Reid, *After the War: A Tour of the Southern States, 1865–1866* (London, 1866; reprint ed., New York: Harper & Row, 1965), p. 355; Doyle, *New Men,* pp. 34–35; Howard N. Rabinowitz, *Race Relations in the Urban South 1865–1890* (New York: Oxford University Press, 1978), pp. 5–17.

4. See James Michael Russell, *Atlanta, 1847–1890: City Building in the Old South and the New* (Baton Rouge: Louisiana State University Press, 1988), pp. 117–128.

5. Frederick Ayers to Rev. George Whipple, 15 February 1866, Georgia, AMA Papers.

6. See Rebecca Craighead to Rev. Samuel Hunt, 30 April 1866, Georgia, AMA Papers; E. T. Ayer to Rev. Samuel Grant, 3 February 1866, Georgia, AMA Papers; Harriet M. Phillips to Rev. Samuel Grant, 15 January 1866, Georgia, AMA Papers; *American Missionary* 13 (January 1869): 4; John T. Trowbridge, *The South: A Tour of Its Battle-Fields and Ruined Cities* (Hartford, 1866; reprint ed., New York: Arno, 1969), p. 453.

7. Frederick Ayers to Rev. George Whipple, 15 February 1866, Georgia, AMA Papers.

8. See Table 1 at the back of the book.

9. Gretchen Ehrmann Maclachlan, "Women's Work: Atlanta's Industrialization and Urbanization, 1879–1929" (Ph.D. diss., Emory University, 1992), p. 29.

10. H. A. Buck to General [Davis Tillson], 2 October 1865, Letters Recd., ser. 732, Atlanta, Ga. Subasst. Comr., Record Group 105: Bureau of Refugees, Freedmen, and Abandoned Lands (hereafter cited as BRFAL), National Archives (hereafter cited as NA), [FSSP A-5153]; Franklin Brown to Gen. Tillson, 30 July 1866, Unregistered Letters Recd., ser. 632, Ga. Asst. Comr., BRFAL, NA, [FSSP A-5327]; clipping from *Augusta Constitutionalist,* 16 February 1866, filed with Lt. Col. D. O. Poole to Brig. Gen. Davis Tillson, 19 February 1866, Unregistered Letters Recd., ser. 632, Ga. Asst. Comr., BRFAL, NA, [FSSP A-5447]. Citations for photo-

copied documents from the National Archives that were consulted at the Freedmen and Southern Society Project, University of Maryland, conclude with the designation "FSSP" and the project's document control number in square brackets: for example, [FSSP A-5447].

11. Quoted in Trowbridge, *South Tour*, pp. 453–454.

12. Jerry Thornbery, "The Development of Black Atlanta, 1865–1885" (Ph.D. diss., University of Maryland, 1977), pp. 48–53; Edmund L. Drago, *Black Politicians and Reconstruction in Georgia: A Splendid Failure* (Baton Rouge: Louisiana State University Press, 1982), pp. 113–116.

13. Brig. Genl. Davis Tillson to Captain George R. Walbridge, 12 March 1866, Letters Recd., ser. 732, Ga. Subasst. Comr., BRFAL, NA, [FSSP A-5153].

14. Rebecca Craighead to Rev. Samuel Hunt, 15 February 1866, Georgia, AMA Papers; see also F. Ayers to Rev. George Whipple, 15 February 1866, Georgia, AMA Papers.

15. Testimony of Abram Colby, 28 October 1871, in 42nd Congress, 2nd Session, House Report no. 22, pt. 6, *Testimony taken by the Joint Select Committee to Inquire into the Condition of Affairs in the Late Insurrectionary States* (Washington, D.C., 1872), vol. 2, p. 700 (hereafter cited as KKK Hearings). See also testimony of Alfred Richardson, 7 July 1871, KKK Hearings, vol. 1, p. 12.

16. Doyle, *New Men*, pp. 38–48, 151; Jonathan W. McLeod, *Workers and Workplace Dynamics in Reconstruction Era Atlanta* (Los Angeles: Center for Afro-American Studies, University of California), pp. 10–16.

17. McLeod, *Workers and Workplace*, pp. 24–31, 45, 61, 75, 81, 91, 94.

18. Ibid., pp. 77–92, 100–103; Thornbery, "Black Atlanta," pp. 191–225.

19. Entry of 27 May 1865, Ella Gertrude Clanton Thomas Journal, William R. Perkins Library, Duke University (hereafter cited as DU).

20. See entries for May 1865, Thomas Journal, DU.

21. Atlanta *Daily Intelligencer*, 25 October 1865.

22. Emma J. S. Prescott, "Reminiscences of the War," typescript, pp. 49–50, 55, Atlanta History Center (hereafter cited as AHC)

23. Atlanta *Daily New Era*, 27 February 1868.

24. Mr. J. T. Ball to Maj. Knox, 19 March 1866, Unregistered Letters Recd., ser. 2250, Meridian, Miss. Subasst. Comr., BRFAL, NA, [FSSP A-9423].

25. Alexa Wynell Benson, "Race Relations in Atlanta, As Seen in a Critical Analysis of the City Council Proceedings and Other Related Works, 1865–1877" (M.A. thesis, Atlanta University, 1966), pp. 43–44; Foner, *Reconstruction*, pp. 199–202; Theodore Brantner Wilson, *The Black Codes of the South* (University, Ala.: University of Alabama Press, 1965); Rabinowitz, *Race Relations*, pp. 34–35; Atlanta *Daily New Era*, 27 February 1868.

26. Virginia Shelton to William Shelton, 20 August 1866, Campbell Family Papers, DU. See also Ellen Chisholm to Laura Perry, 27 July 1867, Perry Family Papers, AHC.

27. Affidavit of Samuel Ellison, 16 Jan 1867 BRFAL, NA.

28. Foner, *Reconstruction*, pp. 425–444; see testimony of Abram Colby, 28 October 1871, KKK Hearings, vol. 2, pp. 699–702.

29. Testimony of Alfred Richardson, 7 July 1871, KKK Hearings, vol. 1, pp. 12, 18.

30. Foner, *Reconstruction*, pp. 87, 290–291; Elsa Barkley Brown, "Negotiating and Transforming the Public Sphere: African American Political Life in the Transition from Slavery to Freedom," *Public Culture* 7 (Fall 1994): 107–126; Thomas C. Holt, *Black Over White: Negro Political Leadership in South Carolina during Reconstruction* (Urbana: University of Illinois Press, 1977), pp. 34–35.

31. Macon *Georgia Weekly Telegraph*, 8 October 1872, as quoted in Edmund L. Drago, "Militancy and Black Women in Reconstruction Georgia," *Journal of American Culture* 1 (Winter 1978): 841.

32. Testimony of Hannah Flournoy, 24 October 1871, KKK Hearings, vol. 1, p. 533. On Ashburn's death see Drago, *Black Politicians*, pp. 145, 153.

33. Testimony of Joe Brown, 24 October 1871, KKK Hearings, vol. 1, p. 502.

34. Henry McNeal Turner's emancipation speech, 1 January 1866, Augusta, as quoted in Herbert G. Gutman, *The Black Family in Slavery and Freedom, 1750–1925* (New York: Pantheon Books, 1977), p. 388. See also Catherine Clinton, "Bloody Terrain: Freedwomen, Sexuality and Violence During Reconstruction," *Georgia Historical Quarterly* 76 (Summer 1992): 318; Atlanta *Weekly Defiance*, 24 February 1883.

35. Eliza Frances Andrews, *The War-Time Journal of a Georgia Girl, 1864–1865*, ed. Spencer Bidwell King, Jr. (Macon, Ga.: Arvidian Press, 1960), p. 349.

36. Gutman, *Black Family*, pp. 387–388.

37. Testimony of Z. B. Hargrove, 13 July 1871, KKK Hearings, vol. 1, p. 83. See also testimony of George B. Burnett, 2 November 1871, KKK Hearings, vol. 2, p. 949. See Jacquelyn Dowd Hall, *Revolt Against Chivalry: Jesse Daniel Ames and the Women's Campaign Against Lynching* (New York: Columbia University Press, 1974).

38. Affidavit of Barbara Price, 15 May 1867, Misc. Court Records, ser. 737, Atlanta, Ga. Subasst. Comr., BRFAL; Bvt. Maj. Fred. Mosebach to Mayor and City Council of Atlanta, 15 May 1867, and Bvt. Maj. Fred. Mosebach to Col. C. C. Sibley, 21 May 1867, vol. 99, pp. 49 and 53–54, Letters Sent, ser. 729, Atlanta, Ga. Subasst. Comr., BRFAL, NA, [FSSP A-5709]. See also James M. Russell and Jerry Thornbery, "William Finch of Atlanta: The Black Politician as Civic Leader," in Howard N. Rabinowitz, ed. *Southern Black Leaders of the Reconstruction Era* (Urbana: University of Illinois Press, 1982), pp. 317, 332.

39. The apprenticeship system was not entirely limited to the conscription of minors; young adults actively providing for themselves were also apprenticed. For example, a turpentine worker with a wife and child was defined as an orphan in North Carolina. See Foner, *Reconstruction*, p. 201.

40. Martin Lee to Mr. Tillson, 7 December 1866, in Ira Berlin et al., "Afro-American Families in the Transition from Slavery to Freedom," *Radical History Review* 42 (Fall 1988): 102–103.

41. Entry of 27 May 1865, Thomas Journal, DU. Evidence from ex-slave narratives suggests a pattern of exploitation of child laborers; they received little or no cash wages. See testimony of Nancy Smith, in George P. Rawick, ed., *The American Slave: A Composite Autobiography* (Westport, Conn.: Greenwood Press, 1941; 1972), *Georgia Narratives*, vol. 13, pt. 3, p. 302 (hereafter cited as WPA Ga. Narr.); testimony of Georgia Telfair, WPA Ga. Narr., vol. 13, pt. 4, p. 5.

42. Rebecca M. Craighead to Bvt. Brig. Gen. J. H. Lewis, 11 May 1866, Ga. Asst. Comr., C-69, 1867, Letters Recd., ser. 631, Ga. Asst. Comr., BRFAL, NA, [FSSP A-415].

43. F. Ayers to Rev. George Whipple, 15 February 1866, Georgia, AMA Papers.

44. Prescott, "Reminiscences of the War," p. 56, AHC. Prescott goes on to reveal that Silvey died penniless, without the help of former owners.

45. Gutman, *Black Family*, pp. 9–23; Berlin et al., "Afro-American Families," pp. 92–93.

46. Corporal Murray, as quoted in J. R. Johnson to Col. S. Lee, 1 June 1866, in Berlin et al., "Afro-American Families," p. 97.

47. For examples of these efforts see Wm. H. Sinclair to Freedmen's Bureau agent at Savannah, Ga., 12 September 1866, Unregistered Letters, ser. 1013, Savannah, Ga. Subasst. Comr., BRFAL, NA, [FSSP A-5762]; R. F. Patterson to Col. D. C. Poole, Letters Recd., ser. 732, Atlanta, Ga. Subasst. Comr., BRFAL, NA, [FSSP A-5704].

48. Gutman, *Black Family*, pp. 418–425.

49. 1st Lt. F. E. Grossmann to the Acting Assistant Adjutant General, 1 October 1866, in Berlin et al., "Afro-American Families," pp. 97–98. Gutman, *Black Family*, pp. 418–425.

50. James D. Anderson, *The Education of Blacks in the South, 1860–1935* (Chapel Hill: University of North Carolina Press, 1988), pp. 4–9, 16; Herbert G. Gutman, "Schools for Freedom: The Post-Emancipation Origins of Afro-American Education," in Herbert G. Gutman, *Power and Culture: Essays on the American Working-Class*, ed. Ira Berlin (New York: Pantheon, 1987), p. 294; Jacqueline Jones, *Soldiers of Light and Love: Northern Teachers and Georgia Blacks 1865–1873* Chapel Hill: University of North Carolina Press, 1980), p. 59.

51. Gutman, "Schools for Freedom," pp. 286, 294; Jones, *Soldiers of Light and Love*, p. 62; Anderson, *Education of Blacks in the South*, pp. 4–32.

52. Drago, *Black Politicians*, pp. 27–28.

53. Russell and Thornbery, "William Finch of Atlanta," pp. 319, 322; Russell, *Atlanta*, p. 181.

54. Mrs. E. T. Ayers to Rev. Samuel Hunt, 1 September 1866, Georgia, AMA Papers.

55. Jennies Barium to Rev. Samuel Grant, 27 January 1866, Georgia, AMA Papers; Andrews, *South Since the War*, p. 338.

56. Sarah J. Thomas to Mr. [Edmund A.] Ware, 11 October 1869, Edmund A. Ware Papers, Robert W. Woodruff Library, Clarke Atlanta University.

DOCUMENTS: After the Civil War: Reconsidering the Law

> *Reconstruction Amendments, 1868, 1870*

Until 1868, the United States Constitution made no explicit distinctions on the basis of gender. Of qualifications for voters, it said only that "the electors in each State shall have the qualifications requisite for electors of the most numerous branch of the State legislature" (Article I, section 2). Reformers merely needed to persuade each state legislature to change its own rules in order to enfranchise women in national elections.

The word *male* was introduced into the Constitution in section 2 of the Fourteenth Amendment, as part of a complex provision—never enforced—intended to constrain former Confederates from interfering with the civil rights of newly freed slaves. Suffragists were bitterly disappointed at the failure to include sex as a category in the Fifteenth Amendment. But until the test case of *Minor* v. *Happersett* (pp. 251–52), they clung to the hope that the first article of the Fourteenth Amendment would be interpreted broadly enough to admit women to the polls.

FOURTEENTH AMENDMENT, 1868

1. All persons born or naturalized in the United States, and subject to the jurisdiction thereof, are citizens of the United States and of the State wherein they reside. No State shall make or enforce any law which shall abridge the privileges or immunities of citizens of the United States; nor shall any State deprive any person of life, liberty, or property, without due process of law; nor deny to any person within its jurisdiction the equal protection of the laws.

2. Representatives shall be apportioned among the several States according to their respective numbers, counting the whole number of persons in each State, excluding Indians not taxed. But when the right to vote at any election for the choice of electors for President and Vice-President of the United States, Representatives in Congress, the executive and judicial officers of a State, or the members of the legislature thereof, is denied to any of the male inhabitants of such State, being twenty-one years of age and citizens of the United States, or in any way abridged, except for participation in rebellion, or other crime, the basis of representation therein shall be reduced in the proportion which the number of such male citizens shall bear to the whole number of male citizens twenty-one years of age in such State. . . .

FIFTEENTH AMENDMENT, 1870

The right of citizens of the United States to vote shall not be denied or abridged by the United States or by any State on account of race, color, or previous condition of servitude. . . .

Bradwell *v.* Illinois, *1873*

Although she could not practice in the courts until the end of her career, Myra Bradwell was perhaps the most notable female lawyer of the nineteenth century. She read law in the office of her husband, a prominent Chicago attorney and county judge. In 1868 she began to publish the *Chicago Legal News,* a weekly newspaper covering developments in courts and legislatures throughout the country. Because she had received a special charter from the state legislature under which she was permitted to act without the usual legal disabilities of a married woman, she ran the *News* as her own business. She wrote vigorous editorials, evaluating legal opinions and new laws, assessing proposed state legislation, and supporting progressive developments like prison reform, the establishment of law schools, and women's rights. She drafted bills improving married women's rights to child custody and to property, including the Illinois Married Woman's Property Act of 1869. Thanks in part to her own lobbying efforts, Illinois permitted women to own property and to control their own earnings.

It was only logical that Myra Bradwell should seek admission to the bar. Although she passed the entrance tests in 1869, although the Illinois Married Woman's Property Act permitted her to own property, and although the law that gave the state supreme court the power to license attorneys did not explicitly exclude women, her application was rejected by the Illinois Supreme Court on the grounds that she was a married woman, and therefore not a truly free agent. Appealing to the United States Supreme Court, her attorney argued that among the "privileges and immunities" guaranteed to each citizen by the Fourteenth Amendment was the right to pursue any honorable profession. "Intelligence, integrity and honor are the only qualifications that can be prescribed . . . the broad shield of the Constitution is over all, and protects each in that measure of success which his or her individual merits may secure."

The Court's decision came in two parts. Speaking for the majority and citing the most recent decision of the Supreme Court in the slaughterhouse cases, Justice Samuel F. Miller held that the right to practice law in the courts of any particular state was a right that had to be granted by the individual state; it was not one of the "privileges and immunities" of national citizenship. This judgment was supplemented by a concurring opinion, in which Justice Joseph P. Bradley offered an ideological justification for the Court's decision that was based on inherent differences between men and women and that was to be widely used thereafter to defend the exclusion of women from professional careers.

While her case was pending before the U.S. Supreme Court, Bradwell and Alta M. Hulett, another woman who had been refused admission to the bar even though she was otherwise qualified, successfully lobbied for a law that granted freedom of occupational choice to all Illinois citizens, both male and female. The bill was passed in 1872; a year later Alta Hulett was sworn in before the Illinois Bar. Bradwell did not think she should have to beg for admission, and she never formally applied for a license to practice law under the new statute. In the *Chicago Legal News* she observed that "having once complied with the rules and regulations of the court . . . [I] declined to . . . again ask for admission." In 1890, twenty years after her initial application, the Illinois Supreme Court admitted Bradwell to the bar. Two years before her death in 1894 she was admitted to practice before the U.S. Supreme Court, but she never did argue a case there.*

MR. JUSTICE JOSEPH P. BRADLEY

The claim of the plaintiff, who is a married woman, to be admitted to practice as an attorney and counselor at law, is based upon the supposed right of every person, man or woman, to engage in any lawful employment for a livelihood. The supreme court of Illinois denied the application on the ground that, by the common law, which is the basis of the laws of Illinois, only men were admitted to the bar, and the legislature had not made any change in this respect. . . .

The claim that, under the 14th Amendment of the Constitution, which declares that no state shall make or enforce any law which shall abridge the privileges and immunities of citizens of the United States, and the statute law of Illinois, or the common law prevailing in that state, can no longer be set up as a barrier against the right of females to pursue any lawful employment . . . assumes that it is one of the privileges and immunities of women as citizens to engage in any and every profession, occupation or employment in civil life.

It certainly cannot be affirmed, as a historical fact, that this has ever been established as one of the fundamental privileges and immunities of the sex. On the contrary, the civil law, as well as nature herself, has always recognized a wide difference in the respective spheres and destinies of man and woman. Man is, or should be, woman's protector and defender. The natural and proper timidity and delicacy which belongs to the female sex evidently unfits it for many of the occupations of civil life. The constitution of the family organization, which is founded in the divine ordinance, as well as in the nature of things, indi-

cates the domestic sphere as that which properly belongs to the domain and functions of womanhood. The harmony, not to say identity, of interests and views which belong or should belong to the family institution, is repugnant to the idea of a woman adopting a distinct and independent career from that of her husband. So firmly fixed was this sentiment in the founders of the common law that it became a maxim of that system of jurisprudence that a woman had no legal existence separate from her husband, who was regarded as her head and representative in the social state; and, notwithstanding some recent modifications of this civil status, many of the special rules of law flowing from and dependent upon this cardinal principle still exist in full force in most states. One of these is, that a married woman is incapable, without her husband's consent, of making contracts which shall be binding on her or him. This very incapacity was one circumstance which the supreme court of Illinois deemed important in rendering a married woman incompetent fully to perform the duties and trusts that belong to the office of an attorney and counselor.

It is true that many women are unmarried and not affected by any of the duties, complications, and incapacities arising out of the married state, but these are exceptions to the general rule. The paramount destiny and mission of woman are to fulfill the noble and benign offices of wife and mother. This is the law of the Creator. And the rules of civil society must be adapted to the general constitution of things, and cannot be based upon exceptional cases. . . .

*See also Frances Olsen, "From False Paternalism to False Equality: Judicial Assaults on Feminist Community, Illinois 1869–1895," *Michigan Law Review* 84 (1986):1518–43.

Comstock Law, 1873

This "Act for the Suppression of Trade in, and Circulation of Obscene Literature and Articles of immoral Use" was passed at the urging of Anthony Comstock, the head of the New York Society for the Suppression of Vice. The first section prohibited the sale of the described materials in the District of Columbia and the territories; subsequent sections prohibited the sending of these materials through the mails or their importation into the United States. Enforcement, as historian Helen Horowitz has explained, was placed in the hands of a newly created "special agent in the United States Post Office with power to confiscate immoral matter in the mails and arrest those sending it."[*] In the 1870s, many states passed their own versions of the federal law.

The link of "obsence literature and articles of immoral use" reflected contemporary practice; erotic literature and pornography were often sold in the same shops that sold condoms and other birth control devices; these devices, and substances offering to induce abortion, were often advertised in the pages of pornographic literature. Anthony Comstock included in this category writings on sexual reform and free love. The law reflected a belief that both contraception and abortion were acts of interference with the natural order and with God's intentions. No distinction was made between drugs used for abortion and materials used for contraception, or indeed, pornographic pictures that encouraged masturbation; all were treated in the same terms. The law may have begun "as a measure to protect children against erotica" but it included "contraceptive information and materials and advertisements for abortion. . . . it was possible to construe this law as banning printed advocacy of free love."[†] Note the heavy penalties provided.

Be it enacted . . . That whoever, within the District of Columbia or any of the Territories of the United States . . . shall sell . . . or shall offer to sell, or to lend, or to give away, or in any manner to exhibit, or shall otherwise publish or offer to publish in any manner, or shall have in his possession, for any such purpose or purposes, any obscene book, pamphlet, paper, writing, advertisement, circular, print, picture, drawing or other representation, figure, or image on or of paper or other material, or any cast, instrument, or other article of an immoral nature, or any drug or medicine, or any article whatever, for the prevention of conception, or for causing unlawful abortion, or shall advertize the same for sale, or shall write or print, or cause to be written or printed, any card, circular, book, pamphlet, advertisement, or notice of any kind, stating when, where, how, or of whom, or by what means, any of the articles in this section . . . can be purchased or obtained, or shall manufacture, draw, or print, or in any wise make any of such articles, shall be deemed guilty of a misdemeanor, and on conviction thereof in any court of the United States . . . he shall be imprisoned at hard labor in the penitentiary for not less than six months nor more than five years for each offense, or fined not less than one hundred dollars nor more than two thousand dollars, with costs of court. . . .

[*]Helen Lefkowitz Horowitz, *Rereading Sex: Battles over Sexual Knowledge and Suppression in Nineteenth Century America* (New York: Alfred A. Knopf, 2002), pp. 381 ff.

[†]Horowitz, p. 385.

Public Laws of the United States of America, Passed at the Third Session of the Forty-Second Congress (Boston, 1873), p. 598.

Minor v. Happersett, 1875

In 1872 suffragists in a number of places attempted to test the possibilities of the first section of the Fourteenth Amendment. "The power to regulate is one thing, the power to prevent is an entirely different thing," observed Virginia Minor, president of the Woman Suffrage Association of Missouri, and she presented herself at the polls in St. Louis in 1872. When the registrar refused to permit her to register to vote, she and her husband sued him for denying her one of the "privileges and immunities of citizenship"; when they lost the case they appealed to the Supreme Court.

In a unanimous opinion the justices held that if the authors of the Constitution had intended that women should vote, they would have said so explicitly. The decision of the Court meant that woman suffrage could not be developed by way of a quiet reinterpretation of the Constitution but would require an explicit amendment to the Constitution or a series of revisions in the laws of the states.

MR. CHIEF JUSTICE MORRISON R. WAITE DELIVERED THE OPINION OF THE COURT:

The question is presented in this case, whether, since the adoption of the fourteenth amendment, a woman, who is a citizen of the United States and of the State of Missouri, is a voter in that State, notwithstanding the provision of the constitution and laws of the State, which confine the right of suffrage to men alone. . . . The argument is, that as a woman, born or naturalized in the United States and subject to the jurisdiction thereof, is a citizen of the United States and of the State in which she resides, she has the right of suffrage as one of the privileges and immunities of her citizenship, which the State cannot by its laws or constitution abridge.

There is no doubt that women may be citizens. They are persons, and by the fourteenth amendment "all persons born or naturalized in the United States and subject to the jurisdiction thereof" are expressly declared to be "citizens of the United States and of the State wherein they reside." But, in our opinion, it did not need this amendment to give them that position . . . sex has never been made one of the elements of citizenship in the United States. In this respect men have never had an advantage over women. The same laws precisely apply to both. The fourteenth amendment did not affect the citizenship of women any more than it did of men . . . Mrs. Minor . . . has always been a citizen from her birth, and entitled to all the privileges and immunities of citizenship.

If the right of suffrage is one of the necessary privileges of a citizen of the United States, then the constitution and laws of Missouri confining it to men are in violation of the Constitution of the United States, as amended, and consequently void. The direct question is, therefore, presented whether all citizens are necessarily voters.

The Constitution does not define the privileges and immunities of citizens. For that definition we must look elsewhere. In this case we need not determine what they are, but only whether suffrage is necessarily one of them.

It certainly is nowhere made so in express terms. The United States has no voters in the States of its own creation. The elective officers of the United States are all elected directly or indirectly by state voters. . . . it cannot for a moment be doubted that if it had been intended to make all citizens of the United States voters, the framers of the Constitution would not have left it to implication. . . .

It is true that the United States guarantees to every State a republican form of government. . . . No particular government is designated as republican, neither is the exact form to be guaranteed, in any manner especially designated. . . . When the Constitution was adopted . . . all the citizens of the States were not invested with the right of suffrage. In all, save perhaps New Jersey, this right was only bestowed upon men and not upon all of them. . . . Under these circumstances it is certainly now too late to contend that a government is not republican, within the meaning of this guaranty in the Constitution, because women are not made voters. . . . If suffrage was intended to be included within its obligations, language better adapted to express that intent would most certainly have been employed. . . .

. . . For nearly ninety years the people have acted upon the idea that the Constitution, when it conferred citizenship, did not necessarily confer the right of suffrage. If uniform practice long continued can settle the construction of so important an instrument as the Constitution of the United States confessedly is, most certainly it has been done here. Our province is to decide what the law is, not to declare what it should be.

We have given this case the careful consideration its importance demands. If the law is wrong, it ought to be changed; but the power for that is not with us. . . . No argument as to woman's need of suffrage can be considered. We can only act upon her rights as they exist. . . .

BARBARA SICHERMAN
Reading *Little Women:* The Many Lives of a Text

> Why should girls be learn'd and wise?
> Books only serve to spoil their eyes.
> The studious eye but faintly twinkles.
> And reading paves the way to wrinkles.
> —*John Trumbull, 1773*

Although there was much skepticism about whether advanced learning was good for women, the early republic was a time of a transformation of educational opportunity. A virtual revolution in literacy was under way, encouraged by the transition of the economy to a print culture and reinforced by a technology that made printed materials more widely available and injected them into new areas of life. Reading was linked to rationality, upward mobility, and control of one's own life. Although literacy did not increase at the same rate for each class or each sex within each class, what might be called a "literacy gap" between free white men and women gradually closed during the years before the Civil War. As early as the 1780s, 80 percent of the white women of urban New England were literate; they seem to have been the most literate women in the Western world.

The gains were specific to region. The South lagged far behind; as late as 1850 one out of five white women in the South was illiterate. Literacy was denied slaves by law;

From *U.S. History as Women's History: New Feminist Essays,* edited by Linda K. Kerber, Alice Kessler-Harris, and Kathryn Kish Sklar. Copyright © 1995 by the University of North Carolina Press. Used by permission of the publisher. Notes have been renumbered and edited.

free blacks lacked both opportunity and institutional support for extended study. Yet urban African Americans quickly narrowed the gap between the races after the Civil War.

In a world in which only a few thousand women were in a college or university in any given year, and in which even high school education was rare, most "higher" education was necessarily self-education. Women shaped their intellectual lives out of their own diary-keeping, letter-writing, and reading. They chose books that had meaning for their lives. One book came to have more meaning for more women than perhaps any other contemporary publication: Louisa May Alcott's *Little Women*. Barbara Sicherman examines this phenomenon.

What elements of *Little Women* did its first readers respond to? Did the meaning of Little Women change over time? What issues in women's lives did it address? How do you account for its continuing popularity? Did you read *Little Women* when you were young? Have you seen any of the films? What differences of emphasis have you seen between the films and the novel?

"I have read and re-read 'Little Women' and it never seems to grow old," fifteen-year-old Jane Addams confided to a friend.[1] Writing in 1876, Addams did not say why she liked *Little Women*. But her partiality was by no means unusual among women, and even some men, of her generation. Louisa May Alcott's tale of growing up female was an unexpected success when it appeared in the fall of 1868. Already a classic when Addams wrote, the book has been called "the most popular girls' story in American literature"; a century and a quarter after publication, there are twenty editions in print.[2]

The early history of this publishing phenomenon is full of ironies. Not the least of them is the author's expressed distaste for the project. When Thomas Niles Jr., literary editor of the respected Boston firm of Roberts Brothers, asked Alcott to write a *"girls' story,"* the author tartly observed in her journal: "I plod away, though I don't enjoy this sort of thing. Never liked girls or knew many, except my sisters, but our queer plays and experiences may prove interesting, though I doubt it."[3] After delivering twelve chapters in June 1868, she claimed that both she and her editor found them *"dull."*[4] Niles assured her that he was "pleased—I ought to be more emphatic & say delighted,—so *please* to consider 'judgement' as favorable"; the following month he predicted that the book would " 'hit.' "[5] Influenced perhaps by the verdict of "some girls" who had pronounced the manuscript " 'splendid!' " Alcott reconsidered while correcting proof: "It

reads better than I expected. Not a bit sensational, but simple and true, for we really lived most of it." Of the youngsters who liked it, she observed: "As it is for them, they are the best critics, so I should be satisfied."[6]

The informal "readers' report" was right on target. Published in early October 1868, the first printing (2,000 copies) of *Little Women, or, Meg, Jo, Beth and Amy* sold out within the month. A sequel appeared the following April, with only the designation *Part Second* differentiating it from the original. By the end of the year some 38,000 copies (of both parts) were in print, with another 32,000 in 1870. Nearly 200,000 copies had been printed by Roberts Brothers by January 1888, two months before Alcott's death.[7] Like it or not, with this book Alcott established her niche in the expanding market for juvenile literature.

Perhaps even more remarkable than *Little Women's* initial success has been its longevity. It topped a list of forty books compiled by the Federal Bureau of Education in 1925 that "all children should read before they are sixteen."[8] . . . On a [1976] bicentennial list of the best eleven American children's books, *Little Women, The Adventures of Tom Sawyer,* and *The Adventures of Huckleberry Finn* were the only nineteenth-century titles. Like most iconic works, *Little Women* has been transmuted into other media, into song and opera, theater, radio, and film. A comic strip even surfaced briefly in 1988 in the revamped *Ms.*[9]

Polls and statistics do not begin to do justice to the *Little Women* phenomenon. Reading the book has been a rite of passage for generations of adolescent and preadolescent females of the comfortable classes. It still elicits powerful narratives of love and passion.[10] In a 1982 essay on how she became a writer, Cynthia Ozick declared: "I read 'Little Women' a thousand times. Ten thousand. I am no longer incognito, not even to myself. I am Jo in her 'vortex'; not Jo exactly, but some Jo-of-the-future. I am under an enchantment: Who I truly am must be deferred, waited for and waited for."[11] Ozick's avowal encapsulates recurrent themes in readers' accounts: the deep, almost inexplicable emotions engendered by the novel; the passionate identification with Jo March, the feisty tomboy heroine who publishes stories in her teens; and—allowing for exaggeration—a pattern of multiple readings. Numerous women who grew up in the 1940s and 1950s report that they read the book yearly or more during their teens or earlier; some confide that they continue to read it as adults, though less frequently. Presumably for them, as for Jane Addams, the story did not grow old.

One of many intriguing questions about *Little Women* is how and why the "dull" book, the girls' story by a woman who claimed she never liked girls, captivated so many readers. An added irony is that Alcott, the product of an unconventional upbringing, whose eccentric transcendentalist father self-consciously tested his child-rearing theories on his daughters, took them to live in a commune, and failed utterly as a breadwinner, should write what many contemporaries considered the definitive story of American family life.[12] . . .

EARLY PUBLISHING AND MARKETING HISTORY

Alcott claimed that she kept on with *Little Women* because "lively, simple books are very much needed for girls, and perhaps I can supply the need."[13] . . . She may have regretted being channeled into one type of literature, but she was extremely well paid for her efforts, a source of considerable pride to a woman whose father was so feckless about money.[14]

Juvenile literature was entering a new phase in the 1860s at the very time Alcott was refashioning her career. . . . In contrast to the overtly religious antebellum stories, in which both sexes were expected to be good and domesticated, the new juvenile market was becoming increasingly segmented by gender. An exciting new adventure literature for boys developed after 1850, featuring escape from domesticity and female authority. Seeking to tap into a new market, Niles asked Alcott to write a "girls' story[.]" . . . Although people of all ages and both sexes read *Little Women*, the book evolved for the emerging female youth market, the "young adults" in the transitional period between childhood and adulthood that would soon be labeled adolescence.[15]

These readers had an unusual say in determining Jo's fate. Eager to capitalize on his experiment, Niles urged Alcott to add a chapter "in which allusions might be made to something in the future."[16] Employing a metaphor well suited to a writer who engaged in theatrical performances most of her life, the volume concludes: "So grouped the curtain falls upon Meg, Jo, Beth and Amy. Whether it ever rises again, depends upon the reception given to the first act of the domestic drama, called 'LITTLE WOMEN.'"[17] Reader response to Alcott's floater was positive but complicated her task. Reluctant to depart from autobiography, Alcott insisted that by rights Jo should remain a "literary spinster." But she felt pressured by readers to imagine a different fate for her heroine. The day she began work on the sequel, she observed: "Girls write to ask who the little women marry, as if that was the only end and aim of a woman's life. I *won't* marry Jo to Laurie to please anyone." To foil her readers, she created a "funny match" for Jo—the middle-aged, bumbling German professor, Friedrich Bhaer.[18]

The aspect of the book that has frustrated generations of readers—the foreclosing of marriage between Jo and Laurie—thus represents a compromise between Alcott and her initial audience. Paradoxically, this seeming misstep has probably been a major factor in the story's enduring success. If Jo had remained a spinster, as Alcott wished, or if she had married the attractive and wealthy hero, as readers hoped, it is unlikely that the book would have had such a wide appeal. Rather, the problematic ending contributed to *Little Women's* popularity, the lack of satisfying closure helping to keep the story alive, something to ponder, return to, reread, perhaps with the hope of a different resolution. Alcott's refusal of the conventionally happy ending represented by a pairing of Jo and Laurie and her insistence on a "funny match" to the rumpled and much older professor effectively subvert adolescent romantic ideals. The absence of a compelling love plot has also made it easier for generations of readers to ignore the novel's ending when Jo becomes Mother Bhaer and to retain the image of Jo as the questing teenage tomboy.[19]

At the same time, an adolescent reader, struggling with her appearance and unruly impulses while contemplating the burdens of future womanhood, might find it reassuring that her fictional counterpart emerges happily, if not perhaps ideally, from similar circumstances. For Jo is loved. And she has choices. She turns down the charming but erratic hero, who consoles himself by marrying her pretty and vain younger sister, Amy. Professor Bhaer is no schoolgirl's hero, but Jo believes that he is better suited to her than Laurie. The crucial point is that the choice is hers, its quirkiness another sign of her much-prized individuality.[20] Jo gives up writing sensation stories because her prospective husband considers them unworthy, but she makes it clear that she intends to contribute to the support of their future family.

By marrying off the sisters in the second part, Alcott bowed to young women's interest in romance. The addition of the marriage to the quest plot enabled *Little Women* to touch the essential bases for middle-class female readers in the late nineteenth century. In this regard, it was unusual for its time. . . . The conjunction of quest and marriage plots helps to account for the book's staying power: it is difficult to imagine large numbers of adolescent female readers in the twentieth century gravitating to a book in which the heroine remained single.[21] *Little Women* took off with the publication of the second part in April 1869. A Concord neighbor called it "the rage in '69 as 'Pinafore' was in '68."[22] A savvy judge of the market, Niles urged Alcott to "'Make hay while the Sunshines'" and did everything he could to keep her name before the public.[23] Shortly after the appearance of *Little Women, Part Second,* Roberts Brothers brought out an augmented edition of her first critical success under the title, *Hospital Sketches and Camp and Fireside Stories,* and in succeeding years published *An Old-Fashioned Girl* (1870) and *Little Men* (1871), a sequel to *Little Women.* . . .

Reviewers stressed the realism of her characters and scenes; readers recognized themselves in her work. Thirteen-year-old Annie Adams of Fair Haven, Vermont, wrote *St. Nicholas,* the most prestigious of the new children's magazines, that she and her three sisters each resembled one of the March sisters (she was Jo): "So, you see, I was greatly interested in 'Little Women,' as I could appreciate it so well; and it seemed to me as if Miss Alcott must have seen us four girls before she wrote the story."[24] Girls not only read themselves into *Little Women,* they elaborated on it and incorporated the story into their lives. In 1872 the five Lukens sisters from Brinton, Pennsylvania, sent Alcott a copy of their home newspaper, "Little Things," which was modeled after "The Pickwick Portfolio" produced by the March sisters. Alcott responded with encouragement, asked for further details, and subscribed to the paper . . . She took their aspirations seriously, providing frank, practical advice about magazines, publishers, and authors' fees to these budding literary women.[25]

There was, then, a reciprocal relationship between the characters and home life depicted in *Little Women* and the lives of middle-class American girls. An unusual feature of this identification was the perception that author and heroine were interchangeable. Alcott's work was marketed to encourage the illusion not only that Jo was Alcott but that Alcott was Jo. When Alcott traveled in Europe in 1870, Niles encouraged her to send for publication "'Jo's Letters from Abroad to the March's [sic] at Home'" . . .

Readers responded in kind. An ad for *Little Women* quotes a letter written by "Nelly" addressed to "Dear Jo, or Miss Alcott": "We have all been reading 'Little Women,' and we liked it so much I could not help wanting to write to you. We think *you* are perfectly splendid; I like you better every time I read it. We were all so disappointed about your not marrying Laurie; I cried over that part,— . . . Blurring the lines between author and character, the writer also requested a picture, wished the recipient improved health, and invited her to visit.[26]

The illusion that she was the youthful and unconventional Jo made Alcott a more approachable author. But the conflation of author and character had its risks. Young readers who formed an image of the author as Jo, a teenager for most of the novel, were startled by Alcott's appearance. When the Lukens sisters informed her that some "friends" had been disappointed in her picture, Alcott replied that she could not understand why people insisted Jo was young "when she is said to be 30 at the end of the book . . . After seeing the photograph it is hardly necessary to say that Jo and L.M.A. are *not* one, & that the latter is a tired out old lady of 42."[27]

With the publication of *Little Women, Part Second,* Alcott became a celebrity. Correspondents demanded her photograph and autograph seekers descended on her home while she "dodge[d] into the woods *à la* Hawthorne."[28] . . . Alcott also drew more serious admirers, some of whom, like the Lukens sisters, sought her literary advice. In the 1860s and 1870s authorship was the most respected female vocation—and the best paid. . . .

Alcott was a well-respected writer during her lifetime, an era of relatively inclusive and nonhierarchical definitions of literature. An American literature course taken by Jane Addams at Rockford Female Seminary in 1878–79 covered authors of domestic fiction, Alcott among them.[29] But her literary reputation transcended the category. A review of *Little Men* pronounced: "Even thus early in her brief history as a country and a nation, America can boast a long list of classics—Prescott, Irving, Hawthorne, Longfellow—and Time, the great sculptor will one day carve Miss Alcott's name among them."[30] . . .

A teenage girl contemplating a literary career could dream of becoming a published author who, like Alcott, might produce a beloved and immortal work. At a time when young women were encouraged, even expected, to take part in the literary activities that suffused middle-class domestic life, such success was not beyond imagining. From James S. Hart's [*Manual of American Literature* (1873)], a reader could learn that Alcott began writing for publication at sixteen and, by hard work and perseverance, became both famous and self-supporting by her pen in her late thirties.[31] The real female American success story was Alcott's, not Jo's.

There were, then, many reasons why a young woman seeking a literary career in the 1870s and early 1880s would look to Alcott as a model. Most important was the story that brought pleasure to so many. . . . The contrast

with Martha Finley's *Elsie Dinsmore* (1867), a story in which strict obedience is exacted from children—to the point of whipping—is striking. In this first of many volumes, the lachrymose and devoutly religious heroine is put upon by relatives and by her father, who punishes her for refusing to play the piano on the Sabbath. Elsie holds fast to her principles but is otherwise self-abnegating in the extreme: it is difficult to imagine her even trying to have fun. . . .

The fictional world of *Little Women* is strikingly different. Despite the use of John Bunyan's *Pilgrim's Progress* as a framing device, an older Calvinist worldview that emphasized sin and obedience to the deity has been replaced by a moral outlook in which self-discipline and doing good to others come first.[32] Consonant with *Little Women's* new moral tone, so congenial to an expanding middle class, are its informal style and rollicking escapades. Aided by her love of the theater and influenced as well by her youthful idol, Charles Dickens, Alcott was a wonderful painter of dramatic scenes; some were heartbreaking, but many were high-spirited depictions of frolics, games, and theatrical productions.[33] She also had an ear for young people's language: her substitution of dialogue for the long passages of moralizing narrative that characterized most girls' books gave her story a compelling sense of immediacy. So did her use of slang, for which critics often faulted her, but which must have endeared her to young readers. Finally, the beautifully realized portrait of Jo March as tomboy, one of the first of its kind, spoke to changing standards of girlhood. Beginning in the 1860s, tomboys were not only tolerated but even admired—up to a point, the point at which they were expected to become women.[34] Perhaps it was fitting after all that it was Alcott, writing of her idiosyncratic childhood in the 1840s, who identified a new type of American girlhood for the 1870s.[35] . . .

JO AS A LITERARY AND INTELLECTUAL MODEL

Reading Alcott became a necessary ritual for children of the comfortable classes. Growing up at a time and in a class that conferred leisure on its young, children devoted considerable time and energy to literary pursuits. *Lit-*

tle Women was a way station en route to more adult books. But it was also a text that acquired its own cachet. Alcott was such an accepted part of childhood that even Theodore Roosevelt declared, "at the cost of being deemed effeminate," that he "worshiped" *Little Men, Little Women,* and *An Old-Fashioned Girl.*[36] . . .

Not all of Alcott's early readers focused on Jo; some were taken with the saga of the entire March family, which invited comparisons with their own. Charlotte Perkins Gilman, for example, who grew up in genteel poverty after her father abandoned the family, liked the fact that in Alcott . . . , "the heroes and heroines were almost always poor, and good, while the rich people were generally bad."[37] . . .

Jo March . . . fueled the literary aspirations of M. Carey Thomas, one of Alcott's early readers, during the critical years of early adolescence. In the fall of 1869, the year of *Little Women's* great success, Thomas and her cousin Frank Smith adopted the personae of Jo and Laurie, although as Quakers they should not have been reading fiction at all. At the ages of twelve and fifteen respectively, Thomas and Smith began addressing each other and signing their letters as Jo and Laurie; they meted out other roles to friends and relatives. . . .

When Thomas began a journal in 1870 at age thirteen, she did so in Jo's name. Declaring at the outset: "Ain't going to be sentimental/'No no not for Jo' (not Joe)," she had much in common with Alcott's heroine.[38] Both were "bookworms" and tomboys; both desired independence. Like Jo, Thomas wished to do something "splendid." In early adolescence her ambitions were still diffuse, but they centered on becoming a famous writer, a famous *woman* writer—"Jo (not Joe)." Her life was suffused with literature, with writing as well as reading: in addition to keeping a journal, she wrote poetry, kept a commonplace book, and complied lists of favorite books and poems, some of them annotated. As she gravitated to such champions of aestheticism as Algernon Charles Swinburne and Dante Gabriel Rossetti, by her early twenties she had outgrown Alcott and other writers who upheld morality in their art. But her close friend Bessie King acknowledged the importance of their childhood play in 1879, when Thomas took the audacious step of starting graduate study in Germany: "Somehow today I went back to

those early days when our horizon was so limited yet so full of light & our path lay as plain before us. It all came of reading over Miss Alcott's books now the quintescence [sic] of Philistinism then a Bible. . . . Doesn't thee remember when to turn out a 'Jo' was the height of ambition"?[39]

At the time Thomas was so engaged with *Little Women,* she was already a feminist. Sensitive to any gender restriction or slight, whether from people she knew or from biblical or scientific sources, she resolved at fifteen to disprove female inferiority by advancing her own education.[40] Despite its inception as a domestic story, then, Thomas read *Little Women* as a female bildungsroman, as did many women after her. This has in many ways been the most important reading, the one that has made the book such a phenomenon for so many years.

With its secular recasting of *Pilgrim's Progress, Little Women* transforms Christian's allegorical search for the Celestial City into the quintessential female quest plot. In a chapter entitled "Castles in the Air," each of the March sisters reveals her deepest ambition. In its loving depictions of the sisters' struggles to attain their goals (Jo to be a famous writer, Amy an artist, and Meg mistress of a lovely house), *Little Women* succeeds in authorizing female vocation and individuality. Nor did Alcott rule out the possibility of future artistic creativity: although married and managing a large household and school, Jo has not entirely given up her literary dreams, nor Amy her artistic ones. Beth, who has no ambition other than "to stay at home safe with father and mother, and help take care of the family," dies because she can find no way of growing up; her mysterious illness may be read as a failure of imagination, her inability to build castles in the air.[41]

In Jo, Alcott creates a portrait of female creativity that was not traditionally available to women:

> Every few weeks she would shut herself up in her room, put on her scribbling suit, and "fall into a vortex," as she expressed it, writing away at her novel with all her heart and soul, for till that was finished she could find no peace. . . .
>
> She did not think herself a genius by any means; but when the writing fit came on, she gave herself up to it with entire abandon, and led a blissful life, unconscious of want, care, or bad

weather, while she sat safe and happy in an imaginary world, full of friends almost as real and dear to her as any in the flesh. Sleep forsook her eyes, meals stood untasted, day and night were all too short to enjoy the happiness which blessed her only at such times, and made these hours worth living, even if they bore no other fruit. The divine afflatus usually lasted a week or two, and then she emerged from her "vortex" hungry, sleepy, cross, or despondent.[42]

Alcott's portrait of concentrated purpose—which describes her own creative practice—is as far removed as it could be from the ordinary lot of women, at least any adult woman. Jo not only has a room of her own; she also has the leisure—and the license—to remove herself from all obligation to others. Jo was important to young women like Thomas because there were so few of her—in literature or in life. . . .

More conventional readers of Thomas's era could find in *Little Women* practical advice on two subjects of growing concern to women: economic opportunities and marriage. Alcott was well qualified to advise on the former because of her long years of struggle in the marketplace. . . . Middle-class women's need to be able to earn a living is a central motif in *Little Women,* as it was in Alcott's life. . . . Mr. March's economic setback, like Bronson Alcott's, forces his daughters into the labor market. Their jobs (as governess and companion) are depicted as mainly unrewarding, although Jo's literary career is described with loving particularity. . . . But although the March sisters marry, Marmee March, who wishes no greater joy for her daughters than a happy marriage, declares that it is better to remain single than to marry without love. Opportunities for self-respecting singlehood and women's employment went hand in hand, as Alcott knew.[43]

If Alcott articulated issues highly pertinent to young women of her era, Jo's continued appeal suggests not only the dearth of fictional heroines to foster dreams of glory but the continued absence of real-life models. Perhaps that is why Simone de Beauvoir was so attracted to *Little Women,* in which she thought she "caught a glimpse of my future self":

I identified passionately with Jo, the intellectual. . . . She wrote: in order to imitate her more completely, I composed two or three short stories. . . . [T]he relationship between Jo an'd Lau-

rie touched me to the heart. Later, I had no doubt, they would marry one another; so it was possible for maturity to bring the promises made in childhood to fruition instead of denying them: this thought filled me with renewed hope. . . . [I]n *Little Women* Jo was superior to her sisters, who were either more virtuous or more beautiful than she, because of her passion for knowledge and the vigor of her thinking. . . . I, too, felt I was entitled to consider my taste in reading and my scholastic success as tokens of a personal superiority which would be borne out by the future. I became in my own eyes a character out of a novel.[44]

De Beauvoir found in Jo a model of authentic selfhood, someone she could emulate in the present and through whom she could read—and invent—her own destiny. It was a future full of possibility, open rather than closed, intellectual and literary rather than domestic. By fictionalizing her own life, de Beauvoir could more readily contemplate a career as a writer and an intellectual, no matter how improbable such an outcome seemed to her family. . . . Although de Beauvoir later claimed that she first learned from *Little Women* that "marriage was not necessary," she responded to the romance as well as the quest plot. Her conviction that Jo and Laurie would marry some day and the "renewed hope" this belief gave her suggest the power of wish fulfillment and the reader's capacity to create her own text. There is no textual basis for this belief: Jo and Laurie each marry someone else; each is a parent by the end of the story. De Beauvoir's reading is therefore not just a matter of filling in gaps but of rewriting the text. Her powerful commentary suggests the creativity of the reading experience and the permeability of boundaries between life and art: lives can be fictionalized, texts can be rewritten, art can become life and life art.

Not all women read with the intensity of Thomas or de Beauvoir. But there is considerable evidence that, from the time of her creation until the recent past, Jo March provided for young women of the comfortable classes a model of female independence and of intellectual and literary achievement. This is not the only way of reading *Little Women,* but it constitutes a major interpretive strand, particularly in the twentieth century. Testimony on this point began as soon as the book was published and persists today among women who grew up in the 1940s and 1950s.[45] Thomas, whose love relations were with women, never mentions the marriage plot, but for de Beauvoir, writing in the twentieth century, it was both important and compatible with a quest plot.

INFLECTIONS OF CLASS AND CULTURE

... For African American women, in the nineteenth century at least, class rather than race was probably the primary determinant of reading practices. Both Mary Church Terrell, a graduate of Oberlin College, and Ida B. Wells, the slave-born daughter of a carpenter and "a famous cook" who became a journalist and reformer, read Alcott. Terrell claimed that her books "were received with an acclaim among the young people of this country which has rarely if ever been equaled and never surpassed," while Wells observed: "I had formed my ideals on the best of Dickens's stories, Louisa May Alcott's, Mrs. A.D.T. Whitney's, and Charlotte Brontë's books, and Oliver Optic's stories for boys." Neither singled out *Little Women*; both seem to have read Alcott as part of the standard fare of an American middle-class childhood.[46]

For African American writer Ann Petry, [who died in 1997 at the age of 89,] *Little Women* was much more than that. On the occasion of her induction into the Connecticut Women's Hall of Fame, she noted her admiration for women writers who had preceded and set the stage for her—" 'Think of Louisa May Alcott.' " *Little Women* was the first book Petry "read on her own as a child." Her comments are reminiscent of those of de Beauvoir and other writers: "I couldn't stop reading because I had encountered Jo March. I felt as though I was part of Jo and she was part of me. I, too, was a tomboy and a misfit and kept a secret diary.... She said things like 'I wish I was a horse, then I could run for miles in this splendid air and not lose my breath.' I found myself wishing the same thing whenever I ran for the sheer joy of running. She was a would-be writer—and so was I."[47] ...

Some working-class women found *Little Women* ... banal. Dorothy Richardson, a journalist, suggests as much in *The Long Day*, an account of her life among the working class. In an arresting episode, Richardson ridicules the reading preferences of her fellow workers in a paper box factory. The plot of a favorite novel, Laura Jean Libbey's *Little Rosebud's*

Lovers; or, A Cruel Revenge, is recounted by one of the workers as a tale of a woman's triumph over all sorts of adversity, including abductions and a false marriage to one of the villains. When Richardson summarizes *Little Women,* a coworker dismisses it: "'[T]hat's no story—that's just everyday happenings. I don't see what's the use of putting things like that in books. I'll bet any money that lady what wrote it knew all them boys and girls. They just sound like real, live people; and when you was telling about them I could just see them as plain as plain could be.... I suppose farmer folks likes them kind of stories.... They ain't used to the same styles of anything that us city folks are.'"[48]

The box makers found the characters in *Little Women* "real"—an interesting point in itself—but did not care to enter its narrative framework. Though they were not class conscious in a political sense, their awareness of their class position may account at least in part for their disinterest in a story whose heroines, despite economic reverses, had the leisure to pursue their interests in art, music, and literature and could expect to live in suburban cottages, conditions out of reach for most working-class women. Since *their* "everyday happenings" were poverty and exhausting work, the attraction of fictions about working girls who preserved their virtue and came into great wealth, either through marriage or disclosure of their middle- or upper-class origins, is understandable. Such denouements would have seemed just as likely—or unlikely—as a future in a suburban cottage. In the absence, in story or in life, of a female success tradition of moving up the occupational ladder, the "Cinderella tale" of marrying up was the nearest thing to a Horatio Alger story for working-class women.[49]

Reading practices depend on cultural as well as class location. It is a telling commentary on class in America that some Jewish immigrant women, who would be defined as working class on the basis of family income and occupation, not only enjoyed *Little Women* but also found in it a vehicle for envisioning a new and higher status.[50] For them, Alcott's classic provided a model for transcending their status as ethnic outsiders and for gaining access to American life and culture. It was a first step into the kind of middle-class family life rejected by Thomas and de Beauvoir. These immigrants found the book liberating and read it as a success story—but of a different kind.

In *My Mother and I,* Elizabeth G. Stern (1889–1954) charts the cultural distance a Jewish immigrant woman traveled from Russia and a midwestern urban ghetto to the American mainstream: she graduates from college, studies social work marries a professional man, and becomes a social worker and writer.[51] *Little Women* occupies a crucial place in the story. After the narrator comes across it in a stack of newspapers in a rag shop, the book utterly engrosses her: "I sat in the dim light of the rag shop and read the browned pages of that ragged copy of 'Little Women.' . . . [N]o book I have opened has meant as much to me as did that small volume telling in simple words such as I myself spoke, the story of an American childhood in New England. I had found a new literature, the literature of childhood." She had also found the literature of America: "I no longer read the little paper-bound Yiddish novelettes which father then sold. In the old rag shop loft I devoured the English magazines and newspapers." Of the books her teachers brought her from the public library, she writes:

> Far more marvellous than the fairy stories were to me in the ghetto street the stories of American child life, all the Alcott and the Pepper books. The pretty mothers, the childish ideals, the open gardens, the homes of many rooms were as unreal to me as the fairy stories. But reading of them made my aspirations beautiful.
>
> My books were doors that gave me entrance into another world. Often I think that I did not grow up in the ghetto but in the books I read as a child in the ghetto. The life in Soho passed me by and did not touch me, once I began to read.[52] . . .

Stern was not unique in reading *Little Women* as a vehicle for assimilation into American middle-class life or in conflating "American" and "middle class." More than half a century later, a Jewish male writer explored the novel's appeal as an "American" book:

> [T]o me, a first generation American, raised in an Orthodox Jewish house-hold where more Yiddish was spoken than English, everything about *Little Women* was exotic. It was all so American, so full of a life I did not know but desperately hoped to be part of, an America full of promises, hopes, optimisms, an America where everyone had a chance to become somebody wonderful like Jo March—Louisa May Alcott who (I had discovered that the Marches and the Alcotts were

almost identical) did become, with this story book that I adored, world famous.[53]

What had been realistic to the early middle- and upper-middle-class WASP readers of *Little Women* was "exotic" to Jewish immigrants a generation or two later. Could there be a better illustration of the importance of historical location in determining meaning? . . .

One of the Jewish immigrants for whom Alcott's success proved inspiring was Mary Antin, a fervent advocate of assimilation into American life. Alcott's were the children's books she "remember[ed] with the greatest delight" (followed by boys' adventure books, especially Alger's). Antin, who published poems in English in her teens and contemplated a literary career, lingered over the biographical entries she found in an encyclopedia. She "could not resist the temptation to study out the exact place . . . where my name would belong. I saw that it would come not far from 'Alcott, Louisa M.'; and I covered my face with my hands, to hide the silly, baseless joy in it."[54] We have come full circle. Eager to assimilate, Antin responded in ways reminiscent of Alcott's early native-born and middle-class readers who admired her success as an author. Antin, too, could imagine a successful American career for herself, a career for which Alcott was still the model.

CONCLUSION

Not all readers of *Little Women* read the same text. This is literally the case, since the story went through many editions. Not until 1880 did it appear in one volume, illustrated in this case and purged of some of its slang.[55] Since then there have been numerous editions and many publishers. I have been concerned here with the changing meaning of the story for different audiences and with historical continuities as well. For many middle-class readers, early and later, *Little Women* provided a model of womanhood that deviated from conventional gender norms, a continuity that suggests how little these norms changed in their essentials from the late 1860s to the 1960s. Reading individualistically, they viewed Jo as an intellectual and a writer, the liberated woman they sought to become. No matter that Jo marries and raises a family; such readers remember the young Jo, the teenager who is far from beautiful, struggles with her temper, is both a book-worm and the center of action, and dreams of literary glory while helping to support her family with her pen. These readers for the most part took for granted their right to a long and privileged childhood, largely exempt from the labor market. Jewish women who immigrated to the United States in their youth could not assume such a childhood. Nor were those raised in Orthodox Jewish households brought up on an individualistic philosophy. Their school experiences and reading—American books like *Little Women*—made them aware of different standards of decorum and material life that we tend to associate with class, but that are cultural as well. For some of these readers, *Little Women* offered a fascinating glimpse into an American world. Of course we know, as they did not, that the world Alcott depicted was vanishing, even as she wrote. Nevertheless, that fictional world, along with their school encounters, provided a vision of what life, American life, could be.

Can readers do whatever they like with texts? Yes and no. As we have seen, *Little Women* has been read in many ways, depending not only on when and by whom it was read but also on readers' experiences and aspirations. It has been read as a romance or as a quest, or both. It has been read as a family drama that validates virtue over wealth. It has been read as a how-to manual by immigrants who wanted to assimilate into American, middle-class life and as a means of escaping that life by women who knew its gender constraints too well. For many, especially in the early years, *Little Women* was read through the life of the author, whose literary success exceeded that of her fictional persona.

At the same time, both the passion *Little Women* has engendered in diverse readers and its ability to survive its era and transcend its genre point to a text of unusual permeability. . . . Most important, readers' testimony in the nineteenth and twentieth centuries points to *Little Women* as a text that opens up possibilities rather than foreclosing them. With its multiple reference points and voices (four sisters, each distinct and recognizable), its depictions of joy as well as sorrow, its fresh and unlabored speech, Alcott's classic has something for almost everyone. For readers on the threshold of adulthood, the text's authorizing of female

ambition has been a significant counterweight to more habitual gender prescriptions.

Little Women is such a harbinger of modern life, of consumer culture and new freedom for middle-class children, it is easy to forget that it was written just a few years after the Civil War, in the midst of Reconstruction and at a time of economic dislocation. For the most part, Alcott left such contemporary markers out of her story, another sign of the text's openness. The Civil War provides an important backdrop and a spur to heroism at home as well as on the battlefield, but it is primarily a plot device to remove Mr. March from the scene. Despite her family's support of John Brown, Alcott does not press a particular interpretation of the war. A final reason *Little Women* has survived so well, despite the chasm that separates Alcott's era from ours, is the virtual absence of references to outside events that would date her story and make it grow old.[56] That way each generation can invent it anew.

NOTES

Citations to the Alcott Family Papers (bMS Am 1130.8 and bMS Am 800.23) are by permission of the Houghton Library, Harvard University.

1. Addams to Vallie Beck, March 16, 1876, *The Jane Addams Papers*, edited by Mary Lynn McGree Bryan (Ann Arbor: University Microfilms International, 1984) (hereafter cited as *Addams Papers*), reel 1.

2. Frank Luther Mott, *Golden Multitudes: The Story of Best Sellers in the United States* (New York: Macmillan, 1947), p. 102: *Books in Print*, 1992–93.

3. May 1868, *The Journals of Louisa May Alcott*, edited by Joel Myerson and Daniel Shealy, associate ed. Madeleine B. Stern (Boston: Little, Brown, 1989), pp. 165–66 (hereafter cited as *Journals*). On reading this entry in later years, Alcott quipped: "Good joke."

4. June [1868], *Journals*, p. 166.

5. Niles to Alcott, June 16, 1868 (#1) and July 25, 1868 (#2), bMS Am 1130.8, Alcott Family Papers, Houghton Library, Harvard University (all citations from Niles's letters are from this collection).

6. August 26 [1868], *Journals*, p. 166. . . .

7. For an account of Alcott's sales through 1909, by which time nearly 598,000 copies of *Little Women* had been printed by Roberts Brothers, see Joel Myerson and Daniel Shealy, "The Sales of Louisa May Alcott's Books," *Harvard Library Bulletin*, n.s., 1 (Spring 1990), esp. pp. 69–71, 86. Sales figures are unreliable for the twentieth century, in part because of foreign sales and the proliferation of editions after the expiration of copyright. Dorothea Lawrence Mann, "When the Alcott Books Were New," *Publishers' Weekly* 116 (September 28, 1929): 1619, claimed sales of nearly three million.

Sales, of course, are only part of the story: library use was high at the outset and remained so.

8. Mann, "When the Alcott Books Were New."

9. See Gloria T. Delamar, *Louisa May Alcott and 'Little Women': Biography, Critique, Publications, Poems, Songs, and Contemporary Relevance* (Jefferson, N.C.: McFarland and Co., 1990), p. 167 and passim.

10. For an intriguing analysis of well-loved texts that takes *Little Women* as a point of departure, see Catharine R. Stimpson, "Reading for Love: Canons, Paracanons, and Whistling Jo March," *New Literary History* 21 (Autumn 1990): 957–76.

11. "Spells, Wishes, Goldfish, Old School Hurts," *New York Times Book Review*, January 31, 1982, p. 24.

12. The classic biography is still Madeleine B. Stern, *Louisa May Alcott* (Norman: University of Oklahoma Press, 1950), which should be supplemented by Stern's extensive criticism on Alcott. See also Sarah Elbert, *A Hunger for Home: Louisa May Alcott and "Little Women"* (Philadelphia: Temple University Press, 1984), and Martha Saxton, *Louisa May: A Modern Biography of Louisa May Alcott* (New York: Avon Books, 1978).

13. June [1868], *Journals*, p. 166.

14. Niles told Alcott that her royalties were higher than any other Roberts Brothers author, including Harriet Beecher Stowe, whom he considered the American writer who could command the highest fees (Alcott possibly excepted). On the redirection of Alcott's career, see Richard H. Brodhead, "Starting Out in the 1860s: Alcott, Authorship, and the Postbellum Literary Field," in *Cultures of Letters: Scenes of Reading and Writing in Nineteenth-Century America* (Chicago: University of Chicago Press, 1993).

15. See Edward G. Salmon, "What Girls Read," *Nineteenth Century* 20 (October 1886): 515–29, and the ad for a series of "Books for Girls" whose intended audience was those "between eight and eighteen. . . . for growing-up girls, the mothers of the next generation." *American Literary Gazette and Publishers' Circular* (ALG) 17 (June 1, 1871): 88.

16. Niles to Alcott, July 25, 1868 (#2).

17. *Little Women* (New York: Random House/Modern Library, 1983), p. 290.

18. November 1, [1868], *Journals*, p. 167; Alcott to Elizabeth Powell, March 20, [1869], in *The Selected Letters of Louisa May Alcott*, edited by Joel Myerson and Daniel Shealy, associate ed. Madeleine B. Stern (Boston: Little, Brown, 1987), p. 125 (hereafter cited as *SL*). Erin Graham, "Books That Girls Have Loved," *Lippincott's Monthly Magazine*, September 1897, pp. 428–32, makes much of Bhaer's foreignness and ungainliness.

19. Jo's standing as a tomboy was recognized— and even respected; an ad for *Little Men* noted that "when a girl, [Jo] was half a boy herself." ALG 17 (May 15, 1871): 49. For girls in early adolescence and/or for lesbian readers, the young Jo may have been the primary romantic interest.

20. A conversation with Dolores Kreisman contributed to this analysis.

21. For an analysis of changes in girls' stories as the heterosexual imperative became stronger, see Martha Vicinus, "What Makes a Heroine?: Nine-teenth-Century Girls' Biographies," *Genre* 20 (Summer 1987): 171–87.

22. Frank Preston Stearns, *Sketches from Concord and Appledore* (New York: Putnam, 1895), p. 82.

23. Niles to Alcott, April 14, 1869 (#4).

24. Letter in *St. Nicholas*, February 1878, p. 300.

25. "Little Things," at first handwritten, then typeset on a small press, was part of a national phenomenon. See Paula Petrik, "The Youngest Fourth Estate: The Novelty Toy Printing Press and Adolescence, 1870–1886," in *Small Worlds: Children and Adolescents in America, 1850–1950*, edited by Elliott West and Paula Petrik (Lawrence: University Press of Kansas, 1992), pp. 125–42. Alcott's correspondence with the Lukens sisters, which extended over fourteen years, is reprinted in SL. . . . The Alcott sisters had their own Pickwick Club in 1849.

26. Letter from "Nelly," dated March 12, 1870, reproduced in Delamar, *Louisa May Alcott*, p. 146.

27. Alcott to the Lukens Sisters, October 2, 1874, SL, pp. 185–86. . . .

28. April [1869], *Journals*, p. 171.

29. "American Literature," [1878–79], *Addams Papers*, reel 27, frames 239–95.

30. Undated review of *Little Men* ("Capital" penciled in), bMS Am 800.23, Alcott Family Papers.

31. See, e.g., Louise Chandler Moulton, "Louisa May Alcott," *Our Famous Women* (1883; reprint, Hartford: A. D. Worthington, 1884), pp. 29–52, which was prepared with Alcott's assistance. Reports of Alcott's financial success appeared frequently in the press.

32. *The Ladies' Repository* ([December 1868], p. 472), while finding *Little Women* "very readable," pointedly observed that it was "not a Christian book. It is religion without spirituality, and salvation without Christ."

33. Alcott's depiction of home theatricals drew the wrath of some evangelicals. Niles to Alcott, October 26, 1868 (#3). . . .

34. On tomboys, see Sharon O'Brien, "Tomboyism and Adolescent Conflict: Three Nineteenth-Century Case Studies," in *Woman's Being, Woman's Place: Female Identity and Vocation in American History*, edited by Mary Kelley (Boston: G. K. Hall, 1979), pp. 351–72, which includes a section on Alcott. . . .

35. The Katy books of "Susan Coolidge," pen name of Sarah Chauncey Woolsey, another Roberts Brothers author, are perhaps closest to Alcott's. But even Katy Carr, who begins as another Jo, an ambitious, harumscarum, and fun-loving girl, is severely punished for disobedience; only after suffering a broken back and several years of invalidism does she emerge as a thoughtful girl who will grow into "true womanhood."

36. Roosevelt, *An Autobiography* (1913; reprint, New York: De Capo Press, 1985), p. 17.

37. Gilman, *The Living of Charlotte Perkins Gilman* (1935; reprint, New York: Harper and Row, 1975), p. 35.

38. M. Carey Thomas Journal, June 20, 1870, *The Papers of M. Carey Thomas in the Bryn Mawr College Archives*, edited by Lucy Fisher West (Woodbridge, Conn.: Research Publications, 1982) (hereafter cited as MCTP), reel 1.

39. Elizabeth King Ellicott to Thomas, November 23, [1879], MCTP, reel 39.

40. See Marjorie Housepian Dobkin, ed., *The Making of a Feminist: Early Journals and Letters of M. Carey Thomas* (N.p.: Kent State University Press, 1979), pp. 66–67 and passim.

41. These remarks draw on Sicherman, "Reading and Ambition: M. Carey Thomas and Female Heroism," *American Quarterly* 45 (March 1993): 82–83.

42. *Little Women,* pp. 328–29.

43. On this subject, see Lee Virginia Chambers-Schiller, *Liberty, a Better Husband: Single Women in America: The Generations of 1780–1840* (New Haven: Yale University Press, 1984). In her next book, *An Old-Fashioned Girl,* Alcott ventures much further in envisioning a life of singlehood and lovingly depicts a community of self-supporting women artists.

44. Simone de Beauvoir, *Memoirs of a Dutiful Daughter,* translated by James Kirkup (1949; reprint, Cleveland: World Publishing Co., 1959), pp. 94–95. . . . According to Deirdre Bair, de Beauvoir had read Little Women by the time she was ten. Bair, *Simone de Beauvoir: A Biography* (New York: Summit Books, 1990), pp. 68–71.

45. These conclusions emerge from my reading and from discussions of *Little Women* with more than a dozen women. They were highly educated for the most part and mainly over fifty, but some women under thirty also felt passionately about the book. Most of my informants were white, but see n. 48 below.

46. Mary Church Terrell, *A Colored Woman in a White World* (1940; reprint, New York: Arno Press, 1980), p. 26; Alfreda M. Duster, ed., *Crusade for Justice: The Autobiography of Ida B. Wells* (Chicago: University of Chicago Press, 1970), pp. 7, 21–22. Wells observed that in her early years, she "never read a Negro book or anything about Negroes."

47. *The Middletown Press,* June 1, 1994, p. B1, and Ann Petry to author, letter postmarked July 23, 1994; I am grateful to Farah Jasmine Griffin for the *Middletown Press* reference. *Little Women* continues to play an important role in the lives of some young black women. A high school student in Jamaica, for example, rewrote the story to fit a local setting. And a young, African American academic felt so strongly about *Little Women* that, on learning about my project, she contended with some heat that Aunt March was unfair in taking Amy rather than Jo to Europe; she seemed to be picking up a conversation she had just left off. Comments like these and Petry's suggest the need for research on the interaction between race and class in African American women's reading practices.

48. Dorothy Richardson, *The Long Day: The Story of a New York Working Girl as Told by Herself* (1905; reprint, New York: Quadrangle Books, 1972), pp. 75–86 (quotation, p. 86). . . . *The Long Day,* which purports to be the story of an educated woman forced by circumstances to do manual labor, must be used with caution. It was initially published anonymously, and many scenes read like sensational fiction. Leonora O'Reilly, a feminist trade unionist, was so outraged at the book's condescension and its insinuations that working-class women were immoral that she drafted a blazing indictment. Leonora O'Reilly Papers, edited by Edward T. James, *Papers of the Women's Trade Union League and Its Principal Leaders* (Woodbridge, Conn.: Research Publications, 1981), reel 9.

49. Michael Denning, *Mechanic Accents: Dime Novels and Working-Class Culture in America* (London: Verso, 1987), pp. 197–200, analyzes *Little Rosebud's Lovers* as a "Cinderella tale." He suggests that stories read by the middle class tended to depict working-class women as victims (of seduction and poverty) rather than as triumphant.

50. I have discussed Jewish immigrants at some length because of the abundance of evidence, not because I view them as the only model for an alternative reading of *Little Women.*

51. *My Mother and I* (New York: Macmillan, 1917) is a problematic book. Some contemporaries reviewed it as autobiographical fiction, but recent critics have tended to view it as autobiography. Theodore Roosevelt must have considered it the latter when he lauded it as a "really noteworthy story" of Americanization in the foreword. . . . Moreover, the facts Stern gave out about her early life—including her status as an Eastern European Jewish immigrant—correspond with the narrator's history. Stern's older son, however, maintains that his mother was native born and Protestant and claimed her Jewish foster parents as her biological parents to hide her out-of-wedlock birth. T[homas] Noel Stern, *Secret Family* (South Dartmouth, Mass.: T. Noel Stern, 1988). Ellen M. Umansky, who generously shared her research materials with me, concludes in "Representations of Jewish Women in the Works and Life of Elizabeth Stern," *Modern Judaism* 13 (1993): 165–76: "[I]t may be difficult if not impossible to ever determine which of Stern's literary self representations reflected her own experiences" (p. 174). Sources that appear to substantiate Elizabeth Stern's foreign and Jewish birth are the U.S. Census for 1900 and for 1910, which both list her birthplace as Russia; the certificate of her marriage, which was performed by a prominent Orthodox rabbi in Pittsburgh; and Aaron Levin's will, which lists Stern as his oldest child.

Despite its contested status, I have drawn on *My Mother and I* because Stern's choice of *Little Women* as a critical marker of American aspirations is consistent with other evidence. The narrative's emphasis on the differences between immigrant and American culture comports with representations in less problematic works by Jewish immigrant writers. Moreover, whatever the facts of Stern's birth, she lived with the Jewish Levin family for many years.

52. *My Mother and I,* pp. 69–71.

53. Leo Lerman, "Little Women: Who's in Love with Miss Louisa May Alcott? I Am," *Mademoiselle,* December 1973, reprinted in Madeleine B. Stern, ed., *Critical Essays on Louisa May Alcott* (Boston: G. K. Hall, 1984), p. 113. See also Stephan F. Brumberg, *Going to America, Going to School: The Jewish Immigrant Public School Encounter in Turn-of-the-Century New York City* (New York: Praeger, 1986), pp. 121–22, 141.

54. Mary Antin, *The Promised Land* (Boston: Houghton Mifflin, 1912), pp. 257, 258–59.

55. Elaine Showalter, "*Little Women:* The American Female Myth," chap. 3 in *Sister's Choice: Tradition and Change in Women's Writing* (Oxford: Clarendon Press, 1991), pp. 55–56; Madeleine B. Stern to author, July 31, 1993. The English edition continued to be published in two volumes, the second under the title *Good Wives.*

56. Elizabeth Young, "Embodied Politics: Fictions of the American Civil War" (Ph.D. diss., University of California, Berkeley, 1993), reading *Little Women* in conjunction with *Hospital Sketches,* views it as a "war novel" (p. 108).

DOCUMENT: The Women's Centennial Agenda, 1876

> *Elizabeth Cady Stanton and Susan B. Anthony, "Guaranteed to us and our daughters forever"*

The capstone of the celebration of the Centennial was a public reading of the Declaration of Independence in Independence Square, Philadelphia, by a descendant of a signer, Richard Henry Lee. Elizabeth Cady Stanton, who was then president of the National Woman Suffrage Association, asked permission to present silently a women's protest and a written Declaration of Rights. The request was denied. "Tomorrow we propose to celebrate what we have done the last hundred years," replied the president of the official ceremonies, "not what we have failed to do."

Led by suffragist Susan B. Anthony, five women appeared at the official reading, distributing copies of their declaration. After this mildly disruptive gesture they withdrew to the other side of Independence Hall, where they staged a counter-Centennial and Anthony read the following address. Compare it to the Declaration of Sentiments (pp. 214–16) of twenty-eight years before. Note the splendid oratorical flourish of the final paragraph.

July 4, 1876

While the nation is buoyant with patriotism, and all hearts are attuned to praise, it is with sorrow we come to strike the one discordant note, on this one-hundredth anniversary of our country's birth. When subjects of kings, emperors, and czars, from the old world join in our national jubilee, shall the women of the republic refuse to lay their hands with benedictions on the nation's head? Surveying America's exposition, surpassing in magnificence those of London, Paris, and Vienna, shall we not rejoice at the success of the youngest rival among the nations of the earth? May not our hearts, in unison with all, swell with pride at our great achievements as a people; our free speech, free press, free schools, free church, and the rapid progress we have made in material wealth, trade, commerce and the inventive arts? And we do rejoice in the success, thus far, of our experiment of self-government. Our faith is firm and unwavering in the broad principles of human rights proclaimed in 1776, not only as abstract truths, but as the corner stones of a republic. Yet we cannot forget, even in this glad hour, that while all men of every race, and clime, and condition, have been invested with the full rights of citizenship under our hospitable flag, all women still suffer the degradation of disfranchisement.

The history of our country the past hundred years has been a series of assumptions and usurpations of power over woman, in direct opposition to the principles of just government, acknowledged by the United States as its foundation. . . .

And for the violation of these fundamental principles of our government, we arraign our rulers on this Fourth day of July, 1876,—and these are our articles of impeachment:

> *Bills of attainder* have been passed by the introduction of the word "male" into all the State constitutions, denying to women the right of suffrage, and thereby making sex a crime—an exercise of power clearly forbidden in article 1, sections 9, 10, of the United States constitution. . . .

Excerpted from Susan B. Anthony, Declaration of Rights for Women by the National Woman Suffrage Association, in *History of Woman Suffrage,* edited by Elizabeth Cady Stanton, Susan B. Anthony, and Matilda Joslyn Gage, vol. 3 (Rochester, N.Y.: Susan B. Anthony, 1886), pp. 31–34.

Nora Stanton Blatch (Barney), Elizabeth Cady Stanton, and Harriot Stanton Blatch (1886) (Courtesy of Elizabeth Cady Stanton Trust/Coline Jenkins-Sahlin.)

Elizabeth Jenkins-Sahlin (age 13), Rhoda Barney Jenkins, and Coline Jenkins-Sahlin (1998) (Courtesy of Joyce Dopkeen/New York Times.)

"Mother believed in pushing," observes Rhoda Barney Jenkins, who became an architect. "You don't question a hurricane." Coline Jenkins-Sahlin has served as a member of the Greenwich, Connecticut, Representative Town Meeting and helped found Third Wave Television, a production company that makes programs on women's issues. "What they did was heroic," observes Elizabeth.

The right of trial by a jury of one's peers was so jealously guarded that States refused to ratify the original constitution until it was guaranteed by the sixth amendment. And yet the women of this nation have never been allowed a jury of their peers—being tried in all cases by men, native, and foreign, educated and ignorant, virtuous and vicious. Young girls have been arraigned in our courts for the crime of infanticide; tried, convicted, hanged—victims, perchance, of judge, jurors, advocates—while no woman's voice could be heard in their defense. . . .

Taxation without representation, the immediate cause of the rebellion of the colonies against Great Britain, is one of the grievous wrongs the women of this country have suffered during the century. Deploring war, with all the demoralization that follows in its train, we have been taxed to support standing armies, with their waste of life and wealth. Believing in temperance, we have been taxed to support the vice, crime and pauperism of the liquor traffic. While we suffer its wrongs and abuses infinitely more than man, we have no power to protect our sons against this giant evil. . . .

Unequal codes for men and women. Held by law a perpetual minor, deemed incapable of self-protection, even in the industries of the world, woman is denied equality of rights. The fact of sex, not the quantity or quality of work, in most cases, decides the pay and position; and because of this injustice thousands of fatherless girls are compelled to choose between a life of shame and starvation. Laws catering to man's vices have created two codes of morals in which penalties are graded according to the political status of the offender. Under such laws, women are fined and imprisoned if found alone in the streets, or in public places of resort, at certain hours. Under the pretense of regulating public morals, police officers seizing the occupants of disreputable houses, march the women in platoons to prison, while the men, partners in their guilt, go free. . . .

Representation of woman has had no place in the nation's thought. Since the incorporation of the thirteen original States, twenty-four have been admitted to the Union, not one of which has recognized woman's right of self-government. On this birthday of our national liberties, July Fourth, 1876, Colorado, like all her elder sisters, comes into the Union with the invidious word "male" in her constitution. . . .

The judiciary above the nation has proved itself but the echo of the party in power, by upholding and enforcing laws that are opposed to the spirit and letter of the constitution. When the slave power was dominant, the Supreme Court decided that a black man was not a citizen, because he had not the right to vote; and when the constitution was so amended as to make all persons citizens, the same high tribunal decided that a woman, though a citizen, had not the right to vote. Such vacillating interpretations of constitutional law unsettle our faith in judicial authority, and undermine the liberties of the whole people.

These articles of impeachment against our rulers we now submit to the impartial judgment of the people. To all these wrongs and oppressions woman has not submitted in silence and resignation. From the beginning of the century, when Abigail Adams, the wife of one president and mother of another, said, "We will not hold ourselves bound to obey laws in which we have no voice or representation," until now, woman's discontent has been steadily increasing, culminating nearly thirty years ago in a simultaneous movement among the women of the nation, demanding the right of suffrage. In making our just demands, a higher motive than the pride of sex inspires us; we feel that national safety and stability depend on the complete recognition of the broad principles of our government. Woman's degraded, helpless position is the weak point in our institutions today; a disturbing force everywhere, severing family ties, filling our asylums with the deaf, the dumb, the blind; our prisons with criminals, our cities with drunkenness and prostitution; our homes with disease and death. It was the boast of the founders of the republic, that the rights for which they contended were the rights of human nature. If these rights are ignored in the case of one-half the people, the nation is surely preparing for its downfall. Governments try themselves. The recognition of a governing and a governed class is incompatible with the first principles of freedom. Woman has not been a heedless spectator of the events of this century, nor a dull listener to the grand arguments for the equal rights of humanity. From the earliest history of our country woman has shown equal devotion with man to the cause of freedom, and has stood firmly by his side in its defense. Together they have made this country what it is. Woman's wealth, thought and labor have cemented the stones of every monument man has reared to liberty.

And now, at the close of a hundred years, as the hour-hand of the great clock that marks the centuries points to 1876, we declare our faith in the principles of self-government; our full equality with man in natural rights; that woman was made first for her own happiness, with the absolute right to herself—to all the opportunities and advantages life affords for her complete development; and we deny that dogma of the centuries, incorporated in the codes of all nations—that woman was made for man—her best interests, in all cases, to be sacrificed to his will. We ask of our rulers, at this hour, no special privileges, no special legislation. We ask justice, we ask equality, we ask that all the civil and political rights that belong to citizens of the United States, be guaranteed to us and our daughters forever.

PATRICIA A. SCHECHTER
Ida B. Wells and *Southern Horrors*

Ida B. Wells's 1892 pamphlet *Southern Horrors: Lynch Law in All Its Phases* launched a critical phase of the African American struggle for civil rights. Its statistical refutation of the rape charge against black men that was used to justify lynching is a sociological breakthrough that has stood the test of time and study in the twentieth century. Wells also demonstrates how the concepts of "race" and "rape" were tied to power relations in the administration of justice, in the media, and in everyday life. Finally, Wells expounds the racial and class dimensions of the sexual double standard in ways that connect to contemporary feminist concerns with violence against all women, communities of color, and the poor in the United States and globally.

The insights expressed in *Southern Horrors* reflect Wells's personal and community survival strategy in the New South. Her situation was shaped by both new opportunities and new oppressions facing the first generation of free African Americans who came of age after the Civil War. Wells's parents, who had been slaves in Mississippi, bequeathed to their children a legacy of strong religious faith, pride in wage-earning, and a commitment to education that echoes through the many projects their daughter undertook over her lifetime. Wells's father, James Wells, was a skilled carpenter and a member of the Masons who, after the war, served on the board of Holly Springs local American Missionary Association school, Rust College, which his daughter attended. Wells's mother, "Lizzie" Warrenton Wells, worked as a cook and was a devout Methodist who made sure her children attended church, where she herself learned to read the Bible. After James and Lizzie's untimely deaths in 1878 from a yellow fever epidemic that swept the Delta, sixteen-year-old Ida B. Wells was left to care for her five siblings, earning money by teaching school.

The prospect of better wages and the presence of extended family soon drew Wells to Memphis, Tennessee. There, her intellectual, social, and political horizons expanded in a burgeoning black community notable for its highly accomplished middle-class and

This essay condenses material from *Ida B. Wells-Barnett and American Reform, 1880–1930* by Patricia A. Schechter (Chapel Hill: University of North Carolina Press, 2001). © by Patricia A. Schechter. Published by permission of the author.

elite members. Aspirations for equality nourished community institutions like schools, newspapers, social clubs, literary lyceums, and churches, especially the Baptist and African Methodist Episcopal denominations. In Memphis, Wells found encouragement to turn her intellectual talents into leadership by teaching Sunday school and by pursuing literary activities, especially journalism. Her first newspaper article appeared in 1883 in a Baptist weekly. It explained how Wells had been unfairly ejected from a first-class "ladies" railroad coach and how she fought racial discrimination by taking her case to court. While tens of thousands of educated women joined the paid labor force as school "ma'ams," religious educators, and journalists in the late nineteenth century, these social roles had particular significance for African American women, whose personal, family, and community well-being was intimately bound up with their wage-earning, educational activities, and community-betterment work.

As *Southern Horrors* emphatically argues, a white racist backlash followed closely upon the achievements of African Americans after Reconstruction. The result of this backlash was "Jim Crow" segregation, a set of laws designed for the economic deprivation, social marginalization, and political disfranchisement of black people. Jim Crow was established and enforced through systematic violence and terror. Ida B. Wells's eight pamphlets, written between 1892 and 1920, painstakingly document the ways in which African Americans were deprived of their rights through mob and police violence, through negative propaganda campaigns in the media, and through the elimination of economic opportunity and political rights. Few aspects of Jim Crow escaped Wells's sharp scrutiny in the press and eventually, while in Memphis, she caught the negative attention of critics. As the passage excerpted below explains, she was forced to leave the South as a kind of political exile, first traveling to New York, then to Great Britain, and finally settling in Chicago in 1895. There, she married lawyer and fellow activist Ferdinand L. Barnett (hypenating her name to Wells-Barnett) and raised a family of four children.

Post-exile, Wells-Barnett's writing and activism were sustained through African-American community networks and by organizations shared by black and white women reformers, like the Woman's Christian Temperance Union. He work with black women's church and club networks nurtured her into a powerful public speaker and political organizer. Between 1892 and 1895, Wells-Barnett organized scores of anti-lynching committees and women's clubs all over the United States and abroad, and helped inaugurate the National Association of Colored Women (NACW), a group that functioned as the preeminent civil rights organization up to World War I. In 1909, Wells-Barnett cofounded the National Association for the Advancement of Colored People (NAACP), which, in 1917, assumed principal leadership of the anti-lynching fight in the United States.

The trajectory of Wells-Bernett's civil rights agitation was neither simple nor smooth. Controversy followed her and her work, especially during its first decade. White supremacists North and South vilified her in the press, slandering her morals and threatening her with violence for speaking out against lynching. While most African American communities embraced Wells-Barnett as a heroine, there was little consensus about how, exactly, to end lynching or resist Jim Crow. Black leaders were a diverse group ideologically and generationally; regional considerations also came into play as black southerners found themselves more circumscribed than their northern peers. Women's roles were also fundamental to the building of black communities and to resistance work. Though black women's families and communities were dependent upon their contributions, any move on their part into official political and intellectual leadership—especially where interactions with whites were concerned—usually sparked controversy. Whether in journalism, public speaking, or institutional leadership—as with her Chicago social settlement, the Negro Fellowship League (1909–1919)—Wells-Barnett's initiatives were always double-edged, affording new spaces for community defense and activism while potentially exposing black men as somehow deficient in their protective or leadership roles. For every celebration of her hard work and successes, there were always powerful voices affirming the propriety of male ministers, business leaders, and elected officials leading the civil rights agenda for African Americans. Wells-Barnett remained staunchly committed to equality for black women, however, fighting hard for suffrage rights in Illinois and nationally. After the passage of the Nineteenth Amendment, she eventually ran for public office herself, in 1930.

Wells-Barnett's steadfast commitment to full equality not just for lynching victims but for "every citizen" rings through *Southern Horrors,* lending the text its prophetic, visionary quality; hers is a plea, to quote further from the pamphlet's preface, that "justice be done though the heavens fall." *Southern Horrors* draws on a number of powerful currents in American thought and style to make its case. As a graphic exposé, *Southern Horrors* shares kinship with muckraking journalism, a hallmark of the U.S. press at the turn of the century. Its empirical bent draws on statistical work to be found in the nascent academic field of sociology. *Southern Horrors* also stands in a tradition of radical pamphleteering in U.S. history that includes Tom Paine's *Common Sense* (1776) and David Walker's *Appeal to the Colored People of the Americas* (1829). Like these texts, *Southern Horrors* is peppered with wilting sarcasm and theatrical asides designed to provoke, starting with its title, a mocking send up of "southern honor." Instead of the neat closure of genteel fiction, *Southern Horrors* is full of questions and commands in a kind of call-and-response engagement with the reader, a pattern of expression at the heart of black worship traditions and one designed to work a deep transformation in participants. Finally, *Southern Horrors* ends with a practical list of strategies for "self-help," including education, boycotts, migration, agitation for protective legislation, suing through the courts, and even armed self-defense, to be "used to give that protection which the law refuses to give." Nearly five thousand Americans, almost three-fourths of them black, were lynched in Wells-Barnett's lifetime. Repeated efforts of African-American activists to pass federal legislation making lynching a crime were defeated in Congress in 1922, 1937, and 1940.

What are the different kinds of violence or threats of violence that Wells documents in *Southern Horrors?* How is violence linked to issues of sexual, racial, and class privilege? How does Wells compare the social and sexual experiences of black and white women under Jim Crow? In what ways does class shape the social behavior and political strategies of the historical actors Wells describes?

PAMPHLETS BY IDA B. WELLS-BARNETT

Southern Horrors: Lynch Law in All Its Phases (New York: New York Age, 1892).

The Reason Why the Colored American Is Not in the World's Columbian Exposition: The Afro-American's Contribution to Columbian Literature (Chicago: Ida B. Wells, 1893).

United States Atrocities: Lynch Law (London: Lux Publishing, 1894).

A Red Record: Tabulated Statistics and Alleged Causes of Lynchings in the United States, 1892–1893–1894 (Chicago: Donahue & Henneberry, 1895).

Lynch Law in Georgia (Chicago: Ida B. Wells-Barnett, 1899).

Mob Rule in New Orleans: Robert Charles and His Fight to the Death (Chicago: Ida B. Wells-Barnett, 1900).

The Arkansas Race Riot (Chicago: Ida B. Wells-Barnett, 1920).

CHAPTER I: THE OFFENSE

Wednesday evening May 24th, 1892, the city of Memphis was filled with excitement. Editorials in the daily papers of that date caused a meeting to be held in the Cotton Exchange Building; a committee was sent for the editors of the *Free Speech,* an Afro-American journal published in that city, and the only reason the open threats of lynching that were made were not carried out was because they could not be found. The cause of all this commotion was the following editorial published in the *Free Speech* May 21st, 1892, the Saturday previous.

> Eight negroes lynched since last issue of the *Free Speech,* one at Little Rock, Ark., last Saturday morning where the citizens broke (?) into the penitentiary and got their man; three near Anniston, Ala., one near New Orleans; and three at Clarksville, Ga., the last three for killing a white man, and five on the same old racket—the new alarm about raping white women. The same programme of hanging, then shooting bullets into the lifeless bodies was carried out to the letter.
>
> Nobody in this section of the country believes the old threadbare lie that Negro men rape white women. If Southern white men are not careful, they will over-reach themselves and public sentiment will have a reaction; a conclusion will then be reached which will be very damaging to the moral reputation of their women.

The Daily Commercial of Wednesday following, May 25th, contained the following leader:

> Those negroes who are attempting to make the lynching of individuals of their race a means for arousing the worst passions of their kind are playing with a dangerous sentiment. The negroes may as well understand that there is no mercy for the negro rapist and little patience with his defenders. A negro organ printed in this city, in a recent issue publishes the following atrocious paragraph: "Nobody in this section of the country believes the old thread-bare lie that negro men rape white women. If Southern white men are not careful they will over-reach themselves, and public sentiment will have a reaction; and a conclusion will be reached which will be very damaging to the moral reputation of their women."
>
> The fact that a black scoundrel is allowed to live and utter such loathsome and repulsive calumnies is a volume of evidence as to the wonderful patience of Southern whites. But we have had enough of it.
>
> There are some things that the Southern white man will not tolerate, and the obscene intimations of the foregoing have brought the writer to the very outermost limit of public patience. We hope we have said enough.

The *Evening Scimitar* of same date, copied the *Commercial's* editorial with these words of comment: "Patience under such circumstances is not a virtue. If the negroes themselves do not apply the remedy without delay it will be the duty of those whom he has attacked to tie the wretch who utters these calumnies to a stake at the intersection of Main and Madison Sts., brand him in the forehead with a hot iron and perform upon him a surgical operation with a pair of tailor's shears."

Acting upon this advice, the leading citizens met in the Cotton Exchange Building the same evening, and threats of lynching were freely indulged, not by the lawless element upon which the deviltry of the South is usually saddled—but by the leading business men, in their leading business centre. Mr. Fleming, the business manager and owning a half interest the *Free Speech,* had to leave town to escape the mob, and was afterwards ordered not to return; letters and telegrams sent me in New York where I was spending my vacation advised me that bodily harm awaited my return. Creditors took possession of the office and sold the outfit, and the *Free Speech* was as if it had never been.

The editorial in question was prompted by the many inhuman and fiendish lynchings of Afro-Americans which have recently taken place and was meant as a warning. Eight lynched in one week and five of them charged with rape! The thinking public will not easily believe freedom and education more brutalizing than slavery, and the world knows that the crime of rape was unknown during four years of civil war, when the white women of the South were at the mercy of the race which is all at once charged with being a bestial one.

Since my business has been destroyed and I am an exile from home because of that editorial, the issue has been forced, and as the writer of it I feel that the race and the public generally should have a statement of the facts as they exist. They will serve at the same time as a defense for the Afro-American Sampsons who suffer themselves to be betrayed by white Delilahs.

The whites of Montgomery, Ala., knew J. C. Duke sounded the keynote of the situation—which they would gladly hide from the world, when he said in his paper, *The Herald,* five years ago: "Why is it that white women attract negro men now more than in former days? There was a time when such a thing was unheard of. There is a secret to this thing, and we greatly suspect it is the growing appreciation of white Juliets for colored Romeos." Mr. Duke, like the *Free Speech* proprietors, was forced to leave the city for reflecting on the "honah" of white women and his paper suppressed; but the truth remains that Afro-American men do not always rape (?) white women without their consent.

Mr. Duke, before leaving Montgomery, signed a card disclaiming any intention of slandering Southern white women. The editor of the *Free Speech* has no disclaimer to enter, but asserts instead that there are many white women in the South who would marry colored men if such an act would not place them at once beyond the pale of society and within the clutches of the law. The miscegnation laws of the South only operate against the legitimate union of the races; they leave the white man free to seduce all the colored girls he can, but it is death to the colored man who yields to the force and advances of a similar attraction in white women. White men lynch the offending Afro-American, not because he is a despoiler of virtue, but because he succumbs to the smiles of white women.

CHAPTER II: THE BLACK AND WHITE OF IT

The *Cleveland Gazette* of January 16, 1892, publishes a case in point. *Mrs. J. S. Underwood,* the wife of a minister of Elyria, Ohio, accused an Afro-American of rape. She told her husband that during his absence in 1888, stumping the State for the Prohibition Party, the man came to the kitchen door, forced his way in the house and insulted her. She tried to drive him out with a heavy poker, but he overpowered and chloroformed her, and when she revived her clothing was torn and she was in a horrible condition. She did not know the man but could identify him. She pointed out William Offett, a married man, who was arrested and, being in Ohio, was granted a trial.

The prisoner vehemently denied the charge of rape, but confessed he went to Mrs. Underwood's residence at her invitation and was criminally intimate with her at her request. This availed him nothing against the sworn testimony of a minister's wife, a lady of the highest respectability. He was found guilty, and entered the penitentiary, December 14, 1888, for fifteen years. Some time afterwards the woman's remorse led her to confess to her husband that the man was innocent.

These are her words: "I met Offett at the Post Office. It was raining. He was polite to me, and as I had several bundles in my arms he offered to carry them home for me, which he did. He had a strange fascination for me, and I invited him to call on me. He called, bringing chestnuts and candy for the children. By this means we got them to leave us alone in the room. Then I sat on his lap. He made a proposal to me and I readily consented. Why I did so, I do not know, but that I did is true. He visited me several times after that and each time I was indiscreet. I did not care after the first time. In fact I could not have resisted, and had no desire to resist."

When asked by her husband why she told him she had been outraged, she said: "I had several reasons for telling you. One was the neighbors saw the fellow here, another was, I was afraid I had contracted a loathsome disease, and still another was that I feared I might give birth to a Negro baby. I hoped to save my reputation by telling you a deliberate lie." Her husband horrified by the confession had Offett, who had already served four years, released and secured a divorce.

There are thousands of such cases throughout the South, with the difference that the Southern white men in insatiate fury wreak their vengeance without intervention of law upon the Afro-Americans who consort with their women. A few instances to substantiate the assertion that some white women love the company of the Afro-American will not be out of place. Most of these cases were reported by the daily papers of the South.

In the winter of 1885–6 the wife of a practicing physician in Memphis, in good social standing whose name has escaped me, left home, husband and children, and ran away with her black coachman. She was with him a month before her husband found and brought her home. The coachman could not be found. The doctor moved his family away from Memphis, and is living in another city under an assumed name. . . .

Sarah Clark of Memphis loved a black man and lived openly with him. When she was indicted last spring for miscegenation, she swore in court that she was *not* a white woman. This she did to escape the the penitentiary and continued her illicit relation undisturbed. That she is of the lower class of whites, does not disturb the fact that she is a white woman. "The leading citizens" of Memphis are defending the "honor" of *all* white women, *demi-monde* included.

Since the manager of the *Free Speech* has been run away from Memphis by the guardians of the honor of Southern white women, a young girl living on Poplar St., who was discovered in intimate relations with a handsome mulatto young colored man, Will Morgan by name, stole her father's money to send the young fellow away from that father's wrath. She has since joined him in Chicago. . . .

The very week the "leading citizens" of Memphis were making a spectacle of themselves in defense of all white women of every kind, an Afro-American, M. Stricklin, was found in a white woman's room in that city. Although she made no outcry of rape, he was jailed and would have been lynched, but the woman stated she bought curtains of him (he was a furniture dealer) and his business in her room that night was to put them up. A white woman's word was taken as absolutely in this case as when the cry of rape is made, and he was freed.

What is true of Memphis is true of the entire South. . . . Frank Weems of Chattanooga who was not lynched in May only because the prominent citizens became his body guard until the doors of the penitentiary closed on him, had letters in his pocket from the white woman in the case, making the appointment with him. Edward Coy who was burned alive in Texarkana, January 1, 1892, died protesting his innocence. Investigation since as given by the Bystander in the *Chicago Inter-Ocean,* October 1, proves: . . . The woman who was paraded as a victim of violence was of bad character; her husband was a drunkard and a gambler. . . . She was compelled by threats, if not by violence, to make the charge against the victim. . . . When she came to apply the match Coy asked her if she would burn him after they had "been sweethearting" so long. . . .

Hundreds of such cases might be cited, but enough have been given to prove the assertion that there are white women in the South who love the Afro-American's company even as there are white men notorious for their preference for Afro-American women.

There is hardly a town in the South which has not an instance of the kind which is well-known, and hence the assertion is reiterated that "nobody in the South believes the old thread-bare lie that negro men rape white women." Hence there is a growing demand among Afro-Americans that the guilt or innocence of parties accused of rape be fully established. They know the men of the section of the country who refuse this are not so desirous of punishing rapists as they pretend. The utterances of the leading white men show that with them it is not the crime but the *class,* Bishop Fitzgerald has become apologist for lynchers of the rapists of *white* women only. . . . But when the victim is a colored woman it is different.

Last winter in Baltimore, Md., three white

ruffians assaulted a Miss Camphor, a young Afro-American girl, while out walking with a young man of her own race. They held her escort and outraged the girl. It was a deed dastardly enough to arouse Southern blood, which gives its horror of rape as excuse for lawlessness, but she was an Afro-American. The case went to the courts, an Afro-American lawyer defended the men and they were acquitted.

In Nashville, Tenn., there is a white man, Pat Hanifan, who outraged a little Afro-American girl, and, from the physical injuries received, she has been ruined for life. He was jailed for six months, discharged, and is now a detective in that city. . . . Only two weeks before Eph. Grizzard, who had only been *charged* with rape upon a white woman, had been taken from the jail, with Governor Buchanan and the police and militia standing by, dragged through the streets in broad daylight, knives plunged into him at every step, and with every fiendish cruelty a frenzied mob could devise, he was at last swung out on the bridge with hands cut to pieces as he tried to climb up the stanchions. . . .

At the very moment these civilized whites were announcing their determination "to protect their wives and daughters," by murdering Grizzard, a white man was in the same jail for raping eight-year-old Maggie Reese, an Afro-American girl. He was not harmed. The "honor" of grown women who were glad enough to be suppported by the Grizzard boys and Ed Coy, as long as the liasion was not known, needed protection; they were white. The outrage upon helpless childhood needed no avenging in this case; she was black. . . .

CHAPTER III: THE NEW CRY

. . . Thoughtful Afro-Americans with the strong arm of the government withdrawn and with the hope to stop such wholesale massacres urged the race to sacrifice its political rights for sake of peace. They honestly believed the race should fit itself for government, and when that should be done, the objection to race participation in politics would be removed.

But the sacrifice did not remove the trouble, nor move the South to justice. One by one the Southern States have legally (?) disfranchised the Afro-American, and since the repeal of the Civil Rights Bill nearly every Southern State has passed separate car laws with a penalty against their infringement. The race regardless of advancement is penned into filthy, stifling partitions cut off from smoking cars. . . . The dark and bloody record of the South shows 728 Afro-Americans lynched during the past eight years; . . . and not less than 150 have been known to have met violent death at the hands of cruel bloodthirsty mobs during the past nine months.

To palliate this record (which grows worse as the Afro-American becomes intelligent) and excuse some of the most heinous crimes that ever stained the history of a country, the South is shielding itself behind the plausible screen of defending the honor of its women. This, too, in the face of the fact that only *one-third* of the 728 victims to mobs have been *charged* with rape, to say nothing of those of that one-third who were innocent of the charge. . . .

Even to the better class of Afro-Americans the crime of rape is so revolting they have too often taken the white man's word and given lynch law neither the investigation nor condemnation it deserved.

They forget that a concession of the right to lynch a man for a certain crime, not only concedes the right to lynch any person for any crime, but (so frequently is the cry of rape now raised) it is in a fair way to stamp us a race of rapists and desperadoes. They have gone on hoping and believing that general education and financial strength would solve the difficulty, and are devoting their energies to the accumulation of both. . . .

PEGGY PASCOE

Ophelia Paquet, a Tillamook Indian Wife: Miscegenation Laws and the Privileges of Property

When Ophelia Paquet's husband died in 1919, the county court recognized her as his widow—the Paquets had been married for thirty years—and appointed Ophelia to administer his estate. As there were no children, Ophelia stood to inherit her late husband's property. It was a just arrangement inasmuch as it was her money that had been used to purchase the land and pay taxes on it. John Paquet, Fred's disreputable brother, thought otherwise. Ultimately the court awarded the estate to him, leaving the sixty-five-year-old widow destitute.

Ophelia's story is a complicated one. It illuminates many issues: the purpose of miscegenation laws, the role of marriage in the transmission of property, the "invisibility" of married women's economic contributions, and the way race can compound gender disadvantage.

In what respects does John Paquet's victory illuminate the convergence of race and class? What parallels does Pascoe draw between the Paquet case and contemporary debates over same-sex marriage? How is the failure to count Ophelia's economic contribution to the marriage related to the "pastoralization" of housework that Jeanne Boydston discussed on pages 153–64.

Although miscegenation laws are usually remembered (when they are remembered at all) as a Southern development aimed at African Americans, they were actually a much broader phenomenon. Adopted in both the North and the South in the colonial period and extended to western states in the nineteenth century, miscegenation laws grew up with slavery but became even more significant after the Civil War, for it was then that they came to form the crucial "bottom line" of the system of white supremacy embodied in segregation.

The earliest miscegenation laws, passed in the South, forbade whites to marry African Americans, but the list of groups prohibited from marrying whites was gradually expanded, especially in western states, by adding first American Indians, then Chinese and Japanese (both often referred to by the catchall term "Mongolians"), and then Malays (or Filipinos). And even this didn't exhaust the list. Oregon prohibited whites from marrying "Kanakas" (or native Hawaiians); South Dakota proscribed "Coreans"; Arizona singled out Hindus; and Georgia prohibited whites from marrying "West" and "Asiatic" Indians.

Many states packed their miscegenation laws with multiple categories and quasi-mathematical definitions of "race." Oregon, for example, declared that "it shall not be lawful within this state for any white person, male or female, to intermarry with any negro, Chinese, or any person having one fourth or more negro, Chinese, or Kanaka blood, or any per-

From *New Viewpoints in Women's History: Working Papers from the Schlesinger Library 50th Anniversary Conference, March 4–5, 1994* edited by Susan Ware. Cambridge, Mass.: Arthur and Elizabeth Schlesinger Library on the History of Women in America, Radcliffe College (1994). Condensed and reprinted by permission of the author. Notes have been renumbered and edited.

son having more than one half Indian blood." Altogether, miscegenation laws covered forty-one states and colonies. They spanned three centuries of American history: the first ones were enacted in the 1660s, and the last ones were not declared unconstitutional until 1967.

Although it is their sexual taboos that have attracted most recent attention, the structure and function of miscegenation laws were . . . more fundamentally related to the institution of marriage than to sexual behavior itself. In sheer numbers, many more laws prohibited interracial marriage than interracial sex. And in an even deeper sense, all miscegenation laws were designed to privilege marriage as a social and economic unit. Couples who challenged the laws knew that the right to marry translated into social respectability and economic benefits, including inheritance rights and legitimacy for children, that were denied to sexual liaisons outside marriage. Miscegenation laws were designed to patrol this border by making so-called "miscegenous marriage" a legal impossibility. Thus criminal courts treated offenders as if they had never been married at all; that is, prosecutors charged interracial couples with the moral offense of fornication or other illicit sex crimes, then denied them the use of marriage as a defense.

Civil courts guarded the junction between marriage and economic privilege. From Reconstruction to the 1930s, most miscegenation cases heard in civil courts were ex post facto attempts to invalidate relationships that had already lasted for a long time. They were brought by relatives or, sometimes, by the state, after the death of one partner, almost always a white man. Many of them were specifically designed to take property or inheritances away from the surviving partner, almost always an African American or American Indian woman. By looking at civil law suits like these (which were, at least in appeals court records, more common than criminal cases), we can begin to trace the links between white patriarchal privilege and property that sustained miscegenation laws.

Let me illustrate the point by describing [a] sample case, *In re Paquet's Estate*, decided by the Oregon Supreme Court in 1921.[1] The Paquet case, like most of the civil miscegenation cases of this period, was fought over the estate of a white man. The man in question,

Fred Paquet, died in 1919, survived by his 63-year-old Tillamook Indian wife, named Ophelia. The Paquet estate included 22 acres of land, some farm animals, tools, and a buggy, altogether worth perhaps $2500.[2] Fred and Ophelia's relationship had a long history. In the 1880s, Fred had already begun to visit Ophelia frequently and openly enough that he had become one of many targets of a local grand jury which periodically threatened to indict white men who lived with Indian women.[3] Seeking to formalize the relationship—and, presumably, end this harrassment—Fred consulted a lawyer, who advised him to make sure to hold a ceremony which would meet the legal requirements for an "Indian custom" marriage. Accordingly, in 1889, Fred not only reached the customary agreement with Ophelia's Tillamook relatives, paying them $50 in gifts, but also sought the formal sanction of Tillamook tribal chief Betsy Fuller (who was herself married to a white man); Fuller arranged for a tribal council to consider and confirm the marriage.[4] Afterwards Fred and Ophelia lived together until his death, for more than thirty years. Fred clearly considered Ophelia his wife, and his neighbors, too, recognized their relationship, but because Fred died without leaving a formal will, administration of the estate was subject to state laws which provided for the distribution of property to surviving family members.

When Fred Paquet died, the county court recognized Ophelia as his widow and promptly appointed her administrator of the estate. Because the couple had no children, all the property, including the land, which Ophelia lived on and the Paquets had owned for more than two decades, would ordinarily have gone to her. Two days later, though, Fred's brother John came forward to contest Ophelia for control over the property.[5] John Paquet had little to recommend him to the court. Some of his neighbors accused him of raping native women, and he had such an unsavory reputation in the community that at one point the county judge declared him "a man of immoral habits . . . incompetent to transact ordinary business affairs and generally untrustworthy."[6] He was, however, a "white" man, and under Oregon's miscegenation law, that was enough to ensure that he won his case against Ophelia, an Indian woman.

The case eventually ended up in the Oregon Supreme Court. In making its decision, the key issue for the court was whether or not to recognize Fred and Ophelia's marriage, which violated Oregon's miscegenation law.[7] The Court listened to—and then dismissed—Ophelia's argument that the marriage met the requirements for an Indian custom marriage and so should have been recognized as valid out of routine courtesy to the authority of another jurisdiction (that of the Tillamook tribe).[8] The Court also heard and dismissed Ophelia's claim that Oregon's miscegenation law discriminated against Indians and was therefore an unconstitutional denial of the Fourteenth Amendment guarantee of equal protection. The Court ingenuously explained its reasoning; it held that the Oregon miscegenation law did not discriminate because it "applied alike to all persons, either white, negroes, Chinese, Kanaka, or Indians."[9] Following this logic, the Court declared Fred and Ophelia's marriage void because it violated Oregon's miscegenation law; it ordered that the estate and all its property be transferred to "the only relative in the state," John Paquet, to be distributed among him, his siblings and their heirs.[10]

As the Paquet case demonstrates, miscegenation law did not always prevent the formation of interracial relationships, sexual or otherwise. Fred and Ophelia had, after all, lived together for more than thirty years and had apparently won recognition as a couple from many of those around them; their perseverance had even allowed them to elude grand jury crackdowns. They did not, however, manage to escape the really crucial power of miscegenation law: the role it played in connecting white supremacy to the transmission of property. In American law, marriage provided the glue which allowed for the transmission of property from husbands to wives and their children; miscegenation law kept property within racial boundaries by invalidating marriages between white men and women of color whenever ancillary white relatives like John Paquet contested them.[11] . . . Property, so often described in legal sources as simple economic assets (like land and capital) was actually a much more expansive phenomenon, one which took various forms and structured crucial relationships. . . . Race is in and of itself a

kind of property.[12] As [legal scholar] Derrick Bell . . . explains, most whites did—and still do—"expect the society to recognize an unspoken but no less vested property right in their 'whiteness.'" "This right," Bell maintains, "is recognized and upheld by courts and the society like all property rights under a government created and sustained primarily for that purpose."[13]

As applied to the Paquet case, this theme is easy to trace, for, in a sense, the victorious John Paquet had turned his "whiteness" (the best—and perhaps the only—asset he had) into property, and did so at Ophelia's expense. This transformation happened not once but repeatedly. One instance occurred shortly after the county judge had branded John Paquet immoral and unreliable. Dismissing these charges as the opinions of "a few scalawags and Garibaldi Indians," John Paquet's lawyers rallied enough white witnesses who would speak in his defense to mount an appeal which convinced a circuit court judge to declare Paquet competent to administer the estate.[14] Another example of the transformation of "whiteness" into property came when the Oregon Supreme Court ruled that Ophelia Paquet's "Indianness" disqualified her from legal marriage to a white man; with Ophelia thus out of the way, John and his siblings won the right to inherit the property.

The second property relationship [is] illuminated by the etymological connection between the words "property" and "propriety." Miscegenation law played on this connection by drawing a sharp line between "legitimate marriage" on the one hand and "illicit sex" on the other, then defining all interracial relationships as illicit sex. The distinction was a crucial one, for husbands were legally obligated to provide for legitimate wives and children, but men owed nothing to "mere" sexual partners: neither inheritance rights nor the legitimacy of children accompanied illicit relationships.

By defining all interracial relationships as illicit, miscegenation law did not so much prohibit or punish illicit sex as it did create and reproduce it. Conditioned by stereotypes which associated women of color with hypersexuality, judges routinely branded long-term settled relationships as "mere" sex rather than marriage. Lawyers played to these assumptions by reducing interracial relationships to interracial sex, then distinguishing interracial sex from marriage by associating it with prostitution. Describing the relationship between Fred and Ophelia Paquet, for example, John Paquet's lawyers claimed that "the alleged 'marriage' was a mere commercial affair" that did not deserve legal recognition because "the relations were entirely meretricious from their inception."[15]

It was all but impossible for women of color to escape the legacy of these associations. Ophelia Paquet's lawyers tried to find a way out by changing the subject. Rather than refuting the association between women of color and illicit sexuality, they highlighted its flip side, the supposed connection between white women and legitimate marriage. Ophelia Paquet, they told the judge, "had been to the man as good a wife as any white woman could have been."[16] In its final decision, the Oregon Supreme Court came as close as any court of that time did to accepting this line of argument. Taking the unusual step of admitting that "the record is conclusive that [Ophelia] lived with [Fred] as a good and faithful wife for more than 30 years," the judges admitted that they felt some sympathy for Ophelia, enough to recommend—but not require—that John Paquet offer her what they called "a fair and reasonable settlement."[17] But in the Paquet case, as in other miscegenation cases, sexual morality, important as it was, was nonetheless still subordinate to channelling the transmission of property along racial ... lines. Ophelia got a judicial pat on the head for good behavior, but John and his siblings got the property.

Which brings me to the third form of property relationship structured by miscegenation laws—and, for that matter, marriage laws in general—and that is women's economic dependence on men. Here the problems started long before the final decision gave John Paquet control of the Paquet estate. One of the most intriguing facts about the Paquet case is that everyone acted as if the estate in question belonged solely to Fred Paquet. In fact, however, throughout the Paquet marriage, Fred had whiled away most of his time; it was Ophelia's basket-making, fruit-picking, milk-selling, and wage work that had provided the income they needed to sustain themselves. And although the deed to their land was made out in Fred Paquet's name, the couple had used Ophelia's earnings, combined with her proceeds from government payments to Tillamook tribal members, both to purchase the property and to pay the yearly taxes on it. It is significant ... that, although lawyers on both sides of the case knew this, neither they nor the Oregon Supreme Court judges considered it a key issue at the trial in which Ophelia lost all legal right to what the courts considered "Fred's" estate.

Indeed, Ophelia's economic contribution might never have been taken into account if it were not for the fact that in the wake of the Oregon Supreme Court decision, United States Indian officials found themselves responsible for the care of the now impoverished Ophelia. Apparently hoping both to defend Ophelia and to relieve themselves of the burden of her support, they sued John Paquet on Ophelia's behalf. Working through the federal courts that covered Indian relations and equity claims, rather than the state courts that enforced miscegenation laws, they eventually won a partial settlement. Yet their argument, too, reflected the assumption that men were better suited than women to the ownership of what the legal system referred to as "real" property. Although their brief claimed that "Fred Paquet had practically no income aside from the income he received through the labor and efforts of the said Ophelia Paquet," they asked the Court to grant Ophelia the right to only half of the Paquet land.[18] In the end, the Court ordered that Ophelia should receive a cash settlement (the amount was figured at half the value of the land), but only if she agreed to make her award contingent on its sale.[19] To get any settlement at all, Ophelia Paquet had to relinquish all claims to actual ownership of the land, although such a claim might have given her legal grounds to prevent its sale and so allow her to spend her final years on the property.

It is not even clear that she received any payment on the settlement ordered by the court. As late as 1928, John Paquet's major creditor complained to a judge that Paquet had repeatedly turned down acceptable offers to sell the land; perhaps he had chosen to live on it himself.[20]

Like any single example, the Paquet case captures miscegenation law as it stood at one moment, and a very particular moment at that, one that might be considered the high water mark of American courts' determination to structure both family formation and property transmission along racial dividing lines.

Today, most Americans have trouble remembering that miscegenation laws ever existed ... [and] are incredulous at the injustice and the arbitrariness of the racial classifications that stand out in [such] ... cases. [Yet] few ... notice that one of the themes raised in the Paquet case—the significance of marriage in structuring property transmission—not only remains alive and well, but has, in fact, outlived both the erosion of traditional patriarchy and the rise and fall of racial classifications in marriage law.

More than a generation after the demise of miscegenation laws ... the drawing of exclusionary lines around marriage [continues]. ... The most prominent—though hardly the only—victims are lesbian and gay couples, who point out that the sex classifications currently embedded in marriage law operate in much the same way that the race classifications embedded in miscegenation laws once did: that is, they allow courts to categorize same-sex relationships as illicit sex rather than legitimate marriage and they allow courts to exclude same-sex couples from the property benefits of marriage, which now include everything from tax advantages to medical insurance coverage.

Both these modern legal battles and the earlier ones fought by couples like Fred and Ophelia Paquet suggest ... that focusing on the connections between property and the political economy of marriage ... offer a revealing vantage point from which to study both the form and power of analogies between race and sex classifications in American law and the relationships between race and gender hierarchies in American history.

NOTES

1. The Paquet case can be followed not only by reading the text of the appeals court decision, In re Paquet's Estate, 200 P 911 (Oregon 1921), but also in the following archival case files: *Paquet v. Paquet*, file No. 4268, Oregon Supreme Court, 1920; *Paquet v. Henkle*, file No. 4267, Oregon Supreme Court, 1920; and Tillamook County Probate file #605, all in the Oregon State Archives; and in *U.S. v. John B. Paquet*, Judgment Roll 11409, Register No. 8-8665, March 1925, National Archives and Records Administration, Pacific Northwest Branch.

2. Initial estimates of the value of the estate were much higher, ranging from $4500 to $12,500. I have relied on the figure of $2528.50 provided by court-appointed assessors. See Tillamook Country Probate file #605, Inventory and Appraisement, June 15, 1920.

3. *Paquet v. Paquet*, Respondent's brief, November 1, 1920, pp. 2–5.

4. Tillamook County Probate file #605, Judge A.M. Hare, Findings of Facts and Conclusions of Law, February 3, 1920; *Paquet v. Paquet*, Appellants Abstract of Record, September 3, 1920, pp. 10–16.

5. *Paquet v. Paquet*, Appellants Abstract of Record, September 3, 1920, p. 3.

6. Tillamook County Probate file #605, Judge A.M. Hare, Findings of Fact and Conclusions of Law, February 3, 1920.

7. Court records identify Fred Paquet as being of French Canadian origin. Both sides agreed that Fred was a "pure" or "full-blooded" "white" man and Ophelia was a "pure" or "full-blooded" "Indian" woman. *Paquet v. Paquet*, Appellant's First Brief, October 8, 1920, p. 1; *Paquet v. Paquet*; Respondent's brief, November 1, 1920, p. 2.

8. The question of legal jurisdiction over Indian tribes was—and is—a very thorny issue. Relations with Indians were generally a responsibility of the U.S. federal government, which, although it advocated assimilating Indian families into white middle-class molds, had little practical choice but to grant general recognition to tribally-determined marriages performed according to Indian custom. In the U.S. legal system, however, jurisdiction over marriage rested with the states rather than the federal government. States could, therefore, use their control over marriage as a wedge to exert some power over Indians by claiming that Indian-white marriages, especially those performed outside recognized reservations, were subject to state jurisdiction. In the Paquet case, for example, the court insisted that, because the Tillamook had never been assigned to a reservation and because Fred and Ophelia lived in a mixed settlement, Ophelia could not be considered part of a recognized tribe nor a "ward" of the federal government. As events would later show, both contentions were inaccurate: Ophelia was an enrolled member of the Tillamook tribe, which was under the supervision of the Siletz Indian Agency; the federal government claimed her as "a ward of the United States." See *U.S. v. John B. Paquet*, Bill of Complaint in Equity, September 21, 1923, p. 3.

9. In re Paquet's Estate, 200 P 911 at 913 (Oregon 1921).

10. In re Paquet's Estate, 200 P 911 at 914 (Oregon 1921).

11. Although the issue did not come up in the Paquet case, ... in miscegenation cases, not only the wife but also the children might lose their legal standing, for one effect of invalidating an interracial marriage was to make the children technically illegitimate. According to the law of most states, illegitimate children automatically inherited from their mothers, but they could inherit from their fathers only if their father had taken legal steps to formally recognize or adopt them. Since plaintiffs could rarely convince judges that fathers had done so, the chil-

dren of interracial marriages were often disinherited along with their mothers.

12. Derrick Bell, "Remembrances of Racism Past," in Hill and Jones, *Race in America: The Struggle for Equality* (Madison: University of Wisconsin Press, 1992), 78. See also Bell, "White Superiority in America: Its Legal Legacy, Its Economic Costs," *Villanova Law Review* 33 (1988), 767–779.

13. *Paquet* v. *Henkle*, Respondent's brief, March 14, 1920, p. 6; *Paquet* v. *Henkle*, Index to Transcript, August 25, 1920, p. 3.

14. *Paquet* v. *Paquet*, Respondent's brief, November 1, 1920, p. 7. Using typical imagery, they added that the Paquet relationship was "a case where a white man and a full blooded Indian woman have chosen to cohabit together illictly [sic], to agree to a relation of concubinage, which is not only a violation of the law of Oregon, but a trans-gression against the law of morality and the law of nature" (p. 16).

15. *Paquet* v. *Paquet*, Appellant's First Brief, October 8, 1920, p. 2.

16. In re Paquet's Estate, 200 P 911 at 914 (Oregon 1921).

17. *U.S.* v. *John B. Paquet*, Bill of Complaint in Equity, September 21, 1923, pp. 4, 6–7.

18. *U.S.* v. *John B. Paquet*, Stipulation, June 2, 1924; *U.S.* v. *John B. Paquet*, Decree, June 2, 1924.

19. Tillamook County Probate file #605, J.S. Cole, Petition, June 7, 1928. Cole was president of the Tillamook-Lincoln County Credit Association.

20. For a particularly insightful analysis of the historical connections between concepts of "race" and "family," see Liu, "Teaching the Differences among Women in a Historical Perspective," *Women's Studies International Forum* 14 (1991): 265–276.

DOCUMENTS: Claiming an Education

> *Mary Tape, "What right! have you to bar my children out of the school because she is a chinese Descend. . . ."*

Until the passage of the Chinese Exclusion Act of 1882, political upheaval and dire poverty in China, contrasted with what appeared to be economic opportunities in the United States, drew thousands of Chinese to "Gold Mountain," their term for California. Those who came initially were men, only a few of whom brought families. For many immigrants, the promise of Gold Mountain proved elusive; the reality was a lifetime of hard work and daily prejudice. Among the women who arrived were merchants' wives whose feet were bound—a painful mark of female subordination in the old country. Impoverished young women also arrived, many of whom had been kidnapped, lured by promises of marriage, or sold by poor parents to procurers in China who supplied prostitutes to the large population of unmarried Chinese men on the West Coast. Considered the property of men in any case, women were not expected to have a public voice. There were, however, exceptions—women who demonstrated what an emancipated Chinese-American woman might become. Mary Tape was one of that number.

Brought up in an orphanage in Shanghai, Mary Tape immigrated to the United States with missionaries when she was eleven years old. She lived for five years at the Ladies' Relief Society outside of Chinatown in San Francisco. Fluent in English and westernized in dress, she married Joseph Tape, with whom she had four children, one of whom was a daughter, Mamie. Mamie's parents wanted her to have an education that would best prepare her for life in the United States. But the San Francisco school system, which was prepared to educate the children of European immigrants, resisted the inclusion of Asians.

Mamie Tape was denied entrance to a neighborhood school outside of Chinatown on the grounds that the association with Chinese children would be "very mentally and morally detrimental" to white children. The Tapes sued the Board of Education and won.

But the School Board circumvented the court's ruling by establishing a separate school for Chinese children in Chinatown. Furious, Mary Tape responded. Her letter, while revealing an imperfect command of English, communicates her sentiments perfectly. Compare her sense of injustice to that expressed by Keziah Kendall (pp. 198–200).

I see that you are going to make all sorts of excuses to keep my child out off the Public Schools. Dear sirs, Will you please to tell me! Is it a disgrace to be Born a Chinese? Didn't God make us all!!! What right! have you to bar my children out of the school because she is a chinese Descend. . . . You have expended a lot of the Public money foolishly, all because of a one poor little Child. Her playmates is all Caucasians ever since she could toddle around. If

Quoted in *Unbound Feet: A Social History of Chinese Women in San Francisco* by Judy Yung (Berkeley, Los Angeles, and London: University of California Press, 1995), p. 49.

she is good enough to play with them! Then is she not good enough to be in the same room and studie with them? . . . It seems no matter how a Chinese may live and dress so long as you know they Chinese. Then they are hated as one. There is not any right or justice for them. . . . May you Mr. Moulder, never be per-

secuted like the way you have persecuted little Mamie Tape. Mamie Tape will never attend any of the Chinese schools of your making! Never!!! I will let the world see sir What justice there is When it is govern by the Race prejudice men!

Zitkala-Ša (Gertrude Simmons Bonnin), ". . . this semblance of civilization . . ."

Zitkala-Ša, whose mother was Sioux and father was Anglo-American, sought throughout her life to bridge the cultures of Native Americans and the United States. She was one of the first American Indian women who built an independent career as a writer; her voice, as the following selection from her early writing shows, could be simultaneously eloquent, sentimental, and bitter. Born in 1876, Zitkala-Ša was eight years old when she left her home on the Yankton Sioux Agency in South Dakota for White's Indiana Manual Labor Institute in Wabash, Indiana, a training school funded by Quakers. She continued her education first at a teacher training school close to her home, then at Earlham College, and finally at the New England Conservatory of Music in Boston where she studied the violin.

Throughout her life, Zitkala-Ša (after her marriage using an anglicized name) worked with her husband, who was an employee of the Bureau of Indian Affairs, advocating citizenship for Indians, exposing corruption in the BIA, insisting on the dignity of Indian religions, and lobbying for the Indian Citizenship Act of 1924 she founded the National Council of American Indians; she sought to shape the Indian policy of the New Deal years.

When she wrote this memoir of her own childhood, Zitkala-Ša had not yet taught at the Carlisle Indian School in Pennsylvania, an experience that would strengthen her criticism of the practice of removing native children from their homes and of the corruption she found among the school's directors, who received federal money for each child they boarded, and whose promotion of "Americanization" could be harsh and cruel. To what extent did her mother anticipate that the experience at the mission school would be difficult? What advantage did the educators think would result from cutting girls' hair? What evidence is there to suggest that she herself was involved in the process of acculturation?

Excerpted from "Impressions of an Indian Childhood," "The School Days of an Indian Girl," and "An Indian Teacher among Indians" by Zitkala-Ša, *Atlantic Monthly* 85 (January, February, and March 1900): 45–47, 186–87, and 386.

Zitkala-Ša in traditional dress. (Courtesy of the Smithsonian Institution.)

The first turning away from the easy, natural flow of my life occurred in an early spring. It was in my eighth year; in the month of March, I afterward learned. At this age I knew but one language, and that was my mother's native tongue.

From some of my playmates I heard that two paleface missionaries were in our village. They were from that class of white men who wore big hats and carried large hearts, they said. Running direct to my mother, I began to question her why these two strangers were among us. She told me, after I had teased much, that they had come to take away Indian boys and girls to the East. My mother did not seem to want me to talk about them. But in a day or two, I gleaned many wonderful stories from my playfellows concerning the strangers.

"Mother, my friend Judéwin is going home with the missionaries. She is going to a more beautiful country than ours; the pale-faces told her so!" I said wistfully, wishing in my heart that I too might go.

Mother sat in a chair, and I was hanging on her knee. Within the last two seasons my big brother Dawée had returned from a three years' education in the East, and his coming back influenced my mother to take a farther step from her native way of living. First it was a change from the buffalo skin to the white man's canvas that covered our wigwam. Now she had given up her wigwam of slender poles, to live, a foreigner, in a home of clumsy logs.

Judéwin had told me of the great tree where grew red, red apples; and how we could reach out our hands and pick all the red apples we could eat. I had never seen apple trees. I had never tasted more than a dozen red apples in my life; and when I heard of the orchards of the East, I was eager to roam among them. The missionaries smiled into my eyes, and patted my head. I wondered how mother could say such hard words against them.

"Mother, ask them if little girls may have all the red apples they want, when they go East," I whispered aloud, in my excitement.

The interpreter heard me, and answered: "Yes, little girl, the nice red apples are for those who pick them; and you will have a ride on the iron horse if you go with these good people."

I had never seen a train, and he knew it.

"Mother, I'm going East! I like big red apples, and I want to ride on the iron horse! Mother, say yes!" I pleaded.

My mother said nothing. The missionaries waited in silence; and my eyes began to blur with tears, though I struggled to choke them back. The corners of my mouth twitched, and my mother saw me.

"I am not ready to give you any word," she said to them. "Tomorrow I shall send you my answer by my son."

With this they left us. Alone with my mother, I yielded to my tears, and cried aloud, shaking my head so as not to hear what she was saying to me. This was the first time I had ever been so unwilling to give up my own desire that I refused to harken to my mother's voice.

There was a solemn silence in our home that night. Before I went to bed I begged the Great Spirit to make my mother willing I should go with the missionaries.

The next morning came, and my mother called me to her side. "My daughter, do you still persist in wishing to leave your mother?" she asked.

"Oh, mother, it is not that I wish to leave you, but I want to see the wonderful Eastern land," I answered....

... My brother Dawée came for mother's decision. I dropped my play, and crept close to my aunt.

"Yes, Dawée, my daughter, though she does not understand what it all means, is anxious to go. She will need an education when she is grown, for then there will be fewer real Dakotas, and many more palefaces. This tearing her away, so young, from her mother is necessary, if I would have her an educated woman. The palefaces, who owe us a large debt for stolen lands, have begun to pay a tardy justice in offering some education to our children. But I know my daughter must suffer keenly in this experiment. For her sake, I dread to tell you my reply to the missionaries. Go, tell them that they may take my little daughter, and that the Great Spirit shall not fail to reward them according to their hearts."

Wrapped in my heavy blanket, I walked with my mother to the carriage that was soon to take us to the iron horse. I was happy. I met my playmates, who were also wearing their best thick blankets. We showed one another our new beaded moccasins, and the width of the belts that girdled our new dresses. Soon we were being drawn rapidly away by the white man's horses. When I saw the lonely figure of my mother vanish in the distance, a sense of regret settled heavily upon me. I felt suddenly weak, as if I might fall limp to the ground. I was in the hands of strangers whom my mother did not fully trust. I no longer felt free to be myself, or to voice my own feelings. The tears trickled down my cheeks, and I buried my face in the folds of my blanket. Now the first step, parting me from my mother, was taken, and all my belated tears availed nothing.

Having driven thirty miles to the ferry-boat, we crossed the Missouri in the evening. Then riding again a few miles eastward, we stopped before a massive brick building. I looked at it in amazement, and with a vague misgiving, for in our village I had never seen so large a house. Trembling with fear and distrust of the palefaces, my teeth chattering from the chilly ride, I crept noiselessly in my soft moccasins along the narrow hall, keeping very close to the bare wall. I was as frightened and bewildered as the captured young of a wild creature.

The first day in the land of apples was a bitter-cold one; for the snow still covered the ground, and the trees were bare. A large bell rang for breakfast, its loud metallic voice crashing through the belfry overhead and into our sensitive ears. The annoying clatter of shoes on bare floors gave us no peace. The constant clash of harsh noises, with an undercurrent of many voices murmuring an unknown tongue, made a bedlam within which I was securely tied. And though my spirit tore itself in struggling for its lost freedom, all was useless.

A paleface woman, with white hair, came up after us. We were placed in a line of girls who were marching into the dining room. These were Indian girls, in stiff shoes and closely clinging dresses. The small girls wore sleeved aprons and shingled hair. As I walked noiselessly in my soft moccasins, I felt like sinking to the floor, for my blanket had been stripped from my shoulders. I looked hard at the Indian girls, who seemed not to care that they were even more immodestly dressed than I, in their tightly fitting clothes. While we marched in, the boys entered at an opposite door. I watched for the three young braves who came in our party. I spied them in the rear ranks, looking as uncomfortable as I felt. . . .

. . . Late in the morning, my friend Judéwin gave me a terrible warning. Judéwin knew a few words of English; and she had overheard the paleface woman talk about cutting our long, heavy hair. Our mothers had taught us that only unskilled warriors who were captured had their hair shingled by the enemy. Among our people, short hair was worn by mourners, and shingled hair by cowards!

We discussed our fate some moments, and when Judéwin said, "We have to submit, because they are strong," I rebelled.

"No, I will not submit! I will struggle first!" I answered.

I watched my chance, and when no one noticed I disappeared. I crept up the stairs as quietly as I could in my squeaking shoes—my moccasins had been exchanged for shoes. Along the hall I passed, without knowing whither I was going. Turning aside to an open door, I found a large room with three white beds in it. The windows were covered with dark green curtains, which made the room very dim. Thankful that no one was there, I directed my steps toward the corner farthest from the door. On my hands and knees I crawled under the bed, and cuddled myself in the dark corner.

From my hiding place I peered out, shuddering with fear whenever I heard footsteps near by. Though in the hall loud voices were calling my name, and I knew that even Judéwin was searching for me, I did not open my mouth to answer. Then the steps were quickened and the voices became excited. The sounds came nearer and nearer. Women and girls entered the room. I held my breath, and watched them open closet doors and peep behind large trunks. Some one threw up the curtains, and the room was filled with sudden light. What caused them to stoop and look under the bed I do not know. I remember being dragged out, though I resisted by kicking and scratching wildly. In spite of myself, I was carried downstairs and tied fast in a chair.

I cried aloud, shaking my head all the while until I felt the cold blades of the scissors against my neck, and heard them gnaw off one of my thick braids. Then I lost my spirit. Since the day I was taken from my mother I had suffered extreme indignities. People had stared at me. I had been tossed about in the air like a wooden puppet. And now my long hair was shingled like a coward's! In my anguish I moaned for my mother, but no one came to comfort me. Not a soul reasoned quietly with me, as my own mother used to do; for now I was only one of many little animals driven by a herder. . . .

. . . Now, as I look back upon the recent past, I see it from a distance, as a whole. I remember how, from morning till evening, many specimens of civilized peoples visited the Indian school. The city folks with canes and eyeglasses, the countrymen with sunburnt cheeks and clumsy feet, forgot their relative social ranks in an ignorant curiosity. Both sorts of these Christian palefaces were alike astounded at seeing the children of savage warriors so docile and industrious.

As answers to their shallow inquiries they received the students' sample work to look upon. Examining the neatly figured pages, and gazing upon the Indian girls and boys bending over their books, the white visitors walked out of the schoolhouse well satisfied: They were educating the children of the red man! They were paying a liberal fee to the government employees in whose able hands lay the small forest of Indian timber.

In this fashion many have passed idly through the Indian schools during the last decade, afterward to boast of their charity to the North American Indian. But few there are who have paused to question whether real life or long-lasting death lies beneath this semblance of civilization.

GLENDA GILMORE

Forging Interracial Links in the Jim Crow South

Anna Julia Cooper—an extraordinary woman in her own right—wrote in 1892, "the colored woman of today . . . is confronted by a woman question and a race problem."* Equality of the sexes, Cooper insisted, would mean that black women should not be passive and subordinate in their relationships with black men; and black men should not criticize women's efforts to obtain equal rights. Equality of the sexes, Cooper continued, meant sharing the leadership burden in the struggle against racism. A remarkable group of African-American women did just that.

Part of a small but growing black middle class in the South, they were prepared by education, professional training, and voluntary work to be the vanguard of their race. Following the disfranchisement of black men in the 1890s, they emerged not only as community activists, but as ambassadors to the white community and astute political strategists. Their political skills were put to the test when, during the most racist era in U.S. history, these black women attempted to forge links with elite white women in an interracial movement. At the forefront of the effort was a remarkable North Carolinian, Charlotte Hawkins Brown.

Glenda Gilmore illuminates Brown's search for fault lines in the system of white supremacy with great sensitivity and insight in the following essay. She also demonstrates just how Brown manipulated class, gender, and even her own identity in the interests of racial justice. In the end, Brown's generation fell short of their goal of racial and sexual equality. The odds against them were overwhelming. In the process, how-

---

*Anna Julia Cooper, *A Voice from the South by a Black Woman of the South* (Xenia, Ohio: Aldine, 1892), p. 135.

Excerpted from "Forging Interracial Links," chapter 7 of *Gender and Jim Crow: Women and the Politics of White Supremacy in North Carolina, 1896–1920* by Glenda Elizabeth Gilmore (Chapel Hill, N.C.: The University of North Carolina Press, 1996). Copyright © 1996 by the University of North Carolina Press. Reprinted by permission of the author and publisher. The author has supplied new paragraphs, and renumbered and edited notes.

ever, they created and nourished a tradition of activism that would emerge with new force and greater success in the 1960s.

Consider Brown's strategy. What were her options? What were the personal costs? Do you agree with Gilmore's characterization of her as a "political genius"?

In the segregated world of the Jim Crow South, laws told black and white people where to eat and where to sit. Undergirding those laws lay a complex web of custom. Its strands separated the races in places beyond the reach of legislation. Custom dictated, for example, which part of the sidewalk belonged to whites and which to blacks. When whites and blacks sometimes occupied the same space, custom demanded that African Americans behave in a subservient manner. Any breach of these codes by a black person could bring an instant response from a white person: a reprimand, a beating, a jail sentence, or even death at the end of a lyncher's rope.

Whites held two unshakable beliefs that gave them the courage and energy to structure such a complicated society, making good on its rules with violence and even murder. First, whites thought that they acted to protect white women from black men's sexual desires. Second, they firmly believed that African Americans should be excluded from the American democratic system. They spoke freely and acted openly against any extension of political rights to blacks. After the turn of the century, restrictive legislation prevented most southern black men from voting and segregation laws crowded the books. White men considered their work done. Henceforth, they thought, African Americans would be a permanent lower caste in southern society: physically separated and politically powerless.

But the white supremacists did not reckon with black women. From behind the borders of segregation and disfranchisement, African American women became diplomats to the white community. They built social service and civic structures that wrested some recognition and meager services from the expanding welfare state. Ironically, as black men were forced from the political sphere, the functions of government expanded, opening a new space for black women to approach officials as good citizens intent on civic betterment.

One of their political strategies was to build contacts with white women. Meager and unequal as they were, these interracial connections often provided black women access to resources for their families, students, and neighbors. Charlotte Hawkins Brown personified such black women across the South who forged invisible careers in interracial politics.

As president of the North Carolina Association of Colored Women's Clubs, Charlotte Hawkins Brown began to direct African American women's formal civic experiences in the state in 1912 and continued to do so for twenty-five years.... No black man could claim prominence to equal hers in ... the state during the period. Brown's work and racialist ideologies illustrate that the decade before woman suffrage constituted a critical period in defining the boundaries of race relations that would remain in place until the post–World War II era.

Charlotte Hawkins Brown's life also provides a parable of the possibilities and the personal costs of interracial cooperation. Her story is so interwoven with myth—fiction that she fashioned to outmaneuver racism—that it is difficult to separate the reality of her experience from the result of her self-creation. The difference between her lived life and her public persona reveals a great deal about her perception of southern whites' racial ideologies and the points at which she saw possibility. Charlotte Hawkins Brown invented herself, repeatedly and with brilliance, but at great personal cost.[1]

According to her account, she was born in Henderson, North Carolina, in 1883 to Caroline Frances Hawkins, the daughter of Rebecca and Mingo Hawkins. Her father was Edmund H. Hight, from "whom fate separated me at birth" and who "belonged to a family that had grown up on the adjoining plantation."[2] Brown characterized her grandmother, Rebecca Hawkins, as a "fair" woman "with blue eyes," the African American sister of her white master, "a great railroad captain whose vision and foresight built up the great Southern Railroad." Brown cast the white master as the Hawkins family's "protector."[3] About the time of my birth, colored people in large numbers were leaving for parts north," she remembered. Charlotte moved with her mother and brother to Cambridge, Massachusetts, where her mother married and the family lived in a large, handsome house near Harvard University.[4] Caroline Hawkins managed a hand laundry in the basement, and Charlotte attended the public schools of Cambridge. Whisked away from the South at an early age, Charlotte was "not conscious of the difference in color and took part in all the activities of my class."[5] She acquired a New England accent, which she kept all of her life.

Charlotte Hawkins's family insisted that she get a practical education and sent her to Massachusetts State Normal School in Salem. Alice Freeman Palmer, the wife of a Harvard professor and the first female president of Wellesley College, was a member of the state board of education that oversaw the school. One day a few months before she entered the normal school, as Charlotte Hawkins was pushing a baby carriage while reading a high school Latin textbook, she chanced to meet Palmer on the street. Hawkins was babysitting to raise money for a silk slip to wear under her new organdy graduation dress, but Palmer assumed that she was an impoverished student, overcoming all odds to get an education. Palmer mentioned Hawkins favorably to the principal of her high school when they next met, and the incident ended. Now, when Hawkins realized that Palmer was an overseer of her normal school, she wrote to her and reminded her of their chance meeting. Palmer responded by paying Hawkins's tuition.[6]

Several months before graduation, Charlotte Hawkins met a supervisor from the American Missionary Association (AMA) on a train. The AMA representative impressed upon Hawkins the needs of the South, and Hawkins left school to accept a position at a one-teacher school in Sedalia, North Carolina, near Greensboro in 1901.[7] The AMA funded the school for two years, then withdrew support. For a year, Hawkins drew no salary, and she and the students survived on what they grew, the produce their parents donated, and a $100 county appropriation. Charlotte Hawkins returned to Cambridge and approached Alice Freeman Palmer for financial help, which Palmer promised to consider when she returned from Europe some months later. Palmer died in

Europe, however, and Hawkins decided to name the school in her memory. With continuing county support and private contributions, Palmer Memorial Institute taught practical vocational skills to its students, and Hawkins became active in the North Carolina Teachers Association and in women's club work. In 1911, Hawkins married Edward S. Brown. But the marriage lasted only a few months since Edward said he could not remain in Sedalia and be "Miss Hawkins's husband."[8]

In the South, Brown tells us, she demanded the respect of whites and received it from the "quality people." She insisted upon being addressed as "Miss," "Mrs.," or, after she gained honorary degrees, "Doctor."[9] She refused to be Jim Crowed and reported that several times she was "put out of Pullman berths and seats during all hours of the night." . . . By 1920, with the support of prominent Greensboro whites, Brown built Palmer Memorial Institute into a sprawling complex. She was proud that the most powerful whites in Greensboro served on the Palmer board, including Lula McIver and Julius Cone, head of the huge Cone Mills.[10]

As Brown rendered it, the theme of her life story is challenge met through interracial cooperation. Brown shaped the narrative in two critical ways: she minimized the restrictions of race in her daily life and exaggerated whites' helpfulness at every critical juncture. She obscured the fact that she was illegitimate by making it seem as if her father, Edmund Hight, was separated from the family by slavery. Brown was born in 1883 and had an older brother, demonstrating that her mother had a long-term relationship with Hight. The Hight family continued to live near Henderson throughout the twentieth century. Brown's grandmother, Rebecca Hawkins, may have been the sister of railroad magnate Captain John Hawkins, Jr., but, far from acting as the family's protector, he retained no contact with his black relatives and was a Democrat of the white supremacist persuasion.[11]

Brown mythologized her birth to remind southern whites of slavery's legacy: their shared kinship with African Americans. At the same time, she drew whites as sympathetic figures, the "protectors" of their African American relatives. Such circumstances did exist in the South; they just did not happen to exist within Charlotte's immediate family. As whites created the fictional "good darky" who treasured the interpersonal relationships that sprang from the close association of whites and blacks during slavery, Brown created a fictional "good master" who realized the responsibilities of miscegenation and loved his family, white and black. She used this good master to assuage whites' guilt about slavery and to argue that even slaves and masters achieved interracial understanding. She did not have to fight whites who melded ancestral ties to romantic class mythologies; she could simply join them. She shared their aristocratic roots.

Brown had moved to Cambridge not "about the time of my birth" but at the age of six. Yet she claimed to have no memory of her early life in North Carolina, no first-hand recollection of discrimination against blacks in the South, indeed no racial consciousness while growing up, even though she spent a great deal of time in the South during her childhood, even entire summers. Brown remade herself as a New Englander. When asked how her name should appear on her high school diploma, she instantly dropped her North Carolina name—Lottie Hawkins—for the more genteel sounding "Charlotte Eugenia Hawkins," which she made up on the spot. She spoke in a manner that "combine[d] the mellow tones of the southern Negro and the quick clipped qualities of New England—people turn[ed] around to see who [was] speaking."[12]

By casting herself as a New Englander, Brown attempted to remain above the southern racial structure. In Greensboro, she occupied a place much like that of African diplomats to the United States—she was an exotic but North Carolina's own exotic. If whites accused her of being an outside agitator, Brown could fall back on her North Carolina roots. Then she presented herself as native stock, a female, black Ulysses who fought her way back to the South and to her own people, where she belonged.

The story of the AMA's dispatch of Charlotte Hawkins to the South to save her people competes with another, more complicated parable that Brown merely hinted at and may have consciously avoided dwelling upon. Rather than seeing herself as a New England missionary to a foreign place, Brown may have construed her return to North Carolina as coming to terms with the realities of race in her own life. One night at a Cambridge meeting, she watched magic lantern slides of the race work being done by African Americans in the South. She was particularly struck by two educators, Joseph Price, the founder of Livingstone College, and Lucy Laney, the founder of Haines Institute in Augusta, Georgia. She noted that both Price and Laney were, like herself, very dark skinned. Price and Laney were also brilliant, and their faces on the screen moved Brown to feel that there was a place where she might belong: the South.[13] Brown never acknowledged publicly that she had any personal reason for wanting to leave New England, choosing rather to emphasize the missionary aspect of her return.

As the years passed, accounts of the relationship between Alice Freeman Palmer and Brown made it seem as if Palmer had sent Brown to the South to found the school and that they had enjoyed a close friendship. . . . Contemporary newspaper accounts, which relied on Brown's own promotional material, reported that Palmer's "efforts" had made the school possible and "until her death she was an ardent supporter of her namesake."[14]

Although Brown did not actually lie about Palmer's interest in her and the school, she embroidered the truth. Brown and Palmer spent less than fifteen minutes together in their lifetimes, and Palmer never promised that she would personally contribute to the school. Instead, Palmer had told Brown upon their second meeting that she was too busy at the moment but that after her return from Europe she would contact friends in Boston to encourage them to support the school. Why, then, when Palmer never returned, did Brown name the school Palmer Memorial Institute? Actually, Brown originally named the school Alice Freeman Palmer Settlement in order to gain support from Palmer's friends in Boston.[15] Palmer, after a brilliant career, had died at a young age and was mourned by her friends, and a memorial to her could prompt contributions. . . .

Around 1910, Brown cannily began to play southern pride against northern dollars when she inspired white leaders in Greensboro to challenge their community to take over the financial support of Palmer.[16] In soliciting southern white support, Brown . . . most often called the school Sedalia rather than Palmer. For example, Brown named the group of students who sang African American spirituals the Sedalia Singers.[17] She understood the white southerners' sense of place, and since her school was the only thing in the crossroads of Sedalia, she did not encroach upon white territory in appropriating the name. The location of Palmer at Sedalia facilitated support from Greensboro whites. It was ten miles outside of the city, surrounded by sparsely populated farmland. Brown never permitted Palmer students to travel alone to Greensboro but instead brought them as a group, with the boys clad in coats and ties and the girls wearing hats and white gloves. Once in the city, they did not mingle with Greensboro's African Americans; rather, Brown negotiated special seating sections for her students at public events.[18]

Although Brown cloaked the curriculum at Palmer in vocational disguises and portrayed it to the press as an industrial school until the late 1930s, the institute offered mostly academic courses from its inception.[19] Booker T. Washington met Brown on a trip to Boston while she was still a student there and pronounced her "the only convert that he made in New England." If he believed her to be a convert, she outfoxed the Wizard himself.[20] . . . Brown never embraced Washington's vocational philosophy past the point of providing for the school's basic needs, but she portrayed the school as industrial, detailing "farm yields" in fund-raising letters.[21] An unidentified Palmer teacher explained the ruse this way: "[Brown] always had a college preparatory class . . . a cultural academic school. All the Negroes had to have that in order to get along in the South." Even though this teacher believed, along with Brown, that African Americans profited most from classical knowledge coupled with reinforcement of middle-class values, support for that sort of training did not exist. So Brown and her teachers positioned Palmer as a "vocational" school. Funding for industrial education "could always get through," the teacher recalled. Despite the vocational exterior, she continued, "you could teach anything you wanted when you got in your school. You came inside your class room and you taught them Latin and French and all the things you knew."[22] Although initially Brown's students were the poor children of the neighborhood, by 1920, Palmer functioned as an academic boarding school that drew students from counties across the state and included secondary grades.[23]

Notwithstanding her vocal cover, at times Brown argued that her approach to "cultural" instruction benefited whites as well as African Americans. She explained, "Recognizing the need of a cultural approach to life, believing absolutely in education through racial contacts, I have devoted my whole life to establish for Negro youth something superior to Jim Crowism." She tried to accomplish this "by bringing the two races together under the highest cultural environment that will increase race pride, mutual respect, confidence, sympathetic understanding, and interracial goodwill."[24]

Why did Brown repeatedly overdraw white understanding and support and minimize the restrictions that her color placed on her? Throughout her life, she operated by a simple rule: it is better to overestimate possibility than to underestimate it. Charlotte Hawkins Brown created a fictional mirror of civility in race relations and held it up to whites as a reflection of their better selves. From slavery, she drew compassion; from the loneliness of Cambridge, racial liberality among her schoolmates; from Alice Freeman Palmer's deferral, a legacy; and from frightened, pinched southern whites, chivalry of a sort. Brown was a political genius, especially suited for interracial work. Her renderings served her own purposes, but she did not . . . delude herself into thinking that they were true. Immune to her own romantic stories, Brown was the consummate pragmatist. So convinced was she of her mission and of her opponent's rigid character, that she could risk the heartbreak of gilding the lily. She expected nothing, received little, and turned that pittance into bounty.

But Charlotte Hawkins Brown was a double agent. When she refused to turn her head toward the "colored" waiting room, she must have felt the stares of its patrons burn into her consciousness. In the decade preceding 1920, Brown immersed herself in social welfare projects and political activity that she kept hidden from whites. After 1920, Brown acquired a national reputation for her interracial work and landed official positions in interracial organizations, success that brought her activities under public scrutiny. Until then, and thereafter when she could, Brown generally said one thing to whites and then did another if it suited her purposes.

Brown's double life left its mark on her.... Living her life as a diplomat to the white community, Brown could never be just Lottie Hawkins. African American women who chose to take up interracial work walked a tightrope that required them to be forever careful, tense, and calculating. One slip would end their careers; they worked without nets.

In Lula Martin McIver, Brown found an exception to her belief that the southern white woman stood at the center of the race "problem." Their first meeting represents a classic case of the Brown treatment. Constantly seeking funds for Palmer Memorial Institute, Brown decided in the spring of 1905 that she must approach prominent white men in Greensboro for support. In Greensboro, Brown had no magic key such as Alice Freeman Palmer's name. Sedalia was a crossroads, Palmer Institute tiny, and Brown unknown. She had no historic connections to white North Carolinians there, no reputation in the black community, no denominational bridge since she had converted to Congregationalism, a faith rare in the South among either African Americans or whites. She had only herself—the New England persona she so carefully cultivated—and courage.

In 1904, she had written a poignant letter to Charles McIver, president of the white women's normal college in Greensboro. It began, "This letter may come to you from a strange source, but it comes from one whose heart is in the educational and moral uplift of our people." It concluded by begging McIver to come to Palmer for a visit. A year later, Brown was still imploring him to the same end, touting the ease of the train ride and signing herself "Very Anxiously Yours."[25] Still McIver did not come. One morning Brown dressed carefully in her customary ankle-length dress, hat, and white gloves and set out to call on him in Greensboro. She had no appointment. Most often Brown did not write or telephone ahead and risk refusal from those she wished to meet but simply appeared on their doorstep. That morning she knocked on the front door of the president's residence and found that he was away. His wife, Lula Mar-

tin McIver, invited Brown in, an unusual act in itself. Lula McIver was stunned by Brown's appearance at the door. "Her daring, her enthusiasm, her faith intrigued me," McIver recalled. The two women talked for over an hour and warmed toward each other. Soon, McIver was advising Brown on "the best way to win friends" and on how to raise money among the Greensboro elite for the school.[26]

When Lula McIver opened the door, Brown chanced upon a valuable connection that would prove enduring. Brown sat in the parlor of the state's foremost white female educational advocate. Graduated from the Moravian academy in Salem, Lula Martin had longed to become a doctor like her father. After she learned that the profession was virtually closed to women, she became an outspoken feminist. As an adolescent, she abandoned the Moravians for the Methodists upon reading that the early Moravian settlers chose wives by lottery. In 1885, strong-willed Lula Martin met Charles Duncan McIver, a dedicated young teacher, who supported her feminist ideas and called her a "most sensible" woman. They married in a ceremony that omitted the word "obey," and Lula refused a wedding ring, which she regarded as a "badge of slavery."[27]

The McIvers worked to build North Carolina's white public educational system one school at a time. While Charles traveled throughout the state promoting graded school education, Lula served as his advance team, preceding him to scrub courthouse venues speckled with tobacco juice, to set up chairs, to post flyers, and to raise a crowd. She was delighted when Charles became first president of the state-supported normal school for white women since both felt that educating women would be the key to building an effective public school system. She helped to found the Woman's Association for the Betterment of Public School Houses, and after Charles's death, she accepted a paying position as its field secretary.[28]

The subtleties of Lula McIver's racial ideology are elusive, but at the center of her thinking about race lay the strongly held belief that African Americans deserved a good education. For nearly a half century after they met, McIver continually raised money for Palmer Memorial Institute. Lula McIver attended meetings of black women's clubs in Greensboro. After the early death of Charles McIver in 1909, and to the eternal perplexity of Greensboro whites, each semester Lula McIver invited a male African American student from nearby North Carolina Agricultural and Technical College to board in the president's residence where she lived until her death. There, surrounded by young white women students, Lula McIver offered an object lesson in race relations.[29]

Both Brown and McIver realized the restrictions on their relationship in the Jim Crow South. For starters, McIver was a woman and thus not powerful in her own right. Moreover, as the normal school's maternal figurehead, she had to act circumspectly since all of her actions reflected upon the school, which was still in the minds of some a dangerous experiment that wasted state money to educate women. Given these restrictions, McIver could do three concrete things for Brown: influence prominent white Greensboro men to support her, introduce leading club women to Palmer's mission, and raise money. She did another intangible and invaluable thing for Brown: Lula McIver publicly referred to Charlotte Hawkins Brown as her friend.[30]

It appears that Lula McIver realized that her husband's influence would be more valuable than her own, and she urged Charles to write an "open letter of endorsement" for Palmer Memorial Institute shortly after she met Brown. Since Charles McIver served on the Southern Education Board, his vote of confidence carried weight in the North as well as the South. The letter went out in June 1905, but Charles McIver admitted in it that he had never been to Palmer.[31] He died four years later. Long after that, Brown named Charles D. McIver as her "first friend" in North Carolina.[32] There is no record that McIver ever made the trip to Sedalia or that Brown ever met him. With Lula McIver's help, Brown appropriated the memory of Charles McIver as she had that of Alice Freeman Palmer.

Local support of Palmer flowered around 1914 when Lula McIver brought a delegation of white women from across the state to visit the school. A member of the delegation wrote an account of the visit that appeared in the *Greensboro Daily Record* and encouraged white women to take an interest in Brown's work. Brown struck just the right note in her solicitation letter: Palmer, she said, "has conducted

its work for the past 13 years without seeking very much help from our southern friends." She claimed friendship and a debt come due in the same breath.[33] The 1914 campaign was the beginning of a steady stream of white visitors to the school and financial support from white North Carolinians.[34] In 1917, Lula McIver conducted some of Greensboro's leading white businessmen on a tour of the school. Many of the men who had ignored Brown's previous appeals converted after that visit. E. P. Wharton recalled that Charlotte Brown had called on him around 1903 to obtain support for Palmer and that he was "ashamed of [him]self for losing sight" of Brown's work. He subsequently served for decades as a Palmer trustee. By 1920, the board of Palmer Memorial Institute included a Greensboro attorney, a banker, and an industrial magnate.[35] McIver sought no publicity for a trip she made to Boston with Charlotte Hawkins Brown two years later. There McIver called upon prominent white women, vouched for Brown's success, and asked for contributions to Palmer. When northern white women visited Palmer, they would not spend the night at the black school but stayed instead with Lula McIver.[36]

In 1919, Charlotte Hawkins Brown, with the endorsement of Lula McIver, published a remarkable novel, *Mammy*. On its face, the appearance of *Mammy* places Brown squarely in the accommodationist camp of African Americans, currying favor from whites by invoking the ties of slavery. The story tells of a loving black woman who nurses a white family and raises its children. Then, when the woman becomes old and ill, the family provides no help beyond an occasional visit to her drafty log cabin. Ultimately, they stand by as Mammy goes to the county home. Brown dedicated the book to "my good friend, Mrs. Charles Duncan McIver." She continued, "It is with gratitude I acknowledge her personal interest in the colored members of her household."[37]

What could Brown have hoped to accomplish by the publication of *Mammy*? At the time, she served as president of the statewide Association of Colored Women's Clubs, refused Jim Crow seating, and was secretly organizing a campaign to interest the state's black women in woman suffrage. She had spent almost twenty years building her dignity in North Carolina. It was amazing that she would play the *Mammy* card now. A close reading of Brown's introduction and McIver's response to the dedication indicates that both saw *Mammy* as a tool to promote their agenda: interracial cooperation among women. Mammies represented the one point of contact between southern black and white women, and white women continually bragged about their love for their Mammies. But Brown's *Mammy* is not a tale of love rewarded; it is an indictment of white neglect of African Americans. Brown calls upon white women to remember their duty to black women and redefines that duty in new ways. It is no longer enough to be fond of ol' Mammy; white women must act on that affection.

McIver framed her endorsement of *Mammy* carefully. She said that today's white woman was not the person her mother was, for in her mother's day, there was "understanding and sympathy" between the races. The problem was the separation of the races since there could be no racial harmony without "knowledge of each other's problems and an active interest in solving them." McIver endorsed the concept of "racial integrity" but reminded white southerners that their "task [was the] training of the uncivilized African." Brown must have winced at that remark, but it preceded McIver's most important statement: "I verily believe that to the most intelligent southern white women we must look for leadership in keeping our 'ship of state' off the rocks of racial antagonism." She signed the piece, "Your friend, Lula Martin McIver."[38]

Interracial cooperation, association among black and white women to solve mutual problems, was the solution that *Mammy* endorsed. McIver did not propose that white women individually care for their mammies but that they enter the public sphere and provide leadership. Male sailors had steered the ship of state onto rocky racial shores. It was time for women to man the lifeboats and rescue government from the oppressive racial politics of the white supremacists. In the same month that *Mammy* appeared, the state's white and black women began to do just that by traveling to Memphis, Tennessee, for a formal interracial summit. The state associations of women's clubs and the YWCAs sent forth those first intrepid female navigators.

Most of the black women who traveled to the Memphis interracial summit learned leadership skills in the National Association of Colored Women, but their experience in working with white women had come from two other sources as well: heretofore racially segregated groups that came together on the homefront in World War I and the interracial work of the Young Women's Christian Association (YWCA). During World War I organizational lines between women's groups of both races blurred when the Council of National Defense chose white women from each southern state to head committees to coordinate work on the homefront. In North Carolina, white women set up integrated county councils that included African American and white women, carefully chosen to represent clubs, YWCAs, and denominational social service programs.[39]

The work of the black YWCA centered on another upheaval of the time: African American migration from farm to town. Southern black women believed strongly in the YWCA's ability to reach poor young women who had moved to the city to find work. The national YWCA board determined that any southern African American branch must be supervised by an existing "central" YWCA. "Central" meant white. Once founded, the black YWCA must be overseen by a management committee of three white women and two black women. The rules mandated interracial "cooperation" of a sort. Despite these humiliating restrictions, two southern black women, Mary McCrorey of Charlotte, North Carolina, and Lugenia Burns Hope of Atlanta, founded Ys in their cities.[40]

On the train to Memphis, a group of white men pulled Brown out of the Pullman car and marched her past "southern white women passing for Christians" who were on their way to the Memphis meeting. The white women sat silent as the men forced Brown to the Jim Crow car.[41] Brown probably recognized among the fellow Memphis delegates North Carolina white women whom she had come to know over the past decade. Among them was the wife of the governor, Fanny Bickett. . . .

When Brown rose to address the white women, the frustration of a decade of interracial work erupted, and she shared the humiliation of being ousted from the Pullman car two nights before. She exhorted white women to fight lynching, to recognize the dignity of the African American woman, and to help black women. Brown ended on an ominous note: "You are going to reach out for the same hand that I am reaching out for but I know that the dear Lord will not receive it if you are crushing me beneath your feet."[42] Most of the white women were profoundly moved.

As it happened, the women's Memphis interracial meeting foundered on the spot that Lula McIver had warned of in *Mammy:* the shoal of politics. Two months before the meeting, a federal amendment had mandated woman suffrage and a month after the meeting women would vote for the first time. Just before Brown left for Tennessee, she had been secretly been organizing black women in North Carolina to register to vote. One faction of black women would not budge on the issue of suffrage at the Memphis meeting. A full year later, the white and black women still had not agreed on a statement of goals for an interracial movement. Brown, McCrorey, and Hope favored a version that included the controversial demand for protection of African American voting rights. Their language was blunt: "We believe that the ballot is the safe-guard of the Nation and that every citizen in the Nation should have the right to use it. We believe that if there is ever to be any justice before the law, the Negro must have the right to exercise the vote."[43] But the white women balked at the suffrage statement and the condemnation of lynching, both points "which the Negro women dared not leave out."[44] Whites suggested the wording, "We believe that the ballot is the safe-guard of the Nation, and that every *qualified* citizen in the Nation should have the right to use it."[45]

Interracial cooperation led straight into politics. As black and white women inched toward cooperation on a grass roots level, they came face-to-face with larger political forces. With a decade of women's interracial experience behind them, many African American women believed that the time had come to take a firm stand on suffrage. Black women looked to their white allies to support their right to vote, a gesture that underscores the success of interracial cooperation. Yet white women's confusion over black women's suffrage reveals the limits of voluntary interracial work. Upon the passage of woman suffrage, white women involved with interracial social service projects had to chose between gender

and race. They could support black women's right to vote as women, or oppose their right to vote as *black* women. Charlotte Hawkins Brown called the question when she used the NACW to organize black women's voter registration drives in urban areas in the fall of 1920. Across the South, other black women did the same thing, reporting back to the National Association for the Advancement of Colored People (NAACP).

In Mobile, Alabama, registrars told black women that they must own property to vote, and when the black juvenile court officer challenged them, court officials fired her.[46] From Birmingham came the news that when a black teacher attempted to register, the registrar "called her an ugly name and ordered her out." Another teacher "answered every question asked her—ex post facto law, habeas corpus proceedings, etc." The frustrated registrar still would not yield and "tore up her card and threw it in her face."[47] Ultimately, in Birmingham, 225 black women succeeded in registering, although 4,500 made the attempt.[48]

It is impossible to judge Charlotte Hawkins Brown's success in the North Carolina registration campaign. Most registration books failed to survive, but those that exist show not only that black women succeeded in urban areas, but that voter registration increased for black men as well. Probably less than 1,000 black women registered in North Carolina that fall.[49] To judge the results of black women's drive for suffrage, however, one must look not just at the few thousand who managed to register in 1920, but at the heritage of interracial work upon which they built and at the example they set for those who followed. The number of black women who voted in 1920 may have been small, but their significance in the South's racial politics was large. For the first time since the nineteenth century in the South, black voters approached the registrars en masse. They assembled as the result of a coordinated, subversive campaign that crossed over the boundaries of voluntary interracial work to reintroduce black civil rights in electoral politics. By their presence at the polls, black women dared whites to use violence and won the dare. In 1921, white supremacy still stood, but black women had found faultlines in its foundations.

NOTES

1. Ceci Jenkins, incomplete notes for "The Twig Bender of Sedalia" ([1946]), unpublished biography of Charlotte Hawkins Brown, reel 1, #12, Brown Collection, Manuscript Collection, Schlesinger Library (SL). See also Stephen Birmingham, *Certain People: America's Black Elite* (Boston: Little, Brown, 1977).

2. "A Biography," reel 1, and "Some Incidents in the Life and Career of Charlotte Hawkins Brown Growing out of Racial Situations, at the Request of Dr. Ralph Bunche," reel 1, #2, both in Brown Collection, SL.

3. "Some Incidents," 1–2, reel 1, #2, ibid.

4. "A Biography," reel 1, ibid. The language of "A Biography" is closely echoed in Sadie L. Daniel, *Women Builders* (Washington, D.C.: Associated Publishers, 1970), 133–63.

5. "A Biography," 13, reel 1, Brown Collection, SL.

6. On Palmer, see Ruth B. Bordin, *Alice Freeman Palmer: The Evolution of a New Woman* (Ann Arbor: University of Michigan Press, 1993). On the Brown/Palmer relationship, see "A Biography," 16–18, reel 1, and Jenkins, "Twig Bender of Sedalia," reel 1, #7, both in Brown Collection, SL.

7. Daniel, *Women Builders*, 139; "A Biography," 19, reel 1, Brown Collection, SL.

8. Charlotte E. Hawkins to Dr. Buttrick, 31 Aug. 1904, folder 1005, box 111, series 1, subseries 1, General Education Board Collection, RAC. Mary Grinnell to Charlotte Hawkins Brown, 4 Oct. 1910, 8 Feb. 1911; H. F. Kimball to Charlotte Hawkins Brown, 2 June 1911; and J. G. Bright to Charlotte Hawkins Brown, 1 Aug. 1911, all on reel 2, #33; Mary T. Grinnell to Charlotte Hawkins Brown, 6 Aug. 1912, 17 Feb. 1913, reel 2, #34; and Charlotte Hawkins Brown Ebony Questionnaire, 16, reel 1, #11, all in Brown Collection, SL.

9. Brown wrote that it was a "big surprise" that the white people in the South refused to "use the term 'Miss'" when they addressed black women. She continued, "Naturally I was constantly being insulting and insulted which merited for me the name 'Yankee Huzzy.'" See "Some Incidents," 5, reel 1, #2, Brown Collection, SL. Leading whites in Greensboro referred to her as "Dr. Brown" after she received honorary degrees from Wilberforce, Lincoln, and Howard universities. See Junius Scales to Glenda Gilmore, 4 Jan. 1990, in author's possession.

10. Letterhead, Palmer Memorial Institute, C. Hawkins Brown to W. E. B. Dubois [sic], to June 1930, W. E. B. Du Bois Papers, reel 33, University of Massachusetts, Amherst.

11. Ruth Anita Hawkins Hughes, *Contributions of Vance County People of Color* (Raleigh: Sparks Press, 1988).

12. Jenkins, "Twig Bender of Sedalia," 1, reel 1, #7, Brown Collection, SL.

13. Ibid., insert B; "Some Incidents," 9, reel 1, #2, Brown Collection, SL.

14. Eva M. Young, "Palmer Memorial Institute Unique," *Charlotte Observer*, 10 Mar. 1940, folder 51, box 94–3, ibid.

15. Jenkins, "Twig Bender of Sedalia," E.F. 16, reel 1, #7, Brown Collection, SL.

16. Ibid., E.F. 16, E.F. 17; "Some Incidents," reel 1, #2, Brown Collection, SL.

17. For an example of the conflation of Sedalia and Palmer Institute, see *Palmer Memorial Institute: The Mission and the Legacy* (Greensboro: Women of Greensboro, [1981]).

18. The description here is from interviews and conversations with Dawn Gilmore, Brooks Gilmore, and Lois MacKenzie, the author's aunt, uncle, and mother, respectively. The author's grandfather, Clyde Manly Gilmore, was Brown's physician, and the author's mother, MacKenzie, was her attorney's secretary in the 1950s.

19. Brown transformed the institute in the late 1930s into a preparatory school for upper-class African Americans. By 1940, the school letterhead read: "The Charm School Idea of the Palmer Memorial Institute, Charlotte Hawkins Brown, President and Promoter." See C. Hawkins Brown to My Dear Friend, 20 Mar. 1940, folder 124, box 112–4, Washington Conservatory of Music Records, Moorland-Spingarn Research Center, Howard University (MRSC).

20. Jenkins, "Twig Bender of Sedalia," insert G, reel 1, #7, Brown Collection, SL.

21. Charlotte Hawkins Brown to Wallace Buttrick, 19 Dec. 1912, folder 1005, box 111, series 1, subseries 1, General Education Board Collection, Rockefeller Archive Center (RAC).

22. "Charlotte Hawkins Brown," Dannett Collection, uncataloged, LC. See also Sylvia G. L. Dannett, *Profiles of Negro Womanhood* (New York: M. W. Lads, 1964–66), 59–63. The notes for Dannett's biographical sketches often do not identify the interviewee and are fragmentary.

23. Map, "Palmer Memorial Institute—Sedalia—Enrol[l]ment—1920–1921," folder 1006, box 111, series 1, subseries 1, General Education Board Collection, RAC.

24. "Some Incidents," reel 1, #2, Brown Collection, SL.

25. Board, 1904, Correspondence G-M, box 14, and C. E. Hawkins to Dr. McIver, 13 Apr. 1905, file Southern Education Board, 1905, Correspondence, E-L, box 15, both in Charles D. McIver Collection, University Archives, Walter Clinton Jackson Library, University of North Carolina, Greensboro (WCJL).

26. Mrs. Charles D. McIver to editor of *Greensboro Daily News*, [ca. 1940], reel 1, #13, and Jenkins, "Twig Bender of Sedalia," reel 1, #7, both in Brown Collection, SL.

27. Rose Howell Holder, *McIver of North Carolina* (Chapel Hill: University of North Carolina Press, 1917), 63–67. See also Virginia T. Lathrop, "Mrs. McIver Believes Greatness of the Past Holds State's Hope for Present and Future," *News and Observer*, 6 Oct. 1940, Clipping File, vol. 94, reel 24, 371–72, North Carolina Collection, University of North Carolina, Chapel Hill (NCC).

28. James Leloudis, "'A More Certain Means of Grace': Pedagogy, Self, and Society in North Car-

olina, 1880–1920" (Ph.D. diss., University of North Carolina at Chapel Hill, 1989), and Pamela Dean, "Covert Curriculum: Class and Gender in a New South Women's College" (Ph.D. diss., University of North Carolina at Chapel Hill, 1995). On the association, see James Leloudis, "School Reform in the New South: The Woman's Association for the Betterment of Public School Houses in North Carolina, 1902–1919," *Journal of American History* 69 (March 1983): 886–909. See also Lula Martin McIver to Charles L. Coon, 4 Feb. 1909, folder 28, box 2, and Lula Martin McIver to Charles L. Coon, 25 Jan. 1910, folder 29, box 2, both in Coon Papers, Southern Historical Collection, University of North Carolina, Chapel Hill (SHC).

29. Sallie Waugh McBryan to Mrs. McIver, 22 Nov. 1913, file Correspondence, 1909–44, box 141, Lula Martin McIver Collection, WCJL; "Famous Landmark at WCUNC Razed," *Durham Morning Herald*, 26 Oct. 1952, Clipping File, vol. 94, reel 24, 343–44, NCC.

30. Lula Martin McIver to Charlotte Hawkins Brown, 6 Apr. 1920, reel 2, #41, Brown Collection, SL.

31. Charles D. McIver letter, 5 June 1905, reel 2, #30, Correspondence, 1902–6, ibid.

32. "Award Will Go to Dr. Brown," *Greensboro Daily News*, 10 Apr. 1947, Clipping File, vol. 18, reel 5, 239, NCC.

33. C. Hawkins Brown to My dear Sir [Professor Julius I. Foust], 25 May 1914, file General Correspondence, 1913–15, box 57, Foust Collection, WCJL.

34. Jenkins, "Twig Bender of Sedalia," 77, reel 1, #12, Brown Collection, SL.

35. E. P. Wharton to Charlotte Hawkins Brown, 12 Jan. 1917, reel 2, #37, Jan.–Apr. 1917; Mrs. Charles D. McIver to editor of *Greensboro Daily News*, n.d., reel 1 #13; and Jenkins, "Twig Bender of Sedalia," 78, reel 1, #12, all in Brown Collection, SL.

36. H. F. Kimball to Charlotte Hawkins Brown, 6 Nov. 1916, reel 2, #36, 1916, and "Notes," copy of notebook maintained by Charlotte Hawkins Brown, reel 1, #8, both in Brown Collection, SL; Annie L. Vickery to My Dear Mrs. McIver, 7 Mar. 1917, file Correspondence, 1909–44, box 141, Lula Martin McIver Collection, WCJL.

37. Charlotte Hawkins Brown, *Mammy* (Boston: Pilgrim Press, 1919).

38. Lula Martin McIver to Charlotte Hawkins Brown, 6 Apr. 1920, reel 2, #41, Brown Collection, SL.

39. Laura Holmes Reilley to D. H. Hill, 18 Oct. 1917, file Women's Committee, box 30, North Carolina Council of Defense, World War I Papers, 1903–33, pt. 2, Military Collection, North Carolina Department of Archives and History.

40. Mary J. McCrorey to Mrs. Hope, 7 May 1920; "Mrs. Hope of the Cleveland Meeting, 1920," 29 May 1920; "What the Colored Women Are Asking of the Y.W.C.A."; "To the National Board of the Young Women's Christian Association"; Minutes of the Cleveland Meeting, 1920; "Minutes of the meeting held in the offices of the South Atlantic Field Committee, Richmond, Virginia, 3 July 1920"; and Mary J. McCrorey to Mrs. Hope, 27 Jan. 1921, all in box 5, NU 14-C-5, Y.W.C.A., Neighborhood Union Papers, Special Collections, Robert Woodruff Library, Atlanta University, Atlanta, Georgia. Mary J. McCrorey to Charlotte Hawkins Brown, 2 Apr. 1920, reel 2, #41, Brown Collection, SL.

41. Jacquelyn Dowd Hall, *Revolt against Chivalry: Jessie Daniel Ames and the Women's Campaign against Lynching*, rev. ed. (New York: Columbia University Press, 1987), 93; "Some Incidents," reel 1, #2, Brown Collection, SL.

42. Brown address, folder 1, box 1, ibid.; Hall, *Revolt against Chivalry*, 93–94.

43. "First Draft," section 2, folder 1, box 1, ibid.

44. "Statement of Negro Women in Session, Mar. 26, 1921," folder 1, box 1.

45. Folder 1, box 1, ibid. (emphasis added).

46. W. E. Morton to NAACP, file Voting, 10–30 Nov. 1920, C284, National Association for the Advancement of Colored People Papers, Library of Congress.

47. H. M. Kingsley to NAACP, 9 Nov. 1920, file Voting, 1–9 Nov. 1920, C284, NAACP Papers.

48. Charles McPerson to NAACP, file Voting, 1–9 Nov. 1920, C284, NAACP Papers. For a summary of reports from across the South, see "Disfranchisement of Colored Americans in the Presidential Election of 1920" ([1920]), file Voting, Dec. 1920, C284, NAACP Papers.

49. Glenda E. Gilmore, *Gender and Jim Crow: Women and the Politics of White Supremacy in North Carolina, 1896–1920* (Chapel Hill: University of North Carolina Press, 1996), 219–224.

III

CREATING THE STATE IN AN INDUSTRIALIZED NATION, 1900–1945

Between 1900 and 1945, American life was reshaped by an influx of immigrants, rapid technological advances, increasing urbanization, and a growing consumer culture. In the midst of these changes, progressives at the turn of the century and New Dealers during the 1930s worked to redefine the responsibility of the federal government to its citizens. No events contributed more to that redefinition than a crippling economic depression and two world wars.

Historians have customarily acknowledged that women were part of the development of the modern American state. Familiar names in textbooks include Mary Harris ("Mother") Jones, the fiery labor agitator who was a symbol of defiance wherever strikers gathered; Jane Addams, the humanitarian reformer who became a relentless foe of economic exploitation and an equally determined advocate of government regulation; and Eleanor Roosevelt, the brilliantly outspoken and activist First Lady. But women were more than just a few notables or an ancillary group. As progressive reformers and grassroots New Deal advocates, women broadened their sphere of influence from the family-centered world of the home into the formerly male world of politics and government, with great impact on public policy. As laborers and as the wives and daughters of laborers, women played a key role in the struggle to organize unions that would protect the rights of American workers. Women also endured the economic devastation of the Depression and exerted great effort and ingenuity to hold their families together. As members of the Roosevelt administration, they shared in the search for solutions. During World War II, women filled critical jobs in both the industrial workforce and the armed forces, contributing to an Allied victory. Women, in short, were *active creators* of America's history, not incidental to it.

This photograph of a young woman, nonchalantly posed atop the framing of a Chicago skyscraper in 1920, conveys both personal daring and a challenge to gender roles. (Photograph by Connie Colliers, courtesy of the Corbis/Bettman Archive.)

Including women's experiences does not in itself refocus history. But by valuing the experiences of both sexes, we get a fuller understanding of American life, creating a history in which, as Gerda Lerner suggests, "both *men and women* are the measure of significance."

DARLENE CLARK HINE
Rape and the Inner Lives of Black Women

The pull of economic opportunity outside the South and the push of disenfranchisement and the Jim Crow system within the South inspired a vast migration of African Americans northward around the turn of the century. Yet for many of the women who made their way to New York, Chicago, or smaller cities along the way, economic circumstances did not vastly improve. They continued to do the same domestic work as they had in Savannah, Birmingham, or Mobile. So why move? For African American women, the need to protect themselves and their daughters from sexual coercion was as pressing an impetus for migration as the need for work.

This particular motive for migration has long been hidden by what Hine calls a "culture of dissemblance." On the one hand, African American women have hesitated to speak about ever-present sexual threats in order to preserve their reputation for respectability. On the other hand, their vulnerability to sexual coercion and violence has a long history easily available in court records, slave narratives, autobiographies, and other sources. Remember Harriet Jacobs in the Block essay?

There were few ways for African American women, whether slave or free, to combat sexual violence. As Sharon Block's essay (pp. 135–45) reminds us, sexual coercion, a term she uses to include a broader range of experiences than suggested by the simpler term rape, was also a problem for white domestics. In what ways do you think the problem of the two groups were comparable? What differences did the legacy of slavery make?

One of the most remarked upon but least analyzed themes in Black women's history deals with Black women's sexual vulnerability and powerlessness as victims of rape and domestic violence. Author Hazel Carby put it baldly when she declared: "The institutionalized rape of black women has never been as powerful a symbol of black oppression as the spectacle of lynching. Rape has always involved patriarchal notions of women being, at best, not entirely unwilling accomplices, if not outwardly inviting a sexual attack. The links between black women and illicit sexuality consolidated during the antebellum years had powerful ideological consequences for the next hundred and fifty years."[1] I suggest that rape and the threat of rape influenced the development of a culture of dissemblance among Black women. By dissemblance I mean the behavior and attitudes of Black women that created the appearance of openness and disclosure but actually shielded the truth of their inner lives and selves from their oppressors. . . .

Virtually every known nineteenth-century female slave narrative contains a reference to rape. . . . Two works come immediately to mind: Harriet Jacob's *Incidents in the Life of a Slave Girl* (1861) and Elizabeth Keckley's *Behind the Scenes; or, Thirty Years a Slave, and Four Years in the White House* (1868).[2] . . . The combined influence of rape (or the threat

Reprinted from "Rape & the Inner Lives of Black Women in the Middle West" by Darlene Clark Hine, in *Signs* 14:4 (1989):912–20. Copyright © 1989 Darlene Clark Hine. Condensed and reprinted by permission of the author and *Signs*. Notes have been renumbered and edited.

of rape), domestic violence, and economic oppression is key to understanding the hidden motivations informing major social protest and migratory movements in Afro-American history.

Second only to Black women's concern for sexual preservation is the pervasive theme of the frustration attendant to finding suitable employment. . . .

Black women faced greater economic discrimination and had fewer employment opportunities than did Black men. Black women's work was the most undesirable and least remunerative of all work available to migrants.

As late as 1930 a little over three thousand Black women, or 15 percent, of the Black female labor force in Chicago were unskilled and semiskilled factory operatives. Thus, over 80 percent of all employed Black women continued to work as personal servants and domestics. . . .

Given that many Black women migrants were doomed to work in the same kinds of domestic service jobs they held in the South, one wonders why they bothered to move in the first place. . . .

In order to understand this historical migratory trend we need to understand the noneconomic motives propelling Black female migration. I believe that many Black women quit the South out of a desire to achieve personal autonomy and to escape both from sexual exploitation from inside and outside of their families and from the rape and threat of rape by white as well as Black males. To focus on the sexual and the personal impetus for Black women's migration in the first several decades of the twentieth century neither dismisses nor diminishes the significance of economic motives. . . .

My own research on the history of Black women in the Middle West had led me to questions about how, when, and under what circumstances the majority of them settled in the region. These questions have led to others concerning the process of Black women's migration across time, from the flights of runaway slaves in the antebellum period to the great migrations of the first half of the twentieth century. The most common, and certainly the most compelling, motive for . . . migrating was a desire to retain or claim some control and

ownership of their own sexual beings and the children they bore. . . .

Two things became immediately apparent as I proceeded with researching the history and reading the autobiographies of late nineteenth- and early twentieth-century migrating, or fleeing, Black women. First, that these women were sexual hostages and domestic violence victims in the South (or in other regions of the country) did not reduce their determination to acquire power to protect themselves and to become agents of social change once they settled in midwestern communities. Second, the fundamental tension between Black women and the rest of the society—referring specifically to white men, white women, and to a lesser extent, Black men—involved a multifaceted struggle to determine who would control their productive and reproductive capacities and their sexuality. . . . Their quest for autonomy, dignity, and access to opportunity to earn an adequate living was (and still is) complicated and frustrated by the antagonisms of race, class, and gender conflict and by differences in regional economics. At heart though, the relationship between Black women and the larger society has always been, and continues to be, adversarial.

. . . Black women, as a rule, developed and adhered to a cult of secrecy, a culture of dissemblance, to protect the sanctity of inner aspects of their lives. The dynamics of dissemblance involved creating the appearance of disclosure, or openness about themselves and their feelings, while actually remaining an enigma. Only with secrecy, thus achieving a self-imposed invisibility, could ordinary Black women accrue the psychic space and harness the resources needed to hold their own in the often one-sided and mismatched resistance struggle.

The inclination of the larger society to ignore those considered "marginal" actually enabled subordinate Black women to craft the veil of secrecy and to perfect the art of dissemblance. . . .

Black women did not possess the power to eradicate negative social and sexual images of their womanhood. Rather . . . in the face of the pervasive stereotypes and negative estimations of the sexuality of Black women, it was imperative that they collectively create alternative self-images and shield from scrutiny these private, empowering definitions of self. . . .

However, the self-imposed secrecy and the culture of dissemblance, coupled with the larger society's unwillingness to discard tired and worn stereotypes, has . . . led to ironic incidences of misplaced emphases. Until quite recently, for example, when historians talked of rape in the slavery experience they often bemoaned the damage this act did to the Black male's sense of esteem and respect. He was powerless to protect his woman from white rapists. Few scholars probed the effect that rape, the threat of rape, and domestic violence had on the psychic development of the female victims. In the late nineteenth and early twentieth centuries . . . lynching, not rape, became the most powerful and compelling symbol of Black oppression. Lynching, it came to be understood, was one of the major noneconomic reasons why southern Black men migrated north.

The culture of dissemblance assumed its most institutionalized form in the founding, in 1896, of the National Association of Colored Women's Clubs (NACW). This association of Black women quickly became the largest and most enduring protest organization in the history of Afro-Americans. Its size alone should have warranted the same degree of scholarly attention paid to Marcus Garvey's Universal Negro Improvement Association.

The primary objects of NACW attack were the derogatory images and negative stereotypes of Black women's sexuality. By 1914 it had a membership of fifty thousand, far surpassing the membership of every other protest organization of the time, including the National Association for the Advancement of Colored People. . . .

Mary Clurch Terrell, the first president of the NACW, declared in her initial presidential address that there were objectives of the Black women's struggle that could be accomplished only by the "mothers, wives, daughters, and sisters of this race." . . . She boldly announced, "We proclaim to the world that the women of our race have become partners in the great firm of progress and reform. . . . We refer to the fact that this is an association of colored women, because our peculiar status in this country. . . . seems to demand that we stand by ourselves."[3]

At the core of essentially every activity of NACW's individual members was a concern with creating positive images of Black women's sexuality. . . .

The twin obsessions with naming and combatting sexual exploitation tinted and shaped Black women's support even of the woman's suffrage movement. Nannie H. Burroughs, famed religious leader and founder of the National Training School for Women and Girls at Washington, D.C., cajoled her sisters to fight for the ballot. She asserted that with the ballot Black women could ensure the passage of legislation to win legal protection against rapists. Calling the ballot a "weapon of moral defense" she exploded, "when she [a Black woman] appears in court in defense of her virtue, she is looked upon with amused contempt. She needs the ballot to reckon with men who place no value upon her virtue."[4]

. . . At least one plausible consequence of this heightened mobilization of Black women was a decline in Black urban birth rates. As Black women became more economically self-sufficient, better educated, and more involved in self-improvement efforts . . . they had greater access to birth control information. As the institutional infrastructure of Black women's clubs, sororities, church-based women's groups, and charity organizations sunk roots into Black communities it encouraged its members to embrace those values, behaviors, and attitudes traditionally associated with the middle classes. To urban Black middle-class aspirants, the social stigma of having many children did, perhaps, inhibit reproduction. . . . Not having children was, perhaps for the very first time, a choice enjoyed by large numbers of Black women.

There were additional burdens placed upon and awards granted to the small cadre of single, educated, professional Black women who chose not to marry or to bear children. The more educated they were, the greater the sense of being responsible, somehow, for the advance of the race and for the elevation of Black womanhood. . . . The increased employment opportunities, whether real or imagined, and the culture of dissemblance enabled many migrating Black women to become financially independent and simultaneously to fashion socially useful and autonomous lives, while reclaiming control over their own sexuality and reproductive capacities.

... At some fundamental level all Black women historians are engaged in the process of historical reclamation. But it is not enough simply to reclaim those hidden and obscure facts and names of Black foremothers. This risks rendering a skewed history focused ... primarily on the articulate, relatively well-positioned members of the aspiring Black middle class. In synchrony with the reclaiming and narrating must be the development of an array of analytical frameworks which allow us to understand why Black women behave in certain ways and how they acquired agency....

NOTES

1. Hazel V. Carby, *Reconstructing Womanhood: The Emergence of the Afro-American Woman Novelist* (New York: Oxford University Press, 1987), p. 39.

2. Harriet A. Jacobs, *Incidents in the Life of a Slave*

Girl Written by Herself, ed. Jean Fagan Yellin (Cambridge, Mass.: Harvard University Press, 1987). Elizabeth Keckley, *Behind the Scenes; or, Thirty Years a Slave, and Four Years in the White House,* introduction by James Olney (New York: Oxford University Press, 1988). See also Rennie Simson, "The Afro-American Female: The Historical Construction of Sexual Identity," in *The Powers of Desire: The Politics of Sexuality,* ed. Ann Snitow, Sharon Thompson, and Christine Stansell (New York: Monthly Review Press, 1983), pp. 229–35.

3. Darlene Clark Hine, "Lifting the Veil, Shattering the Silence: Black Women's History in Slavery and Freedom," in *The State of Afro-American History: Past, Present, and Future,* ed. Darlene Clark Hine (Baton Rouge: Louisiana State University Press, 1986), pp. 223–49, esp. 236–37.

4. Rosalyn Terborg-Penn, "Woman Suffrage: 'First because We Are Women and Second because We Are Colored Women,'" *Truth: Newsletter of the Association of Black Women Historians* (April 1985), p. 9. Evelyn Brooks Barnett, "Nannie Burroughs and the Education of Black Women," in *The Afro-American Woman,* ed. Rosalyn Terborg-Penn and Sharon Harley (Port Washington, N.Y.: Kennikat, 1978), pp. 97–108.

JUDY YUNG

Unbound Feet: From China to San Francisco's Chinatown

The imbalance of men and women in the largest Chinese community on the West Coast was a source of immense frustration, especially after the Immigration Act of 1924 effectively barred Chinese wives, even those married to U.S. citizens, from entering the country. Pany Lowe, an American-born Chinese man, expressed the feelings of men: "I think most Chinese in this country like have their son go to China get married. Under this new law ..., can't do this. No allowed marry white girl. Not enough American-born Chinese to go around. China only place to get wife. Not allowed to bring them back. For Chinaman, very unjust."* Although the act was amended in 1930 to allow the entry of women who had been married to U.S. citizens prior to May 26, 1924, the process of

---

*Quoted in Judy Yung, *Unbound Feet: A Social History of Chinese Women in San Francisco* (Berkeley: University of California Press, 1995), p. 58.

gaining entrance was lengthy, costly, and humiliating for most Chinese women. Many men, like Pany Lowe, chose to visit their wives in China rather than subject them to the ordeal of immigration.

Judy Yung's essay traces the experiences of three women from Guangdong Province who arrived in San Francisco in 1922. Two, Wong Ah So and Law Shee Low, came from impoverished villages to join their husbands in arranged marriages. Wong Ah So was in for a major surprise when she discovered her "marriage" was part of a system of enslaving women in forced prostitution to fill what had become a pressing need in a Chinese bachelor society. The third woman came from a different background with different expectations. Jane Kwong Lee was an urbanized, unmarried "new woman" who came to the United States to further her education. While she would endure many of the same gender and racial restrictions as the other two women, differences in her class and education would make her experience—and the opportunities available to her—significantly different from that of other immigrant Chinese women in the 1920s.

Women's emancipation was heralded in San Francisco's Chinatown on the afternoon of November 2, 1902, when Sieh King King, an eighteen-year-old student from China and an ardent reformer, stood before a theater full of men and women and, according to newspaper accounts, "boldly condemned the slave girl system, raged at the horrors of foot-binding and, with all the vehemence of aroused youth, declared that men and women were equal and should enjoy the privileges of equals."[1] Her talk and her views on women's rights were inextricably linked with Chinese nationalism and the 1898 Reform Movement, which advocated that China emulate the West and modernize in order to throw off the yoke of foreign domination. Elevating the status of women to the extent that they could become "new women"—educated mothers and productive citizens—was part of this nationalist effort to strengthen and defend China against further encroachment.

What Sieh King King advocated on behalf of Chinese women—unbound feet, education, equal rights, and public participation—remained at the heart of social change for Chinese women for the next three decades. This was due largely to the continuous influence of nationalism and women's emancipation in China, the reform work of Protestant missionary women in Chinatown, and Chinese women's entry into the urban economy. By 1929, immigrant women had made considerable progress toward freeing themselves of social restrictions and moving into the public arena. Footbinding was no longer practiced, prostitution had been eradicated, and a substantial number of women were working outside the home, educating themselves and their daughters, and playing a more visible role in community affairs. This discussion of the lives of Chinese immigrant women from 1902, when Sieh King King introduced her feminist views in San Francisco, to 1929, the beginnings of the Great Depression, will illustrate how socioeconomic developments in China and the United States facilitated the unbinding of their feet and of their lives.

JOURNEY TO GOLD MOUNTAIN

At the time of Sieh King King's speech, China was still suffering under the stranglehold of Western imperialism and the inept rule of the Manchus. Life for the ordinary Chinese remained disrupted; survival was precarious. Consequently, many able-bodied peasants in Southeast China continued to emigrate overseas where kinfolk had already settled. Despite the Chinese Exclusion Acts and anti-Chinese hostilities, a good number went to California, the Gold Mountain. As increased numbers of Chinese sojourners became settlers, some found the economic means by which to get married or send for their wives and children from China. American immigration laws and the process of chain migration determined that most Chinese women would continue to come from the rural villages of Guangdong Province, where traditional gender roles still prevailed. Among these women were Wong Ah So and Law Shee Low, who both emigrated as obedient daughters in 1922 to escape poverty at home. Jane Kwong Lee, who also came the same year, was among the small number of urbanized "new women" who emigrated on their own for educational reasons. Together, these three women's stories provide insights into the gender roles and immigration experiences of Chinese women in the early twentieth century.

"I was born in Guangdong Province," begins Wong Ah So's story. "My father was sometimes a sailor and sometimes he worked on the docks, for we were very poor."[2] Patriarchal cultural values often put the daughter at risk when poverty strikes: From among the five children in the family, her mother chose to betroth her, the eldest daughter, to a Gold Mountain man in exchange for a bride price of 450 Mexican dollars.

> I was 19 when this man came to my mother and said that in America there was a great deal of gold. Even if I just peeled potatoes there, he told my mother I would earn seven or eight dollars a day, and if I was willing to do any work at all I would earn lots of money. He was a laundryman, but said he earned plenty of money. He was very nice to me, and my mother liked him, so my mother was glad to have me go with him as his wife.

Out of filial duty and economic necessity, Ah So agreed to sail to the United States with this laundryman, Huey Yow. He had a marriage certificate prepared and told her to claim him as her husband to the immigration officials in San Francisco, although as she admitted later, "I claimed to be the wife of Huey Yow, but in truth had not at any time lived with him as his wife."

In Law Shee Low's case, her family succumbed to poverty after repeated raids by roving bandits in the Chungshan District of Guangdong Province. Conditions became so bad that the family had to sell their land and give up their three servants; all four daughters had to quit school and help at home. Speaking of her arranged marriage to a Gold Mountain man, she said, "I had no choice; we were so poor. We had no food to go with rice, not even soy sauce or black bean paste. Some of our neighbors even had to go begging or sell their

daughters, times were so bad. So my parents thought I would have a better future in Gold Mountain."[3] Her fiancé said he was a clothing salesman in San Francisco and a Christian. He had a minister from Canton preside over the first "modern" wedding in his village. Law was eighteen and her husband, thirty-four. Nine months after the wedding, they sailed for America.

Born in 1902 to wealthy parents of the Toishan District, Guangdong Province (her family owned land and her father and uncle were successful businessmen in Australia), Jane Kwong Lee was able to acquire a Western education in the treaty port of Canton. There she was first exposed to American ideas of democracy and women's emancipation. During her last year in school, she was swept up by the May Fourth Movement, in which students agitated for political and cultural reforms in response to continuing foreign domination. At the time of her graduation from middle school, she observed that classmates were either entering technical institutions or getting married. "I thought otherwise," she said. "I enjoyed studying and I wanted to be economically independent. In that sense, it was clear in my mind that I had to have as much formal education as possible."[4]

Although she wanted to become a doctor, medical school was out of the question, as her father's remittances from Australia could no longer support both her and her younger brother's education. Arguing that graduates trained in American colleges and universities were drawing higher salaries in China than local graduates, Jane convinced her mother to sell some of their land in order to pay her passage to the United States. She then obtained a student's visa and sailed for America, planning to earn a doctorate and return home to a prestigious academic post. Jane Kwong Lee's class background, education, and early exposure to Western ideas would lead her to a different life experience in America than Law Shee Low and Wong Ah So, who came as obedient wives from sheltered and impoverished families.

The San Francisco Chinatown that the three women came to call home was different from the slum of "filth and depravity" of bygone days. After the 1906 earthquake and fire destroyed Chinatown, Chinese community leaders seized the opportunity to create a new "Oriental City" on the original site. The new Chinatown, in stark contrast to the old, was by appearance cleaner, healthier, and more modern with its wider paved streets, brick buildings, glass-plated storefronts, and pseudo-Chinese architecture. In an effort to establish order in the community, nurture business, and protect the growing numbers of families, the merchant elite and middle-class bourgeoisie established new institutions: Chinese schools, churches, a hospital, newspapers, and a flurry of civic and political organizations. Soon after the 1911 Revolution in China, queues and footbinding were eliminated, tong wars and prostitution reduced, and more of Chinatown's residents were dressing in Western clothing and adopting democratic ideas. Arriving in San Francisco's Chinatown at this juncture in time gave immigrant women such as Wong Ah So, Law Shee Low, and Jane Kwong Lee unprecedented opportunities to become "new women" in the modern era of Chinatown.

ESCAPING "A FATE WORSE THAN DEATH"

Upon landing in America, Wong Ah So's dreams of wealth and happiness vanished when she found out that her husband, Huey Yow, had in fact been paid $500 by a madam to procure her as a slave.

> When we first landed in San Francisco we lived in a hotel in Chinatown, a nice place, but one day, after I had been there for about two weeks, a woman came to see me. She was young, very pretty, and all dressed in silk. She told me that I was not really Huey Yow's wife, but that she had asked him to buy her a slave, that I belonged to her, and must go with her, but she would treat me well, and I could buy back my freedom, if I was willing to please, and be agreeable, and she would let me off in two years, instead of four if I did not make a fuss.

For the next year, Wong Ah So worked as a prostitute for the madam in various small towns. She was also forced to borrow $1,000 to pay off Huey Yow, who was harassing her and threatening her life. Soon after, she was sold to another madam in Fresno for $2,500. Meanwhile, her family in China continued to write her, asking for money. Even as her debts piled up and she became ill, she fulfilled her

filial obligation by sending $300 home to her mother, enclosed with a letter that read in part:

> Every day I have to be treated by the doctor. My private parts pain me so that I cannot have intercourse with men. It is very hard. . . . Next year I certainly will be able to pay off all the debts. Your daughter is even more anxious than her mother to do this. Your daughter will do her part so that the world will not look down upon us.

Then one evening at a tong banquet where she was working, Wong Ah So was recognized by a friend of her father's, who sought help from the Presbyterian Mission Home on her behalf. Ten days later, she was rescued and placed in the care of Donaldina Cameron, the director of the home. As she wrote, "I don't know just how it happened because it was all very sudden. I just know that it happened. I am learning English and to weave, and I am going to send money to my mother when I can. I can't help but cry, but it is going to be better. I will do what Miss Cameron says." A year later, after learning how to read Chinese and speak English and becoming a Christian, Ah So agreed to marry Louie Kwong, a merchant in Boise, Idaho.

Wong Ah So's story harks back to the plight of the many Chinese women who were brought to the United States as prostitutes to fill a specific need in the Chinese bachelor society. By the 1920s, however, the traffic had gone underground and was on the decline due to the Chinese exclusion laws, anti-prostitution legislation, and the efforts of Protestant missionaries. In 1870, the peak year of prostitution, 1,426 or 71 percent of Chinese women in San Francisco were listed as prostitutes. By 1900 the number had dropped to 339 or 16 percent; and by 1910, 92 or 7 percent. No prostitutes could be found in the 1920 census, although English- and Chinese-language newspaper accounts and the records of the Presbyterian Mission Home indicate that organized prostitution continued through the 1920s.[5]

Most well known for her rescue work in Chinatown, Donaldina Cameron was a product of the Social Gospel and Progressive movements, which sought to uplift the "uncivilized" throughout the world and eradicate political corruption and social vices in the nation's cities. Unable to work effectively among Chi-

Chinese women and children wait behind fences at the Immigration Station on Angel Island, near San Francisco. (Courtesy of California Historical Society, FN-18240.)

natown bachelors and spurned by white prostitutes, Cameron found her calling among Chinese prostitutes and slave girls. In turn, some Chinese prostitutes, calculating their chances in an oppressive environment with few options for improvement, saw the Mission Home as a way out of their problems. Cameron made it her crusade to free them from "a fate worse than death" by first rescuing them, and then inculcating them with Christian moral values. Numerous accounts in newspapers and religious publications describe in vivid detail the dangerous raids led by Cameron, who was credited with rescuing hundreds of Chinese slave girls during her forty years of service at the Presbyterian Mission Home.[6]

Once rescued, the young women were brought back to the Mission Home to be educated, trained in the domestic arts and industrial skills, and, most importantly, indoctrinated with Victorian moral values. The goal was to regroom them to enter society as Christian women. While some women chose to return to China under Christian escort, others opted to enter companionate marriages, pursue higher education, or become missionary workers. Wong Ah So—a direct beneficiary of the efforts of Protestant missionary women—was among the last to be rescued, Christianized, and married to a Chinese Christian.

IMMIGRANT WIVES AS INDISPENSABLE PARTNERS

Immigrant wives like Law Shee Low also found their lives transformed by the socioeconomic conditions in Chinatown. They did not find streets paved with gold, but practically speaking, they at least had food on the table and hope that through their hard work conditions might improve for themselves and their families. Although women were confined to the domestic sphere within the borders of Chinatown, their contributions as homemakers, wage earners, and culture bearers made them indispensable partners to their husbands in their struggle for economic survival. Their indispensability, combined with changing social attitudes toward women in Chinatown, gave some women leverage to shape gender arrangements within their homes and in the community.

Upon arrival in San Francisco, Law Shee Low moved into a one-room tenement apartment in Chinatown with her husband, where she lived, worked, and gave birth to eleven children, eight of whom survived. While her husband worked in a restaurant that catered to black customers on the outskirts of Chinatown, Law stayed home and took in sewing. Like other immigrant women who followed traditional gender roles, Law believed that the proper place for a woman was at home. As she recalls those days,

> There was no time to feel imprisoned; there was so much to do. We had to cook, wash the clothes and diapers by hand, the floors, and sew whenever we had a chance to sit still. It was the same for all my neighbors. We were all good, obedient, and diligent wives. All sewed; all had six or seven children. Who had time to go out?

Fortunately for Law Shee Low, her husband turned out to be cooperative, supportive, and devoted. Until he developed a heart condition in the 1950s, he remained the chief breadwinner, first cooking at a restaurant, then picking fruit in Suisun [California], sewing at home during the depression, and finally working in the shipyards during World War II. Although he refused to help with housecleaning or childcare, he did all the shopping, cooked the rice, and hung out the wash. In his own way, he showed concern for his wife. "When he was afraid I wasn't eating, he would tell me to eat more. Even though it was an arranged marriage, we got along well. I didn't complain that he went out every day. We hardly talked. Good or bad, we just struggled along as we had work to do."

As far as children were concerned Law Shee Low, like her neighbors, had not known how to interfere with nature. "We didn't know about birth control. We would become pregnant every year without realizing it. Even if we didn't want it, we didn't have the money to go see the doctor." All of Law's children were born at home, with the help of neighbors or the local midwife. Fortunately, her husband wanted children and was more than willing to provide for them all regardless of sex. "Other men would scold their children and beat them.

One woman who had four children told me her husband would drag her out of bed and beat her because she didn't want to have any more children. We heard all kinds of sad stories like that, but my husband never picked on me like that."

It was not until her children were older that Law Shee Low went out to work in the sewing factories and to the Chinese movies on Saturdays, but she still did not leave the confines of Chinatown. Prior to that, she went out so seldom that one pair of shoes lasted her ten years. Since their first responsibility was to their families, many immigrant wives like Law found themselves housebound, with no time to learn English or to participate in social activities outside the home. Their husbands continued to be the chief breadwinner, to hold the purse strings, and to be their liaison to the outside world. But in the absence of the mother-in-law, immigrant wives usually ruled the household and assumed the responsibility of disciplinarian, culture-bearer, and of maintaining the integrity of their families. With few exceptions, they were hardworking, frugal, and tolerant, faithful and respectful to their husbands, and self-sacrificing toward their children. As such, they were indispensable partners to their husbands in their efforts to establish and sustain family life in America. And although they presented a submissive image in public, many immigrant women were known to "wear the pants" at home.

Overall, as compared to their predecessors, immigrant women in the early twentieth century were less tolerant of abuses to their persons and more resourceful in upgrading their status, thanks to the influence of the press, the support of Protestant organizations in the community, and a legal system that was sympathetic toward abused women. Although most immigrant wives like Law Shee Low could not read the Chinese newspapers, they were affected by public opinion as filtered through their husbands, neighbors, and social reformers looking after their interests. Law noted that after the 1911 Revolution it was no longer considered "fashionable" to have bound feet, concubines, or slave girls. And as housebound as Law was, she was aware of the mission homes that rescued prostitutes, helped abused women, and provided education for children and immigrant women.

CHINESE WOMEN
IN THE LABOR MARKET

Compared to Wong Ah So and Law Shee Low, Jane Kwong Lee had an easier time acclimating to life in America. Not only was she educated, Westernized, English-speaking, and unencumbered by family responsibilities, but she also had the help of affluent relatives who provided her with room and board, financial support, and important contacts that enabled her eventually to strike out on her own.

Arriving in the middle of a school semester and therefore unable to enroll in a college, she decided to look for a job. In spite of her educational background and qualifications, she found that only menial jobs and domestic service were opened to her. "At heart I was sorry for myself; I wished I were a boy," she wrote in her autobiography. "If I were a boy, I could have gone out into the community, finding a job somewhere as many newcomers from China had done." But as a Chinese woman, she had to bide her time and look for work appropriate for her race and gender. Thus, until she could be admitted to college, and during the summers after she enrolled at Mills College, Jane took whatever jobs were open to Chinese women. She tried embroidery work at a Chinatown factory, sorting vegetables in the wholesale district, working as a live-in domestic for a white family, peeling shrimp, sorting fruit at a local cannery, and sewing flannel nightgowns at home.

As was true for European immigrant women, the patterns of work for Chinese women were shaped by the intersection of the local economy, ethnic traditions, language and job skills, and family and child-care needs, but in addition, race was an influential factor. At the time of Jane's arrival, San Francisco was experiencing a period of growth and prosperity. Ranked the eighth largest city in the country, it was the major port of trade for the Pacific Coast and touted as the financial and corporate capital of the West. Jobs were plentiful in the city's three largest economic sectors—domestic and personal service, trade and transportation, and manufacturing and mechanical industries—but they were filled according to a labor market stratified by race and gender, with Chinese men occupying the lowest tier as laborers, servants, factory workers, laundrymen, and small merchants, while Chinese women, handicapped further by gender, worked primarily in garment and food-processing factories for low piece-rate wages. With inadequate child-care services in the community, most seamstresses worked with their children close by or had their babies strapped to their backs.

For Jane Kwong Lee, being Chinese and a woman was a liability in the job market, but because she spoke English, was educated, and had good contacts among Chinese Christians, she was better off than most other immigrant women. She eventually got a scholarship at Mills College and part-time work teaching Chinese school and tutoring Chinese adults in English at the Chinese Episcopal Church in Oakland. After earning her bachelor's degree in sociology, she married, had two children, and returned to Mills College, where she received a master's degree in sociology and economics in 1933. She then dedicated herself to community service, working many years as coordinator of the Chinese YWCA and as a journalist and translator for a number of Chinatown newspapers.

For most immigrant women, joining the labor market proved to be a double-edged sword: On the one hand, their earnings helped to support their families and elevate their socioeconomic status; on the other hand, they became exploited laborers in the factory system, adding work and stress to their already burdensome lives. On the positive side, however, working outside the home offered women social rewards—a new sense of freedom, accomplishment, and camaraderie. They were no longer confined to the home, they were earning money for themselves or the family, and they were making new acquaintances and becoming exposed to new ideas. As Jane Kwong Lee observed, having money to spend made the women feel more liberated in America than in China: "They can buy things for themselves, go out to department stores to choose their own clothes instead of sewing them."

FIRST STEPS TOWARD
SOCIAL ACTIVISM

For working-class women like Law Shee Low, family and work responsibilities consumed all their time and energy, leaving little left over for self-improvement or leisure activities, and even less for community involvement. This was not the case for a growing group of educated and professional women like Jane Kwong Lee, who, inspired by Christianity, Chinese nationalism, and Progressivism, took the first steps toward social activism. Prior to the 1911 Revolution in their homeland, Chinese women in America followed the tradition of remaining publicly invisible. They seldom ventured out of their homes except perhaps to shop or go to the Chinese opera, where they sat in a segregated section apart from the men.

The Protestant churches and Chinese YWCA were the first to encourage Chinese women's participation in organized activities outside the home, as evidenced by the small but visible number of them at Sunday services, English classes, meetings, outings, and other church-sponsored programs. Some of the churches also helped organize Chinese women's societies to encourage involvement in Christian activities. Members of these groups met regularly to have lunch or socialize, and paid dues to help support the work of Bible women in their home villages in China.[7]

Aside from Christianity, the intense nationalistic spirit that took hold in the early twentieth century also affected Chinese women in far-reaching ways. Not only did the call for modernization include the need to improve conditions for Chinese women, but reformers also solicited women's active participation in national salvation work. Fund-raising for disaster relief and the revolution in China opened up opportunities for women to become involved in the community, develop leadership abilities, and move into the male-dominated public sphere. The Tongmenghui, the revolutionary party founded by Dr. Sun Yat-sen to overthrow the Qing dynasty and establish a republic in China, was the earliest organization to accept women into its ranks. While women in China participated in benefit performances, enlisted in the army, and engaged in dangerous undercover work, women in San Francisco also did their share for the revolutionary effort—making patriotic speeches, donating money and jewelry for the cause, and helping with Red Cross work—sometimes under the auspices of Protestant churches, other times under the banner of the Women's Young China Society.

Although the success of the revolution and the establishment of a republic in China failed to bring peace and prosperity to the country, it did have a lasting impact on the lives of Chinese American women. As Jane Kwong Lee observed, "After the establishment of the Republic of China, Chinese women in this country picked up the forward-looking trend for equality with men. They could go to school, speak in public places, have their feet free from binding, and go out to work in stores and small factories if they needed to work."[8]

Arriving as a liberated woman at the time when she did, Jane did not hesitate to join other women in becoming socially active in the Chinatown community. In her capacity as a community worker at the Chinese YWCA, she made house visits, wrote articles that were published in the local newspapers, and implemented programs that benefited Chinese women in the community. She was particularly known for her loud and forceful speeches that she delivered in Chinese at churches and street corners in support of Christianity and nationalist causes, and before Chinatown organizations on behalf of the Chinese YWCA. Jane also made presentations in English to groups interested in learning more about Chinese culture, and traveled as a Chinese delegate to YWCA functions outside of Chinatown. On one of these occasions, she was so moved by a discussion on racial discrimination that she surprised herself and African Americans at a YWCA meeting by speaking up for them. "I said, you are all equal; nobody is inferior to another."[9]

CONCLUSION

As Sieh King King had advocated in 1902, Chinese women unbound their feet and began to unbind their lives in America during the first three decades of the twentieth century. Most, like Law Shee Low and Wong Ah So, had immigrated for a better livelihood but found themselves exploited as prostitutes or working wives at the bottom of a labor market stratified by race and gender. Some, like Jane Kwong Lee, had come from a privileged background yet still encountered discrimination in the workplace and in the larger American society. But like many other immigrant women before them, they not only persevered and survived, but took advantage of new circumstances to improve their lives and contribute to the well-being of their families and community. Even as immigrant women began to enjoy their new roles as emancipated women, economic depression set in and war loomed large in their homeland. The challenges of the 1930s and 1940s—economic survival and the war effort on two fronts—would lead to even greater dramatic changes in their lives, allowing them to take the first steps toward fuller participation in American society.

NOTES

1. *San Francisco Chronicle*, November 3, 1902, p. 7.

2. Wong Ah So's story is taken from "Story of Wong Ah So—Experiences as a Prostitute," *Orientals and Their Cultural Adjustment*, Social Science Source Documents, no. 4 (Nashville: Social Science Institute, Fisk University, 1946), pp. 31–35; and Donaldina Cameron, "The Story of Wong So," *Women and Missions* 2, no. 5 (August 1925):169–72.

3. Law Shee Low's story is based on her interview with Sandy Lee, May 2, 1982; and interview with author, October 20, 1988.

4. Jane Kwong Lee's story is based on her unpublished autobiography, "A Chinese American," in the possession of her daughter Priscilla Holmes.

5. See Lucie Cheng Hirata, "Free, Indentured, Enslaved: Chinese Prostitutes in Nineteenth-Century California," *Signs: Journal of Women in Culture and Society* 5, no. 1 (autumn 1979):3–29. The figures for 1900, 1910, and 1920 are based on my computations from the U.S. National Archives, Record Group 29, "Census of U.S. Population" (manuscript), San Francisco, California.

6. See Peggy Pascoe, *Relations of Rescue: The Search for Female Moral Authority in the American West, 1874–1939* (New York: Oxford University Press, 1990).

7. See Wesley Woo, "Protestant Work among the Chinese in the San Francisco Bay Area, 1850–1920," Ph.D. dissertation, University of California, Berkeley, 1983.

8. Jane Kwong Lee, "Chinese Women in San Francisco," *Chinese Digest* (June 1938):8.

9. Jane Kwong Lee, interview with author, November 2, 1988.

ANNELISE ORLECK

From the Russian Pale to Labor Organizing in New York City

The pale of Jewish settlement was a territory within Russia to which Jews were restricted during the eighteenth and nineteenth centuries and where they were frequently subjected to ferocious outbursts of anti-Semitic violence. Crossing from the pale to the teeming streets of Manhattan's Lower East Side was a frontier crossing of major proportions. Yet two million European Jews who came to the United States between 1880 and 1924 made it across, among them the remarkable young women who are the subjects of Orleck's lively and informative essay.

Like so many of their fellow immigrants, Rose Schneiderman, Fannia Cohn, Clara Lemlich, and Pauline Newman gravitated to one of the earliest industries to employ women—the garment industry. Based in New York City, the industry had long provided countless married women with piecework to take back to dimly lit tenements, where they often enlisted the help of grandmothers and children. By the turn of the century, much of the work had been transferred to sweatshops and factories that were notorious for their low wages and squalid working conditions. Because so many of the female employees were young, single women who presumably regarded their work as a temporary necessity until rescued by marriage, labor leaders usually assumed that the

From *Common Sense and a Little Fire: Women and Working-Class Politics in the United States, 1900–1965* by Annelise Orleck. Copyright © 1995 by the University of California Press. Used by permission of the publisher.

women were virtually unorganizable. Yet between 1909 and 1915, women garment workers in New York as well as in other cities exploded in labor militancy. By 1919, half of all women garment workers belonged to trade unions and many had joined the suffrage struggle as well. The role these four young women played in this process is the focus of Orleck's essay.

What experiences shaped their political consciousness and propelled their activism? As young girls forced to work and forego school and college, how did they educate themselves and for what purpose? Who were their allies and why were these alliances so necessary, yet so unstable? How was the balancing act required of the four with respect to male trade unionists and elite female reformers similar to that required of Charlotte Hawkins Brown, albeit in a different context (see pp. 286–96)? What attracted these young working women to suffrage? What is meant by the term "industrial feminists"?

During the summer of 1907, when New York City was gripped by a severe economic depression, a group of young women workers who had been laid off and were facing eviction took tents and sleeping rolls to the verdant Palisades overlooking the Hudson River. While rising rents and unemployment spread panic among the poor immigrants of Manhattan's Lower East Side, these teenagers lived in a makeshift summer camp, getting work where they could find it, sharing whatever food and drink they could afford, reading, hiking, and gathering around a campfire at night to sing Russian and Yiddish songs. "Thus we avoided paying rent or, worse still, being evicted," Pauline Newman later recalled. "Besides which, we liked living in the open— plenty of fresh air, sunshine and the lovely Hudson for which there was no charge."[1]

Away from the clatter of the shops and the filth of Lower East Side streets, the young women talked into the night, refreshed by what Newman called "the cool of the evening, glorious sunsets, the moon and stars." They shared personal concerns as well as shop-floor gripes—worries about love, about the future, and about the pressing problems of housing and food.

Their cliffside village meant more to Newman and her friends than a summer escape. They had created a vibrant alternative to the tenement life they found so oppressive, and their experience of it had set them to wondering. Perhaps the same sense of joy and comradeship could help workers transcend the drudgery of the garment shops and form the basis for effective organizing.[2]

At season's end, they emerged with strengthened bonds and renewed resolve to organize their communities around issues that the recent depression had brought into sharp relief: the need for stabilized rent and food prices, improved working conditions, and housing for the poor.[3]

The spirit of intimacy and solidarity that pervaded the summer of 1907 would inspire much of Pauline Newman's later organizing. Indeed, it became a model for the vision of change that Newman shared with her fellow Jewish immigrant radicals Fannia Cohn, Rose Schneiderman and Clara Lemlich. The four women moved to political struggle not simply by the need for better wages, hours and working conditions but also, in Newman's words, by a need to ensure that "poverty did not deprive us from finding joy and satisfaction in things of the spirit."[4] This essay examines the early careers of these four remarkable organizers and the role they played in building a militant working women's movement during the first decades of the twentieth century.

For even as girls, these marginally educated immigrants wanted to be more than . . . shop-floor drudges. They wanted lives filled with beauty—with friendships, books, art, music, dance, fresh air, and clean water. "A working girl is a human being," Newman would later tell a legislative committee investigating factory conditions, "with a heart, with desires, with aspirations, with ideas and ideals." That image nourished Newman, Schneiderman, Lemlich, and Cohn throughout their long careers. And it focused them on a single goal: to reshape U.S. society so that "working girls" like themselves could fulfill some of their dreams.[5]

The four women moved through strikingly different cultural milieus over the course of long careers that would carry them in different directions. Still, they each bore the imprint of the shared culture in which they were raised, first in Eastern Europe and then in New York City. That common experience gave them a particular understanding of gender, class, and ethnicity that shaped their later activism and political thought.

All four were born in the Russian-dominated pale of Jewish settlement during the last two decades of the nineteenth century. Rose Schneiderman was born in the Polish village of Saven in 1882; Fannia Cohn was born in Kletsk, Poland, in 1885; Clara Lemlich was born in the Ukrainian village of Gorodok in 1886; and Pauline Newman was born in Kovno, Lithuania, around 1890.[6]

They were ushered into a world swept by a firestorm of new ideas, where the contrasting but equally messianic visions of orthodox Judaism and revolutionary Socialism competed for young minds. The excitement of living in a revolutionary era imbued these young women with a faith in progress and a belief that political commitment gave life meaning. It also taught them, at an early age, that gender, class, and ethnicity were fundamental social categories and essential building blocks for political change. Being born into turbulence does not in itself make a child into a political activist. But the changes sweeping the Russian Empire toward the end of the nineteenth century shaped the consciousness of a generation of Eastern European Jews who contributed, in wildly disproportionate numbers, to revolutionary movements in Russia and to the labor and radical movements in the United States.[7]

The four were exposed to Marxist ideas at a tender age. As Eastern Europe shifted uneasily from feudalism to capitalism in the latter part of the nineteenth century, class analysis became part of the common parlance of young people in Jewish towns and villages. "Behind every other volume of Talmud in those years, there was a volume of Marx," one union organizer recalled of his small Polish town. Clara Lemlich grew up on revolutionary tracts and songs; Fannia Cohn considered herself a committed Socialist by the age of sixteen.[8]

Their awareness of ethnicity was even more keen. As Jews in Eastern Europe, the four

learned young that ethnic identity was a double-edged sword. It was a source of strength and solace in their bitterly poor communities, but it also enabled Tsarist authorities to single Jews out and sow seeds of suspicion among their peasant neighbors. Jews living under Russian rule were made painfully aware of their status as permanent "others" in the land where they had lived for centuries. Clara Lemlich's family lived not far from Kishinev, where in 1903 the Tsar's government openly and unabashedly directed an orgy of anti-Jewish violence that shocked the world. In cosmopolitan Minsk, where she had gone to study, Fannia Cohn watched with dismay as the revolutionary populist organization she had joined began mouthing the same anti-Semitic conspiracy theories spewed by the government they despised. Frustration turned to fear when her brother was almost killed in yet another pogrom.[9]

Sex was just as distinct a dividing line as class and ethnicity. Eastern European Jews had observed a strict sexual division of labor for more than a thousand years. But by the late nineteenth century, as political and economic upheaval jolted long-accepted ways of thinking, sex roles too were being questioned. And so the four girls' understandings of gender were informed both by traditional Jewish conceptions of womanhood and by the challenges issued by new political movements.

In traditional Jewish society, mothers were also entrepreneurs. Clara Lemlich, Pauline Newman, and Rose Schneiderman were all raised by mothers who were skilled businesswomen. Jewish mothers' success in this role grew out of and reinforced a belief that women were innately suited to competition in the economic sphere. In contrast to the image of the sheltered middle-class housewife then dominant in the United States, Eastern European Jewish religious tradition glorified strong, economically sophisticated wives and mothers.

But as much as women's entrepreneurship was respected, a far higher premium was placed on study and prayer. And that, religious tradition dictated, could be performed only by men. A woman was expected to be pious, to read the vernacular Yiddish—rather than ancient Hebrew—translation of the Bible, and perhaps to attend women's services at the synagogue. But her primary religious role was

Medical Examination at Ellis Island. "The day of the emigrants' arrival in New York was the nearest earthly likeness to the final day of Judgment, when we have to prove our fitness to enter Heaven." The words are those of a sympathetic journalist who shared the anxiety-ridden experience awaiting immigrants at the port of entry, usually Ellis Island. Failing the medical test could mean deportation. (Courtesy of Brown Brothers, Sterling, Pennsylvania.)

as keeper of the home. Formal religious education was offered only to males.[10] Because Eastern European Jewish women had to fight for every scrap of education they received, many began to see education as the key to independence from all masters. This view would strongly influence their political organizing once in the United States.

The four emigrated as part of the mass movement that brought two million Jews from Eastern Europe to the United States between 1881 and 1924. Schneiderman came in 1890, Newman in 1901, Lemlich in 1903, and Cohn in 1904. Like most of their compatriots, they arrived in New York Harbor and settled on Manhattan's Lower East Side, the largest settlement of Eastern European Jews in the United States.[11] The newcomers were tantalized by the exciting diversions that New York life promised: libraries, theater, music, department stores, and amusement parks. But they had neither time nor money to indulge in such pleasures, for all of them soon found themselves laboring long hours to support their families.

At an age when most girls in the United States were still in grade school, immigrant working girls like Newman spent twelve- to fourteen-hour days in the harshest of atmospheres. Their bodies and minds reeled from the shock of the shops: the deafening noise, the brutal pace, and the rebukes of foremen. Some children were able to slough off the hardship with jokes and games. Others, realizing that they were destined to spend their youth in dank factories rather than in classrooms or schoolyards, grew sullen and withdrawn.

Clara Lemlich, like so many others, was quickly disillusioned by her first job in a New York garment shop: "I went to work two weeks after landing in this country. We worked from sunrise to set seven days a week. . . . Those who worked on machines had to carry the machines on their back both to and from work. . . . The shop we worked in had no central heating, no electric power. . . . The hissing of the machines, the yelling of the foreman, made life unbearable."[12]

Anger drove young women workers like Lemlich and Newman to band together. Untrained and largely unschooled, these young women were drawn to Socialism and trade unionism not because they felt an ideological affinity but because they had a desperate need to improve their working conditions. "I knew very little about Socialism," Lemlich recalled. "[But] the girls, whether Socialist or not, had many stoppages and strikes." Newman too found that for most young women workers, political understanding followed action rather than precipitating it: "We of the 1909 vintage knew nothing about the economics of . . . industry or for that matter about economics in general. All we knew was the bitter fact that, after working seventy and eighty hours in a seven day week, we did not earn enough to keep body and soul together." These assertions reveal much about the political development of the tens of thousands of women garment workers who would soon amaze New York and the nation with their militancy.[13]

Shop-floor culture fed the young women's emerging sense of political identity. Working alongside older men and women who discussed Socialism daily, they began to feel a sense of belonging to a distinct class of people in the world: workers. This allegiance would soon become as important to them as their Judaism. The shops also provided an opportunity for bonding with other women. Slowly, out of their workplace experiences, they began to develop a complex political identity in which class, gender and ethnicity overlapped. Young women workers were moved by the idea of sisterhood. It captured their own experiences in the sex-segregated shops where they worked. The majority of New York's garment workers were little more than girls, and the relationships they forged with factory friends were similar to those of schoolgirls—intense, melodramatic, and deeply loyal. They were teenage confidantes as well as fellow workers, and they relied on shop-floor rapport to soften the harshness of factory life.[14] For young immigrant women trying to build lives in a new land, such bonds were powerful and lasting. From these shop-floor friendships would soon evolve the ties of union sisterhood.[15]

Pauline Newman and her co-workers at the Triangle Shirtwaist Factory literally grew up together. Only twelve when she first came to Triangle, Newman was assigned to a corner known as "the kindergarten," where workers as young as eight, nine, or ten years old trimmed threads from finished garments. They labored, Newman later recalled, "from 7:30 A.M. to 6:30 at night when it wasn't busy.

When the season was on we worked till 9 o'clock. No overtime pay." Their only taste of a normal childhood came through the songs and games they invented to help pass the time, the stories they told and the secrets they shared.[16]

By the early twentieth century, New York State had passed laws prohibiting night work for children. But little attempt was made to enforce them. On the rare occasions when an inspector showed up at her factory, Newman remembered, "the employers were always tipped off.... 'Quick,' they'd say, 'Into the boxes!' And we children would climb into the big box the finished shirts were stored in. Then some shirts were piled on top of us and when the inspector came—No children." In a way it was fun, Newman remembered. They thought they were playing a game like hide and seek.[17]

But it wasn't really a game. Children who had to help support their parents grew up quickly. Rose Schneiderman was thirteen when her mother begged United Hebrew Charities, an organization run by middle-class German Jews, to find her daughter a "respectable job" at a department store. Retail jobs were deemed more respectable than factory work because the environment was more pleasant and sexual harassment was thought to be less common. Deborah Schneiderman worried that factory work would sully Rose's reputation and make her less marriageable. A job as a fashionable salesgirl, she hoped, would usher Rose into the middle class. The single mother who had fed her children on charity food baskets and had been forced to place them in orphanages was grimly determined to help them escape poverty.

But then as now, pink-collar jobs paid significantly less than industrial work. Anxious to free her mother from the rigors of maintaining their tenement building, Schneiderman left her job in Ridley's department store for the harsher and more morally suspect conditions of an industrial shop. Making linings for caps and hats, she immediately raised her weekly income from $2.75 to $6. As the sole supporter of her family, the sixteen-year-old hoped to work her way up quickly to a skilled job in the cap trade.[18]

Clara Lemlich's family also relied on her wages, particularly because her father was unemployed. She aspired to the skilled position of draper, one of the highest-paid positions a woman could attain in the dressmaking trade. Despite terrible working conditions, many ambitious young women chose garment work over other jobs because it seemed to offer their greatest chance to acquire skills and command high wages. When these hopes were dashed, some young workers grew angry. That anger was fanned and channeled by older women in the shops who were itching to challenge the authority of the bosses.[19]

That is what happened to Rose Schneiderman, who, like many skilled women garment workers, was blocked from advancement by the unofficial gender hierarchy at her factory. Finding that all the highest-paid jobs in her cap-making shop were reserved for men, Schneiderman asked around about ways to break through those barriers. When she approached fellow worker Bessie Braut with her concerns, Schneiderman was initiated simultaneously into trade unionism, Socialism, and feminism. Schneiderman recalled, "Bessie was an unusual person. Her beautiful eyes shone out of a badly pockmarked face and the effect was startling. An outspoken anarchist, she made a strong impression on us. She wasted no time in giving us the facts of life—that the men in our trade belonged to a union and were, therefore, able to better their conditions. She added pointedly that it would be a good thing for the lining-makers to join a union along with the trimmers, who were all women."[20]

Schneiderman, Braut, and several other workers called on the secretary-treasurer of the United Cloth Hat and Cap Makers to request union recognition for their fledgling local of trimmers and lining makers. Within a few days they had enough signatures to win a charter for their local, and Schneiderman was elected secretary.[21]

Surprising even herself, the once-shy redhead soon found she could be an eloquent and fierce advocate for her fellow workers. In recognition of her growing reputation, the capmakers elected her to the Central Labor Union of New York. Deborah Schneiderman was disturbed by the turn Rose's life was taking. She warned Rose that if she pursued a public life she would never find a husband. No man wants a woman with a big mouth, her mother said.[22]

In the flush of excitement at the praise and warmth suddenly coming her way, young Rose did not stop to worry. In organizing, she had found both a calling and a world of friends. She had no intention of turning back. "It was such an exciting time," she wrote later. "A new life opened up for me. All of a sudden I was not lonely anymore. . . . It was the beginning of a period that molded all my subsequent life."[23]

Fannia Cohn, too, chose garment work as her path to a career. And like Schneiderman, Lemlich, and Newman, she found a community there. Unlike the others, however, she did not enter a garment factory looking for work that paid well. She was a comfortable middle-class woman in search of a trade ripe for unionizing.

Cohn arrived in New York in 1904 and moved in with her affluent cousins. There was little about her early days in the United States that was comparable to the hard-pressed scrambling for a living that the Schneidermans, Lemlichs, and Newmans experienced. "My family suggested that I complete my studies and then join the labor movement but I rejected this as I did not want to come into it from 'without' but from 'within.' I realized then that if I wanted to really understand the mind, the aspirations of the workers, I should experience the life of the worker in a shop."[24] In 1905, Fannia Cohn became a sleevemaker. For a year she moved from shop to shop until, in the "white goods" trade, she found the organizing challenge she was looking for.

Shops that manufactured white goods— underwear, kimonos, and robes—were considered particularly hard to organize. Production took place in tiny sweatshops, not large factories, and the manufacturing process had been broken down into small tasks that required little skill. The majority of white goods workers were immigrant girls under the age of fifteen. And because they came from a wide range of backgrounds—Jewish, Italian, Syrian, Turkish, and Greek—it was difficult for them to communicate with each other, let alone organize. As a result, these workers were among the lowest paid in the garment trades.

At twenty, Cohn was an elder in the trade. With her high school education and fluency in three languages, she was seen as a mother figure by many of the adolescents in the shops. She and a handful of older women workers began to operate as mentors, meeting with the girls in each shop and identifying potential leaders. Cohn taught her co-workers to read,

write, and speak in public, hoping they would channel those skills into the union struggle. Cohn had already created the role that she would play throughout her career: an educator of younger workers.[25]

Education was a primary driving force in the metamorphosis of all four young women from shop workers to union organizers. From the isolated towns and restive cities of Eastern Europe, where gender, class, and ethnicity stymied Jewish girls' hopes for education, the lure of free public schooling in the United States beckoned powerfully. Having to drop out of school to work was more than a disappointment for many Jewish immigrant girls; it was their first great disillusionment with the dream of America. And they did not give that dream up easily.

"When I went to work," Rose Schneiderman remembered, "I was determined to continue my studies." Her only option was to attend one of the many night schools then open to immigrant workers in New York. Having carried with her from Poland the ideal of education as an exalted, liberating process, she was disgusted by the mediocre instruction she encountered and felt betrayed by teachers who seemed to be patronizing her. "I enrolled and went faithfully every evening for about four weeks. But I found that . . . the instructor seemed more interested in getting one-hundred-percent attendance than in giving one-hundred-percent instruction. He would joke and tell silly stories. . . . I soon realized I was wasting my time." Schneiderman left the evening school but did not stop studying. She asked older co-workers if she could borrow books that she had discussed with them in the shop. In the evenings, she read with her mother at home. Serializations of Emile Zola's J'Accuse and other contemporary writings in the Yiddish evening paper Abendblatt gave Rose a taste for literature. "I devoured everything I could get my hands on."[26]

Clara Lemlich was an equally avid reader. At the end of each twelve-hour day stitching shirtwaists, she would walk from her factory to the East Broadway branch of the New York Public Library. There she read the library's entire collection of Russian classics. "I was so eager to learn things," she later recalled. When she tired of solitary study, Lemlich joined a free night school on Grand Street. She returned home late each night, ate the dinner her mother had kept warm for her, then slept for just a few hours before rising again for work.[27]

Not surprisingly, young women like Schneiderman, Newman, and Lemlich turned to radical politics to fulfill their desire for a life of the mind. If no other school was available, then what Pauline Newman called "the school of solidarity" would have to do. Membership in the Socialist Party and in unions, tenant organizations, and benevolent societies provided immigrant women with an opportunity to learn and study that most would never have gotten otherwise. And as Newman put it, "Because they were hitherto deprived of any tutorship, they at once became ardent students."[28]

Pauline Newman was just fifteen when she first knocked on the doors of the Socialist Literary Society. Although women were not yet allowed to join, she was permitted to attend classes. The Literary Society was a revelation to the young worker. There she was introduced to the writings of Shakespeare, George Eliot, and Thomas Hardy and personally met writers like Jack London and Charlotte Perkins Gilman, who came to speak there. Gratitude, however, didn't stop her from joining a successful petition drive to admit women to the society.

For Newman—as for Clara Lemlich, who attended Marxist theory classes at the Socialist Party's Rand School—studying was more than a distraction from work. The "desire to get out of the shop," Newman wrote later, "to learn, to understand, became the dominant force in my life." But unlike many immigrants, who saw schooling as a ladder out of the working class, both she and Lemlich were committed to helping others rise with them. So Newman and Lemlich formed study groups that met during lunch hours and after work to share what they were learning with their friends.[29]

"We tried to educate ourselves," Newman remembered of her co-workers at the Triangle Shirtwaist Factory. "I would invite the girls to my room and we took turns reading poetry in English to improve our understanding of the language." Because they had to steal the time to study, the young women approached everything they read with a heightened sensitivity. And when something they were reading struck a chord of recognition, seemed to reflect on their own lives, the catharsis was not only emotional; it was political.[30]

The evolution of Lemlich's study group illustrates how study often led to union activity. Older workers, who were teaching Lemlich the craft of draping, invited her to join their lunchtime discussion groups to learn more about trade unionism. Soon Lemlich and a group of young women waistmakers formed their own study group. Discussion quickly escalated to action, and they decided to form a union.[31]

Skilled male workers in the shirtwaist trade had been trying to establish a union since 1900. But after five years the union had managed to attract only ten members. The problem, Lemlich told her male colleagues, was that women workers had to be approached by an organizer who understood their particular needs as women. They bristled at the suggestion that this young girl might know more about their business than they did. But years later, one conceded that the failure of the first waistmakers' union was due at least in part to their ham-fisted tactics: "We would issue a circular reading somewhat as follows: 'Murder the exploiters, the blood-suckers, the manufacturers.... Pay your dues.... Down with the Capitalists!'" Few women or men showed up at their meetings.[32]

During the spring of 1905 the union disbanded and reorganized as Local 25 of the ILGWU, with Clara Lemlich and a group of six young women from her waistmaking shop on the executive board. Taking their cue from Lemlich, the new union used women organizers to attract women workers. Lemlich addressed street-corner meetings in English and Yiddish and found Italian women to address the Italian workers. Soon, like Schneiderman, Newman, and Cohn, she realized that she had found a calling.[33]

In the progressive atmosphere of early-twentieth-century New York City, influential people quickly noticed the militant young working women. Older Socialists, trade unionists, and middle-class reformers offered their assistance. These benefactors helped the young organizers sharpen their arguments, provided financial assistance, and introduced them to politicians and public officials. The protégés recognized the importance of this informal mentoring and would later work to recreate such networks in the unions, schools, and training programs they built for young women workers. Schneiderman, Newman,

Rose Schneiderman at a sewing machine, posed during the capmakers' strike of 1905. (Courtesy of Rose Schneiderman Collection, Robert F. Wagner Labor Archives, New York University.)

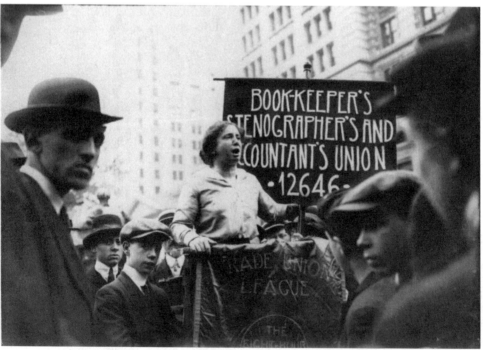

Rose Schneiderman addresses a street rally in New York. (Courtesy of Brown Brothers, Sterling, Pennsylvania.)

Lemlich, and Cohn were keenly aware that young working women needed help from more experienced and more powerful allies. But they also worried that the voices of women workers might be outshouted in the clamorous process of building alliances. From these early days, they battled to preserve the integrity of their vision.

Pauline Newman found her first mentors in the Socialist Party, which she joined in 1906 at the age of fifteen. Older women, including former garment worker Theresa Serber Malkiel, took her on as a protégé. Newman quickly blossomed under their tutelage. Before long she was running street-corner meetings. Armed with a sonorous voice and the certitude of youth, she would take "an American flag and a soapbox and go from corner to corner," exhorting the gospel of Socialism in Yiddish and English. "I, like many of my friends and comrades, thought that socialism and socialism alone could and would someday fill the gap between rich and poor," Newman recalled. In a neighborhood crowded with sidewalk proselytizers, this child evangelist became one of the party's most popular street-corner attractions.[34]

In 1908, nine years before New York State gave women the vote, seventeen-year-old Newman was nominated by the Socialist Party to run for New York's Secretary of State. Newman used her campaign as a platform for suffrage. Her speeches were heckled by some Socialist men, and her candidacy provoked amused commentaries in New York City newspapers; some writers snickered at the prospect of a "skirted Secretary of State." It was a largely symbolic crusade, but Newman felt that she got people talking about the idea of women in government. The highlight of the campaign was her whistlestop tour with presidential candidate and Socialist leader Eugene V. Debs on his "Red Special" train.

The Socialist Party opened up a new world to Newman, who, after all, had never graduated from elementary school. Along with Debs, she met future Congressmen Meyer Berger and Morris Hillquit and leading Socialist intellectuals. Newman later wrote about the excitement of discussions that carried over from meetings and went into the night as she and her friends walked through Central Park, arguing till the sun came up. Those nights made her feel part of a historic moment.[35]

While Newman was being nurtured by the Socialist Party, Rose Schneiderman found her mentors in the United Cloth Hat and Cap Makers. At the union's 1904 convention she was elected to the General Executive Board; she was the first woman to win such a high-level post in the American labor movement. During the winter of 1904–5, Schneiderman's leadership skills were tested when owners tried to open up union shops to nonunion workers. The largely immigrant capmaker's union called for a general strike. The 1905 strike was a watershed event in Schneiderman's emerging career. Her role as the only woman leader in the union won attention from the press and lasting respect from male capmakers, including the future president of the union, Max Zaritsky, who became a lifelong friend and admirer.[36]

It also brought her to the attention of the newly formed Women's Trade Union League (WTUL), an organization of progressive middle- and upper-class women reformers founded in 1903 to help working women organize. Schneiderman had misgivings about the group because she "could not believe that men and women who were not wage earners themselves understood the problems that workers faced." But she trusted the League's best-known working-class member, Irish shirtmaker Leonora O'Reilly. And she could not ignore the favorable publicity that the WTUL won for the strikers. By March 1905, Schneiderman had been elected to the executive board of the New York WTUL. In 1906, the group elected her vice president.[37]

Schneiderman's entrance into the New York WTUL was an important turning point for both her and the organization. Three years after its founding, the WTUL remained dominated by affluent reformers who had dubbed themselves "allies" of the working class. Despite their genuine commitment to trade unionism, League leaders had credibility problems among women workers. Schneiderman had joined the League recognizing that working women lacked the education, the money, and the political clout to organize effectively without powerful allies. Still, she remained ambivalent for a variety of reasons.[38]

The progressive reformers who dominated the League tried to steer workers away from radical influences, particularly the Socialist Party. Yet Schneiderman and O'Reilly, the League's leading working-class organizers, were Socialist Party members and saw unionism as a potentially revolutionary tool. As a result, the pair often felt torn by competing loyalties. Socialists distrusted their work with upper-crust women reformers. Union men were either indifferent or openly hostile to working women's attempts to become leaders in the labor movement. And the League women often seemed to Schneiderman and O'Reilly to act out of a patronizing benevolence that had little to do with real coalition building. The two grew angry at what they saw as attempts by wealthy allies to manipulate them. In January 1906, Leonora O'Reilly announced the first of her many resignations from the League, claiming "an overdose of allies."[39]

There were a few deep friendships between affluent WTUL leaders and working women like Schneiderman, O'Reilly, and Pauline Newman, who joined the League in 1909. Such bonds created hope that intimacy was possible between women of different classes; but cross-class friendships were the exception rather than the rule. Working women like Newman never lost sight of the ways their class background separated them from wealthy reformers. Sisterhood was exhilarating, but outside the WTUL, their lives and political agendas diverged sharply.[40]

Consequently, these women's relations with most wealthy League supporters were marked by deep ambivalence inasmuch as WTUL backers wanted to distance the League from radical working-class activism and to stake out a decidedly middle ground in the struggle for women's rights that was then gathering steam.

Schneiderman tried to counterbalance such influences by encouraging male union leaders to play a more active role in the League, but she had little success. She told them that the WTUL could help the labor movement by successfully organizing women workers, whose low wages might otherwise exert a downward pressure on unionized male wages. A *women's* trade union league was needed, she insisted, because women workers responded to different arguments than did men workers. The League could focus on the particular concerns of women, such as the double shift—having to perform household chores after coming home from long days in the factory. Her suggestions were greeted with indifference.

Addressing the First Convention of American Women Trade Unionists, held in New York on July 14, 1907, Schneiderman reported that she "was very much surprised and not a little disappointed that the attention of men unionists was so small." The truth is, she told her audience, working women needed more than unions. They needed political power. "The time has come," she said firmly, "when working women of the State of New York must be enfranchised and so secure political power to shape their own labor conditions." The convention passed a suffrage resolution, one of the first prosuffrage statements by any organization representing American working-class women.[41]

Schneiderman confronted middle- and upper-class allies with equal frankness. She told the NYWTUL executive board that they were having little success organizing women workers because they approached their task like scholars, not trade unionists. They surveyed conditions in the women's trades, noting which had the lowest salaries, the longest hours, and the worst hygienic conditions. Then they established committees to study the possibilities for unionizing each trade. Finally they went into the shops to explain their findings to the working women. Schneiderman suggested a simpler alternative: take their lead from women workers and respond to requests for aid from women workers who were already trying to organize. It was something they had never thought to do.[42]

Before long, requests for help were pouring in, mostly from immigrant Jewish women. In the dress trade, where Clara Lemlich was working, and in the white goods trade, where Fannia Cohn was organizing, women workers had launched a series of wildcat strikes. "It was not unusual for unorganized workers to walk out without having any direct union affiliation," Schneiderman later recalled.[43]

By 1907, long-simmering anger over speedups, wage cuts, and the requirement that employees pay for their own thread reached a boiling point. Foreshadowing its role in the decades to come, the Women's Trade Union League decided to champion women workers ignored by the male unions. The strike fever soon engulfed Brooklyn, where for two years Fannia Cohn had been struggling against male union leaders' indifference to organize white goods workers. So when three hundred workers in one shop decided to strike in 1908, they bypassed the UGW and called for help from Schneiderman and the WTUL.

Since the ethnic makeup of the Brooklyn white goods trade was far more diverse than any other in the garment industry, this strike raised a new challenge for Schneiderman: how to forge a sense of solidarity between working-class women of many religions and nationalities. Schneiderman decided that the best way to reach immigrant workers was through organizers who literally spoke their language.[44]

She decided to focus first on Italian workers because, after Jews, they comprised the single largest ethnic group in the garment trades. Recognizing the cultural as well as linguistic differences that separated her from Italian immigrant women, Schneiderman tried a strategy she would employ many times over the years to come: to identify and cultivate a leader from within the ranks of the workers. She began working with a Brooklyn priest on ways to approach young Italian women. She also got the League to hire an Italian-speaking organizer who assembled a committee of progressive New York Italians—including prominent women professionals and the editor of a popular evening paper *Bolatino de la Sera*—to popularize trade unionism among Italian women workers.[45]

The strategy proved successful. By 1909 enough workers had enlisted that the ILGWU finally recognized the Brooklyn white goods workers' union. The vast majority of its members were teenage girls; these young women elected their mentor, Fannia Cohn, then twenty-four, to the union's first executive board. Cohn, who stepped off the shop floor to a policy-making position, would remain a paid union official for the rest of her life.[46]

In 1909, Clara Lemlich—then in her twenties and on the executive board of ILGWU Local 25—enlisted Schneiderman's aid in her drive to organize shirt-waist makers. For the past three years, Lemlich had been zigzagging between small shops, stirring up trouble. Her first full-scale strike was at Weisen and Goldstein's Manhattan factory. Like the Triangle Shirtwaist Factory, where Newman worked, Weisen and Goldstein's was considered a model shop. The workrooms were modern and airy—a pleasant contrast to the dark basement rooms where most white goods workers

labored. However, the advantages of working in a clean, new factory were offset by the strains of mechanization. In 1907 the workers at Weisen and Goldstein's went on strike to protest speedups.

Older male strikers proved critical to Lemlich's political education. Confused by an argument between workers at a strike meeting, Lemlich asked one to explain the difference between Socialist unionism and the "pure and simple trade unionism" of the American Federation of Labor (AFL). When the meeting ended, the man took Lemlich for a long walk. He explained Socialism in terms she could use with her fellow workers. "He started with a bottle of milk—how it was made, who made the money from it through every stage of its production. Not only did the boss take the profits, he said, but not a drop of that milk did you drink unless he allowed you to. It was funny, you know, because I'd been saying things like that to the girls before. But now I understood it better and I began to use it more often—only with shirtwaists."[47]

Lemlich returned to the picket line with a more sophisticated view of organizing. She became a regular at Socialist Party meetings and began attending classes at the Rand School. Through the Socialist Party she became friends with Rose Schneiderman, Pauline Newman, and other young women organizers. Both individually and in tandem, this group of radical young women organized strikes across the Lower East Side.

In 1909, after being fired from two more shops for leading strikes, Lemlich began working at the Leiserson shop. Brazenly, she marched uninvited into a strike meeting that had been called by the shop's older male elite—the skilled cutters and drapers. Warning them that they would lose if they attempted to strike without organizing the shop's unskilled women, Lemlich demanded their help in organizing women workers. They bridled at her nerve, but ultimately they helped her unionize the women.[48]

Lemlich's reputation as a leader grew rapidly during the fall of 1909 as stories of her bravery spread. During the Leiserson strike, which began that September, she was arrested seventeen times and had six ribs broken by club-wielding police and company guards. Without complaint, she tended to her bruises and returned to the line. By November 1909, when she stepped onto the stage in Cooper Union's Great Hall of the People to deliver the speech that would spark the largest women's strike the nation had yet seen, Lemlich was not the anonymous "wisp of a girl" that news accounts described. She was a battle-scarred veteran of the labor movement, well known among her fellow workers.[49]

Still, it is worth remembering that in this period, the four women activists were just barely adults. Newman, Schneiderman, and Lemlich still lived with their parents. During the Leiserson strike, Lemlich was so fearful that her parents would try to keep her home if they knew about her injuries that she hid her escapades and bruises from them. Later she explained the events to her grandson: "Like rain the blows fell on me. The gangsters hit me.... The boys and girls invented themselves how to give back what they got from the scabs, with stones and whatnot, with sticks.... Sometimes when I came home I wouldn't tell because if I would tell they wouldn't want me to go anymore. Yes, my boy, it's not easy. Unions aren't built easy."[50]

On November 23, 1909, New York City awoke to a general strike of shirtwaist makers, the largest strike by women workers the United States had ever seen. Overnight, between 20,000 and 40,000 workers—most of them teenage girls—silenced their sewing machines to protest the low wages, long hours, and dangerous working conditions. Though the magnitude of the strike amazed nearly everyone, including Schneiderman, Newman, Cohn, and Lemlich, the four knew that this was no spontaneous uprising: they had been organizing feverishly for almost three years and had noted a transformation in the working women they talked to, a growing sense of collective identity matched by an increasing militancy. They had laid the groundwork through a series of smaller strikes and had trained fellow workers to expect and respond to the violent and divisive tactics used by bosses to break the strike.

Despite their effectiveness, the strike was threatened by the escalation of police violence against the young women picketers. Two weeks after the strike call, Schneiderman and Dreier led ten thousand young waistmakers on a march to city hall to demand that Mayor George McClellan rein in the police. He promised an investigation but did little. One month

into the strike, there had been 771 arrests, many made with undue force.[51]

WTUL leaders decided to try a different tack. They called a mass meeting of all the young women who had been attacked by police. The press and wealthy supporters were invited. One after another, adolescent girls rose to the stage to tell their stories. Mollie Weingast told a cheering crowd that when an officer tried to arrest her, she informed him that she had a constitutional right to picket. Minnie Margolis demanded that a policeman protect her from physical attack by her boss. When he refused, she took down his badge and precinct numbers. It was, she told the audience, an officer's job to protect her right to protest peacefully. Celie Newman, sixteen, said that police had manhandled her and dragged her into court, where her boss told a judge that she was an anarchist and should be deported. At another meeting earlier that week, seventeen-year-old Etta Ruth said that police had taunted her with lewd suggestions.[52]

Implying that picketers were little better than streetwalkers, employers often resorted to sexual innuendos to discredit the strikers. The workers clearly resented the manner in which middle-class standards of acceptable feminine behavior were used to manipulate them even though they enjoyed none of the advantages of middle-class birth. Then as now, society offered a limited range of cultural images of working-class women. They were either "good" girls who listened docilely to fathers, employers, and policemen, or "bad" women whose aggressive behavior made them akin to prostitutes. By walking on picket lines and going public with their demands, they'd forfeited their claims to femininity and respectability—and thus to protection.[53]

Such women were shown little deference by police and company thugs, who attacked them with iron bars, sticks, and billy clubs. And they received little sympathy in court when they attempted to press charges. One young woman appeared in court with a broken nose, a bruised face, and a head swathed in bandages. Yet the judge dropped her assault charge against police. "You are on strike against God and nature," one magistrate told a worker. Only the League's decision to invite college students and wealthy women onto the picket lines ended the violence. Alva Belmont and Anne Morgan led a contingent of New

York's wealthiest women in what newspapers dubbed "mink brigades," which patrolled the dirty sidewalks of the Lower East Side. Fearful of clubbing someone on the Social Register, police grew more restrained.[54]

The socialites' presence generated both money and press for the strikers. The move proved politically wise for the suffrage cause as well, because the constant proselytizing of suffrage zealot Alva Belmont, who often bailed strikers out of jail, got young workers talking about the vote. But rubbing elbows with the mink brigade did not blind workers to the class-determined limits of sisterhood. How far they were from the protected status of more affluent women was made abundantly clear by the violence they encountered at the hands of police and company guards and by the fact that the mink brigades were able to end police brutality simply by joining the picket lines.

Encounters in court and with feminist allies speeded the growth of group consciousness. Telling their stories in court, to reporters, and to sympathetic audiences of college and society women, the strikers grew more confident of their speaking abilities and of their capacity to interpret their world. They became more aware of the distribution of power in the United States. And finally, the violence directed against them intensified their bonds with one another.

For Schneiderman, Newman, and Lemlich, the 1909 shirtwaist uprising sped their maturation as organizers and political leaders. The strike breathed new life into a struggling immigrant labor movement and transformed the tiny ILGWU into a union of national significance. Still, it ended with mixed success for workers. Many won pay increases and union recognition; others did not. And the contracts hammered out by ILGWU negotiators left a devastating legacy, for without consulting the strikers, male union negotiators decided that safety conditions were less important than other issues. Their concessions would come back to haunt the entire labor movement two years later, when the Triangle Shirtwaist Factory burned.[55]

Flames from the volcanic 1909 uprising licked industrial cities from New York to Michigan. Within a matter of weeks, 15,000 women waistmakers in Philadelphia walked off their jobs. The spirit of militancy soon touched the Midwest. In 1910, Chicago women led a strike of 41,000 men's clothing makers. The following year, women workers and the wives of male workers played key roles in a bitter cloakmakers' strike in Cleveland. Meanwhile, in Muscatine, Iowa, young women button makers waged and won a long battle for union recognition. In 1912, corset makers in Kalamazoo, Michigan, launched a campaign for better working conditions that polarized their city and won national press attention. In 1913, a strike of underwear and kimono makers swept up 35,000 young Brooklyn girls and women. Finally, in 1915, Chicago dressmakers capped this period of women's labor militancy by winning recognition of their local union after years of struggle. They elected their organizer, Fannia Cohn, as the first woman vice president of a major American labor union.[56]

Cohn, Rose Schneiderman, Pauline Newman, and Clara Lemlich were at the center of a storm that by 1919 had brought half of all women garment workers into trade unions. Individually and in tandem, the four women participated in all of the major women's strikes between 1909 and 1915, arguably the most intense period of women's labor militancy in U.S. history. This wave of "uprisings" seemed to herald the birth of a working women's movement on a scale never before seen. And it catapulted the four young women into positions of leadership, forcing them, in conjunction with colleagues, to articulate a clearly defined set of goals for the new movement.[57] In the passion and excitement of the years that followed, Schneiderman, Newman, Lemlich, and Cohn would begin to mature as political leaders and to forge a vision of political change that originated in their years on the shop floor. Pauline Newman would later describe this new brand of activism as politics of the 1909 vintage, fermented during a brief era of young women's mass protest. That description expresses the importance of the 1909 strike as both symbol and catalyst for a new working women's politics.

"Industrial feminism," the phrase coined in 1915 by scholar Mildred Moore to describe working women's militancy over the previous six years, evokes the same spirit but focuses more broadly. It simultaneously captures the interaction between women workers and feminist activists and recognizes the profound influence that the shop floor had on shaping working women's political consciousness. Industrial feminism accurately depicts the contours of an emerging political movement that by decade's end would propel the problems and concerns of industrial working women to the center of U.S. political discourse and make them players in the Socialist Party, the suffrage movement, and the politics of progressive reform.[58]

Industrial feminism was not a carefully delineated code of political thought. It was a vision of change forged in an atmosphere of crisis and awakening, as women workers in one city after another "laid down their scissors, shook the threads off their clothes and calmly left the place that stood between them and starvation." These were the words of former cloakmaker, journalist, and Socialist Party activist Theresa Malkiel, a partisan chronicler of women's labor militancy. Once an organizer, later a mentor for Newman, Lemlich, and Schneiderman, Malkiel told readers of the *New York Call* that they should not be surprised by the seemingly sudden explosion of young women workers' discontent. As hard as they might find it to take seriously the notion of a "girl's strike," she warned them, this was no outburst of female hysteria. "It was not . . . a woman's fancy that drove them to it," she wrote, "but an eruption of a long smoldering volcano, an overflow of suffering, abuse and exhaustion."[59]

Common sense, Pauline Newman would later say, dictated the most immediate goals of industrial feminists in the era of women's strikes. Given the dire realities of garment workers' lives, the first order of business had to be to improve their wages, hours, and working conditions. Toward that end the "girl strikers" of 1909–15 followed the most basic tenets of unionism. They organized, struck, and negotiated through their labor unions. But the "long-smoldering volcano" that Malkiel cautioned her readers to heed had been stirred to life by more than dissatisfaction over low wages and poor conditions.

The nascent political philosophy that began to take shape after the 1909 strike was more complex than the bread-and-butter unionism of AFL president Samuel Gompers. Why, young working women reasoned, should unions only negotiate hours and wages? They wanted to build unions that would also offer workers educational and cultural activities,

health care, and maybe even a chance to leave the city and enjoy the open countryside.

Such ambitious goals derived largely from the personal experiences of industrial feminist leaders like Cohn, Schneiderman, Lemlich, and Newman. Political activism had enriched the four young women's lives, exposing them to more interesting people than they would have met had they stayed on the shop floor: writers, artists, professors, people with ideas. Through politics they had found their voices and a forum in which to raise them. The personal excitement and satisfaction they found in activism in turn shaped the evolution of their political vision: they wanted to create institutions that would provide some of the same satisfactions to any working woman who joined.

But alone, working women had none of the political or economic clout needed to open up such doors of opportunity. To build a successful movement, the four knew that they would have to win the support of more powerful allies. So they learned to build coalitions. From the time they left the shop floor until the end of their careers, they operated within a tense nexus of union men, progressive middle- and upper-class women, and the working women they sought to organize. These alliances shifted continuously, requiring the four women to perform a draining and politically hazardous balancing act. But each core group contributed an important dimension to the political education of the four organizers.

With their male counterparts and older women in the labor movement, they shared a class solidarity that would always remain at the heart of their politics. Traveling around the country, they met coal miners, loggers, and railroad workers who shared both their experiences of exploitation as laborers and their exhilaration in the economic and political strength that trade unions gave them.

From the middle- and upper-class women who joined them on the picket lines and lent them both financial and strategic support, they learned that trade union activism was not the only way to fight for improved work conditions. These allies would expose Newman, Cohn, Schneiderman, and Lemlich to a world of power and political influence, encouraging them to believe that through suffrage and lobbying, government could be put to work for their benefit.

Finally, as they began to think in terms of forging a national movement, they were forced to develop new techniques to reach women workers of different races, religions, and ethnicities. They learned from the women they sought to organize that just as women workers were best reached by women organizers, so Italian, Polish, and Hispanic immigrants and native-born black and white Protestant women were better reached by one of their own than by Jewish women steeped in the political culture of Eastern Europe and the Lower East Side. Though each of the four women had some success in bridging racial and ethnic divisions, they were forced to acknowledge their limitations. They could not do it all themselves; they had to nurture women shop-floor leaders from different backgrounds.

The work required to remain politically effective in this nexus of often-conflicting relationships yielded some real rewards, both strategically and personally. But sometimes the constant struggling wore on them. Conflicts and tensions were brought into sharp relief as the four exhausted themselves making speeches and giving pep talks to weary workers, when they themselves needed reassurance: although they had achieved recognition by the end of the 1909 strike, Schneiderman, Cohn, Newman, and Lemlich were still poor, uneducated, and young. Newman was only eighteen years old when the strike began, and Lemlich twenty-three. Even the elders in the circle, Cohn and Schneiderman, were only twenty-five and twenty-eight, respectively.

Letters between Newman and Schneiderman from that era reveal their vulnerability to slights and criticisms by male union leaders and female reformers. Life on "the battlefield," as Newman referred to it, was lonely. At an age when other women were contemplating marriage and family, they spent their nights in smoky union halls or the cheap, dingy hotel rooms that unions rented for their organizers. They sometimes questioned their life choices, for the reality of union work was far less glamorous than it had seemed in their shop-floor days. Indeed, Newman would quit several times before decade's end. Ultimately, though, their disillusionment did not drive the four women from the union movement. Instead, it fueled their desire to broaden the vision of U.S. trade unionism. When Schneiderman said

"The working woman needs bread, but she needs roses, too," she was speaking from personal experience.[60]

NOTES

1. Pauline Newman, "Letters to Hugh and Michael" (1951–69), Box 1, Folder 3, Pauline M. Newman Papers, Schlesinger Library, Radcliffe College, Cambridge, Mass. (hereafter cited as Newman Papers).
2. Ibid.
3. Ibid.; *New York Times*, November 2, 25, December 3, 26, 1907.
4. Newman, "Letters to Hugh and Michael."
5. "The Testimony of Miss Pauline M. Newman," in *Hearings of the New York State Factory Investigating Commission* (Albany: J. B. Lyons Printers, 1915), 2868–71.
6. My estimate of Newman's age is based on evidence suggesting that she was around eighteen years old at the time of the 1909 shirtwaist strike. Newman, like many Jews of her generation, never knew for sure how old she was. Her birthdate was recorded only on the flyleaf of the family Bible. After the Bible was lost in transit, she could only guess at her age.
7. For analyses of the position of Jews in Russian society at the turn of the century, see S. Ettinger, "The Jews at the Outbreak of the Revolution," in *The Jews in Soviet Russia since 1917*, ed. Lionel Kochan, 3d ed. (Oxford: Oxford University Press, 1978), 15–30; see also Salo Baron, *The Russian Jew under Tsars and Soviets* (New York: Macmillan, 1976).
8. Sidney Jonas, interview by author, Brooklyn, N.Y., August 10, 1980; Paula Scheier, "Clara Lemlich Shavelson: Fifty Years in Labor's Front Line," *Jewish Life*, November 1954; Ricki Carole Myers Cohen, "Fannia Cohn and the International Ladies' Garment Workers' Union" (Ph.D. diss., University of Southern California, 1976), 5.
9. Newman, "Letters to Hugh and Michael"; Cohen, "Fannia Cohn," chap. 1; Scheier, "Clara Lemlich Shavelson"; Fannia M. Cohn to "Dear Emma," May 15, 1953, Fannia M. Cohn Papers, Astor, Lenox, and Tilden Foundations, Rare Books and Manuscripts Division, New York Public Library (hereafter cited as Cohn Papers).

In March 1903, gangs organized by Russian police rampaged through the Ukrainian town of Kishinev, killing 51 Jewish men, women, and children, and wounding at least 495 others. Edward H. Judge, *Eastern Kishinev: Anatomy of a Pogrom* (New York: New York University Press, 1992).
10. See Charlotte Baum, Paula Hyman, and Sonya Michel, *The Jewish Woman in America* (New York: NAL/Dutton, 1977), 55–91; Mark Zborowski and Elizabeth Herzog, *Life Is with People* (New York: Schocken, 1962); Jack Kugelmass and Jonathan Bayarin, *From a Ruined Garden: The Memorial Books of Polish Jewry* (New York: Schocken Books, 1985).
11. The Lower East Side continued to receive Jewish immigrants from Eastern Europe into the 1920s. See Ettinger, "Jews at the Outbreak of the Rev-

olution," 19–22; Celia Heller, *On the Edge of Destruction* (New York: Schocken, 1980), 45–55; and Irving Howe, *World of Our Fathers* (New York: Harcourt Brace & Jovanovich, 1976), xix.

12. Clara Lemlich Shavelson to Morris Schappes, March 15, 1965, published in *Jewish Currents* 36, no. 10 (November 1982): 9–11.

13. Clara Lemlich, "Remembering the Waistmakers' General Strike, 1909," *Jewish Currents*, November 1982; Newman, "Letters to Hugh and Michael."

14. Much has been written about the importance of women's colleges to the various social reform movements of the Progressive Era. Stephen Norwood makes a similar argument for high schools. Norwood, *Labor's Flaming Youth: Telephone Workers and Labor Militancy, 1878–1923* (Urbana: University of Illinois Press, 1990).

15. Newman, "Letters to Hugh and Michael"; Pauline Newman, interview by Barbara Wertheimer, New York, N.Y., November 1976; Pauline Newman résumé, n.d., Newman Papers.

16. Pauline Newman, interview by author, New York, N.Y., February 9, 1984; Newman, interview by Wertheimer.

17. Joan Morrison and Charlotte Fox Zabusky, eds., *American Mosaic* (New York: E. P. Dutton, 1980).

18. See Rose Schneiderman, *All for One* (New York: Paul S. Eriksson, 1967), 35–42, and Susan Porter Benson, "The Customers Ain't God: The Work Culture of Department Store Saleswomen, 1890–1940," in *Working Class America*, ed. Michael Frisch and Daniel J. Walkowitz (Urbana: University of Illinois Press, 1983), 185–212.

19. Scheier, "Clara Lemlich Shavelson." See also Susan Glenn, *Daughters of the Shtetl: Work, Unionism and the Immigrant Generation* (Ithaca: Cornell University Press, 1990), 122–31.

20. Schneiderman, *All for One*, 48.

21. Ibid., 48–50.

22. Ibid.

23. Ibid.

24. FMC to Selig Perlman, December 26, 1951, Box 5, Cohn Papers.

25. Information on the problems of organizing the white goods trade is located in Minutes of the Executive Board of the NYWTUL, February 28, August 22, and November 26, 27, 1907, Reel 1, Papers of the New York Women's Trade Union League, Tamiment Institute Library, New York University (hereafter cited as NYWTUL Papers); information on Cohn comes from Cohen, "Fannia Cohn," 11–21.

26. Schneiderman, *All for One*, 39–40.

27. Scheier, "Clara Lemlich Shavelson."

28. Pauline Newman, "The White Goods Workers' Strike," *Ladies' Garment Worker* 4, no. 3 (March 1913):1–4.

29. Scheier, "Clara Lemlich Shavelson"; Pauline Newman, Fragments 1958–61, Box 1, Newman Papers.

30. Newman, interview by Wertheimer; Newman, interview in Morrison and Zabusky, *American Mosaic.*

31. Scheier, "Clara Lemlich Shavelson."

32. Louis Levine [Lewis Lorwin], *The Women's Garment Workers: A History of the International Ladies' Garment Workers' Union* (New York: B. W. Huebsch, 1924), 148–49.

33. This information is pieced together from Scheier, "Clara Lemlich Shavelson"; Dora Smorodin, interview by author, Maplewood, N.J., March 12, 1991; and Levine, *Women's Garment Workers,* 148–49.

34. Newman, interview by Wertheimer; Newman, "Letters to Hugh and Michael."

35. Ibid.

36. Schneiderman, *All for One,* 58–60.

37. Ibid., 73–77; Minutes of the NYWTUL Executive Board, February 24, March 24, 1905. Reel 1, NYWTUL Papers.

38. Nancy Schrom Dye, *As Equals and as Sisters: Feminism, Unionism and the Women's Trade Union League of New York* (Columbia: University of Missouri Press, 1980), 110–22.

39. Ibid.; Minutes of the NYWTUL Executive Board, January 25, 1906, Reel 1, NYWTUL Papers.

40. Newman, interview by Wertheimer; Newman, interview by author, February 9, 1984, New York.

41. See also Alice Kessler-Harris, "Rose Schneiderman," in *American Labor Leaders,* ed. Warren Van Tine and Melvyn Dubofsky (Urbana: University of Illinois Press, 1987), 160–84.

42. Minutes of the NYWTUL Executive Board, February 24, 1905-February 1, 1909, Reel 1, NYWTUL Papers.

43. Schneiderman, *All for One,* 84.

44. Minutes of the NYWTUL Executive Board, February 28, August 22, November 26, 27, 1907, Reel 1, NYWTUL, Papers; Levine, *Women's Garment Workers,* 220.

45. Minutes of the NYWTUL Executive Committee, November 26, 27, 1907, Reel 1, NYWTUL Papers.

46. Levine, *Women's Garment Workers,* 220; Cohen, "Fannia Cohn," 36–43.

47. Scheier, "Clara Lemlich Shavelson."

48. Martha Schaffer, telephone interview by author, March 11, 1989; Joel Schaffer, Evelyn Velson, and Julia Velson, interview by author, Oakland, Calif., September 9, 1992.

49. Scheier, "Clara Lemlich Shavelson."

50. Clara Lemlich Shavelson, interview by Martha and Joel Schaffer, Los Angeles, Calif., February 2, 1974.

51. *New York Call,* November 30, December 4, 5, 6, 7, 8, 29, 1909.

52. *New York Call,* December 5, 7, 8, 1909.

53. *New York Call,* December 29, 1909. For complete coverage of day-to-day events on the picket line, see the *New York Times,* November 5, 6, and 14, 1909, and almost daily from November 23, 1909, through January 28, 1910.

54. Minutes of the New York Women's Trade Union League Membership Meeting, April 20, June 15, 1910, Reel 1, NYWTUL Papers.

55. See Meredith Tax, *The Rising of the Women: Feminist Solidarity and Class Conflict, 1880–1917* (New York: Monthly Review Press, 1980), pp. 230–240. Tax discusses the hierarchical union structure and the ways that union-appointed arbitrators undermined the women workers' control of the strike.

56. For information on the many women's strikes of the period, read the WTUL publication *Life*

and Labor, which covered them all in some detail. The progressive magazine *The Survey* (1909–1914) also has good coverage of most of the strikes. See too, Pauline Newman, "The White Goods Workers' Strike," *Ladies' Garment Worker* 4, number 3 (March 1913):1–4; on the Chicago strike see Mari Jo Buhle, *Women and American Socialism, 1870–1920* (Urbana: University of Illinois Press, 1981), 194–198. On the Kalamazoo strike see Karen Mason, "Feeling the Pinch: The Kalamazoo Corset Makers' Strike of 1912," in *To Toil the Livelong Day: America's Women at Work,* ed. Carol Groneman and Mary Beth Norton (Ithaca: Cornell University Press, 1987), 141–60. On the 1915 strike see *Chicago Day Book* cited in Winifred Carsel, *A History of the Chicago Ladies' Garment Workers' Union* (Chicago: Normandie House, 1940).

57. Gladys Boone, *The Women's Trade Union Leagues* (New York: Columbia University Press, 1942), 112–14.

58. Mildred Moore, "A History of the Women's Trade Union League of Chicago" (M.A. thesis, University of Chicago, 1915), cited in Diane Kirkby, "The Wage-Earning Woman and the State: The National Women's Trade Union League and Protective Labor Legislation, 1903–1923," *Labor History* 28, no. 1 (Winter 1987):58–74.

59. Theresa Malkiel, "The Uprising of the 40,000," *New York Call,* December 29, 1909.

60. Pauline Newman, "From the Battlefield—Some Phases of the Cloakmakers' Strike in Cleveland," *Life and Labor,* October 1911.

KATHRYN KISH SKLAR
Florence Kelley and Women's Activism in the Progressive Era

Florence Kelley was a remarkable woman who lived in a period when attempts to address the problems created by industrialization and urbanization generated both the early social sciences and the foundation of the welfare state. Kathryn Sklar, Kelley's biographer, provides in this authoritative and highly informative essay an account of a single individual that also illuminates the pursuit of social justice in which many progressive women of Kelley's generation were involved. Sklar reveals the factors that made it possible for these women to influence public policy even before they were allowed to vote. She also describes the changing political context that limited their influence following the Red Scare at the end of World War I.

What were the influences, personal and intellectual, that shaped Kelley's vision of social reform? What strategies did she employ in pursuit of that vision? What does Sklar mean when she says that Kelley used gender-specific legislation as a surrogate for class legislation? Precisely how did the Red Scare affect the political agenda of women's organizations? In what respects were at least three of the four significant features of women's power in the Progressive era that Sklar identified highly gendered? As we move into the 1930s and beyond, think about which of the features persist and which do not.

One of the most powerful women in American history deserves to be better known today. Florence Kelley (1859–1932) was well known to her contemporaries as a leading champion of social justice legislation. For most of the 1890s she lived in the nation's leading reform institution, Hull House, a social settlement founded in Chicago by Jane Addams in 1889.

Written expressly for *Women's America.* A revised version of this essay appears in *Historical Encyclopedia of Chicago Women* (Chicago: Indiana University Press, 1999). Copyright © 1998 by Kathryn Kish Sklar.

Between 1899 and 1932 she served as head of the National Consumers' League in New York City.

Living collectively with other women reformers in Chicago and New York, Florence Kelley was able to make the most of her talents; for four decades she occupied the vanguard of social reform. Her forceful personality flourished in the combative atmosphere generated by her struggles for social justice. Jane Addams's nephew, who resided with Kelley at Hull House, was awed by the way she "hurled the spears of her thought with such apparent carelessness of what breasts they pierced." He thought her "the toughest customer in the reform riot, the finest rough-and-tumble fighter for the good life for others, that Hull House ever knew: Any weapon was a good weapon in her hand—evidence, argument, irony or invective." Nevertheless, he said, those who were close to her knew she was "full of love."[1]

Kelley's career, like that of many of her reform contemporaries, was responding to profound changes in American social and economic life. Rapid industrialization was recasting the economy, massive immigration was reconstituting the working class, and sustained urbanization was making cities the focus of social change.[2] In this context, college-educated women reformers often achieved what men and male-dominated organizations could not.

Florence Kelley's life helps us understand how women reformers accomplished their goals. Her reform career exemplified four significant features of women's power in the Progressive era: their access to higher education; their prominence in early social science; the political autonomy of their separate institutions; and their ability to challenge American traditions of limited government. Having experienced these ingredients of women's power in her own life before 1899, thereafter, as the General Secretary of the National Consumers' League, she integrated them into her strategies for pursuing social justice.[3]

WOMEN'S ACCESS TO HIGHER EDUCATION

When she graduated from Cornell University in 1882, Florence Kelley joined thousands of other young women in her generation who received college educations. Two changes in the 1860s and 1870s enabled white, middle-class women to attend college in sufficient numbers to become a sociological phenomenon. Elite women's colleges, such as Vassar, Smith, and Wellesley, began accepting students between 1865 and 1875, providing equivalents to elite men's colleges such as Harvard, Yale, and Princeton. And state universities, established through the allocation of public lands in the Morrill Act of 1862 and required to be "open for all," gradually made college educations accessible for the first time to large numbers of women in the nation's central and western states. By 1880 women, numbering forty thousand, constituted 33 percent of all enrolled students in higher education.[4] Though a small percentage of all women, they exercised an influence disproportionate to their numbers.

To Cornell Kelley brought a social conscience shaped by her family. Born into an elite Philadelphia family with Quaker and Unitarian political traditions, she grew up against the background of the Civil War and Reconstruction—dramas in which her father and her mother's aunt played major roles. Her father, William Durrah Kelley, one of the founders of the Republican Party, was reelected to fifteen consecutive terms in the U.S. Congress between 1860 and 1890. As a Radical Republican, he advanced the cause of black suffrage and tried to forge a biracial Republican Party in the South. Her mother's aunt, Sarah Pugh, served as president of the Philadelphia Female Anti-Slavery Society almost every year between 1838 and 1870. In the 1860s and 1870s, Pugh accompanied her close friend, Lucretia Mott, to early woman suffrage conventions. To young "Florrie," Sarah Pugh was conscience incarnate, a full-time reformer who lived her beliefs, never wearing slave-made cotton or eating slave-produced sugar.[5]

During six mostly schoolless years before she entered Cornell, Florence systematically read through her father's library, imbibing the fiction of Dickens and Thackeray, Louisa May Alcott and Horatio Alger; the poetry of Shakespeare, Milton, Byron, and Goldsmith; the writings of James Madison; histories by Bancroft, Prescott, and Parkman; and the moral and political philosophy of Emerson, Channing, Burke, Carlyle, Godwin, and Spencer. These readings helped her reach out to her moody and distant father. For that purpose she also began reading government reports at the age of ten and, on trips to Washington, began using the Library of Congress by the time she was twelve.

A darker side of Kelley's childhood was shaped by her mother's permanent depression—caused by the death of five of her eight children before they had reached the age of six. Caroline Bonsall Kelley was a descendant of John Bartram, the Quaker botanist. Orphaned at the age of nine, she was raised in the Pugh family. With the death of her infants, Caroline developed a "settled, gentle melancholy" that threatened to envelop her daughter as long as she lived at home.[6] Florence grew up with two brothers, but no sisters survived. Keenly aware of the high social cost of infant mortality to nineteenth-century families, she developed a rage against human suffering that formed her lifelong career as a reformer.

WOMEN'S PROMINENCE
IN EARLY SOCIAL SCIENCE

Like higher education, the newly emerging field of social science served as a critical vehicle by which middle-class women expanded the space they occupied within American civic life between 1860 and 1890. Social science leveled the playing field on which women interacted with men in public life. It offered tools of analysis that enhanced women's ability to investigate economic and social change, speak for the welfare of the whole society, devise policy initiatives, and oversee their implementation. Yet at the same time, social science also deepened women's gender identity in public life and attached their civic activism even more securely to gender-specific issues.[7]

Kelley's early commitment to social science as a tool for social reform built on a generation of women's presence in American social science. Women came with the civic territory that social science embraced. Caroline Dall had been a cofounder of the association in 1865, and other women were especially active in the American Social Science Association's (ASSA) department of education, public health, and social economy, which gave them clear but limited mandates for leadership.

The question of "After college, what?" was as pertinent to Florence Kelley as it was to other women graduates.[8] Barred from admission to graduate study at the University of Pennsylvania because she was a woman, she faced a very limited set of opportunities. First she threw her energies into the New Century Working Women's Guild, an organization that fostered middle-class aid for self-supporting women. She helped found the Guild, taught classes in history, and assembled the group's library. Then, remaining a dutiful daughter, in 1882 she accompanied her brother when his doctor prescribed a winter of European travel to cure temporary blindness. In Europe she encountered M. Carey Thomas, a Cornell acquaintance, who had just completed a Ph.D. at the University of Zurich, the only European university that granted degrees to women. Thomas recommended that Kelley go to Zurich for graduate study.

Initially accompanied by her mother and younger brother, Kelley studied government and law at Zurich between 1883 and 1886. There she promptly befriended exiled socialist students from Russia and Germany. To the shocked amazement of her family and friends, in 1885 she married Lazare Wischnewetzky, a Russian, Jewish, socialist, medical student. She then gave birth to three children in three years.

Cloaked with her new personal identity as a European married woman, she stopped communicating with her family and began to forge a new political identity. Rejecting American public culture because it limited her opportunities for social service and because her father's career revealed so starkly that culture's tolerance of social injustice, she underwent a dramatic conversion to socialism, joined the German Social Democratic Party (SPD), and began to translate the writings of Friedrich Engels and Karl Marx. Outlawed in Germany, the SPD maintained its European headquarters in Zurich, where Kelley met many of its leaders. Since the death of Marx in 1885, Engels had become the chief theoretician of German socialism. Kelley's translation of his 1845 book, *The Condition of the Working Class in England,* is still the preferred scholarly version of that now-classic social science study. This project launched a close but troubled relationship with Engels that persisted until his death in 1895.[9]

When Kelley returned to the United States in 1886 with her small family, she searched without success for a political context capable of sustaining her newfound radicalism. Settling in New York City, within a year she was expelled from the Socialist Labor Party, predominantly a German-speaking immigrant group, for "incessant slander" against party leaders, whom she denounced for failing to recognize the importance of the writings of Marx and Engels.[10] Having reached a political dead-end, Kelley reoriented her use of social science as a vehicle for her activism. She resumed contact with her Philadelphia family and became a self-taught authority on child labor in the United States, as well as a sharp critic of state bureaus of labor, the agencies responsible for monitoring child labor. Writing articles on child labor that deployed both statistical and rhetorical power, she discovered that her most responsive publisher was the Woman's Temperance Publication Association, which printed her lengthy, hard-hitting pamphlet, *Our Toiling Children,* in 1889.

Lazare Wischnewetzky, meanwhile, never having managed to establish a medical practice, began battering her. After enduring this for more than a year, she borrowed money from a friend and fled with her children to Chicago. There she headed for the Woman's Temple, a twelve-story office building and hotel constructed by the Woman's Christian Temperance Union, where she was directed to an even more congenial place—Hull House, the nation's preeminent social settlement founded by Jane Addams and Ellen Gates Starr in 1889.

THE POLITICAL AUTONOMY OF WOMEN'S SEPARATE INSTITUTIONS

"We were welcomed as though we had been invited," Kelley later wrote about her arrival at Hull House. "We stayed."[11] Addams arranged for Kelley's children, Nicholas, Margaret, and John, age seven, six, and five, to live with the family of Henry Demarest Lloyd and his wife, Jessie Bross Lloyd. That winter Kelley cast her lot with Addams and Hull House, remaining until May 1, 1899, when she returned to New York as a figure who had achieved national renown as a reformer of working conditions for women and children.

Chicago and the remarkable political culture of the city's women opened opportunities to Kelley that she had sought in vain in Philadelphia, Germany, and New York.

Exploiting those opportunities to the fullest, she drew on the strength of three overlapping circles of politically active women. The core of her support lay with the community of women at Hull House. This remarkable group helped her reconstruct her political identity within women's class-bridging activism, and provided her with an economic and emotional alternative to married family life. Partly overlapping with this nucleus were women trade unionists. By drawing women and men trade unionists into the settlement community, she achieved the passage of pathbreaking legislation. Toward the end of her years in Chicago, she worked with the circle of middle-class and upper-middle-class women who supported Hull House and labor reform.

Florence Kelley's life in Chicago began with her relationship with Jane Addams. Julia Lathrop, another Hull House resident, reported that Kelley and Addams "understood each other's powers" instantly and worked together in a "wonderfully effective way."[12] Addams, the philosopher with a deep appreciation of the unity of life, was better able to construct a vehicle for expressing that unity in day-to-day living than she was capable of devising a diagram for charting the future. And Kelley, the politician with a thorough understanding of what the future should look like, was better able to invoke that future than to express it in her day-to-day existence. Addams taught Kelley how to live and have faith in an imperfect world, and Kelley taught Addams how to make demands on the future.

At Hull House Kelley joined a community of college-educated women reformers who, like Addams and herself, sought work commensurate with their talents. Julia Lathrop, almost twenty years later the first director of the U.S. Children's Bureau, had joined the settlement before Kelley. Alice Hamilton, who arrived in 1897, developed the field of industrial medicine. These four, with Mary Rozet Smith, Jane Addams's life partner, became the settlement's main leaders. In addition to these women, Kelley forged close ties with Mary Kenney, a trade union organizer affiliated with the settlement, who lived nearby with her mother.

Since her father had lost most of his money before his death in 1890, Kelley had to support herself and her children. She first did so by working for the Illinois Bureau of Labor Statistics and the U.S. Department of Labor, collecting data for governmental studies of working conditions. A good example of the empowerment of her Hull House residence lay in her use of data collected for the U.S. Department of Labor, which in 1895 formed the basis of the maps published in *Hull House Maps and Papers*. She and four government "schedule men" collected responses to sixty-four questions on printed schedules from "each house, tenement, and room" in the ward surrounding Hull House.[13] From this data Carroll Wright, head of the Department of Labor, constructed scores of tables. But Kelley and Hull House associates, using only data about nationalities and wages in conjunction with residential information, created color-coded maps that displayed geographic patterns that told more than Wright's charts. Because the maps defined spatial relationships among human groups, they vividly depicted social and economic relationships: the concentration of certain ethnic groups in certain blocks; the relationship between poverty and race; the distances between the isolated brothel district and the rest of the ward; the very poor who lived in crowded, airless rooms in the rear of tenements and those with more resources in the front; and the omniscient observer and the observed. Expressing the democratic relationship among Hull House residents, *Hull House Maps and Papers* listed only "Residents of Hull House" as the volume's editors.

Kelley described the transformative effect of the Hull House community on her personal life in a letter to her mother a few weeks after her arrival. "In the few weeks of my stay here I have won for the children and myself many and dear friends whose generous hospitality astonishes me. It is understood that I am to resume the maiden name and that the children are to have it."[14] By joining a community of women, she had achieved a new degree of personal autonomy.

CHALLENGING TRADITIONS OF LIMITED GOVERNMENT

In the spring of 1892, Kelley used Hull House as a base to exert leadership within an anti-sweatshop campaign that had been launched in 1888 by the Illinois Woman's Alliance, a class-bridging coalition of women's organizations. At mass meetings that attacked the sweatshop system, Kelley shared the podium with Mary Kenney, Henry Demarest Lloyd, and other Chicago notables such as Reverend Jenkin Lloyd Jones, minister at All Souls' Unitarian Church, the most liberal pulpit in Chicago, and with young trade union organizers in the clothing industry such as Abraham Bisno.

Campaigns against sweatshops were widespread in American cities in the 1890s. These efforts targeted "predatory management" and "parasitic manufacturers" who paid such low wages to their workers as to require them to seek support from relief or charity, thereby indirectly providing employers with subsidies that enabled them to lower wages further.[15] Supported by trade unions, these campaigns used a variety of strategies to shift work from tenement sweatshops to factories. In factories, union organizing could more easily succeed in improving working conditions and raising wages to levels necessary to sustain life.

Outcries raised by anti-sweatshop campaigns prompted government inquiries, and in 1893, after intense lobbying in Springfield by Hull House residents and other well-known Chicago women, the passage of path-breaking legislation drafted by Florence Kelley. That year Governor John Peter Altgeld appointed Kelley to a position the new statute created: Chief Factory Inspector of Illinois. Nowhere else in the Western world was a woman trusted to enforce the labor legislation of a city, let alone of a large industrial region the size of Illinois. With eleven deputies, five of whom were required to be women, and a budget of $28,000, for the next three years Kelley enforced the act's chief clauses. The act banned the labor of children under fourteen years of age; it regulated the labor of children age fourteen to sixteen; it outlawed the production of garments in tenements; it prohibited the employment of women and minors for more than eight hours a day; and it created a state office of factory inspection.

The statute's eight-hour clause made it the most advanced in the United States, equaled only by an eight-hour law for all workers in Australia. The limitation of hours, whether through statutes or union negotiations with employers, was the second most important goal of the labor movement between 1870 and 1910, the first being the recognition of the right of workers to form unions. Skilled workers had acquired the eight-hour day for themselves in many trades by the 1890s, but since women were not admitted to most skilled occupations, their hours remained long, often extending to twelve or even fourteen hours a day. In the late 1880s more than 85 percent of female wage earners were between the ages of fourteen and twenty-five and only about 5 percent were married.[16] Excluded from access to skilled jobs and presumed to leave the paid labor force upon marriage, they were crowded into a few unskilled occupations, where they were easily replaced, and employers exploited them by requiring long hours and paying low wages. Statutes that limited women's hours limited this exploitation. How to achieve such reduction of hours without reducing wages was a challenge that Kelley's office met by promoting the formation of unions among affected women workers, thereby helping them negotiate better wages for the hours they worked.

But the reduction of women's hours by statute had other beneficial effects: in many occupations it also reduced the hours of unskilled men, as was the case in garment-making sweatshops. In this and many other occupations, it proved impossible to keep men working longer than the legal limit of the working day for women. Therefore, hours statutes drove sweatshops out of business, since their profits could only be achieved through long hours. In the United States more than in other industrializing nations, the union movement consisted with few exceptions (miners being the chief exception) of skilled workers who shunned responsibility for the welfare of unskilled workers. Therefore, in the United States more than in elsewhere, gender-specific reforms like Kelley's 1893 legislation—undertaken by women for women—also had the effect of aiding all unskilled workers, men as well as women and children. In the United States, where labor movements were not as strong as they were elsewhere, gender-specific reforms accomplished goals that elsewhere were achieved under the auspices of class-specific efforts.[17]

In an era when courts nullified legislative attempts to intervene in the laissez-faire rela-

tionship between capital and labor, Kelley's enforcement of this new eight-hour law was inevitably challenged in the courts. In 1895 the Illinois Supreme Court found the eight-hour clause of the 1893 law unconstitutional because it violated women's right to contract their labor on any terms set by their employer. This setback made Kelley determined to change the power of state courts to overturn hours laws for women.

The high tide of Kelley's achievements between 1893 and 1896 ebbed quickly when Altgeld lost the election of 1896. His successor replaced her with a person who did not challenge the economic status quo, and she was unable to find work commensurate with her talents. German admirers came to her rescue. For fifty dollars a month she provided a leading German reform periodical with assessments of recent American social legislation. She also worked in the Crerar Library, a reference library specializing in economic, scientific, and medical topics.

Needing to reach beyond the limits of Hull House activities, Kelley began to work more closely with Ellen Henrotin. Wife of a leading Chicago banker, Henrotin had supported Kelley's legislation in 1892, and spoke vigorously at a rally to defend the law in 1894, urging those in attendance to "agitate for shorter hours for women because it means in the end shorter hours for all workers, men and women."[18] Henrotin's organization in 1893 of thirty women's congresses at the Chicago World's Fair catapulted her into the presidency of the General Federation of Women's Clubs (GFWC; founded 1890) from 1894 to 1898. By 1897 the GFWC served as an umbrella organization for more than five hundred women's clubs, including the powerful Chicago Women's Club. Fostering the creation of over twenty state federations to coordinate those clubs, Henrotin moved the GFWC in progressive directions by establishing national committees on industrial working conditions and national health. In this way she directed the path of what was to become one of the largest grass-roots organizations of American women beyond the minimal goals of good government and civil service reform to the more challenging issues of social inequalities and social justice.

Reflecting her growing awareness of the potential power of women's organizations as a vehicle for her social justice agenda, in 1897 Kelley began to work closely with Henrotin in organizing an Illinois Consumers' League. They built on the example of the New York Consumers' League, which had been founded in 1891 to channel consumers' consciousness toward political action on behalf of workers who made the goods that consumers purchased.

THE NATIONAL CONSUMERS' LEAGUE AND NEW STRATEGIES FOR SOCIAL JUSTICE

Kelley's work with Henrotin helped her make the biggest career step of her life when, in 1899, she agreed to serve as Secretary of the newly formed National Consumers' League, a position she held until her death in 1932. With a salary of $1,500 plus traveling and other expenses, the job offered financial stability and a chance to develop a more radical and more focused women's organization than the GFWC.

When she carried her formidable talents into the National Consumers' League in 1899, women's political culture gained a warrior with formidable rhetorical and organizational skills. She quickly made the National Consumers' League (NCL) into the nation's leading promoter of protective labor legislation for women and children. Between 1900 and 1904 she built sixty-four local consumer leagues—one in nearly every large city outside the South. Through a demanding travel schedule, which required her to spend one day on the road for every day she worked at her desk, Kelley maintained close contact with local leagues, urging them to implement the national organization's agenda and inspiring them to greater action within their states and municipalities. At the age of forty she had finally found a platform that matched her talents and goals.

In New York she lived until 1926 at Lillian Wald's nurses' settlement on Henry Street on Manhattan's Lower East Side. Her children moved east with her. Supported by aid from Jane Addams's life partner, Mary Rozet Smith, Nicholas Kelley graduated from Harvard in 1905 and then from Harvard Law School. Living in Manhattan, he became his mother's closest advisor. In a blow that caused Kelley to spend the rest of that year in retirement in Maine, her daughter Margaret died of heart failure during her first week at Smith College in 1905. After this bereavement Kelley maintained a summer home on Penobscot Bay, Maine, where she retreated for periods of intense work with a secretary each summer. John Kelley never found a professional niche, but remained close to his mother and joined her in Maine each summer.

THE WHITE LABEL CAMPAIGN: NEW WAYS OF EDUCATING MIDDLE-CLASS WOMEN ABOUT INDUSTRIAL WORKING CONDITIONS

The national branch of the Consumers' League was formed in 1898 to coordinate the efforts of previously existing leagues in New York, Brooklyn, Philadelphia, Boston, and Chicago, all of which had conducted campaigns against sweatshops. At a convention of the local leagues called to coordinate their anti-sweatshop efforts, Kelley proposed the creation of a consumers' label as a way of identifying goods made under fair conditions. Her proposal galvanized the convention into creating a national organization "for the express purpose of offering a Consumers' League Label" nationally, recognizing that local efforts against sweatshops could never succeed until all producers were "compelled to compete on a higher level," and agreeing that the label could be a means of achieving that goal.[19] The NCL awarded its label to manufacturers who obeyed state factory laws, produced goods only on their own premises, did not require employees to work overtime, and did not employ children under sixteen years of age. To enforce the label, however, factories had to be inspected. Local leagues had employed their own factory inspectors; Kelley became the league's national inspector.

In determining whether local factories qualified for the label, local league members had to educate themselves about local working conditions. They had to pose and answer questions new to middle-class women, though painfully familiar to union organizers: Did the manufacturer subcontract to home workers in tenements? Were children employed? Were state factory laws violated? Could workers live on their wages, or were they forced to augment their pay with relief or charitable donations? How far below the standard set by the consumers' label were their own state laws? Even more technical questions arose when leagues came into contact with factory inspectors, bureaus of labor statistics, state legislatures, and courts. Should the state issue licenses for home workers? What was the relationship between illiteracy in child workers and the enforcement of effective child labor laws? Was their own state high or low on the NCL's ranked list showing the number of illiterate child workers in each? Should laws prohibit the labor of children at age fourteen or sixteen? Should exceptions be made for the children of widows? How energetically were state factory laws enforced? How could local factory standards be improved? These questions, recently quite alien to middle-class women, now held the interest of thousands of the most politically active among them. This was no small accomplishment. State leagues differed in the degree to which they worked with state officials, but wherever they existed they created new civic space in which women used their new knowledge and power to expand state responsibility for the welfare of women and children workers.

On the road steadily between 1900 and 1907, Kelley inspected workshops, awarded the label to qualified manufacturers, and strengthened local leagues. Her efforts were rewarded by the spectacular growth of NCL locals, both in number and location. The NCL's 1901 report mentioned thirty leagues in eleven states; by 1906 they numbered sixty-three in twenty states.

Flourishing local leagues sustained the national's existence, channeling money, ideas, and the support of other local groups into the national office. At the same time, locals implemented the national's agenda at the state level. Most league members were white, urban, northern, middle-class Protestants, but Jewish women held important positions of leadership. Catholic women became more visible after Cardinal James Gibbons of Baltimore consented to serve as vice president of a Maryland league and Bishop J. Regis Canevin of Pittsburgh encouraged members of that city's Ladies Catholic Benevolent Association to join. Two important reasons for the absence of black women from the NCL's membership and agenda were the league's focus on Northern urban manufacturing, and the residence of 90 percent of the nation's black population in the South, employed primarily in agriculture, in 1900.

10-HOUR LAWS FOR WOMEN: NEW USES OF SOCIAL SCIENCE

The work of educating her constituency being achieved by 1907, Kelley implemented a second stage of league work. With the use of social science data, the NCL overcame legal obstacles to the passage of state laws limiting women's hours. The overturning of Illinois's 1893 law by Illinois's Supreme Court in 1895 made Kelley determined to defend such laws before the U.S. Supreme Court. When an Oregon ten-hour law came before the court in 1907, she threw the resources of the NCL into its defense. This case, *Muller* v. *Oregon,* pitted the NCL and its Oregon branch against a laundry owner who disputed the state's ability to regulate working hours in non-hazardous occupations. For what became known as the "Brandeis Brief," Kelley's Research Director, Josephine Goldmark, gathered printed evidence from medical and other authorities (most of whom were British or European) to demonstrate that workdays longer than ten hours were hazardous to the health of women. Goldmark obtained the services of her brother-in-law, Louis D. Brandeis, a leading Boston attorney, who successfully argued the case on sociological rather than legal grounds, using the evidence that Goldmark had compiled. Thus at the same time that this case cleared the way for state hours laws for women, it also established the court's recognition of sociological evidence, a strategy that sustained the court's ruling against segregated schools in *Brown* v. *Board of Education* in 1954.

In the years immediately following the *Muller* decision, inspired by Kelley's leadership, and supported by other groups, local consumer leagues gained the passage in twenty states of the first laws limiting women's working hours. Also responding to the decision, nineteen other states revised and expanded their laws governing women's working hours.

The Supreme Court's 1908 opinion tried to block the possibility of extending such protections to men by emphasizing women's special legal status (they did not possess the same contractual rights as men) and their physiological difference from men (their health affected the health of their future children). Nevertheless, in 1917 Kelley and the NCL again cooperated suc-

Two contrasting photographs intended by photojournalist Lewis Hine to reveal the class-based nature of childhood at the turn of the century. Middle-class girls (top) *are pushing a doll made by child laborers and their mother* (bottom). *(Photos courtesy of the Library of Congress. Caption and photoidentification by Miriam Formanek-Brunell,* Made to Play House: Dolls and the Commercialization of American Girlhood, 1830–1930 *[New Haven, Yale University Press, 1993], p. 110.)*

cessfully with the Oregon league in arguing another case on sociological grounds before the U.S. Supreme Court, *Bunting* v. *Oregon,* in which the Court upheld the constitutionality of hours laws for men in non-hazardous occupations. Viewing laws for women as an entering wedge for improving conditions for all working people, Kelley achieved that goal in the progression from *Muller* to *Bunting.* In this as in other aspects of her work with the League, though nominally focused on gender, her reforms had class-wide effects.

THE MINIMUM WAGE CAMPAIGN: NEW USES OF THE POWER OF WOMEN'S ORGANIZATIONS

As early as 1899, Florence Kelley had hoped "to include a requirement as to minimal wages" in the NCL's White Label. Australia and New Zealand had already organized wage boards as part of compulsory arbitration, but the path to an American equivalent did not seem clear until she and other Consumers' League members in 1908 attended the First International Conference of Consumers' Leagues, in Geneva, where they learned about the proposed British wage law of 1909, which that year implemented minimum wages for all workers in certain poorly paid occupations.

Almost immediately on her return, Kelley established her leadership in what became an enormously successful campaign for minimum wage laws for women in the United States. In her campaign she denounced the large profits made in three industries: retail stores, sweatshop garment making, and textile manufacturers. "Low wages produce more poverty than all other causes together," she insisted, urging that "goods and profits are not ends in themselves to which human welfare may continue to be sacrificed."[20]

Kelley argued that minimum wages would raise the standards in women's employment by recognizing their need to support themselves. "So long as women's wages rest upon the assumption that every woman has a husband, father, brother, or lover contributing to her support, so long these sinister incidents of women's industrial employment (tuberculosis, insanity, vice) are inevitable." She urged that "society itself must build the floor beneath their feet."[21]

Minimum wage legislation was much more difficult to achieve than maximum hours laws because, as one of Kelley's allies put it, wage legislation "pierces to the heart the classic claim that industry is a purely private affair."[22] For this reason, Kelley and the NCL were unaided in their efforts by their male-dominated equivalent, the American Association for Labor Legislation (AALL). When Kelley appealed in 1910 to their executive director, John Andrews, he loftily replied: "I question very seriously the wisdom of injecting the minimum wage proposal into the legislative campaign of this year, because I do not believe our courts would at the present time uphold such legislation, and I am afraid it would seriously jeopardize the splendid progress now being made to establish maximum working hours."[23] Two years later the AALL still opposed wage legislation as premature.

Kelley and the NCL were able to move ahead with this pathbreaking legislation because they could mobilize grass-roots support for it at local and state levels. The AALL had no local branches; instead, their power flowed from a network of male academic experts who advised politicians about legislation. If politicians were not ready to move, neither was the AALL. The NCL, by contrast, had in its sixty-four local branches enough political muscle to take the initiative and lead politicians where they otherwise wouldn't have gone.

In 1912 Massachusetts passed the first minimum wage law for women, followed in 1913 by eight additional states: California, Colorado, Minnesota, Nebraska, Oregon, Utah, Washington, and Wisconsin. By 1919 fourteen states and the District of Columbia and Puerto Rico had enacted minimum wage statutes for women. The success of these laws influenced the inclusion of a minimum wage for men *and* women in the Fair Labor Standards Act (FLSA) of 1938. In 1942, when the U.S. Supreme Court approved the constitutionality of the FLSA, the eight-hour day and the minimum wage became part of the social contract for most American workers. The class-bridging activism of middle-class women in the NCL forged the way with these fundamental reforms.

GAINS AND SETBACKS IN THE 1920s

At Henry Street, Kelley continued to benefit from the same consolidation of female reform talents that had sustained her efforts at Hull House in Chicago. The creation of the U.S. Children's Bureau in 1911 sprang from her discussions with Lillian Wald. The Children's Bureau was the only governmental agency in any industrial society that was headed and run by women. Kelley thought that her most important contribution to social change was the passage in 1921 of the Sheppard-Towner Maternity and Infancy Protection Act, which first allocated federal funds to health care. She was instrumental in the creation of the coalition that backed the act's passage, the Women's Joint Congressional Committee, and in the coalition's successful campaign for the bill in Congress. Although limited to a program administered by the Children's Bureau to combat infant and maternal mortality, Kelley thought the Sheppard-Towner Act marked the beginning of a national health care program.[24]

After this high point in 1921, however, the decade brought a series of reversals that threatened to undo her most of her achievements. In 1923 the U.S. Supreme Court in *Adkins* v. *Children's Hospital* found Washington, D.C.'s wage law for women unconstitutional. Many state wage boards continued to function during the 1920s and 1930s, however, providing ample evidence of the benefits of the law, but no new wage laws were passed. In 1926, Congress refused to allocate new funds for Sheppard-Towner programs, and responsibility for maternal and infant health returned to state and county levels.[25]

Just as important, by 1922 Kelley's strategy of using gender-specific legislation as a surrogate for class legislation had generated opposition from a new quarter—women who did not themselves benefit from gendered laws. The National Woman's Party (NWP), formed in 1916 by the charismatic leadership of Alice Paul and funded almost entirely by Alva Belmont, created a small coalition consisting primarily of professional women with some wage-earning women who worked in male-dominated occupations. Despite Kelley's strong objections over the damage they would do to gender-specific legislation, including the Sheppard-Towner Act, in 1921 the NWP proposed an Equal Rights Amendment to the U.S. Constitution (ERA). Although mainstream organizations such as the General Federation of Women's Clubs and the League of Women Voters continued to support gender-specific

legislation, the NWP's proposed amendment undercut the momentum of such gendered strategies. In the 1920s most wage-earning women opposed the ERA because they stood to lose rather than benefit from it. By the 1970s changes in working conditions and protective labor laws meant that most wage-earning women stood to benefit from the amendment, and many more supported it.[26]

Even more damaging than these reversals, however, were the right-wing attacks launched by hyperpatriots against Kelley and other women reformers during the "red scare" of the 1920s. *The Woman Patriot* exemplified these attacks. Launched in 1916 and published twice a month, before the enactment of the woman suffrage amendment this newsletter was subtitled *Dedicated to the Defense of Womanhood, Motherhood, the Family and the State AGAINST Suffragism, Feminism and Socialism.* After 1920 the newsletter dropped its reference to suffrage, but continued its virulent attacks on the social agenda of women reformers. "SHALL BOLSHEVIST-FEMINISTS SECRETLY GOVERN AMERICA?" their headlines screamed, referring to the Sheppard-Towner Act. When *The Woman Patriot* referred to Kelley as "Mrs. Wischnewtzky" and called her "Moscow's chief conspirator," Kelley urged Addams to join her in a libel suit against them. Addams gently persuaded her to ignore the attacks. Kelley then wrote an impassioned series of autobiographical articles that established her lineage as an inheritor of American ideals and a dedicated promoter of American values.[27]

Attacks on women reformers in the 1920s were in part generated by supporters of American military expansion in the aftermath of World War I, when Kelley and many other women reformers were actively promoting peace and disarmament. For example, *The Woman Patriot* characterized the support that women reformers were giving to disarmament as "an organized internationalist Bolshevist-Feminist plot to embarrass the Limitation of Armaments Conference." Government employees joined the attack in 1924, when Lucia Maxwell of the Chemical Warfare Department of the Department of War issued a "Spider Web Chart" entitled "The Socialist-Pacifist Movement in America Is an Absolutely Fundamental and Integral Part of International Socialism." Depicting the connections between women's organizations and Congressional lobbying for social legislation and for disarmament, the chart sought to characterize as "pacifist-socialist" most women's organizations in the United States, including the National Consumers' League, the National League of Women Voters, the General Federation of Women's Clubs, the Woman's Christian Temperance Union, the National Congress of Mothers and Parent-Teachers Association, the National Women's Trade Union League, the American Home Economics Association, the American Association of University Women, the National Council of Jewish Women, the Girls' Friendly Society, the Young Women's Christian Association, and the National Federation of Business and Professional Women.[28]

Historians have not measured the effect of these attacks on the political agendas of women's organizations, but after these attacks the agendas of many women's organizations, for example that of the League for Women Voters, shifted from social justice to good government projects, from support for a Child Labor Amendment to the U.S. Constitution to advocacy for a city manager form of governance.[29] Such a shift was in keeping with the demise of the Progressive movement after World War I. But that demise was hastened by the rise of "red scare" tactics in American political culture.

Florence Kelley did not live to see many of her initiatives incorporated into federal legislation in the 1930s. Faced with the collapse of the American economy in the Great Depression of 1929–1939, policymakers drew heavily on the legacy of Progressive reforms initiated between 1890 and 1920. Florence Kelley's legacies, including the minimum wage and maximum hours legislation incorporated in the Fair Labor Standards Act of 1938, were strong enough to survive the reversals of the 1920s. In 1933, with the inauguration of Franklin Delano Roosevelt, Kelley's protégée Frances Perkins became the first woman to serve as a cabinet member. Reflecting the power of women's organizations in shaping a new social contract for American working people, Perkins was appointed Secretary of Labor.[30]

But Kelley's legacy reaches beyond any specific policies. U.S. Supreme Court Justice Felix Frankfurter said in 1953 that the nation owed Kelley an "enduring debt for the continuing process she so largely helped to initi-ate, by which social legislation is promoted and eventually gets on the statute books."[31] As Kelley shaped it during her long reform career between 1890 and 1930, that process relied heavily on women's organizations and their ability to act independently of the political status quo.

NOTES

1. James Weber Linn, *Jane Addams: A Biography* (New York, 1938), 138.

2. For an overview of social change in the Progressive era, see Steven J. Diner, *A Very Different Age: Americans of the Progressive Era* (New York, 1998).

3. For more on Kelley before 1900, see Kathryn Kish Sklar, *Florence Kelley and the Nation's Work: The Rise of Women's Political Culture, 1830–1900* (New Haven, 1995). Specific page references are provided for quotations used below.

4. Mabel Newcomer, *A Century of Higher Education for American Women* (New York, 1959), 37, 46. See also Barbara Miller Solomon, *"In the Company of Educated Women": A History of Women and Higher Education in America* (New Haven, 1985), 62–77.

5. For Kelley's childhood, see Kathryn Kish Sklar, ed., *The Autobiography of Florence Kelley: Notes of Sixty Years* (Chicago, 1986).

6. Sklar, *Autobiography of Florence Kelley*, 30.

7. Kathryn Kish Sklar, "Hull House Maps and Papers: Social Science as Women's Work in the 1890s," in Helene Silverberg, ed., *Gender and American Social Science: The Formative Years* (Princeton, 1998).

8. See Joyce Antler, "After College, What?: New Graduates and the Family Claim," *American Quarterly* 32 (Fall 1980):409–34.

9. See Dorothy Rose Blumberg, "'Dear Mr. Engels': Unpublished Letters, 1884–1894, of Florence Kelley (Wischnewetzky) to Friedrich Engels," *Labor History* 5 (Spring 1964), 103–33.

10. Sklar, *Florence Kelley*, 129.

11. Sklar, *Autobiography of Florence Kelley*, 77.

12. Jane Addams, *My Friend Julia Lathrop* (New York, 1935), 77.

13. Residents of Hull House, *Hull House Maps and Papers* (New York, 1895).

14. FK to Caroline B. Kelley, Chicago, Feb. 24, 1892, Nicholas Kelley Papers, New York Public Library.

15. Kathryn Kish Sklar, "Two Political Cultures in the Progressive Era: The National Consumers' League and the American Association for Labor Legislation," in Linda K. Kerber, Alice Kessler-Harris and Kathryn Kish Sklar, eds., *U.S. History as Women's History: New Feminist Essays* (Chapel Hill, N.C., 1995), 58.

16. U.S. Commissioner of Labor, *Fourth Annual Report, Working Women in Large Cities* (Washington, D.C., 1889), 62–64.

17. For a full argument of this point, see Kathryn Kish Sklar, "The Historical Foundations of Women's Power in the Creation of the American Welfare State,

1830–1930," in Seth Koven and Sonya Michel, eds., *Mothers of a New World: Maternalist Politics and the Origins of Welfare States* (New York, 1993).

18. "Hit at Sweat Shops," *Chicago Tribune*, April 23, 1894; Sklar, *Florence Kelley*, 261.

19. Sklar, *Florence Kelley*, 309.

20. Florence Kelley, "Minimum Wage Boards," *American Journal of Sociology* 17 (Nov. 1911), 303–14.

21. Florence Kelley, "Ten Years from Now," *Survey*, March 26, 1910, 978–81.

22. Sklar, "Two Political Cultures," 60.

23. See, for example, John B. Andrews to Erich Stern, New York, Dec. 14, 1910, American Association for Labor Legislation Papers, Cornell University.

24. See Molly Ladd-Taylor, *Mother-Work: Women, Child Welfare, and the State, 1890–1930* (Urbana, Ill., 1994), 167–96.

25. See J. Stanley Lemons, *The Woman Citizen: Social Feminism in the 1920s* (Urbana, Ill., 1973), 169–76.

26. For the opposition of the progressive mainstream of the women's movement, see Kathryn Kish Sklar, "Why Did Most Politically Active Women Oppose the ERA in the 1920s?" in Joan Hoff-Wilson, ed., *Rights of Passage: the Past and Future of the ERA* (Bloomington, Ind., 1986).

27. *The Woman Patriot*, Vol. 5, no. 29, Nov. 1, 1921, 1. For the complete documents of this correspondence between Kelley and Addams, see Anissa Harper, "Pacifism vs. Patriotism in Women's Organizations in the 1920s: How Was the Debate Shaped by the Expansion of the American Military," in *Women and Social Movements in the United States, 1830–1930*, an Internet website edited by Kathryn Kish Sklar and Thomas Dublin, http://womhist. binghamton.edu. See also Nancy F. Cott, *The Grounding of Modern Feminism* (New Haven, 1987), 243–67.

28. The Spider Web Chart is reproduced in Helen Baker, "How Did the Women's International League for Peace and Freedom Respond to Right Wing Attacks in the 1920s?" in *Women and Social Movements* at http://womhist.binghamton.edu.

29. For example, see the furor aroused within the League of Women Voters over the proposed Child Labor Amendment to the U.S. Constitution in 1924, in Louise M. Young, *In the Public Interest: The League of Women Voters, 1920–1970* (New York, 1989), 97–98.

30. For Perkins see Susan Ware, *Beyond Suffrage: Women in the New Deal* (Cambridge, Mass., 1981), *passim*.

31. Felix Frankfurter, "Foreword," in Josephine Goldmark, *Impatient Crusader: Florence Kelley's Life Story* (Urbana, Ill., 1953), v.

DOCUMENT: Protecting Women Wage-Workers

Muller *v.* Oregon, *1908*

The farmer's workday was sunrise to sunset. When the first factories were established in the early nineteenth century, they were operated for equally long hours. It was a particular interest of laborers and of progressive reformers to support enactment of limits on the workday. The ten-hour day was on the agenda of early labor unions, and the federal civil service adopted it shortly after the Civil War.

But in 1905 the United States Supreme Court refused to uphold a state law limiting the hours of bakers to ten hours a day. Ruling in *Lochner* v. *New York* (198 U.S. 45 [1905]), the Court held that such a law was not "a legitimate exercise of the police power of the State, but an unreasonable, unnecessary, and arbitrary interference with the right and liberty of the individual to contract in relation to his labor. . . ."

After the *Lochner* decision progressives were forced to conclude that it was impractical to support limitations on hours that applied to *all* workers. But it occurred to some that a special case might be made in defense of a limit on working hours for women.

When the constitutionality of the Oregon ten-hour law for women was challenged, Florence Kelley committed the National Consumers' League to its defense. As Kathryn Kish Sklar has explained (pp. 327–39), NCL's Research Director, Josephine Goldmark, prepared a pathbreaking brief, of which only two pages consisted of traditional abstract legal reasoning, and over one hundred pages offered sociological evidence. Her brother-in-law, the future Supreme Court Justice Louis D. Brandeis, argued the case in the U.S. Supreme Court.

In 1908 the Supreme Court upheld the constitutionality of the Oregon law, though making it clear that it was swayed primarily by the case made for women's physical vulnerability and couching the decision in terms of traditional sex roles. Fifteen years later, only five states lacked maximum hour legislation of some sort, although provisions varied widely.

Protective legislation for women had complex consequences. Obviously an eight-hour workday was vastly preferable to a longer one. But in the absence of a minimum wage, women living at the margin of subsistence found that limitations on the hours they could work cut their income or speeded up their piecework; some would not have chosen to trade time for money. Maximum hour legislation was often supplemented by restrictions against night work and "heavy" work (the latter often conveniently defined to include well-paying skilled work like iron molding), which further segregated women in the workplace and gave men an advantage in the competition for jobs. There is substantial evidence that male unions understood this when they supported protective legislation.*

---

*See Alice Kessler-Harris, *Out to Work: A History of Wage-Earning Women in the United States* (New York, 1982), pp. 201–5.

Compare the reasoning in *Muller* to that offered in the *Bradwell* case (pp. 248–49) more than thirty-five years before. What were the advantages of pressing the argument of female weakness? What were the disadvantages?

MR. JUSTICE DAVID J. BREWER:

. . . It may not be amiss, in the present case, before examining the constitutional question, to notice the course of legislation, as well as expressions of opinion from other than judicial sources. In the brief filed by Mr. Louis D. Brandeis for the defendant . . . is a very copious collection of all these matters. . . .

The legislation and opinions referred to . . . may not be, technically speaking, authorities, and in them is little or no discussion of the constitutional question presented to us for determination, yet, they are significant of a widespread belief that woman's physical structure, and the functions she performs in consequence thereof, justify special legislation restricting or qualifying the conditions under which she should be permitted to toil. . . .

That woman's physical structure and the performance of maternal functions place her at a disadvantage in the struggle for subsistence is obvious. This is especially true when the burdens of motherhood are upon her. Even when they are not, by abundant testimony of the medical fraternity continuance for a long time on her feet at work, repeating this from day to day, tends to injurious effects upon the body, and, as healthy mothers are essential to vigorous offspring, the physical well-being of woman becomes an object of public interest and care in order to preserve the strength and vigor of the race.

. . . Differentiated by these matters from the other sex, she is properly placed in a class by herself, and legislation designed for her protection may be sustained, even when like legislation is not necessary for men, and could not be sustained. It is impossible to close one's eyes to the fact that she still looks to her brother and depends upon him. . . . her physical structure and a proper discharge of her maternal functions—having in view not merely her own health, but the well-being of the race—justify legislation to protect her from the greed as well as the passion of man. The limitations which this statute places upon her contractual powers, upon her right to agree with her employer as to the time she shall labor, are not imposed solely for her benefit, but also largely for the benefit of all. Many words cannot make this plainer. The two sexes differ in structure of body, in the functions to be performed by each, in the amount of physical strength, in the capacity for long continued labor, particularly when done standing, the influence of vigorous health upon the future well-being of the race, the self-reliance which enables one to assert full rights, and in the capacity to maintain the struggle for subsistence. This difference justifies a difference in legislation, and upholds that which is designed to compensate for some of the burdens which rest upon her.

We have not referred in this discussion to the denial of the elective franchise in the State of Oregon, for while it may disclose a lack of political equality in all things with her brother, that is not of itself decisive. The reason runs deeper, and rests in the inherent difference between the two sexes.

For these reasons, and without questioning in any respect the decision in *Lochner* v. *New York,* we are of the opinion that it cannot be adjudged that the act in question is in conflict with the Federal Constitution, so far as it respects the work of a female in a laundry, and the judgment of the Supreme Court of Oregon is Affirmed.

Pauline Newman, "We fought and we bled and we died . . ."

One of the four young garment industry workers whose organizing activities emerged so vividly from the pages of Annelise Orleck's account, Pauline Newman had started out at the Triangle Shirtwaist Factory, which became the scene of one of the great industrial tragedies in New York City's history. Although the factory contained several elevators and two staircases, the eight-story wooden building had no sprinkler system; the doors to the fire escapes were locked to prevent outdoor relaxation. When fire broke out in 1911, five hundred employees—many of them young Jewish and Italian women—were trapped behind locked doors. Some jumped to their deaths; others burned or asphyxiated inside. Altogether the fire claimed the lives of 146 women. Viewing their charred bodies on the street, one reporter recalled that some of these same women had gone on strike only the year before to demand decent wages, more sanitary working conditions, and safety precautions.

Educational director for the International Ladies Garment Workers' Union until her death in 1986, Newman conveys in her own words what it was like to be a garment worker in the early twentieth century. What does she feel has been gained by organized labor? What does she feel has been lost over the years?

A cousin of mine worked for the Triangle Shirtwaist Company and she got me on there in October of 1901. It was probably the largest shirtwaist factory in the city of New York then. They had more than two hundred operators, cutters, examiners, finishers. Altogether more than four hundred people on two floors. The fire took place on one floor, the floor where we worked. You've probably heard about that. But that was years later.

We started work at seven-thirty in the morning, and during the busy season we worked until nine in the evening. They didn't pay you any overtime and they didn't give you anything for supper money. Sometimes they'd give you a little apple pie if you had to work very late. That was all. Very generous.

What I had to do was not really very difficult. It was just monotonous. When the shirtwaists were finished at the machine there were some threads that were left, and all the youngsters—we had a corner on the floor that resembled a kindergarten—we were given little scissors to cut the threads off. It wasn't heavy work, but it was monotonous, because you did the same thing from seven-thirty in the morning till nine at night.

Well, of course, there were [child labor] laws on the books, but no one bothered to enforce them. The employers were always tipped off if there was going to be an inspection. "Quick," they'd say, "into the boxes!" And we children would climb into the big boxes the finished shirts were stored in. Then some shirts were piled on top of us, and when the inspector came—no children. The factory always got an okay from the inspector, and I suppose someone at City Hall got a little something, too.

The employers didn't recognize anyone working for them as a human being. You were not allowed to sing. Operators would have liked to have sung, because they, too, had the same thing to do and weren't allowed to sing. We weren't allowed to talk to each other. Oh, no, they would sneak up behind if you were found talking to your next colleague. You were admonished: "If you keep on you'll be fired."

There was no morgue in New York City large enough to hold the bodies of the young women who had jumped from the burning buildings of the Triangle Shirtwaist Company. They were laid out on a pier in the open air for families to identify. (Courtesy of UNITE Archives, Kheel Center for Labor-Management Documentation and Archives, School of Industrial and Labor Relations, Cornell University, Ithaca, New York.)

If you went to the toilet and you were there longer than the floor lady thought you should be, you would be laid off for half a day and sent home. And, of course, that meant no pay. You were not allowed to have your lunch on the fire escape in the summertime. The door was locked to keep us in. That's why so many people were trapped when the fire broke out.

My pay was $1.50 a week no matter how many hours I worked. My sisters made $6.00 a week; and the cutters, they were skilled workers, they might get as much as $12.00. The employers had a sign in the elevator that said: "If you don't come in on Sunday, don't come in on Monday." You were expected to work every day if they needed you and the pay was the same whether you worked extra or not. You had to be there at seven-thirty, so you got up at five-thirty, took the horse car, then the electric trolley to Greene Street, to be there on time. . . .

I stopped working at the Triangle Factory during the strike in 1909 and I didn't go back. The union sent me out to raise money for the strikers. I apparently was able to articulate my feelings and opinions about the criminal conditions, and they didn't have anyone else who could do better, so they assigned me. And I was successful getting money. After my first speech before the Central Trade and Labor Council I got front-page publicity, including my picture. I was only about fifteen then. Everybody saw it. Wealthy women were curious and they asked me if I would speak to them in their homes. I said I would if they would contribute to the strike, and they agreed. So I spent my time from November to the end of March upstate in New York, speaking to the ladies of the Four Hundred [the elite of New York's society] and sending money back. . . .

We didn't gain very much at the end of the strike. I think the hours were reduced to fifty-six a week or something like that. We got a 10 percent increase in wages. I think that the best thing that the strike did was to lay a foundation on which to build a union. There was so much feeling against unions then. The judge, when one of our girls came before him, said to her: "You're not striking against your employer, you know, young lady. You're striking against God," and sentenced her to two weeks on Blackwell's Island, which is now Welfare Island. And a lot of them got a taste of the club. . . .

After the 1909 strike I worked with the union, organizing in Philadelphia and Cleveland and other places, so I wasn't at the Triangle Shirtwaist Factory when the fire broke out, but a lot of my friends were. I was in Philadelphia for the union and, of course, someone from here called me immediately and I came back. It's very difficult to describe the feeling because I knew the place and I knew so many of the girls. The thing that bothered me was the employers got a lawyer. How anyone could have *defended* them!—because I'm quite sure that the fire was planned for insurance purposes. And no one is going to con-

vince me otherwise. And when they testified that the door to the fire escape was open, it was a lie! It was never open. Locked all the time. One hundred and forty-six people were sacrificed, and the judge fined Blank and Harris seventy-five dollars!

Conditions were dreadful in those days. But there was something that is lacking today and I think it was the devotion and the belief. We *believed* in what we were doing. We fought and we bled and we died. Today they don't have to.

You sit down at the table, you negotiate with the employers, you ask for 20 percent, they say 15, but the girls are working. People are working. They're not disturbed, and when the negotiations are over they get the increases. They don't really have to fight. Of course, they'll belong to the union and they'll go on strike if you tell them to, but it's the inner faith that people had in those days that I don't see today. It was a terrible time, but it was interesting. I'm glad I lived then.

Even when things were terrible, I always had that faith. . . . Only now, I'm a little discouraged sometimes when I see the workers spending their free hours watching television—trash. We fought so hard for those hours and they waste them. We used to read Tolstoy, Dickens, Shelley, by candlelight, and they watch the *Hollywood Squares*. Well, they're free to do what they want. That's what we fought for.

LINDA GORDON
Orphans and Ethnic Division in Arizona: The Mexican Mothers and the Mexican Town

In 1904, New York nuns brought 40 Irish orphans to an Arizona mining boomtown, to be placed with Catholic families who had volunteered to take them in. This was a far more humane and orderly way of finding homes for them than the usual "orphan train" which, between 1854 and 1929, lined children up at station stops and encouraged local families to claim an extra pair of hands for farm or household.[*]

But although the local priest in Clifton-Morenci, Arizona, had guided the arrangements for placing the children, and although these stable working-class families of Mexican migrants were descended generally from Europeans and Native Americans, the "Anglos" of the towns interpreted the adoption of Irish children by Mexican families as interracial transgression. Anglo women demanded that their husbands "rescue" the children. The men formed a vigilante squad, invaded the homes of the Mexican families, kidnapped the children at gunpoint, and threatened to kill the nuns and the priest. The children were redistributed among the Anglo families, who successfully fought in the U.S. Supreme Court for the right to keep them.

The struggle in Clifton-Morenci is not easy to reconstruct. "From the Mexicans who took in the orphans," writes Linda Gordon, "the historical archives contain exactly two letters, written by one man, to the Sisters of Charity. Not one Mexican testified at the trial. There is no oral history, not a single shard of evidence beyond these two letters of their weeks of preparation, of their one day as foster parents, of how it felt to have their new children kidnapped by vigilantes with Winchesters."[†] Yet working carefully with a wide range of legal records, newspapers, social and political histories, oral histories, and other evidence, Linda Gordon is able to demonstrate how readily ethnic and national difference (in this case between Mexicans and Anglo-Europeans) can be racialized—that is, turned from ethnic difference into race difference. When Anglos observed gender relations and family practices among Mexicans, what differences from their own practices did they find? How did they interpret these differences? Notice the comment on page 352: "Men and women functioned in a patriarchal family culture, yes, but this does

---

[*]For a memoir of her experiences on an orphan train, see the story of Arlene Phelps in Andre Domick, "When Orphan Trains Came to Iowa," *Des Moines Register*, December 22, 2002.

[†]Linda Gordon, *The Great Arizona Orphan Abduction* (Cambridge, Mass.: Harvard University Press, 1999), p. 118.

not mean that one side had all the power and the other side none." What elements of power does Gordon suggest were available to men and women in the same family?

Gordon's close description of the daily lives of the Mexican families is also an opportunity to consider how industrialization changed housekeeping. Compare the housekeeping practices in this early-twentieth-century settlement to the housekeeping practices described for the nineteenth century by Boydston and McCurry (see pp. 145–64). What difference did it make that the men in the families Gordon describes were not farmers?

Orphan trains seem distant from us now, . . . [S]o if we imagine ourselves in the position of these Clifton-Morenci Mexican women who offered themselves as mothers, we admire them but we may also be surprised. They offered to feed, love, and care for one more child although they were poor; they knew nothing about the children, who might be troubled or sick or crippled; and they were not accustomed to the adoption of strangers.[1] One of the criticisms directed against the orphan trains was that they delivered children into virtual servitude, that the "foster" families were often seeking free labor. But these prospective mothers knew that these Catholic orphans were just toddlers, many years from being able to work; and in this mining camp, where few people farmed or ranched, there was little productive work children could do.

As to adoption, it may have been stranger to the Anglos than to the Mexicans. Legal adoption in the contemporary American sense— taking a child into a family so as to legally obliterate the rights and duties of her or his natal family, and so as to make her or him legally undifferentiated from a "natural" child—is an extremely recent phenomenon. Massachusetts passed the first state law allowing this kind of adoption in 1851, and twenty states had followed by 1875, but in most of the United States such adoption were practiced commonly for the first time in the twentieth century. In Latin America the practice of U.S.-style modern legal adoption was an even later development. Traditionally, in most countries . . . , parents could . . . "adopt" a child without the biological parents having to relinquish her or him. In most cultures and among Mexicans in particular it was commonplace to take in the children of kinfolk, [but] taking in strange children was rare. The child-placing agencies did not expect their foster parents to adopt legally, and there was so little paperwork in most agencies' programs that different families could have had

varying understandings of what they were committing themselves to.[2] . . .

Most important, children were a blessing . . . [and] some felt insufficiently blessed. Many Clifton-Morenci families were childless—30 percent of the white and 18 percent of the Mexican—and almost certainly not by choice. Some of this infertility resulted from repeated miscarriages; at least one woman suspected that the sulfurous air around Clifton-Morenci caused her to become sterile.[3] . . .

Families also suffered another kind of loss: in more than half the Mexican families and a fifth of the Anglo families at least one child had died. Mexicans suffered much higher child mortality rates than Anglos [in part because] . . . Mexican infants were usually entirely dependent on breastmilk, and a mother's supply was not always reliable, especially if she was exhausted or malnourished. . . .

Since children did little remunerative labor in Clifton-Morenci, naturally the orphans were sought out mainly by those families who could best afford them. Mexicans in Clifton-Morenci were, of course, economically and socially stratified, as are all modern populations. Mexican men in Clifton divided into three classes: a small group of entrepreneurs— shopkeepers or ranchers mainly—several dozen at most, a middling class who often mixed with the Euro-Latins; proletarians who worked in the mines, mills, or smelters; and the poor self-employed who earned a living through causal labor or peddling. . . . Mexican women were similarly stratified, according to their husbands' earnings and behavior but also in terms of their own standards: they judged themselves and one another with stringent measures of housekeeping, dress, piety, and deportment. . . .

In previous decades, Anglo old-timers, businessmen who dealt with Mexicans, and anyone moderately observant understood these class divisions. . . . [Now, in] a remarkable process of unlearning, many Anglos were primitivizing Mexicans as classless, a pure type, just "Mexican." During the orphan affair most of the Anglos would revert to that decivilizing fallacy. When the Anglos at the Clifton orphan trial referred to the Mexicans always in the aggregate, differentiating neither individuals nor subgroups among Mexicans, their testimony showed that to Anglos, "Mexican" had come to *mean* poor, ignorant, degraded. . . .

The first housing in Clifton consisted of adobe and ocotillo (a cactus with long canes that can be used for fences and roofing), or tents emulating those of some early Indian miners, or gunny sacks stretched over frames of tree branches with brush-and-mud or flattened tin-can roofs (the mud being fixed with a binder such as chopped straw), or caves, partly natural and partly excavated, in the hillsides, usually with an adobe room as a foyer. With the railroads came lumber, which did not wash away in the heavy rains or require constant maintenance like the adobe. . . . Virtually every house had a fenced *corral* for animals, plants, or general use. In town the houses were close together; farther out there would be more room but few men wanted long treks to work.

Inside, the floors were almost always dirt, tightly packed down, regularly sprinkled to suppress dust, and swept. Many of the poor used packing crates of various sizes and shapes for chairs and tables; others relied on homemade rough wooden benches; still others had carved, heavy furniture. The first mattresses were *petates,* made of grass, replaced by American mattresses as soon as possible. There would be a large clay *olla* for water, several five-gallon *tinas,* tins, for carrying water and washing dishes, and many other jars and large cans for storage of *masa* (dough) and *nixtamal* (cooked maize or wheat ready for preparing the *masa*) as well as other liquids and foods. In warm weather, containers storing meat, fruits, and vegetables would be covered with wet cloths to keep them cool, but as soon as they could afford it the women got wooden ice boxes. There would be a heavy iron *comal,* or griddle, for cooking the tortillas, a *metate* for grinding and a smaller *molcajete,* or mortar and pestle, for grinding chiles (they needed two separate tools so the chiles wouldn't stain and flavor the tortillas). Cleaning tools in immigrant homes might include wrapped bundles of cactus fibers for sweeping or grass roots for scouring, but women soon preferred store-bought brooms and soap.[4]

The wives' work and daily lives . . . were dictated by the mine and smelter schedule. The individual jobs women did—the tortilla making, the cooking, the breast-feeding, the sewing—seem preindustrial if examined as separate tasks, in contrast to the industrialized men's work. But that appearance would yield a misunderstanding; industrialization had transformed women's labor and its meanings. The copper companies shaped women's schedule, budget, working conditions and tools, purchases and diet, health and medical care, even family size.

Almost all the plants operated round the clock, so men returned home, slept, and ate at various hours, and depended heavily on women's labor. There was neither electricity nor gas in these homes; women cooked on wood stoves and created light with kerosene lamps and candles. You could see these dim lights at almost any hour of darkness. Women arose as much as several hours before the men and children in order to feed the stove, heat water, and prepare breakfast and lunch buckets; with switching shift work, breakfast might be required at any time of day. With several men in the house working different shifts, a common occurrence, a woman might have to provide a constant succession of substantial meals. Starting in the late morning you could hear the clapping sound of tortilla making wherever you walked.

The labor connected with water was ubiquitous. It had to be fetched in buckets and carried a good distance from wells—this was often a children's chore and could well require a walk of a mile and a half. The drudgery of fetching and heating water for baths and laundry was particularly heavy because the silt from the smokestacks settled everywhere, and the men and their clothes came home filthy every day—they had no showers at work— and it required lots of water to get them clean. There were not many items of clothing, besides, because these were usually made by hand—no one had a sewing machine yet—so doing laundry could not be postponed. It was the hardest piece of housework, the first to be sent out if the family had a cash surplus, and housewives later greeted the possibility of owning a washing machine with nothing short of passion. In these early days of the century the wash was done on a scrub board, in the creek or river if it contained any clean water, or in a tub laboriously filled by the bucket.[5] One Anglo described his memory of his maid doing laundry: "We had large, steel corrugated buckets. These containers were coal black on the outside and snow white on the inside from the soap. After the clothes had boiled for some time she took them out and literally beat them to death with a long piece of wood. It was an all day job to wash and put the clothes out to dry. . . . we [sic] managed to keep very clean."[6]

Local water was not only difficult to get but often dirty with sediment. One pioneer recalled "that on the rare occasion that any one indulged in a bath, a whisk broom was needed to brush the sediment off the body." Those who could afford it bought their drinking water from *aguadores,* who delivered it on burro-back in leather or canvas bags (one Clifton woman sewed all the bags for them); they might charge $4.00 per month or 25¢ a bag.[7] The Clifton Water Company had already begun a city water system, digging a forty-foot-deep well about four miles north of town and installing pumps. Houses with indoor plumbing could pay a connection fee and then a regular charge (there was no metering): the standard rate was $2.25; for households with bathtub or livestock, $3.00; with lawns or trees, $4.90. But in 1904 few Mexicans could afford indoor plumbing, and besides, the pumps did not reliably bring water up to the houses on higher ground. . . .

Even with the water scarcity, housewives were ever scrubbing, sweeping, straightening, and decorating, and the hard work paid them back with pleasure and pride. Mexican women gained a reputation here, as elsewhere, for their dedication to cleanliness—beyond cleanliness, in fact, to beautification.[8] Every woman's home was ornamented with small shrines, pictures of the Virgin or the Virgin of Guadalupe or Christ or Teresita with a small shelf and a candle underneath, or hand-painted *retablos.* Walls were sometimes covered with newspaper or magazine pictures and a calendar.[9] Virtually every woman's home had flowers usually grown in pots or large cans in which the right soil and water could be maintained. Even the most racist Anglo memoir I read commented on Mexican

women's superiority to Anglos in their dedication to beautification, especially with flowers: "the home is blessed with the saving grace of flowers. . . . The Mexican women are ahead in this particular, and it is not uncommon to see in front of their mud-hovels tiny spaces enclosed by cactus or brush fences and blazing with colour."[10]

Mothers were equally proud of their child-raising work, measured by the beauty and *disciplina* of their offspring. These well-behaved children represented substantial maternal labor. Nothing is more draining than pregnancy, nursing, and infant care, especially when combined with the round-the-clock provision for men, yet Mexican women between the ages of eighteen and forty were doing such labor more often than not. The worst burden fell on the younger women, who did not yet have older children to help with the rest of the work. What children could contribute was gendered, and daughters helped more than sons: a son would be expected to fetch water and wood, but a daughter of eight or older could do that work *and* cooking, cleaning, baby care. Some mothers took children back to Mexico to be cared for by kinfolk until they were old enough to marry or work. Clifton-Morenci elementary schools were just beginning to take in Mexican children at the turn of the century but the majority still got no formal schooling. Active young children at home had to be constantly protected from the hazards of the mine, mill, and smelter sites and girls had to be constantly supervised. And they had to be trained to show respect for their elders, defer to their father in all things, and learn their catechism well. The standards for well brought-up children were high and the opprobrium laid on the mothers of *hijos mal criadas,* badly brought-up children, had a sharp bite.[11]

Norteñas felt themselves far from civilization, so they tried to recreate the civilized foods of their homeland; they tried to grow what they could not buy in order to make the traditional *tamales de elote* (fresh corn) in late summer, *tamales de carne* at Christmas, *buñuelos* (fried cakes) for New Year's, and *capirotada* (bread pudding) for Lent. Their horticultural work included not only growing foods—figs, apricots, grapes, pomegranates, squash, chiles, corn, cucumbers, melons, even citrus—but also taming wild plants for healing purposes, such as mesquite pods and wild greens, *ver-*

dolagas (purslane) and *bellotas* (acorns), and *manzanilla* (camomile) for tea.[12] Most families kept chickens, and those with more space might try to keep a goat or pig or two as well.

Supplementing the *tienda de raya,* company store, with what you could grow was essential to the budget. The men's work, especially that in the mines, made them ravenous; their caloric requirements far exceeded those of men performing less demanding labor. Those who cooked knew this well, and their knowledge was confirmed by scientific nutritional calculations offered by efficiency experts to mining employers in the next decades. Calories burnt per hour could triple between "active muscular exercise" (200) and "very hard muscular exercise" (600), so that a miner of only 120 pounds could easily require 6,000 calories a day. Buying that much food would far exceed his income.[13] . . .

Then there were the other necessities. Children's shoes at the Arizona Copper company store were 75¢ and $1.25 a pair, men's undershirts and drawers 75¢ each, flannel was 8.5¢ a yard and gingham 16.5¢. The lowest grade tobacco was 60¢ for eight ounces.[14] It was not easy to manage all this on wages averaging $2.25 a day. Small wonder that pilfering building materials from the companies was standard, a kind of gleaning to which the workers and their families felt entitled.

Shopping in this small town might have led to a great deal of sociability but few women actually went to the stores: most goods were bought from peddlers or ordered from a company-store man . . . who stopped by to take an order in the morning and delivered by wagon in the evening. Numerous peddlers would come by each day: the dairyman, the water man, the wood man, the company-store man, providing a different kind of sociability, a steady stream of visitors it seemed. At times whole herds of burros moved noisily along the streets. . . . Many women patronized the Chinese vegetable men, who sold by far the best produce not only here but in most Arizona and Sonora mining towns. When they walked through the town, they wrapped the vegetables inside wet burlap sacks, loaded in two large bamboo baskets that hung, balanced, weighing about one hundred thirty pounds, from their shoulders on a six-foot pole of tickwood. . . .

Mining camps once seemed to feature classic male-breadwinner families, since these towns, usually far from cities, offered few jobs for women. But there was no way men could support their families single-handedly in a town where the average worker's wage was around two dollars a day and prices were unusually high because of the high cost of transportation. And anyone who had observed the lives of women in mineworkers' families would have known better. Family economic need had a complex relation to family size: at first, the more children, the more the woman needed to bring in; as the children grew older, they could also earn, relieving the pressure on their mother a bit. The logic of the situation, a bit crazy from the standpoint of the modern urban family economy, was that the younger the children, the less the mother was able to devote herself to family care. The housewife's classic "scrimping" would not do; many women and most mothers had to earn. (Anglo women were less pressed because their men's wages were higher.) Mexican men also had to supplement wages, often with the fish and small game they hunted in off hours—virtually every household had a rifle—but the women were small entrepreneurs.

And not all the mothers had male wage-earners to help them. Women commonly ran families on their own, in Clifton-Morenci as in Mexico. In 1900, 9 percent of families were headed by women, 80 percent of them Mexican, and there were numerous other husbandless mothers who did not head households but lived with kinfolk.[15] By 1910, female-headed households were up to 17 percent, a figure consistent with other mining towns.[16] Most female heads were widows, despite the fact that many widows returned to Mexico; some had been deserted, some separated, a few divorced. . . . How did they manage?

For almost all, the answer was that they "took in." Most commonly, washing and sewing. Frequently, boarders and lodgers. Occasionally, someone else's children. Many Arizona Mexican women remembered the labor of taking in laundry: carrying water, heating water, scrubbing, hanging, heating irons, ironing. . . . A widow described her work: "I washed and ironed here for a long time, honey. . . . This porch had a bar from one wall to the other and that's where I ironed and hung the clothes. That was my life, washing and ironing . . . heating the iron on the stove ... At midnight I would be hanging clothes.... By five o'clock I was already up.... I even went for firewood on the hill and carried it on my back."[17] Then "I ironed and ironed and ironed ... standing ... at it and at it and at it with that iron."[18] The children picked up the dirty clothes and delivered the clean to customers. The women made their own children's clothes out of flour sacks but sewed fine linen and woolens for hire. One illiterate seamstress kept her accounts in a neat little book, drawing a circle to stand for one dollar and a half-circle to stand for fifty cents.[19]

Some women took in "tricks." Sixteen women listed in the census as prostitutes, and no doubt more who were unlisted, earned in that manner. Several probably had bosses, such as the two who lived as lodgers in the household of a saloon keeper. One group of four prostitutes in Clifton lived together in interracial partnership: one Mexican, one Japanese, and two Anglo women. Another headed a household with her two young daughters. One lived with her miner father. Assuming that these women were in fact prostitutes, community members probably saw them *both* as disreputable and as honest working women. Other sex workers were able to set limits. One told Manuel Gamio, an extraordinary Mexican anthropologist (twenty years later, but completely relevant to turn-of-the-century Clifton-Morenci), of a dancer-for-hire's delicate balance of feelings:

My work consists of dancing as much as I can with everyone who comes. At the beginning I didn't like this work because I had to dance with anyone, but I have finally gotten used to it and now I don't care, because I do it in order to earn my living.... Each dance is worth ten cents. ... Besides there are some who will give you a present.... This work is what suits me best for I don't need to know any English here.... It is true that some men at times make propositions to me which are insulting, but everything is fixed by just telling them no.... One man whom I liked a lot here in the hall deceived me once.... My mother takes a lot of care of me so that I won't make any bad steps. My sisters do the same.[20]

Two-fifths of Clifton-Morenci's miners and smelter workers were single men, utterly dependent on hiring women not only for sex but for food and rest.... Lodgers usually also got their clothes washed and mended, their socks darned, their bath water heated, their money guarded, their illnesses tended, their loneliness and sadness eased. Women frequently did errands their lodgers could not accomplish because of the limited hours of company stores (typically, 9 to 5 and payday evenings) and other businesses—buying personal necessities, sending letters and money home. Providing board is less visible to the historian today because no one reported it as a "job" to a census taker, but it was the dominant way in which single men got fed. Men would typically arrive for a meal just before and just after work, then leave for the job or for the bars, and sleep at another house. At the entrance to the home would be a table with a water pitcher and bowl and towels for the dirty miners (more laundry); shifts of men seated themselves at long tables and benches, possibly constructed of boards.... Women also sold "box lunches," typically packed in a metal two-layered bucket, for men to take to work, or prepared food they could peddle at the bars.[21] ...

Women sold many other goods and services. Some women provided healing and midwifery skills (although many pregnant women preferred to return to Mexico for confinements) for low fees. Midwives almost certainly also provided abortions; although I have not been told of this practice in Clifton, it was done in other mining towns—and, I would wager, in every community—with herbal abortifacients and knitting needles.[22] Women sold eggs, chickens, home brew, anything they could make. And mothers functioned as general contractors for their children's labor, both directing them in the home and finding out-of-home jobs for them.... Among the very poorest there was out-and-out child labor, most often in the mill in Morenci....

Women who could leave home to earn were limited not only by the scarcity of jobs but also by their family's and community's standards of respectability. Anglo single women could teach or work in copper company offices, but Mexican women were not hired. Working in bars or even in restaurants was out of bounds for most "respectable" Mexican women. This limitation derived from patriarchal customs of women's sequestration: they should remain *casera,* at home, and young women should be always chaperoned.[23] Some women resisted and bent these rules, of course, but they were reinforced by harsh gossip, both

Anglo and Mexican, libeling the morality of women working in service jobs in public places.

What was left? Domestic service and sewing. There were a few small dressmaking shops where several seamstresses worked together. The great majority of those working outside their homes, single or older women, went to other people's homes to cook and clean. Here they encountered the trials typical of domestic servants: low pay—twenty-five to fifty cents per day—poor working conditions, no protection from excessive demands, humiliating supervision. The employing housewives complained of them in exactly the same way that eastern housewives complained of Irish domestics, alleging that they stole and worked slowly and malingered. Employed mothers relied, of course, on their daughters to do all the housework—cooking, cleaning, shopping, child care.

Even play meant work for women, but cherished work, the work that made Clifton home. Women planned, cooked, decorated, and cleaned up for all the many fiestas and religious celebrations, not to mention more casual sociability. . . . [S]ome of the extremely numerous religious fiesta days had to be passed over, but they tried to mark El Día de San Juan, El Día de San Pedro y San Pablo, Sábado de Gloria (Easter), the Fiesta de la Virgen Guadalupana, and Christmas.

Among the most cherished celebrations were baptisms and communions. Just as families lavished all they could afford on these events, at which scores of friends and relatives would be served extravagant meals, so the mothers expressed their love and pride in sewing elaborate clothing for the children: for baptisms, long robes and caps finely stitched and trimmed with lace and ribbon; for the girls' communions, individually designed and fitted dresses with delicate smocking, lace, and ruffles, a flowered bridal-style headpiece and veil. And the boys needed suits. Throughout the year women were raising money and sewing for such events. The funerals also took a lot of work, and they came too frequently, especially considering the relative youth of the population, because of mining deaths and infectious disease.

Clifton's Mexicans also relaxed more spontaneously. On fair evenings you could hear a guitar and folk song or *corrido* no matter where you walked. Several families gathered with beer and singing the Saturday night before the orphans arrived. Music and dance were, along with beer and mescal, the central components of celebration in Mexican Clifton, and there were house parties every week, which could be held anywhere that someone could provide a guitar and a flat space for dancing. Some women turned their *corrales* into patios, surrounding them with plants and candles or *candelarias* (candles in bags), and charged a small fee for parties or even weddings. . . .

Such sociability provided not only the relaxation that allowed work to continue but also the community bonds on which all depended. Here in Arizona almost everyone pined for distant kinfolk in Mexico, Texas, and New Mexico. The loss was economic as well as emotional. How did one survive without the give and take among people whose mutual obligations never ended? By creating an alternative infrastructure of mutual support. . . .

Mexican women . . . established independent women's organizations through the church. At some point two sodalities were organized in Clifton, the Ladies of the Sacred Heart and Los Esclaves de María—neither church records nor memories tell us exactly when. These took on particular projects, usually raising money for church improvements. These groups dignified the activity of women and created for them a sphere of authority. Going to the church, even at night, was always respectable and appropriate for women. The priest's dependence on women was undeniable and his requests uncontestable. In a culture characterized both by anticlericalism and devotion, as this one was, church was a site of women's activism and authority.

The working-class identity developing in Clifton-Morenci exerted a mixed influence on Mexican women's social status. As Clifton-Morenci Mexicans shed their identity as alien "sojourners" and constructed a new one as members of a settled working class, their consciousness was composed simultaneously and inextricably of class and racial-national understandings. . . . One identity, Mexican, was mapped neatly onto another, worker. The solidarity that resulted not only included but also depended on women's sense of membership, to see families through those periods without income, to face down substantial threats, and to pressure other workers not to break that solidarity. . . . But this class identity reinforced women's subordination in some ways. Opportunities for women's economic independence were rare, and those that achieved it usually did so by moving away. Because of the lack of opportunities for women's economic independence and the high level of danger and exertion in the men's work, mining camps seem to have been more patriarchal than other working-class communities. The class organizations—unions and brotherhoods—were men's organizations, and the struggles they fought, victorious or defeated, bonded the men in ways that confirmed their manly sense of themselves as heads of households, *jefes* of the family. There were of course as many ways to be a *jefe* as there were men, and many preferred more egalitarian family relations. What's more, male headship did not by any means imply female subordination on all issues, and as in every society and family, beneath and in between the appearances of traditional male dominance were man-woman and parent-child conflicts, sometimes violent and sometimes so subtle that even the participants were unaware of the power struggle at their core. There were negotiations, haggling, complicated interactions, and sometimes beatings, with outcomes not always predictable.

So we need to hold in our minds a complex picture of the marriages of those who volunteered to take in the orphans: women typically submitted when men insisted on their authority, and sometimes men insisted violently and women were badly hurt, but sometimes women used men's dependence on their labor to negotiate from positions of considerable power. Men and women functioned in a patriarchal family culture, yes, but this does not mean that one side had all the power and the other side none.

Women complained most about men's drunkenness. In earlier decades, when the miners were mainly single and migrant, payday binges were virtually universal, and there were no significant ethnic differences—the whole camp got drunk on "rich day" (payday). In one of Arizona's white camps, the copper company estimated that drunkenness during working hours cost it a thousand dollars per month.[24] With increased family life in Clifton-Morenci, drunkenness declined somewhat as men found other forms of relaxation, but the damages caused by alcohol remained fearsome; the health costs did not stand out because mine and smelter injuries took a high toll first, but alcohol-related violence occurred at least weekly, and drink made men more likely to respond to women's assertions of theirs and their children's needs with beatings. The very fiestas that women so lovingly fashioned created mixed expectations for those with husbands or fathers prone to violence.

The most violent men didn't need a party to set them off; an ordinary night at a saloon was enough, and the most brittle men didn't even need liquor. It is safe to assume that wife beating has gone on in every community in the United States, possibly more extensively in the generally violent culture of mining towns, among all racial-ethnic groups, and we know about only those cases that came to the attention of the courts: some because they led to murder, others because the women actually brought charges. A Metcalf Mexican miner stabbed his wife and ten-year-old daughter to death in July 1903. In Morenci, Tibusia Martínez alleged that Andrés Rodríguez "came home drunk and drove [her] and the children from the house." He was convicted and sentenced to forty days in jail, a heavy sentence for this court.[25] . . . As if to deny Mexican men any appearance of a monopoly on violence, W. H. Carpenter murdered his wife, Rada Carpenter, after she tried to leave him because of his brutality, and then killed himself.[26]

Recorded cases are always just a fragment, of indeterminate proportion, of the incidence of violence against women. But they provide evidence of something else that is equally important: women's willingness to bring legal complaints. Women do not bother when they believe they have nothing to gain, and they have often had nothing to gain. In the United States, women individually and in organizations campaigned to get wife beating criminalized throughout the nineteenth century. . . . Even in extremely patriarchal societies women (and children) resist violence with energy and resourcefulness, relying on gossip, family networks, threats, guns, knives, and occasionally poison to protect themselves or intimidate their assailants. Turning to the courts—or in this case to the justice of the peace—meant using a new country's tool for an old job.

Prosecuting a partner was, however, also a part of a process that by no means yielded only positive benefits. Some call the process Americanization, some modernization, some marketization, and in truth it was all of these— American capital was the closest, most dynamic, irresistible force bringing a commercial-industrial economy to Mexico and the U.S. Southwest.[27] Mexicans of both sexes ardently sought out American consumer goods but also complained about America and lamented the loss of their homeland culture. On the one hand, they did not like the impolite and hurried forms of American speech and interactions, and they missed the fresh fruit and flowers; they were offended by disrespect for women and the elderly. . . . On the other hand, they loved beer, Coca-Cola, blue jeans, higher wages, and opportunity. Both sexes sang this litany of love and hate.

Many observers considered women the Mexicans' primary modernizers, through their desire for new consumer goods. (Some considered this a compliment, others an accusation.) Certainly women longed for American fashions and cosmetics—as well as for health care, indoor plumbing, gas ranges. Adopting the orphans could plausibly be labeled an aspect of this Americanization. . . . Americanization accelerated family and gender change among many immigrant groups as they confronted this land of dollars. Mexicans in the United States displayed a variety of responses, progressive, conservative, and contradictory, and prominent among them was women's exploration of new possibilities. . . .

When [anthropologist] Manuel Gamio interviewed immigrants—two decades later, but his records are still the best source—their views about gender divided to some degree along sex lines. Men disliked American women and what America did to Mexican women. Carlos Ibáñez did not like "the system of the women here. They are very unrestrained . . . control their husband[s] . . . the Mexican women who come here also take advantage of the laws and want to be like the American women."[28] . . .

Elías Sepulveda was born in Nogales, Arizona, but still would not want to marry an American because they are "ambitious and free . . . when the husband comes from his work he has to buy the groceries and then help her in the kitchen and even wash the dishes. . . . The Mexican women are hard workers and do all that one wants."[29] . . .

Strikingly, the women told Gamio exactly the same thing—from a different perspective. Dolores Sánchez de Fuente, a sweatshop worker from Mazatlán, complained that her Mexican husband was domineering, cruel, and arrogant and drank and smoked marijuana too much. "Sometimes when the husband remembers that one doesn't work as hard over there he wants to go, but she remembers that there the women are not as well protected by the law and that if he has never struck her here it has been for fear of going to jail. She thinks that there he would beat her."[30] Beware of translating the Mexico–to–United States transition as one from patriarchy to freedom. Mexican women had their sources of power, and the United States had plenty of male tyrants. But American norms were freer. Señora Campos, of a different class position than Sánchez de Fuente—white and elite—liked the United States because of the goods, comforts, and privacy it offered: "Here she goes with freedom to the grocery store, clothing store . . . and buys whatever she wishes without anyone paying any attention to her." But she disliked "the liberty and way of behaving of the young women . . . by which her daughters have been influenced."[31] . . . Señora Ceballos came to the United States fleeing a husband who beat her and forced sex upon her, a man she'd been forced to marry at fifteen. Arriving in Los Angeles, she told her story of woe to women at a Young Women's Christian Association (YWCA) who sheltered her. "She understands that here woman has come to have a place, like a human being, which is what she really wanted when she was in Mexico."[32]

What women loved about the United States was by no means limited to American men's allegedly greater restraint. They also appreciated a culture that seemed to them, despite its hypocrisy, a bit less punitive and fearful toward female sexuality. They appreciated a different sensibility among women. Several women recalled with bitterness their sexual ignorance and shame about menstruation, sex, and childbirth, an ignorance that continued when they entered marriage, an ignorance imposed upon them by women, albeit women perpetuating a patriarchal helplessness. "Like I say, it's like they kept us completely in the dark. I didn't know, when I was going to have my first child, well, excuse me, I said to her: 'How is this baby going to be born?' . . . I was very desperate. . . . My mother told me: 'Wait daughter, be patient.'" These women admired the greater openness of their American daughters.[33]

Gender is not a system of men stepping on women. It is the social and cultural meanings given to sex, and everyone participates in the construction, confirmation, alteration, and constancy of gender. Precisely because of the sexual division of labor, women are usually more active in communicating gender to other women. They transmit traditions and innovations. In America, immigrants commented, Mexican wives were using contraception, often with husbands' approval; but we can guess that it is not through men that they learned about modern contraception or gained the courage to try it.[34] Many women recalled— with some nostalgia, true—girls' rebellion against the strict chaperonage imposed on them by family members.[35] . . .

The fact that Mexicans associated gender change with Americanness is complicated, in part because it follows a worldwide pattern in which colonial powers sometimes brought "women's liberation" to their colonies. Thus class and ethnic resistance to domination could seem to require loyalty to traditional family relations. Moreover, the rise of Chicano nationalism a few decades later sometimes brought with it a revalorizing and rehonoring of patriarchal family forms; it "idealized the [sexual] division of labor, romanticized the double-standard, ridiculed nontraditional feminine behavior as a form of cultural disloyalty."[36] . . .

Anglo-Mexican intermarriage was common throughout the Southwest, attributed mainly to the shortage of Anglo women. The incidence was highest during the earliest period of U.S. ownership of the region, when Anglo women were scarce; declined thereafter, particularly sharply as Anglos made Mexicans into an alien race; and increased again after about 1945.[37] . . . Throughout this variation there was a continuity: Anglo-Mexican couples consisted almost exclusively of "white" men and Mexican women. In the Clifton-Morenci census and the Sacred Heart Church records for 1900–1904 the Chacóns were the only Mexican man–Anglo woman couple. . . .

In other parts of the Southwest, in the nineteenth century, there were substantial economic inducements for white men to marry into property-owning, politically powerful *hispano* or *californio* families. In this marital commerce, women were the legal tender, exchanged in the process of consolidating ownership and creating new capital. The social outcomes of these exchanges provide further evidence for economic motives, as the "mixed" couples tended to assimilate to Anglo America, perhaps suggesting that women's greater pliability made it their task to acculturate. But these motives and patterns were absent from Clifton-Morenci, where there were few wealthy *hispano* families and many Anglo daughters of wealthy or influential parents. What then explains relationships between working-class whites and Mexicans? Here the economic incentive was women's, because they could benefit from white men's wages. Consider some of the intermarried Mexican women in Clifton-Morenci: Jennie Buttuer was married to a butcher; Carmel Nellton to a smelter foreman. . . . Two-thirds of the intermarried women in Clifton-Morenci in 1900 had husbands with higher-status jobs than a Mexican could get, and to this we must add the likelihood that the other one-third got the usual higher white wage for the same work. The distribution of these economic motives may explain why half of the intermarried couples lived in Mexican neighborhoods and a third in mixed, usually Mexican-Italian neighborhoods; only 17 percent lived in distinctly Anglo neighborhoods, suggesting that here the woman defined the sociability network (as we might expect), or found the housing for the couple, or that the husband had been taken into the Mexican community. Any explanation points to women's influence and initiative.

Add to economics the near constant, near universal attraction of lighter color. But this again provides an incentive only for Mexican women, not Anglo men. Among the upper-class intermarriages in the eighteenth and nineteenth centuries, the *hispanas* involved were usually light-skinned, so at least there was no disincentive for the men. The working-class women of Clifton-Morenci were occasionally darker but perhaps this mattered less to men who did not see themselves as climbing into an elite. There was a significant gender difference in the attitude toward lightness:

among women its value crossed class lines because it was assimilated to standards of beauty, and women seemed to appreciate lighter-skinned children more than men did. So we have another reminder that it is impossible to appraise racial motives or hierarchies without figuring in female as well as male action and subjectivity.

The least certain motives have to do with gender power relations. There are volumes of racialized discourse about Mexican women's passivity, subservience, and sexual availability and Mexican men's machismo. But those volumes come from ill-informed, stereotypical, external, sexist, and often racist perspectives; the critical literature examining gender in Mexican-American relationships is still sparse. Yet how can we ignore gender in thinking about intermarriage? What we are discussing is precisely the meeting of male and female on the most intimate terms, in relations whose rapport or discord derives from gender cultures.

Whites' racist anti-Mexican discourse was directed primarily toward men. Not only did it go softer on Mexican women, but a form of Orientalism rendered Mexican women particularly attractive to men, even trophies, so that marrying a Mexican woman was by no means a low-status move for a white man. The "greaser" label was part of a slander that Mexican people were dirty, but it coexisted with the impression that Mexican women were extraordinary housekeepers, taking great pride in the cleanliness and beauty of their homes and children. Possibly the greatest pull of Mexican women on Anglo men, although the most tricky to delineate, was the belief in their greater submissiveness than "American" women, a belief that remains to this day.[38] . . . But this unilateral story of intermarriage, one that reckons only men's motives, not only works to reinforce women's subordination, but does not fit the facts as well as a bilateral interpretation. Mexican women were also attracted to American men because they saw there the promise of American-style marital behavior—more acceptance of women's autonomy in public and private, a less entrenched double standard regarding sexual and economic fidelity (those mistresses, those *casas chicas*, took money as well as love out of the household), and a lesser emphasis on personal honor and domestic authority. Hardly least

important, white men could bring home white men's wages.

So perhaps these intermarriages represented racial, class, and gender bargains: Men wanted sex appeal, housekeeping, yieldingness; women wanted lighter children, a better standard of living, less machismo. But without much evidence, such speculation is suspect, resting as it does on stereotypes. For example, were Mexican women really more pliable? Could anything be less measurable? Consider the fact that women in Mexico enjoyed more legal rights than most in America, and some of these were incorporated into laws of the Arizona Territory. Sons and daughters usually inherited equally. Property acquired during marriage was community property and women's previously owned holdings did not necessarily fall into their husbands' hands. Women kept their own names. They could sue on their own behalf. In Colorado and New Mexico—where Mexicans were more numerous and their legal culture more established— women were accustomed to turn to courts in marital disputes, and sometimes won. Men as well as women were sometimes punished for adultery,[39] and the Clifton-Morenci court records show that Mexican women tried to use local laws against their male partners. The system of *compadrazgo*, continuing robustly in Clifton-Morenci, provided them with institutionalized networks of support in addition to those of husband or family of origin.

. . . [T]he question about whether Mexican women were subservient is entirely a wrong question; wrong because universalized, abstracted, and perhaps not ever answerable. What we need to know is actually simpler: whether Mexican women saw some opportunity, in some directions, for improving their position by taking what Anglo gender culture offered along with what Mexican gender culture offered.

Was not taking in the orphans a taking in of a piece of Anglo culture? At the least it was another move that marked the limits of patriarchal control over women—and, quite possibly, pushed those limits outward. These women were not, on the whole, accustomed to acting without their husbands' permission, so this orphan plan was a step out of line. This is not to say that the men disapproved or were defied; it is to say only that the women took the initiative in this undertaking, defining it as belonging within their sphere of authority, and that, in taking the initiative, they enlarged that sphere. Questions about that process involve unknowable aspects of these marriages: did the women have to beg and plead to get their husbands' permission? Did their husbands compute that one more mouth to feed would not make much difference? Were the husbands honoring a lonely wife's whim, or did the wives argue that such a child might be an asset? Whatever the answers, the results remind us that the authority of Mexican husbands did not mean the powerlessness of Mexican women.

Whether these were mutual decisions or men's indulgence, it was women's desire that brought the orphans to Clifton. They desired, first, to be good Catholics, to have the opportunity, one not often given to the poor, to help the unfortunate in a truly grand gesture. Surely it seemed to them sad that these motherless children should languish in an orphanage ...

The women also wanted to please the new priest. He was young and they could enjoy flirting, but mostly he brought them into positions of some importance as they helped orient him to his new community and teach him his new language. He was their spiritual father, but they were also his mothers. Through him, too, they could become leaders among women; and through such leadership they could strengthen the church, assure their children's devotion, perhaps even lure their husbands into the little adobe structure on Chase Creek.

They also desired a new child. For some that yearning was a powerful, longstanding loneliness; for others, it was the baby hunger that arose after their children had grown or left; for still others, it was a desire to repeat the greatest satisfaction of a womanly life. An orphan child escalated the importance of their motherhood, made them centers of attention within the community. Those asked to serve as *comadres* and *compadres* were honored and excited to meet their new wards. As any childbirth was an adventure, this was an adventure of multiplied value: comforting an orphan, gaining a child who was a magnet for community interest, without the dread of childbirth—a dread not just of the pain but of staring death in the face.

And then there was the special yearning

for a light child, a yearning they did not know they had—or actually did not have—until one was offered. Appreciation of lightness had been part of their Mexican culture. As girls they longed to be lighter themselves; as mothers they longed for lighter babies. Lightness was not mere aesthetic prejudice but stood, however subconsciously, for material hopes: for prosperity, health, security, status. Today we may contemplate this preference with a shudder and understand it as learned racism. If in turn-of-the-century Mexico a critique of racism was not yet widely articulated, there was no lack of awareness that the light were more and the dark less powerful. But now in Clifton-Morenci light had become "white," not a description but a rank, a caste. Marrying into whiteness was no longer a realistic option, but adopting whiteness—who knew what it might lead to? Such a child might go to school, might learn perfect English, might marry a white man or earn a white man's wage. Perhaps not, but it could hardly lead to anything bad, and the child would at the very least be admired among the Mexicans. Such a child might make the whole family whiter. Such a child might become a true *americano*. If so, it would be an achievement accomplished by the mothers.

Notes

1. Carmina García, descendant of the Navarrete family, explained that when she adopted in the 1950s and 1960s in Morenci, it was difficult, the "talk of the town," because hardly anyone had done it before. Personal interview, February 7–8, 1997.

2. On informal adoption among Mexicans, see Mary Logan Rothschild and Pamela Claire Hronek, *Doing What the Day Brought: An Oral History of Arizona Women* (Tucson: University of Arizona Press, 1992), p. 73.

3. Childlessness figured from the manuscript census. Complaint about the air from Mrs. F. H. Kane, of Clifton, to Mother Superior, New York Foundling Asylum, October 6, 1904, in New York Foundling Hospital Archives, New York.

4. On housekeeping, see Josiah McC. Heyman, *Life and Labor on the Border: Working People of Northeastern Sonora, Mexico, 1886–1986* (Tucson: University of Arizona Press, 1991); Julia Yslas Vélez and Socorro Félix Delgado in Patricia Preciado Martin, *Songs My Mother Sang to Me: An Oral History of Mexican American Women* (Tucson: University of Arizona Press, 1992), pp. 28–29, 59.

5. Rothschild and Hronek, *Doing What the Day Brought*, pp. 22–24; "The Lives of Arizona Women," oral history project, Arizona State University, Tempe, interviews with Ruby Estrada and Lupe Hernández by Maria Hernández.

6. Harold T. Shortridge, *Childhood Memories of a Fabulous Mining Camp, Clifton, Arizona, 1915–1926* (Cottonwood, Ariz.: Harold Shortridge, 1990), p. 53.

7. WPA interviews with Carmen Hillman, Isabel Juárez Hemández, Carmen Escoboza Flynn, WPA Life Histories Collection; quotation from Mrs. E. M. Roscoe, unpublished reminiscence letter, n.d.

8. On the reputation for immaculate housekeeping, see Douglas E. Foley with Clarice Mota, Donald E. Post, and Ignacio Lozano, *From Peones to Politicos: Class and Ethnicity in a South Texas Town, 1900–1987* (Austin: University of Texas Press, orig. 1977, rev. 1988), p. 55.

9. Jorge Durand and Douglas S. Massey, *Miracles on the Border: Retablos of Mexican Migrants to the United States* (Tucson: University of Arizona Press, 1995).

10. Edith M. Nicholl (Mrs. Bowyer), *Observations of a Ranch Woman in New Mexico* (Cincinnati: Editor Publishing, 1901), p. 10.

11. Richard Griswold del Castillo, *La Familia: Chicano Families in the Urban Southwest, 1848 to the Present* (Notre Dame: University of Notre Dame Press, 1984), chap. 6; Martin, *Songs My Mother Sang to Me.*

12. WPA interview with Juanita Gonzales Fellows, by Roberta F. Clayton, WPA Life Histories Collection; Delgado in Martin, *Songs My Mother Sang to Me,* p. 61; Raquel Rubio-Goldsmith, "Seasons, Seeds, and Souls: Mexican Women Gardening in the American Mesilla, 1900–1940," pp. 140–156 in Heather Fowler-Salamini and Mary Kay Vaughan, eds., *Women of the Mexican Countryside, 1850–1990* (Tucson: University of Arizona Press, 1994), pp. 146–148.

13. C. H. Grabill, "Inefficiency and Poor Food of Mexican Miners," *Engineering and Mining Journal* 109, no. 7 (February 14, 1920):448–451.

14. Arizona Copper company store advertisement, *Copper Era,* February 4, 1904, p. 2.

15. Figured from the manuscript census.

16. Elliott West, in "Heathens and Angels: Childhood in the Rocky Mountain Mining Towns," *Western Historical Quarterly* 14 (1983):145–164, reports female-headed households made up one out of eight households in some Colorado and Idaho camps in 1870, and 20 percent in Globe and 25 percent in Tombstone in 1880.

17. Interview with L. Hernández, in Rothschild and Hronek, *Doing What the Day Brought,* p. 11. Carmina Garcia remembers her sister earning this way.

18. Paulina Moreno Montoya in Martin, *Songs My Mother Sang to Me,* p. 50.

19. Vélez in Martin, *Songs My Mother Sang to Me,* p. 32.

20. Manuel Gamio, *The Life Story of the Mexican Immigrant: Autobiographic Documents* (Chicago: University of Chicago Press, 1931), pp. 160–161.

21. Interview with Patricia Preciado Martin, February 11, 1997; interview with Helen Cooper, February 9, 1997; Esperanza Montoya Padilla and Carlotta Silvas Martin in Martin, *Songs My Mother Sang to Me,* pp. 97, 101–105, 201; Rothschild and Hronek, *Doing What the Day Brought,* p. 73.

22. "The Lives of Arizona Women," interview with Elsie Dunn; interviews with Garcia and Ochoa; WPA interview with Casimira Valenzuela, by Romelja Gómez, WPA Life Histories Collection; Rothschild and Hronek, *Doing What the Day Brought,* pp. 68–69; Griswold del Castillo, *La Familia,* p. 81.

23. Padilla in Martin, *Songs My Mother Sang to Me,* p. 99; Vicki L. Ruíz, *From Out of the Shadows: Mexican Women in Twentieth-Century America* (New York: Oxford University Press, 1998), chap. 3.

24. Ramón Eduardo Ruíz, *The People of Sonora and Yankee Capitalists* (Tucson: University of Arizona Press, 1988), pp. 94ff.

25. *Arizona Bulletin,* July 24, 1903, p. 1. Case of September 17, 1901, from Criminal Docket Books, Morenci, Greenlee County Courthouse.

26. August and September cases from Justice's Court of No. 3 Precinct, Graham County, Docket Books, GCHS, pp. 177, 189, 199–200; also reported in *El Labrador,* October 7, 1904, p. 2.

27. George J. Sanchez, *Becoming Mexican American: Ethnicity, Culture, and Identity in Chicano Los Angeles, 1900–1945* (New York: Oxford University Press, 1993); Sarah Deutsch, *No Separate Refuge: Culture, Class, and Gender on the Anglo-Hispanic Frontier in the American Southwest, 1880–1940* (New York: Oxford University Press, 1987).

28. Gamio, *The Life Story,* pp. 45–46.

29. Ibid., p. 271.

30. Ibid., p. 252.

31. Ibid., pp. 234–235.

32. Ibid., p. 249.

33. Interview with L. Hernández, in Rothschild and Hronek, *Doing What the Day Brought,* pp. 7, 45–47.

34. Gamio, *The Life Story,* p. 52.

35. Interviews with García and Ochoa; Rothschild and Hronek, *Doing What the Day Brought,* "Growing Up in Arizona."

36. Alex M. Saragoza, "The Conceptualization of the History of the Chicano Family," in Armando Váldez, Albert Camarillo, and Tomás Almaguer, eds., *The State of Chicano Research on Family, Labor and Migration: Proceedings of the First Stanford Symposium on Chicano Research and Public Policy* (Stanford, Calif.: Stanford Center for Chicano Research, 1983), p. 131.

37. Richard Griswold del Castillo and Arnoldo De Leon, *North to Aztlán: A History of Mexican Americans in the United States* (New York: Twayne, 1996), pp. 45, 110; Griswold del Castillo, *La Familia,* pp. 120–121.

38. Darlis Miller, "Cross-Cultural Marriages in the Southwest: The New Mexico Experience, 1846–1900," in Joan M. Jensen and Darlis A. Miller, eds., *New Mexico Women: Intercultural Perspectives* (Albuquerque: University of New Mexico Press, 1986), p. 105; Griswold del Castillo, *La Familia,* p. 74.

39. Janet Lecompte, "The Independent Women of Hispanic New Mexico, 1821–1846," *Western Historical Quarterly* 12 (January 1981):71–93.

ELLEN CAROL DUBOIS
The Next Generation of Suffragists: Harriot Stanton Blatch and Grassroots Politics

Campaigns to expand suffrage require that voters who are reasonably content with the status quo be persuaded to welcome new and unpredictable constituencies into the political arena. It is perhaps no surprise that the expansion of suffrage met severe resistance, both in the North where there were considerable doubts about the immigrant vote and especially in the South where the franchise had just been restricted to exclude African Americans and, in the process, many poor whites.

The campaign for woman suffrage involved intellectual challenge to established political theory that held a married woman's political interests were represented by her husband. It involved national mass mobilization at a time when even presidential campaigns hardly met that criteria. It required brilliant street theater on a massive scale and, simultaneously, clever and delicate political maneuvering for which women were not noted. Although the accomplishment of woman suffrage in 1920 is well known, the complexity of the work that was required and the high level of political skill that women had to acquire is less appreciated than it deserves to be.

Harriot Blatch, the daughter of Elizabeth Cady Stanton, led the efforts of the Women's Political Union to win suffrage for the women of New York State. From 1910 to 1915, the WPU lobbied state legislators to support the suffrage bill. They also targeted public support with parades, suffrage shops, and films.

Ironically, many suffragists who demanded the vote were deeply skeptical about politics. Believing that women were more pure than men and that politics were corrupt, they insisted that if women had the vote, they would put an end to partisanship. In fact, their views were not so far apart from anti-suffragists who resisted the vote precisely because they felt partisan politics would corrupt American womanhood. To their credit, Harriot Blatch and her colleagues understood that acquiring political skills and understanding partisanship were essential to acquiring the vote and, once acquired, using it effectively.

The battle for women's rights had begun in the state of New York, the birthplace of Elizabeth Cady Stanton and the longtime home of Susan B. Anthony. In Seneca Falls, New York, the Declaration of Rights and Sentiments had been rousingly proclaimed in 1848. In Albany, both Stanton and Anthony testified in the 1850s before the New York Senate's Judiciary Committee. There they argued, with some success, for changes in state law to establish women's guardianship rights over their children, grant property and earnings rights to married women, and deliver woman suffrage. In 1915, nearly seventy years later, the struggle, now led by a new generation, had come to focus on woman suffrage. Fittingly, Harriot Stanton

Blatch, Elizabeth Cady Stanton's daughter, led this major effort to win woman suffrage in its home state. But even in the early twentieth century, success was uncertain.

Harriot Stanton, the second daughter and sixth child of Elizabeth Cady and Henry Brewster Stanton, inherited her role as defender of her sex from her mother. She was born in Seneca Falls in 1856, during a period when Elizabeth Cady Stanton was immersed in women's issues and the development of a convention movement to publicize concerns as revolutionary as liberalizing divorce. . . . While other Victorian girls followed their mothers into quiet lives based on family service, Harriot was taught to be assertive and independent. . . . Her mother prepared her daughters to go out into the world not only to make their individual marks on it but also to embody her convictions about women's untapped capacities. . . .

. . . In 1874, [Harriot] enrolled at Vassar, the first all-female college established in the United States. There, she elected an unconventional course of study focused on science, politics, and history. Upon graduation, she became a member of the first generation of women college graduates, one of only a few thousand women in the United States who held a bachelor's degree. . . .

[In 1882,] she met William Blatch, the handsome, accommodating son of a wealthy brewer from Basingstoke, Hampshire, England. Harriot and William married in 1882, and the couple's first child Nora (named after the heroine of Ibsen's *A Doll's House*) was born in England the next year. A second child, Helen, born in 1892, died of whooping cough in 1896. Like her mother but with fewer children, more money, and a compliant husband, Harriot Blatch managed to combine marriage and motherhood with an energetic commitment to reform activities. She joined with veteran British women activists to revive the British suffrage movement. . . . In 1890, she joined the socialist Fabian Society, where she fought for, but failed to win, strong support for women's rights. For two decades as an [expatriate] in Edwardian England, she honed her political skills and updated her mother's feminist convictions, speaking at meetings, writing for suffrage journals, and becoming involved in local politics as a member of the Women's Local Government Society.

In 1902, with her daughter Nora grown and studying engineering at Cornell, and her husband Henry able to retire, Harriot Blatch moved permanently to New York to take up the task she had inherited—leadership of the American suffrage movement. She joined the Women's Trade Union League, a pioneering effort of elite settlement house women and female wage earners joined together to empower, not patronize, working women. There she came to see that to be modern and effective the suffrage movement in the United States must unite women across the classes in a militant effort. She also saw, as other women activists did not, that women's growing interest in electoral politics was crucial to the reinvigoration of the suffrage movement. Like the English suffragist Emmeline Pankhurst, she was committed to forcing the political parties to address the suffrage issue and winning from them the political support necessary to gain victory. . . .

To enact her vision of a militant, democratic suffrage organization based on a coalition of working-class and middle-class working women, Harriot Blatch organized the Equality League of Self-Supporting Women in 1907, renamed the Women's Political Union (WPU) in 1910. Although it gradually moved away from reliance on wage-earning women for its most active participants, the WPU went on to spearhead a political effort to force the New York legislature to pass a bill authorizing a referendum to amend the state constitution to grant women suffrage.

The WPU suffrage campaign, which ran from 1910 to 1915, involved an exhausting and elaborate two-pronged effort: First, both houses of the state legislature had to pass a bill authorizing a referendum on woman suffrage, and then the state's all-male electorate had to approve the referendum. . . . [S]uffragists in New York took hope from a narrowly won suffrage victory in California in October 1911. . . . By 1912, California was the sixth state in which women were voting in the presidential election. Blatch and her followers were determined that New York women would do the same in the next presidential election. . . .

Harriot Blatch had a talent and taste for partisan politics that was unusual in the movement. Although many of the new generation of suffragists were college-trained professionals, Mary Beard, the historian and a close friend, wrote of Blatch that more than others, "she worked steadfastly to root the suffrage movement in politics, where alone it could reach its goal."[1] She certainly had the lineage. Her mother and Susan B. Anthony had immersed themselves in party politics. From them, from her father, and from her years in England, Harriot had come to see that if suffragists were ever to win, they would have to go behind the scenes and engage in precisely the political maneuvering and lobbying that women had traditionally repudiated as the unhappy consequence of the male monopoly of public life. While such openly political methods distressed many older women reformers, they invigorated Harriot.

In one episode, which became a staple of suffrage legend, Harriot and other WPU leaders tracked down a particularly elusive senator. By this time, opposition to suffrage had moved from ridicule to avoidance. "The chase led up and down elevators in and out of the Senate chamber and committee rooms." Finally, they ferreted out his hiding place and cornered him; he could no longer avoid the issue. The WPU account reversed the standard metaphors of gender to emphasize the senator's humiliation at the hands of women. "Of slight build," he was literally overpowered by the suffragists. "With Mrs. Blatch walking on one side with her hand resting ever so slightly on his sleeve [sic]," the women led him into the committee room and got his vote. "I'll never forgive this," he told Blatch. "Oh yes, you will," she responded, "some day you will be declaring with pride how your vote advanced the suffrage resolution."[2]

The WPU won a similar battle with Robert Wagner, the new Democratic majority leader of the state Senate and one of the most determined opponents of suffrage in the New York legislature. To prevent Wagner from once again employing the delaying legislative tactics of moving to table or returning the referendum resolution to committee for another year, Harriot arranged for three hundred New York City suffragists to go to Albany to pressure him to set a date for a vote. Some fifty or sixty women crowded into the committee room, with the rest gathered in the corridor outside. When Wagner moved to take his place in the chair at the front of the room, the aisle filled with suffragists. "There were no antisuffragists to rescue him," wrote Harriot later.

"There were only all about him, the convinced and ruthless members of the Women's Political Union." He grudgingly agreed to set a date for the state Senate to vote on the suffrage resolution.[3]

In both episodes, the WPU's power rested not only in numbers but also in its willingness to exploit the gendered meanings of power. Wagner yielded because he could not afford to let it be known that he had been physically and politically outmaneuvered by women. The newspapers predictably reported what the women requested, and Wagner graciously granted a date for the Senate vote. But at a time in which accounts of British militant suffragists smashing windows were prominently featured in American papers, the sense of sexual warfare, of women besting men, was close to the surface and hard to overlook.

The Senate debate and vote took place on the date Wagner had guaranteed. Harriot and her followers watched from the gallery. Like good politicians, they had carefully counted their supporters, knew that they had just the right number of votes with not one to spare, and "were full of confidence" that the referendum would carry.[4] Across the hall, the lower house was giving them an unanticipated victory. It looked like the legislative battle might actually be won. But at the last moment a perfidious senator abandoned the public pledge he had given the WPU, shifted his vote, and denied them their victory.

With this undeserved defeat uppermost in her mind, Blatch went to the people. The WPU had organized parades twice before, but the 1912 New York City parade was by far the most carefully organized street demonstration in U.S. suffrage history. The WPU spared no effort at recruiting and educating a large number of marchers and alerting the public to the meaning and significance of the parade. Pledge cards were circulated, committing marchers to take to the streets. Newspapers eagerly covered the clever "stunts" that suffragists devised to advertise the parade: suffragists at the circus, "suffragette hats" for sale at department stores, recruitment booths behind the Public Library.

Harriot was determined that the parade give evidence of a massive, disciplined army of women with which politicians would have to come to terms. She paid great attention to the details of the march, the numbers of marching columns, and the spacing of the lines of marchers. Women were instructed to dress simply, walk erectly, and keep their eyes forward. The spectacle was to be an emotional and sensual evocation of women's power. Opponents, according to Blatch, should be converted through their eyes. "The enemy must see women, marching in increasing numbers year by year out on the public avenues, holding high their banner, Votes For Women." On the appointed day, more than ten thousand took to the streets: women college graduates in their academic gowns, working women by trades and industries, prominent wealthy women, even some men. The president of the national suffrage society marched with a banner that read "Catching Up with China"—a reference to reports that insurgent nationalists in one of China's provincial legislatures had declared women enfranchised. Public demonstrations of this sort were new and a bit daunting to many women. "I marched the whole length," one demonstrator proudly reported to a friend.[5]

In 1912, the emergence of a third national political party, the Progressives, affected the task of getting a suffrage referendum. While Progressive leaders begged women for their support, Blatch was disappointed with the tepid role the party had played in a woman suffrage referendum in Ohio earlier in that year. And former president Theodore Roosevelt, the party's candidate for president in 1912, repeatedly embarrassed himself and his party by sexist declarations that suffragists were "indirectly encouraging immorality."[6] Still, the Progressive Party's support was crucial for the WPU's plans in New York because of the leverage it gave in prying support out of the Republicans, who were struggling to keep voters from bolting to the new party. First the Progressives and then the Republicans endorsed the submission of the suffrage referendum to New York voters at their state conventions. . . . [T]he Democrats followed the other two parties in urging submission of the referendum. Victory, at least in the legislature, was assured. The election of 1912 swept the Democrats . . . into power in the state, and, under the leadership of Woodrow Wilson, into the presidency as well.

There was a last-minute complication when the Republicans added a clause to the referendum subjecting immigrant women, who were citizens by marriage, to special requirements for voting, and the Democrats objected. The issue was a difficult one for Blatch. On the one hand, she had lost her American citizenship by virtue of her marriage to an Englishman and was sympathetic to women whose citizenship was altered by marriage. On the other hand, like her mother decades before, she had her own nativist prejudices, as did many of her middle-class followers. In the end, she decided the issue politically: Keeping the clause would gain the referendum more upstate Republican votes than it would lose downstate Democrats.

Party leaders followed her lead, and in January 1913, both houses passed legislation proposing an amendment to the state constitution striking out the word male and enfranchising citizens over twenty-one "provided that a citizen by marriage should have been an inhabitant of the United States for five years."[7] Blatch had worked three years for this moment, a long time for a single bill. And even with this victory, the most difficult task lay ahead—the winning of the referendum itself. Now the suffrage leaders would have to convince a majority of New York men to vote for woman suffrage.

Harriot Blatch and the leaders of the WPU had no illusions about how difficult this might be. "The task we must accomplish between now and election day 1915 [when the referendum would appear on the ballot] is a Herculean one, compared to that we have just completed," the Executive Committee of the Women's Political Union declared. Harriot had her misgivings about immigrant voters, with their "Germanic and Hebraic attitude toward women," but she counted on the democratic logic of the situation, believing that men who were being allowed to exercise the franchise could be convinced to vote in favor of women's demand to share it. [But a great deal was riding on the New York referendum. "If we win the Empire State all the states will come tumbling down like a deck of cards," she promised.[8]]

To cultivate the voters, the WPU played on its strengths. It based its suffrage advocacy on the proliferating devices of modern mass culture—forms of commercial recreation, methods of advertising, and the pleasures of consumerism. Californians had used billboards, automobile caravans, and suffrage postcards to bring their cause before the electorate in their successful campaign of 1911. New York women had to do the same. ["If we are to reap a victory in 1915, we must cultivate every inch of soil and sow our suffrage seed broadcast in the Empire state," Harriot declared.[9]]

Such an approach conformed to Harriot's view of democracy which, she believed, should be based on the heart rather than the head. Emotions were the key to popular democracy, not reason. "We learned . . . as we toiled in our campaign," she later wrote, "that sermons and logic would never convince. . . . Human beings move because they feel, not because they think."[10] This was not an expression of any special contempt for either women or working-class voters; on the contrary, she considered men (especially politicians) more irrational than women and the rich more prejudiced and conservative than the poor. She believed particularly that changes in women's status and in power relations between the sexes could never be reduced to rational arguments and dispassionate appeals, even to venerable principles of American democracy such as equality and civic virtue.

"Democracy was the keynote" of the grand suffrage ball that the WPU sponsored in January 1913 to inaugurate the referendum campaign. Extensively advertised, it took place in New York City's Seventy-First Street Armory, which was barely large enough for the eight thousand men and women who attended. Rich and poor, working-class and society women alike paid fifty cents to dance the turkey trot and other popular new dances. The event proved, as the WPU put it, "that love of liberty and democracy did not belong to one class or one sex but is deeply rooted in human nature itself."[11] . . .

Given Harriot's appreciation for the role of emotions in mass politics, she was especially intrigued by new technologies of mass communication. "I stand for the achievements of the twentieth century," she declared. "I will make use of . . . anything which civilization places at my command."[12] Lee de Forest, her former son-in-law (Nora's brief marriage to him had ended after a year), was one of the pioneers of modern radio broadcasting. . . . At his invitation, she delivered a radio talk on woman suffrage from the newly opened broadcasting station in downtown Manhattan.

Moving pictures represented another new technology with political possibilities. The WPU arranged for a commercial movie company to produce *The Suffragette and the Man,* a romantic comedy in which the beautiful young heroine, forced to choose between her suffrage principles and her fiancé, first picks principles and then overcomes an anti-suffrage competitor and wins back her lover.

In 1913, the WPU collaborated on a second movie entitled *What 8,000,000 Women Want.* This time the romantic triangle did not involve good and bad men fighting for a heroine's heart but good and bad politics fighting for the hero's soul. Newsreel footage of actual suffrage parades was interspersed with the dramatic action. Harriot played herself and brought to the screen her self-confident authority and her genuine pleasure at conducting the struggle. . . .

[In 1913, as in previous years, the most spectacular suffrage event was the parade organized by the WPU. Each year, the parades had become more stunning affairs, symbolically conveying both the diversity and the unity of modern women.] The 1913 parade was one of the high points of Harriot's suffrage leadership. "We will muster an army fifty thousand strong this year," she predicted. The marchers were arranged by divisions. At the head were two dozen female marshals mounted on horseback and dressed in stylish adaptations of men's evening wear, black cutaways and silk hats with streamers of green, purple, and white, the WPU's colors and those of the movement in England. Leading them, dressed in white and astride a white horse, was Inez Millholand, "the official beauty of the parade." The intention was to provide unforgettable visual images of all kinds of women marching shoulder to shoulder together. "In these times of class wars," Harriot observed, could men really afford "to shut out from public affairs that fine spirit of fellowship" that suffragism represented?[13]

The effectiveness of the parade as political propaganda infuriated antisuffragists, for whom the spectacular aspect of the movement was proof positive of the social and cultural upheaval that votes for women threatened. The antisuffragists charged that the bold stance of the marchers smacked of the deliberate exploitation of "sex appeal." . . . Harriot Blatch found the charges amusing. "Funny idea of sex appeal. Twenty thousand women turn out on a hot day. 87 degrees and march up Fifth Avenue to the blaring music of thirty-five bands; eyes straight to the front; faces red with the hot sun. . . . If it had been mellow moonlight. . . . But a sex appeal set to brass bands! That certainly is a new one."[14] The WPU was determined to finesse the conventional notions of female beauty that had so long restrained women's public activities. . . .

During the legislative lobbying years from 1910 to 1913, Harriot and the WPU had not faced much organizational opposition within the New York suffrage movement. The state suffrage organization was small and ineffective. But once the referendum campaigning began in earnest, the Woman's Political Union, led by the blunt, sometimes undiplomatic Blatch, came into direct conflict with the other great figure of New York suffragism, the moderate, circumspect Carrie Chapman Catt. Within the women's movement, Catt embodied the progressive faith in organizational structure and administrative centralization. In contrast, Harriot celebrated individual initiative, modern invention, and personal freedom. Notwithstanding lofty suffrage rhetoric about the unity of all womanhood and the solidarity of the sex, these two were bound to clash. . . . Catt was always more concerned to unify and reconcile all existing suffragists than to reach out and create new ones. While some activists believed that Blatch was autocratic and high-handed, the ever-diplomatic Catt prized harmony within the movement above all things. Catt's efforts went to creating internal order rather than tackling external obstacles. Unlike Blatch, Catt had little skill or interest in the intricacies of partisan politics and legislative maneuvers.

Catt's plan was to bring all the suffrage societies in New York . . . under one wing, but the Women's Political Union [crucial to her efforts and the richest organization in the state] refused to subsume itself under Catt's leadership. . . . By 1914, it was clear that two parallel suffrage campaigns would be conducted in New York, one by Catt's Empire State Campaign Committee and the other by Harriot Blatch's Women's Political Union. Both raised money for the referendum effort; both sent paid agents around the state; both set up separate offices, sometimes generating considerable conflict among activists in smaller com-

munities in upstate New York. The suffrage movement had survived previous internal divisions and would face others in the future. . . .

In the last six months of the campaign, the WPU flooded the state with publicity-generating gimmicks and stunts. Suffragists played both ends of the gender divide to demonstrate that they could join in traditional male activities as good fellows and at the same time retain their female virtue. On Suffrage Day at the Polo Grounds, New York suffrage organizations competed with each other to sell tickets to a benefit baseball game between the New York Giants and the Chicago Cubs. . . . To counter the anti-suffrage claims that they were bitter women who wanted the ballot as compensation for their inability to find husbands, they even held a series of "married couple days," in which husbands and wives declared their mutual happiness and support of votes for women. . . .

Ten weeks before the end of the campaign, Harriot's single-minded attention to the cause was shattered by the sudden death of her husband, William Blatch, who was accidentally electrocuted. . . . Before leaving [for England to tend to her husband's estate], she took advantage of one benefit of widowhood and resumed her U.S. citizenship. Harriot's decision to leave the country so close to the end of the 1915 campaign is something of a puzzle. She could have postponed the trip a few months. Moreover, England was already at war with Germany, and the transatlantic trip was dangerous. Perhaps she was growing weary of the unrelenting labor of trying to convert New York voters, or perhaps she sensed that she was losing her position as New York's foremost suffragist to Carrie Chapman Catt. . . . By the time she returned in mid-October, the Empire State Campaign Committee . . . had taken over organization of the final suffrage parade. . . .

November 2, 1915, the day toward which Harriot Blatch, Carrie Catt, and thousands of other New York women had been working for years, was the kind of warm, sunny day for which hard-working campaigners pray. When the polls opened at 6 A.M., several thousand suffrage activists were in their places as poll-watchers, guarding against any effort to cheat them of their victory. . . .

By midnight, it was clear that the woman

suffrage amendment had been defeated. Out of 1,200,000 votes cast across the state, woman suffrage had been defeated by 190,000 votes, about 16 percent of the total. All the boroughs of New York City voted against woman suffrage as well as fifty-six of the state's sixty-one counties.

Most New York suffragists kept the bitter disappointment they felt to themselves and declared the referendum a moral triumph. "On the whole we have achieved a wonderful victory," Carrie Chapman Catt proclaimed. "It was short of our hopes but the most contemptuous opponents speak with newly acquired respect for our movement."[15] Catt's wing of the campaign announced the day after the election that a second referendum campaign would begin as soon as state law permitted. . . .

Harriot Blatch was one of the few suffrage leaders who dared to react with open anger. She was "disgusted at the conditions which had forced women to campaign in the streets" and humiliated at having to appeal to immigrant men to gain her native-born rights as an American citizen.[16] She vowed she would never make another street-corner speech. Her retreat into this outraged elitism recalled her mother's reaction to her own crushing disappointment at the failure of the Reconstruction constitutional amendments to include women. Blatch also blamed the suffrage forces themselves for the defeat, at least the Catt wing of the movement, which she thought had neglected upstate New York. She believed a second referendum would be a mistake because the antisuffragists would be even better organized for the next round.

In this she was wrong. In 1917, a second voters' referendum was victorious in New York, thus winning an incalculably important political prize in the battle that was intensifying nationwide. Yet Harriot was correct in a larger way. The era of state suffrage referenda was over; with the exception of New York, no other state was won by this method after 1915. From this point on, attention, energy, and political initiative shifted to the federal arena, to the constitutional amendment Elizabeth Cady Stanton and Susan B. Anthony had first introduced and which had been stalled in congressional committee for almost fifty years. In less than five years, the amendment was moved onto the floor, secured a two-thirds vote in the House and three years later in the Senate, and was ratified by three-quarters of the state legislatures to become the law of the land. . . .

Notes

1. "Foreword" by Mary Beard, in Harriot Stanton Blatch and Alma Lutz, *Challenging Years: The Memoirs of Harriot Stanton Blatch* (New York: G. P. Putnam's Sons, 1940), p. vii.

2. Nora de Forest, "Political History of Women's Political Union," reel 1, Harriot Stanton Blatch Papers, Library of Congress, pp. 13–14; *Challenging Years*, pp. 162–63.

3. *Challenging Years*, pp. 163–64.

4. Ibid., pp. 169–70; Women's Political Union 1912–1913 Annual Report, pp. 7–8.

5. *Challenging Years*, p. 180; "Chinese Women Parade for Suffrage," *New York Times*, April 14, 1912, pt. 7, p. 5; Katherine Devereux Blake to Alice Park, n.d., Susan B. Anthony Memorial Collection, Huntington Library, San Marino, CA.

6. "Roosevelt Is for Woman Suffrage," *New York Times*, February 3, 1912, p. 7.

7. "Official Copy of Proposed Amendment," November 2, 1915, Blatch Papers, Library of Congress.

8. "The Referendum Policy of the Women's Political Union," p. 19, reel 1, Blatch Papers, Library of Congress. "Mrs. Blatch Plans Hot Fight to Win New York to Suffrage," *Chicago Tribune*, March 16, 1913. Blatch to Alice Paul, August 26, 1913, reel 4, National Woman's Party Papers: Suffrage Years.

9. Blatch, "Seed Time and Harvest," *Women's Political World*, June 16, 1913, p. 2.

10. *Challenging Years*, p. 192.

11. "Suffragists Tour City to Boom Ball," *New York Daily Mail*, January 11, 1913; "Charity Versus Votes," *Women's Political World*, January 15, 1913, p. 7.

12. "Barnard Girls Test Wireless Phones," *New York Times*, February 26, 1909, p. 7.

13. ". . . with Suffrage Workers," *New York Post*, March 7, 1913; "Eyes to the Front," *New York Tribune*, May 3, 1913; Blatch, "A Reviewing Stand," *Women's Political World*, May 15, 1913, p. 1.

14. "Answers Anti Attack," *New York Times*, May 13, 1913, p. 3.

15. Catt to Mary Grey Peck, December 12, 1912, Catt Papers, Library of Congress.

16. "Mrs. Blatch Pours Out Wrath . . . ," *New York Times*, November 4, 1915, p. 3.

DOCUMENTS: Dimensions of Citizenship I

Mackenzie *v.* Hare, *1915*

The persistent expansion of Married Women's Property Laws and the development of support for suffrage makes it tempting to conclude that the practice of coverture—women's civic subordination to men—steadily dissolved over the course of the nineteenth and early twentieth centuries. But while it is true that some aspects of coverture eroded, others were sustained and even strengthened.

Although Chief Justice Morrison R. Waite had been right when he observed in *Minor v. Happersett* (1875) (pp. 251–52) "[t]here is no doubt that women may be citizens," he was wrong when he went on to claim that "sex has never been made one of the elements of citizenship. . . . [M]en have never had an advantage over women." According to the common law and early American practice, white women, like men, became citizens either by birth or by their own choice to be naturalized. But in 1855, following practices established in France by the conservative Code Napoleon (1804) and in Britain in 1844, the U.S. Congress extended the principle of marital unity to provide that "any woman who might lawfully be naturalized under the existing laws, married, or shall be married to a citizen of the United States shall be deemed and taken to be a citizen." That is, foreign women who married male citizens did not need to go through a naturalization process or even take an oath of allegiance. The law made no comment about foreign-born men who might marry American women; for the next fifty years, there was little consistency in how courts dealt with the cases that came before them. But when the principle of "marital unity" prevailed, women who were American citizens actually lost their citizenship, and in 1907, Congress passed a statute that explicitly provided that women take the nationality of their husbands.

Expatriation—the loss of citizenship—traditionally has been a very severe punishment, usually reserved for cases of treason. If a married woman had to assume the nationality of her husband, she might become the subject of a king or tsar in a political system that offered her even less protection than did the United States. She might even become stateless. If Americans claimed to base their political system on the "consent of the governed," could women's "consent" be arbitrarily denied? In time of war, the American woman who married, say, a German national, could overnight change her status from a citizen to an alien enemy. President Ulysses S. Grant's daughter lost her citizenship when she married an Englishman in 1874; it required a special act of Congress to reinstate her citizenship when she returned from England as a widow in 1898.

Ethel Mackenzie, who had been born in California, married Gordon Mackenzie, a British subject, in 1909—two years after the passage of the Citizenship Act of 1907. She was active in the woman suffrage movement in California, and when it was successful in 1911 she worked in the San Francisco voter registration drive. It is not surprising that she herself should try to register to vote. When the Board of Election Commissioners denied her application, holding that upon her marriage to a British subject she had "ceased to be a citizen of the United States," she refused to let her husband apply for citizenship and instead challenged the law, claiming that Congress had exceeded its authority. She could not believe that Congress had actually *intended* to deprive her of the citizenship she understood to be her birthright. Why did the Supreme Court deny her claim? What "ancient principle of jurisprudence" did they rely on? Why did the Court think that the marriage of an American woman to a foreign man should be treated differently than the marriage of an American man to a foreign woman?

MR. JUSTICE McKENNA:

... The question ... is, Did [Ethel Mackenzie] cease to be a citizen by her marriage? ... [Mackenzie contends] that it was not the intention [of Congress] to deprive an American-born woman, remaining within the jurisdiction of the United States, of her citizenship by reason of her marriage to a resident foreigner. ... [She is trying to persuade the Court that the citizenship statute was] beyond the authority of Congress. ... [She offered the] earnest argument ... that ... under the Constitution and laws of the United States, [citizenship] became a right, privilege and immunity which could not be taken away from her except as a punishment for crime or by her voluntary expatriation. ...

[But the Court concludes:] ... The identity of husband and wife is an ancient principle of our jurisprudence. It was neither accidental nor arbitrary and worked in many instances for her protection. There has been, it is true, much relaxation of it but in its retention as in its origin it is determined by their

intimate relation and unity of interests, and this relation and unity may make it of public concern in many instances to merge their identity, and give dominance to the husband. It has purpose, if not necessity, in purely domestic policy; it has greater purpose and, it may be, necessity, in international policy. ... Having this purpose, has it not the sanction of power?

... The law in controversy deals with a condition voluntarily entered into. ... The marriage of an American woman with a foreigner has consequences ... [similar to] her physical expatriation. ... Therefore, as long as the relation lasts it is made tantamount to expatriation. This is no arbitrary exercise of government. ... It is the conception of the legislation under review that such an act [marriage to a foreign man] may bring the Government into embarrassments and, it may be, into controversies. ... [Marriage to a foreign man] is as voluntary and distinctive as expatriation and its consequence must be considered as elected.

The decision in *Mackenzie* angered suffragists and energized them; American women needed suffrage to protect themselves against involuntary expatriation and statelessness. The repeal of the Citizenship Act of 1907 was high on the suffragists' agenda, and they turned to it as soon as suffrage was accomplished (see Equal Suffrage [Nineteenth] Amendment). The Cable Act of 1922 provided that "the right of a person to become a naturalized citizen shall not be denied to a person on account of sex or because she is a married woman," but it permitted American women who married foreigners to retain their citizenship only if they married men from countries whose subjects were eligible for U.S. citizenship—that is, not from China or Japan. American-born women who married aliens from China or Japan still lost their citizenship. American-born women who married aliens not from China or Japan were treated as naturalized citizens who would lose their citizenship should they reside abroad for two years. The Cable Act was extended by amendments well into the 1930s, but loopholes remained, and not all of it was made retroactive. As late as the 1950s, some American-born women were denied passports because they had married aliens before 1922. In 2001 the U.S. Supreme Court upheld a practice of different rules by which a child born abroad to an unmarried citizen man and a non-citizen woman, or an unmarried citizen woman and a non-citizen man, could claim citizenship. [*Nguyen* v. *Immigration and Naturalization Service*, 533 U.S. 53 (2001).*]

*This note draws on Candice Lewis Bredbenner, *A Nationality of Her Own: Woman, Marriage and the Law of Citizenship* (Berkeley: University of California Press, 1998) and Linda K. Kerber, *No Constitutional Right to Be Ladies: Women and the Obligations of Citizenship* (New York: Hill and Wang, 1998), ch. 1.

Equal Suffrage (Nineteenth) Amendment, 1920

When the Fourteenth and Fifteenth Amendments (p. 247) failed to provide for universal suffrage, a federal amendment was introduced into the Senate by S. C. Pomeroy of Kansas in 1868 and into the House by George W. Julian of Indiana in March 1869. Historian Ellen DuBois has observed, "Previously the case for suffrage had consistently been put in terms of the individual rights of all persons, regardless of their sex and race. Angered by their exclusion from the Fifteenth Amendment, women's rights advocates began to develop fundamentally different arguments for their cause. They claimed their right to the ballot not as individuals but as a sex. . . . The reason women should vote was not that they were the same as men but that they were different. That made for a rather thorough reversal of classic women's rights premises."*

Arguing for the vote on the basis of women's *difference* from men could be effective in strengthening women's sense of group consciousness, but it also was compatible with racist and nativist arguments that white women needed the vote to counteract the suffrage of black and immigrant men. The old alliance of woman suffrage and abolitionist activism eroded, even though voting rights for black men were increasingly threatened after Reconstruction. The suffrage efforts of 1870 to 1920 continued to display arguments from equality, but younger generations of activists were increasingly likely to emphasize difference—what one activist called "the mother instinct for government."

Woman suffrage was not accomplished easily. One scholar has counted 480 suffrage campaigns between 1870 and 1910, but only seventeen referenda were held, with only two successes. Stanton died in 1902; Anthony in 1906. But a new, younger generation adopted new strategies; Americans were inspired by the militancy of the British suffrage movement; in 1902 Carrie Chapman Catt was simultaneously president of the International Woman Suffrage Alliance and the National American Woman Suffrage Association. By 1910 it was clear that a reinvigorated movement was underway, using door-to-door campaigns, street-corner speakers, poll watchers on election day. For the first time, cross-class suffrage organizations, like New York's Equality League of Inde-

*Ellen Carol DuBois, "Outgrowing the Compact of the Fathers: Equal Rights, Woman Suffrage, and the United States Constitution 1820–1878," *Journal of American History* 74 (1987):848.

pendent Women, were mobilizing support for suffrage. Suffragists staged public parades that attracted tens of thousands of supporters.

Although many suffragists had claimed that when women got the vote there would be no more war, Catt swung NAWSA behind Woodrow Wilson and American support for the Allies and eventually support for American entry into World War I. In 1918, the House of Representatives passed the suffrage amendment, barely achieving the required two-thirds majority, but despite a personal appearance of President Wilson, it failed by only two votes to carry the Senate. As state after state fell into line, the number of congressmen dependent on women's votes increased; when a federal amendment was proposed in Congress, these men were likely to feel they had no choice but to support it. NAWSA targeted four senators in the fall elections; two of them failed to be re-elected. Energetic campaigns in the states to elect prosuffrage people to Congress worked. When the amendment came up in the new Congress, Anne F. Scott and Andrew Scott report, "224 of those voting yes came from suffrage states, and eighty from nonsuffrage states." It squeaked by in the Senate. It was ratified by thirty-five states by August 1920; after a bitter fight in Tennessee, it was ratified by a single vote, just in time to permit women to vote in the elections of 1920.

When Puerto Rican women attempted to register to vote in 1920, however, the U.S. Bureau of Insular Affairs decided that the Nineteenth Amendment did not automatically apply to U.S. territories. Suffragist groups mobilized in Puerto Rico, lobbying throughout the next decade both on the island and in Washington, D.C., with support from the National Women's Party. In 1929 the territorial legislature granted suffrage to women restricted by a literacy requirement; not until 1935 was universal suffrage established in Puerto Rico.

Many southern states had excluded African American men from voting by using literacy tests, poll taxes, and intimidation; in those states black women could vote no more easily than black men, and suffrage was an empty victory. The state of Georgia effectively discouraged white women from voting as well by providing that any woman who did not choose to register to vote did not have to pay the poll tax. This law, which encouraged women—and their husbands—to see voting as an expensive extravagance, was upheld by the U.S. Supreme Court in 1937. [*Breedlove* v. *Suttles*, 302 U.S. 277]

Section 1. The right of the citizens of the United States to vote shall not be denied or abridged by the United States or by any State on account of sex.

Section 2. Congress shall have power to enforce this article by appropriate legislation.

Adkins *v.* Children's Hospital, *1923*

Minimum wage legislation was the counterpart to maximum hour laws. In 1918 Congress authorized the Wage Board of the District of Columbia to fix minimum wages for women and children in order to protect them "from conditions detrimental to their health and morals, resulting from wages which are inadequate to maintain decent standards of living."

This act was attacked, much as maximum hour legislation had been, as an interference with the right of the employer and employee to contract freely. Suit was brought against it by a hospital that employed many women at lower than minimum wages. Arguing for the Wage Board and on behalf of the Consumers' League was Felix Frankfurter, who used a Brandeis Brief researched by Molly Dewson that was a thousand pages long. He convinced Justices William Howard Taft and Oliver Wendell Holmes, Jr., that low wages and long hours were linked. In their dissenting opinion they stated that if Congress could regulate one it could regulate the other. Holmes also observed that the phrase "liberty of contract" did not appear in the Constitution.

The majority of the Court was not persuaded, however. The members of the majority distinguished between maximum hours legislation, which they saw as directly allied to health concerns, and minimum wage legislation, which they thought "simply and exclusively a price-fixing law." The majority also observed that the Nineteenth Amendment obviated the need for protective legislation for women. In taking that position, the Justices were endorsing the arguments of Alice Paul and the National Women's Party, who had no faith in protective labor legislation and who were lobbying for an Equal Rights Amendment.

The *Adkins* decision blocked progress in minimum wage legislation for fifteen years, until there was a new president (Franklin D. Roosevelt) and a new approach in Congress. In 1938 the Fair Labor Standards Act established a federal minimum wage for *both* men and women. However, women continued often to be paid less than men for the same jobs. In 1963 the Equal Pay Act prohibited different pay for men and women when their jobs require "equal skill, effort and responsibility and are performed under similar working conditions." The Court has ruled that jobs meriting equal pay must be substantially equal but not necessarily identical: "Dusting is dusting is dusting" said one court in ruling that the pay of maids and janitors must be equal. More recently, the definition of what constitutes "equal skill, effort and responsibility" has been broadened to a public debate over what constitutes "comparable worth."

MR. JUSTICE GEORGE SUTHERLAND DELIVERED THE OPINION OF THE COURT:

... the ancient inequality of the sexes, otherwise than physical, as suggested in the *Muller Case* has continued "with diminishing intensity." In view of the great—not to say revolutionary—changes which have taken place since that utterance, in the contractual, political and civil status of women, culminating in the Nineteenth Amendment, it is not unreasonable to say that these differences have now come almost, if not quite, to the vanishing point. ... we cannot accept the doctrine that women of mature age, ... require or may be subjected to restrictions upon their liberty of contract which could not lawfully be imposed in the case of men under similar circumstances. To do so would be to ignore all the implications to be drawn from the present day trend of legislation, as well as that of common thought and usage, by which woman is accorded emancipation from the old doctrine that she must be given special protection or be subjected to special restraint in her contractual and civil relationships. . . . What is sufficient to supply the necessary cost of living for a woman worker and maintain her in good health and protect her morals is obviously not a precise or unvarying sum. . . . The amount will depend upon a variety of circumstances: the individual temperament, habits of thrift, care, ability to buy necessaries intelligently, and whether the woman lives alone or with her family. . . . It cannot be shown that well paid women safeguard their morals more carefully than those who are poorly paid. Morality rests upon other considerations than wages. . . .

> *Margaret Sanger, "I resolved that women should have knowledge of contraception. . . ."*

Nowhere does gender matter more than in the area of reproduction. The contrast between the high fertility of newly arriving immigrants and the low birth rate among old-stock Americans around the turn of the century prompted such leaders as Theodore Roosevelt to lament "race suicide" and to exhort women of the "proper sort" to perform their maternal functions in the selfless fashion dictated by time and tradition. Viewed through women's eyes, however, these population trends looked different, as this selection on the beginnings of the birth control movement dramatically illustrates. While a few radicals such as Emma Goldman saw contraception as a means of liberating women by restoring to them control over their own bodies and thereby lessening their economic dependence on men, it was Margaret Higgins Sanger whose name would become most closely linked with the crusade for birth control.

The factors that propelled Sanger—always a complex personality—to leadership were many. One of eleven children, she helped bury her mother, who died of tuberculosis. Young Margaret, however, was convinced that it was the passion of her father who lived to be eighty which was the real cause of her mother's death. A nursing career also shaped Sanger's thinking, as the following account suggests. Arrested under the Comstock Law (p. 250) for publication of a newspaper advocating contraception, she fled in 1914 to England with her husband and three children. There she met the famous British psychologist and sex expert, Havelock Ellis, who further convinced her that sexual experience should be separated from reproduction, enabling couples to enhance the quality of their sexual relationship. Returning to New York, the Sangers continued their activities on behalf of birth control. The opening of the Brownsville clinic in 1916, recounted here, resulted in still further confrontation with authorities. The hunger strike

Excerpted from "Awakening and Revolt," "A 'Public Nuisance,'" and "Hunger Strike." chaps. 3, 12, and 13 of *My Fight for Birth Control* by Margaret Sanger (New York: Farrar & Reinhart, 1931). Copyright © 1931 by Margaret Sanger. Reprinted by permission of Grant Sanger. Cross-references have been adjusted.

Margaret Sanger, following a decision by the New York Court of Appeals in 1918. Although the court upheld her conviction, it interpreted the law in question more broadly, allowing physicians to provide contraceptives to married women "to cure or prevent (venereal) disease." (Photograph reprinted by permission of Planned Parenthood® Federation of America.)

of Sanger's sister, Ethel Byrne, a nurse at the clinic, was followed by Sanger's own trial. Convicted of "maintaining a public nuisance," she was sentenced to thirty days in the workhouse. Ever the iconoclast and rebel, she gave talks to other inmates on sex hygiene when the matrons were out of sight. Divorcing William Sanger, she subsequently married a wealthy oil man who contributed liberally to the American Birth Control League, which she founded in 1921.

Important financial aid would also come in later years from the wealthy feminist Katherine McCormick, who shared Sanger's commitment to research in contraception. In the early 1950s McCormick provided funds for experiments in endocrinology that led to the development of the birth control pill. At a time when few scientists thought an oral contraceptive was possible, the insistence of Sanger and McCormick that every woman had the right to control her own body helped bring about a major breakthrough in medical technology. In 1960 "the pill" became available to the public. The timing was propitious, for it coincided with a period of sexual liberation that, while proving in some respects to be a mixed blessing for women, also coincided with new recognition of the intensity of their sexual drive and capacity for sexual pleasure.

Although Sanger saw the development of an oral contraceptive as another victory in a long and difficult struggle for reproductive freedom, others viewed the birth control movement differently. Arguments that limiting family size could not only free women's energies for social reform but prevent the world's poor from producing children they were unable to care for met with opposition from women themselves in the early years of Sanger's crusade. Some feared that birth control would contribute to promiscuity; others feared it would deny women the dignity that was theirs by virtue of motherhood. The Roman Catholic Church was unrelenting in its opposition, maintaining that the use of contraceptives is a sin. Among groups in the self-styled profamily movement of the present, Sanger is still being angrily attacked. Her contribution to the lives of modern American women remains a matter of political debate. Birth control is not only a technical way of spacing and limiting children so as to benefit both mother and child but is part of a larger debate about the extent to which women should be able to control their own reproductive lives.

AWAKENING AND REVOLT

Early in the year 1912 I came to a sudden realization that my work as a nurse and my activities in social service were entirely palliative and consequently futile and useless to relieve the misery I saw all about me. . . .

It is among the mothers here that the most difficult problems arise—the outcasts of society with theft, filth, perjury, cruelty, brutality oozing from beneath.

Ignorance and neglect go on day by day; children born to breathe but a few hours and pass out of life; pregnant women toiling early and late to give food to four or five children, always hungry; boarders taken into homes where there is not sufficient room for the family; little girls eight and ten years of age sleeping in the same room with dirty, foul smelling, loathsome men; women whose weary, pregnant, shapeless bodies refuse to accommodate themselves to the husbands' desires find husbands looking with lustful eyes upon other women, sometimes upon their own little daughters, six and seven years of age.

In this atmosphere abortions and birth become the main theme of conversation. On Saturday nights I have seen groups of fifty to one hundred women going into questionable offices well known in the community for cheap abortions. I asked several women what took place there, and they all gave the same reply: a quick examination, a probe inserted into the uterus and turned a few times to disturb the fertilized ovum, and then the woman was sent home. Usually the flow began the next day and often continued four or five weeks. Sometimes an ambulance carried the victim to the hospital for a curetage, and if she returned home at all she was looked upon as a lucky woman.

This state of things became a nightmare with me. There seemed no sense to it all, no reason for such waste of mother life, no right to exhaust women's vitality and to throw them on the scrap-heap before the age of thirty-five.

Everywhere I looked, misery and fear stalked—men fearful of losing their jobs, women fearful that even worse conditions might come upon them. The menace of another pregnancy hung like a sword over the head of every poor woman I came in contact with that year. The question which met me was always the same: What can I do to keep from it? or, What can I do to get out of this? Sometimes they talked among themselves bitterly.

"It's the rich that know the tricks," they'd say, "while we have all the kids." Then, if the women were Roman Catholics, they talked about "Yankee tricks," and asked me if I knew what the Protestants did to keep their families down. When I said that I didn't believe that the rich knew much more than they did I was laughed at and suspected of holding back information for money. They would nudge each other and say something about paying me before I left the case if I would reveal the "secret." . . .

I heard over and over again of their desperate efforts at bringing themselves "around"—drinking various herb-teas, taking drops of turpentine on sugar, steaming over a chamber of boiling coffee or of turpentine water, rolling down stairs, and finally inserting slippery-elm sticks, or knitting needles, or shoe hooks into the uterus. I used to shudder with horror as I heard the details and, worse yet, learned of the conditions *behind the reason* for such desperate actions.

. . . Each time I returned it was to hear that Mrs. Cohen had been carried to a hospital but had never come back, that Mrs. Kelly had sent the children to a neighbor's and had put her head into the gas oven to end her misery. Many of the women had consulted midwives, social workers and doctors at the dispensary and asked a way to limit their families, but they were denied this help, sometimes indignantly or gruffly, sometimes jokingly; but always

knowledge was denied them. Life for them had but one choice: either to abandon themselves to incessant childbearing, or to terminate their pregnancies through abortions. Is it any wonder they resigned themselves hopelessly, as the Jewish and Italian mothers, or fell into drunkenness, as the Irish and Scotch? The latter were often beaten by husbands, as well as by their sons and daughters. They were driven and cowed, and only as beasts of burden were allowed to exist. . . .

They claimed my thoughts night and day. One by one these women, with their worried, sad, pensive and aging faces would marshal themselves before me in my dreams, sometimes appealingly, sometimes accusingly. I could not escape from the facts of their misery, neither was I able to see the way out of their problems and their troubles. . . .

Finally the thing began to shape itself, to become accumulative during the three weeks I spent in the home of a desperately sick woman living on Grand Street, a lower section of New York's East Side.

Mrs. Sacks was only twenty-eight years old; her husband, an unskilled worker, thirty-two. Three children, aged five, three and one, were none too strong nor sturdy, and it took all the earnings of the father and the ingenuity of the mother to keep them clean, provide them with air and proper food, and give them a chance to grow into decent manhood and womanhood.

Both parents were devoted to these children and to each other. The woman had become pregnant and had taken various drugs and purgatives, as advised by her neighbors. Then, in desperation, she had used some instrument lent to her by a friend. She was found prostrate on the floor amidst the crying children when her husband returned from work. Neighbors advised against the ambulance, and a friendly doctor was called. The husband would not hear of her going to a hospital, and as a little money had been saved in the bank a nurse was called and the battle for that precious life began.

. . . The three-room apartment was turned into a hospital for the dying patient. Never had I worked so fast, so concentratedly as I did to keep alive that little mother. . . .

. . . July's sultry days and nights were melted into a torpid inferno. Day after day, night after night, I slept only in brief snatches, ever too anxious about the condition of that feeble heart bravely carrying on, to stay long from the bedside of the patient. With but one toilet for the building and that on the floor below, everything had to be carried down for disposal, while ice, food and other necessities had to be carried three flights up. It was one of those old airshaft buildings of which there were several thousands then standing in New York City.

At the end of two weeks recovery was in sight, and at the end of three weeks I was preparing to leave the fragile patient to take up the ordinary duties of her life, including those, of wifehood and motherhood. . . .

But as the hour for my departure came nearer, her anxiety increased, and finally with trembling voice she said: "Another baby will finish me, I suppose."

"It's too early to talk about that," I said, and resolved that I would turn the question over to the doctor for his advice. When he came I said: "Mrs. Sacks is worried about having another baby."

"She well might be," replied the doctor, and then he stood before her and said: "Any more such capers, young woman, and there will be no need to call me."

"Yes, yes—I know, Doctor," said the patient with trembling voice, "but," and she hesitated as if it took all of her courage to say it, "what can I do to prevent getting that way again?"

"Oh ho!" laughed the doctor good naturedly, "You want your cake while you eat it too, do you? Well, it can't be done." Then, familiarly slapping her on the back and picking up his hat and bag to depart, he said: "I'll tell you the only sure thing to do. Tell Jake to sleep on the roof!"

With those words he closed the door and went down the stairs, leaving us both petrified and stunned.

Tears sprang to my eyes, and a lump came in my throat as I looked at that face before me. It was stamped with sheer horror. I thought for a moment she might have gone insane, but she conquered her feelings, whatever they may have been, and turning to me in desperation said: "He can't understand, can he?— he's a man after all—but you do, don't you? You're a woman and you'll tell me the secret and I'll never tell it to a soul."

She clasped her hands as if in prayer, she leaned over and looked straight into my eyes and beseechingly implored me to tell her something—something *I really did not know.* . . .

I had to turn away from that imploring face. I could not answer her then. I quieted her as best I could. She saw that I was moved by the tears in my eyes. I promised that I would come back in a few days and tell her what she wanted to know. The few simple means of limiting the family like *coitus interruptus* or the condom were laughed at by the neighboring women when told these were the means used by men in the well-to-do families. That was not believed, and I knew such an answer would be swept aside as useless were I to tell her this at such a time. . . .

The intelligent reasoning of the young mother—how to prevent getting that way again—how sensible, how just she had been— yes, I promised myself I'd go back and have a long talk with her and tell her more, and perhaps she would not laugh but would believe that those methods were all that were really known.

But time flew past, and weeks rolled into months. . . . I was about to retire one night three months later when the telephone rang and an agitated man's voice begged me to come at once to help his wife who was sick again. It was the husband of Mrs. Sacks, and I intuitively knew before I left the telephone that it was almost useless to go.

. . . I arrived a few minutes after the doctor, the same one who had given her such noble advice. The woman was dying. She was unconscious. She died within ten minutes after my arrival. It was the same result, the same story told a thousand times before—death from abortion. She had become pregnant, had used drugs, had then consulted a five-dollar professional abortionist, and death followed.

The doctor shook his head as he rose from listening for the heart beat. . . . The gentle woman, the devoted mother, the loving wife had passed on leaving behind her a frantic husband, helpless in his loneliness, bewildered in his helplessness as he paced up and down the room, hands clenching his head, moaning "My God! My God! My God!"

The Revolution came—but not as it has been pictured nor as history relates that revolutions have come. . . .

After I left that desolate house I walked and walked and walked; for hours and hours I kept on, bag in hand, thinking, regretting, dreading to stop; fearful of my conscience, dreading to face my own accusing soul. At three in the morning I arrived home still clutching a heavy load the weight of which I was quite unconscious.

. . . As I stood at the window and looked out, the miseries and problems of that sleeping city arose before me in a clear vision like a panorama: crowded homes, too many children; babies dying in infancy; mothers overworked; baby nurseries; children neglected and hungry—mothers so nervously wrought they could not give the little things the comfort nor care they needed; mothers half sick most of their lives—"always ailing, never failing"; women made into drudges; children working in cellars; children aged six and seven pushed into the labor market to help earn a living; another baby on the way; still another; yet another; a baby born dead—great relief; an older child dies—sorrow, but nevertheless relief—insurance helps; a mother's death— children scattered into institutions; the father, desperate, drunken; he slinks away to become an outcast in a society which has trapped him.

. . . There was only one thing to be done: call out, start the alarm, set the heather on fire! Awaken the womanhood of America to free the motherhood of the world! I released from my almost paralyzed hand the nursing bag which unconsciously I had clutched, threw it across the room, tore the uniform from my body, flung it into a corner, and renounced all palliative work forever.

I would never go back again to nurse women's ailing bodies while their miseries were as vast as the stars. I was now finished with superficial cures, with doctors and nurses and social workers who were brought face to face with this overwhelming truth of women's needs and yet turned to pass on the other side. They must be made to see these facts. I resolved that women should have knowledge of contraception. They have every right to know about their own bodies. I would strike out—I would scream from the housetops. I would tell the world what was going on in the lives of these poor women. *I would* be heard. No matter what it should cost. *I would be heard.* . . .

I announced to my family the following day that I had finished nursing, that I would never go on another case—and I never have.

I asked doctors what one could do and was told I'd better keep off that subject or Anthony Comstock would get me. I was told that there were laws against that sort of thing. This was the reply from every medical man and woman I approached. . . .

A "PUBLIC NUISANCE"

The selection of a place for the first birth control clinic was of the greatest importance. No one could actually tell how it would be received in any neighborhood. I thought of all the possible difficulties: The indifference of women's organizations, the ignorance of the workers themselves, the resentment of social agencies, the opposition of the medical profession. Then there was the law—the law of New York State.

Section 1142 was definite. It stated that *no one* could give information to prevent conception to *anyone* for any reason. There was, however, Section 1145, which distinctly stated that physicians (*only*) could give advice to prevent conception for the cure or prevention of disease. I inquired about the section, and was told by two attorneys and several physicians that this clause was an exception to 1142 referring only to venereal disease. But anyway, as I was not a physician, it could not protect me. Dared I risk it?

I began to think of the doctors I knew. Several who had previously promised now refused. I wrote, telephoned, asked friends to ask other friends to help me find a woman doctor to help me demonstrate the need of a birth control clinic in New York. None could be found. No one wanted to go to jail. No one cared to test out the law. Perhaps it would have to be done without a doctor. But it had to be done; that I knew.

Fania Mindell, an enthusiastic young worker in the cause, had come on from Chicago to help me. Together we tramped the streets on that dreary day in early October, through a driving rainstorm, to find the best location at the cheapest terms possible . . .

Finally at 46 Amboy Street, in the Brownsville Section of Brooklyn, we found a friendly landlord with a good place vacant at fifty dollars a month rental; and Brownsville was settled on. It was one of the most thickly populated sections. It had a large population of working class Jews, always interested in health measures, always tolerant of new ideas, willing to listen and to accept advice whenever the health of mother or children was involved. I knew that here there would at least be no breaking of windows, no hurling of insults into our teeth; but I was scarcely prepared for the popular support, the sympathy and friendly help given us in that neighborhood from that day to this. . . .

With a small bundle of handbills and a large amount of zeal, we fared forth each morning in a house-to-house canvass of the district in which the clinic was located. Every family in that great district received a "dodger" printed in English, Yiddish and Italian. . . .

Women of every race and creed flocked to the clinic with the determination not to have any more children than their health could stand or their husbands could support. Jews and Christians, Protestants and Roman Catholics alike made their confessions to us, whatever they may have professed at home or in the church. Some did not dare talk this over with their husbands; and some came urged on by their husbands. Men themselves came after work; and some brought timid, embarrassed wives, apologetically dragging a string of little children. . . .

When I asked a bright little Roman Catholic woman what she would say to the priest when he learned that she had been to the Clinic, she answered indignantly: "It's none of his business. My husband has a weak heart and works only four days a week. He gets twelve dollars, and we can barely live on it now. We have enough children."

Her friend, sitting by, nodded a vigorous approval. "When I was married," she broke in, "the priest told us to have lots of children, and we listened to him. I had fifteen. Six are living. Nine baby funerals in our house. I am thirty-six years old now. Look at me! I look sixty."

As I walked home that night, I made a mental calculation of fifteen baptismal fees, nine funeral expenses, masses and candles for the repose of nine little souls, the physical suffering of the mother, and the emotional suffer-

ing of both parents; and I asked myself, "Was it fair? Is this the price of Christianity?" . . .

Ethel Byrne, who is my sister and a trained nurse, assisted me in advising, explaining, and demonstrating to the women how to prevent conception. As all of our 488 records were confiscated by the detectives who later arrested us for violation of the New York State law, it is difficult to tell exactly how many more women came in those days to seek advice; but we estimate that it was far more than five hundred. As in any new enterprise, false reports were maliciously spread about the clinic; weird stories without the slightest foundation of truth. We talked plain talk and give plain facts to the women who came there. We kept a record of every applicant. All were mothers; most of them had large families.

It was whispered about that the police were to raid the place for abortions. We had no fear of that accusation. We were trying to spare mothers the necessity of that ordeal by giving them proper contraceptive information. . . .

The arrest and raid on the Brooklyn clinic was spectacular. There was no need of a large force of plain clothes men to drag off a trio of decent, serious women who were testing out a law on a fundamental principle. My federal arrest, on the contrary, had been assigned to intelligent men. One had to respect the dignity of their mission; but the New York city officials seem to use tactics suitable only for crooks, bandits and burglars. We were not surprised at being arrested, but the shock and horror of it was that a *woman*, with a squad of five plain clothes men, conducted the raid and made the arrest. A woman—the irony of it!

I refused to close down the clinic, hoping that a court decision would allow us to continue such necessary work. I was to be disappointed. Pressure was brought upon the landlord, and we were dispossessed by the law as a "public nuisance." In Holland the clinics were called "public utilities."

When the policewoman entered the clinic with her squad of plain clothes men and announced the arrest of Miss Mindell and myself (Mrs. Byrne was not present at the time and her arrest followed later), the room was crowded to suffocation with women waiting in the outer room. The police began bullying these mothers, asking them questions, writing down their names in order to subpoena them to testify against us at the trial. These women, always afraid of trouble which the very presence of a policeman signifies, screamed and cried aloud. The children on their laps screamed, too. It was like a panic for a few minutes until I walked into the room where they were stampeding and begged them to be quiet and not to get excited. I assured them that nothing could happen to them, that I was under arrest but they would be allowed to return home in a few minutes. That quieted them. The men were blocking the door to prevent anyone from leaving, but I finally persuaded them to allow these women to return to their homes, unmolested though terribly frightened by it all.

. . . The patrol wagon came rattling through the streets to our door, and at length Miss Mindell and I took our seats within and were taken to the police station. . . .

HUNGER STRIKE

Out of that spectacular raid, which resulted in an avalanche of nation-wide publicity in the daily press, four separate and distinct cases resulted:

Mrs. Ethel Byrne, my sister, was charged with violating Section 1142 of the Penal Code, designed to prevent dissemination of birth control information.

Miss Fania Mindell was charged with having sold an allegedly indecent book entitled "What Every Girl Should Know" written by Margaret Sanger.

I was charged with having conducted a clinic at 46 Amboy Street, Brooklyn, in violation of the same section of the Penal Code.

Having re-opened the clinic, I was arrested on a charge of "maintaining a public nuisance," in violation of Section 1530 of the Penal Code.

The three of us were held for trial in the Court of Special Sessions, with bail fixed at $500 each. This meant that our cases would be decided by three judges appointed by the Mayor and not by a jury. . . .

My sister was found guilty, and on January 22 she was sentenced to thirty days in the Workhouse. A writ of habeas corpus as a means of suspending sentence during appeal

was refused by Supreme Court Justice Callahan. She spent the night in jail.

Ethel Byrne promptly declared a hunger strike. I knew that she would not flinch. Quiet, taciturn, with a will of steel hidden by a diffident air, schooled by her long training as a professional nurse, she announced briefly that she would neither eat, drink, nor work until her release. Commissioner of Correction Burdette G. Lewis promptly announced that she would be permitted to see no one but her attorney.

While the newspapers were reporting—always on the front page—the condition of the hunger striker, plans were hastened for a monster mass meeting of protest, to be held in Carnegie Hall. Helen Todd acted as chairman, and Dr. Mary Halton was an additional speaker. The hall was crowded by a huge audience of all classes. The women patients of the Brownsville clinic were given places of honor on the platform. The salvos of applause which greeted me showed that intelligent opinion was strongly behind us, and did much to give me the courage to fight with renewed strength for the immediate release of Ethel Byrne.

This meeting was acclaimed by the press as a "triumph of women, for women, by women." The meeting was said to have struck the right note—that of being instructive and persuasive, instead of agitational.

In the meantime, Ethel Byrne's refusal to eat and drink was crowding all other news off the front pages of the New York papers. Her defiance was sharpening the issue between self-respecting citizens and the existing law, which was denounced on every street corner as hypocritical. In the subway crowds, on street-corners, everywhere people gathered, the case was discussed. "They are imprisoning a woman for teaching physiological facts!" I heard one man exclaim. . . .

"It makes little difference whether I starve or not," she replied, through her attorney, "so long as this outrageous arrest calls attention to the archaic laws which would prevent our telling the truth about the facts of life. With eight thousand deaths a year in New York State from illegal operations on women, one more death won't make much difference."

All this served to convince the now panic-stricken Mr. Lewis [Commissioner of Correction in charge of Blackwell's Island] that Mrs.

Byrne was different, after all, from the alcoholics and drug addicts who had given him his previous experience, and with whom he had gallantly compared her. When she had gone 103 hours without food, he established a precedent in American prison annals. He ordered her forcibly fed. She was the first woman so treated in this country. . . .

The truth was that Mrs. Byrne was in a critical condition after being rolled in a blanket and having milk, eggs and a stimulant forced into her stomach through a rubber tube. I realized this as soon as I heard that she was "passive under the feeding." Nothing but loss of strength could have lessened the power of her resistance to such authority. Nothing but brutality could have reduced her fiery spirit to acquiescence. I was desperate; torn between admiration for what she was doing and misery over what I feared might be the result.

On January 31st, a committee headed by Mrs. Amos Pinchot, Jessie Ashley and myself went to Albany for the purpose of asking Governor Whitman to appoint a commission to investigate birth control and make a report to the state legislature. Governor Whitman, a wise, fair, intelligent executive and statesman, received us, and listened to our exposition of the economic and moral necessity for birth control; the medical theory behind its justification. He promised to consider appointing the commission. During the interview Miss Jessie Ashley introduced the subject of Mrs. Byrne's treat-

ment on Blackwell's Island and the anxiety we felt about her condition. We tried to make him see the outrage committed by the state in making anyone suffer for so just a cause. The Governor offered Mrs. Byrne a pardon on condition that she would not continue to disseminate birth control information. . . .

When we left Albany that day, I had the promise of a provisional pardon for Mrs. Byrne, but best of all I had in my purse a letter from the Governor to the authorities at Blackwell's Island authorizing me to see her. I was shocked and horrified when, in the late afternoon of February 1st, I saw my sister. She was lying semi-conscious on a cot in a dark corner of the prison cell. . . .

There was not time to inform her of the conditions of her pardon, and moreover she was too ill to face the question. I still believe that I was right in accepting the conditions which the Governor imposed. There was no other course. I saw that she was dangerously ill, that nothing further was to be gained by her keeping on, and that her death would have been a terrible calamity. Her life was what mattered to me, regardless of her future activities. . . .

At any rate, by the time she was released the subject was a burning issue. Newspapers which previously had ignored the case, had to mention a matter important enough to bring the Governor of the State from Albany to New York.

NANCY F. COTT

Equal Rights and Economic Roles: The Conflict over the Equal Rights Amendment in the 1920s

The vote achieved, former suffragists turned their attention to sex-based discrimination in the law. The proper strategy, as in suffrage, seemed to be a constitutional amendment affirming equal rights; men and women would have to be treated under the law as equals and as individuals. Suffragists who had struggled to pass legislation shortening hours and improving working conditions for women in industry had achieved that goal only because the Supreme Court was prepared to regard women as a special class of workers in need of governmental protection because of their childbearing role. (See *Muller* v. *Oregon,* pp. 340–41.) An equal rights amendment would invalidate sex-based labor laws, they feared, since comparable protection would not be extended to men. The ensuing debate was a critical one creating deep and lasting divisions. Unable to agree on a unified agenda for four decades, veterans of the first women's movement expended energy in internal conflict, thereby diluting their political effectiveness. Not surprisingly women's issues made little headway until the 1960s.

The debate over ERA was critical not only because of its long-term consequences, but because it highlighted differing views within feminism of the social significance of gender and the meaning of equality. Does equality require that men and women have the "same" rights and be subject to the "same" treatment or does equality require "different" treatment? How should the law treat the difference created by women's unique reproductive system? With these questions in mind, Nancy Cott carefully assesses the initial debate over ERA, making clear the assumptions and limitations inherent in the arguments of each side.

THE CONFLICT OVER THE EQUAL RIGHTS AMENDMENT IN THE 1920s

Campaigning for ratification of the Equal Rights Amendment during the 1970s, feminists who found it painful to be opposed by other groups of women were often unaware that the first proposal of that amendment in the 1920s had likewise caused a bitter split between women's groups claiming, on both sides, to represent women's interests. The 1920s conflict itself echoed some earlier ideological and tactical controversies. One central strategic question for the women's rights movement in the late nineteenth century had concerned alliances: should proponents of "the cause of woman" ally with advocates for the rights for freed slaves, with temperance workers, or labor reformers, or a political party, or none of them? At various times different women leaders felt passionately for and against such alliances, not agreeing on what they meant for the breadth of the women's movement and for the priority assigned to women's issues.[1] The 1920s contest over the equal rights amendment reiterated that debate insofar as the National Woman's Party, which proposed the ERA, took a "single-issue" approach, and the opposing women's organizations were committed to maintaining multiple alliances. But in even more striking ways than it recapitulated nineteenth-century struggles the 1920s equal rights conflict also predicted lines of fracture of the later twentieth-century women's movement. The advantages or compromises involved in "multi-issue" organizing are matters of contemporary concern, of course. Perhaps more important, the 1920s debate brought into sharp focus (and left for us generations later to resolve) the question whether "equal rights"— a concept adopted, after all, from the male political tradition—matched women's needs. The initial conflict between women over the ERA set the goal of enabling women to have the same opportunities and situations as men against the goal of enabling women freely to be different from men without adverse consequences. As never before in nineteenth-century controversies, these two were seen as competing, even mutually exclusive, alternatives.

The equal rights amendment was proposed as a legal or civic innovation but the intrafeminist controversy it caused focused on the economic arena. Indeed, the connection between economic and political subordination in women's relation to men has been central in women's rights advocacy since the latter part of the nineteenth century. In the Western political tradition, women were historically excluded from political initiatives because they were defined as dependent—like children and slaves—and their dependence was read as fundamentally economic. Nineteenth-century advocates, along with the vote, claimed women's "right to labor," by which they meant the right for women to have their labor recognized, and diversified. They emphasized that women, as human individuals no less than men, had the right and need to use their talents to serve society and themselves and to gain fair compensation. Influential voices such as Charlotte Perkins Gilman's at the turn of the century stressed not only women's service but the necessity and warrant for women's economic independence. Gilman argued simultaneously that social evolution made women's

move "from fireside to factory" inevitable, and also that the move ought to be spurred by conscious renovation of outworn tradition.

By the 1910s suffragists linked political and economic rights, and connected the vote with economic leverage, whether appealing to industrial workers, career women or housewives. They insisted on women's economic independence in principle and defense of wage-earning women in fact. Since the vast majority of wage-earning women were paid too little to become economically independent, however, the two commitments were not identical and might in practice be entirely at odds.[2] The purpose to validate women's existing economic roles might openly conflict with the purpose to throw open economic horizons for women to declare their own self-definition. These tensions introduced by the feminist and suffrage agitation of the 1910s flashed into controversy over the equal rights amendment in the 1920s.

The ERA was the baby of the National Woman's Party, yet not its brainchild alone. As early as 1914, a short-lived New York City group called the Feminist Alliance had suggested a constitutional amendment barring sex discrimination of all sorts. Like the later NWP, the Feminist Alliance was dominated by highly educated and ambitious women in the arts and professions, women who believed that "equal rights" were their due while they also aimed to rejuvenate and reorient thinking about "rights" around female rather than only male definition. Some members of the Feminist Alliance surely joined the NWP, which emerged as the agent of militant and political action during the final decade of the suffrage campaign.[3]

A small group (engaging perhaps 5 percent of all suffragists), the NWP grew from the Congressional Union founded by Alice Paul and Lucy Burns in 1913 to work on the federal rather than the state-by-state route to woman suffrage. Through the 'teens it came to stand for partisan tactics (opposing all Democrats because the Democratic administration had not passed woman suffrage) and for flamboyant, symbolic, publicity-generating actions— large parades, pickets in front of the White House, placards in the Congress, hunger-striking in jail, and more. It gained much of its energy from leftwing radical women who were attracted to its wholesale condemnation of gender inequality and to its tactical adaptations from the labor movement; at the same time, its imperious tendency to work from the top down attracted crucial financial and moral support from some very rich women. When the much larger group, the National American Woman Suffrage Association, moved its focus to a constitutional amendment in 1916, that was due in no little part (although certainly not solely), to the impact of the NWP. Yet while imitating its aim, NAWSA's leaders always hated and resented the NWP, for the way it had horned in on the same pro-suffrage turf while scorning the NAWSA's traditional nonpartisan, educative strategy. These resentments festered into deep and long-lasting personal conflicts between leaders of the two groups.

Just after the 19th Amendment was ratified in August of 1920, the NWP began planning a large convention at which its members would decide whether to continue as a group and, if so, what to work for. The convention, held six months later and tightly orchestrated by chairman Alice Paul, brushed aside all other suggestions and endorsed an ongoing program to "remove all remaining forms of the subjection of women," by means of the elimination of sex discrimination in law.[4] At the outset, NWP leaders seemed unaware that this program of "equal rights" would be much thornier to define and implement than "equal suffrage" had been. They began surveying state legal codes, conferring with lawyers, and drafting numerous versions of equal rights legislation and amendments at the state and federal levels.

Yet the "clean sweep" of such an approach immediately raised a problem: would it invalidate sex-based labor legislation—the laws regulating women's hours, wages, and conditions of work, that women trade unionists and reformers had worked to establish over the past thirty years? The doctrine of "liberty of contract" between employer and employed had ruled court interpretations of labor legislation in the early twentieth century, stymying state regulation of the wages and hours of male workers. State regulation for women workers, espoused and furthered by many women in the NWP, had been made possible only by differentiating female from male wage-earners on the basis of physiology and reproductive functions. Now members of the NWP had to grapple with the question whether such legislation

was sex "discrimination," hampering women workers in the labor market. Initially, there was a great deal of sentiment within the NWP, even voiced by Alice Paul herself, that efforts at equal rights legislation should not impair existing sex-based protective labor legislation. However, there was also contrary opinion, which Paul increasingly heeded; by late November 1921 she had come to believe firmly that "enacting labor laws along sex lines is erecting another handicap for women in the economic struggle." Some NWP affiliates were still trying to draft an amendment that would preserve special labor legislation, nonetheless, and continued to introduce equal rights bills with "safeguards" in some states through the following spring.[5]

Meanwhile women leaders in other organizations were becoming nervous and distrustful of the NWP's intentions. Led by the League of Women Voters (successor to the NAWSA), major women's organizations in 1920 formed a national lobbying group called the Women's Joint Congressional Committee. The LWV was interested in eliminating sex discrimination in the law, but more immediately concerned with the extension of sex-based labor legislation. Moreover, the LWV had inherited NAWSA's hostility to Alice Paul. The first president of the LWV, Maud Wood Park, still smarted from the discomfiture that NWP picketing tactics had caused her when she headed the NAWSA's Congressional Committee from 1916 to 1920.[6] Other leading groups in the Women's Joint Congressional Committee were no less suspicious of the NWP. The National Women's Trade Union League since the mid-1910s had concentrated its efforts on labor legislation to protect women workers. Florence Kelley, director of the National Consumers' League, had been part of the inner circle of the NWP during the suffrage campaign, but on the question of protective labor laws her priorities diverged. She had spent three decades trying to get state regulation of workers' hours and conditions, and was not about to abandon the gains achieved for women.[7]

In December 1921, at Kelley's behest, Paul and three other NWP members met for discussion with her and leaders of the League of Women Voters, the National Women's Trade Union League, the Woman's Christian Temperance Union, and the General Federation of

Women's Clubs. All the latter objected to the new constitutional amendment now formulated by the NWP: "No political, civil or legal disabilities or inequalities on account of sex, or on account of marriage unless applying alike to both sexes, shall exist within the United States or any place subject to their jurisdiction." Paul gave away no ground, and all left feeling that compromise was unlikely. Each side already thought the other intransigent, though in fact debate was still going on within the NWP.[8]

By mid-1922 the National Consumers' League, the LWV, and the Women's Trade Union League went on record opposing "blanket" equal rights bills, as the NWP formulations at both state and federal levels were called. About the same time, the tide turned in the NWP. The top leadership accepted as definitive the views of Gail Laughlin, a lawyer from Maine, who contended that sex-based labor legislation was not a lamented loss but a positive harm. "If women can be segregated as a class for special legislation," she warned, "the same classification can be used for special restrictions along any other line which may, at any time, appeal to the caprice or prejudice of our legislatures." In her opinion, if "protective" laws affecting women were not abolished and prohibited, "the advancement of women in business and industry will be stopped and women relegated to the lowest, worst paid labor."[9] Since NWP lobbyists working at the state level were making little headway, a federal constitutional amendment appeared all the more appealing. In November 1923, at a grand conference staged in Seneca Falls, New York, commemorating the seventy-fifth anniversary of Elizabeth Cady Stanton's Declaration of Sentiments, the NWP announced new language: "Men and women shall have equal rights throughout the United States and every place subject to its jurisdiction." The constitutional amendment was introduced into Congress on December 10, 1923.[10]

In the NWP view, this was the logical sequel to the 19th Amendment. There were so many different sex discriminations in state codes and legal practices—in family law, labor law, jury privileges, contract rights—that only a constitutional amendment seemed effective to remove them. The NWP took the language of liberal individualism, enshrined in the catchphrase of "equal rights," to express its feminism. As Alice Paul saw it, what women as a gender group shared was their subordination and inequality to men as a whole; the legal structure most clearly expressed this subordination and inequality, and therefore was the logical point of attack. The NWP construed this agenda as "purely feminist," that is, appealing to women as women, uniting women around a concern common to them regardless of the other ways in which they might differ. Indeed, at its founding postsuffrage convention the NWP leadership purposely bypassed issues it saw as less "pure," including birth control, the defense of black women's voting rights in the South, and pacifism, which were predictably controversial among women themselves.

The NWP posited that women could and would perceive self-interest in "purely" gender terms. Faced by female opponents, its leaders imagined a fictive or abstract unity among women rather than attempting to encompass women's real diversity. They separated the proposal of equal rights from other social and political issues and effects. Although the campaign for equal rights was initiated in a vision of inclusiveness—envisioned as a stand that all women could take—it devolved into a practice of exclusiveness. The NWP's "appeal for conscious sex loyalty" (as a member once put it) went out to members of the sex who could subordinate identifications and loyalties of class, ethnicity, race, religion, politics, or whatever else to a "pure" sense of themselves as women differentiated from men. That meant principally women privileged by the dominant culture in every way except that they were female.[11]

In tandem with its lobbying for an equal rights amendment, the NWP presented its opposition to sex-based labor legislation as a positive program of "industrial equality." It championed women wage-earners who complained of "protective" legislation as restrictive, such as printers, railroad conductors, or waitresses hampered by hours limitation, or cleaning women fired and replaced by men after the passage of minimum-wage laws. Only a handful of working-class women rose to support for the ERA, however.[12] Mary Anderson, former factory worker herself and since 1919 the director of the U.S. Women's Bureau, which was founded to guide and assist women workers, threw her weight into the fight against the amendment. Male trade

Women used suffrage for a wide range of political expressions. These women of the Ku Klux Klan would not have supported the agendas of the League of Women Voters or of the National Women's Party. Here they parade down Pennsylvania Avenue in 1928. (Photograph courtesy of the Library of Congress.)

unionists—namely leaders of the American Federation of Labor—also voiced immediate opposition to the NWP aims, appearing at the very first U.S. Senate subcommittee hearings on the equal rights amendment. Male unionists or class-conscious workers in this period put their faith in collective bargaining and did not seek labor legislation for themselves, but endorsed it for women and child workers. This differentiation derived partly from male workers' belief in women's physical weakness and veneration of women's "place" in the home, partly from presumptions about women workers being difficult to organize, and also from the aim to keep women from competing for men's jobs. Male unionists tended to view wage-earning women first as women—potential or actual wives and mothers—and only secondarily as workers. For differing reasons women and men in the labor movement con-

verged in their support of sex-based legislation: women because they saw special protection necessary to defend their stake in industry and in union organizations, limited as it was; men to hold at bay women's demands for equal entry into male-controlled union jobs and organizations.[13]

The arguments against the equal rights amendment offered by trade unionists and by such women's organizations as the League of Women Voters overlapped. They assumed that an equal rights amendment would invalidate sex-based labor laws or, at least, destine them for protracted argument in the courts, where judges had shown hostility to any state regulation of employer prerogatives. They insisted that the greatest good for the greatest number was served by protective labor laws. If sex-based legislation hampered some—as the NWP claimed, and could be shown true, for instance, in the case of women linotypists, who needed to work at night—then the proper tactic was to exempt some occupations, not to eliminate protective laws whole. They feared that state welfare legislation in place, such as widows' pensions, would also be at risk. They contended that a constitutional amendment was too undiscriminating an instrument: objectionable sex discriminations such as those concerning jury duty, inheritance rights, nationality, or child custody would be more efficiently and accurately eliminated by specific bills for specific instances. Sometimes, opponents claimed that the ERA took an unnecessarily federal approach, overriding states' rights, although here they were hardly consistent for many of them were at the same time advocating a constitutional amendment to prohibit child labor.

Against the ERA, spokeswomen cited evidence that wage-earning women wanted and valued labor legislation and that male workers, too, benefitted from limits on women's hours in factories where men and women worked at interdependent tasks. Before hours were legally limited, "we were 'free' and 'equal' to work long hours for starvation wages, or free to leave the job and starve!" WTUL leader Pauline Newman bitterly recalled. Dr. Alice Hamilton, pioneer of industrial medicine, saw the NWP as maintaining "a purely negative program, . . . holding down in their present condition of industrial slavery hundreds of thousands of women without doing anything to alleviate their lot."[14] Trade-unionist and Women's Bureau colleagues attacked the NWP's vision as callously class-biased, the thoughtless outlook of rich women, at best relevant to the experience of exceptional skilled workers or professionals. They regularly accused the NWP of being the unwitting tool (at best) or the paid servant of rapacious employers, although no proof of the latter was ever brought forward. They heard in the NWP program the voice of the ruling class and denounced the equal rights amendment as "class" legislation, by and for the bourgeoisie.[15]

Indeed, at the Women's Bureau Conference on Women in Industry in 1926, the NWP's opposition to sex-based labor legislation was echoed by the president of the National Association of Manufacturers, who declared that the "handful" of women in industry could take care of themselves and were not served by legislative "poultices." In this controversy, the positions also lent themselves to, and inevitably were colored by, male "allies" whose principal concerns dealt less with women's economic or legal protection or advancement than political priorities of their own. At the same conference the U.S. Secretary of Labor appointed by President Coolidge took the side of sex-based protective legislation, proclaiming that "The place fixed for women by God and Nature is a great place," and "wherever we see women at work we must see them in terms of motherhood." What he saw as the great danger of the age was the "increasing loss of the distinction between manliness and true femininity."[16]

Often, ERA opponents who supported sex-based labor legislation—including civic-minded middle-class women, social welfare reformers, government officials, and trade union men—appeared more concerned with workingwomen's motherhood than with economic justice. "Women who are wage earners, with one job in the factory and another in the home have little time and energy left to carry on the fight to better their economic status. They need the help of other women and they need labor laws," announced Mary Anderson. Dr. Hamilton declared that "the great inarticulate body of working women . . . are largely helpless, . . . [and] have very special needs which unaided they cannot attain. . . ."[17] Where NWP advocates had before their eyes women who were eager and robust, supporters of protective legislation saw women overburdened and vulnerable. The former claimed that protective laws penalized the strong; the latter claimed that the ERA would sacrifice the weak. The NWP looked at women as individuals and wanted to dislodge gender differentiation from the labor market. Their opponents looked at women as members of families—daughters, wives, mothers, and widows with family responsibilities—and believed that the promise of "mere equality" did not sufficiently take those relationships into account. The one side tacitly positing the independent professional woman as the paradigm, the other presuming the doubly burdened mother in industry or service, neither side distinguished nor addressed directly the situation of the fastest-growing sector of employed women, in white-collar jobs. At least half of the female labor force—those in manufacturing and in domestic and personal service—worked in taxing, menial jobs with long hours, unpleasant and often unhealthy conditions, very low pay, and rare opportunities for advancement. But in overall pattern women's employment was leaving these sectors and swelling in clerical, managerial, sales, and professional areas. White-collar workers were fewer than 18 percent of all women employed in 1900, but the proportion more than doubled by 1920 and by 1930 was 44 percent.[18]

The relation of sex-based legislation to women workers' welfare was more ambiguous and complicated than either side acknowledged. Such laws immediately benefitted far larger numbers of employed women than they hindered, but the laws also had a negative impact on women's overall economic opportunities, both immediately and in the long term. Sex segregation of the labor market was a very significant factor. In industries monopolizing women workers, where wages, conditions, and hours were more likely to be substandard, protective legislation helped to bring things up to standard. It was in more desirable crafts and trades more unusual for women workers, where skill levels and pay were likely to be higher—that is, where women needed to enter in order to improve their earnings and economic advancement— that sex-based protective legislation held women back. There, as a contemporary inquiry into the issue said, "the practice of enacting laws covering women alone appears to discourage their employment, and thereby fosters the prejudice against them." The segregation of women into low-paid, dead-end jobs that made protective laws for women workers necessary, was thus abetted by the legislation itself.[19]

By 1925, all but four states limited workingwomen's hours; eighteen states prescribed rest periods and meal hours; sixteen states prohibited night work in certain occupations; and thirteen had minimum wage regulations. Such regulation was passed not only because it served women workers, but also because employers, especially large corporate employers, began to see benefits in its stabilization of the labor market and control of unscrupulous competition. Although the National Association of Manufacturers, fixed on "liberty of contract," remained opposed, large employers of

women accepted sex-based labor legislation on reasoning about "protection of the race," or could see advantages for themselves in it, or both. A vice-president of Filene's, a large department store in Boston, for instance, approved laws regulating the hours, wages, and conditions of women employees because "economies have been effected by the reduction of labor turnover; by reduction of the number of days lost through illness and accidents; and by increase in the efficiency of the working force as well as in the efficiency of management." He appreciated the legislation's maintaining standards as to hours, wages, and working conditions "throughout industry as a *whole,* thus preventing selfish interests from indulging in unfair competition by the exploitation of women. . . ."[20]

While the anti-ERA side was right in the utilitarian contention that protective laws meant the greatest good to the greatest number of women workers (at least in the short run), the pro-ERA side was also right that such laws hampered women's scope in the labor market and sustained the assumption that employment advantage was not of primary concern to women. Those who advocated sex-based laws were looking at the labor market as it was, trying to protect women in it, but thereby contributing to the perpetuation of existing inequalities. They envisaged wage-earning women as veritable beasts of burden. That group portrait supplanted the prior feminist image of wage-earning women as a vanguard of independent female personalities, as equal producers of the world's wealth. Its advocates did not see that their conception of women's needs helped to confirm women's second-class position in the economy. On the other hand, the ERA advocates who opposed sex-based "protections" were envisioning the labor market as it might be, trying to ensure women the widest opportunities in that imagined arena, and thereby blinking at existing exploitation. They did not admit to the vulnerabilities that sex-based legislation addressed, while they overestimated what legal equality might do to unchain women from the economic stranglehold of the domestic stereotype.

Women on both sides of the controversy, however, saw themselves as legatees of suffragism and feminism, intending to defend the value of women's economic roles, to prevent economic exploitation of women and to open the doors to economic opportunity. A struggle over the very word feminism, which the NWP had embraced, became part of the controversy. For "us even to use the word feminist," contended Women's Trade Union League leader Ethel Smith, "is to invite from the extremists a challenge to our authenticity." Detractors in the WTUL and Women's Bureau called the NWP "ultra" or "extreme" feminists. Mary Anderson considered herself "a good feminist" but objected that "over-articulate theorists were attempting to solve the working women's problems on a purely feministic basis with the working women's own voice far less adequately heard." Her own type of feminist was moderate and practical, Anderson declared; the others, putting the "woman question" above all other questions, were extreme and abstract. The bitterness was compounded by a conflict of personalities and tactics dragged on from the suffrage years. Opponents of the ERA, deeply resenting having to oppose something called equal rights, maligned the NWP as "pernicious," women who "discard[ed] all ethics and fair play," an "insane crowd" who espoused "a kind of hysterical feminism with a slogan for a program."[21] Their critiques fostered public perception of feminism as a sectarian and impracticable doctrine unrelated to real life and blind to injustices besides sex inequality. By the end of the 1920s women outside the NWP rarely made efforts to reclaim the term feminist for themselves, and the meaning of the term was depleted.

Forced into theorizing by this controversy, not prepared as philosophers or legal theorists, spokeswomen on either side in the 1920s were grappling with definitions of women's rights as compared to men's that neither the legal nor economic system was designed to accommodate. The question whether equality required women to have the same rights as men, or different rights, could not be answered without delving into definitions. Did "equality" pertain to opportunity, treatment, or outcome?[22] Should "difference" be construed to mean separation, discrimination, protection, privilege— or assault on the very standard that the male was the human norm?[23]

Opponents of the ERA believed that sex-based legislation was necessary because of women's biological and social roles as mothers. They claimed that "The inherent differences are permanent. Women will always need

many laws different from those needed by men"; "Women as such, whether or not they are mothers present or prospective, will always need protective legislation"; "The working mother is handicapped by her own nature."[24] Their approach stressed maternal nature and inclination as well as conditioning, and implied that the sexual division of labor was eternal.

The NWP's approach, on the other hand, presupposed that women's differentiation from men in the law and the labor market was a particular, social-historical, and not necessary or inevitable construction. The sexual division of labor arose from archaic custom, enshrined in employer and employee attitudes and written in the law. The NWP approach assumed that wives and mothers as well as unencumbered women would want and should have open access to jobs and professions. NWP proponents imagined that the sexual division of labor (in the family and the marketplace) would change if women would secure the same rights as men and have free access to wage-earning. Their view made a fragile potential into a necessary fact. They assumed that women's wage-earning would, by its very existence, challenge the sexual division of labor, and that it would provide the means for women's economic independence— although neither of these tenets was necessarily being realized.

Wage-earning women's experience in the 1910s and 1920s, as documented by the Women's Bureau, showed that the sexual division of labor was budged only very selectively and marginally by women's gainful employment. Most women's wages did not bring them economic independence; women earned as part of a plan for family support (as men did, though that was rarely stressed). Contrary to the NWP's feminist visions, in those places in the nation where the highest proportions of wives and mothers worked for pay, the sexual division of labor was most oppressively in place. To every child growing up in the region of Southern textile and tobacco mills, where wives and mothers worked more "jobs" at home and in the factory than any other age or status group—and earned less—the sexual division of labor appeared no less prescriptive and burdensome than it had before women earned wages.[25]

Critiques of the NWP and its ERA as

"abstract" or "extreme" or "fanatical" represented the gap between feminist tenets and harsh social reality as an oversight of the NWP, a failure to adjust their sights. Even more sympathetic critics, such as one Southern academic, asked rhetorically, "Do the feminists see in the tired and haggard faces of young waitresses, who spend seventy hours a week of hard work in exchange for a few dollars to pay for food and clothing, a deceptive mask of the noble spirit within?" She answered herself, "Surely it is not an increasing army of jaded girls and spent women that pours every day from factory and shop that the leaders of the feminist movement seek. But the call for women to make all labor their province can mean nothing more. They would free women from the rule of men only to make them greater slaves to the machines of industry."[26] Indeed, the exploitation of female service and industrial workers at "cheap" wages cruelly parodied the feminist notion that gainful employment represented an assertion of independence (just as the wifely duties required of a secretary parodied the feminist expectation that wage-earning would challenge the sexual division of labor and reopen definitions of feminity). What such critics were observing was the distance between the potential for women's wage-earning to challenge the sexual division of labor, and the social facts of gender and class hierarchy that clamped down on that challenge.

Defenders of sex-based protective legislation, trying to acknowledge women's unique reproductive endowments and social obligations, were grappling with problems so difficult they would still be present more than half a century later. Their immediate resolution was to portray women's "difference" in merely customary terms. "Average American women prefer to make a home for husbands and children to anything else," Mary Anderson asserted in defense of her position. "They would rather fulfill this normal function than go into the business world."[27] Keeping alive a critique of the class division of wealth, protective legislation advocates lost sight of the need to challenge the very sexual division of labor that was the root of women's "handicap" or "helplessness." As compared to the NWP's emphasis on the historical and social construction of gender roles, advocates of sex-based protective legislation echoed customary

public opinion in proposing that motherhood and wage-earning should be mutually exclusive. They easily found allies among such social conservatives as the National Council of Catholic Women, whose representatives testified against the ERA because it "seriously menaced . . . the unity of the home and family life" and contravened the "essential differences in rights and duties" of the two sexes which were the "result of natural law." Edging into plain disapproval of mothers of young children who earned, protective legislation supporters became more prescriptive, less flexible, than wage-earning mothers themselves, for whom cash recognition of their labor was very welcome. "Why should not a married woman work [for pay], if a single one does?" demanded a mill worker who came to the Southern Summer School for Women Workers. "What would men think if they were told that a married man should not work? If we women would not be so submissive and take everything for granted, if we would awake and stand up for our rights, this world would be a better place to live in, at least it would be better for the women. . . ."[28]

The onset of the Depression in many ways worsened the ERA controversy, for the one side thought protective legislation all the more crucial when need drove women to take any jobs available, and the other side argued that protective legislation prevented women from competing for what jobs there were. In the 1930s it became clear that the labor movement's and League of Women Voters' opposition to the equal rights amendment ran deeper than concern for sex-based legislation as an "entering wedge." The Fair Labor Standards Act of 1938 mandated wages and hours regulation for all workers, and the U.S. Supreme Court upheld it in 1941; but the labor movement and the LWV still opposed the ERA. Other major women's organizations, however—most importantly the National Federation of Business and Professional Women's Clubs and the General Federation of Women's Clubs—and the national platforms of both the Republican [Party] and the Democratic Party endorsed the ERA by 1944.[29]

We generally learn "winners'" history—not the history of lost causes. If the ERA passed by Congress in 1972 had achieved ratification by 1982, perhaps historians of women would read the trajectory of the women's movement from 1923 to the present as a steady upward curve, and award the NWP unqualified original insight. The failure of the ERA this time around (on new, but not unrelated, grounds) compels us to see the longer history of equal rights in its true complexity.[30] The ERA battle of the 1920s seared into memory the fact of warring outlooks among women while it illustrated the inevitable intermeshing of women's legal and political rights with their economic situations. If the controversy testified to the difficulty of protecting women in the economic arena while opening opportunities to them, even more fundamentally the debate brought into question the NWP's premise that the articulation of sex discrimination—or the call for equal rights—would arouse all women to mobilize as a group. What kind of a group were women when their occupational and social and other loyalties were varied, when not all women viewed "women's" interests, or what constituted sex "discrimination," the same way? The ideological dimensions of that problem cross-cut both class consciousness and gender identity. The debate's intensity, both then and now, measured how fundamental was the revision needed if policies and practices of economic and civic life deriving from a male norm were to give full scope to women—and to women of all sorts.

Notes

1. A good introduction to the issue of alliances in the nineteenth-century women's movement, and an essential text on the mid-nineteenth-century split, is Ellen Carol DuBois, *Feminism and Suffrage: The Emergence of an Independent Women's Movement, 1848–1869* (Ithaca, N.Y.: Cornell, 1978).

2. See Leslie Woodcock Tentler, *Wage-Earning Women: Industrial Work and Family Life in the U.S., 1900–1930* (New York: Oxford University Press, 1979), chap. 1, on industrially employed women's wages, keyed below subsistence.

3. On feminists in the final decade of the suffrage campaign, see Nancy F. Cott, *The Grounding of Modern Feminism* (New Haven: Yale University Press, 1987), pp. 23–66.

4. For more detailed discussion of the February 1921 convention, see Nancy F. Cott, "Feminist Politics in the 1920s: The National Woman's Party," *Journal of American History* 71, no. 1 (June 1984).

5. Paul to Jane Norman Smith, Nov. 29, 1921, folder 110, J. N. Smith Collection, Schlesinger Library (hereafter SL). See NWP correspondence of Feb.–Mar. 1921 in the microfilm collection "The National Woman's Party, 1913–1974" (Microfilm Corp. of America), reels #5–7 (hereafter NWP with

reel no.), and Cott, *Grounding*, pp. 66–74, 120–25, for more detail.

In Wisconsin, prominent NWP suffragist Mabel Raef Putnam put together a coalition which successfully lobbied through the first state equal rights bill early in 1921. This legislation granted women the same rights and privileges as men *except for* "the special protection and privileges which they now enjoy for the general welfare." ...

6. Maud Wood Park, *Front Door Lobby*, ed. Edna Stantial (Boston: Beacon Press, 1960), p. 23.

7. Historians' treatments of women's organizations' differing views on the ERA in the 1920s include William N. O'Neill, *Everyone Was Brave* (Chicago: Quadrangle, 1969), pp. 274–94; J. Stanley Lemons, *The Woman Citizen: Social Feminism in the 1920s* (Urbana: University of Illinois Press, 1973), pp. 184–99; William Chafe, *The American Woman: Her Changing Social, Economic and Political Roles* (New York: Oxford University Press, 1972), pp. 112–32; Sheila M. Rothman, *Woman's Proper Place: A History of Changing Ideals and Practices, 1870 to the Present* (New York: Basic Books, 1978), pp. 153–65; Susan Becker, *Origins of the Equal Rights Amendment: American Feminism between the Wars* (Westport, Conn.: Greenwood Press, 1981), pp. 121–51; Alice Kessler-Harris, *Out to Work: A History of Wage-Earning Women in the U.S.* (New York: Oxford University Press, 1982), pp. 194–95, 205–12; Judith Sealander, *As Minority Becomes Majority* (Westport, Conn.: Greenwood Press, 1983). Fuller documentation of my reading of both sides can be found in Cott, *Grounding*, pp. 122–29 and accompanying notes.

8. "Conference on So-Called 'Equal Rights' Amendment Proposed by the National Woman's Party Dec. 4, 1921," ts. NWTUL Papers, microfilm reel 2. . . .

9. NWP National Council minutes, Dec. 17, 1921, Feb. 14, 1922, Apr. 11, 1922, NWP #114. To the NWP inner circle Laughlin's point was borne out by a 1923 ruling in Wisconsin, where, despite the Equal Rights Bill, the attorney general declined to strike down a 1905 law which prohibited women from being employed in the state legislature. He likened the prohibition to an hours-limitation law, because legislative service required "very long and often unreasonable hours." Alice Paul read his decision as "an extremely effective argument against" drafting equal rights bills with exemptions for sex-based protective legislation. Anita L. Pollitzer to Mrs. Jane Norman Smith, Jan. 5, 1922, folder 110, and Paul to Jane Norman Smith, Feb. 20, 1923, folder 111, J. N. Smith Coll.

10. National Council Minutes, June 19, 1923, NWP #114. Before 1923 the ERA went through scores of drafts, recorded in part F, NWP #116. Versions akin to the suffrage amendment—e.g., "Equal rights with men shall not be denied to women or abridged on account of sex or marriage . . ."—were considered in 1922, but not until 1943 was the amendment introduced into Congress in the form "Equality of rights under the law shall not be denied or abridged by the United States or by any state on account of sex," modeled on the Nineteenth Amendment, which in turn was modeled on the Fifteenth Amendment.

11. Quotation from Edith Houghton Hooker, Editor's Note, *Equal Rights* (the NWP monthly publication), Dec. 22, 1928, p. 365. See Cott, *Grounding*, pp. 75–82.

12. The two most seen on NWP platforms were Josephine Casey, a former ILGWU organizer, suffrage activist, later a bookbinder, and Mary Murray, a Brooklyn Railway employee who had resigned from her union in 1920 to protest its acceptance of laws prohibiting night work for women.

13. Kessler-Harris, *Out to Work*, 200–5; and "Problems of Coalition-Building: Women and Trade Unions in the 1920s," in *Women, Work and Protest*, ed. Ruth Milkman (Boston: Routledge and Kegan Paul, 1985), esp. p. 132.

14. . . . More extensive documentation of the debate can be found in the notes in Cott, *Grounding*, pp. 325–26.

15. Kessler-Harris, *Out to Work*, pp. 189–94, reveals ambivalent assessments of labor legislation by ordinary wage-earning women.

16. Printed release from the National Association of Manufacturers, "Defend American Womanhood by Protecting Their Homes, Edgerton Tells Women in Industry," Jan. 19, 1926, in folder 1118, and ts. speech by James Davis, U.S. Secretary of Labor, Jan. 18, 1926, in folder 1117, Box 71, Mary Van Kleeck Collection, Sophia Smith Collection, Smith College.

17. Mary Anderson, "Should There Be Labor Laws for Women? Yes," *Good Housekeeping*, Sept. 1925. . . .

18. See Valerie K. Oppenheimer, *The Female Labor Force in the U.S.* (Westport, Conn.: Greenwood Press, 1976), pp. 3, 149; Lois Scharf, *To Work and to Wed* (Westport, Conn.: Greenwood Press, 1980), pp. 15–16; Winifred Wandersee, *Women's Work and Family Values 1920–1940* (Cambridge Mass.: Harvard, 1981), pp. 85, 89.

19. Elizabeth F. Baker, "At the Crossroads in the Legal Protection of Women in Industry," *Annals of the American Academy of Political and Social Science* 143 (May 1929):277. . . .

Recently historians have stressed the regressive potential of sex-based protective laws. See . . . Nancy Schrom Dye, *As Equals and as Sisters: Feminism, Unionism and the Women's Trade Union League of New York* (Columbia: University of Missouri Press, 1980), pp. 159–60; Olive Banks, *Faces of Feminism: A Study of Feminism as a Social Movement* (New York: St. Martin's, 1981), p. 115; Judith A. Baer, *The Chains of Protection: The Judicial Response to Women's Labor Legislation* (Westport, Conn.: Greenwood Press, 1978). . . .

20. T. K. Cory to Mary Wiggins, Nov. 10, 1922, folder 378, Consumers' League of Mass. Coll., SL. See n. 16, above.

21. Ethel M. Smith, "What Is Sex Equality and What Are the Feminists Trying to Accomplish?" *Century Monthly Magazine* 118 (May 1929):96. . . . Mary Anderson, *Woman at Work: The Autobiography of Mary Anderson as Told to Mary N. Winslow* (Minneapolis: University of Minnesota Press, 1951), p. 168.

22. There is a valuable discussion of differing meanings for "equality" between the sexes in Jean Bethke Elshtain, "The Feminist Movement and the Question of Equality," *Polity* 7 (Summer 1975): 452–77.

23. This is, of course, the set of issues that has preoccupied feminist lawyers in the 1980s. For a sense of the recent debate, see, e.g., Wendy Williams, "The Equality Crisis: Some Reflections on Culture, Courts, and Feminism," *Women's Rights Law Reporter* 7, no. 3 (Spring 1982):175–200; Nadine Taub, "Will Equality Require More Than Assimilation, Accommodation or Separation from the Existing Social Structure?" *Rutgers Law Review* 37 (1985):825–44; Lucinda Finley, "Transcending Equality Theory: A Way out of the Maternity and the Workplace Debate," *Columbia Law Review* 86, no. 6 (Oct. 1986): 1118–82; and Joan Williams, "Deconstructing Gender," *Michigan Law Review* 87, no. 4 (Feb. 1989):797–845.

24. Florence Kelley, "Shall Women Be Equal before the Law?" (debate with Elsie Hill), *Nation* 114 (Apr. 12, 1922):421. . . .

25. Dolores Janiewski, *Sisterhood Denied: Race, Gender and Class in a New South Community* (Philadelphia: Temple University Press, 1985), pp. 30–32, 127–50; Table 26 (p. 134) shows less than 40% of Durham women above age 12 engaged only in unpaid housework.

26. Guion G. Johnson, "Feminism and the Economic Independence of Woman," *Journal of Social Forces* 3 (May 4, 1925):615; cf. Tentler, *Wage-Earning Women*, esp. pp. 25, 45–46, and Wandersee, *Women's Work*, on motivations and psychological results of women's wage-earning.

27. Mary Anderson quoted in unidentified newspaper clipping, Nov. 25, 1925, in folder 349, Bureau of Vocational Information Collection, SL. Cf. Ethel Smith's objection that the NWP's feminism required that "men and women must have exactly the same things, and be treated in all respects as if they were alike," as distinguished from her own view that "men and women must each have the things best suited to their respective needs, which are not all the time, nor in all things, alike." Smith, "What Is Sex Equality?", p. 96.

28. National Council of Catholic Women testimony at U.S. Congress (House of Representatives) subcommittee of Committee on the Judiciary, hearings, 1925, quoted in Robin Whittemore, "Equality vs. Protection: Debate on the Equal Rights Amendment, 1923–1937" (M.A. thesis, Boston University, 1981), p. 19; mill worker quoted in Mary Frederickson, "The Southern Summer School for Women Workers," *Southern Exposure* 4 (Winter 1977):73. See also Maurine Greenwald, "Working-Class Feminism and the Family Wage Ideal: The Seattle Debate on Married Women's Right to Work, 1914–1920," *Journal of American History* 76, no. 1 (June 1989):118–49.

29. For the history of the NWP in the 1930s and 1940s see Becker, *Origins of the Equal Rights Amendment*. On the initiatives of the National Federation of Business and Professional Women and other groups to forward the equal rights amendment, see Lemons, *Woman Citizen*, pp. 202–4, and the papers of Lena Madesin Phillips and Florence Kitchelt at SL.

30. Jane L. Mansbridge's astute analysis, *Why We Lost the ERA* (Chicago: University of Chicago Press, 1986), is essential reading on the failed 1970s campaign for ratification.

JOAN JACOBS BRUMBERG

Fasting Girls: The Emerging Ideal of Slenderness in American Culture

Although anorexia nervosa is generally considered a modern disease, appetite control has long been an important dimension of female experience. Joan Jacobs Brumberg's pioneering study of anorexia nervosa traces changing cultural pressure on women to control their appetite. Exploring the links between food and femininity in the nineteenth century, Brumberg found that by 1890 thinness had become a way in which young privileged women could distance themselves from their working-class counterparts. More important, food preferences and thin bodies also sent moral and aesthetic messages. The young woman whose frail, delicate frame demonstrated her rejection of all carnal appetites more closely approached the Victorian ideal of femininity than did her more robust counterpart whose heavier physique signaled sexual craving. The twentieth century brought additional pressures to control body weight, according to Brumberg, with the development of scientific nutrition and the standard sizing of clothes. By 1920, fat had become a moral issue. Combined with social changes having to do with food and sexuality occurring in the 1960s, the stage was set for the epidemic of eating disorders evident in the 1980s and 1990s. What evidence is there of the persistence of these disorders in the twenty-first century? What is it that we expect our bodies to convey?

Within the first two decades of the twentieth century, even before the advent of the flapper, the voice of American women revealed that the female struggle with weight was under way and was becoming intensely personal. As early as 1907 an *Atlantic Monthly* article described the reaction of a woman trying on a dress she had not worn for over a year: "The gown was neither more [n]or less than anticipated. But I . . . *the fault was on me* . . . I was more! Gasping I hooked it together. The gown was hopeless, and I . . . I am fat."[1] . . . By the twentieth century . . . overweight in women was not only a physical liability, it was a character flaw and a social impediment.

Early in the century elite American women began to take body weight seriously as fat became an aesthetic liability for those who followed the world of haute couture. Since the mid-nineteenth century wealthy

Americans—the wives of J. P. Morgan, Cornelius Vanderbilt, and Harry Harkness Flagler, for instance—had traveled to Paris to purchase the latest creations from couturier collections such as those on view at Maison Worth on the famed rue de la Paix. The couturier was not just a dressmaker who made clothes for an individual woman; rather, the couturier fashioned "a look" or a collection of dresses for an abstraction—the stylish woman. In order to be stylish and wear couturier clothes, a woman's body had to conform to the dress rather than the dress to the body, as had been the case when the traditional dressmaker fitted each garment.[2] . . .

In 1908 the world of women's fashion was revolutionized by Paul Poiret, whose new silhouette was slim and straight. . . . Almost immediately women of style began to purchase new kinds of undergarments that would crimes than to be guilty of the sin of growing fat." By 1930 there was no turning back. Helena Rubenstein, a high priestess of the faith, articulated in *The Art of Feminine Beauty* the moral and aesthetic dictum that would govern the lives of subsequent generations of women: "An abundance of fat is something repulsive and not in accord with the principles that rule our conception of the beautiful.[13] . . .

In adolescence fat was considered a particular liability because of the social strains associated with that stage of life. In the 1940s articles with titles such as "What to Do about the Fat Child at Puberty," "Reducing the Adolescent," and "Should the Teens Diet?" captured the rising interest in adolescent weight control.[14] Women's magazines, reflecting the concerns of mothers anxious to save their daughters from social ostracism, for the first time promoted diets for young girls. According to the *Ladies' Home Journal:* "Appearance plays too important a part in a girl's life not to have her grow up to be beauty-conscious. Girls should be encouraged to take an interest in their appearance when they are very young."[15] . . . Adolescent weight control was also promoted by popular magazines hoping to sell products to young women. . . . *Seventeen's* adoption of the cause of weight control confirmed that slimness was a critical dimension of adolescent beauty and that a new constituency, high school girls, was learning how to diet. From 1944 [when it was founded] to 1948, *Seventeen* had published a full complement of articles on nutrition but almost nothing on weight control. Following the mode of earlier home economists and scientific nutritionists, the magazine had presented basic information about food groups and the importance of each in the daily diet; balance but not calories had been the initial focus. In 1948, however, *Seventeen* proclaimed overweight a medical problem and began educating its young readers about calories and the psychology of eating. Adolescent girls were warned against using eating as a form of emotional expression (do not "pamper your blues" with food) and were given practical tips on how to avoid food bingeing. No mention was made of the new "diet pills" (amphetamines) introduced in the 1930s for clinical treatment of obesity. Instead, teenagers were encouraged to go on "sensible" and "well-rounded" diets of between 1,200 and 1,800 calories. By the 1950s advertisements for "diet foods" such as Ry-Krisp were offering assistance as they told the readership "Nobody Loves a Fat Girl."[16] Girls, much as adult women, were expected to tame the natural appetite.

Although adolescent girls were consistently warned against weight reduction without medical supervision, dieting was always cast as a worthwhile endeavor with transforming powers. "Diets can do wonderful things. When dispensed or approved by your physician . . . all you have to do is follow whither the chart leads."[17] The process of metamorphosis from fat to thin always provided a narrative of uplift and interest. "The Fattest Girl in the Class" was the autobiographical account of Jane, an obese girl who, after suffering the social stigma associated with teenage overweight, went on a diet and found happiness.[18] Being thin was tied to attractiveness, popularity with the opposite sex, and self-esteem—all primary ingredients in adolescent culture. Nonfiction accounts of "make-overs" became a popular formula in all the beauty magazines of the postwar period and provided a tantalizing fantasy of psychological and spiritual transformation for mature and adolescent women alike.[19]

The popularization of adolescent female weight control in the postwar era is a prime component of the modern dieting story and a critical factor in explaining anorexia nervosa as we know it today. . . . Since the 1960s the dieting imperative has intensified in two noticeable and important ways. . . . First, the ideal female body size has become considerably slimmer. After a brief flirtation with full-breasted, curvaceous female figures in the politically conservative postwar recovery of the 1950s, our collective taste returned to an ideal of extreme thinness and an androgynous, if not childlike, figure.[20] A series of well-known studies point to the declining weight since the 1950s of fashion models, Miss America contestants, and *Playboy* centerfolds.[21] Neither bosoms, hips, nor buttocks are currently in fashion as young and old alike attempt to meet the new aesthetic standard. A Bloomingdale's ad posits, "Bean lean, slender as the night, narrow as an arrow, pencil thin, get the point?"[22] It is appropriate to recall Annette Kellerman who, at 5 feet $3\frac{3}{4}$ inches and 137 pounds, epitomized the body beautiful of 1918. Obviously, our cultural tolerance for body fat has diminished over the intervening years.

Second, notably since the middle to late 1970s, a new emphasis on physical fitness and athleticism has intensified cultural pressures on the individual for control and mastery of the body. For women this means that fitness has been added to slimness as a criterion of perfection.[23] Experts on the subject, such as Jane Fonda, encourage women to strive for a lean body with musculature. The incredible popularity among women of aerobics, conditioning programs, and jogging does testify to the satisfactions that come with gaining physical strength through self-discipline, but it also expresses our current urgency about the physical body. Many who are caught up in the exercise cult equate physical fitness and slimness with a higher moral state.... Compulsive exercising and chronic dieting have [thus] been joined as twin obsessions.... [In the] 1980s clinical reports and autobiographical statements show a clear-cut pattern of anorexic patients who exercise with ritualistic intensity. How much one runs and how little one eats is the prevailing moral calculus in present-day anorexia nervosa....

The proliferation of diet and exercise regimens in the past decade, although an important context for understanding the increase in anorexia nervosa, is not the whole story. For a more complete explanation we must turn to some other recent social changes, keeping in mind that no one factor has caused the contemporary problem. Rather, it is the nature of our economic and cultural environment, interacting with individual and family characteristics, which exacerbates the social and emotional insecurities that put today's young women at increasing risk for anorexia nervosa. Two very basic social transformations are relevant to the problem: one has to do with food; the other, with new expectations between the sexes.

Since World War II, and especially in the last two decades, middle-class Americans have experienced a veritable revolution in terms of how and what we eat, as well as how we think about eating.[24] The imperatives of an expanding capitalist society have generated extraordinary technological and marketing innovations, which in turn have transformed food itself, expanded our repertoire of foods, and affected the ways in which we consume them. Even though much contemporary food is characterized by elaborate processing and conservation techniques that actually reduce and flatten distinctive textures and flavors, the current array of food choices seems to constitute an endless smorgasbord of new and different tastes. [Since] the 1980s an individual in an urban center looking for a quick lunch [has been] able to choose from tacos with guacamole and salsa, hummus and falafel in pita, sushi, tortellini, quiche, and pad thai—along with more traditional "American" fare such as hamburgers. Thirty years ago this diversified international menu was as unknown to most Americans as were many of the food products used to create it.... As a consequence of [the expansion of our food repertoire], we are faced with an abundance of food which, in our obesophobic society, necessitates ever greater self-control.... It is no wonder, then, that we talk so incessantly about food and dieting.

The food revolution is a matter of ideas and manners as much as technology and markets.... In our society food is chosen and eaten not merely on the basis of hunger. It is a commonplace to observe that contemporary advertising connects food to sociability, status, and sexuality. In an affluent society, in particular, where eating appears to involve considerable individual choice, food is regarded as an important analogue of the self.

In the 1960s, for example, many young people in the counterculture gave up goods associated with their bourgeois upbringing and turned instead to a diet of whole grains, unprocessed foods, and no meat. This new diet made a statement about personal and political values and became a way of separating one generation from another.... In the 1980s, the extent to which the choice of cuisine dominates and defines the sophisticated life-style [among well-to-do urbanites] is reflected in a recent *New Yorker* cartoon, which shows a young professional couple after a dinner party given by friends. In complete seriousness they say to each other, "We could get close with David and Elizabeth if they didn't put béarnaise sauce on everything."[25] The anorectic is obviously not alone in her use of food and eating as a means of self-definition. There are many others who internalize the dictum "You are what you eat"—or, for that matter, what you don't eat.[26]

Along with the expansion of our food repertoire and our extraordinary attention to food selection, the eating context has changed. Eating is being desocialized. In American society today, more and more food is being consumed away from the family table or any other fixed center of sociability. This process began in the postwar period with the introduction of convenience foods and drive-in restaurants, precursors of the fast-food chains that now constitute a $45-billion-a-year industry. . . . Americans [now] eat everywhere—in the classroom; in theaters, libraries, and museums; on the street; at their desks; on the phone; in hot tubs; in cars while driving. . . . Signs saying "no food and drink," infrequent in other parts of the world, adorn our public buildings, a clear sign of our pattern of vagabond eating.[27]

On college and university campuses, where eating disorders are rampant, the situation is exaggerated. By the early 1970s most undergraduate students were no longer required to take any sit-down meals at fixed times in college dormitories. . . . Typically, students frequent a series of university cafeterias or commercial off-campus restaurants where they can obtain breakfast, lunch, or dinner at any time of the day. Some campus food plans allow unlimited amounts, a policy that fuels the behavior of the bulimic: "I used to go to Contract, eat a whole bunch of stuff, go to the bathroom, throw it up, come back, eat again, throw it up, eat again."[28] In addition, the availability of nearly any kind of food at any time contributes to a pattern of indiscriminate eating. Traditions of food appropriateness—that is, that certain foods are eaten at particular times of the day or in a certain sequence—disappear in this unstructured climate. Thus, an ice-cream cone, a carbonated soft drink, and a bagel constitute an easy popular "meal" that may be eaten at any time of day. Most colleges and the surrounding communities have made provisions to gratify student appetites no matter what the hour. Snack bars and vending machines adorn nearly every free alcove in classroom buildings and residence halls; pizza and Chinese food are delivered hot in the middle of the night.

In a setting where eating is so promiscu-ous, it is no wonder that food habits become problematic. This is not to say that our universities, on their own, generate eating-disordered students. They do, however, provide fertile ground for those who carry the seeds of disorder with them from home. In the permissive and highly individualized food environment of the post-1970 college or university, overeating and undereating become distinct possibilities.[29]

For those young women with either incipient or pronounced anorexia nervosa, the unstructured college life . . . often accentuates the anorectic's physical and emotional problems. [As one young anorectic explained]:

> I don't know any limits here at all. At home, I have my mom dishing out my food . . . But when I'm here it's a totally different story—I can't tell portion size at all. I always get so afraid afterwards, after eating. Oh my God did I eat that much or this much? So I just pass things up altogether and don't eat.[30]

The anorectic's preoccupation with appetite control is fueled by incessant talk about dieting and weight even among friends and associates who eat regularly. Diet-conscious female students report that fasting, weight control, and binge eating are a normal part of life on American college campuses.[31] . . . In our obesophobic society women struggle with food because, among other things, food represents fat and loss of control. For a contemporary woman to eat heartily, energetically, and happily is usually problematic (and, at best, occasional). As a result, some come to fear and hate their own appetite; eating becomes a shameful and disgusting act, and denial of hunger becomes a central facet of identity and personality. . . .

Among adolescents concerned with the transition to adulthood, an intense concern with appetite control and the body [also] operates in tandem with increasing anxiety over sexuality and the implications of changing sex roles. For sex is the second important arena of social change that may contribute to the rising number of anorectics. There are, in fact, some justifiable social reasons why contemporary young women fear adult womanhood. The "anorexic generations," particularly those born since 1960, have been subject to a set of insecurities that make heterosexuality an anxious rather than a pleasant prospect. Family insecurity, reflected in the frequency of divorce, and changing sex and gender roles became facts of life for this group in their childhood. . . . Although there is no positive correlation between divorced families and anorexia nervosa, family disruption is part of the world view of the anorexic generations. Its members understand implicitly that not all heterosexual relationships have happy endings.

As a consequence of these social changes, some young women are ambivalent about commitments to men and have adopted an ideal of womanhood that reflects the impact of post-1960 feminism. Although they generally draw back from an explicitly feminist vocabulary, most undergraduate women today desire professional careers of their own without forsaking the idea of marriage and a family. A 1985 study of college women by sociologist Mirra Komarovsky reveals that finding one's place in the world of work has become essential for personal dignity in this generation—yet a career without marriage was the choice of only 2 percent of the sample.[32] Convinced that individuality can be accommodated in marriage, these young women are interested in heterosexuality, but admit that "relationships with guys" are difficult even in college. Komarovsky describes conflict over dating rituals (who takes the initiative and who pays), decision making as a couple, intellectual rivalries, and competition for entrance into graduate school. Unlike Mother, who followed Dad to graduate school and supported him along the way, today's undergraduate—whether she is a declared feminist or not—wants her own professional career both as a ticket to the good life and as a protection for herself in case of divorce.

Sexual activity also requires an extraordinary degree of self-protection in the modern world of AIDS. While premarital sex is acceptable (if not desirable), it is an understandable source of worry among female undergraduates. An advertisement in a 1986 issue of *Ms.*, aimed at selling condoms to young women, captured the current ambivalence about the physical side of heterosexuality: "Let's face it, sex these days can be risky business, and you need all the protection you can get. Between the fear of unplanned pregnancy, sexually transmitted diseases, and the potential side effects of many forms of contraception, it may seem like sex is hardly worth the risk anymore."[33] For some students the unprecedented privacy and freedom of modern university life generates as much fear as pleasure. It bears repeating that clinical materials suggest an *absence* [emphasis is the editors'] of sexual activity on the part of anorectics.

Even though feminine dependency is no longer in fashion, these same young women combine traditional expectations with a quest for equity and power. To be brainy and beautiful; to have an exciting $75,000-a-year job; to nurture two wonderful children in consort with a supportive but equally high-powered husband—these are the personal ambitions of many in the present college generation. In order to achieve this level of personal and social perfection, young women must be extremely demanding of themselves: there can be no distracting personal or avocational detours—they must be unrelenting in the pursuit of goals. The kind of personal control required to become the new Superwoman (a term popularized by columnist Ellen Goodman)[34] parallels the single-mindedness that characterizes the anorectic. In sum, the golden ideal of this generation of privileged young women and their most distinctive pathology appear to be flip sides of the same record.

My assertion that the post-1960 epidemic of anorexia nervosa can be related to recent social change in the realm of sexuality [and gender roles] is not an argument for turning back the clock. . . . [H]istorical investigation demonstrates that anorexia nervosa was latent in the economic and emotional milieu of the bourgeois family as early as the 1950s. It makes little sense to think a cure will be achieved by putting women back in the kitchen, reinstituting sit-down meals on the nation's campuses, or limiting personal and professional choices to what they were in the Victorian era. On the basis of the best current research on anorexia nervosa, we must conclude that the disease develops as a result of the intersection of external and internal forces in the life of an individual. External forces such as those described here do not, by themselves, generate psychopathologies, but they do give them shape and influence their frequency.

In the confusion of this transitional moment, when a new future is being tentatively charted for women but gender roles and sexuality are still constrained by tradition, young women on the brink of adulthood are feeling the pain of social change most acutely.[35] They look about for direction, but find little in the way of useful experiential guides. What parts of women's tradition do they want to carry into the future? What parts should be left behind? These are difficult personal and political decisions, and most young women are being asked to make them without benefit of substantive education in the history and experience of their sex. In effect, our young women are being challenged and their expectations raised without a simultaneous level of support for either their specific aspirations or for female creativity in general.

Sadly, the cult of diet and exercise is the closest thing our secular society offers women in terms of a coherent philosophy of the self.[36] This being the case, anorexia nervosa is not a quirk and the symptom choice is not surprising. When personal and social difficulties arise, a substantial number of our young women become preoccupied with their bodies and control of appetite. Of all the messages they hear, the imperative to be beautiful and good, by being thin, is still the strongest and most familiar. Moreover, they are caught, often at a very early age, in a deceptive cognitive trap that has them believing that body weight is entirely subject to their conscious control. Despite feminist influences on the career aspirations of the present college-age generation, little has transpired to dilute the basic strength of this powerful cultural prescription that plays on both individualism and conformity. The unfortunate truth is that even when she wants more than beauty and understands its limitations as a life goal, the bourgeois woman still expends an enormous amount of psychic energy on appetite control as well as on other aspects of presentation of the physical self.

And what of the future? . . .

We can expect to see eating disorders continue, if not increase, among young women in those postindustrial societies where adolescents tend to be under stress. For both young men and young women, vast technological and cultural changes have made the transition to adulthood particularly difficult by transforming the nature of the family and community and rendering the future unpredictable.

According to psychologist Urie Bronfenbrenner and others, American adolescents are in the worst trouble: we have the highest incidence of alcohol and drug abuse among adolescents of any country in the world; we also have the highest rate of teenage pregnancy of any industrialized nation; and we appear to have the most anorexia nervosa.[37]

Although the sexually active adolescent mother and the sexually inactive adolescent anorectic may seem to be light-years apart, they are linked by a common, though unarticulated, understanding. For adolescent women the body is still the most powerful paradigm regardless of social class. Unfortunately, a sizable number of our young women—poor and privileged alike—regard their body as the best vehicle for making a statement about their identity and personal dreams. This is what unprotected sexual intercourse and prolonged starvation have in common. Taken together, our unenviable preeminence in these two domains suggests the enormous difficulty involved in making the transition to adult womanhood in a society where women are still evaluated primarily in terms of the body rather than the mind.

NOTES

1. "On Growing Fat," *Atlantic Monthly* (Mar. 1907):430–31.

2. Jo Ann Olian, *The House of Worth: The Gilded Age, 1860–1918* (New York: Museum of the City of New York, 1982); Jane Beth Abrams, "The Thinning of America: The Emergence of the Ideal of Slenderness in American Popular Culture, 1870–1930," B.A. thesis, Harvard University, 1983, chap. 2.

3. Michael Batterberry and Ariane Batterberry, *Mirror Mirror: A Social History of Fashion* (New York: Holt, Rinehart and Winston, 1977), pp. 289–97; Diane DeMarly, *The History of Haute Couture, 1850–1950* (New York: Holmes & Meier, 1980), pp. 81–83.

4. P. Rostaine, "How to Get Thin," *Medical Press and Circular* 149 (Dec. 23, 1914):643–44.

5. Stuart Ewen and Elizabeth Ewen, *Channels of Desire: Mass Images and the Shaping of American Consciousness* (New York: McGraw-Hill, 1982), pt. 4; Claudia Kidwell and Margaret C. Christman, *Suiting Everyone: The Democratization of Clothing in America* (Washington, D.C.: Smithsonian Institution Press, 1974).

6. *Vogue* (Jan. 1, 1923):63.

7. Lois W. Banner, *American Beauty* (New York: Random House, 1983), p. 262; Ewen and Ewen, *Channels of Desire*, pp. 193–98.

8. Banner, *American Beauty*, p. 287; Anne Hollander, *Seeing through Clothes* (New York: Viking Press, 1975).

9. Lulu Hunt Peters, *Diet and Health with a Key to the Calories* (Chicago: The Reilly & Britton Company, 1918), pp. 24, 39.

10. Ibid., pp. 12, 104, 110.

11. Ibid., pp. 85, 94.

12. Ibid., pp. 85, 93, 94.

13. "On Her Dressing Table," *Vogue* (Apr. 24, 1902):413; ibid. (July 1, 1918):78.

14. Mildred H. Bryan, "Don't Let Your Child Get Fat!" *Hygeia* 15 (1937):801–3; G. D. Schultz, "Forget That Clean-Plate Bogey!" *Better Homes and Gardens* 21 (Sept. 1942):24.

15. Louise Paine Benjamin, "I Have Three Daughters," *Ladies Homes Journal* 57 (June 1940):74.

16. "You'll Eat It Up at Noon," *Seventeen* (Sept. 1946):21–22; Irma M. Phorylles, "The Lost Waistline," ibid. (Mar. 1948):124; "Overweight?" ibid. (Aug. 1948):184.

17. Ibid.

18. "Fattest Girl in the Class," ibid. (Jan. 1948):21–22.

19. "Psychology of Dieting," *Ladies' Home Journal* (Jan. 1965):66.

20. Banner, *American Beauty*, pp. 283–85.

21. David M. Garner et al., "Cultural Expectations of Thinness in Women," *Psychology Reports* 47 (1980):483–91.

22. Rita Freedman, *Beauty Bound* (Lexington: Lexington Books, 1986), p. 150.

23. "Coming on Strong: The New Ideal of Beauty," *Time* (Aug. 30, 1983):71–77.

24. William Chafe, *The Unfinished Journey: America since World War II* (New York: Oxford University Press, 1986).

25. *New Yorker* (July 21, 1986):71.

26. "What's Your Food Status Because the Way You Live Has a Lot to Do with the Way You Eat," *Mademoiselle* (Sept. 1985):224–26; "Food as Well as Clothes, Today, Make the Man—As a Matter of Life and Style," *Vogue* (June 1985):271–73.

27. "Severe Growing Pains for Fast Food," *Business Week* (Mar. 22, 1985):225.

28. Greg Foster and Susan Howerin, "The Quest for Perfection: An Interview with a Former Bulimic," *Iris: A Journal about Women* [Charlottesville, Va.] (1986):21.

29. Before they even arrive on campus, during their senior year in high school and the summer before entering college, many girls began to talk about the "freshmen 10 or 15." This is the weight gain predicted as a result of eating starchy institutional food and participating in late-night food forays with friends.

30. Elizabeth Greene, "Support Groups Forming for Students with Eating Disorders," *Chronicle of Higher Education* (Mar. 5, 1986):1, 30.

31. K. A. Halmi, J. R. Falk, and E. Schwartz, "Binge-Eating and Vomiting: A Survey of a College Population," *Psychological Medicine* 11 (1981):697–706; R. L. Pyle et al., "The Incident of Bulimia in Freshman College Students," *International Journal of Eating Disorders* 2, 3 (1983):75–86.

32. Mirra Komarovsky, *Women in College: Shaping the New Feminine Identities* (New York: Basic Books, 1985), pp. 89–92, 225–300.

33. *Ms.* (Sept. 1986):n.p. The condom is called Mentor.

34. Ellen Goodman, *Close to Home* (New York: Fawcett Crest, 1979).

35. In *Theories of Adolescence* (New York: Random House, 1962), R. E. Muuss wrote: "Societies in a period of rapid transition create a particular adolescent period; the adolescent has not only the society's problem to adjust to but his [or her] own as well" (p. 164).

36. My view of this issue complements ideas presented in Robert Bellah et al., *Habits of the Heart: Individualism and Commitment in American Life* (New York: Harper & Row, 1986).

37. These data are synthesized in Urie Bronfenbrenner, "Alienation and the Four Worlds of Childhood," *Phi Delta Kappan* (Feb. 1986):434.

RUTH SCHWARTZ COWAN

The "Industrial Revolution" in the Home: Household Technology and Social Change in the Twentieth Century

The industrial technology that changed factory work also changed housework; the washing machine replaced the washtub just as the power loom replaced the handloom. Yet the impact of changing household technology on household workers has been little explored. In the following essay, Ruth Schwartz Cowan examines how housework changed with the introduction of a variety of laborsaving appliances and the aggressive use of advertising designed to promote their sale. What emerges is a job that has changed in structure. Less burdensome physically, housework became no less time consuming as new duties were added and the work itself invested with new expectations and greater emotional content. What Cowan describes, in part, is the transition from the nineteenth-century mistress of the household who directed a servant's work to the twentieth-century middle-class housewife who, as jane-of-all-trades—laundress, scrub woman, gardener, nursemaid, chauffeur, and cook—was expected to find self-fulfillment in housework. What does this assumption suggest about the role of ideology as well as technology in defining work? Is the job of housework becoming redefined in a way that serves to domesticate the "new woman" rather than liberate her to pursue publicly her talent and abilities? In what sense is the individual housewife more isolated than ever?

When we think about the interaction between technology and society, we tend to think in fairly grandiose terms: massive computers invading the workplace, railroad tracks cutting through vast wildernesses, armies of women and children toiling in the mills. These grand visions have blinded us to an important and rather peculiar technological revolution which has been going on right under our noses: the technological revolution in the home. This revolution has transformed the conduct of our daily lives, but in somewhat unexpected ways. The industrialization of the home was a process very different from the industrialization of other means of production, and the impact of that process was neither what we have been led to believe it was nor what students of the other industrial revolutions would have been led to predict.

Some years ago sociologists of the functionalist school formulated an explanation of the impact of industrial technology on the modern family. Although that explanation was not empirically verified, it has become almost universally accepted.[1] Despite some differences in emphasis, the basic tenets of the traditional interpretation can be roughly summarized as follows:

Before industrialization the family was the basic social unit. Most families were rural, large, and self-sustaining; they produced and processed almost everything that was needed for their own support and for trading in the marketplace, while at the same time performing a host of other functions ranging from mutual protection to entertainment. In these preindustrial families women (adult women, that is) had a lot to do, and their time was almost entirely absorbed by household tasks. Under industrialization the family is much less important. The household is no longer the focus of production; production for the marketplace and production for sustenance have been removed to other locations. Families are smaller and they are urban rather than rural. The number of social functions they perform is much reduced, until almost all that remains is consumption, socialization of small children, and tension management. As their functions diminished, families became atomized; the social bonds that had held them together were loosened. In these postindustrial families women have very little to do, and the tasks with which they fill their time have lost the social utility that they once possessed. Modern women are in trouble, the analysis goes, because modern families are in trouble; and modern families are in trouble because industrial technology has either eliminated or eased almost all their former functions, but modern ideologies have not kept pace with the change. The results of this time lag are several: Some women suffer from role anxiety, others land in the divorce courts, some enter the labor market, and others take to burning their brassieres and demanding liberation.

This sociological analysis is a cultural artifact of vast importance. Many Americans believe that it is true and act upon that belief in various ways: Some hope to reestablish family solidarity by relearning lost productive crafts—baking bread, tending a vegetable garden—others dismiss the women's liberation movement as "simply a bunch of affluent housewives who have nothing better to do with their time." As disparate as they may seem, these reactions have a common ideological source—the standard sociological analysis of the impact of technological change on family life.

As a theory this functionalist approach has much to recommend it, but at present we have very little evidence to back it up. Family history is an infant discipline, and what evidence it has produced in recent years does not lend credence to the standard view.[2] Phillippe Ariès has shown, for example, that in France

the ideal of the small nuclear family predates industrialization by more than a century.[3] Historical demographers working on data from English and French families have been surprised to find that most families were quite small and that several generations did not ordinarily reside together; the extended family, which is supposed to have been the rule in preindustrial societies, did not occur in colonial New England either.[4] Rural English families routinely employed domestic servants, and even very small English villages had their butchers and bakers and candlestick makers; all these persons must have eased some of the chores that would otherwise have been the housewife's burden.[5] Pre-industrial housewives no doubt had much with which to occupy their time, but we may have reason to wonder whether there was quite as much pressure on them as sociological orthodoxy has led us to suppose. The large rural family that was sufficient unto itself back there on the prairies may have been limited to the prairies—or it may never have existed at all (except, that is, in the reveries of sociologists).

Even if all the empirical evidence were to mesh with the functionalist theory, the theory would still have problems, because its logical structure is rather weak. Comparing the average farm family in 1750 (assuming that you knew what that family was like) with the average urban family in 1950 in order to discover the significant social changes that had occurred is an exercise rather like comparing apples with oranges; the differences between the fruits may have nothing to do with the differences in their evolution. Transferring the analogy to the case at hand, what we really need to know is the difference, say, between an urban laboring family of 1750 and an urban laboring family 100 and then 200 years later, or the difference between the rural nonfarm middle classes in all three centuries, or the difference between the urban rich yesterday and today. Surely in each of these cases the analyses will look very different from what we have been led to expect. As a guess, we might find that for the urban laboring families the changes have been precisely the opposite of what the model predicted; that is, that their family structure is much firmer today than it was in centuries past. Similarly, for the rural nonfarm middle class the results might be equally surprising; we might find that married women of that class rarely did any housework at all in 1890 because they had farm girls as servants, whereas in 1950 they bore the full brunt of the work themselves. I could go on, but the point is, I hope, clear: In order to verify or falsify the functionalist theory it will be necessary to know more than we presently do about the impact of industrialization on families of similar classes and geographical locations.

With this problem in mind I have, for the purposes of this initial study, deliberately limited myself to one kind of technological change affecting one aspect of family life in only one of the many social classes of families that might have been considered. What happened, I asked, to middle-class American women when the implements with which they did their everyday household work changed? Did the technological change in household appliances have any effect upon the structure of American households, or upon the ideologies that governed the behavior of American women, or upon the functions that families needed to perform? Middle-class American women were defined as actual or potential readers of the better-quality women's magazines, such as the *Ladies' Home Journal, American Home, Parents Magazine, Good Housekeeping,* and *McCall's*.[6] Nonfictional material (articles and advertisements) in those magazines was used as a partial indicator of some of the technological and social changes that were occurring.

The *Ladies' Home Journal* has been in continuous publication since 1886. A casual survey of the nonfiction in the *Journal* yields the immediate impression that that decade between the end of World War I and the beginning of the depression witnessed the most drastic changes in patterns of household work. Statistical data bear out this impression. Before 1918, for example, illustrations of homes lit by gaslight could still be found in the *Journal*; by 1928 gaslight had disappeared. In 1917 only one-quarter (24.3 percent) of the dwellings in the United States had been electrified, but by 1920 this figure had doubled (47.4 percent—for rural nonfarm and urban dwellings), and by 1930 four-fifths of all households had been electrified.[7] If electrification had meant simply the change from gas or oil lamps to electric lights, the changes in the housewife's routines might not have been very

great (except for eliminating the chore of cleaning and filling oil lamps); but changes in lighting were the least of the changes that electrification implied. Small electric appliances followed quickly on the heels of the electric light, and some of those augured much more profound changes in the housewife's routine.

Ironing, for example, had traditionally been one of the most dreadful household chores, especially in warm weather when the kitchen stove had to be kept hot for the better part of the day; irons were heavy and they had to be returned to the stove frequently to be reheated. Electric irons eased a good part of this burden.[8] They were relatively inexpensive and very quickly replaced their predecessors; advertisements for electric irons first began to appear in the ladies' magazines after the war, and by the end of the decade the old flatiron had disappeared; by 1929 a survey of 100 Ford employees revealed that ninety-eight of them had the new electric irons in their homes.[9]

Data on the diffusion of electric washing machines are somewhat harder to come by; but it is clear from the advertisements in the magazines, particularly advertisements for laundry soap, that by the middle of the 1920s those machines could be found in a significant number of homes. The washing machine is depicted just about as frequently as the laundry tub by the middle of the 1920s; in 1929, forty-nine out of those 100 Ford workers had the machines in their homes. The washing machines did not drastically reduce the time that had to be spent on household laundry, as they did not go through their cycles automatically and did not spin dry; the housewife had to stand guard, stopping and starting the machine at appropriate times, adding soap, sometimes attaching the drain pipes, and putting the clothes through the wringer manually. The machines did, however, reduce a good part of the drudgery that once had been associated with washday, and this was a matter of no small consequence.[10] Soap powders appeared on the market in the early 1920s, thus eliminating the need to scrape and boil bars of laundry soap.[11] By the end of the 1920s Blue Monday must have been considerably less blue for some housewives—and probably considerably less "Monday," for with an electric iron, a washing machine, and a hot water heater, there was no reason to limit the washing to just one day of the week.

Like the routines of washing the laundry, the routines of personal hygiene must have been transformed for many households during the 1920s—the years of the bathroom mania.[12] More and more bathrooms were built in older homes, and new homes began to include them as a matter of course. Before the war most bathroom fixtures (tubs, sinks, and toilets) were made out of porcelain by hand; each bathroom was custom-made for the house in which it was installed. After the war industrialization descended upon the bathroom industry; cast iron enamelware went into mass production and fittings were standardized. In 1921 the dollar value of the production of enameled sanitary fixtures was $2.4 million, the same as it had been in 1915. By 1923, just two years later, that figure had doubled to $4.8 million; it rose again, to $5.1 million, in 1925.[13] The first recessed, double-shell cast iron enameled bathtub was put on the market in the early 1920s. A decade later the standard American bathroom had achieved its standard American form: the recessed tub, plus tiled floors and walls, brass plumbing, a single-unit toilet, an enameled sink, and a medicine chest, all set into a small room which was very often 5 feet square.[14] The bathroom evolved more quickly than any other room of the house; its standardized form was accomplished in just over a decade.

Along with bathrooms came modernized systems for heating hot water: 61 percent of the homes in Zanesville, Ohio, had indoor plumbing with centrally heated water by 1926, and 83 percent of the homes valued over $2,000 in Muncie, Indiana, had hot and cold running water by 1935.[15] These figures may not be typical of small American cities (or even large American cities) at those times, but they do jibe with the impression that one gets from the magazines: After 1918 references to hot water heated on the kitchen range, either for laundering or for bathing, become increasingly difficult to find.

Similarly, during the 1920s many homes were outfitted with central heating; in Muncie most of the homes of the business class had basement heating in 1924; by 1935 Federal Emergency Relief Administration data for the city indicated that only 22.4 percent of the dwellings valued over $2,000 were still heated by a kitchen stove.[16] What all these changes

meant in terms of new habits for the average housewife is somewhat hard to calculate; changes there must have been, but it is difficult to know whether those changes produced an overall saving of labor and/or time. Some chores were eliminated—hauling water, heating water on the stove, maintaining the kitchen fire—but other chores were added, most notably the chore of keeping yet another room scrupulously clean.

It is not, however, difficult to be certain about the changing habits that were associated with the new American kitchen—a kitchen from which the coal stove had disappeared. In Muncie in 1924, cooking with gas was done in two out of three homes; in 1935 only 5 percent of the homes valued over $2,000 still had coal or wood stoves for cooking.[17] After 1918 advertisements for coal and wood stoves disappeared from the Ladies' Home Journal; stove manufacturers purveyed only their gas, oil, or electric models. Articles giving advice to home-makers on how to deal with the trials and tribulations of starting, stoking, and maintaining a coal or a wood fire also disappeared. Thus it seems a safe assumption that most middle-class homes had switched to the new method of cooking by the time the depression began. The change in routine that was predicated on the change from coal or wood to gas or oil was profound; aside from the elimination of such chores as loading the fuel and removing the ashes, the new stoves were much easier to light, maintain, and regulate (even when they did not have thermostats, as the earliest models did not).[18] Kitchens were, in addition, much easier to clean when they did not have coal dust regularly tracked through them; one writer in the Ladies' Home Journal estimated that kitchen cleaning was reduced by one-half when coal stoves were eliminated.[19]

Along with new stoves came new foodstuffs and new dietary habits. Canned foods had been on the market since the middle of the nineteenth century, but they did not become an appreciable part of the standard middle-class diet until the 1920s—if the recipes given in cookbooks and in women's magazines are a reliable guide. By 1918 the variety of foods available in cans had been considerably expanded from the peas, corn, and succotash of the nineteenth century; an American housewife with sufficient means could have purchased almost any fruit or vegetable and quite a surprising array of ready-made meals in a can—from Heinz's spaghetti in meat sauce to Purity Cross's lobster à la Newburg. By the middle of the 1920s home canning was becoming a lost art. Canning recipes were relegated to the back pages of the women's magazines; the business-class wives of Muncie reported that, while their mothers had once spent the better part of the summer and fall canning, they themselves rarely put up anything, except an occasional jelly or batch of tomatoes.[20] In part this was also due to changes in the technology of marketing food; increased use of refrigerated railroad cars during this period meant that fresh fruits and vegetables were in the markets all year round at reasonable prices.[21] By the early 1920s convenience foods were also appearing on American tables: cold breakfast cereals, pancake mixes, bouillon cubes, and packaged desserts could be found. Wartime shortages accustomed Americans to eating much lighter meals than they had previously been wont to do; and as fewer family members were taking all their meals at home (businessmen started to eat lunch in restaurants downtown, and factories and schools began installing cafeterias), there was simply less cooking to be done, and what there was of it was easier to do.[22]

Many of the changes just described—from hand power to electric power, from coal and wood to gas and oil as fuels for cooking, from one-room heating to central heating, from pumping water to running water—are enormous technological changes. Changes of a similar dimension, either in the fundamental technology of an industry, in the diffusion of that technology, or in the routines of workers, would have long since been labeled an "industrial revolution." The change from the laundry tub to the washing machine is no less profound than the change from the hand loom to the power loom; the change from pumping water to turning on a water faucet is no less destructive of traditional habits than the change from manual to electric calculating. It seems odd to speak of an "industrial revolution" connected with housework, odd because we are talking about the technology of such homely things, and odd because we are not accustomed to thinking of housewives as a labor force or of

housework as an economic commodity—but despite this oddity, I think the term is altogether appropriate.

In this case other questions come immediately to mind, questions that we do not hesitate to ask, say, about textile workers in Britain in the early nineteenth century, but we have never thought to ask about housewives in America in the twentieth century. What happened to this particular workforce when the technology of its work was revolutionized? Did structural changes occur? Were new jobs created for which new skills were required? Can we discern new ideologies that influenced the behavior of the workers?

The answer to all of these questions, surprisingly enough, seems to be yes. There were marked structural changes in the workforce, changes that increased the workload and the job description of the workers that remained. New jobs were created for which new skills were required; these jobs were not physically burdensome, but they may have taken up as much time as the jobs they had replaced. New ideologies were also created, ideologies which reinforced new behavioral patterns, patterns that we might not have been led to expect if we had followed the sociologists' model to the letter. Middle-class housewives, the women who must have first felt the impact of the new household technology, were not flocking into the divorce courts or the labor market or the forums of political protest in the years immediately after the revolution in their work. What they were doing was sterilizing baby bottles, shepherding their children to dancing classes and music lessons, planning nutritious meals, shopping for new clothes, studying child psychology, and hand stitching color-coordinated curtains—all of which chores (and others like them) the standard sociological model has apparently not provided for.

The significant change in the structure of the household labor force was the disappearance of paid and unpaid servants (unmarried daughters, maiden aunts, and grandparents fall in the latter category) as household workers—and the imposition of the entire job on the housewife herself. Leaving aside for a moment the question of which was cause and which effect (did the disappearance of the servant create a demand for the new technology, or did the new technology make the servant obsolete?), the phenomenon itself is relatively easy to document. Before World War I, when illustrators in the women's magazines depicted women doing housework, the women were very often servants. When the lady of the house was drawn, she was often the person being served, or she was supervising the serving, or she was adding an elegant finishing touch to the work. Nursemaids diapered babies, seamstresses pinned up hems, waitresses served meals, laundresses did the wash, and cooks did the cooking. By the end of the 1920s the servants had disappeared from those illustrations; all those jobs were being done by housewives—elegantly manicured and coiffed, to be sure, but housewives nonetheless.

If we are tempted to suppose that illustrations in advertisements are not a reliable indicator of structural changes of this sort, we can corroborate the changes in other ways. Apparently, the illustrators really did know whereof they drew. Statistically the number of persons throughout the country employed in household service dropped from 1,851,000 in 1910 to 1,411,000 in 1920, while the number of households enumerated in the census rose from 20.3 million to 24.4 million.[23] In Indiana the ratio of households to servants increased from 13.5/1 in 1890 to 30.5/1 in 1920, and in the country as a whole the number of paid domestic servants per 1,000 population dropped from 98.9 in 1900 to 58.0 in 1920.[24] The business-class housewives of Muncie reported that they employed approximately one-half as many woman-hours of domestic service as their mothers had done.[25]

In case we are tempted to doubt these statistics (and indeed statistics about household labor are particularly unreliable, as the labor is often transient, part-time, or simply unreported), we can turn to articles on the servant problem, the disappearance of unpaid family workers, the design of kitchens, or to architectural drawings for houses. All of this evidence reiterates the same point: Qualified servants were difficult to find; their wages had risen and their numbers fallen; houses were being designed without maid's rooms; daughters and unmarried aunts were finding jobs downtown; kitchens were being designed for housewives, not for servants.[26] The first home with a kitchen that was not an entirely separate room was designed by Frank Lloyd Wright in 1934.[27] In 1937 Emily Post invented a new character for her etiquette books: Mrs. Three-in-One, the woman who is her own cook, waitress, and hostess.[28] There must have been many new Mrs. Three-in-Ones abroad in the land during the 1930s.

As the number of household assistants declined, the number of household tasks increased. The middle-class housewife was expected to demonstrate competence at several tasks that previously had not existed at all. Child care is the most obvious example. The average housewife had fewer children than her mother had had, but she was expected to do things for her children that her mother would never have dreamed of doing: to prepare their special infant formulas, sterilize their bottles, weigh them every day, see to it that they ate nutritionally balanced meals, keep them isolated and confined when they had even the slightest illness, consult with their teachers frequently, and chauffeur them to dancing lessons and evening parties.[29] There was very little Freudianism in this new attitude toward child care: Mothers were not spending more time and effort on their children because they feared the psychological trauma of separation, but because competent nursemaids could not be found, and the new theories of child care required constant attention from well-informed persons—persons who were willing and able to read about the latest discoveries in nutrition, in the control of contagious diseases, or in the techniques of behavioral psychology. These persons simply had to be their mothers.

Consumption of economic goods provides another example of the housewife's expanded job description; like child care, the new tasks associated with consumption were not necessarily physically burdensome, but they were time consuming, and they required the acquisition of new skills.[30] Home economists and the editors of women's magazines tried to teach housewives to spend their money wisely. The present generation of housewives, it was argued, had been reared by mothers who did not ordinarily shop for things like clothing, bed linens, or towels; consequently modern housewives did not know how to shop and would have to be taught. Furthermore, their mothers had not been accustomed to the wide variety of goods that were now available in the modern marketplace; the new housewives had to be taught not just to be consumers, but to be informed consumers.[31] Several contemporary observers believed that shopping and shopping wisely were occupying increasing amounts of housewives' time.[32]

Several of these contemporary observers also believed that standards of household care changed during the decade of the 1920s.[33] The discovery of the "household germ" led to almost fetishistic concern about the cleanliness of the home. The amount and frequency of laundering probably increased, as bed linen and underwear were changed more often, children's clothes were made increasingly out of washable fabrics, and men's shirts no longer had replaceable collars and snap cuffs.[34] Unfortunately all these changes in standards are difficult to document, being changes in the things that people regard as so insignificant as to be unworthy of comment; the improvement in standards seems a likely possibility, but not something that can be proved.

In any event we do have various time studies which demonstrate somewhat surprisingly that housewives with conveniences were spending just as much time on household duties as were housewives without them—or, to put it another way, housework, like so many other types of work, expands to fill the time available. A study comparing the time spent per week in housework by 288 farm families and 154 town families in Oregon in 1928 revealed 61 hours spent by farm wives and 63.4 hours by town wives; in 1929 a U.S. Department of Agriculture study of families in various states produced almost identical results.[35] Surely if the standard sociological model were valid, housewives in towns, where presumably the benefits of specialization and electrification were most likely to be available, should have been spending far less time at their work than their rural sisters. However, just after World War II economists at Bryn Mawr College reported the same phenomenon: 60.55 hours spent by farm housewives, 78.35 hours by women in small cities, 80.57 hours by women in large ones—precisely the reverse of the results that were expected.[36] A recent survey of time studies conducted between 1920 and 1970 concludes that the time spent on housework by nonemployed house-

wives has remained remarkably constant throughout the period.[37] All these results point in the same direction: mechanization of the household meant that time expended on some jobs decreased, but also that new jobs were substituted, and in some cases—notably laundering—time expenditures for old jobs increased because of higher standards. The advantages of mechanization may be somewhat more dubious than they seem at first glance.

As the job of the housewife changed, the connected ideologies also changed; there was a clearly perceptible difference in the attitudes that women brought to housework before and after World War I.[38] Before the war the trials of doing housework in a servantless home were discussed and they were regarded as just that—trials, necessary chores that had to be got through until a qualified servant could be found. After the war, housework changed: It was no longer a trial and a chore, but something quite different—an emotional "trip." Laundering was not just laundering, but an expression of love; the housewife who truly loved her family would protect them from the embarrassment of tattletale gray. Feeding the family was not just feeding the family, but a way to express the housewife's artistic inclinations and a way to encourage feelings of family loyalty and affection. Diapering the baby was not just diapering, but a time to build the baby's sense of security and love for the mother. Cleaning the bathroom sink was not just cleaning, but an exercise of protective maternal instincts, providing a way for the housewife to keep her family safe from disease. Tasks of this emotional magnitude could not possibly be delegated to servants, even assuming that qualified servants could be found.

Women who failed at these new household tasks were bound to feel guilt about their failure. If I had to choose one word to characterize the temper of the women's magazines during the 1920s, it would be "guilt." Readers of the better-quality women's magazines are portrayed as feeling guilty a good lot of the time, and when they are not guilty they are embarrassed: guilty if their infants have not gained enough weight, embarrassed if their drains are clogged, guilty if their children go to school in soiled clothes, guilty if all the germs behind the bathroom sink are not eradicated, guilty if they fail to notice the first signs of an oncoming cold, embarrassed if accused of having body odor, guilty if their sons go to school without good breakfasts, guilty if their daughters are unpopular because of old-fashioned, or unironed, or—heaven forbid—dirty dresses. In earlier times women were made to feel guilty if they abandoned their children or were too free with their affections. In the years after World War I, American women were made to feel guilty about sending their children to school in scuffed shoes. Between the two kinds of guilt there is a world of difference.

Let us return for a moment to the sociological model with which this essay began. The model predicts that changing patterns of household work will be correlated with at least two striking indicators of social change: the divorce rate and the rate of married women's labor force participation. That correlation may indeed exist, but it certainly is not reflected in the women's magazines of the 1920s and 1930s; divorce and full-time paid employment were not part of the life-style or the life pattern of the middle-class housewife as she was idealized in her magazines.

There were social changes attendant upon the introduction of modern technology into the home, but they were not the changes that the traditional functionalist model predicts; on this point a close analysis of the statistical data corroborates the impression conveyed in the magazines. The divorce rate was indeed rising during the years between the wars, but it was not rising nearly so fast for the middle and upper classes (who had, presumably, easier access to the new technology) as it was for the lower classes. By almost every gauge of socioeconomic status—income, prestige of husband's work, education—the divorce rate is higher for persons lower on the socioeconomic scale—and this is a phenomenon that has been constant over time.[39]

The supposed connection between improved household technology and married women's labor force participation seems just as dubious, and on the same grounds. The single socioeconomic factor which correlates most strongly (in cross-sectional studies) with married women's employment is husband's income, and the correlation is strongly negative; the higher his income, the less likely it will be that she is working.[40] Women's labor force participation increased during the 1920s but this increase was due to the influx of single women into the force. Married women's participation increased slightly during those years, but that increase was largely in factory labor—precisely the kind of work that middle-class women (who were, again, much more likely to have laborsaving devices at home) were least likely to do.[41] If there were a necessary connection between the improvement of household technology and either of these two social indicators, we would expect the data to be precisely the reverse of what in fact has occurred: Women in the higher social classes should have fewer functions at home and should therefore be more (rather than less) likely to seek paid employment or divorce.

Thus for middle-class American housewives between the wars, the social changes that we can document are not the social changes that the functionalist model predicts; rather than changes in divorce or patterns of paid employment, we find changes in the structure of the workforce, in its skills, and in its ideology. These social changes were concomitant with a series of technological changes in the equipment that was used to do the work. What is the relationship between these two series of phenomena? Is it possible to demonstrate causality or the direction of that causality? Was the decline in the number of households employing servants a cause or an effect of the mechanization of those households? Both are, after all, equally possible. The declining supply of household servants, as well as their rising wages, may have stimulated a demand for new appliances at the same time that the acquisition of new appliances may have made householders less inclined to employ the laborers who were on the market. Are there any techniques available to the historian to help us answer these questions?

In order to establish causality, we need to find a connecting link between the two sets of phenomena, a mechanism that, in real life, could have made the causality work. In this case a connecting link, an intervening agent between the social and the technological changes, comes immediately to mind: the advertiser— by which term I mean a combination of the manufacturer of the new goods, the advertising agent who promoted the goods, and the periodical that published the promotion. All the new devices and new foodstuffs that were being offered to American households were being manufactured and marketed by large companies which had considerable amounts of capital invested in their production: General Electric, Procter & Gamble, General Foods, Lever Brothers, Frigidaire, Campbell's, Del Monte, American Can, Atlantic & Pacific Tea—these were all well-established firms by the time the household revolution began, and they were all in a position to pay for national advertising campaigns to promote their new products and services. And pay they did; one reason for the expanding size and number of women's magazines in the 1920s was no doubt the expansion in revenues from available advertisers.[42]

Those national advertising campaigns were likely to have been powerful stimulators of the social changes that occurred in the household labor force; the advertisers probably did not initiate the changes, but they certainly encouraged them. Most of the advertising campaigns manifestly worked, so they must have touched upon areas of real concern for American housewives. Appliance ads specifically suggested that the acquisition of one gadget or another would make it possible to fire the maid, spend more time with the children, or have the afternoon free for shopping.[43] Similarly, many advertisements played upon the embarrassment and guilt which were now associated with household work. Ralston, Cream of Wheat, and Ovaltine were not themselves responsible for the compulsive practice of weighing infants and children repeatedly (after every meal for newborns, every day in infancy, every week later on), but the manufacturers certainly did not stint on capitalizing upon the guilt that women apparently felt if their offspring did not gain the required amounts of weight.[44] And yet again, many of the earliest attempts to spread "wise" consumer practices were undertaken by large corporations and the magazines that desired their advertising; mail-order shopping guides, "product-testing" services, pseudoinformative pamphlets, and other such promotional devices were all techniques for urging the housewife to buy new things under the guise of training her in her role as skilled consumer.[45]

Thus the advertisers could well be called the "ideologues" of the 1920s, encouraging certain very specific social changes—as ideologues are wont to do. Not surprisingly, the changes that occurred were precisely the ones that would gladden the hearts and fatten the purses of the advertisers; fewer household servants meant a greater demand for labor- and time-saving devices; more household tasks for women meant more and more specialized products that they would need to buy; more guilt and embarrassment about their failure to succeed at their work meant a greater likelihood that they would buy the products that were intended to minimize that failure. Happy, full-time housewives in intact families spend a lot of money to maintain their households; divorced women and working women do not. The advertisers may not have created the image of the ideal American housewife that dominated the 1920s—the woman who cheerfully and skillfully set about making everyone in her family perfectly happy and perfectly healthy—but they certainly helped to perpetuate it.

The role of the advertiser as connecting link between social change and technological change is at this juncture simply a hypothesis, with nothing much more to recommend it than an argument from plausibility. Further research may serve to test the hypothesis, but testing it may not settle the question of which was cause and which effect—if that question can ever be settled definitively in historical work. What seems most likely in this case, as in so many others, is that cause and effect are not separable, that there is a dynamic interaction between the social changes that married women were experiencing and the technological changes that were occurring in their homes. Viewed this way, the disappearance of competent servants becomes one of the factors that stimulated the mechanization of homes, and this mechanization of homes becomes a factor (though by no means the only one) in the disappearance of servants. Similarly, the emotionalization of housework becomes both cause and effect of the mechanization of that work; and the expansion of time spent on new tasks becomes both cause and effect of the introduction of time-saving devices. For example, the social pressure to spend more time in child care may have led to a decision to purchase the devices; once purchased, the devices could indeed have been used to save time—although often they were not.

If one holds the question of causality in abeyance, the example of household work still has some useful lessons to teach about the general problem of technology and social change. The standard sociological model for the impact of modern technology on family life clearly needs some revision: at least for middle-class nonrural American families in the twentieth century, the social changes were not the ones that the standard model predicts. In these families the functions of at least one member, the housewife, have increased rather than decreased and the dissolution of family life has not in fact occurred.

Our standard notions about what happens to a workforce under the pressure of technological change may also need revision. When industries become mechanized and rationalized, we expect certain general changes in the workforce to occur: Its structure becomes more highly differentiated, individual workers become more specialized, managerial functions increase, and the emotional context of the work disappears. On all four counts our expectations are reversed with regard to household work. The workforce became less rather than more differentiated as domestic servants, unmarried daughters, maiden aunts, and grandparents left the household and as chores which had once been performed by commercial agencies (laundries, delivery services, milkmen) were delegated to the housewife. The individual workers also became less specialized; the new housewife was now responsible for every aspect of life in her household, from scrubbing the bathroom floor to keeping abreast of the latest literature in child psychology.

The housewife is just about the only unspecialized worker left in America—a veritable jane-of-all-trades at a time when the jacks-of-all-trades have disappeared. As her work became generalized the housewife was also proletarianized: Formerly she was ideally the manager of several other subordinate workers; now she was idealized as the manager and the worker combined. Her managerial functions have not entirely disappeared, but they have certainly diminished and have been replaced by simple manual labor; the middle-class, fairly well-educated housewife ceased to be a personnel manager and became,

instead, a chauffeur, charwoman, and short-order cook. The implications of this phenomenon, the proletarianization of a workforce that had previously seen itself as predominantly managerial, deserve to be explored at greater length than is possible here, because I suspect that they will explain certain aspects of the women's liberation movement of the 1960s and 1970s which have previously eluded explanation: why, for example, the movement's greatest strength lies in social and economic groups who seem, on the surface at least, to need it least—women who are white, well-educated, and middle-class.

Finally, instead of desensitizing the emotions that were connected with household work, the industrial revolution in the home seems to have heightened the emotional context of the work, until a woman's sense of self-worth became a function of her success at arranging bits of fruit to form a clown's face in a gelatin salad. That pervasive social illness, which Betty Friedan characterized as "the problem that has no name," arose not among workers who found that their labor brought no emotional satisfaction, but among workers who found that their work was invested with emotional weight far out of proportion to its own inherent value: "How long," a friend of mine is fond of asking, "can we continue to believe that we will have orgasms while waxing the kitchen floor?"

NOTES

1. For some classic statements of the standard view, see W. F. Ogburn and M. F. Nimkoff, *Technology and the Changing Family* (Cambridge, Mass., 1955); Robert F. Winch, *The Modern Family* (New York, 1952); and William J. Goode, *The Family* (Englewood Cliffs, N.J., 1964).

2. This point is made by Peter Laslett in "The Comparative History of Household and Family," in *The American Family in Social Historical Perspective*, ed. Michael Gordon (New York, 1973), pp. 28–29.

3. Phillippe Ariès, *Centuries of Childhood: A Social History of Family Life* (New York, 1960).

4. See Laslett, pp. 20–24; . . .

5. Peter Laslett, *The World We Have Lost* (New York, 1965), passim.

6. For purposes of historical inquiry, this definition of middle-class status corresponds to a sociological reality, although it is not, admittedly, very rigorous. Our contemporary experience confirms that there are class differences reflected in magazines, and this situation seems to have existed in the past as well. . . .

7. *Historical Statistics of the United States,*

Colonial Times to 1957 (Washington, D.C., 1960), p. 510.

8. The gas iron, which was available to women whose homes were supplied with natural gas, was an earlier improvement on the old-fashioned flat-iron, but this kind of iron is so rarely mentioned in the sources that I used for this survey that I am unable to determine the extent of its diffusion.

9. Hazel Kyrk, *Economic Problems of the Family* (New York, 1933), p. 368, reporting a study in *Monthly Labor Review* 30 (1930):1209–52.

10. Although this point seems intuitively obvious, there is some evidence that it may not be true. Studies of energy expenditure during housework have indicated that by far the greatest effort is expended in hauling and lifting the wet wash, tasks which were not eliminated by the introduction of washing machines. In addition, if the introduction of the machines served to increase the total amount of wash that was done by the housewife, this would tend to cancel the energy-saving effects of the machines themselves.

11. Rinso was the first granulated soap; it came on the market in 1918. . . .

12. I take this account, and the term, from Robert S. Lynd and Helen M. Lynd, *Middletown: A Study in Contemporary American Culture* (New York, 1929), p. 97. . . . The rural situation was quite different from the urban; the President's Conference on Home Building and Home Ownership reported that in the late 1920s, 71 percent of the urban families surveyed had bathrooms, but only 33 percent of the rural families did. . . .

13. The data above came from Siegfried Giedion, *Mechanization Takes Command* (New York, 1948), pp. 685–703.

14. For a description of the standard bathroom see Helen Sprackling, "The Modern Bathroom," *Parents Magazine* 8 (Feb. 1933):25.

15. *Zanesville, Ohio and Thirty-Six Other American Cities* (New York, 1927), p. 65. Also see Robert S. Lynd and Helen M. Lynd, *Middletown in Transition* (New York, 1936), p. 537. Middletown is Muncie, Indiana.

16. Lynd and Lynd, *Middletown*, p. 96, and *Middletown in Transition*, p. 539.

17. Lynd and Lynd, *Middletown*, p. 98, and *Middletown in Transition*, p. 562.

18. On the advantages of the new stoves, see *Boston Cooking School Cookbook* (Boston, 1916), pp. 15–20; and Russell Lynes, *The Domesticated Americans* (New York, 1957), pp. 119–20.

19. "How To Save Coal While Cooking," *Ladies' Home Journal* 25 (Jan. 1908):44.

20. Lynd and Lynd, *Middletown*, p. 156.

21. Ibid.; see also "Safeway Stores," *Fortune* 26 (Oct. 1940):60.

22. Lynd and Lynd, *Middletown*, pp. 134–35, 153–54.

23. *Historical Statistics*, pp. 16, 77.

24. For Indiana data, see Lynd and Lynd, *Middletown*, p. 169. For national data, see D. L. Kaplan and M. Claire Casey, *Occupational Trends in the United States, 1900–1950*, U.S. Bureau of the Census Working Paper no. 5 (Washington, D.C., 1958), table 6. . . .

25. Lynd and Lynd, *Middletown*, p. 169.

26. On the disappearance of maiden aunts, unmarried daughters, and grandparents, see Lynd and Lynd, *Middletown*, pp. 25, 99, 110; Edward Bok, "Editorial," *American Home* 1 (Oct. 1928):15; . . .

27. Giedion, p. 619. . . .

28. Emily Post, *Etiquette: The Blue Book of Social Usage*, 5th ed. rev. (New York, 1937), p. 823.

29. This analysis is based upon various child-care articles that appeared during the period in the *Ladies' Home Journal*, *American Home*, and *Parents Magazine*. . . .

30. John Kenneth Galbraith has remarked upon the advent of woman as consumer in *Economics and the Public Purpose* (Boston, 1973), pp. 29–37.

31. . . . On consumer education see, for example, "How to Buy Towels," *Ladies' Home Journal* 45 (Feb. 1928):134; "Buying Table Linen," *Ladies' Home Journal* 45 (Mar. 1928):43; . . .

32. See, for example, Lynd and Lynd, *Middletown*, pp. 176, 196; and Margaret G. Reid, *Economics of Household Production* (New York, 1934), chap. 13.

33. See Reid, pp. 64–68; and Kyrk, p. 98.

34. See advertisement for Cleanliness Institute—"Self-respect thrives on soap and water," *Ladies' Home Journal* 45 (Feb. 1928):107. On changing bed linen, see "When the Bride Goes Shopping," *American Home* 1 (Jan. 1928):370. . . .

35. As reported in Kyrk, p. 51.

36. Bryn Mawr College Department of Social Economy, *Women During the War and After* (Philadelphia, 1945); and Ethel Goldwater, "Woman's Place," *Commentary* 4 (Dec. 1947):578–85.

37. JoAnn Vanek, "Keeping Busy: Time Spent in Housework, United States, 1920–1970" (Ph.D. diss., University of Michigan, 1973).

38. This analysis is based upon my reading of the middle-class women's magazines between 1918 and 1930. For detailed documentation see my paper "Two Washes in the Morning and a Bridge Party at Night: The American Housewife between the Wars," *Women's Studies* 3 (1976):147–72. . . .

39. For a summary of the literature on differential divorce rates, see Winch, p. 706; and William J. Goode, *After Divorce* (New York, 1956), p. 44. . . .

40. For a summary of the literature on married women's labor force participation, see Juanita Kreps, *Sex in the Marketplace: American Women at Work* (Baltimore, 1971), pp. 19–24.

41. Valerie Kincaid Oppenheimer, *The Female Labor Force in the United States*, Population Monograph Series, no. 5 (Berkeley, 1970), pp. 1–15; and Lynd and Lynd, *Middletown*, pp. 124–27.

42. On the expanding size, number, and influence of women's magazines during the 1920s, see Lynd and Lynd, *Middletown*, pp. 150, 240–44.

43. See, for example, the advertising campaigns of General Electric and Hotpoint from 1918 through the rest of the decade of the 1920s; both campaigns stressed the likelihood that electric appliances would become a thrifty replacement for domestic servants.

44. The practice of carefully observing children's weight was initiated by medical authorities, national and local governments, and social welfare agencies, as part of the campaign to improve child health which began about the time of World War I.

45. These practices were ubiquitous. *American Home,* for example, which was published by Doubleday, assisted its advertisers by publishing a list of informative pamphlets that readers could obtain; devoting half a page to an index of its advertisers; specifically naming manufacturer's and list prices in articles about products and services; allotting almost one-quarter of the magazine to a mail-order shopping guide which was not (at least ostensibly) paid advertisement; and as part of its editorial policy, urging its readers to buy new goods.

JACQUELYN DOWD HALL

Disorderly Women: Gender and Labor Militancy in the Appalachian South

In the 1920s Eleanor Roosevelt and other elite women continued the political activism that reformers and suffragists such as Florence Kelley had initiated. Working-class women had little choice but to continue the labor militancy exemplified by Schneiderman, Newman, Cohn, and Lemlich. This was especially true in the South. Unionization had never taken hold in the former states of the Confederacy as it had in heavily industrialized areas of the Northeast and Midwest. Moreover, working conditions had worsened as factory owners introduced new innovations designed to improve productivity. Southern textile mills, as employers of large numbers of poorly paid women, were especially vulnerable to strikes.

Jacquelyn Dowd Hall focuses on one of the many strikes exploding across the South in that tumultuous decade, exploring female activism in an essay that calls into question old stereotypes about southern workers as individualistic, docile, and "hard to organize." In this important study, Hall illuminates the distinctive style of collective action that the women of Elizabethton, Tennessee, employed and the self-concepts and family networks on which that style relied.

In what respects did working conditions resemble those confronting the young immigrant women in New York's garment district about whom Orleck wrote? What were the critical differences? Were the factors that inspired and sustained resistance similar? How does Hall view the actions of Trixie Perry and Texas Bill?

The rising sun "made a sort of halo around the crown of Cross Mountain" as Flossie Cole climbed into a neighbor's Model T and headed west down the gravel road to Elizabethton, bound for work in a rayon plant. Emerging from Stoney Creek hollow, the car joined a caravan of buses and self-styled "taxis" brimming with young people from dozens of tiny communities strung along the creek branches and nestled in the coves of the Blue Ridge Mountains of East Tennessee. The caravan picked up speed as it hit paved roads and crossed the Watauga River bridge, passing beneath a sign advertising the county seat's new-found iden-

Excerpted from "Disorderly Women: Gender and Labor Militancy in the Appalachian South" by Jacquelyn Dowd Hall, in *Journal of American History* 73 (1986):354–82. Copyright © 1986 by Jacquelyn Dowd Hall. Condensed and reprinted by permission of the author. Notes have been renumbered and edited.

tity as a "City of Power." By the time Cole reached the factory gate, it was 7:00 A.M., time to begin another ten-hour day as a reeler at the American Glanzstoff plant.[1]

The machines whirred, and work began as usual. But the reeling room stirred with anticipation. The day before, March 12, 1929, all but seventeen of the 360 women in the inspection room next door had walked off their jobs. Now they were gathered at the factory gate, refusing to work but ready to negotiate. When 9:00 A.M., approached and the plant manager failed to appear, they broke past the guards and rushed through the plant, urging their co-workers out on strike. By 1:40 P.M. the machines were idle and the plant was closed.

The Elizabethton conflict rocked Carter County and made national headlines. Before March ended, the spirit of protest had jumped the Blue Ridge and spread through the Piedmont. Gastonia, Marion, and Danville saw the most bitter conflicts, but dozens of towns were shocked by an unexpected workers' revolt.[2]

The textile industry has always been a stronghold of women's labor, and women were central to these events. They were noted by contemporaries, sometimes as leaders, more often as pathetic mill girls or as "Amazons" providing comic relief.[3] In historical renditions they have dropped out of sight. The result has been thin description: a one-dimensional view of labor conflict that fails to take culture and community into account.

Elizabethton, of course, is not unusual in this regard. Until recently, historians of trade unionism, like trade unionists themselves, neglected women, while historians of women concentrated on the Northeast and the middle class. There were few scholarly challenges to the assumption that women workers in general and southern women in particular were "hard to organize" and that women as family members exercised a conservative pull against class cohesion. Instances of female militancy were seen and not seen.[4] Because they contradicted conventional wisdom, they were easily dismissed.

Recent scholarship has revised that formulation by unearthing an impressive record of female activism. But our task is not only to describe and celebrate but also to contextualize, and thus to understand. In Elizabethton the preindustrial background, the structure of the work force and the industry, the global forces that impinged on local events—these particularities of time and place conditioned women's choices and shaped their identities. Equally important was a private world traditionally pushed to the margins of labor history. Female friendships and sexuality, cross-generational and cross-class alliances, the incorporation of new consumer desires into a dynamic regional culture—these too energized women's participation. Women in turn were historical subjects, helping to create the circumstances from which the strike arose and guiding by their actions the course the conflict took.

With gender at the center of analysis, unexpected dimensions come into view. Chief among them is the strike's erotic undercurrent, its sexual theme. The activists of Elizabethton belonged to a venerable tradition of "disorderly women," women who, in times of political upheaval, embody tensions that are half-conscious or only dimly understood.[5] Beneath the surface of a conflict that pitted workers and farmers against a new middle class in the town lay an inner world of fantasy, gender ideology, and sexual style.

The melding of narrative and analysis that follows has two major goals. The first is a fresh reading of an important episode in southern labor history, employing a female angle of vision to reveal aspects of the conflict that have been overlooked or misunderstood. The second is a close look at women's distinctive forms of collective action, using language and gesture as points of entry to a culture.

The Elizabethton story may also help to make a more general point. Based as it is on what Michel Foucault has termed "local" or "subjugated" knowledge, that is, perceptions that seem idiosyncratic, naive, and irrelevant to historical explanation, this study highlights the limitations of conventional categories.[6] The women of Elizabethton were neither traditionalists acting on family values nor market-oriented individualists, neither peculiar mountaineers nor familiar modern women. Their irreverence and inventiveness shatter stereotypes and illuminate the intricacies of working-class women's lives.

In 1925 the J. P. Bemberg Company of Barmen, Germany, manufacturer of high-quality rayon yarn by an exclusive stretch spinning process, began pouring the thick concrete floors of its first United States subsidiary. Three years later

Germany's leading producer of viscose yarn, the Vereinigte Glanzstoff Fabriken, A.G., of Elberfeld opened a jointly managed branch nearby. A post-World War I fashion revolution, combined with protective tariffs, had spurred the American rayon industry's spectacular growth. As one industry publicist put it, "With long skirts, cotton stockings were quite in order; but with short skirts, nothing would do except sheer, smooth stockings. . . . It was on the trim legs of post-war flappers, it has been said, that rayon first stepped out into big business." Dominated by a handful of European giants, the rayon industry clustered along the Appalachian mountain chain. By World War II, over 70 percent of American rayon production took place in the southern states, with 50 percent of the national total in Virginia and Tennessee alone.[7]

When the Bemberg and Glanzstoff companies chose East Tennessee as a site for overseas expansion, they came to a region that has occupied a peculiar place in the American economy and imagination. Since its "discovery" by local-color writers in the 1870s, southern Appalachia has been seen as a land "where time stood still." Mountain people have been romanticized as "our contemporary ancestors" or maligned as "latter-day white barbarians." Central to both images is the notion of a people untouched by modernity. In fact, as a generation of regional scholars has now made clear, the key to modern Appalachian history lies not in the region's isolation but in its role as a source of raw materials and an outlet for investment in a capitalist world economy.[8]

Frontier families had settled the fertile Watauga River Valley around Elizabethton before the Revolution. Later arrivals pushed farther up the mountains into the hollows carved by fast-falling creeks. Stoney Creek is the oldest and largest of those creek-bed communities. Here descendants of the original settlers cultivated their own small plots, grazed livestock in woods that custom held open to all, hunted and fished in an ancient hardwood forest, mined iron ore, made whiskey, spun cloth, and bartered with local merchants for what they could not produce at home.

In the 1880s East Tennessee's timber and mineral resources attracted the attention of capitalists in the United States and abroad, and an era of land speculation and railroad building began. The railroads opened the way to timber barons, who stripped away the forests, leaving hillsides stark and vulnerable to erosion. Farmers abandoned their fields to follow the march of the logging camps. Left behind, women and children did their best to pick up the slack.[9] But by the time Carter County was "timbered out" in the 1920s, farm families had crept upward to the barren ridge lands or grown dependent on "steady work and cash wages." Meanwhile, in Elizabethton, the county seat, an aggressive new class of bankers, lawyers, and businessmen served as brokers for outside developers, speculated in land, invested in homegrown factories, and looked beyond the hills for their standards of "push, progress and prosperity."[10]

Carter County, however, lacked Appalachia's grand prize: The rush for coal that devastated other parts of the mountains had bypassed that part of East Tennessee. Nor had county farmers been absorbed into the cotton kingdom, with its exploitative credit system and spreading tenancy. To be sure, they were increasingly hard pressed. As arable land disappeared, farms were divided and redivided. In 1880 the average rural family had supported itself on 140 acres of land; by 1920 it was making do on slightly more than 52 acres. Yet however diminished their circumstances, 84.5 percent still owned their own land.[11] The economic base that sustained traditional expectations of independence, production for use, and neighborly reciprocity tottered but did not give way.

The coming of the rayon plants represented a coup for Elizabethton's aspiring businessmen, who wooed investors with promises of free land, tax exemptions, and cheap labor. But at first the whole county seemed to share the boomtown spirit. Men from Stoney Creek, Gap Creek, and other mountain hamlets built the cavernous mills, then stayed on to learn the chemical processes that transformed the cellulose from wood pulp and cotton linters (the short fibers that remain on cotton seeds after longer, spinnable fibers are removed) into "artificial silk." Women vied for jobs in the textile division where they wound, reeled, twisted, and inspected the rayon yarn. Yet for all the excitement it engendered, industrialization in Carter County retained a distinctly rural cast. Although Elizabethton's population tripled (from 2,749 in 1920 to 8,093 in 1930), the rayon workers confounded predictions of spectacular urban growth, for most remained in the countryside, riding to work on chartered buses and trains or in taxis driven by neighbors and friends.

Women made up approximately 37 percent of the 3,213 workers in the mills. Most were under twenty-one, but many were as young as twelve, or more commonly, fourteen. By contrast, the work force contained a large proportion of older, married men. Those men, together with a smaller number of teenage boys, dominated the chemical division, while young women processed the finished yarn.[12]

Whether married or single, town- or country-bred, the men who labored in the rayon plants followed in the footsteps of fathers, and sometimes grandfathers, who had combined farming with a variety of wage-earning occupations. To a greater extent than we might expect, young women who had grown up in Elizabethton could also look to earlier models of gainful labor. A search of the 1910 manuscript census found 20 percent (97/507) of women aged fourteen and over in paid occupations. The largest proportion (29.6 percent) were cooks and servants. But close behind were women in what mountain people called "public work": wage-earning labor performed outside a household setting. For rayon workers from the countryside it was a different story. Only 5.2 percent of adult women on Stoney Creek were gainfully employed (33/638). Nineteen of these were farmers. The rest—except for one music teacher—were servants or washerwomen.[13]

These contrasts are telling, and from them we can surmise two things. The first is that industrialization did not burst upon a static, conflict-free "traditional" world. The women who beat a path to the rayon plants came from families that had already been drawn into an economy where money was a key to survival. The second is that the timber industry, which attracted Carter County's men, undermined its agricultural base, and destroyed its natural resources, created few opportunities for rural women. No wonder that farm daughters in the mills counted their blessings and looked on themselves as pioneers.

Whether they sought work out of family need or for more individualistic reasons, these "factory girls" saw their jobs as a hopeful gamble rather than a desperate last resort, and they remembered the moment with astounding

precision. "I'll never forget the day they hired me at Bemberg," said Flossie Cole. "We went down right in front of it. They'd come out and they'd say, 'You and you and you,' and they'd hire so many. And that day I was standing there and he picked out two or three more and he looked at me and he said, 'You.' It thrilled me to death." She worked 56 hours that week and took home $8.16.[14]

Such pay scales were low even for the southern textile industry, and workers quickly found their income eaten away by the cost of commuting or of boarding in town. When the strike came it focused on the issue of Glanzstoff women's wages, which lagged behind those at the older Bemberg plant. But workers had other grievances as well. Caustic chemicals were used to turn cellulose into a viscous fluid that was then forced through spinnerets, thimble-shaped nozzles pierced with tiny holes. The fine, individual streams coagulated into rayon filaments in an acid bath. In the chemical division men waded through water and acid, exposed all day to a lethal spray. Women labored under less dangerous conditions, but for longer hours and less pay. Paid by the piece, they complained of rising production quotas and what everyone referred to as "hard rules."[15]

Women in particular were singled out for petty regulations, aimed not just at extracting labor but at shaping deportment as well. They were forbidden to wear makeup; in some departments they were required to purchase uniforms. Most galling of all was company surveillance of the washroom. According to Bessie Edens, who was promoted to "forelady" in the twisting room, "men could do what they wanted to in their own department," but women had to get a pass to leave the shop floor. "If we went to the bathroom, they'd follow us," Flossie Cole confirmed, "'fraid we'd stay a minute too long." If they did, their pay was docked; one too many trips and they lost their jobs.[16]

Complaints about the washroom may have had other meanings as well. When asked how she heard that a strike was brewing, Nettie Reece cited "bathroom gossip."[17] As the company well knew, the women's washroom, where only a forelady, not a male supervisor, could go, might serve as a communications center, a hub of gossip where complaints were aired and plans were formulated.

The German origins of the plant managers contributed to the tension. Once the strike began, union organizers were quick to play on images of an "imported Prussian autocracy." The frontier republicanism of the mountains shaded easily into post–World War I Americanism as strikers demanded their rights as "natural-born American citizens" oppressed by a "latter day industrialism." In that they had much in common with other twentieth-century workers, for whom the democratic values articulated during the war became a rallying cry for social justice at home. The nationality of the managers helped throw those values into sharp relief.[18]

The strike came on March 12, 1929, led by women in Glanzstoff inspection department, by what one observer called "girls in their teens [who] decided not to put up with the present conditions any longer." The county court immediately issued injunctions forbidding all demonstrations against the company. When strikers ignored the injunctions, the governor sent in the National Guard. The strikers secured a charter from the American Federation of Labor's United Textile Workers union (UTW). Meeting in a place called the Tabernacle, built for religious revivals, they listened to a Baptist preacher from Stoney Creek warn: "The hand of oppression is growing on our people. . . . You women work for practically nothing. You must come together and say that such things must cease to be." Each night more workers "came forward" to take the union oath.[19]

Meanwhile, UTW and Federal Conciliation Service officials arrived on the scene. On March 22 they reached a "gentlemen's agreement" by which the company promised a new wage scale for "good girl help" and agreed not to discriminate against union members. The strikers returned to work, but the conflict was far from over. Higher paychecks never materialized; union members began losing their jobs. On April 4 local businessmen kidnapped two union organizers and ran them out of town. Eleven days later the workers responded with what most observers agreed was a "spontaneous and complete walkout."[20]

This time the conflict quickly escalated. More troops arrived, and the plants became fortresses, with machine guns on the rooftops and armed guardsmen on the ground. The company sent buses manned by soldiers farther up the hollows to recruit new workers and

escort them back to town. Pickets blocked narrow mountain roads. Houses were blown up; the town water main was dynamited. An estimated 1,250 individuals were arrested in confrontations with the National Guard.[21]

As far as can be determined, no women were involved in barn burnings and dynamitings—what Bessie Edens referred to as "the rough . . . stuff" that accompanied the second strike. Men "went places that we didn't go," explained Christine Galliher. "They had big dark secrets . . . the men did." But when it came to public demonstrations women held center stage. At the outset "hundreds of girls" had ridden down main street "in buses and taxis, shouting and laughing at people who watched them from windows and doorsteps." Now they blocked the road at Gap Creek and refused soldiers' orders that they walk twelve miles to jail in town. "And there was one girl that was awful tough in the bunch. . . . She said, 'No, by God. We didn't walk out here, and we're not walking back!' And she sat her hind end down in the middle of the road, and we all sat down with her. And the law used tear gas on us! . . . And it nearly put our eyes out, but we still wouldn't walk back to town." In Elizabethton after picket duty, women marched down the "Bemberg Highway . . . draped in the American flag and carrying the colors"—thereby forcing the guardsmen to present arms each time they passed. Inventive, playful, and shrewd, the women's tactics encouraged a holiday spirit. They may also have deflected violence and garnered community support.[22]

Laughter was among the women's most effective weapons. But beneath high spirits the terms of battle had begun to change. Local organizers were hobbled by a national union that lacked the resources and commitment to sustain the strike. Instead of translating workers' grievances into a compelling challenge, the UTW pared their demands down to the bone. On May 26, six weeks after the strike began, the union agreed to a settlement that made no mention of wages, hours, working conditions, or union recognition. The company's only concession was a promise not to discriminate against union members. The workers were less than enthusiastic. According to one reporter, "It took nine speeches and a lot of question answering lasting two and a half hours to get the strikers to accept the terms."[23]

The press, for the most part, greeted the

settlement as a workers' victory, or at least a satisfactory resolution of the conflict. Anna Weinstock, the first woman to serve as a federal conciliator, was credited with bringing the company to the bargaining table and was pictured as the heroine of the event. "SETTLED BY A WOMAN!" headlined one journal. "This is the fact that astounds American newspaper editors." "Five feet five inches and 120 pounds of femininity; clean cut, even features"—and so on, in great detail. Little was made of Weinstock's own working-class origins. She was simply a "new woman," come to the rescue of a backward mountain folk. The strikers themselves dropped quickly from view.[24]

From the outside, the conflict at Elizabethton looked like a straightforward case of labor-management strife. But it appeared quite different from within. Everyone interviewed put the blame for low wages on an alliance between the German managers and the "leading citizens" of the town. Preserved in the oral tradition is the story of how the "town fathers" promised the company a supply of cheap and unorganized labor. Bessie Edens put it this way: They told the company that "women wasn't used to working, and they'd work for almost nothing, and the men would work for low wages. That's the way they got the plant here." In this version of events the strike was part of a long-term struggle, with development-minded townspeople on one side and workers, farmers, and country merchants on the other.[25]

Workers' roots in the countryside encouraged resistance and helped them to mobilize support once the strike began. "These workers have come so recently from the farms and mountains . . . and are of such independent spirit," Alfred Hoffman observed, "that they 'Don't care if they do lose their jobs' and cannot be scared." Asked by reporters what would happen if strike activity cost them their jobs, one woman remarked, "I haven't forgotten how to use a hoe," while another said, "We'll go back to the farm."[26] Such threats were not just bravado. High levels of farm ownership sustained cultural independence. Within the internal economy of families, individual fortunes were cushioned by reciprocity; an orientation toward subsistence survived side by side with the desire for cash and store-bought goods.

Stoney Creek farmers were solidly behind the sons and daughters they sent to the factories, as were the small shopkeepers who relied on farmers for their trade. In county politics Stoney Creekers had historically marshaled a block vote against the town. In 1929 Stoney Creek's own J.M. Moreland was county sheriff, and he openly took the strikers' side. A strike leader in the twisting room ran a country store and drove his working neighbors into town. "That's why he was pretty well accepted as their leader," said a fellow worker. "Some of them were cousins and other relations. Some of them traded at his store. Some of them rode in his taxi. All intertwined."[27]

The National Guard had divided loyalties. Parading past the plants, the strikers "waved to and called the first names of the guardsmen, for most of the young men in uniforms [were friends of] the men and girls on strike." Even when the local unit was fortified by outside recruits, fraternizing continued. Nettie Reece, like a number of her girlfriends, met her future husband that way; she saw him on the street and "knew that was mine right there." Some guardsmen went further and simply refused to serve. "The use of the National Guard here was the dirtiest deal ever pulled," one protested. "I turned in my equipment when I was ordered to go out and patrol the road. I was dropped from the payroll two weeks later."[28]

In this context of family-and-community-based resistance, women had important roles to play. Farm mothers nurtured the strikers' independence simply by cleaving to the land, passing on to their children a heritage at odds with the values of the new order and maintaining family production as a hedge against the uncertainties of a market economy. But the situation of farm mothers had other effects as well, and it would be a mistake to push the argument for continuity too far. As their husbands ranged widely in search of wage labor, women's work intensified while their status—now tied to earning power—declined. The female strikers of Elizabethton saw their mothers as resourceful and strong but also as increasingly isolated and hard pressed. Most important, they no longer looked to their mothers' lives as patterns for their own.[29]

The summer after the strike, Bessie Edens attended the Southern Summer School for Women Workers, a workers' education project in North Carolina, where she set the group on its ear with an impassioned defense of women's rights:

> It is nothing new for married women to work. They have always worked.... Women have always worked harder than men and always had to look up to the man and feel that they were weaker and inferior.... If we women would not be so submissive and take every thing for granted, if we would awake and stand up for our rights, this world would be a better place to live in, at least it would be better for the women.
>
> Some girls think that as long as mother takes in washings, keeps ten or twelve boarders or perhaps takes in sewing, she isn't working. But I say that either one of the three is as hard work as women could do. So if they do that at home and don't get any wages for it, why would it not be all right for them to go to a factory and receive pay for what they do?

Edens had been the oldest of ten children. She had dreamed of going to nursing school, but her poverty-stricken parents had opposed her plan. At fifteen, she had gone to work as a servant. "Then I'd come back when Momma had a baby and wait on her, and help if she needed me in any way." Asked fifty years later about a daughter's place on a hardscrabble farm, Edens replied: "The girls were supposed to do housework and work in the fields. They were supposed to be slaves."[30]

Bessie Edens was unusual in her articulation of a working-class feminism. But scattered through the life histories written by other students are echoes of her general themes. Read in the context of farm daughters' lives—their first-hand exposure to rural poverty, their yearnings for a more expansive world—these stories reflect the "structure of feeling" women brought to the rayon plants and then to the picket line and union hall.[31] Women such as Edens, it seems, sensed the devaluation of women's handicraft labor in the face of cheap consumer goods. They feared the long arm of their mothers' fate, resented their fathers' distant authority, and envied their brothers' exploits away from home. By opting for work in the rayon plants, they struck out for their own place in a changing world. When low wages, high costs, and autocratic managers affronted their dignity and dashed their hopes, they were the first to revolt.

The Elizabethton story thus presents another pattern in the female protest tradition.

In coal-mining communities a rigid division of labor and women's hardships in company towns have resulted, paradoxically, in the notable militancy of miners' wives. By contrast, tobacco factories have tended to employ married women, whose job commitments and associational lives enable them to assume leadership roles in sustained organizing drives. In yet other circumstances, such as the early New England textile mills or the union insurgency of the 1920s and 1930s, single women initiated independent strikes or provided strong support for male-led, mixed-sex campaigns. Where, as in Elizabethton, people were mobilized as family and community members rather than as individual workers, non-wage-earning women could provide essential support. Once in motion, their daughters might outdo men in militancy, perhaps because they had fewer dependents than their male co-workers and could fall back more easily on parental resources, perhaps because the peer culture and increased independence encouraged by factory labor stirred boldness and inspired experimentation.[32]

The fact of women's initiative and participation in collective action is instructive. Even more intriguing is the gender-based symbolism of their protest style. Through dress, language, and gesture, female strikers expressed a complex cultural identity and turned it to their own rebellious purposes.

Consider, for instance, Trixie Perry and a woman who called herself "Texas Bill." Twenty-eight-year-old Trixie Perry was a reeler in the Glanzstoff plant. She had apparently become pregnant ten years before, had married briefly and then divorced, giving her son her maiden name. Her father was a butcher and a farmer, and she lived near her family on the edge of town. Trixie later moved into Elizabethton. She never remarried but went on to have several more children by other men. Texas Bill's background is more elusive. All we know is that she came from out of state, lived in a boardinghouse, and claimed to have been married twice before she arrived in town. These two friends were ringleaders on the picket line. Both were charged with violating the injunction, and both were brought to trial.[33]

Trixie Perry took the stand in a dress sewn from red, white, and blue bunting and a cap made of a small American flag. The prosecuting attorney began his cross-examination:

"You have a United States flag as a cap on your head?"

"Yes."

"Wear it all the time?"

"Whenever I take a notion."

"You are dressed in a United States flag, and the colors?"

"I guess so, I was born under it, guess I have a right to."

The main charge was that Perry and her friend had drawn a line across the road at Gap Creek and dared the soldiers to cross it. Above all they were accused of taunting the National Guard. The defense attorney, a fiery local lawyer playing to a sympathetic crowd, did not deny the charges. Instead, he used the women to mock the government's case. Had Trixie Perry threatened a lieutenant? "He rammed a gun in my face and I told him to take it out or I would knock it out." Had she blocked the road? "A little thing like me block a big road?" What had she said to the threat of a tear gas bomb? "That little old fire cracker of a thing, it won't go off."[34]

Texas Bill was an even bigger hit with the crowd. The defense attorney called her the "Wild Man from Borneo." A guard said she was "the wildest human being I've ever seen." Texas Bill both affirmed and subverted her reputation. Her nickname came from her habit of wearing "cowboy" clothes. But when it was her turn to testify, she "strutted on the stand" in a fashionable black picture hat and a black coat. Besides her other transgressions, she was accused of grabbing a soldier's gun and aiming it at him. What was she doing on the road so early in the morning? "I take a walk every morning before breakfast for my health," Texas replied with what a reporter described as "an assumed ladylike dignity."[35]

Witnesses for the prosecution took pains to contradict Texas Bill's "assumed ladylike dignity." A guardsman complained that she called him a "'God damned yellow son-of-a-bitch,' and then branched out from that." Texas offered no defense: "When that soldier stuck his gun in my face, that did make me mad and I did cuss a little bit and don't deny it." Far from discrediting the strikers, the soldiers' testimony added to their own embarrassment and the audience's delight. In tune with the crowd, the defense attorney "enjoyed making the guards admit they had been 'assaulted' ... by 16- and 18-year-old girls."[36]

Mock gentility, transgressive laughter, male egos on the line—the mix made for wonderful theater, and proved effective in court as well. The judge reserved maximum sentences for three especially aggressive men; all the women and most of the men were found not guilty or were lightly fined. In the end even those convictions were overturned by the state court of appeals.[37]

Trixie Perry and Texas Bill certainly donned the role of "disorderly woman." Since, presumably, only extraordinary circumstances call forth feminine aggression, women's assaults against persons and property constitute a powerful witness against injustice. At the same time, since women are considered less rational and taken less seriously than men, they may meet less resistance and be punished less severely for their crimes.[38]

But Trixie Perry and Texas Bill were not just out of line in their public acts; they also led unconventional private lives. It was this erotic subtext that most horrified officialdom and amused the courtroom crowd. The only extended discussion of the strike that appears in the city council minutes resulted in a resolution that read in part:

> WHEREAS, it has come to [our] attention . . . that the moral tone of this community has been lowered by reason of men and women congregating in various houses and meeting-places in Elizabethton and there practicing lewdness all hours of the night, in defiance of morality, law and order. . . .
>
> NOW, THEREFORE, BE IT RESOLVED, that the police force of the City arrest and place in the City Jail those who are violating the laws by practicing lewdness within the City of Elizabethton. . . .[39]

Union representatives apparently shared, indeed anticipated, the councilmen's concern. Worried by rumors that unemployed women were resorting to prostitution, they had already announced to the press that 25 percent of the strikers had been sent back to their hillside homes, "chiefly young single girls whom we want to keep off the streets." The townsmen and the trade unionists were thus united in drawing a line between good women and bad, with respectability being measured not only by chastity but by nuances of style and language as well.[40] In the heat of the trial, the question of whether or not women—as workers—had violated the injunction took second place to questions about their status *as women*, as members of their sex. Had they cursed? Had they been on the road at odd hours of the day or night? Was Texas Bill a lady or a "wild man from Borneo"? Fearing that "lewd women" might discredit the organizing drive, the organizers tried to send them home. To protect the community's "moral tone," the city council threatened to lock them up.

There is nothing extraordinary about this association between sexual misbehavior and women's labor militancy. Since strikers are often young single women who violate gender conventions by invading public space customarily reserved for men (and sometimes frequented by prostitutes)—and since female aggressiveness stirs up fears of women's sexual power—opponents have often undercut union organizing drives by insinuations of prostitution or promiscuity. Fearing guilt by association, "respectable" women stay away.[41]

What is impressive here is how Trixie Perry and Texas Bill handled the dichotomy between ladyhood and lewdness, good girls and bad. Using words that, for women in particular, were ordinarily taboo, they refused deference and signaled disrespect. Making no secret of their sexual experience, they combined flirtation with fierceness on the picket line and adopted a provocative courtroom style. And yet, with the language of dress—a cap made of an American flag, an elegant wide-brimmed hat—they claimed their rights as citizens and their place in the female community.

Moreover, that community upheld their claims. The defense attorney chose unruly women as his star witnesses, and the courtroom spectators enthusiastically cheered them on. The prosecuting attorney recommended dismissal of the charges against all the women on trial except Trixie Perry, Texas Bill, and a "hoodlum" named Lucille Ratliffe, on the grounds that the rest came from "good families." Yet in the court transcripts, few differences can be discerned in the behavior of good girls and bad. The other female defendants may have been less flamboyant, but they were no less sharp-tongued. Was Vivian King a member of the UTW? "Yes, and proud of it." Had she been picketing? "Yes, proud of that." What was a young married woman named Dorothy Oxindine doing on Gap Creek at five o'clock in the morning? "Out airing." Did Lena May Jones "holler out 'scab'"? "No, I think the

statement made was 'I wouldn't be a scab' and 'Why don't you come and join our organization.'" Did she laugh at a soldier and tell him his gun wouldn't shoot? "I didn't tell him it wouldn't shoot, but I laughed at him ... and told him he was too much of a man to shoot a lady."[42]

Interviewed over fifty years later, strike participants still refused to make invidious distinctions between themselves and women like Trixie Perry and Texas Bill. Bessie Edens was a settled, self-educated, married woman. But she was also a self-described "daredevil on the picket line," secure in the knowledge that she had a knife hidden in her drawstring underwear. To Edens, who came from a mountain hamlet called Hampton, the chief distinction did not lie between herself and rougher women. It lay between herself and merchants' wives who blamed the trouble on "those hussies from Hampton." When asked what she thought of Trixie Perry and Texas Bill, she answered simply, "There were some girls like that involved. But I didn't care. They did their part."[43]

Nettie Reece, who lived at home with parents who were "pretty particular with [their] daughters," shared Bessie Edens's attitude. After passing along the town gossip about Trixie Perry, she was anxious to make sure her meaning was not misconstrued. "Trixie was not a woman who sold her body," she emphasized. "She just had a big desire for sex. ... And when she had a cause to fight for, she'd fight." Reece then went on to establish Perry's claim to a certain kind of respectability. After the strike Perry became a hard-working restaurant cook. She was a good neighbor: "If anybody got sick, she was there to wait on them." The children she bore out of wedlock did well in life, and they "never throwed [their mother] aside."[44]

Industrialization, as we know, changed the nature of work, the meaning of time. In Carter County it entailed a shift of economic and political power from the countryside to the town. At issue too were more intimate matters of fantasy, culture, and style.

Implicit in the conflict were two different sexual systems. One, subscribed to by union officials and the local middle class, mandated chastity before marriage, men as breadwinners, and women as housewives in the home. The other, rooted in a rural past and adapted to working-class life, recognized liaisons established without the benefit of clergy or license fees and allowed legitimacy to be broadly construed. It was unfamiliar with—or pragmatic about—prostitution. It circumscribed women's roles without investing in abstract standards of femininity. It was, in short, a society that might produce a Trixie Perry or defend "hussies from Hampton" against the snubs of merchants' wives.

This is not to say that the women of Elizabethton were simply acting on tradition. On the contrary, the strikers dressed the persona of the disorderly woman in unmistakably modern garb. Women's behavior on the witness stand presupposed a certain sophistication: A passing familiarity allowed them to parody ladyhood and to thumb a nose at the genteel standards of the town. Combining garments from the local past with fragments of an expansive consumer culture, the women of Elizabethton assembled their own version of a brash, irreverent Jazz Age style.

By the early 1920s radios and Model Ts had joined railroads and mail-order catalogs as conduits to the larger world. Record companies had discovered hill-country music and East Tennessee's first country-music stars were recording hits that transformed ballad singing, fiddle playing, and banjo picking into one of America's great popular-music sounds. The banjo itself was an Afro-American instrument that had come to the mountains with the railroad gangs. Such cultural interchanges multiplied during the 1920s as rural traditions met the upheavals of industrial life. The result was an explosion of musical creativity—in the hills of Tennessee no less than in New York City and other cosmopolitan centers.[45] Arriving for work in the rayon plants, young people brought with them the useable past of the countryside, but they quickly assimilated the speeded-up rhythms of a changing world.

Work-related peer groups formed a bridge between traditional loyalties and a novel youth culture. Whether married or single, living with parents or on their own, women participated in the strike in same-sex groups. Sisters boarded, worked, and demonstrated together. Girlfriends teamed up in groups or pairs. Trixie Perry and Texas Bill were a case in point. But there were others as well. Nettie Reece joined the union with her parents' approval but also with her whole

school girl gang in tow. Ethel and M. C. Ashworth, ages eighteen and seventeen, respectively, came from Virginia to work in the plants. "Hollering and singing [in a] Ford touring car," they were arrested in a demonstration at Watauga Point. Ida and Evelyn Heaton boarded together on Donna Avenue. Evelyn Heaton was hit by a car on the picket line, swore out a warrant, and had the commander of the National Guard placed under arrest. After the strike she was blacklisted, and Ida attended the Southern Summer School.[46]

The sudden gathering of young people in the town nourished new patterns of heterosociability, and the strike's erotic undercurrent surfaced not only in Trixie Perry's "big desire for sex" but also in the behavior of her more conventional peers. The loyalties of the national guardsmen were divided, but their sympathy was obvious, as was their interest in the female strikers. Most of the Elizabethton women were in their teens or early twenties, the usual age of marriage in the region, and the strike provided unaccustomed opportunities for courtship. Rather than choosing a neighbor they had known all their lives, under watchful parental eyes, women flirted on the picket lines or the shop floor. Romance and politics commingled in the excitement of the moment, flowering in a spectrum of behavior—from the outrageousness of Trixie Perry to a spate of marriages among other girls.

What needs emphasis here is the dynamic quality of working-class women's culture—a quality that is sometimes lost in static oppositions between modernism and traditionalism, individualism and family values, consumer and producer mentalities. This is especially important where regional history has been so thoroughly mythologized. Appalachian culture, like all living cultures, embraced continuity and discontinuity, indigenous and borrowed elements.[47] As surely as Anna Weinstock—or Alabama's Zelda Fitzgerald—or any city flapper, the Elizabethton strikers were "new women," making their way in a world their mothers could not have known but carrying with them values handed down through the female line.

Two vignettes may serve to illustrate that process of grounded change.

Flossie Cole's mother, known by everyone on Stoney Creek as "Aunt Tid," was Sheriff Moreland's sister, but that didn't keep her from harboring cardplayers, buckdancers, and whiskey drinkers in her home. Aunt Tid was also a seamstress who "could look at a picture in a catalog and cut a pattern and make a dress just like it." But like most of her friends, Cole jumped at the chance for store-bought clothes: "That first paycheck, that was it . . . I think I bought me some new clothes with the first check I got. I bought me a new pair of shoes and a dress and a hat. Can you imagine someone going to a plant with a hat on? I had a blue dress and black shoes—patent leather, honey, with real high heels—and a blue hat." Nevertheless, before Cole left home in the morning for her job in the rayon plant, Aunt Tid made sure that around her neck—beneath the new blue dress—she wore a bag of asafetida, a strong-smelling resin, a folk remedy to protect her from diseases that might be circulating in the town.[48]

Second, there is visual evidence: a set of sixteen-millimeter films made by the company in order to identify—and to blacklist—workers who participated in the union. In those films groups of smiling women traipse along the picket line dressed in up-to-date clothes.[49] Yet federal conciliator Anna Weinstock, speaking to an interviewer forty years later, pictured them in sunbonnets, and barefooted. "They were," she explained, "what we would normally call hillbillies": women who "never get away from their shacks."[50] This could be seen as the treachery of memory, a problem of retrospection. But it is also an illustration of the power of stereotypes, of how cultural difference is registered as backwardness, of how images of poverty and backwardness hide the realities of working-class women's lives.

The strike, as we know, was defeated. Participants were blacklisted. The Great Depression settled over the mountains, rekindling reliance on older ways of making do. Flossie Cole, for instance, had been new to factory labor, but she was no stranger to women's work. While her brothers had followed their father's lead to the coal mines, she had pursued the two most common occupations of the poorest mountain girls: agricultural labor and domestic service. "We would hire out and stay with people until they got through with us and then go back home. And when we got back home, it was workin' in the corn or wash for people."

When Cole lost her job after the strike she went back to domestic service, "back to the drudge house," as she put it.[51]

Young women had poured eagerly into the rayon mills, drawn at least in part by the promise of independence, romance and adventure. As hard times deepened, such motives paled beside stark necessity. Two statistics make the point: The percentage of Carter County women who were gainfully employed held steady through the thirties. But by the end of the period a larger proportion than before worked as servants in other people's homes. When Flossie Cole went "back to the drudge house," she had plenty of company.[52]

Still, despite subsequent hardships, the spirit of the 1920s flickered on. Setting out to explore the strike through oral-history interviews, we expected to find disclaimers or silences. Instead, we heard unfaded memories and no regrets. "I knew I wasn't going to get to go back, and I didn't care," said Bessie Edens. "I wrote them a letter and told them I didn't care whether they took me back or not. I didn't! If I'd starved I wouldn't of cared, because I knew what I was a'doing when I helped to pull it. And I've never regretted it in any way. . . . And it did help the people, and it's helped the town and the country."[53] For those, like Edens, who went on to the Southern Summer School or remained active in the union, the strike was a pivot around which the political convictions and personal aspirations of a lifetime turned. For them, there were intangible rewards: a subtle deepening of individual power, a belief that they had made history and that later generations benefited from what they had done.

The strike, of course, made a fainter impression on other lives. Women's rebelliousness neither redefined gender roles nor overcame economic dependency. Their desire for the trappings of modernity could blur into a self-limiting consumerism. An ideology of romance could end in sexual danger or a married woman's burdensome double day. Still, the women of Elizabethton left a legacy. A norm of female public work, a new style of sexual expressiveness, the entry of women into public space and political struggles previously monopolized by men—all these pushed against traditional constraints even as they created new vulnerabilities. The farm daughters who left home for the rayon plants pioneered a new pattern of female experience, and they created for their post-World War II daughters an environment far different from the one they, in their youth, had known. It would be up to later generations to wrestle with the costs of commercialization and to elaborate a vision that embraced economic justice and community solidarity as well as women's liberation.

Notes

This study began as a collaborative endeavor with Sara Evans of the University of Minnesota, who helped to gather many of the interviews on which I have relied. Rosemarie Hester and Jennifer Dowd also joined me on trips to the mountains, and I benefited from their companionship, ideas, and research. I owe a special debt to Christopher Daly, Lu Ann Jones, Robert Korstad, James Leloudis, and Mary Murphy, with whom I have co-written *Like a Family: The Making of a Southern Cotton Mill World* (Chapel Hill, 1987).

1. Dan Crowe, *Old Town and the Covered Bridge* (Johnson City, Tenn., 1977), pp. 32, 71; Florence (Cole) Grindstaff interview by Jacquelyn Hall, July 10, 1981 (in Hall's possession).

2. For this strike wave, see Tom Tippett, *When Southern Labor Stirs* (New York, 1931); James A. Hodges, "Challenge to the New South: The Great Textile Strike in Elizabethton, Tennessee, 1929," *Tennessee Historical Quarterly* 23 (Dec. 1964):343–57; . . .

3. Contemporary observations include, *Knoxville News Sentinel*, May 17, 1929; Florence Kelley, "Our Newest South," *Survey*, June 15, 1929, pp. 342–44; . . .

4. Anne Firor Scott, "On Seeing and Not Seeing: A Case of Historical Invisibility," *Journal of American History* 71 (June 1984):7–8.

5. Natalie Zemon Davis, *Society and Culture in Early Modern France* (Stanford, 1975), pp. 124–51. . . .

6. Michel Foucault, *Power/Knowledge: Selected Interviews and Other Writings, 1972–1977*, trans. and ed. Colin Gordon (New York, 1980), p. 81.

7. Joseph Leeming, *Rayon: The First Man-Made Fiber* (Brooklyn, 1950), pp. 1–82; Jesse W. Markham, *Competition in the Rayon Industry* (Cambridge, Mass., 1952), pp. 1–38, 97, 186, 193, 209.

8. Bruce Roberts and Nancy Roberts, *Where Time Stood Still: A Portrait of Appalachia* (New York, 1970); William Goodell Frost, "Our Contemporary Ancestors in the Southern Mountains," *Atlantic Monthly* 83 (March 1899):311; Arnold J. Toynbee, *A Study of History*, 2 vols. (New York, 1947), II:312; . . .

9. For this preindustrial economy, and its transformation, see Eller, *Miners, Millhands, and Mountaineers*, pp. 3–38, 86–127. . . .

10. *Mountaineer*, Dec. 28, Dec. 31, 1887.

11. U.S. Department of the Interior, Census Office, *Report on the Productions of Agriculture as Returned at the Tenth Census* (June 1, 1880) (Washington, 1883), pp. 84–85, 132, 169; U.S. Department of Commerce, Bureau of the Census, *Fourteenth Census of the United States Taken in the Year 1920: Agri-*

culture, vol. VI, pt. 2 (Washington, [D.C.] 1922), pp. 446–47.

12. Holly, "Elizabethton, Tennessee," pp. 123, 133–38, 156, 198; U.S. Congress, Senate, Committee on Manufactures, *Working Conditions of the Textile Industry in North Carolina, South Carolina, and Tennessee*, 71 Cong., 1 sess., May 8, 9, and 20, 1929, p. 95; Henry Schuettler interview by Hall, n.d. [1981] (in Hall's possession).

13. Thirteenth Census of the United States, 1910, Manuscript Population Schedule, Carter County, Tenn., district 7; ibid., district 15; ibid., district 10; ibid., district 12.

14. Grindstaff interview.

15. *Scraps of Work and Play*, Southern Summer School for Women Workers in Industry, Burnsville, N.C., July 11-Aug. 23, 1929, typescript, pp. 21–22, 24, box 111, American Labor Education Service Records (Martin P. Catherwood Library, New York State School of Industrial and Labor Relations, Cornell University, Ithaca, N.Y.); Bessie Edens interview by Mary Frederickson, Aug. 14, 1975, pp. 1–2, 31–32, Southern Oral History Program Collection, Southern Historical Collection (Wilson Library, University of North Carolina at Chapel Hill) [hereafter SOHP].

16. Edens interview, Aug. 14, 1975, p. 32; Grindstaff interview.

17. Nettie Reece [pseud.] interview by Hall, May 18 and 19, 1983 (in Hall's possession).

18. *Knoxville News Sentinel*, May 13, 1929; *American Bemberg Corporation* v. *George Miller, et al.*, East Tennessee District Supreme Court, Jan. 29, 1930, record of evidence, typescript, box 660 (Tennessee State Library and Archives, Nashville) [hereafter Record of Evidence]. . . .

19. *Knoxville News Sentinel*, Mar. 14, 1929; Christine (Hinkle) Galliher and Dave Galliher interview by Hall, Aug. 8, 1979, pp. 8–9, SOHP; Tom Tippett, "Southern Situation," speech typescript, meeting held at the National Board, May 15, 1929, p. 3, box 25, Young Women's Christian Association Papers, Sophia Smith Collection (Smith College, Northampton, Mass.); Tom Tippett, "Impressions of Situation at Elizabethton, Tenn., May 10, 11, 1929," typescript, p. 1, ibid.

20. *Knoxville News Sentinel*, Mar. 20, Mar. 29, 1929; "Instructions for Adjustment of Wage Scale for Girl Help," Mar. 15, 1929, Records of the Conciliation Service, RG 280 (National Archives); Committee of Striking Workers[,] Members of United Textile Workers of America to the Honorable Herbert Hoover, Apr. 16, 1929, ibid; "Preliminary Report of Commissioner of Conciliation," Apr. 16, 1929, ibid.

21. Dr. J. A. Hardin to Hon. H. H. Horton, May 16, 1929, box 12, Governor Henry H. Horton Papers (Tennessee State Library and Archives); *Knoxville News Sentinel*, May 6, May 10, May 12, May 14, May 19, May 24, 1929.

22. Edens interview, Aug. 14, 1975, pp. 40, 49; Galliher interview, 33; *Knoxville News Sentinel*, Mar. 15, May 16, 1929.

23. *Knoxville News Sentinel*, May 27, 1929; Ina Nell (Hinkle) Harrison interview by Hall, Aug. 8, 1979, p. 2, SOHP; Mary Heaton Vorse, "Rayon Strikers Reluctantly Accept Settlement," press release, May 27, 1929, box 156, Mary Heaton Vorse Papers,

Archives of Labor and Urban Affairs (Walter P. Reuther Library, Wayne State University, Detroit, Mich.).

24. "Rays of Sunshine in the Rayon War," *Literary Digest*, June 8, 1929, p. 12; *Charlotte Observer*, June 2, 1929; *Raleigh News and Observer*, May 24, 1929.

25. Edens interview, Aug. 14, 1975, pp. 43–44; Myrtle Simmerly interview by Hall, May 18, 1983 (in Hall's possession); Ollie Hardin interview by Hall and Sara Evans, Aug. 9, 1979 (in Hall's possession); Effie (Hardin) Carson interview by Hall and Evans, Aug. 6, 1979, p. 41, SOHP; Holly, "Elizabethton, Tennessee," 306–7.

26. James Myers, "Field Notes: Textile Strikes in the South," box 374, Archive Union Files (Martin P. Catherwood Library); *Raleigh News and Observer*, Mar. 15, 1929.

27. Hoffmann, "Mountaineer in Industry," 2–5; Robert (Bob) Moreland and Barbara Moreland interview by Hall, July 11, 1981 (in Hall's possession); *Knoxville News Sentinel*, Mar. 15, 1929; Honard Ward interview by Hall, n.d. [1981] (in Hall's possession).

28. *Knoxville News Sentinel*, May 15, 1929; Reece interview; . . .

29. For the argument that precisely because they are "left behind" by the economic developments that pull men into wage labor, woman-centered families may harbor alternative or oppositional values, see Mina Davis Caulfield, "Imperialism, the Family, and Cultures of Resistance," *Socialist Revolution* 4 (Oct. 1974):67–85; . . .

30. Bessie Edens, "Why a Married Woman Should Work," in *Scraps of Work and Play*, pp. 30–31; Edens interview, Aug. 14. 1975, pp. 14, 21, 34–35; Bessie Edens interview by Hall, Aug. 5, 1979 (in Hall's possession); Millie Sample, "Impressions," Aug. 1931, box 9, American Labor Education Service Records.

31. Mirion Bonner, "Behind the Southern Textile Strikes," *Nation*, Oct. 2, 1929, pp. 351–52; "Scraps From Our Lives," in *Scraps of Work and Play*, pp. 5–11; . . .

32. Corbin, *Life, Work, and Rebellion*, pp. 92–93; Louise A. Tilly, "Paths of Proletarianization: Organization of Production, Sexual Division of Labor, and Women's Collective Action," *Signs* 7 (Winter 1981):400–17; . . .

33. *Elizabethton Star*, Nov. 14, 1953, Jan. 31, 1986; Reece interview; Carson interview, 25; Nellie Bowers interview by Hall, May 15, 1983 (in Hall's possession); *Knoxville News Sentinel*, May 17, May 18, 1929.

34. Record of Evidence.

35. *Knoxville News Sentinel*, May 17, 1929.

36. Ibid.; Record of Evidence.

37. *American Bemberg Corporation* v. *George Miller, et al.*, minute books "Q" and "R," Chancery Court minutes, Carter County, Tenn., July 22, 1929 (Carter County Courthouse, Elizabethton, Tenn.); *American Bemberg Corporation* v. *George Miller, et al.*, Court of Appeals, #1, Sept. 5, 1930 (Supreme Court and Courts of Appeal, State of Tennessee, Knoxville).

38. Davis, *Society and Culture in Early Modern France*, pp. 124–51; Laurel Thatcher Ulrich, *Good Wives* (New York, 1982), pp. 191–97.

39. Elizabethton City Council, Minutes, May 23, 1929, Minute Book, vol. 5, pp. 356–57 (City Hall, Elizabethton, Tenn.).

40. *Knoxville News Sentinel*, May 5, 1929; Myers, "Field Notes." . . .

41. See, for instance, Alice Kessler-Harris, "The Autobiography of Ann Washington Craton," *Signs* 1 (Summer 1976):1019–37.

42. *Knoxville News Sentinel*, May 18, 1929; Record of Evidence.

43. Edens interview, Aug. 5, 1979.

44. Reece interview, May 19, 1983.

45. Charles K. Wolfe, *Tennessee Strings: The Story of Country Music in Tennessee* (Knoxville, 1977), pp. 22–90; Barry O'Connell, "Dick Boggs, Musician and Coal Miner," *Appalachian Journal* 11 (Autumn-Winter 1983–84):48.

46. *Miller's Elizabethton, Tenn., City Directory*, 1930; Reece interview; Record of Evidence; *Knoxville News Sentinel*, May 16, May 17, 1929; . . .

47. David E. Whisnant, *All That Is Native and Fine: The Politics of Culture in an American Region* (Chapel Hill, 1983), p. 48.

48. Grindstaff interview; Moreland interview.

49. *Knoxville Journal*, Apr. 22, 1929; sixteen-millimeter film (1 reel), ca. 1929, Helen Raulston Collection, Archives of Appalachia (East Tennessee State University, Johnson City); sixteen-millimeter film (20 reels), ca. 1927–1928, Bemberg Industry Records (Tennessee State Library and Archives). . . .

50. Anna Weinstock Schneider interview by Julia Blodgett Curtis, 1969, pp. 161, 166, 172–3, 177, Anna Weinstock Schneider Papers, box 1 (Martin P. Catherwood Library).

51. Grindstaff interview.

52. Bureau of the Census, *Fifteenth Census of the United States: 1930. Population*, vol. III, pt. 2 (Washington, [D.C.], 1932), p. 909; U.S. Department of Commerce, Bureau of the Census, *Sixteenth Census of the United States: 1940. Population*, vol. II, pt. 6 (Washington, [D.C.], 1943), p. 616.

53. Edens interview, Aug. 14, 1975, p. 50. . . .

LESLIE J. REAGAN
When Abortion Was a Crime: Reproduction and the Economy in the Great Depression

The frequency with which women—especially those who were married, native-born Protestant, and middle- or upper-middle-class—resorted to abortion fueled a movement to criminalize the practice, as James Mohr discussed in Part II. Motivated by a variety of factors that had little to do with the protection of women's health, which was the primary reason advanced by the physicians who led the movement, anti-abortionists succeeded in making the practice illegal in the post–Civil War era. Some states did allow physicians to perform therapeutic abortions if the woman's life was threatened by carrying the pregnancy to term. In many states, however, the requirements for getting clearance to perform a therapeutic abortion in a hospital setting made this loophole virtually meaningless, especially when a vigilant district attorney was prepared to pit his interpretation against the physician's.

Leslie Reagan's prizewinning study of the practice and policing of abortion during the century it was criminalized (1867–1973) reveals that, despite the law, millions of abortions were performed during those years—and by no means all by "back-alley" butchers.

"My husband has been out of work for over six months and no help is in sight," wrote one mother to Margaret Sanger and the American Birth Control League; "I can't afford more children." Every year she performed two abortions upon herself, and she reported, "I have just now gotten up from an abortion and I don't want to repeat it again."[1] The disaster of the Great Depression touched all aspects of women's lives, including the most intimate ones, and brought about a new high in the incidence of abortion. As jobs evaporated and wages fell, families found themselves living on insecure and scanty funds. Many working people lost their homes; tenants had their belongings put out on the street. Married couples gave up children to orphanages because they could not support them.

As women pressured doctors for help, the medical practice of abortion, legal and illegal, expanded during the 1930s. Physicians

granted, for the first time, that social conditions were an essential component of medical judgment in therapeutic abortion cases. Medical recognition of social indications reveals the ways in which political and social forces shaped medical thinking and practice. A handful of radical physicians, who looked to Europe as a model, raised the possibility of liberalizing the abortion law. . . .

If we move away from the dramatic narratives about abortion produced at inquests or in newspapers, which tell of the deaths and dangers of abortion, and step into the offices of physician-abortionists, a different story can be discerned. Abortion was not extraordinary, but ordinary. The proverbial "back-alley butcher" story of abortion overemphasizes fatalities and limits our understanding of the history of illegal abortion. Case studies of the "professional abortionists" and their practices in the 1930s provide a unique opportunity to analyze the experiences of the tens of thousands of women who went to physician-abortionists. Many women had abortions in a setting nearly identical to the doctors' offices where they received other medical care. These doctors specialized in a single procedure, abortion. They used standard medical procedures to perform safe abortions routinely and ran what may be called abortion clinics. Furthermore, abortion specialists were an integral part of regular medicine, as the network of physicians who referred patients to these physician-abortionists demonstrates. . . .

The Depression years make vivid the relationship between economics and reproduction. Women had abortions on a massive scale. Married women with children found it impossible to bear the expense of another, and unmarried women could not afford to marry. As young working-class women and men put off marriage during the Depression to support their families or to save money for a wedding, marriage rates fell drastically. Yet while they waited to wed, couples engaged in sexual relations, and women became pregnant. Many had abortions.[2]

During the Depression, married women were routinely fired on the assumption that jobs belonged to men and that women had husbands who supported them. Discrimination against married women forced single women to delay marriage and have abortions in order to keep their jobs. One such woman was a young teacher whose fiancé was unemployed. As her daughter recalled fifty years later, "She got pregnant. What were her choices? Marry, lose her job, and bring a child into a family with no means of support? Not marry, lose her job and reputation, and put the baby up for adoption or keep it?" As this scenario makes clear, she had no "choice." Furthermore, it points to the limitations of the rhetoric of "choice" in reproduction: Social forces condition women's reproductive options.[3] . . .

Medical studies and sex surveys demonstrated that women of every social strata turned to abortion in greater numbers during the Depression. Comparative studies by class and race appeared for the first time in the 1930s. Induced abortion rates among white, middle- and upper-class married women rose during the Depression years. The Kinsey Insti-

tute for Sex Research, led by Paul H. Gebhard, analyzed data from over five thousand married, white, mostly highly educated, urban women. The researchers found that "the depression of the 1930's resulted in a larger proportion of pregnancies that were artificially aborted." For every age group of women, born between 1890 and 1919, the highest induced abortion rate occurred during "the depth of the depression." White, married women were determined to avoid bearing children during the Depression: They reduced their rate of conception as well.[4] . . . The findings of Kinsey researchers suggest that aborting first pregnancies early in marriage might have been a growing trend, particularly among more educated, urban white women.[5]

Married black women, like their white counterparts, used abortion more during the Depression. . . . Dr. Charles H. Garvin, an esteemed black surgeon from Cleveland, commented in 1932 "that there has been a very definite increase in the numbers of abortions, criminally performed, among the married."[6] . . . In 1935, Harlem Hospital, which cared for mostly poor black patients, opened a separate ward, "The Abortion Service," to treat the women who came for emergency care following illegal abortions. . . .

A study of reproductive histories collected from forty-five hundred women at a New York clinic between 1930 and 1938 suggested that when class was controlled, working-class women, black and white alike, induced abortions at the same rate.[7] . . .

The key difference between black and white women was in their response to pregnancy outside of marriage, not their use of abortion. Unmarried white women who became pregnant were more likely to abort their pregnancies than were African American women in the same situation. Instead, more black women bore children out of wedlock and did so without being ostracized by their families and community. . . .

The tolerance of illegitimacy among African Americans was tempered by class. As African Americans advanced economically, they held their unwed daughters and sons to more rigid standards of chastity. Similarly, by the time the Kinsey Institute interviewed black women in the 1950s, there were clear class differences in the use of abortion by unmarried black women: Those with more education (and presumably more affluence) aborted at a higher rate than those with less education.[8]

... A study of working-class women in New York in the 1930s found almost identical abortion rates among Catholic, Jewish, and Protestant women.[9] However, researchers found striking differences in the reproductive patterns followed by women of different religious groups, a finding that seems to reflect class differences. Catholic and Jewish women tended to have their children earlier in their lives and began aborting unwanted pregnancies as they got older; Protestant women tended to abort earlier pregnancies and bear children later.[10] The Kinsey Report found for both married and unmarried white women, the more devout the woman, the less likely she was to have an abortion; the more religiously "inactive" a woman, the more likely she was to have an abortion.[11]

Access to physician-induced abortions and reliance upon self-induced methods varied greatly by class and race. Most affluent white women went to physicians for abortions, while poor women and black women self-induced them. Physicians performed 84 percent of the abortions reported by the white, urban women to Kinsey researchers. Fewer than 10 percent of the affluent white women self-induced their abortions, though black women and poor white women, because of poverty or discrimination in access to medical care, often did so. According to the Kinsey study on abortion, 30 percent of the lower-income and black women reported self-inducing their abortions.[12] ...

Low-income women's and black women's greater reliance upon self-induced methods of abortion meant that the safety of illegal abortion varied by race and class. ...

Since poor women and black women were more likely to try to self-induce abortions and less likely to go to doctors or midwives, they suffered more complications. ... Women reported having no complications after their abortions in 91 percent of the abortions performed by doctors and 86 percent of those performed by midwives. In contrast, only 24 percent of the self-induced abortions were without complications.[13] ...

As more women had abortions during the Depression, and perhaps more turned to self-induced measures because of their new poverty, growing numbers of women entered the nation's hospitals for care following their illegal abortions. The Depression deepened an earlier trend toward the hospitalization of women who had abortion-related complications in public hospitals. As childbirth gradually moved into the hospital, so too did abortion. ... One intern at Cook County Hospital recalled that in 1928 she saw at least thirty or forty abortion cases in the month and a half she worked there; or, one woman a day and several hundred women a year entered the hospital because of postabortion complications. In 1934, the County Hospital admitted 1,159 abortion cases, and reported twenty-two abortion-related deaths that year.[14] ...

Doctors and public health reformers began to realize the importance of illegal abortion as a contributor to maternal mortality. ... [Obstetrician Frederick J.] Taussig estimated that approximately fifteen thousand women died every year in the United States because of abortion.[15] ... In hospital wards, doctors saw women with septic infections, perforations of the uterus, hemorrhages, and mutilation of intestines and other organs caused by self-induced abortions or ineptly performed operations.

The hospital atmosphere ... helped forge a liberal consensus within a section of the medical profession about the horrors of self-induced and poorly performed criminal abortions, together with an acceptance of performing abortions for needy patients or referring them to abortionists. ...

Most cities had several physicians who "specialized" in abortion, and many small towns had at least one physician-abortionist. ...

In the mid-1930s one businessman set up a chain of abortion clinics in cities on the West Coast. Doctors Gabler, Keemer, and Timanus, of Chicago, Detroit, and Baltimore respectively, were physician-abortionists who performed abortions for tens of thousands of women during the 1930s. The decades-long existence of these specialty practices points to the tolerance and accessibility of abortion during these years.

Physician-abortionists practiced in a legally and medically gray area. It was not always clear whether they performed illegal abortions or legal, therapeutic abortions. As physicians, the law allowed them to perform therapeutic abortions in order to preserve a woman's life, but abortion was illegal and frowned upon by the profession. What made physician-abortionists different from other doctors was the volume of abortions performed, often to the exclusion of other medical practice. As long as these physicians received referrals from other physicians, practiced safely, and avoided police interference, they might consider the abortions to be therapeutic. Yet any physician who regularly performed abortions also knew that the procedure was criminal and that he or she practiced on a fine line. . . .

It is difficult for the historian to gain access to patient records, and this is particularly true for an illegal procedure. Yet I have uncovered records of abortion patients and have reconstructed, for the first time, the daily practice of an underground abortion clinic and the characteristics of its clientele. Seventy patient records of women who had abortions at a Chicago clinic owned by Dr. Josephine Gabler have been preserved in legal documents. . . . The Gabler clinic (later run by Ada Martin) serves as a case study of a specialty practice and reveals the abortion experiences of many women who found physician-abortionists.[16]

Dr. Josephine Gabler was a major source of abortions for Chicago women and other Midwesterners in the 1930s. She graduated from an Illinois medical school in 1905 and received her Illinois medical license that year. She established herself as a specialist in abortion by the late 1920s, perhaps earlier. Over eighteen thousand abortions were performed at her State Street office between 1932 and 1941.[17] In other words, the clinic provided approximately two thousand abortions a year—about five a day, if it operated seven days a week. Dr. Gabler, and other doctors who worked at the State Street office, provided needed abortion services to women from the entire region, including patients from Illinois, Indiana, Michigan, and Wisconsin. . . .

The Gabler-Martin clinic demonstrates that doctors have been more responsive to the demands of their female patients—even demands for an illegal procedure—than previously suspected. Over two hundred doctors,

including some of Chicago's most prominent physicians and AMA members, referred patients to Gabler and Martin for abortions.[18] . . .

When Mrs. Helen B. learned of her pregnancy in 1940, she wanted an abortion. She "finally persuaded" her doctor that she needed an abortion and was given Dr. Josephine Gabler's business card.[19] The use of business cards itself emphasizes the openness of abortion practice in this period. . . .

Gabler and Martin showed their appreciation for referrals—and encouraged their colleagues and allies to keep referring—by paying commissions to those who sent patients. Investigators reported that the payments were usually fifteen dollars each, which was about a quarter of the average fee for abortion. . . .

The other major path to an abortionist's office was through women's personal networks. An abortionist's name and address were critical information, which women shared with each other. In this sample, of the cases where the source of the referral is identifiable, almost a third of the patients found their way to the clinic through friends. . . . Every woman who went to 190 North State Street for an abortion became a potential source of information for others in the same predicament. . . .

In many ways, the experience of getting an abortion at the State Street clinic was like going into any other doctor's office for medical care. Referrals from physicians, note taking by a receptionist, women dressed in white uniforms, instruments and delivery tables, and the instructions for after-care were all typical in a doctor's office—and familiar to women who had previously delivered babies in hospitals. The women received anesthesia and, apparently, a dilation and curettage of the uterus—the same procedure they would have had if they had a legal, therapeutic abortion in the hospital.

Nonetheless, the criminality of abortion made its practice clandestine. Two safeguards designed to shield the people performing abortions made the procedures in Martin's office different from legal, hospital procedures: covering the eyes of patients in order to make identifying the physician-abortionist impossible and warning women not to go to anyone else if they experienced complications. The clinic did not abandon its clients if problems developed following the abortion, but they did not want them going to physicians or local hospitals who might alert authorities.

The majority of women in the State Street patient records were married when they had their abortions.... Over half of the married women (thirty-two women, or 57 percent) had children. Over a third of these women had children under two years old. Mothers seemed strongly motivated to avoid having two babies in diapers at once....

A second, and large, group of the married women (twenty-four, or 43 percent) had no children at all. This is not what we would expect; we have learned that married women used birth control and abortion after they had children, not before....

Could they represent a significant number of married couples who intended to have no children at all? Since the records do not say how long they had been married, it is possible that these were abortions of prebridal pregnancies. Perhaps some worried about extramarital affairs. Some may have been college students or married to students. Perhaps they needed an abortion because they could not risk losing their jobs. Probably most who had abortions in the early years of their marriages had children later. Class could shape reproduction in complicated ways. Working women and more affluent college women found it necessary to delay childbearing for different reasons and at different times.

The age range of the State Street patients reflected the diversity of women's reproductive patterns and needs. The ages of the women having abortions in this sample ranged from eighteen to forty-eight years.... Their average age was twenty-seven years, but over half were under twenty-five. In 1992, for comparison, most of the women who had abortions were unmarried and under twenty-five years old.[20] ... The difference is that most of the women in the Martin case records ended their pregnancies within the context of marriage: 80 percent of the Gabler-Martin clinic patients were married; now, 80 percent are unmarried. Today, most of the women who have abortions do so when they are single and finishing high school or college and expect to bear children later.[21] ...

It is difficult to determine the class of ... the patients at 190 North State Street, but it seems to have been a mixed group. The records of this office show we cannot assume that working-class women were never able to get safe abortions from physicians.... Information about income or the occupation of the woman's husband, if married, was not included in the patient records, but the records show that at least a third of the women worked for wages....

The racial composition of the women who relied upon the abortion services of Dr. Gabler is even more obscure. There is no racial information in the patient records....

Gabler and Martin could provide illegal abortions openly because they paid for protection from the law. Bribery of police and prosecutors underpinned the abortion practice. We only know of the corruption of legal authorities in Chicago because police officer Daniel Moriarity tried to kill Martin in order to silence her.[22] ...

The office at 190 North State Street where thousands of women obtained abortions from a skilled practitioner was not a rarity.[23] ...

In Detroit, African American physicians might refer patients to Dr. Edgar Bass Keemer Jr.... Throughout his career as an abortionist, which lasted into the 1970s, Keemer served primarily poor women and black women. In thirty-five years, he performed over thirty thousand abortions.[24] ...

In Baltimore, reputable physicians referred their patients to Dr. George Loutrell Timanus, one of two well-known physician-abortionists in [the city]. Dr. Timanus had a close relationship to Baltimore's white medical elite at Johns Hopkins University, where the faculty taught Timanus's techniques to their students and called him a friend....

Doctors Gabler, Keemer, and Timanus represent a larger pattern of medical involvement in illegal abortion and an expansion of the medical provision of abortions during the 1930s.... [Their practices were not temporary, but established; they were not located in back alleys, but on main streets. Dr. Gabler had a business card; Dr. Timanus was listed in the phone book and his office had a sign in front.]

Thousands of women obtained abortions from physicians in conventional medical settings and suffered no complications afterwards.... A mixed group of patients—working-class and middle-class women, white and black—reached these trusted physicians. . . .

NOTES

1. "Unemployment," *Birth Control Review (BCR)* 5 (May 1931):131.

2. Lois Rita Helmbold, "Beyond the Family Economy: Black and White Working-Class Women During the Great Depression," *Feminist Studies* 13 (Fall 1987):640–641; A. J. Rongy, *Abortion: Legal or Illegal?* (New York: Vanguard Press, 1933), p. 111.

3. Alice Kessler-Harris, *Out to Work: A History of Wage-Earning Women in the United States* (Oxford: Oxford University Press, 1982), pp. 256–257; quotations from typed letter from Charleston, IL 61920, April 20, 1985, "Silent No More" Campaign, National Abortion Rights Action League (NARAL), Chicago.

4. Paul H. Gebhard et al., *Pregnancy, Birth and Abortion* (New York: Harper and Brothers and Paul B. Hoeber Medical Books, 1958), pp. 113–114, 140, table 55. Since much of the data comes from the earlier Kinsey studies on sexuality and this report came out of his institute, hereafter I refer to this book in the text as the Kinsey report or study on abortion.

5. The percentage of first pregnancies aborted in this young generation was no more than 10 percent, but it was more than double the rate of earlier generations of women.

6. Charles H. Garvin, "The Negro Doctor's Task," *BCR* 16 (November 1932):270.

7. Endre K. Brunner and Louis Newton, "Abortions in Relation to Viable Births in 10,609 Pregnancies: A Study Based on 4,500 Clinic Histories," *American Journal of Obstetrics and Gynecology* 38 (July 1939):82–83, 88.

8. Gebhard et al., *Pregnancy, Birth and Abortion*, p. 162. Regina G. Kunzel also finds class difference among African-Americans in their use of maternity homes; Kunzel, *Fallen Women, Problem Girls: Unmarried Mothers and the Professionalization of Social Work, 1890–1945* (New Haven: Yale University Press, 1993), p. 73.

9. Brunner and Newton, "Abortions in Relation to Viable Births," pp. 85, 90.

10. Ibid., p. 87, fig. 4.

11. Gebhard et al., *Pregnancy, Birth and Abortion*, pp. 64–65, 114–118.

12. Ibid., pp. 194–195, 198.

13. Regine K. Stix, "A Study of Pregnancy Wastage," *Milbank Memorial Fund Quarterly* 13 (October 1935):362–363.

14. Dr. Gertrude Engbring in Transcript of *People v. Heissler*, 338 Ill. 596 (1930), Case Files, vault no. 44783, Supreme Court of Illinois, Record Series 901, Illinois State Archives, Springfield; Augusta Weber, "Confidential Material Compiled for Joint Commission on Accreditation, June 1964," box 5, "Obstetrics Department—Accreditation 1964," Office of the Administrator, Cook County Hospital Archives. An "Abortion Service" was opened at Harlem Hospital in 1935. Peter Marshall Murray and L. B. Winkelstein, "Incomplete Abortion: An Evaluation of Diagnosis and Treatment of 727 Consecutive Cases of Incomplete Abortions," *Harlem Hospital Bulletin* 3 (June 1950):31.

15. Fred J. Taussig, "Abortion in Relation to Fetal and Maternal Welfare," *American Journal of Obstetrics and Gynecology*, p. 872.

16. This case study is based on patient records and other legal documents discovered in the Transcript of *People v. Martin*, 382 Ill. 192 (1943), Case Files, vault no. 51699, Supreme Court of Illinois, Record Series 901.

17. Supplemental Report, Statement of Gordon B. Nash, Assistant State's Attorney, April 23, 1942, in Transcript of *People v. Martin*.

18. Of the eighteen doctors named in the patient records, eleven could be identified. (Sometimes only a last name was included on the record.) All eleven were AMA members and eight were specialists of various types.

19. Mrs. Helen B. in transcript of *People v. Martin*.

20. "Abortion Surveillance: Preliminary Data— United States, 1992," *Morbidity and Mortality Weekly Report: CDC Surveillance Summaries* 43 (December 23, 1994):930, 932, table I.

21. Recent abortion data show the trend to delaying childbearing. Teenagers make up a smaller proportion of the women having abortions than in the past: in 1972, 33 percent of the women who had abortions were nineteen years old or less; in 1992, teenagers were only 20 percent of the women having abortions, and women twenty-five or older made up 45 percent of the women having abortions. "Abortion Surveillance," p. 932, table I.

22. As a police officer, Moriarity received a little less than $2,500 per year. Quotations in George Wright, "Tells Bribe Behind Killing," *Chicago Daily Tribune*, May 2, 1941, p. 1.

23. Other doctors who appear to have specialized in abortion in Chicago include Dr. William E. Shelton, who may have been involved with Martin ("Dr. William Eugene Shelton," *Daily Tribune*, September 27, 1928; "Loop Physician Held in Abortion Conspiracy Case," *Daily Tribune*, November 21, 1940); Dr. Joseph A. Khamis ("Doctor Accused Second Time as an Abortionist," *Daily Tribune*, August 18, 1942); Dr. Justin L. Mitchell (*People v. Mitchell*, 368 Ill. 399); and Dr. Edward Peyser (*People v. Peyser*, 380 Ill. 404). All newspaper clippings in Abortionists Files, Historical Health Fraud Collection, American Medical Association, Chicago.

24. Ed Keemer, *Confessions of a Pro-Life Abortionist* (Detroit: Vinco Press, 1980), pp. 13, 18, 27, 29, 89–93.

JACQUELINE JONES
Harder Times: The Great Depression

The chronic scarcity of jobs that characterized the Appalachian South where the Elizabethton strike occurred became a national phenomenon in the 1930s. As the Great Depression tightened its hold on the economy, the plight of America's working people generated protest in the farm belt as well as industrial centers. Government aid eventually alleviated some of the suffering while New Deal legislation and a revitalized labor movement brought improved working conditions. Nevertheless many workers, agricultural as well as industrial, struggled daily to survive. They, especially, remained at the mercy of any employers who would hire them.

African Americans were especially vulnerable. Jacqueline Jones's study of black women reminds us once again of the extent to which race and class shape women's experience. Consider the difference that race made in both the job opportunities available to women in the 1930s and the debate about whether married women should work. Observe how the experience of black domestics demonstrated the power of race and class to override "the bonds of womanhood." Note, too, how the speed-ups generating such dissatisfaction among the textile workers in the 1920s described by Hall were extended in the 1930s to private household service.

High unemployment rates among their husbands and sons forced many white wives to enter the labor market for the first time in the 1930s.[1] But black men experienced even higher rates of joblessness, causing their wives to cling more desperately to the positions they already had, despite declining wages and deteriorating working conditions. During the Great Depression, most black women maintained only a precarious hold on gainful employment; their positions as family breadwinners depended upon, in the words of one social worker, "the breath of chance, to say nothing of the winds of economic change."[2] Unemployment statistics for the 1930s can be misleading because they do not reveal the impact of a shifting occupational structure on job options for women of the two races. Just as significantly, the relatively high rate of black females' participation in the labor force obscures the highly temporary and degrading nature of their work experiences. Specifically, most of these women could find only seasonal or part-time employment; racial and sexual discrimination deprived them of a living wage no matter how hard they labored; and they endured a degree and type of workplace exploitation for which the mere fact of having a job could not compensate. During the decade, nine out of ten black women workers toiled as agricultural laborers or domestic servants. Various pieces of federal legislation designed to protect and raise the purchasing power of workers (most notably the National Industrial Recovery Act [1933], the Social Security Act [1935], and the Fair Labor Standards Act [1938]) exempted these two groups of workers from their provisions. In essence, then, no more than 10 percent of gainfully employed black women derived any direct benefit from the new federal policies related to minimum wages, maximum hours, unemployment compensation, and social security.[3]

Despite the rapid decline in a wide variety of indicators related to production and economic growth in the early 1930s, and despite the sluggishness of the pre-1941 recovery period, the numbers and kinds of job opportunities for white women expanded, as did their need to help supplement household income. The clerical sector grew (as it had in the 1920s) and would continue to do so in the 1940s, and in the process attracted more and more women into the work force and employed a larger proportion of all white women workers. (The percentage of white women who were gainful workers steadily increased throughout the period 1920 to 1940 from 21.3 to 24.1 percent of all adult females.) Recent historians have stressed the "benefits of labor segregation" for women, arguing that, at least during the early part of the depression decade, unemployment in the male-dominated industrial sector was generally greater than in the female-dominated areas of sales, communications, and secretarial work. But this was a race-specific phenomenon. In a job market segmented by both race and sex, black women had no access to white women's work even though (or perhaps because) it was deemed integral to both industrial capitalism and the burgeoning federal bureaucracy. In 1940 one-third of all white, but only 1.3 percent of all black, working women had clerical jobs. On the other hand, 60 percent of all black female workers were domestic servants; the figure for white women was only 10 percent.[4] . . .

KITCHEN SPEED-UPS: DOMESTIC SERVICE

Contemporary literary and photographic images of a stricken nation showed dejected white men waiting in line for food, jobs, and relief. Yet observers sensitive to the racial dimensions of the crisis provided an alternative symbol—that of a middle-aged black woman in a thin, shabby coat and men's shoes, standing on a street corner in the dead of winter and offering her housecleaning services for 10 cents an hour. If the migrant labor camp symbolized the black agricultural worker's descent into economic marginality, then the "slave markets" in northern cities revealed a similar fate for domestic servants.

"The 'mart' is but a miniature mirror of our economic battle front," wrote two investigative reporters in a 1935 issue of the NAACP's monthly journal, *The Crisis*. A creature of the depression, the slave market consisted of groups of black women, aged seventeen to seventy, who waited on sidewalks for white women to drive up and offer them a day's work. The Bronx market, composed of several small ones—it was estimated that New York City had two hundred altogether—received the most attention from writers during the decade, though the general phenomenon recurred throughout other major cities. Before 1929, many New York domestics had worked for wealthy white families on Long Island. Their new employers, some of them working-class women themselves, paid as little as $5.00 weekly for full-time laborers to wash windows and clothes, iron (as many as twenty-one shirts a shift), and wax floors. The black women earned radically depressed wages: lunch and 35 cents for six hours of work, or $1.87 for an eight-hour day. They had to guard against various ruses that would deprive them of even this pittance—for example, a clock turned back an hour, the promised carfare that never materialized at the end of the day. As individuals they felt trapped, literally and figuratively pushed to the limits of their endurance. A thirty-year-old woman told federal interviewer Vivian Morris that she hated the people she worked for: "Dey's mean, 'ceitful, an' 'ain' hones'; but what ah'm gonna do? Ah got to live—got to hab a place to steh," and so she would talk her way into a job by boasting of her muscle power. But some days groups of women would spontaneously organize themselves and "run off the corner" those job seekers "who persist[ed] in working for less than thirty cents an hour."[5]

Unlike their country cousins, domestics contended directly with white competitors pushed out of their factory and waitressing jobs. The agricultural labor system served as a giant sieve; for the most part, displaced farm families went to the city rather than vying for the remaining tenant positions. The urban economy had no comparable avenues of escape; it was a giant pressure cooker, forcing the unemployed to look for positions in occupations less prestigious than the ones they held formerly or, in the event of ultimate failure, to seek some form of charity or public assistance. A 1937 Women's Bureau survey of destitute women in Chicago revealed that, although only 37 percent of native-born white women listed their "usual occupation" as domestic service, a much greater number had tried to take advantage of employers' preferences for white servants before they gave up the quest for jobs altogether and applied for relief. Meanwhile, the 81 percent of black women who had worked in service had nowhere else to go. Under these circumstances, the mere act of hiring a black woman seemed to some to represent a humanitarian gesture. In 1934 an observer of the social-welfare scene noted approvingly, with unintentional irony, that "From Mistress Martha Washington to Mistress Eleanor Roosevelt is not such a long time as time goes. There may be some significance in the fact that the household of the first First Lady was manned by Negro servants and the present First Lady has followed her example."[6]

The history of domestic service in the 1930s provides a fascinating case study of the lengths to which whites would go in exploiting a captive labor force. Those who employed live-in servants in some cases cut their wages, charged extra for room and board, or lengthened on-duty hours. But it was in the area of day work that housewives elevated labor-expanding and money-saving methods to a fine art. General speed-ups were common in private homes throughout the North and South. Among the best bargains were children and teenagers; in Indianola, Mississippi, a sixteen-year-old black girl worked from 6 A.M. to 7 P.M. daily for $1.50 a week. In the same town a maid could be instructed to do her regular chores, plus those of the recently fired cook, for less pay than she had received previously. (A survey of Mississippi's domestics revealed that the average weekly pay was less than $2.00.) Some women received only carfare, clothing, or lunch for a day's work. Northern white women also lowered wages drastically. In 1932 Philadelphia domestics earned $5.00 to $12.00 for a forty-eight- to sixty-seven-hour work week. Three years later they took home the same amount of money for ninety hours' worth of scrubbing, washing, and cooking (an hourly wage of 15 cents).[7]

The deteriorating working conditions of domestic servants reflected the conscious choices of individual whites who took advantage of the abundant labor supply. Social workers recorded conversations with potential employers seeking "bright, lively" domestics (with the very best references) to do all the cooking, cleaning, laundry, and childcare for very little pay, because, in the words of one Pittsburgh woman, "There are so many people out of work that I am sure I can find a girl for $6.00 a week." Indeed, at times it seemed as if there existed a perversely negative relationship between expectations and compensation. An eighty-three-year-old South Carolina black woman, Jessie Sparrow, resisted working on Sundays because, she told an interviewer in 1937, "when dey pays you dat little bit of money, dey wants every bit your time." A southern white man demonstrated his own brand of logic when he "admitted as a matter of course that his cook was underpaid, but explained that this was necessary, since, if he gave her more money, she might soon have so much that she would no longer be willing to work for him."[8]

The field of domestic service was virtually unaffected by national and state welfare policies. In the 1930s Women's Bureau officials tried to compensate for this inaction with a flurry of correspondence, radio and luncheon-meeting speeches, and voluntary guidelines related to the "servant problem." In her talks on the subject, bureau head Mary Anderson tried to appeal to employers' sense of fairness when she suggested that they draw up job descriptions, guard against accidents in the workplace, and establish reasonable hours and wages. But the few housewives privy to Anderson's exhortations were not inclined to heed them, especially when confronted by a seemingly accommodating "slave" on the street corner. Consequently, black domestic workers in several cities, often under the sponsorship of a local Young Women's Christian Association, Urban League branch, or labor union, made heroic attempts to form employees' organizations that would set uniform standards for service. However, they remained a shifting, amorphous group immune to large-scale organizational efforts. For example, founded in 1934 and affiliated with Building Service Union Local 149 (AFL), the New York Domestic Workers Union had only 1,000 (out of a potential of 100,000) members four years later. It advocated two five-hour shifts six days a week and insisted, "last but not least, no window washing." Baltimore's Domestic Workers Union (in the CIO fold) also welcomed members of both races and remained a relatively insignificant force in the regulation of wages and working conditions. Without adequate financial resources, leaders like New York's

Dora Jones labored to organize women who "still believe in widespread propaganda that all unions are rackets." As a result, efforts by domestics to control wage rates informally through peer pressure or failure to report for work as promised represented spontaneous job actions more widespread and successful than official "union" activity.[9]

During the depression, a long life of work was the corollary of a long day of work. Black women between the ages of twenty-five and sixty-five worked at consistently high rates; they simply could not rely on children or grandchildren to support them in their old age. The Federal Writers Project interviews with former slaves recorded in the late 1930s contain hundreds of examples of women in their seventies and eighties still cooking, cleaning, or hoeing for wages on a sporadic basis in order to keep themselves and their dependents alive. An interviewer described the seventy-seven-year-old widow Mandy Leslie of Fairhope, Alabama, as "a pillar of strength and comfort to several white households" because she did their washing and ironing every week. Living alone, her children gone, this elderly woman boiled clothes in an iron pot heated by a fire, and then rubbed them on a washboard and hung them on lines so they could be ironed the following day. Such was the price exacted from black women for the "strength and comfort" they provided whites.[10]

NOTES

1. Lois Scharf, *To Work and to Wed: Female Employment, Feminism, and the Great Depression* (Westport, Conn.: Greenwood Press, 1980), pp. 107–8. . . .

2. Marion Cuthbert, "Problems Facing Negro Young Women," *Opportunity* 14 (Feb. 1936):47–49.

3. U.S. Department of Commerce, Bureau of the Census, *The Labor Force*, Pt. 1, U.S. Summary, p. 90; Mary Elizabeth Pidgeon, "Employed Women Under N.R.A. Codes," United States Department of Labor, Women's Bureau, *Bulletin*, no. 130 (1935); "Women at Work: A Century of Industrial Change," United States Department of Labor, Women's Bureau, *Bulletin*, no. 161 (1939). . . .

4. Alice Kessler-Harris, *Out to Work: A History of Wage-Earning Women in the United States* (New York: Oxford University Press, 1982), pp. 250–72; Ruth Milkman, "Women's Work and Economic Crisis: Some Lessons of the Great Depression," *Review of Radical Political Economics* 8 (Spring 1976):73–97; Winifred D. Wandersee, *Women's Work and Family*

Values, 1920–1940 (Cambridge, Mass.: Harvard University Press, 1981), pp. 84–102; U.S. Dept. of Commerce, Bureau of the Census, *The Labor Force*, Pt. 1, U.S. Summary, p. 90.

5. Ella Baker and Marvel Cooke, "The Bronx Slave Market," *Crisis* 42 (Nov. 1935):330, 340; Vivian Morris, "Bronx Slave Market," Dec. 6, 1938, Federal Writers Project, Negro Folklore Division (New York), p. 1, Archive of Folk Song, Manuscript Division, Library of Congress, Washington, D.C. . . .

6. Harriet A. Byrne and Cecile Hillyer, "Unattached Women on Relief in Chicago, 1937," United States Department of Labor, Women's Bureau, *Bulletin*, no. 158 (1938); Elmer Anderson Carter, "The Negro Household Employee," *Woman's Press* 28 (July–Aug. 1934):351.

7. John Dollard, *Caste and Class in a Southern Town* (New Haven, Conn.: Yale University Press, 1937), pp. 107–8; Jean Collier Brown, "The Negro Woman Worker," United States Department of Labor, Women's Bureau, no. 165 (1938), pp. 3–4, 7; Charles T. Haley, "To Do Good and Do Well: Middle-Class Blacks and the Depression, Philadelphia, 1929–1941" (Ph.D. diss., State University of New York at Binghamton, 1980), p. 59. . . .

8. Harold A. Lett, "Work: Negro Unemployed in Pittsburgh" *Opportunity* 9 (Mar. 1931):79–81; "Women Workers in Indianapolis," *Crisis* 37 (June 1930):189–91; *The American Slave: A Composite Autobiography*, ed. George Rawick, 41 vols., Series 1, Supp. Series 1 and 2 (Westport, Conn.: Greenwood Press, 1972, 1978, 1979), Series 1, *South Carolina Narratives*, pt. IV, vol. 3, p. 146; Hortense Powdermaker, *After Freedom: A Cultural Study in the Deep South* (New York: Viking, 1939), pp. 117–18.

9. "The Domestic Worker of Today," Radio Talk by Miss Mary Anderson, Sept. 21, 1932, Station WJAY, sponsored by Cleveland Parent Teachers Association, Speeches No. 112 (Box 71), Women's Bureau Collection, Department of Labor Archives, Record Group 86, National Archives, Washington, D.C.; Dora Jones quoted in "The Domestic Workers' Union," in *Black Women in White America: A Documentary History*, ed. Gerda Lerner, (New York: Pantheon, 1972), pp. 231–34. On the New York union, see Evelyn Seeley, "Our Feudal Housewives," *The Nation* 46 (May 28, 1938):613–15; on Baltimore, see article reprinted from *Baltimore Afro-American*, Oct. 1936, in *The Black Worker: A Documentary History from Colonial Times to the Present*, vol. 6, *The Era of Post-War Prosperity and the Great Depression, 1920–1936*, eds. Philip S. Foner and Ronald L. Lewis (Philadelphia: Temple University Press, 1981), pp. 184–85; Roderick N. Ryon, "An Ambiguous Legacy: Baltimore Blacks and the CIO, 1936–1941," *Journal of Negro History* 65 (Winter 1980):29. For evidence of the Urban League's efforts in this area, see "Program of Mass Meeting of General House Work Employees, Sept. 21, 1933 (St. Louis)" in Correspondence—Household (Domestic) File, General Correspondence Prior to 1934 (Box 926), Women's Bureau Collection, RG 86, National Archives.

10. Rawick, ed., *American Slave, Alabama Narratives*, vol. 6, p. 251.

DOCUMENT: Struggling to Unionize

> *Genora Johnson Dollinger, " . . . Once she understands she is standing in defense of her family—well, God, don't fool around with that woman then"*

The 1930s were a period of intense labor organizing. The American Federation of Labor (AFL) had found it could survive in a period of unrestricted immigration (when the supply of unskilled labor was inexhaustible) only by organizing highly skilled workers in particular crafts. The Congress of Industrial Organizations (CIO), as its name implies, tried a different and very difficult approach: organizing all the workers in an entire industry, such as the automobile industry or the electrical industry. To attempt this during the Depression was an enormous challenge. The one advantage organizers had was that President Franklin Roosevelt, unlike his predecessors, refused to use the power of the federal government against the workers, believing they had a right to unionize. His position generated biting criticism in the business community and cost him heavily among more prosperous constituents; however, it brought organized labor solidly into Democratic ranks.

The huge difficulty of the CIO's task, the severe hardships that the workers and their families were suffering, and the preponderance of power which employers had at their disposal—all are illuminated in this powerful account of the famous 1936 strike at General Motors in Flint, Michigan. But that is only part of the story. What Dollinger reveals so powerfully is her own role and that of the women who joined her in the Women's Emergency Brigade.

What propelled Dollinger to assume leadership, and what inspired the women who answered her call to perform such acts of courage? How do you account for the union's response to their actions once victory had been won? What does this suggest about the potential ability of women at the grassroots level, with few resources at their disposal, to help change the course of history?

. . . When the strike started, my mother—without my father's knowledge—agreed to take care of my two little boys. . . . I was then relatively free, and immediately went to Roy Reuther and Robert Travis—those were the UAW organizers—and I volunteered to help. I was told to go to the kitchen and peel potatoes, but I said there were plenty of others who could do that, including some of the men. So they gave me a job setting up a press clipping bureau. . . . I decided anyone sitting with a pair of shears could handle that job, so I organized a sign painting department. . . . I remember one sign, my own little snow-suited two-year-old holding it high: "My daddy strikes for us little tykes." . . .

. . . On December 30, the police attempted to break the strike at Fisher 2. . . . People came to watch the police shooting us with rifle bullets, buckshot, and tear gas. We had nothing but rocks and car door hinges, but we picked up the tear gas bombs and heaved them back

From Jeane Westin, *Making Do: How Women Survived the '30s* (Chicago: Follett Publishing Company, 1976), pp. 312–318.

at the police before they exploded. Men were going down, and fourteen people were shot that night, one seriously. I saw blood flowing.

But before this happened union men had herded all the women to safety—all except me. I said, "I've got just as strong weapons as you've got. You've got no guns, neither have I. I can fight as well as you." I was the only woman too stubborn to leave, so I stayed down there. . . .

At this point Victor [Reuther] privately told some of us, "We may have lost this battle, but we're not losing the war." He seemed to be preparing us for defeat on this night. It was then I asked him: "Victor, can I speak to them?" And he replied, "We've got nothing to lose." He was a fine person, but still I could feel that he didn't think a woman could do much in this situation.

I got up on the sound car—I know it was an electrifying thing . . . a woman's voice calling to the people of Flint after so many hours of fighting . . . and I said, "I'm talking especially to you women out there. You didn't know that mothers"—I meant myself—"are being fired on by the police. The police are cowards enough to fire into the bellies of unarmed men. Aren't they also cowards to fire at mothers of little children? I'm asking you women out there behind the barricades to break through those police lines. Come down here and stand with your brothers, your sons, your sweethearts, your husbands and help us win this fight."

And so help me, I could hardly believe it—one woman started walking toward us. The police grabbed at her and she walked right out of her coat. She marched down, other women following her—the police didn't dare shoot all those women in the back. Then the union men broke through. The battle was over and the union had won.

The women had saved the day. It was then that I realized how much power women had, and I proceeded to organize the Women's Emergency Brigade. . . . We bought red berets and made arm bands with the white letters "EB" for Emergency Brigade. . . .

Listen, I met some of the finest women I have ever come across in my life. When the occasion demands it of a woman and once she understands that she's standing in defense of her family—well, God, *don't fool around with that woman then*. . . .

I saw women stand up under circumstances where big men ran around the corner and hid under a car. I have seen them rise up when I would not have believed they could. . . .

Finally, you know, everything just came to a head. With so many workers' homes without sufficient food and heat in the freezing January temperatures, and powerful General Motors benefiting from the unequal contest . . . well, it came time for a major decision. Plant 4, the largest plant in the Chevrolet division of ten plants, produced all the motors for Chevrolet throughout the country. That plant became our target. . . .

We pretended to strike one of the other Chevrolet plants, Plant 9, which was far removed on the other side of the whole complex and had that action drawing all the company police, city police, and Pinkerton agents . . . a diversionary tactic, you see. The Women's Emergency Brigade was there and they broke the windows to allow air to get in to the tear-gassed union men. Women just played a fantastic role over there at Plant 9.

Now, my husband Kermit's assignment was to shut down Plant 4, the target plant. But I dared not let the brigade know about it because it had to be such a tight secret. The whole union movement had been infiltrated with company spies. After the Plant 9 action, I sent the brigade back to headquarters and with my five lieutenants, walked around the city streets that paralleled the big Chevrolet compound. . . .

We strolled over to Plant 4 which the union men were attempting to shut down. I was very nervous because I knew it was a life and death matter for my husband and the other men inside. By the time we got over there there was a great deal of confusion. . . .

The plant foreman and his hired agents were giving them trouble. . . . The men yelled to us, "My God, we're having an awful time. Don't let anybody come in through the front gate on Chevrolet Avenue." Naturally, that was a big order, so I sent one of my lieutenants to call headquarters. "Tell the brigade to come at once," I told her. And the five of us left strung ourselves across the front gate.

When the city police got word what was happening they came, seventy-five of them, and found us women on the gate. We defied them . . . told them they would have to go in over our dead bodies. . . . Eighty percent had relatives working under those horrible conditions in the plants. "Look," I said, "if you worked in this plant, and you were being driven crazy, and your health was broken down, wouldn't you expect your wife to come down here to see what she could do?"

It threw them off their guard and they began answering my arguments, just long enough. By the time they got provoked and said, "Well, we've got a job to do," and started pushing us, at that point the brigade came down Chevrolet Avenue. There came hundreds of those red berets bobbing up and down with the American flag at their head, singing "Solidarity Forever." The sound of it, from all those voices, just flooded the whole area.

They quickly set up an oval picket line in front of the main gate. This meant the police would have to club and shoot these women,

and they had no stomach for that. Then the truck arrived filled with union men, and God, it dawned on me, *we'd saved the gate.*

The union had closed the huge and valuable Plant 4 with another sit-down strike. Soon after, Governor Frank Murphy declared martial law and ordered negotiations started. On February 11th, an agreement was reached recognizing unions in GM plants across the nation. That was a much greater victory than our small, inexperienced union ever expected to win. . . .

It's a measure of the strength of those women of the Red Berets that they could perform so courageously in an atmosphere that was often hostile to them. We organized on our own without the benefit of professional leadership, and yet, we played a role, second to none, in the birth of a union and in changing working families' lives forever.

ALICE KESSLER-HARRIS
Designing Women and Old Fools: Writing Gender into Social Security Law

One historian has called the Social Security Act of 1935 "the most important single piece of social legislation in all American history . . . in terms of historical decisiveness and direct influence upon the lives of individual Americans."* It continues to sustain the modern welfare state, providing the basic foundation for old-age pensions and for unemployment insurance. Its conceptualization of how needy mothers and children could claim government assistance was not replaced for sixty years, and continues to haunt debates over welfare. (President Franklin Delano Roosevelt also hoped to include a national system of health care but could not find congressional support.)

*Kenneth S. Davis, *FDR, the New Deal Years, 1933–1937: A History* (New York: Random House, 1986), p. 437; see also, David M. Kennedy, *Freedom from Fear: The American People in Depression and War 1929–1945* (New York: Oxford University Press, 1999), pp. 257–273.

Excerpted from "Maintaining Self Respect" and "Questions of Equity," chs. 2 and 3 of *In Pursuit of Equity: Women, Men, and the Quest for Economic Citizenship in 20th Century America* by Alice Kessler-Harris (New York: Oxford University Press, 2001). © 2001 by Alice Kessler-Harris. Reprinted by permission of the author and Oxford University Press. Notes have been edited and renumbered.

The drive to design the legislation and shepherd it through Congress was led by Frances Perkins, secretary of labor and the first woman cabinet member. It was not easy; anything resembling charity was widely resented. Many compromises were made in order to get enough votes in Congress. Perhaps the most significant was the decision not to conceptualize benefits as entitlement to all citizens. Instead, benefits were linked to payroll taxes paid by employers and employees, who could conclude that they were only getting back what they had put in. The strategy left nearly half the working population—those who were seasonally or marginally employed—not covered. In the short run, there was a deflationary effect, as money paid into the Social Security Administration was pulled out of circulation. By 1937, efforts to amend the law were underway.

Politicians, economists, and other experts struggled to reform the law. They worked, for the most part, in good faith; they understood themselves to be seeking fairness and equity. They spoke of "the people" or "the worker"; their words were general and generic. But, as historian Alice Kessler-Harris read the minutes of meetings and considered the conversations and arguments, she found that the words they chose inadvertently revealed that the reformers' ideas of fairness rested on their own assumptions about work, family, and citizenship. Behind what they would have called "the common sense of the matter" lurked unspoken beliefs: that women are not serious or long-term workers and that African Americans were doomed to marginal employment.

What were the bureaucrats and legislators trying to accomplish by reforming the social security law? What were they trying to avoid? How did the law reflect their understanding of fairness? How did the new law reflect their understanding of the appropriate relationship between men and women? Between husbands and wives? Between blacks and whites? How did the new law reflect their understanding of the appropriate relationship between the citizen and the state? Why were concepts that had lasted since the 1930s attacked at the beginning of the 1970s?

[In the 1930s,] Americans moved from staunch opposition to federal government intervention in the lives of most men (but not women) to eager experiments with government mediation of every kind. Newly adopted social policies had many goals, but among the most dramatic were those connected with earning wages and keeping jobs. . . .

Achieving consensus on issues of who deserved employment and who could languish in uncompensated unemployment required some hard decisions, especially around questions of inclusion and exclusion. For the government to regulate working conditions and monitor benefits for those without jobs, legislators would have to agree on, and administrators determine, eligibility. Someone would have to decide who could be described as a "worker" and who didn't fit the picture; what jobs counted as work and what didn't; how many hours constituted full-time work

and how few precluded the activity from being called "work" at all. Innovative programs and policies demanded clarifications and classifications, precisely placing individuals in their relationships to paid and unpaid activities of different sorts. Each categorization opened or closed a door to the status, social rights, and economic security that measured progress toward economic citizenship for someone. Not only did benefits and entitlements rest on symbols of belonging, but so, ultimately, did the identities of workers, as well as their self-respect, political participation, and a newly differentiated set of meanings for crucial concepts like breadwinning, manhood, and citizenship.

The social constraints that guided these decisions had many roots, including most crucially ideologies of race and of American freedom and liberty. Historians are only now beginning to understand the degree to which they reflected a fundamental consensus around issues of race. But the new policies were also deeply embedded in a widespread and widely shared set of assumptions about gender. The Social Security Act of 1935 provides a case in point.

The pressing need of old people in the 1930s was for assistance or relief, not insurance. Advocates ranging from Abraham Epstein, whose American Association for Old Age Security proposed federal grants to the states, to Francis Townsend, whose plan to give everyone over sixty-five two hundred dollars a month to spend at will exceeded all others in popularity, stimulated the public to believe that the federal government could and should help the states solve this problem. Over this, there was little controversy. The very first title of the Social Security Act, Title I, provided states with matching grants to give relief to the needy aged and to care for unemployable old people. It replaced the mostly inadequate state-based programs with uniform federal standards and more generous grants than all but a handful of states had been able to provide. But Old Age Assistance came at a price: it subjected recipients to the indignities of means testing, fostering an unmanly spirit of dependency. . . .

Social insurance advocates sought to circumvent this anxiety with insurance rather than relief: They sought to prevent destitution and "obviate the necessity of public charity" by protecting family breadwinners against the potential hazards of industrial life. . . .

In the United States, the idea of government-subsidized insurance ran counter to the American grain, which reified independence and self-reliance. If there were to be any old age insurance program at all, its designers faced a formidable challenge: to remove aging workers from the labor force (which required that they be adequately supported) while affirming the dignity of pension recipients (which required that the program be self-supporting). To solve the labor force problem, policy makers imagined a program tied to work rather than to citizenship. Deciding which workers would be covered, however, created two classes of citizens: those who participated regularly in the kind of wage work where resolving unemployment seemed most important, and those who did not. In 1930,

men made up the vast majority of gainfully employed persons (75 percent of the total); about 12 percent of this number were classified by the census as "Negro." But most African American men did not work in the core industrial sectors, where issues of unemployment and labor force stability mattered most. And while women made up a quarter of all wage earners, their tenuous rights to work led many to assume they had little commitment to wage labor. . . . Despite women's own efforts to seek jobs during the depression, public opinion resolutely condemned wage work for those with husbands and fathers who could support them. Through the depression years, less than 15 percent of married women earned wages. Consciously or not, policy makers imagined a program available to most white wage-earning men that would omit "as a matter of course" most African Americans, by virtue of their positions in the labor market, and most women, whose positions appeared derivative of their marital partners.

Efforts to preserve the dignity of beneficiaries participated in the same gendered imagination. In the battle over unemployment compensation, men fought to maintain a sense of themselves as self-sufficient, independent, free, and capable of providing for their families and especially for the dependent women within them. In the struggle for Old Age Insurance (which we now call Social Security), participants deployed gender in more subtle but equally aggressive ways, not only to promote a conception of fairness that relied on the language of male dignity and female dependence but to ensure adequate support for all the aged. Gendered constructs helped to soothe a public increasingly enamored of government-funded assistance (which seemed to some policy makers an appropriate and to others a short-sighted and short-term solution). And they provided the language of family normalcy that convinced reluctant policy makers who remained skeptical of the capacity of an insurance program to solve employment problems without depending on general taxation. Ultimately, gendered conceptions provided the keystone that maintained public confidence in the core old age program and justified its redistributive goals. By providing economic security in particular ways and to particular people, old age insurance defined a new category of economic citizenship; at the same time . . . it fueled the desires of the excluded for fuller participation. . . .

No sooner had the Social Security Act been signed into law on August 14, 1935, than issues of adequacy began to surface. The bill provided for a 1 percent payroll tax, payable by employers, to be instituted in 1936 and matched by an equivalent contribution from every employee; benefits would not be payable until January 1942. The lag produced a surplus that, in a depression economy, threatened to exercise a deflationary effect. Most important, the exclusions written into the old age insurance provisions of the Social Security Act exempted nearly half the working population, evoking questions about its fairness as well as about its capacity to provide for the aged.[1] Because the program did not provide benefits to those who worked intermittently or for only a few years even when they worked in covered occupations, more than three-fifths of fully employed African Americans were denied coverage. Sixty percent of the excluded workers were female. . . . Probably as many as 85 percent of wage-earning black women were deprived of participation and benefits.[2]

At the same time, powerful popular support continued to build for the state-run, noncontributory old age assistance pensions that provided more generous benefits to the needy aged than those envisioned under Social Security for most contributors. . . . [These fueled] a sense of entitlement to old age pensions as a matter of justice. . . . Everyone knew that even when the insurance program started paying benefits in 1942, they would go at first to only three hundred thousand people, compared to the estimated two million needy elderly who would then be receiving noncontributory assistance.

. . . What was to be done? The solution seemed to be to spend the surplus. But how? And on whom? Despite the sharp and purposeful distinctions between adequacy and equity, the principle was violated by the very first set of amendments, which added old age insurance benefits for wives and widows who had not paid for them. No charitable impulse toward women motivated this act; no concern for their poverty inspired it. Rather, Congress added dependent wives and aged widows in order to shore up the legitimacy of a system

in trouble. It did this by enhancing the benefits of already covered (mostly white) males to ensure extra income to those who had aged wives to support and extra insurance to those with young children who survived them. These amendments, adopted in 1939, reinforced the prerogatives, self-images, and citizenship rights of some males while reaffirming racialized conceptions of gender. They redefined equity to incorporate more adequate and appropriate provision for some men, infusing the American system of entitlements with the peculiar imbalance from which it has struggled to release itself since the early 1970s.

In the spring of 1937, the Senate Finance Committee pressured the Social Security Board into creating a federal Advisory Council to suggest remedies. In May, when the new Advisory Council, which J. Douglas Brown agreed to chair, was announced, it consisted of twenty-four members. Six represented employers; six came from the labor movement; and twelve were designated as "public" participants, most of them academics and businessmen. [The public members included three women.][3] . . .

Together with the Social Security Board and several congressional committees, the Advisory Council worked through the following year and a half to recommend basic changes. Their charge from Congress was clear: They had to recommend a permanent way of dealing with ballooning reserves. They were to do this by beginning old age insurance benefits earlier than the originally mandated January 1942 start-up date and by making them larger. They were to explore the possibility of extending benefits to the disabled, to survivors, and to excluded groups. In the end, the council sidestepped the challenge of significantly extending insurance to most of the excluded groups, including the disabled, domestic servants, and agricultural workers and chose to rely instead on a new and expensive package of benefits for aged wives and survivors to reduce the surplus.[4]

The discussions over these alternatives tell us something about how invisible assumptions about men and women informed an entire network of social policy. For when the council moved toward emphasizing expanding benefits to those already covered, it utilized gender to mediate the conflict between adequacy and equity—a conflict in which women played little role but issues of manliness and womanliness assumed paramount importance. . . . The council, as its chairman, Douglas Brown, put it, had adopted "the principle of family protection."

The conversations within the Advisory Council and in Congress clarify the meaning of that principle. The council quickly agreed on pensions for fatherless children—an idea that already had popular support.[5] The Advisory Council adopted the notion rapidly because it promised to significantly reduce the numbers receiving means-tested assistance under both Title I (Old Age Assistance) and Title IV (Aid to Dependent Children) and strengthen the entire Social Security program by providing the illusion that their support was a product of insurance, the provenance of thoughtful and thrifty fathers. . . .

The Advisory Council relied on the same ideas of fairness to provide benefits for the widowed mothers of young children. These widows were to have benefits only as long as their children were young. The sums granted, and the restrictions on them, suggest that insurance for widowed mothers was conceived of as a matter of peace of mind for the husband. The widowed mother was to get three fourths of what her husband's pension would have been. The pension was granted as a matter of need, to enable "the widow to remain at home and care for the children."[6] It was to be reduced or eliminated if her earnings exceeded fifteen dollars a month (a tiny sum, even in 1939), thus encouraging her not to try to earn wages. In the likely event a widow's children reached eighteen before she reached sixty-five, the council recommended that all support end, to be resumed again when she became sixty-five, if in the meantime she had not remarried.[7] A young widow without children lacked any "rights" in her husband's contribution and got no benefits until and unless she grew old without remarrying.

Tying the dignity of men (defined by their capacity to provide) to the virtue of women (their willingness to remain dependent on men and to rear children) proved to be a continuing problem for young and old widows alike. The Social Security Board was fully cognizant of what it called the "widow's gap," noting at congressional hearings that "middle aged widows find it more difficult to become self-supporting." Still, . . . it deferred the annuity of

an under-sixty-five widow until she reached that age, on the grounds that "there is some likelihood that the widow may reenter covered employment."[8] Its sympathies for widows whose children were grown could not overcome internalized portraits of the family that fully rationalized its position: "They are likely to have more savings than younger widows and many of them have children who are grown and able to help them until they reach 65 years of age."[9]

The conversations within the council and the provisions finally adopted suggest that old age insurance was never imagined in terms of fair treatment to women—a product of the joint efforts of a marriage partnership. Consistent with the notion of sustaining male provision for the family, and over the objections of some members of the Social Security Board, the council voted to eliminate any annuity to a widow who remarried lest it construct a system that, in the words of one member, constituted widows "a prize for the fellow that has looked for it."[10] It recommended a plan that gave a wife no rights at all in the husband's insurance in consequence of his contributions to it, though demanding that she forfeit everything if she remarried clearly violated the equity principle that promised a return for what had been put in. . . .

. . . Once a woman was no longer dependent on the earnings of a particular male (dead or alive), the council contended, his support for her should cease, "rendering the woman ineligible whether she is the widow of an annuitant or the widow of a worker who dies before 65."[11] As long as she remained dependent on him, the level of the surviving widow's benefits . . . would be tied to the earnings of the deceased male, feeding the illusion that families deprived of a father or husband would nevertheless conceive him in the abstract as a continuing provider. . . .

We have no need to guess at the gendered images that sustained these seemingly arbitrary decisions. They pop up everywhere. For example, halfway through its eighteen months of deliberations, the Advisory Council confronted the question of what allowance to provide to aged widows. Should it be half of what their provider-husbands would have received? Two thirds? Three quarters? After several hours of debate over what proportion of a husband's benefit might appropriately descend to his widow, one member thought to ask a question that had escaped scrutiny: "Why should you pay the widow less than the individual himself gets if unmarried?" "She can look after herself better than he can," shot back the group's actuary.[12] But the question would not die. Two months later the Advisory Council returned to the issue. This time the chairman, prodded by one of its three female members, took up the defense. "A single woman" he suggested, can "adjust herself to a lower budget on account of the fact that she is used to doing her own housework whereas the single man has to go out to a restaurant."[13] By now, though, others had joined the fray. When the argument resumed at the next meeting, Douglas Brown tried to end it by painting a portrait everyone could accept. Lower rates for women made sense, he argued, his patience clearly worn thin,

> on the principle that it is more costly for the single man to live than for the single woman if she is able to avail herself of the home of the child. A woman is able to fit herself into the economy of the home of the child much better than the single man, that is, the grandmother helps in the raising of the children and helps in home affairs, whereas the aged grandfather is the man who sits out on the front porch and can't help much in the home.[14]

Such homely images shaped decisions that influenced the lives of almost everyone. They appeared at sporadic moments of unguarded conversation. Imagining women as irresponsible, the council voted to remove the original act's lump-sum death benefit to widows. "Such settlements," its minutes recorded, "are likely to be used for many other purposes long before her old age." Women could also be greedy and unprincipled. To avoid what it referred to as "deathbed marriages," the council adopted a clause requiring a pair to have been married and living together for at least a year before the husband died or reached sixty for his widow to be eligible for benefits on his account.[15] No benefits accrued to the woman who married a man over the age of sixty, unless she had lived with him for at least a year before he died.

The imagery became more complicated around the question of whether to increase benefits by providing more to every contributor or by enhancing the benefits of married men. Here the council clearly had in mind the

normative 1930s household in which wives earned little or nothing, and it wanted to protect the economic well-being of the husbands who supported them. No one noted that its image failed to account for the more than 15 percent of white and at least 33 percent of African American households in which women earned regular wages. Rather, members noted that even the original bill had been criticized by social insurance advocates like Abraham Epstein for its failure to include additional benefits for men with aged wives. . . . Advisory Council staff members, including Wilbur Cohen and Isadore Falk, . . . claimed that old age insurance would be perceived as more fair if it treated married men with greater generosity. . . .

[After considering a number of suggestions for an aged wives' allowance, the Advisory Council] explicitly proposed "that the enhancement of early old-age benefits under the system be attained, not by increasing the amount of benefit now payable to an individual, but by the method of paying to a married annuitant on behalf of an aged wife a supplementary allowance equivalent to fifty percent of the husband's own benefit."[16] . . .

None of the three women on the Advisory Council (Theresa McMahon, Elizabeth Wisner, and Josephine Roche, who seems to have been there only rarely) raised a question about gender equity or the rights of women. Neither did political activist and reformer, Mary Dewson, who attended council meetings as a member of the Social Security Board. . . .

We can speculate that under the historical circumstances the proposals of the Advisory Council offered far more security to the families of covered workers than most women could expect to provide through earnings. . . . [I]nfluential women social reformers had long since accepted that providing security for the family was the most likely way to safeguard women. . . . With the exception of McMahon, the women engaged in the Advisory Council's deliberations had been involved in some part of the effort to develop state-run welfare systems, and all were more or less hostile to the efforts of more radical feminists to fight for women's individual rights. . . . In addition, at least some members of the women's reform network (including perhaps Dewson herself) had become convinced of the need to abandon an earlier strategy of seeking benefits for women only and to focus instead on an integrated system of security. Family benefits would encourage this direction.

If the suggestion to provide dependents' allowances for aging wives appealed to some because it recognized the family responsibilities of men, it appealed to others because it retained equity among covered men by maintaining a relationship between contributions and benefits. This strategy was essential to garnering the votes of southern racists. . . .

[As one council member argued,] "It is impractical to have a level benefit in this country because of the differences between the colored workers of the south and the skilled workers of the north. A single flat figure for everybody would not work."[17] . . . [It was important to the council that it not transgress the] relative expectations of income based on occupation or race. . . .

In adopting the program, Congress accepted, with little debate, the relatively rigid definition of the family it demanded. For covered workers, the 1939 amendments provided benefits, without means tests, to fatherless children, widowed mothers of small children, and aged wives and widows. It did not extend benefits to the surviving children of covered women or to aged husbands, aged widowers, or widowed fathers of small children. Thus fatherless children might learn the sweet lesson of continuing parental support beyond the grave, and aging wives would continue to be dependent, though on phantom earnings. But motherless children and aged husbands without resources received quite another lesson in citizenship rights.[18] . . .

Three million domestic workers (including two and a quarter million in private households) counted themselves among the women who learned bitter lessons. Like three and a half million agricultural workers, mostly male, they found themselves among the still "uncovered" workers when the 1939 amendments emerged from Congress.[19] In fact, as a group, they had received a slap in the face. Following the Advisory Council's recommendations, Congress incorporated more than a million seamen and bank employees into the old age insurance program. At the same time, it excluded an equal number of mostly female and largely African American workers by eliminating even the few who had crept under the wire. Three hundred thousand domestic workers in clubs, fraternities, and large households and about seven hundred thousand food-processing workers lost their coverage. . . .

When Congress agreed to save the old age insurance system by changing its financing and using the funds generated annually to provide family protection, legislators altered expectations of the Social Security program and provoked a set of new, vaguely anticipated pressures toward universal coverage. Abandoning the idea that each generation of recipients would build a reserve fund that would support its own retirement in favor of a pay-as-you-go system required each generation of working people to subsidize the retirements of its predecessors. The shift turned a program that had originally been perceived primarily as a labor regulation device meant to preserve the dignity of workers who made way for the next generation into something more clearly approximating a promise of economic security freed of its rigid requirement for an equitable return on individual contributions. Adequate insurance for families displaced individual equity as the primary measure of fairness.

The inexorable logic of a system tilted toward adequacy fueled the hopes of policy makers and the excluded that old age insurance could more quickly include everyone and effectively replace the costly and demeaning charity offered by old age assistance. Advisory Council member Paul Douglas warned his colleagues that the changes made there raised the question of why the council could not recommend an "all-inclusive universal system": "If everybody is in from the standpoint of benefits, then everybody is in from the standpoint of contributions, and if there is to be a government subsidy . . . for only the industrial part of the population, it is going to be difficult to have the entire population pay taxes for benefits designed for only half of the population."[20] As Douglas noticed, by enhancing the value of social insurance for some groups of relatively privileged wage earners without extending coverage to significant numbers of additional workers, the program, which was now called Old-Age and Survivors Insurance (OASI), created two classes of citizens. For one of these, the "right to work" had become a more valuable commodity, carrying with it

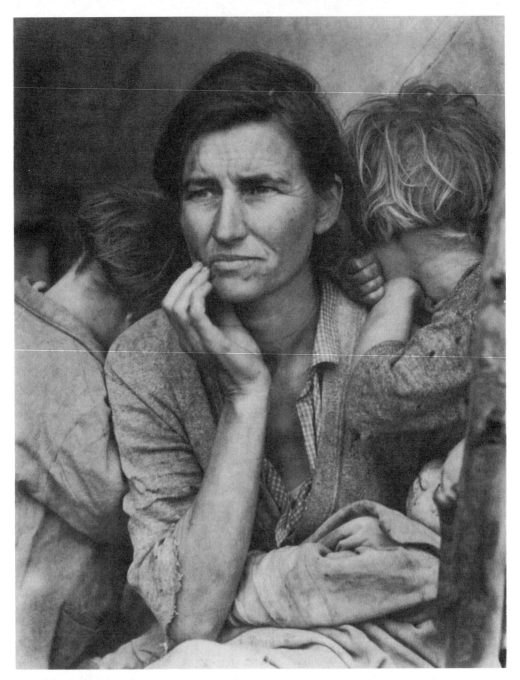

Dorothea Lange was working for the Farm Security Administration in the mid-1930s. Along with her colleagues Russell Lee and Roy Stryker, she documented the problems of farm tenancy in images that would become classic. This photograph was taken at a pea-picker's camp in Nipomo, California. Later Lange recalled, "I saw and approached the hungry and desperate mother, as if drawn by a magnet. I do not remember how I explained my presence or my camera to her, but I do remember she asked me no questions. I made five exposures, working closer and closer. . . . I did not ask her name or her history. She told me her age, that she was thirty-two. She said that they had been living on frozen vegetables from the surrounding fields, and birds that the children killed. She had just sold the tires from their car to buy food. There she sat in that lean-to tent with her children huddled around her, and seemed to know that my picture might help her, and so she helped me. There was a sort of equality about it." (Quoted in Milton Meltzer, Dorothea Lange: A Photographer's Life *[New York: Farrar Straus Giroux, 1978]. Photograph courtesy of the Library of Congress.)*

significant economic benefits and social rights for which the other half was indirectly paying. A large proportion of this other half consisted of self-supporting women (black and white) and African Americans of both sexes.

Afterward, the implications of these distinctions became clear. For one thing, some survivors benefited more than others. The family benefits offered under contributory social insurance slowly removed most widows and their children from the public assistance rolls.[21] By 1960, OASDI (disability insurance was added in 1941) covered 93 percent of widows with children. Most of these were the dependents of men who had held covered jobs, leaving only a tiny number of children and their widowed mothers to rely on relief, or what quickly became known as welfare. The result was to produce an invidious distinction between those said to have earned benefits as of right and those for whom benefits remained a matter of public charity. Both systems exercised some controls over the behavior of mothers caring for children, restricting the amount of income a mother could earn before benefits were lost and removing benefits on remarriage, but charitable provision subjected women to stringent moral and supervisory controls as well.[22] At the same time, the promise of more immediate and more reasonable provenance for the aged, anchored in their own virtue and thrift, successfully undermined public support for noncontributory old age assistance schemes, which soon suffered from derogatory labels. Because so many of the poorest and least stable workers could not collect Social Security benefits, these changes also made racial exclusion more visible.

For another, women quickly learned the costs of a gender-segregated labor market, and black women learned the bitterest lessons of all.[23] The poorest-paid workers, invariably women and people of color, appeared to have been multiply disadvantaged. As workers, they would see their intermittent contributions captured by an insurance program that excluded them, to be used to subsidize more stable workers. As consumers, they would pay higher prices as employers factored their share of taxes into the prices of goods and services. As citizens, they were not only deprived of the dignity attached to a contributory program, but they were compelled to support a dual system of noncontributory and contributory

relief, producing the apparent injustice of some receiving a demeaning "free" benefit while others received a due return on their investment. . . .

The system's planners had anticipated that some part of the contributions of intermittent workers would be captured and returned to beneficiaries. In their imagination, these workers were single women who would soon marry or married women who, though they worked intermittently, would ultimately reap enhanced benefits earned by their husbands. Policy makers frequently articulated these assumptions. With congressional concurrence, the council agreed on the irrelevance of most women's wage work with respect to this new citizenship right. "A married woman whether she works or no," it decided, "will receive an allowance because of her husband's earning." Its intent could not have been plainer. While "a single woman earns her own benefit rights," it concluded that "a married woman who works will not get advantage . . . of her own earnings, as in any case she will receive the 50% allowance for her husband."[24]

The actual situation was even worse. The council fully expected that married women would work occasionally and that their contributions, as well as the early contributions of single women who then married, would be absorbed by the system and help to sustain its financial health without necessarily yielding any direct benefit to the female contributor. There is no question that this was intentional, done, as Douglas Brown told the House Ways and Means Committee that affirmed the council's recommendations, "in order to control the cost of the system."[25] . . .

While some members of the council deplored its failure to provide equitable treatment to wives who earned wages, suggesting, for example, that "women who work all their lives should have a larger return than those who don't," most symbolically shrugged their shoulders along with Paul Douglas, who declared: "Of course, wives work too." Congress apparently concurred that wives who worked would simply have to sacrifice because, as one put it, "most wives in the long run will build up wage credits on their own account."[26] . . .

The 1939 council that designed this trade-off also aimed to discourage family members from taking advantage of the insurance program. Fearing inflated claims to benefits by women who falsely maintained they had worked for their husbands, Congress excluded "service performed by an individual in the employ of his spouse." . . . The issue of "forfeited" contributions had lasting resonance, for wives were not the only ones who forfeited their contributions. "Scrubwomen on their knees" fell victim, too, as well as all those who earned less than two hundred dollars a year from a single employer.[27] This hit African Americans particularly hard, as a special 1941 Senate report lamented when it deplored the unfairness to "contributors who fail to qualify because of insufficient employment or low wages. . . . Money thus forfeited by the dispossessed of the act will flow into the insurance fund and from there it will be distributed to workers everywhere."[28]

The architects of the 1939 amendments surely never intended to harm poor women, but the particular ways in which their gendered imagination infused the legislation nevertheless produced negative consequences. In 1940, the male-breadwinner family remained the modal family. Only 15 percent of wives with husbands present earned wages. If countless numbers of others hid the incomes they earned by taking in sewing, laundry, and boarders, still, most white women and men gratefully accepted the derivative benefits offered to wives and widows. Not so for African American women. As the depression deepened throughout the 1930s, racial segregation made wage work an absolute necessity for many black women, regardless of their marital status. At the same time, gender segregation confined more and more women of color to domestic service jobs, most often in private households. Of the two and a quarter million private household workers in the United States in 1940, about 90 percent were women.[29] A little less than half were African Americans. In contrast, men made up 94 percent of agricultural workers. Yet viewed from the perspective of the prospective worker, the figures take on a different cast. Nearly a third of all black workers (1.6 million men and women) and two-thirds of black working women (compared to less than 18 percent of white women workers) were in domestic service.[30] Of the five and a half million African Americans in the labor force in 1935, fully two-thirds were excluded from old age insurance because they belonged to noncovered occupations. No constitutional impediments stood in the way of including them, especially after the Supreme Court sustained the Social Security Act on the grounds of the welfare clause. In contrast to agricultural workers, whom farm interests desperately wanted excluded, and unlike some other groups, such as nonprofits, retail clerks, and the self-employed, no large interest group lobbied to keep domestic workers out of the old age insurance provisions of the new law. Race alone united them.[31] . . .

. . . [The Committee on Economic Security] sent its proposal to Congress with domestic and agricultural workers included. They were eliminated again by the House Ways and Means Committee on the probably specious grounds that their contributions could not buy sufficient benefits and that in any event collecting their taxes and administering benefits would be costly.[32] Agitation to include both groups continued even as the Social Security Act made its way through Congress. Mary Anderson wrote hopefully that she expected, regardless of what happened to the unemployment provisions, that "all workers regardless of occupation will be eligible to share in the old age benefits of the Economic Security Bill."[33]

Her hopes, of course, did not materialize. . . . A racialized conception of gender created the double jeopardy of black women. The policy committees publicly cited putative administrative difficulties that stood in the way of enrolling workers employed in single-person workplaces; in private they admitted the difficulties of offending southern sensibilities. In public, legislators repeatedly sought to protect white housewives, whose ability to handle the paperwork they denigrated; at the same time, they labeled household workers as "girls" and fostered disrespect for the occupation. Over more than a decade, they deployed race to exaggerate the differences between household workers and their employers while seeking to attach to each the special attributes of gender. . . .

Providing benefits for domestics would offer tangible benefits to poorly paid workers, enhance the appearance of fairness, and solve some of the program's financial problems as well. Yet, for many years, pleas to extend coverage to domestic workers, including the recommendation of the Social Security Board, fell on deaf ears. What had made it possible to ignore domestics, argued a piece in the AFL's journal, *American Federationist*, in the fall of 1939, is that they were thought of as different. Ninety percent female, 45 percent African American, with greater proportions married, widowed, deserted, or divorced, and still working in their older years, they simply did not fit the profile of the stable industrial worker for whom social legislation was constructed.[34] Nor did they conform to the restricted images of womanhood within which the 1939 Advisory Council constructed its system of benefits. So they had been left out partly because they were different and mostly because "we have gotten into the habit of excluding them." ...

Still, for most purposes, most members of Congress and officials of the Social Security Administration continued to support programs that radically distinguished between men and women as contributors. From the perspective of contributors, women's taxes continued to buy far less insurance protection than those of men.... From that of beneficiaries, men lacked the protections that their wives had. In 1961, Congress changed the law so that a wife's contributions covered aged husbands and widowers as well. Once again Congress insisted that they demonstrate financial dependency.

... The debate rendered voiceless a significant minority of women who believed that if they contributed at the same level as men, their contributions ought to buy their spouses and their children the same protection.

In the 1970s, these women found their voices. The rapidly rising numbers of wage-earning women and of women who did not marry, and the emergence of a dynamic and angry women's movement, soon rendered the discrepancies questionable and led some men and women to wonder if they were discriminatory. "The income security programs of this nation were designed for a land of male and female stereotypes," wrote Representative Martha Griffiths in 1973.[35] A series of court decisions confronted the issue, peaking on March 19, 1975, in the landmark decision of *Weinberger* v. *Wiesenfeld*. Eight justices of the U.S. Supreme Court (the ninth abstaining) agreed that Stephen Wiesenfeld, a widower and lone parent of an infant child, was enti-

tled to Social Security benefits. Wiesenfeld claimed the benefits on the basis of contributions made by his wife, Paula, who had been a schoolteacher before she died in childbirth. But the Social Security Administration had turned him down: widows' benefits were available only to women. Now the Supreme Court demurred. "A father no less than a mother," said the Court, "has a constitutionally protected right to the companionship, care, custody, and management of children he has sired and raised."[36] On this basis, the Court struck down forty years of "archaic and overbroad generalizations," accepting the argument put forth in Wiesenfeld's defense that such generalizations unfairly discriminated against women because their contributions to Social Security did not buy as much as the contributions of men. Wisenfeld's lawyer, Ruth Bader Ginsburg, had done her part to draw a new image of gender to the Court's attention.

The Court's majority decision, written by Justice William J. Brennan, explicitly challenged assumptions about men's and women's wage-earning that underlay the Social Security Act and anchored its old age insurance provisions. As late as 1971, an Advisory Council on Social Security had insisted that men rarely became homemakers after the death of a spouse and that, given their attachment to the workforce, widowed fathers did not require benefits to enable them to provide a home for their children. Acknowledging the truth of the generalization that men had been, and were more likely to be, the principal supporters of their families, Brennan nevertheless argued that this assumption did not "suffice to justify the denigration of efforts of women who do work and whose earnings contribute significantly to families' support." Dismissing the government's claim that benefits were unrelated to contributions, the Court held that statutory rights to benefits were directly "related to years worked and amount earned by a covered employee, and not to the need of the beneficiaries directly." Benefits had to be related to some reasonable classification; they could not be based solely on sex. Wiesenfeld's wife had not only been deprived of the security "a similarly situated male" would have received, she had been "deprived of a portion of her own earnings in order to contribute to the fund out of which benefits would be paid to others." As Justice Lewis Powell put it in a concurring opinion, the statute "discriminates against one particular category of family—that in which the female spouse is a wage-earner covered by social security."[37]

The decision in *Wiesenfeld* was followed by others. An aged widower was entitled to benefits on his wife's earnings whether or not he had been dependent on her, just as a widow was entitled to benefits earned by her husband, the Court declared two years later.[38] . . . With the Department of Health, Education, and Welfare and the Social Security Administration fighting every step, the Court methodically overturned a carefully structured set of images about women's roles in the family. Henceforth, the Court concluded, classifications by gender "must serve important governmental objectives."[39] Imaging women as nonworkers no longer met that test.

NOTES

1. Paul H. Douglas, *Social Security in the United States: An Analysis and Appraisal of the Federal Social Security Act* (New York: McGraw-Hill, 1936), estimates that 47 percent of those working would not come under the old age insurance features and thus would require old age assistance.

2. The most careful analysis of the data concludes that 86.69 percent of black female workers and 53.6 percent of black male workers were excluded; F. Davis, "The Effects of the Social Security Act upon the Status of the Negro," Ph.D. diss., University of Iowa, 1939, p. 99, n. 211, and 102, tables 21, 23.

3. "Social Security Advisory Council Is Appointed," typescript of press release, May 10, 1937, File 025: Advisory Council 1937, Box 10, Chairman's Files, RG47, NA2.

4. Typescript, I. S. Falk to the Advisory Council, November 5, 1937, "Benefits for Disabled Persons and Survivors, and Supplemental Allowances for Dependents," ibid., passim.

5. See, for example, Abraham Epstein, *Insecurity: A Challenge to America, a Study of Social Insurance in the United States and Abroad* (New York: Random House, 1938[1933]), part 9.

6. Advisory Council on Social Security, *Final Report*, Senate Document no. 4, 76th Cong., 1st sess., December 10, 1938 (Washington, D.C.: GPO, 1939), p. 18; hereafter, Advisory Council, *Final Report*.

7. Advisory Council Minutes, April 29, 1938, morning session, pp. 8–10 and ff.

8. Advisory Council, *Final Report*, p. 17.

9. House, *Hearings on Social Security Act Amendments of 1939*, p. 6.

10. Advisory Council Minutes, April 29, 1938, second half of morning session, p. 9, A. L. Mowbray of the University of California, Berkeley, speaking.

11. Ibid., pp. 3, 40.

12. Ibid., February 19, 1938, afternoon session, p. 18. The actuary was William Williamson.

13. Ibid., April 29, 1938, first half of morning session, p. 41.

14. Ibid., April 29, 1938, second half of morning session, pp. 5–6.

15. Ibid., first half of morning session, pp. 37–38.

16. Typescript headed "Strictly Confidential," October 22, 1938, File 025, Box 138, Executive Director's Files, Advisory Council on Social Security, RG47, NARA.

17. Jill Quadagno, *The Transformation of Old Age Security: Class and Politics in the American Welfare State* (Chicago: University of Chicago Press, 1988), p. 39, and see ch. 6 on the influence of southern politicians on the old age assistance portion of the Social Security Act.

18. These amendments also included altering the fiscal plan to a pay-as-you-go system, paying benefits on the basis of a wage-averaging device rather than on the basis of accumulated benefits, and expanding the categories of agricultural and domestic workers excluded from coverage. See Edward D. Berkowitz, "The First Social Security Crisis," *Prologue* 15, no. 3 (1983):133–49, for a summary of their full contents.

19. These figures come from the testimony of Sumner Slichter, *Hearings on the Social Security Act Amendments of 1939*, p. 1512. Slichter estimated that eleven million self-employed farmers and others, and about a million employees of nonprofit corporations, also remained uncovered.

20. Advisory Council Minutes, February 19, 1938, afternoon session, p. 20.

21. Gwendolyn Mink, *The Wages of Motherhood: Inequality in the Welfare State, 1917–1942* (Ithaca: Cornell University Press, 1995), p. 175.

22. The best discussion of this issue is in ibid., chs. 6–7.

23. Edward J. McCaffery, *Taxing Women* (Chicago: University of Chicago Press, 1997), ch. 4.

24. Brown, Advisory Council Minutes, February 18, 1938, morning session, p. 14.

25. House, *Hearings on the Social Security Act Amendments of 1939*, p. 1218.

26. Testimony of Sen. Sheridan Downey of California, *Congressional Record—Senate*, July 13, 1939, p. 9012.

27. Downey, *Congressional Record—Senate*, July 13, 1939, p. 9012.

28. *Senate Resolution Preliminary Report, 1941*, p. 8.

29. Thus, though African Americans made up about 10 percent of the labor force, they constituted nearly half of the women in domestic service. Cf. Testimony of Margaret Plunkett, chief, Division of Legislation, Women's Bureau, Department of Labor, U.S. Congress, House, *Hearings before the Committee on Ways and Means, House of Representatives on Social Security Legislation, Amendments to the Social Security Act of 1946*, 79th Cong., 2nd sess. (Washington, D.C.: GPO, 1946), p. 542; hereafter, House, *Hearings on Amendments to the Social Security Act of 1946*. Plunkett also says that 6 percent of agricultural workers were women (p. 545).

30. Figures from Albion Hartwell, "The Need of Social and Unemployment Insurance for Negroes," *Journal of Negro Education* 5 (January 1936), pp. 79–87.

31. This argument appears in the testimony of Edgar G. Brown, director, National Negro Council, Washington, D.C., at U.S. Congress, House, *Hearings on Social Security Act Amendments of 1949*, p. 1878.

32. See the account of this incident in Edwin E. Witte, *The Development of the Social Security Act: A Memorandum on the History of the Committee on Economic Security and Drafting and Legislative History of the Social Security Act* (Madison: University of Wisconsin Press, 1962), pp. 152–53.

33. Mary Anderson, "The Plight of Negro Domestic Labor," *Journal of Negro Education* 5 (January 1936), p. 71.

34. Rae Needleman, "Are Domestic Workers Coming of Age," *American Federationist* 46 (October 1939), pp. 1070–75.

35. Martha W. Griffiths, "Sex Discrimination in Income Security Programs," *Notre Dame Lawyer* 49 (February 1974), p. 534.

36. *Weinberger* v. *Wiesenfeld*, 420 U.S. 636 (1975), p. 652.

37. Ibid., pp. 645, 647.

38. *Califano* v. *Goldfarb*, 97 S.Ct. 1021 (1977), p. 1023. Justice William J. Brennan for the Court.

39. *Califano* v. *Goldfarb*, p. 1028.

BLANCHE WIESEN COOK

Storms on Every Front: Eleanor Roosevelt and Human Rights at Home and in Europe

A woman of limitless energy, compassion, and humanitarian zeal, Eleanor Roosevelt was the most active and controversial First Lady in the nation's history. A fascinating figure, her ability to grow in understanding never ended. She began her adult life as a shy, insecure woman who had imbibed the racism and anti-Semitism of the privileged world to which she was born. She ended her life a feminist and a political champion of civil rights, civil liberties, social justice, and world peace—a woman whose activism was played out on a world stage.

The transformation was well underway by the 1920s. Indeed, it was accelerated when Franklin Delano Roosevelt was paralyzed by polio in 1921 and Eleanor began serving as his representative in the political arena. Long a political activist, she became an increasingly shrewd analyst of the political scene. When FDR became president, ER found herself in an increasingly complex political context. She could try to persuade the president in private conversation; she could also use public pulpits of her own. She was the only First Lady ever to write a long-running daily syndicated newspaper column, "My Day." She could choose (or refuse) speaking invitations, and use her opportunities to speak about issues that mattered to her. As the Nazi threat grew, ER found that the State Department insisted on her silence; she would have to find other ways of expressing her commitment to human rights.

Excerpted and revised by the author from ch. 27 of *Eleanor Roosevelt: The Defining Years, 1933–1938* by Blanche Weisen Cook (New York: Viking/Penguin, 1999). © Blanche Weisen Cook, 1999. Published by permission of the author and publisher. Readers will find ch. 16, "A Silence Beyond Repair," a critical framework for this selection.

Between 9 and 15 November [1938], Jewish homes, schools, hospitals, synagogues, businesses, and cemeteries were invaded, plundered, burned. Kristallnacht, the night of broken glass, was a week of contempt, abuse, destruction.

If anybody doubted the intent of Hitler's words, so clearly revealed in his writings, speeches, and previous outrages, those November days in Germany, Austria, and the Sudetenland shattered any illusion. The violence coincided with Armistice Day, 11 November, when the Allies ended World War I. The defeat of that war was for Hitler to be avenged with new blood, and unlimited terror.

The violence began on 28 October, when Germany expelled thousands of Polish Jews who had lived for decades within the historically changing borders of Germany. Nazis rounded up children and old people on the streets, emptied houses and apartment buildings, allowed people to take nothing with them except 10 marks ($4) and the clothes they wore, shoved them into waiting trucks and trains, and dumped them across the border onto the desolate flats of Poland's borderlands. More than ten thousand Jews were deported in this manner.

Among the deportees was the family of Zindel Grynszpan, whose seventeen-year-old son, Heschel, had previously fled the family home in Hanover to Paris. When he received a letter from his father recounting his family's ordeal, Heschel Grynszpan bought a gun and on 7 November walked to the German embassy in Paris to assassinate the ambassador. Ironically, he was detained by a minor official, Ernst vom Rath, who was himself under investigation by the Gestapo for his opposition to the increasing anti-Semitic violence, and shot him. This murder was the immediate excuse used to launch the well-orchestrated burnings, lootings, and round-ups known as Kristallnacht.

Then on 12 November, German Jews were fined a billion marks—$400 million—as penalty for the murder. This "money atonement" was astronomical and rendered it virtually impossible for most Jews to retain sufficient savings to emigrate. Yet another decree ordered the victims to pay for the repair and restoration of their former shops, buildings, and homes—from which they were permanently banished.

These fines had another, more sinister purpose. Hitler had announced: "If there is any country that believes it has not enough Jews, I shall gladly turn over to it all our Jews." Now, if they left, they left penniless. Moreover, most countries had closed their doors, and those who would accept Jews would not accept paupers.

It was a major challenge for FDR, whose policy was to do nothing to involve the United States in European affairs, but who wanted to respond somehow to the thousands of refugees who stood for hours before the U.S. embassy seeking asylum, only to be routinely turned away.

Within days, Jews were stripped of their remaining human rights. They were no longer permitted to drive cars, travel on public transportation, walk in parks, go to museums, attend theaters or concerts. Passports and visas were canceled. They were stateless and impoverished. Charged for the violence and fined for the damage, the Jewish community now owed the Reich, collectively, one billion Reichsmarks. For a time, they were not molested in their homes. But there was nothing to do, no work to be had; no place to pray; no recourse from agony. Many committed suicide; most tried to leave.

For all moral and political purposes, Kristallnacht was the terminal event. Civility in the heart of western Europe lay in ruins, surrounded by broken glass, bloodied streets, desecrated temples, burned Torahs, ripped books of prayer to the one shared God. Hitler's intentions were flagrant, and the whole world was invited to witness. Twenty thousand Jews were removed to concentration camps, which the Anglo-American press named: Dachau near Munich, Oranienburg-Sachsenhausen north of Berlin, Buchenwald near Weimar. . . .

ER's formerly private protests against bigotry were increasingly for public attribution. Although she had resigned in silence from the Colony Club for its discrimination against Elinor Morgenthau, she now canceled a speaking engagement at a country club in Lancaster, Pennsylvania, with a statement of distress that it excluded Jews.

While she counseled complete assimilation and urged Jews to "wipe out in their own consciousness any feeling of difference by joining in all that is being done by Americans" for justice and democracy, she also spoke on behalf of support for refugees in Palestine.... On 6 December 1938, ER appealed to fifteen hundred people assembled at the Hotel Astor under the auspices of a national committee for refugees chaired by William Green, president of the American Federation of Labor, to help promote the Léon Blum colony in Palestine for the settlement of one thousand Jewish refugee families....

While ER called for demonstrations of "thought and example," little was done, or said, by FDR's administration to indicate official outrage at Hitler's violence. No message of protest warning of boycott or economic reprisal was sent. Yet history abounds in such protests on behalf of victimized peoples. In 1903 and 1906, Theodore Roosevelt protested against Jewish pogroms in Russia, after Jacob Schiff lobbied for an official U.S. condemnation of the massacre of Jews in Odessa....

FDR sent no similar message to Germany.

FDR did respond to the pitiless carnage and massacre in China. In December 1937, Japan destroyed Nanking in a vicious episode of rape, horror, and death. Half the population, an estimated 300,000 people, were tortured and killed. Whether the details were immediately known to FDR, even of Japan's 12 December sinking of the U.S. gunboat *Panay*, remains controversial. But on 11 January 1938, FDR sent a memo to Cordell Hull and Admiral Cary T. Grayson, head of the American Red Cross. He called for additional relief funds for the "destitute Chinese civilians" and for medical aid. "I think we could raise $1,000,000 without any trouble at all." On 17 January, the U.S. Red Cross launched an appeal for aid to the Chinese people, initiated by FDR's formal request for such a drive.[1]

No similar appeal was made by FDR to the Red Cross on behalf of Europe's Jews.*

Since he was considered by many the best friend American Jews ever had, FDR's reactions to the European events of 1938 are unexplainable.... Except for Father Charles E.

Coughlin, who hailed the violence against "Jewish-sponsored Communism," the press was unanimous in its condemnation....

... FDR agreed to allow all German aliens on visitor visas to remain in the United States for six months "and for other like periods so long as necessary." At the time there were between twelve thousand and fifteen thousand political refugees covered by his order, and "not all Jews, by any means," the president assured the press. "All shades of liberal political thought and many religions are represented."[2]

Anti-Semitism in FDR's State Department increased after Hitler's November atrocities. Breckenridge Long now dedicated himself to keeping refugees out of America. Curiously, FDR continually promoted Breckenridge Long, who had life-and-death control over visas and passports. Nevertheless, in 1938, for the first time, the United States filled its refugee quota.

ER and her asylum-seeking circle faced the urgent refugee crisis in a lonely political environment. Thousands of the earliest refugees who left in 1933 were still wandering Europe seeking safety and political asylum. After 31 January 1933, over 30 percent of Germany's 500,000 Jews had become refugees. After the March 1938 Anschluss, Germany's annexation of Austria, when the Nazis began to expel Austria's 190,000 Jews, the situation became critical. The flight of Czech Jews compounded the problem, and Kristallnacht ignited refugee panic.

FDR expanded his search for underpopulated and suitable lands upon which to place the world's unwanted Jews ... but told his press conference that he had no intention of asking Congress to alter existing immigration quotas....

During her own press conference, ER called for temporary emergency measures to do whatever was possible "to deal with the refugee problem, and at home, for renewed devotion to ... the American way of life." Wary of her husband's strategies, she [rarely criticized] him directly.... "For ourselves," "[she said]," I hope we will do, as individuals, all we can to preserve what is a traditional right in this country—freedom for different races and different religions." ...

[From 1938 to 1940, a committee of geographers, scholars, and members of the State

---

*During the 1940s, the International Red Cross deflected complaints about its neglect of Jewish needs, given the magnitude of the mounting tragedy, with the explanation that the Red Cross "could not interfere in the internal affairs of a belligerent nation." Blood plasma for U.S. troops was segregated into "white" and "colored," "Christian" and "Hebrew." It was not desegregated until 1954.

Department explored the possibilities of sanctuary for Jews outside the United States, without success. ER was staggered by the contempt for human suffering expressed by the failure of other nations to welcome refugees.] In the bitter time before the burning time there was hope for rescue country by country. But there was no official objection to Hitler's intention to remove Jews from Germany and all his new territories. ER increasingly bypassed State Department restrictions; she worked, often covertly, with private groups and individuals. She campaigned for a less restrictive refugee policy, pursued visas for individuals, and answered and passed on to government officials every appeal sent to her.

Revolted by world events, ER called for entirely new levels of action. Her speeches became more pointed and vigorous, and she spent more time in the company of radical activists, especially members of the American Youth Congress whose ardent views now coincided most completely with her own.

For ER, AYC leaders represented hope for the best of liberal America. Christian theology students, Jewish children of immigrants, black and white activists from the rural South and urban North imagined a nation united for progressive antifascist action.

A week after Kristallnacht, ER . . . defended the AYC at the annual luncheon of New York's branch of the American Association of University Women and spoke of the need for courage and fearlessness in perilous times. . . . ER's speech was bold: She rejected the current Red Scare tactics which branded the AYC communist and her a dupe or fool: Such name-calling had destroyed democracy in Europe, and she wanted democracy to survive here.

"People whose opinions I respect" had warned her not to attend the AYC convention.

[But] I didn't think that those youngsters could turn me into a Communist, so I went just the same. . . .

I listened to speeches which you and I could easily have torn to shreds. The Chinese listened while the Japanese spoke; the boy from India spoke with the British delegates. . . . Nobody hissed or left the room. I have been in lots of gatherings of adults who did not show that kind of respect. . . .

She spoke with many delegates, asked what they thought of the Soviet Union; she left convinced that there was interest in communism, but not domination by communists: "We who have training, and have minds that we know how to use must not be swept away" by fear and propaganda. The urgent problems before the United States and the world required scrutiny, debate, honest disagreement, democratic participation, not a wild and fearful flight from controversy. . . .

On 22 November 1938, ER embarked on a dangerous mission when she keynoted the radical biracial Southern Conference on Human Welfare, in Birmingham, Alabama. For the first time since the Civil War, Southern liberals were determined to face the race issue embedded within the region's struggling economy. Since 1890 there had been talk of a "New South," but always before, racial cruelties at the heart of peonage and poverty had been ignored in the interest of white supremacy. . . .

In the aftermath of Kristallnacht, there was a new level of commitment and urgency at the Birmingham meeting. Regional race and antiunion violence was behind the call for the SCHW, first conceived as a civil liberties conference by [pioneering progressive activists] Joseph Gelders and Lucy Randolph Mason. According to Virginia Durr, they wanted to deal with the "terrible things happening" to CIO organizers in Mississippi. Many people were beaten [and run out of town,] crosses were burned. . . .

While the South "led the world" in cotton, tobacco, paper, and other products, it was a disaster area. The average per capita income was half the nation's; the poll tax limited voting rights to 12 percent of the population in eight Southern states, including Virginia; the region's children were being undereducated. The South was hampered by backward and colonial customs; and its entrenched leaders wanted no changes.

The Southern Conference on Human Welfare determined to change the South and challenge segregation. Fifteen hundred delegates, black and white, sat anywhere they wanted Sunday night, 21 November 1938, in the city auditorium of downtown Birmingham. According to Virginia Durr: "Oh, it was a love feast. . . . Southern meetings always include a lot of preaching and praying and hymn singing. . . . The whole meeting was just full of love and hope. It was thrilling. . . . The whole South was coming together to make a new day."[3]

Somebody reported the integrated seating at the opening-night gala, and the next morning the auditorium was surrounded. . . . Every police van in the city and county was there. Policemen were everywhere, inside and out. And there was Eugene "Bull" Connor "saying anybody who broke the segregation law of Alabama would be arrested." Tensions escalated; violence was in the air. The delegates complied and arranged themselves into separate sections.

ER, Mary McLeod Bethune, and Aubrey Williams arrived late that day, out of breath. ER "was ushered in with great applause," looked at the segregated audience—and took her seat on the black side. One of Bull Connor's police officers tapped ER on the shoulder and told her to move. . . .

As if to announce fascism would not triumph here, ER refused to "give in" and placed her chair between the white and black sections. Pauli Murray recalled that ER's demonstration of defiance and courage meant everything to the young people of the South, who now knew they were not alone. Although the national press did not report ER's brave action, the weekly *Afro-American* editorialized: "If the people of the South do not grasp this gesture, we must. Sometimes actions speak louder than words."[4]

ER was given a little folding chair and sat in the middle of whatever meeting hall or church she attended for the rest of the four-day meeting. She said she refused to be segregated, and carried the folding chair with her wherever she went. According to Durr: "Policemen followed us everywhere to make sure the segregation laws were observed, but they didn't arrest Mrs. Roosevelt."

ER's address to the SCHW stirred the packed auditorium:

We are the leading democracy of the world and as such must prove to the world that democracy is possible and capable of living up to the principles upon which it was founded. The eyes of the world are upon us, and often we find they are not too friendly eyes.

ER emphasized "universal education" in which "every one of our citizens, regardless of nationality, or race," might be allowed to flourish.[5] . . .

The 1938 SCHW adopted thirty-six resolutions, all of which involved the plight of African Americans, and eight of which directly concerned racial issues, including freedom for the four Scottsboro boys who remained in prison; availability of medical services by African American physicians in all public health facilities; more funding for public housing and recreation facilities for African Americans; equal funding for graduate education in state-supported colleges; and—inspired by ER's demonstration—a resolution to support fully integrated SCHW meetings.

Perceived as "one of the gravest sins that a white southerner could commit," that direct assault against tradition created a furor. The antisegregation resolution divided the delegates, some of whom withdrew, and was branded communist, subversive, and un-American. On the other hand, it transformed national assumptions about the unspeakable: White supremacy, and its primary bulwark, segregation, were forevermore on the nation's agenda—put there by an integrated conference, led by Southern New Dealers.[6]

Traditional "race etiquette" was also challenged when Louise Charlton called on Mary McLeod Bethune to speak. According to Virginia Durr:

She said, "Mary, do you wish to come to the platform?" Mrs. Bethune rose. She looked like an African queen. . . . "My name is Mrs. Bethune." So Louise had to say, "Mrs. Bethune, will you come to the platform?" That sounds like a small thing now, but that was a big dividing line. A Negro woman in Birmingham, Alabama, was called Mrs. at a public meeting. . . .

Virginia Durr, wife of Clifford Durr, the assistant general counsel of the Reconstruction Finance Corporation, and sister-in-law of Justice Hugo Black, addressed the meeting to denounce the South's refusal to educate its people and the prevailing ignorance so general throughout the country. The reasons for an uninformed public, she declared, were propaganda and a controlled press dominated by Wall Street. She accused the National Manufacturers Association of being a "huge propaganda machine" intent on the "liquidation of organized labor." . . .

[A week after the SCHW], the Nazi press announced that Germany had embarked upon "the final and unalterably uncompromising solution" to the Jewish question. In the Gestapo's official paper, *Das Schwarze Korps*, on 24 November, the front-page feature announced that it should have been done immediately, brutally, and completely in 1933. But "it had to remain theory" for lack of the "military power we possess today."

> Because it is necessary, because we no longer hear the world's screeching and because, after all, no power on earth can hinder us, we will now bring the Jewish question to its totalitarian solution.[7]

Two weeks after Kristallnacht, accepted without notable "screeching" from any government, Hitler felt sufficiently unrestrained to publish his intentions for all Jews caught in his widening web. First would come pauperization, isolation, ghettoization. They would all be marked for positive identification. Nobody would escape. Then, the starving, bedraggled remnant would become a scrounging, begging scourge. They would be forced to crime, would be an "underworld" of "politico-criminal subhumans," breeders of Bolshevism. At that stage "we should therefore face the hard necessity of exterminating the Jewish underworld. . . . The result will be the actual and definite end of Jewry . . . and its complete extermination."

While the announcement was made two years and eight months before it was actually implemented, the time to protest and resist was at hand. After it was reprinted in the U.S. and European press, many understood the implications of such crude words given the reality of the cruelties under way in Germany, Austria, and Czechoslovakia. Since Kristallnacht, race hatred had triumphed completely and Jews had been removed from all German institutions, doomed to a pariah existence in complete segregation. Jews could no longer dine with Gentiles—not in restaurants, not anywhere; nor could they buy food in the same stores. Nazis established separate stores where Jews were restricted in the purchase of life's staples—milk, bread.

Such laws cast a torchlight on American traditions. ER made the connections: brown shirts, white sheets; the twisted cross, the burning cross. Yet the internal affairs of a nation were deemed sacrosanct, nobody else's business. ER and other citizens no longer agreed with that diplomatic principle.

FDR remained virtually silent about human rights abuses, and did not end trade with Ger-

many, but he began a vigorous rearmament program, emphasizing military planes and naval construction. Immediately after Kristallnacht, on 14 November, he reported to Josephus Daniels, his Wilson-era boss, that he was working on "national defense—especially mass production of planes." By December, he ordered the navy yards to run full-time, "two shifts or even three" wherever possible. It "is time to get action."

While ER approved of all defense programs, she also called for a worldwide educational crusade to address prejudice. . . . After the SCHW meetings, ER wrote her first articles specifically about Jews and race hatred. One, initially called "Tolerance," was for the *Virginia Quarterly* and attacked the kind of anticommunist hysteria that had resulted in fascist triumph and appeasement throughout so much of Europe. The other, which addressed the mounting hatred against Jews, was dated 25 November 1938. . . .

Untitled, ER's "Jewish article" called for a campaign of understanding to confront "the present catastrophe for Jew and Gentile alike. . . . In books . . . schools, newspapers, plays, assemblies we want incessant truth telling about these old legends that divide and antagonize and waste us."

As she struggled to understand "the kind of racial and religious intolerance which is sweeping the world today," ER rejected her former emphasis on assimilation. . . . Now ER assessed the historic hatred of Jews, their isolation, and forced ghettoization in the Middle Ages, and the ongoing contempt for Jews. . . . ER now pointed out that even when Jews attempted to assimilate they were condemned for "being too ostentatiously patriotic and of pushing themselves forward as nationals," as in Austria and Germany.

ER was also sensitive to the difficulties assimilated Jews faced among their coreligionists, who resented those who strayed from tradition. Never quite accepted into the majority culture, they were everywhere marginalized. . . . ER rejected ghettoization and deplored signs that appeared in many American neighborhoods that read "No Dogs or Jews Allowed."

Written from within the veil of her own stereotypes, ER concluded that the future was not up to the Jews.

The Jew is almost powerless today. It depends almost entirely on the course of the Gentiles what the future holds.... If they perish, we perish sooner or later....

She recalled that as a child her uncle Theodore Roosevelt once said "that when you are afraid to do a thing, that was the time to go and do it. Every time we shirk making up our minds or standing up for a cause in which we believe, we weaken our character and our ability to be fearless." ...

ER challenged Americans to think and act politically, to engage in activist citizenship, to become their best selves. A sense of personal unimportance was encouraged by dictators. Democracy depended on "freedom from prejudice, and public awareness." It required education, economic security, and personal devotion, "a real devotion to freedom.... Freedom is something to guard jealously," but it can never be "freedom for me and not for you."

The bolder ER became, the tougher and more adamant her statements, the higher her public approval rating soared. On 16 January 1939, the *New York Times* published a poll taken by George Gallup regarding America's feelings about ER during 1938. The results were astounding. Two voters in every three voted in her favor (67 percent approved of her conduct, 33 percent disapproved).... According to the poll she had a greater approval rating than FDR.... Given the nature of the controversies ER engaged in and her challenge to work for the transformation of customs and traditions that subjected so many to poverty and powerlessness, America's response indicated a commitment to the very democracy she spoke about so earnestly. ER touched a nerve center in America, and the country would never be the same.

On 10 February 1938, ER [had] commemorated the seventy-fifth anniversary of the Emancipation Proclamation by asserting that while Abraham Lincoln took the "first step toward the abolition of slavery ... we still do tolerate slavery in several ways." Her words, addressed to nine thousand people at a meeting sponsored by the National Negro Congress, were electrifying:

> There are still slaves of many different kinds, and today we are facing another era in which we have to make certain things become facts rather than beliefs.

As Europe fell to fascism, ER and her new network of youth and race radicals heralded the greatest changes in America since the betrayal of Reconstruction.

In her 8 December 1938 column, ER criticized liberals, smug partisans, and patriots for celebrating incomplete victories....

"As I listened [to speeches to promote the Leon Blum colony for refugees in Palestine] ... I could not help thinking how much all human beings like to fool themselves.... [They] made us feel that ... we were more virtuous and fortunate than any other people in the world. Of course, I concede this, and I feel for me it is true, for I have been free and fortunate all my life. While I listened, however, I could not help thinking of some of the letters which pass through my hands.

"Are you free if you cannot vote, if you cannot be sure that the same justice will be meted out to you as to your neighbor, ... if you are barred from certain places and from certain opportunities? ...

"Are you free when you can't earn enough, no matter how hard you work, to feed and clothe and house your children properly? Are you free when your employer can turn you out of a company house and deny you work because you belong to a union?"

Her thoughts turned to refugees in this country, "of the little girl who wrote me not long ago: 'Why do other children call me names and laugh at my talk? I just don't live in this country very long yet.'" ER concluded:

"There are lots and lots of things which make me wonder whether we ever look ourselves straight in the face and really mean what we say when we are busy patting ourselves on the back...."

With grit, determination, and a very high heart, ER helped launch America's crusade for freedom in the fascist era. She was fortified every day by her new allies, her abiding partnership with FDR, love for the people in her life, and love of the world.

Notes

1. FDR to Cordell Hull, Jan. 11, 1938, in *FDR: His Personal Letters, 1928–1945*, Elliott Roosevelt and Joseph P. Lash, eds. (Millwood, N.Y.: Kraus Reprint, 1970), IV, pp. 744–45; see also Iris Chang, *The Rape of Nanking: The Forgotten Holocaust of World War II* (New York: Penguin, 1997).

2. *New York Times*, Nov. 19, 1938.

3. Linda Reed, *Simple Decency and Common Sense: The Southern Conference Movement, 1938–1945* (Bloomington: Indiana University Press, 1991), pp. 15–16 and passim; Virginia Durr, *Outside the Magic Circle: The Autobiography of Virginia Durr* (Tuscaloosa: Univ. of Alabama Press, 1985).

4. Pauli Murray, *Song in a Weary Throat: An American Pilgrimage* (New York: Harper & Row, 1987), p. 113.

5. For ER's Nov. 22, 1938 speech at the SCHW, see Allida Black, ed., *Courage in a Dangerous World: The Political Writings of Eleanor Roosevelt* (New York: Columbia University Press, 1999).

6. Reed, pp. 46–48.

7. *New York Times*, Nov. 24, 1938; Arthur D. Morse, *While Six Million Died: A Chronicle of American Apathy* (New York: Random House, 1968); Michael Berenbaum, *The World Must Know* (Boston: Little Brown, 1993), p. 35.

GERDA LERNER

Life Interrupted: A Young Refugee Arrives in America

Gerda Lerner is a pioneer in the field of women's history and one of its leading practitioners. She is the author and editor of many books, among them *Black Women in White America* (1972), *The Creation of Patriarchy* (1986), and *Why History Matters* (1997). Yet this distinguished professor, writer, and intellectual was once a frightened young immigrant to this country. Her experience has much in common with other new arrivals previously encountered in this volume; however, there was also a critical difference.

Gerda Kronstein was born in Vienna, Austria, in 1920. When her father, a Jewish pharmacist, fled Austria to avoid arrest by the Nazis in 1938, the Gestapo imprisoned mother and daughter for six weeks, releasing them only on the condition that they leave Austria immediately. Gerda's mother, desiring to work as an independent artist, would spend much of the war in Nice, France. Gerda sailed for New York City, where she joined her fiancé, a Viennese medical student whose American relatives had brought him to the United States a few months earlier. Despite their previous long friendship, the couple's prompt marriage, which was a condition for her admittance, was a troubled one that ended a few years later. Afterward she met and married Carl Lerner, an American screenwriter and editor.

Gerda's initial struggles in New York City in 1939 and her frantic and ultimately unsuccessful endeavor to gain U.S. entrance visas for her parents and sister are related in her compelling autobiography, *Fireweed*. With her customary clarity, Lerner's story conveys both the special burden that refugees from fascism faced even as they simultaneously coped with the ordinary traumas of transition that confront every immigrant group that enters the United States.

I arrived in the United States in April 1939 after a terrible voyage of seasickness, loneliness, and fearful anticipation. As the ship passed within sight of the Statue of Liberty, immigration officials processed all passengers in the large social room below deck. I waited and waited; the hours seemed to pass slowly and when my turn came and I was asked to step aside and wait some more, I became very frightened. Almost everyone had left the ship by now and still I was waiting with a handful of others. As the others were processed before me, I realized that we were the problem cases—some were handed their papers, others were led away in tears by an officer. I was sure now that something was terribly wrong—they would deny me entry; they would send me back.

The official who endlessly examined my papers questioned me closely about each of the six affidavits of support I had submitted. They had already been approved by the U.S. Consul in Switzerland, but apparently this official had the right to cancel the Consul's decision. Did I know any of these people who were sponsoring me? Who was this person, Bernard Jensen, who was my main sponsor but only had an income of fifty dollars a month. No, I had no relatives here, except my father's second cousin who had not given me an affidavit. Bernard Jensen [also called Bobby] was my fiance and his relatives had given me an affidavit. On and on and over the same ground again. Finally, a strange question—where did I expect to stay on my arrival?

I instantly became cautious; this was some kind of trap. I don't know; I expect my fiance will have made some sort of arrangement for me. Did I have hotel reservations? No.

Long pause and much shuffling of paper. Consultation among the two officials. I began to panic. Is something wrong, I asked. Are you saying I can't land?

"Did you ever hear of the Mann Act?" the official asked.

"No."

"You are eighteen years old?"

"I'll be nineteen next month. Why, what is the matter?"

"The Mann Act forbids the entry of unattached female minors into the U.S.A."

I did not understand anything about that law, but I understood they were making serious trouble. What did unattached mean? What

were they worried about? "I'm meeting my fiance and his family, what's wrong with that?"

"I'm afraid you may have to go to Ellis Island," the official said. "We may have to deny you entry."

"You can't do that. I have no place to go. I was deported from Austria by the Nazis, they'll kill me if I come back. You can't do that—please, don't do that." He finally had me in tears.

"Well, just a minute, Miss. Don't get excited. I have to go by my regulations. Just wait."

I don't know if I was alone in that great hall or if there were others still waiting to be processed. It seemed to me I was alone at the end of the world—totally helpless and abandoned. I had no one to advise me, no Consul to whom I could appeal. If they sent me back to Austria, which is what I thought they would do, because I came with a German passport, I'd be sent straight to the concentration camp—the police had told me that often enough. In my German passport, with the swastika on the outside cover, my name was doubly underlined and I knew that was the signal for customs that I was a Jew and was to be jailed on reentry. Later, the Germans would attach the name Sarah and Israel to every Jewish person's passport, but when I traveled that was not yet done. As I sat there, I had no hope whatsoever that U.S. immigration officials would be merciful and let me stay. From all I knew, nothing had been done by the U.S. government to make any special allowances for Jewish refugees. To whom could I appeal? The Swiss Consul? The League of Nations? Truly, I felt doomed.

When the official came back, Bobby was with him, agitated and arguing. He shouted at me from across the table: "Don't worry, I'll get you out."

I was too afraid to move. The official sat down and addressed me sternly, like a schoolteacher. "Your cousins are here to take you home," he said. "Why didn't you tell me in the first place?"

What cousins? I kept my mouth shut. Bobby had worked out something, but what? "Joseph and Hilda," he said helpfully. "You know they live in New York."

"Oh, yes. I forgot." Joseph and Hilda were acquaintances from Vienna. I had no idea they lived in New York, but anyway—maybe there was some hope ...

But it was clear the official did not believe us. He turned to Bobby. "I explained the Mann Act provisions to you, Mr. Jensen," he said sternly. "Violation thereof is a deportable offense. You claim to be engaged to this young lady. Very well, Immigration will require her to bring proof of marriage before we will grant her permission to stay."

"Certainly," said Bobby. "We plan to get married." He stood there as I remembered him, short, combative, ugly, and utterly reliable. I felt so grateful to him for rescuing me, for having waited all this year for me.

"Step forward," the official said. "I will ask you to sign this paper, which specifies that you will submit proof of marriage to Immigration within one week of today. Failure to do so will mean immediate deportation." I signed without reading what he put in front of me. I would have signed anything. . . .

The next year and a half was a period of transition and of incessant learning. First of all, being poor. It was different from the way we had been poor in Europe in the months right after our emigration, because there was always enough to eat, there was a decent apartment and if one really needed something desperately there were relatives with some money to whom one could appeal. In New York it was poverty without a fallback. Neither Bobby nor I had any idea of the resources New York City offered to the poor, such as employment services, counseling, retraining, and temporary welfare. We were convinced, and rightly so, that our immigrant status obliged us to be self-supporting and that any contact with any agency whatsoever was dangerous to our status. Although we later learned that the Hebrew Immigrant Aid Society (HIAS) and Jewish welfare agencies helped thousands of refugees like us, we never contacted them. Suddenly, then, I was poor the way the poor are—without any reserve money in the bank, without any relatives to fall back on, without the network of support one usually has if one lives long in a community.

We could just about manage. Bobby's princely salary of fifty dollars a month with occasional overtime secured our room (fifteen dollars a month) and minimal food. He got a hot meal at the hospital at noon and usually managed to bring some leftovers home for me. Carfare for job-seeking was a big expense and I learned to save a nickel a day by first riding the subway to Times Square where the *New York Times* want ads were displayed on large billboards in the Times Building. I would note down all the openings and do all my midtown job applications on foot. I tried for every kind of work but did not get very far. My English was poor and my expensive, well-cut European clothes—the only clothes I had—marked me at once as a recent immigrant. Usually, the second question asked was my undoing. Where have you worked before? I truthfully answered, Nowhere in this country and I was a governess in Europe for a year. "Sorry, we need references." My try-outs at factory jobs were equally hopeless. I had never seen machinery, much less worked at it, and my finger skills have never been good. I was usually fired the first hour. After a few months of this I was so desperate for work, I tried housework. That, too, failed. I went out for a few day-work jobs, tried to follow all instructions and worked hard at scrubbing and cleaning. But usually by lunchtime the lady of the house would get suspicious of me and start questioning me about my past, previous experience, etcetera. When I answered truthfully, I was fired. "You wouldn't be happy in this kind of work, with your education." ...

It took six months of unemployment for me to learn to lie. . . .

As I struggled with the harsh reality of immigrant life, straining all my energies toward survival, toward making a success of my marriage and toward assimilating to my new culture, Europe kept pulling at me with a thousand strands.

Shortly after Germany invaded Czechoslovakia in May 1939, over the feeble and ineffectual protest of the Western powers, the Spanish civil war ended with Franco's victory. Defeated Loyalists swarmed across the French border, only to be arrested and placed in internment camps. I worried about my mother in Nice—once the French started interning some foreigners, it might not take them long to intern all foreigners.

My mother, meanwhile, had other concerns. Her young man had left her, taking a hundred dollars she had lent him. She had moved from the little village where I had last seen her to Nice, where there were many German and Austrian refugee artists. She was happy in her new apartment. My father came to visit her in May 1939 and she made plans with him about emigrating to England in case the situation in Europe got too dangerous for them. She assured me she was being realistic. She asked me to visit several people in New York who owed her money. She wanted me to take some of her pictures to New York galleries so she could secure an exhibit.

My father wrote in a different vein. He had serious health problems, which required a more restful lifestyle than he could now afford. The fact that he had to provide separate living arrangements for each member of the family put a great strain on his finances. He expected war to break out in Europe and felt it was essential for the family to leave Europe as soon as possible. The obstacles to emigration were enormous, but he worried most about his ability to support his family in a new land. He had finally decided that he would come to America, but only if he could be sure to support himself and his family. He had some medications on which he owned the patents and which he would try to market in the U.S.A. He, too, sent me lists of friends of his whom I should visit to secure outstanding small debts or other tangible favors.

It was clear from this correspondence that my parents had no idea of my actual situation. They thought I was comfortably married to a man who adequately supported me; his wealthy family would surely be interested in helping my family, if only I were nice enough to them; they thought I knew my way around, had numerous wealthy contacts and could, if only I wanted to, find sponsors for them, move the State Department to act more quickly and favorably on their behalf, and look after their various friends, acquaintances, and contacts from Europe. They thought I had access to relief agencies, refugee support networks, and the like.

I suppose I could and should have told them the truth in blunt terms: that I was living in poverty; that I had no way of personally contacting Bobby's relatives who lived in Florida; that Florida was as far from New York as Vienna was from London; that his relatives had already given twenty affidavits of support to various relatives and friends before our turn had come; that having given so many affidavits already, any they now might give

would have little value in the eyes of the U.S. Consul; that I had no contact with refugee agencies and was afraid of them; that all the refugees I knew were young and poor. Possibly this might have helped, but I could not do it. I could not risk upsetting my father with his bad heart by bringing bad news. My mother needed above all to keep to a steady course and have some hope in the future—I could not see myself taking that away from her. Besides which, I needed to hold out some hope myself, for my mind and political sense told me that disaster was not far off. . . .

. . . I was frantic. With my limited contacts, I tried to secure affidavits and letters of support for them so that they might be classified as "immigrants" by the U.S. Consul in Zurich. With such a certification European governments were willing to give transit visas and even residence permits. U.S. consulates all over Europe were swamped with immigration applications, but they proceeded with infinite slowness on a business-as-usual policy while Europe was disintegrating. With the hindsight of half a century and with new documentation now available, we can now say that this was a deliberate policy to discourage immigration. It was also arbitrarily carried out by the different Consuls in different countries. The U.S. Consul in Switzerland was known to go strictly by the book.

Securing an affidavit of support for my parents was only the first step in a seemingly endless bureaucratic process. The immigrant who had secured an affidavit of support acceptable to the U.S. Consul and who had passed a medical examination was then obliged to wait until his/her quota number came up. My mother was born in Hungary and therefore, according to immigration regulations, she fell under the Hungarian quota, while my father and sister, both born in Vienna, fell under the more favorable Austrian quota. The Hungarian quota had an eight-year waiting period on it. In July of 1939 we were mere amateurs at the immigration business. We still hoped that once I secured the proper affidavits, the U.S. Consul in Zurich would make allowances "to unite family members," as the law required.

I cannot think with anything but bitterness of the fact that the U.S. government under the presidency of Franklin Delano Roosevelt never did anything to change the racist and anti-Semitic quota system built into the 1924 Immigration Act. Had it done so, hundred of thousands of Jews might have been saved out of Europe, my mother among them. The fact that it could be done, with the stroke of a presidential pen, was shown when the Hungarian quota was suspended after the 1956 Hungarian rebellion in order to save anti-Communist Hungarians by the tens of thousands. None of this was done by the Roosevelt administration, except for the rescue of a thousand prominent intellectuals and artists. My mother was not famous enough to fall under that eligibility. I still have a thick folder in my files, filled with pleading letters I wrote to various people, including Mrs. Roosevelt, to ask them to intercede on behalf of my mother. I was turned down everywhere. . . .

AUGUST 23, 1939—HITLER AND STALIN SIGN "NON-AGGRESSION PACT."

. . . Five days later [my mother] wrote to me:

> God give us strength to persevere. Send me an affidavit . . . At this moment the U.S. embassy here handles only the affairs of U.S. citizens. . . . The border is closed.
>
> No telephone; telegrams are censored. The iron plate has been lowered, we are trapped. It is hopeless . . .

SEPTEMBER 1, 1939—GERMANS INVADE POLAND FROM THE WEST; RUSSIANS INVADE POLAND FROM THE EAST, POLAND SURRENDERS.

SEPTEMBER 3, 1939—ENGLAND AND FRANCE DECLARE WAR ON GERMANY.

As my mother had said, the iron plate had been lowered. They were trapped, my family and all the others. With the fall of Czechoslovakia an entire branch of our family disappeared from view and many of them perished during the holocaust. My mother's sisters were in Holland. The Hungarian branch of the family seemed as yet relatively safe, since Hungary was an Axis partner. Some of the lucky ones of our Vienna relatives and friends were then in England—with the outbreak of the war they would, once again, be in direct danger. Looking at the daily changing map of Europe it seemed like an enormous trap in which my relatives and friends, my teachers, all the people I had loved and admired were rabbits around whom a huge net was being drawn, tighter and tighter. . . .

Nothing I could do would have the slightest impact on their lives and on their safety. . . . [Each time my parents came to some decision about their lives,] some bureaucrat in one or the other countries on whose existence they now depended—Liechtenstein, Switzerland, France, the U.S.A.—pulled a string, wrote notations on some record, cited an obscure law or regulation, and whatever they had come to decide in such agony and turmoil was rendered null and void. All of us were jerked around like puppets on invisible strings. Power and self-determination were nonexistent. That is what it means to be stateless, to be a refugee. Your life is out of your own control, in the hands of people to whom you are nothing but a cipher, a number.

VALERIE MATSUMOTO
Japanese American Women during World War II

On no group of U.S. citizens did the war have greater impact than upon Japanese Americans. Fearful of a Japanese fifth column on American shores, military and civilian leaders urged Franklin Roosevelt to issue an executive order removing Americans of Japanese decent on the West Coast to relocation camps inland. Despite the fact that a vast majority of the nearly 120,000 Japanese Americans in the United States were citizens with the same rights and obligations as any other citizen, the president succumbed to pressure and issued Executive Order 9066 in February 1942, which ultimately resulted in the establishment of ten concentration camps in remote areas of the West. Forced to leave their homes and businesses at great financial cost, both Japanese-born parents, the Issei, and their American-born children, the Nisei, faced the trauma of removal and the shame of implied disloyalty. Not until 1990 would the nation acknowledge the magnitude of its offense and begin providing financial redress for survivors of the camps.

The following essay explores what life in the camps was like for women and the efforts of younger ones to reconstruct a life after internment.

> The life here cannot be expressed. Sometimes, we are resigned to it, but when we see the barbed wire fences and the sentry tower with floodlights, it gives us a feeling of being prisoners in a "concentration camp." We try to be happy and yet oftentimes a gloominess does creep in. When I see the "I'm an American" editorial and write-ups, the "equality of race etc."—it seems to be mocking us in our faces. I just wonder if all the sacrifices and hard labor on [the] part of our parents has gone up to leave nothing to show for it?
> Letter from Shizuko Horiuchi,
> Pomona Assembly Center, May 24, 1942

Overlying the mixed feelings of anxiety, anger, shame, and confusion [of the Japanese Americans who were forced to relocate] was resignation. As a relatively small minority caught in a storm of turbulent events that destroyed their individual and community security, there was little the Japanese Americans could do but shrug and say, "*Shikata ga nai,* " or "It can't be helped," the implication being that the situation must be endured. The phrase lingered on many lips when the Issei, Nisei [second generation], and the young Sansei [third generation] children prepared for the move—which was completed by November 1942—to the ten permanent relocation camps organized by the War Relocation Authority: Topaz, Utah; Poston and Gila River, Arizona; Amache, Colorado; Manzanar and Tule Lake, California; Heart Mountain, Wyoming; Minidoka, Idaho; Denson and Rohwer, Arkansas.[1] Denson and Rohwer were located in the swampy lowlands of Arkansas; the other camps were in desolate desert or semi-desert areas subject to dust storms and extreme temperatures reflected in the nicknames given to the three sections of the Poston Camp: Toaston, Roaston, and Duston.

The conditions of camp life profoundly altered family relations and affected women of all ages and backgrounds. Family unity deteriorated in the crude communal facilities and cramped barracks. The unceasing battle with the elements, the poor food, the shortages of

Excerpted from "Japanese American Women during World War II" by Valerie Matsumoto in *Frontiers* 8 (1984):6, 8–13. Copyright © 1984 by Frontiers Editorial Collective. Reprinted by permission of the author and *Frontiers*. Notes have been renumbered.

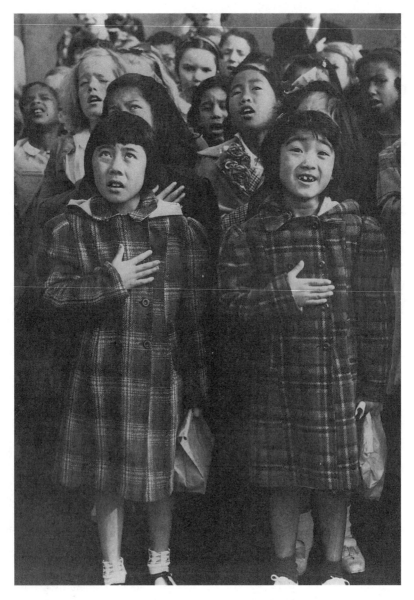

Pledge of Allegiance, 1942. Dorothea Lange had a keen eye for irony, as in this photograph of Japanese American girls in California a few weeks before they were deported to relocation camps. (Photograph courtesy of the National Archives.)

toilet tissue and milk, coupled with wartime profiteering and mismanagement, and the sense of injustice and frustration took their toll on a people uprooted, far from home.

The standard housing in the camps was a spartan barracks, about twenty feet by one hundred feet, divided into four to six rooms furnished with steel army cots. Initially each single room or "apartment" housed an average of eight persons; individuals without kin nearby were often moved in with smaller families. Because the partitions between apartments did not reach the ceiling, even the smallest noises traveled freely from one end of the building to the other. There were usually fourteen barracks in each block, and each block had its own mess hall, laundry, latrine, shower facilities, and recreation room. . . . The even greater lack of privacy in the latrine and shower facilities necessitated adjustments in former notions of modesty. There were no partitions in the shower room, and the latrine consisted of two rows of partitioned toilets "with nothing in front of you, just on the sides."[2] . . . A married woman with a family wrote from Heart Mountain:

Last weekend, we had an awful cold wave and it was about 20° to 30° below zero. In such a weather, it's terrible to try going even to the bath and latrine house. . . . It really aggravates me to hear some politicians say we Japanese are being coddled, for *it isn't so!!* We're on ration as much as outsiders are. I'd say welcome to anyone to try living behind barbed wire and be cooped in a 20 ft. by 20 ft. room. . . . We do our sleeping, dressing, ironing, hanging up our clothes in this one room.[3]

After the first numbness of disorientation, the evacuees set about making their situation bearable, creating as much order in their lives as possible. With blankets they partitioned their apartments into tiny rooms and created benches, tables, and shelves as piles of scrap lumber left over from barracks construction vanished; victory gardens and flower patches appeared. . . .

Despite the best efforts of the evacuees to restore order to their disrupted world, camp conditions prevented replication of their prewar lives. Women's work experiences, for example, changed in complex ways during the years of internment. Each camp offered a wide range of jobs, resulting from the organization

of the camps as model cities administered through a series of departments headed by European American administrators. The departments handled everything from accounting, agriculture, education, and medical care to mess hall service and the weekly newspaper. The scramble for jobs began early in the assembly centers and camps, and all able-bodied persons were expected to work.

Even before the war many family members had worked, but now children and parents, men and women all received the same low wages. In the relocation camps, doctors, teachers, and other professionals were at the top of the pay scale, earning $19 per month. The majority of workers received $16, and apprentices earned $12. The new equity in pay and the variety of available jobs gave many women unprecedented opportunities for experimentation, as illustrated by one woman's account of her family's work in Poston:

First I wanted to find art work, but I didn't last too long because it wasn't very interesting . . . so I worked in the mess hall, but that wasn't for me, so I went to the accounting department—time-keeping—and I enjoyed that, so I stayed there. . . . My dad . . . went to a shoe shop . . . and then he was block gardener. . . . He got $16. . . . [My sister] was secretary for the block manager; then she went to the optometry department. She was assistant optometrist; she fixed all the glasses and fitted them. . . . That was $16.[4]

As early as 1942, the War Relocation Authority began to release evacuees temporarily from the centers and camps to do voluntary seasonal farm work in neighboring areas hard hit by the wartime labor shortage. The work was arduous, as one young woman discovered when she left Topaz to take a job plucking turkeys:

The smell is terrific until you get used to it. . . . We all wore gunny sacks around our waist, had a small knife and plucked off the fine feathers.

This is about the hardest work that many of us have done—but without a murmur of complaint we worked 8 hours through the first day without a pause.

We were all so tired that we didn't even feel like eating. . . . Our fingers and wrists were just aching, and I just dreamt of turkeys and more turkeys.[5]

Work conditions varied from situation to situation, and some exploitative farmers refused to pay the Japanese Americans after they had finished beet topping or fruit picking. One worker noted that the degree of friendliness on the employer's part decreased as the harvest neared completion. Nonetheless, many workers, like the turkey plucker, concluded that "even if the work is hard, it is worth the freedom we are allowed." . . .

Like their noninterned contemporaries, most young Nisei women envisioned a future of marriage and children. They—and their parents—anticipated that they would marry other Japanese Americans, but these young women also expected to choose their own husbands and to marry "for love." This mainstream American ideal of marriage differed greatly from the Issei's view of love as a bond that might evolve over the course of an arranged marriage that was firmly rooted in less romantic notions of compatibility and responsibility. The discrepancy between Issei and Nisei conceptions of love and marriage had sturdy prewar roots; internment fostered further divergence from the old customs of arranged marriage. In the artificial hothouse of camp, Nisei romances often bloomed quickly. As Nisei men left to prove their loyalty to the United States in the 442nd Combat Team and the 100th Battalion, young Japanese Americans strove to grasp what happiness and security they could, given the uncertainties of the future. Lily Shoji, in her "Fem-a-lites" newspaper column, commented upon the "changing world" and advised Nisei women: "This is the day of sudden dates, of blind dates on the up-and-up, so let the flash of a uniform be a signal to you to be ready for any emergency. . . . Romance is blossoming with the emotion and urgency of war."[6]

In keeping with this atmosphere, camp newspaper columns like Shoji's in *The Mercedian*, *The Daily Tulean Dispatch's* "Strictly Feminine," and the *Poston Chronicle's* "Fashionotes" gave their Nisei readers countless suggestions on how to impress boys, care for their complexions, and choose the latest fashions. These evacuee-authored columns thus mirrored the mainstream girls' periodicals of the time. Such fashion news may seem incongruous in the context of an internment camp whose inmates had little choice in clothing beyond what they could find in the Montgomery Ward or Sears and Roebuck mailorder catalogues. These columns, however,

reflect women's efforts to remain in touch with the world outside the barbed wire fence; they reflect as well women's attempt to maintain morale in a drab, depressing environment. "There's something about color in clothes," speculated Tule Lake columnist "Yuri"; "Singing colors have a heart-building effect. . . . Color is a stimulant we need—both for its effect on ourselves and on others."[7] . . .

RESETTLEMENT: COLLEGE AND WORK

Relocation began slowly in 1942. Among the first to venture out of the camps were college students, assisted by the National Japanese American Student Relocation Council, a nongovernmental agency that provided invaluable placement aid to 4,084 Nisei in the years 1942–46.[8] Founded in 1942 by concerned educators, this organization persuaded institutions outside the restricted Western Defense zone to accept Nisei students and facilitated their admissions and leave clearances. A study of the first 400 students to leave camp showed that a third of them were women.[9] Because of the cumbersome screening process, few other evacuees departed on indefinite leave before 1943. In that year, the War Relocation Authority tried to expedite the clearance procedure by broadening an army registration program aimed at Nisei males to include all adults. With this policy change, the migration from the camps steadily increased.[10]

Many Nisei, among them a large number of women, were anxious to leave the limbo of camp and return "to normal life again."[11] . . . An aspiring teacher wrote: "Mother and father do not want me to go out. However, I want to go so very much that sometimes I feel that I'd go even if they disowned me. What shall I do? I realize the hard living conditions outside but I think I can take it."[12] Women's developing sense of independence in the camp environment and their growing awareness of their abilities as workers contributed to their self-confidence and hence their desire to leave. Significantly, Issei parents, despite initial reluctance, were gradually beginning to sanction their daughters' departures for education and employment in the Midwest and East. One Nisei noted: "[Father] became more broad-minded in the relocation center. . . . At first he didn't want me to relocate, but he gave in. . . . He didn't say I could go . . . but he helped me pack, so I thought, 'Well, he didn't say no.'"[13]

The decision to relocate was a difficult one.... Many internees worried about their acceptance in the outside world. The Nisei considered themselves American citizens, and they had an allegiance to the land of their birth.... But evacuation had taught the Japanese Americans that in the eyes of many of their fellow Americans, theirs was the face of the enemy. Many Nisei were torn by mixed feelings of shame, frustration, and bitterness at the denial of their civil rights.... "A feeling of uncertainty hung over the camp; we were worried about the future. Plans were made and remade, as we tried to decide what to do. Some were ready to risk anything to get away. Others feared to leave the protection of the camp."[14]

Thus, those first college students were the scouts whose letters back to camp marked pathways for others to follow. May Yoshino sent a favorable report to her family in Topaz from the nearby University of Utah, indicating that there were "plenty of schoolgirl jobs for those who want to study at the University."[15] Correspondence from other Nisei students shows that although they succeeded at making the dual transition from high school to college and from camp to the outside world, they were not without anxieties as to whether they could handle the study load and the reactions of the European Americans around them. One student at Drake University in Iowa wrote to her interned sister about a professor's reaction to her autobiographical essay, "Evacuation": "Today Mr.—, the English teacher that scares me, told me that the theme that I wrote the other day was very interesting.... You could just imagine how wonderful and happy I was to know that he liked it a little bit.... I've been awfully busy trying to catch up on work and the work is so different from high school. I think that little by little I'm beginning to adjust myself to college life."[16] ... Lillian ... Ota, a Wellesley student, reassured [her interned friends contemplating college:] "During the first few days you'll be invited by the college to teas and receptions. Before long you'll lose the awkwardness you might feel at such doings after the months of abnormal life at evacuation centers."[17] Although Ota had not noticed "that my being a 'Jap' has made much difference on the campus itself," she offered

cautionary and pragmatic advice to the Nisei, suggesting the burden of responsibility these relocated students felt, as well as the problem of communicating their experiences and emotions to European Americans.

> It is scarcely necessary to point out that those who have probably never seen a nisei before will get their impression of the nisei as a whole from the relocated students. It won't do you or your family and friends much good to dwell on what you consider injustices when you are questioned about evacuation. Rather, stress the contributions of [our] people to the nation's war effort.[18] ...

Armed with [such] advice and drawn by encouraging reports, increasing numbers of women students left camp.[19] ... The trickle of migration from the camps grew into a steady stream by 1943, as the War Relocation Authority developed its resettlement program to aid evacuees in finding housing and employment in the East and Midwest.... [But] leaving camp meant [more changes.] Even someone as confident as Marii Kyogoku ... found that reentry into the European American-dominated world beyond the barbed wire fence was not a simple matter of stepping back into old shoes. Leaving the camps—like entering them—meant major changes in psychological perspective and self-image.

> I had thought that because before evacuation I had adjusted myself rather well in a Caucasian society, I would go right back into my former frame of mind. I have found, however, that though the center became unreal and was as if it had never existed as soon as I got on the train at Delta, I was never so self-conscious in all my life.

Kyogoku was amazed to see so many men and women in uniform and, despite her "proper" dining preparation, felt strange sitting at a table set with clean linen and a full set of silverware.

> I felt a diffidence at facing all these people and things, which was most unusual. Slowly things have come to seem natural, though I am still excited by the sounds of the busy city and thrilled every time I see a street lined with trees, I no longer feel that I am the cynosure of all eyes.[20] ...

Many relocating Japanese Americans received moral and material assistance from a number of service organizations and religious groups, particularly the Presbyterians, the Methodists, the Society of Friends, and the Young Women's Christian Association. One such Nisei, Dorcas Asano, enthusiastically described to a Quaker sponsor her activities in the big city:

> Since receiving your application for hostel accommodation, I have decided to come to New York and I am really glad for the opportunity to be able to resume the normal civilized life after a year's confinement in camp. New York is really a city of dreams and we are enjoying every minute working in offices, rushing back and forth to work in the ever-speeding subway trains, counting our ration points, buying war bonds, going to church, seeing the latest shows, plays, operas, making many new friends and living like our neighbors in the war time. I only wish more of my friends who are behind the fence will take advantage of the many helpful hands offered to them.[21]

The Nisei also derived support and strength from networks—formed before and during internment—of friends and relatives. The homes of those who relocated first became way stations for others as they made the transition into new communities and jobs. In 1944, soon after she obtained a place to stay in New York City, Miné Okubo found that "many of the other evacuees relocating in New York came ringing my doorbell. They were sleeping all over the floor!"[22] Single women often accompanied or joined sisters, brothers, and friends as many interconnecting grapevines carried news of likely jobs, housing, and friendly communities. . . .

For Nisei women, like their non-Japanese sisters, the wartime labor shortage opened the door into industrial, clerical, and managerial occupations. Prior to the war, racism had excluded the Japanese Americans from most white-collar clerical and sales positions, and, according to sociologist Evelyn Nakano Glenn, "the most common form of nonagricultural employment for the immigrant women (Issei) and their American-born daughters (Nisei) was domestic service."[23] The highest percentage of job offers for both men and women continued to be requests for domestic workers. In July 1943, the Kansas City branch of the War Relocation Authority noted that 45 percent of requests for workers were for domestics, and the Milwaukee office cited 61 percent.[24] However, Nisei women also found jobs as secre-

taries, typists, file clerks, beauticians, and factory workers. By 1950, 47 percent of employed Japanese American women were clerical and sales workers and operatives; only 10 percent were in domestic service.[25] The World War II decade, then, marked a turning point for Japanese American women in the labor force. . . .

[Improved opportunities could not compensate for the] uprooting [of] communities and [the] severe psychological and emotional damage [inflicted upon Japanese Americans by internment.] The vast majority returned to the West Coast at the end of the war in 1945— a move that, like the initial evacuation, was a grueling test of flexibility and fortitude. Even with the assistance of old friends and service organizations, the transition was taxing and painful; the end of the war meant not only long-awaited freedom but more battles to be fought in social, academic, and economic arenas. The Japanese Americans faced hostility, crude living conditions, and a struggle for jobs. Few evacuees received any compensation for their financial losses, estimated conservatively at $400 million, because Congress decided to appropriate only $38 million for the settlement of claims.[26] It is even harder to place a figure on the toll taken in emotional shock, self-blame, broken dreams, and insecurity. One Japanese American woman still sees in her nightmares the watchtower searchlights that troubled her sleep forty years ago.

The war altered Japanese American women's lives in complicated ways. In general, internment and resettlement accelerated earlier trends that differentiated the Nisei from their parents. Although most young women, like their mothers and non-Japanese peers, anticipated a future centered on a husband and children, they had already felt the influence of mainstream middle-class values of love and marriage and quickly moved away from the pattern of arranged marriage in the camps. There, increased peer group activities and the relaxation of parental authority gave them more independence. The Nisei women's expectations of marriage became more akin to the companionate ideals of their peers than to those of the Issei.

As before the war, many Nisei women worked . . . , but the new parity in wages they received altered family dynamics. And though they expected to contribute to the family economy, a large number did so in settings far from the family, availing themselves of opportunities provided by the student and worker relocation programs. In meeting the challenges facing them, Nisei women drew not only upon the disciplined strength inculcated by their Issei parents but also upon firmly rooted support networks and the greater measure of self-reliance and independence that they developed during the crucible of the war years.

NOTES

1. Many of the Japanese community leaders arrested by the FBI before the evacuation were interned in special all-male camps in North Dakota, Louisiana, and New Mexico. Some Japanese Americans living outside the perimeter of the Western defense zone in Arizona, Utah, etc., were not interned.

2. Chieko Kimura, personal interview, Apr. 9, 1978, Glendale, Arizona.

3. Shizuko Horiuchi to Henriette Von Blon, Jan. 24, 1943, Henriette Von Blon Collection, Hoover Institution Archives ([hereafter] HIA).

4. Ayako Kanemura, personal interview, Mar. 10, 1978, Glendale, Arizona.

5. Anonymous, Topaz Times, Oct. 24, 1942, p. 3.

6. Lily Shoji, "Fem-a-lites," The Mercedian, Aug. 7, 1942, p. 4.

7. "Yuri," "Strictly Feminine," The Daily Tulean Dispatch, Sept. 29, 1942, p. 2.

8. From 1942 to the end of 1945 the Council allocated about $240,000 in scholarships, most of which were provided through the donations of the church and the World Student Service Fund. The average grant for student for was $156.73, which in that area was a major contribution towards the cost of higher education. Source: National Japanese American Student Relocation Council, Minutes of the Executive Committee Meeting, Philadelphia, Pennsylvania, Dec. 19, 1945.

9. Robert O'Brien, The College Nisei (Palo Alto: Pacific Books, 1949), pp. 73–74.

10. The disastrous consequences of the poorly conceived clearance procedure had been examined by Robert Wilson and Bill Hosokawa, East to America: A History of the Japanese in the United States (New York: Morrow, 1980), pp. 226–27, and Audrie Girdner and Anne Loftis, The Great Betrayal: The Evacuation of the Japanese-Americans during World War II (New York: Macmillan, 1969), pp. 342–43.

11. May Nakamoto to Mrs. Jack Shoup, Nov. 20, 1943, Mrs. Jack Shoup Collection, HIA.

12. Toshiko Imada to Margaret Cosgrave Sowers, Jan. 16, 1943, Margaret Cosgrave Sowers Collection, HIA.

13. Ayako Kanemura, personal interview, Mar. 24, 1978, Glendale, Arizona.

14. Mine Okubo, Citizen 13660 (New York: Columbia University Press, 1946), p. 66.

15. Topaz Times, Oct. 24, 2942, p. 3.

16. Masako Ono to Atsuko Ono, Sept. 28, 1942, Margaret Cosgrave Sowers Collection, HIA. Prior to the war, few Nisei had college experience: the 1940 census lists 674 second-generation women and 1,507 men who had attended or who were attending college.

17. Lillian Ota, "Campus Report," Trek (Feb. 1943), p. 33.

18. Ota, pp. 33–34.

19. O'Brien, p. 84.

20. Marii Kyogoku, Resettlement Bulletin (July 1943), p. 5.

21. Dorcas Asano to Josephine Duveneck, Jan. 22, 1944, Conard-Duveneck Collection, HIA.

22. Mine Okubo, Miné Okubo: An American Experience, exhibition catalogue (Oakland: Oakland Museum, 1972), p. 84.

23. Evelyn Nakano Glenn, "The Dialectics of Wage Work: Japanese American Women and Domestic Servants, 1905–1940," Feminist Studies 6, no. 3 (Fall 1980):412.

24. Advisory Committee of Evacuees, Resettlement Bulletin (July 1943), p. 3.

25. 1950 United States Census, Special Report.

26. Susan M. Hartmann, The Home Front and Beyond, American Women in the 1940s (Boston: Twayne Publishers, 1982), p. 126. There is some debate regarding the origins of the assessment of evacuee losses at $400 million. However, a recent study by the Commission on Wartime Relocation and Internment of Civilians has estimated that the Japanese Americans lost between $149 million and $370 million in 1945 dollars, and between $810 million and $2 billion in 1983 dollars. See the San Francisco Chronicle, June 16, 1983, p. 12.

RUTH MILKMAN

Gender at Work: The Sexual Division of Labor during World War II

As the nation, struggling with economic depression, began to fight its second world war, unemployment lines quickly vanished. Manpower shortages meant that women would once again move into jobs in industry and experience new vocational opportunities; a lessening of discrimination based on marital status, age, and race; and public praise for their wartime contribution as workers. The potential provided by the war for refashioning gender roles was enormous, but the results were disappointing. The expectation was that once the men came home, women would happily exchange industrial tools for the broom and mop or new vacuum cleaner and the baby bottle. Polls showed that up to 85 percent of these women needed to continue working and expected that job seniority would entitle them to return after veterans had been absorbed in the work force.

The redefining of "men's jobs" and "women's jobs" precipitated by wartime mobilization and the rapid return to the prewar sexual division of labor is the subject of Ruth Milkman's study. Focusing especially on the auto and electronics industry, she provides unmistakable evidence of the persistence of occupational segregation at a time when the very survival of democracy was at stake. Note how job segregation demonstrates the double meaning of Milkman's title *Gender at Work*. What was the rationale for segregating jobs by sex? What evidence does Milkman provide to suggest that the designation of jobs as "male" or "female" was often arbitrary? Given management's assessment of women's job performance during the war, how does she explain the reversion to old patterns? What factors were involved? What explanation is offered for the fact that black men were able to hold on to wartime gains in industry whereas white and black women were not?

If it is true that occupational sex typing becomes even more important when women's labor force participation increases, what trends do you foresee for the postwar decades given the changes in the pattern of women's labor force participation noted by Jones for the 1930s and by Milkman for the 1940s? How does job segregation help to explain the fact that women have yet to close the earnings gap with men when both are full-time workers?

Frances Green, Reg Kirchner, Ann Waldner, and Blanche Osborne emerging from their four-engine Flying Fortress. They were among the 1,074 Women's Airforce Service Pilots (WASPs) who flew noncombat missions during World War II. Although several died in the line of duty, WASPs were not eligible for military insurance or for G.I. benefits. At the end of the war, the WASPs were disbanded. Not until 1978 were the survivors offered veteran's status. (Courtesy of the U.S. Army Museum.)

Conversion to war production involved redefinition of the entire employment structure. Some civilian automobile production jobs were also necessary for the production of tanks, aircraft, engines and ordnance; other war jobs were completely new. The changeover to war production in electrical manufacturing was less dramatic, but also involved shifts in the character and distribution of jobs. Thus, many of the war jobs that had to be filled (in both industries) were not clearly labeled as "women's" or "men's" work, at least at first. . . .

While the government had actively pressured some firms to hire women, it made no effort whatsoever to influence their placement within industry once management complied. The U.S. Employment Service routinely filled employer job openings that called for specific numbers of women and men. Although ceilings were imposed on the number of men who could be allocated to each plant, employers had a free hand in placing women and men in particular jobs within this constraint.[1] Although the unions sometimes contested the sexual division of labor after the fact, the initial job assignments were left entirely to management.

Women were not evenly distributed through the various jobs available in the war plants, but were hired into specific classifications that management deemed "suitable" for women and were excluded from other jobs. Some employers conducted special surveys to determine the sexual division of labor in a plant; probably more often such decisions were made informally by individual supervisors.[2] Although data on the distribution of women through job classifications in the wartime auto and electrical industries are sketchy, there is no mistaking the persistence of segregation by sex. A 1943 survey of the auto industry's Detroit plants, for example, found more than one-half of the women workers clustered in only five of seventy-two job classifications. Only 11 percent of the men were employed in these five occupations.[3]

Jobs were also highly segregated in the electrical industry during the war. A 1942 study of electrical appliance plants (most of which had already been converted to military production when surveyed) found women, who were 30 percent of the workers, in only twenty-one job classifications, whereas men

were spread across seventy-two of them. Nearly half of the women (47 percent) were employed in a single job category, and 68 percent were clustered in four occupations. Only 16 percent of the men were in these four job classifications.[4] . . .

Job segregation by sex was explicitly acknowledged in many war plants: Jobs were formally labeled "male" and "female." The two largest electrical firms, GE and Westinghouse, continued this practice until the end of the war. And in 45 percent of the auto plants with sexually mixed work forces responding to a survey conducted in mid-1944 by the UAW Women's Bureau, jobs were formally categorized as "male" or "female."[5] Available records suggest that sex segregation also existed elsewhere, even if it was not formally acknowledged. . . .

Segregation appears to be a constant across both industries during the war years. However, in both industries there was considerable plant-to-plant variation in patterns of employment by sex. In the Detroit area, for example, there was a wide range in the proportion of women employed, even among plants manufacturing the same products. In April 1943, women were 29 percent of the workers at the GM Cadillac plant, which was producing engine parts, but women made up 59 percent of the work force at the Excello Corporation's Detroit plant, which made the same product. Similarly, although women were only 2 percent of the workers at Continental Motors, they were 27 percent of those at the Jefferson Avenue plant of the Hudson Motor Car Company. Both plants made aircraft motors.[6] In the electrical industry, too, there was considerable variation of this sort, even among plants owned by the same company and producing similar goods. . . .

Whatever the sexual division of labor happened to be at a given point in time, management always seemed to insist that there was no alternative. When a War Department representative visited an airplane plant where large numbers of women were employed, he was told that the best welder in the plant was a woman. "Their supervisors told me that their work is fine, even better than that of the men who were formerly on those jobs," he reported. "In another plant in the same area, I remarked on the absence of women and was told that women just can't do those jobs—the very same jobs. It is true, they can't do that type of work—as long as the employer refuses to hire and train them."[7]

Although the specifics varied, everywhere management was quick to offer a rationale for the concentration of women in some jobs and their exclusion from others. . . . "Woman-power differs from manpower as oil fuel differs from coal," proclaimed the trade journal *Automotive War Production* in October 1943, "and an understanding of the characteristics of the energy involved was needed for obtaining best results." Although it was now applied to a larger and quite different set of jobs, the basic characterization of women's abilities and limitations was familiar. As *Automotive War Production* put it:

> On certain kinds of operations—the very ones requiring high manipulative skill—women were found to be a whole lot quicker and more efficient than men. Engineering womanpower means realizing fully that women are not only different from men in such things as lifting power and arm reach—but in many other ways that pertain to their physiological and their social functions. To understand these things does not mean to exclude women from *the jobs for which they are peculiarly adapted*, and where they can help to win this war. It merely means using them as women, and not as men.[8]

The idiom of women's war work in the electrical industry closely paralleled that in auto. "Nearly every Westinghouse plant employs women, especially for jobs that require dexterity with tiny parts," reported an article in *Factory Management and Maintenance* in March 1942. "At the East Pittsburgh plant, for instance, women tape coils. The thickness of each coil must be identical to within close limits, so the job requires feminine patience and deft fingers. Another job that calls for unlimited patience is the inspection of moving parts of electric instruments. . . ." Repeatedly stressed, especially in auto, was the lesser physical strength of the average woman worker. "Woman isn't just a 'smaller man,'" *Automotive War Production* pointed out. "Compensations in production processes must be made to allow for the fact that the average woman is only 35 percent muscle in comparison to the average man's 41 percent. Moreover, industrial studies have shown that only 54 percent of woman's weight is strength, as against man's 87 percent, and that the hand squeeze

of the average woman exerts only 48 pounds of pressure, against man's 81 pounds."[9]

Accompanying the characterization of women's work as "light" was an emphasis on cleanliness. "Women can satisfactorily fill all or most jobs performed by men, subject only to the limitations of strength and physical requirements," a meeting of the National Association of Manufacturers concluded in March 1942. "However . . . jobs of a particularly 'dirty' character, jobs that subject women to heat process or are of a 'wet' nature should not be filled by women . . . despite the fact that women could, if required, perform them."[10]

The emphasis in the idiom of sex-typing on the physical limitations of women workers had a dual character. It not only justified the sexual divison of labor, but it also served as the basis for increased mechanization and work simplification. "To adjust women's jobs to such [physical] differences, automotive plants have added more mechanical aids such as conveyors, chain hoists, and load lifters," reported *Automotive War Production*. A study by Constance Green found job dilution of this sort widespread in electrical firms and other war industries in the Connecticut Valley as well. "Where ten men had done ten complete jobs, now . . . eight women and two, three, or possibly four men together would do the ten split-up jobs," she noted. "Most often men set up machines, ground or adjusted tools, and generally 'serviced' the women who acted exclusively as machine operators."[11]

Although production technology was already quite advanced in both auto and electrical manufacturing, the pace of development accelerated during the war period. Management attributed this to its desire to make jobs easier for women, but the labor shortage and the opportunity to introduce new technology at government expense under war contracts were at least as important. However, the idiom that constructed women as "delicate" and, although poorly suited to "heavy" work, amenable to monotonous jobs, was now marshaled to justify the use of new technology and work "simplification." At Vultee Aircraft, for example, a manager explained:

> It definitely was in Vultee's favor that the hiring of women was started when production jobs were being simplified to meet the needs of fast, quantity production. . . . Special jigs were added

to hold small tools, such as drills, so that women could concentrate on employing more effectively their proven capacity for repetitive operations requiring high digital dexterity.

Unlike the man whom she replaced, she as a woman, had the capacity to withstand the monotony of even more simplified repetitive operations. To have suspended the air wrench from a counterbalanced support for him would have served merely to heighten his boredom with the job. As for the woman who replaced him, she now handles two such counterbalanced, air-driven wrenches, one in each hand.[12] . . .

There was a contradiction in the management literature on women's war work. It simultaneously stressed the fact that "women are being trained in skills that were considered exclusively in man's domain" and their special suitability for "delicate war jobs."[13] These two seemingly conflicting kinds of statements were reconciled through analogies between "women's work" at home and in the war plants. "Note the similarity between squeezing orange juice and the operation of a small drill press," the Sperry Gyroscope Company urged in a recruitment pamphlet. "Anyone can peel potatoes," it went on. "Burring and filing are almost as easy." An automotive industry publication praised women workers at the Ford Motor Company's Willow Run bomber plant in similar terms. "The ladies have shown they can operate drill presses as well as egg beaters," it proclaimed. "Why should men, who from childhood on never so much as sewed on buttons," inquired one manager, "be expected to handle delicate instruments better than women who have plied embroidery needles, knitting needles and darning needles all their lives?"[14] The newsreel *Glamour Girls of '43* pursued the same theme: "Instead of cutting the lines of a dress, this woman cuts the pattern of aircraft parts. Instead of baking cake, this woman is cooking gears to reduce the tension in the gears after use. . . ."[15] In this manner, virtually any job could be labeled "women's work."

Glamour was a related theme in the idiom through which women's war work was demarcated as female. As if calculated to assure women—and men—that war work need not involve a loss of femininity, depictions of women's new work roles were overlaid with allusions to their stylish dress and attractive appearance. "A pretty young inspec-

tor in blue slacks pushes a gauge—a cylindrical plug with a diamond-pointed push-button on its side—through the shaft's hollow chamber," was a typical rendition.[16] Such statements, like the housework analogies, effectively reconciled woman's position in what were previously "men's jobs" with traditional images of femininity.

Ultimately, what lay behind the mixed message that war jobs were at once "men's" and "women's" jobs was an unambiguous point: Women *could* do "men's work," but they were only expected to do it temporarily. The ideological definition of women's war work explicitly included the provision that they would gracefully withdraw from their "men's jobs" when the war ended and the rightful owners returned. Women, as everyone knew, were in heavy industry "for the duration." This theme would become much more prominent after the war, but it was a constant undercurrent from the outset.

Before the war, too, women had been stereotyped as temporary workers, and occupational sex-typing had helped to ensure that employed women would continue to view themselves as women first, workers second. Now this took on new importance, because the reserves of "womanpower" war industries drew on included married women, even mothers of young children, in unprecedented numbers. A study by the Automotive Council for War Production noted that of twelve thousand women employed during the war by one large automotive firm in Detroit, 68 percent were married, and 40 percent had children. And a 1943 WPB study found that 40 percent of one hundred fifty thousand women war workers employed in Detroit were mothers. "With the existing prejudice against employing women over forty, the overwhelming majority of these women workers are young mothers with children under 16."[17]

This was the group of women least likely to have been employed in the prewar years. "In this time of pressure for added labor supply," the U.S. Women's Bureau reported, "the married women for the first time in this country's history exceeded single women in the employed group."[18] . . .

Some firms made deliberate efforts to recruit the wives and daughters of men whom they had employed before the war. A 1942 study by Princeton University's Industrial

Relations Section reported on the reasons given by employers for this policy: "(1) It increases the local labor supply without affecting housing requirements; (2) it brings in new employees who are already acquainted with the company and who are likely to be as satisfactory employees as their male relatives; and (3) it may help to minimize postwar readjustment since wives of employed men are not looking for permanent employment."[19] Similarly, the Detroit Vickers aircraft plant had a policy of hiring "members of men's families who have gone to forces so that when these men come back there will be less of a problem in getting the women out of the jobs to give them back to the men."[20]

The dramatic rise in married women's employment during the war raised the longstanding tension between women's commitment to marriage and family and their status as individual members of the paid work force to a qualitatively different level. Before the war, the bulk of the female labor force was comprised of unmarried women; young wives with no children; and self-supporting widowed, divorced, and separated women. When married women and mothers went to work during the war, the occupational sex-typing that linked women's roles in the family and in paid work, far from disintegrating, was infused with new energy. . . .

DEMOBILIZATION AND THE RECONSTRUCTION OF "WOMAN'S PLACE" IN INDUSTRY

The war's end generated renewed upheaval in the sexual division of labor. As reconversion brought massive layoffs and then new hiring, the issue of women's position in industry came to the fore. . . . Would there be a return to the "traditional," prewar sexual division of labor as the mobilization-era ideology of "woman's place" in the war effort had promised? Or would the successful wartime deployment of women in "men's jobs" lead to a permanent shift in the boundaries between women's and men's jobs? Or—a third alternative—would completely new, postwar exigencies reshape, or even eliminate, the sexual division of labor?

Reversion to prewar patterns, which ultimately did occur, might appear to have been the only real possibility. Had not the nation been repeatedly assured that women's entrance into industry was a temporary adaptation to the extraordinary needs of war? . . . Such a view is consistent with the prevailing ideology of the demobilization period, but it obscures the significance of the war years themselves. Wartime conditions were indeed transitory, yet the extraordinary period between Pearl Harbor and V-J Day left American society permanently transformed. One legacy of the war years, from which no retreat would be possible, was the increase in female labor force participation. On an individual basis, to be sure, many women faced conflicting pressures after the war—to continue working for pay on the one hand, and to go back to the home on the other. Yet a permanent shift had occurred for women as a social group. Despite the postwar resurgence of the ideology of domesticity, by the early 1950s the number of gainfully employed women exceeded the highest wartime level. And as early as 1948, the labor force participation rate of married women was higher than in 1944, the peak of the war boom. The rise in female employment, especially for married women, would continue throughout the postwar period, and at a far more rapid rate than in the first half of the century. In this respect, far from being a temporary deviation, the war was a watershed period that left women's relationship to work permanently changed.[21]

The crucial issue, then, was not whether women would remain in the work force, but rather which women would do so and on what terms. What would the postwar sexual division of paid labor look like? Would women retain their wartime foothold in basic industries like auto and electrical manufacturing? To what extent would they be able to find work in fields that had been predominantly male before the war? For women who worked for pay, whether by choice or necessity, exclusion from "men's jobs" did not mean the housewifery first celebrated and later decried as the "feminine mystique." Instead, it meant employment in low-wage "female" jobs, especially clerical, sales, and service work—all of which expanded enormously in the postwar decades.

That the war brought a permanent increase in female employment made the demobilization transition particularly consequential. The opportunity was there for incorporating the dramatic wartime changes in women's position in industry into the fabric of a postwar order in which paid work would become increasingly central to women's lives. In the absence of any events affecting the labor market as fundamentally and cataclysmically as the war, there has been no comparable occasion for a wholesale restructuring of the sexual division of labor since the 1940s. The fact that the opportunity the wartime upheaval presented was lost had enormous implications for the entire postwar era.

Why, then, was the potential for an enduring transformation in the sexual division of labor not fulfilled in the 1940s? There are two standard explanations. One focuses on the postwar resurgence of domesticity, both as a practice and as an ideology, and suggests that women war workers themselves relinquished the "men's jobs" they held during the war—either because of the genuine appeal of traditional family commitments or because they were ideologically manipulated. The second explanation, in contrast, suggests that the key problem was the operation of union-instituted seniority systems, and their manipulation by male unionists, to exclude women and to favor returning male veterans in postwar employment.

... [B]oth these accounts of the postwar transition, while partially correct, are inadequate.... A large body of evidence demonstrates that management took the lead both in purging women from "men's jobs" after the war and in refusing to rehire them (except in traditionally "female" jobs) as postwar production resumed. Management chose this course despite the fact that most women war workers wanted to keep doing "men's work," and despite the fact that refusing to rehire women often violated seniority provisions in union contracts....

I will offer a two-part explanation for management's postwar policy. First, in both auto and electrical manufacturing, the "traditional" sexual division of labor had a historical logic embodied in the structure of each industry, which remained compelling in the demobilization period. At one level, indeed, reconstructing the prewar sexual division of labor was a foregone conclusion from management's perspective. Wartime female substitution was an experiment that employers had undertaken unwillingly and only because there was no alternative. Despite the success

with which women were integrated into "men's jobs," the war's end meant an end to the experiment, and management breathed a collective sigh of relief.

But that is only half of the story. The postwar purge of women from men's jobs also reflected management's assessment of labor's position on the issue. For one thing, the CIO's wartime struggles for equal pay for women workers, which narrowed sex differentials in wages considerably, made permanent female substitution less appealing than it might otherwise have been. Moreover, in the reconversion period, male workers displayed a great deal of ambivalence about the postwar employment rights of women war workers, even those with seniority standing. The CIO's official policy was to defend women's job rights in line with the seniority principle, but in practice there was substantial opposition to retaining women in "men's jobs." This, I will suggest, effectively reinforced management's determination to reconstruct the prewar sexual division of labor....

MANAGERIAL POLICY TOWARD WOMEN WORKERS DURING THE WAR— AND AFTER

... Why was management so determined to oust women from the positions that they had occupied during the war? Women war workers wanted to keep their jobs, and union seniority policies did not stand in the way of hiring women, yet they were purged. The problem is all the more puzzling in light of contemporary evidence that management was highly satisfied with women war workers' abilities and performance. While initially employers had strenuously resisted replacing men with women in war industries, once having reconciled themselves to the inevitable, they seemed very pleased with the results. Moreover, because sex differentials in wages, although smaller than before, persisted during the war, one might expect management to have seriously considered the possibility of permanent female substitution on economic grounds.

There is no doubt that women's wartime performance proved satisfactory to management. Under the impact of the "manpower" crunch in the seven months following Pearl Harbor, the proportion of jobs for which the nation's employers were willing to consider women rose from 29 to 55 percent. And management praised women's industrial performance extravagantly during the mobilization period. "Women keep piling up evidence that they *can do,* and *do well,* a multitude of jobs," proclaimed the American Management Association in a 1943 report. "The distribution of basic aptitudes between the two sexes does not differ to any appreciable extent. . . . What is needed is *training*—training to develop latent aptitudes, to increase mechanical knowledge and skill, and to overcome any fear of the machine."[22] . . .

. . . In a 1943 National Industrial Conference Board survey of 146 executives, nearly 60 percent stated without qualification that women's production was equal to or greater than that of men on similar work. Similarly, a study by the Bureau of Employment Security of several California war plants found an increase in production per hour of workers of both sexes, and a lowering of costs per hour when women were employed, in every plant studied. The BES study also found that women were easier to supervise, and that labor turnover and accident rates decreased with the introduction of women.[23]

Many traditional management policies toward women workers were revised or eliminated with their successful incorporation into war industry. For example, physical segregation of the sexes was no longer deemed necessary; the belief "that men and women could work satisfactorily side by side" was held by the majority of executives questioned by the magazine *Modern Industry* as early as mid-1942. There were also many efforts to promote women to supervisory posts, especially at the lower levels, although women were almost never given authority over male workers, and there was a lingering conviction that women workers themselves preferred male bosses.[24]

Women workers' wartime performance, then, stood as evidence that they could be successfully incorporated into the industrial labor force. In addition, wage differentials between the sexes persisted during the war years—a consideration that one might expect to have enhanced management's interest in retaining women permanently in the postwar era. The unions, to be sure, had successfully contested sex discrimination in wages in many "equal pay for equal work" cases before the War

Labor Board. But although sex differentials were narrowed as a result of these struggles, they were not eliminated. The Conference Board's composite earnings index for twenty-five manufacturing industries registered only a modest increase in the ratio of female to male average hourly earnings, from 61.5 percent in 1941 to 66.4 percent in 1945.[25] . . .

Still, because men and women rarely did "equal work" even during the war, the outcome of successful WLB equal pay cases was to narrow sex differentials in wages, not to eliminate them. And the Board's equal pay policy was not fully enforced, so that even when jobs were identical, or nearly so, women were often paid less than men. The Conference Board found differentials in starting rates paid to men and to "women hired for men's jobs" in nearly half the 148 plants that it surveyed in 1943, well after equal pay "for comparable quality and quantity of work" had become official WLB policy. Of the ninety-two plants in the survey that had systems of automatic progression in wage rates, twenty-five had sex differentials built into the progression systems despite the fact that the WLB had declared this practice improper.[26]

Similarly, a study of women's wages by the New York State Department of Labor found that 40 percent of the 143 plants surveyed had different starting rates for men and women on "men's jobs." When the state's investigators asked employers to account for such differences, most simply referred to "tradition," standard practice, prevailing wage rates, and custom. "It's also cheaper," said one manager.[27] . . .

There were some extra costs associated with the employment of women, to be sure, particularly in previously all-male plants. Women's absenteeism was generally higher than men's, especially if they were married and had domestic responsibilities, although employers succeeded in narrowing or even eliminating the gap in some plants.[28] UAW President R. J. Thomas, summarizing the reasons auto industry employers were reluctant to hire women for postwar jobs, noted other costs associated with expanding or introducing female employment in a plant. "First is that as you know on most jobs equal rates are paid for equal jobs today," he pointed out. "Management doesn't want to pay women equal rates with men. Not only that but in many of these plants additional facilities have to be put in, such as toilet facilities to take care of women. More space has to be taken to give an opportunity of changing clothes and more safety measures have to be instituted. I think it is pretty well recognized that it is an additional expense to a management to have women."[29]

This is an accurate rendition of the reasons auto industry managers themselves adduced for their reluctance to employ women. Yet it is an inadequate explanation for managerial hostility toward female employment. The costs of maintaining special "facilities" for women were largely absorbed by the government during the war, and could hardly have been a major financial consideration in any event. Surely the savings associated with sex differentials in pay would outweigh any expense firms would incur in continuing to maintain such facilities. Indeed, if only the direct economic costs and benefits of female employment are taken into account, one would expect management to have consistently discriminated *in favor of* women and against men in postwar layoffs and rehiring. Particularly in view of the vigorous efforts of employers to increase labor productivity in the reconversion period, management should have preferred to retain women permanently in the "men's jobs" they had just demonstrated their ability to perform.[30]

Industrial employers chose the opposite course, however, defying not only the apparent imperatives of economic rationality, but also the stated preference of women war workers to keep their war jobs and the unions' official policy that layoffs and rehiring be done strictly by seniority. Rather than institutionalizing the wartime incorporation of women into male jobs, management returned to its prewar practices. . . .

THE ROOTS OF MANAGEMENT'S POSTWAR POLICY

In retrospect, then, management's determination to restore the status quo ante seems altogether irrational. Yet from the perspective of employers themselves at the time, it was a foregone conclusion. Management viewed the successful performance of women war workers as, at best, the fortunate outcome of an experiment in which it had participated with

great trepidation and only because there was no alternative. To be sure, women had proved better workers than anyone had expected during the war. But now men's jobs were men's jobs once more. The ideology of sex-typing emerged triumphant again, defining the postwar order along prewar lines in both auto and electrical manufacturing.

In part, the explanation for management's postwar policy involves the logic of the sexual division of labor as it had first developed within the auto and electrical industries a half-century earlier. Not only did the traditions of sex-typing established then have a continuing influence in the post–World War II period, but the factors that had originally shaped those traditions remained salient. In auto, wage levels were still high relative to other industries and would continue to increase in the postwar decades. As in the prewar years, automotive management's efforts to boost productivity focused on tightening control over labor, not on reducing pay levels.[31] Under these conditions, female substitution had little to recommend it, and employers continued to indulge the conviction . . . that women simply were not suitable for employment in automotive production jobs.

In electrical manufacturing, too, prewar traditions of sex-typing persisted in the postwar [era]. But in this industry, the prewar sexual division of labor was historically rooted in a logic of feminization linked to labor-intensity and piecework systems. So why should the further extension of feminization during the war have been rolled back? Even in the case of the automobile industry, why was there a permanent departure from prewar tradition in regard to black employment while the sexual division of jobs persisted virtually unaltered? The historical, industry-specific logic of sex-typing seems to constitute only a partial explanation for management's postwar determination to reconstruct the prewar order.

It is tempting to look outside of the industrial setting to the arena of family and social reproduction in seeking a better solution to the conundrum of management's postwar policies. The interest of capital in reconstructing a family structure in which women are responsible for the generational and daily reproduction of the working class, one might argue, ruled out the permanent employment of women in the well-paid manufacturing jobs that they had during the war. In this view, if women—and more significantly, married women—were to be employed outside the home in ever-increasing numbers in the post-war era, it was crucial that they be confined to poorly paid, secondary jobs that would not jeopardize their primary allegiance to family.

The difficulty with this line of argument is in specifying how the presumed interest of collective capital in reconstituting traditional family forms was translated into the actual employer policies with respect to women workers that emerged in this period. The historical record offers no evidence that such familial considerations played a role in shaping managerial policy in the postwar transition.[32] Although the idea that "woman's place is in the home" was pervasive in the postwar period, it was seldom invoked by employers as a justification for restoring the prewar sexual division of jobs. Instead, management tended to define the issue in economic terms and, above all, by reference to women's physical characteristics and supposed inability to perform "men's jobs."

Although it would be extremely difficult to demonstrate that management policy was rooted in conscious concern over social reproduction, there is evidence for a different kind of explanation: that the postwar purge of women from "men's jobs" involved employers' assessment of the implications of their policies toward women for labor relations. The wartime struggles over equal pay indicated that the unions were committed to resisting any effort to substitute women for men in order to take advantage of their historically lower wages. If wage savings could not be garnered from substitution, or if they could only be garnered at substantial political cost, then why attempt to preserve the wartime sexual division of jobs after the war? In addition, given the widespread fear of postwar unemployment, management might reasonably have anticipated that unemployed male workers would be a source of potential political instability, given the working-class cultural ideal of the "family wage" and the obvious ambivalence of male unionists about women's postwar employment rights.

In short, management had good reason to believe that a wholesale postwar reorganization of the sexual division of labor, in defiance of the wartime assurances that women were in

"men's jobs" only for the duration, could precipitate widespread resistance from labor. The unions were at the peak of their strength at this time, and at the war's end they were no longer constrained by the no-strike pledge. As one contemporary analyst noted, consideration of labor's reaction figured prominently in employers' postwar policies:

> Employers in plants where women had long been assigned to some jobs were disposed favorably to widening the fields of work open to women, unless the job dilutions had proved complicated and costly. In fact, union men declared that some companies, unless prevented by organized labor, would try to continue to use women on men's work because they could be hired at lower initial base pay, be upgraded more slowly, and would be throughout more docile. With the installation of mechanical aids, which using women had necessitated, already paid for out of war profits, management had frequently no particular reason to oppose keeping women on.... Yet most companies frankly admitted that, given full freedom of choice after the war, if only out of deference to prevailing male opinion in the shops, management would revert to giving men's jobs, so called, only to men. *And employers generally assumed that labor would permit no choice.*[33]

Understanding management's postwar policy in these terms helps explain why, in the auto case, women and blacks were treated differently. Despite their common history of exclusion from most auto jobs in the prewar era, the two groups stood in very different positions at the war's end. Organized feminism was at its nadir in the 1940s, and the labor movement's commitment to sexual equality was limited, so that management had little reason to fear that purging women from the industry would meet with substantial political opposition. In contrast, at least in the North, there was a large and vital black civil rights movement, which enjoyed substantial UAW support and from which management could expect vigorous protests if it pursued racially discriminatory employment policies.[34]

Only a few years earlier, when blacks were first hired in large numbers in Detroit's auto factories during the war mobilization, white workers had been vocal in their opposition, most notably in the numerous hate strikes which erupted in the plants and in the race riot of the summer of 1943.[35] But during the war, Detroit became a stronghold of the civil rights movement. The Motor City had the largest branch of the National Association for the Advancement of Colored People (NAACP) of any city in the nation, with a membership of twenty thousand by 1943, and the UAW had become a strong ally of the NAACP and other civil rights groups. While racial discrimination persisted in the auto industry in regard to promotion to the elite skilled trades, no one contested blacks' claims to semi-skilled jobs in the aftermath of the war.[36]

The sharp regional variation in racial patterns of hiring within the auto industry suggests the critical importance of the political dimension in shaping management's employment policies. Although the proportion of blacks in Detroit's auto plants rose dramatically in the 1940s and 1950s, reaching well over 25 percent of the production work force by 1960, in the nation as a whole the percentage of nonwhite auto workers grew much more modestly, from 4 percent in 1940 to only 9 percent in 1960. The national figures reflect the continuing practice of excluding blacks from employment in southern plants. As a manager at a GM plant in Atlanta told the *Wall Street Journal* in 1957, "When we moved into the South, we agreed to abide by local custom and not hire Negroes for production work. This is no time for social reforming and we're not about to try it."[37]

The situation of women auto workers was entirely different from that of northern blacks. Although the incorporation of women into the industry during the war had not provoked riots or hate strikes, this was primarily because female employment was explicitly understood to be a temporary expedient, "for the duration" only. After the war, women were expected to go "back to the home." There was no parallel expectation regarding black men. And while women war workers wanted to remain in the auto industry, as we have seen, their preferences (unlike blacks') lacked legitimacy. While black workers had the civil rights movement behind them, there was no mass feminist movement or even popular consciousness of women's job rights at this critical juncture, when the sexual division of labor that would characterize the postwar period was crystallizing. . . .

NOTES

1. U.S. Senate Hearings, *Manpower Problems in Detroit*, 79th Cong. 1st sess., pp. 9–13 (Mar. 1945), pp. 13534, 13638; interview with Edward Cushman.

2. Reference to such a survey made "to determine those operations which were suitable for female operators" is made on pp. 2–3 of the Summary Brief Submitted by Buick Motor Division, Melrose Park, General Motors Corporation, "In the Matter of GMC–Buick, Melrose Park, Ill., and UAW-CIO," 14 June 1943, Walter Reuther Collection, WSU Archives, box 20, folder: "WLB, GM Women's Rates." A survey of this type was also conducted at the Ford Willow Run plant; see the section on "Training of Women" in *Willow Run Bomber Plant, Record of War Effort* (notebook), vol. 2, pt. 2, Jan.–Dec. 1942, p. 30, La Croix Collection, Accession 435, Ford Archives, Dearborn, Michigan, box 15.

3. Computed from data in U.S. Department of Labor, Bureau of Labor Statistics, Division of Wage Analysis, Regional Office no. 8-A, Detroit, Michigan, Dec. 3, 1943, serial no. 8-A-16 (mimeo), "Metalworking Establishments, Detroit, Michigan, Labor Market Area, Straight-Time Average Hourly Earnings, Selected Occupations, July, 1943." UAW Research Department Collection, WSU Archives, box 28, folder: "Wage Rates (Detroit) Bureau of Labor Statistics, 1943–45." . . .

4. Computed from data in "Earnings in Manufacture of Electrical Appliances, 1942," p. 532.

5. Regarding GE and Westinghouse, see U.S. National War Labor Board, *War Labor Reports*, vol. 28, pp. 677–78. . . .

6. See "Summary Employment Status Report for Michigan," Apr. 30, 1943, Records of the U.S. Employment Service, National Archives, Record Group 183, box 181, folder: "Michigan Statewide."

7. Press release of Office of Production Management, Labor Division, Dec. 5, 1941, UAW Research Department Collection, WSU Archives, box 32, folder: "Women Employment 1941."

8. "Engineers of Womanpower," *Automotive War Production* 2 (Oct. 1943):4–5 (emphasis added). . . .

9. "What Women Are Doing in Industry," *Factory Management and Maintenance* 100 (March 1942):63; "Provisions in Plants for Physical Differences Enable Women to Handle Variety of War Jobs," *Automotive War Production* 2 (Sept. 1943):7.

10. "Report of Two Special Meetings on Employing and Training Women for War Jobs," attended by executives from 85 N.A.M. companies from the East and Midwest, Mar. 27 and 30, 1942, in Records of the Automotive Council for War Production, Detroit Public Library, folder: "Manpower: Source Material: New Workers," p. 1.

11. "Provisions in Plants"; Constance Green, "The Role of Women as Production Workers in War Plants in the Connecticut Valley," *Smith College Studies in History* 28 (1946):32. . . .

12. W. Gerald Tuttle, "Women War Workers at Vultee Aircraft," *Personnel Journal* 21 (Sept. 1942):8–9.

13. "Women Work for Victory," *Automotive War Production* 1 (Nov. 1942):4; "Engineers of Womanpower," p. 4.

14. "There's a Job for You at Sperry . . . Today" (pamphlet), Records of UE District 4, UE Archives, University of Pittsburgh folder 877; "Hiring and Training Women for War Work," *Factory Management and Maintenance* 100 (Aug. 1942):73; "Engineers of Womanpower," p. 4.

15. The transcript of this newsreel was made available to me by the Rosie the Riveter Film Project, Emeryville, California.

16. "Engineers of Womanpower," p. 4.

17. "New Workers," *Manpower Reports* 10 (published by the Manpower Division of the Automotive Council for War Production), p. 4; Anne Gould, "Problems of Woman War Workers in Detroit," Aug. 20, 1943, Records of the War Production Board, National Archives, RG 179, box 203, folder: "035.606 Service Trades Divisions, WPB Functions," p. 2.

18. U.S. Department of Labor, Women's Bureau, Special Bulletin no. 20, *Changes in Women's Employment During the War* (1944), p. 18.

19. Helen Baker, *Women in War Industries* (Princeton: Princeton University Press, 1942), p. 15.

20. "Report of Mrs. Betty Sturges Finan on Cleveland Detroit Trip, Feb. 9–17 [1943] inclusive," pp. 3–4, Records of the War Manpower Commission, National Archives, Record Group 211, Series 137, box 977, folder. "Consultants—Betty Sturges Finan." See also "Report of Two Special Meetings," p. 6.

21. See U.S. Bureau of the Census, *Historical Statistics of the U.S.: Colonial Times to 1970* (1975), pp. 131, 133. This claim is considerably more modest than William Chafe's controversial thesis that the wartime changes in female labor force participation make the 1940s a key "turning point in the history of American women." See William H. Chafe, *The American Woman: Her Changing Social, Economic, and Political Role, 1920–1970* (New York: Oxford University Press, 1972), p. 195. . . .

22. Chafe, *The American Woman*, p. 137; American Management Association, Special Research Report no. 2, *Supervision of Women on Production Jobs: A Study of Management's Problems and Practices in Handling Female Personnel* (1943), pp. 8–10 (emphasis in the original).

23. National Industrial Conference Board, "Wartime Pay of Women in Industry," *Studies in Personnel Policy*, no. 58 (1943):27; "Woman's Place," *Business Week* (May 16, 1942):20–22. . . .

24. *Modern Industry*, July 15, 1942, summarized in *Management Review* 31 (Sept. 1942):303–4. Regarding the use of women as supervisors, see *Supervision of Women on Production Jobs*, pp. 24–27. . . .

25. Computed from data in *The Management Almanac 1946* (New York: National Industrial Conference Board, 1946), p. 77.

26. "Wartime Pay of Women in Industry," pp. 18–19. . . .

27. New York State Department of Labor, Division of Women in Industry, *Women's Wages on Men's Jobs* (1944), p. 26.

28. See New York State Department of Labor, Division of Women in Industry, *Absenteeism in New York State War Production Plants* (1943); National Industrial Conference Board, "The Problem of Absenteeism," *Studies in Personnel Policy*, no. 53 (1943); "Women Workers on War Production," *UAW Research Report* 3 (Mar. 1943):3. . . .

29. *Manpower Problems in Detroit*, pp. 13112–13.

30. See Howell John Harris, *The Right to Manage: Industrial Relations Policies of American Business in the 1940s* (Madison: University of Wisconsin Press, 1982), pp. 66–67, 91–93.

31. Ibid. This is Harris's main thesis.

32. Denise Riley, "The Free Mothers': Pronatalism and Working Women in Industry at the End of the Last War in Britain," *History Workshop* II (Spring 1981):59–118, presents the most convincing case for this argument in regard to the postwar transition for the British case, but she relies on evidence about state policy with virtually none directly from employers.

33. Green, "Role of Women as Production Workers," pp. 64–65 (emphasis added).

34. August Meier and Elliot Rudwick, *Black Detroit and the Rise of the U.A.W.* (New York: Oxford University Press, 1979).

35. Ibid.; Robert C. Weaver, *Negro Labor: A National Problem* (New York: Harcourt, Brace, and World, 1946).

36. Meier and Rudwick, *Black Detroit*, p. 113. See also Karen Anderson, "Last Hired, First Fired: Black Women Workers during World War II," *Journal of American History* 69 (June 1982), especially pp. 86–87, where white male workers' attitudes toward women and blacks are compared.

37. Both the employment figures and the quote are cited in Herbert R. Northrup, Richard L. Rowan, et al., *Negro Employment in Basic Industry*, Industrial Research Unit, Wharton School of Finance and Commerce, University of Pennsylvania (1970), pp. 65–75. The national employment figures are from the U.S. Census, and because (unlike the figures for Detroit) they include both production and nonproduction workers, they overstate the difference between Detroit and the nation as a whole, for the vast majority of nonproduction workers were white in this period. The quote is from the *Wall Street Journal*, Oct. 24, 1957.

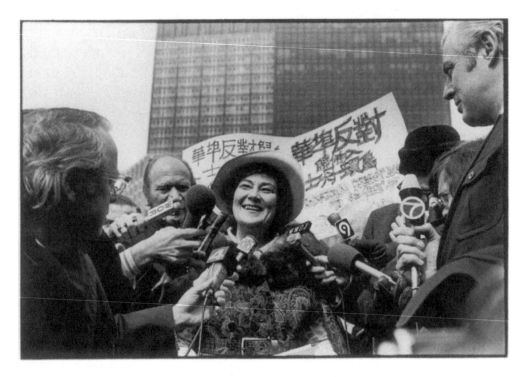

Congresswoman Bella Abzug addressing a crowd in New York City in 1972. (Copyright © 1972 by Diana Mara Henry.)

I V

STRUGGLES AGAINST INJUSTICE, 1945–2000

On the surface, at least, America of the postwar years was a nation of prosperity and opportunity. Indeed, the new atomic age was marked by a greater affluence and heightened consumerism. Enrollment in universities swelled, more and more Americans moved to the suburbs, and the birthrate soared.

But these images mask the reality of life in the United States during an era marked by a "cold" war. Residential discrimination made the move to the suburbs difficult, if not impossible, for most families of color. Although the domestic ideal cast women as full-time mothers and housewives, most women continued to work outside the home. Fearing domestic subversion, anticommunists during the McCarthy era purged the government, organized labor, the entertainment industry, and universities of communists—real and imagined. Labeled as security risks due to their "un-American" identity, gays and lesbians became favored targets of the purges. Like feminists, they were increasingly silenced, as dissent became tantamount to disloyalty.

The election of John F. Kennedy in 1960 promised energy and optimism. The young leader urged his fellow citizens to "ask not what your country can do for you; ask what you can do for your country." Women eagerly answered this call to action. Within a few years, they were on the front lines in the civil rights war in the South. They played key roles in the student movements that rocked college campuses across the nation, challenging everything from restrictive curfews to the narrow focus of the curricula. Women served their nation as nurses and volunteers in Vietnam; at home, they protested against the war. Soon, a feminist consciousness re-emerged. Women fought for equal pay for equal work, access to safe and legal abortions, and an end to sexual violence.

By the mid-1980s, however, the time for social reform appeared to be over. The expansive mood of the 1960s disintegrated in the face of anxiety over unemployment, inflation, rising energy costs, and declining productivity. Yet women continued to challenge conventional definitions of womanhood. They fought in the 1990–91 Gulf War in an integrated military. They continued the battle against sexism and fought to protect their reproductive rights. In 1992, the number of women in the U.S. House of Representatives leaped from 28 to 47, and the new president nominated six women to his cabinet and a second woman to the Supreme Court. In 1996, Madeline Albright became the first woman to serve as secretary of state. Four years later, Hillary Rodham Clinton continued to redefine the role of the First Lady by successfully campaigning for and winning a seat in the U.S. Senate.

Nevertheless, those who would exploit racial, class, and gender injustice have persisted in their attempts to roll back these gains. This ongoing struggle dramatizes the need for a new generation of feminists—male as well as female—who will forge a better future for all Americans.

DANIEL HOROWITZ

Betty Friedan and the Origins of Feminism in Cold War America

The years immediately after World War II were marked by a resurgent domesticity. The average age at marriage of women dropped sharply—by the end of the 1950s it was 20. Women's age at the birth of their first child also dropped precipitously; the number of children per family increased sharply. The proportion of women in college fell in comparison to men; many others dropped out of college to marry or because they saw no advantage in increased education.

In 1963 Betty Friedan published *The Feminine Mystique*, a searing indictment of the triviality and frustrations of postwar domesticity (pp. 573–76). She wrote in the voice of an author who located herself in the middle-class suburbs and whose ethnicity was unmarked. But as Daniel Horowitz explains in the essay that follows, Friedan's analysis emerged not only from her experience of suburban life, but also from her experience in left-wing politics and in the labor movement—experiences she did not mention in *The Feminine Mystique*. The execution of Ethel and Julius Rosenberg for spying in 1952 frightened many progressive Jewish organizations lest they be tainted as Communist sympathizers; they would subsequently be inhospitable to reformers from the left.* The House Un-American Activities Committee investigations that Amy Swerdlow describes on pages 517–32 continued in the late 1950s and early 1960s. Many elements of Cold War politics and culture may have contributed to the choices Friedan made as she developed her voice.

In 1951, a labor journalist with a decade's experience in protest movements described a trade union meeting where rank-and-file women talked and men listened. Out of these conversations, she reported, emerged the realization that the women were "fighters—that they refuse any longer to be paid or treated as some inferior species by their bosses, or by any male workers who have swallowed the bosses' thinking."[1] The union was the UE, the United Electrical, Radio and Machine Workers of America, the most radical American union in the postwar period and in the 1940s what historian Ronald Schatz . . . has called "the largest communist-led institution of any kind in the United States."[2] In 1952 that same journalist wrote a pamphlet, *UE Fights for Women Workers,* that the historian Lisa Kannenberg, unaware of the identity of its author, has called "a remarkable manual for fighting wage discrimination that is, ironically, as relevant today as it was in 1952." At the time, the pamphlet helped raise the consciousness of Eleanor Flexner, who in 1959 would publish *Century of*

---

*Stanley Svonkin, *Jews against Prejudice: American Jews and the Fight of Civil Liberties* (New York: Columbia University Press, 1997).

Daniel Horowitz, "Rethinking Betty Friedan and *The Feminine Mystique:* Labor Union Radicalism and Feminism in Cold War America." *American Quarterly* 48 (1998): 1–42. Copyright © The American Studies Association. Reprinted with permission of the Johns Hopkins University Press. Notes have been renumbered and edited.

Struggle, the first scholarly history of American women. In 1953–54, Flexner relied extensively on the pamphlet when she taught a course at the Jefferson School of Social Science in New York on "The Woman Question." Flexner's participation in courses at the school, she later said, "marked the beginning of my real involvement in the issues of women's rights, my realization that leftist organizations—parties, unions—were also riddled with male supremacist prejudice and discrimination."[3] The labor journalist and pamphlet writer was Betty Friedan.

In 1973 Friedan remarked that until she started writing *The Feminine Mystique* (1963), "I wasn't even conscious of the woman problem." In 1976 she commented that in the early 1950s she was "still in the embrace of the feminine mystique."[4] Although in 1974 she revealed some potentially controversial elements of her past, even then she left the impression that her landmark book emerged only from her own captivity by the very forces she described. Friedan's portrayal of herself as so totally trapped by the feminine mystique was part of a reinvention of herself as she wrote and promoted *The Feminine Mystique.* Her story made it possible for readers to identify with its author and its author to enhance the book's appeal. However, it hid from view the connection between the union activity in which Friedan participated in the 1940s and early 1950s and the feminism she inspired in the 1960s. In the short term, her misery in the suburbs may have prompted her to write *The Feminine Mystique;* a longer term perspective makes clear that the book's origins lie much earlier—in her college education and in her experiences with labor unions in the 1940s and early 1950s.[5] . . . Friedan's life provides evidence of. . . . continuity. . . . between the struggle for justice for working women in the 1940s and the feminism of the 1960s. This connection gives feminism and Friedan, both long under attack for a lack of interest in working class and African American women, a past of which they should be proud. . . . Moreover, a new reading of *The Feminine Mystique* sheds light on the remaking of progressive forces in America, the process by which a focus on women and the professional middle and upper middle classes supplemented, in some ways replaced a focus on unions. Finally, an examination of *The Feminine Mystique* reminds

us of important shifts in the ideology of the left: from an earlier economic analysis based on Marxism to one developed in the 1950s that also rested on humanistic psychology, and from a focus on the impact of conditions of production on the working class to an emphasis on the effect of consumption on the middle class.

In print and in interviews, Friedan has offered a narrative of her life that she popularized after she became famous in 1963.[6] A full biography might begin in Peoria, where Bettye Naomi Goldstein was born February 4, 1921 and grew up with her siblings and their parents: a father who owned a jewelry store and a mother who had given up her position as a society editor of the local paper to raise a family.[7] My analysis of Friedan's political journey starts with her years at Smith College, although it is important to recognize Friedan's earlier sense of herself as someone whose identity as a Jew, a reader, and a brainy girl made her feel freakish and lonely.[8]

As an undergraduate, she has suggested, her lonely life took a turn for the better. "For the first time," she later remarked of her years in college, "I wasn't a freak for having brains." Friedan has acknowledged that she flourished at Smith, with her editorship of the student newspaper, her election to Phi Beta Kappa in her junior year, and her graduation *summa cum laude* among her most prominent achievements. She has told the story of how Gestalt psychology and Kurt Koffka (one of its three founders) were critical in her intellectual development.[9]

Friedan has described the years between her graduation from Smith in 1942 and the publication of her book twenty-one years later as a time when the feminine mystique increasingly trapped her. In her book and in dozens of speeches, articles, and interviews beginning in 1963, she mentioned a pivotal moment in her life, one that she felt marked the beginning of the process by which she succumbed. She told how, while in graduate school at Berkeley in the year after her graduation from college, the university's offer of a prestigious fellowship forced her to make a painful choice. Her first serious boyfriend, a graduate student who had not earned a similarly generous award, threatened to break off the relationship unless she turned down her fellowship. "I never could explain, hardly knew myself, why" she turned away from a career in psychology, she wrote in 1963. She decided to reject the fellowship because she saw herself ending up as an "old maid college teacher" in part because at Smith, she said, there were so few female professors who had husbands and children.[10] The feminine mystique, she insisted, had claimed one of its first victims.[11]

After leaving Berkeley, the copy on the dust jacket of The Feminine Mystique noted, Friedan did some "applied social-science research" and free-lance writing for magazines. Friedan's biography in a standard reference book quotes her as saying that in the 1940s, "for conscious or unconscious reasons," she worked at "the usual kinds of boring jobs that lead nowhere."[12] This story continues in 1947 with her marriage to Carl Friedan, a returning vet who would eventually switch careers from theater to advertising and public relations. She has told of how she gave birth to three children between 1948 and 1956 and the family moved to the suburbs, with these experiences making her feel trapped. Friedan's picture of her years in the suburbs is not one of contentment and conformity.[13] Though she acknowledged her role in creating and directing a program that brought together teenagers and adult professionals, Friedan portrayed herself as someone who felt "freakish having a career, worried that she was neglecting her children."[14] In an oft-repeated story whose punch line varied, Friedan recounted her response to the census form. In the space where it asked for her occupation, she put down "housewife" but remained guilty, hesitant, and conflicted about such a designation, sometimes pausing and then adding "writer."[15]

Friedan laced The Feminine Mystique with suggestions of how much she shared with her suburban sisters. In the opening paragraph, she said that she realized something was wrong in women's lives when she "sensed it first as a question mark in my own life, as a wife and mother of three small children, half-guiltily, and therefore half-heartedly, almost in spite of myself, using my abilities and education in work that took me away from home." Toward the end of the paragraph, when she referred to "a strange discrepancy between the reality of our lives as women and the image to which we were trying to conform," she suggested that she experienced the feminine mystique as keenly and in the same way as her

readers. Using the second person plural, she wrote that "all of us went back into the warm brightness of home" and "lowered our eyes from the horizon, and steadily contemplated our own navels." Her work on newspapers, she wrote in The Feminine Mystique, proceeded "with no particular plan." Indeed, she claimed that she had participated as a writer in the creation of the image of the happy housewife.[16]

Friedan asserted she embarked on a path that would lead to The Feminine Mystique only when, as she read over the responses of her college classmates to a questionnaire in anticipation of their fifteenth reunion in 1957, she discovered what she called "The Problem That Has No Name," the dissatisfaction her suburban peers felt but could not fully articulate. When she submitted articles to women's magazines, Friedan said, editors changed the meaning of what she had written or rejected outright her suggestions for pieces on controversial subjects. Then at a meeting of the Society of Magazine Writers, she heard Vance Packard recount how he had written The Hidden Persuaders (1957) after Reader's Digest turned down an article critical of advertising. Friedan decided to write her book.[17]

In "It Changed My Life": Writings on the Women's Movement (1976), a book that included a 1974 autobiographical article, Friedan suggested some of what she had omitted from earlier versions of her life.[18] Perhaps responding to attacks on her for not being sufficiently radical, she acknowledged that before her marriage and for several years after she participated in radical activities and worked for union publications.[19] She and the friends with whom she lived before marrying considered themselves in "the vanguard of the working-class revolution," participating in "Marxist discussion groups," going to political rallies, and having "only contempt for dreary bourgeois capitalists like our fathers." Without getting much more specific, Friedan noted that right after the war she was "very involved, consciously radical. Not about women, for heaven's sake!" but about African Americans, workers, the threat of war, anti-communism, and "communist splits and schisms." This was a time, Friedan reported briefly, when, working as a labor journalist, she discovered "the grubby economic underside of American reality."[20]

"I was certainly not a feminist then—none of us," she remarked in the mid-1970s, "were a bit interested in women's rights." She remembered one incident, whose implications she said she only understood much later. Covering a strike, she could not interest anyone in the fact that the company and the union discriminated against women. In 1952, she later claimed, pregnant with her second child, she was fired from her job on a union publication and told that her second pregnancy was her fault. The Newspaper Guild, she asserted, was unwilling to honor its commitment to grant pregnancy leaves. This was, Friedan later remembered, as she mentioned her efforts to call a meeting in protest, "the first personal stirring of my own feminism, I guess. But the other women were just embarrassed, and the men uncomprehending. It was my own fault, getting pregnant again, a *personal* matter, not something you should take to the union. There was no word in 1949 for 'sex discrimination.'"[21]

Though in the 1970s Friedan suggested this more interesting version of her life in the 1940s and 1950s, she distracted the reader from what she had said. She began and ended the 1974 piece with images of domestic life. Even as she mentioned participation in Marxist discussion groups, she talked of how she and her friends read fashion magazines and spent much of their earnings on elegant clothes. Describing what she offered as a major turning point in her life, she told of how, after campaigning for Henry Wallace in 1948, all of a sudden she lost interest in political activity. The 1940s and 1950s were a period, she later asserted, when she was fully exposed to what she would label the feminine mystique as she learned that motherhood took the place of career and politics. She gave the impression of herself in the late 1940s as a woman who embraced domesticity, motherhood, and housework, even as she admitted that not everything at the time resulted from the feminine mystique.[22]

In her 1974 article Friedan filled her descriptions of the late 1940s and 1950s with a sense of the conflicts she felt over her new roles, as she surrendered to the feminine mystique with mixed emotions. She reported how wonderful was the time in Parkway Village, Queens, a period when she experienced the pleasure of a spacious apartment, edited the community newspaper, and enjoyed the camaraderie of young marrieds. Yet, having read

Benjamin Spock's *Child and Baby Care,* she felt guilty when she returned to work after a maternity leave. With her move to a traditional suburb, she said, the conflicts intensified. She spoke of driving her children to school and lessons, participating in the PTA, and then, when neighbors came by, hiding "like secret drinking in the morning" the book she was working on.[23]

Accomplishing practical, specific tasks around the house and in local politics was "somehow more real and secure than the schizophrenic and even dangerous politics of the world revolution whose vanguard we used to fancy ourselves." Friedan remarked that by 1949 she realized that the revolution was not going to happen in the United States as she anticipated, in part because workers, like others, wanted kitchen gadgets. She reported that she found herself disillusioned with what was happening in unions, in Czechoslovakia, and in the Soviet Union, despite the fact that cries about the spread of Communism merely provided the pretext for attacks on suspected subversives. In those days, she continued, "McCarthyism, the danger of war against Russia and of fascism in America, and the reality of U.S. imperial, corporate wealth and power" combined to make those who once dreamed of "making the whole world over uncomfortable with the Old Left rhetoric of revolution." Using the first person plural as she referred to Margaret Mead's picture in *Male and Female* (1949) of women fulfilled through motherhood and domesticity, Friedan wrote, "we were suckers for that apple." It hardly occurred to any of those in her circle, who themselves now wanted new gadgets, that large corporations profited from marketing household appliances by "overselling us on the bliss of domesticity."[24]

The new information Friedan offered in 1974 did not dislodge the accepted understanding of how she became a feminist . . . [Yet] what the written record reveals of Friedan's life from her arrival at Smith in the fall of 1938 until the publication of *The Feminine Mystique* makes possible a story different from the one she has told. To begin with, usually missing from her narrative is full and specific information about how at college she first developed a sense of herself as a radical.[25] Courses she took, friendships she established with peers and professors, events in the United States and abroad, and her campus leadership all turned Friedan from a provincial outsider into a determined advocate of trade unions as the herald of progressive social change, a healthy skeptic about the authority and rhetorical claims of those in power, a staunch opponent of fascism, a defender of free speech, and a fierce questioner of social privilege expressed by the conspicuous consumption of some of her peers.[26]

What and with whom she studied points well beyond Gestalt psychology and Koffka.[27] Though Friedan acknowledged the importance of James Gibson, she did not mention his activity as an advocate of trade unions.[28] Moreover, her statement that at Smith there were few role models is hard to reconcile with the fact that the college had a number of them; indeed she took courses from both James Gibson and Eleanor Gibson, husband and wife and parents of two children, the first of them born in 1940.[29] As a women's college, and especially one with an adversarial tradition, Smith may well have fostered in Friedan a feminism that was at least implicit—by enabling her to assume leadership positions and by encouraging her to take herself seriously as a writer and thinker.

In the fall of her junior year, Friedan took an economics course taught by Dorothy W. Douglas, Theories and Movements for Social Reconstruction. Douglas was well known at the time for her radicalism.[30] In what she wrote for Douglas, and with youthful enthusiasm characteristic of many members of her generation, Friedan sympathetically responded to the Marxist critique of capitalism as a cultural, economic, and political force.[31]

Friedan also gained an education as a radical in the summer of 1941 when, following Douglas's suggestion, she participated in a writers' workshop at the Highlander Folk School in Tennessee, an institution active in helping the CIO organize in the South. The school offered a series of summer institutes for fledgling journalists which, for 1939 and 1940 (but not 1941), the communist-led League of American Writers helped sponsor. For three years beginning in the fall of 1939, opponents of Highlander had sustained a vicious redbaiting attack, but a FBI investigator found no evidence of subversive activity.[32] In good Popular Front language, Friedan praised Highlander as a truly American institution that was attempting to help America to fulfill its democratic ideals. She explored the contradictions of her

social position as a Jewish girl from a well-to-do family who had grown up in a class-divided Peoria, gave evidence of her hostility to the way her parents fought over issues of debt and extravagance, and described the baneful influence of the mass media on American life. Though she also acknowledged that her Smith education did "not lead to much action," she portrayed herself as someone whose radical consciousness relied on the American labor movement as the bulwark against fascism.[33]

At Smith Friedan linked her journalism to political activism. She served as editor-in-chief of the campus newspaper for a year beginning in the spring of 1941. The campaigns she undertook and the editorials she wrote reveal a good deal of her politics. Under Friedan's leadership, the newspaper's reputation for protest was so strong that in a skit a fellow student portrayed an editor, perhaps Friedan herself, as "a strident voice haranguing from a perpetual soap-box.[34] While at Smith, a Peoria paper reported in 1943, Friedan helped organize college building and grounds workers into a union.[35] Under her leadership, the student paper took on the student government for holding closed meetings, fought successfully to challenge the administration's right to control what the newspaper printed, campaigned for the relaxation of restrictions on student social life, censured social clubs for their secrecy, and published critiques of professors' teaching.[36] In response to an article in a campus humor magazine that belittled female employees who cleaned the students' rooms and served them food, an editorial supported the administration's censorship of the publication on the grounds that such action upheld "the liberal democratic tradition of the college."[37]

The editorials written on her watch reveal a young woman who believed that what was involved with almost every issue—at Smith, in the United States and abroad—was the struggle for democracy, freedom, and social justice. Under Friedan's leadership the editors supported American workers and their labor unions in their struggles to organize and improve their conditions. . . . The inequality of power in America, the editorial argued in good social democratic terms, "has to be admitted and dealt with if democracy is to have meaning for 95% of the citizens of this country."[38]

Above all, what haunted the editorials was the spread of fascism and questions about

America's involvement in a world war. In April of 1941, the editors made it clear that the defeat of fascism was their primary goal and one that determined their position on questions of war or peace. In the fall of 1941, after the German invasion of the Soviet Union during the preceding summer, the editors increasingly accepted the inevitability of war even as they made it clear that they believed "fighting fascists is only one part of fighting fascism."[39] Some Smith students responded with redbaiting to the newspaper's anti-fascism and reluctance to support intervention wholeheartedly, accusing the editorial board of being dominated by communists, at a time when the Party reached its greatest membership in the years after Pearl Harbor while the United States and the Soviet Union were allies. Though one editor denied the charge of communist influence, like many newspapers at American colleges in these years, on the paper's staff were students attracted to the political analysis offered by radical groups. In the fall of 1940 one columnist argued against lumping communists and Nazis together, remarking that communism was not a "dark terror" but "a precarious scheme worked out by millions of civilized men and women."[40]

When America entered the war in December of 1941, the editors accepted the nation's new role loyally, albeit soberly. The central issue for them was how American students, especially female ones, could "contribute actively to the American cause." . . .

Friedan's experiences at Smith cast a different light on her decision to leave Berkeley after a year of graduate school. The editorials she and her peers had written immediately after Pearl Harbor revealed an impatience to be near the action. A 1943 article in the Peoria paper reported that Friedan turned down the fellowship because "she decided she wanted to work in the labor movement—on the labor press."[41] . . . Off and on from October 1943 until July 1946 she was a staff writer for the Federated Press, a left-wing news service that provided stories for newspapers, especially union ones, across the nation.[42] Here Friedan wrote articles that supported the aspirations of African Americans and union members. She also criticized reactionary forces that, she believed, were working secretly to undermine progressive social advances.[43] As early as 1943,

she pictured efforts by businesses, coordinated by the National Association of Manufacturers (NAM), to develop plans that would enhance profits, diminish the power of unions, reverse the New Deal, and allow businesses to operate as they pleased.[44]

At Federated Press, Friedan also paid attention to women's problems. Right after she began to work there, she interviewed UE official Ruth Young, one of the clearest voices in the labor movement articulating women's issues. In the resulting article, Friedan noted that the government could not solve the problem of turnover "merely by pinning up thousands of glamorous posters designed to lure more women into industry." Neither women, unions, nor management, she quoted Young as saying, could solve problems of escalating prices or inadequate child care that were made even more difficult by the fact that "women still have two jobs to do." Action of the federal government, Friedan reported, was needed to solve the problems working women faced.[45]

She paid special attention to stories about protecting the jobs and improving the situation of working women, including married ones with children.

For about six years beginning in July, 1946, precisely at the moment when the wartime Popular Front came under intense attack, Friedan was a reporter for the union's paper *UE News.*[46] At least as early as 1943, when she quoted Young, Friedan was well aware of the UE's commitments to equity for women.[47]

. . . In 1949–50, union activists who followed the recommendations of the Communist Party . . . advocated the automatic granting of several years of seniority to all African Americans as compensation for their years of exclusion from the electrical industry. If the UE pioneered in articulating what we might call affirmative action for African Americans, then before and during World War II it advocated what a later generation would label comparable worth. Against considerable resistance from within its ranks, the UE also worked to improve the conditions of working-class women in part by countering a seniority system which gave advantage to men.[48] After 1949, with the UE out of the CIO and many of the more conservative union members out of

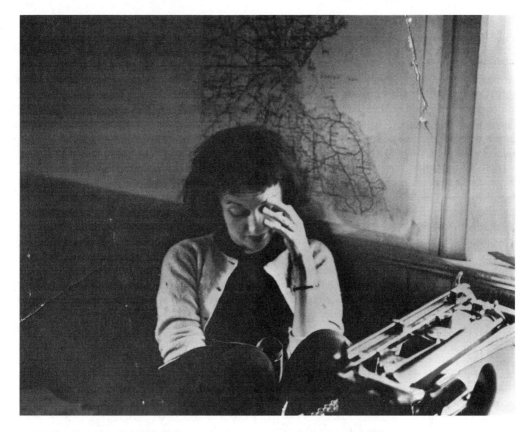

Betty Friedan as labor journalist, late 1940s. (Courtesy of the Schlesinger Library, Radcliffe College, Harvard University.)

the UE, women's issues and women's leadership resumed the importance they had in the UE during World War II, when it had developed, Ruth Milkman has written, a "strong ideological commitment to gender equality."[49]

Beginning in 1946, Friedan [also] witnessed the efforts by federal agencies, congressional committees, major corporations, the Roman Catholic Church, and the CIO to break the hold of what they saw as the domination of the UE by communists. The inclusion of a clause in the Taft-Hartley Act of 1947, requiring union officers to sign an anticommunist affidavit if they wished to do business with the National Labor Relations Board, helped encourage other unions to challenge the UE, whose leaders refused to sign.[50] Internecine

fights took place within the UE, part of a longer term fight between radicals and anticommunists in its ranks. . . . Before long, . . . the UE was greatly weakened: in 1949, its connection with the CIO was severed and the newly-formed and CIO-backed IUE recruited many of its members. Membership in UE, numbering more than 600,000 in 1946, fell to 203,000 in 1953 and to 71,000 four years later.[51]

At *UE News,* from her position as a middle-class woman interested in the lives of the working class, Friedan continued to articulate a progressive position on a wide range of issues. She again pointed to concerted efforts, led by big corporations under the leadership of the NAM, to increase profits, exploit labor, and break labor unions.[52] In 1951, she contrasted the extravagant expenditures of the wealthy with the family of a worker who could afford neither fresh vegetables nor new clothes.[53] Friedan also told the story of how valiant union members helped build political coalitions to fight Congressional and corporate efforts to roll back gains workers made during the New Deal and World War II.[54] She drew parallels between the United States in the 1940s and Nazi Germany in the 1930s as she exposed the way HUAC and big business were using every tactic they could to destroy the UE. Friedan hailed the launching of the Progressive Party in 1948.[55] She exposed the existence of racism and discrimination, even when they appeared among union officials and especially when directed against Jews and African Americans. Praising heroic workers who struggled against great odds as they fought monopolies, Friedan, probably expressing her hopes for herself, extolled the skills of a writer "who is able to describe with sincerity and passion the hopes, the struggle and the romance of the working people who make up most of America."[56]

Throughout her years at UE News, Friedan participated in discussions on women's issues, including the issue of corporations' systematic discrimination against women. Going to factories to interview those whose stories she was covering, she also wrote about working women, including African Americans and Latinas.[57] In the worlds Friedan inhabited in the decade beginning in 1943, as the historian Kathleen Weigand has shown, people often discussed the cultural and economic sources of women's oppression, the nature of discrimination based on sex, the special difficulties African American women faced, and the dynamics of discrimination against women in a variety of institutions, including the family.[58] Moreover, for the people around Friedan and doubtlessly for Friedan herself, the fight for justice for women was inseparable from the more general struggle to secure rights for African Americans and workers.[59] As she had done at the Federated Press, at UE News in the late 1940s and early 1950s she reported on how working women struggled as producers and consumers to make sure their families had enough to live on.[60]

Friedan's focus on working women's issues resulted in her writing the pamphlet, UE Fights for Women Workers, published by the UE in June of 1952.[61] She began by suggesting the

contradiction in industry's treatment of women as consumers and as producers. "In advertisements across the land," Friedan remarked, "industry glorifies the American woman—in her gleaming GE kitchen, at her Westinghouse laundromat, before her Sylvania television set. Nothing," she announced as she insightfully explored a central contradiction women faced in the postwar world, "is too good for her—unless" she worked for corporations, including GE, or Westinghouse, or Sylvania.[62]

The central theme of the piece was how, in an effort to improve the pay and conditions of working women, the UE fought valiantly against greedy corporations that sought to increase their profits by exploiting women. Friedan discussed a landmark 1945 National War Labor Board decision on sex-based wage discrimination in favor of the UE. Remarking that "fighting the exploitation of women is men's business too," she emphasized how discriminatory practices corporations used against women hurt men as well by exerting downward pressure on wages of all workers. To back up the call for equal pay for equal work and to fight against segregation and discrimination of women, she countered stereotypes justifying lower pay for women: they were physically weaker, entered the work force only temporarily, had no families to support, and worked only for pin money. She highlighted the "even more shocking" situation African American women faced, having to deal as they did with the "double bars" of being female and African American.[63] Friedan set forth a program that was, Lisa Kannenberg has noted, "a prescription for a gender-blind workplace."[64]

The conditions under which she left Federated Press and UE News are not entirely clear. In May of 1946, during her second stint at Federated Press, she filed a grievance with the Newspaper Guild, saying she had lost her job in June of 1945 to a man she had replaced during the war. Later she claimed she was "bumped" from her position "by a returning veteran." There is evidence, however, that Friedan had to give up her position to a man who returned to the paper after two years in prison because he refused to serve in the military during what he considered a capitalists' war.[65] Friedan later claimed that she lost her job at the UE during her second pregnancy because the labor movement failed to honor its commitment to maternity leaves. Yet a knowledgeable observer has written that when the union had to cut the staff because of the dramatic drop in its membership, something that resulted from McCarthyite attacks, Friedan "offered to quit so another reporter," a man with more seniority, could remain at *UE News*.[66] Although her experience with unions may have provided a negative spur to her feminism, it also served as a positive inspiration. Friedan was indebted to the UE for major elements of her education about gender equity, sex discrimination, and women's issues.

The reason Friedan left out these years in her life story is now clear. Her stint at the *UE News* took place at the height of the anti-communist crusade, which she experienced at close quarters. When she emerged into the limelight in 1963, the issue of affiliation with communists was wracking SANE, SDS, and the civil rights movement. In the same years, HUAC was still holding hearings, the United States was pursuing an anti-communist war in Vietnam, and J. Edgar Hoover's FBI was wiretapping Martin Luther King, Jr., ostensibly to protect the nation against communist influence. Had Friedan revealed all in the mid-1960s, she would have undercut her book's impact, subjected herself to palpable dangers, and jeopardized the feminist movement, including the National Organization for Women (NOW), an institution she was instrumental in launching. Perhaps instead of emphasizing continuities in her life, she told the story of her conversion in order to heighten the impact of her book and appeal to white middle-class women. Or . . . Friedan may have come to believe a narrative that outlived the needs it originally fulfilled.

Until 1952, almost everything Friedan published as a labor journalist appeared under the name Betty Goldstein, though she had married in 1947. When she emerged as a writer for women's magazines in 1955, it was as Betty Friedan. Aside from indicating her marital status, the change in name was significant. It signaled a shift from an employee for a union paper who wrote highly political articles on the working class to a free-lance writer for mass circulation magazines who concentrated on the suburban middle class in more muted tones [and in the 1950s became a suburbanite herself. In 1957, the Freidans moved into an] eleven-room Victorian house, which they

bought with the help of the GI Bill and some money Friedan inherited from her father.[67]

What Friedan wrote for mass circulation women's magazines [during those years] belies her claim that she had contributed to what she later attacked in *The Feminine Mystique*.

Sylvie Murray has demonstrated that Friedan drafted, but was unable to get into print, articles that fully celebrated women's political activism, expressed skepticism about male expertise, and described blue collar and lower middle-class families, not generic middle-class ones. Yet Friedan was able to sell articles that went against the grain of the cold war celebration by criticizing middle-class conformity. . . . Friedan critiqued suburban life by drawing a dismal picture of those who conformed, by offering alternatives to conventional choices, and by exploring the strength of cooperative communities.[68] She drew portraits of American women that opposed the picture of the happy, suburban housewife who turned her back on a career in order to find satisfaction at home.[69] Friedan also portrayed women accomplishing important tasks as they took on traditionally feminine civic roles, thus implicitly undercutting the ideal of the apolitical suburban housewife and mother.[70]

In one particularly revealing piece, Friedan prefigured some of the issues she later claimed she only began to discover when she started to work on *The Feminine Mystique*. In "I Went Back to Work," published in *Charm* in April 1955, she wrote that initially she did not think highly of housework or of housewives and was guilty about what she was doing. Eventually she decided that her commitment to being a good mother was not "going to interfere with what I regarded as my 'real' life." Finding it necessary to be away from home for nine hours a day in order to work, she solved the problem of child care by hiring "a really good mother-substitute—a housekeeper-nurse." In the end, Friedan had no regrets about her decision or apparently about her privileged position. She believed her work outside the home improved her family's situation and acknowledged that her "whole life had always been geared around creative, intellectual work" and "a professional career."[71]

In what ways, then, was Friedan a captive of the feminine mystique? There is no question but that she was miserable in the suburbs. Her emphasis on her captivity may have expressed one part of her ambivalence. Yet, though she claimed that she shared so much with her suburban, white, middle-class sisters in the postwar world, during much of the two decades beginning in 1943 Friedan was participating in left-wing union activity, writing articles that went against the grain of cold war ideology, and living in a cosmopolitan, racially integrated community. During most of the time between her marriage in 1947 and the publication of *The Feminine Mystique,* Friedan combined career and family life. As a woman who worked with her at Federated Press later noted, at the time Friedan and her female colleagues expected to have professional careers.[72] Caution about the predominantly suburban origins of her book is also in order because Friedan's move to suburban Rockland County in 1956 preceded by only a few months her initial work on the survey for her reunion that was so critical to *The Feminine Mystique.*[73]

To be sure, in the postwar world Friedan experienced at first hand the trials of a woman who fought against considerable odds to combine marriage, motherhood, and a career.[74] Yet in critical ways her difficulties did not stem from the dilemmas she described in her book: lack of career and ambition, a securely affluent household, and absence of a political sensibility. Friedan experienced psychological conflicts over issues of creativity in writing and motherhood.[75] Researching and writing her free-lance articles was a laborious process.[76] She had three young children, hardly felt comfortable in the suburbs, had no local institutions to provide a supportive environment for an aspiring writer, and continually faced financial difficulties. Her income from writing articles was unpredictable, a situation exacerbated by the pressure she was under to help support the household and justify the expenses for child care. Tension persisted between the Friedans over a wide range of issues, including who was responsible for earning and spending the family's income. Moreover, she was in a marriage apparently marked by violence.[77]

Friedan was largely right when she said "all the pieces of my own life came together for the first time in the writing" of *The Feminine Mystique.* The skills as a journalist she had developed beginning as a teenager stood her in good stead as she worked to make what she had to say accessible to a wide audience. Her identity as a Jew and an outsider gave her a distinctive perspective on American and suburban life. Her years at Smith boosted her confidence and enhanced her political education. Her life as a wife and mother sensitized her to the conflicts millions of others experienced but could not articulate. Her education as a psychologist led her to understand the gestalt, the wholeness of a situation, and to advocate self-fulfillment based on humanistic psychology. Above all, her work as a labor journalist and activist provided her with the intellectual depth, ideological commitments, and practical experiences crucial to her emergence as a leading feminist in the 1960s.

Why did a woman who had spent so much energy advocating political solutions focus in *The Feminine Mystique* largely on adult education and self-realization and turn social problems into psychological ones? How did a woman who had fought to improve the lives of African Americans, Latinas, and working-class women end up writing a book that saw the problems of America in terms of the lives of affluent, suburban white women?[78]

Even at the time, at least one observer, Gerda Lerner, raised questions about what Friedan emphasized and neglected. Active in the trade union movement in the 1940s, present at the founding meeting of NOW, and after the mid-1960s one of the nation's leading historians of women, in February 1963 Lerner wrote Friedan. "I have just finished reading your splendid book and want to tell you how excited and delighted I am with it. . . . You have done for women," she remarked as she referred to the author who had warned about the destruction of the environment, "what Rachel Carson did for birds and trees." Yet, Lerner continued:

> I have one reservation about your treatment of your subject: you address yourself solely to the problems of middle class, college-educated women. This approach was one of the shortcomings of the suffrage movement for many years and has, I believe, retarded the general advance of women. Working women, especially Negro women, labor not only under the disadvantages imposed by the feminine mystique, but under the more pressing disadvantages of economic discrimination. To leave them out of consideration of the problem or to ignore the contributions they can make toward its solution, is something we simply cannot afford to do. By their desperate need, by their numbers, by their organizational experience (if trade union mem-

bers), working women are most important in reaching *institutional* solutions to the problems of women.[79]

The dynamics of Friedan's shifts in attention from working-class to middle-class women are not entirely clear. At some point after May 1953, when she followed the proceedings at the UE conference on the problems of women workers, Friedan turned away from working-class and African American women, something that undercut the power of *The Feminine Mystique*. An important question is whether the shift from her UE radicalism and focus on working-class women was a rhetorical strategy designed for the specific situation of *The Feminine Mystique* or part of a longer-term deradicalization. Until her personal papers are fully open and extensive interviewing is carried out, and perhaps not even then, we may not know the dynamics of this change.

NOTES

1. Betty Goldstein, "UE Drive on Wage, Job Discrimination Wins Cheers from Women Members," *UE News*, 16 Apr. 1951, 6. My interview of Friedan in 1987 first brought to my attention the possibility of this alternative story, as did the research my colleague, Helen L. Horowitz, carried out in the late 1980s. The appearance of the article by Joanne Meyerowitz in 1993, cited below, added an important piece of evidence. Because Friedan has denied me permission to quote from her unpublished papers and has not responded to my request that she grant me an opportunity to interview her or to have her respond to my questions, I have not been able to present as full and perhaps as accurate a story as I wished to do.
2. Ronald W. Schatz, *The Electrical Workers: A History of Labor at General Electric and Westinghouse, 1923–60* (Urbana, Ill., 1983), xiii.
3. Lisa Kannenberg, "The Impact of the Cold War on Women's Trade Union Activism: The UE Experience," *Labor History* 34 (spring-summer 1993): 318; Jacqueline Van Voris, interview with Eleanor Flexner, Northampton, Mass., 16 Oct. 1982, 70–71, Eleanor Flexner Papers, Schlesinger Library, Radcliffe College, Cambridge, Mass. [hereinafter cited as FP-SLRC]; [Eleanor Flexner], "The Woman Question," Syllabus for course at Jefferson School of Social Science, 1953–54, 1, 2, 5. For information on Flexner. I am relying on Ellen C. DuBois, "Eleanor Flexner and the History of American Feminism," *Gender and History* 3 (spring 1991): 81–90. On the Jefferson School, see Annette T. Rubinstein, "David Goldway," *Science and Society* 54 (winter 1990–91): 386–89; Daniel F. Ring, "Two Cultures: Libraries, the Unions, and the 'Case' of the Jefferson School of

Social Science," *Journal of Library History* 20 (1985): 287–88.
4. Betty Friedan, "Up From the Kitchen Floor," *New York Times Magazine*, 4 Mar. 1973, 8; Betty Friedan, *"It Changed My Life": Writings on the Women's Movement* (New York, 1976), 304.
5. For evidence of the continuing importance of Friedan and her book, see, for example, Elaine T. May, *Homeward Bound: American Families in the Cold War Era* (New York, 1988), 209–17, 219 and Joanne Meyerowitz, "Beyond the Feminine Mystique: A Reassessment of Postwar Mass Culture, 1946–1958," *Journal of American History* 79 (Mar. 1993): 1455–82. For textbooks, see John M. Faragher et al., *Out of Many: A History of the American People* (Englewood Cliffs, N.J., 1994), 2:865, 943: James A. Henretta et al., *America's History*, 2d ed. (New York, 1993), 2:909, 910, 911, 968; William H. Chafe, *The Unfinished Journey: America Since World War II*, 3d ed. (New York, 1995), 124, 330, 433. A widely-used reader in American women's history contains a selection from Friedan's book, introducing its author as "a suburban housewife": Linda K. Kerber and Jane S. De Hart, *Women's America: Refocusing the Past*, 4th ed. (New York, 1995), 512.
6. For biographical information, in addition to what Friedan has said in print, I am relying on Kathleen Wilson, "Betty (Naomi) Friedan," *Contemporary Authors*, New Revision Series (New York, 1995) 45: 133–36; David Halberstam, *The Fifties* (New York, 1993), 592–98; Marilyn French, "The Emancipation of Betty Friedan," *Esquire* 100 (Dec. 1983): 510, 512, 514, 516, 517; Jennifer Moses, "She's Changed Our Lives: A Profile of Betty Friedan," *Present Tense* 15 (May–June 1988): 26–31; Lyn Tornabene, "The Liberation of Betty Friedan," *McCall's* 98 (May 1971): 84, 136–40, 142, 146; Paul Wilkes, "Mother Superior to Women's Lib," *New York Times Magazine*, 29 Nov. 1970, 27–29, 140–43, 149–50, 157; Marcia Cohen, *The Sisterhood: The True Story of the Women Who Changed the World* (New York, 1988), 25, 54–71, 83–84, 89–99; Lisa Hammel, "The 'Grandmother' of Women's Lib," *New York Times*, 19 Nov. 1971, 52; Friedan, *Changed My Life*, 5–16; Jacqueline Van Voris, interview of Betty Friedan, New York, N.Y., 17 Apr. 1973, College Archives, Smith College, Northampton, Mass. [hereinafter cited as CA-SC]; Daniel Horowitz, interview of Betty Friedan, Santa Monica, Calif., 18 Mar. 1987. As late as 6 Nov. 1995, the date she sent me a letter denying me permission to quote from her unpublished papers, Friedan reiterated key elements of her story: I am grateful to Rachel Ledford for reporting to me on Friedan's 6 Nov. 1995 talk at the Smithsonian Institution, Washington, D.C. Ironically, two biographies aimed at children provide fuller stories than do other treatments (for instance, they are the only published sources I have been able to locate that make clear that Friedan worked for the UE): Sondra Henry and Emily Taitz, *Betty Friedan: Fighter for Women's Rights* (Hillside, N.J., 1990) and Milton Meltzer, *Betty Friedan: A Voice for Women's Rights* (New York, 1985).
7. This article is based on considerable but hardly exhaustive examination of the available written record. When other researchers examine the Friedan papers (including those to which access is

restricted) and are able to carry out extensive interviews, they will be able to offer a fuller exploration of several issues, especially the shifts in Friedan's commitments as a radical at a time of great factionalism, when and how the feminine mystique did or did not trap her, how she interpreted the research on which *The Feminine Mystique* relied, and the pressures Friedan faced from her publisher to shape her 1963 book in certain ways.

8. An examination of what Friedan wrote for her high school paper reveals someone less lonely than she has often portrayed herself: see articles by Friedan in *Peoria Opinion* from the fall of 1936 until the spring of 1938. For one political piece that reveals an early anti-fascism, see Bettye Goldstein, "Long, Coughlin, Roosevelt in 'It Can't Happen Here,' " *Peoria Opinion*, 18 Sept. 1936, 8.

9. Friedan, quoted in Wilkes, "Mother Superior," 140; Betty Friedan, *The Feminine Mystique* (New York, 1963), 12.

10. Friedan, *Feminine Mystique*, 70; Friedan, quoted in Wilkes, "Mother Superior," 140. On the paucity of role models at Smith, see Van Voris, Friedan interview.

11. Horowitz, interview.

12. Dust jacket of 1963 copy of *The Feminine Mystique*, author's possession. See also, "About Betty Friedan . . . ," biographical note accompanying Betty Friedan, "How to Find and Develop Article Ideas," *The Writer* 75 (Mar. 1962), 13.

13. Friedan, quoted in "Betty Friedan," *Current Biography Yearbook 1970*, ed. Charles Moritz (New York, 1971), 146; Betty Friedan, "New York Women: Beyond the Feminine Mystique," *New York Herald Tribune*, 21 Feb. 1965, 7–15, women's liberation, biographics, individuals, box 4, folder 31, clippings on Betty Friedan, Sophia Smith Collection, Smith College [hereinafter referred to as SSC-SC]; Wilkes, "Mother Superior," 141; Friedan, quoted in Wilkes, "Mother Superior," 141; Tornabene, "Liberation," 138; and Friedan, "Kitchen Floor," 8.

14. Tornabene, "Liberation," 138. See Betty Friedan, "The Intellectual Pied Pipers of Rockland County," unpublished paper, written in 1960–61, FP-SLRC, carton 9, folder 347, Friedan Collection, Schlesinger Library, Radcliffe College, Cambridge, Mass. [hereinafter cited as BF-SLRC; unless otherwise noted, the references are to collection 71–62 . . . 81-M23].

15. Rollene W. Saal, "Author of the Month," *Saturday Review*, 21 Mar. 1964, women's liberation, biographies, individuals, box 4, folder 31, SSC-SC; *Hackensack Record*, 2 May 1963, Class of 1942 folders, Betty Goldstein folder, CA-SC; Friedan, "Kitchen Floor," 8.

16. Friedan, *Feminine Mystique*, 9, 20, 66, 70, 186–87.

17. Horowitz, interview: Betty Friedan, "Introduction to the Tenth Anniversary Edition" of *Feminine Mystique* (New York, 1974), 1–5. For early articles with the themes that would emerge in the book, see Betty Friedan, "I Say: Women are *People* Too!" *Good Housekeeping* 151 (Sept. 1960): 59–61, 161–62; Betty Goldstein Friedan, "If One Generation Can Ever Tell Another," *Smith Alumnae Quarterly*, Feb. 1961, 68–70.

18. The 1974 article, which in the book was called "The Way We Were—1949," was originally published with some relatively unimportant differences, but with a more revealing title, as Betty Friedan, "In France, de Beauvoir Had Just Published 'The Second Sex,' " *New York* 8 (30 Dec. 1974–6 Jan. 1975): 52–55. In Horowitz, interview, which covered mainly the years up to 1963, Friedan discussed her move to a radical politics even as she emphasized captivity by the feminine mystique beginning in the Berkeley years. Though Friedan has revealed a good deal about her life, to the best of my knowledge she has not acknowledged in print the full range of reasons she left Berkeley, that she worked for the UE, her authorship of the 1952 pamphlet, and her leadership of the rent strike. Moreover, she has insisted that in the late 1940s and early 1950s, she had interest neither in a career nor in women's problems.

19. I am grateful to Judith Smith for helping me to think through this and other issues.

20. Friedan, *Changed My Life*, 6, 8–9.

21. Friedan, *Changed My Life*, 6, 9, 16; Halberstam, *Fifties*, 593; French, "Emancipation," 510. Horowitz, interview, dates the firing in 1952. In the immediate postwar years, the term "feminist" often referred to women who were Republicans, independent businesswomen, and professionals.

22. Friedan, *Changed My Life*, 5, 6–7, 8–9, 15, 16. She gave 1949 as the turning point because she had been asked to do a piece in 1974 on what had happened a quarter of a century earlier: Horowitz, interview.

23. Friedan, *Changed My Life*, 14–16.

24. Friedan, *Changed My Life*, 12, 16.

25. Cohen, *Sisterhood*, 63 and Wilkes, "Mother Superior," 140 briefly draw a picture of Friedan as a college rebel but to the best of my knowledge, the politics of that rebellion have remained largely unknown.

26. This summary relies on unsigned editorials that appeared under Friedan's editorship, which can be found in *SCAN* [*Smith College Associated News*] from 14 Mar. 1941 to 10 Mar. 1942, p. 2. Although members of the editorial board held a wide range of opinions, I am assuming that as editor-in-chief Friedan had a significant role in shaping editorials. Friedan placed four editorials in her papers: "They Believed in Peace," "Years of Change and Unrest," "Behind Closed Doors," and "Answer No Answer": carton 7, folder 310, BF-SLRC.

27. For the article she published on the basis on her honors thesis, see H. Israel and B. Goldstein, "Operationism in Psychology," *Psychological Review* 51 (May 1944): 177–88.

28. See James J. Gibson, "Why a Union For Teachers?" *Focus* 2 (Nov. 1939): 3–7.

29. I am grateful to Margery Sly, Archivist of Smith College, for providing this information. She has also pointed out that teaching at Smith in Friedan's years were several married, female faculty members who had children and that Harold Israel and Elsa Siipola, two of Friedan's mentors, were married but without children.

30. In 1955 Douglas took the Fifth Amendment before HUAC as she was redbaited, accused of hav-

ing been a member of a communist teachers union in the late 1930s. I am grateful to Margery Sly and Jacquelyn D. Hall for providing this information on Douglas. See also, Betty Friedan, "Was Their Education UnAmerican?" unpublished article, 1953 or 1954, carton 11, folder 415, BF-SLRC, 3. For Friedan's continued use of Marxist analysis, see Friedan, *It Changed My Life*, 110.

31. Bettye Goldstein, "Discussion of Reading Period Material," paper for Economics 319, 18 Jan. 1941, carton 1, folder 257, BF-SLRC, 1, 2, 4, 8. See also "Questions on *Communist Manifesto*" and "Questions on Imperialism," papers for Economics 319, carton 1, folder 257, BF-SLRC.

32. John M. Glen, *Highlander: No Ordinary School, 1932–1962* (Lexington, Ky., 1988), 47–69. I am grateful to Professor Glen for a letter in which he clarified the timing of the League's sponsorship. Meltzer, *Friedan*, 20 says that Friedan's economics professor pointed her to Highlander but identifies that professor as a male; since the only economics course Friedan took was from Douglas, I am assuming that it was she who urged her student to attend the workshop. Meltzer thinks that is a reasonable assumption: Milton Meltzer, phone conversation with Daniel Horowitz, 24 Sept. 1995.

33. Bettye Goldstein, "Highlander Folk School—American Future," unpublished paper, 1941, carton 6, folder 274, BF-SLRC; Goldstein, "Learning the Score," 22–24.

34. "Epilogue of Failure," *SCAN*, 10 Mar. 1942, 2.

35. "Betty Goldstein, Local Girl, Makes Good in New York," clipping from Peoria newspaper, probably 10 Dec. 1943 issue of *Labor Temple News*, carton 1, folder 86, BF-SLRC.

36. "Behind a Closed Door," *SCAN*, 3 Oct. 1941, 2; "Declaration of Student Independence," *SCAN*, 5 Dec. 1941, 1–2; "SCAN Protests Against Censorship," *SCAN*, 5 Dec. 1941, 1; "A Few Hours More," *SCAN*, 10 Oct. 1941, 2; "Review of Philosophy Courses," *SCAN*, 10 Mar. 1942, 2.

37. "The Tatler Suspension," *SCAN*, 7 Nov. 1941, 2; for the article in question see "Maids We Have Known and Loved," *Tatler*, Oct. 1941, 9, 21. When the administration moved against *SCAN*, over a different incident, the editors changed their minds about the earlier suspension of the *Tatler*: *SCAN*, 5 Dec. 1941, 1–2.

38. "Education in Emergency," *SCAN*, 15 Apr. 1941, 2; "The Right to Organize," *SCAN*, 21 Oct. 1941, 2; "Comment," *SCAN*, 14 Nov. 1941, 2; Filene's advertisement, *SCAN*, 21 Oct. 1941, 2. Bettye Goldstein, "For Defense of Democracy," *Smith College Monthly* 1 (Oct. 1940): 11, 12, 28 is a passionate defense of democracy and a warning about the possibility of American fascism.

39. "They Choose Peace," *SCAN*, 22 Apr. 1941, 2; for the minority opinion, see "The Case for Intervention," *SCAN*, 2 May 1941, 2; "War Against Fascism," *SCAN*, 24 Oct. 1941, 2. Placing the editorials written on Friedan's watch in the national context of student politics makes clear that after the Nazi-Soviet pact the student movement was more active and radical at Smith than elsewhere. In addition, the commitment of Friedan and her fellow editors to anti-fas-

cism and their reluctance to embrace interventionism fully after the German invasion of the Soviet Union suggests that they dissented from the Communist Party position. On the national context see Robert Cohen, *When The Old Left Was Young: Student Radicals and America's First Mass Student Movement, 1929–1941* (New York, 1993), especially 315–37.

40. J. N., "The Red Menace," *SCAN*, 14 Oct. 1941, 2; Neal Gilkyson, "The Gallery," *SCAN*, 21 Oct. 1941, 2.

41. "Betty Goldstein, Local Girl," Meltzer, *Friedan*, 21 provides explanations for Friedan's decision that do not rely on the standard story.

42. To date her work for the Federated Press, see Betty Friedan, job application for Time Inc., 1 July 1951, carton 1, folder 61, BF-SLRC. For information on the Federated Press, see Doug Reynolds, "Federated Press," *Encyclopedia of the American Left*, ed. Mari Jo Buhle, Paul Buhle, and Dan Georgakas (New York, 1990), 225–27.

43. Betty Goldstein, "Negro Pupils Segregated, Parents Strike; Issue Headed for Courts," Federated Press, 15 Sept. 1943, carton 8, folder 328, BF-SLRC; Betty Goldstein, "Peace Now: Treason in Pious Garb," Federated Press, 16 Feb. 1944, carton 8, folder 328, BF-SLRC; Betty Goldstein, "Well-Heeled 'White Collar League' Seen as Disguised Native Fascist Threat," Federated Press, 16 Mar. 1944, carton 8, folder 328, BF-SLRC.

44. Betty Goldstein, "Big Business Getting Desperate, Promising Postwar Jobs," Federated Press, 19 Nov. 1943, carton 8, folder 328, BF-SLRC; Betty Goldstein, "NAM Convention Pro-War—For War on Labor, New Deal, Roosevelt," Federated Press, 14 Dec. 1943, carton 8, folder 328, BF-SLRC; Betty Goldstein, "Details of Big Business Anti-Labor Conspiracy Uncovered," Federated Press, 11 Feb. 1946, carton 8, folder 328, BF-SLRC. For the larger story, see Elizabeth A. Fones-Wolf, *Selling Free Enterprise: The Business Assault on Labor and Liberalism, 1945–60* (Urbana, 1994).

45. Betty Goldstein, "Pretty Posters Won't Stop Turnover of Women in Industry," Federated Press, 26 Oct. 1943, and Ruth Young quoted in same, carton 8, folder 328, BF-SLRC.

46. Job application, 1951.

47. For information on women in the UE see Schatz, *Electrical Workers*; Ruth Milkman, *Gender at Work: The Dynamics of Job Segregation by Sex During World War II* (Urbana, 1987); Kannenberg, "Impact"; Lisa A. Kannenberg, "From World War to Cold War: Women Electrical Workers and Their Union, 1940–1955," M.A. thesis, University of North Carolina, Charlotte, 1990. Robert H. Zieger, *The CIO, 1935–1955* (Chapel Hill, N.C., 1995), 253–93 assesses the role of communists in the CIO, including the UE and discusses the vagueness of the line between sympathy and Party membership in unions like the UE; Ronald L. Filippelli and Mark McCulloch, *Cold War in the Working Class: The Rise and Decline of the United Electrical Workers* (Albany, N.Y., 1994) charts the attack on the UE and discusses the issue of communist presence in the UE.

48. Schatz, *Electrical Workers*, 30, 89, 116–27, 129–30.

49. Milkman, *Gender at Work*, 77–78; see also Kannenberg, "Impact," esp. 311, 315. Nancy B. Palmer, "Gender, Sexuality, and Work: Women and Men in the Electrical Industry, 1940–1955," Ph.D. diss., Boston College, 1995, more skeptical of women's gains in the UE, focuses on how the construction of gender in labor unions, including the UE, limited women's advances: see esp. chap. 4.

50. Zieger, *CIO*, 251.

51. This summary relies on Schatz, *Electrical Workers*, 167–240. The 1946 quote is from Harry Block in Schatz, *Electrical Workers*, 181. For the impact of the attack on UE on women's issues, see Kannenberg, "From World War to Cold War," 95.

52. Betty Goldstein, "NAM Does Gleeful War Dance to Profits, Wage Cuts, Taft Law," *UE News*, 13 Dec. 1947, 4. What follows relies on the more than three dozen articles signed by Betty Goldstein in the *UE News* from the fall of 1946 until early 1952.

53. Betty Goldstein, "A Tale of 'Sacrifice': A Story of Equality in the United States, 1951," *March of Labor*, May 1951, 16–18, carton 8, folder 334, BF-SLRC. This also appeared in *UE News*, 12 Mar. 1951, 6–7.

54. Betty Goldstein, "It'll Take a Strong Union To End Winchester Tyranny," *UE News*, 7 Dec. 1946, 9; Betty Goldstein, "Fighting Together: We Will Win!" *UE News*, 31 May 1947, 5, 8; Betty Goldstein, "Labor Builds New Political Organization To Fight for a People's Congressman," *UE News*, 23 Aug. 1947, 4.

55. Betty Goldstein, "People's Needs Forgotten: Big Business Runs Govt.," *UE News*, 12 May 1947, 5; Betty Goldstein, "In Defense of Freedom! The People Vs. the UnAmerican Committee," *UE News*, 8 Nov. 1947, 6–7; Betty Goldstein, "They Can't Shove the IBEW Down Our Throats," *UE News*, 4 Sept. 1948, 6–7; Betty Goldstein, "UnAmerican Hearing Exposed as Plot By Outsiders to Keep Grip on UE Local," *UE News*, 22 Aug. 1949, 4; Betty Goldstein, "New NAM Theme Song: Labor-Management Teamwork," *UE News*, 9 Jan. 1950, 5; Betty Goldstein, "Plain People of America Organize New Political Party of Their Own," *UE News*, 31 July 1948, 6–7.

56. B. G., review of Sinclair Lewis, *Kingsblood Royal*, *UE News*, 6 Sept. 1947, 7; B. G., review of the movie "Gentleman's Agreement," *UE News*, 22 Nov. 1947, 11; B. G., review of movie "Crossfire," *UE News*, 9 Aug. 1947, 8–9; Betty Goldstein, "CIO Sold Out Fight for FEPC, T-H Repeal, Rep. Powell Reveals," *UE News*, 17 Apr. 1950, 4; B. G., review of Fielding Burke, *Sons of the Stranger*, *UE News*, 24 Jan. 1948, 7.

57. These two sentences rely on James Lerner, interview. For treatments of the relationship between communism and women's issues, see Ellen K. Trimberger, "Women in the Old and New Left: The Evolution of a Politics of Personal Life," *Feminist Studies* 5 (fall 1979): 432–61; Van Gosse, "'To Organize in Every Neighborhood, in Every Home': The Gender Politics of American Communists Between the Wars," *Radical History Review* 50 (spring 1991): 109–41; Kannenberg, "From World War to Cold War"; and Kathleen A. Weigand, "Vanguards of Women's Liberation: The Old Left and the Continuity of the Women's Movement in the United

States, 1945–1970s," Ph.D. diss., Ohio State University, 1995. For her coverage of Latinas, see Betty Goldstein, "'It's a Union That Fights for All the Workers,'" *UE News*, 3 [?] Sept. 1951, 6–7.

58. Though she does not discuss Friedan's situation, the best treatment of the prominent role of women's issues in radical circles in the 1940s and 1950s is Weigand, "Vanguards." In working on *The Feminine Mystique*, Friedan may have been influenced by writings she may have encountered in the 1940s, such as Mary Inman, *In Women's Defense* (Los Angeles, 1940) and Betty Millard, "Woman Against Myth," *New Masses*, 30 Dec. 1947, 7–10 and 6 Jan. 1948, 7–20. There is evidence that Friedan was well aware of *New Masses*. Under a pseudonym, she published two articles in *New Masses*: Lillian Stone, "Labor and the Community," *New Masses* 57 (23 Oct. 1945): 3–5; Lillian Stone, "New Day in Stamford," *New Masses* 58 (22 Jan. 1946): 3–5. In identifying Friedan as the author, I am relying on a 22 Sept. 1995 conversation with Kathy Kraft, an archivist at the Schlesinger Library and on a letter in carton 49, folder 1783, BF-SLRC.

59. Chinoy, interview.

60. Betty Goldstein, "Price Cuts Promised in Press Invisible to GE Housewives," *UE News*, 1 Feb. 1947, 7; Betty Goldstein, "Union Members Want to Know—WHO Has Too Much Money to Spend," *UE News*, 26 Mar. 1951, 8.

61. [Betty Goldstein], *UE Fights for Women Workers*, UE Publication no. 232, June 1952 (New York, 1952). To authenticate her authorship, I am relying on the following: Horowitz, interview; James Lerner, interview; Betty Friedan, postcard to author, late August, 1995; Meltzer, *Friedan*, 25. Meltzer, who knew Friedan in the 1940s, discusses her work on women's issues at the UE. Friedan may also have written *Women Fight For a Better Life!* (New York, 1953): see Friedan, postcard.

62. [Goldstein], *UE Fights*, 5.

63. [Goldstein], *UE Fights*, 9–18, 26–27, 38.

64. Kannenberg, "Impact," 318.

65. Betty Goldstein to Grievance Committee of Newspaper Guild of New York, 23 May 1946, carton 8, folder 330, BF-SLRC; Friedan, *Changed My Life*, 9; Mim Kelber, phone conversation with Daniel Horowitz, 16 Sept. 1995, identified the man as James Peck; obituary for James Peck, *New York Times* 13 July 1993, B7.

66. Meltzer, *Friedan*, 29. For additional perspectives on Friedan's departure from the *UE News*, see Kelber, conversation and James Lerner, interview. Lerner, who had more seniority than Friedan, worked for the UE for more than 40 years, eventually becoming managing editor of *UE News*. He shared an office with Friedan during her years at *UE News* and has noted that the union protected Friedan's position during her first pregnancy: James Lerner, interview.

67. To date these moves, I am relying on a number of sources, including Betty Friedan to Mrs. Clifford P. Cowen, 5 Aug. 1957, carton 7, folder, 313, BF-SLRC; Friedan, "New York Women"; "About the Author," in "New York Women"; "Friedan," *Current Biography*, 146; *Smith College Bulletin*.

68. Betty Friedan, "Two Are an Island," *Mademoiselle* 41 (July 1955): 88–89, 100–101; Betty Friedan, "Teenage Girl in Trouble," *Coronet* 43 (Mar. 1958): 163–68; Betty Friedan. "The Happy Families of Hickory Hill," *Redbook*, Feb. 1956, 39, 87–90; Stone, Marian and Harold Stone [fictitious names], as told to Betty Friedan, "With Love We Live. . . ." *Coronet* 42 (July 1957): 135–44. For another article on a suburban development that relied on cooperation, see Betty Friedan, "'We Built a Community for Our Children,'" *Redbook,* Mar. 1955, 42–45, 62–63. Friedan's papers contain information on scores of articles that she was working on; this analysis focuses on those actually published. Sylvie Murray's "Suburban Citizens: Domesticity and Community Politics in Queens, New York, 1945–1960," Ph.D. diss., Yale University, 1994 ably contrasts the adversarial politics of Friedan's unpublished pieces with the milder tone of her published ones; on the difficulty of getting into print articles on women who were not middle-class, I am relying on Sylvie Murray, phone conversation with Daniel Horowitz, 9 Oct. 1995.

69. Betty Friedan, "The Gal Who Defied Dior," *Town Journal,* Oct. 1955, 33, 97–98; Betty Friedan, "Millionaire's Wife," *Cosmopolitan,* Sept. 1956, 78–87; Betty Friedan, "New Hampshire Love Story," *Family Circle,* June 1958, 40–41, 74–76. An influential book on the origins of 1960s feminism begins with a discussion of Friedan's magazine articles without seeing how they might connect parts of her career: Sara Evans, *Personal Politics: The Roots of Women's Liberation in the Civil Rights Movement and the New Left* (New York, 1979), 3.

70. Betty Friedan, "Now They're Proud of Peoria," *Reader's Digest* 67 (Aug. 1955): 93–97.

71. Betty Friedan, "I Went Back to Work," *Charm,* Apr. 1955, 145, 200.

72. Kelber, conversation.

73. Parkway Village had some suburban characteristics and was marketed on the basis of its suburban qualities: Murray, conversation. Yet Friedan has made it clear that she was happy there: Friedan, *Changed My Life,* 14. Moreover, being in Parkway Village did not involve inhabiting a single-family home or living individualistically among conformists.

74. Especially crucial but nonetheless elusive is the period from May 1953, when she appears to have ended her union work, and 1955, when her first article appeared in a woman's magazine.

75. Friedan, "How to Find and Develop Article Ideas," 12–15 has some discussion of these conflicts.

76. This becomes clear through an examination of her files on her free-lance work, especially when compared with the files of Vance Packard in the same years.

77. Wilkes, "Mother Superior," 141. On violence in the marriage, see also Tornabene, "Liberation," 138; Cohen, *Sisterhood,* 17–18; Meyer, "Friedan," 608; Myra MacPherson, "The Former Mr. Betty Friedan Has Scars to Prove It," probably 1971, newspaper article from unidentified source, women's liberation, biographies, individuals, box 4, folder 31, clippings on Betty Friedan, SSC-SC.

78. On this problem, see Elizabeth V. Spelman, *Inessential Woman: Problems of Exclusion in Feminist Thought* (Boston, 1988).

79. Gerda Lerner to Betty Friedan, 6 Feb. 1963, box 20a, folder 715, BF-SLRC; quoted with permission of Gerda Lerner. For information on Lerner's participation in the labor movement, the Congress of American Women, and at the founding meeting of NOW, I am relying on Daniel Horowitz, phone conversation with Gerda Lerner, 18 Oct. 1995; Amy Swerdlow, "The Congress of American Women: Left-Feminist Peace Politics in the Cold War," in *U.S. History as Women's History: New Feminist Essays,* ed. Linda K. Kerber, Alice Kessler-Harris, and Kathryn Kish Sklar (Chapel Hill, 1995), 306.

GERDA LERNER
Neighborhood Women and Grassroots Human Rights

Gerda and Carl Lerner met when he was a marginally employed theater director and she worked for a garment industry wholesaler in New York City. By the time they had completed work on their first joint project—an amateur pageant celebrating the history of progressive German-American immigrants—they knew themselves to be in love. In 1941 they moved to Hollywood and married; two children were born, in 1945 and 1947.

After Pearl Harbor, Gerda was required to register weekly as an "enemy alien" despite the fact that her homeland had expelled her. Carl was physically disqualified from the draft; manpower shortages ironically gave him the break he needed. Hired as an apprentice, his career as a film editor developed rapidly. (Eventually he would be nationally known for films like *Twelve Angry Men*, *The Fugitive Kind*, and *Klute*.) "[H]aving lived half my life under dictatorships," Gerda observed, she was thrilled to meet Carl's friends, actors and writers committed to progressive politics. "Their ability to work openly for progressive causes was something I could not simply take for granted." Many were members of the Communist Party, which they supported less out of a defense of the Soviet Union than for its support of struggles to build unions, "the fight against racism, the resistance to nuclear weapons and war . . . the availability of decent housing, adequate low-cost childcare—these were my issues. The Communists I knew were stronger, more consistent fighters for these issues than other people I knew."

By 1949, attacks by the House Un-American Activities Committee on Communists in the film industry made it impossible for Carl to get work in Hollywood. Carl and Gerda—who by then had become an American citizen—returned to New York. After a few years of living in rented apartments, they decided to buy a house.

In the pages that follow, Gerda Lerner encounters difficult local choices that have national political significance. Ethical choices face housewives daily. What challenges did Gerda Lerner find? What did she learn about the women of her neighborhood? How effective was their grassroots organizing against blockbusting? What equivalent challenges exist today?

We could not afford Manhattan. The subway lines to the Bronx and to Brooklyn were ancient, the cars dirty and decrepit. The trains to Queens were newer, ran more frequently, and seemed less crowded. We had friends in Queens and liked some of the neighborhoods. We decided to search in an old neighborhood in Queens, and we were determined to live in a racially mixed neighborhood. We had strong feelings about that, after our year in an all-white community with nearly all-white schools. We wanted our children to mix naturally and on a daily basis with children of color so that they would grow up as free from prejudices as possible. That narrowed our choice considerably. There were a number of

Excerpted from ch. 19 of *Fireweed: A Political Autobiography* by Gerda Lerner (Philadelphia: Temple University Press, 2002). © 2002 by Gerda Lerner. Reprinted by permission of the author and Temple University Press.

racially integrated apartment-house projects in Queens, several of them middle income, but when it came to houses the racial boundaries were firmly drawn.

The two major areas where African Americans lived were Jamaica, a concentration of low-income projects and low-income tenants, and the upper- and middle-class black community in St. Albans, which clustered around the huge Veterans Administration Hospital. We looked on the fringes of the St. Albans community and soon found a few streets we liked, mostly because they had rows of old trees. The streets were all white, a typical working-class neighborhood of modest homes, all at least twenty years old, but two blocks away there were black homeowners and we figured the children would be going to the same school. There were quite a few houses for sale on these streets. We soon found a house that seemed to fit our needs as to size and that seemed suitable as to price. After we had made an offer and put a small deposit down, the real-estate agent, a pleasant young woman, told us with an air of painful concern that she had to be honest with us, we seemed such a nice couple and she wouldn't want us to be disappointed later. . . . In good conscience, she had to tell us that a black family had just bought a house on the street behind us, in fact *the* house directly behind us. So, if we moved, we would have black neighbors. . . . Of course, she said, you have a backyard fence and your street is okay—

We assured her the prospect of having black neighbors was not unpleasant to us. In fact, we were looking forward to it.

The young woman was obviously relieved that she was not going to lose a sale. Nothing further was said on the subject and we bought the house. We realized that had we looked for a house five or six blocks away, we might have saved two to three thousand dollars on the sale price. Contrary to common mythology, when blacks moved into a neighborhood the real-estate prices did not fall; they rose. Real-estate agents advised the white sellers to raise their prices so that only "the better kind" of blacks would move into the neighborhood. The kind of "warning" our real-estate agent had given us would usually scare off potential white buyers. Sellers and real-estate agents reaped the benefit. We were, in effect, paying "black prices."

The house itself lacked charm or individuality, but it was solid and in good repair. A poor imitation of imitation-Tudor row houses in the more genteel sections of the borough, it stood flat-chested and stolid behind a tiny plot of front lawn. Separated from its neighbors by a narrow cement driveway, at the end of which a small wooden garage provided space for just one car, the house offered respectability without privacy. Six steps leading up to the front door and six steps leading down from the kitchen into the tiny backyard offered room for neighborly "stoop-sitting" and little else. From the front stoop one could observe the comings and goings of neighbors, their careful lawn-mowing of their postage-stamp front lawns, their hedge-trimming, their car-washing. Inside, the rooms were good-sized and airy, even though our living room was always dark. The upstairs bedrooms looked out on the tree-tops, which meant a lot to me, but compared to our great old house in L.A. and the wonderful house in the woods we had just left, this was a come-down. It was simply that it was a house we could afford even if things should get worse financially. And that was our main concern in those days.

In the fall of 1952 we moved in. Stephanie entered second grade and Dan kindergarten in the nearby public school. I walked them to school and picked them up and I drove Carl to the subway. In that sense, it was a great improvement, since he could spend more time at home during the children's waking hours.

The people on the street were postal clerks and government employees, men and women working in the Veterans Hospital, a few craft workers, a bus driver. The neighbors on our right were an elderly couple, unfriendly and resentful of having neighbors with small children. We were barely on speaking terms with them during our entire stay there. The neighbors on our left were a couple about our age with three boys, ages nine, seven, and five. The father was a carpenter working for a construction company, the mother a full-time housewife. They were Catholics, but sent their children to public school. We were quite different in education, lifestyle, and political convictions, but we were good neighbors. The boys next door were playmates for our children and their mother and I helped each other out with child-minding, babysitting, and shopping.

I made it my business to introduce myself

to the neighbor in the back. The Prices had two daughters, one of them Stephanie's age, the other younger, and since their mother, too, walked them to school and picked them up, it was easy to move from a neighborly acquaintance to inviting the girls to play in our house and inviting the mother to share a cup of coffee. Sarah Price was a highly educated woman, a high-school music teacher whose ambition was to make a career as an opera singer. She had a great voice, a fine stage presence, and coffee-colored skin, but she was labeled a "Negro" and that, in the 1950s, made an operatic career an unlikely dream. She sang in church concerts and gave voice lessons.

Before long we organized an interracial playgroup, which included the two Price girls and two Indian girls, originally from Calcutta; the boys next door; the four Hartmann children (white, Jewish); and Billy, a science whiz kid without social skills. The playgroup was an informal child-minding club for the mothers, who could take turns leaving their children once a week under the care of the other mothers. It was also a group designed to break down cultural and racial barriers. We celebrated each child's birthday, then Christmas, Chanukka, Easter, and Passover, and we learned about Indian holidays and ate Indian food. Such superficial multicultural exchanges have become much more common in recent decades and are now part of the experience of many children in schools. At the time we did this, such contacts were unusual.

Shortly after we moved in, we noticed that several houses on our block and in the neighboring streets had FOR SALE signs. This development turned out to be part of a well-organized campaign by real-estate agents to turn our neighborhood into a black neighborhood. Several times a week, real-estate agents would knock on our door to inquire whether we wanted to put up our house for sale. When we said no, they explained, in the same bereaved tone our own real-estate saleswoman had used, that they simply wished to let us know that "colored people" had begun to move into the neighborhood—just one street away, as a matter of fact—and that this would undoubtedly decrease the value of our property. We would be well advised to sell, as soon as possible.

These forays were followed up by stronger tactics. Real-estate agents would appear at your door with a black couple in tow to show them your house. When told that the house was not on the market, they would profusely apologize for "the error" and move on down the street. A few weeks of this and the FOR SALE signs went up.

This kind of campaign was known as "block-busting," and it apparently worked well to "turn" neighborhoods. The white working-class families who had put their entire cash reserves into their homes were truly panicked at the prospect of losing their real-estate investments. Even if they would not have had any objections to living on an interracial street, the fear of economic loss convinced them to sell and move. When two or three houses on a block had been sold to African Americans, the street would be "redlined" in the banking and real-estate community; that is, it would be treated as a "black" street. House prices would go up and mortgages would become more expensive, presumably to compensate the lender for a more risk-prone population. People living in "redlined" neighborhoods would pay higher car and medical insurance rates and find it difficult to get credit. All of this based on racist myths—that any influx of non-white people meant lower real-estate prices, more crime and drugs, and a deterioration of public schools. Block-busting and red-lining were practices the banking and real-estate companies denounced publicly, but which flourished unchecked. Nobody admitted to doing it, but it was done in neighborhood after neighborhood. And in a way, the dire predictions of the realtors turned into a self-fulfilling prophecy. Because real-estate prices were so much higher for African Americans and mortgages for them were so much more expensive, many families could afford a house only by sharing with relatives. Thus, one-family houses were often occupied by extended families or by several families, with both parents working in order to be able to afford their home. This meant that children were often unsupervised after school hours and more conspicuous on the streets, a fact that, even if such children did not get into any trouble, fed racist myths and beliefs.

After a little checking around with neighborhood organizations and churches, I found out that there was a sort of resistance movement in effect, which had been able to win a few victories in the past. We joined in this effort, in which I was quite active.

We went door to door to speak to our neighbors. When I told people that we had just moved into the neighborhood, they were impressed, because it refuted the real-estate agents' claim that no whites would move in. Our main argument was that we could keep the neighborhood as it was and welcome the few black families that were moving into it if we did not give in to panic-selling. Sometimes we went from door to door, white and black together, and introduced the old neighbors to their new neighbor. People were usually quite friendly when we did this, but it is hard to tell how much impact we had. People who responded to our appeal were asked to refuse to talk to real-estate agents. We put signs in our front windows that read WE LOVE OUR HOME AND OUR NEIGHBORS. THIS HOUSE IS NOT FOR SALE. After several months of our resistance campaign, about half of the houses on our street had our signs and the real-estate agents stopped coming to the door. If we did not stop the block-busting, at least we slowed it down.

We made great efforts in the PTA to welcome the new black neighbors and to make the PTA an organization in which ethnic and racial differences were celebrated. Our luncheon meetings always featured varied ethnic foods and our school parades and celebrations were quite inclusive.

Still, the onward march of racist real-estate practices could not be stopped. I know of no white family that moved into my neighborhood after we did. A good way to chart the racial change in home ownership is to look at the children's class pictures, year after year. The year after we moved in, there were a handful of black children in each class. Four years later, there were a handful of white children amidst all the black faces.

The new black neighbors on our street were economically more advantaged than the white residents. They were predominantly middle class and certainly better educated than the people they replaced. They were "house-proud" and outdid each other in home improvements and neatness of front gardens. Their cars were distinctly better and higher priced than was customary on the street, and they spent as much time as their neighbors washing and polishing them. In short, by all definitions of white standards, they were

"good" neighbors. Ironically, our family was censured more by the black neighbors than by the white. We were not known for great neatness of front lawn or house, and our car, an aged Chevrolet, was distinctly inferior to those of the neighbors. And yet Carl claimed to be working in TV and motion pictures.... This upset a set of stereotypes held by our black neighbors, namely that all people working in the media must be rich and status-proud. We were asked direct and pointed questions about this by some of our new neighbors and I'm not sure our answers were satisfactory. I think several of them thought of us as some sort of "hippies" and remained cool and formal in their contacts with us. Trying to break down cultural stereotypes is always an ambiguous undertaking. One of the things I learned by living in an interracial community is that hierarchies and prejudices against those who are "different" exist among all groups, not only among whites.

Our white neighbors on the right, the elderly couple, responded to our appeal to stay and put an appropriate sign on the door. I understand they stayed for years, until they were the only white family on the block. They did not become much friendlier toward us or anyone else with children, but give credit where credit is due.

Our new African American neighbor, four houses down the street, bought an expensive snow blower. He drove a Buick and put shutters on all the front windows of his house, transforming it into the best house on the block. He was an accountant, and when it snowed, he made it a point to clear the entire sidewalk on his side of the street with his snow blower. We were all obliged to him, but he would not visit with the Lerners. Probably because of the Chevy.

Sarah and I had become close friends. We shared our interest in music, in education, in books. Now her husband's mother had come for a visit and was staying for a month. She was from South Carolina and Sarah introduced her to me as a leader in the state's NAACP. I knew that meant she was a person at great risk in her hometown and Sarah confirmed that. I was eager to get to know her, but she was distinctly cool to me when we first met. About a week later, after she had been at our playgroup meeting and had once visited, quite formally, at my house, I sat at Sarah's kitchen table, drinking coffee with her and Sarah. Suddenly she faced me with the authority of a schoolteacher over a pupil, an older woman over the young.

"How come you folks moved in here, after the neighborhood turned?" she asked sternly.

"We wanted our children to be raised in an interracial community."

She didn't buy it. "That sounds too good to be true."

"Just the same, that's the reason."

"Are you Commies?" she asked.

"I don't ask how you vote."

"Republican. Baptist. NAACP. Sorry," she said, "that was out of line. I've been called a Commie many times, myself."

"Well, we have that in common. But maybe you'd understand better if I say, it's because we're Jewish. And I, in particular, am a refugee from Hitler."

"Yeah. Sarah told me that. I'm sorry to hear it. I haven't had much contact with Jewish people. So I can't understand—"

"You've lived in the Jim Crow South. You've been excluded from public rest rooms, restaurants, trains. Segregated because of race. Well, after Hitler came, Jews in Vienna were not only excluded from schools, public places, parks, but fired from their jobs, imprisoned without cause, many sent to concentration camps. And as you know, six million were killed, deliberately, men, women, and children. So to me, any kind of discrimination is evil. I can't stand it. I want my children free of it."

"I can believe that," she said, for the first time with real warmth.

I felt I had passed the test. That such a test should be necessary at all I found not surprising. For fifty years after World War II, whenever I met a German or an Austrian old enough to have been an adult during that time, I needed to know what they were doing THEN and, more or less overtly, I would give them a similar test. Suffering oppression does not make you into an open, trusting person.

After that, during the years we lived in the neighborhood, Sarah's mother-in-law accepted me as a family friend.

ESTELLE FREEDMAN
Miriam Van Waters and the Burning of Letters

Miriam Van Waters belonged to that elite group of women reformers that included Florence Kelley and Eleanor Roosevelt. She was also part of a transitional generation, having grown up in an era when many educated women seeking public careers rejected marriage and family for a woman-centered existence. The female networks they created enhanced their public as well as private lives, providing professional mentors and allies and personal relationships that were supportive and intimate. Even if the intimacy extended to sexual expression, couples often lived together for extended periods attracting little comment. Prior to the 1920s, many people simply assumed that these were the intense female friendships described in Carroll Smith-Rosenberg's essay "The Female World of Love and Ritual" (pp. 168–83). Tolerance lessened markedly, however, with the pathologizing of homosexuality in the 1920s.

From "The Burning of Letters Continues" by Estelle Freedman in *Journal of Women's History*, 9.4. Reprinted by permission of the author and Indiana University Press. Notes have been renumbered and edited.

As Estelle Freedman makes clear, Miriam Van Waters was very much aware of the new construction of lesbianism as deviant behavior. As the head of a women's correctional institution and a leading reformer in her field, she was also highly informed about the increasing attention to prison lesbianism. How she understood her own sexuality is the subject of this sensitive and perceptive essay.

Van Waters's problems were compounded by the fact that as a penal administrator, she was on the public payroll during the heyday of domestic containment. In Cold War America, lesbianism, like unwed motherhood, represented the dangers of female sexuality and intolerable deviations from the family norm. Used since the 1920s to label and stigmatize nonconforming women, especially feminists, "lesbian" in the 1950s came to signify an aggressive deviance that verged on criminality.

Why did Van Waters resist labeling her long-term romantic partnership with Geraldine Thompson as a lesbian relationship? In what sense was class a factor?

On a clear June morning in 1948, the controversial prison reformer Miriam Van Waters made a painful and momentous decision. For months she had been embroiled in a political struggle with conservative state officials who wished to dismiss her as the liberal superintendent of the Massachusetts Reformatory for Women. Local newspapers headlined the claims that Van Waters coddled prisoners, hired ex-inmates, and condoned homosexual behavior in prison. Investigators from the Department of Corrections interrogated her staff and seized inmate files as evidence.

As she sat before a glowing fireplace in her home that June morning, Miriam Van Waters fueled the blaze with some of her most precious possessions. "The Burning of Letters continues," she wrote in her journal that day. "One can have no personal 'life' in this battle, so I have destroyed many letters of over 22 years." Van Waters had met her patron and romantic partner, Geraldine Thompson, twenty-two years earlier. Since the late 1920s they had corresponded almost daily, sharing their thoughts, their activities, and their love during the weeks between their regular visits with one another. All but a few of the daily letters Thompson had addressed to her "Old Sweet," her "Dearest Dearest Love," went up in flames that day. As she burned the letters, Van Waters recorded her sense of loss: "They might have been inspiration, history, joy, style—to me in 'old age.'" Instead, she resolved to keep their message within herself. "The letters are bone and sinew now in my carnage. Doubtless my character has been formed by them."[1] ...

[To understand] Van Waters's conscious effort to conceal her relationship with Thompson, [we need to understand how Van Waters understood her own sexuality. Did she identify herself as lesbian? What would she have known about same-sex relationships?] ...

In the early twentieth century, highly-educated women such as Miriam Van Waters might be exposed to published literature that clearly named both male and female homosexuality. Only a generation earlier, even romantic female friends and women who passed as men perceived their experiences within frameworks largely devoid of sexual references. The "female world of love and ritual" mapped by historian Carroll Smith-Rosenberg allowed same-sex attractions to "pass" as sexually innocent, whether they were or not. Beginning in the late nineteenth century, a modern conception of homosexuality emerged, articulated first as a form of gender inversion and later as an expression of erotic desire.[2] Gradually an explicitly sexual language characterized the literature on same-sex relationships. Helen Horowitz' insightful interpretation of M. Carey Thomas provides a good example of the transition. In the 1870s, Thomas' reading of romantic and pre-Raphaelite poets afforded her an initial and asexual framework for understanding passion between women; after the 1890s, however, the Oscar Wilde trial and the availability of works by sexologists such as Richard von Krafft-Ebing allowed Thomas to name sexual acts between women as well. ...

As a graduate student at Clark University between 1910 and 1913, Van Waters easily discovered the scholarly literature on sexuality. She read Havelock Ellis, Krafft-Ebing, and some Sigmund Freud, as well as the work of her advisor, psychologist G. Stanley Hall. Her own writing recognized the power of sexuality and stressed the importance of sex education and the strategy of channeling youthful energies into recreation and social service. She also became curious about gender identity and same-sex relationships, as a questionnaire she designed reveals. The survey of adolescent girls asked, for example, "did you wish to be a boy?" and was your first "love for some one you knew closely, or for some distant person ... or for some older woman or girl friend?" A separate questionnaire for teachers asked if "crushes" between girls were "based on mutuality of interest and inclination; or are they more likely to exist between 'masculine,' and excessively 'feminine' types?"[3] The questions suggest Van Waters' interest in whether same-sex attractions correlated with gender identity, an inquiry prompted in part by Ellis' notion of sexual inversion, which associated "mannish" women with lesbianism.

Although Van Waters never conducted this survey, her intellectual curiosity about gender nonconformity and its relationship to homosexuality recurred in her doctoral dissertation, "The Adolescent Girl among Primitive People." At this time she consciously rejected Freudian interpretations of sexuality and adopted Ellis' language of inversion—albeit without the pathological notions of deviant sexuality. Her views also reflected the cultural relativism of Franz Boas. After describing institutionalized gender-crossing among North American Indians, for example, Van Waters concluded that "among primitive peoples, a useful and appropriate life-role is commonly furnished the inverted individual. . . . It is quite possible that modern policy could profitably go to school to the primitive in this regard."[4] Similarly, in an appendix on contemporary American approaches to adolescent delinquents, Van Waters analyzed the case of a cross-dressing young woman accused of being a "white slaver" because she brought girls to her rooms at night. Reluctant to label the girl a "true homosexual," she reported that "it is impossible for her to earn an honest and adequate living while dressed as a woman," and claimed that sympathy for women of the underworld rather than sexual proclivities accounted for her behavior.[5]

During her subsequent career working in juvenile and adult female reformatories, Van Waters retained a liberal tolerance for homosexuality, even as she increasingly incorporated Freudian views of sexual psychopathology. When she discussed the management of "'crushes' and sentimental attachment" among reformatory inmates in her 1925 book, *Youth in Conflict,* she advised that a trained social worker could draw out the girl and replace unhealthy attachments with healthy ones through a beneficial "transference." A harsher passage reflected conservative medical views of sex and gender when she labeled as the most perverse juvenile case she had encountered a narcissistic girl whose "emotional life will be self-centered or flow toward those of her own sex," and who would "never wish to live the biologically normal life."[6]

Despite these published critiques of unhealthy homosexual attachments, as superintendent of the Framingham, Massachusetts, reformatory for women from 1932 to 1957, Miriam Van Waters consistently resisted the labeling of prison relationships as homosexual. Her liberal administration emphasized education, social welfare services, psychiatric counseling, and work opportunities outside prison for the three to four hundred women inmates, the large majority of whom were young, white, Catholic, and working-class. Although the criminological literature then identified black women in prison as the aggressors in interracial sexual relationships, Van Waters and her staff did not draw a racial line around prison homosexuality. Rather, they tried to distinguish between "true homosexuality" and temporary attractions. They believed the former could be detected by the Rorschach test; in the absence of such "positive evidence" they assumed that only the boredom of prison routine stimulated "unnatural" interest in same-sex relationships. Thus an active program of classes and clubs attempted to channel the energies of both black and white prisoners into what the staff considered healthier recreations. Even when staff discovered two women in bed together—of any racial combination—they hesitated to label them as homosexual.

Van Waters' tolerance of prison homosexual liaisons contributed to the conservative assault on her administration in the 1940s. In 1949, when the Commissioner of Corrections dismissed Van Waters from office, he charged:

> That you have known of and failed to prevent the continuance of, or failed to know and recognize that an unwholesome relationship has existed between inmates of the Reformatory for Women which is called the "doll racket" by inmates and some officer personnel; the terms "stud" and "queen" are used with implied meanings, and such association has resulted in "crushes", "courtships", and homosexual practises [sic] among the inmates in the Reformatory.[7]

During several months of public hearings, Van Waters successfully defended her policies, in part by minimizing the existence of homosexuality at the reformatory, in part by deferring to psychiatric authorities when asked about homosexual tendencies among inmates. Typical of her strategic evasion was this response to hostile interrogation about whether certain acts or personal styles revealed homosexual tendencies:

> That, sir, is so distinctly a medical and technical question that I would not presume to answer it. One of the first things we are taught is that a homosexual tendency must be distinguished from a homosexual act. A homosexual tendency may be completely repressed and turned into a variety of other expressions, including a great aversion to emotion.[8]

By invoking the power of psychiatry, Van Waters acknowledged the shifting meaning of homosexuality—from an act to an identity. At the same time, she tried to avoid a labeling process that would mark close friends, mannish women, and those who had crushes on other inmates as confirmed homosexuals, a category she reserved for a treatable psychopathological condition that posed problems only when characterized by aggressive sexual behaviors.

Whether consciously or not, Van Waters' testimony represented a form of resistance to the use of accusations of homosexuality to discredit nonconforming women. Rather than sacrifice some "mannish" women or close female friends by calling them either "homosexuals," "latent homosexuals," or "women with homosexual tendencies," she firmly opposed labeling. At the same time, like psychologists of the period, she did so by accepting a definition of true homosexuality as pathology. In the 1950s,

partly in response to her reading of the Kinsey Reports, and partly in the wake of the accusations about prison lesbianism during her dismissal hearings, Van Waters' public lectures urged greater tolerance. Homosexuality, she explained, could be "found in all levels of society," in all types of people. Her emphasis, however, was on treatment. Once revealed through use of the Rorschach test, she believed, homosexual tendencies could be reversed with the aid of psychiatry.[9]

In short, for Miriam Van Waters, lesbianism was a curable social problem not unlike alcoholism. Although she initially encountered lesbianism among working-class, immigrant, and black reformatory inmates, she recognized that it occurred within other groups, as well. Rather than emphasizing a heterosexual solution, Van Waters placed great faith in "healthy" female bonding as an alternative to lesbianism. In this sense, whether or not she had internalized modern medical categories, she strategically invoked an earlier discourse of sexually innocent and nurturing female friendships as a corrective to the increasing stigmatization of women's love for women as a form of perversion.

When Superintendent Van Waters evaded the labeling of homosexuality during her dismissal hearings, she also sidestepped implicit questions about her own sexual identity. In her personal life, Van Waters had refused to label her love for a woman as a form of homosexuality, despite her long-term romantic partnership with Geraldine Thompson, a New Jersey philanthropist who was known publicly only as a wealthy benefactor and a supporter of Van Waters' reforms. So, too, she hesitated to assume that other women who appeared to fit the medical definition really were homosexuals, a term she reserved for women's pathological, though curable, sexual aggression toward other women.[10]

What of her internal consciousness of her own sexuality? The private story of Miriam Van Waters' own relationships with women both parallels and contradicts her public pronouncements. Beginning in adolescence, she fell deeply in love with other women and, for the most part, preferred their company to the attentions of male suitors. Never a sexual prude, Van Waters recognized the importance of the erotic, especially within the poetry and fiction she wrote in her late twenties. But she also placed great stock in the power of sublimation for harnessing erotic energy into expression as art, spirituality, or public service. Thus, upon reading Radclyffe Hall's *The Well of Loneliness* in 1929, Van Waters commented in her journal that had Stephen Gordon's parents been more loving, instead of becoming a lesbian Gordon might have "run a girls camp," become a high school counselor, or supervised a juvenile protective agency, all activities remarkably similar to those Van Waters chose.[11]

The detailed introspective journals Van Waters kept as an adult provide further clues about her subjective experience of sexuality, despite the frequently coded and intentionally obscure nature of her writing. Tantalizing passages in Van Waters' journals made little sense to me until late into my research, when I gained access to a cache of personal papers that had not been deposited in the archives. Literally locked away within a rusting trunk and forgotten in an attic, that cache included passionate letters from two of Van Waters' ardent admirers: one set from Hans Weiss, a young Swiss social worker who wished to marry Van Waters; the other, a year's worth of daily letters from Geraldine Thompson, the older, wealthy, married philanthropist whose subsequent correspondence Van Waters burned in 1948. Working with both the journals and the "courtship letters," as I called them, I learned how Van Waters struggled to balance the erotic, the emotional, and the spiritual in each of these relationships.

Despite significant differences between the Weiss and Thompson correspondence—his letters were more erotic, hers more spiritual; he was more emotionally demanding, she longed to be of service to her beloved—I was struck by the consistency in Van Waters' response to her male and female suitors. In each case, she remained publicly silent, restrained in her responses to passion, and conflicted about making any lifelong commitment. The two relationships did present separate challenges to Van Waters' sexuality. The younger, less established Weiss frequently articulated his erotic longings; in response, Van Waters struggled to incorporate physical passion while subsuming it to her ideal of a spiritualized romantic friendship. The older, wealthier, and more powerful Thompson longed for "the Justice of the Peace

and church bells" to signify their commitment; in response, Van Waters feared the dependency that could result from their union.[12]

In both cases, the management of passion was a recurrent theme for Miriam Van Waters. Although her journals were characteristically obscure about sexual experiences, one passage written after a visit with Weiss alluded to an unidentified young "Beloved" with whom she had experienced both a spiritual epiphany and a "yielding to love." In one entry, she recalled a candlelit scene in which her "hands were flung up by a strong clasp of young hands on my wrists—and with another soul—I plunged down a glittering waterfall immeasurably high, and sunk at last—into a pool—where two floated in weariness and content."[13] More typical, however, was her insistence on limiting their intimacy. "As a lover I yield to no one in sustained worship," she wrote in her journal. To Weiss she explained that their spiritual union transcended the need for physical proximity, suggesting that unrequited love could yield the "deepest spiritual gain."[14] By 1930, she had successfully encouraged Weiss to wed someone else; she had already informed him of another, unnamed attraction.

The Thompson courtship, begun during the late 1920s, overlapped with the waning of Van Waters' intimacy with Weiss. Both women valued romantic and spiritual intimacy, and neither wrote explicitly about their sexual experiences. Yet Van Waters left hints about her consciousness of lesbianism and her continuing management of erotic impulses. In 1930, she read an article about Katherine B. Davis' 1929 study of female sexuality, which found that a quarter of unmarried women college graduates acknowledged a sexual component within their intense emotional relationships with other women. Van Waters starred the point that these were normal, not pathological, women, as if to differentiate her experience from the perversions she had earlier identified among juvenile delinquents. As in her relationship with Weiss, however, Van Waters continued to place limits on erotic expression. Thus when Thompson expressed a desire "to 'catch your soul's breath' in kisses," Van Waters questioned the impulse in her journal: "What one calls appetite—satisfaction of warmth needs—hunger needs—is not just that. . . . In maturity some times in some circumstances—to feed hunger fully—is to lose hunger. There are other ways of quenching the fire—and all must be escaped." Professionally she had recommended channeling youthful sexual energies, whether heterosexual or homosexual. But her personal ideal suggested not simply sublimation but rather that desire could be maintained best by leaving it largely unfulfilled. While staying at Thompson's home, she again alluded to the value of control: "The secret of life is manifested in hunger—it can't safely be quenched—neither by denial, nor complete feeding, nor running away, nor escape—but by a new way."[15]

Whether or not she discovered this "new way" of managing desire, by the time she and Thompson pledged their love at the end of 1930, Van Waters recognized that she had crossed some line. "The object which arouses love—cannot be foreseen or controlled," she wrote in her journal. "All we know is—that same force which engulfs us, and makes us ready for service to husband and children—some times—to some persons—flows out to a man, woman, child, animal, 'cause,' idea." Van Waters did not, however, acknowledge her love publicly nor claim a lesbian identity. When Geraldine longed to "shout about" their love so that her family would "know what life through you is giving me," Miriam counseled discretion.[16] Similarly, when an acquaintance who lived openly with another woman later asked Van Waters in public about the ring she wore—a gift from Thompson—Van Waters seethed at the impudence of this inquiry into her private life. Perhaps her status as a civil service employee, and as the guardian and later adoptive mother of a child, made Van Waters more cautious than her independently wealthy partner, Thompson. Equally likely, Van Waters struggled to reconcile her passion with the psychological construction of lesbianism she had already formed.

Another cryptic journal entry suggests how powerfully that psychological construction influenced her. In a dream, she wrote, she had enjoyed a feeling of "Understanding" that derived in part from "the recent Rorshak [sic] and integration." Van Waters used the Rorschach test to detect "innate homosexuality" among inmates; in 1938, a trusted friend administered the test to her and the results made Van Waters feel confident and optimistic. One line in this passage was crossed out heavily in pencil, especially over some-

one's name, but the entry continued, "Geraldine and I shall learn together."[17] In my reading, the Rorschach test proved to Van Waters that she was not an innate homosexual, thus freeing her of the deviant label and, ironically, granting her permission to integrate her love for Thompson, without adopting a lesbian identity.

Why, then, the burning of letters? Even if Van Waters did not consider herself a lesbian, the world around her was not as thoroughly convinced. Although her close associates insisted to me that the relationship was much too spiritual to have been homosexual, Van Waters' partnership with Geraldine Thompson made her increasingly vulnerable to the insinuations of her political opponents.

In the conformist atmosphere after World War II, accusations of Communism, often conflated with homosexuality, fueled an attack on liberalism. Thus, in 1948, claims that Van Waters tolerated homosexuality at the Massachusetts women's reformatory facilitated her dismissal from office. Aside from the widely publicized claims about the "doll racket" among inmates, rumors about Van Waters' sexuality circulated underground, though never in print. For example, Eleanor Roosevelt—a friend of Thompson and supporter of Van Waters—learned of the whispering campaign when she received several "vile" letters that were so disturbing that she destroyed most of them. Similarly, a hostile postcard sent to supporters referred to Van Waters as "supt. (or Chief Pervert)" of the reformatory.[18] It was at this time that Van Waters burned most of Thompson's correspondence, carefully locking away only that one year of "courtship" letters.

Despite the private insinuations that led her to burn Thompson's letters, Van Waters survived the attempt to fire her. The publicity surrounding prison lesbianism during her hearings, however, contributed to a national preoccupation with homosexuality and to the naming of lesbianism as a social threat. No matter how confident Van Waters may have been that she was not a lesbian, outside observers often assumed that she was. Late in my research, after years of waiting to receive Van Waters' FBI file, I found a 1954 document that seemed to place an official government seal upon Van Waters' identity. While carrying out surveillance on Helen Bryan, a suspected Communist sympathizer with whom

Van Waters had a romantic friendship later in life, a local FBI informant read the correspondence between the two women. Shocked by the "unusual" nature of the letters, which contained "numerous repeated terms of endearment and other statements," he came to "the definite opinion that Dr. VAN WATERS and BRYAN are Lesbians."[19] It was to prevent just such a conclusion from being drawn that Van Waters had earlier burned Thompson's letters.

That identity formation is often a social as much as an individual phenomenon is further revealed by a final anecdote from my research on Van Waters, a coda of sorts that brings the story into the 1990s. My book completed, I turned to the task of acquiring permission to quote from sources, including Geraldine Thompson's courtship letters. With trepidation I sent the permission form to Thompson's eldest surviving granddaughter, who soon called to discuss the request. Her initial words, "I will not grant permission," struck further terror in me, until I absorbed the completion of her sentence: "I will not grant permission to repeat any lies; I want the truth." Too much had been concealed in her family, she explained, too much smoothed over. By the end of our conversation, she had told me with confidence that her grandmother had been a lesbian and that she was sure that Thompson and Van Waters were lovers, for they had shared a bed during family vacations. "Do you know what we grandchildren called Miriam when she came to visit?" she asked. "Grammy Thompson's yum-yum." She gladly granted permission to quote when I seemed willing to reveal "the truth."[20] . . .

Van Waters came of age in a transitional moment, when the social possibilities for romantic and sexual love between women increased, but also while medical labeling pathologized these relationships. As an educated, professional woman, exposed to such sexologists as Ellis and Freud, she was both conscious of the erotic and aware of the psychopathic label then attached to same-sex relationships. At the same time, Van Waters was attracted to women; she was able to live outside of heterosexual institutions; and she could and did take advantage of the opportunity to establish a partnership with another woman, even as she fiercely resisted lesbian identification.

Perhaps the fear of losing her job, and her social standing, kept Van Waters from identifying as a lesbian. But her rejection of lesbianism as an identity was not merely self-serving, for she just as fiercely resisted the labeling of working-class prison inmates as lesbians, and during her dismissal hearings in 1949 she more or less placed her class and race privilege on the line to defend these women from such charges. In the end, it was Van Waters' privileges—combined with her distinguished career of service and her upper-class political connections—that protected her from public disgrace. The working-class women she tried to protect would forge their own public lesbian identity, one that equally rejected the pathological discourse of the early twentieth century.

. . . To contemporary feminists, who value our own historically constructed ideal of the openly lesbian sexual subject, Van Waters seems anything but progressive. Yet if we are serious about . . . recognizing women's historical agency, we have to be willing to accept it when beliefs, and possibly behaviors, go against the grain of a "progressive" narrative that embraces categories we have claimed for ourselves. And we must keep in mind that this narrative rests heavily upon a highly class- and race-specific lesbian identity constructed since the 1960s, one that depathologized white, middle-class women's love for women but simultaneously failed to recognize a range of other sources of identity. . . . [Ultimately] Miriam Van Waters' case suggests the ways that some women could simultaneously internalize, resist, manipulate, and ignore the cultural constructions of sexuality in their times. Above all, her story reminds us to look beyond our sources, to read both silences and speech, and, at times, to accept the historical integrity of elusive personal identities.

NOTES

1. Miriam Van Waters Journal (hereafter MVW Journal), 16 June 1948, 19 June 1948, and 22 June 1948, file 220v, Anne Gladding-Miriam Van Waters Papers, Schlesinger Library, Radcliffe College (hereafter Gladding-MVW Papers). A handful of surviving letters were scattered through Van Waters' correspondence in the papers she donated to the Schlesinger Library. For a full account of her life, see Estelle B. Freedman, *Maternal Justice: Miriam Van Waters and the Female Reform Tradition* (Chicago: University of Chicago Press, 1996).

2. MVW to parents, 10 October 1911, file 42 (misdated, probably 9 October 1911), MVW Papers; MVW, "Topical Syllabus No. 44 (A) and No. 44 (B)

[for teachers], Psychology of Adolescence," 15 November 1911, Box 37, file 464, G. Stanley Hall Papers, Clark University, Worcester, Massachusetts.

3. MVW, "The Adolescent Girl among Primitive People," *Journal of Religious Psychology* 6, no. 4 (1913): 375–421, and 7, no. 1 (1914): 75–120 (esp. pt. 1, 377–78 and pt. 2, 102–5). Her advisor, Alexander Chamberlain, had been Franz Boas' first doctoral student at Clark.

4. MVW, "Adolescent Girl," pt. 2, 108–12.

5. MVW, *Youth in Conflict* (New York: New Republic, 1925), 35–36.

6. McDowell to MVW, 7 January 1949, file 201, MVW Papers.

7. John O'Connor, "Van Waters Rejects Inmate Sex Charge," *Boston Herald,* 1 January 1949, 1.

8. MVW, Boston University lecture transcript, 24 October 1951 (in possession of author).

9. Rumors about Van Waters' sexuality are discussed in MVW to Ethel Sturges Dummer, 26 September 1948, file 825, Ethel Sturges Dummer Papers, Schlesinger Library, Radcliffe College; and in letters from a former inmate to MVW, 1 June 1948, file 195, and from Harry R. Archbald to MVW, 7 February 1949, file 203, both in MVW Papers. For a full discussion of Van Waters' interpretation of lesbian identity and the political response to rumors of her own homosexuality, see Freedman, *Maternal Justice,* esp. chaps. 9, 12, 14, and 15.

10. MVW Journal, 30 March 1929, file 208, Gladding-MVW Papers. MVW's phrasing suggests an ambivalence about the experience of marriage and reproductive, as opposed to social, motherhood: Gordon, she wrote might have been "anything—everything in fact but a stupid wife and mother—Wife she co[uld] have been and mother too."

11. See, for example, Geraldine Thompson (GT) to MVW, 31 October 1930, 4 November 1930, and 14 November 1930, file 261, Gladding-MVW Papers.

12. MVW Journal, 28 June 1928, file 206, Gladding-MVW Papers; compare Hans Weiss' (HW) sweet memory of "what you did for me when you had the tremendous courage of giving yourself to me." HW to MVW, 24 July 1930, file 279, Gladding-MVW Papers.

13. MVW Journal, 19 February 1928, 14 June 1928, file 206, and 23 November 1928, file 208; HW to MVW, 7 August 1930, file 280, all in Gladding-MVW Papers. For complex reasons, Van Waters refused to consider marrying Weiss. Aside from the emotional distance she kept, the formal obstacle to

their marriage was his "tremendous longing for a home and for children." He accepted "the cruel reality" that he could not have this with her, for like many professional women, she had chosen career over marriage. Although some women reformers did try to combine the two, having a job and children would be too physically taxing for her and, given her history of tuberculosis, possibly life-threatening. HW to MVW, 19 January 1929, file 276, Gladding-MVW Papers.

14. MVW to Edna Mahan, 20 July 1930, file 253, Gladding-MVW Papers; and Katherine B. Davis, *Factors in the Sex Life of Twenty-Two Hundred Women* (New York: Harper and Row, 1929), 312, 295, 280. The data showed that 28 percent of the women's college graduates and 20 percent of those from coeducational schools recognized sexual components in their relations; in addition, almost equal numbers had enjoyed intense emotional attachments that involved kissing and hugging.

15. GT to MVW, 31 October 1930, file 261, 10 November and 6 November 1930, file 262, all in Gladding-MVW Papers; MVW Journal, 27 September 1930, and 11 June 1931, file 211, Gladding-MVW Papers.

16. MVW Journal, 27 September 1930, and GT to MVW, 13 November 1930, file 262, both in Gladding-MVW Papers.

17. On Rorschach, see, for example, Inmate record, 21 February 1949, file 251, MVW Journal, 11 June 1938, 213v, Gladding-MVW Papers; MVW Journal, vol. 5, 26 June 1938, MVW Papers.

18. Eleanor Roosevelt (ER) letter, 19 December 1948, file 200; GT to Dorothy Kirchwey Brown, 4 January 1949, file 201; ER to GT, n.d., in response to an enclosed letter from GT dated 5 January 1949, all in Box 3820, ER Papers. ER to GT, 13 January 1949, file 8, Friends of Framingham Papers (hereafter FOF Papers), Schlesinger Library, Cambridge, Massachusetts; Miriam Clark Nichols to ER, 18 January 1949, file 8, FOF Papers (the letter was reprinted in *The Civil Service Reporter* [8 February 1949]: 5); George Hooper to Friends of Framingham, 1 January 1949, file 8, FOF Papers.

19. SAC, Boston (100-15782) to Director, FBI (100-206852), "Office Memorandum," Re: Helen Reid Bryan, 20 January 1954, declassified 12 April 1994 pursuant to Freedom of Information Act Request (emphasis in original).

20. Telephone interview with Geraldine Boone, 17 February 1995; and Boone to author, 6 March 1995.

SUSAN K. CAHN
"Mannishness," Lesbianism, and Homophobia in U.S. Women's Sports

Miriam Van Waters, like many white middle-class women who loved other women, chose not to acknowledge her lesbianism. To do so would have meant acknowledging an affiliation with working-class lesbians. Their butch-femme roles and bar culture, like the aggressive prison lesbian, had been so thoroughly pathologized in the 1950s as to seem quite alien to women of a different class and culture. Others made a different choice. Some even tried to organize to gain rights, only to discover subsequently that the Daughters of Bilitis had been infiltrated with informants who were supplying names to the FBI and CIA. In an era when sexual conformity was seen as essential to national security, it is hardly surprising that *all* women engaged in any same-sex activity were suspect. Women athletes were particularly vulnerable.

In the following article, Susan Cahn explores the suspicions and the reality behind those suspicions in women's athletics. Note the persistence of concerns about feminine sexuality, whether heterosexual or homosexual, throughout the history of women's sports. What measures did colleges and universities take to protect women's sports from charges of lesbianism? What was the price of such actions? Since those athletes who were lesbian could no more afford to proclaim their sexual identity publicly than Van Waters, why does Cahn argue that athletics nonetheless afforded them social and psychic space to affirm their identity and find community? Do you agree?

In 1934, *Literary Digest* subtitled an article on women's sports, "Will the Playing Fields One Day Be Ruled by Amazons?" The author, Fred Wittner, answered the question affirmatively and concluded that as an "inevitable consequence" of sport's masculinizing effect, "girls trained in physical education to-day may find it more difficult to attract the most worthy fathers for their children."[1] The image of women athletes as mannish, failed heterosexuals represents a thinly veiled reference to lesbianism in sport. At times, the homosexual allusion has been indisputable, as in a journalist's description of the great athlete Babe Didrikson as a "Sapphic, Brobdingnagian woman" or in television comedian Arsenio Hall's more recent witticism, "If we can put a man on the moon, why can't we get one on Martina Navratilova?"[2] More frequently, however, popular commentary on lesbians in sport has taken the form of indirect references, surfacing through denials and refutations rather than open acknowledgment. When in 1955 an *Ebony* magazine article on African American track stars insisted that "off track, girls are entirely feminine. Most of them like boys, dances, club affairs," the reporter answered the implicit but unspoken charge that athletes, especially Black women in a "manly" sport, were masculine manhaters, or lesbians.[3]

The figure of the mannish lesbian athlete has acted as a powerful but unarticulated "bogey woman" of sport, forming a silent foil for more positive, corrective images that attempt to rehabilitate the image of women

Susan K. Cahn, " 'Mannishness,' Lesbianism, and Homophobia in U.S. Women's Sports," was originally published in *Feminist Studies* 19, no. 2 (Summer 1993):343–368. Reprinted by permission of the publisher, Feminist Studies, Inc.

athletes and resolve the cultural contradiction between athletic prowess and femininity. As a stereotyped figure in U.S. society, the lesbian athlete forms part of everyday cultural knowledge. Yet historians have paid scant attention to the connection between female sexuality and sport.[4] This essay explores the historical relationship between lesbianism and sport by tracing the development of the stereotyped "mannish lesbian athlete" and examining its relation to the lived experience of mid-twentieth-century lesbian athletes.

I argue that fears of mannish female sexuality in sport initially centered on the prospect of unbridled heterosexual desire. By the 1930s, however, female athletic mannishness began to connote heterosexual failure, usually couched in terms of unattractiveness to men, but also suggesting the possible absence of heterosexual interest. In the years following World War II, the stereotype of the lesbian athlete emerged full blown. The extreme homophobia and the gender conservatism of the postwar era created a context in which longstanding linkages among mannishness, female homosexuality, and athletics cohered around the figure of the mannish lesbian athlete. Paradoxically, the association between masculinity, lesbianism, and sport had a positive outcome for some women. The very cultural matrix that produced the pejorative image also created possibilities for lesbian affirmation. Sport provided social and psychic space for some lesbians to validate themselves and to build a collective culture. Thus, the lesbian athlete was not only a figure of discourse but a living product of women's sexual struggle and cultural innovation.

The athletic woman sparked interest and controversy in the early decades of the twentieth century. In the United States and other Western societies, sport functioned as a male preserve, an all-male domain in which men not only played games together but also demonstrated and affirmed their manhood.[5] The "maleness" of sport derived from a gender ideology which labeled aggression, physicality, competitive spirit, and athletic skill as masculine attributes necessary for achieving true manliness. This notion found unquestioned support in the dualistic, polarized concepts of gender which prevailed in Victorian America. However, by the turn of the century, women

had begun to challenge Victorian gender arrangements, breaking down barriers to female participation in previously male arenas of public work, politics, and urban nightlife. Some of these "New Women" sought entry into the world of athletics as well. On college campuses students enjoyed a wide range of intramural sports through newly formed Women's Athletic Associations. Off-campus women took up games like golf, tennis, basketball, swimming, and occasionally even wrestling, car racing, or boxing. As challengers to one of the defining arenas of manhood, skilled female athletes became symbols of the broader march of womanhood out of the Victorian domestic sphere into once prohibited male realms.

The woman athlete represented both the appealing and threatening aspects of modern womanhood. In a positive light, she captured the exuberant spirit, physical vigor, and brazenness of the New Woman. The University of Minnesota student newspaper proclaimed in 1904 that the athletic girl was the "truest type of All-American coed."[6] Several years later, *Harper's Bazaar* labeled the unsportive girl as "not strictly up to date," and *Good Housekeeping* noted that the "tomboy" had come to symbolize "a new type of American girl, new not only physically, but mentally and morally."[7]

Yet, women athletes invoked condemnation as often as praise. Critics ranged from physicians and physical educators to sportswriters, male athletic officials, and casual observers. In their view, strenuous athletic pursuits endangered women and threatened the stability of society. They maintained that women athletes would become manlike, adopting masculine dress, talk, and mannerisms. In addition, they contended, too much exercise would damage female reproductive capacity [interfering with menstruation and causing reproductive organs to harden or atrophy]. And worse yet, the excitement of sport would cause women to lose [sexual] control, . . . unleash[ing] nonprocreative, erotic desires identified with male sexuality and unrespectable women. . . . These fears collapsed into an all-encompassing concept of "mannishness," a term signifying female masculinity . . .

The public debate over the merits of women's athletic participation remained lively throughout the 1910s and 1920s. On all sides of the issue, however, the controversy about sports and female sexuality presumed hetero-sexuality. Neither critics nor supporters suggested that "masculine" athleticism might indicate or induce same-sex love. And when experts warned of the "amazonian" athlete's possible sexual transgressions, they linked the physical release of sport with a loss of hetero sexual *control*, not of *inclination*.

In the 1930s, however, the heterosexual understanding of the mannish "amazon" began to give way to a new interpretation which educators and promoters could not long ignore. To the familiar charge that female athletes resembled men, critics added the newer accusation that sport-induced mannishness disqualified them as candidates for heterosexual romance. In 1930, an *American Mercury* medical reporter decried the decline of romantic love, pinning the blame on women who entered sport, business, and politics. He claimed that such women "act like men, talk like men, and think like men." The author explained that "women have come closer and closer to men's level," and, consequently, "the purple allure of distance has vamoosed."[8] . . . Although the charges didn't exclusively focus on athletes, they implied that female athleticism was contrary to heterosexual appeal, which appeared to rest on women's difference from and deference to men.

The concern with heterosexual appeal reflected broader sexual transformations in U.S. society. Historians of sexuality have examined the multiple forces which reshaped gender and sexual relations in the first few decades of the twentieth century. Victorian sexual codes crumbled under pressure from an assertive, boldly sexual working-class youth culture, a women's movement which defied prohibitions against public female activism, and the growth of a new pleasure-oriented consumer economy. In the wake of these changes, modern ideals of womanhood embraced an overtly erotic heterosexual sensibility. At the same time, medical fascination with sexual "deviance" created a growing awareness of lesbianism, now understood as a form of congenital or psychological pathology. The medicalization of homosexuality in combination with an antifeminist backlash in the 1920s against female autonomy and power contributed to a more fully articulated taboo against lesbianism. The modern heterosexual woman stood in stark opposition to her threatening sexual counterpart, the "mannish" lesbian.[9]

By the late 1920s and early 1930s, with a modern lesbian taboo and an eroticized definition of heterosexual femininity in place, the assertive, muscular female competitor roused increasing suspicion. It was at this moment that both subtle and direct references to the lesbian athlete emerged in physical education and popular sport. Uncensored discussions of intimate female companionship and harmless athletic "crushes" disappear from the record, pushed underground by the increasingly hostile tone of public discourse about female sexuality and athleticism. Fueled by the gender antagonisms and anxieties of the Depression, the public began scrutinizing women athletes—known for their appropriation of masculine games and styles—for signs of deviance.

Where earlier references to "amazons" had signaled heterosexual ardor, journalists now used the term to mean unattractive, failed heterosexuals. Occasionally, the media made direct mention of athletes' presumed lesbian tendencies. A 1933 *Redbook* article, for example, casually mentioned that track and golf star Babe Didrikson liked men just to horse around with her and not "make love," adding that Babe's fondness for her best girlfriends far surpassed her affection for any man.[10] The direct reference was unusual; the lesbian connotation of mannishness was forged primarily through indirect links of association. . . .

Tentatively voiced in the 1930s, these accusations became harsher and more explicit under the impact of wartime changes in gender and sexuality and the subsequent panic over the "homosexual menace." In a post–World War II climate markedly hostile to nontraditional women and lesbians, women in physical education and in working-class popular sports became convenient targets of homophobic indictment.

World War II opened up significant economic and social possibilities for gay men and women. Embryonic prewar homosexual subcultures blossomed during the war and spread across the midcentury urban landscape. Bars, nightclubs, public cruising spots, and informal social networks facilitated the development of gay and lesbian enclaves. But the permissive atmosphere did not survive the war's end. Waving the banner of Cold War political and social conservatism, government leaders acted at the federal, state, and local levels to purge gays and lesbians from government and military posts, to initiate legal investigations and prosecutions of gay individuals and institutions, and to encourage local police crackdowns on gay bars and street life. The perceived need to safeguard national security and to reestablish social order in the wake of wartime disruption sparked a "homosexual panic" which promoted the fear, loathing, and persecution of homosexuals.[11]

Lesbians suffered condemnation for their violation of gender as well as sexual codes. The tremendous emphasis on family, domesticity, and "traditional" femininity in the late 1940s and 1950s reflected postwar anxieties about the reconsolidation of a gender order shaken by two decades of depression and war. As symbols of women's refusal to conform, lesbians endured intense scrutiny by experts who regularly focused on their subjects' presumed masculinity. Sexologists attributed lesbianism to masculine tendencies and freedoms encouraged by the war, linking it to a general collapsing of gender distinctions which, in their view, destabilized marital and family relations.[12]

Lesbians remained shadowy figures to most Americans, but women athletes—noted for their masculine bodies, interests, and attributes—were visible representatives of the gender inversion often associated with homosexuality. Physical education majors, formerly accused of being unappealing to men, were increasingly charged with being uninterested in them as well. The 1952 University of Minnesota yearbook snidely reported: "Believe it or not, members of the Women's Athletic Association are normal" and found conclusive evidence in the fact that "at least one . . . of WAA's 300 members is engaged."[13]

The lesbian stigma began to plague popular athletics too. . . . The career of Babe Didrikson, which spanned the 1920s to the 1950s, illustrates the shift. In the early 1930s the press had ridiculed the tomboyish track star for her "hatchet face," "door-stop jaw," and "button-breasted" chest. After quitting track, Didrikson dropped out of the national limelight, married professional wrestler George Zaharias in 1938,

and then staged a spectacular athletic comeback as a golfer in the late 1940s and 1950s. Fascinated by her personal transformation and then, in the 1950s, moved by her battle with cancer, journalists gave Didrikson's comeback extensive coverage and helped make her a much-loved popular figure. In reflecting on her success, however, sportswriters spent at least as much time on Didrikson's love life as her golf stroke. Headlines blared, "Babe Is a Lady Now: The World's Most Amazing Athlete Has Learned to Wear Nylons and Cook for Her Huge Husband," and reporters gleefully described how "along came a great big he-man wrestler and the Babe forgot all her man-hating chatter."[14] . . . The challenge for women athletes was not to conquer new athletic feats, which would only further reduce their sexual appeal, but to regain their womanhood through sexual surrender to men.

Media coverage in national magazines and metropolitan newspapers typically focused on the sexual accomplishments of white female athletes, but postwar observers and promoters of African American women's sport also confronted the issue of sexual normalcy. In earlier decades, strong local support for women's sport within Black communities and the racist gender ideologies that prevailed outside Black communities may have weakened the association between African American women athletes and "mannish" lesbianism. Historically, European American racial thought characterized African American women as aggressive, coarse, passionate, and physical—the same qualities assigned to manliness and sport.[15] Excluded from dominant ideals of womanhood, Black women's success in sport could therefore be interpreted not as an unnatural sexual deviation but, rather, as the natural result of their reputed closeness to nature, animals, and masculinity.[16] . . . Moreover, stereotypes of Black females as highly sexual, promiscuous, and unrestrained in their heterosexual passions further discouraged the linkage between mannishness and lesbianism. . . .

Although Black athletes may initially have encountered few lesbian stereotypes . . . circumstances in the broader society eventually pressed African American sport promoters and journalists to address the issue of mannish sexuality. The strong postwar association of sports with lesbianism developed at the same time as Black athletes became a dominant presence in American sport culture. . . . Therefore, while there was no particular correlation between Black women and lesbianism, the association of each with mannishness and sexual aggression potentially linked the two. . . . In the late 1950s, Black sport promoters and journalists joined others in taking up the question of sexual "normalcy." One Black newspaper in 1957 described tennis star Althea Gibson as a childhood "tomboy" who "in later life . . . finds herself victimized by complexes."[17] The article did not elaborate on the nature of Gibson's "complex," but lesbianism is inferred in the linkage between "tomboys" and psychological illness. This connotation becomes clearer by looking at the defense of Black women's sport. Echoing *Ebony's* avowal that "entirely feminine" Black female track stars "like boys, dances, club affairs," in 1962 Tennessee State University track coach Ed Temple asserted, "None of my girls have any trouble getting boy friends. . . . We don't want amazons."[18]

Constant attempts to shore up the heterosexual reputation of athletes can be read as evidence that the longstanding reputation of female athletes as mannish women had become a covert reference to lesbianism. By midcentury, a fundamental reorientation of sexual meanings fused notions of femininity, female eroticism, and heterosexual attractiveness into a single ideal. Mannishness, once primarily a sign of gender crossing, assumed a specifically lesbian-sexual connotation. In the wake of this change, the strong cultural association between sport and masculinity made women's athletics ripe for emerging lesbian stereotypes. This meaning of athletic mannishness raises further questions. What impact did the stereotype have on women's sport? And was the image merely an erroneous stereotype, or did lesbians in fact form a significant presence in sport? . . .

The image of the mannish lesbian athlete had a direct effect on women competitors, on strategies of athletic organizations, and on the overall popularity of women's sport. The lesbian stereotype exerted pressure on athletes to demonstrate their femininity and heterosexuality, viewed as one and the same. Many women adopted an apologetic stance toward their athletic skill. Even as they competed to win, they made sure to display outward signs of femininity in dress and demeanor. They took special care in contact with the media to reveal "feminine" hobbies like cooking and sewing, to mention current boyfriends, and to discuss future marriage plans.[19]

Leaders of women's sport took the same approach at the institutional level. In answer to portrayals of physical education majors and teachers as social rejects and prudes, physical educators revised their philosophy to place heterosexuality at the center of professional objectives. . . . Curricular changes implemented between the mid-1930s and mid-1950s institutionalized the new philosophy. In a paper on postwar objectives, Mildred A. Schaeffer explained that physical education classes should help women "develop an interest in school dances and mixers and a desire to voluntarily attend them."[20] To this end, administrators revised coursework to emphasize beauty and social charm over rigorous exercise and health. They exchanged old rationales of fitness and fun for promises of trimmer waistlines, slimmer hips, and prettier complexions. . . . Some departments also added coeducational classes to foster "broader, keener, more sympathetic understanding of the opposite sex."[21] Department heads cracked down on "mannish" students and faculty, issuing warnings against "casual styles" which might "lead us back into some dangerous channels."[22] They implemented dress codes which forbade slacks and men's shirts or socks, adding as well a ban on "boyish hair cuts" and unshaven legs.[23]

Popular sport promoters adopted similar tactics. Martialing sexual data like they were athletic statistics, a 1954 AAU poll sought to sway a skeptical public with numerical proof of heterosexuality—the fact that 91 percent of former female athletes surveyed had married.[24] Publicity for the midwestern All-American Girls Baseball League included statistics on the number of married players. . . . Behind the scenes, teams passed dress and conduct codes. For example, the All-American Girls Baseball League prohibited players from wearing men's clothing or getting "severe" haircuts.[25] That this was an attempt to secure the heterosexual image of athletes was made even clearer when league officials announced that AAGBL policy prohibited the recruitment of "freaks" and "Amazons."[26]

In the end, the strategic emphasis on heterosexuality and the suppression of "mannishness" did little to alter the image of women in sport. The stereotype of the mannish lesbian athlete grew out of the persistent common-sense equation of sport with masculinity. Opponents of women's sport reinforced this belief when they denigrated women's athletic efforts and ridiculed skilled athletes as "grotesque," "mannish," or "unnatural." Leaders of women's sport unwittingly contributed to the same set of ideas when they began to orient their programs around the new feminine heterosexual idea. As physical education policies and media campaigns worked to suppress lesbianism and marginalize athletes who did not conform to dominant standards of femininity, sport officials embedded heterosexism into the institutional and ideological framework of sport. The effect extended beyond sport to the wider culture, where the figure of the mannish lesbian athlete announced that competitiveness, strength, independence, aggression, and physical intimacy among women fell outside the bounds of womanhood. As a symbol of female deviance, she served as a powerful reminder to all women to toe the line of heterosexuality and femininity or risk falling into a despised category of mannish (non-women) women. . . .

[But] was the mannish lesbian athlete merely a figure of homophobic imagination, or was there in fact a strong lesbian presence in sport? When the All-American Girls Baseball League adamantly specified, "*Always appear in feminine attire* . . . MASCULINE HAIR STYLING? SHOES? COATS? SHIRTS? SOCKS, T-SHIRTS ARE BARRED AT ALL TIMES," and when physical education departments threatened to expel students for overly masculine appearance, were administrators merely responding to external pressure?[27] Or were they cracking down on women who may have indeed enjoyed the feel and look of a tough swagger, a short haircut, and men's clothing? And if so, did mannishness among athletes correspond to lesbianism, as the stereotype suggested? In spite of the public stigmatization, [is it probable that] some women may have found the activities, attributes, and emotions of sport conducive to lesbian self-expression and community formation?

As part of a larger investigation of women's athletic experience, I conducted oral histories with women who played competitive

amateur, semiprofessional, and professional sports between 1930 and 1970. The interviews included only six openly lesbian narrators and thirty-six other women who either declared their heterosexuality or left their identity unstated.[28] Although the sample is too small to stand as a representative study, the interviews . . . and scattered other sources indicate that sport, particularly softball, provided an important site for the development of lesbian subculture and identity in the United States.[29] Gay and straight informants alike confirmed the lesbian presence in popular sport and physical education. Their testimony suggests that from at least the 1940s on, sport provided space for lesbian activity and social networks and served as a path into lesbian culture for young lesbians coming out and searching for companions and community.

Lesbian athletes explained that sport had been integral to their search for sexual identity and lesbian companionship. Ann Maguire, a softball player, physical education major, and top amateur bowler from New England, recalled that as a teenager in the late 1950s,

I had been trying to figure out who I was and couldn't put a name to it. I mean it was very— no gay groups, no literature, no characters on *Dynasty*—I mean there was just nothing at that time. And trying to put a name to it. . . . I went to a bowling tournament, met two women there [and] for some reason something clicked and it clicked in a way that I was not totally aware of.

She introduced herself to the women, who later invited her to a gay bar. Maguire described her experience at age seventeen:

I was being served and I was totally fascinated by the fact that, oh god, here I am being served and I'm not twenty-one. And it didn't occur to me until after a while when I relaxed and started realizing that I was at a gay bar. I just became fascinated. . . . And I was back there the next night. . . . I really felt a sense of knowing who I was and feeling very happy. Very happy that I had been able to through some miracle put this into place.[30] . . .

For women like Maguire, sport provided a point of entry into lesbian culture.

The question arises of whether lesbians simply congregated in athletic settings or whether a sports environment could actually "create" or "produce" lesbians. Some women fit the first scenario, describing how, in their struggle to accept and make sense out of lesbian desire, sport offered a kind of home that put feelings and identities into place. For other women, it appears that the lesbian presence in sport encouraged them to explore or act on feelings that they might not have had or responded to in other settings. Midwestern baseball player Nora Cross remembered that "it was my first exposure to gay people. . . . I was pursued by the one I was rooming with, that's how I found out." She got involved with her roommate and lived "a gay lifestyle" as long as she stayed in sport. Dorothy Ferguson Key also noticed that sport changed some women, recalling that "there were girls that came in the league like this . . . yeah, gay," but that at other times "a girl came in, and I mean they just change. . . . When they've been in a year they're completely changed. . . . They lived together."[31]

The athletic setting provided public space for lesbian sociability without naming it as such or excluding women who were not lesbians. This environment could facilitate the coming-out process, allowing women who were unsure about or just beginning to explore their sexual identity to socialize with gay and straight women without having to make immediate decisions or declarations. Gradually and primarily through unspoken communication, lesbians in sport recognized each other and created social networks. Gloria Wilson, who played softball in a mid-sized midwestern city, described her entry into lesbian social circles as a gradual process in which older lesbians slowly opened up their world to her and she grew more sure of her own identity and place in the group.

A lot was assumed. And I don't think they felt comfortable with me talking until they knew me better. Then I think more was revealed. And we had little beer gatherings after a game at somebody's house. So then it was even more clear who was doing what when. And then I felt more comfortable too, fitting in, talking about my relationship too—and exploring more of the lesbian lifestyle, I guess.[32]

In an era when women did not dare announce their lesbianism in public, the social world of popular sport allowed women to find each other as teammates, friends, and lovers. But if athletics provided a public arena and social activity in which lesbians could recognize and affirm each other, what exactly was it that they recognized? This is where the issue of mannishness arises. Women athletes consistently explained the lesbian reputation of sport by reference to the mannishness of some athletes. . . . Suspected lesbians were said to "act like a man, you know, the way they walked, the way they talked, the things they did."

Such comments could merely indicate the pervasiveness of the masculine reputation of athletes and lesbians. However, lesbian narrators also suggested connections, although more complicated and nuanced, between athletics, lesbianism, and the "mannish" or "butchy" style which some lesbians manifested. None reported any doubt about their own gender identification as girls and women, but they indicated that they had often felt uncomfortable with the activities and attributes associated with the female gender. They preferred boyish clothes and activities to the conventional styles and manners of femininity.

Several spoke of . . . their relief upon finding athletic comrades who shared this sensibility. Josephine D'Angelo recalled that as a lesbian participating in sport, "you brought your culture with you. You brought your arm swinging . . . , the swagger, the way you tilted or cocked your head or whatever. You brought that with you." She explained that this style was acceptable in sports: "First thing you did was to kind of imitate the boys because you know, you're not supposed to throw like a girl." Although her rejection of femininity made her conspicuous in other settings, D'Angelo found that in sport "it was overlooked, see. You weren't different than the other kids. . . . Same likeness, people of a kind."[33]

These athletes were clearly women playing women's sports. But in the gender system of U.S. society, the skills, movements, clothing, and competition of sport were laden with impressions of masculinity. Lesbianism too crossed over the bounds of acceptable femininity. Consequently, sport could relocate girls or women with lesbian identities or feelings in an alternative nexus of gender meanings, allowing them to "be themselves"—or to express their gender and sexuality in an unconventional way. This applied to heterosexual women as well, many of whom also described themselves as "tomboys" attracted to boyish games and styles. As an activity that incorporated prescribed "masculine" physical activity into a way of being in the female body, athletics provided a social space and practice for reorganizing conventional meanings of embodied masculinity and femininity. *All* women in sport gained access to activities and expressive styles labeled masculine by the dominant culture. However, because lesbians were excluded from a concept of "real womanhood" defined around heterosexual appeal and desire, sport formed a milieu in which they could redefine womanhood on their own terms. . . .

However, the connections among lesbianism, masculinity, and sport require qualification. Many lesbians in and out of sport did not adopt "masculine" markers. And even among those who did, narrators indicated that butch styles did not occlude more traditionally "feminine" qualities of affection and tenderness valued by women athletes. Sport allowed women to combine activities and attributes perceived as masculine with more conventionally feminine qualities of friendship, cooperation, nurturance, and affection. Lesbians particularly benefited from this gender configuration, finding that in the athletic setting, qualities otherwise viewed as manifestations of homosexual deviance were understood as inherent, positive aspects of sport.[34] Aggressiveness, toughness, passionate intensity, expanded use of motion and space, strength, and competitiveness contributed to athletic excellence. With such qualities defined as athletic attributes rather than psychological abnormalities, the culture of sport permitted lesbians to express the full range of their gendered sensibilities while sidestepping the stigma of psychological deviance. For these reasons, athletics, in the words of Josephine D'Angelo, formed a "comforting" and "comfortable" place.[35]

Yet lesbians found sport hospitable only under certain conditions. Societal hostility toward homosexuality made lesbianism unspeakable in any realm of culture, but the sexual suspicions that surrounded sport made athletics an especially dangerous place in which to speak out. Physical educators and sport officials vigilantly guarded against signs of "mannishness," and teams occasionally expelled women who wore their hair in a "boyish bob" or engaged in obvious lesbian relationships. Consequently, gay athletes avoided naming or verbally acknowledging their sexuality. Loraine Sumner explained that "you never talked about it. . . . You never saw anything in public amongst the group of us. But you knew right darn well that this one was going with that one. But yet it just wasn't a topic of conversation. Never."[36] Instead, lesbian athletes signaled their identity through dress, posture, and look, reserving spoken communication for private gatherings among women who were acknowledged and accepted members of concealed communities.

Although in hindsight the underground nature of midcentury lesbian communities may seem extremely repressive, it may also have had a positive side. Unlike the bars where women's very presence declared their status as sexual outlaws, in sport athletes could enjoy the public company of lesbians while retaining their membership in local communities where neighbors, kin, and coworkers respected and sometimes even celebrated their athletic abilities. The unacknowledged, indefinite presence of lesbians in sport may have allowed for a wider range of lesbian experience and identity than is currently acknowledged in most scholarship. For instance, among women who did not identify as lesbian but were sexually drawn to other women, sport provided a venue in which they could express their desires without necessarily having articulated their feelings as a distinct sexual identity. The culture of sport provided space for some women to create clearly delineated lesbian identities and communities, at the same time allowing other women to move along the fringes of this world, operating across sexual and community lines without a firmly differentiated lesbian identity.

Women in sport experienced a contradictory array of heterosexual imperatives and homosexual possibilities. The fact that women athletes disrupted a critical domain of male power and privilege made sport a strategic site for shoring up existing gender and sexual hierarchies. The image of the mannish lesbian confirmed both the masculinity of sport and its association with female deviance. Lesbian athletes could not publicly claim their identity without risking expulsion, ostracism, and loss of athletic activities and social networks that had become crucial to their lives. Effectively silenced, their image was conveyed to the dominant culture primarily as a negative stereotype in which the mannish lesbian athlete represented the unfeminine "other," the line beyond which "normal" women must not cross.

The paradox of women's sport history is that the mannish athlete was not only a figure of homophobic discourse but also a human actor engaged in sexual innovation and struggle. Lesbian athletes used the social and psychic space of sport to create a collective culture and affirmative identity. The pride, pleasure, companionship, and dignity lesbians found in the athletic world helped them survive in a hostile society. The challenge posed by their collective existence and their creative reconstruction of womanhood formed a precondition for more overt, political challenges to lesbian oppression which have occurred largely outside the realm of sport.

NOTES

1. Fred Wittner, "Shall the Ladies Join Us?" *Literary Digest* 117 (19 May 1934):43.

2. Jim Murray, *Austin American Statesman* (n.d.), Zaharias scrapbook, Barker Texas History Center ([hereafter] BTHC), University of Texas, Austin; Arsenio Hall Show, 1988.

3. "Fastest Women in the World," *Ebony* 10 (June 1955):28.

4. Helen Lenskyj, *Out of Bounds: Women, Sport, and Sexuality* (Toronto: Women's Press, 1986); Yvonne Zipter, *Diamonds Are a Dyke's Best Friend: Reflections, Reminiscences, and Reports from the Field on the Lesbian National Pastime* (Ithaca: Firebrand Books, 1988).

5. J. A. Mangan and Roberta J. Park, eds., *"Fair Sex" to Feminism: Sport and the Socialization of Women in the Industrial and Post-Industrial Era* (London: Frank Cays, 1987).

6. 1904–5 Scrapbooks of Anne Maude Butner, Butner Papers, University of Minnesota Archives, Minneapolis (UMA).

7. Violet W. Mange, "Field Hockey for Women," *Harper's Bazaar* 44 (Apr. 1910):246; Anna de Koven, "The Athletic Woman," *Good Housekeeping* 55 (Aug. 1912):150.

8. George Nathan, "Once There Was a Princess," *American Mercury* 19 (Feb. 1930):242.

9. This is an extremely brief and simplified summary of an extensive literature. For a good synthesis, see Estelle Freedman and John D'Emilio, *Intimate Matters: A History of Sexuality in America* (New York: Harper & Row, 1988), chaps. 8–10.

10. William Marston, "How Can a Woman Do It?" *Redbook* (Sept. 1933):60.

11. John D'Emilio, *Sexual Politics, Sexual Communities: The Making of a Homosexual Minority in the United States, 1940–1970* (Chicago: University of Chicago Press, 1983), pp. 9–53; Alan Berube, *Coming Out Under Fire: The History of Gay Men and Women in World War Two* (New York: Free Press, 1990).

12. Donna Penn, "The Meanings of Lesbianism in Post-War America," *Gender and History* 3 (Summer 1991):190–203; Wini Breines, "The 1950s: Gender and Some Social Science," *Sociological Inquiry* 56 (Winter 1986):69–92.

13. Gopher Yearbook (1952), p. 257, UMA.

14. Paul Gallico, *Houston Post*, 22 Mar. 1960; Pete Martin, "Babe Didrikson Takes Off Her Mask," *Saturday Evening Post* 20 (Sept. 1947):26–27.

15. Paula Giddings, *When and Where I Enter: The Impact of Black Women on Race and Sex in America* (New York: William Morrow, 1984), chaps. 1, 2, 4; Patricia Hill Collins, *Black Feminist Thought: Knowledge, Consciousness, and the Politics of Empowerment* (Boston: Unwin Hyman, 1990), chaps. 4, 8.

16. Elizabeth Lunbeck, "'A New Generation of Women': Progressive Psychiatrists and the Hypersexual Female," *Feminist Studies* 13 (Fall 1987): 513–43.

17. *Baltimore Afro-American*, 29 June 1957.

18. "Fastest Women in the World," pp. 28, 32; *Detroit News* 31 (July 1962):1.

19. Patricia Del Rey, "The Apologetic and Women in Sport," in Carole Oglesby, ed., *Women and Sport* (Philadelphia: Lea & Febiger, 1978), pp. 107–11.

20. Mildred A. Schaeffer, "Desirable Objectives in Post-war Physical Education," *Journal of Health and Physical Education* 16 (Oct. 1945):44–47.

21. "Coeducational Classes," *Journal of Health, Physical Education, and Recreation* 26 (Feb. 1955):18. For curricular changes, I examined physical education records at the universities of Wisconsin, Texas, and Minnesota, Radcliffe College, Smith College, Tennessee State University, and Hampton University.

22. Dudley Ashton, "Recruiting Future Teachers," *Journal of Health, Physical Education, and Recreation* 28 (Oct. 1957):49.

23. The 1949–50 Physical Training Staff Handbook at the University of Texas stated, "Legs should be kept shaved" (p. 16). Box 3R213 of Department of Physical Training for Women Records, BTHC.

24. Roxy Andersen, "Statistical Survey of Former Women Athletes," *Amateur Athlete* (Sept. 1954):10–11.

25. All-American Girls Baseball League (AAGBL) 1951 Constitution, AAGBL Records.

26. Morris Markey, "Hey Ma, You're Out!" (n.d.), 1951 Records of the AAGBL; and "Feminine Sluggers," *People and Places* 8 (1952), AAGBL Records.

27. AAGBL 1951 Constitution, AAGBL Records.

28. The sample included forty-two women, ranging in age from their forties to their seventies, who had played a variety of sports in a range of athletic settings in the West, Midwest, Southeast, and Northeast. The majority were white women from urban working-class and rural backgrounds.

29. Zipter, *Diamonds Are a Dyke's Best Friend*; Lillian Faderman, *Odd Girls and Twilight Lovers: A History of Lesbian Life in Twentieth-Century America* (New York: Columbia University Press, 1991), pp. 154, 161–62.

30. Ann Maguire, interview with the author, Boston, 18 Feb. 1988.

31. Nora Cross (pseudonym), interview with

the author, 20 May 1988; Dorothy Ferguson Key, interview with the author, Rockford, Ill., 19 Dec. 1988.

32. Gloria Wilson (pseudonym), interview with the author, 11 May 1988.

33. Josephine D'Angelo, interview with the author, Chicago, 21 Dec. 1988.

34. Joseph P. Goodwin, *More Man Than You'll Ever Be! Gay Folklore and Acculturation in Middle America* (Bloomington: Indiana University Press, 1989), p. 62.

35. D'Angelo interview.

36. Loraine Sumner, interview with the author, West Roxbury, Mass., 18 Feb. 1988.

AMY SWERDLOW
Ladies' Day at the Capitol: Women Strike for Peace versus HUAC

In the years surrounding World War I, women played a significant role in the peace movement, often justifying their activism in maternalist rhetoric. As mothers and potential mothers, they had a responsibility to save children from the horrors of war. Nearly half a century later, American women would again invoke their role as mothers to urge the end of nuclear testing on behalf of the world's children. The women's peace movement, which Swerdlow explores in the following article, coalesced at a time when the Cuban Missile Crisis had brought the United States and the Soviet Union to the brink of war. It also occurred during a period when virtually any form of political protest was automatically labeled by its critics as "communist inspired." Although the most virulent phase of McCarthyism had subsided by 1962, the machinery of repression was still intact; the women's peace movement was promptly investigated by the House Un-American Activities Committee.

Note the prior involvement of some of the women strikers in radical and liberal causes. Combine this information with Horowitz's point about the persistence of concern about the status of women workers in key unions such as the UE in the aftermath of World War II. Add the growing attention on the part of liberal women to race reconciliation. How does our view of the Cold War years change? Does this suggest that some women may have retained a willingness to criticize and subvert dominant power relationships? Might minority women be especially eager to fight injustice?

Note how participants in the peace strike challenged committee tactics by manipulating traditional gender stereotypes. Who were these women? How can their emergence as political activists be explained?

Amy Swerdlow, "Ladies Day at the Capitol: Women Strike for Peace versus HUAC," was originally published in *Feminist Studies* 8, no. 3 (Fall 1982):493–520. Reprinted by permission of the publisher, Feminist Studies, Inc.

The assumption that women found their true happiness in domesticity could be carried to extremes; here film star Joan Crawford posed for a publicity photograph that showed her engaged in household tasks. She does not look very happy. (Photograph courtesy of the Museum of Modern Art/Film Stills Archive.)

In mid-December of 1962 in the Old House Office Building of the United States Congress, a confrontation took place between a recently formed women's peace movement called Women Strike for Peace (WSP) and the House Committee on Un-American Activities (HUAC). The confrontation took place at a HUAC hearing to determine the extent of Communist party infiltration into "the so-called 'peace movement' in a manner and to a degree affecting the national security."[1] This three-day battle of political and sexual adversaries, which resulted in a rhetorical victory for the women of WSP and a deadly blow to the committee, occurred only twenty-five years ago.[2] It is a moment in the history of peace movements in the United States in which women led the way by taking a more courageous and principled stand in opposition to cold war ideology and political repression than that of their male counterparts.[3] However, in keeping with the historical amnesia which besets both the history of women and radical movements in America, the WSP-HUAC struggle is largely forgotten.[4]

This article seeks to reconstruct the WSP-HUAC confrontation and the reasons it took the form it did. By analyzing the ideology, consciousness, political style, and public demeanor of the WSP women as they defended their right as mothers "to influence the course of government," we can learn a great deal about the strengths and weaknesses of women's movements for social change that build on traditional sex role ideology and on female culture.[5]

WSP burst upon the American political scene on November 1st, 1961, when an estimated fifty thousand women in over sixty cities across the United States walked out of their kitchens and off their jobs in a one-day women's strike for peace. As a radioactive cloud from a Russian nuclear test hung over the American landscape, these women strikers staged the largest female peace action in the nation's history.[6] In small towns and large cities from New York to California, the women visited government officials demanding that they take immediate steps to "End the Arms Race—Not the Human Race."[7] Coming on the heels of a decade noted for cold war consensus, political conformity, and the celebration of female domesticity, this spontaneous women's initiative baffled both the press and

the politicians. The women seemed to have emerged from nowhere. They belonged to no unifying organizations, and their leaders were totally unknown as public figures.

The women strikers were actually responding to a call from a handful of Washington, D.C., women who had become alarmed by the acceleration of the nuclear arms race. So disheartened were they by the passivity of traditional peace groups, that they had sent a call to women friends and contacts all over the country urging them to suspend their regular routine of home, family, and job to join with friends and neighbors in a one-day strike to end the nuclear arms race.[8]

The call to strike spread rapidly from Washington through typical female networks: word of mouth and chain letter fashion from woman to woman, from coast to coast, through personal telephone calls, and Christmas card lists. Contacts in Parent Teacher Associations (PTAs), the League of Women Voters, church and temple groups, as well as the established peace organizations such as the Women's International League for Peace and Freedom (WILPF) and the Committee for a Sane Nuclear Policy (SANE), also spread the word.

The nature of the strike in each community depended entirely on what the local women were willing, and able, to do. Some marched, others lobbied local officials, a few groups took ads in local newspapers. Thousands sent telegrams to the White House and to the Soviet embassy, calling upon the two first ladies of the nuclear superpowers, Jacqueline Kennedy and Nina Khrushchev, to urge their husbands on behalf of all the world's children to "stop all nuclear tests— east and west." Amazed by the numbers and composition of the turnout on November 1st, *Newsweek* commented:

They were perfectly ordinary looking women, with their share of good looks; they looked like the women you would see driving ranch wagons, or shopping at the village market, or attending PTA meetings. It was these women by the thousands, who staged demonstrations in a score of cities across the nation last week, protesting atomic testing. A "strike for peace," they called it and—carrying placards, many wheeling baby buggies or strollers—they marched on city halls and Federal buildings to show their concern about nuclear fallout.[9]

The strikers' concern about the nuclear arms race did not end with the November 1st actions. Within only one year, the one-day strike for peace was transformed by its founders and participants into a national women's movement with local groups in sixty communities and offices in ten cities. With no paid staff and no designated leaders, thousands of women in different parts of the country, most of them previously unknown to each other, managed to establish a loosely structured communications network capable of swift and effective direct action on both a national and international scale.

From its inception, the WSP movement was a non-hierarchical participatory network of activists opposed both to rigid ideologies and formal organizational structure. The WSP women called their format simply "our unorganization." It is interesting to note that the young men of Students for a Democractic Society (SDS), a movement founded in the same year as WSP, more aware of their place in the radical political tradition, more aware of the power of naming, and more confident of their power to do so, named their loose structure "participatory democracy." Eleanor Garst, one of the Washington founders, explained the attractions of the un-organizational format:

> No one must wait for orders from headquarters—there aren't any headquarters. No one's idea must wait for clearance through the national board. No one waits for the president or the director to tell her what to do—and there is no president or director. Any woman who has an idea can propose it through an informal memo system; if enough women think it's good, it's done. Those who don't like a particular action don't have to drop out of the movement; they just sit out that action and wait for one they like. Sound "crazy"?—it is, but it also brings forth and utilizes the creativity of thousands of women who could never be heard from through ordinary channels.[10]

The choice of a loose structure and local autonomy was a reaction to hierarchical and bureaucratic structures of traditional peace groups like WILPF and SANE to which some of the early leaders belonged. These women perceived the WILPF structure, which required that all programmatic and action proposals be cleared with state and national

offices, as a roadblock to spontaneous and direct responses to the urgent international crisis.[11] The willingness of the Washington founders to allow each group to act in the way that suited its particular constituency was WSP's greatest strength and the source of the confidence and admiration that women across the country bestowed on the Washington founders. Washington came to be considered the WSP national office not only because it was located in the nation's capital, but also because the Washington group was trusted by all.

There was also another factor militating against a traditional membership organization. Only the year before the WSP strike, Linus Pauling, the Nobel Laureate in physics and opponent of nuclear testing, had been directed by the Senate Internal Security Subcommittee to turn over the names of those who had helped him gather signatures on a scientists' antinuclear petition. The commandeering of membership lists was not an uncommon tactic of political intimidation in the 1950s. Membership lists of radical organizations could therefore be a burden and responsibility. As they served no purpose in the WSP format, it was a sensible strategy to eliminate them. Another benefit was that WSP never had to assess accurately its numerical strength, thus allowing its legend to grow even when its numbers did not.

From its first day onward, WSP tapped a vast reservoir of moral outrage, energy, organizational talent, and sisterhood—female capacities that had been submerged and silenced for more than a decade by McCarthyism and the "feminine mystique." Using standard pressure group tactics, such as lobbying and petitioning, coupled with direct demonstrative action and civil disobedience, executed with imagination and "feminine flair," the WSP women succeeded in putting women's political demands on the front pages of the nation's newspapers, from which they had largely disappeared since the days of the suffrage campaign. WSP also managed to influence public officials and public policy. At a time when peace marchers were ignored, or viewed as "commies" or "kooks," President John F. Kennedy gave public recognition to the women strikers. Commenting on WSP's first antinuclear march at the White House, on January 15, 1962, the president told the nation that he thought the WSP women were "extremely earnest."

> I saw the ladies myself. I recognized why they were here. There were a great number of them, it was in the rain. I understand what they were attempting to say, therefore, I consider their message was received.[12]

In 1970, *Science* reported that "Wiesner (Jerome Wiesner, Pres. Kennedy's Science Advisor) gave the major credit for moving President Kennedy toward the limited Test Ban Treaty of 1963, not to arms controllers inside the government but to the Women Strike for Peace and to SANE and Linus Pauling."[13]

Although WSP, in its first year, was well received by liberal politicians and journalists, the surveillance establishment and the right-wing press were wary. They recognized early what the Rand Corporation described obliquely as the WSP potential "to impact on military policies."[14] Jack Lotto, a Hearst columnist, charged that although the women described themselves as a "group of unsophisticated wives and mothers who are loosely organized in a spontaneous movement for peace, there is nothing spontaneous about the way the pro-Reds have moved in on our mothers and are using them for their own purposes."[15] On the West Coast, the *San Francisco Examiner* claimed to have proof that "scores of well-intentioned, dedicated women . . . were being made dupes of by known Communists . . . operating openly in the much publicized Women Strike for Peace demonstrations."[16]

That WSP was under Federal Bureau of Investigation (FBI) surveillance from its first public planning meeting in Washington in October 1961, is abundantly evidenced in the forty-three volumes of FBI records on WSP which have been made available to the movement's attorneys under the provisions of the Freedom of Information Act. The records show that FBI offices in major cities, North, East, South, and West—and even in such places as Mobile, Alabama; Phoenix, Arizona; and San Antonio, Texas; not known for WSP activities—were sending and receiving reports on the women, often prepared in cooperation with local "red squads."[17]

Having just lived through the Cuban Missile Crisis of October 1962, WSP celebrated its first anniversary in November with a deep sense of urgency and of heightened political efficacy. But, as the women were making plans to escalate their commitment and their protests, they were stopped in their tracks in the first week of December by HUAC subpoenas to thirteen women peace activists from the New York metropolitan area, as well as Dagmar Wilson of Washington, D.C., the WSP national spokesperson.[18]

It is difficult today to comprehend the emotions and fears such a summons could invoke in individuals and organizations. Lillian Hellman's *Scoundrel Time* gives a picture of the tension, isolation, and near hysteria felt by an articulate and prominent public figure, as she prepared her defense against the committee in 1953.[19] By 1962, cold war hysteria had abated somewhat, as the United States and the USSR were engaged in test ban negotiations, but HUAC represented those forces and those voices in American politics that opposed such negotiations. As a congressional committee, it still possessed the awesome power of an agency of the state to command headlines; cast suspicion; and by labeling individuals as subversives, to destroy careers, lives, and organizations.

The HUAC subpoenas gave no indication of the subject of the hearings, or of their scope. So there was, at first, some confusion about whether it was the WSP connection or other aspects of the subpoenaed women's political lives that were suspect. To add to the confusion, it was soon discovered that three of the women called were not even active in WSP. They were members of the Conference of Greater New York Peace Groups, an organization founded by New Yorkers who had either been expelled from, or who had willingly left, SANE because of its internal red hunt. Of these three women, two had already been named by the committee informers as communists in previous HUAC hearings. One of these women, Elizabeth Moss, had achieved considerable notoriety when she was identified by accused Russian spy William Remington as his mother-in-law and a card-carrying communist. Given these circumstances it was clear that the WSP leadership had some important decisions to make regarding their response to the HUAC hearings. There were two important questions to be faced. First, as WSP had no official membership list, would the movement embrace any woman working for peace even if she were not directly involved in WSP activity? Second, would WSP disavow its members who had past or present communist affiliations, and if WSP did not disavow them, would the movement lose its following and its effectiveness?

The key to WSP unity in the face of the "communist issue" which had divided and disrupted peace, labor, and even civil liberties organizations in the previous decade, was the fact that WSP had previously decided to handle forthrightly and in advance of any attack, the issue of communist inclusion. WSP had, even before the HUAC hearings, decided to reject political screening of its members, deeming it a manifestation of outdated cold war thinking. This decision, the women claimed, was based not on fear or expediency, but on principle. The issue of accepting communists in the movement was brought to the floor of the first national WSP conference in June 1962 by the Los Angeles coordinating council. A prepared statement by the Los Angeles group declared: "Unlike SANE and Turn Toward Peace, WSP must not make the error of initiating its own purges." Treating the issue of communist membership as a question of personal conscience, the Los Angeles group asked, "If there are communists or former communists working in WSP, what difference does that make? We do not question one another about our religious beliefs or other matters of personal conscience. How can we justify political interrogation?" The Los Angeles statement continued, "If fear, mistrust and hatred are ever to be lessened, it will be by courageous individuals who do not hate and fear and can get together to work out tolerable compromises."[20] The argument that "this is a role women would be particularly equipped to play," won over the conference and resulted in the inclusion of a section in the WSP national policy statement which affirmed, "we are women of all races, creeds and political persuasions who are dedicated to the achievement of general and complete disarmament under effective international control."[21]

An emergency meeting of about fifty New York area "key women," along with Dagmar Wilson and other representatives from Washington, was called a few days after the HUAC summonses began to arrive.[22] The first decision made at this meeting was that WSP would live up to the national policy statement that had been arrived at six months earlier and make a reality of the phrase, "We are women of all ... political persuasions." Following from this decision it was clear that WSP would support and embrace every woman summoned before HUAC, regardless of her past or present affiliations, as long as she supported the movement's campaign against both Russian and American nuclear policies. This meant that in addition to supporting its own women, the three women not active in WSP would also come under the movement's protection if they so desired. They would be given access to the same lawyers as the WSP activists. They would not be isolated or attacked either for their affiliations or for the way they chose to conduct themselves at the hearing. This decision was in sharp contrast to the action taken by SANE in 1960 when it expelled a leading member of its New York chapter after he invoked the Fifth Amendment at a Senate Internal Security Subcommittee hearing, and then refused to tell Norman Cousins, a cochairman of SANE, whether or not he had ever been a communist.[23]

The decision made by the New York and Washington women not "to cower" before the committee, to conduct no internal purges, to acknowledge each woman's right to act for peace and to conduct herself according to the dictates of her conscience was bold for its day. It was arrived at within the movement, by the women themselves, without consultation with the male leaders of traditional peace and civil liberties groups, many of whom disagreed with this WSP policy.[24] It was based not only on the decision to resist the demonology of the cold war, but also on a sense of sisterhood, on feelings of identification with and empathy for the women singled out for attack. Even the subpoenaed women themselves turned for counsel and support more to each other and the WSP leadership than to their families and lawyers. Working together at a feverish pace, night and day for three weeks, writing, phoning, speaking at rallies, the key women seemed to be acting as if they were a family under attack, for which all personal resources, passions, and energies had to be marshaled. But the family, this time, was "the movement" and it was the sisters, not the fathers, who were in charge.

In response to the subpoenas, a massive

campaign was organized for the cancellation of the hearings and for support of WSP from national organizations and public figures. An anti-HUAC statement was composed in New York and Washington which spoke so well to the concerns and the consciousness of "the women" that it succeeded in unifying a movement in shock. The WSP statement on the HUAC inquisition was quoted widely by the press, used by local groups in ads and flyers, in letters to editors, and in speeches. "With the fate of humanity resting on a push button," the statement declared, "the quest for peace has become the highest form of patriotism."[25] In this first sentence, the women set the ground rules for their confrontation with the committee: it was going to be a contest over which group was more patriotic. But the test of "Americanism," according to the WSP rules, was the extent of one's dedication to saving America's children from nuclear extinction. Addressing the issue of communism in the movement, WSP declared: "Differences of politics, economics or social belief disappear when we recognize man's common peril . . . we do not ask an oath of loyalty to any set of beliefs. Instead we ask loyalty to the race of man. The time is long past when a small group of censors can silence the voice of peace." These words would be the WSP *leitmotif* in the Washington hearings. The women were saying, once again, as they had throughout their first year, that for them, the arms race, cold war ideology, and cold war politics, were obsolete in the nuclear age, as was the committee itself. This is the spirit Eric Bentley caught and referred to when he wrote: "In the 1960s a new generation came to life. As far as HUAC is concerned it began with Women Strike for Peace."[26]

The WSP strategy against HUAC was innovative. An organizing memorandum from the Washington office declared, "the usual response of protest and public statements is too traditional and ineffectual. . . . Let's Turn the Tables! Let's meet the HUAC challenge in the Good New WSP way!"[27] The "new way" suggested by women all over the country was to insist that WSP had nothing to hide. Instead of refusing to testify, as radicals and civil libertarians had done in the 1950s, large numbers of WSP participants volunteered to "talk." Approximately one hundred women sent wires to Representative Francis Walter, chair-

man of HUAC, offering to come to Washington to tell all about their movement. The offers were refused by HUAC. But this new WSP tactic pointed up the fact that the committee was less interested in securing information than in exposing and smearing those it chose to investigate. Some WSP groups objected to the free testimony strategy on the grounds that there was a contradiction between denying the right of the committee to exist, and at the same time offering to cooperate with it. But these groups were in a minority. Carol Urner of Portland, Oregon, spoke for all those who volunteered to testify, making it clear that she would not be a "friendly witness." "I could not, of course, divulge the names of others in the movement," she wrote to Representative Walter. "I suppose such a refusal could lead one to 'contempt' and prison and things like that . . . and no mother can accept lightly even the remote possibility of separation from the family which needs her. But mankind needs us too. . . ."[28]

Only three weeks' time elapsed between the arrival of the first subpoenas from HUAC and the date of the Washington hearings. In this short period, the WSP key women managed to develop a legal defense, a national support system for those subpoenaed, and a broad national campaign of public protest against the committee. The women's performance at the hearings was so original, so winning, and so "feminine" in the traditional sense, that it succeeded in capturing the sympathy and the support of large sections of the national media and in strengthening the movement instead of destroying it.

The hearings opened on December 11, 1962, at 10:00 A.M. in the caucus room of the Old House Office Building of the United States Congress in Washington, D.C. Fear, excitement, and exhilaration were in the air as each WSP woman in the audience looked around to see every seat in the room occupied by sisters who had come from eleven states, some from as far as California, in response to a call for their presence from the national leadership. Clyde Doyle, chairman of the subcommittee of HUAC conducting the WSP hearings, opened with a statement of their purpose. Quoting from Lenin, Stalin, Khrushchev, and Gus Hall, he explained:

> Communists believe that there can be no real peace until they have conquered the world. . . .

The initiated Communist, understanding his Marxist-Leninist doctrine, knows that a Moscow call to intensify the "fight for peace" means that he should intensify his fight to destroy capitalism and its major bastion, the United States of America.[29]

The WSP women in the audience rose as one as the committee called its first witness, Blanche Posner, a retired schoolteacher who was the volunteer office manager for New York WSP. The decision to rise with the first witness, to stand *with* her, was spontaneous. It was proposed only a few minutes before Posner was called, as a note from an unknown source was circulated around the room. Posner refused to answer any questions about the structure or personnel of WSP. She resorted to the Fifth Amendment forty-four times, as the press pointed out in dozens of news stories covering the first day of the hearings. They also reported the way in which Posner took matters into her own hands, lecturing the committee members as though they were recalcitrant boys at DeWitt Clinton High School in the Bronx, where she had taught. Talking right through the interruptions and objections raised by the chairman and by committeee counsel, Alfred Nittle, Posner declared:

> I don't know, sir, why I am here, but I do know why you are here, I think . . . because you don't quite understand the nature of this movement. This movement was inspired and motivated by mothers' love for children. . . . When they were putting their breakfast on the table, they saw not only the wheaties and milk, but they also saw strontium 90 and iodine 131. . . . They feared for the health and life of their children. That is the only motivation.[30]

Each time Posner resorted to the Fifth Amendment, she did it with a pointed criticism of the committee or a quip that endeared her to the women in the hearing room who needed to keep their spirits up in the face of charges that Posner had been identified by an FBI informer as a Communist party member while working in New York City as a schoolteacher. One prize exchange between Nittle and Posner led to particularly enthusiastic applause and laughter from WSP women. Nittle asked, "Did you wear a colored paper daisy to identify yourself as a member of the Women

Strike for Peace?" Posner answered, "It sounds like such a far cry from communism it is impossible not to be amused. I still invoke the Fifth Amendment."[31]

Most of the witnesses were called because the committee believed it had evidence to link them with the Communist party through identification by FBI informers or the signing of party nominating petitions. But the strategy backfired with Ruth Meyers, of Roslyn, Long Island. She stepped forward, according to Mary McGrory's report in the Washington (D.C.) *Evening Star,* "swathed in red and brown jersey, topped by a steeple crowned red velvet hat," and "she was just as much of a headache to the committee as Posner had been."[32] There was much sparring between Meyers and the committee about the nature and structure of WSP. "Are you presently a member of a group known as Women Strike for Peace?" Nittle asked. "No, sir, Women Strike for Peace has no membership," Meyers answered. Nittle then asked, "You are familiar, I understand, with the structural organization of Women Strike for Peace as evidenced by this plan?" Meyers replied, "I am familiar to the extent of the role that I play in it. I must say that I was not particularly interested in the structure of Women Strike for Peace. I was more involved in my own community activities. . . . I felt that structure, other than the old telephone, has not much of what I was interested in." Nittle then proceeded to deliver what he believed would be the coup de grâce for Meyers. "Mrs. Meyers," he barked, "it appears from the public records that a Ruth Meyers, residing at 1751 East 10th Street, Brooklyn, New York, on July 27, 1948, signed a Communist Party nominating petition. . . . Are you the Ruth Meyers who executed that petition?" Meyers shot back, "No, sir." She then examined the petition carefully, and announced, "I never lived in Brooklyn, and this is not my signature."[33] Although the official transcript does not contain this statement, many, including the author, remember that she added, "My husband could never get me to move there." This female remark brought an explosion of laughter and applause. Meyers also invoked the Fifth Amendment. As she left the witness stand, Meyers received a one-minute ovation for humor, grace, and mistaken identity. In the corridor outside the caucus room in front of the TV cameras, she told reporters that she had never been a Communist. "But I'll never acknowledge the Committee's right to ask me that question."[34]

Another witness, Lyla Hoffman, chose to tell the committee of her past communist affiliation, asserting that she had left the Communist Party, but would not cooperate in naming names or in citing the cause of her resignation. In a statement written after the hearings Hoffman explained, "I felt that it was high time to say, 'What difference does it make what anyone did or believed many years ago? That's not the problem facing humanity today.' But I had to say this in legal terms." She found it very difficult to do so, as the committee was interested only in whether she was a genuine anticommunist or a secret fellow-traveler.[35] Hoffman invoked the Fifth Amendment.

The witnesses that followed Posner, Meyers, and Hoffman, each in her own style, invoked whatever legal and rhetorical strategy her conscience and her situation dictated. They lectured the committee eloquently and courageously on the danger of nuclear holocaust, on women's rights and responsibility to work for peace. In attempting to explain the nonstructured format of WSP, several witnesses suggested that the movement was too fluid and too unpredictable to be comprehended by the masculine mind.

In their most optimistic projections, the WSP women could not have predicted the overwhelmingly favorable press and public response they would receive, and the support and growth for the movement that would result from the HUAC episode. From the outset, the WSP leadership understood that HUAC needed the press to make its tactics of intimidation and punishment work. So, WSP played for the press—as it had done from its founding—and won! The Washington and New York leadership knew that it had two stories; both were developed to the hilt. The first was "motherhood under attack" and the second was the age-old "battle of the sexes." The contest between the sexes, according to the WSP version, involved female common sense, openness, humor, hope and naiveté versus male rigidity, solemnity, suspicion, and dark theories of conspiracy and subversion. The WSP women, in their middle-class, feminine, political style turned the hearings into an episode of the familiar and funny "I Love

Lucy," rather than the tragic and scary inquisition of Alger Hiss.

For the first time, HUAC was belittled with humor and treated to a dose of its own moral superiority. Headlines critical of the committee and supportive of WSP were featured on the front pages of prominent newspapers from coast to coast. The *Chicago Daily News* declared: "It's Ladies' Day at Capitol: Hoots, Howls—and Charm; Congressmen Meet Match." Russell Baker's column was headed "Peace March Gals Make Red Hunters Look Silly" and a *Detroit Free Press* story was entitled, "Headhunters Decapitated." A cartoon by Herblock in the *Washington* (D.C.) *Post* of December 13th showed three aging and baffled committee members: One is seated at the hearing table. One is holding a gavel. Another turns to him and says, "I Came in Late, Which Was It That Was Un-American—Women or Peace?"[36] A story in the *Vancouver* (B.C.) *Sun* of December 14 was typical of many other reports:

> The dreaded House Un-American Activities Committee met its Waterloo this week. It tangled with 500 irate women. They laughed at it. Klieg lights glared, television cameras whirred, and 50 reporters scribbled notes while babies cried and cooed during the fantastic inquisition.

Bill Galt, author of the *Vancouver Sun* story, gave a blow-by-blow description of WSP civil disobedience in the Old House Office Building:

> When the first woman headed to the witness table, the crowd rose silently to its feet. The irritated Chairman Clyde Doyle of California outlawed standing. They applauded the next witness and Doyle outlawed clapping. Then they took to running out to kiss the witness. . . . Finally, each woman as she was called was met and handed a huge bouquet. By then Doyle was a beaten man. By the third day the crowd was giving standing ovations to the heroines with impunity.[37]

The hearings were a perfect foil for the humor of Russell Baker, syndicated columnist of the *New York Times*.

> If the House Un-American Activities Committee knew its Greek as well as it knows its Lenin, it would have left the women peace strikers alone. . . . Instead with typical male arrogance it has subpoenaed 15 of the ladies, . . . spent several

days trying to show them that women's place is not on the peace march route, and has come out of it covered with foolishness.

Baker, a liberal columnist, understood the committee's purpose and also the "drama of the absurd" that WSP had staged to defeat that purpose. "The Committee's aim was simple enough," Baker pointed out,

> their sleuths studying an organization known as Women Strike for Peace had learned that some of the strikers seemed to have past associations with the Communist Party or its front groups. Presumably if these were exposed, right thinking housewives would give up peace agitation and go back to the kitchen.

The committee had reckoned without female logic, according to Baker:

> How could WSP be infiltrated, witness after witness demanded, when it was not an organization at all? . . . Try as he might, Alfred Nittle, the committee counsel, never managed to break through against this defense.[38]

The *Detroit Free Press* commented: "The House Committee can get away with attacking college students in California, government flunkies who are forced to shrive their souls to save their jobs, and assorted misguided do-gooders. But when it decides to smear an estimated half-million angry women, it's in deep trouble. We wish them nothing but the worst."[39]

Mary McGrory in the *Washington* (D.C.) *Evening Star* played up the difference between the male, HUAC perceptions and those of the female, WSP:

> "Why can't a woman be like a man?" sings Henry Higgins in *My Fair Lady*. That is precisely the question the House Committee on Un-American Activities is asking itself today. . . . The committee is trying to find out if the ladies' group is subversive. All it found out was that their conduct in the caucus room certainly was.

"The leader of the group kept protesting that she was not really the leader at all," McGrory observed. Pointing out that few men would deny being leaders, or admit they didn't know what was going on, Mary McGrory reported that:

> Dagmar Wilson of Washington, when asked if she exercised control over the New York chapter merely giggled and said, "Nobody controls anybody in the Women Strike for Peace. We're all leaders."

Characterizing Wilson's appearance as the "coup de grâce in the battle of the sexes," McGrory noted that the ladies had been using the Congress as a babysitter, while their young crawled in the aisles and noisily sucked their bottles during the whole proceedings. With a mixture of awe and wonder McGrory described how the ladies themselves, as wayward as their babies, hissed, gasped, clapped entirely at will. When several of their number took the Fifth Amendment, to McGrory's surprise, the women applauded, and

> when Mrs. Wilson, trim and beguiling in red wool, stepped up to take the stand, a mother with a baby on one hip worked her way through the crowd and handed her a bouquet of purple and white flowers, exactly as if she were the principal speaker at a ladies' luncheon.

McGrory caught the flavor of Wilson's testimony which was directed not only at the committee, but also at her sisters in the audience. She reported that when Mr. Nittle asked whether the New York chapter had played a dominant role in the group, Wilson replied, "Other cities would be mortified if you said that."

> "Was it," Mr. Nittle wanted to know, "Mrs. Wilson's idea to send delegates to a Moscow peace conference?" "No," said Mrs. Wilson regretfully, "I wish I'd thought of that." When Mr. Nittle pursued the question of whose idea it was to send observers to Moscow, Dagmar Wilson replied, "This is something I find very difficult to explain to the masculine mind."

And, in a sense, it was. "Mr. Nittle pressed forward to the clutch question," one, according to McGrory, "that would bring a man to his knees with patriotic protest: 'I would like to ask you whether you would knowingly permit or encourage a Communist Party member to occupy a leadership position in Women Strike for Peace.'" Wilson replied:

> Well, my dear sir, I have absolutely no way of controlling, do not desire to control, who wishes to join in the demonstrations and the efforts that women strikers have made for peace. In fact, I would also like to go even further. I would like to say that unless everybody in the whole world joins us in this fight, then God help us.

"Would you knowingly permit or welcome Nazis or Fascists?" asked Mr. Nittle. Mrs. Wilson replied, "if we could only get them on our side."[40] Mr. Doyle then thanked Wilson for appearing and being so helpful. "I want to emphasize," he said,

that the Committee recognizes that there are many, many, many women, in fact a great great majority of women, in this peace movement who are absolutely patriotic and absolutely adverse to everything the Communist Party stands for. We recognize that you are one of them. We compliment you on your leadership and on your helpfulness to us this morning.

Dagmar Wilson tried to get the last word: "I do hope you live to thank us when we have achieved our goal." But Doyle replied, "Well, we will."[41]

The way in which WSP, a movement of middle-class, middle-aged, white women, mobilized to meet the attack by a feared congressional committee was energetic and bold, politically nontraditional, pragmatic rather than ideological, moralistic and maternal. It was entirely consistent with the already established program, tactics, rhetoric, and image of this one-year-old movement, labeled by the University of Wisconsin's student newspaper as "the bourgeois mother's underground."[42]

Were these courageous women who bowed to traditional notions of female behavior merely using the politics of motherhood for political advantage? Or had they internalized the feminine mystique? It is useful to examine the backgrounds of the WSP women in seeking to understand their use of their own female culture to legitimate a radical critique of national, foreign, and military policies. The WSP key women were mostly in their late thirties to mid forties at the inception of the movement in 1961. Most of them, then, had come into adulthood in the late 1930s and early 1940s. They were students or workers in the years of political ferment preceding World War II. Many had married just before, during, or right after the war. The majority of these women participated in the postwar baby boom, the rise of middle-class affluence, and the privatism and consumerism connected with suburban life. It was during the 1950s that they made their adjustment to family, parenting, community, and consensus politics.

As a movement born out of, and responding to, the consciousness of the 1950s, WSP projected a middle-class and politically moderate image. In an article celebrating WSP's

first anniversary, Eleanor Garst, one of WSP's early image makers, proclaimed:

Breaking all the rules and behaving with incredible disorder and naivete, "the women" continue to attract recruits until the movement now numbers hundreds of thousands.... Furthermore, many of the women behaving in these unaccustomed ways are no odd-ball types, but pillars of the community long courted by civic organizations. Others—perhaps the most numerous—are apolitical housewives who have never before lifted a finger to work for peace or any other social concern.[43]

Although the movement projected an image of political innocence and inexperience, WSP was actually initiated by five women who were already active members of SANE. The women—Dagmar Wilson, Jeanne Bagby, Folly Fodor, Eleanor Garst, and Margaret Russell—had gravitated toward each other because of their mutual distaste for SANE's internal red hunt, which they felt contributed to an escalation, rather than an end to cold war hysteria. Perhaps, more important, they shared a frustration over the slow pace with which the highly structured SANE reacted to international crises. They also resented the reluctance of SANE's male leadership to deal with "mother's issues" such as the contamination of milk by radioactive fallout from nuclear tests.

Dagmar Wilson was forty-five years old, and a political novice when she was moved to call a few friends to her home in the late summer of 1961 to discuss what could be done about the nuclear crisis. At this meeting WSP was born. Wilson was at that time a successful freelance children's book illustrator, the mother of three daughters and wife of Christopher Wilson, a commercial attaché at the British embassy. Wilson had been born in New York City, had moved to Germany as a very young child, and had spent most of her adult years in England where her father, Cesar Searchinger, was a well-known broadcast correspondent for the Columbia Broadcasting System and the National Broadcasting Company.

Wilson came to the United States prior to World War II, held a variety of professional jobs as an artist and teacher, and finally became a freelance illustrator. She worked in a studio at home, so as to be available to her children and to ensure a smooth-running household. Despite the fact that Wilson was so successful an artist that one of her children's books had become a best-seller, she nevertheless identified herself as a housewife.

> My idea in emphasizing the housewife rather than the professional was that I thought the housewife was a downgraded person, and that we, as housewives, had as much right to an opinion and that we deserved as much consideration as anyone else, and I wanted to emphasize . . . this was an important role and that it was time we were heard.[44]

A gifted artist, an intelligent person of good sense, good grace, and charm, Wilson possessed the charisma of those who accurately represent the feelings and the perceptions of their constituency, but excel them in passion and the capacity for creative articulation. Having been most of her life a "nonjoiner" Wilson was, as the *New York Times Magazine* reported in a feature story in May 1962, a "political neophyte."[45] Because Wilson had not been involved in U.S. radical politics of the 1940s, she was free from the self-conscious timidity that plagued those who had been involved in leftist organizations and who feared either exposure or a repetition of the persecution and the political isolation they had experienced in the 1950s.

Among the women who met at Wilson's house to plan the emergency peace action was Eleanor Garst, whose direct, friendly, practical, yet passionate political prose played a powerful role in energizing and unifying the WSP women in their first year. It was she who drafted the call for November 1st, and later helped create most of the anti-HUAC rhetoric.

Garst came from a conservative Baptist background. She recalls that everything in her upbringing told her that the only thing a woman should do was to marry, have babies, care for her husband and babies, and "never mind your own needs." Despite this, Garst was the only one of the inner circle of Washington founders, who in 1961 was a completely self-supporting professional woman, living on her own. She was the mother of two grown children. At the time of the founding of WSP, Garst was employed as a community organizer for the Adams Morgan Demonstration Project, administered by American University, working to maintain integrated neighborhoods in Washington, D.C. She had become a pacifist in her early childhood after reading about war in novels and poems. Her husband,

a merchant seaman, refused to be drafted prior to World War II, a decision that he and Eleanor made together without consulting any other pacifists because they knew none. They spent their honeymoon composing an eighty-page brief against peacetime conscription.

After the war, Garst became a professional political worker, writer, and peace activist on the West Coast before coming to Washington. She had been a founder of the Los Angeles SANE and editor of its newsletter. A forceful and easy writer, Garst had already been published in the *Saturday Evening Post, Reporter, Ladies' Home Journal,* and other national publications when she was asked to draft the letter that initiated the successful November 1st strike.

Folly Fodor, a leading figure in the founding group, had come to Washington in 1960 to follow her husband's job with the U.S. Labor Department. She joined SANE on her arrival in Washington and had been elected to the board. Thirty-seven years old at the time of the founding of WSP, Fodor was the mother of two. Folly Fodor was not new to politics. She was the daughter of parents who had been involved in liberal-to-communist political causes and had herself been a leader in political organizations since her youth. As an undergraduate at Antioch College, in Yellow Springs, Ohio, Folly Fodor had become active in the Young People's Socialist League, eventually becoming "head of it," as she put it. In retrospect she believes she spent too much time fighting the communists on campus, and "never did a goddamn thing." Fodor had been chairperson of the Young Democrats of California and as a Democrat she had clandestinely supported Henry Wallace in 1948. During the mid-1950s, after the birth of her second child, Fodor organized a mother's group to oppose nuclear testing. So Fodor, like Garst, was not new to radical causes, to peace activity, or to women's groups. She was ready and eager for a separate women's peace action in the fall of 1961.

Two other women who founded WSP, Jeanne Bagby and Margaret Russell, were also already active in the peace cause at the time of the founding of WSP. Bagby was a frequent contributor to *Liberation* magazine. Together the founders possessed research, writing, organizing, and speaking talents that were not unusual for women active in a variety of community, civic, and church groups in the 1950s. All the founders shared a conviction that the men in the peace movement and the government had failed them and that women had to take things into their own hands.

But what of the thousands of women who joined the founders? What was their social and political background and their motivation to take to the streets in peace protest? Elise Boulding, a sociologist and longtime pacifist activist, who became involved in the WSP communications network right after November 1st, decided to try to find out. During the six months in which Boulding edited the *Women's Peace Movement Bulletin,* an information exchange for WSP groups, she kept asking herself whether the WSP women were really political neophytes as they claimed, or "old pros with a well defined idea of some kind of world social order?" Using the resources of the Institute for Conflict Resolution in Ann Arbor, Michigan, where she was working, and with the help of WSP colleagues in Ann Arbor, she composed a questionnaire that was sent to every eighth name on the mailing lists of forty-five local groups. By the fall of 1962, shortly before the summonses from HUAC, 279 questionnaires had been returned from thirty-seven localities in twenty-two states. According to Boulding, the respondents represented a cross-section of the movement—not only leaders.[46]

Boulding found that the overwhelming majority of the WSP women were well-educated mothers, and that 61 percent were not employed outside the home. But she concluded that the women who went out on strike for peace on November 1, 1961, and stayed on in the movement in the following months, appeared to be a more complex and sophisticated group than the "buggy-pushing housewife" image the movement conveyed. She characterized the early WSP participants as "largely intellectual and civic-minded people, mostly of the middle class"—very much like the Washington founders themselves.[47]

Most of the women strikers had been liberals, radicals, or pacifists in the 1940s. Although few had been political leaders of any kind, they shared the 1940s belief that society could be restructured on humanistic lines through the direct political action of ordinary people. Dorothy Dinnerstein described the psychological process of depoliticization and privatization that many politically active people experienced in the 1950s. Many radicals, according to Dinnerstein, spent the 1950s in a state of moral shock, induced by the twin catastrophes of Stalinism and McCarthyism. They lost their capacity for social connectedness and, "in this condition they withdrew from history—more or less totally, more or less gradually, more or less blindly into intensely personalistic, inward-turning, magically thing-and-place-oriented life." According to Dinnerstein they withdrew their passion from the larger human scene and sought to invest in something less nightmarish, more coherent and mentally manageable.[48] What the WSP women withdrew into, with society's blessing and encouragement, was the domestic sphere, the management of family, children, home, and local community. Many, when their school-aged children no longer required full-time care, were propelled into the PTAs, League of Women Voters, Democratic party politics, church, synagogue, or cultural activities by their earlier social, political, and humanitarian concerns.

It took the acceleration of nuclear testing by both the capitalist United States and the socialist USSR to convince the WSP women of something they already suspected: that there was no political force in the world acting morally and humanely in the interest of the preservation of life. It took a series of international crises, the example of the civil rights sit-ins, and the Aldermarston antibomb marches in Britain to give the WSP women both the sense of urgency, and of possibility, that are the necessary ingredients for a political movement. Once out in the political arena, the women found that their moral outrage, their real fear for their children's future, and their determination never to be pushed back into the non-political domestic sphere, made them unafraid of a mere congressional committee before which others had quaked.

The women who were drawn to WSP certainly took the job of motherhood seriously. They had willingly chosen to sacrifice careers and personal projects to raise society's children because they had been convinced by the post-Freudians that the making of human beings is a far more important vocation than anything else; and that the making of human beings was a sex-specific vocation requiring the full-time duties of a resident mother.[49] But where the WSP women differed from the majority of their middle-class cohorts was that they saw motherhood not only as a private function, but also as a contribution to society in general and to the future. When they built on their rights and responsibilities to act politically in defense of the world's children, they were invoking not only their maternal consciousness, but their social conscience as well. They were women of heart, emotion, ingenuity, wit, and guile, but they were also serious political thinkers and activists. They chose to rely on their femininity, as most women did in the fifties and early sixties, to create whatever space and power they could carve out for themselves.

The Birmingham (England) Feminist History Group in an article, "Feminism as Femininity in the Nineteen Fifties?" suggests that feminism of the fifties seemed to be more concerned with integrating and foregrounding femininity than in transforming it in a fundamental way.[50] The conduct of WSP before the House Committee on Un-American Activities follows this pattern. The WSP women were not concerned with transforming the ideology of femininity, but rather with using it to enhance women's political power. But in so doing they were transforming that ideology and foreshadowing the feminism that emerged later in the decade.

Very much in the way that the concept of Republican motherhood was used in the late eighteenth century to justify the demand for women's education, and the cult of true womanhood was built upon to project women into the ante-bellum reform movements, WSP used the feminine mystique of the 1950s to legitimize women's right to radical dissent from foreign and military policies. In the repressive political climate of the early 1960s, WSP relied heavily upon sex role stereotypes to legitimize its opposition to cold war policies. But by emphasizing the fact that the men in power could no longer be counted on for protection in the nuclear age, WSP implied that the traditional sex-gender contract no longer worked. And by stressing global issues and international sisterhood, rather than domestic responsibilities, WSP challenged the privatization and isolation of women which was a key element of the feminine mystique. Most important, by performing in relation to HUAC with more courage, candor, and wit than most men

had done in a decade of inquisitions, WSP raised women's sense of political power and self-esteem. One of the negative effects for WSP of relying so heavily on the politics of motherhood to project its political message was that it alienated a new generation of younger women who admired the movement's stand for peace, but saw its acquiescence to sex role stereotypes as regressive. In the late 1960s these younger women insisted upon working for peace not as wives, mothers, and sisters, but as autonomous persons.

Sara Evans, in *Personal Politics*, points out that those few young women in the civil rights movement who first raised feminist issues within the movement had to step *outside* the sex role assumptions on which they were raised in order to articulate a radical critique of women's position.[51] For WSP it was obviously different. The founders and leaders of WSP certainly did not step outside the traditional sex role assumptions; rather, they stood squarely upon them, with all their contradictions. By using these contradictions to present a radical critique of man's world, WSP began the transformation of woman's consciousness and woman's role.

NOTES

1. U.S. Congress, House, Committee on Un-American Activities, *Communist Activities in the Peace Movement (Women Strike for Peace and Certain Other Groups), Hearings before the Committee on Un-American Activities on H.R. 9944.* 87th Cong., 2d. sess., 1962, p. 2057.

2. Historians and political opponents of HUAC agree that the WSP hearing marked the beginning of the end of the committee's power. Eric Bentley called the WSP-HUAC confrontation, "the fall of HUAC's Bastille." See Eric Bentley, *Thirty Years of Treason* (New York: Viking Press, 1971), p. 951. . . .

3. In May 1960, Senator Thomas Dodd, vice-chairman of the Senate International Security Subcommittee, threatened SANE with congressional investigation if it did not take steps to rid itself of communist infiltrators. SANE responded by voting to exclude all those with communist sympathies. Whole chapters that did not go along with internal red hunts were expelled, as was Henry Abrams, a leading New York activist who refused to tell the Senate committee whether or not he was a communist. Turn Toward Peace also rejected communists or former communists. See Milton S. Katz, "Peace, Politics, and Protest: SANE and the American Peace Movement, 1957–1972" (Ph.D. diss., St. Louis University, 1973), pp. 109–130. . . .

4. The way in which WSP's militant role in the peace movement has been either ignored or trivial-

ized by journalists, peace movement leaders, and historians is illustrated by the following examples. Mary McGrory in her syndicated column described a WSP visit to the White House in the following manner: "This week's Cinderella story has to do with Women Strike for Peace, which after 15 years of drudgery in the skullery of anti-war activity has been invited to the White House" (*New York Post,* 8 Mar. 1977, p. 27). Dave Dellinger, one of the most prominent of the male leaders of the 1960s peace movement, devoted about 10 lines to WSP in a 317-page book on the history of the civil rights and peace movements from 1965 to 1973. He described WSP as a group fearful of engaging in civil disobedience in the 1967 "Mobilization March on the Pentagon." Nowhere in the book did Dellinger mention that nine months earlier 2,500 WSP women broke through police barricades to bang their shoes on the Pentagon doors which had been shut in their faces. See Dave Dellinger, *More Power Than We Know* (Garden City, N.Y.: Anchor Press, 1975). . . .

5. For a symposium on the relationship of feminism, women's culture, and women's politics, see Ellen DuBois, Mari Jo Buhle, Temma Kaplan, Gerda Lerner, and Carroll Smith-Rosenberg, "Politics and Culture in Women's History: A Symposium," *Feminist Studies* 6 (Spring 1980):26–64. . . .

6. The figure of fifty thousand claimed by the Washington founders after November 1st was accepted in most press accounts and became part of the WSP legend. It was based on reports from women in sixty cities and from newspapers across the country. . . .

7. "End the Arms Race—Not the Human Race" was the central slogan of the November 1st "strike": "Help Wanted" flyer, 25 Oct. 1961, Washington, D.C. See WSP Document Collection in custody of the author. (Mimeographed.)

8. "Dear—, Last night I sat with a few friends in a comfortable living room talking of atomic war." Draft of call to strike by Eleanor Garst, Washington, D.C., 22 Sept. 1961. WSP Document Collection. (Mimeographed.)

9. *Newsweek,* 13 Nov. 1961, p. 21.

10. Eleanor Garst, "Women: Middle-Class Masses," *Fellowship* 28 (1 Nov. 1962):10–12.

11. Minutes of the WILPF National Executive Committee stated: "Each branch taking direct action should clear with the National Action Projects Committee. The committee should have, and send out to branches, a list of approved action and a list of the organizations with which we formally cooperate." Women's International League for Peace and Freedom, Minutes of the National Executive Committee meeting of 28–29 Sept. 1961. Swarthmore College Peace Collection, DG 43, Series A-2, Box 18, p. 5.

12. "Transcript of the President's News Conference on World and Domestic Affairs," *New York Times,* 16 Jan. 1962, p. 18.

13. *Science* 167 (13 Mar. 1970):1476.

14. A. E. Wessel, *The American Peace Movement: A Study of Its Themes and Political Potential* (Santa Monica: Rand Corporation, 1962), p. 3.

15. *New York Journal American,* 4 Apr. 1962, p. 10.

16. *San Francisco Examiner,* 21 May 1962, p. 10.

17. The FBI files on WSP are located in the offices of the Washington, D.C., law firm of Gaffney, Anspach, Shember, Klimasi, and Marx. These contain hundreds of documents from security officers in major cities to the director of the FBI and from the directors to the security officers. For instance, as early as 23 Oct. 1961, one week before the November 1st strike, the Cleveland office of the FBI already identified one of the WSP planning groups as communist. (FBI Document 100-39566-8). . . .

18. Those subpoenaed were (in order of appearance) Blanche Posner, Ruth Meyers, Lyla Hoffman, Elsie Neidenberg, Sylvia Contente, Rose Clinton, Iris Freed, Anna Mackenzie, Elizabeth Moss, Ceil Gross, Jean Brancato, Miriam Chesman, Norma Spector, and Dagmar Wilson. Spector never testified; she was excused due to illness. *Hearings before Committee on Un-American Activities,* p. iii.

19. Lillian Hellman, *Scoundrel Time* (Boston: Little, Brown & Co., 1976), p. 99.

20. Los Angeles WISP, Statement I, Ann Arbor Conference, June 9–10, 1962 (WSP Document Collection); . . .

21. "WSP National Policy Statement," *Women Strike for Peace Newsletter,* New York, New Jersey, Connecticut, Summer 1962, pp. 1–2.

22. "Key women" was the name used by WSP for those women who were part of the national and local communications network. They were the ones who were called upon to initiate actions or who called upon others to so.

23. Katz, "Peace, Politics, and Protest," pp. 122–26.

24. Homer Jack, "The Will of the WISP versus the Humiliation of HUAC," transcript of a talk on Radio Station WBAI, New York, 28 Dec. 1962 (WSP Document Collection).

25. The anti-HUAC statement by WSP was composed by the New York and Washington leadership in their usual collaborative fashion, with no pride or claim of authorship, so it is difficult to know which group wrote what part. It was distributed through official WSP channels via the national office in Washington.

26. Bentley, *Thirty Years of Treason,* p. 951.

27. Women Strike for Peace, Washington, D.C. to "Dear WISP's," 6 Dec. 1962 (WSP Document Collection).

28. Carol Urner to Representative Francis Walter reprinted in the *Women's Peace Movement Bulletin* 1 (20 Dec. 1962):5.

29. *Hearings before Committee on Un-American Activities,* pp. 2064–65.

30. Ibid., p. 2074.

31. Ibid., p. 2085.

32. Mary McGrory, "Prober Finds 'Peacemakers' More Than a Match," *Washington* (D.C.) *Evening Star,* 12 Dec. 1962, p. A-1.

33. *Hearings before Committee on Un-American Activities,* pp. 2095, 2101.

34. McGrory, "Prober Finds 'Peacemakers' More Than a Match," p. A-1.

35. Lyla Hoffman, undated typewritten statement (WSP Document Collection).

36. Thirty-seven favorable news stories, columns and editorials were reprinted in a hastily

prepared WSP booklet, published less than two weeks after the hearings. . . .

37. *Vancouver* (B.C.) *Sun*, 14 Dec. 1962, p. 2.

38. "The Ladies Turn Peace Quiz into Greek Comedy," *Detroit Free Press*, 16 Dec. 1962, p. 1.

39. *Detroit Free Press*, 13 Dec. 1962, p. A-8.

40. Mary McGrory, "Nobody Controls Anybody," *Washington* (D.C.) *Evening Star*, 14 Dec. 1962, pp. A-1, A-9.

41. *Hearings before Committee on Un-American Activities*, p. 2201.

42. *Madison* (Wis.) *Daily Cardinal*, 14 Dec. 1962, p. 2.

43. Garst, "Women: Middle-Class Masses," pp. 10–11.

44. Interview with Dagmar Wilson, Leesburg, Va., Sept. 1977.

45. *New York Times Magazine*, 6 May 1962, p. 32.

46. On a WSP activity measure, 38 percent rated themselves as "very active," 10 percent as "active," and 42 percent rated themselves as "not active," or only "slightly active." The profile of the majority of the WSP participants that emerged was indeed that of middle-class, well-educated housewives. . . .

Thirty-eight percent of the women who responded claimed to belong to no other organizations, or at least did not record the names of any organizations in response to questions concerning other community activities. Forty percent of the women were active in a combination of civic, race relations, civil liberties, peace, and electoral political activity. Only 11 percent were members of professional organizations. . . .

47. Ibid., p. 15.

48. Dorothy Dinnerstein, *The Mermaid and the Minotaur: Sexual Arrangements and Human Malaise* (New York: Harper Colophon Books, 1976), pp. 259–62.

49. Ashley Montagu, "The Triumph and Tragedy of the American Woman," *Saturday Review*, 27 (Sept. 1958):14; . . .

50. "Feminism as Femininity in the Nineteen Fifties?" Birmingham (England) Feminist History Group, *Feminist Review*, no. 3 (1979):48–65.

51. Sara Evans, *Personal Politics: The Roots of Women's Liberation in the Civil Rights Movement and the New Left* (New York: Alfred A. Knopf, 1979), p. 23.

CHARLES PAYNE

A Woman's War: African American Women in the Civil Rights Movement

Ask most people who made the civil rights movement happen and the names that come to mind are those of male leaders. Brilliant legal minds like Charles Houston and the inimitable Thurgood Marshall of the NAACP (National Association for the Advancement of Colored People) Legal Defense Fund and, of course, Roy Wilkins, also of the NAACP. Best known is the articulate and charismatic Reverend Martin Luther King, Jr., who reached out to white and black alike with his vision of a beloved community. Other names include Andrew Young and Jesse Jackson, who started out in King's SCLC (Southern Christian Leadership Conference); John Lewis and James Forman of SNCC (Student Nonviolent Coordinating Committee); and James Farmer, who orchestrated the Freedom Rides for CORE (Congress of Racial Equality).

Women's historians noted that women played important roles in the movement as well, pointing to, among others, Ella Baker, a veteran organizer who was the founding mother of SNCC; Fannie Lou Hamer, who went from sharecropper to civil rights activist

From *I've Got the Light of Freedom: The Community Organizing Tradition in the Mississippi Freedom Struggle* by Charles Payne. Copyright © 1995 The Regents of the University of California. Reprinted by permission of the University of California Press and the author. Notes have been renumbered and edited.

to founding member of the Mississippi Freedom Democratic Party; Septima Clark, who organized citizenship schools for SCLC; Jo Ann Robinson, head of the Women's Political Council, which started the bus boycott that King took over in Montgomery; Diane Nash, organizer of sit-ins and freedom rides for SNCC; and Ruby Doris Smith Robinson, SNCC's executive secretary and a powerful figure in the organization, which was at the vanguard of the movement.

While historians such as Kathryn Nasstrom* have probed the way memory shapes perception of participants' contributions to the civil rights movement, Charles Payne has used a different tactic in order to assess more accurately the role of women. He has looked at black women in rural Mississippi who were not leaders, but rather grassroots participants. In this selection, he seeks to explain their widespread involvement.

Since sex seems not to have insulated these women from white violence, and families as well as individuals were the focus of reprisals, why did these women take such risks? Are there factors you would add or expand upon in explaining their motivation? Do you see any similarities with the women of Flint, Michigan, who joined Genora Johnson Dollinger's Emergency Brigade during the CIO's unionizing effort in the 1930s?[†]

Asked to name all the women they can think of who were associated with the civil rights movement of the 1960s, most audiences are hard-pressed after Rosa Parks and Coretta King. In the South, a few may remember Mrs. Hamer. That so few women are remembered is ironic, to understate it. In the Delta, in the rural South generally, women were in fact much more politically active than men, at least in the early sixties. According to COFO (Council of Federated Organizations) organizers, women took civil rights workers into their homes, of course, giving them a place to eat and sleep, but women also canvassed more than men, showed up more frequently at mass meetings and demonstrations, and more frequently attempted to register to vote. There appears to be no disagreement with Lawrence Guyot's comment that "It's no secret that young people and women led organizationally."[1] Another organizer called the war in the Delta a woman's war.

The greater responsiveness of women represents a departure from the 1950s. Traditional wisdom among political scientists holds that across the Western world men are more politically involved than women.[2] The pattern in Mississippi during the 1950s appears consistent with that. In that especially dangerous period, Black political activism in rural Mississippi seems to have been dominated by men. There were women at all levels of the state NAACP hierarchy, but when they had official positions they tended to have those traditionally assigned to women—hospitality committee, secretary, membership committee—and they did not dominate the membership rolls in the way they would come to dominate many COFO-initiated movements.

The gender-related pattern of participation in the 1960s seems to have been age-specific. That is, among older folks, there is no clear imbalance. . . . Similarly, there does not seem to be any clear difference between teenage boys and teenage girls. The gender difference appears to be strongest in the years in between, the "settle-aged" years from, roughly, thirty to fifty. In that age range, some

---

*See Kathryn Nasstrom, "Down to Now: Memory, Narrative, and Women's Leadership in the Civil Rights Movement in Atlanta, Georgia," in *Gender and History* 11 (April 1999).

---

†One point of similarity between the two movements is that the sit-in, which the workers tried successfully for the first time in Dollinger's account, was borrowed by the civil rights movement and used by SNCC demonstrators at lunch counters and other segregated facilities, with equal success.

Young Elizabeth Eckford faces the gauntlet of racial heckling and hatred at the Court-ordered integration of schools in Little Rock, Arkansas in 1957. When the Arkansas governor defied the Supreme Court order, President Dwight Eisenhower reluctantly sent in federal troops to enforce it. Even with military protection, the young people who actually integrated public schools had to put up with racist slurs, harassment, and intimidation that required of them daily displays of uncommon courage and self-possession. Summoning up such courage became commonplace for thousands of rank-and-file African Americans, many of them girls and women. Indeed, it was women who carried the civil rights struggle at the grass-roots level, often at considerable risk to their physical safety and even their lives. As this picture makes clear, white women were promi-nent among the harassers. Other white women worked for integration in practice by keeping the schools open. (Photo by Will Counts.)

of my respondents estimated that women were three or four times more likely to participate than men. . . .

While there was virtually no disagreement among the people I spoke with about the nature of the pattern, there was no consensus at all about what explains it. . . . These gender differences were not something to which people had given a lot of thought, even though they were aware of them. This is not surprising, given that in 1962 or 1963 gender was not as politicized a social category as it became a few years later.

Joyce Ladner [a Black SNCC veteran and a sociologist] offered an explanation that made sense to several people:

> . . . Women in the rural South have a long history of being doers. This is what set them apart from a lot of white women who came into the movement. . . . If they were employed it was as a maid and not necessarily as major breadwinners in their families. They weren't as beholden to a paycheck. White people considered them less threatening. . . . Because Southern white men discounted women, period. Because of their strong sexism, they didn't see Black women as much more threatening than they did white women. . . .

Although not mentioned by anyone I interviewed, one factor that probably played some role was SNCC's operating style. Founded by a woman, in its early years, women were always involved in the development of policy and the execution of the group's program. . . . SNCC organizers were concerned with finding and helping to develop nontraditional sources of leadership. Women obviously represented an enormous pool of untapped leadership potential. . . . SNCC, despite the traditional expectations of sex roles held by many of its members,[3] was structurally and philosophically open to female participation in a way that many older organizations would not have been. . . . Still, SNCC's openness to the participation of women does not explain why women were so responsive. . . .

As Joyce Ladner noted, historically, Black women, especially poor Black women in rural areas, have had to fulfill social roles not commonly played by more privileged women. [Acclaimed Black writer] Zora Neale Hurston called southern Black women the mules of the world; they did whatever needed doing. Still, that has not always led to the kind of domi-

nance of political activity that we seem to have [had] in the rural South in the sixties. . . .

The notion that women were less exposed to reprisals than men has a certain plausibility. Southern whites, the argument goes, were less afraid of Black women and thus less likely to initiate either physical violence or economic reprisals against women. Even when economic reprisals were used, the wife's salary was likely to be less important to the family than the husband's. If anyone was going to be fired, better it be the wife. In short, it was simply safer, more cost-effective, for women to participate. . . . [But] the differential-exposure thesis minimizes the very substantial risks that women who joined the movement were running. . . . SNCC's newsletters in 1962 and 1963 suggest that some of the most violent incidents of reprisals took place against women. Women who were even rumored to be a part of the movement lost their jobs. . . . Any woman in Greenwood who contemplated joining the early movement had to be aware of all this. She would have also been aware of the absolutely brutal beating[s] that Annell Ponder, Mrs. Hamer, June Johnson, and Euvester Simpson had received in jail. . . .

Moreover, it is misleading to think of reprisals as being directed against merely the individual who was involved. Anyone who joined the movement placed his or her whole family at risk. . . . The Citizens' Council in particular made it a point to put pressure on the entire family. If anyone in a family was known to be a part of the movement, any adult in that family might have trouble finding work or getting credit. Similarly, the most popular forms of violence in that period—arson, drive-by shootings into homes, and bombings—were reprisals against family units, not just individuals. . . .

When explaining their own decision to join the movement, my respondents constructed answers primarily in terms of either religious belief or pre-existing social networks of kinship and friendship. For many women, both factors seem operative. Thus, Lou Emma Allen was drawn into the movement by her son, a junior-college student. Though she was often afraid, she was sure the Lord would see her through. Lula Belle Johnson got involved after June, her fourteen-year-old daughter, was arrested along with Fannie Lou Hamer and beaten. . . . Susie Morgan was drawn in partly by the activity of her daughters. She prayed and prayed over the decision to join, and finally she could see that it was what the Lord wanted her to do. . . .

The religious issue raises a series of important questions. One line of explanation for the overparticipation of women might go as follows: The movement grew out of the church. Women participate in the church more than men do. (One contemporary estimate is that across all varieties of Black religious activities, women represent seventy-five to ninety percent of the participants.)[4] . . .

This argument is probably more applicable to the urban South. In urban areas, the churches certainly were an early focal point of organizing activity.[5] It is not surprising that there would be a high level of participation by women in the activities of the Southern Christian Leadership Conference, because many of that organization's affiliates were large, urban churches populated largely by women. Their rural counterparts, however, were far less supportive of the movement. In Greenwood, . . . the early movement grew despite the opposition of the church. . . . Nonetheless, if the church as an organization did not lead people into the movement, the religiosity of the population may have been much more important. . . .

Those who joined the movement in its early days could not have known that things would work out as they did. What they knew for certain was that those who joined were going to suffer for it. From the viewpoint of most rural Black southerners in 1962 or 1963, the overwhelming preponderance of evidence must have suggested that the movement was going to fail. Joining a movement under such circumstances may literally require an act of faith. Faith in the Lord made it easier to have faith in the possibility of social change. As the slaves of a century ago, according to Du Bois, saw the fulfillment of Biblical prophecy in the coming of the Civil War, residents of the Delta may have seen the civil rights movement as a sign that God was stirring. . . .

NOTES

1. Howell Raines, *My Soul Is Rested* (New York: Putnam, 1977), p. 241.

2. See Seymour Lipset, *Political Man* (New York: Doubleday, 1960), pp. 189, 193–94. The book, considered a classic, is aptly named; its index contains no entry for "women."

3. Sara Evans, *Personal Politics* (New York: Vintage, 1980). The degree of sexism among men in SNCC has recently become an ongoing controversy, with Black women who participated saying that some white women participants have blown male chauvinism in the movement out of proportion and that they—Black women—were always able to exercise authority in some rough correspondence to their abilities and desires, and that they ignored or didn't care much about some expressions of chauvinism. See Joyce Ladner, "A Sociology of the Civil Rights Movement: An Insider's Perspective," presented at the annual meeting of the American Sociological Association, August 1988. Ladner points out that while Stokely Carmichael's remark about the position of women in the movement being prone has been much quoted, during his tenure as chair "he encouraged and supported women as project directors and as members of SNCC's Central Committee."

4. Cheryl Gilkes, "Together and In Harness: Women's Traditions in the Sanctified Church," *Signs* 10 (Summer 1985):679.

5. Aldon Morris, *Origins of the Civil Rights Movement* (New York: Free Press, 1984), esp. chs. 1, 4.

DOCUMENTS: Dimensions of Citizenship II

> *Pauli Murray, "I had entered law school preoccupied with the racial struggle . . . but I graduated an unabashed feminist as well. . . ."*

Pauli Murray was a remarkable woman. Born into a family that blended slaves, slave-owning whites, Cherokee Indians, freeborn African Americans—a family whose history she would later celebrate in her book *Proud Shoes*—she grew up an orphan in her grand-parents' home in Durham, North Carolina. Bright and energetic but poor, Murray graduated from the city's segregated schools in 1926. In a display of characteristic determination, she applied to Hunter College in New York City. Rejected because she was so poorly prepared, she moved in with a cousin, enrolled in high school in New York, and entered Hunter a year later. The struggle to find work and stay in school in the midst of the Great Depression was so intense, however, that Murray, already suffering from malnutrition, nearly succumbed to tuberculosis. Shortly after her graduation from Hunter in 1933, she found brief sanctuary in Camp Tera, one of the handful of women's camps established by the New Deal as a counterpart to the men's Civilian Conservation Corps, and then as an employee of remedial reading and workers' education projects funded by the WPA.

"World events were breeding a new militancy in younger Negroes like me," she would write; "One did not need Communist propaganda to expose the inescapable parallel between Nazi treatment of Jews in Germany and the repression of Negroes in the American South. Daily occurrences pointed up the hypocrisy of a United States policy that condemned Fascism abroad while tolerating an incipient Fascism within its own borders." In 1938, she applied to the law school at the University of North Carolina at Chapel Hill, attracted by the work of its sociologists on race relations and farm tenancy. Many law school students supported her admission, as did Frank Porter Graham, the president of the university, but state law mandated her rejection because of race.

Torn between her writing and law, Murray threw herself into working for social justice. Her involvement in the unsuccessful struggle to obtain clemency for Odell Waller, a black sharecropper whose right to be tried by a representative jury had been denied because Virginia called to jury service only those who had paid a poll tax, brought her to the attention of Leon Ransom of Howard University Law School in Washington, D.C. When Howard University offered her a scholarship in 1941, she entered law school "with the single-minded intention of destroying Jim Crow."

The following selections from her autobiography include an account of Murray's discovery of sexism amidst her battle with racism during her years at Howard University,

Excerpted from "Writing or Law School?," "Jim Crow in the Nation's Capital," and "Don't Get Mad, Get Smart" in *Song in a Weary Throat: An American Pilgrimage* (New York: Harper & Row, 1987), pp. 183–85, 205–9, 238–45, 361–62. Reprinted courtesy of the Charlotte Sheedy Agency, Inc.

and her leadership, eighteen years before the famous sit-ins in Greensboro, North Carolina, of a successful sit-in to desegregate a restaurant in Washington, D.C. Perhaps more than any other single person, Murray linked the civil rights movement with the federal quest for equity for women. After the establishment of New Deal wages and hours legislation, liberals began to recognize that the old protective labor laws (see pp. 340–41) were increasingly "protecting" women from better-paying "men's" jobs, just as the label of "privilege" was sustaining many inequalities, among them unequal access to professions and permissive rather than mandatory jury service (see pp. 546–50).

As early as 1947, Pauli Murray had begun to call discrimination on the basis of sex a system of "Jane Crow." In a biting and deeply personal essay published in *Negro Digest* entitled "Why Negro Girls Stay Single," Murray insisted that the "minority status" of women is suffered "despite their numerical size," and "independently of race, religion or politics." As a staff member of John F. Kennedy's Commission on the Status of Women in 1962, Murray grew firm in her conviction that "Jane Crow" and "Jim Crow" were twin evils. She welcomed the passage of the Civil Rights Act of 1964, with its notable Title VII outlawing employment discrimination on the basis of sex as well as race. With a colleague, Mary Eastwood, she wrote what would become a classic essay, "Jane Crow and the Law." The arguments made there would help make it possible for the Supreme Court to rule in 1971 that discrimination on the basis of sex was discrimination, not privilege.

Murray would go on to have an extraordinary legal career as a champion of racial and gender justice, serving on the National Board of the American Civil Liberties Union. In January 1977, she became one of the first women to be ordained as an Episcopal priest. Not long after, she was invited to celebrate her first Holy Eucharist in the Chapel of the Cross in Chapel Hill, the same church where the daughter of a prominent slave-holding family had many years before brought for baptism an infant whose father was her own lawyer brother, and whose mother was her own servant, Harriet. The infant was Pauli Murray's grandmother. On that occasion, "all the strands of my life came together," Murray wrote in an autobiography aptly subtitled "Activist, Feminist, Lawyer, Priest, and Poet." For Pauli Murray, the personal was indeed political.

Ironically, if Howard Law School equipped me for effective struggle against Jim Crow, it was also the place where I first became conscious of the twin evil of discriminatory sex bias, which I quickly labeled Jane Crow. In my preoccupation with the brutalities of racism, I had failed until now to recognize the subtler, more ambiguous expressions of sexism. In the all-female setting of Hunter College, women were prominent in professional and leadership positions. My awareness of the additional burden of sex discrimination had been further delayed by my WPA experience. Hilda Smith, national director of the WPA Workers' Education Project, was a woman, my local project director and my immediate supervisor were both women, and it had not occurred to me that women as a group received unequal treatment. Now, however, the racial factor was removed in the intimate environment of a Negro law school dominated by men, and the factor of gender was fully exposed.

During my first year at Howard there were only two women in the law school student body, both of us in the first-year class. When the other woman dropped out before the end of the first term, I was left as the only female for the rest of that year, and I remained the only woman in my class for the entire three-year course. While I was there, not more than two or three women enrolled in the lower classes of the law school. We had no women on the faculty, and the only woman professional on staff was . . . the registrar, who had graduated from the law school many years earlier.

The men were not openly hostile; in fact, they were friendly. But I soon learned that women were often the objects of ridicule disguised as a joke. I was shocked on the first day of class when one of our professors said in his opening remarks that he really didn't know why women came to law school, but that since we were there the men would have to put up with us. His banter brought forth loud laughter from the male students. I was too humiliated to respond, but though the professor did not know it, he had just guaranteed that I would become the top student in his class. Later I began to notice that no matter how well prepared I was or how often I raised my hand, I seldom got to recite. It was not that professors deliberately ignored me but that their freewheeling classroom style of informal discussion allowed the men's deeper voices to obliterate my lighter voice, and my classmates seemed to take it for granted that I had nothing to contribute. For much of that first year I was condemned to silence unless the male students exhausted their arguments or were completely stumped by a professor's question.

My real awakening came several months after school began, when I saw a notice on the official bulletin board inviting "all male students of the First Year Class" to a smoker at the residence of Professor Leon A. Ransom. The exclusion of women from the invitation was so pointed that I went to Dr. Ransom's office to seek an explanation. He told me blandly that Sigma Delta Tau, a legal fraternity limited to male students and members of the legal profession, had established a chapter at the law school and that the purpose of the smoker was to look over first-year men for likely prospects. Through their association with experienced lawyers these young men would enhance their professional development. I had not yet become aware of the sexist bias of the English language, and recalling that the national professional English "fraternity" to which I had been elected while in college included both sexes, I asked Dr. Ransom, "What about us women?"

To my surprise, Dr. Ransom merely chuckled and said that if we women wanted an organization we could set up a legal sorority. Angrily, I said it was ridiculous to speak of a legal sorority for two women, but he did not seem concerned about our plight. I left Dr. Ransom's office feeling both bewildered and

betrayed, especially because he was one of the most liberal professors on the university campus and had always treated me as a person. He had encouraged me to come to law school and used his influence to have me awarded a scholarship. Yet he did not seem to appreciate fully that barring women from an organization purporting to promote professional growth had the same degrading effect upon women as compelling us as Negroes to sit in the back of a bus or refusing to admit black lawyers to white bar associations. The discovery that Ransom and other men I deeply admired because of their dedication to civil rights, men who themselves had suffered racial indignities, could countenance exclusion of women from their professional association aroused an incipient feminism in me long before I knew the meaning of the term "feminism." . . .

The fact that an accident of gender exempted me from military service and left me free to pursue my career without interruption made me feel an extra responsibility to carry on the integration battle. Many other Howard University women were feeling a similar responsibility, which was heightened by the dramatic leave-taking of sixty-five Howard men, who marched off campus in a body to report for military duty. We women reasoned that it was our job to help make the country for which our black brothers were fighting a freer place in which to live when they returned from wartime service.

From the nightly bull sessions in Truth Hall a plan of action emerged. . . . It was designed to attract the widest possible support from all segments of the university community, with direct action reserved for the last of a series of steps. My role as student "legal adviser" was to make sure that our proposed actions were within the framework of legality so as not to arouse the official disapproval of the university administration. . . . Although we were engaged in serious business, our planning sessions were fun and challenged our power of imagination. The fact that we were doing something creative about our racial plight was exhilarating and increased our self-esteem. The Direct Action subcommittee attracted some of the leading students on campus, for it was important that those undertaking unorthodox activities maintain academic excellence. Also, we proceeded cautiously, aware that a misstep would compromise our goal. Instead of rushing precipitously into "hostile" territory, a group of students surveyed public eating places in the neighboring, mostly Negro community on Northwest U Street that still catered to the "White Trade Only." One of the most notorious of these lily-white establishments was the Little Palace Cafeteria, located at the busy intersection of Fourteenth and U streets, N.W., and run by a Mr. Chaconas. Because of its strategic location, the Little Palace had long been a source of mortification for countless unsuspecting Negroes, who entered it assuming that at least they would be served in the heart of the Negro section of the city.

The Little Palace Cafeteria was selected as our first target. For a week prior to our move against the cafeteria we held campus pep rallies and drummed up support for our effort through noon-hour broadcasts from the tower of Founder's Library. We decorated hot-chocolate cups and used them around campus as collection cans to solicit the funds we needed for paper, postage, and picket signs. We held a midweek Town Hall meeting and brought in experienced political leaders . . . to lead a forum on civil rights legislation and methods of achieving it. We conducted classes on the legal aspects of picketing and disorderly conduct in the District of Columbia, spent hours in small groups discussing public decorum, anticipating and preparing for the reactions of the black public, the white public, white customers, and white management respectively. We stressed the importance of a dignified appearance, and the subcommittee directed that all participants dress well for the occasion. We also pledged ourselves to exemplary nonviolent conduct, however great the provocation.

Finally, on April 17, a rainy Saturday afternoon, we assembled on campus and began to leave the Howard University grounds in groups of four, about five minutes apart, to make the ten-minute walk to the Little Palace Cafeteria. The demonstration was limited to a carefully selected group of volunteers—less than twenty students—who felt confident they could maintain self-restraint under pressure. As each group arrived, three entered the cafeteria while the fourth remained outside as an "observer." Inside, we took our trays to the steam table and as soon as we were refused service carried our empty trays to a vacant seat at one of the tables, took

out magazines, books of poetry or textbooks, notebooks and pencils, and assumed an attitude of concentrated study. Strict silence was maintained. Minutes later the next group arrived and repeated the process. Outside, the observers began to form a picket line with colorful signs reading "Our Boys, our Bonds, our Brothers are Fighting for YOU! Why Can't We Eat Here?"; "We Die Together—Why Can't We Eat Together?"; "There's No Segregation Law in D.C. What's Your Story, Little Palace?" Two pickets carried posters (prepared for the War Manpower Commission by the Office of War Information) depicting two workers—one black and the other white—working together as riveters on a steel plate. The inscription on the poster read "UNITED WE WIN!"

My heart thumped furiously as I sat at a table awaiting developments. The management was stunned at first, then after trying unsuccessfully to persuade us to leave, called the police. Almost immediately a half-dozen uniformed officers appeared. When they approached us we said simply, "We're waiting for service," and since we did not appear to be violating any law, they made no move to arrest us.

After forty-five minutes had passed and twelve Negro students were occupying most of the tables of the small cafeteria, Chaconas gave up and closed his restaurant eight hours earlier than his normal closing time. Those of us who were inside joined the picket line and kept it going for the rest of the afternoon. Chaconas told reporter Harry McAlpin, who covered the demonstration for the *Chicago Defender:* "I'll lose money, but I'd rather close up than practice democracy this way. The time is not ripe." When Juanita Morrow, a journalism student, interviewed Chaconas several days later, he admitted that he had lost about $180 that Saturday afternoon and evening, a considerable sum for a small business.

Actually, the incident did not arouse the furor we had feared but revealed the possibilities for change. When told why the place was closed and being picketed, a white customer named Raymond Starnes, who came from Charlotte, North Carolina, said, "I eat here regularly, and I don't care who eats here. All I want is to eat. I want the place to stay open. After all, we are all human." Another white bystander, asked what he thought of the students' action, replied, "I think it's reasonable.

Negroes are fighting to win this war for democracy just like whites. If it came to a vote, it would get my vote."

When Chaconas opened his place on Monday morning, our picket line was there to greet him, and it continued all day. Within forty-eight hours he capitulated and began to serve Negro customers. We were jubilant. Our conquest of a small "greasy spoon" eating place was a relatively minor skirmish in the long battle to end segregation in the nation's capital—a battle that was ended by a Supreme Court decision ten years later—but it loomed large in our eyes. We had proved that intelligent, imaginative action could bring positive results and, fortunately, we had won our first victory without an embarrassing incident. (One other small restaurant in the area was desegregated that spring before final examinations and summer vacation interrupted our campaign.)

Significantly, the prominent role of women in the leadership and planning of our protest was a by-product of the wartime thinning of the ranks of male students. Twelve of the nineteen Howard University demonstrators at the Little Palace on April 17 were female. . . . Many of those young women who had joined together to defy tradition would continue to make breakthroughs in their respective fields after their college days. . . . The youngest member of that little band of demonstrators, Patricia Roberts, carried the impact of her civil rights experiences from Howard University to the cabinet level of the federal government, [Patricia Roberts Harris served as President Carter's Secretary of Housing and Urban Development from 1977 to '79]. . . .

I had entered law school preoccupied with the racial struggle and single-mindedly bent upon becoming a civil rights attorney, but I graduated an unabashed feminist as well. Ironically, my effort to become a more proficient advocate in the first struggle led directly into the second through an unanticipated chain of events which began in the late fall of my senior year.

One day Dean Hastie called me into his office to discuss what I planned to do after graduation. To my utter surprise, he spoke of the possibility of my returning to teach at the law school after a year of graduate study, and with that possibility in mind he recommended that I apply for a Rosenwald fellowship. For a number of reasons, "graduate study" meant to me "graduate study at Harvard University." At least half of the Howard Law School faculty had studied at Harvard, both Hastie and Ransom held doctorates from its law school, and it had become a tradition at Howard to groom an exceptionally promising law graduate for a future faculty position by sending him to Harvard "to put on the gloss" of a prestigious graduate degree in law. My greatest rival in the preceding class, Francisco Carniero, who had graduated with top honors and as Chief Justice of the Court of Peers, was now completing his year of graduate law there. We had run neck and neck in courses we took together, he topping me by a couple of points in one and I topping him in another.

Naively unaware of Harvard's policy toward women, I was stunned when my schoolmates began kidding me. "Murray," someone said, "don't you know they're not going to let you into Harvard?" Harvard, it became clear, did not admit women to its law school.

Then my hopes were raised by a rumor which circulated around campus that Harvard was opening up to women students. Accordingly, when filling out my application to the Rosenwald Fund, I wrote in the space provided for choice of law school: "I should like to obtain my Master's degree at Harvard University, in the event they have removed their bar against women students. If not, then I should like to work at Yale University or at any other University which has advanced study in the field of labor law." I also wrote to the secretary of Harvard Law School, requesting confirmation or denial of the rumor I had heard. The answer was prompt. On January 5, 1944, the secretary's office wrote back: "Harvard Law School . . . is not open to women for registration."

This verdict was disappointing, of course, but with all the other preoccupations of my senior year, the matter probably would have rested there if I had not won the Rosenwald fellowship or at least if the names of the award winners had not been published nationwide. The announcement, made in late spring, listed me among fifteen white Southerners and twenty-two Negroes (including such notables as E. Franklin Frazier, Adelaide Cromwell Hill, Chester Himes, Rayford W. Logan, Dorothy Porter, and Margaret Walker) who received awards "for creative talent or distinguished scholarship." Mine was the only award in the field of law, and all the news stories reported that I was to do graduate study in labor law at Harvard University.

I was embarrassed to receive congratulatory messages from a number of people who were either unaware of Harvard's restrictive policy or assumed I had broken the barrier. At the same time, some of the men at Howard stepped up their banter, not without a touch of malicious glee. Until then I had been able to lick my wounds in private, but the public disclosure of my dilemma mortified me and presented a challenge I could not pass over lightly. If my schoolmates expected me to dissolve into tears under their stinging gibes, they were disappointed. I simply sat down and wrote a letter of application to Harvard Law School, which was duly processed, and I received a written request for my college transcript and a photograph.

In due course there came from Professor T. R. Powell, who chaired Harvard Law School's Committee on Graduate Studies, a letter that must have been dictated with an impish smirk. As nearly as I can recall, it ran: "Your picture and the salutation on your college transcript indicate that you are not of the sex entitled to be admitted to Harvard Law School." To appreciate the impact of this letter upon me, it is only necessary to remember the similar letter of rejection I had received in 1938 from the dean of the graduate school of the University of North Carolina in Chapel Hill: "Under the laws of North Carolina and under the resolutions of the Board of Trustees of the University of North Carolina, members of your race are not admitted to the University."

The personal hurt I felt now was no different from the personal hurt I had felt then. The niceties of distinction that in one case rejection was based upon custom and involved my sex and in the other was grounded in law and involved my race were wholly irrelevant to me. Both were equally unjust, stigmatizing me for a biological characteristic over which I had no control. But at least in the case of racial rebuffs long experience had taught me some coping mechanisms and I did not feel alone in that struggle. The fact that Harvard's rejection was a source of mild amusement rather than outrage to many of my male colleagues who were ardent civil rights advocates made it all the more bitter to swallow.

The harsh reality was that I was a minority within a minority, with all the built-in disadvantages such status entailed. Because of the considerable snobbery that—even apart from race and sex—existed in the highly competitive field of law, one's initial entry into the profession was profoundly affected by the law school one attended. This was particularly true for anyone who had ambitions to teach law. Since in my case the most common hurdles— lack of funds and a poor scholastic record— did not apply, I felt the injustice of the rejection even more strongly. I knew that however brilliant a record I had made at Howard, among my teaching colleagues I would never be considered on equal academic footing with someone who could boast of Harvard training. I also knew that the school of my second choice, Yale, had suspended its graduate program in law during the wartime emergency. [Professors William H.] Hastie and [Leon] Ransom, my law school mentors, understood my academic dilemma and were quietly supportive of my decision to pursue the Harvard matter further. Dr. [Caroline] Ware, whose great-great-grand-father Henry Ware had been the first dean of Harvard Divinity School and who grew up surrounded by the Harvard tradition, identified with me wholly in my fight. The only one of five generations of Phi Beta Kappas in her family not to take a Harvard degree, she held a Ph.D. from Radcliffe.

Then began the disheartening effort to budge a sluggishly corpulent bureaucracy on which my protests and appeals made about as much impression as a gnat on an elephant's hide. Harvard, being a private institution, was immune from legal attack and thus I had only the force of reason and logic with which to plead my case. A letter to Professor Powell asking what procedure to follow in appealing the law school's policy brought the information that the law school was bound by the rule of the Harvard Corporation not to admit women, and any appeal from that ruling would have to be submitted to the Corporation through its secretary, A. Calvert Smith.

Since my exclusion from Harvard was based solely on gender, my appeal necessarily was strongly feminist in tone:

> I have met a number of women and have heard of many more who wished to attend Harvard and yet were refused. This fight is not mine, but

that of women who feel they should have free access to the very best of legal education. . . .

Women are practicing before the Supreme Court, they have become judges and good lawyers, they are represented on the President's Cabinet and greater demand is being made for women lawyers in administrative positions as the men move into the armed forces. They are proving themselves worthy of the confidence and trust placed in them. . . . They are taking an intelligent view toward the political events at home and abroad, and statistics show they are in the majority of the voting population this year. A spot-check on memory would indicate there are only four important places they are not now holding—(1) As graduates of Harvard University, (2) as President of the United States, (3) as a member of the United States Supreme Court, and (4) as workers in the mines. Although [by admitting women] Harvard might lose in the sense of a loss of tradition, it might gain in the quality of the law school student personnel.

Meanwhile, two influential (if wholly unanticipated) male supporters sympathetic to the rights of women materialized. One was President Franklin D. Roosevelt! I had sent copies of the correspondence with Harvard to Mrs. Roosevelt, suggesting that the President might be amused at this attempt to storm the walls of his alma mater, never dreaming it would evoke more than a chuckle on his part. FDR was not merely amused; he actually wrote a letter on my behalf to President James B. Conant of Harvard University.

It would take more than one of that institution's most illustrious graduates to overturn a three-hundred-year tradition of male exclusiveness, however. President Conant's reply, sent on to me by FDR's secretary, only confused the issue. The letter assured President Roosevelt that I was free to do graduate work at Radcliffe, and even sent along a Radcliffe catalogue—never mind the obvious fact that Radcliffe did not offer graduate courses in law. I was flattered that the President of the United States had intervened on my behalf, but I was no nearer my goal. Mrs. Roosevelt was unequivocally in my corner, and wrote me a note saying: "I loved your Harvard appeal."

Lloyd K. Garrison, who was to become a lifelong friend and sponsor, was my second unexpected supporter. Mr. Garrison, former dean of the University of Wisconsin School of Law, was then a member of the National War Labor Board, which he later chaired. He was also a member of the Harvard Board of Overseers. I first met him through an ambitious undertaking of our student organization, the First Annual Court of Peers Dinner, jointly sponsored by the faculty and the Student Guild of Howard University School of Law. Mr. Garrison was our guest speaker, and as chief officer of the Student Guild it was my function to preside over the dinner and sit next to him at the speakers' table.

The great-grandson of abolitionist William Lloyd Garrison, Lloyd K. Garrison bore a striking resemblance to his famous ancestor and had inherited his commitment to human freedom. Unlike the fiery nineteenth-century Garrison, however, Lloyd K. Garrison combined a gentleness of disposition with a tough-minded pragmatism. . . . He was intensely interested in my effort to get into Harvard but warned me that I did not have a chance against the arch-conservative Harvard Corporation. Under the circumstances he encouraged me to follow an alternative plan for graduate study elsewhere, in the meantime pressing my appeal.

A. Calvert Smith informed me that the Harvard Corporation would review my appeal on July 10, by which time I had already applied to Boalt Hall [School] of Law, University of California at Berkeley, one of the few schools in the country whose wartime faculty of distinguished scholars remained relatively intact. On July 12, Mr. Smith wrote me to say that since I was asking, in effect, for a change in the long-established practice of the law school not to admit women, and since the conditions of admission to any department were in general set up by the faculty governing that department, "Whether or not women should be admitted to the Law School is . . . a decision for the Faculty of the Law School." Mr. Smith indicated that since no recommendation from the faculty of the law school was then before the Corporation, "it does not feel itself in a position to take any action on your application."

By sidestepping my appeal, the Harvard Corporation had rid itself temporarily of an annoying question, but it had also called into play a theory about the significance of individual action I had once announced half-seriously to Dr. Ware: "One person plus one typewriter constitutes a movement." If I could not compel admission to Harvard, at least I could raise the issue in such a way that its law school would be unable to avoid it. I was also learning the process of patiently following whatever administrative procedure was available even when there was every reason to believe the result would be futile.

My next letter was addressed to the Faculty of the Harvard Law School, summarizing the correspondence to date and requesting a meeting of the faculty "to reconsider my application and to decide whether it will recommend a change of the policy now in practice." I included a copy of my appeal to the Harvard Corporation and closed on a humorous note:

> [G]entlemen, I would gladly change my sex to meet your requirements but since the way to such change has not been revealed to me, I have no recourse but to appeal to you to change your minds on this subject. Are you to tell me that one is as difficult as the other?

As I had learned in the case of the University of North Carolina, correspondence could accomplish little more than stir up interest among a few key individuals and keep the issue flickering feebly. At the suggestion of Dr. Ware, I wrote to Judge Sarah T. Hughes of the United States District Court of Texas, who also chaired the Committee on Economic and Legal Status of Women. She replied that this was not a matter her committee had considered, but she said, "I shall be glad to discuss the problem at the next meeting which is in September," and asked that I keep her informed. After I left Washington, Dean Hastie wrote: "My best information on the Harvard situation is that the faculty is sharply divided on the matter of admitting women and will probably take the position that no action should be taken while a majority of the permanent faculty are on leave for war work." Lloyd K. Garrison's analysis prepared me for the inevitable. He wrote:

> From what I could pick up in Cambridge, my guesses are:
> (1) That the corporation will do nothing unless the Law School takes the initiative in asking that the rules be changed to admit women.
> (2) That the Law School will do nothing . . . , certainly not until Dean Landis gets back next fall and probably not then.
> (3) That this is due to combination of long tradition, an excessively high enrollment which has become an increasing headache [and]
> (4) A touch of some undefinable male egoism, which is, I think, rather particularly strong

in and around Boston as compared let us say with the middle west where we take our co-education for granted.

At my last meeting on the Board of Overseers [at Harvard] there was a great debate as to whether women should be admitted to the Medical School and, so I was told (I had to leave the meeting early), the proposal mustered only two votes out of a dozen. . . .

I was in California when the faculty of the Harvard School of Law met on August 7, 1944, and took action on my petition for review. A few days later, Acting Dean E. M. Morgan informed me of their decision. His letter said in part:

> In October, 1942, the Faculty thoroughly considered a proposal to request the University authorities to change the general rule. The first proposition was to admit women only during the emergency. This was almost immediately and unanimously rejected. The second proposal was for a permanent policy admitting women on exactly the same basis as men. This was debated by the Faculty at intervals for about three months, and the views of all members fully considered. There was much difference of opinion, but it was finally unanimously voted that no action looking to a change in the present practice be taken until after the emergency and after the School has returned to normal conditions with its full Faculty in residence. At that time the question will be debated anew. Accordingly it has been necessary to deny all applications for admission by women.
> At its meeting on August 7, the Faculty determined to abide by its previous decision.

Having lost my first battle against "Jane Crow," I was somewhat comforted to learn indirectly that the effort was not entirely wasted. That fall when I registered at the University of California's Boalt Hall [School] of Law, I was surprised to discover that news of the Harvard affair had traveled across country, and I was greeted with the remark, "So you're the woman who caused the Harvard Law School faculty to split 7-7 on your application." I also learned later of Harvard's announcement that women would be admitted to its medical school in 1945.

Fortunately, my controversy with Harvard was unresolved when I graduated from Howard in June, and it did not affect the high excitement of the ceremonies. Aunt Pauline came from Durham and Uncle Lewis Murray from Baltimore, each filled with proprietary pride and vying to share the honor of a niece who had "turned out so well." The high point of Aunt Pauline's visit was having tea at the White House with Mrs. Roosevelt. Then on Commencement Day an unexpected recognition electrified the huge outdoor gathering. Harry McAlpin, a reporter for the *Pittsburgh Courier*, captured the mood of the occasion in a story headlined "Flowers from the First Lady." He wrote:

> Flowers—a huge bouquet of them—delivered near the close of the Howard University commencement exercises last Friday, overshadowed all the previous proceedings of the impressive occasion. They were from Mrs. Roosevelt, wife of the President of the United States. They were for brilliant, active, strong-willed Pauli Murray, graduate cum laude of the Howard Law School.

According to McAlpin—no stranger to hyperbole—the arrival of the flowers overshadowed the commencement address . . . [and] the conferring of honorary degree[s]. . . .

Actually, the flowers had been delivered to the law school a half hour before the ceremonies began. When I came in to get my cap and gown, I glanced at them admiringly. . . . When someone finally made me realize it was my name on the card, I removed it, suggesting the flowers be placed on the platform for all the graduates to share. A few minutes later, the sight of University Secretary . . . parading across campus with the spectacularly beautiful display only moments before the academic procession began created an extra touch of excitement and added a special luster to the pageantry of the event. . . .

My intense involvement with the early stirrings of the resurgent feminist movement called on all my professional skills and kept me so busy I had no time to become demoralized. In 1965 and 1966, Title VII was the principal issue that fueled the movement, especially among business and professional women, as we battled against public attitudes ranging from ridicule to disregard of the new law. The Equal Employment Opportunity Commission (EEOC), charged with administration of the statute, was one of the chief offenders in that respect. A warning of what women might expect came shortly after the law went into effect, on July 2, 1965. EEOC Chairman Franklin D. Roosevelt, Jr., declared

in his first public statement that "the whole issue of sex discrimination is terribly complicated," and indicated that the Commission had not yet come to grips with most of the problems involved. Along with this lukewarm approach, Chairman Roosevelt announced the appointment of his seven key aides who would head the EEOC staff, giving a further clue to official indifference toward women's issues. All seven appointees to the staff were men, and not one of them had functioned on the President's Commission on the Status of Women or any of its study committees that had canvassed sex-based discrimination in employment. The prevailing attitude of the EEOC staff (with a few exceptions) seemed to be that of its executive director, Herman Edelsburg, who stated some months later at New York University's Annual Conference on Labor that the sex provision of Title VII was a "fluke" and "conceived out of wedlock." The newly appointed EEOC deputy general counsel had recently published a lengthy law review article on Title VII, offering an unduly restrictive interpretation of the sex provision as a prohibited ground of discrimination.

Only two of the EEOC's five commissioners responded sympathetically to representations made by women's groups: Richard Graham, a Republican appointed for a term of one year, who had been given responsibility for reviewing cases of sex discrimination, and Aileen Clarke Hernandez, the lone female member of the Commission, an honors graduate of Howard University and a former official of the International Ladies' Garment Workers' Union, with extensive experience in the administration of the California fair employment practices law. No pressure group existed to press for implementation of women's employment rights under the statute, and members of our feminist network who had fought to keep the word "sex" in Title VII were powerless to do more than sound an alarm. . . .

In the absence of organized group actions, we had to rely upon maximizing our individual efforts. Mary Eastwood and I coauthored a law review article entitled "Jane Crow and the Law: Sex Discrimination and Title VII," setting forth ways in which the Fifth and Fourteenth amendments and the sex provisions of Title VII could be interpreted to accord women equality of rights. We equated the evil of antifeminism (Jane Crow) with the evil of racism (Jim Crow), and we asserted that "the rights of women and the rights of Negroes are only different phases of the fundamental and indivisible issue of human rights." Published in the *George Washington Law Review* in Decem-

ber 1965, at a time when few authoritative legal materials on discrimination against women existed, our article broke new ground and was widely cited.

Hoyt *v.* Florida, *1961*; Taylor *v.* Louisiana, *1975*

When Pauli Murray surveyed the American landscape in 1962 for examples of sex discrimination, jury service was the first contemporary example to which she turned. Jury service was, she thought, the issue that most clearly illustrated widespread "confusion" about whether women had been oppressed by the law and required emancipation, or favored by the law and permitted easy exemption from an onerous duty.

Some members of the founding generation had believed that service on juries is a more significant aspect of citizenship than voting; voting, after all, is complete in a moment, while service on juries requires extended periods of time, debate, and deliberation among the jurors, and ultimately the exercise of judgment, which can result in important consequences—including the death sentence—for an accused fellow citizen. The Constitution promises an "impartial" jury drawn from "the district wherein the crime shall have been committed." The conditions of impartiality are not spelled out; the Constitution promises neither "a jury of one's peers," nor one drawn from a "cross-section" of the community. It is tradition that has linked the concept of the jury with "peers," neighbors, and the community in which the crime is committed and from which the jury is chosen.

When women achieved the vote in Wyoming in 1869, it seemed to follow that they could hold office and serve on juries, but after only a few years the objection of male voters and officeholders was so severe that the law was changed to exclude them.

In some states, the achievement of jury service followed painlessly on the heels of suffrage. In Iowa, Michigan, Nevada, and Pennsylvania, where statutes defined as competent jurors "all qualified electors . . . of good moral character, sound judgment, and in full possession of the senses of hearing and seeing, and who can speak, write and read the English language," the admission of women to the electorate automatically defined them as competent jurors. When these interpretations were tested in state courts, judges usually upheld them. Not all state courts, however, thought it was obvious that "electors" could be properly construed to mean women as well as men. In 1925 the Illinois Supreme Court ruled that because only men had been voters in 1874 when the jury statute had been passed, the terms "legal voters" and "electors" referred only to male persons. Not until 1939 did the Illinois state legislature permit women to serve on juries.

Hoyt v. *Florida* 368 U.S. 57 (1961); *Taylor* v. *Louisiana* 419 U.S. 522 (1975); *J.E.B.* v. *Alabama ex rel. T.B.* No. 92–1239 (April 19, 1994). For a full treatment of the history of women and jury service, see Linda K. Kerber, *No Constitutional Right to Be Ladies: Women and the Obligations of Citizenship* (New York: Hill and Wang, 1998), ch. 4.

In most states, new statutes were required. By 1923, eighteen states and the territory of Alaska had arranged for women to serve on juries. But then the momentum ran out; subsequently the issue had to be debated afresh in each state. A few states continued to exclude women completely, but most developed some form of "voluntary" jury service, in which women could be called to serve but could easily decline. In Florida, no women at all served on juries until 1949, when the legislature passed a law providing that women who wished to be eligible could go to their county courthouses and register their willingness to have their names placed in the jury pool.

When Gwendolyn Hoyt came to trial in Tampa in 1957, charged with manslaughter for killing her husband, only 218 women of the more than 46,000 women voters in Hillsborough County had registered to serve; the jury commissioner placed only 10 of those women's names in a pool of 10,000 names. It was no surprise that she was tried—and found guilty—by an all-male jury. It took the six-man jury only twenty-five minutes to convict Gwendolyn Hoyt of second-degree murder; on January 20, 1958, she was sentenced to imprisonment at hard labor for thirty years.

Hoyt appealed, first to the Florida Supreme Court, and then to the U.S. Supreme Court, which heard the case in 1961. Hoyt claimed temporary insanity, brought on by her suspicions of her husband's infidelity, his rejection of her offer of reconciliation, and her own vulnerability to epilepsy. She believed that women would understand her distress better than would men. Her lawyers did not claim that a fair jury was required to have women as members; rather, they claimed that a fair jury would have been drawn at random from a list of names from which women had not been excluded. Hoyt claimed that in order to have enjoyed the right to a trial by a jury of her peers, other women would have to be obligated to serve on juries. To grant other women the privilege of easy avoidance of jury duty, she and her lawyers thought, was to diminish Hoyt's right to a fair trial. The prosecution argued, instead, that if men and women were truly equal, Hoyt should have no objection to being judged by men.

MR. JUSTICE JOHN MARSHALL HARLAN:

At the core of appellant's argument is the claim that the nature of the crime of which she was convicted peculiarly demanded the inclusion of persons of her own sex on the jury. She was charged with killing her husband . . . in the context of a marital upheaval involving, among other things, the suspected infidelity of appellant's husband, and culminating in the husband's final rejection of his wife's efforts at reconciliation. It is claimed, in substance, that women jurors would have been more understanding or compassionate than men in assessing the quality of appellant's act and her defense of "temporary insanity." No claim is made that the jury as constituted was otherwise afflicted by any elements of supposed unfairness.

. . . [T]he right to an impartially selected jury assured by the Fourteenth Amendment . . . does not entitle one accused of crime to a jury tailored to the circumstances of the particular case, whether relating to the sex or other condition of the defendant, or to the nature of the charges to be tried. It requires only that the jury be indiscriminately drawn from among those eligible in the community for jury service, untrammelled by any arbitrary and systematic exclusions. . . . The result of this appeal must therefore depend on whether such an exclusion of women from jury service has been shown.

. . . Florida's [law] does not purport to exclude women from state jury service. Rather, the statute "gives to women the privilege to serve but does not impose service as a duty." It accords women an absolute exemption from jury service unless they expressly waive that privilege. . . . [W]e [cannot] . . . conclude that

THEY AUGUR NO GOOD FOR LOVE SLAYERS

When New York State *passed a voluntary jury service law for women in 1937, hundreds of women lined up to register. The* New York World Telegram *treated the story as cute; the caption identifying these women read: "Women jurors registering in the Hall of Records, and do they like it!" Dorothy Kenyon, a feminist attorney who had fought for fifteen years for mandatory jury service, welcomed the new statute as a first step: "This gives a new lease of life to the jury system." In the 1960s, Kenyon and Pauli Murray would lead the efforts of the American Civil Liberties Union to establish equitable jury service throughout the nation. (Courtesy of the Library of Congress.)*

Florida's statute is . . . infected with unconstitutionality. Despite the enlightened emancipation of women from the restrictions and protections of bygone years, and their entry into many parts of community life formerly considered to be reserved to men, woman is still regarded as the center of home and family life. We cannot say that it is constitutionally impermissible for a State, acting in pursuit of the general welfare, to conclude that a woman should be relieved from the civil duty of jury service unless she herself determines that such service is consistent with her own special responsibilities.

II

. . . Finding no substantial evidence whatever in this record that Florida has arbitrarily undertaken to exclude women from jury service . . . we must sustain the judgment of the Supreme Court of Florida.

JUSTICES WARREN, BLACK, AND DOUGLAS:

We cannot say from this record that Florida is not making a good faith effort to have women perform jury duty without discrimination on the ground of sex. Hence we concur in the result, for reasons set forth in Part II of the Court's opinion.

Why do you think Warren, Black, and Douglas wrote a separate concurring opinion? To what extent was the Court's opinion based on arguments from equality? on arguments from difference?

When Ruth Bader Ginsburg began to work on the ACLU's Women's Rights Project (see *Frontiero* v. *Richardson*, pp. 628–29), she was committed to persuading the Supreme Court to reverse its decisions on several major cases that had sustained sex discrimination; one of those cases was *Hoyt*. Not until 1975, in a case arising in Louisiana, a state in which women were still required to file a written declaration of their desire to be subject to jury service, was *Hoyt* reversed by the Supreme Court. Billy Taylor, convicted of rape and kidnapping, successfully appealed his conviction on the grounds that women had been systematically excluded from the jury pool. His lawyers drew an analogy between his experience and the Court's decision three years before that a white man was entitled to have a jury from which blacks had not been systematically barred. The majority opinion upheld Taylor's claim. It made extensive use of an opinion written by Justice William O. Douglas in 1946. What did Douglas mean when he said, "the two sexes are not fungible"? Do you agree?

MR. JUSTICE BYRON R. WHITE DELIVERED THE OPINION OF THE COURT:

The Louisiana jury-selection system does not disqualify women from jury service, but in operation its conceded systematic impact is that only a few women, grossly disproportionate to the number of eligible women in the community, are called for jury service. In this case, no women were on the venire from which the petit jury was drawn. . . .

The State first insists that Taylor, a male, has no standing to object to the exclusion of women from his jury. . . . Taylor was not a member of the excluded class; but there is no rule that claims such as Taylor presents may be made only by those defendants who are members of the group excluded from jury service. In [1972] . . . a white man [successfully] challenged his conviction on the ground that Negroes had been systematically excluded from jury service. . . .

We are . . . persuaded that the fair-cross-section requirement is violated by the systematic exclusion of women, who in the judicial district involved here amounted to 53 percent of the citizens eligible for jury service. . . . This very matter was debated in *Ballard* v. *U.S.* [1946]. . . . The . . . view that an all-male panel drawn from various groups in the community would be as truly representative as if women were included, was firmly rejected:

> . . . who would claim that a jury was truly representative of the community if all men were intentionally and systematically excluded from the panel? The truth is that the two sexes are not fungible; a community made up exclusively of one is different from a community composed of both; the subtle interplay of influence one on the other is among the imponderables. . . . The exclusion of one may indeed make the jury less representative of the community than would be true if an economic or racial group were excluded. [Justice William O. Douglas, 1946]

. . . It is untenable to suggest these days that it would be a special hardship for each and every woman to perform jury service . . . it may be burdensome to sort out those who should be exempted from those who should serve. But that task is performed in the case of men, and the administrative convenience in dealing with women as a class is insufficient justification for diluting the quality of community judgment represented by the jury in criminal trials.

The decision in *Taylor* addressed only the problem of who is included in the panels from whom jurors are chosen. Not until 1994 did the Supreme Court rule that the Fourteenth Amendment's equal protection clause prohibits the use of peremptory jury challenges on the basis of gender. Overturning a paternity suit in which a woman challenged virtually all the men in the jury pool, leaving an all-female jury to decide on her claims for child support, the majority held "that gender, like race, is an unconstitutional proxy for juror competence and impartiality."*

*J.E.B. v. *Alabama* 511 U.S. 127 (1994).

Civil Rights Act, Title VII, 1964

The Civil Rights Act of 1964 was a comprehensive law of enormous significance. It was a complex statute, twenty-eight printed pages long and divided into eleven major sections, or *Titles*. Title I dealt with voting rights; Title III with the desegregation of public facilities; Title V established a Commission on Civil Rights. Title VII defined a long list of practices that would be forbidden to employers and labor unions, obliged the federal government to undertake an "affirmative" program of equal employment opportunity for all employees and job applicants, and created an Equal Employment Opportunity Commission (EEOC) to monitor compliance with the law.

Title VII was notable in that it outlawed discrimination on the basis of gender as well as race. Sex was added to the categories "race, color, religion and national origin" by Congressman Howard Smith, a conservative Democrat from Virginia, who was a vigorous opponent of civil rights legislation. He introduced his motion after urging from Republican supporters of the National Women's Party, who had been lobbying for an Equal Rights Amendment whether or not it would undermine protective labor legislation, and who wanted to equate discrimination on the basis of race and discrimination on the basis of sex. The debate on Smith's motion was filled with misogyny; Smith joked that his amendment would guarantee the "right" of every woman to a husband. But it passed, supported by conservative members who were more comfortable voting for a civil rights bill if there was something in it for white women.

The Equal Employment Opportunity Commission, which began to operate in the summer of 1965, anticipated that virtually all its complaints would come from blacks. They were surprised to discover that 25 percent of the complaints received during the

U.S. Statutes at Large, 78:253–66. For a discussion of the circumstances of the passage of Title VII, see Jo Freeman, "How 'Sex' Got into Title VII: Persistent Opportunism as a Maker of Public Policy," *Law and Inequality* IX (1991): 163–84.

first year were from women. In the course of responding to these complaints, both the commission and the courts were driven to a more subtle analysis of female job categories and work patterns. Section 703(e)1 required that employers wishing to define a job category by sex had to show that sex was a "bona fide occupational qualification"; it was not enough to say that men or women had traditionally filled any given job.

In the decade that followed, most states developed their own versions of Title VII, establishing laws that prohibited sex discrimination in employment. The federal statute was amended in 1972 and again in 1978; on both occasions the EEOC was given substantial additional powers and responsibilities. The three major areas of EEOC activity are: (1) furnishing assistance to comparable state agencies, (2) furnishing advice to employers and labor unions about compliance, and (3) enforcing compliance by conciliation and by legal action. In 1978 Congress passed the Pregnancy Discrimination Act, which amplified the definition of sex to include pregnancy, childbirth, or related medical conditions. EEOC has been willing to view sexual harassment as a form of sex discrimination but has not endorsed the concept of comparable worth.

Sec. 703.(a) It shall be an unlawful employment practice for an employer—

(1) to fail or refuse to hire or to discharge any individual, or otherwise to discriminate against any individual with respect to his compensation, terms, conditions, or privileges of employment, because of such individual's race, color, religion, sex, or national origin; or

(2) to limit, segregate, or classify his employees in any way which would deprive or tend to deprive any individual of employment opportunities or otherwise adversely affect his status as an employee, because of such individual's race, color, religion, sex, or national origin.

(b) It shall be an unlawful employment practice for an employment agency to fail or refuse to refer for employment, or otherwise to discriminate against, any individual because of his race, color, religion, sex, or national origin, or to classify or refer for employment any individual on the basis of his race, color, religion, sex, or national origin.

(c) It shall be an unlawful employment practice for a labor organization—

(1) to exclude or to expel from its membership, or otherwise to discriminate against, any individual because of his race, color, religion, sex, or national origin;

(2) to limit, segregate, or classify its membership, or to classify or fail or refuse to refer for employment any individual, in any way which would deprive or tend to deprive any individual of employment opportunities, or would limit such employment opportunities or otherwise adversely affect his status as an employee or as

an applicant for employment, because of such individual's race, color, religion, sex, or national origin; or

(3) to cause or attempt to cause an employer to discriminate against an individual in violation of this section. . . .

(e) Notwithstanding any other provision of this title, (1) it shall not be an unlawful employment practice for an employer to hire and employ employees, for an employment agency to classify, or refer for employment any individual, for a labor organization to classify its membership or to classify or refer for employment any individual, or for an employer, labor organization, or joint labor-management committee controlling apprenticeship or other training or retraining programs to admit or employ any individual in any such program, on the basis of his religion, sex, or national origin in those certain instances where religion, sex, or national origin is a bona fide occupational qualification reasonably necessary to normal operation of that particular business or enterprise. . . .

Sec. 705.(a) There is hereby created a Commission to be known as the Equal Employment Opportunity Commission, which shall be composed of five members, not more than three of whom shall be members of the same political party, who shall be appointed by the President by and with the advice and consent of the Senate. . . .

(g) The Commission shall have power—

(1) to cooperate with and, with their consent, uti-

lize regional, State, local, and other agencies, both public and private, and individuals; ...

(3) to furnish to persons subject to this title such technical assistance as they may request to further their compliance with this title or an order issued thereunder;

(4) upon the request of (i) any employer, whose employees or some of them, or (ii) any labor organization, whose members or some of them, refuse or threaten to refuse to cooperate in effectuating the provisions of this title, to assist in such effectuation by conciliation or such other remedial action as is provided by this title;

(5) to make such technical studies as are appropriate to effectuate the purposes and policies of this title and to make the results of such studies available to the public;

(6) to refer matters to the Attorney General with recommendations for intervention in a civil action brought by an aggrieved party under section 706, or for the institution of a civil action by the Attorney General under section 707, and to advise, consult, and assist the Attorney General on such matters. . . .

FELICIA KORNBLUH

A Human Right to Welfare? Social Protest among Women Welfare Recipients after World War II

In the Cold War years, racial justice became a new and compelling terrain for progressive white women; for black women it had always been an imperative. In the aftermath of the historic Supreme Court decision banning school segregation, black and white women in Southern cities such as Atlanta and Little Rock worked to keep public schools open so as to begin the process of integration. By the 1960s, the civil rights movement elicited the involvement of young college-age women of both races and the leadership of remarkable African American women.

Rights talk was contagious. As the focus of the civil rights movement shifted from the South to the urban areas of the North, it became increasingly clear to national leaders of both races that there could be no racial justice without economic justice. It was in this context that the Johnson administration declared its war on poverty.

As Martin Luther King turned his attention to the poor, so did another civil rights activist, George Wiley. Wiley's focus was on a particular segment of the poor—those on welfare. In his quest for welfare rights, he found allies in a new breed of "poverty lawyers" who mounted a legal campaign to persuade the Supreme Court that there was a constitutional right to welfare. But the story of the welfare rights movement was never just the story of a litigation strategy that ultimately failed. The National Welfare Rights Organization (NWRO) that Wiley formed was intended to mobilize the poor at the grassroots level. While the organization was interracial, its rank-and-file members were overwhelmingly black and female. Most were recipients of funds through the government program known as Aid to Families with Dependent Children (AFDC), which had its

Prepared especially for *Women's America*. Copyright © 1998 by Felicia Kornbluh.

origins in mothers' pensions. (Mothers' pensions were government stipends paid to eligible widows to enable them to stay at home and care for their children.) As was the case with mothers' pensions, AFDC was means-tested and involved supervision of recipients by social workers.

This mobilization of welfare mothers, especially poor African American women, marked a first in American history. As these women marched on local welfare offices and ultimately on the national capital under the banner of "Mother Power," they demonstrated that maternalism knew no color. The realities of welfare that brought these women into the NWRO, how they understood their goals and "rights," and what tactics they used to achieve them is the focus of Felicia Kornbluh's essay.

To what extent did the consumerism that had permeated American culture since the end of World War II influence NWRO members' definition of "basic needs"? How were these relatively powerless women attempting to reconfigure basic American understanding of right and obligations? Do you see any continuities in their understanding of life's necessities and that of an earlier generation of young labor organizers and working-class reformers encountered in Part III? To what extent do the concerns of NWRO mothers remain relevant in an era of shrinking government aid to the poor? Is there a "right" to basic survival?

Welfare gives us enough for food and rent and second-hand clothes for us and our children, and in some states, not even enough for food. But food and rent is not all of life. Why shouldn't we be able to buy perfume once in a while—or a ring—or even a watch? Every woman wants and needs some of these things—particularly when we see all other women having them. If we put money in the collection plate at church, we're taking food out of our children's mouths. Our children drop out of school because they don't have decent clothes, let alone the things that other children take for granted—enough school supplies, money for a class trip, a graduation suit or dress.

—Mrs. Juliet Greenlaw,
Indiana State Representative,
National Welfare Rights
Organization, 1968[1]

Between 1963 and 1973 a grass-roots movement of welfare recipients changed the political conversation about welfare in the United States. This movement has not received much attention in history books, including accounts of 1960s organizing and histories of women.[2] However, for several years it captured public attention, inspired heated debates,

and compelled both national and local government officials to recognize the perspectives of some of their poorest constituents. The welfare rights effort crossed paths with other social change campaigns, including those of white feminists, black civil rights activists, and members of the New Left who organized against the Vietnam War. Welfare rights activists differed from their counterparts in the other movements in their intense focus on economic inequality and their lack of faith in the private labor market to fill the gaps between the material needs of poor people and their resources.

Beginning in 1967, a National Welfare Rights Organization (NWRO) with headquarters in Washington, D.C., represented this movement and coordinated many of its activities. At its height in 1969, NWRO membership reached approximately 25,000 welfare recipients and other poor people. Thousands more participated in actions sponsored by NWRO's local affiliates or organized for welfare rights with unaffiliated groups.[3] By 1971, NWRO encompassed 540 local Welfare Rights Organizations (WROs), located primarily in big cities in the Northeast, Midwest, and California. A majority of welfare rights activists were African American women. Smaller numbers were Puerto Rican, Chicana/o, Native American, or white. Perhaps 10% of them were men.[4] Although low-income mothers with children

Johnnie Tillmon addressing a Mother's Day March on Washington, circa 1968 or 1969. George Wiley sits directly behind her, on the left; Ethel Kennedy looks on. (Courtesy State Historical Society of Wisconsin. Whi (x3) 62064. Lot 5025.)

predominated in the movement, smaller numbers of senior citizens, disabled people, public housing tenants, and tenant farmers—recipients of such government programs as Aid to Families with Dependent Children (AFDC), Old Age Assistance, Aid to the Disabled, food stamps, and Indian Welfare—rallied to the cry of rights for clients of the welfare state.

These activists made four primary arguments about why they had a right to welfare. First, they argued that access to welfare in times of need was part of their inheritance as American citizens. Second, they argued that as women of color, welfare was essential to their equality—a means to narrow the economic gap between themselves and those Mrs. Juliet Greenlaw in the epigraph identified as "all other women." Third, some welfare rights activists claimed that they deserved benefits because they did the difficult, but socially necessary, work of raising young children. Fourth, many others argued that they deserved benefits because they were human beings who possessed a "right to live." This "right to live" encompassed not only a right to base survival, but also a right to the goods and services that

signified normality in postwar America, including many of the things that Greenlaw pointed out: "[D]ecent clothes" or "money for a class trip" for school-aged children, and for adult women, not only "food and rent" but also "perfume . . . a ring—or even a watch."

As part of the argument that they possessed a "right to live" in modern terms, activists criticized the welfare system for underestimating the needs of families. They fought welfare authorities over the contents of the welfare budget, the breakdown of welfare families' needs that formed the basis of their biweekly welfare grants. They also fought over the assessments that case workers and other welfare authorities made of what they called the "basic" and "special needs" of clients—charging in general that clients' basic needs were more profound, and their special needs more frequent, than welfare officials recognized.[5] Welfare rights activists utilized loopholes in the rules that governed welfare practice, legal challenges, and confrontational tactics to gain what they saw as the material substance of their human rights from reluctant welfare administrations.

"I SHOULD AT LEAST BE TREATED LIKE A HUMAN BEING": BUDGETS AND NEEDS

The welfare budget of a public assistance recipient in the 1960s was a complex entity. Although all recipients had the same right to aid as specified under the federal program AFDC, states and localities had wide discretion in the way they administered the program. They, in turn, directed caseworkers to calculate the budget of each individual or family separately, based on the caseworker's understanding of the particular situation.[6] Caseworkers had one major guide in making their determinations, the Welfare Manual that the local department issued to all employees. The manual was full of details about the basic welfare budget—scaled to family size and children's ages, dependent upon whether the people in question received AFDC, Home Relief,[7] or Old Age Assistance,[8] on what they paid for rent, and on whether they had a washing machine or needed to pay separately for laundry.[9] The manual also detailed the numerous goods welfare departments expected families to have to bring them "up to standard." These were the "basic needs" that welfare administrators thought all families required as a prerequisite before they could provide for their families with the biweekly grant. In New York City, welfare officials determined that an "adequate basic supply" of clothing that would bring an adult woman "up to standard" included:

1 hat	2 cotton dresses
1 "dressy dress"	3 pairs of panties
1 girdle	2 pairs of stockings, etc.[10]

The manual contained specified appropriate "unit prices" for each of the items, for both regular and large sizes. The basic supply of furniture and household equipment that would bring a family "up to standard" included:

Living Room:

Couch ("spring on legs with new cotton linters mattress")

"Table—drop leaf or extension (wood)"

Kitchen:

"Dinette set (table and 4 chairs)"

"Linoleum (new)"

Cooking Equipment:

"Paring knife"

"Egg beater, rotary type"

"Fruit reamer, glass"[11]

In addition to these "basic needs," Welfare Manuals itemized various "special needs" that welfare clients might encounter, which the welfare department might pay for on a one-time-only basis or under certain circumstances. These ran the gamut from a special diet for a diabetic welfare recipient, to transportation to a doctor's visit, to baby-sitting or child care help for an "overburdened mother" who was certified as such by a Case Supervisor.[12] The total amount a family or individual received in the welfare check was to be a combination of its basic budget, plus any "basic needs" that the welfare department was meeting to bring the case "up to standard," plus payment to fulfill various "special needs," minus amounts earned from employment; received in gifts, alimony, or child support; or due the welfare department because of a prior overpayment.

Although Welfare Manuals stipulated an enormous array of consumer goods (from a fruit reamer to a "dressy dress") that families were supposed to receive to bring them "up to standard," welfare departments almost never brought their clients fully up to standard. Neither did they fully meet recipients' "special needs." They were able to maintain wide gaps between what they theoretically maintained welfare clients should have and what they in fact offered these clients by tightly controlling the information in the manual.

The welfare rights movement exploited the ambiguities of this system. The first strategic objective of most WROs was to get hold of the Welfare Manual. Next, WRO members sought collectively to make welfare departments narrow the gap between manual and reality, by making good on their stated standards for "basic" and "special needs"—that is, by distributing enormous quantities of cash or in-kind benefits to recipients. Often the WRO would distribute a simple one-page flier to all of its members asking them to check off the things they did not have, but which the welfare department claimed every family needed if it was to survive on a welfare budget. Members would submit these "basic needs" forms to welfare departments together in large batches.

Complaints and protests about the welfare budget were widespread within the welfare rights movement. In Columbus, Ohio, for example, an AFDC recipient and movement poet named Mary Spurlock did her own rendition of the welfare budget. Whereas welfare administrators presented budgets as adequate to cover the food and other expenses of thirty families, Spurlock associated the welfare budget with terms such as "Wanting," "Envy," "Losing," "Begging," "Underfed," and "Tears."[13] On the occasion of a Sunday morning welfare rights protest at the church of the Governor of Ohio, Spurlock contributed "Ten Welfare Commandments," which pointed up many of the things she believed should be included in welfare cost accounting:[14]

1— Thou shall give thy children what they need—but don't spend over 73c. a day.
2— Thou shall have furniture—if glue will hold it together.
3— Thou shall live in a real nice house—in the slums.
4— Thou shall clothe thy children—as long as their clothes are rags.
5— Thou shall send thy children to school but don't give them any supplies.
6— Thou shall feed thy children—but don't give them meat.
7— Thou shall not buy any underclothes—no one sees them.
8— Thou shall not give thy children spending money—let them beg.
9— Thou shall not ride a bus up-town—Walk!
10— Thou shall not get sick—just die.[15]

Spurlock registered her protest at the low figures the Ohio welfare department budgeted for items such as clothing, especially underclothes ("no one sees them"), transportation ("Walk!") and food. The official symbol of the Columbus Welfare Rights Organization was an empty horn of plenty, turned upside down, perhaps symbolizing how little welfare recipients such as Spurlock believed they received from the bounty of postwar America.[16]

Welfare activists also had more discrete complaints regarding needs that welfare budgets failed to cover. Mrs. Andrea Keyes, an NWRO member from Meriden, Connecticut, expressed her concerns about welfare cuts in her state in a letter to the NWRO staff in Wash-

ington. "With a total of $6.41 left monthly after expenses," she asked, "where will I get the money to buy women's monthly needs, clothing for my sons & myself, household needs, and appliance repairs[?] I feel that I should at least be treated like a human being."[17] In New York City, a neighborhood activist lampooned the hypocrisy he saw in the welfare department's suggestions to recipients about how to attain a healthy diet:

> The heighth of bureaucratic idiocy has finally been reached.... The D[epartment of] W[elfare] has large, beautiful, colored posters in the various centers, illustrating many food items, with the advice to welfare clients that in order to maintain a balanced healthy diet, the pictured items should become a part of their daily fare.
>
> With the price of fruits and vegetables today ... and with the present welfare allotments (would you believe $1.12 cents a day for a single man?) to follow the DW advice would call for a more than tripling of food allotments [in the budget] ...
>
> Welfare recipients can't even afford the paper the poster is made of, let alone the items pictured.[18]

The implication here was that welfare department employees did not understand consumer prices as well as did recipients themselves. Moreover, it suggested that welfare employees constructed budgets ("would you believe $1.12 cents a day for a single man?") that made it impossible for recipients to have such ordinary amenities as fresh fruits and vegetables.

Welfare recipients complained about specific goods that they felt they needed, but that welfare departments denied or called into question. Mrs. Eliza Williams, a WRO leader, wrote in 1969 to Health, Education, and Welfare Secretary Robert Finch. She complained that some of her elderly neighbors "have been badly mistreated by the Welfare department." As for one, Mr. Moses Hemingway, Williams explained: "He is in need of clothing, has to go to the hospital and he doesn't have any pajamas ... This is what the elderly has to go through. This is their last plea for their rightly needs. If you can't help then the next step is to demolish the whole Welfare program."[19] In a letter she mailed to New York City Mayor John Lindsay and other officials, AFDC recipient Annie Frett complained: "There is no protection for people on welfare who trie [sic] to help themselves, or justice." She wrote of the welfare department's refusal to help her move to what she considered a decent apartment and its reluctance to help pay her bills, and then asked:

WHAT LAW OR RULE IS THERE THAT SAYS THAT A NEGRO WOMAN MUST USE ONE BOX OF SANITARY NAPKINS A MONTH AND NO MORE? I WAS QUESTIONED BY A [CASE] WORKE[R] ABOUT THAT.[20]

Frett appears to have reached the end of her tether with a welfare department that she saw as denying her the basics in terms of shelter, utilities, and even personal hygiene.

LEGAL APPEALS: THE CASE OF THE CHROME DINETTE

When welfare recipients such as Annie Frett, Eliza Williams, or Andrea Keyes were dissatisfied with the decisions of their local welfare departments, they could formally appeal the decisions. These appeals were also available to welfare rights groups that were dissatisfied with the responses they received to collective requests for "basic" and "special needs." From the early 1960s through the early 1970s, both individual welfare recipients and organized welfare rights organizations made increasing use of these appeals, called "Fair Hearings." Fair hearings became a particularly effective backup tool for protests over the budgeting decisions of local welfare departments. When caseworkers and welfare department directors failed to fulfill clients' stated needs, dragged their heels on responding to clients' requests, or refused requests without explanation, the clients could always appeal. At least initially, the hearings were costly to welfare departments in terms of money, bureaucratic attention, and negative publicity. Often welfare departments chose to fulfill clients' demands for new budgets, or "basic" and "special needs," rather than pay these costs.

The role of fair hearings as backups to efforts by welfare recipients to compel welfare departments to meet what they saw as their needs appears in the case of Margaret Hayes. This case also illustrates the degree to which battles over such needs amounted to battles between welfare recipients and welfare department personnel over the question of who would determine the specifics of welfare fam-

ilies' needs. Margaret Hayes was an NWRO activist from Newport News, Virginia, and a recipient of supplementary welfare benefits, which she received in addition to her salary as a school bus driver.[21] Hayes requested a grant to fulfill her "basic need" for a dinette set. Department personnel agreed to pay for a dinette, but determined that the reasonable set cost $100, while the one Mrs. Hayes wanted cost almost three times more. Hayes decided to accept the $100 and to find the rest of the money for the furniture she wanted from another source, but welfare officials refused to give her the money. She brought a fair hearing, which she lost. She then appealed to the Commonwealth of Virginia's Director of Welfare and Institutions to reopen the case. The official summary of Mrs. Hayes's fair hearing notes that she:

Stated that she was ... informed by [case] worker, Supervisor and Superintendent that the estimates [she obtained] were too high and that the agency would sanction a chrome [dinette] set in the price range of $100.00. Stated that she would not accept a chrome set (would not say why), that she wanted a wood set and this was the reason for her appeal. Stated that the agency has "lowered her dignity" by not giving her a check for the furniture so that she could buy the kind of set she wanted to suit her specifications.

Appellant stated that she had read the Manual and in her opinion the estimates for a wooden set were not unreasonable ... Appellant queried Superintendent as to what her check would be if she didn't work at all. Stated that if she didn't get a wood dinette set of her own choice she would go to "Richmond" [i.e., to the Commonwealth Welfare Department], that she was sick and tired of getting the "run around" by the Local Department.

Agency representative attempted to explain to appellant that the need for a dinette set was recognized, but that the agency was obligated to authorize those items sold for a reasonable price ... That the Department kept a file on local sales and that chrome dinette set could be bought for approximately $100.00.[22]

The conflict between Margaret Hayes and the authorities in Newport News emerged from the context of a welfare system that gave the authority to define clients' needs to local officials and not to the clients themselves. As much as it concerned the dinette set, Hayes's appeal may have concerned her claim as a mother, and a welfare recipient with rights, to define her material needs. What "'lowered her dignity'" in particular may have been the department's insistence that she buy only the set her case-worker thought was offered "for a reasonable price"—especially since "in her opinion the estimates" she obtained "for a wooden set were not unreasonable." In correspondence to the Virginia Director of Welfare and Institutions, Hayes further explained her position:

> The furniture which I desired to purchase costs more than the $100 which the Department feels welfare recipients should be satisfied with. I told my caseworker that if $100 was all that the Department would allow, then I would accept the $100 and apply it toward the dining set of my choice . . . In your letter you say that the State Board found that the $100 offered by the welfare was not acceptable to me. This is not true. The whole question is whether the Department will give me the $100 not whether I will accept it.[23]

In response, an welfare official advised Mrs. Hayes that when she found "a dinette set of your choice which will not cost more than the amount of $100.00, we believe the local agency will be willing to reconsider your request."[24] The welfare departments, at both the county and state levels, were as fixed in their position as Mrs. Hayes was in hers. As much as she considered it a component of her dignity to choose the furniture she wanted instead of set-tling for what "the Department feels welfare recipients should be satisfied with," welfare administrators apparently considered it im-perative that Hayes buy what they considered "reasonable" merchandise instead of using public money to do what she liked in the con-sumer marketplace.

Beyond their needs for basic food and cloth-ing, welfare rights activists who mobilized in the 1960s saw as part of their human rights a range of additional goods and services that would help round out their lives. For Juliet Greenlaw it was "perfume" or "a watch," for Mary Spurlock a little meat in her children's diets, and for Margaret Hayes a wood dinette set that represented the material minimum for being "a human being" in the affluent United States. These and other public assistance recip-ients did what few poor people had ever done before: They formed a national movement that placed its own political perspectives on the public agenda.

The essence of this perspective was an insistence that the recipients of public benefits had rights—rights as Americans, rights as peo-ple of color who had never yet enjoyed the fruits of full citizenship, rights as mothers, and rights as human beings. Unlike the women who formed the nucleus of the feminist move-ment of the 1960s, they did not ask for greater access to the wage labor market. Unlike virtu-ally all parties to the welfare reform debates of the years since then, welfare rights activists did not generally believe that they needed to work outside their homes in order to justify receiv-ing welfare. In light of these later debates, the political vision of the welfare rights movement seems almost irremediably far off. However, while the historical moment that shaped the welfare rights movement will not come again, remembering the concerns that welfare recipi-ents voiced at the high-water mark of their political influence may help us imagine alter-natives to the narrowness that has prevailed when welfare policy proceeded as though their perspectives did not matter.[25]

NOTES

1. Mrs. Juliet Greenlaw, "Statement of National Welfare Rights Organization to the Democratic Plat-form Hearing," August 16, 1968, from Box 2101, file titled "Demo Platform August 19, 1968," NWRO papers, Moorland-Spingarn Research Center, Howard University.

2. Exceptions include such histories of black women as Paula Giddings, *When and Where I Enter: The Impact of Black Women on Race and Sex in Amer-ica* (New York, 1984), pp. 312–13; Jacqueline Jones, *Labor of Love, Labor of Sorrow: Black Women, Work, and the Family from Slavery to the Present* (New York, 1985), pp. 306–7; and such histories of social welfare as Michael Katz, *In the Shadow of the Poorhouse: A Social History of Welfare in America* (New York, 1986), pp. 253–54, and James Patterson, *America's Struggle Against Poverty 1900–1980* (Cambridge, Mass., 1981), pp. 153, 180–81, 195–96.

3. Thirty thousand was the official membership figure that NWRO leaders utilized most frequently. However, my study of NWRO records reveals some-what lower figures. See National Welfare Rights Organization, "Table, Annual Membership Figures, by State, for 1968, 1969, 1970, 1971," n.d., "Table, WROs and Members, by State, for 1967, 1968, and 1969, through 5/27," and "Membership Report for August, 1969," all in Box 8, Folder 4, George Wiley papers, State Historical Society of Wisconsin (SHSW).

4. "1971 Membership Lists, by Region," no author, Box 1971, file titled "Regional Group Lists—1971," NWRO Papers, Moorland-Spingarn Research Center, Howard University.

5. For the complicated politics of needs and rights see Nancy Fraser, "Struggle Over Needs: Outline of a Socialist-Feminist Critical Theory of Late-Capitalist Political Culture," in *Women, The State, and Welfare*, ed. Linda Gordon (Madison, Wis., 1990), pp. 199–225. I am also indebted to Jeremy Waldron's suggestion that needs and rights are not competing, but complementary, and that meaningful social and political struggle can involve battles over needs within a framework of rights.

6. For the origins of such "differential diagnoses" in the social work theories of the early twentieth century, see Linda Gordon, "Social Insurance and Public Assistance: The Influence of Gender in Welfare Thought in the United States, 1890–1935," *American Historical Review* 97 1 (February 1992): 19–54.

7. Home Relief was, and is, the term in many states for the assistance program for adults who have no children or who do not qualify for AFDC for some other reason. Home Relief is not a federal program, but is funded and administered exclusively by the states. The same program is known in some states as General Assistance.

8. Old Age Assistance (OAA) was a federal program for the low-income elderly who were not covered by the Old-Age Insurance program (what we usually call "Social Security"). Created by the Social Security Act of 1935, OAA was supplanted in 1974 by Supplementary Security Insurance (SSI), which was designed to serve both disabled and elderly people; unlike OAA, which, like AFDC, had combined state–federal administration, SSI was to be funded and administered entirely by the federal government.

Frances Fox Piven argues that the welfare rights movement should be given credit for the creation of SSI, which had all the features that NWRO sought in a welfare program while not covering the people who formed the bulk of the NWRO membership (discussion with the author, City University of New York Graduate Center, December 5, 1995).

9. Social Service Employees Union (SSEU), New York City, "Tables of Minimum Standards from Information Found in the Handbook for Case Units in Public Assistance," n.d., "Basic Budget" (no page), Box 2010, file titled "SSEU-NY," NWRO papers. At the time that NWRO was most active, SSEU was an independent union of welfare caseworkers, which had on its staff a liaison to the welfare activists. For discussion see Daniel J. Walkowitz, *The Muddle of the Middle Classes* (Chapel Hill, N.C., 1997). SSEU probably drew up these tables specially for NWRO or its New York affiliate, the Citywide Coordinating Committee of Welfare Rights Groups.

10. Basic clothing chart, "Woman," no page, in SSEU manual, in ibid.

11. "Household Furnishings and Equipment (not included in the regular check)," no page, in SSEU manual, in ibid. Former Lindsay Administration official Charles Morris, who generally treats the welfare rights movement with disdain, also emphasizes the variations from client to client in welfare grants, adding that welfare codes "stipulated living conditions in such detail—for example, a kitchen should have a fruit reamer—that almost everyone could qualify for additional special grants to meet standards." Charles Morris, *The Cost of Good Intentions: New York City and the Liberal Experiment, 1960–1975* (New York, 1980), p. 69.

12. SSEU manual, p. 13, in Box 2010, file titled "SSEU-NY," NWRO papers.

13. Mary Spurlock, "Welfare Budget," from Columbus Welfare Rights Organization pamphlet, "Got Welfare Problems? Join WRO," n.d., Box 2167, file titled "Columbus WRO," NWRO papers.

14. I borrow the idea of "cost accounting" from Nell Irvin Painter, "Soul Murder and Slavery: Toward a Fully Loaded Cost Accounting," in *U.S. History as Women's History: New Feminist Essays*, ed. Linda K. Kerber, Alice Kessler-Harris, and Kathryn Kish Sklar (Chapel Hill, N.C., 1995), pp. 125–46.

15. Mary Magdalene Spurlock, "Ten Welfare Commandments," from the Ohio Steering Committee for Adequate Welfare, "Notice for the Ohio Crusade for Adequate Welfare," November 5, 1967, Box 2167, file titled "Ohio Steering Committee for Adequate Welfare," NWRO papers.

16. "The [Columbus] WRO has adopted as its symbol an empty horn of plenty circled by the words 'Welfare: a right—not a privilege,'" from Ohio Steering Committee for Adequate Welfare, *Adequate Welfare News,* January 9, 1967, 3, from Box 2167, file titled "Ohio Steering Committee for Adequate Welfare," NWRO papers.

17. Letter from Mrs. Andrea Keyes, Meriden, Connecticut, to the National Welfare Rights Organization, Washington, D.C., October 13, 1971, Box 1971, file titled "Connecticut," NWRO papers.

18. [Henry Pollack], "Mama, What's a Strawberry?" *Newsletter, West Side Welfare Council, The Voice of Poverty Midst Plenty,* vol. 1, no. 5, September 1966: 3, Box 2167, file titled "Upper West Side Council," NWRO papers. Home economists on the staffs of local welfare departments drew up schedules of standard prices for goods, as well as of the retinue of goods that constituted consumption by the normal American family.

19. Letter from Mrs. Eliza Williams, Co-chairman, Waterbury Welfare Rights Organization, Waterbury, Conn., to Secretary of Health, Education and Welfare Robert Finch, Washington, D.C., June 3, 1969, Box 2017, file titled "Letters of Complaint," NWRO papers.

20. Letter from Annie Frett, Brooklyn, New York, to Mayor Lindsay, [New York City Welfare] Commissioner Ginsberg, and [New York State Welfare] Commissioner Louch[heim], August 28, 1967, Fox 47, Folder 118, papers of the Scholarship, Education, and Defense Fund for Racial Equality (SED-FRE), SHSW.

21. In a 1969 membership tally, Hayes appeared as the contact person for the Newport News WRO, which had a total of 36 members. Membership list, 1969, in Box 1952, file titled "Local Groups—WRO," NWRO papers.

22. Summary of Appeal, Case of Margaret Beatrice Hayes, May 20, 1970, 5–6, Box 2063, file titled "Margaret Hayes," NWRO papers. For similar issues raised in a Fair Hearing, see Fair Hearing

Transcript, Case of Joanne Smitherman, October 24, 1967, pp. 80–82, in Box 49, Folder 1, SEDFRE papers. Smitherman, a Harlem welfare rights activist, spoke in the hearing of her right to keep "[d]emitasse cups and saucers . . . goblets and wine glasses."

23. Letter from Mrs. Margaret Hayes, Newport News, Va., to Mr. Otis L. Brown, Director, Department of Welfare and Institutions, Richmond, Va., August 12, 1970, in ibid.

24. Letter from (Miss) Mary Kilcullen, Assistant to the Chief, Bureau of Assistance and Service Programs, Commonwealth of Virginia Department of Welfare and Institutions, Richmond, Va., to Mrs. Margaret Hayes, August 27, 1970, in ibid.

25. This is not to suggest that welfare recipients in more recent years have not tried to make their voices heard in the making of social policy. For discussions of more recent efforts among college students who are also welfare recipients, see my article "Class Dismissed: Welfare Recipients Fight to Stay in College," In These Times, October 5, 1997:18–20. For a more general discussion of the relationship between welfare rights and contemporary politics, see my "The Goals of the National Welfare Rights Movement: Why We Need Them Thirty Years Later," Feminist Studies 24/1 (Spring 1998): 65–78.

BETH L. BAILEY

Prescribing the Pill: The Coming of the Sexual Revolution in America's Heartland

In this fascinating bit of historical detective work, Beth Bailey explodes the myth that the advent of the oral contraceptive in 1960 ushered in the Sexual Revolution, freeing women—especially those who were unmarried—to engage in sex without fears of unwanted pregnancies. Bailey tells a different story, one in which use of the new contraceptive is closely linked to concerns about overpopulation and poverty. By narrowing her focus to Lawrence, Kansas, home to the University of Kansas, she provides a clear view of the complex process by which college women gained access to the pill.

Why does Bailey refer to this process as "elite-managed, gradual change"? At what point did young women demand access on their own behalf? Why were their voices virtually mute throughout the 1960s, even though Bailey provides clear evidence that their behavior was changing? Is this silencing on the part of heterosexual young women related in any way to the silencing that Betty Friedan, Miriam Van Waters, or various lesbians imposed on themselves in the postwar era?

American women went "on the pill" in the 1960s. The oral tablets that most Americans called simply "the pill" were approved for contraceptive use by the FDA in 1960. By early 1969, eight and a half million women were using the pill; their numbers had grown by about one million each year from 1961.[1] Every day for three weeks out of their monthly menstrual cycle, millions of women popped the tiny tablet through the foil package that fit into the daisywheel container that somewhat resembled a compact—if one didn't know bet-

Excerpted from "Prescribing the Pill," ch. 4 of Sex in the Heartland by Beth L. Bailey (Cambridge, Mass.: Harvard University Press, 1999). Copyright © 1999 by President and Fellows of Harvard College. Notes have been renumbered and edited.

ter. The high hormonal doses of the early oral contraceptives had pronounced side effects, which mimicked pregnancy: breast tenderness, weight gain, some nausea. But the pill was more than 99 percent effective, in no way dependent on the direct cooperation of the woman's partner, and completely separate from the act of sexual intercourse. A great many women were willing to accept some side effects in exchange for freedom from fear of pregnancy. By giving women greater control over their sexual and reproductive lives, this new contraceptive technology helped change the meaning and experience of sex in America.

The great majority of the women who went on the pill in its early years, however, were not the young single women who lived "the revolution." Most were married. . . . Nonetheless, by the mid-1960s the pill symbolized the revolution in sex. . . . In America, talk of the sexual revolution inevitably turned to talk of the pill, and discussions of the pill often centered on its possible effects on America's sexual mores.

Largely because of its symbolic role, the pill frequently appears in discussions (both then and now) as a sort of *deus ex machina*, bringing about the sexual revolution. In 1968 a no less distinguished figure than Pearl S. Buck, writing for the mass market in *Reader's Digest*, linked a crisis in sexual morality to the pill: "It is a small object—yet its potential effect upon our society may be even more devastating than the nuclear bomb."[2] . . . [But Buck's analogy to the bomb] overlooks a key fact. The pill was not simply a new technology available in the free marketplace of postwar America. It had to be prescribed by a physician.

Doctors, then as now, controlled access to oral contraceptives. And at that time only a small minority of physicians would prescribe birth control pills to women who were not married. Most believed, along with a large majority of the American public, that it was wrong for unmarried women to have sex. Thus, before the pill could play any significant role in the sexual behavior of America's unmarried youth, something had to change. Unmarried women—in large numbers—had to have access to oral contraceptives. How did single women get the pill?

Once again, revolutionary change in Americans' sexual mores and behavior was made possible inadvertently. . . . The pill did not become available to single women because they raised their voices and demanded the right to sexual freedom and control of their own bodies. Instead, it became available to them as a byproduct of two political movements that were at the heart of sixties liberalism and its attempts to ameliorate the difficult social problems that plagued America and the world.

One of these movements was driven by concern about population growth, both international and domestic, which reached near-panic proportions in the United States during the 1960s and early 1970s. The other, Lyndon Johnson's Great Society, used federal funds and programs to attack the causes and consequences of poverty and racism in the United States. Neither set of efforts, by any stretch of the imagination, was intended to foster a sexual revolution. However, these two movements helped make the pill available to single women, in large part by providing rationales for prescribing contraceptives that did not employ a language of morality. . . .

[In Kansas, population control advocates urged the state senate to] vote on legislation allowing public agencies to distribute information about contraceptives to Kansas citizens. Senate Bill 375 stemmed largely from the intense lobbying efforts of Patricia Schloesser, M.D., head of the state division of maternal and child services, who was motivated by a frightening vision of unrestrained world population growth. . . . [T]he senate voted unanimously in favor of the measure. The house vote the following April, however, was close enough to require a roll call. . . . While it was now legal for public institutions to offer birth control and contraceptive information to citizens of Kansas, the legislature had offered no . . . funding. Without money for birth control services, the change in law had little practical impact. . . .

Among the most vocal and vehement advocates of birth control in Kansas was the director of Lawrence's public health department, Dr. Dale Clinton. . . . Like Dr. Schloesser, Clinton believed that the world population explosion was a greater threat to public health than any contagious disease or environmental hazard. . . . In 1959 the professional organization for public health workers, the 20,000-member American Public Health Association (APHA), had adopted a resolution that called for attention, at "all levels of government," to "the impact of population change on health." And in 1963 the APHA called population growth "one of the world's most important health problems" and began lobbying government officials for action.[3]

[While the population advocates pressed for maximum dissemination of both information about contraceptives and the contraceptives themselves, the Johnson administration pursued a similar strategy as part of a very different objective.] President Johnson pledged in his state of the union address "to seek new ways to use our knowledge to help deal with the explosion in world population and the growing scarcity of world resources." In April [1965], Senator Gruening of Alaska introduced a bill that led to the funding of birth control programs through the Department of Health, Education, and Welfare. Earlier, the Office of Economic Opportunity (OEO) had funneled some money to family planning programs under the "local option" policy that allowed community groups to initiate welfare programs. (Initially the OEO did not allow its funds to be used for contraceptives for unmarried women; that restriction was lifted in 1966.)[4] The federal government's decisions to spend taxpayers' money on public family planning programs were not based on concern about women's reproductive health or a wish to promote sexual freedom. Rather, the funding was a result of the confluence of alarm about the "population problem" and increased federal involvement in programs intended to alleviate the effects of poverty in the United States. Limiting the number of children born to poor women (or allowing poor women to avoid unplanned and unwanted pregnancies) was a priority for these programs.

The political implications of linking Johnson's Great Society (with its strong focus on poverty) and population control were as apparent at the time as they are today. In the early twentieth century, many advocates of birth control had worked closely with the eugenics movement, which sought to limit childbearing among people the eugenicists deemed genetically and racially inferior and so preserve the dominance of white, Anglo-Saxon Americans. Those uncomfortably close links between the birth control movement and the eugenics movement were not so far in the past. . . .

The politics of the Johnson administration's "war on poverty" and welfare programs were complicated at best, and those who attempted to implement policies struggled with opposition from widely divergent sources. In the case of birth control, the administration faced both the suspicions of targeted groups such as poor African Americans *and* voters' reservations about the costs of burgeoning social welfare programs. . . . The American Association of Public Health consistently focused on the dangers of world population growth, an argument that was more compelling to Americans who rejected the idea of "benefits" for the poor and underprivileged. But throughout the 1960s, authors also attempted to demonstrate that contraception for America's poor was fully in keeping with "broadly democratic principles of equal opportunity for all." Birth control, one prominent activist wrote in an attempt to shift the grounds for suspicion, should not be the "special privilege" of the "well-to-do."[5]

Many Americans, however, drew connections between birth control and antipoverty programs that were exactly what government agencies had tried to avoid. For example, when *Good Housekeeping* sampled its 20,000-member "consumer panel" in 1967 on the question "Should Birth Control Be Available to Unmarried Women," its editors discovered that the negative responses (significantly, a strong majority) were based on "moral" arguments, while the affirmative responses were "practical." An Arizona woman wrote: "It would eliminate many dollars in child-welfare payments." A more vehement response came from a woman in the Midwest, who supported birth control for unmarried women because "I deeply resent having to deprive my family of privileges I cannot afford because I have to pay support for others not of my choosing."[6] . . .

Once the Kansas legislature made funding available, Dr. Clinton moved quickly and Lawrence's health department began to offer contraceptive services—something fewer than 20 percent of local health departments in the United States did at that time. Clinton, however, was decidedly uninterested in the professional debate about birth control for the indigent and the related directives. Though the framework provided by state (and eventually federal) guidelines indicated an implicit, but clear, association of these programs with services for the poor, Clinton made it equally clear that his birth control clinic was not "indigent-oriented," nor did he consider it the appropriate site for clinical medicine. He did not intend to focus on the poor, and he did not mean to provide women (of any income level) with health care. Instead, he intended to combat the scourge of unrestrained population growth by offering contraceptives to any and all.

. . . Kansas's laws restricting birth control, in effect from 1870 through 1963, had applied only to public agencies. Even before 1963 a married woman in Lawrence had ready access to birth control if she could afford a private doctor. When the pill became available for contraceptive purposes in 1960, Lawrence doctors had begun prescribing it to married women. . . .

As private doctors in Lawrence were already meeting the needs of their patients, the health department, naturally, would draw from a different constituency. Married women who could afford private doctors were more or less out of the pool. Who was left? Those for whom medical fees were too expensive. . . .

There was also another constituency, one that the state and federal governments had not intended to target: unmarried women. And because of the University of Kansas and Haskell Indian Junior College, Lawrence had a disproportionately high number of young, unmarried women. The Kansas legislature had mandated access to contraceptive information and services only for *married* women 18 years and older. Parental permission was required for women under 18, no matter what their marital status. But the legislature also provided a back door to access: Any woman might receive contraceptives at a public clinic if she was "referred to said center by a licensed physician." Clinton interpreted this law in the broadest terms. He was a licensed physician, legally authorized to make such referrals. Thus, as he made clear in newspaper interviews and public talks, any woman who wanted birth control might receive her referral at the clinic itself, at the time of her appointment. With virtually no exceptions, women seeking contraceptives at the health department came away with the pill.

[At the University of Kansas,] the question was whether the University Health Service should prescribe the pill to unmarried women students. This debate . . . centered around issues of morality. It was precipitated by a 1966 forum on the topic: "Should unmarried undergraduates be given birth control information and/or materials through Watkins Hospital [the student health service]?"

The panelists were three: Rev. Simmons, the campus minister who had helped form the family planning clinic [affiliated with Planned Parenthood] and who focused on sexuality counseling and birth control in his ministry at KU; Father Falteisch, chairman of the moral theology department at St. Louis University and a Roman Catholic priest; and Dr. Raymond Schwegler, director of KU's student health service. According to coverage by the *University Daily Kansan,* Simmons argued that population control was desperately needed. Father Falteisch agreed, and suggested that the Church was moving toward accepting the "responsible use" of contraceptives as legitimate, though not for the unmarried. In the context of 1966 America and their respective churches, both men of the cloth took liberal to progressive positions. The hard line, however, came from the man of medicine.

The *Kansan* described Dr. Schwegler, then about 60 years old, as a "small, white-haired man" with a soft voice, but he certainly never minced words. Watkins would not, Schwegler insisted, give contraceptives to unmarried students "under any circumstances." "I know this is old fashioned, mid-Victorian, and the *Kansan* will cut us to ribbons," he is quoted in the *Kansan* as saying, "but I don't want to do it and my staff backs me completely." Rev. Simmons pushed, arguing that unless premarital intercourse was grounds for expulsion, Schwegler's policy was unfair. Schwegler replied: "We'd have trouble keeping the student population up [if we expelled students for premarital intercourse]. But Watkins will not contribute to the recreational activities of the campus." When a student asked about the possibility of a "rebel doctor," Schwegler deemed it impossible: "All the doctors are handpicked—by me." He continued: "If I had somebody over there who I thought was as far out as some of the teaching faculty, I'd fire him. I want a conservative hospital that can be respected."[7]

The 1966 forum on birth control prompted a flood of letters to the *Kansan.* The letters contained no dire predictions about the earth's future if population growth continued uncontrolled. Instead, students used a language of morality to dispute Schwegler's stance. . . .

The first response to Schwegler published in the *Kansan* was . . . from a graduate student from Iola, Kansas. . . . Noting that the health service did provide the pill to married women, he argued that by so doing the administration had defined the issue as moral, not medical. Thus, he said, the question was, "Who should make the moral decision, the university or the students themselves?" Another graduate student (from Gettysburg, South Dakota) questioned "the irresponsible use of the concept 'morality' as employed primarily by the 'anti-pill' proponents." Morality, he insisted, existed only in a situation in which there was "opportunity for choice." Without "free access" to contraceptives, students were not making a moral—or immoral—choice about premarital intercourse. Instead, their choices were constrained by fear or coercion.

The "anti-pill" faction was represented by only one letter. The writer, a male sophomore from Nebraska, argued that because the university was a "public servant," it must follow the "doctrines of the society." He warned that premarital sex would be likely to increase if single women could get the pill, for without fear of pregnancy, "restraining factors would be few and far between." Reaching for an analogy, he asked: "If the possibility of punishment for murder were eliminated," would there not be "a substantial increase in the number of murders committed every year?" . . .

What was largely missing in this flurry of letters was a statement embracing sexual freedom—an affirmative voice. . . . [M]ost of the writers shifted the focus away from sex in making their arguments. . . . While their central claim—that the university should provide contraceptives to unmarried women students—was quite radical, their arguments were not. These were not yet the voices of revolution.

In the forum and in the ensuing debate, there were no arguments centering around the rights of women to control their own bodies. In fact, only two women participated in this public debate, and their names do not appear, effaced in the signatures "Mr. and Mrs. James Cooley" and "Mr. and Mrs. Angus Wright." . . . Why didn't women speak out in the paper? After all, the debate was about

women's choices—it was not men who might go "on the pill."

Women did not write because the stakes for them were so high. Discussions about morality and the pill in the larger society did not center on the morality of existential choice, but on the immorality of premarital sex. In the February 1967 *Good Housekeeping* poll on unmarried women and the pill, respondents made comments such as: "I truly pity a generation growing up with the morals of alley cats"; and "Making birth control available to unmarried girls to me would mean lowering our moral standards and destroying our culture." These women were not policymakers or experts. . . . [T]heir voices represent a different sort of authority. These are the voices of mothers—mothers of the sort whose daughters went to state colleges in the Midwest. The *Kansan* was a student paper, but news of a daughter's making public claims about her right to birth control was very likely to travel fast and to travel home.

. . . Writings in the *Journal of the American College Health Association, School and Society,* and the *Journal of School Health* at the time were equally emphatic about the evils of premarital sex. . . . The director of the Princeton health service . . . warned against prescribing contraceptives to unmarried women, as "the student's unconscious mind might interpret such prescriptions as a signal from 'authority' giving permission for sexual freedom."[8] [A] physician at the Ohio State University health service . . . made an unfortunate analogy to sex: "It is all a bit like cars: Some choose a new one and break it in with loving care; others buy from a used car lot—it is just as nice and shiny but you are not sure what problems the previous drivers have left you."[9]

Mass-circulation magazines and professional journals would not have devoted so much space to debates over premarital sex if there had been no audience for them. . . . Nonetheless, these are essentially prescriptive discourses. What of the students themselves?

In the spring semester of 1964 the "Roles of Women" committee of the Associated Women Students (AWS) surveyed its constituency. Presented with descriptions of behavior ("using race as one basis for choosing your associates"; "showing disrespect for those in authority"; "wearing short shorts in town"; "feeling very angry with someone"), students were asked to judge each item. Categories were "morally or ethically right," "generally acceptable," "generally unacceptable," and "morally or ethically wrong." The instructions emphasized that each student should indicate what was right or wrong "for *you*." More than 1,900 women completed the survey.

Questions about sex provoked the strongest responses. Significantly higher percentages of women students disapproved of "mixed swimming parties in the nude" than of using an exam "which has been illegally obtained." ... [M]ost of the respondents (77 percent of the freshmen and 68 percent of the seniors) rated premarital sex with a fiancé as "morally or ethically wrong," not merely as "generally unacceptable." Even stronger was the students' disapproval of sexual intercourse when the couple was not engaged to be married. A striking 91 percent of both freshmen and seniors labeled it unacceptable or wrong. Only 2 percent of each group deemed premarital sex for those who were not engaged "morally or ethically right."

... In 1967 a student union forum offered three professors addressing the question "Is Free Love a Bargain?" ... This forum was dominated by a professor of English, who accused the audience of coming in search of "some rationalization for the sex you've indulged in." ... [In] such a climate, with the threat of moral condemnation from peers and authorities alike, few students wished to make public their private decisions about sex.

In 1967, following the "Is Free Love a Bargain?" forum, an unmarried woman finally wrote to the editor of the campus newspaper, claiming her right to both sex and the pill: "I take the pill because I'd rather express my love than repress it. I'm not promiscuous, but once in a while I meet a 'special' guy. I've seen too many girls on campus totally disregard school for several weeks as they suffer anxiety over a missed menstrual period. ... If a girl takes one chance a year, that's enough to warrant taking the pill." ... Her letter, which had begun, "I'm a woman and I'm glad," employed a feminist language, emphasizing women's right and capacity to choose. It was a powerful and affirmative statement. But it was unsigned. An editor's note below the letter read: "Contrary to established editorial page policy, we are printing this letter without signature." All letters, no matter how controversial their claims, required signature—except this one. A woman's claiming her right to sex and the pill was understood as a whole different category of risk.

That this woman remained anonymous and was allowed to do so by the *Kansan* editorial board in violation of its policy, that women's voices were so conspicuously silent in the previous year's debate on the pill, that 91 percent of the women students surveyed *said* they believed premarital sex to be "ethically or morally wrong"—all this is strong evidence that it wasn't only the prescriptive voices of adults denying the legitimacy of the culture of youth. Even within student culture, there was a gulf between public claims and private behavior. For the women of KU were having sex. And they were, in increasing numbers, on the pill.

Actually getting the pill could be complicated, however. When a young, single woman sought a prescription for contraceptives in the 1960s, she was making a statement about her sexual status. Virgins didn't need birth control pills unless they did not plan to remain virgins much longer. ... When a single woman went to a doctor to request any sort of contraceptive device, she risked refusal, embarrassment, even lectures on morality and appropriate behavior. Some women bought cheap rings and tried to pass them off as wedding bands. Others claimed they were coming in for a "premarital exam," with the wedding pending. Still others complained of menstrual cramps or heavy bleeding and came away with the pill, prescribed to "regulate" their periods. But many doctors, especially those in small towns and university communities, saw through such pretexts and often treated young women with suspicion. Single women were not guaranteed, by law or custom, access to birth control.

As women learned through informal networks, alternative newspapers, and the completely mainstream *Journal World*, the quickest, cheapest, and least complicated place to get birth control pills in Lawrence was the public health department. The university student health service refused to "contribute to the recreational activities of the campus," in its director's colorful words, and many students worried about having such information about their sex lives in what were, after all, official university records at the health service. ...

[The Planned Parenthood–affiliated] clinic was open only two nights a month, and simply could not serve large numbers of women. . . .

The number of women obtaining oral contraceptives at the public health department grew dramatically from year to year, and the vast majority of the new patients each year were KU students. The patient load closely followed the academic year. In 1971, for example, there were only 44 new patients in August, but in September, with the beginning of the fall semester, there were 300. That year the Lawrence-Douglas County health department served 8,529 birth control patients and dispensed or prescribed almost 38,000 months of pills. . . . The pill was a wonder drug not simply because of its effectiveness for women but also because of its possible convenience for those who prescribed it. Women went to the health department and walked out a few minutes later "on the pill." Stories of young women who were offered virtual armloads of free pills and told to pass them on to their friends still circulate today. . . .

The Planned Parenthood–affiliated clinic took a very different approach. Prescription of the pill was contingent upon not only a physical examination but also a time-consuming process of education and counseling. . . . The clinic, which had opened in early 1967, closed its doors permanently on the first day of 1970. Though it had been founded to serve low-income residents of Lawrence, the president of its sponsoring group explained, it had been used almost exclusively by KU students (she did not say whether they were married or single). Many of the volunteers were frustrated by what they saw as a misdirection of resources, and upon closing the clinic the directors sent a letter to Dr. Schwegler at the student health service and to the chancellor arguing that the university must take responsibility for its students' birth control needs instead of allowing students to overwhelm community resources needed by and for a different population.[10]

. . . In 1970, after the closing of the Planned Parenthood clinic, a student group approached top-level administrators about the health service's birth control policies. The administrators responded sympathetically, promising that two upcoming vacancies at Watkins would be filled with doctors who would prescribe the pill without using marital

status or "morality" as criteria. This never happened. . . . In 1970, 53 percent of American college health services offered no gynecological care to women students, and 72 percent did not prescribe contraceptives (to single *or* married students).[11]

Thus far, the story of the pill in Lawrence, Kansas, has been one of elite-managed, gradual change. . . . Until the 1970s, Lawrence's youth also fit into this model. . . . While thousands of young women went on the pill during the 1960s, public acknowledgment of that private behavior lagged behind. [Although the] pill may have been revolutionary in its results, it was not especially revolutionary in its introduction.

In the early 1970s the women's movement captured the pill, in both its symbolic and its physical manifestations. Women in Lawrence—and not only young women—interrupted the process of gradual change within the paradigms of population control and sexual morality and offered, instead, revolutionary claims about gender equality, cultural authority, and sexual freedom.

By 1972 any woman in Lawrence—married or unmarried—could obtain birth control pills, free if necessary. This had been true, and widely known, for at least five years. But it wasn't simply access to the pill that was at stake. It was the nature of the access, and the meaning attributed to it, that angered some women. In 1972 two different groups of women in Lawrence challenged the medical men who controlled access to the pill.[12] Though the two groups used different methods and different vocabularies . . . both made claims based on the rights and needs of women themselves and not on those of the larger society. In so doing they stepped outside the discourses of morality and of the population problem and centered the debate over access to the pill in a discourse on women, rights, and freedom.

. . . KU's dean of women, Emily Taylor, was a NOW-style feminist who lobbied for political legislation and university policies supporting equal rights for women. Her office had supported a form of liberal feminism on campus, including a commission on the status of women, and had served as a center of action for some women students and administrators throughout her tenure.

On the other end of the continuum,

women in Lawrence's large and diverse counterculture had begun to draw connections between the oppression of minorities and the oppression of women. The women of *Vortex* (the most important underground newspaper) published a women's issue in 1970, and soon afterward the *Lavender Luminary*, a lesbian paper, appeared. W.I.T.C.H. (Women's International Terrorist Conspiracy from Hell) emerged briefly as a local group. Consciousness-raising groups formed. In Lawrence, women were talking with other women about their lives, and those conversations would have repercussions in the world they inhabited.

[In February 1972,] a lecture by radical feminist Robin Morgan inspired these two groups of women to unite as the February Sisters. They took over a university building to voice their demands for] full health care for women students, a federally funded child care center on campus, an end to discriminatory employment practices at KU, more women in high-level administrative positions, an affirmative action program, and a department of women's studies. . . . When the Sisters emerged from the building early the next morning, they had won commitments from the administration on a substantial portion of their demands, including the women's health program.

[The Sisters] couched their argument in language echoing the American tradition of rights and freedoms. "We, the February Sisters," their proposal for a human sexuality clinic began, in an invocation of the U.S. Constitution. Arguing that "control of her reproductive functions is a fundamental right of every woman," the Sisters insisted: "The University cannot view the action proposal . . . as a request for additional privileges, but rather as a demand to recognize right [*sic*] which have been neglected."[13]

It was not simply the right to access these women claimed. . . . More important, these women were rejecting the frameworks of sexual morality and population control that had governed access to contraceptives for more than a decade. The February Sisters condemned the ways that many Americans used concepts of sexual morality to deny women's autonomy and dignity—a fairly obvious and expected critique—but also criticized the efforts of population control groups. . . . These women understood that rationales for contraception based on population control, no less than those based on morality, left room for comments like the one made by the irritated director of student health, Dr. Schwegler, who said that he did so many pelvic exams he sometimes felt like he worked in a whorehouse. The February Sisters and their allies meant to provide a new framework for prescribing the pill that centered around the needs of women themselves and left no room for such demeaning and disrespectful remarks.[14]

After the actions of the February Sisters in February 1972, Watkins student health center officially began prescribing the pill to unmarried women. Somewhat ironically, the following month the Supreme Court ruled that women could not be denied contraceptives on the basis of marital status.

The struggles over the pill in Lawrence were not yet over, however. Even though Watkins offered contraceptives, students still sought the quick access to birth control and the relative anonymity offered by Dr. Clinton's clinic at the public health department. . . . In August 1972, however, the Kansas State Department of Health cut off funding for Clinton's birth control program. The state agency received its funding from the Department of Health, Education, and Welfare (HEW), and it came with federal mandates [that] committed doctors to follow a specified procedure in prescribing the pill, including performing a complete physical exam, pap smear, visual exam for cancer, tuberculin test, hemoglobin, and urinalysis. Clinton . . . refused to perform these tests. . . . Comprehensive medical services for the indigent were not his mandate, he insisted, and he would continue to provide birth control as before, funding it through donations from patients, not to exceed $1 per woman each month. Dr. Schwegler, the director of KU's student health service, who was also serving as chairman of the public health committee, told the *Journal World* that he was "irritated as a private citizen" over the state health department's action. Clinton prevailed with Lawrence's Board of Health, and his refusal stood. Though the local clinic lost a $12,000 federal grant, it was soon running a $10,000 surplus from donations by birth control patients.[15]

Young women who took the pill Clinton prescribed had sex without fear of pregnancy.

They obtained the pill simply by request, without the demeaning act of lying about an impending marriage or the purchase of a cheap gold ring at a drugstore. They were, by and large, grateful. By prescribing the pill, Dr. Clinton inadvertently facilitated the sexual revolution in Lawrence and changed the lives of thousands of young women and their partners. . . .

NOTES

1. Elizabeth Rose Siegel Watkins, in "On the Pill: A Social History of Oral Contraceptives in America, 1950–1970" (Ph.D. diss., Harvard University, 1996), pp. 130–131.

2. Pearl S. Buck, "The Pill and the Teen-Age Girl," *Reader's Digest* 92 (April 1968):111, quoted in Watkins, "On the Pill," p. 138.

3. Donald Harting and Leslie Corsa, "The American Public Health Association and the Population Problem," *American Journal of Public Health* 59 (Oct. 1969):1927–29. For a history of population control initiatives, see James Reed, *From Private Vice to Public Virtue* (New York: Basic Books, 1978).

4. Leslie Corsa, "Public Health Programs in Family Planning," *American Journal of Public Health* 56 (Jan. 1966, supplement); Reed, *From Private Vice*, p. 378; Watkins, "On the Pill," pp. 141–142. For statistics on federal funding see "Family Planning Services," Hearing before the Subcommittee on Public Health and Welfare of the Committee on Interstate and Foreign Commerce, House of Representatives, serial no. 91–70 (Washington: GPO, 1970), pp. 190–193.

5. Mary Calderone, "Health Education for Responsible Parenthood: Preliminary Considerations," *American Journal of Public Health* (Jan. 1964):1735–40.

6. "Should Birth Control Be Available to Unmarried Women?" *Good Housekeeping*, Feb. 1967, p. 14.

7. Will Hardesty, "Birth Control Practices Debated," *University Daily Kansan (UDK)*, Nov. 4, 1966.

8. Willard Dalrymple, M.D., "A Doctor Speaks of College Students and Sex," *Journal of the American College Health Association* 15 (Feb. 1967):286.

9. W. Roy Mason Jr., M.D., "Problems of Married College Students: Health Education Implications," ibid., 14 (April 1966):273–274. Frances K. Harding, M.D., "The College Unmarried Population Explosion," *Journal of School Health* 35 (Dec. 1965):450–457.

10. "Over-Interest Closes County Clinic," *UDK*, Feb. 3, 1970; "Birth Control Clinic Closes," *UDK*, Feb. 5, 1970.

11. The student request was in conjunction with the Commission on the Status of Women at KU, sponsored by the dean of women's office. Information here is from "February Sisters Position Statement on a Health Care Program for Women," Addendum II, in Lorna Zimmer personal files, Lawrence, Kan.; "Women—February First Movement," Women's Studies Program Archives, KU (WSPA); Judy Browder, "Women's Decade of History," WSPA; "Campus Problems for Consideration," Council on Student Affairs files, University of Kansas Archives.

12. There was at least one woman physician in Lawrence, and she had been quoted in the *UDK* refusing to prescribe contraceptives to unmarried women. But in this controversy the divisions that appeared publicly were strictly along gender lines.

13. "February Sisters Position Statement on a Health Care Program for Women," in Zimmer files.

14. Judy Henry, "Groups Urge Birth Control," *UDK*, April 4, 1971. Browder, "Women's Decade," and transcript of "February Sisters Panel Discussion," 1987, statement by Mary Coral, in WSPA.

15. "State Drops Birth Control Funding Here," *Lawrence Daily Journal World (JW)*, Sept. 22, 1972; "Birth Control Funding Possible," *JW*, Sept. 27, 1972; Tim Pryor, "Health Agency Says Changes Due," *JW*, Jan. 10, 1973; Toby MacIntosh, "Policy on Pills is Controversial," *JW*, Feb. 9, 1973.

SUSAN J. DOUGLAS
Why the Shirelles Mattered: Girl Groups on the Cusp of a Feminist Awakening

Worrying about the moral impact of rock 'n' roll on one's teenage children was a conversational staple among white, middle-class parents in the 1950s and early 1960s. Concern about the sexual message Elvis's pelvic gyrations sent to viewers was so widespread that when he appeared on *The Ed Sullivan Show,* there were no shots from the waist down of the rock star, who seemed more black than white. What parents did not realize was that their daughters, while Elvis fans, took as their role models of female liberation icons such as the Supremes and the Shirelles, all of whom were, in fact, black. In her insightful essay, Susan J. Douglas explores why the music of these girl groups resonated so intensely with so many American teens. In particular, she examines the meanings of the very mixed messages these teens received about gender and sexuality.

Does Douglas make her case for why the Shirelles and other girl groups "mattered"? Do you agree with her conclusion about their role in the rise of fans' feminist consciousness? What role does the music of today play in the lives of young women?

OK—here's a test. Get a bunch of women in their thirties and forties and put them in a room with a stereo. Turn up the volume to the "incurs temporary deafness" level and play "Will You Love Me Tomorrow" and see how many know the words—all the words—by heart. If the answer is 100 percent, these are bona fide American baby boomers. Any less, and the group has been infiltrated by impostors, pod people, Venusians. But even more interesting is the fact that non–baby boomers, women both older and younger than my generation, adore this music too, and cling to the lyrics like a life raft.

Why is it that, over thirty years after this song was number one in the country, it still evokes in us such passion, such longing, such euphoria, and such an irresistible desire to sing very loudly off-key and not care who hears us? And it's not just this song, it's girl group music in general, from "He's So Fine" to "Nowhere to Run" to "Sweet Talkin' Guy." . . .

First of all, girl group music was really about us—girls. When rock 'n' roll swiveled

onto the national scene in the mid-1950s and united a generation in opposition to their parents, it was music performed by rebellious and sexually provocative young men. Elvis Presley was, of course, rock 'n' roll's most famous and insistently masculine star—in 1956, five of the nine top singles of the year were by Elvis. At the same time, there would be weeks, even months, when no woman or female group had a hit among the top fifteen records.[1] . . .

Then, in December 1960, the Shirelles hit number one with "Will You Love Me Tomorrow"; it was the first time a girl group, and one composed of four black teenagers, had cracked the number one slot.[2] And these girls were not singing about doggies in windows or old Cape Cod. . . . They were singing about whether or not to go all the way and wondering whether the boyfriend, so seemingly full of heartfelt, earnest love in the night, would prove to be an opportunistic, manipulative, lying cad after he got his way, or whether he would, indeed, still be filled with love in the morning. . . . "Will You Love Me Tomorrow" was about a traditional female topic, love, but it was also about female longing and desire, including sexual desire. And, most important, it was about having a choice. . . .

[T]his was new. This was, in fact, revolutionary. Girl group music gave expression to our struggles with the possibilities and dangers of the Sexual Revolution.

What were you to do if you were a teenage girl in the early and mid-1960s, your hormones catapulting you between desire and paranoia, elation and despair, horniness and terror? You didn't know which instincts to act on and which ones to suppress. . . .

For answers—real answers—many of us turned to the record players, radios, and jukeboxes of America. . . .

By the late 1950s, Tin Pan Alley realized that Perry Como, Doris Day, and Mantovani and his orchestra weren't cutting it with the fastest-growing market segment in America, teenagers. . . . Music publishers and producers grasped two key trends: Rock 'n' roll was here to stay, and there was this flourishing market out there, not just boys, but girls, millions of them, ready and eager to buy. . . . At the same time, the proliferation of transistor radios meant that this music could be taken and heard almost everywhere, becoming the background music. . . .

. . . [I]n the aftermath of the Shirelles hit, all kinds of girl groups and girl singers appeared, from the pouf-skirted Angels ("My Boyfriend's Back") to the cute and innocent Dixie Cups to the eat-my-dirt, in-your-face, badass Shangri-Las. . . .

The most important thing about this music, the reason it spoke to us so powerfully, was that it gave voice to all the warring selves inside us struggling, blindly and with a crushing sense of insecurity, to forge something resembling a coherent identity. Even though the girl groups were produced and managed by men, it was in their music that the contradictory messages about female sexuality and rebelliousness were most poignantly and authentically expressed. . . . They sang about the pull between the need to conform and the often overwhelming desire to rebel, about the tension between restraint and freedom, and about the rewards—and costs—of prevailing gender roles. They sang, in other words, about getting mixed messages and about being

ambivalent in the face of the upheaval in sex roles. . . .

Some girl group songs, like "I Will Follow Him," allowed us to assume the familiar persona Cinderella had trained us for, the selfless masochist whose identity came only from being some appendage to a man. As we sang along with Dionne Warwick's "Walk On By," we were indeed abject martyrs to love, luxuriating in our own self-pity. But other songs addressed our more feisty and impatient side, the side unwilling to sit around and wait for the boy to make the first move. In "tell him" songs like "Easier Said Than Done," "Wishin' and Hopin'," and, of course, "Tell Him," girls were advised to abandon the time-wasting and possibly boy-losing stance of passively waiting for him to make the first move. . . . Girls were urged to take up a previously male prerogative—to be active agents of their own love lives and to go out and court the boy. . . .

Girl group songs were, by turns, boastful, rebellious, and self-abnegating, and through them girls could assume different personas, some of them strong and empowering and others masochistic and defeating. . . . The songs were about escaping from yet acquiescing to the demands of a male-dominated society, in which men called the shots but girls could still try to give them a run for their money. . . .

In girl group music, girls talked to each other confidentially, primarily about boys and sex. The songs took our angst-filled conversations, put them to music, and gave them a good beat. Some songs, like "He's So Fine" (doo lang, doo lang, doo lang), picked out a cute boy from the crowd and plotted how he would be hooked. In this song the choice was clearly hers, not his. Songs also re-created images of a clot of girls standing around in their mohair sweaters assessing the male talent and, well, looking over boys the way boys had always looked over girls. . . .

The absolute necessity of female collusion in the face of thoughtless or mystifying behavior by boys bound these songs together, and bound the listeners to the singers in a knowing sorority. . . . And while boys were often identified as the love object, they were also identified as the enemy. So while some of the identities we assumed as we sang along were those of the traditional, passive, obedient, lovesick girl, each of us could also be a sassy, assertive, defiant girl who intended to have more control over her life—or at least her love life. In numerous advice songs, from "Mama Said" to "You Can't Hurry Love," the message that girls knew a thing or two, and that they would share that knowledge with one another to beat the odds in a man's world, circulated confidently.

Other songs fantasized about beating a different set of odds—the seeming inevitability, for white, middle-class girls, of being married off to some boring, respectable guy with no sense of danger or adventure. . . .

Here we come to the rebel category—"Leader of the Pack" . . . and "He's Sure the Boy I Love." Academic zeros, on unemployment, clad in leather jackets, sporting dirty fingernails, and blasting around on motorcycles, the boy heroes in these songs were every suburban parent's nightmare, the boys they loved to hate. By allying herself romantically and morally with the rebel hero, the girl singer and listener proclaimed her independence from society's predictable expectations about her inevitable domestication. There is a role reversal here, too—the girls are gathered in a group, sharing information about their boyfriends, virtually eyeing them up and down, while the rebel heroes simply remain the passive objects of their gaze and their talk. And the girls who sang these songs, like the Shangri-Las, dressed the part of the defiant bad girl who stuck her tongue out at parental and middle-class authority. The Ronettes, whose beehives scraped the ceiling and whose eyeliner was thicker than King Tut's, wore spiked heels and skintight dresses with slits up the side as they begged some boy to "Be My Baby." They combined fashion rebellion with in-your-face sexual insurrection. . . .

While a few girl groups and individual singers were white—the Angels, the Shangri-Las, Dusty Springfield—most successful girl groups were black. Unlike the voices of Patti Page or Doris Day, which seemed as innocent of sexual or emotional angst as a Chatty Cathy doll, the vibrating voices of black teenagers, often trained in the gospel traditions of their churches, suggested a perfect fusion of naivete and knowingness. And with the rise of the civil rights movement, which by 1962 and 1963 dominated the national news, black voices conveyed both a moral authority and a spir-

ited hope for the future. These were the voices of exclusion, of hope for something better, of longing. They were not, like Annette [Funicello] or the Lennon Sisters, the voices of sexual repression, of social complacency, or of homogenized commercialism.

From the Jazz Age to rap music, African American culture has always kicked white culture upside the head for being so pathologically repressed; one consequence, for black women, is that too often they have been stereotyped as more sexually active and responsive than their white-bread sisters. Because of these stereotypes, it was easier, more acceptable, to the music industry and no doubt to white culture at large that black girls, instead of white ones, be the first teens to give voice to girls' changing attitudes toward sex. But since the sexuality of black people has always been deeply threatening to white folks, black characters in popular culture also have been desexualized, the earth-mother mammy being a classic example. The black teens in girl groups, then, while they sounded orgiastic at times, had to look feminine, innocent, and as white as possible. Berry Gordy, the head of Motown, knew this instinctively, and made his girl groups take charm school lessons and learn how to get into and out of cars, carry their handbags, and match their shoes to their dresses.[3] They were trapped, and in the glare of the spotlight, no less, between the old and new definitions of femininity. But under their crinolined skirts and satin cocktail dresses, they were also smuggling into middle-class America a taste of sexual liberation. . . .

The Shirelles paved the way for the decade's most successful girl group, the Supremes, who had sixteen records in the national top ten between 1964 and 1969. But of utmost importance was the role Diana Ross played in making African American beauty enviable to white girls[:] as slim as a rail with those cavernous armpits, gorgeous smile, and enormous, perfectly made-up eyes. . . . The Supremes—who seemed to be both girls and women, sexy yet respectable, and a blend of black and white culture—made it perfectly normal for white girls to idolize and want to emulate their black sisters.

Another striking trend that grew out of the girl group revolution was the proliferation of the male falsetto. From Maurice Williams in "Stay" to . . . Randy and the Rainbows in "Denise" (ooo-be-ooo), and most notably with the Four Seasons and the Beach Boys, boys sang in high-pitched soprano ranges more suited for female than for male sing-along. What this meant was that girls belting out lyrics . . . had the opportunity to assume *male* roles, male subjective stances as they sang, even though they were singing in a female register.

This was nothing less than musical cross-dressing. . . .

While girl group music celebrated love, marriage, female masochism, and passivity, it also urged girls to make the first move, to rebel against their parents and middle-class conventions, and to dump boys who didn't treat them right. Most of all, girl group music—precisely because these were groups, not just individual singers—insisted that it was critically important for girls to band together, talking about men, singing about men, trying to figure them out.

What we have here is a pop culture harbinger in which girl groups, however innocent and commercial, anticipate women's groups, and girl talk anticipates a future kind of women's talk. The consciousness-raising groups of the late sixties and early seventies came naturally to many young women because we'd had a lot of practice. We'd been talking about boys, about loving them and hating them, about how good they often made us feel and how bad they often treated us, for ten years. The Shirelles mattered because they captured so well our confusion in the face of changing sexual mores. And as the confusion of real life intersected with the contradictions in popular culture, girls were prepared to start wondering, sooner or later, why sexual freedoms didn't lead to other freedoms as well. . . .

The Shirelles and the other girl groups mattered because they helped cultivate inside us a desire to rebel. The main purpose of pop music is to make us feel a kind of euphoria that convinces us that we can transcend the shackles of conventional life and rise above the hordes of others who do get trapped. It is the euphoria of commercialism, designed to get us to buy. But this music . . . generated another kind of euphoria as well. For when tens of millions of young girls started feeling, at the same time, that they, as a generation, would not be trapped, there was planted the tiniest seed of a social movement. . . .

NOTES

1. See the chart listings in Norm N. Nite, *Rock On Almanac* (New York: Harper & Row, 1989).

2. Charlotte Greig, *Will You Still Love Me Tomorrow?* (London: Virago Press, 1989), p. 33.

3. Ibid., p. 121.

DOCUMENTS: Making the Personal Political

> *Betty Friedan, "The problem that has no name . . . I understood first as a woman . . ."*

If the teenagers singing along with the Shirelles were vocalizing more than the usual adolescent discontent, the mothers who worried about their daughters had their own set of frustrations. However, despite some grumbling on the part of adults, mothers seemed no better than their daughters at articulating their discomfort and malaise. It was 1963 when Betty Friedan, identifying herself as a suburban housewife, did the job for them, exposing the triviality and frustrations of a resurgent domesticity. Friedan's indictment, a brief portion of which appears here, was the subject of much controversy. Women who found the gratification associated with child care and housework vastly overemphasized applauded Friedan's forceful articulation of their own dissatisfactions. Other women objected vehemently, insisting that, as wives and mothers and perhaps community activists, they enjoyed a life style that not only benefited both their families and communities, but also provided them personally with freedom, pleasure, and a sense of self-worth. How are we to explain such different responses? Is the housewife described by Friedan foreshadowed in Ruth Schwartz Cowan's article on housework? Is "the problem" that Friedan identifies a universal one?

The problem lay buried, unspoken, for many years in the minds of American women. It was a strange stirring, a sense of dissatisfaction, a yearning that women suffered in the middle of the twentieth century in the United States. Each suburban wife struggled with it alone. As she made the beds, shopped for groceries, matched slipcover material, ate peanut butter sandwiches with her children, chauffeured Cub Scouts and Brownies, lay beside her husband at night, she was afraid to ask even of herself the silent question—"Is this all?"

For over fifteen years there was no word of this yearning in the millions of words written about women, for women, in all the columns, books and articles by experts telling women their role was to seek fulfillment as wives and mothers. Over and over women heard in voices of tradition and of Freudian sophistication that they could desire no greater destiny than to glory in their own femininity.

Experts told them how to catch a man and keep him, how to breast-feed children and handle their toilet training, how to cope with sibling rivalry and adolescent rebellion; how to buy a dishwasher, bake bread, cook gourmet snails, and build a swimming pool with their own hands; how to dress, look, and act more feminine and make marriage more exciting; how to keep their husbands from dying young and their sons from growing into delinquents. They were taught to pity the neurotic, unfeminine, unhappy women who wanted to be poets or physicists or presidents. They learned that truly feminine women do not want careers, higher education, political rights—the independence and the opportunities that the old-fashioned feminists fought for. Some women, in their forties and fifties, still remembered painfully giving up those dreams, but most of the younger women no longer even thought about them. A thousand expert voices applauded their femininity, their adjustment, their new maturity. All they had to do was devote their lives from earliest girlhood to finding a husband and bearing children.

By the end of the 1950s, the average marriage age of women in America dropped to 20, and was still dropping, into the teens. Fourteen million girls were engaged by 17. The proportion of women attending college in comparison with men dropped from 47 percent in 1920 to 35 percent in 1958. A century earlier, women had fought for higher education; now girls went to college to get a husband. By the mid-fifties, 60 percent dropped out of college to marry, or because they were afraid too much education would be a marriage bar. Colleges built dormitories for "married students," but the students were almost always the husbands. A new degree was instituted for the wives—"Ph.T." (Putting Husband Through).

Then American girls began getting married in high school. And the women's magazines, deploring the unhappy statistics about these young marriages, urged that courses on marriage, and marriage counselors, be installed in the high schools. Girls started going steady at twelve and thirteen, in junior high. Manufacturers put out brassieres with false bosoms of foam rubber for little girls of ten. And an advertisement for a child's dress, size 3–6x, in the *New York Times* in the fall of 1960, said: "She Too Can Join the Man-Trap Set."

By the end of the fifties, the United States birthrate was overtaking India's. The birth-control movement, renamed Planned Parenthood, was asked to find a method whereby women who had been advised that a third or fourth baby would be born dead or defective might have it anyhow. Statisticians were especially astounded at the fantastic increase in the number of babies among college women. Where once they had two children, now they had four, five, six. Women who had once wanted careers were now making careers out of having babies. So rejoiced *Life* magazine in a 1956 paean to the movement of American women back to the home.

In a New York hospital, a woman had a nervous breakdown when she found she could not breast-feed her baby. In other hospitals, women dying of cancer refused a drug which research had proved might save their lives: Its side effects were said to be unfeminine. "If I

have only one life, let me live it as a blonde," a larger-than-life-sized picture of a pretty, vacuous woman proclaimed from newspaper, magazine, and drugstore ads. And across America, three out of every ten women dyed their hair blonde. They ate a chalk called Metrecal, instead of food, to shrink to the size of the thin young models. Department-store buyers reported that American women, since 1939, had become three and four sizes smaller. "Women are out to fit the clothes, instead of vice-versa," one buyer said.

Interior decorators were designing kitchens with mosaic murals and original paintings, for kitchens were once again the center of women's lives. Home sewing became a million-dollar industry. Many women no longer left their homes, except to shop, chauffeur their children, or attend a social engagement with their husbands. Girls were growing up in America without ever having jobs outside the home. In the late fifties, a sociological phenomenon was suddenly remarked: A third of American women now worked, but most were no longer young and very few were pursuing careers. They were married women who held part-time jobs, selling or secretarial, to put their husbands through school, their sons through college, or to help pay the mortgage. Or they were widows supporting families. Fewer and fewer women were entering professional work. The shortages in the nursing, social work, and teaching professions caused crises in almost every American city. Concerned over the Soviet Union's lead in the space race, scientists noted that America's greatest source of unused brainpower was women. But girls would not study physics: It was "unfeminine." A girl refused a science fellowship at Johns Hopkins to take a job in a real-estate office. All she wanted, she said, was what every other American girl wanted—to get married, have four children, and live in a nice house in a nice suburb.

The suburban housewife—she was the dream image of the young American women and the envy, it was said, of women all over the world. The American housewife—freed by science and labor-saving appliances from the drudgery, the dangers of childbirth, and the illnesses of her grandmother. She was healthy, beautiful, educated, concerned only about her husband, her children, her home. She had found true feminine fulfillment. As a housewife and mother, she was respected as a full and equal partner to man in his world. She was free to choose automobiles, clothes, appliances, supermarkets; she had everything that women ever dreamed of.

In the fifteen years after World War II, this mystique of feminine fulfillment became the cherished and self-perpetuating core of contemporary American culture. Millions of women lived their lives in the image of those pretty pictures of the American suburban housewife, kissing their husbands good-bye in front of the picture window, depositing their station wagons full of children at school, and smiling as they ran the new electric waxer over the spotless kitchen floor. They baked their own bread, sewed their own and their children's clothes, kept their new washing machines and dryers running all day. They changed the sheets on the beds twice a week instead of once, took the rug-hooking class in adult education, and pitied their poor frustrated mothers, who had dreamed of having a career. Their only dream was to be perfect wives and mothers; their highest ambition to have five children and a beautiful house, their only fight to get and keep their husbands. They had no thought for the unfeminine problems of the world outside the home; they wanted the men to make the major decisions. They gloried in their role as women, and wrote proudly on the census blank: "Occupation: housewife."

For over fifteen years, the words written for women, and the words women used when they talked to each other, while their husbands sat on the other side of the room and talked shop or politics or septic tanks, were about problems with their children, or how to keep their husbands happy, or improve their children's school, or cook chicken or make slipcovers. Nobody argued whether women were inferior or superior to men; they were simply different. Words like "emancipation" and "career" sounded strange and embarrassing; no one had used them for years. When a Frenchwoman named Simone de Beauvoir wrote a book called *The Second Sex*, an American critic commented that she obviously "didn't know what life was all about," and besides, she was talking about French women. The "woman problem" in America no longer existed.

If a woman had a problem in the 1950s and 1960s she knew that something must be wrong with her marriage, or with herself. Other women were satisfied with their lives, she thought. What kind of a woman was she if she did not feel this mysterious fulfillment waxing the kitchen floor? She was so ashamed to admit her dissatisfaction that she never knew how many other women shared it. If she tried to tell her husband, he didn't understand what she was talking about. She did not really understand it herself. For over fifteen years women in America found it harder to talk about this problem than about sex. Even the psychoanalysts had no name for it. When a woman went to a psychiatrist for help, as many women did, she would say, "I'm so ashamed," or "I must be hopelessly neurotic." "I don't know what's wrong with women today," a suburban psychiatrist said uneasily. "I only know something is wrong because most of my patients happen to be women. And their problem isn't sexual." Most women with this problem did not go to see a psychoanalyst, however. "There's nothing wrong really," they kept telling themselves. "There isn't any problem."

But on an April morning in 1959, I heard a mother of four, having coffee with four other mothers in a suburban development fifteen miles from New York, say in a tone of quiet desperation, "the problem." And the others knew, without words, that she was not talking about a problem with her husband, or her children, or her home. Suddenly they realized they all shared the same problem, the problem that has no name. They began, hesitantly, to talk about it. Later, after they had picked up their children at nursery school and taken them home to nap, two of the women cried, in sheer relief, just to know they were not alone.

Gradually I came to realize that the problem that has no name was shared by countless women in America. As a magazine writer I often interviewed women about problems with their children, or their marriages, or their houses, or their communities. But after a while I began to recognize the telltale signs of this other problem. I saw the same signs in suburban ranch houses and split-levels on Long Island and in New Jersey and Westchester County; in colonial houses in a small Massachusetts town; on patios in Memphis; in suburban and city apartments; in living rooms in the Midwest. Sometimes I sensed the problem, not as a reporter, but as a suburban housewife, for during this time I was also bringing up my own three children in Rockland County, New York. I heard echoes of the problem in college dormitories and semi-private maternity wards, at PTA meetings and luncheons of the League of Women Voters, at suburban cocktail parties, in station wagons waiting for trains, and in snatches of conversation over-heard at Schrafft's. The groping words I heard from other women, on quiet afternoons when children were at school or on quiet evenings when husbands worked late, I think I understood first as a woman long before I understood their larger social and psychological implications.

Carol Hanisch, "The protest of the Miss America Pageant . . . told the nation a new feminist movement is afoot. . . ."

Women of Friedan's generation were divided as to whether they saw domesticity as sufficient to their fulfillment or if there truly was "a problem that had no name," and, if so, what it involved. Many young women, who had joined in the protest movements of the 1960s, had no such doubts. The group who gathered in Atlantic City in 1968 to protest the Miss America Pageant instantly caught the eye of the national and world media. Contrary to myth, no bras were burned; however, demonstrators hurled what they called "items of female torture" into a large "Freedom Trash Can," including false eyelashes, hair curlers, girdles, high-heel shoes, Toni home permanents (a sponsor of the pageant), *Playboy* and *Good Housekeeping* magazines, and even some bras. The pro-testers called for the end of beauty competitions, the pressure to conform to false beauty standards and buy related products, and the elevation of appearance over more impor-tant human qualities.

Despite all the media attention and the flood of new members into women's liber-ation groups, one of the action's originators felt that that the basic message had been overshadowed and distorted by some of the protesters' activity, as Carol Hanisch makes clear in this astute analysis.

Were the concerns of the 1968 protesters valid? Are they relevant to today's women? In what sense are they among the body issues Brumberg introduces in "Fasting Girls" (pp. 390–98)? Why does Hanisch consider some of the actions employed by her sister protesters counterproductive? What was the message of the protest that she believed they failed to get across?

The protest of the Miss America Pageant in Atlantic City told the nation that a new femi-nist movement is afoot in the land.

Due to the tremendous coverage in the mass media, millions of Americans now know there is a Women's Liberation Movement. The action brought many new members into our group and many requests from women out-

---

side the city for literature and information. A recurrent theme was, "I've been waiting so long for something like this."

But no action taken in the Women's Liberation struggle will be all good or all bad. We must analyze each step to see what was effective, what was not, and what was downright destructive.

At this point in our struggle, our actions should be aimed primarily at doing two interrelated things: (1) awakening the latent consciousness of women about our own oppression, and (2) building sisterhood. With these in mind, let us examine the Miss America protest.

The idea for the protest came out of the method used first in New York Radical Women of analyzing women's oppression by analyzing our own experiences, called consciousness-raising. One night at a meeting we were watching *Schmearguntz,* a feminist movie which contains flashes of the Miss America Pageant. I found myself remembering the powerful feelings the pageant had evoked in me as a child, an adolescent, and a college student. When I proposed the action to our group, we decided to go around the room with each woman telling how she felt about the pageant. We discovered that many of us who had always put down the contest still watched it. Others had consciously identified with it.

From our communal thinking came the concrete plans for the action. The original planning group agreed that the main point in the demonstration would be that all women are hurt by beauty competition—Miss America as well as ourselves. We opposed the pageant in our own self-interest, e.g., the self-interest of all women.

Yet one of the biggest mistakes of the whole pageant was our anti-womanism. A spirit of every woman "doing her own thing" began to emerge as women not in the original meetings came to the planning meetings. Some just went ahead and did what they wanted to do, even though it was something we had decided against. Because of this egotistic individualism, a definite strain of anti-womanism was presented to the public to the detriment of the action.

Posters that read "Up against the Wall, Miss America," "Miss America Sells It," and "Miss America Is a Big Falsie" hardly raised any woman's consciousness and really harmed the cause of sisterhood. Miss America and all beautiful women came off as our enemy instead of as our sisters who suffer with us.

A more complex situation developed around the decision of a few women to use an "underground" disruptive tactic. The group approved this activity only after its adherents said they would do it anyway as an individual action. We learned there is no such thing as "individual action" in a movement. There is, at this time, no real need to do "underground" actions anyway. We need to reach as many women as possible as quickly as possible with a clear message that has the power of our person behind it. Women need to see other women standing up together and saying these things. That's why draping a women's liberation banner over the balcony and yelling our message was much clearer than spraying a smelly chemical in the audience. The problem of how to enforce group decisions is one we haven't solved.

Another way we came off as anti-woman was our lack of clarity. We didn't say clearly enough that we women are all *forced* to play the Miss America role—not by beautiful women but by men who we have to act that way for, and by a system that has so well institutionalized male supremacy for its own ends. This was not very clear in our guerrilla theater. Women chained to a replica, red, white, and blue bathing-suited Miss America could have been misinterpreted as our blaming beautiful women. Also, crowning a live sheep Miss America sort of said that beautiful women *are* sheep. However, the action did say to some that women are *viewed as* auction-block, docile animals. The grandmother of one of the participants really began to understand the action when she was told about the sheep, and she ended up joining the protest.

There is as great a need for clarity in our language as there is in our actions. The leaflet that was distributed as a press release and flyer was too long, too wordy, too complex, too hippy-yippee-campy. Instead of an "in" phrase like "Racism with Roses," we could have just called the pageant "racist" and everybody would have understood our opposition on that point.

We should avoid the temptation to say everything there is to say about what is wrong with the world and thereby say nothing that a new person can really dig into and understand. Women's liberation itself is revolutionary dynamite. When other issues are interjected, we should clearly relate them to our oppression as women.

We tried to carry the democratic means we used in planning the action into the actual doing of it. We didn't want leaders or spokesmen. It makes the movement not only *seem* stronger and larger if everyone is a leader, but it actually *is* stronger if not dependent on a few. And, of course, many voices are more powerful than one. We must learn how to fight against the media's desire to make leaders— and some women's desire to appoint themselves spokesmen.

The Miss America protest was a zap action, which means using our presence as a group to make women's oppression into a social issue. In such actions we speak to men as a group as well as to women. It is a rare opportunity to talk to men in a situation where they can't talk back. (Men must learn to listen.) Our power of solidarity, not our individual intellectual exchanges will change men.

The reaction of many of the women we talked to about the protest was, "But I'm not oppressed" or "I don't care about Miss America." If more than half the television viewers in the country watch the pageant, somebody cares! While much of the Left was putting us down for attacking something so "silly and unimportant" or "reformist," the Right saw us as a threat and yelled such things as "Go back to Russia" and "Mothers of Mao" at the picket line. Ironically enough, what the Left/Underground press seemed to like best about our action was what was really our worst mistake—our anti-woman signs.

Surprisingly and fortunately, some of the mass media ignored our mistakes and concentrated on our best points. To quote the *Daily News*, "Some women who think the whole idea of such contests is degrading to femininity, took their case to the people.... During boardwalk protest, gals say they're not anti-beauty, just anti-beauty contest." Shana Alexander wrote in a *Life* magazine editorial that she "wished they'd gone farther."

The best slogan for the action came up afterward, when Ros Baxandall blurted out on the David Susskind television show that "Every day in a woman's life is a walking Miss America Contest!" But we shouldn't wait for the perfect slogan; we should go ahead to the best of our understanding.

> *Redstockings, "Male supremacy is the oldest, most basic form of domination."*

Another radical New York group which formed in 1969 called itself Redstockings. The name was a blending of "blue stocking," which had long been used to refer to women with intellectual and literary interests, with "red," which signaled revolution. In its "Manifesto," the group indicated that "the problem" went far beyond Friedan's resurgent domesticity. Friedan's "problem which had no name" indeed had a name, and that name was male supremacy, the most ancient form of oppression—older even than class oppression. That sexual oppression was the most basic form of oppression would become *the* fundamental tenet for women who would come to be known as radical feminists.

The Redstockings Manifesto was issued in New York City on July 7, 1969. It appeared as a mimeographed flier, designed for distribution at women's liberation events. It is reprinted by permission of Redstockings. A catalog containing ordering information for this and other documents from the 1960s rebirth years of feminism is available from the Redstocking Women's Liberation Archives for Action Distribution Project, P.O. Box 2625, Gainesville, FL 32602-2625. The catalog is also available on the web at: http://www.redstockings.org.

To what extent were the Redstockings using Marxist theory, substituting women for the working class? What did they believe had prevented women from recognizing their oppression and doing something about it? What was it they wanted to change with respect to men? What did they imply were (and are) the barriers among and between women that have to be overcome to achieve the female solidarity required if women are to be a collective entity—a class prepared to undertake revolutionary action on its own behalf?

REDSTOCKINGS MANIFESTO

I After centuries of individual and preliminary political struggle, women are uniting to achieve their final liberation from male supremacy. Redstockings is dedicated to building this unity and winning our freedom.

II Women are an oppressed class. Our oppression is total, affecting every facet of our lives. We are exploited as sex objects, breeders, domestic servants, and cheap labor. We are considered inferior beings, whose only purpose is to enhance men's lives. Our humanity is denied. Our prescribed behavior is enforced by the threat of physical violence.

Because we have lived so intimately with our oppressors, in isolation from each other, we have been kept from seeing our personal suffering as a political condition. This creates the illusion that a woman's relationship with her man is a matter of interplay between two unique personalities, and can be worked out individually. In reality, every such relationship is a *class* relationship, and the conflicts between individual men and women are *political* conflicts that can only be solved collectively.

III We identify the agents of our oppression as men. Male supremacy is the oldest, most basic form of domination. All other forms of exploitation and oppression (racism, capitalism, imperialism, etc.) are extensions of male supremacy: men dominate women, a few men dominate the rest. All power structures throughout history have been male-dominated and male-oriented. Men have controlled all political, economic and cultural institutions and backed up this control with physical force. They have used their power to keep women in an inferior position. *All men* receive economic, sexual, and psychological benefits from male supremacy. *All men* have oppressed women.

IV Attempts have been made to shift the burden of responsibility from men to institutions or to women themselves. We condemn these arguments as evasions. Institutions alone do not oppress; they are merely tools of the oppressor. To blame institutions implies that men and women are equally victimized, obscures the fact that men benefit from the subordination of women, and gives men the excuse that they are forced to be oppressors. On the contrary, any man is free to renounce his superior position provided that he is willing to be treated like a woman by other men.

We also reject the idea that women consent to or are to blame for their own oppression. Women's submission is not the result of brainwashing, stupidity, or mental illness but of continual, daily pressure from men. We do not need to change ourselves, but to change men.

The most slanderous evasion of all is that women can oppress men. The basis for this illusion is the isolation of individual relationships from their political context and the tendency of men to see any legitimate challenge to their privileges as persecution.

V We regard our personal experience, and our feelings about that experience, as the basis for an analysis of our common situation. We cannot rely on existing ideologies as they are all products of male supremacist culture. We question every generalization and accept none that are not confirmed by our experience.

Our chief task at present is to develop female class consciousness through sharing experience and publicly exposing the sexist foundation of all our institutions. Consciousness-raising is not "therapy," which implies the existence of individual solutions and falsely assumes that the male-female relationship is purely personal, but the only method by which we can ensure that our program for liberation is based on the concrete realities of our lives.

The first requirement for raising class consciousness is honesty, in private and in public, with ourselves and other women.

VI   We identify with all women. We define our best interest as that of the poorest, most brutally exploited woman.

We repudiate all economic, racial, educational or status privileges that divide us from other women. We are determined to recognize and eliminate any prejudices we may hold against other women.

We are committed to achieving internal democracy. We will do whatever is necessary to ensure that every woman in our movement has an equal chance to participate, assume responsibility, and develop her political potential.

VII   We call on all our sisters to unite with us in struggle.

We call on all men to give up their male privileges and support women's liberation in the interest of our humanity and their own.

In fighting for our liberation we will always take the side of women against their oppressors. We will not ask what is "revolutionary" or "reformist," only what is good for women.

The time for individual skirmishes has passed. This time we are going all the way.

July 7, 1969
REDSTOCKINGS
P.O. Box 748
Stuyvesant Station
New York, N.Y. 10009

Radicalesbians, "What is a lesbian?"

This question mattered in the late 1960s and early 1970s. Was it a label used contemptuously to belittle and isolate radicals like the protesters who had "burned" their bras at the Miss America pageant? Was the charge a form of rhetorical retaliation to be wielded by opponents against the "man-hating" women who wrote the Redstockings "Manifesto"? Or did it refer to the sexual preferences and behavior of specific women who identified themselves as feminists? Fearing that the presence of the latter would be used by opponents to discredit the growing women's movement, Betty Friedan worried about what she allegedly referred to as the "lavender menace." The "lavender menace" went public in 1970 when a group of lesbians on both coasts stepped forward to demand discussion of homophobia within the emerging feminist movement. In the years to follow, as they increasingly insisted that being a lesbian is fundamentally sexual, not political, and that sexual orientation may not be a matter of choice, the separatist pull became stronger—a phenomenon evident especially among feminists of color, who also had differences with the movement over race. In the meantime, a group known as Radicalesbians issued the controversial statement that follows, describing the lesbian as a "woman-identified woman."

Note the reaction to the enduring tendency to equate feminists generally with "unnatural women" or lesbians. Do the authors see lesbianism as a political choice or a biological preference for sexual partners of the same sex (a matter still far from settled)?

Radicalesbians, "The Woman-Identified Woman," 1970, Susan O'Malley personal collection; reprinted in *Dear Sisters: Dispatches from the Women's Liberation Movement*, ed. Rosalyn Baxandall and Linda Gordon (New York: Basic Books, 2000).

What would be the advantage of viewing lesbianism as a political stance only? What would be the drawbacks of that position? Who would object and why?

What is a lesbian? A lesbian is the rage of all women condensed to the point of explosion. She is the woman who, often beginning at an extremely early age, acts in accordance with her inner compulsion to be a more complete and freer human being than her society—perhaps then, but certainly later—cares to allow her. She may not be fully conscious of the political implications of what for her began as personal necessity, but on some level she has not been able to accept the limitations and oppression laid on her by the most basic role of her society—the female role. The turmoil she experiences tends to induce guilt proportional to the degree to which she feels she is not meeting social expectations, and eventually drives her to question and analyse what the rest of her society more or less accepts. She is forced to evolve her own life pattern, often living much of her life alone, learning usually much earlier than her "straight" (heterosexual) sisters about the essential aloneness of life (which the myth of marriage obscures). For she is caught somewhere between accepting society's view of her—in which case she cannot accept herself, and coming to understand what this sexist society has done to her and why it is functional and necessary for it to do so. Those of us who work that through find ourselves on the other side of a tortuous journey through a night that may have been decades long. The perspective gained from that journey, the liberation of self, the inner peace, the real love of self and of all women, is something to be shared with all women—because we are all women.

It should first be understood that lesbianism, like male homosexuality, is a category of behaviour possible only in a sexist society characterized by rigid sex roles and dominated by male supremacy. Those sex roles dehumanize women by defining us as a supportive/serving caste *in relation to* the master caste of men, and emotionally cripple men by demanding that they be alienated from their own bodies and emotions in order to perform their economic/political/military functions effectively. Homosexuality is a by-product of a particular way of setting up roles (or approved patterns of behaviour) on the basis of

sex; as such it is an inauthentic (not consonant with "reality") category. In a society in which men do not oppress women, and sexual expression is allowed to follow feelings, the categories of homosexuality and heterosexuality would disappear.

But lesbianism is also different from male homosexuality, and serves a different function in the society. "Dyke" is a different kind of put-down from "faggot," although both imply you are not playing your socially assigned sex role—are not therefore a "real woman" or a "real man." The grudging admiration felt for the tomboy, and the queasiness felt around a sissy boy point to the same thing: the contempt in which women—or those who play a female role—are held. And the investment in keeping women in that contemptuous role is very great. Lesbian is the word, the label, the condition that holds women in line. When a woman hears this word tossed her way, she knows she is stepping out of line.

Lesbian is a label invented by the Man to throw at any woman who dares to be his equal, who dares to challenge his prerogatives, who dares to assert the primacy of her own needs. To have the label applied to people active in women's liberation is just the most recent instance of a long history; older women will recall that not so long ago, any woman who was successful, independent, not orienting her whole life about a man, would hear this word. For in this sexist society, for a woman to be independent means she *can't be* a woman—she must be a dyke. It says as clearly as can be said: Woman and person are contradictory terms. And yet, in popular thinking, there is really only one essential difference between a lesbian and other women: that of sexual orientation—which is to say, when you strip off all the packaging, you must finally realize that the essence of being a "woman" is to get fucked by men.

"Lesbian" is one of the sexual categories by which men have divided up humanity. For women, especially those in the movement, to perceive their lesbian sisters through this male grid of role definitions is to accept this male cultural conditioning and to oppress their sisters much as they themselves have been oppressed by men. Are we going to continue the male classification system of defining all females in sexual relation to some other category of people? Affixing the label lesbian not only to a woman who aspires to be a person, but also to any situation of real love, real solidarity, real primacy among women is a primary form of divisiveness among women: It is the condition which keeps women within the confines of the feminine role, and it is the debunking/scare term that keeps women from forming any primary attachments, groups, or associations among ourselves.

Women in the movement have in most cases gone to great lengths to avoid discussion and confrontation with the issue of lesbianism. It puts people uptight. They are hostile, evasive, or try to incorporate it into some "broader issue." They would rather not talk about it. If they have to, they try to dismiss it as a "lavender herring." But it is no side issue. It is absolutely essential to the success and fulfillment of the women's liberation movement that this issue be dealt with. As long as the label "dyke" can be used to frighten women into a less militant stand, keep her separate from her sisters, keep her from giving primacy to anything other than men and family—then to that extent she is controlled by the male culture. Until women see in each other the possibility of a primal commitment which includes sexual love, they will be denying themselves the love and value they readily accord to men, thus affirming their second-class status. As long as male acceptability is primary—both to individual women and to the movement as a whole—the term lesbian will be used effectively against women. Insofar as women want only more privileges within the system, they do not want to antagonize male power. They instead seek acceptability for women's liberation, and the most crucial aspect of the acceptability is to deny lesbianism—i.e., deny any fundamental challenge to the basis of the female.

It should also be said that some younger, more radical women have honestly begun to discuss lesbianism, but so far it has been primarily as a sexual "alternative" to men. This, however, is still giving primacy to men, both because the idea of relating more completely to women occurs as a negative reaction to men, and because the lesbian relationship is being characterized simply by sex, which is divisive and sexist. It must be understood that what is crucial is that women begin disengaging from male-defined response patterns in the privacy of our own psyches; we must cut those cords to the core. For irrespective of where our love and sexual energies flow, if we are male-identified in our heads, we cannot realize our autonomy as human beings.

As the source of self-hate and the lack of real self are rooted in our male-given identity, we must create a new sense of self. As long as we cling to the idea of "being a woman," we will sense some conflict with that incipient self, that sense of I, that sense of a whole person. It is very difficult to realize and accept that being "feminine" and being a whole person are irreconcilable. Only women can give to each other a new sense of self. That identity we have to develop with reference to ourselves, and not in relation to men. As long as women's liberation tries to free women without facing the basic heterosexual structure that binds us in one-to-one relationship with our oppressors, tremendous energies will continue to flow into trying to straighten up each particular relationship with a man, how to get better sex, how to turn his head around—into trying to make the "new man" out of him, in the delusion that this will allow us to be the "new woman." This obviously splits our energies and commitments, leaving us unable to be committed to the construction of the new patterns which will liberate us.

It is the primacy of women relating to women, of women creating a new consciousness of and with each other which is at the heart of women's liberation, and the basis for the cultural revolution. Together we must find, reinforce, and validate our authentic selves. As we do this, we confirm in each other that struggling incipient sense of pride and strength, the divisive barriers begin to melt, we feel this growing solidarity with our sisters. We see ourselves as prime, find our centers inside of ourselves. We find receding the sense of alienation, of being cut off, of being behind a locked window, of being unable to get out what we know is inside. We feel a real-ness, feel at last we are coinciding with ourselves. With that real self, with that consciousness, we begin a revolution to end the imposition of all coercive identifications, and to achieve maximum autonomy in human expression.

Jennie V. Chavez, "It has taken . . . a long time . . . to realize and speak out about the double oppression of Mexican-American women"

Jennie Chavez, like thousands of young women of color, joined liberation movements in the 1960s and 1970s. In this account of her experience in the Chicano movement, Chavez describes the resistance she faced when, recognizing the double oppression of Mexican American women, she organized "Las Chicanas." Incipient feminists, these women of color recognized early on that gender was not the only factor subordinating women. What insights does she have into power relationships between Mexican Americans and Anglos as well as between men and women within her own ethnic group? Note her disdain for the consumer goods that signal middle-class status. What evidence is there to suggest that Chavez and her Chicana generation had also been affected by the sexual revolution of the 1960s? How did males in the movement respond to women asserting themselves? To what does Chavez attribute their machismo?

As one of the first members of the United Mexican American Students [UMAS] when it got started in 1969 on the UNM [University of New Mexico] campus, I was given special attention, being fairly attractive and flirtatious. But as soon as I started expounding my own ideas the men who ran the organization would either ignore my statement or make a wisecrack about it and continue their own discussion. This continued for two years until I finally broke away because of being unable to handle the situation. I turned to student government. There I was considered a radical racist Mexican militant, yet with the Chicano radicals I was considered a sellout. I was caught in the middle, wanting to help but with neither side allowing me.

The summer of 1970, after the Cambodia crisis, I traveled extensively, "getting my head together," [and formed] Las Chicanas the following December. [The result was that I] caught more shit than I knew existed from both males and females in the movement. Some felt I was dividing the existing UMAS; some were simply afraid of displeasing the men. Some felt that I was wrong and my ideas were "white," and still others felt that their contribution to La Causa or El Movimiento was in giving the men moral support from the kitchen. It took two months of heartbreak on both sides for the organization to be recognized as valid. Now, however, because a few women were willing to stand strong against some of the macho men who ridiculed them, called them white and avoided them socially, the organization has become one of the strongest and best-known in the state.

It has taken what I consider a long time for [Chicanas] to realize and to speak out about the double oppression of the Mexican-American woman. Chicanas traditionally, have been tortilla-makers, baby-producers, to be touched but not heard. In order to someday obtain those middle-class goods (which in my eyes oppress more people than they liberate from "drudgery") our women have not only been working at slave jobs for the white society as housemaids, hotel maids and laundry workers, but have tended also to the wants of a husband and many children—many children because contraceptives have been contrary to the ethnic idea of La Familia (with all its socio-political economic implications).

As the social revolution for all people's freedoms has progressed, so Chicanas have caught the essence of freedom in the air. The change occurred slowly. Mexican-American women have been reluctant to speak up, afraid that they might show up the men in front of the white man—afraid that they may think our men not men. Now, however, the Chicana is becoming as well-educated and as aware of oppression, if not more so, as the Mexican-American male.

The women are changing their puritanical mode of dress, entering the professions of law, business, medicine and engineering. They are no longer afraid to show their intellect, their capabilities and their potential. More and more they oppose the Catholic Church, to which a large majority of our ethnic group belongs, challenging its sexual taboos as well as the idea that all Catholic mothers must be baby-producing factories, and that contraceptives are a sin.

Out of the workshop on "Sex and La Chicana" at the first National Mujeres Por la Raza conference in Houston, Texas came the following resolutions:

(1) that Chicanas should develop a more healthy attitude toward sex and get rid of the misconceptions about its "evil," thus allowing ourselves to be as aggressive as men; (2) that we object to the use of sex as a means of exploiting women and for commercial purposes; (3) that no religious institution should have the authority to sanction what is moral or immoral between a man and a woman.

As the new breed of Mexican-American women, we have been, and probably will continue to be, ridiculed by our men for attempting the acrobatics of equality. We may well be ostracized by La Familia for being vendidos, sell-outs to the "white ideas" of late marriage, postponing or not wanting children and desiring a vocation other than tortilla-rolling, but I believe that this new breed of bronze womanhood, as all women today, will be a vanguard for world change.

Naturally, there are liberated Chicanos who respect and treat women as equals, but they are so few that at this point I still have to generalize. Mexican-American men, as other men of oppressed groups, have been very reluctant to give up their machismo [exaggerated assertion of masculinity] because it has been a last retention of power in a society which dehumanizes and mechanizes them. But now they are comprehending the meaning of carnalismo (brotherhood) in the feminine gender as well . . . a new revolution within a revolution has begun.

"Women in the Asian movement find that . . . stereotypes are still hovering over their heads . . . that [they] must play [the] old role[s] in order to get things done"

Like their Chicana sisters, women in the Asian movement fought against old stereotypes and encountered new ones when they tried to exercise leadership in the Asian movement. They too found that their men were prone to male chauvinism and that as women they had to deal with racism, sexism, and imperialism, and deal with them simultaneously.

On the basis of this document (first published in 1971), compare the stereotypes that exist about women of both ethnic groups in the larger culture. Do both encounter the same resistance from men in the movement? With respect to their movements and the men in them, the options of these third world women or women of color, as they are sometimes called, are basically two. What are these options and what, on the basis of the two documents you have read, do both Chicanas and Asian women initially hope for?

ASIAN WOMEN AS LEADERS

American society is broken up into different levels based on economic income, education, politics, color, and sex. Each level has a pre-scribed set of rules for action and interplay—roles that are enforced by the levels above. At the bottom of these varying gradations are women of color. Third World women face domination by both racism and sexism (dis-crimination based on sex). Both racism and sexism are means by which American society controls and oppresses everyone. Everyone is forced to conform to the values and roles established by the dominant group in order to "succeed." For the Asian movement to progress, it must have a clear understanding of sexism, racism, and imperialism; and deal with them simultaneously.

For Asian women in general, the stereo-types or roles have been of two major kinds: either docile, submissive Oriental dolls who will cater to the whims of any man; or the Suzie Wong, sexpot, exotic bitch-body. Between these two are the efficient secretary, sexy stewardess, the good housekeeper and domestic, the girl any guy would like to marry.

Women in the Asian movement find that these stereotypes are still hovering over their heads. Not only these but new stereotypes, too: i.e., Asian men have tried to define for "their women" what it means to be "heavy." Men in the Asian movement also find them-selves tied down to stereotypes. Perhaps they may feel that to be a MAN one must have authority and responsibility. In the same light, they will frown on women who take on a lot of responsibility (and the authority that goes along with it), labelling them as "unfeminine." Women then tend to fear this loss of "femi-ninity" and so they do the clerical work and the cleaning up, activities for which intellect is not essential or expected. Women may also ful-fill these jobs because they do them best: And why do they do the best? Because

women are never encouraged to do anything else; women's potential abilities as a leader are left untapped and undeveloped. She loses her confidence in being able to handle such responsibility.

The sisters who have achieved a position of authority in the movement are a minority and are still trapped by the stereotypes that society has created. It is a struggle for women to attain the top leadership positions. Women who "make it" into such positions have had to reject the stereotypes already imposed upon them. But because the new definition of "the Asian woman" has not yet evolved, women find themselves in a "limbo." Some find them-selves being labelled as Bitches—women who speak out loudly and strongly; who are authoritarian, who boss people around, and command some form of respect. Some must resort to being overly diligent and efficient to prove themselves as worthy of the same lead-ership positions as the men. Others gain respect by appearing to accomplish work in a multitude of projects but actually only com-plete a few tasks. And still others attain their leadership positions as token gestures. Some women can gain respect only by putting up with put-downs on other women, i.e., "you're not one of those bird-brained little girls," or "You're as strong as a man!"

Once women do get into leadership posi-tions, they find that their ideas are usurped by the men, who then take credit for the idea as being their own. Women are often heard but not listened to. Many times, the woman must play her old role in order to get things done: "Oh, please, can you help me carry this. It's much too heavy for little old me. . . ."

How can these problems be solved? Peo-ple must recognize that women are half of the working force in the movement against oppression, exploitation, and imperialism. They are half of the working force in creating the new revolutionary lifestyle. Men and women in the movement must therefore begin to live the ideals and goals they are working for. To do this, they must not let chauvinist acts slide by. People cannot work together effectively if there are hidden tensions or if people let little annoyances build up inside themselves. They must deal with racism or imperialism. They must be able to develop as human beings, not subject to categorizations and stereotypes. Developing as people confident in themselves, in their ideas, they will not be afraid of criticism; they will see the need for criticism, and self-criticism, in order to move forward. The struggle is not men against women nor women against men, but it is a united front striving for a new society, a new way of life.

> If I go forward,
> Follow me.
> Push me if I fall behind.
> If I betray you,
> If they take me,
> Avenge me then in kind.

The Combahee River Collective, "We also find it difficult to separate race from class from sex oppression"

The Combahee River Collective, a black feminist group founded in Boston in 1974, took its name from a guerrilla action planned and led by Harriet Tubman during the Civil War that freed more than 750 South Carolina slaves. The group, which consisted of battle-scarred veterans of the civil rights, New Left, and early women's movements, had done some hard thinking before writing this statement. In it, they stated what they believed to be the limitations of their white feminist sisters as well as their own problems in organizing black feminists.

What were the Collective's specific criticisms of other feminists—radical, liberal, as well as lesbian separatists? Why did they think that black feminism was (and is) so threatening to the black community, especially to black males who identified with black nationalism? What do you regard as their most important insights?

We are a collective of Black feminists who have been meeting together since 1974. During that time we have been involved in the process of defining and clarifying our politics, while at the same time doing political work within our own group and in coalition with other progressive organizations and movements. The most general statement of our politics at the present time would be that we are actively committed to struggling against racial, sexual, heterosexual, and class oppression, and see as our particular task the development of integrated analysis and practice based upon the fact that the major systems of oppression are interlocking. The synthesis of these oppressions creates the conditions of our lives. As Black women we see Black feminism as the logical political movement to combat the manifold and simultaneous oppressions that all women of color face. . . .

1. THE GENESIS OF CONTEMPORARY BLACK FEMINISM

Before looking at the recent development of Black feminism, we would like to affirm that we find our origins in the historical reality of Afro-American women's continuous life-and-

Excerpts from The Combahee River Collective Statement in *Home Girls: A Black Feminist Anthology* edited by Barbara Smith (Latham, NY: Kitchen Table: Women of Color Press, 1983), pp. 272–82. Reprinted by permission of Barbara Smith.

death struggle for survival and liberation. Black women's extremely negative relationship to the American political system (a system of white male rule) has always been determined by our membership in two oppressed racial and sexual castes. As Angela Davis points out in "Reflections on the Black Woman's Role in the Community of Slaves," Black women have always embodied, if only in their physical manifestation, an adversary stance to white male rule and have actively resisted its inroads upon them and their communities in both dramatic and subtle ways. There have always been Black women activists—some known, like Sojourner Truth, Harriet Tubman, Frances E. W. Harper, Ida B. Wells Barnett, and Mary Church Terrell, and thousands upon thousands unknown—who have had a shared awareness of how their sexual identity combined with their racial identity to make their whole life situation and the focus of their political struggles unique. Contemporary Black feminism is the outgrowth of countless generations of personal sacrifice, militancy, and work by our mothers and sisters.

A Black feminist presence has evolved most obviously in connection with the second wave of the American women's movement beginning in the late 1960s. Black, other Third World, and working women have been involved in the feminist movement from its start, but both outside reactionary forces and racism and elitism within the movement itself have served to obscure our participation. In 1973, Black feminists, primarily located in New York, felt the necessity of forming a separate Black feminist group. This became the National Black Feminist Organization (NBFO).

Black feminist politics also have an obvious connection to movements for Black liberation, particularly those of the 1960s and 1970s. Many of us were active in those movements (Civil Rights, Black nationalism, the Black Panthers), and all of our lives were greatly affected and changed by their ideologies, their goals, and the tactics used to achieve their goals. It was our experience and disillusionment within these liberation movements, as well as experience on the periphery of the white male left, that led to the need to develop a politics that was anti-racist, unlike those of white women, and anti-sexist, unlike those of Black and white men.

There is also undeniably a personal genesis for Black feminism, that is, the political realization that comes from the seemingly personal experiences of individual Black women's lives. Black feminists and many more Black women who do not define themselves as feminists have all experienced sexual oppression as a constant factor in our day-to-day existence. As children we realized that we were different from boys and that we were treated differently. For example, we were told in the same breath to be quiet both for the sake of being "ladylike" and to make us less objectionable in the eyes of white people. As we grew older we became aware of the threat of physical and sexual abuse by men. However, we had no way of conceptualizing what was so apparent to us, what we *knew* was really happening.

Black feminists often talk about their feelings of craziness before becoming conscious of the concepts of sexual politics, patriarchal rule, and most importantly, feminism, the political analysis and practice that we women use to struggle against our oppression. The fact that racial politics and indeed racism are pervasive factors in our lives did not allow us, and still does not allow most Black women, to look more deeply into our own experiences and, from that sharing and growing consciousness, to build a politics that will change our lives and inevitably end our oppression. Our development must also be tied to the contemporary economic and political position of Black people. The post–World War II generation of Black youth was the first to be able to minimally partake of certain educational and employment options, previously closed completely to Black people. Although our economic position is still at the very bottom of the American capitalistic economy, a handful of us have been able to gain certain tools as a result of tokenism in education and employment which potentially enable us to more effectively fight our oppression.

A combined anti-racist and anti-sexist position drew us together initially, and as we developed politically we addressed ourselves to heterosexism and economic oppression under capitalism.

2. WHAT WE BELIEVE

Above all else, our politics initially sprang from the shared belief that Black women are inherently valuable, that our liberation is a necessity not as an adjunct to somebody else's but because of our need as human persons for autonomy. This may seem so obvious as to sound simplistic, but it is apparent that no other ostensibly progressive movement has ever considered our specific oppression as a priority or worked seriously for the ending of that oppression. Merely naming the pejorative stereotypes attributed to Black women (e.g., mammy, matriarch, Sapphire, whore, bulldagger), let alone cataloguing the cruel, often murderous, treatment we receive, indicates how little value has been placed upon our lives during four centuries of bondage in the Western hemisphere. We realize that the only people who care enough about us to work consistently for our liberation are us. Our politics evolve from a healthy love for ourselves, our sisters, and our community, which allows us to continue our struggle and work.

This focusing upon our own oppression is embodied in the concept of identity politics. We believe that the most profound and potentially most radical politics come directly out of our own identity, as opposed to working to end somebody else's oppression. In the case of Black women this is a particularly repugnant, dangerous, threatening, and therefore revolutionary concept because it is obvious from looking at all the political movements that have preceded us that anyone is more worthy of liberation than ourselves. We reject pedestals, queenhood, and walking ten paces behind. To be recognized as human, levelly human, is enough.

We believe that sexual politics under patriarchy is as pervasive in Black women's lives as are the politics of class and race. We also often find it difficult to separate race from class from sex oppression because in our lives they are most often experienced simultaneously. We know that there is such a thing as racial-sexual oppression which is neither solely racial nor solely sexual, e.g., the history of rape of Black women by white men as a weapon of political repression.

Although we are feminists and Lesbians, we feel solidarity with progressive Black men and do not advocate the fractionalization that white women who are separatists demand. Our situation as Black people necessitates that we have solidarity around the fact of race, which white women of course do not need to have with white men, unless it is their negative solidarity as racial oppressors. We struggle together with Black men against racism, while we also struggle with Black men about sexism.

We realize that the liberation of all oppressed peoples necessitates the destruction of the political-economic systems of capitalism and imperialism as well as patriarchy. We are socialists because we believe that work must be organized for the collective benefit of those who do the work and create the products, and not for the profit of the bosses. Material resources must be equally distributed among those who create these resources. We are not convinced, however, that a socialist revolution that is not also a feminist and anti-racist revolution will guarantee our liberation. We have arrived at the necessity for developing an understanding of class relationships that takes into account the specific class position of Black women who are generally marginal in the labor force, while at this particular time some of us are temporarily viewed as doubly desirable tokens at white-collar and professional levels. We need to articulate the real class situation of persons who are not merely raceless, sexless workers, but for whom racial and sexual oppression are significant determinants in their working/economic lives. Although we are in essential agreement with Marx's theory as it applied to the very specific economic relationships he analyzed, we know that his analysis must be extended further in order for us to understand our specific economic situation as Black women.

A political contribution which we feel we have already made is the expansion of the feminist principle that the personal is political. In our consciousness-raising sessions, for example, we have in many ways gone beyond white women's revelations because we are dealing with the implications of race and class as well as sex. Even our Black women's style of talking/testifying in Black language about what we have experienced has a resonance that is both cultural and political. We have spent a great deal of energy delving into the cultural and experiential nature of our oppression out of necessity because none of these matters has ever been looked at before. No one before has ever examined the multilayered texture of Black women's lives. An example of this kind of revelation/conceptualization occurred at a meeting as we discussed the ways in which our early intellectual interests had been attacked by our peers, particularly Black males. We discovered that all of us, because we were "smart" had also been considered "ugly," i.e., "smart-ugly." "Smart-ugly" crystallized the way in which most of us had been forced to develop our intellects at great cost to our "social" lives. The sanctions in the Black and white communities against Black women thinkers is comparatively much higher than for white women, particularly ones from the educated middle and upper classes.

As we have already stated, we reject the stance of Lesbian separatism because it is not a viable political analysis or strategy for us. It leaves out far too much and far too many people, particularly Black men, women, and children. We have a great deal of criticism and loathing for what men have been socialized to be in this society: what they support, how they act, and how they oppress. But we do not have the misguided notion that it is their maleness, per se—i.e., their biological maleness—that makes them what they are. As Black women we find any type of biological determinism a particularly dangerous and reactionary basis upon which to build a politic. We must also question whether Lesbian separatism is an adequate and progressive political analysis and strategy, even for those who practice it, since it so completely denies any but the sexual sources of women's oppression, negating the facts of class and race.

3. PROBLEMS IN ORGANIZING BLACK FEMINISTS

During our years together as a Black feminist collective, we have experienced success and defeat, joy and pain, victory and failure. We have found that it is very difficult to organize around Black feminist issues, difficult even to announce in certain contexts that we *are* Black feminists. We have tried to think about the reasons for our difficulties, particularly since the white women's movement continues to be strong and to grow in many directions. In this section we will discuss some of the general reasons for the organizing problems we face and also talk specifically about the stages in organizing our own collective.

The major source of difficulty in our political work is that we are not just trying to fight oppression on one front, or even two, but instead to address a whole range of oppressions. We do not have racial, sexual, heterosexual, or class privilege to rely upon, nor do we have even the minimal access to resources and power that groups who possess any one of these types of privilege have.

The psychological toll of being a Black woman and the difficulties this presents in reaching political consciousness and doing political work can never be underestimated. There is very low value placed upon Black women's psyches in this society, which is both racist and sexist. As an early group member once said, "We are all damaged people merely by virtue of being Black women." We are dispossessed psychologically and on every other level, and yet we feel the necessity to struggle to change the condition of all Black women. In "A Black Feminist's Search for Sisterhood," Michele Wallace arrives at this conclusion:

> We exist as women who are Black who are feminists, each stranded for the moment, working independently because there is not yet an environment in this society remotely congenial to our struggle—because, being on the bottom, we would have to do what no one else has done: We would have to fight the world.[1]

Wallace is pessimistic but realistic in her assessment of Black feminists' position, particularly in her allusion to the nearly classic isolation most of us face. We might use our position at the bottom, however, to make a clear leap into revolutionary action. If Black women were free, it would mean that everyone else would have to be free, since our freedom would necessitate the destruction of all the systems of oppression.

Feminism is, nevertheless, very threatening to the majority of Black people because it calls into question some of the most basic assumptions about our existence, i.e., that sex should be a determinant of power relationships. Here is the way male and female roles were defined in a Black nationalist pamphlet from the early 1970s:

> ... The man is the head of the house. He is the leader of the house/nation because his knowledge of the world is broader, his awareness is greater, his understanding is fuller and his application of this information is wiser. ... Women cannot do the same things as men—they are made by nature to function differently. Equality of men and women is something that cannot happen even in the abstract world.[2] ...

The material conditions of most Black women would hardly lead them to upset both economic and sexual arrangements that seem to represent some stability in their lives. Many Black women have a good understanding of both sexism and racism, but because of the everyday constrictions of their lives, cannot risk struggling against them both.

The reaction of Black men to feminism has been notoriously negative. They are, of course, even more threatened than Black women by the possibility that Black feminists might organize around our own needs. They realize that they might not only lose valuable and hardworking allies in their struggles but that they might also be forced to change their habitually sexist ways of interacting with and oppressing Black women. Accusations that Black feminism divides the Black struggle are powerful deterrents to the growth of an autonomous Black women's movement. . . .

4. BLACK FEMINIST ISSUES AND PROJECTS

During our time together we have identified and worked on many issues of particular relevance to Black women. The inclusiveness of our politics makes us concerned with any situation that impinges upon the lives of women, Third World, and working people. We are of course particularly committed to working on those struggles in which race, sex, and class are simultaneously factors in oppression. We might, for example, become involved in workplace organizing at a factory that employs Third World women or picket a hospital that is cutting back on already inadequate health care to a Third World community, or set up a rape crisis center in a Black neighborhood. Organizing around welfare and daycare concerns might also be a focus. The work to be done and the countless issues that this work represents merely reflect the pervasiveness of our oppression.

Issues and projects that collective members have actually worked on are sterilization abuse, abortion rights, battered women, rape, and health care. We have also done many workshops and educationals on Black feminism on college campuses, at women's conferences, and most recently for high school women.

One issue that is of major concern to us and that we have begun to publicly address is racism in the white women's movement. As Black feminists we are made constantly and painfully aware of how little effort white women have made to understand and combat their racism, which requires among other things that they have a more than superficial comprehension of race, color, and Black history and culture. Eliminating racism in the white women's movement is by definition work for white women to do, but we will continue to speak to and demand accountability on this issue.

In the practice of our politics we do not believe that the end always justifies the means. Many reactionary and destructive acts have been done in the name of achieving "correct" political goals. As feminists we do not want to mess over people in the name of politics. We believe in collective process and a nonhierarchical distribution of power within our own group and in our vision of a revolutionary society. We are committed to a continual examination of our politics as they develop through criticism and self-criticism as an essential aspect of our practice. . . .

As Black feminists and Lesbians we know that we have a very definite revolutionary task to perform and we are ready for the lifetime of work and struggle before us.

NOTES

1. Michele Wallace, "A Black Feminist's Search for Sisterhood," *Village Voice*, July 28, 1975, pp. 6–7.
2. Mumininas of Committee for Unified Newark, Mwanamke Mwananchi (The Nationalist Woman), Newark, NJ, 1971, pp. 4–5.

Kay Weiss, "One of the cruelest forms of sexism we live with today is . . . [that] of many doctors"

Critiques of physicians came not only from female patients and medical students, but from health care workers at every level. Gynecologists and obstetricians who treated women on matters relating to sexual activity, abortion, and childbirth received the severest scrutiny. Many were patronizing, moralistic, and infantilizing in their treatment of female patients. Critics emphasized that the problem was not just the personal shortcomings of individual doctors. Nor was it merely the result of their training. At the heart of the problem was a fundamental devaluation of women that led physicians to feel that it was their responsibility to make health care decisions for their female patients, since women were simply not competent to participate in informed decisions regarding their own health. Medical scientists under the imprimatur of the National Institutes of Health, operating under their own masculinist bias, tested drugs on men and mistakenly assumed the results would apply to women, whom they didn't bother to include in the tests.

Many of these early critiques, like the one that follows, were published and distributed through women's movement networks. In calling for women to take greater responsibility for their own health care, they were forerunners of the classic *Our Bodies, Ourselves.* The book had its origins in 1969 in the discussion of a small group of Boston women who felt frustrated about doctors whom they considered "condescending, paternalistic, judgmental, and non-informative."* (On your next trip to a bookstore, take a look at the book's most recent edition, *Our Bodies, Ourselves for the New Century,* and try to imagine what it would have been like to encounter the text and illustration in the chapters on sexuality and birth control in 1971.)

While these early indictments, including the one that follows, may have verged on exaggeration, they also provide a window into psychotherapy in the age of the feminine mystique. It should come as no surprise that feminists would challenge a sexist psychiatric and psychological establishment that recommended treatment for any woman who displayed mental and physical symptoms that suggested she was not behaving as a "mature adult" who found sexual fulfillment in vaginally induced orgasm and personal fulfillment in marriage and maternity.

In your own experience with the medical community, have most of the problems of which young women complained a quarter of a century ago been remedied as both sexes have come to take greater responsibility for their medical treatment? What vestiges linger?

---

*The Boston Women's Health Book Collective, *The New Our Bodies, Ourselves* (New York: Simon & Schuster, 1984), quoted from the preface of the original edition, xvii.

Kay Weiss, "What Medical Students Learn," KNOW pamphlet #310, Pittsburgh; reprinted in *Dear Sisters: Dispatches from the Women's Liberation Movement,* ed. Rosalyn Baxandall and Linda Gordon (New York: Basic Books, 2000).

One of the cruelest forms of sexism we live with today is the unwillingness of many doctors to diagnose people's diseases with equality. The education of doctors can explain this. [Consider the messages in] the recently revised text *Obstetrics and Gynecology* (1971, 4th edition), which is used this year [1975] in 60 of the nation's medical schools.

SHE'S A CHILD

In *Obstetrics and Gynecology,* women are childlike, helpless creatures with animal-like or "instinctive" natures, who can't get through intercourse, pregnancy, labor or child-raising without "enlightened" physician intervention. The woman in childbirth is just a child herself. Her doctor, even if he is a novice and she is an old pro, is a fount of knowledge while she is "anxious," "fearful," afraid of "getting messy" and may feel "ashamed" and "guilty." The medical student is taught to believe that many symptoms of illness in pregnancy (excessive nausea, headache) are really a result of her "fear of pregnancy" rather than any physical condition he (all medical students and physicians are "he" in *Obstetrics and Gynecology*) need test for. . . .

SHE LOVES RAPE

Many gynecology texts reveal a greater concern with the patient's husband than with the patient herself and tend to maintain sex-role stereotypes in the interest of men and from a male perspective. But *Obstetrics and Gynecology* clearly spells out the attitudes that other texts only imply:

> The normal sexual act . . . entails a masochistic surrender to the man . . . there is always an element of rape.
>
> The traits that compose the core of the female personality are feminine narcissism, masochism, and passivity.
>
> Every phase of a woman's life is influenced by narcissism. Women then love in a different way from men. The woman falls in love with the idea of being loved; whereas the man loves an object for the pleasure it will give. She says, "I am valuable, important, etc. because he loves me. . . ." This type of narcissism finds expression in . . . her interest in clothes, personal appearance, and beauty. Too much feminine narcissism without masochism produces a self-centered woman.

The idea of suffering is an essential part of her life.

SHE FEELS LIKE AN ANIMAL

Women are described in the text alternately as psychopathic and idiotic: "She is likely to feel that she is animal-like . . . to think of the vagina as a 'dirty cavity.' Black patients will think that the source of sexual desires is in the uterus; white patients think that it is in the ovaries. . . . Orgasm represents the woman's ability to accent her own feminine role in life. . . . Menstruation symbolizes her role in life. . . ."

The medical student is persuaded by the authors that women with dysmenorrhea (menstrual dysfunctions including painful uterine contractions) have no organic disease they need test for; these women simply have "personality disorders," "emotional difficulty in the home," or "neurotic predispositions." They need "sex education" and "mental hygiene" . . . if not "intensive psychotherapy." . . . A brief concession is made to the possible physical causes for menstrual pain, but the authors then quickly return to the problem of diagnosis:

> It is important to ascertain how crippling the symptom and how much emotional gain the patient is deriving from it. For example, does the whole household revolve around whether or not the mother is having menstrual cramps? . . .
>
> The adult woman who presents this symptom very often is resentful of the feminine role. Each succeeding period reminds her of the unpleasant fact that she is a woman. . . .

SHE NEEDS A PSYCHIATRIST

. . . Frigidity is defined as "occasional failure to obtain orgasm," placing 99 percent of women in the category of abnormal. If pleasure is only felt from clitoral stimulation, she may be referred to a psychiatrist. . . . Her frigidity may develop because she "resents her husband's preoccupation with his work or his recreational activities." The physician, a "parental figure," should "discover the problem in the patient's personality" and "encourage her to mature sexually."

Twenty-seven gynecology texts written over the past three decades were reviewed by Diana Scully and Pauline Bart in the *American*

Journal of Sociology in January 1973. . . . No text Scully and Bart examined incorporated Kinsey's 1953 findings that orgasm without stimulation "is a physical and physiological impossibility for nearly all females" or Masters and Johnson's 1966 findings that portions of the vagina have no nerve endings and lack sensation and that although orgasm is felt in the vagina, the feeling derives from stimulation of clitoral nerves.

With doctors like these for friends, who needs enemies?

Phyllis Schlafly, "The thoughts of one who loves life as a woman . . ."

Not all well-educated, white middle-class family women with energy and ability to spare reacted to the resurgent domesticity of Cold War years as did Betty Goldstein Friedan. Phyllis Stewart Schlafly is a case in point. The two had much in common. Separated in age by only three years, both were the first child born to their respective families, the Goldsteins, who were Jewish, and the Stewarts, who were Roman Catholic. Both grew up during the depression years in Illinois and were valedictorians of their high school classes. Both attended women's colleges, Goldstein choosing prestigious Smith College in Massachusetts and Stewart attending College of the Sacred Heart in Maryville, Illinois, before transferring to Washington University in St. Louis. Excelling in college, both entered graduate school, Goldstein studying for an M.A. in psychology at the University of California, Berkeley, Stewart earning an M.A. in political science at Radcliffe College and Harvard University. (She would later return to Washington University for a law degree.)

Both went on to interesting jobs, Stewart as a congressional researcher in Washington, Goldstein as a journalist in New York City. Both subsequently married, Stewart choosing John Fred Schlafly, Jr., a lawyer and fellow conservative, and Goldstein choosing Carl Friedan, a theatrical producer and later an advertising executive. Both women had children, Schlafly six and Friedan three, whom they reared in suburbia along with the millions of other middle-class families caught up in the resurgent domesticity of the postwar years.

Energetic and intelligent, neither found domesticity sufficient. Friedan continued to write, as did Schlafly, who also became a community volunteer, Republican party activist, and, in 1952, a congressional candidate, winning her primary but losing in the general election. In the early 1960s, both published first books that became best-sellers— Friedan *The Feminine Mystique* (see pp. 573–76) and Schlafly *A Choice Not an Echo*, a political endorsement of conservative Arizona senator Barry Goldwater, the Republican presidential candidate in 1964.

Yet despite these similarities, the personal became political for these two women in ways that would lead them in sharply divergent directions in the years ahead.

Friedan's name would become synonymous with a resurgent feminism, Schlafly's with antifeminism. Friedan, as a founder and the first president of the National Organization for Women (NOW), would champion equal rights for women. Schlafly, creator and author of the *Phyllis Schlafly Report,* would devote her extraordinary energy as well as formidable organizational and speaking skills to defeat of the Equal Rights Amendment (see p. 624). Equality between the sexes, she insisted, would harm rather than help women.

While Schlafly's states' rights stance partially explains her opposition to using the federal government on behalf of sexual equality, more is involved, as is evident in the following document.

The cry of "women's liberation" leaps out from the "lifestyle" sections of newspapers and the pages of slick magazines, from radio speakers and television screens. Cut loose from past patterns of behavior and expectations, women of all ages are searching for their identity—the college woman who has new alternatives thrust upon her via "women's studies" courses, the young woman whose routine is shattered by a chance encounter with a "consciousness-raising session," the woman in her middle years who suddenly finds herself in the "empty-nest syndrome," the woman of any age whose lover or lifetime partner departs for greener pastures (and a younger crop).

All of these women, thanks to the women's liberation movement, no longer see their predicament in terms of personal problems to be confronted and solved. They see their own difficulties as a little cog in the big machine of establishment restraints and stereotypical injustice in which they have lost their own equilibrium. Who am I? Why am I here? Why am I just another faceless victim of society's oppression, a nameless prisoner behind walls too high for me to climb alone? . . .

For a woman to find her identity in the modern world, the path should be sought from the Positive Women who have found the road and possess the map, rather than from those who have not. In this spirit, I share with you the thoughts of one who loves life as a woman and lives love as a woman, whose credentials are from the school of practical experience, and who has learned that fulfillment as a woman is a journey, not a destination.

Like every human being born into this world, the Positive Woman has her share of sorrows and sufferings, of unfulfilled desires and bitter defeats. But she will never be crushed by life's disappointments, because her positive mental attitude has built her an inner security that the actions of other people can never fracture. To the Positive Woman, her particular set of problems is not a conspiracy against her, but a challenge to her character and her capabilities.

The first requirement for the acquisition of power by the Positive Woman is to understand the differences between men and women. Your outlook on life, your faith, your behavior, your potential for fulfillment, all are determined by the parameters of your original premise. The Positive Woman starts with the assumption that the world is her oyster. She rejoices in the creative capability within her body and the power potential of her mind and spirit. She understands that men and women are different, and that those very differences provide the key to her success as a person and fulfillment as a woman.

The women's liberationist, on the other hand, is imprisoned by her own negative view of herself and of her place in the world around her. . . . Someone—it is not clear who, perhaps God, perhaps the "Establishment," perhaps a conspiracy of male chauvinist pigs—dealt women a foul blow by making them female. It becomes necessary, therefore, for women to agitate and demonstrate and hurl demands on society in order to wrest from an oppressive male-dominated social structure the status that has been wrongfully denied to women through the centuries. . . . Confrontation replaces cooperation as the watchword of all relationships. Women and men become adver-

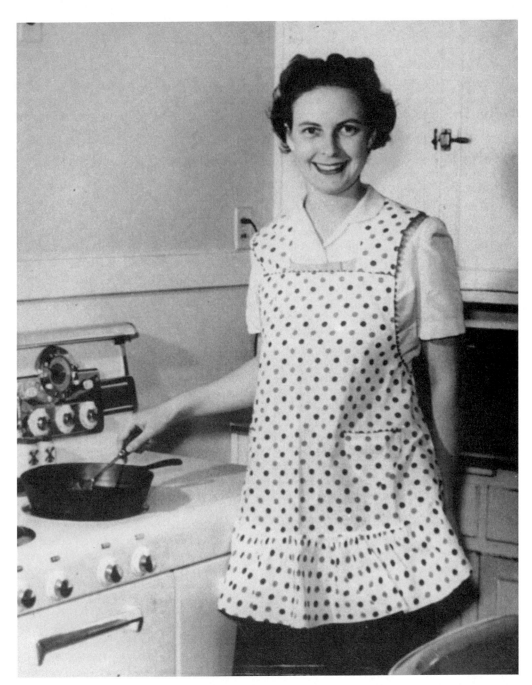

Phyllis Schlafly demonstrated the domestic ideal by posing cooking her husband's breakfast the morning after her victory in the 1952 Republican congressional primary. She would lose her bid for a congressional seat but continue to be active as a party volunteer. In 1964, she was a strong supporter of Republican presidential candidate Barry Goldwater, and the author of one of the most effective pieces of his campaign literature, A Choice, Not an Echo. *The first printing sold more than 600,000 copies and made her national reputation; there were two more printings before election day. In 1967, she lost her bid for the presidency of the National Federation of Republican Women. In the early 1970s, the NFRW endorsed the ERA. Independently, Schlafly mobilized women behind conservative issues like free enterprise and support for nuclear weapons development. When she began to publicize her opposition to the ERA, the circulation of* The Phyllis Schlafly Report *bounced quickly from 3,000 to 35,000 and continued to grow. Her organization, the Eagle Forum, took the lead in developing opposition to the ERA and to feminism generally. (St. Louis Globe-Democrat photo. Courtesy of The Collections of the St. Louis Mercantile Library at the University of Missouri-St. Louis. Caption courtesy of Catherine Rymph.)*

saries instead of partners. . . . Within the confines of the women's liberationist ideology, therefore, the abolition of this overriding inequality of women becomes the primary goal.

This goal must be achieved at any and all costs—to the woman herself, to the baby, to the family, and to society. Women must be made equal to men in their ability *not* to become pregnant and *not* to be expected to care for babies they may bring into the world. This is why women's liberationists are compulsively involved in the drive to make abortion and child-care centers for all women, regardless of religion or income, both socially acceptable and government-financed. . . .

If man is targeted as the enemy, and the ultimate goal of women's liberation is independence from men and the avoidance of pregnancy and its consequences, then lesbianism is logically the highest form in the ritual of women's liberation. . . .

The Positive Woman will never travel that dead-end road. It is self-evident to the Positive Woman that the female body with its baby-producing organs was not designed by a conspiracy of men but by the Divine Architect of the human race. Those who think it is unfair that women have babies, whereas men cannot, will have to take up their complaint with God because no other power is capable of changing that fundamental fact. . . . The Positive Woman looks upon her femaleness and her fertility as part of her purpose, her potential, and her power. She rejoices that she has a capability for creativity that men can never have.

The third basic dogma of the women's liberation movement is that there is no difference between male and female except the sex organs, and that all those physical, cognitive, and emotional differences you *think* are there, are merely the result of centuries of restraints imposed by a male-dominated society and sex-stereotyped schooling. The role imposed on women is, by definition, inferior, according to the women's liberationists. . . .

There are countless physical differences between men and women. The female body is 50 to 60 percent water, the male 60 to 70 percent water, which explains why males can dilute alcohol better than women and delay its effect. The average woman is about 25 percent fatty tissue, while the male is 15 percent, making women more buoyant in water and able to swim with less effort. Males have a tendency to color blindness. Only 5 percent of persons who get gout are female. Boys are born bigger. Women live longer in most countries of the world, not only in the United States where we have a hard-driving competitive pace. Women excel in manual dexterity, verbal skills, and memory recall. . . .

Does the physical advantage of men doom women to a life of servility and subservience? The Positive Woman knows that she has a complementary advantage which is at least as great—and, in the hands of a skillful woman, far greater. The Divine Architect who gave men a superior strength to lift weights also gave women a different kind of superior strength. . . . A Positive Woman cannot defeat a man in a wrestling or boxing match, but she can motivate him, inspire him, encourage him, teach him, restrain him, reward him, and have power over him that he can never achieve over her with all his muscle. How or whether a Positive Woman uses her power is determined solely by the way she alone defines her goals and develops her skills.

The differences between men and women are also emotional and psychological. Without woman's innate maternal instinct, the human race would have died out centuries ago. . . . The overriding psychological need of a woman is to love something alive. A baby fulfills this need in the lives of most women. If a baby is not available to fill that need, women search for a baby-substitute. This is the reason why women have traditionally gone into teaching and nursing careers. They are doing what comes naturally to the female psyche. The schoolchild or the patient of any age provides an outlet for a woman to express her natural maternal need. . . . The Positive Woman finds somebody on whom she can lavish her maternal love so that it doesn't well up inside her and cause psychological frustrations. Surely no woman is so isolated by geography or insulated by spirit that she cannot find someone worthy of her maternal love. . . .

One of the strangest quirks of women's liberationists is their complaint that societal restraints prevent men from crying in public or showing their emotions, but permit women to do so, and that therefore we should "liberate" men to enable them, too, to cry in public. The public display of fear, sorrow, anger, and irritation reveals a lack of self-discipline that should be avoided by the Positive Woman just as much as by the Positive Man. Maternal love, however, is not a weakness but a manifestation of strength and service, and it should be nurtured by the Positive Woman. . . .

Another silliness of the women's liberationists is their frenetic desire to force all women to accept the title *Ms* in place of *Miss* or *Mrs*. If Gloria Steinem and Betty Friedan want to call themselves *Ms* in order to conceal their marital status, their wishes should be respected. But most married women feel they worked hard for the *r* in their names; and they don't care to be gratuitously deprived of it. . . .

Finally, women are different from men in dealing with the fundamentals of life itself. Men are philosophers, women are practical, and 'twas ever thus. Men may philosophize about how life began and where we are heading; women are concerned about feeding the kids today. No woman would ever, as Karl Marx did, spend years reading political philosophy in the British Museum while her child starved to death. Women don't take naturally to a search for the intangible and the abstract. . . . Where man is discursive, logical, abstract, or philosophical, woman tends to be emotional, personal, practical, or mystical. Each set of qualities is vital and complements the other. Among the many differences explained in [Amaury] de Riencourt's book, [*Sex and Power in History*], are the following:

> Women tend more toward conformity than men—which is why they often excel in such disciplines as spelling and punctuation where there is only one correct answer, determined by social authority. Higher intellectual activities, however, require a mental independence and power of abstraction that they usually lack, not to mention a certain form of aggressive boldness of the imagination which can only exist in a sex that is basically aggressive for biological reasons.

> To sum up: The masculine proclivity in problem solving is analytical and categorical; the feminine, synthetic and contextual. . . . Deep down, man tends to focus on the object, on external results and achievements; woman focuses on subjective motives and feelings. If life can be compared to a play, man focuses on the theme and structure of the play, woman on the innermost feelings displayed by the actors.

De Riencourt provides impressive refutation of two of the basic errors of the women's liberation movement: (1) that there are no emotional or cognitive differences between the sexes, and (2) that women should strive to be like men. . . . An effort to eliminate the differences by social engineering or legislative or constitutional tinkering cannot succeed, which is fortunate, but social relationships and spiritual values can be ruptured in the attempt. . . .

JANE SHERRON DE HART
Second-Wave Feminists and the Dynamics of Social Change

The dissatisfactions that simmered just beneath the surface during the 1950s and early 1960s erupted in the late 1960s into unconcealed anger as small groups of women, many of them movement veterans, gathered to protest their treatment as women. Their actions marked the resurgence of feminism. "As an *ism* (an ideology) *[feminism]* presupposed a set of principles not necessarily belonging to every woman—nor limited to women," wrote historian Nancy Cott of first-wave feminism.[1] Her observation held. Some men, but not all women, once again embraced its core principles, joining an ongoing struggle to dismantle gender hierarchy.

While this resurgence had many tributaries and flowed into various feminisms, the focus of this essay on what is sometimes referred to as mainstream feminism is of necessity partial. My purpose is to identify the long-term developments that created conditions conducive to the emergence of a mass-based feminist movement as well as the resources these feminists-in-the-making brought with them from other protest movements. The ideological issues these second-wave feminists wrestled with, the changes they initiated, and the opposition they encountered (especially in their efforts to secure an amendment to the Constitution guaranteeing equal rights for women) also are explored. So, too, is the extent to which, by 1980, the movement's agenda was at the mercy of larger changes in the political climate over which feminists and their allies had little control. How feminism itself changed over the years and what happened to it as a movement are fitting questions to pose about a social movement from which so many women have benefited and with which so few young women seem willing to identify.

Fifty years after gaining the right to vote, women who had been suffragists and women young enough to be their great-granddaughters embarked on a new feminist movement. Referred to as feminism's second wave, to distinguish it from an earlier surge that had occurred around 1910, the goals and membership of this new movement reflected fundamental changes in American life that had developed in the intervening decades, as well as unresolved issues from the past. Medical advances that lengthened life expectancy also provided greater reproductive control; despite the "baby boom" of the postwar years, the nation's birthrate and family size continued to decline; the continuing influx of women, including married women with children, into the workplace produced new patterns of workforce participation among white women; and finally, the restraints of second-class citizenship chafed—even when rationalized as "that's the way things are." These changes alone did not generate a new feminist consciousness. But they enlarged the distance between old gender norms and ideals and new circumstances, creating greater receptivity to feminist perspectives and concerns. What had been regarded as personal problems and grievances could, with a new lens, be seen as political, and thus susceptible to change.

From the outset the new movement was vigorous, diffused, ideologically varied, geographically decentralized, and highly controversial. It was in fact many movements, some predominantly white and middle-class, others comprised largely of women of color, and still others that were low-income and multiracial. The various factions of the movement formed interweaving strands of thought and action. Some of these strands acquired the labels *liberal, radical, socialist*, and, by 1975, *cultural feminism*. Others identified themselves as black, Chicana, Asian American, Native American, or U.S. third world feminists. One cannot make simplistic assumptions about which variant an individual woman might embrace. (For example, Pauli Murray, an African American lawyer and writer, would have been more likely to describe herself as a liberal feminist rather than a black feminist.) Nor should one make the mistake of allowing the differences between and among groups to overshadow interconnections. For example, marking the distinction between liberal feminists and radical feminists by associating the former with advocacy of equal rights and the latter with the belief that male supremacy was the primary form of oppression is an unfair oversimplification. Many equal rights advocates adopted radical feminists' insight into gender oppression, just as they later came to appreciate the insights of feminists of color, who argued that gender was one of several interacting forms of oppression, among them race and class. Liberal feminists could also respond that preempting radicalism for radical feminists only masked the radical potential of liberal feminism. Indeed, as sociologists Myra Marx Ferree and Beth B. Hess have demonstrated in their study of the movement, it was both the "controversies" and the "coalitions" that sustained second-wave feminism.[2]

THE ROOTS OF SECOND-WAVE FEMINISM

At first glance, many of the groups of second-wave feminism seem to have sprouted overnight like mushrooms after a hard rain. But closer investigation reveals deeper roots. Feminism in the African American community reached back to the turn-of-the-century South, where author Anna Julia Cooper first identified the double challenge facing her sisters: "a race problem" and "the woman question." Black women's emphasis on self-definition and empowerment had long suffused their activism on behalf of community development, anti-lynching laws, and civil rights. Furthermore, the existence of a local black and low-income group in New York's Mount Vernon/New Rochelle community, founded in 1960, belied the conventional assumption that second-wave feminism did not exist until the late 1960s. Union women—black and white—had forged their own feminism in the labor movement, especially in the years after World War II. Fighting for equal pay for equal work, their leaders championed equal treatment in the workplace as well as the special needs of working women.[3]

Women of the Old Left, determined to make the Communist Party take seriously "the woman question" in the immediate postwar years, had expanded traditional Marxist understanding of women's oppression as deriving from economic structures. Insisting that social and cultural components were also important and that male domination extended to personal relationships, they forged a new understanding of women's oppression and liberation. When McCarthyism forced their retreat from organized Party activity, some concealed their past affiliations. But they did not hide their commitment to improving women's status in the new organizations they joined, the families they created, and the literary works they produced.[4]

The political experience of these Old Leftists also remained intact. In Seattle, for example, the approximately twenty-five women who met in the home of a graduate student in 1967 to discuss the formation of an activist women's group ranged in age from fifty-one to eighteen. Among the organizers of the meeting were women whose political past included years of activism in both the Communist Party and the Socialist Workers Party as well as in more recent labor, civil rights, and welfare struggles. It was these veterans who provided theoretical and political direction to the group until the women's liberation movement exploded on the Seattle scene in 1970.[5]

Links to second-wave feminism were not always so obvious. Daughters who were their mothers' heirs ideologically would bring to the new movement terminology that their parents had used in talking about women's secondary status. Writers—Eleanor Flexner, Gerda Lerner, Aileen Kraditor, Tillie Olson, and Eve Merriam, among others— would bequeath a body of literature shaped by Communist Party perspectives on women's oppression and women's history. Reflecting a race- and class-conscious feminism, the origins and influence of which have long been obscured by the impact of McCarthyism, this work would feed a new generation hungry for authentic feminist writing.[6]

White, middle-class suburbanites, stifled by the triviality and frustrations of a resurgent domesticity, found a voice for their discontent in 1963 with the publication of Betty Friedan's best-seller, *The Feminine Mystique*. But Friedan's portrayal of herself as just another well-educated suburban housewife, whose consciousness of "the woman problem" gelled as she began writing her book, was misleading. It obscured her debt to the French intellectual Simone de Beauvoir, whose inspiring classic *The Second Sex*, published in 1952, had already raised compelling questions that would preoccupy a new generation of feminists. More important, as historian Daniel Horowitz discovered, Friedan's account obscured her debt to the Old Left. A labor journalist in the 1940s and early 1950s, she too had been part of a cross-class, racially integrated feminism that emerged in progressive circles in the aftermath of World War II. Just as McCarthyism had deflected that struggle, so it silenced Friedan on this critical aspect of her past. But what mattered to the women who devoured *The Feminine Mystique* was not full disclosure of the author's political past or intellectual debts. Rather, it was her ability to articulate and thereby legitimate their own discontents with domesticity.[7]

If the roots of second-wave feminism were deep, gnarled, and intertwined, this was not yet apparent in the late 1960s. What was clear was that in a decade when Americans had been thrust into the throes of self-examination by a movement for racial equality, women of diverse experiences were beginning to acquire a feminist consciousness. Although the media and the public did not always differentiate, referring to them collectively as "women's libbers," there were distinct differences between the most visible groups in the vanguard—women's rights advocates and women's liberationists—and within the strands of women's liberationists. The latter included young veterans of the civil rights movement and the New Left who were steeped in commitment to equality and the techniques of protest. Others were young professionals, many of whom were aware of their secondary status in their professions by virtue of the fact that they were women. Women's rights advocates were often more established professionals and veteran activists who had used organizations such as the American Civil Liberties Union (ACLU), the Young Women's Christian Association (YWCA), and the United Auto Workers (UAW) to fight sex-based discrimination. Included, too, were those whose outwardly conformist lives belied an intense awareness of the malaise of domesticity and the untenably narrow boundaries of their prescribed roles. To explore how they came self-consciously to appraise women's condition as one demanding collective action is to explore the process of radicalization that helped to create a new feminist movement.

THE CREATION OF A FEMINIST CONSCIOUSNESS

Although the differences between women's rights advocates and women's liberationists began to blur as the movement matured, initial distinctions were sharp. Women's rights advocates were likely to have been older, to have had professional training or work experience, to have been more inclined to form or join organized feminist groups. Reform oriented, these organizations used traditional pressure group tactics to achieve changes in laws and public policy that would guarantee women equal rights. Emphasis on "rights" meant extending to women in life outside the home the same "rights" men had, granting them the same options, privileges, and responsibilities that men enjoyed. There was little suggestion initially of personal or cultural transformation.

Women's liberationists were younger women, often less highly educated, whose ideology and political style, shaped in the dissent and violence of the 1960s, led them to look at women's predicament differently. Instead of relying upon traditional organizational structure and lobbying techniques, they developed a new style of politics. Instead of limiting their goals to changes in public policy, they embraced a transformation in private, domestic life as well. They sought liberation from ways of thinking and behaving that they believed stunted or distorted women's growth and kept them subordinate to men. Through the extension of their own personal liberation they hoped to remake the male world, changing it as they had changed themselves. For women's liberationists as for women's rights advocates, however, the first step toward becoming feminists demanded a clear statement of women's position in society, one that called attention to the gap between the egalitarian ideal and the actual position of women in American culture. There also had to be a call to action from women themselves, *for* women, *with* women, *through* women. Redefining themselves, they had to make being a woman a political fact; and, as they did so, they had to live with the radical implications of what could only be called a rebirth.

The Making of Liberal Feminists: Women's Rights Advocates

For some women, the process of radicalization began with the appointment of a Presidential Commission on the Status of Women in 1961. Presidents, Democrat and Republican, customarily discharged their political debt to female members of the electorate, especially to those who had loyally served the party, by appointing a few token women, usually party stalwarts, to highly visible posts. John Kennedy was no exception. He was, however, convinced by Esther Peterson, the highest-ranking woman in his administration, that the vast majority of women would be better served if he also appointed a commission charged with investigating obstacles to the full participation of women in society. Peterson, who was assistant secretary of labor and head of the Women's Bureau, believed that the report of such a commission could sensitize the public to barriers to equality just as her own experience as a labor organizer had sensitized her to the particular problems confronting women workers. Citizens thus informed could then be mobilized on behalf of governmental efforts at reform.[8] Accordingly, the commission was appointed with Eleanor Roosevelt serving as chair until her death a year later. Its report, *American Women* (1963), was conservative in tone, acknowledging the importance of women's traditional roles within the home and the progress they had made in a "free democratic society." Acknowledging also that women were an underutilized resource that the nation could ill afford to ignore, the report provided extensive documentation of discriminatory practices in government, education, and employment, along with substantial recommendations for change.[9] Governors, replicating Kennedy's move, appointed state commissions on the status of women. In these commissions hundreds of men and women encountered further evidence of the economic, social, and legal disabilities that encumbered the nation's "second sex." For some, the statistics were old news; for others, they were a revelation.

Aroused by growing evidence of "the enormity of our problem," members of state commissions gathered in Washington in 1966 for the Third National Conference of the Commissions on the Status of Women. Individuals who were coming to know and rely on one another as they pooled their growing knowledge of widespread inequities, they were a network in the making. They were also women who wanted something done. This time they encountered a situation that transformed at least some of those present into activists in a new movement for women's equality. The catalyst proved to be a struggle involving Representative Martha Griffiths and the Equal Employment Opportunity Commission (EEOC), the federal agency in charge of implementing the Civil Rights Act of 1964.

Despite the fact that the law proscribed discrimination on the basis of sex as well as race, the commission refused to take seriously the problem of sexual discrimination. The first executive director of EEOC, believing that "sex" had been injected into the bill by opponents seeking to block its passage, regarded the sex provision as a "fluke" best ignored. Representative Griffiths from Michigan thought otherwise. The inclusion of sex discrimination, while used by civil rights opponents to sabotage the bill, had been initiated by the venerable and elitist National Woman's Party. Support was also strong among women in the House whom Griffiths had mobilized. While liberals had initially objected, fearing that so encumbering a bill would prevent passage of much-needed legislation on behalf of racial equality, Griffiths had prevailed. Without the sex provision, she had reminded her colleagues, the Civil Rights Act would give black women advantages that white women were denied. A racist appeal that revealed the exclusivity of Griffiths's vision of sisterhood, it had worked. Once the bill passed she was determined to see the new law enforced in its entirety. When EEOC failed to do so, she lambasted the agency for its inaction in a biting speech delivered on the House floor only days before the Conference of the Commissions on the Status of Women met.

Griffiths's concern was shared by a group of women working within EEOC. Echoing an argument made the year before by a black trade unionist in the Women's Bureau,[10] they insisted that the agency could be made to take gender-related discrimination more seriously if women had a civil rights organization as adept at applying pressure on their behalf as was the National Association for the Advancement of Colored People (NAACP) on behalf of blacks. Initially the idea was rejected. Conference participants most upset by EEOC's inaction decided instead to propose a resolution urging the agency to treat sexual discrimination with the same seriousness it applied to racial discrimination. When the resolution was ruled inappropriate by conference leaders, they were forced to reconsider. After a whispered conversation over lunch they concluded the time for discussion of the status of women was over. It was time for action. Before the day was out twenty-eight women had paid five dollars each to join the National Organization for Women (NOW), including author Betty Friedan, who happened to be in Washington at the time of the conference.[11]

Friedan's presence in Washington was auspicious; her involvement in NOW, virtually inevitable. By articulating heretofore inarticulated grievances, *The Feminine Mystique* had advanced a process initiated by more dispassionate investigations of women's status and the discriminatory practices which made that status inferior. That process was the collective expression of discontent. It is not surprising that the voices initially heard were those of women who were overwhelmingly white, educated, and middle or upper middle class. College women who regarded themselves the equals of male classmates by virtue of intellect and training were, as Jo Freeman points out, more likely to develop expectations they saw realized by their male peers but not, in most cases, by themselves. The frustrations were even greater for women with professional training. The very fact that many had sought advanced training in fields not traditionally "female" meant that they were less likely to find in traditional gender roles the identity and self-esteem such roles provided other women. Moreover, when measuring themselves against fellow professionals who happened to be men, the greater rewards enjoyed by their white male counterparts seemed especially galling. Privileged though they were, such women *felt* more deprived in many cases than did those women who were in reality less privileged. By 1966 this sense of deprivation had been sufficiently articulated and shared and the networks of like-minded women sufficiently developed so that collective discontent could be translated into collective action. The formation of NOW signaled a feminist resurgence.[12]

The three hundred men and women who gathered in October for the organizational meeting of NOW included mainly professionals, some of them veterans of commissions on the status of women as well as a few feminist union activists, notably Dorothy Haener. Adopting bylaws and a statement of purpose, they elected officers, naming Friedan president. Her conviction that intelligent women needed purposeful, generative work of their own was reflected in NOW's statement of purpose, which attacked "the traditional assumption that a woman has to choose between marriage and motherhood on the one hand and serious participation in industry or the professions on the other." Determined that women should be allowed to develop their full potential as human beings, the organization's goal was to bring them into "full participation in the mainstream of American society NOW, exercising all the privileges and responsibilities thereof in truly equal partnership with men." To that end NOW developed a Bill of Rights, adopted at its 1967 meeting, that exhorted Congress to pass an equal rights amendment to the Constitution, called on EEOC to enforce antidiscrimination legislation, and urged federal and state legislators to guarantee equal and unsegregated education. To ensure women control over their reproductive lives, these new feminists called for removal of penal codes denying women contraceptive information and devices as well as safe, legal abortions. To ease the double burden of working mothers, they urged legislation that would ensure maternity leaves without jeopardizing job security or seniority, permit tax deductions for child care expenses, and create public, inexpensive day care centers. To improve the lot of poor women, they urged reform of the welfare system and equality with respect to benefits, including job-training programs.[13]

Not content simply to call for change, NOW leaders, following the lead of equality advocates within the labor movement, worked to make it happen. Using persuasion, pressure, and even litigation, they, with other newly formed women's rights groups such as the Women's Equity Action League (WEAL), launched a massive attack on sex discrimination. By the end of the 1960s NOW members had filed legal suits against newspapers listing jobs under the headings "Help Wanted: Male" and "Help Wanted: Female," successfully arguing that such headings discouraged women from applying for jobs they were perfectly capable of doing. Building on efforts begun in the Kennedy administration such as the passage of the Equal Pay Act, they pressured the federal government to intensify its commitment to equal opportunity. They urged congressmen and labor leaders to persuade the Department of Labor to include women in its guidelines designed to encourage the hiring and promotion of blacks in firms holding contracts with the federal government. They persuaded the Federal Communications Commission to open up new opportunities for women in broadcasting. Tackling the campus as well as the marketplace, WEAL filed suit against more than three hundred colleges and universities, ultimately securing millions of dollars in salary raises for women faculty members who had been victims of discrimination. To ensure that women receive the same pay men received for doing the same work, these new feminists lobbied for passage of a new Equal Employment Opportunity Act that would enable EEOC to fight discrimination more effectively.

NOW also scrutinized the discriminatory practices of financial institutions, persuading them to issue credit to single women and to married women in their own—not their husband's—name. WEAL, in turn, filed charges against banks and other lending institutions that refused to grant mortgages to single women, or in the case of married couples, refused to take into account the wife's earnings in evaluating the couple's eligibility for a mortgage. Colleges and universities that discriminated against female students in their sports programs came under fire, as did fellowship programs that failed to give adequate consideration to female applicants.

While NOW and WEAL attacked barriers in industry and education, the National Women's Political Caucus (NWPC) focused on government and politics. Formed in 1971, the caucus was initiated by Friedan, New York congresswomen Bella Abzug and Shirley Chisholm—both outspoken champions of women's rights—and Gloria Steinem, soon to become founding editor of the new mass-circulation feminist magazine *Ms.* Abzug, a lawyer and veteran activist for peace and civil rights, and Chisholm, the first black woman elected to Congress, were especially concerned about the small numbers of women in government. Accordingly the caucus concentrated on getting women elected and appointed to public office while also rallying support for issues such as the Equal Rights Amendment (see p. 624). Meanwhile, women in the professions, aware of their small numbers and inferior status, began to organize as well. Physicians, lawyers, and university professors fought for equal opportunity in the meetings of such overwhelmingly male groups as the American Medical Association, the American Association of University Professors, and the American Historical Association. Union women also mobilized. In 1974, three thousand women from fifty-eight unions attended the founding convention of the Coalition of Labor Union Women (CLUW), resolving to fight for equality in the workplace and within organized labor.[14]

Collectively such protests served notice that more women were becoming radicalized. The particular combination of events that transformed these women into feminists varied with the individual. A southern legislator, describing the process that brought home the reality of her own second-class citizenship, wrote:

> As a State Senator, I succeeded in getting Mississippi women the right to sit on juries (1968); the opposition's arguments were appalling. When women began hiring me in order to get credit, I became upset at the discrimination I saw. After I was divorced in 1970, I was initially denied a home loan. The effect was one of the worst traumas I've suffered. Denial of a home loan to one who was both a professional and a member of the legislature brought things to a head.[15]

Although the number of women who understood what it meant to be the "second sex" was still only a tiny minority, they were nonetheless a minority whose energy, talents, and experience enabled them to work for changes necessary to ensure equal rights. And they were gaining important allies in liberal organizations. The American Civil Liberties Union (ACLU) was a case in point. Best known for its defense of civil liberties, the ACLU put its considerable resources behind a newly created Women's Rights Project, headed by Ruth Bader Ginsberg, then a professor at Columbia School of Law. Her task was to devise a litigation strategy designed to persuade the Supreme Court (of which she is now a member) that gender discrimination in the law was unconstitutional. Since even the liberal Warren Court had been unable to move beyond judicial paternalism and gender stereotypes, the challenge was formidable. But Ginsberg had "high hopes for significant change," as, no doubt, did strategically placed feminists in trade unions, the National Council of Churches, foundations, and other organizations whose support helped legitimate this fledgling movement.[16]

The Making of Women's Liberationists

The process of radicalization that transformed some individuals into liberal feminists occurred simultaneously—but in different fashion and with somewhat different results—among a younger generation of women who initially were also predominantly white and middle class. Many of them veterans of either the civil rights movement or of the New Left, these were the activists who would initially become identified as women's liberationists. Differing in perspective as well as style, they would ultimately push many of their older counterparts beyond the demand for equal rights to recognition that true emancipation would require a far-reaching transformation of society and culture.

The experiences awakening in this 1960s generation a feminist consciousness have been superbly described by Sara Evans in her book, *Personal Politics*.[17] "Freedom, equality, love and hope," the possibility of new human relationships, the importance of participatory democracy—letting the people decide—were, as Evans points out, part of an egalitarian ideology shared by both the southern-based Student Nonviolent Coordinating Committee (SNCC) in its struggle for racial equality and the Students for Democratic Society (SDS) in its efforts to mobilize an interracial organization of the urban poor in northern ghettos. Membership in both organizations—"the movement"—thus reinforced commitment to these ideals among the women who joined. In order to translate ideals into reality, however, young, college-age women who had left the shelter of middle-class families for the hard and dangerous work of transforming society found themselves doing things that they would never have thought possible. Amidst the racial strife of the South, they joined picket lines, created freedom schools, and canvassed for voter registration among blacks, often enduring arrest and jailing. SDS women from affluent suburbs entered decaying tenements and were surrounded by the grim realities of the ghetto. They trudged door-to-door in an effort to reach women whose struggle to survive made many understandably suspicious of intruding strangers. In the process, not only did these young activists achieve a heightened sense of self-worth and autonomy, they also learned the skills of movement building and the nuts and bolts of organizing.

Particularly important was the problem of getting people, long passive, to act on their own behalf. SDS women began by encouraging ghetto women to come together to talk about their problems. This sharing of experiences, they believed, would lead these women to recognize not only that their problems were common but that solutions required changes in the system. In the process of organizing, the organizers also learned. They began to understand the meaning of oppression and the valor required of those who fought it. They found new role models, Evans suggests, in extraordinary southern black women whose courage seemed never to waver in the face of violence and in those welfare mothers of the North who confronted welfare bureaucrat and slum lord after years of passivity.

But if being in the movement brought a new understanding of equality, it also brought new problems. Men who were committed to equality for one group were not necessarily committed to equality for another group. Women in SNCC, as in SDS, found themselves frequently relegated to domestic chores and treated as sex objects, denied most leadership positions, and refused a key voice in the formulation of policy. Moreover, the sexual freedom that had been theirs as part of the cultural revolution taking place in the 1960s soon began to feel more like sexual exploitation as they saw their role in the movement spelled out in the draft resister's slogan: "Girls Say Yes to Guys Who Say No." Efforts to change the situation were firmly rebuffed. When SNCC leader Stokely Carmichael joked that the only "position for women in SNCC is prone," he encapsulated views which, while not his own, reflected all too accurately the feelings of males in the New Left as well as many in SNCC.[18]

By 1967, the tensions had become so intense that white women left the movement, propelled, in part, by the ascendancy of black power. They would soon be joined by SDS women aggrieved by their subordinate position within that organization as well as veterans of various other New Left and anti-war groups. Black women, whose own tradition of feminism was venerable, stayed. Fully aware of the double jeopardy involved in being both black and female, many would embrace varieties of feminism that reflected their own problems and priorities. Other women of color would repeat the pattern, torn by conflicting loyalties to the ethnic liberation movement in which they had come of age politically and to the need to act on behalf of their own liberation as women. Lesbians too would part company with male activists in the gay liberation movement that erupted in 1969 with the Stonewall Riots in New York City.[19]

Neither SNCC (renamed the Student National Coordinating Committee) nor SDS veterans left empty-handed. Radicals all, these women were impatient with liberalism, critical of capitalism, and profoundly suspicious of authority. "Never trust anyone over thirty" was the maxim of a generation disillusioned with government officials who handed out disinformation on the war in Vietnam. Accustomed to challenging prevailing ideas and practices, fluent in the language of protest, and skilled in the art of organizing, they also shared a deep-seated conviction, as had many Old Left feminists, that the personal was political—that is, problems customarily understood as personal and private were often rooted not in the individual but rather in society and in culture. The solutions required were public and political. How that legacy would shape this burgeoning new movement became evident as small women's liberation groups began to spring up spontaneously in major cities and university communities across the country.

STRUCTURE, LEADERSHIP, AND CONSCIOUSNESS-RAISING

Initially, at least, the two branches of mainstream feminism seemed almost to be two different movements, so unlike were they in structure and style. Linked only by newsletters, notices in underground newspapers, and networks of friends, women's liberation groups rejected both traditional organizational structure and leadership. Unlike NOW and the other women's rights groups associated with liberal feminism, they had no central headquarters, no elected officers, no bylaws. There was no legislative agenda and little of the activism that transformed the more politically astute women's rights leaders into skilled lobbyists and tacticians. Instead this younger generation of feminists, organizing new groups wherever they found themselves, concentrated on a kind of personal politics rooted in movement days. Looking back on male-dominated meetings in which, however informal the gathering, a few highly verbal, aggressive men invariably controlled debate and dictated strategy and left less articulate and assertive women effectively excluded, they recalled the technique they had used in organizing the poor. They remembered how they had encouraged those women to talk among themselves until the personal became political, that is, until problems which, at first glance, seemed to be personal were finally understood to be social in cause—rooted in society rather than in the individual—and political in solution. Applying this same process in their own informal "rap groups," women's liberationists developed the technique of "consciousness-raising." Adopted by women's rights groups such as local chapters of NOW, consciousness-raising sessions became one of the most important innovations of mainstream feminism.

The immediate task of the consciousness-raising session was to bring together in a caring, supportive, noncompetitive setting women accustomed to relating most intimately not with other women but with men—husbands, lovers, "friends." As these women talked among themselves, exchanging confidences, reassessing old options, and mentally exploring new ones, a sense of shared problems began to emerge. The women themselves gradually gained greater understanding of how profoundly their lives had been shaped by the constraints of culture. Personal experience with those constraints merged with intellectual awareness of women's inferior status and the factors that made it so. By the same token, new understanding of problems generated new determination to resolve them. Anger, aggression, and frustration formerly turned inward in unconscious self-hatred began to be directed outward, becoming transformed into new energy directed toward constructive goals. If society and culture had defined who women were through their unconscious internalization of tradition, they could reverse the process, and, by redefining themselves, redefine society and culture. Or, to put it another way, if woman was a *social construct*—the product not so much of biology, but of what people in a particular society and culture believed to be the implications of biology—then women themselves would re-create the construct. At work was a process of discovery so radicalizing that the individuals undergoing it ultimately emerged in a very real sense as different people. Now feminists, these were women with a different understanding of reality—a new "consciousness," a new sense of "sisterhood," and a new commitment to change.

Consciousness-raising was an invigorating and sometimes frightening experience. As one young woman wrote, "This whole movement is the most exhilarating thing of my life. The last eight months have been a personal revolution. Nonetheless, I recognize there is dynamite in this and I'm scared shitless."[20] "Scared" or not, such women could no longer be contained. Veterans of one rap group fanned out, creating others, often with arresting names such as Cell 16, the Furies, Redstockings, Radicalesbians, and WITCH (Women's International Terrorist Conspiracy from Hell).

TOWARD A FEMINIST IDEOLOGY: OPPRESSION, SEXISM, AND CHANGE

To explain the significance of the discovery that woman is both a biological being and a social construct *and* that subordination was built into that construct was no simple process. The concept itself was complex. Moreover, some feminists were basically pragmatists. They were eager to talk about what it took to sustain a movement over time, or how to resolve differences; they wanted to discuss critical issues—abortion, childcare, sterilization abuse, an expanded and more participatory welfare—but not the origins of women's oppression. Results, please, not theory, they insisted. Others retorted that results depended on the correct understanding of the problem. Theory mattered. But even among women's liberationists who were more theoretically oriented, ideological perspectives reflected different political stances, experiences, and sexual preferences. Manifestos, position papers, and books began to pile up among these ideologically fractious sisters as liberationists searched for the historical origins of female oppression. Those whose primary loyalty was still to the New Left—soon dubbed "politicos"—attributed women's oppression to capitalism. Others, who would come to be known as socialist-feminists, insisted that both male supremacy and capitalism were responsible for women's subordination and that feminists must be allied with, but apart from, the left. Still other liberationists argued that male supremacy, not class or race, was the more fundamental and universal form of oppression and that women as a group constituted an oppressed class. Known as radical feminists, their emphasis on the primacy of gender would prevail, although it would be ultimately challenged by feminists of color, who insisted on multiple forms of oppression. In the meantime, however, radical feminists' identification of the family as the basic unit in the system of oppression led to new debates among radical feminists themselves. If marriage as an intersexual alliance divided women, leading them to identify with the oppressor from whom they derived economic advantages rather than each other, ought marriage to be abolished? If so, what new structure should take its place? Pushing the logic of this position, lesbian feminists argued that the ultimate rejection of male domination required not just the rejection of marriage, but the rejection of sexual intimacy with men. Heterosexuality, they insisted, was at the very core of patriarchy. Other feminists disagreed. Family, while a source of gender hierarchy, could also be a site of support. Moreover, collective struggle against male supremacy did not mean rejecting the men with whom one was intimately connected; the challenge ought to be to make them allies.

But the lesbian issue would not go away. Feminists, seeking to desexualize lesbianism, argued that it was a political stance—being a woman-identified woman. Lesbians were quick to reject this position, declaring that who one slept with mattered and that sexual preference was not simply a matter of choice. But did this mean that only women whose sexual preference and behavior involved same-sex partners could be authentic feminists? Surely not, insisted heterosexuals. The more sociologically oriented pointed to sex-based role differentiation as a source of oppression, arguing that work and family roles should be restructured in ways that would encourage greater mutuality and fulfillment for both sexes. Others argued that personality—men and women's psychic identity—were also overly differentiated by sex. Only by merging role and personality characteristics of both sexes within each individual could androgynous men and women be developed and real liberation achieved.[21]

Given the great variety of perspectives and positions even among women's liberationists alone, it is impossible to talk about *a* feminist ideology to which all those who identified with the women's movement subscribed. The ascendancy of radical feminism among women's liberationists in the early 1970s and the eventual embrace of many of their insights by liberal feminists, however, does make it possible to talk about a common conceptual framework shared by mainstream feminists. Most believed that *gender hierarchy* is a primary factor essential to any understanding of why women *as a group* suffer from an unequal distribution of power and resources in a society. They agreed that men have been the dominant sex and that women as a group are subordinate. While not all mainstream feminists were comfortable talking about a *system* of oppression or even using the word "oppression," they were quick to list the many areas where inequities were—and still are—evident.

At the top of the list was the economy. Men, they agreed, are more likely to be economically independent than women because the latter work within the home where their labor has no monetary value and/or outside the home in sex-segregated jobs for wages too meager to ensure economic self-sufficiency. Society and culture also provided numerous examples of the higher status, greater options, and greater power conferred upon men by virtue of their sex. Just as traditional male roles provide access to power and independence, whereas female roles do not, so, feminists pointed out, masculine values define what attributes are admired and rewarded. The very fact that strength, competence, independence, and rationality are considered masculine values, that they are more highly regarded by both sexes, *and* that they constitute the standard by which mental health is judged these new feminists found revealing indeed. The problem, they insisted, is not simply that the qualities themselves, intrinsically neither "male" or "female," are the product of gender socialization. It is the preference, conscious and unconscious, for whatever society regards as "masculine" that is so persistent and so objectionable—a preference feminists termed *sexism*.

Sexism, they believed, is persistent, pervasive, and powerful. It is internalized by women as well as men. It is most dramatically evident in the programmed-to-please women who search for happiness through submissiveness to men and in the men who use their power to limit women's options and keep them dependent. It is also evident in a more subtle fashion among women who emulate male models and values, refusing to see those aspects of women's lives that are positive and life-affirming, and among men who are unaware of the unconscious sexism permeating their attitudes and actions. Internalized in individuals, sexism is also embedded in institutions—the family, the education system, the media, the economy, politics, law, organized religion, language, and sexual morality.

Given the pervasiveness of sexism, many feminists saw no possibility for real equality short of transformation not only of individuals but also of social institutions and cultural values. Even what was once seen as the relatively simple demand of women's rights advocates for equal pay for equal work no longer looked so simple. What seemed to be a matter of obtaining equal rights *within* the existing system in reality demanded changes that *transform* the system. Involved was:

> a reevaluation of women as workers, of women as mothers, of mothers as workers, of work as suitable for one gender and not for the other. The demand implies equal opportunity and thus equal responsibilities. It implies a childhood in which girls are rewarded for competence, risk taking, achievement, competitiveness and independence—just like boys. Equal pay for equal work means a revision in our expectations about women as equal workers and it involves the institutional arrangements to make them so.

"There is nothing small here," a feminist scholar observed.[22] And indeed there was not.

FEMINISM IN ACTION

How feminists chose to enact their new commitment varied. For some the changes consisted largely of private actions—relationships renewed, careers resumed. Others, preferring public statements, used flamboyant methods to dramatize their newfound understanding of the subtle ways in which society defined and thereby confined women. As part of the confrontational politics of the 1960s, radical feminists picketed the 1968 Miss America contest, protesting the commercialization of beauty and our national preoccupation with bust size and "congeniality" rather than brain power and character. (In the process they were dubbed "bra burners," despite the fact that no bras were burned.) Activists pushed their way into all-male bars and restaurants as a way of forcing recognition of how these bastions of male exclusivity were themselves statements about "man's world/woman's place." They sat in at the offices of *Ladies' Home Journal* and *Newsweek* protesting the ways in which the media's depiction of women perpetuated old stereotypes at the expense of new realities. Others focused on abortion, mindful that mishandled illegal abortions claimed the lives of an estimated ten thousand women each year. Organizing "speakouts," they talked publicly about their own humiliating and dangerous encounters with the netherworld of abortion, thereby transforming this heretofore taboo and explosive subject into a matter of public debate and an issue of women's rights. Feminist lawyers, no less convinced that forcing a woman to bear a child against her will was a violation of her fundamental rights, used their legal skills to advance the cause of abortion law repeal in the courts.

Still other feminists chose to work for social change in a different fashion. They created nonsexist day care centers, wrote and published nonsexist children's books, monitored sex stereotyping in textbooks, lobbied for women's studies programs in high schools and colleges, and founded women's health clinics. They formed rape crisis centers so that rape victims could be treated by caring females; they agitated for more informed, sympathetic treatment on the part of hospital staffs, the police, and the courts. They created shelters for battered women, insisting that physical abuse was not a private family matter but a social problem requiring a public response. Feminist scholars used their talents to recover and interpret women's experience, opening new areas for research and in the process furthering change.

Feminist legislators, especially black Congresswoman Shirley Chisholm, sponsored legislation to extended minimum wage coverage to domestic workers. Other lawmakers sponsored bills, not always successful, to help housewives to secure some form of economic recognition for work performed, to enable women workers to obtain insurance that would give them the same degree of economic security afforded male coworkers, and to protect them from violence, which is the most blatant form of male oppression.

Trade union feminists, concerned with their dual identity as women and as wage workers, struggled to keep the needs of working women in the forefront. Black feminists, by their own admission "the most pressed down of us all," focused on issues of special concern to many minority women: media depictions of black women, racially coded credit policies, public housing, household workers' rights, and welfare and prison reform. Their sisters on the left in the Third World Women's Alliance, convinced that imperialism as well as sexism, racism, and classism oppressed women, organized demonstrations of solidarity with the women of Cuba and Vietnam. Actions, like voices, differed. Such diversity, however, was basic to the movement.[23]

FEMINISM: THE PUBLIC IMPACT

In a society in which the media, with their hunger for sensationalism, create instant awareness of the more dramatic aspects of social protest movements, feminism burst upon the public consciousness with all the understated visibility of a fireworks display on the Fourth of July. The more radical elements of the movement, with their talk of test tube conception, the slavery of marriage, and the downfall of capitalism, might be dismissed out of hand. But it was hard to ignore 50,000 women parading down New York's Fifth Avenue, the presence of *Ms.* magazine on newsstands, feminist books on the best-seller lists, women in hard hats on construction jobs, or the government-mandated affirmative action programs that put them there. It was harder still to ignore the publicity that accompanied the appointment of women to the Carter cabinet, the enrollment of coeds in the nation's military academies, and the ordination of women to the ministry. A Harris poll of December 1975 reported that 63 percent of the women interviewed favored most changes designed to improve the status of women, although some were quick to insist that they were not "women's libbers." Black women, recognizing that equality is indivisible, viewed feminism even more positively than did their white counterparts, although the feminists among them often preferred their own organizations.[24]

Evidence of changing views was everywhere. The list of organizations lined up in support of ratification of the Equal Rights Amendment included not only such avowedly feminist groups as NOW, WEAL, and NWPC as well as longtime supporters such as the National Woman's Party and the National Federation of Business and Professional Women's Clubs, but also well-established women's organizations such as the General Federation of Women's Clubs, the American Association of University Women, the League of Women Voters, the National Council of Jewish Women, the National Council of Negro Women, and the YWCA.

Even more potent evidence that feminism had "arrived" was the 1977 International Women's Year Conference in Houston. Before more than two thousand delegates from every state and territory in the United States and twenty thousand guests, three First Ladies—Lady Bird Johnson, Betty Ford, and Rosalynn Carter—endorsed the Equal Rights Amendment and the goals of the Houston Conference, their hands holding a lighted torch carried by women runners from Seneca Falls where, in 1848, the famous Declaration of Sentiments had been adopted. Confessing that she once thought the women's movement belonged more to her daughters than to herself, Lady Bird Johnson added, "I have come to know that it belongs to women of all ages." Such an admission, like the presence of these three women on the platform, proclaimed a message about feminists that was boldly printed on balloons throughout the convention hall: "We Are Everywhere."[25]

OPPOSITION TO FEMINISM

For some women the slogan was not a sign of achievement but of threat. Gathered at a counter-convention in Houston were women who shared neither the critique nor the goals of the movement. They were an impressive reminder that social change generates opposition and that opposition to feminism had crystalized in the struggle for ratification of the Equal Rights Amendment. ERA—as the amendment is called—simply stated: "Equality of rights under the law shall not be denied or abridged by the United States or by any State on account of sex." First suggested in 1923 as the logical extension of suffrage, the amendment had long been opposed by those who feared it would be used to strike down laws intended to protect women in the workplace. By the 1960s, those concerns no longer applied. Prodded by NOW, Congress once again turned its attention to a constitutional amendment removing sexual bias from common, statutory, and constitutional law. After a massive lobbying effort by women's rights advocates and their allies, the Senate finally joined the House and sent ERA to the states for ratification by a lopsided vote of eighty-four to eight in 1972. Almost immediately twenty-one states rushed to ratify. Within a year, however, opponents of ratification had begun a

The Torch Relay, opening the International Women's Year Conference, Houston, Texas, 1977. The torch, brought by runners from Seneca Falls to Houston, symbolized the link between those early feminists who drafted the Declaration of Sentiments and their contemporary counterparts who assembled to present new proposals designed to achieve the still-elusive goal of equality. (The Houston Conference was the last major bipartisan feminist public event of the twentieth century held in the United States.) From left to right: Billie Jean King, Susan B. Anthony II, Bella Abzug, Sylvia Ortiz, Peggy Kokernot, Mechele Cearcy, Betty Friedan. (Copyright © 1978 by Diana Mara Henry.)

counterattack that ultimately stalled the number of ratified states at thirty-five, three short of the needed three-fourths majority when the deadline for ratification expired on June 30, 1982. Opponents even induced some ratifying states to rescind their approval. Early successes indicated a majority of Americans favored ERA—but not a large enough majority.

Opposition to ERA is starkly paradoxical. A constitutional amendment proposed especially to benefit women was opposed by women. The paradox is resolved in part by remembering that many Americans who claim to believe in equality become profoundly apprehensive when the principle is identified with specific governmental policies they consider to be intrusive and unreasonable. When supporters of ERA said that implementation of a constitutional ban on sex discrimination would be left to the Supreme Court, conservatives of both sexes were reminded that this was the same Supreme Court that had not only mandated racial integration, but prohibited prayer in the public schools and struck down bans on birth control, abortion, and pornography. Court-enforced sexual equality, like racial equality, many people believed, would further diminish the power of state and local governments and the right of individuals to live as they chose. As one women wrote her U.S. senator: "*Forced* busing, *forced* mixing, *forced* housing. Now *forced* women! No thank you!"[26]

Such logic also illuminates antiratificationist charges, mystifying to ratificationists, that ERA would destroy the family. Although ERA supporters correctly pointed out that the amendment had nothing to do with private relationships, social conservatives were not convinced; they had seen what a federal agenda in feminist hands looked like at the International Women's Year Conference in Houston. A meeting subsidized by the U.S. government had endorsed not only women's rights and ERA, but government-sponsored child care, federal funding of abortions for poor women, contraception for minors without parental consent, and gay rights. If Big Brother or, more appropriately, Big Sister, had her way in Washington, women might well be forced to live in the kind of post-ERA world invoked by anti-ERA spokeswoman Phyllis Schlafly—a world in which mothers, no longer financially able to remain at home, would be forced to surrender their children to government-sponsored daycare centers. There child-care personnel would supplant parental authority and family identification with loyalty to the state.

The danger, as anti-ERA women saw it, was not just to family, but to women themselves. Feminists believed that theirs was a struggle for justice and liberation—liberation from economic inequities, social roles, and cultural values that denied rights and limited autonomy. To require *all* women to endure constraints dictated not by biology (sex) but by culture (gender) was, from the standpoint of feminists, to deny freedom and self-determination to half the population simply because they were born female. To women who did not believe they were oppressed, feminists' efforts at liberation, especially the rhetoric of radical feminists, appeared *not* as an attack on traditional gender categories, but rather an assault on familiar patterns that provided security, identity, and meaning. Fusing feminism and ERA, an antiratificationist begged her senator not to vote for the amendment, insisting that she did not want to be liberated. "My husband," she wrote, "works for me and takes care of me and our three children, doesn't make me do things that are hard for me (drive in town), loves me and doesn't smoke, drink, gamble, run around or do anything that would upset me. I do what he tells me to do. I like this arrangement. *It's the only way I know how to live.*" Insisted another: "I am a widow, have three children, and work to make ends meet. I am still against ERA. I am a woman—and want to be treated as a woman."[27]

When ERA supporters responded that treating women as individuals legally rather than classifying them by sex had nothing to do with the division of labor between husbands and wives, social etiquette, or the masculinization of women, their reassurances fell on deaf ears. The free-floating anxiety aroused by the enormity of the social change inherent in feminism had acquired concrete focus in ERA. Opponents' predictions of the terrible consequences that would result from ratification of the amendment were not so important as the function such statements served—an indictment of what Schlafly called the "unisex" society and an affirmation of traditional gender categories. For women living in a world in which personal identity, social legitimacy, economic viability, and moral order were rooted in traditional gender categories, calling those categories into question in the name of gender-neutral law meant that feminists must want men and women to be "the same." Finding it difficult to separate gender from sex—to see gender as a social construction—ERA opponents could only conclude that this latest drive for equality was not only absurd ("you can't fool Mother Nature") but dangerous. By rallying women to this danger, Schlafly revealed that the issue was not whether women should stay at home minding the children and cooking the food—Schlafly herself did not do that. The issue was the *meaning* of sexual differences between men and women.

In the early years of the movement, both radical and liberal feminists minimized those differences, believing reproductive control and work in the public sector have made women's lives more like men's. Antifeminists inflated those differences. Their response is a measure both of their belief that women are "eternal in their attributes and unchanged by events" and their anger and distress at changes that had already occurred.[28]

Although supporters managed to persuade Congress to extend the deadline for ratification of ERA from 1979 to 1982, only one state ratified after 1975. By the mid-seventies, the political climate that had sustained the reforms of the sixties had changed. Despite the tall ships and fireworks with which Americans lavishly celebrated the nation's two-hundredth birthday, the wars of Watergate, defeat in Vietnam, economic woes, and finally the Iranian hostage crisis had shaken citizens' confidence. A disaffected and angry segment of white Americans believed that a liberal elite in Washington, engaged in misguided social engineering, had led the country astray politically, and also severed its moral moorings. They ticked off a list of liberal "sins": school busing to achieve racial balance, affirmative action programs and hiring goals that advantaged minorities and women at the expense of white men, a constitutional amendment mandating gender equality, court rulings allowing abortion and forbidding school prayer, and a war on poverty that used hardworking taxpayers' dollars to support people too lazy to work. By the mid-1970s, skillful opinion-mobilizers and politicians welded the people who held these convictions, anxieties, and resentments with older constituencies, forging them all into a resurgent right. Flexing their political muscle in the Republican Party, this New Right was poised to put pro-life candidate Ronald Reagan in the White House in 1980, dropping the party's historic endorsement of ERA. Pro-choice feminists in the Republican Party were, with good reason, alarmed, as were their sisters who bore no allegiance to the GOP. Clearly, feminism's first decade had come to an end; it was time to take stock.

TAKING STOCK

There were gains to be sure. New reproductive freedom came in 1973 with the Supreme Court's liberalization of abortion laws that removed the danger of the illegal, back-alley abortions so long the recourse of desperate women. Sexual preference and practice became less an occasion for denial of civil rights and more a matter of individual choice. Evidence of expanding educational and employment opportunities seemed to be everywhere. Women assumed high-level posts in government, the judiciary, the military, business, and labor. In a new batch of female "firsts," Sandra Day O'Connor assumed a seat on the Supreme Court, NASA's Sally Ride zoomed into space, and Geraldine Ferraro won the vice-presidential slot on the 1984 Democratic ticket. From an expanding population of female college graduates, younger women moved in record numbers into professional school, dramatically changing enrollment patterns in such fields as law, medicine, and business. Their blue-collar counterparts, completing job training programs, trickled into the construction industry and other trades, finding in those jobs the decent wage that had eluded them as waitresses, hairdressers, salesclerks, or domestics. Political participation also increased. Women emerged from years of lobbying for ERA with a new understanding of the political process. (So, too, did their opponents.) More female candidates filed for office and more female politicians worked themselves into positions of power. Revision of discriminatory statutes, while by no means completed, brought a greater measure of legal equality. A heightened public consciousness of sexism ushered in other changes. School officials began admitting boys to home economics classes, girls to shop. Some employers transformed maternity leaves into child-care leaves, making them available to fathers as well as mothers. Liberal religious leaders talked of removing gender-related references from prayer books.

Such gains, while in some cases smacking of tokenism, are not to be minimized. Most required persistent pressure from feminists, from government officials, and often from both. They were by no means comprehensive, however. As in the case of the civil rights movement, the initial beneficiaries of the feminist movement were predominantly middle-class, often highly educated, and relatively young. The increase in the number of single women, the older age at which women married for the first time, the declining birth rate—changes characteristic of the entire female population during the 1970s—were especially characteristic of a younger generation of career-oriented women. But even for these women and their partners, financial as well as personal costs were sometimes high: couples living apart for some portion of the week or year in order to take advantage of career opportunities; married women devoting virtually all of their salaries to domestic and child-care costs, especially during their children's preschool years. Perhaps the personal recognition, independence, and sense of fulfillment associated with career success made the costs "affordable"—especially given the alternatives.

The women who stood to gain most from the implementation of feminists' efforts to change the nation's economic and social structure were not those who were young, talented, and educated but those who were less advantaged. Yet by the 1990s the latter could with good reason argue that two decades of feminist activity had left their lives little changed in ways that really count. While the number of women in the work force continued to rise from less than 20 percent in 1920 to just below 70 percent in 2000, working women in the 1970s and 1980s saw the gap between male and female income remain virtually unchanged. By 2003, female workers earned 78 cents for every dollar earned by males, although the gap has narrowed among younger women, who are currently earning more college degrees and MBAs than men. Significant numbers of younger women are also breaking into better-paying professions with the result that around 30 percent are earning more than their husbands.[29] For most women, however, especially older women, the pay gap still persists. Part of the explanation for its persistence lies in pay inequities. More fundamental, however, is the continuation of occupational segregation and the undervaluation of work done by women. Around 80 percent of all working women still cluster in gender-segregated occupations in which wages are artificially low. That women made up two-thirds of all minimum-wage workers in the United States is, therefore, hardly surprising.[30]

With the dramatic rise in the number of female-headed households—33 percent of all working mothers are their family's breadwinners—the continuation of this occupational ghetto has disturbing implications not only for women workers but also for their children. Female heads of households, often lacking both child-care facilities and skills that would equip them for better-paying jobs if such jobs were available, earn enough to enable less than two-thirds to stay above the poverty level. Their struggle for economic survival is shared by other women, especially older women—widows or divorcées whose years of housework have left them without employment skills. Indeed divorce often contributes to the problem, for with the breaking up of a marriage, the standard of living for most women falls dramatically. The fact that child support, if awarded, is frequently inadequate, unpaid, and uncollectible further exacerbates the economic plight of those women who have custody of their children. Thus, ironic as it may seem, the decade that witnessed the revival of the feminist movement also saw the feminization of poverty. By the end of the 1970s, two out of every three poor persons in the United States were female. At the beginning of the twenty-first century, women remain a disproportionately higher percent of those Americans below the poverty line—a trend that has shown no signs of changing.[31]

Ironic, too, given the feminist insistence that child-care and household responsibilities should be shared by working spouses, is the persistence of the double burden borne by women working outside the home. Working women continue to do 80 to 90 percent of the chores related to running a household, with husbands and elder children "helping out." For all the talk about the changing structure of family roles, major shifts have occurred slowly, even in households in which women were informed and engaged enough to be familiar with current feminist views.[32] Although some fathers, especially among the middle class, have become more involved in parenting, the primary responsibility for children still remains the mother's.[33] And working mothers still receive little institutional help despite the fact that by 2000, 65 percent of all mothers with children under six worked outside the home.[34] Without a fundamental rethinking of both work and family, women will continue to participate in the labor force in increasing numbers. Many, however, will remain in its lower echelons as marginal members.[35]

In sum, economic and demographic change has been the basis of important changes in attitudes and behavior. As a result, life is more challenging for many women, but the feminization of poverty reminds the nation of its failures. We have yet to see the new social policies necessary to create the egalitarian and humane society envisioned by feminists. Indeed, in the climate of political conservatism of the 1980s feminists had to fight hard to maintain gains already won. The reproductive freedom of poor women had already been eroded by limitations on federal funding of abortions, and the reproductive freedom of all women had been threatened by congressional advocates of the Human Life Bill. Although that bill never received the votes necessary to become law, an increasingly conservative Supreme Court dealt reproductive rights a further blow. The 1989 *Webster* and the 1992 *Planned Parenthood* decisions, while not overturning the right to an abortion, upheld the right of states to limit access. With reproductive rights now a contested issue in state legislatures, the struggle to keep abortion legal and unrestricted has escalated dramatically.

During the 1980s legislation mandating equal opportunity in education and employment was also weakened by the courts and assaulted by the Reagan and Bush administrations, whose budget cuts further hampered EEOC's antidiscrimination efforts. There were also cuts in funds for Title IX, which seeks to ensure sex equality on campus; cuts in grants for traditionally female programs such as nursing; and cuts in Small Business Administration funding for programs benefiting women. Day care centers, battered women's shelters, and legal aid centers had their work curtailed by budget cuts as well. Also under attack was comparable worth, a policy designed to reduce pay inequities by evaluating skills, effort, and responsibilities associated with jobs traditionally held mainly either by men or by women so that pay could be equalized for jobs that are indeed comparable. Defeat of the Equal Rights Amendment left determination of the meaning of discrimination in the law to Supreme Court justices with varying understandings of legal equality.

The election of 1992 brought to the White House a pro-choice President and a feminist First Lady, new feminist legislators to Capitol Hill, and the subsequent appointment of a pioneer feminist litigator to the Supreme Court. The gains of the 1990s, however, were accompanied by sharp reminders of the elusiveness of full equality. The Supreme Court opened the doors of Virginia Military Institute and The Citadel to women and clarified the law on sexual harassment, while Congress offered block grants to states outlawing marital rape. Yet that same Congress passed a welfare reform law that presupposes a society in which there is full employment, living wages, child care, and health care for all.

While some women were able to make the transition from welfare to employment, many found themselves in an ever-deepening economic crisis without the safety net that offered them a modicum of security in the past. While the robust economy of the 1990s accelerated the flow of women into the workplace and allowed more to own their own businesses and increase their earnings—one in five women in the U.S. earned more than her husband—the economic downtown in the new century has diminished expectations, jobs, and income. The wage gap remains even as the government safety net continues to shrink, hitting hardest less skilled workers, who are disproportionately women of color. Lower pay usually means lower or no benefits and smaller pensions upon retirement, contributing further to the feminization of poverty. Meanwhile, the war on affirmative action threatens the educational and occupational mobility of black and Hispanic women. Whatever their occupational level, few working mothers are spared a high level of stress. Unlike their European and Japanese counterparts, women in the U.S. continue to make do with only brief time off for childbirth and a patchwork quilt of child care that is as good as they can afford, and frequently not good enough.

Gains in other areas have also come with reminders of parity yet to be achieved. Americans can now point to two female Supreme Court justices and varying numbers of women who hold positions in the president's cabinet. President William Clinton even appointed Madeline Albright secretary of state. In Congress, however, women are proportionately underrepresented. In 2000, 73 women served in the 107th Congress, holding only 13 of the 100 seats in the Senate and 60 of the 435 seats in the House—an all-time high. A little over 22 percent of state legislators are women—a five-fold increase since 1969, when only 4 percent of all state legislators were women.[36] Here too feminists have made a difference, symbolized by their change in the old maxim "a woman's place is in the home" to the bold new proclamation "a woman's place is in the House." At the executive level, five of the fifty states have women as governors and women hold almost 28 percent of statewide elective offices.[37] Women of color, while included, are, like all women, proportionately underrepresented. It is also worth noting that often the positions women do attain are not the ones in which greatest power resides. For example, several women have held lower-level cabinet appointments, such as secretary of energy. But this is hardly the equivalent of serving as secretary of state or defense. It is no coincidence in recent years that only one woman has headed the state department and none has run the treasury or defense departments. Nor is being a member of a citizen's legislature like the General Court of New Hampshire—where members are less well paid and have less power—comparable to being a member of a professional legislature in Pennsylvania and other states where a seat holds the promise of upward political mobility. Of the New Hampshire legislature, which has a comparatively high percentage of women as compared to Pennsylvania, one lawmaker observed, "men can no longer afford to [serve]." Another explained the presence of women more bluntly: "It's just a continuation of the volunteer bullshit."[38] Parity, in short, involves more than numbers. Yet progress once again should not be discounted.

In the military, women won combat medals in the Gulf War and the War in Iraq even as the armed services gained new notoriety as a continuing site of gender warfare and sexual harassment. The nation's female athletes continued to scoop up medals at the Olympic games. Yet the celebration of the twenty-fifth anniversary of Title IX, which mandated equity in money spent by N.C.A.A. colleges, saw money spent on women still dwarfed by that spent on men's—$663,000 on average was budgeted for women and $2.4 million for men.[39] On another twenty-fifth anniversary, pro-choice women celebrated the survival of *Roe* v. *Wade* while mourning the death of an Indiana teenager who died from an illegal abortion after her state mandated parental consent.[40] In the twenty-first century, the right to legal abortion stands even more imperiled. (See pp. 691–96.)

THE EVOLUTION AND FUTURE OF FEMINISM

This seemingly contradictory view of feminism reminds us that social change is complex and results from the interplay of many factors. Nowhere is this truer than in the women's movement. The swiftness with which a resurgent feminism captured the imagination of millions of American women dramatized the need for change. The inability of feminists to win ratification of ERA dramatized the limits of change. The irony of the polarization, however, was that the failure of ERA did not and could not stop feminism in its tracks and that antifeminist women, in mobilizing to fight the amendment, were themselves assuming a new role whether they acknowledged that fact or not. They organized lobbies, political action committees, and conventions; they also ran for and won public office. Where feminists had led, antifeminists would not be too far behind, defining themselves within the context of change they could not stop. But the rhetoric of liberation that had been so important to the awakening and maturation of women in the 1970s seemed by the 1980s to be less appealing. Women could happily benefit from the achievements of feminism without understanding or embracing its critique. Transformational politics seemed to have given way to a bevy of career women armed with a copy of *Savvy* or *Working Woman*, "dressed for success," and busily playing "games their mothers never taught them" with scant realization, as one observer noted, that "only a decade ago they would never have been allowed to play."[41] Commentators, speculating that feminism had become careerism, pronounced the movement dead.

Although press speculation was off the mark, feminism had changed. By the mid-seventies, radical feminism had given way to cultural feminism. The appeal that alternative institution-building held for cultural feminists in the conservative eighties was understandable. But the kind of celebrating of the female reflected in the search for lost matriarchies and goddess worship seemed to radical and liberal feminists to represent not only female separatism but a retreat from political struggle. Both seemed alien to women whose aim had been to transcend gender, not reaffirm it. Valorization of female difference was also at the heart of still newer varieties of feminism such as eco-feminism: women as natural nurturers were presumed to be uniquely concerned with ecological ruin. If eco-feminism focused on issues that radical and liberal feminists of the 1960s would have regarded as broad human issues rather than distinctively feminist ones, the groups themselves functioned as a sharp reminder that second-wave feminism had always been an ideologically pluralistic, decentralized, and structurally amorphous movement. Indeed diversity is a source of strength—a point made with renewed intensity in the 1980s by women of color. Their insistence that racism, classism, and sexism are multiple and interlocking forms of oppression has served to remind mainstream feminists that women speak in different voices from multiple historical, cultural, racial, economic, and sexual locations. The need to move beyond totalizing notions of "sisterhood," recognizing the extent to which women have themselves been oppressors of other women, requires of mainstream feminism further transformation. There can be no mistaking black poet and feminist Audre Lorde's meaning when she asked, "What woman here is so enamored of her own oppression that she cannot see her heelprint upon another woman's face?"[42] If feminism is to become genuinely egalitarian and multicultural, mainstream feminists who bear the greater responsibility for that transformation will have much to do.

Meanwhile the movement continues to expand even in the midst of antifeminist backlash as women continue to make the connection between the personal and political as they confront in their own lives or the lives of others the trauma of sexual harassment, job discrimination and sexual violence. For every woman who disdains the label "feminist," there is another who proclaims, as does the young Anastasia Higgenbotham: "The one word all phallocrats most fear (and well they should), I wear like a badge of honor, my pride, my work, my glowing, spiked tiara."[43] It is on this youngest generation of feminists that the future of feminism depends. They understand that the battle is not over. Indeed, a resurgent right has made it abundantly clear that older patterns of inequality have not lost their force and that contemporary efforts to secure women's full emancipation can be challenged, slowed, even interrupted. But they cannot be extinguished. To stop struggling is to allow dominance justified by appeals to constructed differences of gender, ethnicity, race, class, and sexual preference to limit our lives and what connects us to each other.

NOTES

1. Nancy F. Cott, *The Grounding of Modern Feminism* (New Haven: Yale University Press, 1987), p. 3.
2. Myra Marx Ferree and Beth B. Hess demonstrate the utility of describing the various movements as

strands rather than branches in their volume *Controversy and Coalition: The New Feminist Movement across Four Decades of Change*, 3rd edition (New York: Routledge, 2000), pp. 56–57.

3. If one begins dating feminism among African American women with resistance to gendered violence, then enslaved women enacted an early form of feminist resistance and Harriet Jacobs, *Incidents in the Life of a Slave girl: Written by Herself*, ed. Jean Fagin Yellin (Cambridge: Harvard University Press, 1987), becomes a feminist memoir inasmuch as the narrative reflects Jacobs's consciousness of oppression as a slave and as a woman. Anna Julia Cooper, *A Voice from the South by a Black Woman of the South* (Xenia, Oh.: Aldine, 1892), quote, p. 135. On the distinctive African American feminist tradition, see Patricia Hill Collins, "The Social Construction of Black Feminist Thought," *Signs* 14 (1989):745–73; and idem, *Black Feminist Thought: Knowledge, Consciousness, and the Politics of Empowerment* (New York: Routledge, 1990). On industrial feminism see Annelise Orleck, *Common Sense and a Little Fire: Women and Working-Class Politics in the United States, 1900–1965* (Chapel Hill: University of North Carolina Press, 1991); Nancy F. Gabin, *Feminism in the Labor Movement: Women and the United Auto Workers, 1935–1975* (Ithaca: Cornell University Press, 1990); and Dennis A. Deslippe, *"Rights, Not Roses": Unions and the Rise of Working-Class Feminism, 1945–1980* (Urbana: University of Illinois Press, 2000). Examples of black and low-income women's groups include Mothers Working Along and the Mt. Vernon/New Rochelle group. On the latter, see Rosalyn Baxandall, "Re-visioning the Women's Liberation Movement's Narrative: Early Second Wave African American Feminists," *Feminist Studies* 27 (2001):225–45.

4. "Old Left" refers to those left-wing political organizations such as the Communist Party, Trotskyist organizations such as the Socialist Workers' Party, independent Socialist clubs, and the Freedom Socialist Party, as well as anarchist groups. On the links between the Old Left and new feminists, see Kate Weigand, *Red Feminism: American Communism and the Making of Women's Liberation* (Baltimore: Johns Hopkins University Press, 2001).

5. Barbara Winslow, "Old Left/New Left: The Origins and Development of the Women's Liberation Movement in Seattle, Washington, 1966–1970," paper delivered at the American Historical Association, Seattle, January, 1998. See also Baxandall, "Re-visioning the Women's Liberation Movement's Narrative."

6. Weigand, *Red Feminism*.

7. Daniel Horowitz, *Betty Friedan and the Making of the Feminine Mystique: The American Left, the Cold War, and Modern Feminism* (Amherst: University of Massachusetts Press, 1998). The origins of the feminist movement in the Cold War are also explored extensively in Ruth R. Rosen, *The World Split Open: How the Modern Women's Movement Changed America* (New York: Viking, 2000).

8. Cynthia E. Harrison, "A 'New Frontier' for Women: The Public Policy of the Kennedy Administration," *Journal of American History* 67 (1980):630–46.

9. U.S. President's Commission on the Status of Women, *American Women* (Washington, D.C., 1963).

10. Gabin, *Feminism in the Labor Movement*, p. 188.

11. For events leading to the founding of NOW, see Jo Freeman, *The Politics of Women's Liberation: A Case Study of an Emerging Social Movement and Its Relation to the Social Policy Process* (New York: Longman, 1975), pp. 53–55; and Cynthia Harrison, *On Account of Sex: The Politics of Women's Issues, 1945–1968* (Berkeley: University of California Press, 1988), pp. 192–209.

12. Freeman, *Politics of Women's Liberation*, pp. 35–37.

13. National Organization of Women, Statement of Purpose, 1966, reprinted in *Up from the Pedestal*, ed. Aileen S. Kraditor (Chicago: Quadrangle, 1968), pp. 363–64; National Organization of Women, Bill of Rights, 1967, reprinted in *Sisterhood Is Powerful: An Anthology of Writings on the Women's Liberation Movement*, ed. Robin Morgan (New York: Random House, 1970), pp. 512–14.

14. Freeman, *Politics of Women's Liberation*, chap. 3; Maren Lockwood Carden, *The New Feminist Movement* (New York: Russell Sage, 1974), chaps. 8–10; also Gayle Graham Yates, *What Women Want: The Ideas of the Movement* (Cambridge, Mass.: Harvard University Press, 1975), chap. 2; Gabin, *Feminism in the Labor Movement*, p. 226.

15. Quoted in Carolyn Hadley, "Feminist Women in the Southeast," *Bulletin of the Center of the Study of Southern Culture and Religion* 3 (1979):10.

16. Quoted in "Ruth Bader Ginsburg," *1994 Current Biography*, p. 214.

17. Sara Evans, *Personal Politics: The Roots of Women's Liberation in the Civil Rights Movement and the New Left* (New York: Vintage, 1979); see also Evans, "Tomorrow's Yesterday: Feminist Consciousness and the Future of Women," in *Women of America: A History*, ed. Carol Ruth Berkin and Mary Beth Norton (Boston: Houghton Mifflin, 1979), pp. 390–415. The following paragraphs rely heavily on this essay and on Evans's *Personal Politics*.

18. Mary King, one of the authors of the manifesto protesting the treatment of women in SNCC, insists that Carmichael was personally responsive to their concerns if others were not. See Mary King, *Freedom Song* (New York: Morrow, 1987), pp. 450–52. On the treatment of women in the New Left, see Ellen Willis, "Sequel: Letter to a Critic," *Notes from the Second Year* n.v. (1970): 55–58. In a previous article, Willis had argued that the New Left was dominated by men and its theory, priorities, and strategy reflected male interests. See her "Women and the Left," *Notes from the Second Year* n.v. (1970):5–56. See also Alice Echols, *Daring to be Bad: Radical Feminism in America, 1965–1975* (Minneapolis: University of Minnesota Press, 1989).

19. On the early organization of feminists of color, see Esther Ngan-Ling Chow, "The Development of Feminist Consciousness Among Asian American Women," *Gender and Society* 1 (1987): 284–299; William Wei, *The Asian American Movement* (Philadelphia: Temple University Press, 1993); Naomi Barry, "Women's Participation in the Chicano Movement," *Latino Studies Journal* 8 (1997):47–82; Alma Garcia, *Chicano Feminist Thought:*

The Basic Historical Writings (New York: Routledge, 1997). Black feminists in SNCC formed a Black Women's Caucus in 1968 to discuss the problems of women in SNCC. Reaching out to non-SNCC, some members of the Black Women's Caucus formed an independent feminist group, the Black Women's Alliance. Other SNCC feminists formed a Black Women's Liberation Committee, which was part of SNCC. See "Memo, From the National Office of SNCC to All SNCC workers and Programs, Regarding Minutes of the National SNCC Workers Meeting," June 1970; "Just What Is the SNCC Black Women's Liberation Committee?"; Frances Beal to Julia, April 23, 1969; "Memo, Francie Beal to All SNCC Workers," October 9, 1970; "Third World Women's Alliance History and Goals," all in Box 4, Third World Women's Alliance Papers, Records of the National Conference of Negro Women, Mary McLeod Bethune Museum and Archives, Washington, D.C. On the exodus of lesbians, see Radicalesbians, "Leaving the Gay Men Behind," in Karla Jay and Allen Young, eds., *Out of the Closets: Voices of Gay Liberation* (New York: Douglas Book Co., 1972).

20. Quoted in Evans, "Tomorrow's Yesterday," p. 407.

21. See *Notes from the Second Year,* the Redstockings Manifesto and other writing in Robin Morgan, ed., *Sisterhood Is Powerful: An Anthology of Writings from the Women's Liberation Movement* (New York: Random House, 1970); Deborah Babcox and Madeline Belkin, eds., *Liberation Now: Writings from the Women's Liberation Movement* (New York: Dell, 1971); Alexander Bloom and Wini Breines, eds. *'Takin' It to the Streets': A Sixties Reader* (New York: Oxford, 1995); Kate Millett, *Sexual Politics* (Garden City, N.Y.: Doubleday, 1970); Shulamith Firestone, *The Dialectic of Sex: The Case for a Feminist Revolution* (New York: Morrow, 1970); Germaine Greer, *The Female Eunuch* (New York: McGraw Hill, 1970); Juliet Mitchell, *Women's Estate* (New York: Vintage, 1971); Evelyn Reed, *Problems of Women's Liberation: A Marxist Approach* (New York: Pathfinder, 1971); Mary Daly, *Beyond God the Father: Toward a Philosophy of Women's Liberation* (Boston: Beacon, 1973); Carolyn Heilbrun, *Toward a Recognition of Androgyny* (New York: Knopf, 1973); and *The Black Woman: An Anthology,* ed. Toni Cade (New York: Signet, 1970).

22. Judith M. Bardwick, *In Transition: How Feminism, Sexual Liberation and the Search for Self-Fulfillment Have Altered America* (New York: Holt, 1979), p. 26.

23. On CWLU, see its newspaper *Womankind,* published between 1970 and 1974, as well as "A Critical History of the CWLU," "CWLU Background History of CWLU, 1968–1976," and Hyde Park Chapter of CWLU, "Socialist Feminism: A Strategy for the Women's Movement," Box 1, Chicago Women's Liberation Union Collection, Chicago Historical Society, Chicago, IL. See also Barbara Ehrenreich, speech at the National Conference on Socialist Feminism, box 2, CWLU Papers. Black feminists belonged to organizations such as the short-lived National Black Feminist Organization and the National Alliance of Black Feminists. This characterization of black feminists as the most pressed down is from Patricia Haden, Donna Middleton, and Patricia Robinson, "A Historical and Critical Essay for Black Women," in *Voices from Women's Liberation,* ed. Leslie B. Tanner (New York: American Library, 1971), pp. 316–24. For the differing concerns of black feminists, see Carol Kleiman, "When Black Women Rap, the Talk Sure is Different," *Chicago Tribune,* June 1, 1975, sec. 5, p. 13. Information on the Third World Women's Alliance is based on my research in its papers, which are located in the Records of the National Congress of Negro Women, Bethune Museum and Archives, Washington, D.C.

24. Louis Harris, "Changing Views on the Role of Women," *The Harris Survey,* Dec. 11, 1975.

25. Caroline Bird and the Members and Staff of the National Commission on the Observance of International Woman's Year, *What Women Want: From the Official Report to the President, the Congress, and the People of the United States* (New York: Simon & Schuster, 1979), p. 68 for Johnson's statement.

26. Violet S. Devieux to Senator Sam J. Ervin, Jr., Mar. 23, 1972, Samuel J. Ervin Papers, #3847 Southern Historical Collection, Library of the University of North Carolina at Chapel Hill. For a fuller analysis of the significance of the struggle over ERA and the debate over feminism, see Donald G. Mathews and Jane S. De Hart, *Sex, Gender, and the ERA: A State and the Nation* (New York: Oxford, 1990).

27. For analysis of these and other anti-ERA women's quotes, see also De Hart, "Gender on the Right: Meanings behind the Existential Scream," *Gender and History* 3 (1991):246–67.

28. This apt characterization is William Chafe's; see *The Paradox of Change* (New York: Oxford, 1991) p. 209.

29. U.S. Bureau of the Census, *Statistical Abstract of the United States: 2000* (120th ed.). (Washington, D.C., 2000); Peg Tyre and Daniel McGinn, "She Works, He Doesn't," *Newsweek,* May 12, 2003, pp. 46–52.

30. For a fuller discussion, see *Women's Work, Men's Work: Sex Segregation on the Job,* eds. Barbara F. Reskin and Heidi I. Hartmann (Washington, D.C.: National Academy Press, 1986).

31. Diane Pearce, "The Feminization of Poverty: Women, Work, and Welfare," *Urban and Social Change Review* 11 (1978):28–36; Barbara Ehrenreich and Francis Fox Piven, "The Feminization of Poverty: When the 'Family Wage System' Breaks Down," *Dissent* 31 (1984):162–70; Leonore J. Weitzman, *The Divorce Revolution and the Unanticipated Consequences for Women and Children in America* (New York: Free Press, 1985); Census Bureau, Historical Poverty Tables, Table 7. Poverty of People, by Sex: 1966 to 2001: http://www.census.gov/hhes/poverty/histpov/hstpov7.html.

32. *The American Woman, Status Report 1988–1989,* ed. Sara E. Rix (New York: W. W. Norton, 1988), p. 151.

33. Arlie Hochschild, *Second Shift: Working Parents and the Revolution at Home* (New York: Viking, 1989).

34. *Statistical Abstracts of the United States: 2000.*

35. Joan William, *Unbending Gender: Why Family and Work Conflict and What to Do About It* (New York: Oxford, 2000).

36. For data on women governors and state legislators, see CAWP Fact Sheet Summaries: Women in Elective Office in 2000, compiled by the Center for the American Woman and Politics, Eagleton Institute for Politics, Rutgers University; New Brunswick, N.J.

37. Ibid.

38. Jane Sherron De Hart, "Rights and Representation: Women, Politics, and Power in the Contemporary United States," in *U.S. History as Women's History*, eds., Linda K. Kerber, Alice Kessler-Harris, and Kathryn Kish Sklar (Chapel Hill, N.C. University of North Carolina Press, 1995), pp. 214–42, esp. 235–36.

39. *New York Times*, June 16, 1997, p. A1.

40. On the celebration of *Roe*, see "NARAL News" 28:2 (Fall, 1997): 1.

41. *New York Times*, December 12, 1997, p. A3.

42. Quoted in Verta Taylor, "The Future of Feminism in the 1980s: A Social Movement Analysis," in *Feminist Frontiers*, eds. Laurel Richardson and Verta Taylor (Reading, Mass.: Addison-Wesley, 1983), p. 442.

43. The quote is from Audre Lorde, *Sister Outsider* (Trumansburg, N.Y.: Crossing Press, 1984), p. 60. See also Angela Y. Davis, *Women, Race, and Class* (New York: Vintage, 1981). For a more theoretical discussion, see Patricia Hill Collins, *Black Feminist Thought*, and Nancie Caraway, *Segregated Sisterhood: Racism and the Politics of American Feminism* (Knoxville, Tenn.: University of Tennessee Press, 1991).

44. Quoted in *Listen Up: Voices From the Next Feminist Generation*, ed. Barbara Findlen (Seattle: Seal Press, 1995), p. 6.

DOCUMENTS: Dimensions of Citizenship III

Equal Rights Amendment, 1972

An equal rights amendment, with wording slightly different from that passed by Congress in 1972, was sponsored in 1923 by the National Woman's Party. It seemed to party members the logical corollary to suffrage. But that amendment was vigorously opposed by the League of Women Voters and other progressive reformers, lest it undermine the protective legislation for which they had fought so hard.

An equal rights amendment was introduced regularly in Congress virtually every year thereafter, but it received little attention until after World War II. In 1950 and 1953 it was passed by the Senate but ignored by the House.

By 1970 much protective legislation had been applied to both men and women. It was possible to support an equal rights amendment without risking the undoing of labor law reforms. The hope that the Supreme Court would apply the Fourteenth Amendment's "equal protection of the laws" clause to cases involving discrimination on the basis of sex as firmly as it applied the clause to cases involving racial discrimination had not been fulfilled. When the current Equal Rights Amendment was introduced in 1970, it was endorsed by a wide range of organizations, some of which had once opposed it; these organizations included groups as disparate as the United Automobile Workers and the Woman's Christian Temperance Union. Its main sponsor in the House was Martha Griffiths of Michigan; in the Senate, Birch Bayh of Indiana.

The ERA was passed by Congress on March 22, 1972, and sent to the states for ratification. There was much initial enthusiasm; within two days six states had ratified. But the pace of ratification slowed after 1975, and only thirty-five of the needed thirty-eight states had ratified it by 1978. (Four state legislatures voted to rescind ratification, although the legality of that move was open to question.) In October 1978 Congress extended the deadline for ratification to June 30, 1982; the extension expired with no additional ratifications. The amendment was reintroduced in Congress in 1983 but has not been passed.

Section 1. Equality of rights under the law shall not be denied or abridged by the United States or by any State on account of sex.

Section 2. The Congress shall have the power to enforce, by appropriate legislation, the provisions of this article.

Section 3. The amendment shall take effect two years after the date of ratification.

Title IX, Education Amendments of 1972

In 1972, women received 9 percent of the M.D. degrees awarded by universities in the United States, 7 percent of the law degrees, and 15 percent of the doctoral degrees. Women were 2 percent of college varsity athletes. It was common practice to encourage women students into specialties marked as appropriate for women: teaching rather than scientific research, for example, or nursing rather than medicine. In athletics, it was usual practice for the travel budgets of male athletic teams to be paid for from student fees (paid by both women and men), while women's teams received 0.5 percent of the school's athletic budgets and there were no athletic scholarships for women. Women's teams often had to raise their own travel funds, sometimes from bake sales and raffles. Title IX of the Education Amendments of 1972 was brief but far-reaching.

No person in the United States shall, on the basis of sex, be excluded from participation in, be denied the benefits of, or be subjected to discrimination under any education program or activity receiving Federal financial assistance . . .

Each Federal department and agency which is empowered to extend Federal financial assistance to any education program or activity, by way of grant, loan, or contract . . . is authorized and directed to effectuate the provisions of . . . this title with respect to such program or activity by issuing rules, regulations, or orders of general applicability which shall be consistent with achievement of the objectives of the statute . . .

Title IX was enforced by the Office of Civil Rights and by the Department of Education. Enforcement was gradual; two years after the passage of Title IX it was estimated that colleges offered athletic scholarships to 50,000 men and fewer than 50 women. Not until 1975 were there full federal regulations applying to secondary schools and colleges and universities; other regulations were subsequently developed. Although Title IX applies to all elements of university programs, its impact on athletic programs had high visibility, and has been followed attentively by the public and the press. Equality in athletics has been taken by much of the public as the marker of equality in higher education in general. Participation in athletics has been linked to benefits to health and to self-confidence and self-esteem.

Title IX regulations require that the total amount of athletic financial assistance awarded to men and women be proportionate to their respective participation rates in intercollegiate athletic programs. They require that male and female athletes receive *equivalent* benefits, treatment, services, and opportunities; *identical* benefits and opportunities are not required. It does not require that all teams be coeducational, or that the same number of teams be provided for men and women, or that men's teams be cut in order for the institution to come into compliance with the law.

In the years since the passage of Title IX, the number of women participating in NCAA intercollegiate athletics has more than tripled, from approximately 32,000 in 1971

Title IX of Public Law 92–318 (1972) and subsequent amendments. See also *Hearing on Title IX of the Education Amendments of 1972 Before the Subcommittee on Post Secondary Education . . . of the Committee on Economic and Educational Opportunities*, 104th Congress, House of Representatives, 1st Session, May 9, 1995, Serial No. 104–31.

Diversity in admissions and more equitable funding for women's athletics have made new opportunities for women to hone their skills and overcome challenges, as the players at the University of California happily attest. (Photo courtesy of Department of Athletics, University of California, Santa Barbara.)

to roughly 157,000 in at the turn of the twenty-first century. (The number of men in intercollegiate athletics has remained relatively stable, at 205,000.) At the high school level, the change is even more striking: in 1972, only 1 in 27 high school women participated in a sport; in 2000 the ratio was 1 in 3.* But at Division I schools (with major football and basketball teams), the amount of money spent on men's athletics is now twice as much as the money spent on women's athletics.

Argument continues about what constitutes equitable treatment. Is it fair for men to hold the great majority of athletic scholarships (an imbalance largely due to the size of men's football and basketball teams)? Is it fair for a university to support a women's varsity rowing team but not a men's varsity rowing team? What is the proper relationship between women's sports and men's sports? Between women's sports and men's "minor" sports? Perhaps most significantly, what is the wise relationship between expenditures on athletics and expenditures on academic programs?

In 2002, the U.S. secretary of education established the Commission on Opportunity in Athletics. At issue were the measures of fairness. Title IX's basic rule has been that the ratio of male and female athletes should be about equal to the ratio of all male and female undergraduates. Institutions can also be found in compliance if they have a "history and continuing practice" of expanding opportunities for women, or they must be able to demonstrate that they are "fully and effectively accommodating" the "interests and abilities" of women on their campus. More than three-quarters of colleges and universities are in comfortable compliance with Title IX, having added women's teams and continued to support men's teams. It is Division I schools, which reserve substantial numbers of slots for revenue-producing sports (even at the expense of cutting men's minor sports) that have found it most difficult to meet Title IX's expectations. Yet in 1999–2000, a period when men worried about the lack of support for minor sports, women varsity athletes in Division I schools represented 53 percent of the student body but received only 32 percent of the money budgeted to athletics overall.† After more than a year of intense public debate, the Department of Education reaffirmed the established regulations by which schools measured compliance with Title IX.

Title IX also provides that "no person shall, on the basis of sex . . . be subjected to discrimination under any education program." In 1999 the Supreme Court responded to the appeal of the fifth-grade girl who had been subjected to explicit sexual teasing by a classmate. He attempted to touch her breasts and genital area, he told her "I want to get into bed with you," and he rubbed his body against her in the hallway. Her grades plummeted as she lost the ability to concentrate on her studies. Although she and her mother complained repeatedly to teachers and the principal, no action was taken. The Court ruled that school districts may be liable for damages when administrators are indifferent to repeated and known acts of student-to-student sexual harassment, during school hours and on school grounds. (*Davis* v. *Monroe County Board of Education*, 119 S. Ct. 1661). The case raised the question of responsibility of schools to provide a harassment-free environment (cf. *Meritor Savings Bank* v. *Vinson*, pp. 643–45). Critics charged that remedies should have been sought, if at all, against the offending student, not against the school administration. Do you agree?

New York Times, May 9, 2002.

†Commission on Intercollegiate Athletics, "Report of the Knight Foundation," June 2001.

Frontiero *v.* Richardson, *1973*

Sharron A. Frontiero was an Air Force officer who was dismayed to discover that she could not claim dependent's benefits for her husband on the same terms that her male colleagues could for their wives. She and her husband brought suit, claiming that statutes requiring spouses of female members of the uniformed services to receive more than half of their support from their wives to be considered dependents, while all spouses of male members were treated as dependents, violated the due process clause of the Fifth Amendment and the equal protection clause of the Fourteenth Amendment.

Until 1971, the Supreme Court had never ruled that discrimination on the basis of sex was a violation of the equal protection clause of the Fourteenth Amendment. So long as a legislature had a "reasonable" basis for making distinctions between men and women, discriminatory laws were upheld. Between 1971 and 1975, in a stunning series of decisions, the Supreme Court placed the burden of proof that discrimination on the basis of sex was reasonable on those who tried to discriminate. Ruth Bader Ginsburg was a 38-year-old law professor working with the American Civil Liberties Union in 1971 when the Court accepted her argument that an Idaho law requiring that fathers, rather than mothers, always be preferred as executors of their children's estates was unconstitutional. (*Reed* v. *Reed* 404 U.S. 71 [1971].)

The ACLU set up a Women's Rights Project in 1973 with Ginsburg at its head to follow up on the implications of the *Reed* decision. Ginsburg wrote the brief and managed the argument in *Frontiero;* it was one of a brilliant series of cases that she argued in the early 1970s. With her colleagues, she helped persuade the Court that a wide range of discriminatory practices were illegal. Her career as a litigator would lead to her appointment as a judge on the U.S. Court of Appeals in 1980 and, in 1993, to her appointment to the U.S. Supreme Court.

The Supreme Court ruled in favor of the Frontieros in a complex decision that used statistical information about woman's place in the work force in a manner reminiscent of the Brandeis Brief. Speaking for three of his colleagues Justice William J. Brennan, Jr., prepared a historically based argument, explaining the distance American public opinion had traveled since the *Bradwell* case (see *Bradwell* v. *Illinois,* pp. 248–49). He drew analogies between discrimination on the basis of race, which the court subjected to strict scrutiny, and discrimination on the basis of sex.

In concurring with Brennan's opinion, three justices observed that although they agreed with the Frontieros in this particular case, they were not yet persuaded that sex ought to be regularly treated as a "suspect category." Only when—or if—the Equal Rights Amendment were passed could the Court be sure that the public agreed that discrimination on the basis of sex ought to be evaluated as critically as discrimination on the basis of race. Note that the facts in *Frontiero* relate to discrimination against the husband of the wage earner, not directly against a woman. It is the family of the wage earner that is discriminated against. A similar case, also argued by Ginsburg, is *Weinberger* v. *Weisenfeld* (420 U.S. 636 [1975]), in which the husband of a dead woman successfully demanded survivor's benefits equal to those available to widows. Ginsburg and her colleagues stressed that both men and women benefited from gender-blind equal treatment under the law.

MR. JUSTICE WILLIAM J. BRENNAN, JR. DELIVERED THE OPINION OF THE COURT:

The question before us concerns the right of a female member of the uniformed services to claim her spouse as a "dependent." . . .

At the outset, appellants contend that classifications based upon sex, like classifications based upon race, alienage, and national origin, are inherently suspect and must therefore be subjected to close judicial scrutiny. We agree. . . .

There can be no doubt that our Nation has had a long and unfortunate history of sex discrimination. Traditionally, such discrimination was rationalized by an attitude of "romantic paternalism" which, in practical effect, put women, not on a pedestal, but in a cage. Indeed, this paternalistic attitude became so firmly rooted in our national consciousness that, 100 years ago, a distinguished Member of this Court was able to proclaim. . . . "The natural and proper timidity and delicacy which belongs to the female sex evidently unfits it for many of the occupations of civil life." . . .

It is true, of course, that the position of women in America has improved markedly in recent decades. Nevertheless, it can hardly be doubted that, in part because of the high visibility of the sex characteristic, women still face pervasive, although at times more subtle, discrimination in our educational institutions, in the job market, and perhaps most conspicuously, in the political arena. . . .

Moreover, since sex, like race and national origin, is an immutable characteristic determined solely by the accident of birth, the imposition of special disabilities upon the member of a particular sex because of their sex would seem to violate "the basic concept of our system that legal burdens should bear some relationship to individual responsibility. . . . " And what differentiates sex from such non-suspect statuses as intelligence or physical disability, and aligns it with the recognized suspect criteria, is that the sex characteristic frequently bears no relation to ability to perform or contribute to society. . . .

. . . over the past decade, Congress has itself manifested an increasing sensitivity to sex-based classification. In Tit[le] VII of the Civil Rights Act of 1964, for example, Congress expressly declared that no employer, labor union, or other organization subject to the provisions of the Act shall discriminate against any individual on the basis of "race, color, religion, sex, or national origin." Similarly, the Equal Pay Act of 1963 provides that no employer covered by the Act "shall discriminate . . . between employees on the basis of sex." . . .

With these considerations in mind, we can only conclude that classifications based upon sex, like classifications based upon race, alienage, or national origin, are inherently suspect, and must therefore be subjected to strict judicial scrutiny. Applying the analysis mandated by that stricter standard of review, it is clear that the statutory scheme now before us is constitutionally invalid. . . .

MR. JUSTICE LEWIS F. POWELL, JR., WITH WHOM THE CHIEF JUSTICE AND MR. JUSTICE HARRY A. BLACKMUN JOIN, CONCURRING IN THE OPINION:

I agree that the challenged statutes constitute an unconstitutional discrimination against servicewomen . . . but I cannot join the opinion of Mr. Justice Brennan, which would hold that all classifications based upon sex . . . are "inherently suspect and must therefore be subjected to close judicial scrutiny." . . . The Equal Rights Amendment, which if adopted will resolve the substance of this precise question, has been approved by the Congress and submitted for ratification by the States. If this Amendment is duly adopted, it will represent the will of the people accomplished in the manner prescribed by the constitution. . . . It seems to me that this reaching out to pre-empt by judicial action a major political decision which is currently in process of resolution does not reflect appropriate respect for duly prescribed legislative processes.

Roe *v.* Wade, *1973;* Planned Parenthood of Southeastern Pennsylvania *v.* Casey, *1992*

The Comstock Law had been echoed by a series of anticontraception and antiabortion laws throughout the country. James Mohr observes, "Every state in the Union had [by 1900] an antiabortion law of some kind on its books . . . except Kentucky, where the state courts outlawed the practice anyway."* In 1962 the ethics of abortion became a pressing problem when it was revealed that thalidomide, a drug extensively used in Europe and occasionally in the United States, resulted in the birth of thousands of babies with phocomelia (deformed or missing arms and legs). Sherry Finkbine, an Arizona woman who had taken the drug, demanded a legal abortion. Although her doctors supported her, the county medical society refused to approve the procedure, and, lacking confidence that she and her doctors would be spared immunity from prosecution, she fled to Sweden, where abortion was legal.

Her plight, and her challenge to hospital practice, helped to shift public opinion, both within the medical profession, which would subsequently be instrumental in advocating liberalization of abortion legislation, and among women's groups, who began to articulate dismay that women were generally denied access to safe abortion services. Estimates of the number of illegal abortions performed each year before 1973 range from 200,000 to 1,200,000; it is estimated that 200 women died each year as a result. Abortion was virtually the only medical procedure to which middle-class women did not have access. The issue was less intense for black women's groups; working-class minority women lacked a wide range of medical services, and abortion was only one among many which they needed. Thus at the beginning of the reinvigorated women's movement of the late 1960s, black and white women were divided about the place that access to legal abortion should hold in their list of priorities for legal change.

In 1970, Alaska, Hawaii, New York, and Washington legalized abortion. Texas law, like the law of most states, continued to prohibit abortion except for the purpose of saving the mother's life. In 1970, Norma McCorvey, a single pregnant woman, known as Jane Roe to protect her privacy, brought a class action suit challenging the constitutionality of that law as a violation of her right to liberty as guaranteed by the due process clause of the Fourteenth Amendment.

The Supreme Court's decision in *Roe* v. *Wade* marked a sharp change from long-established practice. As the opening lines of the majority decision make clear, the justices were aware they were making a sensitive and important decision.

MR. JUSTICE HARRY A. BLACKMUN DELIVERED THE OPINION OF THE COURT:

We forthwith acknowledge our awareness of the sensitive and emotional nature of the abor-tion controversy, of the vigorous opposing views, even among physicians, and of the deep

---

*James C. Mohr, *Abortion in America: The Origins and Evolution of National Policy, 1800–1900* (New York: Oxford University Press, 1978), pp. 229–30.

and seemingly absolute convictions that the subject inspires. One's philosophy, one's experiences, one's exposure to the raw edges of human existence, one's religious training, one's attitudes toward life and family and their values, and the moral standards one establishes and seeks to observe, are all likely to influence and to color one's thinking and conclusions about abortion.

In addition, population growth, pollution, poverty, and racial overtones tend to complicate and not to simplify the problem.

Our task, of course, is to resolve the issue by constitutional measurement, free of emotion and of predilection. We seek earnestly to do this. . . .

The principal thrust of the appellant's attack on the Texas statutes is that they improperly invade a right, said to be possessed by the pregnant woman, to choose to terminate her pregnancy. Appellant would discover this right in the concept of personal "liberty" embodied in the Fourteenth Amendment's Due Process Clause; or in personal, marital, familial and sexual privacy said to be protected by the Bill of Rights . . . or among those rights reserved to the people by the Ninth Amendment. . . .

It perhaps is not generally appreciated that the restrictive criminal abortion laws in effect in a majority of States today are of relatively recent vintage. Those laws, generally proscribing abortion or its attempt at any time during pregnancy except when necessary to preserve the pregnant woman's life, are not of ancient or even of common-law origin. Instead, they derive from statutory changes effected, for the most part, in the latter half of the nineteenth century. . . . At common law, at the time of the adoption of our Constitution, and throughout the major portion of the nineteenth century . . . a woman enjoyed a substantially broader right to terminate a pregnancy than she does in most states today. . . .

When most criminal abortion laws were first enacted, the procedure was a hazardous one for the woman. This was particularly true prior to the development of antisepsis. . . . Abortion mortality was high. . . . Modern medical techniques have altered this situation. Appellants . . . refer to medical data indicating that abortion in early pregnancy, that is, prior to the end of the first trimester, although not without its risk, is now relatively safe. Mortality rates for women undergoing early abortions, where

the procedure is legal, appear to be as low as or lower than the rates for normal childbirth. Consequently, any interest of the State in protecting the woman from an inherently hazardous procedure . . . has largely disappeared. . . . The State has a legitimate interest in seeing to it that abortion, like any other medical procedure, is performed under circumstances that insure maximum safety for the patient. . . .

The Constitution does not explicitly mention any right of privacy. In a line of decisions, however . . . the Court has recognized that a right of personal privacy, or a guarantee of certain areas or zones of privacy, does exist under the Constitution. . . . This right . . . whether it be founded in the Fourteenth Amendment's concept of personal liberty . . . or . . . in the Ninth Amendment's reservation of rights to the people, is broad enough to encompass a woman's decision whether or not to terminate her pregnancy. . . . We . . . conclude that the right of personal privacy includes the abortion decision, but that this right is not unqualified and must be considered against important state interests in regulation. . . .

. . . the State does have a important and legitimate interest in preserving and protecting the health of the pregnant woman . . . and . . . it has still *another* important and legitimate interest in protecting the potentiality of human life. These interests are separate and distinct. Each grows in substantiality as the woman approaches term, and, at a point during pregnancy, each becomes "compelling."

With respect to the State's important and legitimate interest in the health of the mother, the "compelling" point, in the light of present medical knowledge, is at approximately the end of the first trimester. This is so because of the now-established medical fact . . . that until the end of the first trimester mortality in abortion may be less than mortality in normal childbirth. It follows that . . . for the period of pregnancy prior to this "compelling" point, the attending physician, in consultation with his patient, is free to determine, without regulation by the State, that in his medical judgment, the patient's pregnancy should be terminated.

. . . For the state subsequent to approximately the end of the first trimester, the State, in promoting its interest in the health of the mother, may, if it chooses, regulate the abortion procedure in ways that are reasonably related to maternal health.

For the state subsequent to viability, the State in promoting its interest in the potentiality of human life may, if it chooses, regulate, and even proscribe, abortion except where it is necessary, in appropriate medical judgment, for the preservation of the life or health of the mother.

Our conclusion . . . is . . . that the Texas abortion statutes, as a unit, must fall. . . .

In the years before 1973, when abortion was generally illegal, commonly performed in the private offices of doctors and unlicensed practitioners without emergency medical support, and generally without anesthesia, death from abortion was substantial. In 1985, it was estimated that only two deaths occurred from illegal abortion and only six deaths resulted from legal abortion.

The issues that were raised by *Roe* v. *Wade* have not been fully settled and are not likely to be easily resolved, touching as they do on basic religious and ethical beliefs. Because only women become pregnant, and because there is no obvious parallel to pregnancy in male experience, arguments about abortion are less easily made on the equal treatment grounds that served women's rights activists well in *Frontiero* (see *Frontiero* v. *Richardson*, pp. 628–29). and other similar cases. Advocates must ask what equal treatment would mean for men and women, who are differently situated in relation to abortion.

In the 1980s, a number of states tested what boundaries would be considered reasonable limits on the abortion rights sustained in Roe. In 1980, the Supreme Court upheld the "Hyde Amendment" by which Congress refused to fund even medically necessary abortions for indigent women (*Harris* v. *McRae*, 448 U.S. 297). This decision was not the focus of massive public protest, and it was replicated in the laws of many states. An effort to defeat the Hyde Amendment failed in Congress in 1993, but some states did revise their practice, covering some abortions for indigent women, usually in the case of rape or incest.

Missouri legislators developed further the position that the state could deny any form of public support or facilities for the performance of abortions. A 1986 law prohibited the use of public employees and facilities to perform or assist abortions not necessary to save the life of the mother and also prohibited the use of public funds for counseling a woman in abortion decisions not necessary to save her life. It included a preamble that claimed that the life of each human being begins at conception and a provision that required that medical tests of fetal viability—tests whose efficacy was disputed—be performed before any abortion on a fetus estimated to be twenty weeks or more in gestation. Since 97 percent of all late abortions (done at an estimated sixteen-week gestational age) were performed at a single hospital in Kansas City that, although private, received public aid and was located on public property, the practical impact of the law was great.

In deciding *Webster* v. *Reproductive Health Services* in July 1989, by a 5–3 vote, the Supreme Court majority claimed that the conclusions of *Roe* had not been changed.* Missouri law left a pregnant woman free to terminate her pregnancy so long as neither public funds nor facilities were used for it; this was, the Court majority said, a "value

---

*William L. Webster, Attorney General of Missouri v. Reproductive Health Services, 109 Sup. Ct. 3040 (1989).

judgment" favoring childbirth over abortion. But the majority raised a general question about *Roe*. "[T]he rigid Roe framework," wrote Chief Justice Rehnquist in the majority opinion, "is hardly consistent with the notion of a Constitution cast in general terms, as ours is, and usually speaking in general principles, as ours does. The key elements of the *Roe* framework—trimesters and viability—are not found in the text of the Constitution or in any place else one would expect to find a constitutional principle . . . the result has been a web of legal rules that . . . [resemble] a code of regulations rather than a body of constitutional doctrine." Justice Anthony Scalia concurred, adding that in his view, *Roe* should have been overturned; abortion is, he thought, a field in which the Court "has little proper business since the answers to most of the cruel questions posed are political and not juridical." He was appalled at efforts to bring the pressure of public opinion to bear on the decisions of the Court, notably the March on Washington of some 200,000 people that had been sponsored by pro-choice groups shortly before the *Webster* case was argued in April 1989.

Justice Harry A. Blackmun, who had written the Court's opinion in *Roe*, now wrote a bitter dissent for the minority. He denied that Rehnquist's opinion left *Roe* "undisturbed." Rather it challenged a large body of legal precedent that had established a "private sphere of individual liberty," which although not explicitly specified in the Constitution had long been taken to have been implied by the Fourth Amendment guarantee against unreasonable searches. The right to privacy had been invoked in the 1960s when the Court protected the sale and use of birth control devices; the *Webster* decision, Blackmun feared, bypassed "the true jurisprudential debate underlying this case: . . . whether and to what extent . . . a right to privacy extends to matters of childbearing and family life, including abortion." Justice John Paul Stevens argued that the preamble's claim that life begins at conception was a religious view, and to write it into law was to ignore First Amendment requirements for the separation of church and state. Finally, Blackmun argued that the state had a distinct interest in maintaining public health, and that as safe and legal abortions became more difficult to get, an increase in deaths from illegal abortions could be predicted. "For today," he concluded, "the women of this Nation still retain the liberty to control their destinies. But the signs are evident and very ominous, and a chill wind blows."

The Court's decision in *Webster* left many questions open. If states could deny public funds for abortions, what other limitations was it reasonable for state legislatures to impose? Was it reasonable to require a waiting period? Was it reasonable to require minors to get the consent of one parent? of both parents? The Court had ruled in 1976 that a state could not require a married woman to get her husband's consent before having an abortion (*Planned Parenthood* v. *Danforth*, 428 U.S. 52 [1976]); could a state require a married woman to *notify* her husband?

In 1988 and 1989 Pennsylvania amended its Abortion Control Act of 1982 extensively, requiring a twenty-four-hour waiting period and the provision of "certain information" twenty-four hours before the abortion is performed. Minors were required to have the consent of one parent, and married women to have notified their husbands, although it was possible for a court to waive that requirement and all requirements could be waived in the event of a "medical emergency." Because most of the Justices had made public substantial reservations about the decision in *Roe*, it seemed to many observers not unreasonable to predict that the Court would uphold the entire Pennsylvania statute and, possibly, overturn *Roe* v. *Wade*. Instead, a plurality organized by Justices Sandra Day O'Connor, Anthony Kennedy, and David Souter, joined by Harry Blackmun and John Paul Stevens, wrote a complex opinion that began with a ringing affirmation of *Roe*. But O'Connor, Kennedy, and Souter also made it clear that they shared Rehnquist's skepticism of the trimester framework of *Roe*. How does the plurality think the principle of equal protection of the laws should be applied in abortion decisions?

Note the comments on coverture at the end of the plurality opinion; this statement marks the first explicit recognition by the Court of the end of coverture.

Why do the dissenting Justices think *Roe* should be overturned?

PLANNED PARENTHOOD OF SOUTHEASTERN PENNSYLVANIA v. CASEY

JUSTICES O'CONNOR, KENNEDY, SOUTER:

Liberty finds no refuge in a jurisprudence of doubt. Yet 19 years after our holding that the Constitution protects a woman's right to terminate her pregnancy in its early states . . . that definition of liberty is still questioned. . . . After considering the fundamental constitutional questions resolved by *Roe*, principles of institutional integrity, and the rule of *stare decisis* [the principle that decisions of previous courts should be let stand unless there is overwhelming reason to change them], we are led to conclude this: the essential holding of *Roe* v. *Wade* should be retained and once again reaffirmed. . . . Constitutional protection of the woman's decision to terminate her pregnancy derives from the Due Process Clause of the Fourteenth Amendment. It declares that no State shall "deprive any person of life, liberty, or property, without due process of law." . . . It is a premise of the Constitution that there is a realm of personal liberty which the government may not enter. We have vindicated this principle before. Marriage is mentioned nowhere in the Bill of Rights and interracial marriage was illegal in most States in the 19th century, but the Court was no doubt correct in finding it to be an aspect of liberty protected against state interference by the substantive component of the Due Process Clause in *Loving* v. *Virginia* 388 U.S. 1 (1967). . . .

Men and women of good conscience can disagree, and we suppose some always shall disagree, about the profound moral and spiritual implications of terminating a pregnancy, even in its earliest stage. Some of us as individuals find abortion offensive to our most basic principles of morality, but that cannot control our decision. Our obligation is to define the liberty of all, not to mandate our own moral code. . . .

Our law affords constitutional protection to personal decisions relating to marriage, procreation, contraception, family relationships, child rearing, and education. . . . These matters, involving the most intimate and personal choices a person may make in a lifetime, choices central to personal dignity and autonomy, are central to the liberty protected by the Fourteenth Amendment. At the heart of liberty is the right to define one's own concept of existence, of meaning, of the universe, and of the mystery of human life. Beliefs about these matters could not define the attributes of personhood were they formed under compulsion of the State. The woman's right to terminate her pregnancy before viability is the most central principle of *Roe* v. *Wade*. It is a rule of law and a component of liberty we cannot renounce.

On the other side of the equation is the interest of the State in the protection of potential life. The *Roe* Court recognized the State's "important and legitimate interest in protecting the potentiality of human life." . . . That portion of the decision in *Roe* has been given too little acknowledgment and implementation by the Court in its subsequent cases. . . . Though the woman has a right to choose to terminate or continue her pregnancy before viability, it does not at all follow that the State is prohibited from taking steps to ensure that this choice is thoughtful and informed. Even in the earliest stages of pregnancy, the State may enact rules and regulations designed to encourage her to know that there are philosophic and social arguments of great weight that can be brought to bear in favor of continuing the pregnancy to full term.... We reject the trimester framework, which we do not consider to be part of the essential holding of *Roe*.... Measures aimed at ensuring that a woman's choice contemplates the consequences for the fetus do not necessarily interfere with the right recognized in *Roe* ... not every law which makes a right more difficult to exercise is, ipso facto, an infringement of that right....

...We ... see no reason why the State may not require doctors to inform a woman seeking an abortion of the availability of materials relating to the consequences to the fetus.... Whether the mandatory 24-hour waiting period is ... invalid because in practice it is a substantial obstacle to a woman's choice to terminate her pregnancy is a closer question. [We do not agree with the District Court] that the waiting period constitutes an undue burden.... [From Part D: We have already established the precedent, and] we reaffirm today, that a State may require a minor seeking an abortion to obtain the consent of a parent or guardian, provided that there is an adequate judicial bypass procedure....

... Pennsylvania's abortion law provides, except in cases of medical emergency, that no physician shall perform an abortion on a married woman without receiving a signed statement from the woman that she has notified her spouse that she is about to undergo an abortion. The woman has the option of providing an alternative signed statement certifying that her husband is not the man who impregnated her; that her husband could not be located; that the pregnancy is the result of spousal sexual assault which she had reported [or that she fears bodily harm from him]. A physician who performs an abortion on a married woman without receiving the appropriate signed statement will have his or her license revoked, and is liable to the husband for damages.

... In well-functioning marriages, spouses discuss important intimate decisions such as whether to bear a child. But there are millions of women in this country who are the victims of regular physical and psychological abuse at the hands of their husbands.... Many may have a reasonable fear that notifying their husbands will provoke further instances of child abuse [or psychological abuse]....

... [A]s a general matter ... the father's interest in the welfare of the child and the mother's interest are equal. Before birth, however, the issue takes on a very different cast. It is an inescapable biological fact that state regulation with respect to the child a woman is carrying will have a far greater impact on the mother's liberty than on the father's. [That is why the Court has already ruled that when the wife and husband disagree on the abortion decision, the decision of the wife should prevail.]

... There was a time, not so long ago, when a different understanding of the family and of the Constitution prevailed. In *Bradwell* v. *Illinois* [pp. 248–49], three Members of this Court reaffirmed the common-law principle that "a woman had no legal existence separate from her husband." ... Only one generation has passed since this Court observed that "woman is still regarded as the center of home and family life," with attendant "special responsibilities" that precluded full and independent legal status under the Constitution (*Hoyt* v. *Florida* [pp. 547–49]). These views, of course, are no longer consistent with our understanding of the family, the individual, or the Constitution.... [The Pennsylvania abortion law] embodies a view of marriage consonant with the common-law status of married women but repugnant to our present understanding of marriage and of the nature of the rights secured by the Constitution. Women do not lose their constitutionally protected liberty when they marry.

CHIEF JUSTICE REHNQUIST, WITH WHOM JUSTICE WHITE, JUSTICE SCALIA, AND JUSTICE CLARENCE THOMAS JOIN:

The joint opinion . . . retains the outer shell of *Roe* v. *Wade* . . . but beats a wholesale retreat from the substance of that case. We believe that *Roe* was wrongly decided, and that it can and should be overruled consistently with our traditional approach to *stare decisis* in constitutional cases. We would . . . uphold the challenged provisions of the Pennsylvania statute in their entirety. . . . [B]y foreclosing all democratic outlet for the deep passions this issue arouses, by banishing the issue from the political forum that gives all participants, even the losers, the satisfaction of a fair hearing and an honest fight, by continuing the imposition of a rigid national rule instead of allowing for regional differences, the Court merely prolongs and intensifies the anguish.

We should get out of this area, where we have no right to be, and where we do neither ourselves nor the country any good by remaining.

Abortion is an issue of concern to men as well as to women. It is an issue on which women and men hold a wide variety of views. Among the questions raised are:

1. What are the limits of a woman's right to make her own reproductive decisions?
2. Should the unborn be afforded legal rights?
3. What rights does the father have? In 1976 the Supreme Court held that a state could not require a married woman to get her husband's consent before having an abortion (*Planned Parenthood* v. *Danforth*, 428 U.S. 52 [1976]). Is the husband's claim of a role in an abortion decision a reinstatement of the old law of coverture?
4. What rights does the community have to set general policy? What are the appropriate limits of government intervention? The state may not require a woman to conceive a child; can the state require a woman to bear a child?
5. Will any of these rights change as improvements are made in the technology for the discovery of birth defects and genetic abnormalities, for the implantation of embryos, and for caring for premature infants at earlier ages?

DOCUMENTS: Dimensions of Citizenship IV

> *"We were the first American women sent to live and work in the midst of guerrilla warfare . . ."*

The American ships and planes that went to Vietnam carried women as well as men. There were approximately 10,000 military women and more than 13,000 Red Cross women, as well as smaller numbers of women foreign service officers, staff of the U.S. Agency for International Development, and employees of the USO. In 1980, Congress authorized a memorial to be built "in honor and recognition of the men and women of the Armed Forces of the United States who served in Vietnam." The competition for the design of the memorial was won by 21-year-old Maya Lin, an undergraduate architecture student at Yale. The memorial stands today in Washington, visited by millions of people each year. They leave offerings as at a shrine: flowers, photographs, mementos.

The design of the memorial—whose black granite walls bear the names of 58,000 Americans who died, including eight women—was controversial from the beginning. Many veterans groups insisted on a more traditional, representational design. In 1984 an additional statue that depicted three soldiers was placed in a grove of trees nearby. When the additional statue failed to include the figure of a woman, women veterans began to urge the addition of another statue honoring the women who had served.

In 1988 Congress authorized a statue recognizing women, to be constructed on federal property at the Vietnam Veterans Memorial from funds (like those of the other memorials) raised from private donations. The comments that follow were made at hearings conducted by Senator Dale Bumpers of Arkansas, chair of the Senate Subcommittee on Public Lands, National Parks and Forests.

Each of the veterans had complex memories of their experience in Vietnam, twenty years before. How do the women explain the meaning of their service? How is Robert Doubek's testimony affected by concerns about class, race, and gender?

Both Karen Johnson's testimony and the arguments of the Supreme Court in *Rostker* v. *Goldberg* (pp. 641–43) address the issue of whether men and women have an equal obligation to serve in the military. Do you think men and women have an equal obligation to serve in the military in time of war, as Karen Johnson believes? Does that obligation extend to service in combat? Does the exclusion of women from combat suggest that American society attaches greater value to women's lives than men's? What other factors might also be relevant in explaining the exclusion of women from combat?

100th Congress, 2nd Session, U.S. Senate. Committee on Energy and Natural Resources. *Vietnam Women's Memorial.* Hearing before the Subcommittee on Public Lands, National Parks and Forests to consider S. 2042, February 23, 1988.

STATEMENT OF DONNA-MARIE BOULAY, CHAIRMAN, VIETNAM WOMEN'S MEMORIAL PROJECT

Mr. Chairman, people who serve in wars have unique experiences. War was never meant to be. War makes death. Day after day, even hour after hour, we lived and worked amidst the wounded, the dead, and the dying.

I arrived in Vietnam at the end of February 1967. A few days later I was assigned to triage for the first time. The medevac helicopters brought twelve soldiers into our emergency room. Ten were already dead. Two were bleeding to death.

Mr. Chairman, our daily duty was to care for the badly wounded, the young men whose legs had been blown off, whose arms had been traumatically amputated, whose bodies and faces had been burned beyond recognition.

We eased the agony of a young marine, his legs amputated, his wounds dangerously infected. We worked hard to stop the bleeding of a sailor who had been shot in his liver. He died three days after, in immense pain.

We cared for a young Army lieutenant from New York named Pat who had been admitted with a badly mangled leg and later evacuated to Japan, like many of the other seriously wounded soldiers we treated. I do not know whether Pat's leg was saved. I hope so. Pat was a good soldier.

Mr. Chairman, "Pat" is not short for "Patrick." Pat is a nurse. Patty was a nurse. She was stationed at the 24th Evacuation Hospital in Long Binh.

We were the first American women sent to live and work in the midst of guerrilla warfare. The month-long Tet offensive was especially frightening. The Viet Cong blew up the ammunition dump down the street, causing a wall in our unit to collapse on some patients.

VC snipers shot at us. The North Vietnamese Army artillery roared throughout the nights. Those of us not at work huddled in our bunkers, wondering if we would survive until dawn.

At work, listening to the thundering sounds around us, we tried to keep our hands from shaking, the fear out of our voices and off of our faces, so that the wounded would not see or hear it.

Women served in Vietnam in many capacities. We served as personnel specialists, journalists, clerk-typists, intelligence officers, and nurses. There was no such thing as a generic woman soldier, as there was no such thing as a generic male soldier. Men served as mechanics, engineers, pilots, divers, and infantrymen.

The design of the men's statue at the Veterans Memorial was selected, according to Frederick Hart, the sculptor, because they "depict the bonds of men at war and because the infantry bore the greatest burden."

Mr. Chairman, we are proposing that the design for the women's statue be that of a nurse who served in Vietnam. The statue of a nurse is so compatible with the existing trio of figures because the nurses' experience so closely parallels the experience of the infantrymen—the intensity, the trauma, the carnage of war.

The statue design which we are proposing is an easily recognizable symbol of healing and hope, consistent with the spirit and the experience of the Vietnam Veterans Memorial. . . .

STATEMENT OF KAREN K. JOHNSON, LITTLE ROCK, AR

I was born in Petersburg, Virginia. My father was in the military. He was killed in France on November the 11th, 1944.

I was raised in Oklahoma. I graduated from college in 1964 and explored the military as a career and joined the Army in 1965.

My family was very patriotic because of the trials and tribulations that we had to go through because of being raised without a father. Considering that everyone in my family had experienced all that patriotism, when I said that I was going to join the Army it was not a new thought, even though I was the first woman to have joined.

My family felt that all Americans owed their country any sacrifice needed for the national good, regardless of their race or sex, that patriotism should be a blind emotion, and it should be accepted by our country without any thought or qualm as to who offered such patriotism.

Consequently, after I served in Germany from 1966 to 1968, when my country asked me to go overseas again to Vietnam, I went. I served in Vietnam from July of 1970 to March of 1972, for a total of 20 months in country.

When I tell people these facts, they always ask me, was I a nurse, that I did not see any combat, and that I must have volunteered.

When I tell them that I was awarded a Bronze Star, they ask me what for.

For 18 years I have answered these questions with several long-winded explanations which were really an apology for my Vietnam service, because I was not a nurse and I was not a combat soldier, and there were many others who had served who the public much better understood their service in their traditional roles.

I have kept silent on what I did in Vietnam because it was easier than making the apologies or trying to educate my listener. I know now that I have done many Vietnam veterans a great disservice by my silence. Thanks to the support of the Arkansas Vietnam Veterans, my husband and my grandchildren, I have made my last apology, felt my last twinge of embarrassment, and I will not remain silent to the detriment of my comrades in arms.

I am a veterans' veteran and I am proud of it. I was not a nurse. I saw very little full-fledged combat, and when my country called I went willingly. I see no disgrace in answering such a call or in volunteering to serve in the United States Army.

I served as the Command Information Officer of the United States Army, Vietnam Headquarters, located at Long Binh. However, my job entailed finding out what Army troops were doing, photographing those troops, writing news reports, and printing the internal publications to keep the troops informed.

I could not do that from Long Binh. I traveled all over Vietnam. Wherever there were Army troops, I went, too. I have flown in attack helicopters, been shot at in jeeps, and I went over the Hay Van Pass in several convoys.

Whatever it took to get the news out to the troops is what I and my staff did, and we did it very well. "Uptight Magazine," one of our publications, was awarded the Thomas Jefferson Award for the outstanding military publication in its field, an award that was given to me by "Time Magazine."

Our office published a twice-daily news bulletin, a weekly Long Binh paper, the weekly "Army Reporter," "Uptight Magazine Quarterly"; and "Tour 364," the history of the war, was updated every six months so that troops rotating home had a written history of their service. We were also responsible for the free distribution of "Stars and Stripes" to ensure that every U.S. military personnel serving in Vietnam had daily access to a newspaper.

There were a lot of obstacles to resolve to make all of this happen. My staff made it happen every day for 20 months, in 12 hour shifts, seven days a week, including Christmas, when we worked harder because we were responsible for making Operation Jingle Bells work so that the troops could see Bob Hope.

I am here today to tell you that I am very proud of that staff, and especially of Spec. 5 Steven Henry Warner, who gave his life so the American soldier could be the best informed and most motivated soldier in the world. I do not believe they would want me to apologize for our service or the fact that Steve Warner gave his life as a journalist and not as a combat soldier.

If there is any apology owed, it is the one I owe my staff for not standing up for them for the last 18 years because I did not like the questions my admission to being a Vietnam veteran elicited because I was a woman, something not well understood by the American public.

Their service and mine should be given equal recognition with all who served, not diminished because of the non-traditional position I held.

I come before you today to ask you to legislate equal dignity for the women who served their country by answering the call to arms. The Vietnam Women's Memorial would do much to give women veterans a new sense of self-respect and it will make a strong public statement that bias, prejudice, or ignorance of the sacrifices that women veterans have made for their country will no longer be tolerated.

Today the flag that covered my father's casket when he was put to final rest in 1948 lies in front of me, because I have always wanted him to be proud of me, his only child. And I believe he would be proudest of me today when I say, after 18 long years of silence: I was an American soldier; I answered my country's call to arms; and I am an American veteran, a title I should be able to share with equal dignity with all who have served before me and will serve after me. . . .

STATEMENT OF ROBERT W. DOUBEK . . .

Mr. Chairman, my name is Robert W. Doubek of Washington, D.C. I am a Vietnam veteran.

I am employed in the private sector. I was a founder of the Vietnam Veterans Memorial Fund. I served as its Executive Director and Project Director. I was responsible for building the memorial. I did the work. In recognition of my achievement, I was nominated for a Congressional Gold Medal which was a bill passed by the Senate on November 14, 1985.

The fact is that women are not represented by the Vietnam Veterans Memorial. The fact is also that the memorial does not represent anyone. It is not a legislative body. It is a symbol of honor, and as such, it is complete as a tribute to all who served their country in the Vietnam War.

It is a basic rule of common sense that mandates that something which is not broken should not be fixed. The genius of the wall is its equalizing and unifying effect. All veterans are honored, regardless of rank, service branch, commission, sex, or any other category. The names of the eight women casualties take their rightful places of honor. To ensure that this fact is never overlooked, the inscription on the first panel of the wall states that the memorial is in honor of the men and women of the Armed Forces. The reason I know this is because I was instrumental in drafting the inscription.

In 1982, politics required that we add a figurative sculpture as a more specific symbol of the Vietnam veteran. Even with the heroic and dangerous service rendered by other combatants such as Air Force and Navy pilots, Navy swiftboat crews, and the life saving efforts of nurses, helicopter pilots and medics, there was only one possible choice of what category would be literally depicted to symbolize the Vietnam veteran, and that could only be the enlisted infantrymen, grunts. They account for the majority of names on the wall; they bore the brunt of the battle. The fact is all grunts were men.

The addition of a statue of a woman or of any other category, for that matter, would reduce the symbolism of the existing sculpture from honoring or symbolizing the Vietnam veterans community as a whole to symbolizing only enlisted infantrymen. This in turn would open a Pandora's box of proliferating statuary toward the goal of trying to depict every possible category. The National Park Service has already received requests for a statue to literally depict Native Americans and even for scout dogs, and in fact, I want to say that the figure for Native American casualties was 225.

The addition of a statue solely on the basis of gender raises troubling questions about proportion. Is gender of such overriding importance among veterans that we should have a specific statue to women who suffered eight casualties, and none for the Navy which suffered over 2,500, nor for the Air Force which suffered over 2,400? Is gender of such importance to outweigh that some 90 percent of the women who served in Vietnam in the military were officers [nurses were commissioned officers], while over 87 percent of all casualties were enlisted? . . . Approval . . . would set the precedent that strict literal depiction of both genders is an absolute requirement of all military related memorials. What about the new Navy memorial? Will Congress mandate an additional figure at the Iwo Jima Memorial?

STATEMENT OF COL. MARY EVELYN BANE, USMC (RETIRED), ARLINGTON, VA

Mr. Chairman, my name is Mary Evelyn Bane. I live in Arlington, Virginia, and I have lived in the Washington metropolitan area for a total of almost 19 nonconsecutive years. I retired in 1977 from a 26-year career in the United States Marine Corps in the grade of colonel. I never served in Vietnam, only a few women Marines did, and they were in Saigon, but I was in active service during the entire period of the war there. My career was in personnel management and, like most Marine officers, I had a variety of assignments and experiences, including two tours at our famous or infamous Parris Island training recruits, and an assignment with the Joint Staff in France. All of my male Marine colleagues did serve in Vietnam, many of them more than once, and some of their names are on the Vietnam Veterans Memorial.

I am opposed to the installation of a statue of a woman at the site of the VVM for both artistic and philosophical reasons, artistically, because it is at odds with the design as well as the theme of the memorial. . . . [and] philosophically simply because I am a woman. This may seem unfathomable to the statue's proponents, but perhaps I can explain. From the beginning of my chosen career in what most will agree is a macho outfit, I tried hard to be the best Marine I was capable of being. When I was commissioned, fewer than 1 percent of the officers in the Marine Corps were female. Women were assigned to women's billets, and restricted to a handful of occupational specialties considered appropriate for women. Over the years, through the combined efforts of many, many people, of which I am happy to say I am one, the concept of how women could and should serve their country has changed. The huge increase in the military's population required by the Vietnam War hastened the changes.

Nevertheless, in 1973 when I, then a lieutenant colonel, was assigned as the Marine Corps member of a Department of Defense ad hoc group studying the recruitment and processing of non-prior service personnel, the Civil Service GS-15 chair of the group complained to the Commandant of the Marine Corps that he had not appointed a real Marine.

My point here is that sex is an accident of birth. I chose to be a Marine and worked hard at it, and spent a career combatting discrimination based on sex. I feel every service person should be recognized for what he or she accomplished as a soldier, sailor, Marine or airman. The Vietnam Veterans Memorial recognizes American military members for their service in Vietnam, irrespective of sex, rank, service, race, or occupational specialty. To single out one of these criteria for special recognition in the form of a statue on the site of the Vietnam Veterans Memorial would not only violate the integrity of the design, but would be discriminatory.

Rostker v. Goldberg, *1981*

Classical republican tradition linked political identity with property holding and military obligation. In the United States, the obligations of male citizens include military service; the obligations of female citizens do not. Although women had been employed by the army and navy as nurses, not until World War II were they involved in military service in substantial numbers. Women's sections of the Army, Navy, and Air Force accepted volunteers under strict regulations which excluded them from combat duty, limited the numbers who could be accepted and the rank to which they could rise (until 1967 no woman could serve in a command position), and offered fewer fringe benefits than were received by servicemen of the same rank (see *Frontiero* v. *Richardson,* pp. 628–29). Partly in response to the Vietnam War, many of these restrictions were eased; in 1976 women were admitted to West Point, Annapolis, and the Air Force Academy.

When President Jimmy Carter recommended the resumption of peacetime selective service registration in 1980, he proposed registering women as well as men. The president and his supporters on the Armed Services Committees of the Senate and the House sought to separate the issue of registration, the actual draft, and the use of women in combat. They argued that decision on whether women would actually be drafted (and, if so, whether mothers would be exempted) and whether women would be placed in combat positions could be left for future debate. They also argued that registration did

---

101 Sup Ct. 2646. For extended comment see Linda K. Kerber, *No Constitutional Right to Be Ladies: Women and the Obligations of Citizenship* (New York: Hill and Wang, 1998), ch. 5.

not necessarily mean that one would be drafted, for men who planned to request exemption as conscientious objectors were still required to register.

Opponents insisted that the issues were linked: if the sexes were treated equally in registration, it would be impossible to reject equity in future treatment. Since the primary goal of Selective Service was to identify combat-ready men, opponents also argued that if women were not used in combat there was no need to register them. In the course of debate contrasting ideas of the role of women in American society were expressed.* This debate overlapped with the debate on the Equal Rights Amendment, taking place at the same time; probably the single most effective argument used by opponents of the ERA was that it would involve women in the draft. In the end, Congress approved registration for men but not for women.

The Military Selective Service Act of 1980 was challenged by a group of men who argued that they had been denied the equal protection of the laws guaranteed by the Fifth Amendment. The Carter administration was now placed in the odd position of having to defend the statute it had opposed.

Note the reasoning of the Supreme Court and its emphasis on the exclusion of women from combat positions. Although the argument was not offered in *Rostker*, some men have argued that if women are drafted but not placed in combat positions, the likelihood that any specific man would be assigned to a noncombat job diminishes and men are therefore placed at greater risk for combat assignments. Moreover, some men in similar situations, such as police or prison guards, have demanded the exclusion of women on the grounds that women can not back men up effectively in physical confrontation; thus giving women equal opportunity to become prison guards actually increases the risks to men. Yet another perspective is offered by the legal historian Leo Kanowitz, who argues that "the equanimity with which men's exclusive liability for military service is regarded by the general population, even during times of violent combat . . . [suggests] the philosophy that a man's life is less precious than that of a woman." Do you agree?

MR. JUSTICE WILLIAM H. REHNQUIST DELIVERED THE OPINION OF THE COURT:

The question presented is whether the Military Selective Service Act . . . violates the Fifth Amendment to the United States Constitution in authorizing the President to require the registration of males and not females. Whenever called upon to judge the constitutionality of an Act of Congress—"the gravest and most delicate duty that this Court is called upon to perform," . . . the Court accords "great weight to the decisions of Congress."

. . . This case is quite different from several of the gender-based discrimination cases we have considered in that . . . Congress did not act "unthinkingly" or "reflexively and not for any considered reason." . . . The question of registering women for the draft not only received considerable national attention and was the subject of wide-ranging public debate, but also was extensively considered by Congress in hearings, floor debate, and in committee. Hearings held by both Houses of Congress in response to the President's request for authorization to register women adduced extensive testimony and evidence concerning the issue. . . . the decision to exempt women from registration was not the "accidental by-product of a traditional way of thinking about women. . . ."

Women as a group, however, unlike men as a group, are not eligible for combat. The restrictions on the participation of women in combat in the Navy and Air Force are statutory. . . . The Army and Marine Corps preclude the use of women in combat as a matter

*See the *Congressional Record*, June 10, 1980.

of established policy.... The existence of the combat restrictions clearly indicates the basis for Congress' decision to exempt women from registration. The purpose of registration was to prepare for a draft of combat troops. Since women are excluded from combat, Congress concluded that they would not be needed in the event of a draft, and therefore decided not to register them.... This is not a case of Congress arbitrarily choosing to burden one of two similarly situated groups, such as would be the case with an all-black or all-white, or an all-Catholic or all-Lutheran, or an all-Republican or all-Democratic registration. Men and women, because of the combat restrictions on women, are simply not similarly situated for purposes of a draft or registration for a draft.... The Constitution requires that Congress treat similarly situated persons similarly, not that it engage in gestures of superficial equality.

MR. JUSTICE BYRON WHITE, DISSENTING:

I assume ... that excluding women from combat positions does not offend the Constitution ... [but] I perceive little, if any, indication that Congress itself concluded that every position in the military, no matter how far removed from combat, must be filled with combat-ready men.

MR. JUSTICE THURGOOD MARSHALL, DISSENTING:

The Court today places its imprimatur on one of the most potent remaining public expressions of "ancient canards about the proper role of women." It upholds a statute that requires males but not females to register for the draft, and which thereby categorically excludes women from a fundamental civic obligation.

Meritor Savings Bank *v.* Mechelle Vinson et al., *1986*

The term "sexual harassment" was unknown before the mid-1970s. One legal scholar has written, "the term was invented by feminist activists, given legal content by feminist litigators and scholars, and sustained by a wide-ranging body of scholarship generated largely by feminist academics." Another legal scholar observes "[f]or the first time in history, women have defined women's injuries in a law."*

Consider Part 1 of Section 703 of Title VII of the Civil Rights Act of 1964 (pp. 550–51). The authors of the statute were defining economic injuries, and for more than a decade the Equal Employment Opportunity Commission supported only economic claims of sex discrimination. But working women had long put up with behavior that, beginning in the 1970s, they began to say was also sex discrimination: supervisors who referred to all women as "whores," whether or not in joking tones; workplaces that had cheesecake or frankly pornographic calenders on the walls; and, worst of all, covert or explicit

---

*Martha Chamallas, "Writing About Sexual Harassment: A Guide to the Literature," *UCLA Women's Law Journal* IV (1993):37–38; Catharine MacKinnon, *Feminism Unmodified: Discourses on Life and Law* (Cambridge, Mass.: Harvard University Press, 1987), p. 105; Vicki Schultz, "Reconceptualizing Sexual Harassment," *Yale Law Journal* 107 (1998):1683–1805.

pressure to have sex with supervisors or employers for fear of losing their jobs if they refused.

Legal scholar Catharine MacKinnon gave names to two forms of sexual harassment: (1) "quid pro quo": when sexual submission to a supervisor becomes, either implicitly or explicitly, a condition of employment; and (2) "offensive working environment": when the conduct of a supervisor, co-employee, or client unreasonably interferes with an individual's work or creates an intimidating and hostile workplace. By the late 1970s, many behaviors that men had described as flirting, and that women had "put up with" because they saw no alternative, could be named and challenged. In 1980, the EEOC published an official set of guidelines describing behavior it would challenge as sexual harassment, even if the actors claimed they were merely flirting or "joking around."

In 1986, a unanimous Supreme Court for the first time formally recognized sexual harassment as a violation of Title VII. Catharine MacKinnon was one of the attorneys for Mechelle Vinson, who complained that she had been hired in 1974 as a teller-trainee by a vice president of Meritor Savings Bank and was steadily promoted for four years until she became assistant branch manager. During those four years, however, she had a sexual relationship with the man (Mr. Taylor) who had hired her; when she tried to decline his attentions, he exposed himself to her, and even forcibly raped her.

Vinson claimed that she had been the victim of both "quid pro quo" and offensive environment forms of sexual harassment. Vinson told the court "that because she was afraid of Taylor she never reported his harassment to any of his supervisors and never attempted to use the bank's complaint procedure." But when she was fired for what the bank claimed was excessive use of sick leave, she sued the bank, claiming sexual harassment and asking for punitive damages. The bank claimed that "any sexual harassment by Taylor was unknown to the bank and engaged in without its consent or approval."

A unanimous Court agreed with Vinson. What analogies do they see with race discrimination? Why do they hold Meritor Bank guilty as well as Mr. Taylor? Taylor argued that Vinson wore sexually provocative clothing. How much responsibility do you think the victim of sexual harassment should be expected to take for avoiding the harassment?

JUSTICE WILLIAM REHNQUIST:

This case presents important questions concerning claims of workplace "sexual harassment" brought under Title VII of the Civil Rights Act of 1964 . . . [Vinson] argues . . . that unwelcome sexual advances that create an offensive or hostile working environment violate Title VII. Without question, when a supervisor sexually harasses a subordinate because of the subordinate's sex, that supervisor "discriminate[s]" on the basis of sex. [Meritor Bank] does not challenge this proposition. It contends instead that in prohibiting discrimination with respect to "compensation, terms,

conditions, or privileges" of employment, Congress was concerned with what petitioner describes as "tangible loss" of "an economic character," not "purely psychological aspects of the workplace environment."

We reject petitioner's view. First, the language of Title VII is not limited to "economic" or "tangible" discrimination. The phrase "terms, conditions, or privileges of employment" evinces a congressional intent "to strike at the entire spectrum of disparate treatment of men and women" in employment. . . . As the Court of Appeals for the Eleventh Circuit wrote . . . in 1982: "Sexual harassment which creates a hostile or offensive environment for members of one sex is every bit the arbitrary barrier to sexual equality at the workplace that racial harassment is to racial equality. Surely a requirement that a man or woman run a gauntlet of sexual abuse in return for the privilege of being allowed to work and make a living can be as demeaning and disconcerting as the harshest of racial epithets."

. . . [W]e reject the . . . view that the mere existence of a grievance procedure and a policy against discrimination, coupled with respondent's failure to invoke that procedure, must insulate petitioner from liability. . . . the bank's grievance procedure apparently required an employee to complain first to her supervisor, in this case Taylor. Since Taylor was the alleged perpetrator, it is not altogether surprising that respondent failed to invoke the procedure and report her grievance to him. . . . [W]e hold that a claim of "hostile environment" sex discrimination is actionable under Title VII. . . .

A wave of attention to sexual harassment in the workplace took place after the fall of 1991, when hearings on the nomination of Clarence Thomas to the Supreme Court were interrupted by the charges of Anita Hill that he had sexually harassed her a decade earlier. Ironically, their encounter had taken place within the EEOC itself, where Thomas had been director and Hill had been a lawyer on his staff. In response, Thomas charged that he was himself victimized by the media attention. Adrienne Davis and Stephanie Wildman observe, "in a stunning sleight of hand, [Thomas] managed to convince all involved, including the Senate, that white racism, rather than a Black woman, had accused him of harassment."[*] Thomas's nomination to the Supreme Court was confirmed by the Senate.

Over the years since the *Meritor* decision, increasing numbers of workers have filed sexual harassment complaints, and a massive body of doctrine has developed on the details of the law's protection. In 1998 the Supreme Court ruled that harassment based on an employee's homosexuality could constitute sex discrimination, and that male-on-male harassment could be a cause of action (*Oncale* v. *Sundowner Offshore Services, Inc.*). The definition of an "offensive working environment" remains under debate. Legal theorist Vicki Schultz has proposed:

> Many of the most prevalent forms of harassment are actions that are designed to maintain work—particularly the more highly rewarded lines of work—as bastions of masculine competence and authority. Every day, in workplaces all over the country, men uphold the image that their jobs demand masculine mastery by acting to undermine their female colleagues' perceived (or sometimes even actual) competence to do the work. The forms of such harassment are wide-ranging. They include characterizing the work as appropriate for men only; denigrating women's performance or ability to master the job; providing patronizing forms of help in performing the job; withholding the training, information, or opportunity to learn to do the job well; engaging in deliberate work sabotage; . . . isolating women from the social networks that confer a sense of belonging . . . much of the time, harassment assumes a form that has little or nothing to do with sexuality but everything to do with gender.[†]

---

[*]Adrienne D. Davis and Stephanie M. Wildman, "The Legacy of Doubt: Treatment of Sex and Race in the Hill-Thomas Hearings," *Southern California Law Review* 65 (1992):1367.

[†]Schultz, p. 1687.

Violence against Women Act, 1994, 2000

The Violence against Women Act (VAWA) was part of the comprehensive Violent Crime Control and Law Enforcement Act, passed in 1994. It was pathbreaking in establishing a new right: "All persons within the United States shall have the right to be free from crimes of violence motivated by gender." Congress was persuaded that the states fail to treat violent assaults against women as seriously as they treat other forms of violent assault. As one member of the Senate observed, "Typically we do not ask whether the victim of a barroom brawl is a real victim; we do not comment that the victim deserved to be hit; we do not inquire whether there was resistance or whether the victim said 'no' persistently enough."

VAWA provided funding to states for criminal law enforcement against perpetrators of violence. It also created (based on the commerce clause of the Fourteenth Amendment) a new federal civil rights remedy for victims of violence resulting from "animus based on the victim's gender." It defined domestic violence and sexual assault as potential infractions of the victim's civil rights. It overrode the inadequate remedies that persist in many states (for example, several states exempt cohabiting companions from rape laws). A victim of a violent crime motivated by gender was permitted to bring a civil lawsuit in federal or state court, seeking money damages or an injunction.

(a) PURPOSE.—Pursuant to the affirmative power of Congress to enact this subtitle under section 5 of the Fourteenth Amendment to the Constitution, as well as under section 8 of Article I of the Constitution, it is the purpose of this subtitle to protect the civil rights of victims of gender motivated violence and to promote public safety, health, and activities affecting interstate commerce by establishing a Federal civil rights cause of action for victims of crimes of violence motivated by gender.

(b) RIGHT TO BE FREE FROM CRIMES OF VIOLENCE.—All persons within the United States shall have the right to be free from crimes of violence motivated by gender (as defined in subsection (d)).

(c) CAUSE OF ACTION.—A person (including a person who acts under color of any statute, ordinance, regulation, custom, or usage of any State) who commits a crime of violence motivated by gender and thus deprives another of the right declared in subsection (b) shall be liable to the party injured, in an action for the recovery of compensatory and punitive damages, injunctive and declaratory relief, and such other relief as a court may deem appropriate.

(d) DEFINITIONS.—For purposes of this section—

(1) the term "crime of violence motivated by gender" means a crime of violence committed because of gender or on the basis of gender, and due, at least in part, to an animus based on the victim's gender; and

(2) the term "crime of violence" means—

(A) an act or series of acts that would constitute a felony against the person or that would constitute a felony against property if the conduct presents a serious risk of physical injury to another, and that would come within the meaning of State or Federal offenses described in section 16 of title 18, United States Code, whether or not these acts have actually resulted in criminal charges, prosecution, or conviction and whether or not those acts were committed in the special maritime, territorial, or prison jurisdiction of the United States; and

(B) includes an act or series of acts that would constitute a felony described in subparagraph (A) but for the relationship between the person who takes such action and the individual against whom such action is taken.

Not long after VAWA was passed, Christy Brzonkala charged that she had been raped by two college football players in her dorm during her first semester at Virginia Polytechnic Institute. The athletes were not suspended from school, even though they'd boasted about what they'd done and had been found guilty of "abusive conduct" by the university's judicial committee. Virginia Tech sentenced one of the players to two semesters suspension, but upon appeal the provost set the suspension aside, calling it excessive punishment.

Brzonkala dropped out of school, fearing its dangers, and sued Virginia Tech, claiming damages equal to what the school earned from the Sugar Bowl, in which the athletes played. In May 2000, the U.S. Supreme Court upheld an appeals court ruling that Congress had reached too far in its interpretation of a right to regulate interstate commerce. The Court invalidated the part of the VAWA that permitted victims of rape, domestic violence, and other crimes "motivated by gender" to sue their attackers in federal court.*

Congress acted quickly: Within a few months it had reauthorized all but the contested section of VAWA. It provided more than $3 billion to fight violence against women: (1) $1 billion over five years to help prosecutors track down domestic abusers; (2) $875 million to expand shelters for battered women; (3) $95 million over two years to protect foreign women brought into the country by the international sex trade; and (4) $140 million to stop violent crimes against women on college campuses. The amount of money required is itself an indictment of the extent to which gender-motivated crimes, international trafficking in women, and the conditions on college campuses are major threats to women. This last point is particularly chilling to those of us who work and study on college campuses.

*U.S. v. Morrison, 529 U.S. 598 2000.

LINDA BIRD FRANCKE
Women in the Gulf War

In 1990, women made up 11 percent of the all-volunteer armed forces. They were placed in positions on patrol ships and stationed on the fringes of the defense perimeter. They were also placed in "combat support" units; in the Panama invasion of 1989 Army captain Linda Bray led a military police unit in an exchange of fire while conducting what had been expected to be a routine police mission. Five women were killed in the Gulf War of 1991 and, as Linda Bird Francke describes in the essay that follows, two were taken prisoner. In 1994 the "risk rule" was lifted; women now serve in hostile zones. Two women pilots based on the *U.S.S. Enterprise* flew successful combat missions in the Arabian Gulf in December 1998. In 2003, at the time of the war in Iraq, 200,000 women made up more than 15 percent of the U.S. armed forces. Although women may not serve on submarines, in the Special Forces, or in the infantry, armor, and artillery divisions, some 90 percent of military jobs are open to them. Two women were taken prisoner in Iraq and Pfc. Lori Piestewa was killed. What implications, if any, do these developments have for the reasoning of the Supreme Court in *Rostker?*

On January 30, 1991, almost two weeks into the air war against Iraq, NBC's Pentagon correspondent Fred Francis made one of his twice daily calls to Riyadh, Saudi Arabia. Iraqi troops were battling U.S., Qatari and Saudi troops for control of the Saudi border town of Khafji. In what would prove to be the fiercest battle of the war, three hundred Iraqis and eleven Marines would be killed. But the news tip Francis got from an Army colonel in Riyadh set up the dynamic the Pentagon feared most. "We've got a white female missing and probably snatched by the Iraqis," the colonel told Francis. "Holy shit, do we have problems now."

Francis hurried down the hall in the Pentagon to Defense Department spokesman Pete Williams's office to confirm the tip. "Pete got on the phone and called Powell's office," recalls Francis. "Powell's office confirmed it and I went on the air with it. It was boom-boom-boom. There was no hesitation at all." NBC's bombshell led the evening news: an American servicewoman attached to an Army transportation company was missing near Khafji in the northern Saudi desert.

The news was particularly ominous in concert with the Iraqi announcement shortly thereafter that a "number of male and female transcripts" had been captured. The Iraqi government's assurance that any female prisoners would receive "good treatment in accordance with the spirit of lofty Islamic laws" was questionable in light of the stories circulating about the Iraqi brutality toward women in Kuwait.

The Pentagon was less concerned about the well-being of the missing servicewoman than it was about the effect of a female prisoner of war on the national psyche. Fifty years had passed since the nurses had been captured by the Japanese and they had been officers. The servicewoman, who was soon identified as Melissa Rathbun-Nealy, a twenty-year-old Army truck driver with the 233rd Transportation Company, would be the first enlisted American woman to be captured by an enemy in history.

If indeed she had been captured, there was concern that the Iraqis would publicly exploit her, potentially eroding public support for the conflict during the buildup to the ground war. Such speculation about the negative effect of female POWs on the "national will" had circulated for years, though there had been no such erosion over the nurses in World War II.

The unanswerable question lay in the potential propaganda visuals of women POWs being marched through the streets of Baghdad, women being among the downed, battered Allied pilots captured by the Iraqis and displayed on Iraqi television in January, a woman's face replacing the swollen, scratched face of captured Navy pilot Jeffrey Zaun which ran on the cover of *Newsweek*. Similar images of blindfolded American diplomatic hostages in Iran had helped bring down Jimmy Carter's presidency in 1980. The political effect of women POWs was incalculable.

"Will it cause such a public outcry that our leaders will be forced to terminate the conflict under less than desirable terms and in spite of any national goals which may not have been attained?" Air Force Major Wayne Dillingham had written the year before the Gulf war. "Or, in the alternative, will the outcry incite us to conduct reprisal-type operations which, in turn, may unnecessarily escalate the conflict?"[1]

Perhaps that is why the Pentagon professed not to know what had happened to Specialist Rathbun-Nealy and her co-driver, Specialist David Lockett, or how they had ended up in Khafji. The scuttlebutt going around the Pentagon involved a sexual tryst. "They thought they'd gotten lost for the purpose of being alone," says a Pentagon observer. "They still do." And a new round of military gender politics began.

Instead of declaring Rathbun-Nealy and Lockett as POWs or missing in action, the Army's accounting of their disappearance merely classified them as DUSTWUN, or duty status whereabouts unknown, a low-level categorization that simply meant the Army had no idea where they were or what had happened to them. "They found her truck and she and a man in her truck had disappeared," Pentagon spokesman Lieutenant Colonel Douglas Hart would say a year after the fact. "We make no assumptions."

Leo Rathbun, Rathbun-Nealy's father, was convinced the Pentagon was covering up his daughter's capture. All the evidence pointed toward her and her partner being taken prisoner by the Iraqis. Not only had Iraq reported "female transcripts" captured, but on February 10, ten days after Rathbun-Nealy's disappearance, NBC News reported that a captured Iraqi said he had transported two American prisoners—a white woman and a black man—to the city of Basra.

"There was never any doubt that they'd been taken prisoner, never a question among reporters covering the story that she was believed by senior leadership to be missing and a POW," says Fred Francis.

But the Pentagon stuck to its low-level story. "The [rescuers] found the truck she was in and it appeared to be an accident," insisted Lieutenant Colonel Hart. "So we couldn't say what the reasons were. The truck wasn't blown up or anything. It couldn't be proven that they had engaged the enemy, so to speak."

Rathbun hounded the Pentagon to have Melissa declared either MIA or POW. Not only was he worried that his daughter might be left behind when the war ended because she wasn't on an official list, he also wanted her to get whatever benefits were due her. "I told them, if she survives this thing and gets home, she won't receive any MIA or POW benefits because you bastards won't say she is one, even if you know she really is," says Rathbun.

It wasn't until February 14, two weeks after Rathbun-Nealy and Lockett had disappeared, that the Rathbuns got an official accounting of their daughter's disappearance. The bare facts in the Army casualty report noted only that Melissa was "last seen" on January 30, 1991, when the two trucks in her convoy "took a wrong turn." When Melissa's truck "became stuck in the sand trying to turn around," the second truck "went for assistance." A Marine Corps patrol found her 22-wheel vehicle "in the vicinity of Ras Al Khafji, Saudi Arabia," but "could not locate the soldier."[2]

The more telling details were in the Army letter accompanying the casualty report and came from the truck drivers who had been following Rathbun-Nealy and Lockett in the second truck. By their account, the young soldiers had thought they were heading back to their base when they were headed toward the fighting in Khafji. Their error became apparent when the two trucks maneuvered around a freshly destroyed Saudi tank partially blocking the road north of Khafji only to be met by two explosions and "the sound of debris hitting their vehicle." Seeing "what they perceived to be enemy troops" ahead near the archway into Khafji, the soldiers tried to turn their 22-wheel trucks around to escape. The second truck made it, but Rathbun-Nealy and Lockett's lead truck crashed into a wall. The last sight the escaping soldiers had of Rathbun-Nealy and Lockett was of the pair still sitting in their crippled truck as Iraqi soldiers approached. When a rescue party of Marines arrived soon thereafter, they found the truck with a flat tire and its engine still running, but "no trace of Melissa or Specialist Lockett."

More clues to Rathbun-Nealy's status in the Army letter came from Saudi interrogation reports of Iraqi soldiers captured during the battle for Khafji. An Iraqi lieutenant told Saudi interrogators he had "witnessed the capture of an American male and female" and that "both had been injured." The "white female," he reported, had "sustained an injury to her arm." Two other Iraqi prisoners of war told their Saudi interrogators what had already been reported by NBC News: the POWs had seen a "white female and a black male" near the city of Basra in southern Iraq.

Based on these reports, the Army notified the Rathbuns, the Army was changing Melissa's status from duty status whereabouts unknown to missing, which put her under the jurisdiction of the National Prisoner of War Information Center. The Army stopped short, however, of declaring Melissa a POW or even MIA, a designation reserved for personnel missing involuntarily as a result of "hostilities directed against the United States."[3] "While there are indications that Melissa and Specialist Lockett may have been captured, the reports received are unconfirmed and unsubstantiated," read the letter from the Army chief of POW/MIA Affairs.[4]

The Army's letter made Leo Rathbun even more furious. Not only had it taken the

Army two weeks to at least declare his daughter missing, he was convinced that the Pentagon was denying her POW or MIA status because of her gender. "Bush was afraid of adverse publicity with a woman captured," he says.

The Defense Department denied the charge of gender politics. "There was a long delay in declaring them MIA and I can't remember exactly the reason," says Pete Williams, who joined NBC News after the war. "I don't recall that it was a sensitivity about women. No one ever told me, 'let's hold off on this because she's a woman.'"

But Rathbun-Nealy's presumed capture was all about gender politics. While the Pentagon was playing down her military status, the civilian sector was playing up her sexual status. Though the International Red Cross had predicted that any U.S. woman taken POW would be treated in accordance with the Geneva Conventions and shown the respect afforded women in the Iraqi culture, Rathbun-Nealy became a presupposed rape victim.[5]

Historically, no U.S. servicewomen had been sexually molested as POWs, including the nurses in the Pacific and Lieutanant Reba Whittle, an Army flight nurse who was captured by the Germans in September 1944 after her hospital plane was shot down. The North Vietnamese had not molested Monika Schwinn, a German nurse who had endured forced marches, disease and near starvation in her three and a half years of captivity in Vietnam, including a stint in 1973 as the only woman prisoner at the infamous "Hanoi Hilton."[6] But Rathbun-Nealy's projected sexual molestation overshadowed all other concerns about her disappearance, including her reported injuries.

"I was asked by a reporter what I thought about that little girl's chances of being mistreated in Iraq," says former World War II POW Sally Millett. "I said I would doubt that. I would be inclined to think that she would be treated quite well. The Muslims aren't that mean. And they don't hate women any more or as much as American men hate women."

Rathbun-Nealy as symbolic rape victim was seized on by both sides of the growing debate about women in combat. The National Organization for Women adopted the position of [the female students at the Defense's survival, evasion, resistance, and escape (SERE) schools] in trying to preempt any reaction that would jeopardize servicewomen's future roles. "We don't think rape is a problem peculiar to women," said NOW vice president Rosemary Dempsey only four day after Melissa vanished. "Men also are victims of rape and sodomy. We'd strongly hope all POWs would be treated in accord with the Geneva Convention and would consider any kind of brutalization affecting either sex equally horrible."[7]

Conservatives were just as quick to adopt the position of SERE's male students in order to limit the future utilization of servicewomen. "It's not a good idea to try to obliterate concerns about a woman's reproductive system and the kinds of humiliation she could be forced to endure," said Jean Yarborough, a professor at Bowdoin College who used the POW issue to question the combat support jobs women had held for almost twenty years. Phyllis Schlafly, president of the Eagle Forum, added: "It's absolutely ridiculous to have women in combat. It's an embarrassment to our country."[8]

While the debate raged in Washington over her reproductive organs and her official status, the twenty-year-old truck driver was very much a POW in the Gulf. Suffering from shrapnel wounds and a bullet through the upper arm, she had been taken first to a prison cell in Basra, then on to a prison in Baghdad. She was, in fact, safer from sexual abuse in Baghdad than were her fellow female soldiers in the field. At least twenty-five servicewomen were sexually assaulted in the Gulf, while Rathbun-Nealy had only one minor and brief sexual incident as a POW. En route by truck from Khafji to Baghdad, she would tell her father, one of her guards had reached over and touched her breasts. When she slapped him, he stopped and did not try again.

Her guards in Baghdad were sympathetic. One, an Arab Christian, gave her a crucifix and another, an Iraqi with relatives in Detroit, gave her a rosary. An English-speaking officer took a particular shine to her, chasing away the Iraqis who gawked at her in her cell and bringing her food. "I'm probably the only POW who gained weight in prison," she would say after her release. Instead of abusing her, the Iraqi officer ended up proposing to her. "She told him she was already married and that her country didn't allow multiple husbands," says her father.

On March 4, 1991, Melissa Rathbun-Nealy was among the first group of U.S. POWs to be exchanged for Iraqi POWs. She was still officially listed as missing by the Army, though U.S. pilots flying over Baghdad had reported seeing her in her prison compound. The Pentagon's stubbornness, whether calculated or not, would make the first television pictures of Rathbun-Nealy still wearing Iraq's yellow prisoner-of-war uniform doubly sweet to Leo Rathbun. "I called that jackass in the Pentagon at 3 a.m. in the morning," says Rathbun. "'Now, you asshole, will you declare her a prisoner of war?'"

The World War II nurses, who themselves had still been classified as missing a year and a half into their three-year captivity, were more impressed by Rathbun-Nealy's bearing, regardless of what she had endured. "When she came off the plane, she had her head up and her hair combed and she walked like a real American woman," says former Navy nurse Mary Nelson. "I was so proud of her."

The nurses were equally proud two days later when a civilian jet chartered by the International Red Cross flew the last load of fifteen U.S. POWs from Baghdad to Riyadh. Among them, with both her arms in slings, was Army Flight Surgeon Major Rhonda Cornum. No one knew yet that Cornum's weeklong experience as a POW would be reduced to a single incident and prove pivotal in the debate over women in combat.

On February 27, 1991, the last day of the four-day ground war, "Doc" Cornum and seven other crew members were flying low and fast over the Iraqi desert in a Black Hawk search-and-rescue helicopter. Accompanied by two Apache attack helicopters and directed by an AWACS radar plane overhead, they were answering an emergency call to retrieve a downed and injured Air Force pilot. "He was worth getting before the Iraqis got to him," says Cornum, who was planning to jump out of the helicopter to quickly stabilize the pilot on the ground before he was loaded and whisked away. "He was flying a mission for the Army. He was the highest decorated guy in the Air Force. And he was my husband's classmate at the Air Force Academy."

The Black Hawk crew was startled when the seemingly empty desert suddenly erupted into flashes of green light and the crack of anti-aircraft guns. "It was as if we were a lawn mower that had run over a beehive, and the bees were coming up to sting," Cornum wrote later in her Gulf war memoir.[9] While the door gunners sprayed return machine-gun fire, the protective infantrymen aboard the Black Hawk pushed Cornum to the floor. In misguided chivalry they covered her body with theirs, thus pinning Cornum in a direct line with the Iraqi fire coming from below.

The last words Cornum heard after the Black Hawk took a thunderous hit came from a pilot yelling, "We're going in." By the time she regained consciousness on the desert floor and saw five Iraqi officers looking down at her, both her arms had been broken between the elbow and the shoulder, a bone in her little finger had been shot away, the ligaments in her right knee were torn beyond repair and she had lost half the blood in her body from a bullet lodged in her shoulder. Even at that, Cornum was lucky. She was one of three crew members to be taken prisoner. The other five crew members—the two pilots, one of the door gunners and two of the infantrymen—died in the crash.

As Cornum's Iraqi captors led her by the hair from one command bunker to the next in their desert compound, she was well aware she had not had any prisoner-of-war training. SERE school was reserved primarily for high-flying aircraft crews whose return to earth by parachute made them prime targets for enemy capture. Army helicopters flew so fast and low in combat that the crews didn't even wear parachutes and were more or less expected to die if their helicopters went down.

The Code of Conduct was also just a dim thirteen-year-old memory to Cornum from Officer Basic Course. What little she remembered came from old war movies and from her husband, Kory, who had been a SERE instructor at the Air Force Academy. She did know that under the terms of the Geneva Conventions, a flight surgeon shouldn't be taken prisoner of war at all. But she had purposely left her medical identity card behind. Not only did she think it would do her little good if she were captured on a combat search-and-rescue mission, she also didn't want to be treated any differently from the rest of the crew. Forced to kneel on her one good leg in the enemy compound with a gun pressed into the back of her head, Cornum, thirty-six, was as much a POW as the surviving twenty-year-old infantryman kneeling beside her.

For the next seven days Cornum was shuttled blindfolded between Iraqi bunkers in the desert, the Baath Party office and a health clinic in Basra, a military hospital and a final cell in Baghdad. Like Melissa Rathbun-Nealy, she had only one, though very unpleasant, sexual incident. On her first night of captivity, as she and the young infantryman, Troy Dunlap, were being transported to Basra in the back of a truck, an Iraqi guard suddenly unzipped her flight suit and started kissing and mauling her. "I was manually molested, anally and vaginally," Cornum would tell me later. While Dunlap sat helplessly on the other side of the truck, only Cornum's broken arms and screams of pain kept the Iraqi from consummating the assault. "I would have gotten raped but he couldn't get my flight suit off," says Cornum.

Cornum was not physically molested again. Indeed, her experience in captivity seems a benchmark in international cross-gender sensitivity. With her broken arms dangling and tied in front of her Cornum persuaded her next Iraqi guards to cut off her flight suit with a knife and pull down her underpants so she could go to the bathroom. They then voluntarily reclothed her in a blue wool bathrobe. "All three of them averted their eyes, or looked me straight in the eye, so I would know they weren't leering," Cornum wrote later.

In Basra, she depended on Dunlap and, later, other male POWs not only to feed and clothe her, but also for the most intimate help. "I had my period and they helped me go to the bathroom and remove the tampons and all that stuff," says Cornum. "It was bad planning to have my period. I'm not sure what good planning would be, but it just happened that way. I didn't want to die of toxic shock out there. I wanted to make it home."

On the fifteen-hour bus ride with other blindfolded POWs to Baghdad on her fourth day of captivity, Cornum developed chills and a fever from blood poisoning and had to manipulate her broken finger to drain the pus. She was cheered, however, when she looked out from under her blindfold and saw the name tag on a fellow prisoner with a broken leg: it was the Air Force pilot she and her crew had been on their way to save.

At home, Cornum's father was as worried about his daughter as Leo Rathbun was about his. In the brave new world of role reversals, Cornum's father was sending furious telegrams to George Bush and Norman Schwarzkopf saying, "You've lost my daughter. What are you going to do about it?" while his daughter was in Baghdad listening to Troy Dunlap being interrogated and beaten. "Shouting. Silence. Whap, the sound of a hand across Troy's face," Cornum writes. "I felt terrible, helpless."

But Norrington's prognosis turned out to be correct. [Giles Norrington was a Navy combat reconnaissance pilot and a former POW in Vietnam.] While the U.S. prisoners in Cornum's group could hear each other's interrogation, they were interrogated separately. Cornum braced for the worst when she was brought in for her interrogation and saw Dunlap sitting on a chair with his head between his knees and tied with a rope to his boots before he was led away. But whether it was her obvious injuries, her status as a medical officer or her gender, she was not beaten.

Norrington was also correct in predicting that a woman would be more apt to answer the interrogator's questions. But Cornum deliberately gave the wrong answers. After lying about such inquiries as to what direction her helicopter had been headed when it was shot down (straight north, she had answered, instead of due east), she was abruptly dismissed by the interrogating officer. "Was that it? Was it over?" Cornum would write. "The officer said nothing."

Her release came just as abruptly. On March 5, day 7 of her captivity, Cornum was awakened at 3 a.m. in her military hospital room, blindfolded and taken by bus to a cement block of cells somewhere in Baghdad. A guard threw a pair of sneakers and a plastic bag into her cell containing a yellow suit with the words PW stencilled on the pocket. She was then reblindfolded and bused to another location. But this time when the blindfolds were removed, she and at least twenty other yellow-suited prisoners were in the lobby of a luxury hotel. "You are safe. You are now in the custody of the International Committee of the Red Cross," someone called out. "It's over and you are going home." Not until the Red Cross plane left Iraqi airspace the next day, however, and entered the air over Saudi Arabia, did the POWs erupt into cheers.

Cornum and Rathbun-Nealy came home to the same disproportionate attention which was showered on all servicewomen in the Gulf. Rathbun-Nealy, who had been missing for over a month, had become an international celebrity. In France, a photograph of the twenty-year-old truck driver ran on the cover of *Paris-Match*. The president of Italy sent her a huge bouquet of flowers and she was declared an honorary citizen of an Italian town named Melissa. Newspapers around the world carried her photo on the front page and a special edition of *Life* magazine ran a cover photograph of Norman Schwarzkopf hugging her in Riyadh. "Survivor of 32 Too Many Arabian Nights, Melissa Rathbun-Nealy Heads Home from Baghdad" ran a story in *People*.

The attention upset Rathbun-Nealy, who was just one of the ten prisoners of war released on March 4. "She was very embarrassed that she was considered a hero. 'I just got stuck on the sand,'" she told her father. "She literally disappeared as much as she could. She didn't want publicity."

But Saddam Hussein and his armed forces had given U.S. servicemen a gift. By taking Rathbun-Nealy and Cornum prisoners of war, by not exploiting them for propaganda as they had the captured male pilots, by returning Rathbun-Nealy in apparent good health and Cornum in better shape than she was when she was shot down, the Iraqi forces had reassured the American public about the viability of women in combat.

For all the trepidation and the Pentagon over women POWs, the public had not overreacted. "Women did get captured," says Pete Williams, "but I don't recall at the time any more great public outrage about that other than the general mistreatment of American POWs by the Iraqis."

Cornum did not reveal the groping episode in her press interviews. Both she and Rathbun-Nealy did tell the SERE agency about their respective incidents in their POW debriefings, but no one else. Like her female counterparts at SERE school, Cornum resented the issue of sexual abuse being seen solely as a woman's issue. "None of the male POWs asked me whether I got molested. I didn't ask any of the guys, either," says Cornum. "The only people who asked were inquisitive reporters." Cornum insisted her feelings of helplessness listening to Troy Dunlap being beaten were no different from his feelings when she was being molested on the truck. "I don't think Troy liked it," she says. "But I didn't like it when they beat him up, either."

It was religion, Cornum told me, that was far more of a danger to her fellow male POWs in Iraq than her gender was to her. "If we're going to pick people to send to war based on cultures, we should have taken out all the Jewish soldiers and left them home," she says. "The Iraqis asked me my religion, but they made all the male POWs drop their pants so they could see if they were circumcised. These guys had to do a lot of talking to convince the Iraqis that circumcision was an American tradition, not Jewish, or they would have shot them. No question of that."

It would be another year before Cornum's episode in the back of the truck would become public knowledge and deemed so explosive in the debate over women in combat that it merited a front-page story in the *New York Times*. Lost in the public frenzy over the sexual groping was the far greater slight to Cornum.

For her voluntary participation in the search for the downed pilot, for all the injuries she suffered in the downing of the Black Hawk, she alone among the surviving crew did not get a medal for the search-and-rescue mission in Iraq. The Army refused to admit she had been in combat. "I got put in for a Distinguished Flying Cross and a Bronze Star," says Cornum. "Everyone else on my mission got a DFC. I got nothing."

The World War II nurses were not surprised. For their service under constant shelling in the Pacific and their three years of internment by the Japanese, the nurses, too, had come home to public, but not military recognition. "The eighty-four women were all but ignored when they came back," says Giles Norrington, the ex-Vietnam POW. "There were press things, to be sure. But the military ignored them. The history books, and that's what really counts, ignored them." . . .

[But] the Gulf war marked the end of

women's invisibility in the military. The women who died or were taken prisoners of war, combined with the seemingly painless rout of the enemy, elevated women's military contribution and cemented their new public status. [Congress established a Presidential Commission on the Assignment of Women in the Armed Forces; it held hearings in the summer of 1992.]

Female prisoners of war had dominated the combat debate from the moment Hays Parks, chief of the Army's International Law Branch, testified on June 8, 1992, that each of the Army women taken prisoner of war in the Gulf had been "treated more favorably than their U.S. and Coalition male counterparts," though each had been the "victim of indecent assaults."[10]

Five former prisoners of war had given testimony later the same day, including three men held in Vietnam, a World War II Navy nurse interned by the Japanese and Desert Storm POW Major Rhonda Cornum. The commissioners had not asked the male POWs to elaborate on the torture they had endured which had left one unable to lift his arm above the height of his shoulder. Elaine Donnelly zeroed in on Cornum, however, demanding to know the nature of her "indecent assault." Cornum's reply, that she had been "violated manually, vaginally and rectally" the year before in Iraq, had provided an emotional argument against women in combat and generated public interest in the hearings for the first time.[11]

"Sexual Assaults of Female POW's Withheld from Panel," read the story headline in *USA Today.* "Women in War: Ex-Captive Tells of Ordeal" read the front-page story in the *New York Times.*[12] While male POWs had traditionally been viewed as heroes, Cornum had become a victim.

The cultural divide over female POWs was the most graphic to come out of the presidential commission. The female pilots monitoring the commission had been furious at Donnelly for invading Cornum's privacy. "Mrs. Donnelly's disgraceful conduct was an attempt to exploit Major Cornum's courage to further her well-known political agenda oposing women in combat," WMA [Women Military Advisors] president Rosemary Mariner wrote to the *Washington Times.*[13] Commis-

sioner Mimi Finch was angry that Donnelly had pressed Cornum for details about her treatment as a POW, but not the male POWS. "Why didn't they call in Jeffrey Zaun and ask him what it was like or what made him talk?" said Finch. "It just seemed very sexist that Cornum would be asked that question and nobody else would."

Cornum had been the least disturbed. "Getting raped or abused or whatever is one more bad thing that can happen to you as a prisoner of war. There's about four hundred bad things I can think of and it's not the worst of them," Cornum had testified, calling her incident an "occupational hazard." The other female POW, Army truck driver Melissa Rathbun-Nealy, dismissed her designation as a "victim of indecent assault." A letter sent on her behalf to the presidential commission reiterated that she "at all times steadfastly maintained that she was not the victim of sexual abuse and continues to so maintain this position."[14]

But another "difference" had been identified between servicemen and servicewomen, another perceived threat to unit cohesion. "There is no question in my mind that I would certainly lean toward giving the enemy something if I knew they were raising hell with a fellow female prisoner," former Vietnam POW and Air Force Colonel Norman McDaniel testified.[15]

The POW issue became a matter of white male "values" in their protectionist arguments against women in combat. "I am not prepared to see America's mothers and daughters paraded down the streets of Baghdad and subjected to abuse, when it's not necessary," testified Rhonda Cornum's battalion commander, Lieutenant Colonel William Bryan. "Now those are my values as an American citizen."[16]

"Values" would motivate General Maxwell Thurman's commision vote against the female pilots. "No people want women to get victimized," Thurman would tell me. "Even if the pilots want to get victimized, we don't want to get them victimized. You follow me? It's not our American value system." The word "values" was never attached to the American concept of equal opportunity or individual choice or the meritocracy in which the military took such pride, but was being denied women.

The POW issue was never about women,

but about men. In the commission's final report to the president, every argument against women in combat would revolve around the pain women's capture would cause, not to the women themselves but to their male colleagues. "The mistreatment of women taken as POWs could have a negative impact on male captives," read one rationale against women in ground combat. "The presence of women might cause additional morale problems for male prisoners," read an argument against women in combat aircraft.[17]

The philosophical battle over women in combat was so incendiary that the conservative bloc staged a walkout in the midst of the commission's final votes in November. "The Fadeout Five," as the Navy Times called them, demanded, and would get, their own section in the final report titled "Alternative Views: The Case Against Women in Combat," written before a single vote on combat had been taken.... One white male commissioner would cite the Scriptures, the Bible, God and his identity as a "Christian" in his combat case against women.[18]

The presidential commission voted resoundingly against women in ground combat, and even called on Congress to enact a new combat exclusion law shielding the Army and Marine Corps from women and a hypothetical draft. (During the Vietnam War, 99.7 percent of draftees had gone to the Army or Marine Corps; during the Korea War, 100 percent, presumably as ground combat troops.) For extra insurance against women, the commission voted to retain the DOD's "Risk Rule" that supposedly distanced women in support roles from combat and against the nonissue of requiring women to register for the draft.[19]

By one vote, the commission voted to lift the combat exclusion law against women on Navy combat vessels, save for submarines and amphibious ships. By the same margin, they voted to reinstate the combat exclusion law against women pilots. The deciding vote against the pilots was based on menstruation.[20]

"I'd like to know, is it true or false that flight schedules are adjusted for menstrual cycles?" asked Commissioner Charles Moskos, who would author the controversial "Don't Ask, Don't Tell" policy for gays in the military.[21]

A chorus of noes came from the pilots in the back of the room.

No, confirmed Commissioner Meredith Neizer.

Commissioner Finch, an Army helicopter pilot, explained that aviators, male or female, had the discretion to adjust their peacetime flight schedules if they hadn't slept well, had hangovers or felt under the weather so as not "to sacrifice the aircraft or themselves." "I do not believe menstruation in any way, shape or form is an issue here," she said.

But pilots' menstrual cycles continued to be a prime concern to the white male commissioners. Commissioner Darryl Henderson, an expert on male cohesion, suggested that during "the highest rate of flow," one study showed that women had an increased susceptibility to decompression sickness and hypoxia.

Commissioner Hogg questioned "menstrual considerations" as well, but reported he had heard it might be a problem for a forty-five-year-old woman pilot, but not for younger women.

The pilots sitting in the back of the room were incredulous at the turn the debate had taken. After nine months of military testimony about their qualifications as aviators, the hundreds of hours they had spent in the air in the Gulf refueling fighter planes and ferrying combat troops, the lives lost like Marie Rossi's, it had all come down to making men feel bad if women were taken prisoners of war and their menstrual periods. [Marie Rossi was an Army pilot and company commander who was killed in the Gulf War.]

The Clinton administration threw out the presidential commission recommendations on combat in April 1993. Adopting the DEOMI approach to diversity and replacing the defining category of gender with individual qualifications, Secretary of Defense Les Aspin removed the Risk Rule as "no longer appropriate," and ordered the services to open combat cockpits to women and the eager, post-Tailhook Navy to seek congressional repeal of the 1948 law against women on combat ships.[22] In 1994 the Navy opened combat ships to women and the Army, under pressure from its black male secretary, Togo D. West Jr., muscled the white male club of the Army into opening over 32,000 new jobs to women. Only Army and Marine units engaged in direct combat with an enemy—infantry, armor and much of field artillery—remained closed to women.

NOTES

1. Wayne E. Dillingham, "The Possibility of American Military Women Becoming POWs: Justification for Combat Exclusion Rules?" *Federal Bar News & Journal*, May 1990, p. 228.

2. Department of the Army, "Report of Casualty D-0702," Feb. 11, 1991.

3. Response to a Freedom of Information Act request from the U.S. Total Army Personnel Command, Alexandria, VA, July 26, 1993.

4. Letter to Mr. and Mrs. Leo Rathbun from the POW/MIA Division of the U.S. Total Army Personnel Command, Alexandria, VA, Feb. 14, 1991, from Lt. Col. J. G. Cole, chief, POW/MIA Affairs.

5. "Panel One Report to the Presidential Commission," p. 92.

6. Monika Schwinn, "Break Your Teeth on Me," *Der Spiegel*, March 26, 1973, pp. 46–57, from the library archives at Fort Belvoir, VA.

7. Joyce Price, "NOW Cites Woman POW," *Washington Times*, Feb. 4, 1991.

8. Ibid.

9. Rhonda Cornum as told to Peter Copeland, *She Went to War: The Rhonda Cornum Story* (Novato, CA: Presidio, 1992), p. 9. The quotations in the next paragraphs are from pp. 13, 54, 174, 113, 115, and 162.

10. Testimony of Hays Parks, chief of the International Law Branch of the International and Operational Law Division Office of the Judge Advocate General, USA, to the presidential commission, June 8, 1992, Washington, DC.

11. Testimony of Rhonda Cornum to the presidential commission, June 8, 1992.

12. Laurence Jolidonin, "Sexual Assaults of Female POW's Withheld from Panel," *USA Today*, June 11, 1992. Elaine Sciolino, "Women in War: Ex-Captive Tells of Ordeal," *New York Times*, June 29, 1992, p. A1.

13. Letter from Cmdr. Rosemary Mariner to the *Washington Times*, June 28, 1992.

14. Letter to the presidential commission, June 11, 1992.

15. Air Force Col. Norman McDaniel was one of the prisoners of war giving testimony to the presidential commission on June 8, 1992.

16. Testimony of Lt. Col. William Bryan, USA, attack helicopter battalion commander, U.S. Army Aviation Center, to the presidential commission, Aug. 7, 1992, Los Angeles.

17. "Issue K: Ground Combat," "Issue L: Combat Aircraft," presidential commission report, pp. 25, 28.

18. George Wilson, "Opinion/Commentary," *Navy Times*, Nov. 30, 1991, Commissioner Ronald D. Ray, Commissioner Statements in the presidential commission report, p. 116.

19. Presidential commission report, pp. 24–27, 22, 36, 40, 41.

20. "Issue M: Combatant Vessels," presidential commission report, p. 31.

21. Commissioners' discussion and vote on women in combat cockpits, Nov. 3, 1992.

22. Memorandum from Secretary of Defense Les Aspin to the Secretaries of the Army, Navy and Air Force, the chairman of the Joint Chiefs of Staff, and the Assistant Secretaries of Defense for Personnel and Readiness and Reserve Affairs, Jan. 13, 1994.

DOCUMENTS: The Changing Workplace

> *Lucille Schmidt, " . . . It's such a waste—such a waste of people. The way they put in word processing there, you had a lot of smart women getting dumb very fast"*

In the late nineteenth and early twentieth centuries, "efficiency experts" such as Frederick Winslow Taylor and Henry Ford strove to make employees as productive as humanly possible. This trend soon ventured beyond the factory assembly line and into the corporate office. "Turn-of-the-century time-and-motion studies calculated by the tenth of a second how long it took to open envelopes, how long it took to close file drawers, and even how long it took ink to dry."* Although "back office" departments such as bookkeeping, payroll, and inventory control became increasingly mechanized, the "front office" remained characterized by a one-to-one personal relationship between manager and secretary. This distinction persisted until the 1970s, when the introduction of the personal computer coincided with a move to reorganize the front office along the same model of efficiency as the back office. Lucille Schmidt, an employee of Procter & Gamble, one of the top fifty "Fortune 500" companies, had worked for the company's Cincinnati, Ohio, operation for over a decade when the computerized automation of its offices began. The process significantly altered the work and status of large numbers of female secretaries. Schmidt recounted her experience in this 1981 letter to Barbara Garson, the author of an article she had just read in an issue of *Mother Jones*.

Was Lucille Schmidt suffering from a loss of status or did computerized automation result in actual de-skilling of workers and job loss? What alternatives do workers have in such conditions?

I have been employed with The Procter & Gamble Company for 13 years now. Four years ago I was promoted from secretary to manager. About that time, our Division brought in Word Processing equipment. All the secretaries and quite a few of us managers were very interested in the new technology and eager to utilize it to streamline the work. But then something very strange happened.

There was a reorganization. . . . all secretaries and clerks now became part of an organization called Administrative Services. . . .

One of the first visible signs that Administrative Services had arrived was the removal of the Executive Secretaries from the offices they had shared with their male bosses. No longer would there be 1:1 relationships as this did not "meet the needs of the business." All secretaries regardless of status, experience, or rank were now "equal" and shared an office or "work center" with two or three others.

. . . Women whose typing was considered excellent became Information Processors and typed eight hours a day. Others were Support

---

*Barbara Garson, *The Electronic Sweatshop: How Computers Are Transforming the Office of the Future into the Factory of the Past* (New York: Simon & Schuster, 1988), p. 170.

From Barbara Garson, *The Electronic Sweatshop: How Computers Are Transforming the Office of the Future into the Factory of the Past* (New York: Simon & Schuster, 1988), pp. 179–181. Reprinted by permission of Simon & Schuster.

Secretaries. They were told they must learn to work as a team. . . .

Secretaries were transferred from one job to another, from one location to another, with little warning and no prior discussion. This was called career planning. . . .

A monthly newsletter extolled the virtues of the new system. "Production reports" displayed the weekly output—pages typed. There were team meetings, not to discuss the work or how to effectively get it done, but to learn the "team concept." . . . Administrative Services was the office of the future . . . improving productivity for managers and providing a challenging and rewarding work life for the secretaries and clerks. . . .

[Lucille Schmidt was asked repeatedly to become a manager in Administrative Services, the new bureaucracy that provided clerical support for almost 3,000 engineers. But Lucille was already a manager. She didn't think of supervising secretaries as a step up.]

"After all, my position as Personnel Manager provided regular interaction with the Paper hierarchy." [At Procter & Gamble there's a soup hierarchy, a soap hierarchy, a cosmetics hierarchy, and so on.] "I represented our division at various meetings at Corporate headquarters, I was respected for my technical and interpersonal skills and had well-established credibility. . . . For two years I was able to resist a transfer to Administrative Services. Then I was told it's this or the front door—there was no option.

I am now an Administrative Supervisor.

I am to take attendance (I forego the "bed-check"), report any absence or overtime, and arrange for LOs [Temps are called Low Overheads at Procter & Gamble] to cover any planned or unplanned absences. . . . I am to hand out the 3 × 5 cards notifying of a salary increase. I am to call meetings to share (read) organizational announcements. . . .

Of course I know why I was transferred here. . . . Few positions in Personnel carry much responsibility and much authority. I held such a position but I am female, a former secretary, and my father's collar is blue. Now I am a leader of secretaries, all female, in an organization of female secretaries. Now I am "back" in my proper "place" and I can grow and progress all the hell I want. . . .

Susan Eisenberg, "Entering construction . . . was a little like falling in love with someone you weren't supposed to"

For women trying to escape traditionally "female" jobs that carried low pay and, in Lucille Schmidt's case, the added peril of de-skilling and loss of status, a new alternative was better-paying "male" jobs. Since the expulsion of Rosie the Riveter in the aftermath of World War II, electricians, plumbers, welders, carpenters, and machinists had been almost entirely male and white. But with the passage of the Civil Rights Act in 1964 and executive orders promoting affirmative action, women gained access to jobs in the construction industry. Making sexual harassment illegal eventually helped. Nevertheless, despite these major pressures on the construction industry from the federal government, the number of hard-hatted women has remained pitifully small in subsequent decades—less than 2 percent.

Excerpted from "Susan Eisenberg, Electrician," in *Hard-Hatted Women: Life on the Job*, edited by Molly Martin (Seattle: Seal Press, 1988, 1997), pp. 216–224. Reprinted by permission of Seal Press.

For Susan Eisenberg and the other women who entered the trades in the 1970s and stuck it out, the experience has been both challenging and rewarding. Her account shows how being pregnant on the job added a new dimension to the challenges. Above all, Eisenberg's is a story of enormous pride in her work and her young daughter's pride in a mother who builds buildings.

Like many of the first women in their locals I've met across the country, I started in 1978, when affirmative action guidelines were mandated. I graduated four years later in the first apprenticeship class of IBEW Local 103 (Boston), to include women. Of the six women who started together, five of us graduated, a higher percentage than the men in our class. We owed that largely to the support, information-sharing, and prodding we gave each other. . . .

I remember, particularly in those first years, the enormous encouragement I felt from women on the outside, as though I represented them as well. Not only friends, but strangers, too. Women driving past my jobsite who would notice me and honk and give me a raised fist. The neighbor who rode to work on the same early morning bus and always cheered me on. The older black woman I met once in the bathroom of a remodel job, who had noticed my tool pouch on the sink and told me about her own unfulfilled ambitions of a job in the skilled trades, and how she had taught herself radio electronics from books. I felt indebted and privileged that I was able to live out a dream of generations of women who had been locked out. . . .

My initial experience in union construction was my worst. In the first shop that I worked for, the journeymen were extremely hostile and unwilling to train me. There was even a foreman I worked under who tried to get me injured. Fortunately, I was laid off, and went to work for another shop where my experience was just the opposite. I was able to work on small jobs with some good mechanics who took me seriously and gave me a chance to learn the trade. They taught me how to mount boxes, pull and connect wires, and lay out the circuitry from a panel in an electric closet to the receptacles and lights in a room. After a lot of insisting, I got a chance to do the bigger and heavier work: wiring motors; cutting, threading, and bending pipe; mounting equipment. I learned how to climb and carry ladders, use power tools, and maneuver my-self around the debris and dangers on a construction site.

Even though the work and its newness were exhilarating, I also found myself often overcome with anger, depression, or the feeling that I was in over my head. Working outside in a New England winter, or even by the water in the fall, is *cold*. And there were a lot of times I just had to grit my teeth and plunge across fear to do what I was asked: climb a crane, walk across a beam, work on scaffolding.

The hardest part of the job for me to get used to, though, was the talk on a construction site. Not the swearing—which guys often apologized for when I hadn't even noticed it—but jokes about beating up wives, racist and anti-Semitic slurs, degrading remarks about each other's girlfriends or some woman who happened to pass by, and comments about each others' personal lives that I found incredibly cruel. . . . On one remodel job, a residence for elders, one of the electricians joked about pulling the fire alarm and raping all the women residents . . . When I tried to say why a comment like that wasn't funny, he suggested that I could rape all the men. . . . I had to learn to harden myself, to expect little support from co-workers in group conversations, and to be selective about who and what was worth responding to. It quickly became clear that responding to all the comments I found offensive would guarantee not being heard. . . .

I worked into the sixth month of my first pregnancy without telling anyone except the general foreman and a woman elevator installer that I was pregnant. I told most people on the day I stopped working. . . . [S]ince I wore baggy clothes to work (what I called my maternity overalls) and since no one *expected* to see a pregnant woman on a construction sight—they didn't. I presented myself as I always had—as an electrician there to work and earn a paycheck. . . .

Not talking about my pregnancy exaggerated the feeling I often have in construction of feeling split in two. At coffee break, I would be intently aware of the kicking in my womb while having a conversation about the Red Sox. It also meant making a clear pact with myself to ask for help when I needed it or refuse to do things I felt I shouldn't do—that I *would* put health and safety ahead of ego. . . .

Driving around Boston, I love pointing out to my daughter and son "the jobs we worked together." It brings back the times when I felt like I carried a delicious secret: lying on a plank across an open airshaft on the roof of a building, tying in a fan motor, talking to the baby-in-utero. It gave me a powerful appreciation for the changes we have brought about. "We built that, Susie?" my daughter asks as we drive by a big hotel. "You bet!" I tell her.

SUSAN BORDO

"Material Girl": Madonna as Postmodern Heroine

"Postmodern" is a term that has been used by artists and writers in many different ways. In the longer essay from which this excerpt was taken, Susan Bordo uses it to describe the late-twentieth-century view of the human body as "cultural plastic," made infinitely pliable and transformable by technologies from colored contact lenses to body sculpting to cosmetic surgery. Over the course of the 1990s, pop singer Madonna perfectly exemplified this postmodern ethos as she continually reimagined and reshaped her sexual persona, and her body. For some of her fans, including many academic theorists, this made Madonna into something of a feminist icon—a symbol of female self-determination and "resistance" to sexual norms. Bordo, as you'll see, is more skeptical. She questions whether Madonna's toned and sculpted body can truly be seen as a "choice" in the fitness-obsessed culture of the nineties, and whether her sexual persona became more free or more objectified.

Reading this excerpt ten years after it was originally published is an invitation to think about how routine—even required—it has become for pop stars to shape their bodies to fat-free perfection, as Madonna was the first to do. (In recent years, female stars are likely to have breasts implants as well.) Consider, too, how tame "Open Your Heart," the video discussed in this excerpt, now seems. Undulating, nearly nude bodies on overt sexual display, with gestures and expressions lifted straight from the strip clubs, now barely raise an eyebrow. What message is being sent to young women—and young men—by these developments? Are there any signs of "resistance" to them? Any new "heroines" on the horizon?

John Fiske's conception of "difference" . . . imagines resistance as challenging specifiable historical forms of dominance. Women, he argues, connect with subversive "feminine" values leaking through the patriarchal plot of soap operas; blacks laugh to themselves at the glossy, materialist-cowboy culture of *Dallas*. Such examples suggest a resistance directed against *particular* historical forms of power and subjectivity. . . . "Your Body is a Battleground," declares a famous Barbara Kruger poster, urging women to support reproductive rights. Resistance involves choice, commitment, standing one's ground. . . . For some postmodern theorists, however, resistance is imagined as the refusal to embody *any* positioned subjectivity at all; what is celebrated is continual creative escape from location, containment, and definition. . . . From this perspective, the truly resistant female body is, not the body that wages war on feminine sexualization and objectification, but the body that, as Cathy Schwichtenberg has put it, "uses simulation strategically in ways that challenge the stable notion of gender as the edifice of sexual difference . . . [in] an erotic politics in which the female body can be refashioned in the flux of identities that speak in plural styles."[1] For this erotic politics, . . . the body is a playground not a battleground, and . . . the new postmodern heroine is Madonna.

This celebration of Madonna as postmodern heroine does not mark the first time Madonna has been portrayed as a subversive culture-figure. Until the early 1990s, however, Madonna's resistance has been interpreted along "body as battleground" lines, as deriving from her refusal to allow herself to be constructed as a passive object of patriarchal desire. John Fiske, for example, argues that . . . Madonna demonstrated the possibility of a female heterosexuality that was independent of patriarchal control, a sexuality that defied rather than rejected the male gaze, teasing it with her own gaze, deliberately trashy and vulgar, challenging anyone to call her a whore, and ultimately not giving a damn how she might be judged. Madonna's rebellious sexuality, in this reading, offered itself, not as coming into being through the look of the "other," but as self-defining and happy with itself—an attitude that is rather difficult for women to achieve in this culture and that

helps to explain, as Fiske argues, her enormous appeal for pre-teen girls.[2] . . .

Madonna herself, significantly and unlike most sex symbols, has never advertised herself as disdainful of feminism or constructed feminists as man-haters. Rather, in a 1985 *Time* interview, she suggests that her lack of inhibition in "being herself" and her "luxuriant" expression of "strong" sexuality constitute her brand of feminist celebration.[3] Some feminist theorists would agree. Molly Hite, for example, argues that "asserting female desire in a culture in which female sexuality is viewed as so inextricably conjoined with passivity" is "transgressive."[4] . . .

. . . An argument similar to Fiske's can be made concerning Madonna's refusal to be obedient to dominant and normalizing standards of female *beauty*. I am now talking, of course, about Madonna in her more fleshy days. In those days, Madonna saw herself as willfully out of step with the times. "Back in the fifties," she says in the *Time* interview, "women weren't ashamed of their bodies." (The fact that she is dead wrong is not relevant here.) Identifying herself with her construction of that time and what she calls its lack of "suppression" of femininity, she looks down her nose at the "androgynous" clothes of our own time and speaks warmly of her own stomach, "not really flat" but "round and the skin is smooth and I like it." . . .

Of course, this is no longer Madonna's body type. Shortly after her 1987 marriage to Sean Penn she began a strenuous reducing and exercise program, now runs several miles a day, lifts weights, and has developed, in obedience to dominant contemporary norms, a tight, slender, muscular body. . . . Why did she decide to shape up? "I didn't have a flat stomach anymore," she has said. "I had become well-rounded." Please note the sharp about-face here, from pride to embarrassment. My goal here, however, is not to suggest that Madonna's formerly voluptuous body was a non-alienated, freely expressive body, a "natural" body. While the slender body is the current cultural ideal, the voluptuous female body is a cultural form, too (as are all bodies), and was a coercive ideal in the fifties. My point is that in terms of Madonna's own former lexicon of meanings—in which feminine voluptuousness and the choice to be round in a culture of the lean were clearly connected to spontaneity, self-definition, and defiance of the cultural gaze—the terms set by that gaze have now triumphed. Madonna has been normalized; more precisely, she has self-normalized. . . . So have the increasing numbers of young girls who are making rigorous dieting and exercise the organizing discipline of their lives. They do not require Madonna's example, of course, to believe that they must be thin to be acceptable. But Madonna clearly no longer provides a model of resistance or "difference" for them.

None of this "materiality"—that is, the obsessive body-praxis that regulates and disciplines Madonna's life and the lives of the young (and not so young) women who emulate her—makes its way into the representation of Madonna as postmodern heroine. In the terms of this representation . . . Madonna is "in control of her image, not trapped by it"; the proof lies in her ironic and chameleon-like approach to the construction of her identity, her ability to "slip in and out of character at will," to defy definition, to keep them guessing.[5] In this coding of things . . . control and power, words that are invoked over and over in discussions of Madonna, have become equivalent to self-creating. Madonna's new body has no material history; it conceals its continual struggle to maintain itself, it does not reveal its pain. (Significantly, Madonna's "self-exposé," the documentary Truth or Dare, does not include any scenes of Madonna's daily workouts.) It is merely another creative transformation of an ever-elusive subjectivity. "More Dazzling and Determined Not to Stop Changing," as Cosmopolitan describes Madonna: ". . . whether in looks or career, this multitalented dazzler will never be trapped in any mold!"[6] The plasticity of Madonna's subjectivity is emphasized again and again in the popular press, particularly by Madonna herself. It is how she tells the story of her "power" in the industry: "In pop music, generally, people have one image. You get pigeonholed. I'm lucky enough to be able to change and still be accepted . . . play a part, change characters, looks, attitudes."[7]

Madonna claims that her creative work, too, is meant to escape definition. "Everything I do is meant to have several meanings, to be ambiguous," she says. She resists, however (in true postmodern fashion), the attribution of

serious artistic intent; rather (as she told Cosmo), she favors irony and ambiguity, "to entertain myself" and (as she told Vanity Fair) out of "rebelliousness and a desire to fuck with people."[8] It is the postmodern nature of her music and videos that has most entranced academic critics, whose accolades reproduce in highly theoretical language the notions emphasized in the popular press. Susan McClary . . . describes "Open Your Heart" which features Madonna as a porn star in a peep show, as creating "an image of open-ended jouissance—an erotic energy that continually escapes containment." . . . She points to the video's use of parody and play, its portrayal of the male patrons of the show as leering and pathetic, and its "destabilizing" of power-relations by having Madonna, at the end of the video, changing her clothes to those of a little boy and tripping off . . . leaving the manager of the porno house sputtering behind her. McClary reads this ending as "turn[ing] sexual identity into a kind of play."[9]

Now, many feminist viewers may find this particular video quite disturbing, for a number of reasons. First, unlike many of Madonna's older videos, "Open Your Heart" does not visually emphasize Madonna's subjectivity or desire—as "Lucky Star," for example, did through frequent shots of Madonna's face and eyes, flirting with and controlling the reactions of the viewer. Rather, "Open Your Heart" places the viewer in the position of the voyeur by presenting Madonna's body as object, now perfectly taut and tightly managed for display. To be sure, we do not identify with the slimy men, drooling over Madonna's performance, who are depicted in the video; but, as E. Ann Kaplan has pointed out, the way men view women in the filmic world is only one species of objectifying gaze. There is also the viewer's gaze, which may be encouraged by the director to be either more or less objectifying.[10] In "Open Your Heart," as in virtually all rock videos, the female body is offered to the viewer purely as a spectacle, an object of sight, a visual commodity to be consumed. Madonna's weight loss and dazzling shaping-up job make the spectacle of her body all the more compelling; we are riveted to her body, fascinated by it. Many men and women may experience the primary reality of the video as the elicitation of desire for that perfect body;

women, however, may also be gripped by the desire (very likely impossible to achieve) to *become* that perfect body....

I would argue . . . [that] there *is* a dominant position in this video: It is that of the objectifying gaze. One is not *really* decentered and confused by this video, despite the "ambiguities" it formally contains. Indeed, the video's postmodern conceits, I would suggest, facilitate rather than deconstruct the presentation of Madonna's body as an object on display. For in the absence of a coherent critical position telling us how to read the images, the individual images themselves become preeminent, hypnotic, fixating. Indeed, I would say that ultimately this video is entirely about Madonna's body, the narrative context virtually irrelevant, an excuse to showcase the physical achievements of the star, a video centerfold. On this level, any parodic or destabilizing element appears as cynically, mechanically tacked on, in bad faith, a way of claiming trendy status for what is really just cheesecake—or, perhaps, soft-core pornography.

Indeed, it may be worse than that. If the playful "tag" ending of "Open Your Heart to Me" is successful in deconstructing the notion that the objectification, the sexualization of women's bodies is a serious business, then Madonna's *jouissance* may be "fucking with" her youthful viewers' perceptions in a dangerous way. Judging from the proliferation of rock and rap lyrics celebrating the rape, abuse, and humiliation of women, the message—not Madonna's responsibility alone, of course, but hers among others, surely—is getting through. The artists who perform these misogynist songs also claim to be speaking playfully, tongue-in-cheek, and to be daring and resistant transgressors of cultural structures that contain and define....

My argument here is a plea, not for censorship, but for recognition of the social contexts and consequences of images from popular culture, consequences that are frequently effaced in postmodern and other celebrations of "resistant" elements in these images.... The notion that one can play a porno house by night and regain one's androgynous innocence by day does not seem to me to be a refusal of essentialist categories about gender, but rather a new inscription of mind/body dualism. What the body does is immaterial, so long as the imagination is free. This abstract, unsituated, disembodied freedom . . . glorifies itself only through the effacement of the material praxis of people's lives, the normalizing power of cultural images, and the continuing social realities of dominance and subordination.

NOTES

1. Cathy Schwichtenberg, "Postmodern Feminism and Madonna: Toward an Erotic Politics of the Female Body," paper presented at the University of Utah Humanities Center, National Conference on Rewriting the (Post)Modern: (Post)Colonialism/Feminism/Late Capitalism, March 30–31, 1990.

2. John Fiske, "British Cultural Studies and Television," in Robert C. Allen, ed., *Channels of Discourse* (Chapel Hill: University of North Carolina Press, 1987), pp. 254–90.

3. Quoted in John Skow, "Madonna Rocks the Land," *Time* (May 27, 1985):77,81.

4. Molly Hite, "Writing—and Reading—the Body: Female Sexuality and Recent Feminist Fiction," in *Feminist Studies* 14, no. 1 (Spring 1988):121–22.

5. Catherine Texier, "Have Women Surrendered in MTV's Battle of the Sexes?" *New York Times*, April 22, 1990, p. 31.

6. *Cosmopolitan* (July 1987):cover.

7. David Ansen, "Magnificent Maverick," *Cosmopolitan* (May 1990):311.

8. Ibid.; Kevin Sessums, "White Heat," *Vanity Fair* (April 1990):208.

9. Susan McClary, "Living to Tell: Madonna's Resurrection of the Fleshy," *Genders*, no. 7 (Spring 1990):12.

10. E. Ann Kaplan, "Is the Gaze Male?" in Ann Snitow, Christine Stansell, and Sharon Thompson, eds., *Powers of Desire: The Politics of Sexuality* (New York: Monthly Review Press, 1983), pp. 309–27.

DOCUMENTS: Rethinking Marriage in the Late
Twentieth Century

| Loving *v.* Virginia; Griswold *v.* Connecticut; *Defense of Marriage Act* |

Although marriage is generally understood to be the most private of matters, it has been subjected to regulation by colonies and the states since the founding era (see pp. 55–58). The national government has also been deeply involved in defining which marriages would be legally recognized. It has enacted laws on areas ranging from polygamy, to immigration policy, to the family structures that would be eligible for social security and aid to dependent children. As World War II ended, more old rules were ignored in practice, and pressures for legislative change grew. American military personnel successfully claimed the right to bring spouses in to the United States more easily than established quotas permitted (or than Gerda Lerner had experienced, see pp. 454–58). Federal laws that made Asians ineligible for citizenship proved embarrassing when China was a U.S. ally during World War II; the exclusion of Chinese was ended in 1943. American military personnel stationed in Japan during the Occupation repeatedly challenged the rule that Asians were ineligible for citizenship. The Soldier Brides Act of 1947, which cautiously facilitated the entry of foreign fiancées and spouses regardless of race, was a response to this situation.

The democratic, inclusive rhetoric of a war against fascism made American practices of segregation increasingly anomalous and an international embarrassment. Among the civil rights that increasing numbers of citizens claimed was the right to marry the person of their choice despite state laws defining interracial marriage between whites and others as miscegenation. (Generally, these statutes permitted interracial marriage among other groups.) Challenges built state by state. Although the California Supreme Court struck down that state's miscegenation statute in 1948 and thirteen other legislatures repealed their laws, bans continued to be enforced with serious penalties in many other states.

Virginia's law made it illegal for "any white person in the state to marry any save a white person, or a person with no other admixture of blood than white and American Indian." (The link between whiteness and Native Americans was arranged in order to include all those white Virginians who proudly claimed descent from Pocohontas.) In 1958, two Virginians, Mildred Jeter, who was black, and Richard Loving, who was white, married in a ceremony in Washington, D.C. When they returned to Virginia to live they were indicted for violating Virginia's ban on interracial marriages. They were found guilty and sentenced to one year in jail, which would be suspended if they left the state and did not return for twenty-five years. The aptly named Lovings moved to Washington, D.C., and challenged the conviction; eventually their case reached the U.S. Supreme Court.

How did the state of Virginia defend its practice? On what grounds did the Supreme Court declare the miscegenation law illegal? How did the Court describe "freedom to marry"?

LOVING v. *VIRGINIA*, 1967

CHIEF JUSTICE EARL WARREN WROTE THE OPINION FOR A UNANIMOUS COURT:

. . . the State [of Virginia] argues that the meaning of the Equal Protection Clause [of the Fourteenth Amendment, see p. 247] . . . is only that state penal laws containing an interracial element as part of the definition of the offense must apply equally to whites and Negroes in the sense that members of each race are punished to the same degree. Thus the State contends that, because its miscegenation statutes punish equally both the white and the Negro participants in an interracial marriage, these statutes, despite their reliance on racial classifications, do not constitute an invidious discrimination based upon race. . . .

Because we reject the notion that the mere "equal application" of a statute containing racial classifications is enough to remove the classifications from the Fourteenth Amendment's proscription of all invidious racial discriminations, we do not accept the State's contention. . . . There is patently no legitimate overriding purpose independent of invidious racial discrimination which justifies this classification. The fact that Virginia prohibits only interracial marriages involving white persons

87 S. Ct. 1817 (1967).

demonstrates that the racial classifications must stand on their own justification, as measures designed to maintain White Supremacy. . . . There can be no doubt that restricting the freedom to marry solely because of racial classification violates the central meaning of the Equal Protection Clause.

These statutes also deprive the Lovings of liberty without due process of law in violation of the Due Process Clause of the Fourteenth Amendment. The freedom to marry has long been recognized as one of the vital personal rights essential to the orderly pursuit of happiness by free men.

Marriage is one of the "basic civil rights of man," fundamental to our very existence and survival. To deny this fundamental freedom on so unsupportable a basis as the racial classifications embodied in these statutes . . . is surely to deprive all the State's citizens of liberty without due process of law. . . . Under our Constitution, the freedom to marry or not marry, a person of another race resides with the individual and cannot be infringed by the state.

These convictions must be reversed. It is so ordered.

Meanwhile, debate over the appropriate limits of contraception—dating at least from the Comstock Act (see p. 250)—continued in the postwar era. Long after they were legal in other states, Connecticut continued to forbid the use of contraceptives. Seeking to test the statute, the Planned Parenthood League of Connecticut established a center in New Haven where a physician offered counsel and prescriptions to married couples. It opened on November 1, 1961; within ten days it had served seventy-five patients. But on the tenth day detectives arrived to arrest its volunteer physician, Dr. C. Lee Buxton, who was the chairman of the Yale Medical School's department of obstetrics and gynecology, and Estelle Griswold, the executive director of the PPL. They were quickly convicted and fined. They appealed their conviction. When their case reached the U.S. Supreme Court they won on a 7–2 decision.

Note the discussion of marital privacy in Justice Douglas's opinion. Why did Justice Stewart disagree?

GRISWOLD v. CONNECTICUT, 1965

JUSTICE WILLIAM O. DOUGLAS WROTE THE MAJORITY OPINION:

... The association of people is not mentioned in the Constitution nor in the Bill of Rights ... [but] specific guarantees in the Bill of Rights have penumbras, formed by emanations from those guarantees that help give them life and substance. Various guarantees create zones of privacy.

The right of association contained in the penumbra of the First Amendment is one. ... The Third Amendment in its prohibition against the quartering of soldiers "in any house" in time of peace without the consent of the owner is another facet of that privacy. The Fourth Amendment explcitly affirms the "right of the people to be secure in their persons, houses, papers, and effects, against unreasonable searches and seizures." ... We deal with a right of privacy older than the Bill of Rights—older than our political parties, older than our school system. Marriage is a coming together for better or for worse, hopefully enduring, and intimate to the degree of being sacred. It is an association that promotes a way of life, not causes; a harmony in living, not political faiths, a bilateral loyalty, not commercial or social projects. Yet it is an association for as noble a purpose as any involved in our prior decisions.

JUSTICE BYRON WHITE, CONCURRING

In my view this Connecticut law as applied to married couples deprives them of "liberty" without due process of law ... the liberty entitled to protection under the Fourteenth Amendment includes the right "to marry, establish a home and bring up children." ... These [prior] decisions affirm that there is a "realm of family life which the state cannot enter" without substantial justification.

JUSTICE POTTER STEWART, DISSENTING

Since 1879 Connecticut has had on its books a law which forbids the use of contraceptives by anyone. I think this is an uncommonly silly law. As a practical matter, the law is obviously unenforceable ... as a philosophical matter, I believe the use of contraceptives in the relationship of marriage should be left to personal and private choice, based upon each individual's moral, ethical and religious beliefs. ... But we are not asked in this case to say whether we think this law is unwise, or even asinine. We are asked to hold that it violates the United States Constitution. And that I cannot do. ...

What provision of the Constitution, then, does make this state law invalid? The Court says it is the right of privacy "created by several fundamental constitutional guarantees." With all deference I can find no such general right of privacy in the Bill of Rights, in any other part of the Constitution. ... It is the essence of judicial duty to subordinate our own personal views, our own ideas of what legislation is wise and what is not. If, as I should surely hope, the law before us does not reflect the standards of the people of Connecticut, the people of Connecticut can freely exercise their true Ninth and Tenth Amendment rights to persuade their elected representatives to repeal it. That is the constitutional way to take this law off the books.

381 U.S. 479.

Griswold v. *Connecticut* limited its decision to married couples, recognizing for them a zone of privacy in their intimate relations into which the state could not intrude. Not until 1971 did the Supreme Court rule that unmarried people also had a right to contraceptives. That decision, as historian Nancy F. Cott has observed, "pronounced a historic reversal, since it denied the state's right to distinguish between citizens of differing marital status." The Court recognized "the right of the *individual*, married or single, to be free from unwarranted governmental intrusion into matters so fundamentally affecting a person as the decision whether to bear or beget a child."* That decision made state practice congruent with the sexual revolution that characterized American society in the 1960s and 1970s, sustained by new developments in contraceptive technology, notably the widely available birth control pill. (See Beth Bailey, pp. 560–68.)

But the Supreme Court was not prepared to recognized intimate privacy for same-sex couples. Over the course of the 1980s and 1990s, gay men and lesbians challenged criminal sodomy laws, usually written in generic terms but only enforced against gay couples, which denied intimate privacy. In 1986 the Atlanta police, acting on a tip, entered the apartment of Michael Hardwick and found him in bed with another man. When they were arrested for violating Georgia's sodomy statutes, they claimed—unsuccessfully—that their constitutional right to equal protection of the laws had been violated. Chief Justice Warren Burger observed that "Decisions of individuals relating to homosexual conduct have been subject to state intervention throughout the history of Western civilization."† The vote was 5–4; voting with the majority was Justice Lewis Powell, who stated publicly several years later that the decision was one he regretted.

In the aftermath of *Bowers* v. *Hardwick*, gay men and lesbians argued with increasing conviction that they were marked as criminals for behavior covered by the protections of privacy when engaged in by heterosexuals. They argued that they too fulfilled one of the major social reasons for the practice of marriage—the choice of committed relationships rather than transient ones. Lesbians and gay men also identified ways in which the status of marriage gave privileges and rights to heterosexual couples, including tax advantages in the form of joint-income tax returns; the ability to share health insurance coverage (often paid for in part by employers); and rights related to the acquisition and inheritance of property, awards of child custody, and companionship as next of kin when partners were hospitalized or dying. And they resented the stigma of being marked as criminals.

By the late twentieth century, these claims developed dynamism of their own. Between 1986 and 2003, the number of states that had laws criminalizing sodomy declined from twenty-five to thirteen, and virtually none enforced these laws against private consensual heterosexual conduct. The European Court of Human Rights has sustained the right of homosexual adults to engage in intimate, consensual conduct. European practices of state recognition of registered same-sex domestic partnerships offered a model: Partners are entitled to state benefits in Denmark, Norway, Sweden, Iceland, France, Germany, and Finland; the Netherlands and Belgium recognize same-sex mar-

---

*Nancy F. Cott, *Public Vows: A History of Marriage and the Nation* (Cambridge, Mass.: Harvard University Press, 2000), pp. 198–99.

†478 U.S. 186 (1986).

riages. In 1993, the Hawaii Supreme Court held that although it was not prepared to say that the claim of gay men and lesbians to same-sex marriage was a fundamental right "rooted in the traditions and collective conscience of our people," it did agree that by limiting the rights and benefits that were associated with marriage to heterosexual couples, the state had established a sex-based classification, reserving "a multiplicity of rights and benefits" for a single class of people, and therefore presumed to be unconstitutional unless it could be justified by "compelling state interests." The logic of the decision established twenty years before in *Frontiero* v. *Richardson* (see pp. 628–29)—that illegality must turn on the act, not the gender of the actor—opened the door to claims on behalf of same-sex partnerships. In 2000, Vermont extended the rights and protections of marriage to same sex couples who had established a "civil union," and in 2002, the law of Quebec, Canada, gave sweeping rights and protections to same-sex couples.

In 2003, the U.S. Supreme Court heard arguments in *Lawrence* v. *Texas,* a case with many similarities to *Bowers*. Acting on what turned out to be a false report of a disturbance, Houston police entered John Lawrence's apartment and found him in bed with Tyron Garner. Lawrence and Garner challenged the Texas law that criminalized private homosexual intimacy. Writing for the majority in a sweeping 6–3 decision, Justice Anthony Kennedy placed the matter in the center of constitutional understandings of liberty: "As the Constitution endures, persons in every generation can invoke its principles in their own search for greater freedom." The protection against intrusion should be broadly understood; liberty is traditionally the protection from unwarranted government intrusions into a dwelling or other private places. In our tradition the state is not omnipresent in the home. Liberty is also the right to "an autonomy of self that includes freedom of thought, belief, expression, and certain intimate conduct. [This case] involves liberty of the person both in its spatial and more transcendent dimensions. . . . To say that the issue in *Bowers* was simply the right to engage in certain sexual conduct demeans the claim [of John Lawrence] . . . just as it would demean a married couple were it to be said marriage is simply about the right to have sexual intercourse . . . [this] personal relationship . . . is within the liberty of persons to choose without being punished as criminals."

The Court explicitly overturned *Bowers*. It recognized that the decision in *Bowers* had relied on historical misunderstandings and overstatements. The Court was persuaded that laws directed specifically against homosexual conduct are of a relatively recent vintage; in the nineteenth century, laws against sodomy criminalized heterosexual as well as homosexual conduct and were enforced generally only when the activity was public or involved a minor or the victim of assault. "It was not until the 1970s that any state singled out same-sex relations for criminal prosecution." And the Court pointed to changing international understandings: "the right the petitioners seek has been accepted as an integral part of human freedom in many other countries."*

Many people, however, were deeply dismayed by these moves toward treating marriage as malleable. Polls in 2000 showed strong popular support for the extension of health insurance, Social Security benefits, and insurance rights to same-sex partners. But strong majorities—as high as two-thirds—opposed "marriage." Hawaii voters, who supported the extension of benefits, also overwhelmingly supported a constitu-

---

Lawrence v. *Texas,* 539 U.S. ___ (2003).

tional amendment to bar same-sex marriages. Predicting that once a single state recognized same-sex marriage, gay and lesbian couples would travel there to solemnize their relationship and then return to their home states to live (much as couples had made use of Nevada's "quickie" divorce laws in the 1940s and 1950s), Congress quickly passed the Defense of Marriage Act in 1996. It was a brief statute with two major parts.

AN ACT TO DEFINE AND PROTECT THE INSTITUTION OF MARRIAGE, 1996

. . . No State, territory or possession of the United States, or Indian tribe, shall be required to give effect to any public act, record, or judicial proceeding of any other State, territory possession or tribe respecting a relationship between persons of the same sex that is treated as a marriage under the laws of such other State, territory, possession or tribe, or a right or claim arising from such relationship . . .

In determining the meaning of any Act of Congress, or of any ruling, regulation, or interpretation of the various administrative bureaus and agencies of the United States, the word "marriage" means only a legal union between one man and one woman as husband and wife, and the word "spouse" refers only to a person of the opposite sex who is a husband or a wife.

This statute is likely to be challenged. As this book goes to press, a decision by an appeals court in Ontario, Canada, extended full marriage rights to gay and lesbian couples, and the Canadian parliament is considering rewriting the definition of marriage as "the lawful union of two persons." The Supreme Judicial Court in Massachusetts is scheduled to hand down a decision sometime in 2003 on the legal recognition of same-sex marriage.

It is interesting to note that a half-century marked by steadily rising divorce rates—which roughly doubled between 1950 and 1990—was also marked by widened recognition of the social meanings of sexual intimacy and widened boundaries for its practice.

ROBIN TOLMACH LAKOFF

Sexual Harassment on Trial: The Anita Hill/Clarence Thomas Narrative(s)

In 1986, the Supreme Court for the first time formally recognized sexual harassment as a violation of the law (pp. 643–45). An old problem more joked about than taken seriously, the subject was suddenly the topic of choice five years later. In the summer of 1991, the Hollywood hit *Thelma & Louise* sparked heated conversations about sexual exploitation. Just a few months later, the action shifted from big screen to small as shocked television viewers watched composed young law professor Anita Hill accuse former boss and Supreme Court nominee Clarence Thomas of sexual harassment. Transfixed, the public saw the Hill/Thomas confrontation unfold before a Senate Judiciary Committee that seemed unevenly weighted between Thomas's Republican advocates and Democrats who should have been Hill's defenders.

    In this essay, Lakoff does more than recount the narrative with insight. She explores criticisms, poses alternative scenarios, and analyzes the varying responses of black women. How does she deal with the question of where the truth lies? What does she suggest is the answer to the question of who "won"?

The movie everyone was going to see, and heatedly discussing, in the summer of 1991 was *Thelma & Louise*. In it two women (played by Susan Sarandon and Geena Davis) . . . go off together without their partners for a couple of days' vacation. They stop off for dinner; Thelma, the younger and prettier married one, is hit on, responds positively, drinks too much, and is helped outside for some fresh air by the guy she has been flirting with. He proceeds to try to rape her, at which moment Louise appears with Thelma's gun and, when he insults her, shoots him dead. They take off in a panic, with Louise gradually evolving a plan to get to Mexico. In the course of their flight they are harassed, threatened, taken advantage of, and variously mistreated by virtually every male with whom they come in contact. They kill a couple and disable a few others. The plan is thwarted by Thelma's irresponsibility, and they end up (in all probability) committing suicide by driving off a cliff to avoid capture.

    This picaresque plot is not unfamiliar to Hollywood audiences, yet the movie was shocking: Instead of guys (who can be expected to behave this way), it was two *women*. . . . Critics and audiences were split about how to take the story. Was it right to show women responding to adversity with violence? Even though the protagonists (probably) got killed in the end, did the movie send women the wrong message? One thing was striking: Women tended to respond much more positively to the action than men; and at each scene in which the women turned violently on their harassers, the female members of the audience responded with lusty cheers.

    If *Thelma & Louise* did nothing else, it brought up in the most graphic and unavoidable way, on the big screen where it couldn't be avoided, the fact that too many men treat women as children, sex objects, or possessions. It brought the topic of sexual harassment into sharp focus as a subject of impassioned arguments between and within the sexes, and presented the possibility of retribution (if not necessarily of exactly this kind). The popularity of the movie, and the reactions of audiences, made it clear that harassment and other gender-related mistreatment were neither a dirty secret in which the woman was at fault nor something that only happened to *you*: it universalized the problem, presenting it from a female perspective, and gave us a language, visual and verbal, in which to discuss it. Of course, it was just entertainment, a summer flick, and the excitement would simmer down as the weather cooled off. . . .

In June, Thurgood Marshall, the only African American on the Supreme Court and a strong liberal, announced his retirement. With a presidential election coming up in 1992, the Bush administration realized that Marshall would have to be replaced by another black jurist. They naturally preferred a conservative. . . . [Their nominee was a] . . . forty-three-year-old federal appellate justice, former head of the Equal Employment Opportunity Commission (E.E.O.C.) named Clarence Thomas.

The candidate's selection had little to do with professional distinction or civil rights background. There was immediate protest, both from legal circles concerned about his competence and from civil rights and other liberal groups concerned about his worse than lackluster record. But the administration persisted, and Senate Judiciary Committee confirmation hearings began on September 10. . . . On September 27 the committee split 7–7 on whether to recommend Thomas's confirmation to the Senate as a whole. The hearings were officially concluded.

Meanwhile, other problems with the nominee were slowly oozing to the surface. A former subordinate of Thomas's at the E.E.O.C., Anita Hill, a law professor at the University of Oklahoma . . . [alleged that] on numerous occasions . . . Thomas had asked her out on dates; rejected, he had spoken to her in his office several times using graphic and often disgusting sexual terminology. Twenty-four at the time she took the position, conservatively reared in rural Oklahoma, Hill had found the assaults so distressing that she had at one

point been hospitalized with gastrointestinal symptoms. Eventually she had left to take a position at Oral Roberts University. But she had remained on the job, without making any formal complaint, for a few years (though she had spoken of the incidents with distress to a couple of friends), and had kept in contact with her former boss, calling him once a year or so on professional business.

Exactly how Hill's allegations made it to the Judiciary Committee is still not clear. Reluctant to be brought to public attention, she agreed only under pressure to testify if called. If, in fact, the head of the E.E.O.C.—the government office charged with investigating and dealing with sexual harassment complaints— was himself a harasser, that was no trivial matter. And if a nominee to the Supreme Court had knowingly behaved illegally (since sexual harassment is illegal), that in itself might constitute grounds for disqualification. . . .

. . . Participants were pushing the envelope before the reopened hearings even began, with an astonishing statement from one member of the committee, Alan Simpson, ordinarily a genial if sharp-tongued senator. Speaking to the media on Tuesday, October 8 [three days before the televised hearings began], Simpson said of Hill: "She will be injured and destroyed and belittled and hounded and harassed—real harassment, different than the sexual kind— just plain old Washington-variety harassment, which is pretty—pretty—unique in itself."[1] . . . In her September 1997 *Dateline* interview, Hill says that she saw Simpson's utterance as "a threat," an interpretation that is perfectly reasonable under the circumstances. . . .

. . . While technically Simpson's words could be construed as a kindly warning or a simple prediction, the fact that Simpson was in a position to make the prophecy come true and had a motive to do so makes them interpretable in this context as a threat. . . . In a normal trial, such behavior—on nationwide TV, no less—would occasion at the very least his removal from the deliberative body and perhaps criminal sanctions. . . . The purpose of a hearing is to find the truth through sworn witness testimony. Anything that is likely to interfere with this aim should be subject to penalty and render the proceedings null and void, just as, in a real trial, it provides grounds for a mistrial. . . .

Even more seriously, Simpson appears to be prejudging a very important part of the testimony he is to hear. A lot hinges on the decision: What is sexual harassment, and how seriously should it be taken? Juror-equivalents should be entering the proceedings with an open mind on these questions. Yet Simpson refers to "real harassment, different than the sexual kind," a statement that makes the presupposition that the "sexual kind," the kind Hill is alleging, isn't "real." . . .

. . . In these hearings, Hill was pretty clearly in a weaker position (despite claims to the contrary by Thomas's partisans). For one thing . . . her side was sociopsychologically less defensible. In a struggle that was played as feminism vs. civil rights, race trumped gender. In theory, both women and blacks are equally disadvantaged in late-twentieth-century American society, so each was equally deserving of special consideration. But events proved that Hill's champions, the Democrats, were terrified of being cast as racist, a fear both Thomas and his defenders hastened to exploit. Thomas on a couple of occasions referred to the proceedings as a "lynching"; he and the Republicans regularly emphasized his race and the disadvantages that that had exposed him to in life, playing "the race card" for all it was worth. On their part, the Democrats were unwilling or unable to place corresponding emphasis on a "gender card." Or perhaps there is no "gender card." Certainly the Republicans didn't worry about sounding sexist. . . .

The two sides had achieved very different degrees of organization in preparation for the fight. While the Democrats held a majority in the Senate, and therefore on the committee, which was also chaired by a Democrat, the Republicans acted and voted as a bloc, while the Democrats were split. . . .

Thomas had a strong advocate in Senator John Danforth, while Hill had no personal champion. . . .

A conservative Democrat, Howell Heflin of Alabama, was selected to lead the questioning of Hill as a sympathetic partisan. But reading the colloquy between him and Hill in the hearing transcript, it is difficult not to see him as a fifth column, his questions undercutting Hill and offering the Republicans an opening wedge. The Democrats . . . left her on her own to twist slowly in the wind. That nonetheless she created a spellbinding story and made a persuasive case attests to her sincerity and personal strength. Thomas, on the other hand, had been coached heavily from the moment of his nomination. . . .

Finally, Thomas was a long-time Washington insider. That meant not only that he had friends inside the Beltway, but that he knew the ropes, was conversant with the procedures of the Senate, and was familiar with members of the media. . . . The procedure clearly was adversarial from the start—as Senator Simpson's veiled threat made perfectly clear. And while Thomas's proponents were permitted great latitude in questioning witnesses about Hill's character and mental health, Thomas was allowed to exclude all "personal" topics—such as his reputed interest in pornography, a claim that bore directly on Hill's charges. . . .

. . . Competent lawyers look out for their clients' interests. But Hill's putative defenders often seemed to be doing just the reverse, especially Howell Heflin. . . . Heflin seemed to be illustrating the phrase "you just don't get it." His questioning of Hill rehashed misogynistic stereotypes which, once brought up, could be and were eagerly made use of by the Republicans.

Sen. Heflin: [to Anita Hill] Now, in trying to determine whether you are telling falsehoods or not, I have got to determine what your motivation might be. Are you a scorned woman?

Ms. Hill: No.

Sen. Heflin: Are you a zealoting civil rights believer that progress will be turned back, if Clarence Thomas goes on the Court?

Ms. Hill: No, I don't—I think that—I have my opinion, but I don't think that progress will be turned back. I think that civil rights will prevail, no matter what happens with the Court.

Sen. Heflin: Do you have a militant attitude relative to the area of civil rights?

Ms. Hill: No, I don't have a militant attitude.

Sen. Heflin: Do you have a martyr complex?

Ms. Hill: No, I don't. [Laughter.][2]

Whatever Heflin believed he was doing here, his questions raised suspicions about Hill that the Republicans could capitalize on later. The "Snark Rule" is at work—the more times it is alleged that someone might be telling "falsehoods," the harder that accusation will be to dislodge.

... Racial stereotyping—the myth of the hypersexual and threatening black male—is explicitly explored and thus at least partially defused as a threat to Thomas; but many stereotypes of women, black and white, are invoked without explicit examination: women as liars, fantasizers, hysterics, and malleable dupes. Typically, Hill is damned if she conforms to one of these stereotypes and damned if she doesn't (because if she doesn't, she's not a good—i.e., normal—woman).[3] ...

The blackness of Hill and Thomas is treated and mythologized in different ways.... In this society ... we remain afraid that sexuality reduces us to animality and deprives us of rational control. So for a very long time the culture has situated uncontrolled "hypersexuality" in ... both women and blacks.[4] The awareness of this country's horrible history of attributing hypersexuality to black males and punishing them for it by lynching made many Democrats wary of finding a black man guilty of an apparently sexual offense.[5] It is less well appreciated that black women are also the victims of white sexual stereotyping.... The Republicans, anxious to desexualize Thomas, worked to hypersexualize Hill ... deliberately flogg[ing] "pubic hair" in order to play down "Long Dong Silver," attributing the former to Hill's hypersexual "fantasies." And since pubic hair is grosser than a penis, she comes out doubly the loser.... At the same time the white committee has created her as the representative of black female hypersexuality ... Hill is construed by the black community as a renegade, "functionally white." To appreciate Thomas's repeated references to "lynching," the hearer must imagine the woman whose assault justifies the lynching. The only woman available to us is Hill. But lynching was only done to avenge injury to a white woman. So ... Hill must be white! And since, to many in the black community, she participated in the sexual disgracing of a black man before an all-white tribunal, she can no longer be black—she must be not merely white, but a traitor to African Americans....

Some critics of Hill and her performance suggest that she orchestrated her own downfall by being genteel, polite, and calm. Especially combined with her failure to act strongly to stop the harassment when it first occurred, her gentleness now conveys not rationality and reasonableness, but "aloofness," primness, unengagement—a lack of involvement that could only mean the events never took place....

... Why did she put up with it? Why didn't she say something definitively crushing, or retaliate physically, or haul the bastard into court? The possibilities make tasty fantasy fodder, but they ignore the real reality of the workplace and the justice system.... Quite aside from the fact that the defendant was the head of the agency that would normally have been involved on the plaintiff's side in any litigation, myths outrun realities about the working of the justice system. It was essential in the early 1980s—more than now, thanks in great measure to Hill—to have an utterly ironclad case, involving at least one of (1) nonconsensual physical assault; (2) demotion or quid pro quo; (3) repeated verbal assaults in the presence of witnesses. Otherwise ... [it] would have been almost impossible to convince a typical jury that he wasn't "just flirting," or that she wasn't an exaggerating hysteric. Even if we discount these realities, civil cases normally take years to come to court. Could Hill have tolerated the situation that long? And in suing, she might well have rendered herself unemployable in the future, as a troublemaker.

Suppose, for the sake of argument, that there does exist a plausible way to stop harassment without retribution. Even so, Hill should not be penalized for not using it....

Why should the victim of the harassment be expected to run further risks by taking steps to end it? Why is it her fault if, for reasons of upbringing or personality, she feels unable to do so? These interpretations are indulged in by people sitting securely in their homes, at their word processors, writing and reflecting in peaceful serenity. Often these critics are considerably older and more worldly than the then twenty-four-year-old Hill, barely out of law school and just a few years away from conservative Oklahoma, where women don't talk back to their male bosses. The clever retorts a forty- or fifty-year-old woman can think of, and the poise required for delivering them effectively, are a lot to ask of someone in Hill's position. And we know all too well "l'esprit d'escalier"—the tendency to think of the perfect cutting riposte when it's too late to deliver it. . . .

Other second-guessers more charitably see Hill as truthful but undermined by her self-presentation. To them, she failed to fit her testimony into the style of the stereotypical wronged woman: angry, tearful, pleading for redress. In this view, a woman who has suffered as Hill has must act in a particular way—must be "womanly" before she can be credible. . . . We have become a nation of amateur psychoanalysts. We *think* we can read others. . . .

Too often, when jurors are questioned about a guilty verdict after a criminal trial, they tell the reporter that one factor in their decision was that the defendant, sitting there in the courtroom day after day, didn't show "enough" remorse. That in itself is troubling. How do you know when someone feels remorse? "Enough" of it? And how can a defendant who is innocent sincerely express remorse? . . .

We all behave differently, based on the usual suspects: gender, ethnicity, class, age. . . . In some cultures, it is considered appropriate to wear your heart on your sleeve, weep, tear your hair, and snuffle in front of strangers. In others, that would create the presumption that you were out of control and perhaps had something to hide; a good and rational person is one who maintains face by keeping a stiff upper lip. In Hill's case, some analysts have pointed out that many southern black families teach their children—especially their daughters—to maintain a calm, unreadable demeanor in public. Since black women are doubly subject—as women and as black—to interpretation by others, it is safest to offer observers as little as possible to work with. . . . If she had shown anger, she would have been seen as a "bitch."

Thomas, on the other hand, ran no risk in showing anger and received only positive notices for it. It seemed to enhance his credibility. . . .

What if she tried another tack—suppose she broke down and cried, became inarticulate, overwhelmed by the horror of her memories? Then she would have triggered the other discrediting characterization: She would have been seen as "hysterical." . . .

Whatever else can be said about Hill/Thomas . . . the amount of media (and public) attention given to the hearing was extraordinary. . . . Sex always sells. But it took more than mere titillation to keep people glued to the TV that weekend and discussing it heatedly for months thereafter. . . .

For many Americans, *Thelma & Louise* had brought the issues examined in Hill/Thomas to fever-pitch intensity. The movie established the topic of sexual harassment in the collective public mind, so that when Hill came to tell her story, it seemed familiar and reasonable. But the response to the movie, too, did not arise out of nothing. *Thelma & Louise* would not have been a hit—perhaps could not even have been made—had the social climate not been receptive. . . .

The question—who is telling the truth?—is typically framed as a polarized either/or: *One* of them must be lying. But I see a plausible middle ground. Perhaps both are reporting their memories accurately, as they existed in 1991, years after the events in dispute. Her recollections are in accord with what actually happened . . . [and] Thomas is telling the truth *as he remembers it.* To him, the interchanges seared so painfully into Hill's memory are just idle chit-chat, joking around, the kind of small talk that no one remembers five minutes later. Who recalls the topics of conversation from a dinner party ten years ago? . . .

Black women found themselves painfully torn during the hearing and its aftermath. Many black women are reluctant to identify with the causes or rhetoric of white, middle-class feminism. . . . Some of these women supported Thomas either because they mistrusted Hill and her white supporters or because they acknowledged that Hill's story might be true but saw it as irrelevant to the goal of confirming a black Supreme Court justice. They felt racial solidarity trumped gender solidarity.

Other black women identified as feminists. Some expressed outrage at the interpretations being made of Hill, black women, and women generally by black (and other) men. . . . Some black feminists saw Thomas's behavior as analogous to the misogynistic rant of rappers like Ice-T and Snoop Doggy Dogg, and saw no reason to tolerate that treatment. They questioned whether it was a good idea, even in the name of black solidarity and political progress, for women to cover up their mistreatment by black men. . . .

In Hill/Thomas we have to deal with an irreparably frayed and fragmented cultural narrative. There is irreconcilable disagreement on all sides about every aspect of the story: whether the events in Hill's story happened; why Hill behaved as she had, both before and during her Senate testimony; whether the harassment, if it did occur, was significant enough to disrupt Thomas's confirmation; what the uproar was really about; what relations between the sexes, and the races, in the workplace and elsewhere, are really like in the late twentieth century; who "won" Hill/Thomas and why. The last question is open to several answers.

ARGUMENT A: THE RIGHT WON

According to this view, the right maintained its dominance. Thomas was, finally, confirmed; the polls, at least initially, supported his confirmation.[6] . . . But if they had won so resoundingly, why were right-wingers . . . endlessly apoplectic about the hearing and its aftermath? If they had won, why couldn't they let it go? And why hadn't the issue of sexual harassment melted away as the triviality conservatives claimed it was?

ARGUMENT B: THE LEFT WON

According to this view, the right won the battle but not the war: It was a Pyrrhic victory. By forcing the issue of sexual harassment into public notice via the Thomas nomination fight, the right gave women a more prominent public voice and made it clear that many women had opinions different from those of the majority of men.

The laws on sexual harassment have changed, undoubtedly as a result of the public interest aroused by the hearings. More harassment lawsuits were filed, and more were successful. In May of 1992 there was a prolonged inquiry into "Operation Tailhook," in which a group of male Naval aviators were charged with indecent conduct toward female colleagues at their yearly conventions. . . .

Perhaps most significant was the election of 1992. Not only did Bill Clinton win resound-ingly over George Bush (an outcome deemed impossible just a year before), but 20 women were running for Senate seats, of whom 4 succeeded, 150 for the House, of whom 47 were elected. The "ultimate men's club" was a little less of one.

The new respect accorded the concept of sexual harassment culminated in two Supreme Court decisions in June 1998 (*Burlington Industries* v. *Ellerth* and *Farragher* v. *Boca Raton*) which defined relatively precisely the responsibilities of both employers and workers in preventing harassment and specified the circumstances under which employers could be found liable. . . .

ARGUMENT C: NOBODY WON

. . . Some have suggested that the current widespread public disenchantment with and cynicism about government was accelerated by the opportunity to watch the Judiciary Committee come apart on television. . . .

Even if this is true, it's not necessarily a bad thing. If watching our lawmakers in action provokes cynicism, that seems less a problem arising from the televising of government process than a critique of the performers of that process, a realization that could conceivably bring this country closer to a more fully responsive and competent government.[7]

If one aftereffect of Hill/Thomas was to divide the sexes in the workplace more obviously than had been so before, another was to heighten interest in close encounters of the adulterous kind in high places, like the military, Congress, and the Oval Office. . . . And while the public might be split on whether Thomas had actually done what he had been accused of doing, and whether it mattered, there was wide recognition that such behavior was no longer to be construed as "just fooling around." Actions and words that had formerly gone beneath the radar were now out there on public display, and claims had to be either credibly disposed of or acted on by those in positions of power. . . .

. . . The most important aftermath of Hill/Thomas is that it gave women and others the interpretive power they had lacked and gave it to them publicly in front of everyone at the very highest level of public discourse. Anita Hill forced us to accept not merely the term "sexual harassment" and what it implied, but also the right of women to define male behavior for everyone and to give that definition legal standing. The potency and permanence of the slogan "They just don't get it" attests to this. Because of Hill's testimony, women can now contribute fully to the decision about what *it* is and how you *get* it.

NOTES

1. Shown on NBC's *Dateline*, September 29, 1997.

2. *The Complete Transcripts of the Clarence Thomas–Anita Hill Hearings*, Anita Miller, ed. (Chicago: Academy Chicago, 1994), p. 66.

3. If you don't find these differences in the treatment of Hill and Thomas startling, or convincing, try a thought experiment: Imagine Thomas being expected to submit to examinations of his dating behavior, fantasy life, and video preferences, and his mental health becoming a topic of open discussion, while Hill could choose to deflect all such discussions, expressing anger that anyone would even *think* of bringing up her personal life.

4. It is of course true that, at the same time, European culture traditionally desexualized "ladies," that is, "nice" women. But in religion, mythology, and literature, women are sexual predators and destroyers, evil temptresses always bringing good men down (think of Eve, Delilah, and Salome—just for starters).

5. Sexual harassment is better seen as *harassment via the sexual channel* than as sexual behavior per se.

If we could keep this in mind, we would find it much easier to take sexual harassment seriously, as it is intended: as a threat rather than as "just flirting." But since the word "sexual" is attached to the behavior, we permit ourselves to make a dirty joke of it and of those who are involved in it. If they could have seen sexual harassment as sexual merely in surface form, the Democrats might have been less leery of exploring the possibility that Thomas engaged in it. An intriguing and unanswerable question is, would the outcome of the hearing have been different had Hill been white? Quite possibly, I think. The older "chivalrous" male senators might have found the image of Thomas harassing a *white* woman harder to overlook, and might have been reluctant to hypersexualize a white woman in this context.

6. See Ronald Brownstein, "The *Times* Poll: Public Tends to Believe Thomas by 48% to 35%," *Los Angeles Times*, October 14, 1991. This poll sampled 1,264 Americans on October 12 and 13. According to Jane Mayer and Jill Abramson another (unspecified) poll taken in October 1991 showed a 47 percent vs. 24 percent split on the credibility of Thomas vs. Hill. See Mayer and Abramson, *Strange Justice: The Selling of Clarence Thomas* (New York: Houghton Mifflin, 1994), p. 354. Actually, poll data in this case are notoriously hard to interpret. There were many polls, and many communities in which they were taken. So there are different results for black men, black women, white men, white women, and "all." Different polls ask different questions. A poll taken in October 1992 found that a majority of Americans still felt that Thomas should have been confirmed, but 44 percent of Americans believed Hill and only 34 percent Thomas.

7. And pigs fly.

VIVYAN C. ADAIR

Inscriptions of Poverty on the Female Body in the Era of Welfare Reform

In 1996 Congress passed the Welfare Reform Act, ending welfare "as we know it." Getting rid of AFDC (Aid to Families with Dependent Children) and putting welfare recipients to work were two of new law's best-known features. Although there was much about the old welfare system that needed fixing (as the welfare recipients in the National Welfare Rights Organization (NWRO) about whom Kornbluh wrote were the first to point out), the climate in this country had grown more hostile toward welfare recipients with the demise of the NWRO and the backlash against the protests of the 1960s.

With the resurgence of conservatism in the 1970s and especially the emergence of the New Right, welfare recipients who allegedly refused to work or to wed became popular targets of resentment. According to critics, they lived off the tax dollars of hardworking, patriotic whites, who had become victims of government programs that benefited minorities. The particular target in mind was clearly the recipient of an AFDC check—the single mother of several children who, in the minds of welfare critics, was black and sexually promiscuous. Indeed one of the ways welfare detractors succeeded in undercutting support for AFDC was by racializing welfare mothers so they were perceived by the public as nonwhite and morally suspect, and therefore undeserving of public assistance.

This line-drawing between the deserving and the undeserving, the worthy poor and the unworthy poor, the independent and the dependent—and the stigmatizing of the latter—has been an enduring part of our history. In this article Vivyan Adair explores the stigmata evident on the body of the female poor.

How does she suggest bodies are "read"? Do you agree that the "broken and scarred body becomes proof of . . . [the welfare woman's] inner pathology . . . unchecked sexuality . . . and lawlessness"? How do you account for the assumption on the part of many government officials that marriage is the solution? Why the belief that a man—any man—will automatically introduce order and stability into "chaotic" households? Is there a problem, as Adair suggests, with a welfare reform program that shoves adults, especially single mothers of families, into minimum-wage jobs that provide an income too small to pay for adequate housing, nutrition, health care, child care, and heating? What credentials does she bring to her assessment? Do you find it persuasive?

Excerpted from "Branded with Infamy: Inscriptions of Poverty and Class in the United States," by Vivyan C. Adair, *Signs: A Journal of Women in Culture and Society*, vol. 27 (2002): 451–471.

My kids and I been chopped up and spit out just like when I was a kid. My rotten teeth, my kids' twisted feet. My son's dull skin and blank stare. My oldest girl's stooped posture and the way she can't look no one in the eye no more. This all says we got nothing and we deserve what we got. On the street good families look at us and see right away what they'd be if they don't follow the rules. They're scared too, real scared.

—*Welfare recipient and activist, Olympia, Washington, 1998*

I begin with the words of a poor, white, single mother of three. Although officially she has only a tenth-grade education, she expertly reads and articulates a complex theory of power, bodily inscription, and socialization that arose directly from the material conditions of her own life. She sees what many far more "educated" scholars and citizens fail to recognize: that the bodies of poor women and children are produced and positioned as texts that facilitate the mandates of a didactic, profoundly brutal, and mean-spirited political regime. . . .

Recycled images of poor welfare women permeate and shape our national consciousness.[1] Yet—as is so often the case—these images and narratives tell us more about the culture that spawned and embraced them than they do about the object of the culture's obsession. Simple, stable, and often widely skewed cover stories tell us what is "wrong" with some people, what is normative, and what is pathological; by telling us who "bad" poor women are, we reaffirm and reevaluate who we, as a nation and as a people—of allegedly good, middle-class, white, able-bodied, independent, male citizens—are. At their foundations, stories of the welfare mother intersect with . . . and reproduce myriad mythic American narratives associated with a constellation of beliefs about capitalism, male authority, the "nature" of humans, and the sphere of individual freedom, opportunity, and responsibility. These narratives . . . promise to tell the story of who poor women are in ways that allow Americans to maintain a belief in both an economic system based on exploitation and an ideology that claims that we are all beyond exploitation.

These productions orchestrate the story of poverty as one of moral and intellectual lack and of chaos, pathology, promiscuity, illogic, and sloth, juxtaposed always against the order, progress, and decency of "deserving" citizens. . . . These narratives reduce and collapse the lives and experiences of poor women to deceptively simplistic dramas, which are then offered for public consumption. The terms of these dramas are palatable because they are presented as simple oppositions of good and bad, right and wrong, independent and dependent, deserving and undeserving. . . .

I am, and will probably always be, marked as a poor woman. I was raised by a poor, single, white mother who had to struggle to keep her four children fed, sheltered, and clothed by working at what seemed like an endless stream of minimum-wage, exhausting, and demeaning jobs. As a child, poverty was written onto and into my being at the level of private and public thought and body. At an early age my body bore witness to and emitted signs of the painful devaluation carved into my flesh; that same devaluation became integral to my being in the world. . . .

For many poor children this double exposure results in debilitating—albeit politically useful—shame and lack. As Carolyn Kay Steedman reminds us in *Landscape for a Good Woman* (1987 [p. 8]), the mental life of poor children flows from material deprivation. Steedman speaks of the "relentless laying down of guilt" she experienced as a poor child living in a world where identity was shaped through envy and unfulfilled desire and where her own body "told me stories of the terrible unfairness of things, of the subterranean culture of longing for that which one can never have." . . .

In spite of my mother's heroic efforts, at an early age my brothers and sister and I were stooped, bore scars that never healed properly, and limped with feet mangled by ill-fitting, used Salvation Army shoes. When my sister's forehead was split open by a door slammed in frustration, my mother "pasted" the angry wound together on her own, leaving a mark of our inability to afford medical attention, of our lack, on her very forehead. . . . And when throughout elementary school we were sent to the office for mandatory and very public yearly checkups, the school nurse sucked air through her teeth as she donned surgical gloves to check only the hair of poor children for lice.

We were read as unworthy, laughable, and often dangerous. Our schoolmates laughed at our "ugly shoes," our crooked and ill-serviced teeth, and the way we "stank," as teachers excoriated us for our inability to concentrate in school, our "refusal" to come to class prepared with proper school supplies, and our unethical behavior when we tried to take more than our allocated share of "free lunch."[2] . . .

When we sat glued to our seats, afraid to stand in front of the class in ragged and ill-fitting hand-me-downs, we were held up as examples of unprepared and uncooperative children. And when our grades reflected our otherness, they were used to justify even more elaborate punishment that exacerbated the effects of our growing anomie. . . .

As children, our disheveled and broken bodies were produced and read as signs of our inferiority and undeservedness. As adults, our mutilated bodies are read as signs of inner chaos, immaturity, and indecency as we are punished and then read as proof of the need for further discipline and punishment. When my already bad teeth started to rot and I was out of my head with pain, my choices as an adult welfare recipient were either to let my teeth fall out or to have them pulled out. In either case the culture would then read me as a "toothless illiterate," as a fearful joke. . . .

A neighbor of mine went back to the man who continued to beat her and her scarred children after being denied welfare benefits when she realized that she could not adequately feed, clothe, and house her family on her own minimum-wage income. My good friend sold her ovum to a fertility clinic in a painful and potentially damaging process. Other friends exposed themselves to all manner of danger and disease by selling their bodies for sex in order to feed and clothe their babies.

Poverty becomes a vicious cycle that is written on our bodies and intimately connected with our value in the world. Our children need healthy food so that we can continue working; yet working at minimum-wage jobs, we have no money for wholesome food and very little time to care for our families. So our children get sick, we lose our jobs to take care of them, we fall deeper and deeper into debt before our next unbearable job, and then we really cannot afford medical care. . . . The food banks we gratefully drag our exhausted children to on the weekends hand out bags of rancid candy bars, hot dogs that have passed their expiration dates, stale broken pasta, and occasionally a bag of wrinkled apples. We are either fat or skinny, and we seem always irreparably ill. Our emaciated or bloated bodies are then read as a sign of lack of discipline and as proof that we have failed to care as we should.[3]

Exhaustion also marks the bodies of poor women in indelible script. Rest becomes a privilege we simply cannot afford. After working full shifts each day, poor mothers trying to support themselves at minimum-wage jobs continue to work to a point of exhaustion that is inscribed on their faces, their bodies, their posture, and their diminishing sense of self and value in the world. . . .

. . . Those who need the respite less go away for weekends, take drives in the woods, take their kids to the beach. . . .

Ultimately, we come to recognize that our bodies are not our own, that they are rather public property. State-mandated blood tests, interrogation of the most private aspects of our lives, the public humiliation of having to beg officials for food and medicine, and the loss of all right to privacy, teach us that our bodies are only useful as lessons, warnings, and signs of degradation that everyone loves to hate. In "From Welfare to Academe: Welfare Reform as College-Educated Welfare Mothers Know It," Sandy Smith-Madsen describes the erosion of her privacy as a poor welfare mother:

> I was investigated. I was spied upon. A welfare investigator c[a]me into my home and after thoughtful deliberation granted me permission to keep my belongings. . . . Full-fledged citizens have the right to deny an officer entry into their home unless they possess a search warrant; welfare mothers fork over citizenship rights for the price of a welfare check. In Tennessee, constitutional rights go for a cash value of $185 per month for a family of three. [In press, 185.]

Welfare reform policy is designed to publicly expose, humiliate, punish, and display "deviant" welfare mothers. "Workfare" and "Learnfare"—two alleged successes of welfare reform—require that landlords, teachers, and employers be made explicitly aware of the second-class status of these very public bodies. In Ohio, the Department of Human Services uses tax dollars to pay for advertisements on the side of Cleveland's RTA buses that show a "Welfare Queen" behind bars with a logo that proclaims "Crime does not pay. Welfare fraud is a crime."[4] . . . In Eugene, recipients who cannot afford to feed their children adequately on their food stamp allocations are advised through fliers issued by a contractor for Oregon's welfare agency to "check the dump and the residential and business dumpsters" in order to save money.[5] . . . And welfare reform legislation enacted in 1996 as the Personal Responsibility and Work Opportunities Reconciliation Act (PRWORA) requires that poor mothers work full-time, earning minimum-wage salaries with which they cannot support their children. Since these women are often denied medical, dental, and child-care benefits and are unable to provide their families with adequate food, heat, or clothing, through this legislation the state mandates child neglect and abuse. The crowds of good parents and their growing children watch and learn. . . .

Spectacular cover stories of the "Welfare Queen" play and replay in the national mind's eye, becoming a prescriptive lens through which the American public as a whole reads the individual dramas of the bodies of poor women and their place and value in the world. These dramas produce "normative" citizens as independent, stable, rational, ordered, and free. . . . The poor welfare mother is . . . the embodiment of dependency, disorder, disarray, and otherness. Her broken and scarred body becomes proof of her inner pathology and chaos, suggesting the need for further punishment and discipline.

In contemporary narratives welfare women are imagined to be dangerous because they refuse to sacrifice their desires and fail to participate in legally sanctioned heterosexual relationships; theirs is read, as a result, as a selfish, "unnatural," and immature sexuality. . . . In this androcentric equation fathers become the sole bearers of order and of law, defending poor women and children against their own unchecked sexuality and lawlessness.

For Republican senator [and future attorney general] John Ashcroft writing in the *St. Louis Dispatch,* the inner city is the site of "rampant illegitimacy" and a "space devoid of discipline" where all values are askew. For Ashcroft, what is insidious is not material poverty but an entitlement system that has allowed "out-of-control" poor women to rupture traditional patriarchal authority, valuation, and boundaries.[6] Impoverished communities then become a site of chaos because without fathers they allegedly lack any organizing or patrolling principle. George Gilder agrees with Ashcroft when he writes in the conservative *American Spectator* that "the key problem of the welfare culture is not unemployed women and poor children. It is the women's skewed and traumatic relationships with men. In a reversal of the pattern of civilized societies, the women have the income and the ties to government authority and support." . . .

William Raspberry frames poor women as selfish and immature, when in "Ms. Smith Goes after Washington," he claims, "Unfortunately AFDC [Aid to Families with Dependent Children] is paid to an unaccountable, accidental, and unprepared parent who has chosen her head of household status as a personal form of satisfaction, while lacking the simple life skills and maturity to achieve love and job fulfillment from any other source. I submit that all of our other social ills—crime, drugs, violence, failing schools—are a direct result of the degradation of parenthood by emotionally immature recipients."[7] Raspberry goes on to assert that, like poor children, poor mothers must be made visible reminders to the rest of the culture of the "poor choices" they have made. He claims that rather than "coddling" her, we have a responsibility to "shame her" and to use her failure to teach other young women that it is "morally wrong for unmarried women to bear children," as we "cast single motherhood as a selfish and immature act." . . .

Race is clearly written on the body of the poor single mother. The welfare mother, imagined as young, never married, and black (contrary to statistical evidence), is positioned as dangerous and in need of punishment because she "naturally" emasculates her own men, refuses to service white men, and passes on— rather than appropriate codes of subservience and submission—a disruptive culture of resistance, survival, and "misplaced" pride to her children.[8] In stark contrast, widowed women with social security and divorced women with child support and alimony are imagined as white, legal, and propertied mothers whose value rests on their abilities to stay in their homes, care for their own children, and impart traditional cultural mores to their offspring, all for the betterment of the dominant culture. . . .

Here the welfare mother is read as both the product and the producer of a culture of disease and disorder. These narratives imagine poor women as a powerful contagion capable of infecting, perhaps even lying in wait to infect, their own children as raced, gendered, and classed agents of their "diseased" nature. . . .

These representations position welfare mothers' bodies as sites of destruction and as catalysts for a culture of depravity and disobedience; in the process they produce a reading of the writing on the body of the poor woman that calls for further punishment and discipline. In New York City, "Workfare" programs force *lazy* poor women to take a job—"any job"—including working for the city wearing orange surplus prison uniforms picking up garbage on the highway and in parks for about $1.10 per hour.[9]

"Bridefare" programs in Wisconsin give added benefits to *licentious* welfare women who marry a man—"any man"—and publish a celebration of their "reform" in local newspapers. "Tidyfare" programs across the nation allow state workers to enter and inspect the homes of poor *slovenly* women so that they can monetarily sanction families whose homes are not deemed to be appropriately tidied.[10] . . . Despite the rhetoric and policy that mark and mutilate our bodies, poor women survive. Hundreds of thousands of us are somehow good parents despite the systems that are designed to prohibit us from being so. We live on the unlivable and teach our children love, strength, and grace. . . .

If we somehow manage to find a decent pair of shoes, or save our food stamps to buy our children a birthday cake, we are accused of being cheats or living too high. If our children suffer, it is read as proof of our inferiority and bad mothering; if they succeed, we are suspect for being too pushy, for taking more than our share of free services, or for having too much free time to devote to them. Yet, as former welfare recipient Janet Diamond says in the introduction to *For Crying Out Loud*: "In spite of public censure, welfare mothers graduate from school, get decent jobs, watch their children achieve, make good lives for themselves. Welfare mothers continue to be my inspiration, not because they survive, but because they dare to dream. Because when you

are a welfare recipient, laughter is an act of rebellion."[11] . . .

NOTES

1. Throughout this essay I use the terms *welfare recipient* and *poor working women* interchangeably because as the recent Urban Institute study made clear, today these populations are, in fact, one and the same. See Pamela Loprest, "Families Who Left Welfare: Who Are They and How Are They Doing?" Urban Institute, Washington, D.C. (August 1991), B1.

2. As recently as 1993, in my daughter's public elementary school cafeteria, "free lunchers" (poor children who could not otherwise afford to eat lunch, including my daughter) were reminded with a large and colorful sign to "line up last."

3. Adolescent psychologist Martha Root claims that a beautiful or "fit" body becomes equated with "purity, discipline—basically with goodness." See Joan DeClaire, "Body by Barbie," *View* (October 1993):36.

4. Valerie Robinson, "State's Ad Attacks the Poor," *Plain Dealer* (November 2, 1999):B8.

5. Women's Enews, 2001a. "Civil Rights Bad for Welfare Moms." Mailing list, available online at http://www.womensenews.org, May 4.

6. John Ashcroft, "Illegitimacy Rampant," *St. Louis Dispatch* (July 2, 1995):A23.

7. William Raspberry, "Ms. Smith Goes After Washington," *Washington Post* (February 1, 1995):A19.

8. See Patricia Hill Collins, *Black Feminist Thought: Knowledge, Consciousness, and the Politics of Empowerment* (New York: Routledge, 2000). In the two years directly preceding the passage of the PRWORA, as a part of sweeping welfare reform, in the United States the largest percentage of people on welfare were white (39 percent), and fewer than 10 percent were teen mothers (U.S. Department of Health and Human Services, 1994).

9. Peter Dreier, "Treat Welfare Recipients Like Workers," *Los Angeles Times* (August 29, 1999):M6.

10. "Tidyfare" programs additionally required that caseworkers inventory the belongings of Aid to Families with Dependent Children (AFDC; welfare) recipients so that they could require them to "sell-down" their assets. In my own case, in 1994 a Section 8 inspector from the U.S. Department of Housing and Urban Development came into my home, counted my daughter's books, checked them against his list to see that as a nine-year-old she was entitled to have only twelve books, calculated what he perceived to be the value of the excess books, and then had my welfare check reduced by that amount the following month.

11. Diane Dujon and Ann Withorn, *For Crying Out Loud: Women's Poverty in the United States* (Boston: South End, 1996), p. 1.

CARMEN TERESA WHALEN
Sweatshops Here and There: The Garment Industry, Latinas, and Labor Migrations

Long before the industrial revolution, women worked in the garment trades. As clothing production was mechanized, women were employed in small shops and large factories. Their demands for decent wages and livable hours have been behind many of the most effective labor reforms: federal and state minimum wage and maximum hour legislation of the early twentieth century, occupational health and safety standards of the post–World War II decades. But pressures to erode those standards have been and continue to be strong.

In this essay, Carmen Whalen considers the impact of global markets on the clothing industry in the United States in the second half of the twentieth century. What connections does she find between economic development in the United States and the growth of low-wage jobs at home and in Latin America? Compare the conditions she finds in contemporary workplaces to those described by Pauline Newman on pp. 342–44. To what extent has the garment industry in New York City provided opportunity for women workers? How does she describe the impact of globalization on women's jobs?

In 1991, an advertisement in a trade magazine sought to lure the U.S. garment industry to El Salvador. The ad revealed key elements that had come to define the globalization of the garment industry and its impact on Latinas. Across the top in bold print, it announced, "Quality, Industriousness, and Reliability Is What El Salvador Offers You!" Just beneath this was the picture of a young woman working at a sewing machine, her eyes focused on the machine in front of her. She was surrounded by piles of material on one side and neatly folded shirts complete with tags on the other. The ad continued, "Rosa Martinez produces apparel for U.S. markets on her sewing machine in El Salvador. *You* can hire her for thirty-three cents an hour." Rosa's wages had declined, as the same ad the previous year had boasted wages of fifty-seven cents an hour. In addition to low wages, there were other advantages, "Rosa is more than just colorful.

She and her co-workers are known for their industriousness, reliability and quick learning. They make El Salvador one of the best buys." El Salvador also offered potential investors "excellent road and sea transportation," Central America's "most modern airport," and "*no* quotas," indicating that U.S. companies could produce and export as much as they wished. Placed by an organization that was funded in large part by the U.S. government through the U.S. Agency for International Development, the ad highlighted the U.S. government's role in promoting export processing zones, as well as the centrality of the garment industry, and the key combination of low wages and women's labor.[1]

From the post–World War II era to the present, the U.S. garment industry has turned to Latinas as a source of low-wage workers in their countries of origin and as migrants to the United States. The globalization of the gar-

Excerpted from "Sweatshops Here and There: The Garment Industry, Latinas, and Labor Migrations," by Carmen Teresa Whalen, *International Labor and Working-Class History* 61 (April 2002, Cambridge University Press):45–68. Notes have been edited and renumbered. Reprinted by permission of the author, *International Labor and Working-Class History*, and Cambridge University Press.

ment industry has meant the proliferation of export processing zones overseas and of sweatshops in U.S. cities. . . .

[After World War II] the garment industry relocated to Puerto Rico, [as] Puerto Rican women migrated and found garment industry jobs . . . in urban areas in Puerto Rico, [in New York City,] and elsewhere in the States. Yet the postwar economic boom in New York gave way to the industry's continued relocation to lower-wage areas, and Puerto Rican women confronted fewer jobs and deteriorating working conditions. Dominican women then encountered this changed labor market, as they became the next group of Latinas incorporated into New York's garment industry, while also experiencing the impact of export processing in the Dominican Republic.

Immigration is often portrayed as something that happens *to* the United States and that is problematic precisely because the United States does *not* control the process. . . . [Yet] the globalization of the garment industry provides an example of the economic and political connections between the United States and countries of origin that shape migrations, particularly from the region that the United States has historically defined as its backyard. In addition, the experiences of Puerto Rican and Dominican women provide an important basis for exploring how the globalization of labor-intensive industries, like the garment industry, fostered the labor migrations of women and deteriorating economic conditions in the inner cities. . . .

[After World War II] the political ties between the United States and Puerto Rico facilitated the emergence of patterns of investment and migration that would be repeated in other countries. Puerto Rico's policymakers crafted an economic development strategy based on industrialization by invitation, and the U.S. garment industry relocated to Puerto Rico to take advantage of low wages for women, as well as tax and other incentives. . . .

. . . Because of the political ties between Puerto Rico and the United States, Puerto Rico provided a safe and profitable investment site for U.S. capital. The United States took control of Puerto Rico in 1898 at the end of the Spanish American War and has retained sovereignty to the present day. In 1917, the U.S. Congress made Puerto Ricans U.S. citizens and

exempted individuals and businesses in Puerto Rico from federal income taxes. In 1947, Puerto Rico's policymakers extended this tax break by instituting their own tax exemptions. . . . U.S. companies could now manufacture goods in Puerto Rico tax-free and then "export" those goods to the States without having to pay "import" duties. As a former employee of Puerto Rico's Economic Development Administration, David Ross suggested in 1969, it was "freedom from taxes without leaving the United States."[2] Despite political ties, federal minimum wages were not applied in Puerto Rico until the late 1970s, so that wages were significantly lower than those in the States.[3] . . .

The garment industry came to Puerto Rico to reap the potential profits. . . .

The home needlework industry was, as economist Harvey Perloff noted in 1950, "developed chiefly by mainland capital" and "based essentially on cheap labor." Through a system of contractors and subcontractors, materials were shipped from the U.S. mainland, contractors in Puerto Rico handled the distribution and collection of materials, and rural women added the hand details at home, earning piecework wages. The finished products were shipped back to the States for marketing.[4] By the late 1950s, the home needlework industry declined, and factory work increased. Yet, these key dynamics remained . . .

The garment industry was central to Puerto Rico's industrialization, and women's labor was central to the garment industry. . . .

By 1963, plants established by Puerto Rico's Economic Development Administration, or Fomento, employed 70,000 workers, with 60 percent of the new jobs filled by women. In 1970, apparel was the largest industrial employer and 87 percent of the workers were women. Women's labor force participation increased as a result, from 21 to 25 percent between 1950 and 1970, while men's declined from 71 to 59 percent.[5] Wage differentials, tax exemptions, and profits remained central to Fomento's efforts to recruit the U.S. apparel industry. . . .

[In] 1972 . . . garment workers earned an average of $2.67 an hour in the United States compared to $1.76 in Puerto Rico . . . [and] firms in Puerto Rico were almost two-and-a-half times more profitable than those in the

States before taxes, and were more than four and a half times more profitable after taxes.[6] . . . [But] Puerto Rico demonstrated that economic development based on export processing and labor-intensive industries failed to generate sufficient employment. New manufacturing jobs in urban areas did not replace the jobs lost in rural areas, as Puerto Rico's agriculture and home needlework industry declined. As Ross noted, "No one could greatly lament the passing of an industry which made a sweatshop of every poor man's home in some sections of the island; except that this industry provided desperately needed income for several times the number of families that had been benefitted by the Development Company."[7] Total employment in Puerto Rico declined during the 1950s. As a result, Puerto Rico's industrialization coincided with massive migration.

As Puerto Rico's rural economies declined, Puerto Rican women became labor migrants, going to nearby towns, as well as to urban areas in Puerto Rico and the States in search of work. Doña Genara, who was born in 1926 in a rural area, recalled, "We started to leave the *barrio* little by little and to look for work." For Doña Genara, moving to the nearby town to live with her sister in the early 1950s enabled her to attend a vocational training program that taught embroidering, knitting, and sewing by machine. After the training program, she explained, "I stayed mostly at my sister's house because in the country there still wasn't any electricity. So I stayed to do my work." Her first job was in a knitting shop, where she earned $12.80 for the week, "But we had to work fast, if not, they fired you." After two years, the shop closed. Doña Genara turned to knitting homework, working longer hours and earning less money, "Three dozen, it was thirty-six hats to earn four dollars. . . . I didn't have time for anything. I worked about ten or twelve hours [a day]." She saw few options, "I always worked in knitting, because there wasn't anything else, I mean in my town."[8]

Seeing few options in Puerto Rico's rural areas and towns, other women migrated to urban areas in Puerto Rico and the States. . . . Sixty-four percent of women were migrating [to the States] because they had a job offer or were looking for work, according to a 1952 survey. The others were joining family members, and perhaps would look for work as well.[9] . . .

According to needlework employers in San Juan in a 1953 survey, migration to the States was one of the primary reasons their workers quit. A year later a study in Philadelphia found that 48 percent of women had last worked as operatives in Puerto Rico and only 28 percent identified themselves as housewives.[10] . . . Policymakers fostered migration, providing training programs and alerting potential migrants to the availability of jobs in the States. As one policymaker commented in 1948, "Any man or woman who can earn a substandard living at needle work in Puerto Rico can earn a standard living at the hosiery plants around Philadelphia."[11] . . . [Doña Genara] found work easily, "As soon as I arrived from Puerto Rico, I started in that factory." . . . "I wanted to come for a better life," . . . said Doña Genara, adding, "I earned more money. . . . In Puerto Rico I earned twelve dollars a week and here I earned forty, they took out two, I kept thirty-eight."

Finding jobs readily available, Puerto Rican women helped each other migrate and get garment industry jobs. . . . Doña Juanita came to Philadelphia with the help of her sister . . . in 1953 because "there wasn't any work." Doña Juanita's first job was in the garment factory where her sister worked, making men's suits. Their neighbors from Naguabo, a family of twelve, gradually made their way to Philadelphia. . . . They all worked in the garment industry, as Doña Juanita explained, "because there were a lot of garment factories in Philadelphia. You would get a factory job anywhere."[12]

At the end of World War II, Puerto Rican women in New York City were entering what was still the center of the U.S. garment industry.[13] . . . In 1947, New York City accounted for 40 percent of U.S. employment in women and children's apparel, and the New York metropolitan region accounted for 49 percent. . . . In 1953, New York City still produced 78 percent of unit-priced dresses, 73 percent of coats and suits, 72 percent of blouses, and 68 percent of underwear.[14] . . .

As a result of their labor migrations, Puerto Rican women became concentrated in New York City's garment industry, but only within certain trades. During the 1940s, Puerto Ricans became the "major new source" of labor for the undergarments trade, and constituted half of the skirt industry's labor force. Puerto Ricans, along with African Americans, constituted half of the new members of the unit-priced dresses local by 1948. Puerto Ricans became the largest ethnic group in dressmaking, skirts, and blouses. The skirt and dress trades, however, were the lowest skilled and lowest paid trades. Puerto Ricans had not found work in the skilled and higher paid suit trades; nor had they entered the skilled cutters' and pressers' locals.[15] . . .

Nevertheless, contemporary observers failed to consider Puerto Rican women as labor migrants. . . . [For example,] economist Raymond Vernon excluded Puerto Rican women from the ranks of labor migrants. . . . "Some of the Puerto Rican women, for instance, probably came to the mainland because of their husband's job opportunities, not their own, then joined the labor force when they discovered that some apparel plants were begging for their services." From this perspective, labor migration was a male phenomenon, while women followed "their" men and "discovered" work in the receiving society.[16]

Even with the postwar boom in the garment industry . . . journalist Dan Wakefield [wrote,] "The seventy-two hour week, at less than a dollar an hour, sounds like a tale of life in the New York sweatshops of thirty years ago. To the lady at the Sano garment shop, it was not a remote fact of history but a fact of life in Spanish Harlem in 1958." She earned \$.35 per garment, regardless of the difficulty of the piece, and the most she had ever earned was seventy dollars in a week, a feat she accomplished by working from 7:00 A.M. to 7:00 P.M. for six days. In union shops, piece rates were set based on the difficulty of the piece, with some set at \$.70 to \$.90. . . .

Wakefield considered the "farmed-out needlework of garment shops" and "the small often fly-by-night dress shops" as "the main chance of employment within the neighborhood," and concluded that "very few girls grow up in these streets without getting a touch of it."[17] In Philadelphia, most of Doña Genara's shops were represented by the Amalgamated Clothing Workers of America, and she considered these good jobs, "The factory was good. The bosses were good. It was good work." Yet in one of her shops, "They didn't turn in social security, they found themselves

in trouble. . . . It seems they didn't pay taxes or something, I don't know. And we had to go to another factory." Others did homework, "I didn't sew at home . . . but I saw a lot of people sewing at home. . . . They got homework . . . because the factory gave them clothes to sew at home." . . .

The availability of garment industry jobs gave women a certain leverage in the labor market, enabling them to switch jobs for better conditions or to struggle to improve conditions in their shops. Doña María, who had confronted her boss about piecework rates, did not appreciate being fired in front of fifty coworkers. Returning to work with the help of the union, she waited until her skills on the machine were needed and then quit, creating a predicament for her boss. "I worked Monday and Tuesday and on Wednesday I didn't report to work. I went next door and I find another job, this time in bathing suits. . . . They paid me about seventy-five cents a garment which at that time, this was in 1956, was good money."[18] . . .

Similarly, Doña Anastasia left her first job. "So when I found that I wasn't satisfied but already had the experience to work on any machine, I said 'No, I'm not staying here. I'm going somewhere else.'" As the "chairlady" in one of her factories, Doña Anastasia helped other women and took their complaints to the union, contrary to her boss's wishes.[19] . . .

Women also learned to sew on the job. . . .

Upon arriving in New York in 1948, Doña María realized, "All the jobs available were for sewing machine operators and I said to myself. 'My God, I have to learn to sew.'" She taught herself to sew by getting jobs and getting fired after fifteen minutes or less, but with more practice each time.[20] . . .

As Puerto Ricans entered the garment industry in large numbers, wages declined. The garment industry was shifting from a higher paying to a lower paying industry, and New York City itself was changing from a high to a low wage area.[21] Between 1946 and 1949, wages in the dress trade, a major employer of Puerto Rican women, decreased from \$1.44 to \$1.37, while wages for all manufacturing increased from \$1.08 to \$1.40.[22] The deskilling of the industry continued. As consumer demand shifted to casual wear, the more simple, standardized garments could be produced by unskilled workers. Garment production was broken down into particular tasks or section work, with each worker responsible for a single task. These tasks were increasingly parceled out to contracting shops, which relied heavily on the labor of Puerto Rican and African American women. . . .

[D]eskilling, section work, and contracting lessened the industry's dependence on New York City, with its skilled labor force. . . . [As] improvements in transportation lowered the costs of conducting business beyond . . . [New York City's] limits . . . high rents, limited manufacturing space, and traffic congestion increased the cost of doing business in the city.

Employment in New York's apparel industry plummeted. . . . Between 1947 and 1982, New York City's share of production of women and children's apparel decreased from 42 to 16 percent. Employment in the apparel industry decreased by 54,000 jobs between 1947 and 1958, and the next decade witnessed the loss of another 72,000 jobs. . . . By 1975, fewer than 150,000 people worked in apparel, just one-third of the 1969 labor force.[23] . . . Wages in the apparel industry continued to decline relative to other manufacturing wages. In 1977 garment workers earned just 64 percent of average manufacturing wages, a sharp contrast to 95 percent in 1947. Nevertheless, labor still constituted 27 percent of the production costs in apparel, in contrast to 10 percent for manufacturing as a whole, propelling the industry's search for cheaper labor.[24]

The continued globalization of the garment industry meant that Puerto Rican women in New York City confronted fewer jobs, economic displacement, and deteriorating working conditions.

In 1969, the *New York Times* reported "an increase in illegal home work."[25] During the 1970s, an estimated 400 to 600 nonunion shops operated in the Bronx, employing primarily Puerto Rican and Dominican workers, according to one union organizer. A Puerto Rican woman, who worked a forty-five hour week with days up to fifteen hours, averaged fifty-four dollars per week without any benefits, at a time when union wages ranged from eighty-five to ninety-five dollars for a thirty-five hour week. . . .

As the garment industry continued its search for cheap labor via sweatshops in the States and continued relocation, Puerto Rican

women became displaced labor migrants. . . . Poverty among Puerto Ricans in the inner city increased, and Puerto Rican women turned to the state for the financial assistance they needed to sustain their households.[26] In Philadelphia, Doña Genara described the change. "All those lots that are vacant over there, those were factories." Some jobs disappeared, while as anthropologist Judith Goode notes, "A somewhat clandestine garment industry has developed based on Korean and Chinese capital and using newcomer Asian labor."[27] . . .

This was the labor market that Dominican women then confronted. . . . The growth of export processing zones in the Dominican Republic echoed Puerto Rico's economic development. Policymakers in the Dominican Republic lured foreign investment through incentives that resembled those in Puerto Rico, while U.S. policymakers instituted trade policies to promote the assembly of manufactured goods abroad. . . .

U.S. policymakers facilitated overseas investment in ways that made the Dominican Republic and other Caribbean nations more like Puerto Rico. Trade policies reduced tariffs and hence the costs for U.S. firms doing business beyond the boundaries of the United States. Beginning with Tariff Item 807, the U.S. reduced the duties on imports that were made from U.S. components but processed or assembled abroad. Tariffs were collected only on the "value added" or on the low-wage labor that companies had sought. From 1965 to 1983, the value of Item 807 imports increased from $578 million to $9,226 million. Mexico sent the most in 1983, over $156 million worth of Item 807 clothing exports, and the Dominican Republic was second, sending almost $130 million.[28] . . .

[In 1986] the Caribbean Basin Textile Access Program provided unlimited [tariff-free] access to the U.S. market for apparel products provided that the fabric was made and cut in the United States. . . . In addition to favorable trade policies, the U.S. government has provided financial assistance to firms that invest overseas, as well as to the governments of host countries that welcome them. . . .

As in Puerto Rico, policymakers in the Dominican Republic . . . exempted industries from local taxes, from customs duties on imported capital and semi-finished goods, and from export duties on finished or semi-finished goods. Employment in manufacturing increased from 20,000 to 47,562 between 1968 and 1977. More than 125 subsidiaries of U.S. firms were among those providing manufacturing jobs.[29] The number of free-trade zones, foreign investment, and imports to the United States all increased dramatically between the mid-1980s and the early 1990s. By 1988, garments accounted for 78 percent of manufacturing exports. In that same year, 63 percent of export-processing firms were U.S. owned, while only 10 percent were Dominican owned. Indeed, most garment factories were direct subsidiaries of U.S. transnational corporations rather than subcontractors.[30]

The U.S. garment industry relied on the low-wage labor of Dominican women in the export processing zones. . . . In 1984, U.S. apparel workers earned an average of $7.00 an hour. Between 1984 and 1990, wages in the Dominican Republic plummeted from $1.33 to $.56 an hour. Meanwhile, industrial exports grew to $850 million in 1991. By 1991, women held three-fourths of the 135,000 jobs in the free-trade zones. Between 1960 and 1990, women's labor force participation increased from 9 to 38 percent, while men's decreased from 76 to 72 percent. This was a more dramatic increase in women's labor force participation than among Puerto Rican women.[31] . . .

Economic development via export-oriented industrialization fostered internal and international migration. . . . During the first half of the 1990s, [Dominican] immigration averaged over 26,000 per year, and by 1997, 832,000 Dominicans lived in the United States. Sixty percent lived in New York City, where Dominicans were the fastest growing ethnic group and constituted the second-largest Latino group after Puerto Ricans.[32]

Dominican women became labor migrants. As early as 1970, anthropologist Nancie L. González observed that ". . . women find jobs more easily from afar than men. . . . Most of the women work as domestics or in the garment industry." For undocumented workers, "there are many jobs available in New York where employers are glad to avoid having to pay their own share and can thus lower the wages since the employee then has no deductions."[33] . . .

Dominican women found garment industry jobs readily available in New York City.

The garment industry, according to González, was one of "the few avenues open to these women to improve their situation." "For the working-class woman, work is available, regular, and though poorly paid by United States standards, nevertheless enables her to live better than at home."[34] . . . As Dominican women continued to migrate to New York City, they became concentrated in the now downgraded garment industry. As Sherri Grasmuck and Patricia Pessar explain . . . "Our female informants voiced concern that garment work was virtually the only avenue of 'honorable' employment opened to female immigrants with little or no proficiency in English."[35] . . .

Still, women's labor migration continued. . . . Women accounted for 59 percent of all Dominican immigrants in the United States in 1996, and most immigrants were young. . . . Like Puerto Rican women, Dominican women who migrated in search of work, found themselves concentrated in low-wage jobs and then displaced.

. . . While changes in the garment industry may have created some opportunities for ethnic entrepreneurs, most Dominican women . . . found low-paid, dead-end jobs, less demand for labor, and deteriorating working conditions. Their options and leverage in the garment industry were much more circumscribed than those initially encountered by Puerto Rican women in the postwar era. . . .

In describing their shop, workers emphasized the long hours, strict supervision, the tiring pace of the work, and the low wages. One worker summarized the conditions as, "a lot of work and a little money."[36] Their regular work week was Monday through Fridays from 7:30 A.M. to 5:30 P.M., with breaks from 12:00 to 12:30 and from 4:00 to 4:15; and Saturdays from 7:30 A.M. to 4:00 P.M., with just the one break from 12:00 to 12:30, a total of fifty-three-and-a-half hours. During busy times, they were expected to work late and occasionally on Sundays and holidays, as Nerida [who left the Dominican Republic in search of work in 1993] recounted, "Maybe until 7:00 at night, or 7:30, or 8:00, until the time they say that there's work, depending on whether I want to stay. . . . If there is enough work in the factory, almost always there is enough work until after 5:30 and there is work seven days a week or six. . . . The latest I have stayed, not always, until 10:00 at night." While stating that overtime was optional, workers suggested that there were repercussions for those unwilling to work overtime and added that they needed the money.[37]

The work pace is intense . . . compared to working in stores, Nerida found.

> It was a bit more difficult, because when you are used to working with people, it is more difficult to work in a shop where you have to be quiet, you can't talk, you can't go to the bathroom as many times as you could in the store. You have to be standing in the same place—in the store you are walking, you get less tired.

The faster pace also increased the potential for injuries.

> The machine that is used for packing, if you put your hand in, it can cut it. If it doesn't completely catch your hand, it will burn it. . . . I have burned myself many times, many times. . . . Almost always it happens when you are more pressured because there is a lot of work. In trying to do the work a little faster, you forget yourself and you forget that your hand is there.

Workers who pressed also suffered from burns. . . .

For Nerida meeting her household expenses as well as balancing her job and household responsibilities presented challenges. She had remarried [since arriving in] the U.S. and was living with her husband and their daughter, while sending money to the Dominican Republic to support her first child. Household finances were tight. "If the work is good, I work the whole week, for example until 7:00 at night, I can pay my bills. . . . If this week I don't work much, I pay the babysitter, I can't pay any bills. So, yeah, it depends on how the work is." Her husband contributed financially, working as a wholesale delivery driver, and shared in household chores and childcare. She described their daily routine:

> I leave the factory at 7:00. I get home at 8:00, 8:15. I get a bath and I eat. Basically, I get together the things for the baby for the next day. I prepare lunch, look for clothes, it's already time to go to bed. Before I leave [in the morning], I don't have to do anything because . . . he gets the baby ready to take her to the babysitter because he leaves later than I do.

Her husband also picked up their daughter after work and cooked dinner, as he came home earlier than she did. Nerida and her hus-

band were both taking English classes, on different nights so that one of them was home with their daughter. They barely saw each other. "He arrives from class at 10:00, I arrive home more or less at 10:00 . . . about half an hour, an hour, we go to bed."

In defining a "sweatshop," Nerida pointed to the physical conditions, exploitation, and oppressive supervision. Her current shop paid the minimum wage of $5.15, and time-and-a-half for overtime. Workers were paid weekly, by check, their shop had never missed a payroll, and workers were not owed back wages. Workers had been paid off the books and in cash only on rare occasions, mostly for holidays, Sundays, and excessive overtime. But there were no benefits, except unemployment once workers were eligible. Seasonal fluctuations meant overwork at times, and layoffs at others, decreasing workers' incomes and providing supervisors with a means to reprimand workers. Was it a sweatshop? Nerida answered:

> That term, I believe means because where you work that is where you leave your sweat. . . . I think that word should be used for when there is exploitation in the shops. Even though all of them are exploiters, but some are more extreme than others. But I suppose that term should be used where it is really believed that the workers are being exploited. . . . I think that [my shop] would fall in the middle. . . .

Nerida concluded:

> . . . It's sort of difficult to know that you are sacrificing so much for work and at the end of the year you say, "Let me see how much I've saved." When you see it's a pittance. . . . That's the bad thing about this country.

Long hours, low wages, and layoffs strained her household economy and her aspirations.

Dominicans' economic status has parallels to that of Puerto Ricans, suggesting the impact of the garment industry in shaping not only women's migration patterns, but also the well-being of migrants in the city. . . . Like Puerto Rican women, Dominican women had gone from higher than average to lower than average labor-force participation. And Dominicans were still overrepresented as operators, laborers, and fabricators: 36 percent of all Dominicans in contrast to 12 percent of workers citywide. Dominican women were especially concentrated in manufacturing: 33 percent compared to 18 percent of Dominican men in 1990. As New York began to witness a growing disparity in incomes during the 1990s, Dominicans' earnings decreased. Poverty levels increased from 37 to 46 percent for Dominicans and from 17 to 24 percent citywide between 1989 and 1996.[38]

While their low-wage labor may have kept some garment industry jobs in New York City, for Dominican women, working in the garment industry has increasingly meant a life of working poverty for individuals, as well as households and communities confronting poverty.

Parallels in the experiences of Puerto Rican and Dominican women suggest that the globalization of the garment industry is resulting in repeating patterns of economic displacement, labor migration, and sweatshop jobs in U.S. cities. The garment industry continues to be marked by relocation and by the persistence of sweatshops here and there. The garment industry figures prominently in a particular model of economic development based on export-oriented industrialization and foreign, often U.S., investment. In both Puerto Rico and the Dominican Republic this model was accompanied by internal and international migration as insufficient employment and wages too low to sustain households sent people in search of work; Latinas became labor migrants. These economies remain dependent and mired in low-wage assembly jobs that are always poised to relocate to even lower-wage areas. . . . As the ad at the beginning of this essay suggests, export-processing zones and the garment industry have spread to Central American countries and elsewhere, bringing the same model of economic development to different countries at different times. Displaced, Latinas will likely continue their search for paid employment that will sustain their households.

Meanwhile, Latinas working in New York City's garment industry have become more diverse, with many coming from countries where the U.S. garment industry and export processing zones have taken hold. Here too, competition and contracting exert a relentless downward pressure on wages, creating jobs that are notable for their low wages, long hours, pressured pace, harsh supervision, poor working conditions, and instability, as the possibility of shop relocation to lower-wage areas remains

a constant and very real threat. For Puerto Rican and Dominican women, as well as for newcomer Latinas, the garment industry has been one of few avenues for employment. Yet garment industry jobs have translated into working poverty, offering few opportunities for improvements. For Puerto Rican and Dominican women, concentration in the garment industry was followed by economic displacement as employment continued to decline, at the same time that employers' search for the lowest-wage labor appears unrelenting. The repercussions for Puerto Rican and Dominican women, their households, and their communities have had sobering parallels. The U.S. model for economic development in inner cities seems a repeating pattern as well, based on recruiting low-wage labor and then displacing it, abandoning communities in its wake. Here too, Latinas will likely continue their efforts to provide for their households and to improve conditions for their communities.

NOTES

1. *Bobbin* (August 1991) as reproduced in Charles Kernaghan, "Paying to Lose Our Jobs," in *No Sweat: Fashion, Free Trade, and the Rights of Garment Workers*, ed. Andrew Ross (New York: Verso, 1997), p. 88. According to Kernaghan, U.S. assistance accounted for 94 percent of the budget for the Salvadoran Foundation for Economic and Social Development (FUSADES), who placed the ad. Between 1984 and 1991, the U.S. government provided $102,397,000 in funding.

2. David Ross, *The Long Uphill Path: A Historical Study of Puerto Rico's Program of Economic Development* (San Juan, P.R.: Editorial Edil, 1969), p. 98.

3. See Whalen, *From Puerto Rico to Philadelphia: Puerto Rican Workers and Postwar Economics* (Philadelphia: Temple University Press, 2001), Chapters 1 and 2.

4. Harvey S. Perloff, *Puerto Rico's Economic Future: A Study in Planned Development* (Chicago: University of Chicago Press, 1950), pp. 184, 99. See also Eileen Boris, "Needlewomen under the New Deal in Puerto Rico, 1920–1945," in *Puerto Rican Women and Work: Bridges in Transnational Labor*, ed. Altagracia Ortiz (Philadelphia: Temple University Press, 1996), pp. 33–54.

5. Palmira N. Ríos, "Export-Oriented Industrialization and the Demand for Female Labor: Puerto Rican Women in the Manufacturing Sector, 1953–1980," in *Colonial Dilemma: Critical Perspectives on Contemporary Puerto Rico*, eds. Edwin Meléndez and Edgardo Meléndez (Boston: South End Press, 1993), pp. 95, 97, 93, 92.

6. Puerto Rico, Economic Development Administration (Fomento), Continental Operations Branch, New York, N.Y., "The Apparel and Related Prod-

ucts Industry" (August 1973), La Colección Puertor-riqueña, University of Puerto Rico, Río Piedras, P.R.

7. Ross, *Long Uphill Path*, p. 119.

8. Genara Aponte, interview by author, October 9, 1997, November 6 and 20, 1997, Philadelphia, Penn., tape recording, translated by author except for words in italics.

9. Puerto Rico, Office of the Governor, Division of Statistics, "Estudio Sobre La emigración" (San Juan, 1952), Centro de Estudios Puertorriqueños, Hunter College, New York, N.Y.

10. Lloyd G. Reynolds and Peter Gregory, *Wages, Productivity and Industrialization in Puerto Rico* (Homewood, Ill: R. D. Irwin, 1965), p. 158; Philadelphia, Commission on Human Relations, *Puerto Ricans in Philadelphia: A Study of Their Demographic Characteristics, Problems, and Attitudes*, by Arthur Siegel, Harold Orlans and Loyal Greer of the Institute for Research in Human Relations (April 1954; reprint ed., New York: Arno Press, 1975), p. 35.

11. Donald J. O'Connor, "Memorandum: Mainland Labor Force Needs in 1948–1949 and Puerto Rico's Opportunities to Exploit Them," August 10, 1948, Record Group 126, File 9-8-116, National Archives, Washington, D.C.

12. Juanita Rodríguez, interview by author, June 18, 1997, Palmyra, N.J., tape recording, translated by author.

13. On Puerto Rican women's earlier history in New York's garment industry, see Altagracia Ortiz, "En la aguja y el pedal eché la hiel: Puerto Rican Women in the Garment Industry of New York City, 1920–1980," in Ortiz, *Puerto Rican Women and Work*, pp. 55–81, and Robert Laurentz, "Racial/Ethnic Conflict in the New York City Garment Industry, 1933– 1980" (Ph.D. diss., State University of New York at Binghamton, 1980).

14. Laurentz, "Racial/Ethnic Conflict," p. 248.

15. Roy B. Helfgott, "Women's and Children's Apparel," in *Made in New York: Case Studies in Metropolitan Manufacturing*, ed. Max Hall (Cambridge, Mass.: Harvard University Press, 1959), pp. 94–95.

16. Raymond Vernon, *Metropolis 1985: An Interpretation of the Findings of the New York Metropolitan Region Study* (Cambridge, Mass.: Harvard University Press, 1960), pp. 8, 90. In explaining New York's higher labor force participation rates relative to the national average, Vernon included white women among the labor migrants, as they were "coming into the area for work," but he excluded Puerto Rican women, referring to "the tide of Puerto Rican and Negro males."

17. Dan Wakefield, *Island in the City: Puerto Ricans in New York* (New York: Arno Press, 1975), pp. 199, 195, 198.

18. Blanca Vázquez Erazo, "The Stories Our Mothers Tell: Projections of Self in the Stories of Puerto Rican Garment Workers," in *Stories to Live By: Continuity and Change in Three Generations of Puerto Rican Women*, ed. Rina Benmayor, Ana Juarbe, Celia Alvarez, and Blanca Vázquez Erazo (New York: Centro de Estudios Puertorriquenos Working Paper Series, 1987), p. 47.

19. Ana Juarbe, "Anastasia's Story: A Window into the Past—A Bridge to the Present," in *Stories to Live By*, p. 59 in translation, p. 22.

20. Vázquez Erazo, "Stories Our Mothers Tell," pp. 47, 48, 64 in translation.

21. Kathie Friedman Kasaba, "New York City: The Underside of the World's Capital," in *Creating and Transforming Households: The Constraints of the World-Economy*, eds. Joan Smith and Immanuel Wallerstein (Cambridge: Cambridge University Press, 1992), p. 63.

22. Laurentz, "Racial/Ethnic Conflict," p. 188.

23. Roger D. Waldinger, *Through the Eye of the Needle: Immigrants and Enterprise in New York's Garment Trades* (New York: New York University Press, 1986), pp. 56, 76.

24. Saskia Sassen-Koob, "Changing Composition and Labor Market Location of Hispanic Immigrants in New York City, 1960–1980," in *Hispanics in the U.S. Economy*, eds. George J. Borjas and Marta Tienda (Orlando, Fla.: Academic Press, 1985), pp. 302, 312.

25. "Major Labor Shortage Squeezing N.Y. Garment Center," *New York Times*, August 10, 1969, III, 1. Twenty employers had been picked up for home work violations and seven had been prosecuted and fined during the first half of 1969.

26. See Alice Colon-Warren, "The Impact of Job Losses on Puerto Rican Women in the Middle Atlantic Region, 1970–1980," in Ortiz, *Puerto Rican Women and Work*, pp. 103–138; Rosa M. Torruellas, Rina Benmayor, and Ana Juarbe, "Negotiating Gender, Work and Welfare: *Familia* as Productive Labor among Puerto Rican Women in New York City," in Ortiz, *Puerto Rican Women and Work*, pp. 184–208; and Carol Smith, "Immigrant Women, Work, and Use of Government Benefits: A Case Study of Hispanic Women Workers in New York's Garment Industry" (Ph.D. diss., Adelphia University School of Social Welfare, 1980).

27. Judith Goode, "Polishing the Rustbelt: Immigrants Enter a Restructuring Philadelphia," in *Newcomers in the Workplace: Immigrants and the Restructuring of the U.S. Economy* (Philadelphia: Temple University Press, 1994), p. 208.

28. Waldinger, *Through the Eye*, p. 77.

29. David Bray, "Economic Development: The Middle Class and International Migration in the Dominican Republic," *International Migration Review* 18 (1984):226.

30. Helen I. Safa, "Export Manufacturing, State Policy, and Women Workers in the Dominican Republic," in *Global Production: The Apparel Industry in the Pacific Rim*, eds. Edna Bonacich, Lucie Chen, Norma Chinchilla, Norma Hamilton, and Paul Ong (Philadelphia: Temple University Press, 1994), pp. 251, 253.

31. Edna Bonacich and David V. Waller, "Mapping a Global Industry: Apparel Production in the Pacific Rim Triangle," in Bonacich, *Global Production*, p. 29; Helen I. Safa, *The Myth of the Male Breadwinner: Women and Industrialization in the Caribbean* (Boulder, Colo.: Westview Press, 1995), p. 101; Safa, "Export Manufacturing," pp. 250, 257.

32. Ramona Hernández and Francisco Rivera-Batiz, *Dominican New Yorkers: A Socioeconomic Profile, 1997* (New York: CUNY Dominican Studies Institute, Dominican Research Monographs, 1997), pp. 9, 1–2.

33. Nancie L. González, "Peasant's Progress: Dominicans in New York," *Caribbean Studies* 10 (October 1970): 162, 161, 165.

34. Nancie L. González, "Multiple Migratory Experiences of Dominican Women," *Anthropological Quarterly* 49 (January 1976):40, 42.

35. Sherri Grasmuck and Patricia R. Pessar, *Between Two Islands: Dominican International Migration* (Berkeley: University of California Press, 1991), p. 191. Their New York data was based on interviews with 301 persons born in the Dominican Republic and working at the time of their survey, and on additional ethnographic data derived from casual conversations and participant observation between 1981 and 1983, see pp. 58–60.

36. Maria, interview, trans. These Interviews were conducted by the author between April and July 1998 as part of a Rockefeller Humanities Institute, The Sweatshop Project, sponsored by the Lower East Side Tenement Museum and UNITE! Nerida and Maria were each interviewed twice, while Manuel and Miriam were each interviewed once. Their names and identifying details have been changed. The interviews were conducted in Spanish and have been translated, except for words in italics, and edited for clarity.

37. Nerida, interview, trans.

38. Hernández and Rivera-Batiz, *Dominican New Yorkers*, pp. 54, 42, 51, 57, 37.

JANE SHERRON DE HART
AND CAROLYN HERBST LEWIS

Thirty Years after *Roe*: The Continued Assault on a Woman's Right to Choose

A woman's right to decide for herself whether or not to carry a pregnancy to term was guaranteed by the 1973 Supreme Court decision *Roe* v. *Wade* (pp. 630–32). Opposition to the decision was immediate and fueled a rapidly growing grassroots movement, initially populated primarily by Roman Catholics and later joined by fundamentalist Protestants. Together with anti-choice church leaders and politicians, they have vigorously and continuously challenged the extent to which women are able to exercise this right, using a wide variety of tactics. In the last quarter-century, their efforts have successfully restricted access to federally funded abortions for poor women; restricted access to governmental hospitals for women in the military and wives of servicemen stationed overseas seeking to terminate a pregnancy; inhibited physicians from prescribing mifepristone, the "abortion pill"; limited late-term abortions; and proposed measures that would, if enacted, grant legal rights to fetuses.

Many of the greatest restrictions on access to abortion affect women under the age of 25, the age group into which falls the majority of women seeking abortions in the United States. Twenty percent of all women receiving abortions in this country are between the ages of 11 and 19, and another 32 percent are in the 20 to 24 age range.[1] Not only is this the age group directly affected by laws passed in thirty-two states requiring minors to seek parental notification and consent, it is also the age group with least access to the financial resources required to obtain an abortion. In 1997, the average cost

"Thirty Years after *Roe:* The Continued Assault on a Woman's Right to Choose" by Jane Sherron De Hart and Carolyn Herbst Lewis has been written for this edition of *Women's America.*

of a non-hospital abortion in the first trimester was $316. Since 86 percent of U.S. counties lack an abortion provider, these women also face the added expense and difficulties of having to travel considerable distance to an abortion provider.[2] The trip—and expense—is extended in the nineteen states requiring a minimum twenty-four-hour waiting period after receiving an informational lecture or viewing materials before an abortion can be performed. One state, Tennessee, mandates that a woman may not receive an abortion until the third day after her initial consultation.[3] For young women, many of whom are high school and college students, parental consent requirements and waiting periods make exercising their right to choose virtually impossible. Similarly, women of any age with limited financial resources face restrictions on both public funding and private insurance coverage of abortion procedures. In most states, this ban is lifted only in cases of life endangerment, rape, and incest.

Compounding these challenges to reproductive freedom, a nationwide campaign of intimidation and violence initiated in the mid-1980s by groups within the anti-abortion movement has produced a steady decline in the number of abortion providers. According to the Feminist Majority Foundation's *1999 National Clinic Violence Survey Report,* one in five clinics experiences severe anti-abortion violence including death threats, stalking, bombings, arson, blockades, invasions, and chemical attacks. Although Congressional passage of the Freedom of Access to Clinic Entrances Act in 1994 has reduced such violence, it has not eliminated it. Since 1992, anti-choice violence has claimed the lives of four doctors, two clinic employees, a clinic escort, a security guard, and an off-duty police officer. Add to these numbers the sixteen attempted murders since 1991 and the 203 anthrax threats directed at abortion clinic personnel since 1997, seventy-three of which occurred prior to terrorist attacks on the World Trade Center and the Pentagon and the subsequent anthrax attacks.[4] Abortion providers have had to wage their own "war on terrorism" since long before September 11, 2001.

This ongoing program of intimidation and violence clearly has had the impact intended. By 1999, only 14 percent of all counties in the United States had abortion providers; North Dakota had only one provider in the entire state. Despite anti-choice rhetoric concerning the high incidence of late-term abortions, only 11 percent of abortions are performed after the first trimester, and half of the women involved report that they were delayed because of problems obtaining abortion services—either in affording the cost or finding a provider. Recent studies have shown that waiting periods seem to increase the rate of second-trimester abortions, which have a greater rate of both physical and emotional complications. After Mississippi mandated a 24-hour waiting period, there was a 53 percent increase in the number of second-trimester abortions in the state.

In September 2000, the Food and Drug Administration (FDA) approved the use of mifepristone, also known as RU-486 or the "abortion pill," to induce medical abortions. Often confused with the "morning-after pill," a high dose of contraceptives that can be taken within 72 hours of unprotected sex to prevent a fertilized ovum from implanting in the uterus, mifepristone can only be administered after a woman knows she is pregnant and is hardly the quick and easy form of abortion that anti-choice activists claim it to be.[5] In a three-part regimen, mifepristone first prevents a woman's body from producing the hormones necessary to sustain a pregnancy. Two days later, the at-home self-insertion of misoprostol tablets into a woman's vagina triggers uterine contractions.

A follow-up visit to the physician's office a week later ensures that the abortion was successful. Although the drug had been in use in Europe for over a decade, anti-choice activists had repeatedly blocked its introduction to the United States. While pro-choice advocates lauded the FDA's decision as "an historic moment, comparable to the arrival of the birth control pill forty years ago," anti-choice opponents, such as then Texas governor George W. Bush, condemned the FDA's approval of mifepristone as "wrong." In the midst of the 2000 presidential campaign, Bush expressed his fear that the pill would make abortions "more and more common rather than more and more rare." Laura Echevarria, the spokeswoman for the National Right to Life Committee, voiced her organization's displeasure at the agency's action: "In the past, the FDA has approved drugs to save lives and prolong lives. Now they are approving a drug designed to take life."[6]

But the fears of anti-choice activists and the hopes of their pro-choice counterparts that the availability of these medical abortions would make access to abortions easier and less burdensome to women proved hollow. In a recent survey, only 6 percent of gynecologists and 1 percent of general practitioners reported that they have offered a medical abortion to their patients since FDA approval. Furthermore, 40 percent of gynecologists and 37 percent of general practitioners said that the reason why they do not offer mifepristone is because they "personally oppose" medical abortion. Still others are hindered not by moral objections but rather by restrictions imposed by anti-choice legislators. Almost immediately following the FDA's approval of mifepristone for use in medical abortions, state legislators began introducing restrictions on its prescription and use. For example, since surgical abortion is necessary if medical abortion is unsuccessful, several state legislatures require the prescribing physician to have surgery rights at a local hospital. In addition, the existing statutes on abortion, such as waiting periods and informed consent as well as restrictions on insurance coverage and public funding, continue to apply to medical abortion as well. These factors help account for why 70 percent of mifepristone sales come from not-for-profit clinics, such as Planned Parenthood.[7]

A woman's right to choose has been further eroded by legislation banning late-term abortions, which can be necessary to save the life of the woman or to avert serious health consequences. Although President Clinton vetoed such legislation in 1996 and 1997, by February 2000, forty states had enacted restrictions on late-term abortions to varying degrees based on viability, danger to the woman's life or health, or "serious, grave or irreversible damage."[8]

The anti-abortion movement gained added momentum in the year 2000 with the election of an anti-choice president and Republican control of the U.S. House of Representatives. In June 2003, the House passed the Partial-Birth Abortion Ban Act, which was nearly identical to a Nebraska bill that the U.S. Supreme Court found to be unconstitutional in 2000. In *Stenberg* v. *Carhart*, the Supreme Court ruled that the term "partial-birth abortion" has "no factual, medical, or legal meaning." Furthermore, the Court stated that any future bans on dilation and extraction (the more precise medical term for the procedure) must include exceptions for the health and safety of the mother. The Partial-Birth Abortion Ban Act of 2003, however, does not include such provisions.[9] The bill mandates a two-year prison term and fines for any person who performs a so-called partial-birth abortion under any circumstances. The bill also provides a right to compensation for the husband of a woman or the parents of a minor who undergoes a "partial-birth" abortion. Oddly, the bill makes clear that "a woman upon whom a partial birth abortion is performed" shall not be subject to prosecution.[10] Thus, the Partial-Birth Abortion Ban Act of 2003, once signed into law, will not interfere with a woman's right to choose an abortion, but it will make it impossible for her to get one. With both houses of Congress under control of the Republicans in 2003 and with an anti-choice president in office, past barriers to such legislation have been removed.

Taking a different approach, other anti-choice forces have focused on the fetus itself. Although they failed to pass a constitutional amendment declaring the fetus a "person" so as to provide protection under the Fourteenth Amendment, efforts to provide legal protection to the fetus persist. For example, proposals to extend health insurance to embryos as a means of ensuring that poor pregnant women receive adequate prenatal care are also intended to set a precedent for granting legal rights to fetuses. In the wake of the murder of Laci Peterson and her unborn son, Connor, the Senate passed the Unborn Victims of Violence Act, which makes it a federal offense to cause harm to or the death of "a child, who is in utero at the time the conduct takes place."[11] Further efforts to protect the fetus are visible in regulations denying women in the U.S. military and the wives of servicemen stationed overseas access to abortions in U.S. military hospitals.[12] Instead, they are forced to seek local services, which are often unsafe and illegal. Nor have such efforts been confined to the United States and its citizens. President Bush's revival of the Global Gag Rule on the twenty-eighth anniversary of the *Roe* decision silenced pro-choice physicians and activists around the world. The Global Gag Rule prevents "foreign NGOs that receive U.S. family planning funds from using their own, non-U.S. funds to provide legal abortion services, lobby their own governments for abortion law reform, or even provide accurate medical counseling for referrals regarding abortion."[13] Meanwhile, around the world, more than 80,000 women die each year from unsafe and illegal abortions.[14]

Visual evidence of the impact of abortion opponents is available each year when the National Abortion and Reproductive Rights Action League (NARAL) releases a report card charting each state's efforts to ensure the availability of abortions for its residents. States are given demerits based on requirements for counseling and "informed" consent and waiting periods. Mandated notification of a married woman's husband or of a minor's parents also result in a lower rating. Scores also reflect state-legislated constraints on public funding and insurance coverage, post-viability bans, and restrictions on specific abortion procedures, such as the "partial birth" abortion. Scores improve according to a state's efforts to curtail clinic violence, including specific legal prohibitions against interference with entry to or exit from an abortion facility, trespassing, and bombing.

The map below shows the results of the NARAL study in 2002.[15] Only eight states (California, Connecticut, Hawaii, Maryland, New York, Oregon, Vermont, and Washington) plus the District of Columbia earned an A or A− rating. One-third of the states received an F. The overall rating for the nation was a C−. While the *right* to choose has remained more or less intact for over a quarter of a century, *access* to a safe and legal abortion remains another matter altogether.

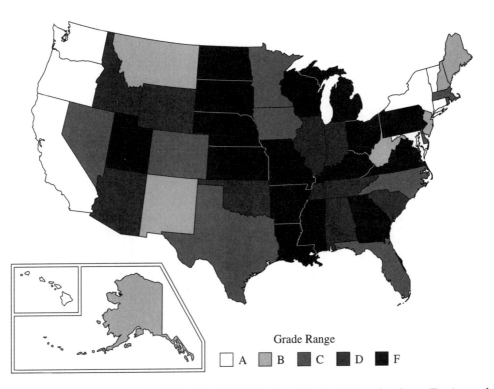

Grade Range

☐ A   ▨ B   ▩ C   ◼ D   ◼ F

This map shows the results of NARAL's 2002 Who Decides? A State-by-State Review of Abortion and Reproductive Rights. *Only nine states received an A or A− rating. (Copyright © Carolyn Lewis.)*

Even the right is more tenuous than it has been at any time since the months immediately preceding the 1992 Supreme Court decision *Planned Parenthood* v. *Casey* (pp. 633–36). In the quarter-century since *Roe,* the court has been the main line of defense for protection of reproductive freedom. In keeping with the Supreme Court's ruling, the lower courts around the country have upheld women's right to choose in the face of persistent legislative efforts to erode that right. In 2002, for example, a federal district court struck down an Oklahoma law requiring parental notification and consent for a minor seeking an abortion. In Florida and Alabama, courts overturned state laws mandating what information abortion providers were required to discuss with a woman before performing an abortion. In Pennsylvania, the Luzerne County Court ruled that a woman's ex-boyfriend had no legal authority to prevent her from obtaining an abortion.

With anti-choice Republicans controlling the White House, the Senate, and the House of Representatives, the courts, too, are now problematic. There are numerous vacancies to fill in the lower courts, especially the federal courts, traditionally a training ground for Supreme Court justices. The high court itself has its share of elderly justices who have talked about retirement. So long as one's position on abortion remains a litmus test for prospective judicial nominees, pro-choice advocates have little reason to believe that a pro-choice nominee, male or female, will even reach the Senate Judicial Committee for official hearings, much less get a full Senate vote.

The current Court has already gone an uncommonly long period without a change in personnel. Justice John Paul Stevens, who supports *Roe* and appears to be in good health, is over eighty years old. The likelihood that the present cast can hold out for many more years is minimal—a prospect that leads supporters of *Roe* to conclude that, at present, not only is access limited, but a woman's right to abortion is potentially endangered as well.

NOTES

1. Alan Guttmacher Institute, *Facts in Brief: Induced Abortion* (2002).

2. Ibid. Thirty-two percent of women between the ages of 15 and 44 reside in these counties.

3. NARAL Foundation, *Who Decides? A State-by-State Review of Abortion and Reproductive Rights* (May 2002).

4. For annual data on restricted access, see NARAL, *Who Decides?* (1997, 1998, 1999, 2000, 2002); *New York Times*, July 2, 1998, A11. On abortion violence and fatalities, see The Feminist Majority Foundation, *1999 National Clinic Violence, Intimidation, and Terrorism* (2000); "Anthrax Attacks Old News for Abortion Providers," *Reproductive Freedom News*, November 2001.

5. The "morning-after pill" is available without a prescription in parts of Alaska, California, and Washington.

6. Marc Kaufman, "Abortion Pill Gets Approval From FDA," *Washington Post*, September 29, 2000.

7. "Women's Access to Early Abortion Pill Blocked by Abortion Politics," *Reproductive Freedom News*, October 2001.

8. For late-term abortion restrictions, see Alan Guttmacher Institute, *Facts in Brief: Induced Abortion* (February 2000). On the broad wording of bans, see "'Partial-Birth Abortion' Bans and Statistics," *Reproductive Freedom News*, January 1999.

9. The bill only contains an exception for cases when the mother's life—but not her health—is at risk. The Senate attached an amendment to the bill that confirms the constitutionality of the *Roe* v. *Wade* decision, but this amendment is expected to be deleted before the legislation is sent to the president to be signed.

10. Partial-Birth Abortion Ban Act of 2003, 108th Cong., 1st session, s. 3.

11. Unborn Victims of Violence Act of 2003, 108th Cong., 1st session, s. 146.

12. Exceptions are made for cases of rape or incest, or if carrying the pregnancy to term puts the woman's life at risk. In May 2002, the U.S. Court of Appeals for the Ninth Circuit upheld an order to the U.S. Navy to reimburse the wife of a serviceman for the abortion of an anencephalic fetus. See "Justice for Military Women," *Of Counsel*, Fall 2002.

13. "Global Gag Rule Renewal Is Bush's First Assault on Women's Reproductive Rights," *Reproductive Freedom News*, January 2002.

14. "Nepal: How the Global Gag Rule Policy Affects Abortion Reform Abroad," *Reproductive Freedom News*, January 2002. Prior to September 2002, when the King of Nepal signed a law legalizing abortion, six women died *each day* from unsafe and illegal abortions in Nepal. The new law, which ends Nepal's 150-year ban on abortion, legalizes all abortions in the first twelve weeks of pregnancy, in the first eighteen weeks for cases of rape or incest, and at any time when the mother's health is at stake.

15. The map is based on information available in NARAL, *Who Decides?* (2002).

SARA EVANS
Women and Global Citizenship

One of the distinctive features of the Declaration of Sentiments, signed at Seneca Falls in 1848 (pp. 215–17), was the claim that issues that were generally treated as private matters—access to education, child custody, "moral delinquencies"—should be subjects for public and political concern. A century and a half later, this challenge is still a vibrant one.

Throughout the nineteenth and twentieth centuries, women in the United States and elsewhere created voluntary associations through which they could seek reform even without the vote. Today, voluntary non-governmental associations (NGOs)—many focused on issues that women have identified—are building worldwide networks and global civic institutions. Indeed, historians are increasingly recognizing these activities as basic to the practice of diplomacy and foreign relations.*

In this essay, Sara Evans sketches the development of women's international grass-roots organizations in the late twentieth century. What issues do feminists in the United States share with women in the rest of the world? On what issues has there been disagreement?

In western societies with democratic civic traditions women have struggled for two centuries for access to full citizenship. The relegation of women to the "private" sphere placed them outside the civic realm and defined their citizenship as secondary, enacted through male representatives (fathers, husbands). Such definitions also placed issues affecting women (child care, domestic violence, women's health, and sexual exploitation) outside the political arena. Because women's demands challenged ancient definitions of public as male and private as female, and potentially represented a shift in fundamental power relations within society and the family, they met great resistance. In the United States during the nineteenth and early twentieth centuries, women responded to their exclusion by creating large numbers of voluntary associations through which they could engage in civic action even without the franchise.

Today, similar struggles continue at a global level, primarily—once again—through voluntary non-governmental associations (NGOs) that have built global networks through the global civic institutions linked to the United Nations.

Global citizenship—enacted through global civic institutions such as the UN and its sponsored conferences (Copenhagen, Mexico City, Nairobi, Beijing) and through growing links between NGOs on issues of women's human rights—has become a critical means of mobilizing and building alliances for the expansion of women's access to fundamental human and civic rights.

In the years following the Second World War, the older generation of international women's organizations—such as the Young Women's Christian Association, the World Association of Girl Guides, and the League of Women Voters—lobbied for and in 1946 won

---

*See, for example, Akira Iriye, *Global Community: The Role of International Organizations in the Making of the Contemporary World* (Berkeley: University of California Press, 2002).

"Women and Global Citizenship" by Sara Evans has been written for *Women's America.* © 2002 by Sara Evans. Published by permission of Sara Evans.

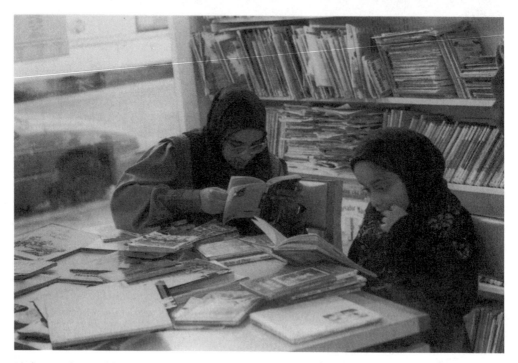

Asefia Patel, age sixteen, and her sister Hafsalo visit the Flushing branch of the Queens Borough Public School Library three or four times a week, "sometimes for school and sometimes for fun." The library has materials in Spanish, Chinese, Korean, Hebrew, Hindi, Urdu, Gujarati, and Russian. The hunger of young women for learning is as strong as it was in Rose Schneiderman's day. (Courtesy of Nancy Siesel/New York Times.)

The Vietnam War created hundreds of thousands of refugees; among them were these Hmong women, shown filling out tax forms in Seattle. (Photo by Nancy D. Donnelly, from her book, Changing Lives of Refugee Hmong Women [Seattle: University of Washington Press, 1994]. Courtesy of the University of Washington Press and Nancy D. Donnelly.)

a United Nations Commission on the Status of Women (CSW) through which they could continue a sustained effort to garner international attention to the barriers to women's equal political and legal rights. At that time, only forty-seven of the seventy-four member states of the UN allowed women to vote. For the next twenty-five years, the CSW worked assiduously to define an agenda regarding women's rights.[1]

Through the 1940s, 1950s, and 1960s, women played key roles in many anti-colonial struggles, gaining both visibility and greater access to politics and education. In the Chinese Revolution, in fact, the mobilization of women by the Communist Party relied heavily on challenges to traditional patriarchal household structures. In anti-colonial struggles, women found a new political voice, learned crucial political skills, and frequently provided a disproportionate share of popular support for anti-colonial movements. But they were most often confined to women's auxiliaries and, following independence, faced severe difficulties in asserting their civic rights in the face of traditional patriarchal norms, high levels of illiteracy, and development strategies that favored men. Indeed, efforts to build the economies of developing third world nations were, on the whole, keyed to western patriarchal assumptions. They placed little priority on educating women, ignored women's traditional roles in agriculture, and diminished women's historic sources of power and influence. Thus, the entry of millions into the global civic arena in the 1950s and 1960s as new nations emerged throughout Asia and Africa was a highly gendered phenomenon.

The growing influence of new members from Africa and Asia sparked the CSW in 1967 to propose a Declaration on the Elimination of All Forms of Discrimination Against Women, broadening the agenda from its original emphasis on political rights to include issues concerning women and development.

In the decades after 1970, the forces set in motion earlier in the century came together to place women's citizenship forcefully on the global agenda, weaving together the older agenda of legal and political equality with the newer emphases on economics, development, and culture. The confluence of two major developments framed this new context:

1. A new wave of feminism emerged in the United States and Europe in the 1960s and 1970s. This massive social movement expressed the hopes and frustrations of women who had achieved high levels of education yet found themselves confined by traditional expectations and discriminatory laws to marginal positions in the labor force and in social and political life. Feminists challenged definitions of "politics" that excluded issues of personal life (child care, domestic abuse, sexual violence, and sexual harassment). They also mobilized to increase women's representation among elected officials and in positions of power and authority across the board. This new movement raised issues of political participation and rights to a new level of visibility.[2]

2. Third World nations, recently admitted to the United Nations Assembly, had begun to place the problem of economic development in poorer regions of the world at the forefront of international debates. For women in the Third World, there was growing concern about the unique impact on women of many development schemes. They challenged the UN Commission on the Status of Women's primary focus on legal equality and sought to broaden its agenda.[3]

At the intersection of these changes grew a new generation of international, non-governmental women's organizations—building blocks for a global civil society. Using this global political structure in new ways, women both changed the international political agenda and dramatically increased their access to fundamental rights of political participation.

The 1975 United Nations International Women's Year (IWY) can be seen as a product of the earlier generation of international women's organizations, which had long pressed for an international conference to address women's legal and political inequities. After 1947 they worked through the UN Commission on the Status of Women to lobby for a conference. In 1972, on the twenty-fifth anniversary of CSW, the UN General Assembly at last agreed to declare IWY and fund a conference. In line with the older agenda, the focus of the conference was intended to be women's legal rights, but the General Assembly added the newer themes of peace and development to its description of the themes for the conference.

As delegates gathered in Mexico City in August 1975, they were startled to realize that 6,000 interested observers, media personnel, and representatives from NGOs had also shown up. Quickly, UN staff and NGO leaders organized a spontaneous and unofficial series of panels and workshops, known as the Tribune, which met simultaneously with the conference. Subsequent descriptions offer different reasons for the organization of the Tribune. Some say that it was simply an effort to provide some programming for the thousands of observers who arrived unexpectedly. Others claim that it was in reaction to the politics of the conference, in which many delegations were headed by men and discussions frequently veered into familiar international debates with no serious effort to make them relevant to the situation of women.[4]

Whatever the reason, the 6,000 observers had come with a passionate desire to engage in an international conversation about women's condition. Participants also went well beyond the traditional list of formally recognized NGOs and international women's organizations. They made visible a new generation of women's organizations—more secular, less structured and hierarchical (networks/alliances), and linked to broader definitions of women's issues including economics, poverty, education, health, and culture. In contrast to the orchestrated politics of the formal conference, the Tribune was open, diverse, female-dominated, and impassioned. Numerous networks formed on the spot. For example, one series of workshops constituted the first international gathering of scholars and students interested in Women's Studies and it spun off a series of conferences in subsequent years. The energy level of that Tribune led to creation of a new structure within the UN— the Women's Tribune Center—charged with coordinating links to grassroots efforts and ultimately providing a new pathway to get women's issues onto UN agendas.[5]

The IWY also sparked the self-organization of women in more than 100 countries that officially observed the year. At least eighty of these appointed national commissions or committees, which organized seminars, conferences, and special events. The experience of the Tribune inspired and empowered women to new efforts. Victoria Mokejwu of Nigeria told a reporter, "There is something called catharsis, sharing and participation. You have pain for so many years, and now I know that women all over the world have this same pain. If this is all I get out of the Tribune, then that's enough." In the United States, delegates to the NGO Forum in Mexico City returned fired up to demand that the U.S. also observe the year with a major national conference. In 1976, Representative Bella Abzug introduced a resolution to that effect in Congress. As a result, preparatory conferences were held in every state leading up to a meeting in November 1977 of 2,000 delegates and 18,000 observers. The Houston conference can be seen as perhaps the high point in the mobilization of American women in the 1970s. It also provoked a right-wing backlash that would also become an international phenomenon by the 1990s.

In the aftermath of IWY, women were sufficiently mobilized internationally to insist that a year was not enough. They lobbied the General Assembly to extend the year into a Decade for Women, with plans for conferences in the middle (Copenhagen, 1980) and at the end (Nairobi, 1985). From that point forward, all such conferences had massive NGO forums which met alongside the official conference, and their attendance soared: 6,000 in Mexico City; 8,000 in Copenhagen; 14,000 in Nairobi; 35,000 in Beijing. They also finally achieved the adoption of the Convention on the Elimination of All Forms of Discrimination Against Women (CEDAW), which defined discrimination on the basis of sex and called for equality between women and men. Fifty-seven nations signed CEDAW at the opening ceremonies of the Copenhagen Conference.

The second conference in Copenhagen, 1980, is remembered as the most conflicted. The official conference was deeply split over political issues linked to conflicts in the Middle East (specifically wording in the plan of action that defined Zionism as racism). Observers were dismayed to realize that governments totally controlled their official delegations—most of which were headed by men. Delegates' inability to explore issues from the point of view of women may have been linked to the continuing power of the public/private dichotomy, understood in this setting as a dichotomy between foreign relations (state-to-state and therefore public) and domestic policies.

The NGO Forum in Copenhagen, however, was no less filled with conflict than the conference. The difference was that it was open, energetic, and not required to reach agreement. One participant argued that the "diversity passion, openness, and largely honest conflict [shown at the NGO forum] were a refreshing counterpoint to the tightly scripted UN arena." Many participants experienced it as fragmented. Workshops on the Middle East degenerated into shouting. Presentations by western feminists on cliterodectomy and female genital mutilation sparked angry defenses from African women. In a post-colonial world, third world women, just beginning to find their own voices, accused western feminists of a kind of imperialism: "To talk feminism to a woman who has no water, no food, and no home is to talk nonsense." But in the free space of the Forum, conflict could coexist with a democratic ethos that allowed many positions to be articulated. In response to attacks on feminism, a multinational group wrote a refutation and called a spontaneous workshop to discuss "feminism as a political perspective that reaches beyond patriarchal political divisions and national boundaries." Three hundred showed up. Because no resolution was required, conversations could continue and positions could remain fluid. A Latin American woman reflected afterwards, "Before Copenhagen, I was not at all interested in feminism, but after seeing how governments and the UN treat women and what has and has not happened in the Forum, I am now considering the potential of feminism seriously."[6] "Networking" was a hallmark of the Forum, central to numerous workshops and meetings ranging from appropriate technology to women's studies, population planning, and lesbian rights. A group of African women decided to form an African women's develop-

ment association. As Nigerian Victoria Okoye told the New York Times, "This was the outcome of our network to discuss rural development at the grass roots. There is a need for this, to discuss our common problems."

By the time of the Nairobi Conference and NGO Forum in 1985, the networks and conversations initiated during the first two meetings had mushroomed. The fact that the meeting was in Africa signaled a new level of self-organization among third world women. Thousands of African women attended and the NGO Forum of 14,000 from across the globe was a massive success. In contrast to Copenhagen, feminists from the north no longer dominated. Rather, women from developing nations displayed a new sensibility, defining their own issues. In Mexico City, for example, family planning had been an issue of the north. In Nairobi, it was articulated as a human right for women in the south. Female physicians from North Africa led workshops in which they described their own efforts to end the practice of female circumcision and genital mutilation. Nadia Atif expressed the dominant view in the conference newspaper:

> The Africans are on the move. What is needed from our Western sisters is not a denigrating, we-know-better approach, but the realization that mutilation of women is the actual order of the day. In the West, it manifests itself as economic, psychological, and spiritual mutilation; in Africa, it includes the physical. Let us then unite against all forms of female mutilation, beginning with ourselves and our children.[7]

The Asian Women's Research and Action Network (AWRAN) organized sessions on sex tourism and labor conditions in export zones in the Philippines and other parts of Southeast Asia.

These and other workshops drove home the point that development politics continued to overlook the essential roles of women and could not succeed unless leaders consulted the people who do the bulk of the productive work on the land. Political scientist and conference participant Amrita Basu observed afterwards that "by 1985 it was clear that third world women were constructing indigenous feminist theory and practice that linked struggles against sexual inequality to other political struggles."[8]

The impact of these conferences is certainly difficult to measure. Yet one can point to the exponential growth of international networks and grassroots organizations, to the increased seriousness with which governments treated both the conferences and the issues affecting women, and to numerous local impulses in the immediate aftermath of each conference. For example, all-women political parties were organized in Iceland in 1975 following the Mexico City Conference and in the Philippines in 1986 after the Marcos regime collapsed. Women from Uganda returned home in 1985 inspired to demand a more effective and less corrupt political process. Women also became a highly visible and effective constituency at UN conferences on many topics, mainstreaming women's issues into the broader international agenda. Prior to the UN Conference on Environment and Development in Rio de Janeiro in 1992 (the Earth Summit), Women's Environment and Development Organization (WEDO) convened a World Women's Congress for a Healthy Planet in 1991. Fifteen hundred women from eighty-three countries came to prepare strategies, and at the Earth Summit's NGO Forum, the women were one of the largest and most effective groups. The resulting plan of action included a chapter on women's issues. The following year, at the 1993 World Conference on Human Rights in Vienna, women's groups articulated the theme that women's rights are human rights. And finally, at the 1994 Conference on Population and Development in Cairo, the plan of action included a chapter on empowering women as a way to improve health.[9]

The Fourth World Conference in Beijing, held ten years after the Decade for Women, was by all accounts a massive success. One hundred eighty-nine governments sent official delegates and nearly 35,000 interested observers participated in the NGO Forum. This time the conference itself demonstrated significant changes in the international agenda as it adopted a platform for action "focused consistently on women's human rights rather than on a welfare model of service delivery." The long-fought transition to treatment of women's issues as issues of human rights finally bore fruit. The sheer size and energy of the NGO Forum and its many preparatory conferences placed on display the enormous variety of grassroots efforts and international networks built over a quarter-century of activism. In Africa, for example, thousands of African women within their respective countries had met with members of their governments as a part of national preparatory committees discussing the issues to be included in the platform. Three thousand African women then came together for a continental preparatory conference in Dakar, defining an agenda focused on growing poverty; women's legal and human rights; access to education, health, and reproductive health services; women's relationship to the environment; involvement in peace processes; and the need for data about women and development.[10]

Those who journeyed to China found there, in the words of Robin Morgan, "A virtual city of female people. Turbans, caftans, saris, abayas, sarongs, kente cloth, blue jeans, T-shirts. Banners, posters, buttons. A twenty-kilometer-long sisterhood ribbon initiated by Cambodian women, added to at the forum, later stretched along the Great Wall. Almost four thousand workshops—on soybeans, sexuality, paid and unpaid labor, reproductive freedom, microcredit, caste, solar stoves, networking techniques, inheritance, health, refugee/displaced women, regional priorities, you name it."[11]

Beijing also witnessed the reality of an international backlash. The self-organization of women clearly challenges a wide range of traditional power relations. It is an unruly and democratic force. The Chinese, for example, initially welcomed the conference, but as the time drew near—and Chinese women held regional preparatory conferences across the country—the potential for empowerment represented a threat. Fearful of the potential for disruption, the Chinese leaders decided at the last minute to isolate the NGO Forum in a distant suburb and to make the logistics of the conference extremely difficult. Yet they were trumped both by the patience and goodwill of 35,000 fervent participants and by the impact of new technologies which spectacularly demolished all efforts at isolation. At the forum, Apple Computer, Hewlett Packard, and the Women's Networking Support Programme of the Association for Progressive Communications set up a computer center that generated 1,700 free e-mail accounts and

100,000 visits to the international World Wide Web. Staff assisted conference participants in the use of e-mail, electronic conferencing, databases, and Internet navigation tools. Conference documents were available on the web almost as soon as they were produced, and networks created during the conference were able to plan for ongoing communication in subsequent years.

Global citizenship becomes possible when individuals and groups have the capacity to think and act on issues of concern from a global perspective. Relegated by tradition and by law to the private arena, women face enormous obstacles to full citizenship at the national level, much less globally. Yet, their new capacity to function as global citizens through non-governmental organizations and the structures and conferences of the United Nations in the late twentieth and early twenty-first centuries has allowed them to mobilize for change at both national and international levels. Scholars and activists have recently taken note of the powerful impact of these new female public arenas. Irene Tinker argues that the expansion of civil society created by the growth of NGOs and women's organizations is "the real arena for citizen participation and the foundation of present or future democracy." The result has been a dramatic expansion of women's legal and political rights.

These changes offer some hope in a world fraught with environmental devastation, murderous violence, and continuing disparities between the wealthy and the poor. Precisely because they allow the voices of those at the grass roots—those most affected and least invested in the power-politics of nation states—to be heard, women have been central to the initiation of a global civic infrastructure that holds the potential for public problem-solving on these seemingly intractable issues. Through voluntary associations and NGOs, women have created avenues through which concerns rooted in private life can reach the broader arenas of public discussion. This linkage of public and private, in turn, may well be central to effective global citizenship on issues such as peace and development.

Swanee Hunt and Cristina Posa, for example, argue that "women are crucial to inclusive security since they are often at the center of non-governmental organizations, popular protests, electoral referendums, and other citizen-empowering movements whose influence has grown with the global spread of democracy." There are numerous examples of women's roles in peacemaking precisely because they are able to claim a civic identity—such as motherhood—which crosses ethnic and national lines; because they have the deepest investment in community stability and safety; and because due to their second-class status, they have learned to communicate "below the radar." In Northern Ireland, the Middle East, Southern Sudan, Pakistan and India, Bosnia, and many other places, women's organizations have been critical to making peace possible. Their organizing skills, however, are continually tested to the limits as traditional patriarchal political structures regularly exclude them. In Bosnia, for example, women were not invited to the peace talks to end the war, though throughout the conflict more than 40 women's associations worked actively across ethnic lines. In Northern Ireland in 1996, when peace activists Monica McWilliams (later elected to the Northern Ireland Assembly) and May Blood (later elected to the House of Lords) learned that no women would be invited to the peace talks made up of leaders of the top ten political parties, they collected ten thousand signatures within six weeks to create a new political party, the Northern Ireland Women's Coalition (NIWC). The NIWC won enough votes to rank in the top ten, giving McWilliams and Blood a place at the table. In subsequent negotiations, it was the women who broke through many a deadlock by reminding people hung up on small points of principle in the name of past suffering that success would create a violence-free future for their children and loved ones.[12]

Similarly critical roles of women in grass-roots organizations have placed new issues on the political agenda and pioneered new forms of development. In many African countries, for example, women are critical to the success of "rounds"—organizations that systematize a process of collective capital accumulation. Each member saves an agreed-upon amount every month and each month one member receives the savings of the entire group. This rotates until everyone has had a turn. In Zimbabwe there are ten thousand such organizations with fifty thousand members, 97 percent of whom are women.

Through the free spaces of international networks and organizations, women have developed a new, and global, sense of themselves as *women* citizens, challenging traditional assumptions that women's place remains private, familial, and outside of politics. They have learned critical political skills, found bonds of commonality despite massive differences, and successfully introduced a range of new issues into the international public agenda, ranging from domestic violence and sexual slavery to the importance of clean water and efficient, appropriate technologies for household use. In doing so, they have challenged the public/private dichotomy on a global level, broadening the definition of politics and the on-the-ground, activist meaning of citizenship as well.

Global citizenship, like national citizenship, cannot be understood as passive, simply a status, but must be highly engaged and participatory if we are to address the overwhelming problems which face us. We must find a way to respect differences while recognizing that we are, in fact, inextricably linked. I believe that the global citizenship of women—half of humanity—is one of the most promising steps in this direction. This ability to engage in public conversation across difference, to find common ground in the fundamentals of their lives—work, children, education, health, human dignity, and the earth that we share—is a gift and a foundation upon which we can build in the twenty-first century.

NOTES

1. Margaret E. Galey, "Women Find a Place," in *Women, Politics, and the United Nations*, ed. Anne Winslow (Westport, Conn.: Greenwood Press, 1995), pp. 14–16.

2. Sara M. Evans, *Tidal Wave: How Women Changed America at Century's End* (New York: Free Press, 2003).

3. Irene Tinker and Jane Jaquette, "UN Decade for Women: Its Impact and Legacy," *World Development* 15 (March 1987):419–427; Arvonne S. Fraser, *The UN Decade for Women* (Boulder, Colo.: Westview Press, 1987).

4. Lois A. West, "The United Nations Women's Conferences and Feminist Politics," in *Gender Politics in Global Governance*, ed. Mary K. Meyer and Elizabeth Prugl (New York: Rowan & Littlefield, 1999), p. 179.

5. Virginia Allen et al., "World Conference of International Women's Year," in Winslow, pp. 40–41; Tinker and Jaquette, p. 426.

6. Georgina Ashworth, "The United Nations 'Women's Conference' and International Linkages in the Women's Movement," in *Pressure Groups in the Global System: The Transnational Relations of Issue-Orientated Non-Governmental Organizations*, ed. Peter Willetts (New York: St. Martin's Press, 1982), pp. 125–45; Charlotte Bunch, *Passionate Politics: Feminist Theory in Action—Essays 1978–1986* (New York: St. Martin's Press, 1987), pp. 298–300.

7. Tinker and Jacquette, p. 423; Tami Hultman, "Reflections on Forum '85 in Nairobi, Kenya," *Signs: Journal of Women in Culture and Society* 11 (1986):592.

8. Amrita Basu, "Reflections on Forum '85 in Nairobi, Kenya," *Signs* 11 (1986):604.

9. Irene Tinker, "Nongovernmental Organizations: An Alternative Power Base for Women?" in Meyer and Prugl, p. 99; Marsha A. Freeman, "International Institutions and Gendered Justice," *Journal of International Affairs* 52 (1999):513–32.

10. Mary Johnson Osirim, "Making Good on Commitments to Grassroots Women," *Women's Studies International Forum* 24 (2001):172.

11. Robin Morgan, "The NGO Forum: Good News and Bad," *Women's Studies Quarterly* 24 (1996):46–53.

12. Swanee Hunt and Cristina Posa, "Women Waging Peace," *Foreign Policy* 124 (May/June 2001): 38–47.

REFERENCE WORKS

Important references containing excellent short biographies and a brief bibliography for many of the women appearing in this book are *Notable American Women, 1607–1950: A Biographical Dictionary*, ed. Edward T. James, Janet Wilson James, and Paul Boyer, 3 vols. (Cambridge, Mass., 1971); *Notable American Women: The Modern Period*, ed. Barbara Sicherman and Carol Hurd Green (Cambridge, Mass., 1980); *Black Women in America: An Historical Encyclopedia*, ed. Darlene Clark Hine, 2 vols. (Brooklyn, N.Y., 1993); and *Jewish Women in America: An Historical Encyclopedia*, ed. Paula Hyman and Deborah Dash Moore, 2 vols. (New York, 1997). An annually updated reference, first published in 1987, which surveys all aspects of the status of women in the United States, is the series sponsored by the Women's Research and Education Institute in Washington, D.C., *The American Woman: A Status Report*.

PART I: TRADITIONAL AMERICA, 1600–1820

Biology

James Axtell, ed., *The Indian Peoples of Eastern America: A Documentary History of the Sexes* (New York, 1981), is organized in terms of life cycle and includes sections on birth, puberty, marriage, and death. Elaine Forman Crane has edited *The Diary of Elizabeth Drinker*, 3 vols. (Boston, 1991), and a single-volume edition, *The Diary of Elizabeth Drinker: The Life Cycle of an Eighteenth Century Woman* (Boston, 1994); both include extensive comments on Drinker's experience of childbearing and motherhood. The intersection of biology and economics is clarified in Laurel Thatcher Ulrich's insightful study of a woman who delivered nearly nine hundred infants safely in a record comparable to that achieved in modern medical practice: *A Midwife's Tale: The Life of Martha Ballard Based on Her Diary, 1785–1812* (New York, 1990). Daniel Scott Smith and Michael S. Hindus, "Premarital Pregnancy in America, 1640–1971: An Overview and Interpretation," *Journal of Interdisciplinary History* 5 (1975):537–70, remains the classic study.

For the ways early Americans understood women's bodies, see Susan Klepp, "Colds, Worms, and Hysteria: Menstrual Regulation in Eighteenth-Century America," in *Regulating Menstruation,* ed. Etienne van de Walle and Elisha Renne (Chicago, 2001), and essays in Janet Moore Lindman and Michele Lise Tarter, eds., *A Centre of Wonders: The Body in Early America* (Ithaca, N.Y., 2001). For the relationship of biological choices to social change, see Susan E. Klepp, "Revolutionary Bodies: Women and the Fertility Transition in the Mid-Atlantic Region, 1760–1820," *Journal of American History* 85 (1998):910–45. Joyce Chaplin considers science and bodies in *Subject Matter: Technology, the Body, and Science on the Anglo-American Frontier, 1500–1676* (Cambridge, Mass., 2001).

Economics

A good place to begin is Betty Wood, *Women's Work, Men's Work: The Informal Slave Economies of Lowcountry Georgia* (Athens, Ga., 1995). David Barry Gaspar and Darlene Clark Hine, eds., *More Than Chattel: Black Women and Slavery in the Americas* (Blooming-ton, In., 1996), includes essays on many subjects related to work from the colonial period through the antebellum era. Judith Carney, *Black Rice: The African Origins of Rice Culti-vation in the Americas* (Cambridge, Mass., 2001), establishes the centrality of West Africans, particularly female West Africans, to the introduction and cultivation of rice in the Americas.

Susan Sleeper-Smith, *Indian Women and French Men: Rethinking Cultural Encounter in the Western Great Lakes* (Amherst, Mass., 2001), positions women as key to interna-tional contact. Other histories of economies and cultures in collision are Ann Marie Plane, *Colonial Intimacies* (Ithaca, N.Y., 2000), and James F. Brooks, *Captives and Cousins* (Chapel Hill, N.C., 1996).

Julia Cherry Spruill, *Women's Life and Work in the Southern Colonies* (Chapel Hill, N.C., 1938), is rich in descriptive detail and still repays reading. Carole Shammas, "The Domestic Environment in Early Modern England and America," *Journal of Social History* 31(1980):3–24, clarifies the economics of household management. For a thoughtful intro-duction to the handicraft that occupied most women much of the time, see Susan Bur-rows Swan, *Plain and Fancy: American Women and Their Needlework 1750–1850* (New York, 1977). Laurel Thatcher Ulrich offers a fresh interpretation in *The Age of Homespun: Objects and Stories in the Creation of an American Myth* (New York, 2001).

Biographies often make clear the economic setting in which women made their way; an especially readable one is Patricia Cleary's biography of a shopkeeper whose substantial wealth came from international trade with England: *Elizabeth Murray: A Woman's Pursuit of Independence in Eighteenth-Century America* (Amherst, Mass., 2000). Four books, taken together, offer a rich portrait of the political economy the mid-Atlantic: Sharon V. Salinger, *To Serve Well and Faithfully: Labor and Indentured Servants in Penn-sylvania, 1682–1800* (New York, 1987); Jean R. Soderlund and Gary Nash, *Freedom by Degrees: Emancipation in Pennsylvania and Its Aftermath* (New York, 1991); Karin Wulf, *Not All Wives: Women of Colonial Philadelphia* (Ithaca, N.Y., 2000); and Clare Lyons, *Sex Among the "Rabble": Gender and Power in the Age of Revolution,* (Chapel Hill, N.C., 2004).

On the law, see Elizabeth Bowles Warbasse's classic *The Changing Legal Rights of Married Women 1800–1861* (1960; reprint New York, 1987); Marylynn Salmon, *Women and the Law of Property in Early America* (Chapel Hill, N.C., 1986); and Cornelia Hughes

Dayton, *Women Before the Bar: Gender, Law and Society in Connecticut, 1639–1789* (Chapel Hill, N.C., 1995). Essays in *The Many Legalities of Early America,* ed. Christopher Tomlins and Bruce Mann (Chapel Hill, N.C., 2001), point to new directions in historical inquiry; those by Christine Daniels, Linda Sturtz, and John Kolp and Terri Snyder raise new questions about violence inside households and the power of propertied women. Terri Snyder, *Brabbling Women: Gender, Law, and Culture in Seventeenth Century Virginia* (Ithaca, N.Y., 2003), examines women and the law in seventeenth-century Virginia.

Politics

Religious and political concern often mingled. For the southwest, the place to begin is Ramon A. Gutierrez, *When Jesus Came, the Corn Mothers Went Away: Marriage, Sexuality, and Power in New Mexico* (Stanford, Cal., 1991); see also Virginia M. Bouvier, *Women and the Conquest of California, 1542–1840: Codes of Silence* (Tucson, Ariz., 2001). For New England, see Jane Kamensky, *Governing the Tongue: The Politics of Speech in Early New England* (New York, 1998). Religious and political anxieties came together in witchcraft panics; in addition to Carol Karlsen's *The Devil in the Shape of a Woman* (New York, 1998), see Mary Beth Norton, *In the Devil's Snare: The Salem Witchcraft Crisis of 1692* (New York, 2002); Elaine G. Breslaw, *Tituba, Reluctant Witch of Salem* (New York, 1996); John Demos, *Entertaining Satan: Witchcraft and the Culture of Early New England* (New York, 1982); and David D. Hall, ed., *Witch-Hunting in Seventeenth Century New England: A Documentary History 1638–1693,* 2nd ed. (Boston, 1999).

For white women who chose to stay with the Indians who captured them, see James E. Seaver, ed., *A Narrative of the Life of Mrs. Mary Jemison* (1823; reprint Syracuse, N.Y., 1990), and John Demos, *The Unredeemed Captive: A Family Story from Early America* (New York, 1994).

Politics is expressed in regulation of sex, violence, and race relations—Kirsten Fischer, *Suspect Relations: Sex, Race and Resistance in Colonial North Carolina* (Ithaca, N.Y., 2002), is a good place to start. Christine Daniels and Michael V. Kennedy, eds., *Over the Threshold: Intimate Violence in Early America* (New York, 1999), explores explosive relationships between men and women. Sharon Block, "Rape without Women: Print Culture and the Politicization of Rape, 1765–1815," *Journal of American History* 89 (2002): 848–868, opens important new questions.

Ideology

For general overviews, see Carol Berkin, *First Generations* (New York, 1996), and Mary Beth Norton, *Founding Mothers and Fathers* (New York, 1996). For striking examples of the ways in which some representative colonial women interpreted their own lives, see Anne Firor Scott, "Self-Portraits: Three Women," in *Uprooted Americans: Essays to Honor Oscar Handlin,* ed. Richard Bushman et al. (Boston, 1979). For the very high rates of literacy among white New England women, see William J. Gilmore, *Reading Becomes a Necessity of Life: Material and Cultural Life in Rural New England 1780–1835* (Knoxville, Tenn., 1989). For women's religious practices and understandings, see Catherine A. Brekus, *Strangers and Pilgrims: Female Preaching in America 1740–1845* (Chapel Hill, N.C., 1989), and Susan Juster, *Disorderly Women: Sexual Politics and Evangelicalism in Revolutionary New England* (Ithaca, N.Y., 1994). For international religious networks, see

Rebecca Larson, *Daughters of Light: Quaker Women Preaching and Prophesying in the Colonies and Abroad, 1700–1775* (New York, 1999). Janet Wilson James, ed., *Women in American Religion* (Philadelphia, 1980), remains useful, especially Mary Maples Dunn, "Saints and Sisters: Congregational and Quaker Women in the Early Colonial Period."

Essays in Laura F. Klein and Lillian A. Ackerman, eds., *Women and Power in Native North America* (Norman, Ok., 1995), introduce a wide range of cultures and gender practices. Also useful is Theda Purdue, *Cherokee Women: Gender and Culture Change, 1700–1835* (Lincoln, Neb., 1998).

For the interaction of biology, economics, politics, and ideology in early America, see Betty Wood, *Gender, Race, and Rank in a Revolutionary Age: The Georgia Lowcountry, 1750–1820* (Athens, Ga., 2000); Kathleen Brown, *Good Wives, Nasty Wenches and Anxious Patriarchs: Gender, Race, and Power in Colonial Virginia* (Chapel Hill, N.C., 1996); Mary Beth Norton, *Liberty's Daughters: The Revolutionary Experience of American Women, 1750–1800* (Boston, 1980); Linda K. Kerber, *Women of the Republic: Intellect and Ideology in Revolutionary America* (Chapel Hill, N.C., 1980); and essays in Ronald Hoffman and Peter J. Albert, eds., *Women in the Age of the American Revolution* (Charlottesville, Va., 1989). For urban women in the economy of the early republic, see Elizabeth Blackmar, *Manhattan for Rent, 1785–1850* (Ithaca, N.Y., 1989). For the debate over the relationship of women to the state, see Jan Lewis, "The Republican Wife: Virtue and Seduction in the Early Republic," *William and Mary Quarterly* 44 (1987):689–721; Carroll Smith-Rosenberg, "Dis-Covering the Subject of the Great Constitutional Discussion 1786–1789," *Journal of American History* 79 (1992):841–73; Jan Lewis, "'of every age sex & condition': The Representation of Women in the Constitution," *Journal of the Early Republic* 15 (1995): 359–87; Catherine Allgor, *Parlor Politics: In Which the Ladies of Washington Help Build a City and a Government* (Charlottesville Va., 2000); and Linda K. Kerber, *No Constitutional Right to Be Ladies: Women and the Obligations of Citizenship* (New York, 1998), ch. 1.

PART II: THE MANY FRONTIERS OF INDUSTRIALIZING AMERICA, 1820–1900

Biology and Sexuality

For an overview, John D'Emilio and Estelle B. Freedman, *Intimate Matters: A History of Sexuality in America*, 2nd ed. (New York, 1997), remains the place to start. For conflict about the meanings of sexuality, see Helen Lefkowitz Horowitz, *Rereading Sex: Battles over Sexual Knowledge and Suppression in Nineteenth-Century America* (New York, 2002).

For childbirth, see Judith Walzer Leavitt, *Brought to Bed: Childbearing in America, 1750–1950* (New York, 1986). For health and disease in the slave south, see Sharla M. Fett, *Working Cures: Healing, Health and Power on Southern Slave Plantations* (Chapel Hill, N.C., 2002), and Sally G. McMillen, *Motherhood in the Old South: Pregnancy, Childbirth and Infant Rearing* (Baton Rouge, La., 1990). For the relationship of women to the health reform movement, see Susan E. Cayleff, *Wash and Be Healed: The Water Cure Movement and Women's Health* (Philadelphia, 1987).

For contrasting interpretations of the birth control movement, see Linda Gordon, *Woman's Body, Woman's Right: Birth Control in America* (New York, 1977; most recent edition published as *The Moral Property of Women*, Urbana, Il., 2002), and James Reed, *From*

Private Vice to Public Virtue: The Birth Control Movement and American Society Since 1830 (New York, 1978). For abortion, see James Mohr, *Abortion in America* (New York, 1978), and the first chapters of Leslie J. Reagan, *When Abortion Was a Crime* (Berkeley, Cal., 1997). Carl N. Degler, *At Odds: Women and the Family in America from the Revolution to the Present* (New York, 1980), esp. chs. 2–9, has much to say about family relations.

Economics

Good places to begin are Alice Kessler-Harris, *Out to Work: A History of Wage-Earning Women in the United States* (New York, 1982); Claudia Goldin, *Understanding the Gender Gap: An Economic History of American Women* (New York, 1989); and the essays collected in Ava Baron, ed., *Work Engendered: Toward a New History of American Labor* (Ithaca, N.Y., 1991), and Eileen Boris and Cynthia R. Daniels, eds., *Homework: Historical and Contemporary Perspectives on Paid Labor at Home* (Urbana, Il., 1989).

Dorothy Sterling, ed., *We Are Your Sisters: Black Women in the Nineteenth Century* (New York, 1984), includes many well-selected documents of the working lives of black women, slave and free (it also includes documents that have much bearing on politics and ideology), as does Gerda Lerner, ed., *Black Women in White America* (New York, 1972), which includes materials from the full range of U.S. history. Willie Lee Rose, ed., *A Documentary History of Slavery in North America* (New York, 1976), and John Blassingame, ed., *Slave Testimony: Two Centuries of Letters, Speeches, Interviews and Autobiographies* (Baton Rouge, La., 1977), should also be consulted. Many elderly women who had been slaves when young were interviewed by the Federal Writer's Project in the 1930s. Selected interviews appear in B. A. Botkin, ed., *Lay My Burden Down: A Folk History of Slavery* (Chicago, 1945), and Ira Berlin et al., eds., *Remembering Slavery: African Americans Talk about Their Personal Experiences of Slavery and Freedom* (New York, 1998).

Deborah Gray White, *Ar'n't I a Woman?: Female Slaves in the Plantation South* (originally published in New York, 1985) has been reprinted (New York, 1999) with a new introductory essay. Jacqueline Jones, *Labor of Love, Labor of Sorrow* (New York, 1986), is a basic introduction to the history of women and slavery. *Incidents in the Life of a Slave Girl, Written by Herself,* long thought to be fictionalized, has been brilliantly edited by Jean Fagen Yellin, whose detective work establishes firmly that Harriet Jacobs was the author, and provides rich and lively detail about people and places in the extensive footnotes (1860; reprint Cambridge, Mass., 1987). Melton McLaurin, *Celia, A Slave* (Athens, Ga., 1991), is a compelling account of the trial of a woman charged with murder. Elizabeth Keckley, *Behind the Scenes; or, Thirty Years a Slave, and Four Years in the White House* (New York, 1988), includes her career as a seamstress, her experiences during the Civil War, and her friendship with Mary Todd Lincoln.

For free women's work in the domestic economy, and the interrelationship between biology, economics, politics, and gender, see Joan Jensen, *Loosening the Bonds: Mid-Atlantic Farm Women 1750–1850* (New Haven, Conn., 1986) and Jeanne Boydston, *Home and Work* (New York, 1990), as well as Nancy F. Cott, *The Bonds of Womanhood: "Woman's Sphere" in New England 1780–1835* (New Haven, Conn., 1977), ch. 1. For the interrelationship between biology, economics, politics, and gender, see Stephanie McCurry, *Masters of Small Worlds: Yeoman Households, Gender Relations, and the Political Culture of Antebellum South Carolina Low Country* (New York, 1995), and Brenda E. Stevenson, *Life in Black and White: Family and Community in the Slave South* (New York, 1996).

For changing understandings of the labor of caregiving, see Emily Abel, *Hearts of Wisdom: American Women Caring for Kin, 1850–1940* (Cambridge, Mass., 2000). Widowhood is an economic category as well as a demographic one; see Lisa Wilson, *Life After Death: Widows in Pennsylvania 1750–1850* (Philadelphia, 1992). For the influence of economic roles on domestic roles, see Lisa Norling, *Captain Ahab Had a Wife: New England Women and the Whalefishery, 1720–1870* (Chapel Hill, N.C., 2000). For domestic work and the maintenance of gendered roles in a frontier context, see John Mack Faragher's *Women and Men on the Overland Trail* (New Haven, Conn., 1979), and *Sugar Creek: Life on the Illinois Prairie* (New Haven, Conn., 1988), and Paula Petrik, *No Step Backward: Women and Family on the Rocky Mountain Mining Frontier—Helena Montana 1865–1900* (Helena, Mont., 1987). A good overview is Nancy Grey Osterud, *Bonds of Community: The Lives of Farm Women in Nineteenth Century New York* (Ithaca, N.Y., 1991).

For the ways in which federal efforts to "civilize" Native Americans shifted economic conditions and affected Cherokee women and men differently, see Theda Perdue, *Cherokee Women: Gender and Culture Change, 1700–1835* (Lincoln, Neb., 1998). For the economic impact of the U.S. absorption of New Mexico on women's relationship to the state, see Deena J. Gonzalez, *The Spanish-Mexican Women of Santa Fe 1820–1880* (New York, 1999). For alternate cultural understandings of the interaction of gender, culture, and economics, see Sarah A. Deutsch, *No Separate Refuge: Culture, Class and Gender on an Anglo-Hispanic Frontier in the American Southwest* (New York, 1987).

For the impact of industrialization on women, the classic studies are Helen Sumner, *History of Women in Industry in the United States* (Washington, D.C., 1910), and Caroline F. Ware, *The Early New England Cotton Manufacture: A Study in Industrial Beginnings* (1931; reprint New York, 1966). These should be followed by Thomas Dublin, *Women at Work: The Transformation of Work and Community in Lowell, Massachusetts, 1826–1860* (New York, 1979). Other industrial sectors are treated in Judith A. McGaw, *Most Wonderful Machine: Mechanization and Social Change in Berkshire Papermaking, 1801–1885* (Princeton, N.J., 1987); Mary H. Blewett, *Men, Women and Work: Class, Gender and Protest in the New England Shoe Industry, 1780–1910* (Urbana, Ill., 1988); and Lucy Larcom's classic memoir *A New England Girlhood* (1889; reprint New York, 1961). For the post–Civil War period, see Ardis Cameron, *Radicals of the Worst Sort: Laboring Women in Lawrence, Massachusetts 1860–1912* (Urbana, Ill., 1993), and Susan Levine, *Labor's True Woman: Carpet Weavers, Industrialization, and Labor Reform in the Gilded Age* (Philadelphia, 1984).

For the invention of school teaching as a career for women, the place to begin is Kathryn Kish Sklar, *Catherine Beecher: A Study in American Domesticity* (New Haven, Conn., 1973). For the feminization of schooling, see Richard M. Bernard and Maris A. Vinovskis, "The Female School Teacher in Antebellum Massachusetts, 1826–1860," *Journal of Social History* 10 (1977):332–45, and the important essays on teaching in Anne Firor Scott, *Making the Invisible Woman Visible* (Urbana, Ill., 1984). For continuing issues of gender and power in the schools, the classic essay is Myra H. Strober and David Tyack, "Why Do Women Teach and Men Manage? A Report on Research on Schools," *Signs* 5 (1980):494–503.

For the origins of the first workforce in which women and men worked side by side, see Cindy Sondik Aron, *Ladies and Gentlemen of the Civil Service: Middle Class Workers in Victorian America* (New York, 1987). For barriers to women in a wide range of scientific work, see Margaret Rossiter, *Women Scientists in America: Struggles and Strategies to 1940* (Baltimore, 1982); for the rest of the story, see the following volume, *Women Scientists in America: Before Affirmative Action 1940–1972* (Baltimore, 1995). For entry into the medical professions, see Mary Roth Walsh, *"Doctors Wanted, No Women Need Apply": Sexual Barriers in the Medical Profession 1835–1975* (New Haven, Conn., 1977); Regina Morantz-Sanchez, *Sympathy and Science: Women Physicians in America* (New York, 1985); Susan Reverby, *Ordered to Care: The Dilemma of American Nursing, 1850–1945* (New York, 1987); and Ellen S. More, *Restoring the Balance: Women Physicians and the Profession of Medicine, 1850–1995* (Cambridge, Mass., 1999), chs. 1–2. For women physicians as intellectuals, see Susan Wells, *Out of the Dead House: Nineteenth-Century Women Physicians and the Writing of Medicine* (Madison, Wis., 2001).

Politics

Gerda Lerner's classic biography, *The Grimke Sisters from South Carolina: Rebels Against Slavery* (Boston, 1967), shows how a concern for abolition could lead to a concern for women's rights. The connections are more recently pursued in Jean Fagen Yellin, *Women and Sisters: Antislavery Feminists in American Culture* (New Haven, Conn., 1990); Dorothy Sterling, *Ahead of Her Time: Abby Kelley and the Politics of Antislavery* (New York, 1991); and Julie Roy Jeffrey, *The Great Silent Army of Abolitionism: Ordinary Women in the Anti-Slavery Movement* (Chapel Hill, N.C., 1998). Nancy Isenberg, *Sex and Citizenship in Antebellum America* (Chapel Hill, N.C., 1998), links antislavery reform and political change; for women's political expression in the absence of social movements, see Elizabeth Varon, *We Mean to Be Counted: White Women and Politics in Antebellum Virginia* (Chapel Hill, N.C., 1998).

Sojourner Truth's *Narrative* of her life, prepared by Olive Gilbert, has been edited by Margaret Washington (New York, 1993). For biographies of the elusive Sojourner Truth, see Carlton Mabee, *Sojourner Truth: Slave, Prophet, Legend* (New York, 1993), and Nell Irvin Painter, *Sojourner Truth: A Life, a Symbol* (New York, 1996).

Ellen Carol DuBois, *Feminism and Suffrage: The Emergence of an Independent Women's Movement in America: 1848–1869* (Ithaca, N.Y., 1978), stresses the radicalism of the demand for suffrage; it should be read with Rosalyn Terborg-Penn, *African-American Women in the Struggle for the Vote, 1850–1920* (Bloomington, Ind., 1998). Nancy Hewitt, *Women's Activism and Social Change: Rochester, New York* (Ithaca, N.Y., 1984), and Lori Ginzberg, *Women and the Work of Benevolence: Morality and Politics in Nineteenth Century United States* (New Haven, Conn., 1990), incisively examine reformers' tactics and underlying strategies. Estelle Freedman, *Their Sisters' Keepers: Women and Prison Reform in Nineteenth-Century America* (Ann Arbor, Mich., 1981), introduces an important reform movement.

For politics and gender in the far west, see Albert L. Hurtado, *Intimate Frontiers: Sex, Gender and Culture in Old California* (Albuquerque, N.M., 1999), and Susan Yohn, *A Contest of Faiths: Missionary Women and Pluralism in the American Southwest* (Ithaca, N.Y., 1995). For an overview of women's organizations at the local and national levels, see Anne Firor Scott, *Natural Allies: Women's Associations in American History* (Urbana, Ill., 1991). For women's participation in a variety of public sectors, see Mary Ryan, *Women in Public: Between Banners and Ballots, 1825–1880* (Baltimore, 1990).

Ellen Carol DuBois forces a fresh understanding of the meanings of the Thirteenth, Fourteenth, and Fifteenth Amendments in "Outgrowing the Compact of the Fathers:

Equal Rights, Woman Suffrage, and the United States Constitution, 1820–1878," *Journal of American History* 74 (1987):836–62. The best overview of women and the law is Sandra F. VanBurkleo, *"Belonging to the World": Women's Rights and American Constitutional Culture* (New York, 2001), the first eight chapters of which cover the colonial era through the end of the nineteenth century. Readers will want to browse in *The Selected Papers of Elizabeth Cady Stanton and Susan B. Anthony,* vols. I and II, ed. Ann D. Gordon (New Brunswick, N.J., 1997); Stanton had a wicked wit. Selections from the correspondence between Stanton and Anthony and some of their more notable speeches are conveniently available in Ellen Carol DuBois, ed., *Elizabeth Cady Stanton, Susan B. Anthony: Correspondence, Writing and Speeches* (New York, 1981). Six massive volumes of the basic sources on the suffrage movement have been abridged in *A Concise History of Woman Suffrage,* ed. Mari Jo Buhle and Paul Buhle (Urbana, Ill., 1978). For challenges to the continued taxation of women without representation, and to the heightened vulnerability of black women to charges of vagrancy, see Linda K. Kerber, *No Constitutional Right to Be Ladies* (New York, 1998), chs. 2 and 3.

Gerda Lerner examines the process of women's politicization in an international context in *The Creation of Feminist Consciousness: From the Middle Ages to 1870* (New York, 1993). For American suffragists' international connections, see Leila J. Rupp, *Worlds of Women: The Making of an International Women's Movement* (Princeton, N.J., 1998).

There are many memoirs of women's participation in the Civil War, among them *Belle Boyd in Camp and Prison,* ed. Sharon Kennedy-Nolle (Baton Rouge, La., 1998); Susie King Taylor, *A Black Woman's Civil War Memoirs,* ed. Patricia W. Romero and Willie Lee Rose (New York, 1988); *Civil War Nurse: The Diary and Letters of Hannah Ropes,* ed. John R. Brumgart (Knoxville, Tenn., 1980); and Sarah Emma Edmonds, *Nurse and Spy in the Union Army* (Hartford, Conn., 1865). For a northern woman who went south to nurse before she entered the writing career that would make her famous, see Louisa May Alcott, *Hospital Sketches* (New York, 1863). For the perspective of a southern woman on the home front, see the compelling *Mary Chesnut's Civil War,* ed. C. Vann Woodward (New Haven, Conn., 1981).

For treatments of women and the experience of Civil War, see Catherine Clinton and Nina Silber, eds., *Divided Houses: Gender and the Civil War* (New York, 1992); Drew Gilpin Faust, *Mothers of Invention* (New York, 1996), and Elizabeth D. Leonard, *All the Daring of the Soldier: Women of the Civil War Armies* (New York, 1999). Overviews of southern women's experience are Catherine Clinton, *Tara Revisited: Women, War, and the Plantation Legend* (New York, 1995), and Laura Edwards, *Scarlett Doesn't Live Here Anymore: Southern Women in the Civil War Era* (Urbana, Ill., 2000). For northern women and the war, see Jeannie Attie, *Patriotic Toil: Northern Women and the American Civil War* (Ithaca, N.Y., 1998), and Judith Ann Giesberg, *Civil War Sisterhood: The U.S. Sanitary Commission and Women's Politics in Transition* (Boston, 2000).

Many compelling interpretations of the Reconstruction era, which link economics, politics, and ideology in complex ways, have been published in the last decade. See Noralee Frankel, *Freedom's Women: Black Women and Families in Civil War Era Mississippi* (Bloomington, Ind., 1999); Laura Edwards, *Gendered Strife and Confusion: The Political Culture of Reconstruction* (Urbana, Ill., 1997); Lee Ann Whites, *The Civil War as a Crisis in Gender: Augusta, Georgia 1860–1890* (Athens, Ga., 1995); Marlie F. Weiner, *Mistresses and Slaves: Plantation Women in South Carolina, 1830–1880* (Urbana, Ill., 1998); Leslie Schwalm,

A Hard Fight for We: Women's Transition from Slavery to Freedom in South Carolina (Urbana, Ill., 1997); and Tera Hunter, *To 'Joy My Freedom* (Cambridge, Mass., 1997). For black women's challenge to segregation long before *Plessy* v. *Ferguson,* Barbara Welke's essay, "When All the Women Were White, and All the Blacks Were Men: Gender, Class, Race and the Road to *Plessy* 1855–1914," *Law and History Review* 13 (1995):261–316.

The most famous group of reformers were the settlement house women, whose political activism is skillfully probed in Kathryn Kish Sklar's "Hull House in the 1890s: A Community of Women Reformers," *Signs* (1985):658–77, and her *Florence Kelley and the Nation's Work: The Rise of Women's Political Culture 1830–1900* (New Haven, Conn., 1995). The first volume of *The Selected Papers of Jane Addams: Preparing to Lead, 1860–1881,* Mary Lynn McCree Bryan et al., eds., (Urbana Ill., 2002), is indispensable and compelling reading; it should be supplemented by *The Social Thought of Jane Addams,* ed. Christopher Lasch (New York, 1965), and Allen Davis, *American Heroine: The Life and Legend of Jane Addams* (New York, 1973). For one of Addams' colleagues, who developed her own pioneering career in industrial medicine, see Barbara Sicherman, *Alice Hamilton: A Life in Letters* (Cambridge, Mass., 1984).

Ideology

"The Cult of True Womanhood" was given its name in an essay of the same title by Barbara Welter, *American Quarterly* 18 (1966):151–74. A very different interpretation of some of the same sources was offered by Gerda Lerner in her classic essay, "The Lady and the Mill Girl," originally published in 1969 and conveniently reprinted in *The Majority Finds Its Past: Placing Women in History* (New York, 1979), ch. 2. Both should be read along with recent reconsiderations of the concept of separate spheres. See Linda K. Kerber, "Separate Spheres, Female Worlds, Woman's Place: The Rhetoric of Women's History," *Journal of American History* 75 (1988):9–39, and Leila Rupp et al., "Women's History in the New Millenium: A Retrospective Analysis of Barbara Welter's 'The Cult of True Womanhood, 1820–1860,' " *Journal of Women's History* 14:1 (2002):149–173.

The relationship of women's roles to a developing economy is brilliantly dissected in Mary P. Ryan, *Cradle of the Middle Class: The Family in Oneida County, New York* (Cambridge, Mass., 1981), and *Women in Public* (Baltimore, 1990). The social construction of gender is insightfully explored in Carroll Smith-Rosenberg's essays, collected in *Disorderly Conduct: Visions of Gender in Victorian America* (New York, 1985), and Lee Chambers-Schiller, *Liberty, A Better Husband: Single Women in America—The Generations of 1780–1840* (New Haven, Conn., 1984). For the intersections of gender, class, and sexuality in a major city, see Christine Stansell, *City of Women: Sex and Class in New York* (New York, 1986); Timothy Gilfoyle, *City of Eros: New York City, Prostitution and the Commercialization of Sex, 1790–1920* (New York, 1992); and Patricia Cline Cohen, *The Murder of Helen Jewett: The Life and Death of a Prostitute in 19th Century New York* (New York, 1998). For women's cross-dressed performances as political and cultural statements, see Elizabeth Reitz Mullenix, *Wearing the Breeches: Gender on the Antebellum Stage* (New York, 2000). For one startling effort to change the terms of the relationships between men and women, and between women, men, and the economic order, see Maren Lockwood Carden, *Oneida: Utopian Community to Modern Corporation* (Baltimore, 1969).

For resistance to Chinese immigration, see George Anthony Peffer, *If They Don't Bring Their Women Here: Chinese Female Immigration Before Exclusion* (Urbana, Ill., 1999).

For women reformers' responses, see Peggy Pascoe, *Relations of Rescue: The Search for Female Moral Authority in the American West, 1874–1939* (New York, 1990). For the complexity of the immigrant experience, see Suzanne M. Sinke, *Dutch Immigrant Women in the United States 1880–1920* (Urbana, Ill., 2002).

The law of marriage both shapes and reflects gender relations. A good place to begin is Nancy Cott, *Public Vows: A History of Marriage and the Nation* (Cambridge, Mass., 2000), chs. 2–5. See also Michael Grossberg, *Governing the Hearth: Law and the Family in Nineteenth Century America* (Chapel Hill, N.C., 1985); Hendrik Hartog, *Man and Wife in America: A History* (Cambridge, Mass., 2000); and Peter Bardaglio, *Reconstructing the Household: Families, Sex and the Law in the Nineteenth Century South* (Chapel Hill, N.C., 1995). For the ways in which marriage relations have been grounded in economic relations, see Norma Basch, *In the Eyes of the Law: Women, Marriage and Property in Nineteenth Century New York* (Ithaca, N.Y., 1982), and Amy Dru Stanley, *From Bondage to Contract: Wage Labor, Marriage and the Market in the Age of Slave Emancipation* (Cambridge, England, 1998). For violence inside the family, see Elizabeth H. Pleck, *Domestic Tyranny: The Making of Social Policy against Family Violence from Colonial Times to the Present* (New York, 1987), and David Peterson Del Mar, *What Trouble I Have Seen: A History of Violence Against Wives* (Cambridge, Mass., 1998); for the ending of marriage, see Norma Basch, *Framing American Divorce: From the Revolutionary Generation to the Victorians* (Berkeley, Cal., 1999).

In *The Free Women of Petersburg: Status and Culture in a Southern Town* (New York, 1984), Suzanne Lebsock examines the interconnection of biology, economics, politics, and ideology in a single city. The relationship of poor southern white women to state power is analyzed in Victoria Bynum, *Unruly Women: The Politics of Social and Sexual Control in the Old South, 1840–1865* (Chapel Hill, N.C., 1992). For treatments of mistresses and enslaved women as part of the same social order, see Nell Irvin Painter, ed., *The Secret Eye: The Journal of Ella Clanton Thomas, 1848–1889* (Chapel Hill, N.C., 1990). Martha Hodes, *White Women, Black Men: Illicit Sex in the Nineteenth Century South* (New Haven, Conn., 1997), is an important reconsideration of race relations; see also the essays in Martha Hodes, ed., *Sex, Love, Race: Crossing Boundaries in North American History* (New York, 1999).

Women's claims to intellectual authority are examined in Mary Kelley, "Reading Women/Women Reading: The Making of Learned Women in Antebellum America," *Journal of American History* 83 (1996):401–24, and *Private Woman, Public Stage: Literary Domesticity in Nineteenth Century America* (New York, 1984). See also Annette Kolodny, *The Land Before Here: Fantasy and Experience of the American Frontier, 1630–1860* (Chapel Hill, N.C., 1984). For women's philanthropic involvement in the art world, see Kathleen D. McCarthy, *Lady Bountiful Revisited: American Philanthropy and Art, 1830–1930* (Urbana, Ill., 1993).

Religious organizations often provided the context for women's intellectual and reform activism; see, for example, Evelyn Brooks Higginbotham, *Righteous Discontent: The Women's Movement in the Black Baptist Church, 1880–1920* (Cambridge, Mass., 1993). The history of nuns in America is beginning to find its historians; see Eileen Brewer, *Nuns and the Education of American Catholic Women, 1860–1920* (Chicago, 1987), and Carol Coburn, *Spirited Lives: How Nuns Shaped Catholic Culture and American Life, 1836–1920* (Chapel Hill, N.C., 1999). For African American nuns, see Diane Batts Morrow, *Persons of Color and Religious at the Same Time: The Oblate Sisters of Providence, 1820–1860* (Chapel Hill, N.C., 2002), and the journal of Sister Mary Bernard Deggs, *No Cross, No Crown: Black Nuns in Nineteenth Century New Orleans,* ed. V. M. Gould and C. E. Nolan (Bloomington, Ind., 2001).

For the involvement of women for and against American empire in the late nineteenth century, see Joan Jacobs Brumberg, *Mission for Life: The Story of the Family of Adoniram Johnson* (New York, 1980); Louise M. Newman, *White Women's Rights: The Racial Origins of Feminism in the United States* (New York, 1999); and Kristin L. Hoganson, *Fighting for American Manhood: How Gender Politics Provoked the Spanish-American and Philippine-American Wars* (New Haven, Conn., 1998).

PART III: CREATING THE STATE IN AN INDUSTRIALIZED NATION, 1900–1945

For overviews of the period, see William H. Chafe, *The Paradox of Change: American Women in the 20th Century* (New York, 1991), and Rosalind Rosenberg, *Divided Lives: American Women in the Twentieth Century* (New York, 1992). On minority women, see Karen Anderson, *Changing Woman: A History of Racial Ethnic Women in Modern America* (New York, 1997); Judy Yung, *Unbound Feet* (Berkeley, 1995); Vicki L. Ruiz, *From Out of the Shadows: Mexican Women in 20th Century America* (New York, 1995); Jacqueline Jones, *Labor of Love, Labor of Sorrow* (New York, 1986), and *We Specialize in the Wholly Impossible: A Reader in Black Women's History,* ed. Darlene Clark Hine, Alma King, and Linda Reed (New York, 1995). For overviews with a regional focus, see *Writing the Range: Race, Class, and Culture in the Women's West,* ed. Elizabeth Jameson and Susan Armitage (New York, 1997); Christine Anne Farnham, *Women of the American South: A Multicultural Reader* (New York, 1997); and Huping Ling, *Surviving on the Gold Mountain: A History of Chinese American Women and Their Lives* (Ithaca, N.Y., 1998).

Biology and Sexuality

Biology and ideology interacted in the medical treatment of women, a subject much discussed in scholarly articles. On birth control, see David M. Kennedy, *Birth Control in America: The Career of Margaret Sanger* (New Haven, Conn., 1970); Ellen Chesler, *Woman of Valor: Margaret Sanger and the Birth Control Movement in America* (New York, 1992); and Linda Gordon, *Woman's Body, Woman's Right* (New York, 1990), chaps. 5–10. See also John D'Emilio and Estelle B. Freedman, *Intimate Matters* (Chicago, 1997), chaps. 8–11; *Powers of Desire: The Politics of Sexuality,* ed. Anne Snitow, Christine Stansell, and Sharon Thompson (New York, 1983); and *Passion and Power: Sexuality in History,* ed. Kathy Peiss and Christina Simmons (Philadelphia, 1989). On birth control and the black community, see Jessie M. Rodrique, "The Black Community and the Birth Control Movement," in Kathy Peiss and Christina Simmons, eds., *Passion and Power.* Other biologically related issues include: homosexuality, physical abuse of women's bodies in situations of domestic violence, venereal disease, infertility, and unwed motherhood. See Jennifer Terry, *An American Obsession: Science, Medicine, and Homosexuality in Modern Society* (Chicago and London, 1999); Linda Gordon, *Heroes of Their Own Lives: The Politics and History of Family Violence, Boston, 1880–1960* (New York, 1988), chap. 8; Allan M. Brandt, *No Magic Bullet: A Social History of Venereal Disease in the United States Since 1880*

(New York, 1987); and Elaine Tyler May, *Barren in the Promised Land: Childless Americans and the Pursuit of Happiness* (Cambridge, Mass., 1995), chaps. 1–3.

Economics

Housework engaged all women, except for the most privileged. See Ruth Schwartz Cowan, *More Work for Mother: The Ironies of Household Technology from the Open Hearth to the Microwave* (New York, 1983), chaps. 4–6, and Susan Strasser, *Never Done: A History of American Housework* (New York, 1982), chaps. 1–12. Farm women had additional burdens, as described in Deborah Fink, *Agrarian Women: Wives and Mothers in Rural Nebraska, 1880–1940* (Chapel Hill, N.C., 1992); Lu Ann Jones, *Mama Learned Us to Work: Farm Women in the New South* (Chapel Hill, N.C., 2002); and Valerie Matsumoto, *Farming the Home Place: A Japanese American Community in California, 1919–1982* (Ithaca, N.Y., 1982). The impact of technology on farm women's work is described in Katherine Jellison, *Entitled to Power: Farm Women and Technology, 1913–1963* (Chapel Hill, N.C., 1993). Women who engaged in paid labor in the home are the focus of *Homework: Historical and Contemporary Perspectives on Paid Labor at Home*, ed. Eileen Boris and Cynthia R. Daniels (Urbana, Ill., 1989).

Whether women worked outside the home and at what jobs depended on economic need and work options as well as family expectations. How family expectations and work options interacted with different ethnic groups is explored in a variety of studies. For a general study of working-class women who found work options in industry, see Leslie Woodcock Tentler, *Wage-Earning Women: Industrial Work and Family Life in the United States, 1900–1930* (New York, 1979). For those finding new opportunities in other areas, see Patricia A. Cooper, *Once a Cigar Maker: Men, Women, and Work Culture in American Cigar Factories, 1900–1919* (Urbana, Ill., 1987); Jacquelyn Dowd Hall et al., *Like a Family: The Making of a Southern Cotton Mill World* (Chapel Hill, N.C., 1987); Miriam Cohen, *Workshop to Office: Two Generations of Italian Women in New York City, 1900–1950* (Ithaca, N.Y., 1993); and Susan Porter Benson, *Counter Cultures: Saleswomen, Managers, and Customers in American Department Stores: 1890–1940* (Urbana, Ill., 1986). Shoplifters rather than shop workers are the focus of Elaine Abelson's *When Ladies Go A-Thieving: Middle-Class Shoplifters in the Victorian Department Store* (New York, 1989). Prostitution also provided jobs whether women entered such work voluntarily or, as many did, involuntarily, as demonstrated in Ruth Rosen's *Lost Sisterhood: Prostitution in America, 1900–1918* (Baltimore, 1982), and Benson Tong, *Unsubmissive Women: Chinese Prostitutes in Nineteenth Century San Francisco* (Norman, Ok., 1994).

How working-class women used their leisure and whether leisure activities contributed to individual and/or collective self-improvement are issues explored by Kathy Peiss, *Cheap Amusements* (Philadelphia, 1986), and Elizabeth Ewen, *Immigrant Women in the Land of Dollars: Life and Culture on the Lower East Side, 1890–1925* (New York, 1985). For efforts to improve the economic well-being of working-class women through unionization, see Annelise Orleck, *Common Sense and a Little Fire* (Chapel Hill, N.C., 1995), Nan Enstad, *Ladies of Labor, Girls of Adventure: Working Women, Popular Culture, and Labor Politics at the Turn of the Twentieth Century* (New York, 1999); Susan Levine, *Labor's True Woman: Carpet Weavers, Industrialization, and Labor Reform in the Gilded Age* (Philadelphia, 1984); Nancy Schrom Dye, *As Equals and as Sisters: Feminism, the Labor Movement and the*

Women's Trade Union League of New York (Columbia, Mo., 1980); Elizabeth A. Payne, *Reform, Labor, and Feminism: Margaret Dreier Robins and the Women's Trade Union League* (Urbana, Ill., 1988); Stephen H. Norwood, *Labor's Flaming Youth: Telephone Operators and Worker Militancy, 1878–1923* (Urbana, Ill., 1990); as well as selected essays in *Women, Work, and Protest: A Century of U.S. Women's Labor History*, ed. Ruth Milkman (Boston, 1985). On the larger issue of working-class consciousness, see Sarah Eisenstein, *Give Us Bread but Give Us Roses: Working Women's Consciousness in the United States, 1890 to the First World War* (London, 1983).

On the role of gender in determining wage inequities, see Alice Kessler-Harris, *A Woman's Wage: Historical Meanings & Social Consequences* (Lexington, Ky., 1991), chaps. 1–3. On the application of gender analysis to labor history, see Ava Baron, "Gender and Labor History: Learning from the Past, Looking at the Future," in *Work Engendered: Toward a New History of American Labor* (Ithaca, N.Y., 1991), pp. 1–46. On women and labor unions, see Dorothy Sue Cobble, *Dishing It Out: Waitresses and Their Unions in the Twentieth Century* (Urbana, Ill., 1991); Melinda Chateauvert, *Marching Together: Women of the Brotherhood of Sleeping Car Porters* (Urbana, Ill., 1998); and Elizabeth Faue, *Community of Suffering and Struggle: Women, Men, and the Labor Movement in Minneapolis, 1915–1945* (Chapel Hill, N.C., 1991). On Hispanic women and unionization, see Vicki L. Ruiz, *Cannery Women, Cannery Lives: Mexican Women, Unionization, and the California Food Processing Industry, 1930–1950* (Albuquerque, N.M., 1987). For the particular problems facing black women, see Jacqueline Jones, *Labor of Love, Labor of Sorrow* (New York, 1986), chaps. 6–7; Dolores Janiewski, *Sisterhood Denied: Race, Class, and Gender in a New South Community* (Philadelphia, 1985); Elizabeth Clark-Lewis, *"This Work Hada' End": The Transition from Live-in to Day Work* (Memphis, Tenn., 1985); and Phyllis Palmer, *Domesticity and Dirt: Housewives and Domestic Servants in the United States, 1920–1945* (Philadelphia, 1990).

For new opportunities provided by office work, see Margery W. Davies, *Woman's Place Is at the Typewriter: Office Work and Office Workers, 1879–1930* (Philadelphia, 1982); Lisa M. Fine, *The Souls of Skyscrapers: Female Clerical Workers in Chicago, 1890–1930* (Philadelphia, 1990); and Sharon Strom Hartman, *Beyond the Typewriter: Gender, Class, and the Origins of Modern American Office Work, 1900–1930* (Urbana, Ill., 1992). Better educated, middle-class women also discovered new opportunities for employment in a variety of new professions. See, for example, Barbara Melosh, *The Physician's Hand: Work, Culture, and Conflict in American Nursing* (Philadelphia, 1982); Susan M. Reverby, *Ordered to Care* (New York, 1987); Darlene Clark Hine, *Black Women in White: Racial Conflict and Cooperation in the Nursing Profession, 1890–1950* (Bloomington, Ind., 1989); Regina Morantz-Sanchez, *Sympathy and Science* (New York, 1985); Margaret Rossiter, *Women Scientists in America* (Baltimore, 1995); and Virginia G. Drachman, *Sisters in Law: Women Lawyers in Modern American History* (Cambridge, Mass., 1998). Black women found new work in the professions as well as entrepreneurial opportunities in the new beauty business, as did white women. See Stephanie J. Shaw, *What a Woman Ought to Be and to Do: Black Professional Women Workers During the Jim Crow Era* (Chicago, 1995); Beverly Lowry, *Her Dream of Dreams: The Rise and Triumph of Madame C. J. Walker* (New York, 2003); and Kathy Peiss, *Hope in a Jar: The Making of America's Beauty Culture* (New York, 1998). On the first generation of working women to live alone, see Joanne I. Meyerowitz, *Women Adrift: Independent Wage Earners in Chicago, 1880–1930* (Chicago, 1988). For women as educators, see Ruth Jacknow Markowitz, *My Daughter, the Teacher: Jewish Teachers in the New York City Schools* (New Brunswick, N.J., 1993).

The Great Depression and World War II had significant impacts on women's economic opportunities. For the 1930s, see Lois Scharf, *To Work and to Wed: Female Employment, Feminism and the Great Depression* (Westport, Conn., 1980), and Winifred Wandersee, *Women's Work and Family Values, 1920–1940* (Cambridge, Mass., 1981). Karen Anderson explores women's work as part of a larger study of women's status during World War II in *Wartime Women: Sex Roles, Family Relations and the Status of Women during World War II* (Westport, Conn., 1981), as does Susan M. Hartmann in *The Home Front and Beyond: American Women in the 1940s* (Boston, 1982). On those women who served in the armed forces, see Leisa D. Meyer, *Creating G.I. Jane: Sexuality and Power in the Women's Army Corps During World War II* (New York, 1996), and Molly Merryman, *Clipped Wings: The Rise and Fall of the Women Air Force Service Pilots (WASPS) of World War II* (New York, 1998). Job segregation in two key industries is the focus of Ruth Milkman's *Gender at Work* (Urbana, Ill., 1987).

Politics

There is extensive literature on female political activism in the decades before women could vote, especially on women's clubs—black and white, voluntary, and philanthropic associations. Women's voluntary associations and philanthropy are examined in Priscilla Murolo, *The Ground of Womanhood: Class, Gender, and Working Girls' Clubs, 1884–1928* (Champaign, Ill., 1996); Anne Firor Scott, *Natural Allies: Women's Associations in American History* (Urbana, Ill., 1991); and Kathleen D. McCarthy, *Lady Bountiful Revisited: Women, Philanthropy, and Power* (New Brunswick, N.J., 1990). McCarthy also explores women's philanthropic involvement in the art world in *Women's Culture: American Philanthropy and Art, 1830–1930* (Urbana, Ill., 1991). For African-American Women's reform activism, see Paula Giddings, *When and Where I Enter: The Impact of Black Women on Race and Sex in America* (New York, 1984); Evelyn Brooks Higginbotham, *Righteous Discontent: The Women's Movement in the Black Baptist Church, 1880–1920* (Cambridge, Mass., 1993); Susan L. Smith, *Sick and Tired of Being Sick and Tired: Black Women's Health Activism in America, 1890–1950* (Philadelphia, 1995); Judith Weisenfeld, *African American Women and Christian Activism: New York's Black YWCA 1905–1945* (Cambridge, Mass., 1998); and Glenda F. Gilmore, *Gender and Jim Crow* (Chapel Hill, N.C., 1996). Leila J. Rupp, *Worlds of Women: The Making of an International Women's Movement* (Princeton, N.J., 1998), examines the internationalization of the movement.

That the city provided women a laboratory not only for social activism but for professionalization and institutional modernization is demonstrated in Sarah Deutsch's *Women and the City: Gender, Space, and Power in Boston, 1870–1940* (New York, 2000); Clarke A. Chambers, *Seedtime of Reform: Social Service and Social Action, 1918–1933* (Ann Arbor, Mich., 1967); and Robyn Muncy, *Creating a Female Dominion in American Reform, 1890–1935* (New York, 1991). On delinquent girls and the women reformers, see Regina G. Kunzel, *Fallen Women, Problem Girls* (New Haven, Conn., 1993), chaps. 1–4; Ruth M. Alexander, *The "Girl Problem": Female Sexual Delinquency in New York, 1900–1930* (Ithaca, N.Y., 1995); and Mary F. Odum, *Delinquent Daughters: Protecting and Policing Adolescent Female Sexuality in the United States, 1885–1920* (Chapel Hill, N.C., 1995). On courts and correctional institutions, see Elizabeth J. Clapp, *Mothers of All Children: Women Reformers and the Rise of Juvenile Courts in Progressive-Era America* (University Park, Pa., 1998); Anne M. Butler, *Gendered Justice in the American West: Women Prisoners in Men's Penitentiaries* (Urbana, Ill., 1997); and L. Mara Dodge, *"Whores and Thieves of the Worst Kind": A Study of Women, Crime, and Prisons, 1835–2000* (DeKalb, Ill., 2002).

The impact of female activists and social scientists on social policies and welfare state formation is further demonstrated in Ellen Fitzpatrick, *Endless Crusade: Women Social Scientists and Progressive Reform* (New York, 1990); Theda Skocpol, *The Political Origins of Social Policy in the United States* (Cambridge, Mass., 1992); Molly Ladd-Taylor, *Mother-Work: Women, Child Welfare, and the State, 1890–1930* (Urbana, Ill., 1994); Joanne L. Goodwin, *Gender and the Politics of Welfare Reform: Mother's Pensions in Chicago, 1911–1929* (Chicago, 1997); Linda Gordon, *Pitied but Not Entitled: Single Mothers and the History of Welfare, 1890–1935* (New York, 1994); Gwendolyn Mink, *The Wages of Motherhood: Inequality in the Welfare State, 1917–1942* (Ithaca, N.Y., 1995); and Lynne Curry, *Modern Mothers in the Heartland: Gender, Health, and Progress in Illinois, 1900–1930* (Columbus, Oh., 1999). These historians make clear that social policies were themselves gendered, particularly with respect to benefits.

The peace movement and the socialist movement also attracted dedicated activists. On peace movement participation, see Carrie A. Foster, *The Women and the Warriors: The U.S. Section of the Women's International League for Peace and Freedom, 1915–1946* (Syracuse, N.Y., 1995); see also Catherine Foster, *Women for All Seasons: The Story of the Women's International League for Peace and Freedom* (Athens, Ga., 1989). Participation in the socialist movement and its politics was also an important part of the process of political socialization for women, as is ably documented by Mary Jo Buhle in *Women and American Socialism, 1870–1920* (Urbana, Ill., 1983). Biographies of radicals include Candace Falk, *Love, Anarchy and Emma Goldman: A Biography* (New York, 1989); Dee Garrison, *Mary Heaton Vorse: The Life of an American Insurgent* (Philadelphia, 1989); Janice R. MacKinnon and Stephen R. MacKinnon, *Agnes Smedley: The Life and Times of an American Radical* (Berkeley, 1987); Helen C. Camp, *Iron in Her Soul: Elizabeth Gurley Flynn and the American Left* (Pullman, Wash., 1995); Kathleen Kennedy, *Disloyal Mothers and Scurrilous Citizens: Women and Subversion during World War I* (Bloomington, Ind., 1999); and Rhodri Jeffreys-Jones, *Changing Differences: Women and the Shaping of American Foreign Policy, 1917–1994* (New Brunswick, N.J., 1995).

The classic history of suffrage, Eleanor Flexner's *Century of Struggle: The Woman's Rights Movement in the United States* (Cambridge, Mass., 1958), should be supplemented with Ellen Carol DuBois, *Harriot Stanton Blatch and the Winning of Woman Suffrage* (New Haven, Conn., 1997); Sara Hunter Graham, *Women Suffrage and the New Democracy* (New Haven, Conn., 1996); and Suzanne Marilley, *Woman Suffrage and the Origins of Liberal Feminism, 1880–1920* (Cambridge, Mass., 1996). New books on African American women and suffrage include Rosalyn Terborg-Penn, *African-American Women in the Struggle for the Vote, 1850–1920* (Bloomington, Ind., 1998), and *African American Women and the Vote, 1837–1935,* ed. Anne D. Gordon with Bettye Collier-Thomas et al. (Amherst, Mass., 1997). For illuminating regional studies, see Marjorie Spruill Wheeler's *New Women of the New South: The Leaders of the Woman Suffrage Movement in the Southern States* (New York, 1993), and Elna Green, *Southern Strategies: Southern Women and the Woman Suffrage Question*

(Chapel Hill, N.C., 1997). On anti-suffragists, see Susan F. Marshall, *Splintered Sisterhood: Gender and Class in the Campaign Against Woman's Suffrage* (Madison, Wis., 1997).

On the Woman's Party, see Christina A. Leonardi, *From Equal Suffrage to Equal Rights: Alice Paul and the National Woman's Party, 1910–1928* (New York, 1986). For women's involvement in other political parties, see Robert J. Dinkin, *Before Equal Suffrage: Women in Partisan Politics from Colonial Times to 1920* (Westport, Conn., 1995), and Michael Goldberg, *An Army of Women: Gender and Politics in Gilded Age Kansas* (Baltimore, 1997). On the impact of suffrage, see Kristi Anderson, *After Suffrage* (Chicago, 1996). On women in partisan politics in the post-suffrage decades, consult two new studies: Jo Freeman, *A Room at a Time: How Women Entered Party Politics* (New York, 2000), and *We Have Come to Stay: American Women and Political Parties, 1880–1960*, ed. Melanie Gustafson, Kristi Miller, and Elisabeth Israels Perry (Albuquerque, N.M., 1999).

The activities of women in the aftermath of suffrage, first probed in J. Stanley Lemons, *The Woman Citizen: Social Feminism in the 1920s* (Urbana, Ill., 1975), has received attention in more recent works, notably Nancy F. Cott's *The Grounding of Modern Feminism* (New Haven, Conn., 1987). For black women's activism, see Paula Giddings's *When and Where I Enter* (New York, 1996); Jacqueline Anne Rouse, *Lugenia Burns Hope: Black Southern Reformers* (Athens, Ga., 1989); Ula Yvette Taylor, *The Veiled Garvey: The Life and Times of Amy Jacques Garvey* (Chapel Hill, N.C., 2002); and Victoria W. Wolcott, *Remaking Respectability: African American Women in Interwar Detroit* (Chapel Hill, N.C., 2001). On women reformers' continued concern for industrial conditions, see Claudia Clark, *Radium Girls: Women and Industrial Health Reform, 1910–1935* (Chapel Hill, N.C., 1997).

Not all this activism was progressive. On how anti-suffragist women morphed into women of the anti-communist right after World War I, see Kim E. Nielsen, *Un-American Womanhood: Antiradicalism, Antifeminism, and the First Red Scare* (Columbus, Oh., 2001). Women who joined the KKK are the focus of Kathleen M. Blee, *Women of the Klan: Racism and Gender in the 1920s* (Berkeley, Cal., 1991), while Glen Jeansonne, *Women of the Far Right: The Mother's Movement and World War II* (Chicago, 1990), examines yet another group of conservative women who were isolationists.

Important biographies of activists and/or politicians include Jacquelyn Dowd Hall's *Revolt Against Chivalry: Jessie Daniel Ames and the Women's Campaign Against Lynching* (New York, 1974); Christie Miller, *Ruth Hanna McCormick: A Life in Politics, 1880–1944* (Albuquerque, N.M., 1992); Susan Ware, *Partner and I: Mollie Dewson, Feminism, and New Deal Politics* (New Haven, Conn., 1987); Blanche Weisen Cook, *Eleanor Roosevelt, 1884–1933* (New York, 1993) and *Eleanor Roosevelt, The Defining Years, 1933–1938* (New York, 2000); Ingrid Scobie, *Center Stage: Helen Gahagen Douglas, A Life* (New York, 1992); Patricia L. Schmidt, *Margaret Chase Smith: Beyond Convention* (Orono, Me., 1996); and Janann Sherman, *No Place for a Woman: A Life of Senator Margaret Chase Smith* (New Brunswick, N.J., 2000).

Ideology

Carroll Smith-Rosenberg, *Disorderly Conduct* (New York, 1985), extends its sophisticated treatment of gender ideology and social change into the early twentieth century. On ideology and education, see Devon A. Mihesuah, *Cultivating the Rosebuds: The Education of Women at the Cherokee Female Seminary, 1851–1928* (Urbana, Ill., 1993); Barbara Miller

Solomon, *In the Company of Educated Women* (New Haven, Conn., 1985); Helen L. Horowitz, *Alma Mater: Design and Experience in the Women's Colleges from Their Nineteenth Century Beginning to the 1930s* (New York, 1984); Lynn D. Gordon, *Gender and Higher Education in the Progressive Era* (New Haven, Conn., 1990); and Dorothy C. Holland and Margaret A. Eisenhart, *Educated in Romance: Women, Achievement, and Culture* (Chicago, 1990). The way ideology affected both attitudes toward divorce and the debate on changing divorce laws is evident in Glenda Riley, *Divorce: An American Tradition* (New York, 1991). The effect of ideology on changing standards of beauty is explored in Lois Banner, *American Beauty* (New York, 1983). The intersection of ideology and technology is explored in Virginia Scharff, *Taking the Wheel: Women and the Coming of the Motor Age* (New York, 1991). For insight into contemporary feminist thought, see Ann I. Lane, *To "Herland" and Beyond: The Life and Work of Charlotte Perkins Gilman* (New York, 1990), and Nancy F. Cott, *A Woman Making History: Mary Ritter Beard Through Her Letters* (New Haven, Conn., 1991). On the origins of feminism in women's union activism during and after World War II, see Nancy F. Gabin, *Feminism in the Labor Movement: Women and the United Auto Workers: 1935–1975* (Ithaca, N.Y., 1990).

PART IV: THE STRUGGLE AGAINST INJUSTICE, 1945–2000

Biology and Sexuality

On sexuality, see John D'Emilio and Estelle B. Freedman, *Intimate Matters* (Chicago, 1997), chaps. 11–15. On the development of homosexual subcultures, see John D'Emilio, *Sexual Politics, Sexual Communities: The Making of a Homosexual Minority in the U.S., 1940–1970* (Chicago, 1983), and Allan Berube, *Coming Out Under Fire: Gay Men and Women in World War II* (New York, 1990). For recent scholarship on gay and lesbian studies, see Eric Marcus, *Making History: The Struggle for Gay and Lesbian Equal Rights, 1945–1990: An Oral History* (New York, 1992), and Lillian Faderman, *Odd Girls and Twilight Lovers: A History of Lesbian Life in Twentieth-Century America* (New York, 1991). On transsexuals, see Joanne Meyerowitz, *How Sex Changed: A History of Transsexuality in the United States* (Cambridge, Mass., 2002).

For the postwar pressure for children, see Elaine Tyler May, *Barren in the Promised Land: Childless Americans and the Pursuit of Happiness* (New York, 1995) and Judith Walzer Leavitt, *Brought to Bed* (New York, 1986), chaps. 7–8. On single pregnancy, see Rickie Solinger, *Wake Up Little Susie: Single Pregnancy and Race Before Roe v. Wade* (New York, 1992), and Kristin Luker, *Dubious Conceptions: The Politics of Teenage Pregnancy* (Cambridge, Mass., 1996). On the pill and the sexual revolution, see Elizabeth Siegel Watkins, *On the Pill: A Social History of Contraception, 1950–1970* (Baltimore, 1998), and Beth Bailey, *Sex in the Heartland* (Cambridge, Mass., 1999). For the impact of second-wave feminism on women's health care, see Sandra Morgen, *Into Our Own Hands: The Women's Health Movement in the United States, 1969–1990* (New Brunswick, N.J., 2002).

The role of the state in relation to both reproductive freedom and domestic violence cuts across biology, ideology, and politics. On abortion and fetal politics, see Rosalind Pollack Petchesky, *Abortion and Woman's Choice: The State, Sexuality and Reproductive Freedom* (New York, 1984); Leslie J. Reagan, *When Abortion Was a Crime* (Berkeley, Cal., 1997), and Cynthia Daniels, *At Women's Expense: State Power and the Policies of Fetal Rights* (Cambridge, Mass., 1993).

Eating disorders and preoccupation with aging, which began earlier in the century, also involve the intersection of biology and ideology, as is demonstrated in Joan Jacob Brumberg's *Fasting Girls* (Cambridge, Mass., 1988); Sharlene Hess-Biber, *Am I Thin Enough Yet? The Cult of Thinness and the Commercialization of Identity* (New York, 1996); and Lois Banner's *In Full Flower: Aging Women, Power and Sexuality: A History* (New York, 1992), chaps. 7–9.

On sexuality and popular culture in the 1950s and 1960s, see Susan J. Douglas, *Where the Girls Are* (New York, 1994), and Alice Echols, *The Scars of Sweet Paradise: The Life and Times of Janis Joplin* (New York, 1999).

Economics

On new occupations for women, see Dorothy Moses Shulz, *From Social Worker to Crime Fighter: Women in United States Municipal Policing* (Westport, Conn., 1995); Janis Appier, *Policing Women: The Sexual Politics of Law Enforcement and the LAPD* (Philadelphia, 1998); and Susan Eisenberg, *We'll Call You If We Need You: Experiences of Women Working Construction* (Ithaca, N.Y., 1998). A major faction opening up the new occupational categories was affirmative action, which was put in place in the 1960s and early 1970s. Although discrimination in the professions continued, as is made clear in such studies as Mary Beth Walsh's *Doctors Wanted, No Women Need Apply: Sexual Barriers in the Medical Profession, 1835–1975* (New Haven, Conn., 1977), affirmative action had an ameliorating impact, as is demonstrated in Margaret W. Rossiter, *Women Scientists in America: Before Affirmative Action, 1940–1972* (Baltimore, 1995). For important affirmative action cases, see Melvin I. Urofsky, *A Conflict of Rights: The Supreme Court and Affirmative Action* (New York, 1991), which focuses on a 1987 Santa Clara County case. On the Sears case, see Alice Kessler-Harris, "*EEOC v. Sears, Roebuck & Co.*: A Personal Account," *Radical History Review* 35 (Spring 1986); Ruth Milkman, "Women's History and the Sears Case," *Feminist Studies* 12 (1986); and Joan W. Scott, "Deconstructing Equality-versus-Difference: Or, the Uses of Poststructuralist Theory for Feminism," *The Postmodern Turn*, ed. Steven Seidman (Cambridge, England, 1994). A more recent case cracking the last remaining educational institution barring gender equity is Philippa Strum, *Women in the Barracks: The VMI Case and Equal Rights* (Lawrence, Kan., 2002).

Another method of addressing the wage gap association with gender-based occupational segregation was pay equity. See Alice Kessler-Harris, *A Woman's Wage* (Lexington, Ky., 1990), chaps. 4–5, and Linda M. Blum, *Between Feminism and Labor: The Significance of the Comparable Worth Movement* (Berkeley, Cal., 1991).

Despite changes, certain problems have remained enduring. Influential recent studies of the pressures of home and work include Arlie Hochshild, *The Second Shift: Working Parents and the Revolution at Home* (New York, 1989), and *The Time Bind: When Work Become Home and Home Become Work* (New York, 1997); Joan Williams, *Unbending Gender: Why Family and Work Conflict and What To Do About It* (New York, 2000); and Fay J. Crosby, *Juggling, The Unexpected Advantage of Balancing Career and Home for Women and Their Families* (New York, 1993). On child care, see Sonya Michel, *Children's Interests/Mothers' Rights: The Shaping of America's Child Care Policy* (New Haven, Conn., 1999). On the larger problem of economic equity for women, see Alice Kessler-Harris's superb

INDEX

AALL. *See* American Association for Labor Legislation

Abendblatt, 316

Abolitionism, 130, 158
  Garrisonian, 203–4
  political, 203, 204, 208
  Seneca Falls convention and, 203–4, 208–11
  women's rights, religion, and, 193–97

Abortion, 4, 17, 19–20, 350, 479, 604, 610–11, 614, 615, 630–36
  Comstock Law and, 250
  cost of, 691–92
  death rate from illegal, 694
  in the eighteenth century, 97–113
  during the Great Depression, 423–28
  instruments for, 98
  late-term, 691, 692, 693
  legal protection for fetus, 691, 694
  in the nineteenth century, 183–92
  number performed prelegalization, 630
  Planned Parenthood of Southeastern Pennsylvania v. *Casey,* 634–36, 695
  Planned Parenthood v. *Danforth,* 633, 636
  quickening doctrine and, 100, 101, 111n3, 185, 187, 188, 191

Roe v. *Wade,* 19, 619, 630–36, 691, 694, 695, 696
  Sanger on, 372–74, 423
  therapeutic, 426
  threats to access, 617, 619, 691–96
  violence against clinics, 692
  Webster v. *Reproductive Health Services,* 617, 632–33

Abortion Control Act of 1982, 633–36

Abzug, Bella, 604, 613, 700

ACLU. *See* American Civil Liberties Union

Adair, Vivyan C., 677–81

Adams, Abigail, 120

Adams, Annie, 255

Adams Morgan Demonstration Project, 528

Addams, Jane, 10, 253, 254, 256, 297, 327, 328, 330, 333

Adkins v. *Children's Hospital,* 337, 369

"Adolescent Girl among Primitive People, The" (Van Waters), 502

Adultery, 355

Advertisements, 401, 402, 404, 406–8, 410n45

AFDC. *See* Aid to Families with Dependent Children

Affirmative action, 550, 618, 658

AFL. *See* American Federation of Labor

African American men. *See also* Lynching
  post–World War II employment, 474, 475–76
  social security and, 437
  suffrage for, 129, 131, 207, 367, 368

African Americans
  blockbusting and, 496–500
  Roosevelt (Eleanor) and, 450–51, 453

African American women, 2, 7, 14, 309, 382, 618. *See also* Reconstruction; Slavery; individual woman activists
  abortion and, 424–25, 427
  absence from National Consumers' League, 334
  birth control pill and, 562
  in the civil rights movement, 532–36
  in colonial society, 59–66
  feminism and, 17, 537–46, 586–90, 599, 606–7, 611
  forging links with white women, 286–96
  Friedan and, 482, 486, 488, 491
  in the garment industry, 685, 686
  in girl groups, 569, 571
  during the Great Depression, 429–32
  higher education and, 15, 537–46

727